THE NEW TESTAMENT

THE
NEW
TESTAMENT

A TRANSLATION

David Bentley Hart

Yale
UNIVERSITY PRESS
New Haven and London

Published with assistance from the Mary Cady Tew Memorial Fund.

Yale University Press books may be purchased in quantity for educational, business, or promotional use. For information, please e-mail sales.press@yale.edu (U.S. office) or sales@yaleup.co.uk (U.K. office).

Designed by Sonia Shannon.

Set in Janson type by Tseng Information Systems, Inc.

Printed in the United States of America.

Library of Congress Control Number: 2017939708
ISBN 978-0-300-18609-3 (hardcover : alk. paper)
A catalogue record for this book is available from the British Library.

This paper meets the requirements of ANSI/NISO Z39.48-1992 (Permanence of Paper).

10 9 8 7 6 5 4 3 2 1

For John Milbank

λέγει ὁ λόγος:
ἔγειρον τὸν λίθον κἀκεῖ εὑρήσεις με·
σχίσον τὸν ξύλον κἀγὼ ἐκεῖ εἰμί.

Contents

Contents

Acknowledgments

MY THANKS PRINCIPALLY to Jennifer Banks of Yale University Press for suggesting this project, after I—in keeping with a discreditable appetite for the needlessly recherché—had proposed producing a translation of either some of Ronsard's verse or the whole of Quintus of Smyrna's *Posthomerica*. I had not realized how deeply this labor would affect me, and she can have no way of knowing what I owe her for having given it to me. (Ghaṇā ābhāra.) I am also grateful to her and the other editors at Yale for their patience: the translation was interrupted for over a year and a half by a particularly debilitating illness I contracted, and not once did any representative of Yale University Press give me cause to feel I was letting down the side. I am especially indebted to Lawrence Kenney, the copy editor of this book, for his keen diligence and his patience, and for rescuing me from my own omissions.

   My thanks to my brother Addison for our conversations regarding various words in the original Greek, for encouraging me in my resolve to resist the easy path of adopting conventional solutions to difficult interpretive problems, and for agreeing with me on certain translations that otherwise I might have decided were too outlandish (even though correct). My thanks as well to my mother, Marianne Hart, for typing out long portions of this translation when I was too ill to do it for myself. And thanks too to Jacob Prahlow, my research assistant at Saint Louis University, for proofreading the texts of the four Gospels with such care and for removing the typographical errors from those manuscripts for me.

I am especially grateful to Robert L. Wilken, both for the encouragement he offered me with regard to the finished product and for his suggestions on how to reorganize the introductory and critical materials. And I am very grateful indeed to the editors of *Commonweal* for permission to adapt portions of an article that I originally published in the pages of their journal ("Christ's Rabble," 7 October 2016) for my introduction to this volume.

A Note on Transliteration

IN MY INTRODUCTION and footnotes I have many occasions to transliterate Greek words into Latin lettering, and for the most part—
inasmuch as the phonetic correspondences are mostly obvious—I do so
quite conventionally. But I should note that the pronunciation I assume
to be "correct" is that of modern demotic. While it is possible to debate the degree to which modern Greek pronunciation matches that of
late antiquity, there can be no serious doubt that it comes much nearer
to doing so than does the accent invented by sixteenth-century Western European humanists, which corresponds to no version of spoken
Greek—Homeric, Attic, *koinē*, Mediaeval, Katharevousa, Demotic—
ever heard on the lips of a native speaker. It is not difficult to find plays
on words in late antique texts that are entirely invisible unless one is
reading the words as having demotic vowel values; and we have enough
specimens of phonetically induced misspellings (scrawled on certain
ancient Cappadocian monastic walls, for instance) or homophonous
variant spellings of transliterations (for instance, Matthew 27:46 and
Mark 15:34) to confirm that late antique speakers of Greek used an accent at least very close to that of modern Greek. It is something of a
mystery that classicists are still taught to lisp Sophocles or Plato in the
entirely artificial and really rather hideous intonations of what is often
called Erasmian Greek. This affects my text in only a limited way, but
one that needs some clarification. I have not attempted to "demoticize"
every aspect of my transliteration, for fear of producing something un-

intelligible. I have eschewed the classicist habit of rendering a *rho* as "rh" rather than "r," but I have also resisted the demotic temptation to render every *delta* as "dh" rather than "d," however much I might wish to try to capture the lovely, melting, soft "th" sound that the consonant has in spoken Greek. Neither have I rendered *beta* as "v," which would baffle far too many readers, as would also happen if I tried to render the softness of the modern Greek *gamma*, or wrote it as a consonantal "y" before an *epsilon* or *iota*. And sadly there is no intelligible way to represent the diphthong *omicron-iota* in such a way as to make readers hear it as an English long "e" rather than the obnoxious and philologically indefensible "oy" of Western European sixteenth-century convention. I have used a long mark over the "o" that represents *omega*, to distinguish it from *omicron*, even though the latter is "short" more durationally than tonally in modern Greek; to Anglophone ears, it would still sound long. (The long pronunciation of both "e" and "o" is the same as in English.) I have also made the "h" that represents the hard breathing mark over certain vowels a superscript, to make clear that ideally it should be voiced somewhere along the continuum from extremely softly to silently. I have similarly made the iota-subscript of singular datives into a subscript in English also. And I have rendered the letter *ypsilon* (not, as it is often mispronounced, *upsilon*) by three separate letters: "y," "u," and "v." Where the *ypsilon* is simply an isolated vowel it becomes a "y," just as we are accustomed to seeing it rendered in such words as "physics" or "psychology," and it should always be pronounced like an English long "e." And, just as "u" and "v" were really one letter in classical Latin, functioning at times as the vowel and at times as the consonant, something similar is true of the *ypsilon:* It can serve as a vowel, sounded either with its own "y" sound or, after an *omicron*, as producing the diphthong "ou," which sounds like the double-o in "boot"; but it can serve also as a consonant, after an *alpha, eta*, or *epsilon*, where it produces either a "v" or an "f" sound, depending on what letter follows it, and in those cases I have rendered it as a "v" (think of it as sometimes an English "v," sometimes a German).

Introduction

The Purpose of This Translation

To write yet another translation of the New Testament is probably something of a foolish venture. No matter what one produces—recklessly liberal, timidly conservative, or something poised equilibriously in between—it will provoke consternation (and probably indignation) in countless breasts. There are so many traditions, denominations, assemblies, and devotions—so many magisteria, critical schools, theological factions, and assorted individuals with idiosyncratic spiritual commitments—that one can never hope to please everyone at once, or perhaps anyone entirely. And, as scarcely needs be said, there is an entire guild of New Testament scholars, most of whom owe allegiance to some dogmatic tradition or critical theory, and each of whom is likely to favor his or her understanding of the text over every other. Even the doctrinally indifferent or academically uninvolved are apt to have very particular prejudices regarding what style is most appropriate for rendering scripture into a modern language: whether, for example, one's principal concern should be to produce good literature or to provide a stringently faithful gloss; whether one should strive more for explanatory clarity or for literal accuracy; whether one should substitute modern equivalents for the obsolete idioms of the ancient world or remain obedient to the unfamiliar diction of the original despite any awkwardness that might ensue; whether paraphrase is a duty or a sin; and so on. It is a game in which no player prospers.

Yet, even so, here is my attempt at a new translation. In a sense, I have spent years preparing for it. At least, I have often enough found myself retranslating passages of the New Testament for students in a lecture hall, in a rather ad hoc fashion, because whatever printed translation they were using obscured aspects of the original text I thought extremely important. To be honest, I have come to believe that all the standard English translations render a great many of the concepts and presuppositions upon which the books of the New Testament are built largely impenetrable, and that most of them effectively hide (sometimes forcibly) things of absolutely vital significance for understanding how the texts' authors thought. At times this is a result of the peculiarities of the translators' linguistic, historical, or conceptual training. More often it is the result of their commitment to one or another specific theological tradition or predisposition. And occasionally it is the result of their loyalty to some prevailing theory of translation (such as "dynamic equivalence theory") that encourages them to make the line between translation and interpretation perilously hazy. Really, it is usually the result of all these things at once, inasmuch as almost all modern translations of the text have been produced not by single scholars with their own particular visions of the texts but by committees. The inevitable consequence of this is that many of the most important decisions are negotiated accommodations, achieved by general agreement, and favoring only those solutions that prove the least offensive to everyone involved. This becomes, in effect, a process of natural selection, in which novel approaches to the text are generally the first to perish, and only the tried and trusted survive. And this can result in the exclusion not only of extravagantly conjectural readings, but often of the most straightforwardly literal as well. (A sort of "acid test" for me is Judas [or Jude] 1:19, a verse whose meaning is startlingly clear in the Greek but which no collaborative translation I know of translates in any but the vaguest and most periphrastic manner.) I think I have come to be opposed to translation by mass collaboration on principle, even when (as in the case of the King James) the final product is literarily admirable. All such renderings, it seems to me, become ineluctably mired in the anodyne blandness and imprecision of "diplomatic" accord.

Still, all this said, the idea of undertaking a complete translation of my own would probably not have occurred to me without the prompting of an indispensable editor at Yale University Press named Jennifer Banks. The project would not have appealed to me at all, moreover, if it had been only a matter of repeating the efforts of past translators in a slightly different combination of words. But the prospect of writing a version that would be by my lights as scrupulously faithful as I could make it, that would not merely reiterate conventional readings of the text, and that would allow me to call attention to features of the Greek original usually invisible in English versions proved irresistible. After all, most modern readers are separated from the New Testament not only by those obvious differences in language, culture, and intellectual formation that put them at an immense historical remove from the authors, but also to a considerable degree by the doctrinal expectations that have shaped the decisions of translators for centuries. The relation between Christian theology and scriptural translation has a long and complicated history; theology has not only influenced translation, but particular translations have had enormous consequences for the development of theology (it would be almost impossible, for instance, to exaggerate how consequential the Latin Vulgate's inept rendering of a single verse, Romans 5:12, proved for the development of the Western Christian understanding of original sin). In the end even the most conscientious translations tend, at certain crucial junctures, to use language determined as much by theological and dogmatic tradition as by the "plain" meaning of the words on the page. And in some extreme cases doctrinal or theological or moral ideologies drive translators to distort the text to a discreditable degree. Certain popular translations, like *The New International Version* and *The English Standard Version*, are notorious examples of this. These may represent the honest zeal of devout translators to communicate what they imagine to be the "correct" theology of scripture, but the preposterous liberties taken to accomplish this end often verge on a kind of pious fraudulence. Moreover, even where ideology does not intrude quite so violently on the work of translation, a kind of inertia has come to hold sway, from generation to generation, over the making of new versions: Where difficult words or syntactical uncertainties or grammatical obscurities appear in the Greek, the solutions favored by earlier translators are generally carried over by their successors, even where there may be more plausible or more interesting alternatives. At the last, generation upon generation, those who cannot read the original Greek are deprived of any way to see in the text of scripture a vast number of those verbal connections, conceptual ambiguities, and semantic oddities that are, in a very real sense, inseparable from its essence.

This is not to say that I can pretend to be free of intellectual prejudices; I can only say that I have made every effort not to allow them to interpose themselves between me and the text, even when the result has at some level displeased me. In the end it may not be entirely possible to write a translation of scripture not shaped by later theological and doctrinal history. Even so, that is what I have attempted. I am not prompted by any great desire, I hasten to add, to challenge or offend against theological orthodoxies; those, as a rule, can take care of themselves perfectly well, and for the most part would not be threatened by even the most daringly revisionist approach to the text. Some orthodoxies, of course, fare better than others when one returns to the original Greek; but that is not my guiding concern. Neither, in fact, do I think of my translation as "revisionist" so much as reconstructive. It is easy to anticipate the criticisms this version of the text might elicit from those who firmly believe that any rendering should reflect the usages of later doctrinal determinations. But it would be contrary to conscience on my part to try to make the words on the page conform to what later dogmatic reflection found in them (and, after all, if orthodoxy really required that sort of discreet redaction of the record, it would be self-evidently false). My principal aim is to help awaken readers to mysteries and uncertainties and surprises in the New Testament documents that often lie wholly hidden from view beneath layers of received hermeneutical and theological tradition. And I would hope my translation would succeed, in many places, in making the familiar strange, novel, and perhaps newly compelling.

Here, however, I defer discussion of the particulars of some of my more consequential choices to my Concluding Scientific Postscript, at the end of this volume. And I recommend consulting that postscript to any reader who wants some explanations of the decisions I have made regarding how to render various words and phrases. At least, I suspect that many readers will be somewhat taken aback by the absence of many terms they are accustomed to finding in the New Testament—"eternal," "forever," "redemption," "justification," "repentance," "predestination," "world," "hell," and so on—and by the presence of very different terms in their places. My postscript explains the reasoning behind many of these decisions, and constitutes in some sense a kind of manifesto for the understanding of the New Testament's texts that I regard as most convincing.

Matters of Style

I should note that this is not a literary translation of the New Testament, much less a rendering for liturgical use. If it conforms in any degree to any current school of translation theory, it is certainly that of "formal," rather than "dynamic," equivalence—though, in fact, I believe that no translator should entrust his or her choices to the authority of any "theory" whatsoever. Again and again, I have elected to produce an almost pitilessly literal translation; many of my departures from received practices are simply my efforts to make the original text as visible as possible through the palimpsest of its translation. I cannot emphasize this too starkly: I have not chosen to fill in syntactical lacunae, rectify grammatical lapses, or draw a veil of delicacy over jarring words or images (while "uncircumcision," for example, may be the traditional and demure rendering of the Greek ἀκροβυστία [*akrobystia*] it singularly fails to capture the physiological bluntness of the word).

Where the Greek of the original is maladroit, broken, or impenetrable (as it is with some consistency in Paul's letters), so is the English of my translation; where an author has written bad Greek (such as one finds throughout the book of Revelation), I have written bad English. Even then, I have not captured all the idiosyncrasies of the texts. It was common practice in *koinē* Greek, at least when written (perhaps because writing materials were rarer and more precious than they are now), to elide verbs in predicative constructions, as well as some other syntactic ligatures; if done well this can produce an elegant terseness, if poorly a confused heap of grammatical wreckage. Paul's fondness for elision is so pronounced that any translator is bound to supply a large quantity of words only adumbrated in the original Greek (all those italicized words in the King James), and this practice often does as much to determine the meaning of a verse as to elucidate it. I have added the pretermitted verbs where it seemed unproblematic to me, but not nearly as freely as most translators have done. In part to preserve uncertainties that I did not want to presume to dispel, and in part to capture something of the concise, urgent, precipitous quality of Paul's writings, I have reproduced many of his fragmentary formulations without augmentation or "correction." I have, however, also resorted to copious dashes and parentheses and other devices to break up the unbroken flow of his often deeply tangled sentences into discrete intelligible phrases and clauses, though the original texts are devoid of all but the minimal punctuation (which is a common feature of texts of the time). In general, moreover, I have not attempted to clarify these texts by redistributing their often insufferably prolonged periods into discrete sentences, or by supplying proper subjects in place of the personal pronouns that vie wildly with one another in verse after verse; again, these are features both of late antique style and of the peculiar voices of these authors, neither of which I want to dissemble.

Also, throughout the New Testament, where there are sudden shifts of tense in the original Greek, my English usually follows suit. The use of the "historical present" in the books of the time was common enough, and the result of rendering it literally often cannot help but seem awkward in modern English; but the device is employed fairly haphazardly in the Gospels, and my interest is accuracy. And I have to say that I find the effect somewhat enchanting: When the Gospels of Matthew, Mark, and John shift back and forth between past and present tenses—it happens only rarely in Luke—it has something of the immediacy of a person standing among friends and relating a story, perhaps a little breathlessly, lapsing naturally into the present tense at critical moments, then withdrawing into the past again. At times, it endows the text with a peculiar vividness; at least, to me there is a strikingly plain plangency to "They crucify him" that is qualitatively different from the effect of "They crucified him."

I have as well elected generally to translate many words from the Greek by their literal meanings in English, rather than in the forms consecrated by theological tradition. Thus I have not rendered Χριστός (*Christos*) by the Anglicized Greek word "Christ" or, for that matter, by the Anglicized Hebrew or Aramaic word "Messiah," but by the simply literal translation "Anointed"; rather than rendering διάβολος (*diabolos*) by the Anglicized Persian word "devil," I have used "Slanderer"; I have made ἐκκλησία (*ekklēsia*) "assembly" rather than "church," not out of some predisposition toward a low ecclesiology, but simply to make the reader aware that it was once an ordinary word with an ordinary meaning. This is not, I hope, a gesture of pedantry or preciosity on my part; my aim is simply to make the modern English reader "hear" the words of the text as words with common meanings, as early Greek-speaking Christians would have done. I have not been entirely consistent in this regard, admittedly. I considered rendering ἀπόστολος (*apostolos*) as "emissary" rather than "apostle," for instance, but in English the former is still just barely included among the latter's connotations, and in much of the New Testament the apostolate has already emerged as a recognizably distinct office and distinct title among Christ's followers. And I considered translating ἄγγελος (*angelos*) not as "angel" but as "herald" or "messenger," but in many cases the effect would have been absurd (talk of "legions of messengers" would, at least for me, immediately summon up images of massed ranks of mailmen or bicycle letter-carriers or hotel bellhops, and to say that the face of Stephen before the Sanhedrin looked like "the face of a messenger" would lack a certain poetic force). Really, there are only a few instances in the New Testament where the word refers to a human agent; for the most part, it is used as already having the special referent of one of the heavenly host, or occasionally one of the devil's deputies. I have also insistently chosen to render particular words throughout the text by the same English "equivalent" whenever possible, even when the result is less than perfectly attractive or utterly clear or when another course might be recommended by prevailing theories of translation; I have done this especially in those places (John 3:8 is a good example) where an obvious bit of wordplay would be lost if I were to render a single Greek word, used in two distinct but related instances, by two different English words. I have adopted a similar principle in the case where words with the same root are used in what seems like a more than accidental association, as in the case of the substantive *aiōn* and the adjective *aiōnios* (see my postscript at the end of this volume). All that said, it would be disingenuous of me to suggest that what follows is *simply* a literal rendering from the Greek into English. Part of the task of illuminating the original text for Anglophone readers raised on the standard translations is, as I say, to give them a sense of the strangeness of the text: the novelty, the impenetrability, the frequently unfinished quality of the prose and of the theology. To this end, I have on many occasions chosen to offer the more unfamiliar or more baffling interpretation of a difficult passage — in part to apprise readers that the original may differ considerably from what they expect, but also because in most cases I truly believe that the more unsettling rendering is also the more accurate.

All this being said, however, I should note that much of the original Greek of the New Testament can be translated without inordinate difficulty. More important than the small local matters of dealing with multivalent words or vague turns of phrase is the larger matter of rendering the entire text into modern English as gracefully as possible without sacrificing the literal meaning of the original. In the long twilight struggle between felicity and fidelity, the latter should always win out in the end; and, though in many cases a happy compromise between the two is possible, in many cases it is not. But, frankly, any loss of high or mellifluous diction in parts of my rendering does not constitute any great injustice to the source material. The power and beauty of the New Testament are, for the most part, largely unrelated to its literary quality, which is often meager (at least, as these things are conventionally judged). Most of the authors of the New Testament did not write particularly well, even by the forgiving standards of the *koinē*—that is, "common"—Greek in which they worked. The unknown author of the Letter to the Hebrews commanded a fairly distinguished and erudite style, and was obviously an accomplished native speaker of the tongue; and Luke, the author of both the third Gospel and the Acts of the Apostles, wrote in an urbane, unspectacular, but mostly graceful prose; the author of the first letter attributed to Peter was clearly an educated person whose primary language was a fairly refined form of Greek, while the author of the second letter wrote in a somewhat bombastic style, of the kind classically called Asiatic Greek; but the language of most of the canon is anything but extraordinary. Paul's letters possess an elemental power born out of the passion of his faith and the marvel of what he believes has been revealed to him, and his prose occasionally flowers into a plain but startling lyricism; but his Greek is generally rough, sometimes inept, and occasionally incoherent. The Gospel of Mark contains obvious solecisms and is awkwardly written throughout. The prose of the Gospel of Matthew is rarely better than ponderous. Even the Gospel of John, perhaps the most structurally and symbolically sophisticated religious text to have come down to us from late antiquity, is written in a Greek that is grammatically correct but syntactically almost childish (or perhaps I should say, "remarkably limpid"), and—unless its author was some late first-century precursor of Gertrude Stein—its stylistic limitations suggest an author whose command of the language did not exceed mere functional competence. Then, of course, the book of Revelation, the last New Testament text to be accepted into the canon—it was not firmly established there throughout the Christian world until the early fifth century—is, if judged *purely* by the normal standards of literary style and good taste, almost unremittingly atrocious. And, in the most refined pagan critics of the new faith in late antiquity, the stylistic coarseness of Christian literature often provoked the purest kind of patrician contempt.

This is all evidence, however, of a deeper truth about these texts: They are not beguiling exercises in suasive rhetoric or feats of literary virtuosity; rather, they are chiefly the devout and urgent attempts of often rather ordinary persons to communicate something "seen" and "heard" that transcends any language, but that nevertheless demands to be spoken, now, here, in whatever words one can marshal. This is the special amphibology of Christian scripture. Whereas the Jewish Bible represents the concentrated literary genius of an ancient and amazingly rich culture—mythic, epic, lyric, historical, and visionary, in texts assembled over many centuries and then judiciously synthesized, redacted, and polished—the Christian New Testament is a somewhat unsystematically compiled and pragmatically edited compendium of "important documentation": writings from the first generations of witnesses to the new faith, the oldest ambassadors to us from the apostolic and early postapostolic ages, consisting in quickly limned stories, theological discourses, and even a bit of historically impenetrable occasional writing. As such it draws one in by the intensity, purity, and perhaps frequent naïveté of its language, not by the exquisite sheen of its belletristic graces. Romans chapter twelve, for instance, is a syntactical congeries; but its moral beauty is ravishing. Over the centuries, the authors of the New Testament have profited greatly from translation; the King James Bible, among the greatest glories of our tongue, transformed their "common Greek" into a very uncommon, though sublimely uncluttered, English. Even if my intention here were another "literary" translation, my efforts would fall so far short of that achievement as to render them pointless. But, happily, my aim in what follows is something else altogether, and so I have been left relatively unmolested by the "anxiety of influence."

The sole literary claim I make for my version, then, is that my mulish stubbornness regarding the idiosyncrasies of the text allowed me to "do the police in different voices," so to speak. Most translations, in evening out the oddities of the text, tend to flatten the various voices of the writers into a single clean, commodious style (usually the translator's own). And yet in the Greek their voices differ radically; and I like to think that my version is somewhat more successful than most at capturing those differences. I believe, for example, that a reader of this version will get something like an accurate sense of how vastly the style of Romans differs from that of Hebrews in the Greek by seeing how vastly they differ in my English rendering. Obviously, any translator's choices in these matters are dependent upon what he or she wishes to convey: If a translator is interested only in the "inner content" of the authors' messages, then the peculiar qualities of their various voices are at most a distraction and should probably be effaced. But, even if I granted that substance and style could be so neatly discriminated (which I definitely do not), my interest is in something else altogether.

The Community of the New Testament

Finally, something of a personal confession. Before embarking on this project, I doubt I ever truly properly appreciated precisely *how* urgent the various voices of the New Testament authors are, or how profound the provocations of what they were saying were for their own age, and probably remain for every age. Those voices blend, or at least interweave, in a kind of wildly indiscriminate polyphony, as if an early Baroque vocal trio, an Appalachian band, a couple of Viennese tenors piping twelve-tone *Lieder*, and a jazz crooner or two were all singing out together; but what all have in common, and what somehow forges a genuine harmony out of all that ecstatic clamor, is the vibrant certainty that history has been invaded by God in Christ in such a way that nothing can stay as it was, and that all terms of human community and conduct have been altered at the deepest of levels. And perhaps I could never have come to this realization had I not undertaken this task. To translate a text is to be conducted into its mysteries in a way that no mere act of reading—however conscientious or frequent—makes possible. At the very least, a translator is obliged to confront the words on the page not merely as meanings to be received, but as problems to be solved; and this demands an attentiveness to detail for which most of us never quite have the time. For myself, I know that writing this translation caused me to absorb certain conclusions about the world of the early church at a deeper level than I could have anticipated. Most of them I already knew, admittedly, if often as little more than shadows glimpsed through a veil of conventional habits of thought—for instance, how stark the dualism really is, in Paul's letters and elsewhere in the New Testament, between "flesh" and "spirit," or how greatly formulations that seem to imply universal salvation outnumber those very few that appear (and rather nebulously) to threaten an ultimate damnation for the wicked, and so on. Still, none of that *surprised* me; I was learning nothing about these matters for the first time, even if I was learning about them for the first time in an indelible way; the experience merely roused me from my complacent assumption that, simply by virtue of having read the text in Greek for many years, I had a natural feel for its tone.

What perhaps did impress itself upon me with an entirely unexpected force was a new sense of the utter strangeness of the Christian vision of life in its first dawning—by which I mean, precisely, its strangeness in respect to the Christianity of later centuries. When one truly ventures into the world of the first Christians, one enters a company of "radicals" (for want of a better word), an association of men and women guided by faith in a world-altering revelation, and hence in values almost absolutely inverse to the recognized social, political, economic, and religious truths not only of their own age, but of almost every age of human culture. The first Christians certainly bore very little resemblance to the faithful of our day, or to any generation of Christians that has felt quite at home in the world, securely sheltered within the available social stations of its time, complacently comfortable with material possessions and national loyalties and civic conventions. In truth, I suspect that very few of us, in even our wildest imaginings, could ever desire to be the kind of persons that the New Testament describes as fitting the pattern of life in Christ. And I do not mean merely that most of us would find the moral requirements laid out in Christian scripture a little onerous—though of course we do. Therein lies the perennial appeal of the venerable early modern theological fantasy that the Apostle Paul inveighed against something called "works-righteousness" in favor of a purely extrinsic "justification" by grace—which, alas, he did not. He rejected only the notion that one might be "shown righteous" by "works" of the Mosaic Law—that is, ritual *"observances"* like circumcision or keeping kosher—but he also quite clearly insisted, as did Christ, that all will be judged in the end according to their deeds (Romans 2:1-16 and 4:10-12; 1 Corinthians 3:12-15; 2 Corinthians 5:10; Philippians 2:16; and so on). Rather, I mean that most of us would find Christians truly cast in the New Testament mold fairly obnoxious: civically reprobate, ideologically unsound, economically destructive, politically irresponsible, socially discreditable, and really just a bit indecent. Or, if not that, we would at least be bemused by the sheer, unembellished, unremitting otherworldliness of their understanding of the gospel. We are quite accustomed, after all, to thinking of Christianity as a fairly commonsensical creed as regards the practicalities of life. On the matter of wealth, for instance, we take it as given that, while the New Testament enjoins generosity to the poor, it otherwise allows the wealthy to enjoy the fruits of their industry or fair fortune with a clean conscience. Common sense instructs us that it is not wealth as such that the New Testament condemns, but only a spiritually unhealthy preoccupation with it—the idolatry of riches, wealth misused, wealth immorally gained; riches in and of themselves, we assume, are neither good nor bad. But, in fact, one thing in startlingly short supply in the New Testament is common sense, and the commonsensical view of the early church is invariably the wrong one. For instance, the New Testament, alarmingly enough, condemns personal wealth not merely as a moral danger, but as an *intrinsic* evil.

Actually, the biblical texts are so unambiguous on this matter that it requires an almost heroic defiance of the obvious to fail to grasp their import. Admittedly, many translations down the centuries have had an emollient effect on a few of the New Testament's severer pronouncements. But this is an old story. The great theologian Clement of Alexandria (c. 150–c. 215 CE) may have been the first—back when the faith had just begun spreading among the more comfortably situated classes in the empire—to apply a reassuring gloss to the raw rhetoric of scripture on wealth and poverty. He drew a distinction between the poverty that matters (humility, renunciation, spiritual purity, generosity) and the poverty that does not (actual material indigence), and assured propertied Christians that, so long as they cultivated the former, they need never submit to the latter. And throughout Christian history, even among the few who bothered to consult scripture on the matter, this has generally been the tacit interpretation of Christ's (and Paul's and James's) condemnations of the wealthy and acquisitive. In the early modern period, moreover, for obvious reasons, forms of Christianity took shape that were especially well suited to the needs of an emerging prosperous middle class, and to the spiritual complacency that a culture of increasing material security dearly required of its religion. For this vision of the gospel, all moral anxiety became a kind of spiritual pathology, the heresy of "works-righteousness," sheer Pelagianism. Grace had set humanity free not only from works of the Law, but also from the spiritual agony of seeking to become holy by moral deeds. In a sense, the good news announced by scripture was that Christ had come to save humanity from the burden of Christianity.

Or so, at any rate, "our" version of Christianity might have seemed in the eyes of the very first Christians. None of which is to deny the cultural genius of, say, early modern Christianity's sanctification of the ordinary or the countless ways in which it allows for an appreciation of the moral heroism of the everyday. But if, as may be the case, such a vision of Christian life is a genuine unfolding of some logic implicit in the gospel, it was nonetheless a logic largely invisible to those who wrote the Christian scriptures. Again, the New Testament knows very little of common sense. The Gospels, the epistles, Acts, Revelation—all of them are relentless torrents of exorbitance and extremism: commands to become as perfect as God in his heaven and to live as insouciantly as the lilies in their field; condemnations of a roving eye as equivalent to adultery and of evil thoughts toward another as equivalent to murder; injunctions to sell all one's possessions and to give the proceeds to the poor, and demands that one hate one's parents for the Kingdom's sake and leave the dead to bury the dead. This extremism is not merely an occasional hyperbolic presence in the texts or an infrequent intonation sounded only in their most urgent moments; it is their entire cultural and spiritual atmosphere. The New Testament emerges from a cosmos ruled by malign celestial principalities (conquered by Christ but powerful to the end) and torn between spirit and flesh (the one, according to Paul, longing for God, the other opposing him utterly). There are no comfortable medians in these latitudes, no areas of shade. Everything is cast in the harsh light of a final judgment that is both absolute and terrifyingly imminent. In regard to all these texts, the qualified, moderate, commonsense interpretation is always false.

Without question, there are texts in the New Testament that condemn an idolatrous obsession with wealth, and that might be taken as saying nothing more than that. At least, 1 Timothy 6:17–19 is often cited as an example of this—though (see below) it probably should not be. If one confines oneself to such passages, it is possible to imagine that the earliest church thought it sufficient, in order to avoid trying to serve both God and Mammon, simply to have the right *attitude* toward riches. But, if this really were all the New Testament had to say on the matter, then one would expect those texts to be balanced out by others affirming the essential benignity of riches honestly procured and well used. And this is precisely what one does not find. Instead, they are balanced out by still more uncompromising comminations of wealth *in and of itself*. Certainly Christ condemned not only an unhealthy preoccupation with riches, but rather the getting and keeping of riches as such. The most obvious citation from all three synoptic Gospels would be the story of the rich young ruler who could not bring himself to part with his fortune for the sake of the Kingdom, and of Christ's astonishing remark about camels passing more easily through needles' eyes than rich men through the Kingdom's gate. As for the question the disciples then put to Christ, it should probably be translated not as "Who then can be saved?" or "Can anyone be saved?" but rather "Then can any [of them, the rich] be saved?" To which the sobering reply is that it is humanly impossible, but that by divine power *even* a rich man might be spared. But one can look everywhere in the Gospels for confirmation of the message. Christ clearly means what he says when quoting the prophet: He has been anointed by God's Spirit to preach good tidings *to the poor* (Luke 4:18). To the prosperous, the tidings he bears are decidedly grim: "But alas for you who are rich, for you have your comfort. Alas for you who are now replete, for you will be hungry. Alas for those now laughing, for you will mourn and lament" (Luke 6:24–25). As Abraham tells Dives in Hades, "You received your good things during your life . . . and now . . . you are in torment" (Luke 16:25). Again, perhaps many of the practices Christ condemns in the rulers of his time are merely misuses of power and property; but that does not begin to exhaust the rhetorical force of his teachings as a whole. He not only demands that his followers give freely to all who ask from them (Matthew 5:42), and to do so with such prodigality that one hand is ignorant of the other's largesse (Matthew 6:3); he explicitly *forbids* storing up earthly wealth— not merely storing it up too obsessively—and allows instead only the hoarding of the treasures of heaven (Matthew 6:19–20). He tells all who would follow him (as he tells the rich young ruler) to sell all their possessions and give the proceeds away as alms, thereby supplying that same heavenly treasury (Luke 12:33), and explicitly states that "no one of you who does not bid farewell to all his own possessions can be my disciple" (Luke 14:33). It is truly amazing how rarely Christians seem to notice that these counsels are stated, quite decidedly, as commands. Certainly the texts are not in any way unclear on the matter. After all, as Mary says, part of the saving promise of the gospel is that the Lord "has filled the hungry with good things and sent the rich away empty" (Luke 1:53).

Of the compilation of pericopes, however, there is no end. What is most important to recognize is that all these pronouncements on wealth and poverty belong to a moral sensibility that saturates the pages of the New Testament. It is there, for instance, in the epistles' condemnations of πλεονέξια (*pleonexia*) (often translated as "greed" but really meaning all acquisitive desire), and in the Pastoral Epistles' condemnation of αἰσχροκερδής (*aischrokerdēs*) (often translated as "greed for base gain" but really referring to the sordidness of seeking financial profit for oneself). James perhaps states the matter most clearly: "Come now, you who are rich, weep, howling out at the miseries that are coming for you: Your riches have spoiled and your garments have become moth-eaten; Your gold and silver have corroded, and their corrosion will serve as testimony against you and will eat your flesh like fire. You have kept treasure in the last days. Look: The wages of the workers who have reaped your lands, which have been unfairly held back by you, clamor aloud, and the outcries of those who have reaped have entered the ears of the Lord Sabaoth. You lived on the earth in dainty luxury and self-indulgence. You have gorged your hearts on a day of slaughter. You have condemned—have murdered—the upright man; he does not oppose you" (James 5:1-6). Now, perhaps we can read this as a dire warning issued only to those wealthy persons who have acted unjustly toward their employees and who live *too* self-indulgently. But the rest of the letter does not encourage us to do so. Earlier in the epistle, James has already asserted that, while the "poor brother" should exult in how God has lifted him up, the "rich man" (who, it seems, scarcely merits the name of "brother") should rejoice in being "made low" or "impoverished," as otherwise he will wither and vanish away like a wildflower scorched by the sun (1:9–11). He has also gone on to remind his readers that God has "chosen the destitute within the cosmos, as rich in faithfulness and as heirs of the Kingdom he has promised to those who love him," while the rich, by contrast, must be recognized as oppressors and persecutors and blasphemers of Christ's holy name (2:5–7). And this constant leitmotif merely swells to a crescendo and reaches a climax in those later verses quoted above, which plainly condemn not only those whose wealth is gotten unjustly, but all who are rich as oppressors of workers and lovers of luxury. It is almost as if, seen from the perspective of the Kingdom, all property is theft. Fair or not, the text does not distinguish good wealth from bad—any more than Christ did.

This, in all likelihood, explains why the early Christians were (in the strictly technical sense) communists, as the book of Acts quite explicitly states. If these are indeed the Last Days, as James says—if everything is now seen in the light of final judgment—then storing up possessions for ourselves is the height of imprudence. And I imagine this is also why subsequent generations of Christians have *not*, as a rule, been communists: the Last Days in fact are taking quite some time to elapse, and we have families to raise in the meantime. But at the dawn of the faith little thought was given to providing a decent life in this world for the long term. Thus we are told the first converts in Jerusalem after the resurrection, as the price of becoming Christians, sold all their property and possessions and distributed the proceeds to those in need, and then fed themselves by sharing their resources in common meals (Acts 2:43–46). Barnabas, on becoming a Christian, sold his field and handed over all the money to the Apostles (Acts 4:35)—though Ananias and Sapphira did not follow suit, with somewhat unfortunate consequences. To be a follower of "The Way" was to renounce every claim to private property and to consent to communal ownership of everything (Acts 4:32).

Even those verses from 1 Timothy 6 that I mentioned above are not nearly as mild and moderate as they might seem at first glance. Earlier in the chapter, the text reminds Christians that they bring nothing into this world and can take nothing with them when they leave it, and tells them to content themselves simply with having enough food and clothing. It also tells them that all who seek wealth—not simply all who procure it unjustly—have ensnared themselves in desires that will lead to their ruin: "For the love of money is a root of all evils, in reaching out for which some have wandered from the faith and pierced themselves about with many pains" (6:7–10). True, verse 17 merely advises the rich not to be "arrogant" or "in high spirits" (depending on how one interprets it), and not to put their trust in wealth's "uncertainty" (or, better, in "the hiddenness" of their riches) rather than in the lavishness of God's providence. But verse 18 goes further and tells them not only to make themselves rich in good works, but also to become— well, here the customary translations are along the lines of "generous" (εὐμεταδότους [evmetadotous]) and "sharing" (κοινωνικούς [koinōnikous]), but the better renderings would be something like "persons readily distributing" their goods, in the former case, and something like "communalists" or "persons having all their possessions in common," in the latter. (A property that is *koinōnikon* is something held in common or corporately, and therefore a person who is *koinōnikos* is certainly not just someone who occasionally makes donations at his own discretion.) Only thus, says verse 19, can the wealthy now "store up" a good foundation for the age that is coming, and reach out to take hold of "the life that is real." And this would seem to have been the social philosophy of the early church in general. When Christianity arrived in Edessa (to take a very local but very revealing case, more or less at random), its adherents promptly became a kind of mendicant order, apparently owning nothing much at all. In the words of that very early manual of Christian life, *The Didache*, a Christian must never claim that anything is his own property, but must own all things *communally* with his brethren (4:9–12).

In any event, however Christians might be disposed to take such verses today, and regardless of whether they reflect the actual social situation—rather than the professed ideals—of the early church, one cannot begin to understand the earliest Christians or the texts they wrote if one imagines that such language was intended as mere bracing hyperbole. Throughout the history of the church, Christians have keenly desired to believe that the New Testament affirms the kind of people they are, rather than—as is actually the case—the kind of people they are not, and really would not want to be. Again, the first, perhaps most crucial thing to understand about the earliest generations of Christians is that theirs was an association of extremists, radical in its rejection of the values and priorities of society not only at its most degenerate, but often at its most reasonable and decent also. They were rabble. They lightly cast off all their prior loyalties and attachments: religion, empire, nation, tribe, even family. In fact, far from teaching "family values," Christ was remarkably dismissive of the family. And decent civic order, like social respectability, was apparently of no importance to him. Not only did he not promise his followers worldly success (even success in making things better for others); he told them to hope for a Kingdom not of this world, and promised them that in this world they would win only rejection, persecution, tribulation, and failure. Yet he instructed them also to take no thought for the morrow. And this apparently was the pattern of life the earliest Christians believed had been given them by Christ to live out. As I say, I doubt we would think highly of their kind if we met them today. Then again, those who have tried to be like them have always been few. Clement of Alexandria may have been making an honest attempt to accommodate the gospel to the realities of a Christian empire, but it was those other Egyptians, the Desert Fathers, who took the gospel at its word. But, as a rule, very few can live like that, or can imitate that obstinacy and perversity. To live as the New Testament language really requires, Christians would have to become strangers and sojourners on the earth, to have here no enduring city, to belong to a Kingdom truly not of this world. And we surely cannot do that, can we?

Remarks on the Greek Text and on My Footnotes

There is no single definitive text of the New Testament canon. Among the oldest manuscripts we have, no text in the New Testament, nor any complete collection of New Testament texts, wholly agrees with every other version. Among the oldest renditions of its various books there are numerous differences, mostly quite small, but occasionally quite significant. This presents a problem for the literalist believer in "verbal inspiration"; for, if indeed an absolutely *pure* text of scripture somewhere exists, we have no notion whatsoever where it is to be found. That sort of textual fundamentalism, however, is very much a late modern phenomenon; during the first several centuries of the church, it was widely known that there was a great variety of differing versions of biblical texts, and this seemed to perturb no one very much. In fact, it was many centuries before what we regard as the New Testament canon gained universal acceptance; in many places, books we do not now tend to regard as canonical were treated as sacred scripture, while other books that we assume to be part of Christian scripture were either unknown or rejected as dubious. That said, there is (or was) what came to be a sort of generally identifiable standard version of the New Testament in the West that (borrowing the term advanced by Erasmus, in his decidedly synthetic edition) is called the *textus receptus;* this, in turn, is derived from what is called the Byzantine Text-type, or Majority Text, of the New Testament, the version more or less exclusively reproduced from the ninth century onward in the East, but poorly represented among earlier manuscripts; and it is upon this "received text" that most older traditional translations are based. But not only does this version, to the extent it can be isolated, differ in various places from other, often more ancient and better-attested Greek versions (such as those belonging to the Alexandrian Text-type); even among the various iterations of the "received" version there are numerous differences, some occasionally seriously affecting how a passage is to be understood. And, in many places, it seems more than reasonable to conclude that the Byzantine type incorporates certain conscious alterations of the text, sometimes simply to improve the quality and grammar of its Greek, sometimes more nearly to harmonize the language of its synoptic Gospels, and sometimes discreetly to burnish away an irksome flaw from its surface (such as the accidental ascription to Isaiah of a quotation from Malachi in Mark 1:2, an error found in all earlier forms of the Gospel).

For this translation I have worked from the so-called Critical Text, which is based on earlier and different manuscript sources (such as those of the Alexandrian Text-type), though I have also included many verses and phrases found only in the Majority Text (placing them in brackets to set them off from the Critical Text). Even here, I should note, each of these versions exists in differing forms, and I have accorded none of them absolute authority. In the course of my work, though taking the most recent scholarship on the Critical Text as my guide, I consulted editions going as far back as the edition of Hort and Westcott from 1881 and as far forward as the current editions of the Nestle-Aland *Novum Testamentum Graece* (currently in its twenty-eighth edition) and *The Greek New Testament* of the United Bible Societies (currently in its fifth edition), as well as various reproductions of ancient manuscripts (to the degree that my meager palaeographic skills allowed). Where I found evidence of interesting textual variants, I recorded the fact in my footnotes. For the bracketed materials from the Majority Text, I consulted both *The New Testament in the Original Greek According to the Byzantine/Majority Textform* of Maurice A. Robinson and William G. Pierpont, and *The Greek New Testament According to the Majority Text* edited by Zane C. Hodges and Arthur L. Farstad; but ultimately I relied on the official Patriarchal Text of the Greek Orthodox Church from 1904, as it seems to me the most representative of the Majority tradition. I have also enclosed a few other dubious words or passages within brackets in my translation, even if they appear in both the Critical and Majority Texts, to indicate where to my mind the most credible critical consensus identifies an interpolation; in each significant case, I explain my decision in a footnote. The result is that my version agrees with no other scholarly or devotional version perfectly, and that it—like every other, alas—is an attempt at an approximation to an ideal version of the text that in actuality we shall never be able to identify entirely.

As for my footnotes in general, they are not meant to provide anything like an exhaustive critical apparatus of the sort that would please or impress a New Testament scholar. They are meant simply to advance my larger project of attempting to give readers with little or no Greek, and limited or no knowledge of late antique culture, as much access to the original text as possible. For the most part, my notes merely call attention to uncertainties in the text, or in my translation thereof, or explain references or idioms with which a modern reader is unlikely to be familiar. In a very few instances, in Romans in particular, where the complexity of the text and the influence of later tradition have conspired to make the original especially difficult to follow, I have tried to clarify the argument on the page by providing something like a paraphrase in my notes. On the whole, though, my notes should be taken as nothing more than useful information for those who might find some use for it; they do not begin to represent all that might (or should) be said about any of these texts.

THE NEW TESTAMENT

The Gospel
According to Matthew

¹The record of the lineage of Jesus the Anointed, son of David, son of Abraham:

²Abraham sired Isaac, and Isaac sired Jacob, and Jacob sired Judah and his brothers; ³And Judah, by Tamar, sired Perez and Zarah, and Perez sired Hezron, and Hezron sired Ram; ⁴And Ram sired Amminadab, and Amminadab sired Nahshon, and Nahshon sired Salmon; ⁵And Salmon, by Rahab, sired Boaz; and Boaz, by Ruth, sired Obed; and Obed sired Jesse; ⁶And Jesse sired King David. David, by Uriah's wife, sired Solomon; ⁷And Solomon sired Rehoboam, and Rehoboam sired Abijah, and Abijah sired Asa; ⁸And Asa sired Jehosaphat, and Jehosaphat sired Joram, and Joram sired Uzziah; ⁹And Uzziah sired Jotham, and Jotham sired Ahaz, and Ahaz sired Hezekiah; ¹⁰And Hezekiah sired Manasseh, and Manasseh sired Amos, and Amos sired Josiah; ¹¹And Josiah sired Jeconiah and his brothers, in the time of the removal to Babylon. ¹²And, after the removal to Babylon, Jeconiah sired Salathiel, and Salathiel sired Zerubbabel; ¹³And Zerubbabel sired Abiud, and Abiud sired Eliakim, and Eliakim sired Azor; ¹⁴And Azor sired Zadok, and Zadok sired Achim, and Achim sired Eliud; ¹⁵And Eliud sired Eleazar, and Eleazar sired Matthan, and Matthan sired Jacob; ¹⁶And Jacob sired Joseph the husband of Mary, from whom was born Jesus, called the Anointed. ¹⁷Thus there were in all fourteen genera-

tions from Abraham to David, and fourteen generations from David to the removal to Babylon, and fourteen generations from the removal to Babylon to the Anointed.

[18]Now the manner of the birth of Jesus the Anointed was this: His mother Mary was betrothed to Joseph but, before they had been joined, she was discovered to be pregnant from a Holy Spirit. [19]And her husband Joseph, being an upright man and not wishing to make a spectacle of her, resolved to divorce her in private. [20]But look: As he was pondering these matters the Lord's angel appeared to him in a dream, saying, "Joseph, son of David, do not fear to receive your wife Mary; for what has been begotten within her is from a Spirit, the Holy one. [21]And she will bear a son, and you shall declare his name to be Jesus, for he will save his people from their sins. [22]All of this has occurred in order that there might be fulfilled what the Lord spoke through the prophet, saying, [23]'See: The virgin shall conceive in her womb and shall bear a son, and they shall declare his name to be Emmanuel'"—which, being interpreted, means "God with us." [24]And Joseph, having arisen from sleep, did as the Lord's angel had bidden him, and received his wife. [25]But he had no intimacy with her until she bore a son. And he declared his name to be Jesus.

CHAPTER TWO

[1]Now, Jesus having been born in Bethlehem of Judaea in the days when Herod was king, look: Magians[a] arrived in Jerusalem from Eastern parts, [2]Saying, "Where is the newborn King of the Judaeans? For we saw his star at its rising,[b] and came to make obeisance to him."[c]

a. μάγοι (magoi): either "Magians" (men of the Zoroastrian priestly caste of the Persians and Medes, largely associated in the Hellenistic mind with oneiromancy and astrology) or "sorcerers" (in later usage, but obviously not here); it is a word that never merely means "wise" or "learned" men.

b. ἐν τῇ ἀνατολῇ (en tē₁ anatolē₁): perhaps "in the East," but the construction would be unusual.

c. προσκυνῆσαι (proskynēsai): "make obeisance," "prostrate oneself," "bow

³And, hearing this, King Herod was perturbed, and so was all of Jerusalem along with him; ⁴And, having assembled all of the chief priests and scribes of the people, he inquired of them where the Anointed is to be born. ⁵And they said to him, "In Bethlehem of Judaea, for so it has been written by the prophet: ⁶'And you, Bethlehem, land of Judah, are by no means least among the leaders of Judah. For from you will come forth a leader who will shepherd my people Israel.'"

⁷Then Herod, secretly summoning the Magians, ascertained from them the exact time of the star's appearance ⁸And, sending them to Bethlehem, said, "Go and inquire very precisely after the child; and when you find him send word to me, so that I too may come and make my obeisance to him." ⁹And, obeying the king, they departed. And look: The star, which they saw at its rising, preceded them until it came to the place where the child was and stood still above it. ¹⁰And, seeing the star, they were exultantly joyful. ¹¹And, entering the house, they saw the child with his mother Mary and, falling down, made obeisance to him; and, opening their treasure caskets, they proffered him gifts: gold and frankincense and myrrh. ¹²Having been warned in a dream not to return to Herod, however, they departed for their own country by another path.

¹³And when they had departed, look: The Lord's angel appears in a dream to Joseph, saying, "Awaken, and take the child and his mother and flee into Egypt, and remain there till such time as I might speak to you; for Herod intends to seek out the child in order to destroy him." ¹⁴And, waking, he took the child and his mother in the night and departed into Egypt, ¹⁵And was there until Herod's death, in order that there might be fulfilled what the Lord spoke through the prophet, saying, "I have called my son out of Egypt."

¹⁶Then Herod, seeing that he had been made a fool by the Magians, was furious and, dispatching men, he destroyed all the male children in

---

down before," "fall down in adoration"; the classic Eastern gesture of abasement before a superior, originally a kiss of reverence.

Bethlehem and all its environs, two years old and younger, in accord with the time he had so exactly ascertained from the Magi. [17]Then was fulfilled what was spoken by the prophet Jeremiah when he said, [18]"A voice was heard in Rama, a weeping and a great lamentation: Rachel weeping for her children; and she would not be comforted, because they are no more."

[19]But when Herod had died, look: The Lord's angel appears in a dream to Joseph in Egypt, [20]Saying, "Awaken, and take the child and his mother, and go into the land of Israel; for those who sought the child's soul[d] have died." [21]And, waking, he took the child and his mother and entered into the land of Israel. [22]Hearing, however, that Archelaus now reigns over Judaea in place of his father Herod, he was afraid to go there; and, being warned in a dream, he departed into the territories of Galilee, [23]And on arriving took up his dwelling in a city called Nazareth; thus was fulfilled what was spoken by the prophet: that "He shall be called a Nazorean."

CHAPTER THREE

[1]Now in those days comes John the Baptist, making his proclamation in the wilderness of Judaea, [2]Saying, "Change your hearts; for the Kingdom of the heavens has drawn near." [3]For this is the one spoken of by the prophet Isaiah when he said, "A voice of one crying out in the wilderness: 'Prepare the Lord's way, make straight his paths.'" [4]Now this man John had on a garment made from the hairs of a camel, as well as a leather girdle about his loins; and his food was locusts and wild honey. [5]At that time Jerusalem went out to him, and all of Judaea and all of the countryside surrounding the Jordan, [6]And they were baptized by him in the River Jordan, confessing their sins. [7]But seeing many of the Pharisees and Sadducees coming to baptism he said to them, "Brood of vipers, who divulged to you that you should flee from the wrath that

---

d. ψυχή (*psychē*): "soul," "life," "principle of life."

4

is coming? [8]Bear fruit worthy of a change of heart; [9]And do not think to say among yourselves, 'We have Abraham as father'; for I tell you that God has the power to raise up children to Abraham from these stones. [10]And even now the axe is laid to the root of the trees; and thus every tree not bearing good fruit is felled and thrown into fire. [11]I indeed baptize you in water for the sake of transforming hearts; but the one coming after me is mightier than I, whose sandals I am not fit to carry; he will baptize you in a Holy Spirit and fire: [12]He whose winnow is in his hand, and he will thoroughly purge his threshing floor, and will gather his grain into the storehouse, and will burn away the chaff with inextinguishable fire."

[13]Then Jesus arrives at the Jordan, coming from Galilee to John to be baptized by him. [14]But he prevented him, saying, "I need to be baptized by you, yet you come to me?" [15]But in reply Jesus said to him, "Let me pass now; for it is necessary for us to fulfill every right requirement." Then he lets him pass. [16]And, having been baptized, Jesus immediately rose up out of the water; and look: The heavens were opened, and he saw God's Spirit descending as a dove, alighting upon him; [17]And look: a voice out of the heavens, saying, "This is my Son, the beloved, in whom I have delighted."

CHAPTER FOUR

[1]Then Jesus was led up into the wilderness by the Spirit to be tried by the Slanderer. [2]And, having fasted for forty days and forty nights, he was hungry. [3]And, drawing near, the Tempter said to him, "If you are God's Son, command that these stones become loaves of bread." [4]He, however, answered by saying, "It has been written, 'The human being shall live not upon bread alone, but upon every utterance issuing from the mouth of God.'" [5]Then the Slanderer carries him off into the Holy City, and stood him upon the pinnacle of the Temple, [6]And says to him, "If you are God's Son, cast yourself down; for it has been written that 'He will command his angels concerning you' and that 'They will catch

you in their hands, that you may not strike your foot against a stone.'"
⁷"Conversely," said Jesus to him, "it has been written, 'You shall not put
the Lord your God to the test.'" ⁸Again the Slanderer carries him off, to
an extremely high mountain, and displays before him all the kingdoms
of the world and their glory, ⁹And said to him, "All of these things I shall
give to you, were you to prostrate yourself and make obeisance to me."
¹⁰Then Jesus says to him, "Be gone, Accuser:ᵉ for it has been written,
'You shall make obeisance to the Lord your God and him only shall you
adore.'" ¹¹Then the Slanderer leaves him alone, and look: Angels arrived
and ministered to him.

¹²Now, hearing that John had been handed over, he withdrew into
Galilee. ¹³And, departing from Nazareth, he came and took up his
dwelling in Capernaum beside the sea, in the territories of Zebulon
and Naphthali: ¹⁴So that there might be fulfilled what was spoken by
Isaiah the Prophet, saying, ¹⁵"Land of Zebulon and land of Naphthali,
sea road, beyond the Jordan, Galilee of the nations, ¹⁶The people sitting
in darkness saw a great light, and light dawned upon those sitting in the
region and shadow of death."

¹⁷From that time Jesus began to make his proclamation and to say,
"Change your hearts; for the Kingdom of the heavens has drawn near."

¹⁸And, walking beside the Sea of Galilee, he saw two brothers,
Simon (called Peter) and his brother Andrew, casting a net into the sea;
for they were fishermen. ¹⁹And he says to them, "Come follow me and
I shall make you fishers of men." ²⁰And, immediately abandoning the
nets, they followed him. ²¹And, going on from there, he saw another
pair of brothers, James the son of Zebedee and his brother John, mending their nets in the boat with their father Zebedee; and he summoned
them. ²²And, immediately abandoning the boat and their father, they
followed him.

²³And he went about in the whole of Galilee, teaching in their synagogues and proclaiming the good tidings of the Kingdom and healing

e. "Satan," which is to say, "prosecutor," "accuser," "arraigner."

every illness and every infirmity among the people. ²⁴And word of him went out into the whole of Syria. And they brought to him all those who were very sick, suffering from complicated illnesses and enduring torments, demoniacs and lunatics and paralytics, and he healed them. ²⁵And large crowds followed him from Galilee and Decapolis and Jerusalem and Judaea and from beyond the Jordan.

CHAPTER FIVE

¹Now, seeing the crowds, he ascended the mountain; and when he seated himself his disciples approached him; ²And opening his mouth he taught them, saying: ³"How blissfulᶠ the destitute, abjectᵍ in spirit, for theirs is the Kingdom of the heavens; ⁴How blissful those who mourn, for they shall be aided; ⁵How blissful the gentle, for they shall inherit the earth; ⁶How blissful those who hunger and thirst for what is right, for they shall feast; ⁷How blissful the merciful, for they shall receive mercy; ⁸How blissful the pure in heart, for they shall see God; ⁹How blissful the peacemakers, for they shall be called sons of God; ¹⁰How blissful those who have been persecuted for the sake of what is right, for theirs is the Kingdom of the heavens; ¹¹How blissful you when they reproach you, and persecute you and falsely accuse you of every evil for my sake: ¹²Rejoice and be glad, for your reward in the heavens is great; for thus they persecuted the prophets before you.

¹³"You are the salt of the earth; but if the salt should become insipid, by what shall it be made salty? It is no longer of any use except to scatter outside for people to tread upon. ¹⁴You are the light of the world. A city set upon a hill cannot be hidden; ¹⁵Neither do they light a lamp and place it under the dry-goods basket, but rather they place it upon a lampstand, and it illumines all who are in the house. ¹⁶So let your light

f. μακάριος (*makarios*): "blessed," "happy," "fortunate," "prosperous," but originally with a connotation of divine or heavenly bliss.

g. A πτωχός (*ptōchos*) is a poor man or beggar, but with the connotation of one who is abject: cowering or cringing.

shine out before humanity, so that they may see your good works and may glorify your Father in the heavens.

[17]"Do not think that I came to destroy the Law and the prophets; I came not to destroy but to fulfill. [18]For, amen, I tell you, until heaven and earth shall pass away, not a single iota or single serif must vanish from the Law, until all things come to pass. [19]Whoever breaks one of the least of the commandments and teaches people to do likewise shall be called least in the Kingdom of the heavens; but whoever performs and teaches it, this one shall be called great in the Kingdom of the heavens. [20]For I tell you that, unless your uprightness surpass that of the Scribes and Pharisees, you shall not enter into the Kingdom of the heavens.

[21]"You have heard that it was said to those of ancient times: 'You shall not commit murder; and whoever commits murder shall be liable to judgment.' [22]Whereas I say to you that everyone who becomes angry with his brother shall be liable to judgment; and whoever says '*Raka*'[h] to his brother shall be liable to the Council; and whoever says 'worthless reprobate'[i] shall be liable to enter Hinnom's Vale of fire. [23]If, therefore, you bring your gift to the altar and there recall that your brother holds something against you, [24]Leave your gift in front of the altar, and first go and be reconciled with your brother, and then come and offer your gift. [25]Be quick to show good will to the plaintiff against you, while you are out in the street with him, lest that plaintiff deliver you to the judge, and the judge to the guard, and you are thrown into prison. [26]Amen, I tell you, you shall most certainly not emerge from there until you repay the very last pittance.

[27]"You have heard it said, 'You shall not commit adultery.' [28]Whereas I tell you that everyone looking at a married woman[j] in order to lust

---

h. ῥακά (ᵇraka): an Aramaic word meaning "foolish," "empty," "of no account," "worthless."

i. μωρός (mōros): "foolish," "insipid," "dull," "of no account"; occasionally with the connotation of low and deplorable character.

j. γυνή (gynē): "woman" (as distinct from "maiden," "virgin"), "wife." Here

after her has already committed adultery with her in his heart. [29]So if your right eye causes you to falter remove it and fling it away from you; for it is expedient for you that one of your members should perish, rather than that your whole body should be thrown into the Vale of Hinnom. [30]And, if your right hand causes you to falter, cut it off and fling it away from you; for it is expedient for you that one of your members should perish, rather than that your whole body should depart into the Vale of Hinnom. [31]Moreover, it has been said, 'Whoever divorces his wife, he must provide her with a writ of separation.' [32]Whereas I tell you that everyone who divorces his wife, except in cases of whorishness, causes her to commit adultery, and whoever weds a divorced woman commits adultery. [33]Again, you have heard that it was said to those of ancient times, 'You shall not swear oaths falsely,' and 'You shall render up to the Lord what your oaths are sworn upon.' [34]Whereas I tell you not to swear at all: neither by heaven, inasmuch as it is God's throne; [35]Nor by the earth, inasmuch as it is the footstool of his feet; nor by Jerusalem, inasmuch as it is the Great King's city; [36]—Neither swear by your own head, inasmuch as you cannot make a single hair white or black. [37]Rather, let your utterance be 'Yes, yes,' 'No, no'; because it is from the roguish man that anything more extravagant than this comes. [38]You have heard that it was said, 'An eye for an eye and a tooth for a tooth.' [39]Whereas I tell you not to oppose the wicked man by force; rather, whosoever strikes you upon the right cheek, turn to him the other as well; [40]And to him who wishes to bring a judgment against you, so he may take away your tunic, give him your cloak as well; [41]And whoever presses you into service for one mile, go with him for two. [42]Give to the one who begs from you, and do not turn away from one who wishes to borrow from you. [43]You have heard that it has been said, 'You shall love your neighbor and shall hate your enemy'— [44]Whereas I tell you, love your enemies and pray for those who persecute you; [45]In

---

the topic is clearly a man who wishes to violate the marriage covenant of another man's wife.

this way you may become sons of your Father in the heavens, for he makes his sun to rise on the wicked and the good, and sends rain upon the just and the unjust. ⁴⁶For if you love only those who love you, what recompense do you have? Do not even the tax-collectors do the same? ⁴⁷And if you greet only your brothers, what are you doing that is extraordinary? Do not even the gentiles do the same? ⁴⁸So be perfect, as your Heavenly Father is perfect.

CHAPTER SIX

¹"And make certain not to practice your righteousness before men, in order to be watched by them; otherwise you have no recompense with your Father in the heavens. ²When you give alms, therefore, do not trumpet it aloud before you, as those who are playacting do in the synagogues and in the streets so they may be lauded by men; amen, I tell you, they have their recompense in full. ³But when you are giving alms do not allow your left hand to know what it is your right hand does, ⁴So that your almsgiving is in secret. And your Father, who watches what is secret, will reward you. ⁵And when you pray do not be like those who are playacting; for they love to pray while standing in the synagogues and on the corners of streets, so that they may be visible to men; I tell you truly, they have their recompense in full. ⁶But, when you pray, enter into your private room and, having closed your door, pray to your Father who is in secret; and your Father, who watches what is secret, will reward you. ⁷And when praying do not babble repetitious phrases as the gentiles do; for they imagine that they will be listened to by virtue of their prolixity. ⁸So do not be like them; for your Father knows what you need before you ask him. ⁹Therefore, pray in this way: 'Our Father, who are in the heavens, let your name be held holy; ¹⁰Let your Kingdom come; let your will come to pass, as in heaven so also upon earth; ¹¹Give to us today bread for the day ahead; ¹²And excuse us our debts, just as we have excused our debtors; ¹³And do not bring us to trial, but rescue us from him who is wicked. [For yours is the Kingdom and the power and

the glory unto the ages.]' ¹⁴For, if you forgive men their offenses, your heavenly Father will also forgive you; ¹⁵But if you should not forgive men, neither shall your Father forgive your offenses. ¹⁶And when you fast do not adopt a sullen countenance, as do those who are playacting; for they disfigure their faces so that it is apparent to men that they are fasting; amen, I tell you, they have their recompense in full. ¹⁷But when you fast anoint your head and wash your face, ¹⁸So that you show yourself to be fasting not to men, but rather to your Father who is in secret; and your Father, who watches what is secret, will reward you.

¹⁹"Do not store up treasures for yourself on the earth, where moth and rust destroy, and where thieves penetrate by digging and steal; ²⁰Rather, store up for yourself treasure in heaven, where neither moth nor rust destroys, and where thieves neither penetrate by digging nor steal; ²¹For where your treasure is, there your heart will also be. ²²The lamp of the body is the eye. Thus if your eye be pure your entire body will be radiant; ²³But if your eye be baleful your entire body will be dark. So if the light within you is darkness, how very great the darkness. ²⁴No one can be a slave to two lords; for either he will hate the one and love the other, or he will stand fast by the one and disdain the other. You cannot be a slave both to God and to Mammon. ²⁵Therefore I say to you: Do not worry, regarding your soul, what you will eat; nor, regarding your body, what you will wear. Is not your soul more than food and your body more than garments? ²⁶See the birds of the sky—that they neither sow nor reap nor gather into granaries; and your heavenly Father feeds them; are you not more excellent than they? ²⁷But who among you can, by worrying, lengthen the span of his life by a single cubit? ²⁸And why do you worry over clothing? Look closely at the lilies of the field—how they grow; they neither labor nor spin; ²⁹Yet I tell you that not even Solomon in all his glory was garbed like one of them. ³⁰But if God thus clothes the grass of the field, which exists for today and is thrown into an oven tomorrow, will he not much more clothe you, men of little faith? ³¹So do not worry, saying, 'What might we eat?' or 'What might we drink?' or 'What might we wear?' ³²For the gen-

tile peoples seek after all these things—for your heavenly Father knows that you have need of all these things. ³³But first seek his Kingdom and his justice, and all of these things shall be supplied to you. ³⁴So do not worry about tomorrow, for tomorrow will worry about itself; each day has evil enough of its own.

CHAPTER SEVEN

¹"Judge not, that you may not be judged; ²For by whatever verdict you pass judgment you shall be judged, and in whatever measure you measure it shall be meted out to you. ³And why do you look at the straw in your brother's eye, yet do not perceive the beam in your own eye? ⁴How is it that you will say to your brother, 'Let me take that straw out of your eye,' and look: The beam is in your eye? ⁵Charlatan, first pluck the beam out of your eye, and then you will see clearly how to pluck the straw out of your brother's eye. ⁶Do not give what is holy to the dogs, neither cast your pearls before swine, lest they trample them with their feet and, turning, shatter you. ⁷Ask, and it shall be given to you; seek, and you shall find; knock, and it shall be opened to you. ⁸For everyone who asks receives, and everyone who seeks finds, and to everyone who knocks it shall be opened. ⁹Or is it not the case that no man among you, if his son should ask for a loaf of bread, would give him a stone? ¹⁰Or, if he should also ask for a fish, would give him a serpent? ¹¹If you, therefore, who are wicked, know to give good gifts to your children, how much more will your Father in the heavens give good things to those who ask him. ¹²Therefore, all such things as you wish men might do to you, so do to them as well; for this is the Law and the prophets.

¹³"Enter through the narrow gate; for the path leading away to destruction is broad and open, and there are many who enter by it; ¹⁴For narrow is the gate and close-cramped the path leading away to life, and those who find it are few. ¹⁵Beware of false prophets, who come to you garbed as sheep, but who are ravenous wolves within. ¹⁶You will know them from their fruits. Persons do not gather grapes from thorns or

figs from thistles, do they? [17]So every good tree produces good fruits, but the diseased tree produces bad fruits. [18]A good tree cannot bear bad fruits, nor can a diseased tree bear good fruits. [19]Every tree not producing good fruit is felled and cast into fire. [20]From their fruits, therefore, you will know them. [21]Not everyone saying 'Lord, Lord' to me will enter into the Kingdom of the heavens, but rather the one doing the will of my Father who is in the heavens. [22]Many will say to me on that day, 'Lord, Lord, did we not prophesy in your name, and exorcize demons in your name, and perform many acts of power in your name?' [23]And then I will declare to them that: 'I never knew you; go away from me, you workers of lawlessness.'

[24]"Everyone, therefore, who hears these sayings of mine and enacts them shall be likened to a prudent man who built his house upon rock. [25]And the rain descended and the rivers flooded in and the winds blew and fell upon that house, and it did not fall; for it had been founded upon rock. [26]And everyone who hears these sayings of mine and does not enact them shall be likened to a foolish man who built his house upon sand. [27]And the rain descended and the rivers flooded in and the winds blew and beat upon that house, and it fell, and its fall was a great one."

[28]And it happened that, when Jesus completed these sayings, the crowds were astounded at his teaching; [29]For he was teaching them like one possessing authority, and not like their scribes.

CHAPTER EIGHT

[1]And at his descent from the mountain large crowds followed him. [2]And look: A leper approached and bowed down to him, saying, "Lord, if you wish, you are able to cleanse me." [3]And stretching out a hand he touched him, saying, "I wish it; be cleansed." And immediately his leprosy was cleansed away. [4]And Jesus says to him, "See to it that you tell no one, but go and show yourself to the priest and offer the gift that Moses commanded, as a testimony to them."

⁵And on his entry into Capernaum a centurion approached him, imploring him ⁶And saying, "Lord, my servant[k] has been laid low in my house, a paralytic, suffering terribly." ⁷He says to him, "I shall come and heal him." ⁸But in reply the centurion said, "Lord, I am not worthy that you should come in under my roof; but only declare it by a word and my servant will be healed. ⁹For I am also a man under authority, having soldiers under me, and to this one I say, 'Go,' and he goes, and to another, 'Come,' and he comes, and to my slave, 'Do this,' and he does it." ¹⁰And, hearing this, Jesus marveled and said to those following him, "Amen, I tell you, I have found no one in Israel with such faith. ¹¹Moreover, I tell you that many will come from East and West and will recline at table alongside Abraham and Isaac and Jacob in the Kingdom of the heavens; ¹²But the sons of the Kingdom will be thrown out into the darkness outside; there will be weeping and grinding of teeth there." ¹³And Jesus said to the centurion, "Go; as you have had faith, so let it come to pass for you." And in that hour the servant was healed.

¹⁴And coming into Peter's house Jesus saw Peter's mother-in-law laid out and in a fever; ¹⁵And he touched her hand and the fever left her; and she arose and waited on him.

¹⁶And when evening arrived they brought to him many who were possessed by demons; and he exorcized the spirits by word, and healed all those who were suffering; ¹⁷Thus was fulfilled what was spoken by the prophet Isaiah when he said, "He took away our infirmities and bore away our maladies."

¹⁸But, seeing a crowd surrounding him, Jesus gave orders to depart, across to the far shore. ¹⁹And one scribe approached and said to him, "Teacher, I will follow you wherever you may go." ²⁰And Jesus says to him, "The foxes have lairs and the birds of the sky have nests, but the Son of Man[l] has no place where he may rest his head." ²¹Then another,

k. παῖς (pais): "child," "boy," "son," "slave," "servant"; here almost certainly the last.

l. Though "son of man" is simply a good Semitic idiom meaning "a man," by the first century it had long served as the name of a mysterious apocalyptic or

one of the disciples, said to him, "Lord, allow me first to go away and bury my father." ²²But Jesus says to him, "Follow me, and leave the dead to bury their dead."

²³And when he embarked into the boat his disciples followed him. ²⁴And look: There was a great upheaval in the sea, so that the boat was enveloped by the waves; but he was asleep. ²⁵And they went to him and roused him, saying, "Lord, save us, we are perishing." ²⁶And he says to them, "Why are you afraid, you of little faith?" Then rising, he rebuked the winds and the sea, and a great calm came about. ²⁷And the men marveled, saying, "What kind of man is this, that even the winds and the sea obey him?" ²⁸And when he had come across to the far shore, into the country of the Gadarenes, two men possessed by demons came out from among the tombs and met him: men so extremely dangerous that no one was strong enough to pass by that road. ²⁹And look: They cried out, saying, "What do we and you have to do with one another, Son of God? Did you come here to torment us before a due season?" ³⁰Now at a good distance from them a herd of many swine was feeding. ³¹And the demons implored him, saying, "If you exorcize us, send us into the herd of swine." ³²And he said to them, "Go." And they came out and went off into the swine; and look: The whole herd charged down the precipice into the sea and died in the waters. ³³Then the herdsmen fled and, going away into the city, reported it all, including the things concerning the demoniacs. ³⁴And look: The whole city came out to meet Jesus and, on seeing him, begged that he might pass on beyond their borders.

CHAPTER NINE

¹And embarking into the boat he made the crossing, and came into his own city. ²And look: They brought to him a paralytic laid out upon

---

eschatological figure (as in the one "like a son of man" who rides in the chariot of God in Ezekiel), and as Christ uses it in the Gospels it should clearly be read as a distinctive prophetic title (even if its precise significance cannot be ascertained).

a pallet. And Jesus, seeing their faith, said to the paralytic, "Take heart, child, your sins are forgiven you." [3]And look: Some of the scribes said among themselves, "This man blasphemes." [4]And Jesus, perceiving their thoughts, said, "Why do you think wicked things in your hearts? [5]For which is easier: to say, 'Your sins are forgiven you,' or to say, 'Rise and walk'? [6]In order, then, that you may know that the Son of Man has power upon earth to forgive sins . . ."—then he says to the paralytic, "Rise, take your pallet, and go to your house." [7]And rising he departed for his house. [8]And seeing this the crowds were frightened and glorified the God who gave such power to human beings. [9]And passing on from there Jesus saw a man named Matthew sitting at the tax-collection house, and says to him, "Follow me." And rising he followed him. [10]And it happened that, as he was reclining at table in the house, look: Many tax-collectors and sinners came and reclined at table with Jesus and his disciples. [11]And, seeing this, the Pharisees said to his disciples, "Why does your teacher eat with tax-collectors and sinners?" [12]But he heard them and said, "The hale do not have need of a physician, but rather those who are ill. [13]Go then and learn what this means: 'I desire mercy and not sacrifice'; for I came to call not the upright, but sinners."

[14]Then the disciples of John approach him, saying, "How is it that we and the Pharisees fast, but your disciples do not fast?" [15]And Jesus said to them, "Can the sons of the bridal chamber mourn so long as the bridegroom is with them? But the days will come when the bridegroom is taken away from them, and then they will fast. [16]And no one puts a patch of unfulled cloth on an old garment; for the filling tears away from the garment and a worse rent appears. [17]Neither do they put new wine in old wineskins; for if they should the wineskins are burst open, and the wine is spilled out, and the wineskins are destroyed. Rather, they put new wine into fresh wineskins, and both are together preserved."

[18]As he was saying these things to them, look: A ruler approached and bowed down to him, saying that: "My daughter has just died; but come and lay your hand on her and she will live." [19]Jesus, rising, fol-

lowed him, and his disciples also. [20]And look: A woman who had been suffering a discharge of blood for twelve years approached from behind and touched the fringe of his mantle; [21]For she was saying within herself, "If I may but touch his mantle, I shall be healed." [22]And, turning and seeing her, Jesus said, "Take heart, daughter; your faith has healed you." And from that hour the woman was healed. [23]And Jesus, coming into the ruler's house and seeing the flute-players and the clamoring crowd, [24]Said, "Go away; for the girl has not died, but is asleep." And they ridiculed him. [25]But, when the crowd was expelled, he went in and took hold of her hand, and the girl was raised. [26]And this story went into all of that land. [27]And, as Jesus passed on from there, two blind men followed, crying out and saying, "Pity us, Son of David." [28]And, when he came into the house, the blind men approached him, and Jesus says to them, "Do you have faith that I am able to do this?" They say to him, "Yes, Lord." [29]Then he touched their eyes, saying, "According to your faith, let it happen to you." [30]And their eyes were opened. And Jesus sternly commanded them, "See you let no one know of this." [31]But when they departed they spread word of him throughout that whole land. [32]And as they were going out, look: They brought a mute demoniac to him. [33]And when the demon was exorcized the mute man spoke. And the crowds marveled, saying, "Never has anything like this been seen in Israel." [34]But the Pharisees said, "He exorcizes demons through the Archon of the demons."

[35]And Jesus went about all the cities and the villages, teaching in their synagogues and announcing the good tidings of the Kingdom and healing every disease and infirmity. [36]And seeing the crowds he was moved inwardly with compassion for them, because they were in distress and cast down, like sheep having no shepherd. [37]Then he says to his disciples, "Indeed the harvest is abundant, but the laborers few; [38]Pray to the Lord of the harvest, therefore, that he may send forth laborers to his harvest."

CHAPTER TEN

¹And, calling to him his twelve disciples, he gave them power: over impure spirits so as to exorcize them, and to heal every disease and every infirmity. ²Now the names of the twelve disciples are these: first Simon, who is called Peter, and Andrew his brother, and James the son of Zebedee and his brother John, ³Philip and bar-Tholomaeus, Thomas and Matthew the tax-collector, James the son of Alphaeus, and Thaddeus, ⁴Simon the Kananaian,^{m} and Judas the Iscariot—the one also betraying him. ⁵These twelve Jesus sent forth, giving them orders, saying:

"Do not go forth on a road of the gentiles, and do not enter into a city of the Samaritans; ⁶Go rather to the lost sheep of the household of Israel. ⁷And preach as you go along, saying that the Kingdom of the heavens has drawn near. ⁸Heal the ailing, raise the dead, cleanse lepers, exorcize demons. You have received a free gift; give a free gift. ⁹Do not provide yourself with gold or silver or brass in your girdles, ¹⁰Nor with a leather pouch for the road, or two tunics, or sandals, or a staff. For the laborer earns his provisions. ¹¹And, whatever city or village you enter into, carefully ascertain who within it is a worthy man, and stay with him until you should depart. ¹²On entering the household, moreover, give it your salutation; ¹³And if indeed the household should be worthy, may your 'Peace'^{n} come upon it; but if it should be unworthy, may your 'Peace' revert back to you. ¹⁴And whoever should not welcome you, or should not listen to your words, on departing outside that household or that city shake the dust off your feet. ¹⁵Amen, I tell you, it will be more tolerable for the land of Sodom and Gomorrah on the day of judgment than for that city. ¹⁶See: I send you forth as sheep into the midst of wolves; so be as wise as serpents and as guileless as doves. ¹⁷And be-

m. An obscure word, probably a Hellenized form of the Aramaic *qannāyā*, "zealot" (a reading confirmed by Luke's Gospel), but some scholars see it as an eccentric form of "Canaanite."

n. The typical form of salutation being to wish peace upon a person or a household.

ware of men; for they will deliver you up to councils, and they will flog you in their synagogues; [18]And you will be led before leaders and even kings for my sake, as a witness to them and to the gentiles. [19]But when they deliver you up do not worry over how or what you might speak; for whatever you might say will be given to you in that hour; [20]For you are not the ones speaking, but rather the Spirit of your Father is speaking in you. [21]And brother will deliver up brother to death, and father child, and children will rise up against parents and put them to death. [22]And you will be hated by all on account of my name; but whosoever endures to the end, that one will be saved. [23]And when they persecute you in one city, flee to another; for, amen, I tell you, you will most certainly not have finished with the cities of Israel before the Son of Man arrives. [24]A disciple is not above his teacher, nor a slave above his lord. [25]It suffices that the disciple become as his teacher, and the slave as his lord. If they have arraigned the master of the household as 'Beelzebul,' how much more so those who belong to his household? [26]Therefore, do not fear them; for there is nothing that has been veiled that will not be unveiled, and nothing hidden that will not be made known. [27]What I say to you in the dark, speak in the light; and what you hear in your ear, proclaim upon the housetops. [28]And do not fear those who kill the body but cannot kill the soul; but rather fear the one who can destroy both soul and body in the Vale of Hinnom. [29]Are not two sparrows sold for the smallest pittance? And not one of them will fall to earth without your Father. [30]But even the hairs of your head have all been numbered. [31]So do not be afraid; you are of greater worth than a great many sparrows. [32]Therefore, everyone who acknowledges me before men, I also will acknowledge him before my Father in the heavens; [33]And whoever denies me before men, I also will deny him before my Father in the heavens. [34]Do not suppose that I have come to impose peace upon the earth; I came to impose not peace but a sword. [35]For I came to divide a man against his father, and a daughter against her mother, and a bride against her mother-in-law — [36]And a man's enemies: the members of his household. [37]Whoever cherishes father or mother more than me is not

19

worthy of me; and whoever cherishes son or daughter more than me is not worthy of me. ³⁸And whoever does not take up his cross and follow after me is not worthy of me. ³⁹Whoever gains his soul will lose it, and whoever loses his soul for my sake will gain it. ⁴⁰Whoever welcomes you welcomes me, and whoever welcomes me welcomes the one who has sent me forth. ⁴¹Whoever welcomes a prophet because he is called prophet will receive a prophet's reward, and whoever welcomes a just man because he is called just will receive a just man's reward. ⁴²And whoever gives one of these humble ones a cup of cold water solely because he is called disciple, amen, I tell you, he most certainly will not lose his reward."

CHAPTER ELEVEN

¹And it happened that when Jesus finished issuing instructions to his twelve disciples, he went from there to teach and to make proclamation in their cities.

²And John in prison heard of the works of the Anointed. Sending word by two of his disciples, ³He said, "Are you he who is coming, or should we expect another?" ⁴And in reply Jesus said to them, "Go and report to John what you hear and see: ⁵The blind see again and the lame walk, lepers are cleansed and the deaf hear, and dead men are raised and the destitute are given the good tidings; ⁶And blissful is he who is not scandalized by me." ⁷And as they were going on Jesus began to speak to the crowds concerning John: "What did you go out into the wilderness to gaze at? A reed being shaken by the wind? ⁸But then what did you go out to see? A man clothed in soft finery? Look: Those clad in soft finery are in the houses of kings. ⁹But then why did you go out? To see a prophet? Yes, I tell you, and much more than a prophet. ¹⁰This is he concerning whom it has been written, 'See: I send forth my messenger°before your face, who will prepare your path before you.' ¹¹Amen, I tell

o. ἄγγελος (angelos), "angel."

you, among those born of women there has not arisen one greater than John the Baptist; but a lesser man, in the Kingdom of the heavens, is greater than he. ¹²Yet from the days of John the Baptist until now, the Kingdom of the heavens has been violently assailed, and the violent seize it. ¹³For all the prophets and the Law, right up to John, prophesied; ¹⁴And—if you are willing to accept this—he is himself Elijah who is destined to come. ¹⁵Whoever has ears, let him listen. ¹⁶But to what shall I liken this generation? It is like children sitting in the marketplace who, accosting the others, ¹⁷Say, 'We played flutes for you and you did not dance; we wailed in lamentation and you did not beat your breasts.' ¹⁸For John came neither eating nor drinking, and they say, 'He has a demon.' ¹⁹The Son of Man came eating and drinking, and they say, 'Look: a gluttonous and wine-besotted man, a friend of tax-collectors and sinners.' And Wisdom has been vindicated by her works."

²⁰Then he began to reproach the cities in which his many feats of power had taken place, because they did not change their hearts: ²¹"Alas for you, Chorazin; alas for you, Bethsaida; because, if the feats of power that have occurred in you had occurred in Tyre and Sidon, they would long ago have changed their hearts, in sackcloth and ashes. ²²But I tell you, it will be more tolerable for Tyre and Sidon on the day of judgment than for you. ²³And you, Capernaum, were you not exalted as far as heaven? You shall descend as far as Hades; because if the feats of power that occurred in you had occurred in Sodom, it would have endured to this day. ²⁴But I tell you that it will be more tolerable for the land of Sodom on the day of judgment than for you."

²⁵At that time, Jesus spoke out and said, "I give you fullest thanks, Father, Lord of heaven and earth, because you hid these things from the wise and sagacious and revealed them to infants; ²⁶Yes, Father, because such was pleasing before you. ²⁷All things were delivered to me by my Father, and no one knows the Son except the Father, and neither does anyone know the Father except the Son and anyone to whom the Son wishes to reveal him. ²⁸Come to me, all who toil and are burdened, and I shall give you rest. ²⁹Take my yoke upon yourselves and learn from me,

because I am gentle and accommodating in heart, and you will find rest for your souls; ³⁰For my yoke is mild and my burden light."

CHAPTER TWELVE

¹At that time, Jesus passed through fields of grain during the Sabbath; and his disciples were hungry, and they began to pluck ears of grain and to eat. ²But the Pharisees saw, and said to him, "Look: Your disciples are doing what it is not lawful to do on the Sabbath." ³And he said to them, "Have you not read what David did when he and his companions were hungry? ⁴How he entered into the house of God and they ate the loaves of bread of presentation, to eat which was not permitted to him, nor to his companions, but only to the priests? ⁵Or have you not read in the Law that during the Sabbath the priests in the Temple profane the Sabbath and are guiltless? ⁶But I tell you that something greater than the Temple is here. ⁷But if you had known the meaning of 'I desire mercy and not sacrifice' you would not have condemned the guiltless. ⁸For the Son of Man is Lord of the Sabbath."

⁹And passing on from there he entered their synagogue. ¹⁰And look: a man with a withered hand; and they questioned him, saying, "Is it lawful to heal during the Sabbath?"—so that they might bring an accusation against him. ¹¹But he said to them, "Will there be one man among you who will own one sheep and, if it should fall into a pit during the Sabbath, he will not take hold of it and raise it out? ¹²How much more than a sheep is a man. So it is permitted to do good during the Sabbath." ¹³Then he says to the man, "Stretch forth your hand." And he stretched it forth, and it was restored, becoming as healthy as the other. ¹⁴But going outside the Pharisees conferred together against him, so that they might destroy him. ¹⁵But Jesus, knowing this, departed from there. And many followed him, and he healed all of them, ¹⁶And warned them that they should not make him known, ¹⁷So that there might be fulfilled what was spoken by the prophet Isaiah when he said, ¹⁸"See

my servant, whom I have chosen, my beloved in whom my soul has delighted; I shall place my Spirit upon him, and he will proclaim judgment to the nations. [19]He will neither fight nor cry out, nor will anyone hear his voice out in the streets. [20]He will not break the bent reed nor quench the smoldering flax, until he should issue his judgment victoriously. [21]And in his name the nations shall have hope."

[22]Then a blind and mute demoniac was brought to him; and he healed him, thus causing the mute man to speak and to see. [23]And all the crowds were astonished and said, "Is not this the son of David?" [24]But hearing this the Pharisees said, "This man does not exorcize demons except by Beelzebul, the Archon of the demons." [25]But, knowing their thoughts, he said to them, "Every kingdom divided against itself is reduced to desolation, and every city or household divided against itself will not stand. [26]And if the Accuser exorcizes the Accuser, he has been divided against himself; how therefore will his kingdom stand? [27]And, if I exorcize demons by Beelzebul, by what do your sons exorcize? Hence they shall be your judges. [28]But if I exorcize the demons by God's Spirit, then the Kingdom of God has overtaken you. [29]Or how can anyone enter the strong man's house and steal his possessions if he does not first tie the strong man up? And then he can plunder his household. [30]Whoever is not with me is against me, and whoever does not gather together with me scatters. [31]Hence I tell you, every sin and blasphemy will be excused men, but the blasphemy of the Spirit will not be excused. [32]And whoever speaks a word against the Son of Man, it will be excused him; but whoever speaks against the Spirit, the Holy one, it will not be excused him, neither in this age nor in the one that is coming. [33]Either make out the tree to be good and its fruit good, or make out the tree to be rotten and its fruit rotten; for the tree is known by the fruit. [34]You brood of vipers, how can you, being wicked, speak of good things? For the mouth speaks out of what overflows from the heart. [35]The good man issues good things out of his good stores, and the wicked man issues wicked things out of his wicked stores. [36]But I

tell you that every idle word that men will speak, they will render an account of it on the day of judgment; [37]For by your words you shall be vindicated, and by your words you shall be condemned."

[38]Then some of the scribes and Pharisees responded to him, saying, "Teacher, we wish to see a sign from you." [39]But in reply he said to them, "A wicked and adulterous generation seeks a sign and a sign shall not be given it, except the sign of the prophet Jonah. [40]For, just as Jonah was in the bowels of the sea-monster three days and three nights, so will the Son of Man be in the heart of the earth three days and three nights. [41]The men of Ninevah will stand up with this generation at the judgment and will condemn it; because at Jonah's proclamation they changed their hearts, and look: Something more than Jonah is here. [42]The Queen of the South will be raised with this generation at the judgment and will condemn it; because she came from the ends of the earth to listen to Solomon's wisdom, and look: Something more than Solomon is here. [43]And when the unclean spirit comes out of the man it wanders through dry places seeking rest, and does not find it. [44]Then it says, 'I shall go back into my house, from which I came out'; and coming it finds it standing idle, swept clean and furnished in good order. [45]Then it goes off and brings along with itself seven other spirits, more evil than itself, and enters in and takes up residence there; and the man's last circumstances turn out worse than the first. So it shall also be for this wicked generation."

[46]While he was still speaking to the crowds, look: His mother and brothers stood outside seeking to speak to him. [47]And someone said to him, "Look: Your mother and your brothers are standing outside seeking to speak to you." [48]But in reply he said to the one speaking to him, "Who is my mother, and who are my brothers?" [49]And stretching out a hand toward his disciples he said, "Look: my mother and my brothers. [50]For whoever does the will of my Father in the heavens, that one is my brother and sister and mother."

CHAPTER THIRTEEN

¹On that day Jesus, going out of the house, sat down beside the sea; ²And many crowds were gathered before him, so that he embarked into a boat in order to sit down, and the whole crowd stood upon the strand. ³And he told them many things in parables, saying, "Look: A sower went out to sow. ⁴And, as he was sowing seeds, some of course fell beside the path and birds came and devoured them. ⁵Others, however, fell upon stony places where there was not much soil, and it sprang up instantly because there was no depth to the soil; ⁶But when the sun had risen it was parched, and because it had no root it withered away. ⁷But still others fell upon thorns, and the thorns grew up and throttled them. ⁸But still others fell upon the good soil and yielded fruit, some a hundredfold, some sixtyfold, some thirtyfold. ⁹Let him who has ears listen." ¹⁰And the disciples, approaching him, said to him, "Why do you speak to them in parables?" ¹¹And in reply he said, "Because it has been granted to you to know the mysteries of the Kingdom of the heavens, but it has not been granted to them. ¹²For to him who has it shall be given and shall be more than is needed; but from him who does not have even what he has shall be taken away. ¹³Hence I speak to them in parables, because seeing they do not see, and hearing they neither hear nor understand. ¹⁴And in them is fulfilled the prophecy of Isaiah, when he says, 'With your hearing you will hear and in no way understand, and in seeing you will see and in no way perceive. ¹⁵For this people's heart has grown crass, and they have listened with their ears grudgingly, and they have closed their eyes, so that it may never happen that they see with their eyes and hear with their ears and understand with the heart and turn back, and I shall heal them.' ¹⁶But blissful are your eyes because they see, and your ears because they hear. ¹⁷For, amen, I tell you that many prophets and upright men yearned to see the things you see, and did not see, and to hear the things you hear, and did not hear. ¹⁸Listen, therefore, to the parable of the sower. ¹⁹When anyone hears the word of the Kingdom and does not understand, the wicked one comes and seizes

away what has been sown in his heart; this is what was sown beside the path. [20]And the word sown upon stony places: this is the one who hears the word and immediately accepts it with joy; [21]But he does not hold the root within himself and it is temporary, and when tribulation and persecution come on account of the word he immediately falters. [22]But what is sown among the thorns: this is the one who hears the word, and the anxiety of this life and the beguilement of riches throttle the word, and it becomes fruitless. [23]But the word sown upon the good soil: this is the one who, hearing and understanding the word, bears fruit, one a hundredfold, another sixtyfold, another thirtyfold."

[24]He set another parable before them, saying, "The Kingdom of the heavens has been likened to a man sowing good seed in his field. [25]But, when men were asleep, his enemy came and sowed darnel-seeds as well, in among the grain, and departed. [26]And when the crop sprouted and bore fruit the darnel-weeds also appeared. [27]And the householder's slaves, approaching, said to him, 'Lord, did you not sow good seed in your field? Where have the darnel-weeds it contains come from?' [28]And he said to them, 'Someone who is an enemy did this.' So the slaves say to him, 'Do you wish then that we should go out and gather them?' [29]But he says, 'No, lest in gathering the darnel-weeds you should uproot the grain along with them. [30]Let them both grow up together until the harvest; and at the time of the harvest I shall tell the reapers, "First gather the darnel-weeds and tie them in sheaves in order to burn them; but gather the grain into my granary."'" [31]He set another parable before them, saying, "The Kingdom of the heavens is like mustard seed that a man took and sowed in his field, [32]Which is indeed the smallest of all seeds, but when it grows it is larger than garden-herbs and becomes a tree, so that the birds of the sky come and dwell in its branches." [33]He told them another parable: "The Kingdom of the heavens is like yeast, which a woman took and mixed into three measures of flour, until all of it was leavened."

[34]All these things Jesus told the crowds in parables, and he told them nothing apart from a parable; [35]So that there was fulfilled what

was spoken by the prophet, when he said, "I shall open my mouth in parables, I shall utter things that have been hidden since the creation."

[36]Then, sending the crowds away, he went into the house. And his disciples approached him, saying, "Explain the parable of the field's darnel-weeds to us." [37]And in reply he said, "The one sowing the good seed is the Son of Man; [38]And the field is the cosmos; and the good seed—these are the sons of the Kingdom; and the darnel-weeds are the sons of the wicked one, [39]And the enemy who sowed them is the Slanderer; and the harvest is the consummation of the age, and the reapers are angels. [40]Therefore, just as the darnel-weeds are gathered and consumed by fire, so it will be at the consummation of the age; [41]The Son of Man will send forth his angels, and they will gather up out of his Kingdom all the snares that cause stumbling, as well as the workers of lawlessness, [42]And will throw them into the furnace of fire; there will be weeping and grinding of teeth there. [43]Then the just will shine out like the sun in the Kingdom of their Father. Let him who has ears hear.

[44]"The Kingdom of the heavens is like a treasure that had been hidden in a field, which a man found and hid, and from his joy he goes and sells the things he owns and purchases that field. [45]Again, the Kingdom of the heavens is like a merchant looking for lovely pearls; [46]And, finding one extremely valuable pearl, he went away and sold all the things he owned and purchased it. [47]Again, the Kingdom of the heavens is like a large dragnet cast into the sea and gathering in things of every kind: [48]And when it was filled they drew it up onto the strand and, sitting down, collected the good things in vessels, but threw the rancid things away. [49]Thus it will be at the consummation of the age: The angels will go forth and will separate the wicked out from the midst of the just, [50]And will throw them into the furnace of fire; there will be weeping and grinding of teeth there. [51]Did you understand all of these things?" They say to him, "Yes." [52]Then he said to them, "Hence every scribe who has been made a disciple to the Kingdom of the heavens is like a man who is master of a house, who brings forth things new and old from his treasury."

[53]And it happened that when Jesus finished these parables he departed from there. [54]And coming into his native country he taught them in their synagogues, in such a way as astonished them and caused them to say, "From where has this man received this wisdom and these powers? [55]Is not this man the craftsman's son? Is not his mother called Mary, and his brothers James and Joseph and Simon and Judas? [56]And are not all his sisters with us? From where, therefore, does this man receive all these things?" [57]And they took offense at him. But Jesus said to them, "A prophet is not dishonored except in his native country and in his own household." [58]And, on account of their lack of faith, he did not perform many feats of power there.

CHAPTER FOURTEEN

[1]At that time, the tetrarch Herod heard report of Jesus, [2]And said to his servants, "This is John the Baptist; he has been raised from the dead, and for this reason powers are at work in him." [3]For Herod had arrested John and bound him and put him away in prison on account of Herodias, the wife of his brother Philip; [4]For John had said to him, "It is not legal for you to have her." [5]And, though wishing to kill him, he was afraid of the crowd, for they held him to be a prophet. [6]But when Herod's birthday celebrations took place the daughter of Herodias danced in the middle of them and was pleasing to Herod, [7]In consequence of which he promised her with an oath to grant whatever she might request. [8]And she, having been instructed in advance by her mother, says, "Give me, here on a trencher, the head of John the Baptist." [9]And, in distress, the king—on account of his oaths and of those reclining together at table—commanded that it be given, [10]And sent word and had John beheaded in the prison. [11]And his head was brought on a trencher and given to the girl, and she brought it to her mother. [12]And his disciples came and took away the corpse and buried it, and went and told Jesus. [13]And, hearing this, Jesus withdrew from there in a boat to a deserted place by himself; and the crowds, hearing of this,

followed him on foot from the cities. [14]And on disembarking he saw a large crowd, and he was moved inwardly with compassion for them and healed the ill among them. [15]But when evening arrived his disciples approached him, saying, "This is a desert place and the hour is already past; so send the crowd away so that they may go off into the villages and buy foodstuffs for themselves." [16]But Jesus said to them, "They have no need to go away; you give them something to eat." [17]But they say to him, "We have nothing here but five loaves of bread and two fishes." [18]And he said, "Bring them here to me." [19]And, having bidden the crowds to recline upon the grass, he took the five loaves and two fishes, looked up to heaven, pronounced a blessing, and broke the loaves and gave them to the disciples, and the disciples to the crowds. [20]And all ate and ate their fill; and they took up what was left over of the fragments, filling twelve baskets. [21]And those eating were about five thousand men, not counting women and children. [22]Then he insisted that the disciples embark into the boat and precede him to the other side, until he should dismiss the crowds. [23]And having dismissed the crowds he ascended the mountain by himself to pray. And when evening arrived he was there alone. [24]But the boat was now many stadia away from land, being tormented by the waves because the wind was adverse. [25]And in the fourth watch of the night he came toward them, walking upon the sea. [26]And the disciples, seeing him walking upon the sea, were disturbed, saying, "It is a phantom," and they cried out in fear. [27]But at once he spoke to them, saying, "Take heart, it is I; do not be afraid." [28]And, answering him, Peter said, "Lord, if it is you, command me to come to you upon the waters." [29]And he said, "Come." And descending from the boat Peter walked on the waters and came toward Jesus. [30]But seeing the blowing wind he was afraid and, beginning to sink, he cried out, saying, "Lord, save me!" [31]And, immediately stretching out a hand, Jesus took hold of him and says, "You of little faith, why did you waver?" [32]And as they went up into the boat the wind fell. [33]And those in the boat prostrated themselves to him, saying, "Truly you are the Son of God." [34]And, crossing over, they came into the land of Gennesaret. [35]And the men of that place, recognizing him, sent out word to the whole of that region, and brought to him all those who were suffering afflictions, [36]And begged him that they might but touch the fringe of his mantle; and as many as touched it were entirely cured.

CHAPTER FIFTEEN

[1]Then Pharisees and scribes from Jerusalem approach Jesus, saying, [2]"Why do your disciples transgress the tradition of the elders? For they do not wash their hands whenever they eat bread." [3]But in reply he said to them, "And why, on account of your tradition, do you transgress God's commandment? [4]For God said, 'Honor father and mother,' and 'To him who speaks abusively to father or mother let death put an end.' [5]But you say that whoever says to father or mother, 'Anything that might have been owed to you by me is a consecrated offering,' [6]Most certainly must not honor his father or mother; and by your tradition you have made the word of God powerless. [7]You charlatans, Isaiah prophesied well concerning you when he said, [8]'This people honors me with their lips, but their heart is far away from me; [9]And they worship me vainly, teaching doctrines that are the dictates of men.'" [10]And, calling the crowd forward, he said to them, "Listen and understand: [11]It is not what goes into the mouth that defiles a man, but what comes out of the mouth—this defiles the man." [12]Then, approaching, the disciples say to him, "Are you aware that the Pharisees who heard this saying were scandalized?" [13]But in reply he said, "Every plant that my heavenly Father did not plant shall be uprooted. [14]Leave them: They are blind guides to the blind; and if a blind man guides a blind man both will fall into a pit." [15]But in reply Peter said to him, "Explain the parable to us." [16]But he said, "Are you also so unable to understand? [17]Do you not grasp that everything entering the mouth passes on to the bowels and is expelled into a latrine? [18]But the things that come out of the mouth emerge from the heart, and those defile the man. [19]For from the heart emerge wicked thoughts, murders, adulteries, whorings, thefts, perjuries, blasphemies.

²⁰These are the things that defile a man; but to eat with unwashed hands does not defile a man."

²¹And going out Jesus departed from there into the regions of Tyre and Sidon. ²²And look: A Canaanite woman from those bounds came forward and cried out, saying, "Have mercy upon me, Lord, son of David, my daughter is badly demon-possessed." ²³But he answered not a word to her. And, approaching, his disciples implored him, saying, "Send her away, for she is crying out behind us." ²⁴But in reply he said, "I was not sent forth except to the lost sheep of the house of Israel." ²⁵But she came and prostrated herself to him, saying, "Lord, help me." ²⁶But in reply he said, "It is not a good thing to take the children's bread and throw it to the dogs." ²⁷And she said, "Yes, Lord; for the dogs also eat, from the crumbs that fall from their masters' tables." ²⁸Then in reply Jesus said to her, "O woman, your faith is great; as you desire, so let it happen to you." And her daughter was healed from that hour.

²⁹And, moving on from there, Jesus went by the Sea of Galilee and ascended a mountain and seated himself there. ³⁰And many crowds approached him, bringing with them the lame, the maimed, the blind, the mute, and many others, and threw them at his feet; and he healed them; ³¹So that the crowd was astonished when they saw mutes speaking, the maimed made whole and the lame walking and the blind seeing; and they glorified the God of Israel. ³²But Jesus, calling his disciples forward, said, "I am moved inwardly with compassion for the crowd, because they stay with me, three days now, and they do not have anything they might eat; and I do not wish to send them away unfed, for fear they should grow weak on the way." ³³And the disciples say to him, "From where, in a desert, can we get enough loaves of bread fully to feed so great a crowd?" ³⁴And Jesus says to them, "How many loaves do you have?" And they said, "Seven, as well as a few fishes." ³⁵And, having enjoined the crowd to repose upon the ground, ³⁶He took the seven loaves and the fishes and, giving thanks, broke them and gave them to the disciples, and the disciples to the crowds. ³⁷And all ate and ate their fill, and they took up what was left over of the fragments, filling seven bas-

kets. ³⁸And those eating were four thousand men, not counting women and children. ³⁹And, having sent the crowds away, he embarked into the boat and entered the borders of Magadan.ᴾ

¹And the Pharisees and Sadducees approached and, testing him, asked him to show them a sign from heaven. ²But in reply he said to them, "When evening comes, you say, 'Fair weather, for the sky is a fiery red'; ³And in the morning, 'Stormy weather today, for the lowering sky is a fiery red.' You know how to judge the face of the sky, yet can you not judge the signs of the times? ⁴A wicked and adulterous generation seeks out a sign, and a sign shall not be given to it, except the sign of Jonah." And, leaving them behind, he departed. ⁵And the disciples, in crossing to the other shore, forgot to bring along loaves of bread. And Jesus said to them, ⁶"Watch and be wary of the yeast of the Pharisees and Sadducees." ⁷But they talked among themselves, saying, "We did not bring along loaves of bread." ⁸But, knowing this, Jesus said, "Why do you talk among yourselves, you of little faith, because you have no loaves of bread? ⁹Do you not yet understand, and do you not remember the five thousand's five loaves of bread and how many baskets you took up? ¹⁰Nor the four thousand's seven loaves of bread and how many baskets you took up? ¹¹How do you not grasp that I was not speaking to you about loaves of bread? Be wary, rather, of the yeast of the Pharisees and Sadducees." ¹²Then they understood that he was telling them to be wary not of the yeast in loaves of bread, but of the teaching of the Pharisees and Sadducees.

¹³And Jesus, coming into the regions of Caesarea Philippi, questioned his disciples, saying, "Who do men say the Son of Man is?" ¹⁴And they said, "While some say John the Baptist, others say Elijah, and others say Jeremiah or one of the prophets." ¹⁵He says to them, "But

p. Perhaps a faulty transcription of Magdala.

you, who do you say I am?" [16]And, answering, Simon Peter said, [17]"You are the Anointed, the Son of the living God." And in reply Jesus said to him, "Blissful are you, Simon bar-Jonah, for flesh and blood did not reveal this to you, but rather my Father in the heavens. [18]And to you I also say, You are Peter [Rock], and upon this rock I will build my assembly, and the gates of Hades shall have no power against it. [19]I shall give you the keys of the Kingdom of the heavens, and whatever you bind on the earth will have been bound in the heavens, and whatever you unbind on the earth will have been unbound in the heavens." [20]Then he warned the disciples that they should tell no one that he is the Anointed.

[21]From then on, Jesus the Anointed began to explain to his disciples that it was necessary for him to go forth into Jerusalem and to suffer many things from the elders and ruling priests and scribes, and to be put to death and to be raised on the third day. [22]And, taking hold of him, Peter began to remonstrate with him, saying, "Grace to you, Lord; by no means shall this happen to you." [23]But he turned and said to Peter, "Get behind me, Accuser; you are a stumbling-block for me, because you think not the things of God, but those of men." [24]Then Jesus said to his disciples, "If anyone wishes to come along behind me, let him deny himself utterly and take up his cross and follow me. [25]For whoever wishes to save his soul will lose it; and whoever loses his soul for my sake will find it. [26]For what will it profit a man if he should gain the whole cosmos but lose his soul? Or what will a man give in exchange for his soul? [27]For the Son of Man is about to arrive in the glory of his Father with his angels, and then he will reward each according to his conduct. [28]Amen, I tell you that among those standing here there are some who most certainly will not taste of death until they see the Son of Man arriving in his Kingdom."

CHAPTER SEVENTEEN

[1]And after six days Jesus takes Peter, and James, and his brother John, and privately leads them up to a high mountain. [2]And he was

transfigured before them, and his face shone out like the sun, and his garments became as white as light. ³And look: Visible to them were Moses and Elijah conversing with him. ⁴And Peter, speaking out, said, "Lord, it is a good thing that we are here; if you wish, I shall make three tabernacles here, one for you and one for Moses and one for Elijah." ⁵While he was still speaking, look: A shining cloud overshadowed them, and look: a voice from the cloud saying, "This is my Son, the beloved, in whom I have delighted; listen to him." ⁶And, hearing this, the disciples fell on their faces and were extremely afraid. ⁷And Jesus approached and, touching them, said, "Arise and do not be afraid." ⁸And lifting their eyes they saw no one except Jesus alone. ⁹And as they were coming down out of the mountain Jesus enjoined them, saying, "Relate the vision to no one until the Son of Man is raised up from among the dead." ¹⁰And the disciples questioned him, saying, "Why therefore do the scribes say that it is necessary for Elijah to come first?" ¹¹And in reply he said, "Indeed, Elijah is coming and will restore all things; ¹²But I tell you that Elijah already came, and they did not recognize him, but instead did whatever things to him they wished; thus the Son of Man is also about to suffer at their hands." ¹³Then the disciples understood that he was speaking to them about John the Baptist.

¹⁴And as they came to the crowd a man approached him, kneeling before him ¹⁵And saying, "Lord, have mercy upon my son, for he is a lunatic and is in a very bad state; for often he falls into the fire, and often into the water. ¹⁶And I brought him to your disciples, and they were unable to heal him." ¹⁷And, speaking out, Jesus said, "O faithless and perverted generation, for how long shall I be with you? For how long shall I endure you? Bring him here to me." ¹⁸And Jesus rebuked it, and the demon came out of him, and the boy was healed from that hour. ¹⁹Then the disciples, privately coming to Jesus, said, "Why were we not able to exorcize it?" ²⁰And he says to them, "Because of your little faith; for, amen, I tell you, if you possess as much as a mustard seed of faith, you will say to this mountain, 'Move from here to there,' and it will

move, and nothing will be impossible to you. [²¹But this kind does not come out, except by prayer and fasting.]"

²²And when they were gathered together in Galilee, Jesus said to them, "The Son of Man is about to be delivered into the hands of men, ²³And they will put him to death, and on the third day he will be raised." And they were greatly saddened.

²⁴And when they came into Capernaum, the two-drachma fee-collectors approached Peter and said, "Does not your teacher pay the two drachmas?" He says, "Yes." ²⁵And as he was going into the house Jesus anticipated him, saying, "How does it seem to you, Simon? From whom do the kings of the earth exact a toll or tribute? From their sons or from strangers?" ²⁶And when he said, "From strangers," Jesus said to him, "Well then, the sons are free. ²⁷But, so as not to scandalize them, go to the sea, cast a hook and take the first fish drawn up, and opening its mouth you will find a stater; take and give that to them for me and you."

CHAPTER EIGHTEEN

¹At that hour, the disciples approached Jesus, saying, "Who then is the greater in the Kingdom of the heavens?" ²And, calling a child forward, he stood the child in their midst, ³And said, "Amen, I tell you, unless you turn back and become as children, you most certainly may not enter into the Kingdom of the heavens. ⁴He therefore who will make himself small as this child, this one is the greater in the Kingdom of the heavens. ⁵And whoever welcomes one such child in my name welcomes me; ⁶And, whoever causes one of these little ones who have faith in me to falter, it is better for him to have a millstone, of the kind turned by an ass, hung about his neck, and to be drowned in the depths of the sea. ⁷Alas for the cosmos because of the occasions of faltering; for it is a necessity that occasions of faltering come about, but alas for the man through whom the occasion of faltering comes. ⁸Now, if your hand or

your foot causes you to falter, cut it off and fling it away from you; it is good for you to enter into life crippled or limping rather than, having two hands or two feet, to be cast into the fire of the Age. ⁹And if your eye causes you to falter, tear it out and fling it away from you; it is good for you to enter into life with one eye rather than, having two eyes, to be cast into Hinnom's Vale of fire. ¹⁰See to it that you are not contemptuous of one of these little ones; for I tell you that their angels in the heavens forever look upon the face of my Father in the heavens. [¹¹For the Son of Man has come to save the lost.] ¹²How does it seem to you? If there is any man to whom a hundred sheep belong, and one of them wanders off, will he not leave the ninety-nine upon the hillside and go in search of the one that has strayed? ¹³And if he happens to find it, amen, I tell you that he takes more joy over it than over the ninety-nine who have not strayed. ¹⁴So it is not a desire that occurs to your Father in the heavens that one of these little ones should perish. ¹⁵Now, if your brother sins, go and remonstrate with him, between you and him privately. If he listens to you, you gain your brother; ¹⁶If, though, he does not listen, take one or two others along with you, so that everything that is said may be confirmed by the mouths of two or three witnesses; ¹⁷If, though, he refuses to listen to them, tell it to the assembly; and if he refuses to listen even to the assembly, let him be to you as the gentile or the tax-collector. ¹⁸Amen, I tell you, whatever things you bind on the earth will have been bound in heaven, and whatever things you unbind on the earth will have been unbound in heaven. ¹⁹Again, [amen,] I tell you that if two among you agree on earth concerning everything they request, whatever it is, it shall come to pass for them, coming from my Father in the heavens. ²⁰For where there are two or three who have gathered in my name, I am there in their midst."

²¹Then Peter approached and said to him, "Lord, how many times will my brother sin against me and I shall forgive him? As many as seven times?" ²²Jesus says to him, "I tell you, not as many as seven times, but as many as seventy times seven. ²³Thus the Kingdom of the heavens

has been likened to a man who was a king, who wished to reckon up accounts with his slaves. ²⁴And, as he began his reckoning, one who was indebted to him for ten thousand talents was brought forward. ²⁵And, as he was unable to make repayment, the master commanded he be sold, as well as his wife and children and all such things as he owns, and repayment be made. ²⁶Then the slave fell down and made obeisance to him, saying, 'Be patient toward me, and I shall repay you everything.' ²⁷And that slave's master, being inwardly moved with compassion, released him and forgave him his loan. ²⁸But going out that slave found one of his fellow slaves who owed him a hundred denarii, and seized hold of and throttled him, saying, 'Pay me everything you owe.' ²⁹Then his fellow slave fell down and implored him, saying, 'Be patient toward me, and I shall repay you.' ³⁰He would not, though, but went off and threw him into prison until he should repay the debt. ³¹Therefore, seeing the things that had taken place, his fellow slaves were extremely upset and went and explained to their master all the things that had happened. ³²Then, calling him forward, his master says to him, 'You wicked slave, I forgave you all that debt after you implored me; ³³Should you not also have mercy on your fellow slave, even as I had mercy on you?' ³⁴And in anger his master delivered him to the inquisitors until he should repay everything owing to him. ³⁵Thus also my heavenly Father will do to you unless, from your hearts, each one of you forgive his brother."

CHAPTER NINETEEN

¹And it happened that when Jesus had done with these sayings, he moved on from Galilee and entered the borders of Judaea, across the Jordan. ²And many crowds followed him, and he healed them there.

³And Pharisees approached him to test him and said, "Is it lawful for a man to divorce his wife for any reason?" ⁴But in reply he said, "Have you not read that the Creator from the beginning 'made them male and female'? ⁵And said, 'For this cause a man shall leave father and

mother and shall be joined fast to his wife, and they shall be two in one flesh': ⁶So that they are no longer two, but one flesh. What therefore God joined together let no man separate." ⁷They say to him, "Why then did Moses enjoin giving a writ of separation and divorcing?" ⁸He says to them, "Moses, on account of your hardness of heart, allowed you to divorce your wives; but from the beginning it did not happen thus. ⁹And I tell you that whoever divorces his wife, except for whorishness, and marries another woman, commits adultery." ¹⁰The disciples say to him, "If such is the responsibility of a man with a wife, it is not profitable to marry." ¹¹But he said to them, "Not all can accept this saying—save those to whom it is given. ¹²For there are eunuchs who were born so from their mother's womb, and there are eunuchs who were gelded by men, and there are eunuchs who gelded themselves for the sake of the Kingdom of the heavens. Let him who can accept this accept it."

¹³Then small children were brought to him, that he might lay hands upon them and pray. But the disciples rebuked them. ¹⁴But Jesus said, "Leave the little children be and do not prevent them from coming to me; for of such is the Kingdom of the heavens." ¹⁵And, laying hands upon them, he departed from there.

¹⁶And look: Someone approaching him said, "Teacher, what good thing may I do in order that I may have the life of the Age?" And he said to him, ¹⁷"Why do you question me concerning the good? One there is who is good. But if you wish to enter into life keep the commandments." ¹⁸He says to him, "Which ones?" And Jesus said, "You shall not murder, you shall not commit adultery, you shall not steal, you shall not bear false witness, ¹⁹Honor father and mother, and love your neighbor as yourself." ²⁰The young man says to him, "All of these I have kept; what am I still lacking?" ²¹Jesus said to him, "If you wish to be perfect, go sell your possessions and give to the poor, and you shall have a treasury in the heavens, and come follow me." ²²But the young man, hearing the counsel, went away in sorrow, for he was someone who had many possessions. ²³And Jesus said to his disciples, "Amen, I tell you that it will be hard for a rich man to enter into the Kingdom of the heavens.

24And again I tell you, it is easier for a camel[q] to enter in through the
eye of a needle than for a rich man to enter into the Kingdom of God."
25But on hearing this the disciples were greatly astonished, saying, "Can
any of them then be saved?"[r] 26And, looking directly at them, Jesus said
to them, "For men this is impossible, but for God all things are possible." 27Then, in reply, Peter said to him, "Look: We gave up all things
and followed you; what then will there be for us?" 28And Jesus said to
them, "Amen, I tell you, in the Regeneration, when the Son of Man sits
upon the throne of his glory, you who have followed me will yourselves
sit also upon twelve thrones, judging the twelve tribes of Israel. 29And
everyone who gave up houses or brothers or sisters or father or mother
or children or fields for my name's sake will receive many times as much
and will inherit life in that Age. 30But many who are first will be last,
and the last first."

CHAPTER TWENTY

1"For the Kingdom of the heavens is like a man, a master of a household, who went out in the early morning to hire workers for his vineyard. 2And agreeing with the workers upon a denarius for the day he
sent them out into his vineyard. 3And going out at about the third hour
he saw others standing idle in the marketplace, 4And to those men he
said, 'You also go into the vineyard, and I shall give you whatever is fair.'
And they went. 5Going out again at about the sixth and the ninth hours,
he did likewise. 6And at about the eleventh hour he went out and found
others standing about, and he says to them, 'Why do you stand here idle

q. The text speaks of a κάμηλος (*kamēlos*, acc. *kamēlon*), "camel," but from the early centuries it has been an open question whether it should really be the homophonous (but poorly attested) word κάμιλος (*kamilos*), "rope," "hawser": a more symmetrical but less piquant analogy.

r. τίς ἄρα δύναται σωθῆναι (*tis ara dynatai sōthēnai*): often translated as "Who then can be saved?" or "Can anyone then be saved?" but I take the import (specifically as regards the τίς) to be "Can any [rich man] then be saved?"

the whole day?' [7]They say to him, 'Because no one hired us.' He says to them, 'You also go into the vineyard.' [8]And, evening having come, the lord of the vineyards says to his steward, 'Call the workers and pay the wage, beginning from the last and proceeding to the first.' [9]And when those of about the eleventh hour came each received a denarius. [10]And when the first came they supposed they would receive more; and each of them also received a denarius. [11]And on receiving it they murmured against the master of the house, saying, [12]'These last ones labored one hour, and you made them equal to us, who have borne the day's oppressiveness and the heat.' [13]But he, making rejoinder, said to one of them, 'Friend, I am not being unjust to you; did you not agree to a denarius with me? [14]Take what is yours and go; but I wish to give to the last man what I also give to you; [15]Am I not permitted to do what I wish with my own possessions? Or is your eye baleful because I am generous?' [16]Thus the last will be first and the first last."

[17]Then, as Jesus was about to go up to Jerusalem, he took the twelve aside privately and, on the way, said to them, [18]"See: We are going up to Jerusalem, and the Son of Man will be handed over to the chief priests and scribes, and they will condemn him to death, [19]And they will hand him over to the gentiles to mock and to flog and to crucify, and on the third day he will be raised."

[20]Then the mother of the sons of Zebedee approached him with her sons, making her obeisance and asking something from him. [21]And he said to her, "What do you wish?" She says to him, "Say that in your Kingdom these two sons of mine may sit one on your right and one on your left." [22]And in reply Jesus said, "You do not know what you ask. Can you drink the cup that I am about to drink?" They say to him, "We can." [23]He says to them, "You will indeed drink my cup; but to sit on my right and on my left, this is not mine to give, but is for those for whom it has been prepared by my Father." [24]And hearing this the ten were irate over the two brothers. [25]But Jesus, calling them forward, said to them, "You know that the rulers of the gentile peoples dominate them, and that their great men wield power over them. [26]It is not so among

you; rather, whoever among you wishes to be great will be your servant, [27]And whoever among you wishes to be first will be your slave; [28]Just as the Son of Man came not to be served, but to serve and to give his soul as the price of liberation for many."

[29]And as they were departing from Jericho a large crowd followed him. [30]And look: Two blind men sitting beside the road, hearing that Jesus is passing by, cried out, saying, "Lord, have mercy upon us, son of David." [31]But the crowd censured them, demanding that they should be silent; but they cried out the louder, saying, "Lord, have mercy on us, son of David." [32]And coming to a standstill Jesus called to them and said, "What do you wish that I might do for you?" [33]They say to him, "Lord, that our eyes might be opened." [34]And, moved inwardly with compassion for them, Jesus touched their eyes, and immediately they saw again and followed him.

CHAPTER TWENTY-ONE

[1]And when they came near to Jerusalem and arrived at Bethphage, at the Mount of Olives, Jesus then sent two disciples out, [2]Telling them, "Go into the village opposite you, and you will at once find a tethered ass, and a foal with her; untie them and bring them to me. [3]And if anyone says anything to you, you shall say that 'the Lord has need of them'; and he will send them along right away." [4]And this occurred that there might be fulfilled what was spoken by the prophet when he said, [5]"Tell the daughter of Zion: See, your king comes to you, gentle and mounted upon an ass and upon a foal, a son of a beast of burden." [6]And the disciples, going and doing as Jesus directed them, [7]Brought the ass and the foal, and covered them with their cloaks, and he sat down upon them. [8]And the largest crowd spread their own cloaks in the road, but others cut branches from the trees and spread them in the road. [9]And the crowds preceding him and those following him cried out, saying, "Hosanna to the son of David; blessed is he who comes in the name of the Lord; Hosanna in the highest places." [10]And as he entered Jeru-

salem the whole city was in commotion, saying, "Who is this?" [11]And the crowds said, "This is the prophet Jesus, the one from Nazareth in Galilee."

[12]And Jesus entered the Temple and threw out all those selling and buying in the Temple, and overturned the tables of the moneychangers and the seats of those selling doves, [13]And he says to them, "It has been written, 'My house shall be called a house of prayer,' but you make it a robbers' den." [14]And the blind and the lame came to him in the Temple, and he healed them. [15]But, seeing the wonders he performed and the children crying out in the Temple and saying 'Hosanna to the son of David,' the chief priests and the scribes were indignant, [16]And said to him, "Do you hear what they are saying?" And Jesus says to them, "Yes. Have you never read, 'Out of the mouths of infants and nurslings you have provided praise'?" [17]And leaving them he went forth, outside the city to Bethany, and lodged there for the night.

[18]Now, going up in the morning to Jerusalem, he was hungry. [19]And seeing a single fig tree on the way he went over to it and found nothing on it, but only leaves, and he says to it, "May fruit never come forth from you, throughout the age."[s] And at once the fig tree withered. [20]And seeing this the disciples marveled, saying, "How was the fig tree withered in an instant?" [21]And in reply Jesus said to them, "Amen, I tell you, if you have faith and do not doubt, you will not only do what was done to the fig tree, but also if you say to this mountain, 'Be caught up and flung into the sea,' it will happen; [22]And all such things as you might ask in prayer, if you have faith, you shall receive."

[23]And when he went into the Temple, the chief priests and the elders of the people approached him while he was teaching and said, "By what power do you do these things? And who gave you this power?" [24]And in reply Jesus said to them, "I shall also ask you to tell me one thing, if you will tell me which I shall also tell you by what power I do these things: [25]John's baptism, where did it come from? From heaven or from men?"

s. Or "until the Age [to come]."

And they discussed this among themselves, saying, "If we say 'From heaven,' he will say to us, 'Why then did you not trust him?' [26]But if we say, 'From men,' we are afraid of the crowd, for all hold John to be a prophet." [27]And replying to Jesus they said, "We do not know." He said to them in turn, "Neither do I tell you by what power I do these things. [28]But how does it seem to you? A man had two children; going to the first, he said, 'Child, go work in the vineyard today,' [29]But he in answer said, 'I will, Lord,' and did not go. [30]And going to the second he spoke in the same way. And in answer he said, 'I do not wish to,' and later regretted it and went. [31]Which of the two did the father's will?" They said, "The latter." Jesus says to them, "Amen, I tell you that the tax-collectors and prostitutes are going before you into the Kingdom of God. [32]For John came to you on the path of rectitude, and you did not trust him; but the tax-collectors and prostitutes trusted him; yet, having seen this, you did not later feel regret and trust him. [33]Listen to another parable. There was a man, the master of a household, who planted a vineyard and ran a fence around it and dug a winepress in it and constructed a tower and leased it out to husbandmen and went abroad. [34]And when the proper time of fruiting drew near he sent out his slaves to the husbandmen to receive its fruits. [35]And the husbandmen seized his slaves, and one they flogged, and another they killed, and another they stoned. [36]Again he sent other slaves, more than the first lot, and they treated them in the same way. [37]Thereafter he sent his son to them, saying, 'My son they will treat with shamed deference.' [38]But the husbandmen, seeing the son, said among themselves, 'This is the heir; come, let us kill him and let us take possession of his inheritance'; [39]And seizing him they cast him outside the vineyard and killed him. [40]When the lord of the vineyard comes, what therefore will he do to those husbandmen?" [41]They say to him, "He will put those wicked men to a wicked death, and he will lease out the vineyard to other husbandmen, who will render to him the fruits at their proper times." [42]Jesus says to them, "Have you never read in the scriptures 'A stone that the builders rejected, this became the corner's capstone; from the Lord this came to pass, and it is marvelous in our eyes'? [43]Therefore I tell you that the Kingdom of God will be taken from you and will be given to a nation bearing its fruits. [[44]And whoever falls upon this stone will be shattered; but whomever it falls upon, it will crush him.]" [45]And, hearing his parables, the chief priests and Pharisees knew that he is speaking about them; [46]And, seeking how to seize him by force, they were afraid of the crowds: for they held him to be a prophet.

CHAPTER TWENTY-TWO

[1]And in reply Jesus spoke to them in parables again, saying, [2]"The Kingdom of the heavens has been likened to a man, a king, who arranged wedding celebrations for his son. [3]And he sent out his slaves to summon those who had been invited to the wedding celebrations, and they did not wish to come. [4]Again, he sent out other slaves, saying, 'Say to those who have been invited, "Look: I have prepared my luncheon, my bulls and fatted beasts have been sacrificed, and all things are ready; come to the wedding celebrations."' [5]But they went away in indifference, one to his own field, another to his business; [6]But the rest overpowered the slaves, treated them brutally, and killed them. [7]The king was then enraged and, sending his armies, destroyed those murderers and burned their city. [8]Then he says to his slave, 'The wedding is indeed ready, but those who were invited were not worthy; [9]Go, therefore, to where the roads let out, and summon as many as you find to the wedding celebrations.' [10]And those slaves, going out into the streets, gathered together all whom they found, both the bad and the good; and the wedding hall was filled with those reclining at table. [11]But the king, coming in to see those who reclined at table, spied there a man not clothed in a wedding garment; [12]And he says to him, 'Friend, how did you enter here not wearing a wedding garment?' And he was speechless. [13]Then the king said to his servants, 'Bind his feet and hands and throw him into the darkness outside.' There will be weeping and grinding of teeth there. [14]For many are called, but few chosen."

¹⁵Then, going away, the Pharisees took counsel together regarding how they might ensnare him in words. ¹⁶And they send their disciples to him, along with the Herodians, saying, "Teacher, we know that you are truthful and that you teach the way of God in truth, and you harbor no anxiety toward anyone, for you are not a respecter of men's persons; ¹⁷Tell us, then, how does it seem to you? Is it lawful to render the poll-tax to Caesar or not?" ¹⁸But knowing their wickedness Jesus said, "Why do you try me, you charlatans? ¹⁹Show me the coin for the poll-tax." And they brought a denarius to him. ²⁰And he says to them, "Whose image is this and whose inscription?" ²¹They say, "Caesar's." Then he says to them, "Then render the things that are Caesar's to Caesar and the things that are God's to God." ²²And hearing this they were amazed and, leaving him be, they departed.

²³On that day the Sadducees, who say there is no resurrection, approached him and questioned him, ²⁴Saying, "Teacher, Moses said, 'If any man dies having no children, his brother shall marry his wife in turn and shall raise up seed for his brother.' ²⁵But among us there were seven brothers; and the first, having married, died and had no children, and left his wife to his brother; ²⁶Likewise also the second and the third, right up to the seventh of them. ²⁷And, last of all, the wife died. ²⁸In the resurrection, therefore, of which of the seven will she be the wife? For they all had her." ²⁹But in reply Jesus said to them, "You have been led astray, knowing neither the scriptures nor the power of God. ³⁰For in the resurrection they neither marry nor are married, but are as angels in heaven.ᵗ ³¹But regarding the resurrection of the dead have you not read what was told you by God, in saying, ³²'I am God of Abraham and God of Isaac and God of Jacob'? He is not a God of the dead, but of the living." ³³And, hearing this, the crowds were stupefied by his teaching.

³⁴But the Pharisees, hearing that he had rendered the Sadducees speechless, gathered together, ³⁵And one of them who was a lawyer,

---

t. See Acts 23:8; 1 Corinthians 15:40–54; and 1 Peter 3:18–19, 4:6, as well as the footnotes thereto.

testing him, posed him the question, [36]"Teacher, what is the great commandment in the law?" [37]And he said to him, "You shall love the Lord your God with all your heart and with all your soul and with all your reason. [38]This is the great and first commandment. [39]The second is like it: You shall love your neighbor as yourself. [40]All the Law and the prophets depend upon these two commandments."

[41]And while the Pharisees were assembled Jesus questioned them, [42]Saying, "How does it seem to you regarding the Anointed? Whose son is he?" They say to him, "David's." [43]He says to them, "How is it then that David calls him 'Lord' when saying, [44]'The Lord said to my lord, "Sit upon my right until I put your enemies beneath your feet"'? [45]If therefore David calls him 'Lord,' how is he his son?" [46]And no one could answer him a word, nor did anyone dare from that day to interrogate him again.

CHAPTER TWENTY-THREE

[1]Then Jesus spoke to the crowds and to his disciples, [2]Saying, "The scribes and the Pharisees have seated themselves upon the seat of Moses. [3]Therefore, all the things they might tell you, whatever they are, do and observe, but do not act in accord with their deeds; for they speak and do not do. [4]And they tie up heavy loads and place them on men's shoulders, but they are not willing to apply a finger of their own to move them. [5]And they perform all their deeds so as to be seen by men; for they widen their phylacteries and exaggerate their fringes in the synagogues, [6]And they cherish the chief couch at meals and the chief seats in the synagogues, [7]And the salutations in the marketplaces, and to be called Rabbi by men. [8]But do not let yourselves be called Rabbi; for there is one who is your teacher, and you are all brothers. [9]And do not call someone on earth 'Father,' for there is one who is your heavenly Father. [10]Neither let yourself be called instructors, because your one instructor is the Anointed. [11]And the greater among you shall be your servant. [12]And whoever will exalt himself will be humbled, and whoever will

humble himself will be exalted. ¹³But alas for you, scribes and Pharisees, charlatans, because you shut the Kingdom of the heavens in men's faces; for you do not enter, nor do you allow those going in to enter. [¹⁴Alas for you, scribes and Pharisees, charlatans, because you devour the homes of widows and declaim at great length when praying, for which you shall receive condemnation in greater abundance.] ¹⁵Alas for you, scribes and Pharisees, charlatans, because you travel all about the sea and the dry land to make one proselyte, and when it is done you make him twice as much a son of Hinnom's Vale as you yourselves. ¹⁶Alas for you blind guides who say, 'Whoever swears by the Temple sanctuary, it means nothing; but whoever swears by the gold of the Temple sanctuary, he is under obligation.' ¹⁷Fools and blind men! For what is greater, the gold of the Temple sanctuary or the sanctuary that makes the gold holy? ¹⁸And: 'Whoever swears by the altar, it means nothing; but whoever swears by the offering upon it, he is under obligation.' ¹⁹Blind men! For what is greater, the offering or the altar that makes the offering holy? ²⁰Hence the one who swears by the altar swears by it and by all the things upon it; ²¹And the one who swears by the Temple sanctuary swears by the sanctuary and by him who dwells in it. ²²And the one who swears by heaven swears by the throne of God and by him who sits upon it. ²³Alas for you, scribes and Pharisees, charlatans, because you tithe a tenth of the mint and the dill and the cumin, and have neglected the weightier things of the law, the judgment and the mercy and the faith; yet these things you ought to have done, while also not neglecting those others. ²⁴Blind guides, who strain out the gnat but drink down the camel. ²⁵Alas for you, scribes and Pharisees, charlatans, because you clean the outside of the cup and dish, but inside they are filled up with plunder and dissoluteness. ²⁶Blind Pharisee, first clean the inside of the cup, so that its outside may also be clean. ²⁷Alas for you, scribes and Pharisees, charlatans, because you are like whitewashed tombs, which outwardly indeed appear lovely, but within are filled with the bones of the dead and with all uncleanliness. ²⁸Thus you also outwardly indeed appear upright, but within you are full of dissimulation and lawlessness.

²⁹Alas for you, scribes and Pharisees, charlatans, because you build the tombs of the prophets and adorn the monuments of the upright, ³⁰And say, 'If we had lived in the days of our fathers, we should not have had a part with them in the blood of the prophets.' ³¹Thus you bear witness regarding yourselves that you are the sons of the prophets' murderers. ³²And you—you fully measure up to your fathers. ³³Serpents, brood of vipers, how may you escape the verdict of Hinnom's Vale? ³⁴So look: I send prophets and wise men and scribes to you; some of them you will kill and crucify, and some of them you will flog in your synagogues and drive from city to city; ³⁵Thus accrues to you all the righteous blood shed on the earth, from the blood of Abel the upright up to the blood of Zechariah, the son of Barachiah, whom you murdered between the sanctuary and the altar. ³⁶Amen, I tell you, all these things will come upon this generation. ³⁷Jerusalem, Jerusalem, you who kill the prophets and stone those who have been sent to you, how often I have wished to gather your children, the way a bird gathers chicks under her wings, and you did not wish it. ³⁸See: For you, your house is abandoned [to desolation]. ³⁹For I tell you, henceforth you most assuredly will not see me until you say, 'Blessed is he who comes in the name of the Lord.'"

CHAPTER TWENTY-FOUR

¹And going out Jesus departed from the Temple, and his disciples approached him to call his attention to the Temple's buildings. ²And he, in response, said to them, "Do you not see all these things? Amen, I tell you, by no means shall a stone be left upon a stone here that will not be thrown down." ³And as he sat upon the Mount of Olives, the disciples came to him in private, saying, "Tell us, when will these things be, and what the sign of your arrival and of the consummation of the age?" ⁴And in reply Jesus said to them, "Keep watch, so that no one causes you to go astray. ⁵For many will come in my name, saying, 'I am the Anointed,' and will cause many to go astray. ⁶But you will begin to hear about wars and rumors of wars; see that you are not alarmed; for

it is necessary that this occur, but the end is not yet. [7]For nation will be raised against nation, and kingdom against kingdom, and there will be famines and earthquakes in various places; [8]But all these things are the beginning of birth pangs. [9]Then they will deliver you over to affliction and will kill you, and you will be hated by all the nations on account of my name. [10]And then many will be caused to falter and will betray one another and hate one another; [11]And many false prophets will be raised up and will cause many to go astray; [12]And because of the increase of lawlessness the love of many will grow cold. [13]But whoever endures to the end—this one will be saved. [14]And these good tidings of the Kingdom will be proclaimed in the whole of the inhabited world, in witness to all the nations, and then the end will come. [15]When, therefore, you see the abomination of desolation spoken of by the prophet Daniel standing in the holy place . . ." (Let the reader understand) [16]". . . Then those in Judaea, let them flee into the mountains; [17]He who is on the housetop, let him not descend to collect things from his house; [18]And he who is in the field, let him not turn back to fetch his cloak. [19]Alas in those days for pregnant women and for women nursing. [20]And pray that your flight may not occur in winter, nor on a Sabbath; [21]For there will be great affliction then, such as has not occurred from the beginning of the cosmos until now—nor indeed could occur. [22]And, but that those days were shortened, no flesh at all would have been saved; yet, on account of the chosen, those days will be shortened. [23]If anyone says to you then, 'Look: The Anointed is here' or 'here,' do not believe; [24]For false Anointed Ones and false prophets will be raised up, and they will produce great signs and prodigies, so as to lead astray—if possible— even the chosen. [25]See, I have told you in advance. [26]Therefore, if they say to you, 'Look: He is in the desert,' do not venture out; 'Look: He is in the inner rooms,' do not believe. [27]For as the lightning comes forth from the east and shines as far as the west, such shall be the arrival of the Son of Man; [28]Wherever the carcass may be, there the eagles will be gathered. [29]And immediately after the affliction of those days the sun will be darkened, and the moon will not give her light, and the stars will fall from the sky, and the powers of the heavens will be shaken. [30]And then the sign of the Son of Man will appear in the sky, and then all the tribes of the earth will beat their breasts and will see the Son of Man coming upon the clouds of the sky with power and great glory; [31]And he will send forth his angels with a great trumpeting, and they will gather together the chosen from the four winds, from end to end of the heavens. [32]But learn the parable from the fig tree: Now, when its branch softens and produces leaves, you know that the summer is near; [33]So too, when you see all these things you know that he is near, at the doors. [34]Amen, I tell you that this generation most definitely does not pass away until all these things happen. [35]The sky and the earth will pass away, but in no way could my words pass away. [36]But about that day and hour no one knows—neither the angels of the heavens nor the Son— except the Father only. [37]For just as in the days of Noah, so shall be the arrival of the Son of Man. [38]For just as those in the days before the flood were eating and drinking, marrying and giving in marriage, right up to the day on which Noah entered the ark, [39]And knew nothing until the flood came and carried all away, so also will be the arrival of the Son of Man. [40]Then two men will be in the field: one is carried off and one is spared; [41]Two women grinding at the mill: one is carried off and one is spared. [42]Be alert, therefore, because you do not know on what day your Lord is coming. [43]But this you know: that if the master of the house had known in what watch the thief comes, he would have been awake and would not have permitted his household to be breached. [44]For this reason, you too be ready, because the Son of Man comes at the hour you do not expect. [45]Who then is the faithful and prudent slave whom the master appointed over his household slaves, to give them food at the proper time? [46]How blissful that slave whom his master will find so doing when he arrives; [47]Amen, I tell you that he will appoint him over all his possessions. [48]But if that slave, being base, says in his heart, 'My master is taking a long time,' [49]And begins to beat his fellow slaves, and eats and drinks with the wine-sots, [50]That slave's master will come on a day on which he is not expecting him, and at an hour in which he is unaware, [51]And will cut him in two,[u] and will assign him his lot with the dissemblers; there will be weeping and grinding of teeth there.

CHAPTER TWENTY-FIVE

[1]"Then the Kingdom of the heavens shall be likened to ten virgins who, taking their own lamps, went out to meet the bridegroom. [2]And five of them were foolish and five wise. [3]For the foolish, when taking the lamps, did not take oil with them. [4]But the wise took oil in vessels along with their lamps. [5]With the bridegroom taking a long time, however, they all grew drowsy and lay down to sleep. [6]And in the middle of the night there was a cry: 'Look, the bridegroom; go out to meet him!' [7]Then all those virgins were roused and trimmed their lamps. [8]But the foolish ones said to the wise, 'Give us some of your oil, for our lamps are going out.' [9]But the wise ones answered by saying, 'Surely there would not be enough for us and for you; rather than that, go instead to the merchants and buy some for yourselves.' [10]But while they were gone away to make their purchase the bridegroom came, and those who were prepared went in with him to the wedding celebrations, and the door was shut. [11]And afterward the remaining virgins also come, saying, 'Lord, lord, open up for us.' [12]But in reply he said, 'Amen, I tell you, I do not know you.' [13]So be alert, for you do not know the day or the hour. [14]For just as a man leaving home on a journey summoned his own slaves and handed his possessions over to them, [15]And gave five talents to one, and two to another, and one to another, to each according to his peculiar ability, and left home on his journey— [16]Immediately, the one who received five talents employed them in trade and gained another five; [17]Similarly, the one who had two gained another two; [18]But the one who received one went away, dug into the ground, and hid his master's silver. [19]Then after a long time the master of those slaves comes and settles ac-

---

u. A hyperbolic image for severe chastisement, not a literal description of a real punishment.

counts with them. ²⁰And, approaching, the one receiving the five talents brought the other five talents forward, saying, 'Master, you handed over five talents to me; look, I gained another five talents.' ²¹His master said to him, 'Well done, good and trustworthy slave, you were trustworthy over a few things, I shall place you over many; enter into your master's delight.' ²²Also approaching, the one with two talents said, 'Look, I gained another two talents.' ²³His master said to him, 'Well done, good and trustworthy slave, you were trustworthy over a few things, I shall place you over many; enter into your master's delight.' ²⁴And, also approaching, the one who had received one talent said, 'Master, I knew you, that you are a harsh man, reaping where you did not sow and gathering from where you did not scatter; ²⁵And, being afraid, I went away and hid your talent in the earth; see, you have what is yours.' ²⁶But in reply his master said to him, 'You wicked and timorous slave, did you know that I reap where I did not sow and gather from where I did not scatter? ²⁷Then you ought to have placed my silver pieces with the bankers, and when I came I would have recovered what was my own with interest. ²⁸Therefore, take the talent away from him and give it to him who has ten talents; ²⁹For to everyone who has, it shall be given and shall be more than is needed; but from him who does not have even what he has shall be taken away. ³⁰And throw the useless slave into the darkness outside; there will be weeping and grinding of teeth there.' ³¹And when the Son of Man comes in his glory, and all the angels with him, then he will sit on his throne of glory; ³²And all the nations will be assembled before him, and he will separate them from one another, as the shepherd separates the sheep from the kid goats,ᵛ ³³And will set the sheep to his right, but the kid goats to the left. ³⁴Then the King will say to those to his right, 'Come, you blessed by my Father, inherit the Kingdom prepared for you from the foundation of the cosmos. ³⁵For I was

---

v. The noun ἔριφος (*eriphos*), which is used here in the plural, means specifically "kid" or "kid goat"; kids intermingle with sheep in a mixed herd.

hungry and you gave me something to eat, I was thirsty and you gave me drink, I was a stranger and you gave me hospitality, [36]Naked and you clothed me, I was ill and you looked after me, I was in prison and you came to me.' [37]Then the just will answer him, saying, 'When did we see you hungry and feed you, or thirsty and give you drink? [38]And when did we see you a stranger and give you hospitality, or naked and clothe you? [39]And when did we see you ill or in prison and come to you?' [40]And in reply the King will say to them, 'Amen, I tell you, inasmuch as you did it to one of the least of these my brothers, you did it to me.' [41]Then he will say to those to the left, 'Go from me, you execrable ones, into the fire of the Age prepared for the Slanderer and his angels. [42]For I was hungry and you did not give me anything to eat, I was thirsty and you did not give me drink, [43]I was a stranger and you did not give me hospitality, naked and you did not clothe me, ill and in prison and you did not look after me.' [44]Then they too will answer, saying, 'Lord, when did we see you hungry or thirsty or a stranger or naked or ill or in prison, and did not attend to you?' [45]Then he will answer them, saying, 'Amen, I tell you, inasmuch as you did not do it to one of the least of these my brothers, neither did you do it to me.' [46]And these will go to the chastening[w] of that Age, but the just to the life of that Age."

w. The word κόλασις (*kolasis*) originally meant "pruning" or "docking" or "obviating the growth" of trees or other plants, and then came to mean "confinement," "being held in check," "punishment," or "chastisement," chiefly with the connotation of "correction." Classically, the word was distinguished (by Aristotle, for instance) from τιμωρία (*timōria*), which means a retributive punishment only. Whether such a distinction holds here is difficult to say, since by late antiquity *kolasis* seems to have been used by many to describe punishment of any kind; but the only other use of the noun in the New Testament is in 1 John 4:18, where it refers not to retributive punishment, but to the suffering experienced by someone who is subject to fear because not yet perfected in charity. The verbal form, κολάζω (*kolazō*), appears twice: in Acts 4:21, where it clearly refers only to disciplinary punishment, and in 2 Peter 2:9 in reference to fallen angels and unrighteous men, where it probably means "being held in check" or "penned in" [until the day of judgment].

CHAPTER TWENTY-SIX

¹And it happened that, when Jesus had finished all of these utterances, he said to his disciples, ²"You know that after two days the Passover takes place, and the Son of Man is handed over to be crucified." ³Then the chief priests and the elders of the people were assembled in the courtyard of the chief priest named Caiaphas, ⁴And together deliberated on how they might by deceit seize and kill Jesus; ⁵But they said, "Not during the festival, so that no unrest occurs among the people."

⁶Now while Jesus was in Bethany, in the home of Simon the leper, ⁷A woman who had an alabaster phial of precious unguent approached him and poured it upon his head as he reclined at table. ⁸But seeing this the disciples were indignant, saying, "Why this waste? ⁹For this could be sold for a large amount and be given to the destitute." ¹⁰But, knowing this, Jesus said to them, "Why do you subject the woman to abuse? For she has done a beautiful deed for me; ¹¹For you always have the destitute with you, but you do not always have me; ¹²When she shed this unguent upon my body, she did it so as to prepare me for burial. ¹³Amen, I tell you, wherever these good tidings are proclaimed, in the whole world, what this woman did will also be told, as a memorial to her." ¹⁴Then one of the twelve, the one named Judas Iscariot, going to the chief priests, ¹⁵Said, "What are you willing to give me, and I shall hand him over to you?" And they paid him thirty silver pieces. ¹⁶And from then on he sought a good opportunity, so that he might hand him over.

¹⁷Now on the first day of the Unleavened Loaves the disciples approached Jesus, saying, "Where do you wish us to make preparations for you to eat the Passover?" ¹⁸And he said, "Go into the city to a certain man and say to him, 'The teacher says, "My appointed time is near; I am observing the Passover at your place, along with my disciples."'" ¹⁹And the disciples did as Jesus enjoined them and prepared the Passover. ²⁰And when evening came he reclined at table with the twelve. ²¹And as they were eating he said, "Amen, I tell you that one of you will hand me over." ²²And in vehement distress they began, each one of

them, to say to him, "Am I he, Lord?" ²³And in reply he said, "He who dips his hand in the bowl along with me, this one will hand me over. ²⁴True, the Son of Man goes away, just as has been written about him, but alas for that man by whom the Son of Man is handed over; it would have been a good thing for that man had he not been born." ²⁵And in reply Judas, the one handing him over, said, "Is it I, Rabbi?" He says to him, "You have said it." ²⁶And as they were eating, Jesus, taking a loaf and giving thanks, broke it and, giving it to his disciples, said, "Take, eat: This is my body." ²⁷And, taking a cup and giving thanks, he gave it to them, saying, "Drink from this, all of you: ²⁸For this is my blood of the covenant, which is being shed for many, for the forgiveness of sins. ²⁹And I tell you, henceforth I will most surely not drink of this, the yield of the vine, until that day when I drink it with you, new, in the Kingdom of my Father."

³⁰And, having sung a hymn, they went out to the Mount of Olives. ³¹Then Jesus says to them, "During this night, you will all be caused to fail me; for it has been written, 'I shall strike down the shepherd, and the sheep of the flock will be scattered'; ³²But after I am raised, I shall precede you into Galilee." ³³But in reply Peter said to him, "Though all will be made to fail you, I shall never be made to fail." ³⁴Jesus said to him, "Amen, I tell you that on this night, before the cock crows, you will deny me three times." ³⁵Peter says to him, "Even if it is necessary for me to die with you, I most assuredly will not deny you." And so said all the disciples.

³⁶Then Jesus goes with them to a place called Gethsemane, and says to the disciples, "Sit down here while I go apart in order to pray over there." ³⁷And, taking along Peter and the sons of Zebedee, he began to grieve and to suffer distress. ³⁸Then he says to them, "My soul is in anguish, to the point of death; remain here and keep watch with me." ³⁹And going a little ahead he fell on his face, praying and saying, "My Father, if it is possible, let this cup pass from me; yet not as I will, but as you will." ⁴⁰And he comes to the disciples and finds them sleeping, and says to Peter, "So, were you not strong enough to keep watch with

me for one hour? [41]Keep watch and pray that you might not come to trial; truly, the spirit is eager, but the flesh is frail." [42]Going off again a second time, he prayed, saying, "My Father, if it is not possible for it to pass by without my drinking it, let your will be done." [43]And on coming he again found them sleeping, for their eyes were very heavy. [44]And, leaving them alone, he again went away and prayed a third time, speaking the same words again. [45]Then he comes to the disciples and says to them, "Sleep some more and rest—Look: The hour has drawn near and the Son of Man is delivered over into the hands of sinners. [46]Arise, let us be going; look: The one handing me over has come near."

[47]And while he was still speaking, look: Judas—one of the twelve—came, and with him a large crowd with swords and bludgeons from the chief priests and elders of the people. [48]Now the one handing him over gave them a sign, saying, "Whomever I should kiss, that is he; seize him." [49]And immediately approaching Jesus he said, "Greetings, Rabbi," and kissed him affectionately. [50]But Jesus said to him, "Friend, get on to what you are here for." Then coming forward they laid hands on Jesus and forcibly seized him. [51]And look: One of those with Jesus, stretching forth a hand, pulled out his sword and, striking the chief priest's slave, cut off his ear. [52]Then Jesus says to him, "Return your sword to its place; for all who take up a sword will be destroyed by a sword. [53]Or do you imagine that I cannot ask my Father, and he will at this very moment place more than twelve legions of angels beside me? [54]How then would the things written by the prophets be fulfilled: that it must happen thus?" [55]At that hour, Jesus said to the crowds, "You came out with swords and bludgeons to arrest me, as though coming against a bandit? I sat each day in the Temple teaching, and you did not seize me. [56]But all of this has happened so that the writings of the prophets might be fulfilled." Then all the disciples, abandoning him, fled away.

[57]And those who had seized Jesus led him away to Caiaphas the chief priest, where the scribes and the elders were assembled. [58]And Peter followed him from afar to the courtyard of the chief priest, and entering within sat with the attendants in order to see the end. [59]And the chief

priests and the entire Council sought out false evidence against Jesus, so that they might put him to death, ⁶⁰And they found none, though many perjurers came forward. But two came forward later, ⁶¹And said, "This man declared, 'I can tear down God's sanctuary and erect it within three days.'" ⁶²And standing up the chief priest said to him, "Do you have no answer to what these men attest against you?" ⁶³But Jesus remained silent. And the chief priest said to him, "I adjure you by the living God that you tell us if you are the Anointed, the Son of God." ⁶⁴Jesus says to him, "You have said it; but I tell you, you will presently see the Son of Man sitting at the right hand of the Power and coming upon the clouds of the sky." ⁶⁵Then the chief priest tore his mantle, saying, "He blasphemed; what need do we still have for witnesses? See now, you heard the blasphemy. ⁶⁶How does it seem to you?" And in reply they said, "He deserves death." ⁶⁷Then they spat in his face and struck him with their fists, and they slapped him, ⁶⁸Saying, "Prophesy for us, Anointed One, who is it who has slapped you?" ⁶⁹And Peter sat outside in the courtyard, and a lone maidservant came up to him, saying, "You were also with Jesus the Galilaean." ⁷⁰But he denied it before them all, saying, "I do not know what you are saying." ⁷¹And when he went out into the portico another maidservant saw him and says, "This one was with Jesus the Nazorean." ⁷²And again he denied it, with an oath, saying, "I do not know the man." ⁷³And a little later the bystanders, approaching, said to Peter, "Truly you too are one of them, for even your dialect makes you conspicuous." ⁷⁴Then he began to curse and to swear, "I do not know the man." And immediately a cock crowed. ⁷⁵And Peter remembered the words of Jesus, when he had said, "Before the crowing of the cock you will deny me three times"; and, going outside, he wept bitterly.

CHAPTER TWENTY-SEVEN

¹And when early morning came all the chief priests and elders of the people took counsel together against Jesus, so as to put him to death; ²And having bound him they led him away and handed him over to

Pilate the governor. ³Then Judas, the one who betrayed him, seeing that he had been condemned, changed his heart and returned the thirty silver pieces to the chief priests and elders, ⁴Saying, "I sinned by betraying innocent blood." But they said, "What is it to us? You will see to it." ⁵And flinging the silver pieces into the sanctuary he withdrew, and going away he hanged himself. ⁶But the chief priests, taking up the silver pieces, said, "It is not lawful to deposit them in the treasury, because it is a price for blood." ⁷And, taking counsel together, with them they purchased the potter's field for the burial of strangers. ⁸Hence that field has been called Field of Blood up to this day. ⁹Then was fulfilled what had been spoken by the prophet Jeremiah when he said, "And I took the thirty silver pieces, the price of the one on whom a price had been set, whom they prized out from among the sons of Israel, ¹⁰And gave them in exchange for the potter's field, as the Lord commanded me."ˣ ¹¹And Jesus stood before the governor; and the governor interrogated him, saying, "You are the king of the Judaeans?" And Jesus said, "You say it." ¹²And, when he was accused by the chief priests and elders of the people, he made no answer. ¹³Then Pilate says to him, "Do you not hear all the things they attest against you?" ¹⁴And he did not answer him, not a single word, so that the governor was greatly astonished. ¹⁵Now, for the festival it was the governor's custom to release to the crowd one prisoner, whomever they wished. ¹⁶And they had at that time a notable prisoner named bar-Abbas. ¹⁷When therefore they were assembled Pilate said to them, "Whom do you wish I should release to you, bar-Abbas or Jesus, who is called the Anointed?" ¹⁸For he knew that they had handed him over through malice. ¹⁹But as he sat upon the dais his wife sent word to him, saying, "Let there be nothing between you and that just man; for I have suffered many things today in a dream because of him." ²⁰But the chief priests and the elders persuaded the crowds that they should ask for bar-Abbas and should destroy Jesus. ²¹And in reply the governor said

x. This is not in fact a quotation from the book of Jeremiah, but may be a vague reference to Zechariah 11:3.

to them, "Which of the two do you wish that I should release to you?" And they said, "Bar-Abbas." [22]Pilate says to them, "What then should I do with Jesus, who is called the Anointed?" They all say, "Let him be crucified!" [23]But he said, "Why, for what evil did he commit?" But they cried out the more, saying, "Let him be crucified!" [24]And Pilate, seeing that it is bootless, and that unrest is being produced instead, took water and washed his hands in front of the crowd, saying, "I am innocent of this man's blood; you will see to it." [25]And in reply all the people said, "His blood be on us and on our children." [26]Then he released bar-Abbas to them, but having flogged Jesus he handed him over so that he might be crucified.

[27]Then the governor's soldiers, having led Jesus into the Praetorium, gathered the whole cohort around him. [28]And, stripping him, they placed a scarlet cloak about him, [29]And having plaited a crown of thorns they placed it on his head, and a rod in his right hand, and genuflecting before him they derided him, saying, "Hail, King of the Judaeans," [30]And spitting at him they took the rod and battered his head. [31]And when they had mocked him they stripped the cloak from him and put his clothing on him and led him away to crucify him. [32]And going forth they found a Cyrenian man by the name of Simon; and they pressed this man into service so that he might carry his cross. [33]And coming to a place called Golgotha—which is to say, Skull's Place— [34]They gave him wine mixed with gall to drink; and, tasting it, he did not wish to drink. [35]And having crucified him they portioned out his garments, casting lots, [36]And they sat there guarding him. [37]And above his head they set the charge inscribed against him: "THIS IS JESUS THE KING OF THE JUDAEANS." [38]Then two bandits are crucified with him, one to the right and one to the left. [39]And the passersby blasphemed against him, wagging their heads, [40]And saying, "You, the one tearing down the sanctuary and building it up in three days, save yourself if you are God's Son and descend from the cross." [41]Likewise, the chief priests, mocking along with the scribes and the elders, said, [42]"He saved others, himself he cannot save; if he is king of Israel, let him now descend from

the cross and we will believe in him. [43]He has trusted in God—let him now rescue him, if he wants him; for he said, 'I am God's Son.'" [44]And the bandits who were crucified along with him upbraided him also in the same way. [45]And, from the sixth hour to the ninth hour, darkness fell over all the land. [46]And around the ninth hour Jesus cried out in a loud voice, saying, *"Eli, Eli, lema sabachthani?"*—that is, "My God, my God, why did you forsake me?" [47]And some of those who were standing there, hearing this, said, "This man calls to Elijah." [48]And one of them immediately ran and—taking a sponge and filling it with vinegar and putting it on a rod—gave it to him to drink. [49]But the rest said, "Leave off, let us see if Elijah comes to save him." [50]And Jesus, again crying out in a loud voice, gave up the spirit. [51]And look: The veil of the sanctuary was rent in two, from top to bottom, and the earth was shaken, and the rocks were split, [52]And the tombs were opened and many bodies of those holy ones who had fallen asleep were raised; [53]And, coming forth from the tombs, they went into the holy city after his resurrection and appeared to many. [54]And the centurion and those guarding Jesus with him, seeing the earthquake and the things that were happening, were extremely afraid, saying, "Truly this was a god's son." [55]Now there were many women there, watching from afar, who had followed Jesus from Galilee ministering to him; [56]Among them was Mary the Magdalene, and Mary the mother of James and Joseph, and the mother of the sons of Zebedee.

[57]And, evening having come, there came a rich man from Arimathaea by the name of Joseph, who had himself also been a disciple to Jesus; [58]This man, approaching Pilate, requested the body of Jesus. Pilate then ordered that it be given him. [59]And taking the body Joseph wrapped it in clean linen, [60]And placed it in his new tomb, which he had hewn out of rock, and having rolled a great stone before the door he departed. [61]But Mary the Magdalene and the other Mary were there, sitting opposite the tomb. [62]And on the next day, which is after the Preparation, the chief priests and the Pharisees were assembled before Pilate, [63]Saying, "Lord, we have remembered that that deceiver, when he was

still living, said, 'After three days I am raised.' ⁶⁴Therefore command that the tomb be secured until the third day, so that the disciples might not come steal him and say to the people, 'He has been raised from the dead,' and the final deception will be worse than the first." ⁶⁵Pilate said to them, "You have a guard; go make it as secure as you know how." ⁶⁶And going away, along with the guard, they made the tomb secure, sealing up the stone.

CHAPTER TWENTY-EIGHT

¹But after the Sabbath, at the dawn of the first day of the Sabbath-week, Mary the Magdalene and the other Mary came to view the tomb. ²And look: A great earthquake occurred, for an angel of the Lord, descending from the sky and coming forward, rolled away the stone and sat upon it. ³And his appearance was like lightning, and his raiment white as snow. ⁴And those who were standing guard were shaken by terror at him and became as dead men. ⁵And speaking out the angel said to the women, "Do not be afraid; for I know that you seek Jesus who has been crucified; ⁶He is not here; for he was raised, just as he said; come see the place where he lay. ⁷And go quickly, tell his disciples that he was raised from the dead; and look: He precedes you into Galilee, where you will see him. See, I have told you." ⁸And, quickly departing from the tomb with great fear and joy, they ran to announce it to his disciples. ⁹And look: Jesus met them, saying, "Greetings." And, approaching, they took hold of his feet and prostrated themselves before him. ¹⁰Then Jesus says to them, "Do not be afraid; go announce to my brothers that they should depart into Galilee, and there they will see me." ¹¹And as they were going, look: Some of the guard, going into the city, reported to the chief priests all the things that had happened. ¹²And, having met with the elders and taking counsel together, they gave the soldiers a good quantity of silver, ¹³Saying, "Say that 'His disciples, coming by night, stole him while we were sleeping.' ¹⁴And if this is heard of by the governor we shall prevail upon him and see to it that

you are free from trouble." ¹⁵And taking the silver they did as they were instructed. And this is the tale that has been spread about by the Judaeans to this day. ¹⁶But the eleven disciples went into Galilee, to the mountain where Jesus appointed them, ¹⁷And seeing him they prostrated themselves; but some doubted. ¹⁸And, approaching, Jesus spoke to them, saying, "All power in heaven and on earth has been given to me. ¹⁹Go, therefore, instruct all the nations, baptizing them in the name of the Father and the Son and the Holy Spirit, ²⁰Teaching them to observe everything that I have commanded you; and see: I am with you every day until the consummation of the age."

The Gospel
According to Mark

¹The beginning of the good tidings of Jesus the Anointed. ²As has been written by Isaiah the Prophet, "See, I send forth my messengerᵃ before your face, who will prepare your path"ᵇ—³"A voice of one crying out in the wilderness: 'Prepare the Lord's way, make straight his paths'"—⁴John appeared, baptizing in the wilderness, proclaiming a baptism of the heart's transformation, for forgiveness of sins. ⁵And all the region of Judaea and all the Jerusalemites went out to him and were baptized by him in the Jordan River, confessing their sins. ⁶And John was clothed in camel's hairs and a leather girdle about his loins, and would eat locusts and wild honey. ⁷And he made his proclamation, saying, "There comes hereafter one mightier than I, regarding whom I am not fit to bend down and loosen the thong of his sandals. ⁸I baptized you by water, but he will baptize you by a Holy Spirit."

⁹And in those days it happened that Jesus, from Nazareth of Galilee, came and was baptized in the Jordan by John. ¹⁰And, immediately rising

a. ἄγγελος (*angelos*), "angel."

b. Actually, this quotation comes from Malachi 3:1; but the quotation in the following verse is indeed from Isaiah 40:3. In the Byzantine Text-type version of the text, the mention of Isaiah is omitted and replaced by a reference simply to "the prophets."

up out of the water, he saw the heavens being rent apart and the Spirit descending to him as a dove; [11]And a voice out of the heavens: "You are my Son, the beloved, in you I have delighted." [12]And immediately the Spirit cast him out into the wilderness. [13]And he was in the wilderness forty days, being tempted by the Accuser, and was with the wild beasts, and the angels ministered to him.

[14]And after John was handed over Jesus came into Galilee, proclaiming the good tidings of God: [15]That "The proper time has been fulfilled and the Kingdom of God has drawn near; change your hearts and have faith in the good tidings." [16]And, passing along beside the Sea of Galilee, he saw Simon and Simon's brother Andrew trawling in the sea; for they were fishermen. [17]And Jesus said to them, "Come along after me, and I shall make you become fishers of men." [18]And, immediately abandoning the nets, they followed him. [19]And proceeding a little further he saw James, the son of Zebedee, and his brother John, and they were in the boat mending the nets. [20]And immediately he called them; and leaving their father Zebedee in the boat with the hired hands they went away after him.

[21]And they enter Capernaum and, immediately entering the synagogue on the Sabbath, he taught. [22]And they were astonished at his teaching; for he was teaching them as one having authority and not as the scribes. [23]And immediately there was in their synagogue a man in an impure spirit, and he cried out, [24]Saying, "What is there between us and you, Jesus the Nazarene? Did you come to destroy us? I recognize you, who you are, the holy one of God." [25]And Jesus rebuked it: "Be silent and come out." [26]And the impure spirit, convulsing him and shouting with a loud voice, came out of him. [27]And all were astounded, so that they debated among themselves, saying, "What is this? A new teaching, with authority; and he commands the impure spirits and they obey him." [28]And the report of him immediately went forth everywhere, into the whole region of Galilee. [29]And, immediately departing from the synagogue, they went into the house of Simon and Andrew, along with

James and John. [30]And Simon's mother-in-law was laid out, stricken with fever, and immediately they tell him about her. [31]And, approaching, he raised her up, taking hold of her hand; and the fever left her and she waited on them. [32]And, evening coming on, after the sun had set they brought to him all who were ailing and those possessed by demons; [33]And the whole city was assembled at the door. [34]And he healed many who were ailing with various diseases, and he exorcized many demons, and did not allow the demons to speak, because they recognized him. [35]And rising very early in the morning, in the darkness, he went out and departed to a deserted place, and prayed there. [36]And Simon and those with him hunted for him and found him, and they say to him, [37]"Everyone is looking for you." [38]And he says to them, "Let us go somewhere else, into the neighboring towns, that there too I may make my proclamation; for it is for this purpose that I went forth." [39]And he came making his proclamation, into their synagogues, throughout the whole of Galilee, and exorcizing demons.

[40]And a leper comes to him, imploring him and falling to his knees, saying to him, "If you wish it, you are able to cleanse me." [41]And, moved inwardly with compassion,[c] he stretched out his hand and touched him, and says to him, "I wish it, be clean." [42]And the leprosy immediately left him, and he was cleansed. [43]And, sternly admonishing him, he immediately thrust him out, [44]And says to him, "See that you tell nothing to anyone, but go show the priest and offer the things Moses commanded for your cleansing, for a testimony to them." [45]But, on going out, that man began announcing it frequently and spreading the story about, so that he was no longer able to enter a city openly, but was outside in desert places; and they came to him from everywhere.

c. An alternative version of the text, attested by a few ancient witnesses, describes Jesus as moved not by compassion but by anger or vexation (perhaps at the man, perhaps at his affliction).

CHAPTER TWO

¹And, again entering into Capernaum, after some days it was heard that he was in a house. ²And many gathered, so that there was not even room before the door, and he spoke the word to them. ³And they come bearing a paralytic to him, carried by four men. ⁴And, not being able to reach him on account of the crowd, they took away the roof where he was and, having gouged out an opening, they lower the pallet on which the paralytic lay. ⁵And Jesus, seeing their faith, says to the paralytic, "Child, your sins are forgiven." ⁶But some of the scribes were sitting there and reasoning in their hearts, ⁷"Why does this man speak thus? He blasphemes. Who can forgive sins except God alone?" ⁸And Jesus, immediately aware in his spirit that they reasoned thus among themselves, says to them, "Why do you reason over these things in your hearts? ⁹Which is easier, to say to the paralytic, 'Your sins are forgiven,' or to say, 'Rise and take up your pallet and walk'? ¹⁰But in order that you should know that the Son of Man[d] has power to forgive sins on the earth . . ." —He says to the paralytic, ¹¹"I say to you, rise, take up your pallet, and go to your house." ¹²And he arose and, immediately taking up the pallet, went out before everyone, so that all were astonished and glorified God, saying, "We have never seen the like."

¹³And he went out again beside the sea; and the whole crowd came to him, and he taught them. ¹⁴And as he was passing by he saw Levi the son of Alphaeus sitting at the tax-collection house, and he says to him, "Follow me." And getting up he followed him. ¹⁵And it happened that he reclined at table in his house, and many tax-collectors and sinners reclined at table along with Jesus and his disciples; for there were many, and they followed him. ¹⁶And the scribes of the Pharisees, seeing that

d. Though "son of man" is simply a good Semitic idiom meaning "a man," by the first century it had long served as the name of a mysterious apocalyptic or eschatological figure (as in the one "like a son of man" who rides in the chariot of God in Ezekiel), and as Christ uses it in the Gospels it should clearly be read as a distinctive prophetic title (though not one whose precise significance can be ascertained).

he eats with sinners and tax-collectors, said to his disciples, "Does he eat with tax-collectors and sinners?" [17]And, hearing this, Jesus says to them, "Those who are strong have no need of a physician, but rather those who are ill; I came to call not the upright, but sinners." [18]And John's disciples and the Pharisees were fasting. And they come and say to him, "Why do John's disciples and the Pharisees fast, but your disciples do not fast?" [19]And Jesus said to them, "Can the sons of the bridal chamber fast while the bridegroom is with them? For such time as they have the bridegroom with them, they cannot fast. [20]But the days will come when the bridegroom is taken away from them, and then, in that day, they will fast. [21]And no one sews a patch of unfulled cloth on an old garment; otherwise, the filling tears away from it, the new from the old, and a worse rent appears. [22]And no one puts new wine in old wineskins; otherwise, the wine will burst the wineskins, and the wine is lost, and the wineskins also [, but rather new wine into new wineskins]."

[23]And it happened that he passed through fields of grain on the Sabbath, and his disciples began to pluck ears of grain as they made their way. [24]And the Pharisees said to him, "Look: Why do they do what is unlawful on the Sabbath?" [25]And he says to them, "Did you never read what David did when he was in need and hungry, as well as those with him? [26]How he entered the house of God in the days of the chief priest Abiathar and ate the loaves of the bread of Presentation, which it is unlawful for any but the priests to eat, and gave them also to those who were with him?" [27]And he says to them, "The Sabbath came about for the sake of man, not man for the sake of the Sabbath; [28]Thus the Son of Man is Lord even of the Sabbath."

CHAPTER THREE

[1]And he again entered a synagogue. And there was a man who had a hand that had been withered; [2]And they observed him closely to see if he will heal him on the Sabbath, that they might bring an accusation against him. [3]And he says to the man having a withered hand, "Stand

up in our midst." ⁴And he says to them, "Is it permissible on the Sabbath to do good or to do evil? To save a soul or to kill?" But they were silent. ⁵And, looking around at them with anger, mortified at the hardness of their hearts, he says to the man, "Stretch forth the hand." And he stretched it forth and his hand was restored. ⁶And going out the Pharisees immediately exchanged counsel with the Herodians against him, that they might destroy him.

⁷And Jesus withdrew with his disciples to the sea; and a great multitude followed from Galilee, as well as from Judaea ⁸And from Jerusalem and from Idumea and beyond Jordan and the environs of Tyre and Sidon—a great multitude, hearing what things he does, came to him. ⁹And he told his disciples that a boat should be standing by on account of the crowd, so that they should not press in upon him; ¹⁰For he healed many, so that as many as had afflictions fell upon him, in order to touch him. ¹¹And the impure spirits, when they gazed upon him, fell down before him and cried out, saying, "You are the Son of God." ¹²And he gave them many stern admonitions that they should not make him manifest. ¹³And he goes up into the mountain, and summoned to himself those whom he wanted, and they went to him. ¹⁴And he made the number twelve, that they might be with him and that he might send them out to make proclamation ¹⁵And to have power to exorcize demons; ¹⁶And he made them twelve, and to Simon he added the name Peter; ¹⁷And James the son of Zebedee and John the brother of James—to them he also added a name, "Boanerges," which is to say, "Sons of Thunder"— ¹⁸And Andrew, and Philip, and bar-Tholomaeus, and Matthew, and Thomas, and James the son of Alphaeus, and Thaddeus, and Simon the Kananaian,ᵉ ¹⁹And Judas Iscariot, who also betrayed him.

²⁰And he comes into a house; and again a crowd assembles, so that they are not able to eat a loaf of bread. ²¹And his relatives, hearing this,

e. An obscure word, probably a Hellenized form of the Aramaic *qannāyā*, "zealot" (a reading confirmed by Luke's Gospel), but some scholars see it as an eccentric form of "Canaanite."

went out to seize him forcibly; for they said, "He is beside himself." [22]And the scribes coming down from Jerusalem said, "He has Beelzebul in him, and he exorcizes demons by the Archon of the demons." [23]And calling them over he spoke to them in parables: "How can the Accuser[f] exorcize the Accuser? [24]And, if a kingdom be divided against itself, that kingdom cannot stand; [25]And, if a household be divided against itself, that household cannot stand. [26]And, if the Accuser has risen up against himself and has been divided, he cannot stand, but has reached an end. [27]But no one can enter the strong man's household and plunder his possessions unless first he should tie the strong man up, and then he can plunder his household. [28]Amen, I tell you that all will be excused the sons of men, the transgressions and the blasphemies, howsoever they may blaspheme; [29]But whoever blasphemes against the Spirit, the Holy one, has no excuse throughout the age,[g] but is answerable for a transgression in the Age."[h] [30]Because they said, "He has an impure spirit." [31]And his mother and his brothers come, and standing outside they sent word to him, summoning him. [32]And a crowd was seated around him, and they say to him, "Look: Your mother and your brothers and your sisters are outside looking for you." [33]And in reply he says to them, "Who is my mother and who are my brothers?" [34]And looking around at those sitting in a circle about him he says, "Look: my mother and my brothers. [35]Whoever does the will of God, this one is my brother and sister and mother."

CHAPTER FOUR

[1]And again he began to teach beside the sea; and the largest crowd yet gathers to him, so that he embarked in a boat on the sea in order

f. "The Satan," which is to say, "prosecutor," "accuser," "arraigner."
g. Or "until the Age [to come]."
h. An "aeonian transgression": perhaps "answerable for an age-long transgression."

to sit down, and the whole crowd was on land facing the sea. [2]And he taught them many things in parables, and in the course of his instruction he said to them, [3]"Listen, look: A sower went out to sow. [4]And it happened that as he sowed a part fell beside the path and the birds came and devoured it. [5]And another part fell upon the stony place where there was not much soil, and immediately it sprang up because there was no depth to the soil; [6]And when the sun rose it was parched, and because it had no root it was withered. [7]And another part fell among the thorns, and the thorns grew up and throttled it, and it did not yield fruit. [8]And others fell into the good soil and yielded fruit, shooting up and swelling, and bore thirtyfold and sixtyfold and a hundredfold." [9]And he said, "Whoever has ears to hear, let him listen." [10]And, when he was alone, those around him along with the twelve asked him about the parables. [11]And he said to them, "To you the mystery of the Kingdom of God has been granted; but to those outside everything comes in parables, [12]So that seeing they may see and not perceive, and hearing they may hear and not understand, lest they should turn and it should be forgiven them." [13]And he says to them, "Do you not grasp this parable? And how will you understand all the parables? [14]The sower sows the word. [15]And these are those beside the path where the word is sown and, when they hear, the Accuser immediately comes and seizes away the word that has been sown in them. [16]And, similarly, these are those being sown upon the stony places, who when they hear the word immediately accept it with joy, [17]And they do not take root in themselves, but are temporary; then tribulation or persecution comes about on account of the word and they immediately falter. [18]And others are those being sown among thorns: These are those hearing the word, [19]And, the anxieties of the age and the beguilement of riches and longings for other things intrude, throttling the word, and it becomes fruitless. [20]And those sown on the good soil are the ones who hear the word and welcome it and bear fruit, thirtyfold and sixtyfold and a hundredfold." [21]And he said to them: "Does the lamp arrive that it may be placed under the dry-goods basket or under the bed? Not that it may be placed on the lampstand? [22]For there is nothing that is hidden except that it might be made manifest, nor that has become concealed except that it might come out into plain sight. ²³If anyone has ears to hear, let him listen." ²⁴And he said to them, "Pay attention to what you hear. With whatever measure you measure, it shall be meted out to you and will be added to you. ²⁵For he who has, to him it will be given; and he who does not have, even what he has will be taken away from him." ²⁶And he said, "Such is the Kingdom of God: just as a man might cast the seed upon the earth, ²⁷And might sleep and arise night and day, and the seed sprouts and increases while he does not observe. ²⁸The earth bears fruit of itself, first a shoot, then an ear, then the full grain within the ear. ²⁹But, when the fruit permits, he immediately extends the scythe, because the harvest has come." ³⁰And he said, "How may we depict the Kingdom of God, or by what parable may we present it? ³¹As a grain of mustard that, when sown upon the soil, is smaller than all the seeds on earth, ³²And when it is sown it rises up and becomes larger than all the garden-herbs, and produces great branches, so that the birds of the sky are able to shelter under its shade." ³³And he spoke the word to them in many such parables, according to what they were able to hear. ³⁴And he did not speak to them without a parable, but in private he explained everything to his disciples.

³⁵And on that day, when evening had come, he says to them, "Let us cross over to the far shore." ³⁶And dismissing the crowd they take him, as he was in the boat, and other boats were with him. ³⁷And a great windstorm arose, and the waves broke into the boat, so that now the boat was filling. ³⁸And he was sleeping on the pillow in the stern. And they rouse him and say to him, "Teacher, does it not matter to you that we are perishing?" ³⁹And, being woken, he rebuked the wind and said to the sea, "Be silent, quell yourself!" And the wind fell and a great calm came about. ⁴⁰And he said to them, "Why are you so afraid? How is it you do not have faith?" ⁴¹And they were afraid, enormously afraid, and said to one another, "Who then is this man, that even the wind and the sea obey him?"

CHAPTER FIVE

¹And they came to the far shore of the sea, into the region of the Gerasenes. ²And as he disembarked from the boat there came out to meet him from the tombs a man with an impure spirit, ³Who had his dwelling among the tombs, and no one was able any longer to bind him with a chain, ⁴Since he had often been bound with fetters and chains, and the chains had been torn asunder by him and the fetters shattered, and no one had the strength to subdue him; ⁵And always, every night and day, he was among the tombs and in the mountains crying out and gashing himself with stones. ⁶And seeing Jesus from afar he ran and prostrated himself to him, ⁷And crying out with a loud voice he says, "What do I and you have to do with one another, Jesus, Son of the Highest God? I adjure you by God not to torment me." ⁸For he said to him, "Come out from the man, impure spirit." ⁹And he asked him, "What is your name?" And he says to him, "My name is Legion, because we are many." ¹⁰And he vehemently implored him that he not send them out of the land. ¹¹Now there near the mountain a large herd of swine was feeding; ¹²And they entreated him, saying, "Send us into the swine, so that we might enter into them." ¹³And he gave them leave. And coming forth the impure spirits entered into the swine, and the herd charged down the precipice into the sea, about two thousand, and were suffocated in the sea. ¹⁴And those grazing them fled and reported it in the city and in the fields; and they came to see what it is that has happened. ¹⁵And they come to Jesus, and see the demoniac—the one who had had Legion in him—seated, clothed, and in his right mind; and they were afraid. ¹⁶And the eyewitnesses recounted to them how this had happened to the demoniac, and all about the swine. ¹⁷And they began to implore him to pass on beyond their borders. ¹⁸And as he embarked into the boat the former demoniac begged him that he might be with him. ¹⁹And he did not permit him, but says to him, "Go to your house, to your own family, and report to them the things the Lord has done for you, and that he

showed you mercy." ²⁰And he departed and began to proclaim in Decapolis the things Jesus did for him, and everyone was amazed.

²¹And, when Jesus had crossed over in the boat to the far side again, a great crowd congregated about him, and he was beside the sea. ²²And one of the leaders of the synagogue, Jairus by name, comes and, seeing him, falls down at his feet, ²³And implores him urgently, saying: "My little daughter is at the last extremity—so come that you may lay hands upon her, that she may be healed and live." ²⁴And he went with him. And a large crowd followed him, and pressed in upon him. ²⁵And a woman enduring a flow of blood for twelve years, ²⁶And suffering many things under many physicians, and having spent everything she had, and having gained nothing but rather having become worse, ²⁷Hearing things about Jesus, came up behind in the crowd and touched his mantle. ²⁸For she said: "If I may touch even his mantle I shall be healed." ²⁹And immediately the fountain of her blood dried up, and she knew in her body that she was cured of her affliction. ³⁰And immediately Jesus, recognizing in himself the power going forth from him, turning in the crowd, said, "Who touched my mantle?" ³¹And his disciples said to him, "You see the crowd pressing in upon you and you say, 'Who touched me?'" ³²And he looked around to see the woman who had done this. ³³And the woman, afraid and trembling, knowing what had happened to her, came and fell down before him and told him the whole truth. ³⁴And he said to her, "Daughter, your faith has healed you; go in peace and be healed of your affliction." ³⁵As he was still speaking, they come from the home of the leader of the synagogue, saying, "Your daughter has died; why continue to trouble the teacher?" ³⁶But Jesus, overhearing the remark as it was spoken, says to the leader of the synagogue, "Do not be afraid, only have faith." ³⁷And he allowed no one to accompany him except Peter and James and James's brother John. ³⁸And they come into the house of the leader of the synagogue, and he sees a commotion, and people weeping and lamenting a great deal. ³⁹And entering he says to them, "Why do you make a commotion and weep? The

child has not died, but rather sleeps." [40]And they ridiculed him. But he, throwing all of them out, takes the child's father and mother and those who are with him, and goes in where the child was. [41]And seizing the child's hand he says to her, "*Talitha koum*"—which, being interpreted, means, "Little girl, I say to you, arise." [42]And immediately the little girl arose and walked about; for she was twelve years old. And immediately they were astonished, very greatly astonished. [43]And he charged them at length that no one should know of this, and instructed that she be given something to eat.

CHAPTER SIX

[1]And he departed from there, and comes into his native country, and his disciples follow him. [2]And when the Sabbath came he began to teach in the synagogue; and many who heard were astonished, saying, "From where has this man received these things? And what wisdom has been given to this man? And such feats of power brought about by his hands? [3]Is not this man the craftsman, the son of Mary and brother of James and Joses and Judas and Simon? And are not his sisters here with us?" And they were scandalized by him. [4]And Jesus said to them: "A prophet is not dishonored except in his native country and among his own kin and in his household." [5]And he could not perform any feat of power there, except for healing a few sick persons by laying on of hands. [6]And he was amazed at their lack of faith.

And he went round the villages in a circuit, teaching. [7]And he calls the twelve forward and began to send them forth, two by two, and gave them power over impure spirits, [8]And charged them that they should take nothing upon the way, "Except only a staff—not a loaf of bread, not a leather pouch, no copper coin in the girdle—[9]But with sandals bound on, and do not don two tunics." [10]And he said to them, "Wherever you enter a household, remain there until you depart from that place. [11]And whatever place does not receive you or listen to you, on departing from there shake off the dust on the bottom of your feet as a witness to them.

[Amen, I tell you, it will be more tolerable for Sodom and Gomorrah on a day of judgment than for that city.]" ¹²And, going out, they proclaimed that persons should change their hearts, ¹³And exorcized many demons, and anointed with oil many who were ill, and healed them.

¹⁴And King Herod heard of it, for his name became well known, and they said: "John the Baptist has been raised from the dead, and thus feats of power are performed by him." ¹⁵But others said: "It is Elijah." Yet others said: "A prophet, like one of the prophets." ¹⁶But when Herod heard of it he said, "Him whom I beheaded, John—this one has been raised." ¹⁷For Herod himself had sent and arrested John and bound him in prison on account of Herodias, the wife of his brother Philip, because he had married her; ¹⁸For John said to Herod: "It is unlawful for you to have the wife of your brother." ¹⁹And Herodias resented[i] him and wished to kill him, and could not; ²⁰For Herod was afraid of John, knowing him to be a man upright and holy, and protected him, and was very much at a loss when listening to him, yet listened to him with pleasure. ²¹And an opportune day arrived when Herod, for his birthday celebrations, produced a banquet for his grandees and the chiliarchs and the foremost men of Galilee; ²²And, when Herodias's own daughter came in and danced, she pleased Herod and those reclining at table together. And the king said to the girl, "Ask of me whatever you wish, and I will give it to you." ²³And he swore to her: "Whatever you ask I will give you, up to half my kingdom." ²⁴And stepping out she said to her mother, "What should I request?" And she said, "The head of John, the one who baptizes." ²⁵And immediately hastening in to the king she made the request, saying, "I wish that you should at once give me the head of John the Baptist on a trencher." ²⁶And the king, becoming greatly distressed, did not wish to refuse her, on account of his oaths and of those reclining together at table. ²⁷And, immediately sending

---

i. ἐνεῖχεν (*eneichen*): "hold within," "keep fast within" (among other meanings); here it seems to have the sense of χόλον ἐνέχειν (*cholon enechein*): "to harbor anger against," "to resent."

word, the king ordered a guard to bring his head. And going away he beheaded him in prison, [28]And brought his head on a trencher and gave it to the girl, and the girl gave it to her mother. [29]And, hearing of this, his disciples came and took away his corpse and placed it in a tomb.

[30]And those who had been sent out came together to Jesus and reported to him all the things that they had done and taught. [31]And he says to them, "Come by yourselves privately to a deserted place and rest a little." For there were many persons coming and going, and they had no opportunity to eat. [32]And they went away in the boat privately to a deserted place. [33]And many saw them going and knew where, and ran together on foot from all the cities and arrived before them. [34]And disembarking he saw a great crowd, and was moved inwardly with compassion for them because they were like sheep having no shepherd, and he began to teach them many things. [35]And now, the hour getting late, his disciples approached and said: "This place is deserted and the hour is now late; [36]Dismiss them so that, going away to the fields and villages round about, they might buy something to eat for themselves." [37]But in reply he said to them, "You give them something to eat." And they say to him, "How could we go out and buy two hundred denarii's worth of loaves, and give them to them to eat?" [38]And he says to them, "How many loaves do you have? Go look." And finding out they say, "Five, and two fishes." [39]And he instructed all of them to recline, party by party, on the green grass. [40]And they reclined, group by group, a hundred or fifty each. [41]And, taking the five loaves and the two fishes and looking up to heaven, he pronounced a blessing and broke the loaves and gave them to the disciples, to serve to them, and the two fishes he portioned out to everyone. [42]And all ate and ate their fill, [43]And they took up twelve basketfuls of bread fragments and morsels of fish. [44]And those eating the loaves were five thousand men. [45]And immediately he insisted that his disciples embark into the boat and precede him to the other side, to Bethsaida, until he dismisses the crowd. [46]And having taken his leave of them he went away to the mountain to pray. [47]And when evening arrived the boat was in the middle of the sea, and he was upon the land

alone. [48]And seeing them tormented in their rowing, for the wind was against them, he comes toward them at about the fourth watch of the night, walking on the sea; and he intended to pass them by. [49]But, on seeing him walking upon the sea, they thought: "It is a phantom"; and they cried out; [50]For they all saw him and were disturbed. Immediately, however, he spoke with them, and says to them, "Take heart, it is I; do not be afraid." [51]And he went to them, up into the boat, and the wind ceased; and within themselves they were quite overwhelmingly astonished, [52]For they did not understand about the loaves, while their heart was obdurate. [53]And crossing over to the land they came into Gennesaret and moored. [54]And, immediately recognizing him as they disembarked from the boat, [55]They ran about that whole region and began carrying the ill about on pallets, to wherever they heard he was, [56]And wherever he went, into villages or into towns or into fields, they set down the afflicted in the open, and pleaded with him that they might but touch the fringe of his mantle; and as many as touched him were healed.

CHAPTER SEVEN

[1]And the Pharisees and some of the scribes coming out from Jerusalem gather about him. [2]And seeing that some of his disciples eat loaves of bread with impure (that is, unwashed) hands—[3]For the Pharisees and the Judaeans as a whole do not eat unless they wash their hands all the way up the length of the forearm,[j] upholding the tradition of the elders, [4]And coming from the marketplace they do not eat unless they make their ablutions; and there is much else to uphold that they have inherited: immersing drinking vessels, both carven and copper, in

j. The text is obscure; the word here is the dative of $\pi\upsilon\gamma\mu\acute{\eta}$ (*pygmē*), which generally means "fist," and it has been taken variously to mean "with hands clenched together" (and therefore "vigorously" or "thoroughly"), or "with cupped hands," or "palm against fist," or "with a fistful of water." *Pygmē* can also, however, mean a unit of measurement equivalent to the distance from knuckles to elbow: hence my (debatable) translation.

water . . .—⁵And the Pharisees and the scribes inquired of him, "Why do your disciples not walk in accord with the tradition of the elders, but instead eat bread with impure hands?" ⁶But he said to them, "Isaiah prophesied well concerning you, the charlatans, as has been written: 'This people honors me with their lips, but their heart is far away from me; ⁷And they worship me vainly, teaching doctrines that are the dictates of men.' ⁸Forsaking the command of God, you uphold the tradition of men." ⁹And he said to them, "You are quite adept at setting aside God's command so that you may keep your own tradition. ¹⁰For Moses said, 'Honor your father and your mother,' and 'To him who speaks abusively to father or mother let death put an end.' ¹¹But you say if a man says to father or mother, 'Anything that might have been owed you by me is *qurban*'"—which is to say, a consecrated offering—¹²"You no longer allow him to do anything for father or mother, ¹³Making the word of God powerless by your tradition, which you have handed down; and you do many other things of the same kind." ¹⁴And calling the crowd forward again he said to them, "Listen to me, all of you, and understand: ¹⁵There is nothing from outside a man that, entering into him, can defile him; but rather the things that come forth from a man are what defile him." [¹⁶If anyone has ears to listen, let him listen.] ¹⁷And when he went into a house, away from the crowd, his disciples asked him about the parable. ¹⁸And he says to them, "Are you also so unable to understand? Do you not grasp that nothing that enters into a man from without can defile him, ¹⁹Because it enters not into his heart, but into the bowels and is expelled into a latrine, purging away everything that has been eaten?" ²⁰And he said: "That which comes forth from a man, that defiles the man. ²¹For from within, out of the heart of men, emerge evil thoughts, whorings, thefts, murders, ²²Adulteries, acts of greed, iniquities, deceit, licentiousness, a baleful eye, blasphemy, arrogance, recklessness: ²³All these wicked things come forth from within and defile the man."

²⁴And arising from there he departed into the region of Tyre. And he went into a household, wanting no one to recognize him, but he

was unable to stay hidden; ²⁵Rather, immediately hearing about him, a woman whose young daughter had an impure spirit came and cast herself down at his feet; ²⁶And the woman was Greek, by race a Syrophoenician; and she asked him to exorcize the demon from her daughter. ²⁷And he said to her, "First, let the children be fully fed; for it is not a good thing to take the children's bread and throw it to the dogs." ²⁸But she answered and says to him, "Yes, Lord; and the dogs under the table eat from the children's crumbs." ²⁹And he said to her, "On account of this remark, go: the demon has gone out from your daughter." ³⁰And going away to her house she found the child laid out upon the bed, and found that the demon had gone away. ³¹And departing again from the region of Tyre he passed through Sidon to the Sea of Galilee, through the middle of the region of Decapolis. ³²And they bring to him a man who is deaf and can hardly speak, and they implore him that he might lay his hand upon him. ³³Then, privately taking him away from the crowd, he put his fingers into his ears and, spitting, touched his tongue, ³⁴And looking up into the sky he sighed deeply, and says to him, "*Ephphatha*," which means: "Be opened." ³⁵And his ears were opened, and immediately the fetter on his tongue was loosed, and he spoke normally. ³⁶And he commanded them that no one should tell of it; but, as much as he commanded them, they proclaimed it all the more extravagantly. ³⁷And they were astonished beyond all measure, saying, "He has done all things well, and he makes the deaf to hear and the mute to speak."

CHAPTER EIGHT

¹In those days, there being again a great crowd and they not having anything that they might eat, he summons the disciples and says to them, ²"I am moved inwardly with compassion for the crowd, because they remain with me, three days now, and they do not have anything that they might eat, ³And if I send them away home unfed they will grow weak on the way; and some of them come from far away." ⁴And his disciples answered him: "From where, in a desert, will anyone here

be able to get loaves of bread fully to feed these people?" ⁵And he asked them, "How many loaves do you have?" And they said, "Seven." ⁶And he enjoins the crowd to rest upon the ground; and taking the seven loaves, giving thanks, he broke them and gave them to his disciples so that they might serve them out, and they served them to the crowd. ⁷And they had a few small fishes; and blessing these he instructed that they too be served out. ⁸And they ate and were fully fed, and they gathered up the overflow of fragments, seven baskets of them. ⁹And they were about four thousand. And he sent them away. ¹⁰And, immediately embarking in the boat with his disciples, he went into the district of Dalmanoutha.ᵏ

¹¹And the Pharisees came out and began to debate with him, seeking from him a sign from heaven, testing him. ¹²And groaning in his spirit he says, "Why does this generation seek a sign? As if—amen, I tell you—a sign will be given to this generation!" ¹³And leaving them he again embarked and crossed over to the other side. ¹⁴And they forgot to take along loaves of bread, and except for one loaf they had nothing with them in the boat. ¹⁵And he instructed them, saying, "Watch, be wary of the yeast of the Pharisees and of the yeast of Herod." ¹⁶And this, they reasoned with one another, was because they have no loaves of bread. ¹⁷And, knowing this, he says to them, "Why do you reason that it is because you have no loaves of bread? Do you not yet perceive, nor understand? Do you keep an obdurate heart in you? ¹⁸Having eyes, do you not look? And having ears, do you not listen? And do you not remember? ¹⁹When I broke the five loaves of bread among the five thousand, how many baskets filled with fragments did you gather up?" They say to him, "Twelve." ²⁰"When the seven among the four thousand, how many basketfuls of fragments did you gather up?" And they say, "Seven." ²¹And he said to them, "Do you still not understand?"

k. The Greek reads "τὰ μέρη Δαλμανουθά" (*ta merē Dalmanoutha*), "Dalmanoutha's parts" or "the district of Dalmanoutha." No place bearing this name is known to have existed, and many scholars suspect a corruption of an Aramaic phrase meaning nothing more than what the Greek *ta merē* already says: "the district of."

[22]And they come to Bethsaida. And they bring a blind man to him and implore him that he might touch him. [23]And taking the blind man's hands he led him away outside the village, and spitting in his eyes he laid hands upon him and inquired of him: "Do you see anything?" [24]And looking up he said, "I see men, such that it is as if I perceive trees walking about." [25]Then he again laid hands upon his eyes, and he stared hard, and he was restored, and he saw everything clearly. [26]And he sent him away to his house, saying, "You must not even go into the village."

[27]And Jesus and his disciples departed to the villages of Caesarea Philippi; and on the way he questioned his disciples, saying to them, "Whom do people say me to be?" [28]And they told him, saying: "John the Baptist, and others Elijah, and yet others one of the prophets." [29]And he asked them, "But you, whom do you say me to be?" And in reply Peter says to him, "You are the Anointed." [30]And he warned them sternly that they should tell no one about him. [31]And he began to teach them that it is necessary for the Son of Man to suffer many things, and to be rejected by the elders and the chief priests and the scribes, and to be killed, and after three days to rise again. [32]And he made this declaration frankly. And, taking hold of him, Peter began to admonish him. [33]But he, turning about and looking at his disciples, admonished Peter and says, "Get behind me, Accuser, because you think not the things of God but those of men." [34]And summoning the crowd along with his disciples he said to them, "If anyone wishes to come along behind me, let him deny himself utterly and take up his cross and follow me. [35]For whoever wishes to save his soul will lose it; but whoever will lose his soul for the sake of me and of the good tidings will save it. [36]For what does it profit a man to gain the whole cosmos and to forfeit his soul? [37]For what might a man give in exchange for his soul? [38]For whoever is ashamed of me and my words in this adulterous and sinful generation, of him too will the Son of Man be ashamed when he comes in the glory of his Father with the holy angels."

CHAPTER NINE

¹And he said to them, "Amen, I tell you that there are some of those standing here who most certainly shall not taste of death until they see the Kingdom of God come in power."

²And after six days Jesus takes Peter and James and John, and privately leads them up alone to a high mountain. ³And he was transfigured before them, and his garments became an exceedingly brilliant white, a white such as no fuller on earth can produce. ⁴And Moses and Elijah were seen by them, and they were conversing with Jesus. ⁵And Peter, speaking out, says to Jesus, "Rabbi, it is a good thing for us to be here, and let us make three tabernacles, one for you and one for Moses and one for Elijah." ⁶For he did not know what expostulation to make; for they had become extremely afraid. ⁷And a cloud arose, overshadowing them, and there came a voice from the cloud: "This is my Son, the beloved; listen to him." ⁸And, looking around, they all at once saw no one with them any longer, save Jesus alone. ⁹And as they were coming down out of the mountain he enjoined them that they should not relate the things they saw to anyone, except when the Son of Man should rise from among the dead. ¹⁰And they seized upon this phrase for themselves, debating what this "to rise from among the dead" means. ¹¹And they questioned him, saying, "Why do the scribes say that it is necessary for Elijah to come first?" ¹²And he said to them, "Elijah indeed, coming first, will restore all things; and how has it been written about the Son of Man that he should suffer many things and be held in contempt? ¹³But I tell you that Elijah has also come, and they did whatever things to him they wished, as has been written about him."

¹⁴And as they came to the disciples they saw a great crowd around them, and scribes arguing with them. ¹⁵And, on seeing him, all the crowd were greatly amazed and ran up to him and hailed him. ¹⁶And he inquired of them, "What are you arguing about with them?" ¹⁷And one in the crowd answered him, "Teacher, I brought you my son, who has a mute spirit; ¹⁸And wherever it seizes him, it tears at him, and he froths and

grinds his teeth and is withered up; and I told your disciples that they should exorcize it, and they did not have the strength." [19]And in reply he says to them, "O faithless generation, how long shall I be in your presence? Bring him to me." [20]And they brought him to him. And, seeing him, the spirit immediately convulsed him violently, and falling upon the ground he rolled about frothing. [21]And he asked his father, "Over what span of time has this been happening to him?" And he said, "Since early childhood. [22]And it has often flung him both into fire and into waters, so that it might destroy him; but if you are able, moved by compassion for us, help us." [23]And Jesus said to him, "As to 'if you are able'— all things are possible for the one who has faith." [24]Immediately crying out, the child's father said, "I have faith; help my faithlessness!" [25]And Jesus, seeing that the crowd is rapidly gathering, admonished the impure spirit, saying to it, "Spirit mute and deaf, I command you: Come out of him, and never again may you enter into him." [26]And, crying aloud and with many convulsions, it came out; and he became like a corpse, such that many said that he had died. [27]But Jesus, taking hold of his hand, raised him, and he stood up. [28]And when he entered into a house his disciples asked him in private, "Why were we not able to exorcize it?" [29]And he said to them, "By nothing but prayer can this kind come out."

[30]And departing from there they passed through Galilee, and he did not wish that anyone should know it; [31]For he was teaching his disciples, and said to them: "The Son of Man is delivered over into the hands of men, and they will kill him, and having been killed he will arise after three days." [32]But they did not understand this utterance, and were afraid to question him.

[33]And they came to Capernaum. And when he had come into the household he asked them, "What were you debating on the way?" [34]But they were silent; for on the way they debated with one another who was greater. [35]And sitting down he called out to the twelve and says to them, "If anyone wishes to be first, he shall be the last of all and the servant of all." [36]And taking a small child he stood him in their midst, and folding the child in his arms he said to them, [37]"Whoever in my name receives

one of the little children, like this one, receives me; and whoever receives me receives not me but the one having sent me forth." [38]John said to him, "Teacher, we saw someone who does not follow us exorcizing demons in your name, and we forbade him, because he was not following us." [39]But Jesus said, "Do not forbid him, for there is no one who will perform a deed of power in my name who will also be able soon afterward to speak ill of me; [40]For whoever is not against us is for us. [41]For whoever gives you a cup of water to drink in the name, because you belong to the Anointed, amen, I tell you that he most certainly will not lose his reward. [42]And whoever causes one of these little ones who have faith to falter, it is better for him to have a millstone, of the kind turned by an ass, hung about his neck and to be thrown into the sea. [43]And if your hand causes you to falter, cut it off; it is good for you to enter into life maimed rather than, having two hands, to go away into the Vale of Hinnom, into the inextinguishable fire. [[44]'Where their worm does not die and their fire is not quenched.'] [45]And if your foot causes you to falter, cut it off; it is good for you to enter into life limping rather than, having both feet, to be cast into the Vale of Hinnom. [[46]'Where their worm does not die and their fire is not quenched.'] [47]And if your eye causes you to falter, fling it away; it is good for you to enter one-eyed into the Kingdom of God rather than, having two eyes, to be cast into the Vale of Hinnom, [48]'Where their worm does not die and their fire is not quenched.' [49]For everyone will be salted with fire. [50]Salt is good; but if the salt loses saltiness, with what will you season it? Keep salt in yourselves and be at peace with one another."

CHAPTER TEN

[1]And rising up from there he comes into the region of Judaea [and] beyond the Jordan,[1] and again crowds gather to him, and again he taught

---

1. This is geographically inaccurate, unless the (questionable) "and" found in some manuscripts is taken as indicating two separate journeys.

them, as was his normal practice. [2]And Pharisees approached and tested him, asking him whether it is lawful for a man to divorce his wife. [3]But in reply he said to them, [4]"What did Moses command you?" And they said, "Moses permitted inscribing a writ of separation and divorcing." [5]And Jesus said to them, "Because of your hardheartedness he wrote this commandment for you. [6]But from the beginning of creation 'male and female he created them'; [7]'For this cause a man shall leave father and mother, [8]And they shall be two in one flesh'; thus they are no longer two, but rather one flesh. [9]What therefore God joined together, let no man separate." [10]And when they were again in the house the disciples questioned him about this. [11]And he says to them, "Whoever divorces his wife and marries another commits adultery against her; [12]And if she, having divorced her husband, marries another, she commits adultery."

[13]And they brought small children to him that he might touch them; but the disciples scolded them. [14]But seeing this Jesus was deeply annoyed and said to them, "Let the little children come to me, do not prevent them; for of such is the Kingdom of God. [15]Amen, I tell you, whoever does not receive the Kingdom of God like a little child certainly may not enter into it." [16]And, enfolding them in his arms and laying hands upon them, he blesses them.

[17]And, as he went forth into the roadway, someone came running to him and knelt and asked, "Good teacher, what may I do in order that I may inherit the life of the Age?" [18]"Why do you call me good? There is no one good save one: God. [19]You know the commandments: You shall not murder, you shall not commit adultery, you shall not steal, you shall not bear false witness, you shall not defraud, honor your father and mother." [20]And he declared to him, "Teacher, all of these I have kept since my youth." [21]And Jesus, looking at him, loved him and said to him, "You lack a single thing: Go, sell whatever you possess and give to the destitute, and you shall have a treasury in the heavens, and come follow me." [22]But the young man, saddened by the counsel, went away in sorrow, for he was someone who had many possessions. [23]And looking around Jesus says to his disciples, "How hard it will be for those

possessing riches to enter into the Kingdom of God." ²⁴And the disciples were amazed at his words. And Jesus, speaking out again, says to them, "Children, how hard it is to enter into the Kingdom of God; ²⁵It is easier for a camelᵐ to pass through the eye of a needle than for a rich man to enter into the Kingdom of God." ²⁶And they were greatly astonished, saying to themselves, "Can any of them then be saved?"ⁿ ²⁷Looking directly at them, Jesus says, "For men this is impossible, but not for God; for all things are possible with God." ²⁸Peter began to say to him, "See: We gave up all things and followed you." ²⁹Jesus said, "Amen, I tell you, there is no one who gave up house or brothers or sisters or mother or father or children or fields for my sake and for the sake of the good tidings, ³⁰Who does not—along with persecutions—receive a hundredfold, in the present time, houses and brothers and sisters and mothers and children and fields, as well as, in the Age to come, the life of that Age. ³¹But many who are first will be last and last first."

³²And they were on the road, going up to Jerusalem, and Jesus was leading them, and they were astonished, and those following along were afraid. And, again taking the twelve aside, he began to tell them the things that were about to happen to him: ³³"Look: We are going up to Jerusalem, and the Son of Man will be handed over to the chief priests and scribes, and they will condemn him to death, and they will hand him over to the gentiles, ³⁴And they will mock him and spit upon him and flog and kill him, and after three days he will rise again."

³⁵And James and John, the sons of Zebedee, approach him, saying to him, "Teacher, we wish that you would do for us whatever we might request of you." ³⁶And he said to them, "What do you wish that I might

m. The text speaks of a κάμηλος (kamēlos, acc. kamēlon), "camel," but from the early centuries it has been an open question whether it should really be the homophonous (but poorly attested) word κάμιλος (kamilos), "rope," "hawser": a more symmetrical but less piquant analogy.

n. καὶ τίς δύναται σωθῆναι (kai tis dynatai sōthēnai): often translated as "Who then can be saved?" or "Can anyone then be saved?" but I take the import (specifically as regards the τίς) to be "Can any [rich man] then be saved?"

do for you?" [37]And they said to him, "Grant to us that, in your glory, we may sit one on your right and one on your left." [38]But Jesus said to them, "You do not know what you ask. Can you drink the cup that I drink, or be baptized with the baptism with which I am baptized?" [39]And they said to him, "We can." And Jesus said to them, "You shall drink the cup I drink, and be baptized with the baptism with which I am baptized; [40]But to sit on my right and on my left is not mine to give, but is theirs for whom it has been prepared." [41]And hearing this the ten began to be irate about James and John. [42]And, summoning them, Jesus says to them, "You know that those who are supposed to rule the gentile peoples dominate them, and that their great men wield power over them. [43]But it is not so among you; rather, whoever among you wishes to be great will be your servant, [44]And whoever among you wishes to be first will be the slave of all; [45]For even the Son of Man came not to be served, but to serve and to give his soul as the price of liberation for many."

[46]And they come into Jericho. And, as he was departing from Jericho along with his disciples and a considerable crowd, a blind beggar, bar-Timaeus—"son of Timaeus"—sat beside the road. [47]And hearing that it is Jesus the Nazarene he began to cry out and to say, "Son of David, Jesus, have mercy on me." [48]And many persons admonished him to be silent; but he cried out all the more, "Son of David, have mercy on me." [49]And coming to a standstill Jesus said, "Call to him." And they call to the blind man, saying to him, "Take heart, arise, he calls to you." [50]So, throwing off his mantle and springing up, he came to Jesus. [51]And, answering him, Jesus said, "What do you wish that I might do for you?" And the blind man said to him, "Rabbouni, that I might see again." [52]And Jesus said to him, "Go, your faith has healed you." And immediately he saw again and followed him upon the road.

CHAPTER ELEVEN

[1]And when they come near to Jerusalem, to Bethphage and Bethany, at the Mount of Olives, Jesus sends forth two of his disciples, [2]And tells

them, "Go into the village opposite you, and immediately on entering it you will find a tethered colt upon which no one among men has yet sat; untie and bring it. ³And if anyone says to you, 'Why do you do this?' say, 'The Lord has need of it, and he is sending it here again right away.'" ⁴And they went and found a colt tethered at a door, outside in the open street, and they untie it. ⁵And some of the bystanders there said to them, "What are you doing, untying the colt?" ⁶And they spoke to them as Jesus instructed, and they let them go. ⁷And they bring the colt to Jesus, and they place their cloaks upon it, and he sat on it. ⁸And many persons spread their cloaks in the road, but others stalks of straw, cutting them from the fields. ⁹And both those going ahead and those following after cried out, "Hosanna! Blessed is the one coming in the name of the Lord; ¹⁰Blessed is the coming kingdom of our father David; hosanna in the highest places!" ¹¹And he entered into Jerusalem, into the Temple; and on looking around at everything, the hour now being late, he went out to Bethany with the twelve.

¹²And as they went out from Bethany the next day he was hungry. ¹³And seeing from afar a fig tree bearing leaves he went over, seeing whether he will perhaps find something on it, and coming up to it he found nothing except leaves; for it was not the season for figs. ¹⁴And speaking out he said to it, "May no one eat fruit from you again, throughout the age."ᵒ And his disciples heard him. ¹⁵And they come into Jerusalem. And entering the Temple he began to throw out those selling and buying in the Temple, and he overturned the tables of the money-changers and the seats of those selling the doves, ¹⁶And did not permit anyone to carry a container through the Temple, ¹⁷And he taught and said to them, "Has it not been written that 'My house shall be called a house of prayer for all the nations'? But you have made it a robbers' den." ¹⁸And the chief priests and the scribes heard, and sought a way by which they might destroy him; for they were afraid of him, for all the crowd was awestruck at his teaching. ¹⁹And when it grew late they went

o. Or "until the Age [to come]."

forth outside the city. ²⁰And passing by early in the morning they saw the fig tree dried up from the roots. ²¹And Peter, remembering, says to him, "Rabbi, look: The fig tree that you cursed has been withered." ²²And in reply Jesus said to them, "Have faith in God. ²³Amen, I tell you that whoever says to this mountain, 'Be caught up and flung into the sea,' and is not divided in his heart, but rather has faith that what he says is happening, it will be his. ²⁴Therefore I tell you, all such things as you might pray and ask for, have faith that you have received and they will be yours. ²⁵And when you stand praying, forgive anything you might have against anyone, so that your Father in the heavens might also forgive you your transgressions. [²⁶But if you do not forgive, neither will your Father in the heavens forgive your transgressions.]"

²⁷And they come again into Jerusalem. And, as he was walking about in the Temple, the chief priests and the scribes and the elders come to him, ²⁸And said to him, "By what power do you do these things? Or who gave you this power, that you might do such things?" ²⁹And Jesus said to them, "I shall ask you one thing, and you answer me, and I will tell you by what power I do these things: ³⁰John's baptism, was it from heaven or from men? Answer me." ³¹And they discussed this among themselves, saying, "If we say, 'From heaven,' he will say to us, 'Why then did you not trust him?' ³²But may we say, 'From men'?" — They were afraid of the crowd, for all held that John truly was a prophet. ³³And replying to Jesus they say, "We do not know." And Jesus says to them, "Neither do I tell you by what power I do these things."

CHAPTER TWELVE

¹And he began to speak to them in parables: "A man planted a vineyard and ran a fence around it and dug a winepress in it and constructed a tower and leased it out to husbandmen and went abroad. ²And at the proper season he sent a slave to the husbandmen that he might receive from the husbandmen a share of the vineyard's fruits. ³And seizing him they flogged him and sent him away empty. ⁴And again he sent another

slave to them; and that one they struck on the head and treated with contempt. ⁵And he sent another—and that one they killed—then many others—some they flogged, some they killed. ⁶One he still had, a beloved son; he sent him to them last, saying: 'My son they will treat with shamed deference.' ⁷But those husbandmen said to themselves: 'This is the heir; come, let us kill him, and the inheritance will be ours.' ⁸And seizing him they killed him, and flung him outside the vineyard. ⁹What will the lord of the vineyard do? He will come and will destroy the husbandmen and will give the vineyard to others. ¹⁰Have you not read this scripture: 'A stone that the builders rejected, this became the corner's capstone; ¹¹From the Lord this came to pass, and it is marvelous in our eyes'?" ¹²They both desired to seize him by force and were also afraid of the crowd; for they knew that he told the parable in regard to them. And, leaving him be, they departed.

¹³And they send some of the Pharisees and the Herodians to him, in order that they might trap him in words. ¹⁴And approaching they say to him, "Teacher, we know that you are truthful and that you have no anxiety concerning anyone, for you do not regard men's persons, but teach the way of God in truth. Is it lawful to render the poll-tax to Caesar or not? May we render it or may we not render it?" ¹⁵But he, recognizing their pretense, said to them, "Why do you try me? Bring me a denarius so that I see it." ¹⁶And they brought it. And he says to them, "Whose image is this and whose inscription?" And they say to him, "Caesar's." ¹⁷And Jesus said to them, "Render the things that are Caesar's to Caesar and the things that are God's to God." And they were utterly amazed at him.

¹⁸And Sadducees, who say there is no resurrection, approach him and questioned him, saying, ¹⁹"Teacher, Moses wrote to us that 'If the brother of anyone should die and leave behind a wife and leaves no child, his brother should take his wife and should raise up seed for his brother.' ²⁰There were seven brothers; and the first took a wife and, dying, left no seed; ²¹And the second took her and died, leaving no seed behind; and the third likewise; ²²And the seven left no seed. Last of all,

the wife died. [23]In the resurrection, when they rise again, of which of them will she be the wife? For the seven had her as wife." [24]Jesus said to them, "Have you not been led astray, knowing neither the scriptures nor the power of God? [25]For when they rise again from the dead they neither marry nor are married, but are as angels in the heavens.[p] [26]But regarding the dead, that they are raised, have you not read in the book of Moses how at the bush God spoke to him, saying, 'I am God of Abraham and God of Isaac and God of Jacob'? [27]He is not a God of the dead, but of the living. You go far astray."

[28]And one of the scribes, approaching, hearing them debating and perceiving that he answered them well, asked him, "Which commandment is first among all?" [29]Jesus answered: "The first is: 'Hear, Israel, the Lord our God is One Lord, [30]And you shall love the Lord your God out of your whole heart and out of your whole soul and out of your whole reason and out of your whole strength.' [31]The second is this: 'You shall love your neighbor as yourself.' There is not another commandment greater than these." [32]And the scribe said to him, "Well said, teacher, you speak the truth in saying that there is One and there is no other beside him; [33]And to love him out of the whole heart and out of the whole understanding and out of the whole of one's strength, and to love the neighbor as oneself, is more than all holocausts and sacrifices." [34]And Jesus, seeing that he answered wisely, said to him, "You are not far from the Kingdom of God." And no one dared interrogate him anymore.

[35]And Jesus, teaching in the Temple, spoke aloud: "How do the scribes say that the Anointed is the son of David? [36]David himself, in the Holy Spirit, said, 'The Lord said to my lord, "Sit upon my right until I put your enemies beneath your feet."' [37]David himself calls him 'Lord,' and how is he his son?"

And the large crowd heard him with delight. [38]And in the course of

p. See Acts 23:8; 1 Corinthians 15:40–54; and 1 Peter 3:18–19, 4:6, as well as the footnotes thereto.

his teaching he said, "Be wary of the scribes who desire to walk about in long robes, and desire salutations in the marketplaces, [39]And chief seats in the synagogues, and chief couches at meals; [40]Those devouring the homes of the widows and praying at great length for show, these shall receive condemnation in greater abundance." [41]And sitting opposite the treasury he watched how the crowd puts coin into the treasury; and many rich men put in a great deal; [42]And one destitute widow came and put in two lepta, which is a quadrans. [43]And summoning his disciples he said to them, "Amen, I tell you that this widow, the destitute woman, put in more than all those donating to the treasury; [44]For all donated out of what they have in abundance, but out of her poverty this woman donated all she had whatsoever, her whole livelihood."

CHAPTER THIRTEEN

[1]And as he goes out of the Temple one of his disciples says to him, "Teacher, look: such stones and such buildings!" [2]And Jesus said to him, "Do you see these great buildings? By no means shall there be a stone left upon a stone that will not be thrown down." [3]And as he sat upon the Mount of Olives, opposite the Temple, Peter and James and John and Andrew asked him in private, [4]"Tell us: When will these things be? And, when all these things are about to be completed, what will be the sign?" [5]And Jesus began, saying to them, "Keep watch, so that no one causes you to go astray. [6]Many will come in my name, saying: 'I am he,' and will cause many to go astray. [7]But when you hear about wars and rumors of wars, do not be alarmed; it is necessary that this occur, but the end is not yet. [8]For nation will be raised against nation, and kingdom against kingdom. In places there will be earthquakes, there will be famines; these things are the beginning of birth pangs. [9]But you, look to yourselves: They will deliver you over to councils and you will be beaten in synagogues, and you will be arraigned before rulers and kings for my sake — in order to testify to them. [10]And it is necessary first that the good tidings be proclaimed to all the nations. [11]And when, on

delivering you over, they lead you in, do not worry beforehand about what you are saying; rather, whatever is given to you in that hour, say that; for you are not the ones speaking, but rather the Spirit, the Holy one. [12]And brother will deliver up brother to death, and father child, and children will rise up against parents and put them to death; [13]And you will be hated by all on account of my name; but whoever endures to the end, that one will be saved. [14]And when you see the abomination of desolation standing where it ought not . . ." (Let the reader understand) ". . . then those in Judaea, let them flee into the mountains; [15]He who is on the housetop, let him neither descend nor go in to collect things from his household; [16]And he who is in the field, let him not turn back to fetch his cloak. [17]And alas in those days for pregnant women and for women nursing. [18]And pray that it may not occur in winter; [19]For those days will be an affliction such as has not occurred from the beginning of the creation that God created until now—nor indeed could occur. [20]And, but that the Lord shortened those days, no flesh at all would have been saved; yet, because of the chosen whom he chose, he shortened the days. [21]And if anyone says to you then, 'Look: Here is the Anointed,' 'Look: There,' do not believe; [22]False Anointed Ones and false prophets will be raised up, and they will produce signs and prodigies, so as to lead astray—if possible—the chosen. [23]But keep watch: I have told you all things in advance. [24]And in those days, after that affliction, the sun will be darkened, and the moon will not give her light, [25]And the stars will be falling from the sky, and the powers in the heavens will be shaken. [26]And then they will see the Son of Man coming in the clouds with great power and glory; [27]And then he will send forth the angels and they will gather together the chosen from the four winds, from the ends of the earth to the ends of the sky. [28]But learn the parable from the fig tree: Now, when its branch softens and it produces leaves, you know that the summer is near; [29]So you also, when you see these things happening, you know that he is near, at the doors. [30]Amen, I tell you that this generation most certainly does not pass away until all these things happen. [31]The sky and the earth will pass away, but my words will not pass away. [32]But, as for the day and hour, no one knows—neither the angels in heaven nor the Son—except the Father. [33]Keep watch, be alert: For you do not know when the moment is. [34]Just as a man gone abroad, leaving his household and giving power to his slaves—to each a task of his own—also commanded the doorkeeper that he should be vigilant. [35]Be vigilant, therefore—for you do not know when the Lord of the household comes, whether at evening or at midnight or at cockcrow or in the morning—[36]So that, arriving suddenly, he does not find you sleeping. [37]And what I say to you I say to all: Be vigilant."

CHAPTER FOURTEEN

[1]Now it would after two days be the Passover and the feast of Unleavened Bread. And the chief priests and the scribes sought a way in which, seizing him by deceit, they might kill him; [2]For they said, "Not during the festival, so that there will be no unrest among the people."

[3]And when he was in Bethany, in the home of Simon the leper, reclining at table, there came a woman who had an alabaster phial of pure, precious unguent of nard; breaking the alabaster phial, she poured it over his head. [4]But there were some who expressed indignation to one another: "Why has there been this waste of the unguent? [5]For this unguent could be sold for more than three hundred denarii, and that given to the destitute." And they were angry at her. [6]But Jesus said, "Leave her be; why do you subject her to abuse? She has done me a beautiful deed; [7]For you always have the destitute with you, and you can do good to them whenever you wish, but you do not always have me. [8]She did what she could; she has anointed my body, in anticipation, for burial. [9]Amen, I tell you, wherever the good tidings are proclaimed, in the whole world, what this woman did will also be told, as a memorial to her." [10]And Judas Iscariot, one of the twelve, went to the chief priests in order that he might hand him over to them. [11]And hearing this they were grateful and promised to give him silver. And he sought an opportune means by which he might hand him over.

[12]And on the first day of the Unleavened Loaves, when they sacrifice the Passover lamb,[q] his disciples say to him, "Where do you wish us to go make preparations for you to eat the Passover?" [13]And he sends out two of his disciples and says to them, "Go into the city, and a man carrying an earthen vessel of water will meet you; follow him, [14]And, wherever he goes inside, tell the master of the house, 'The teacher says, "Where are my quarters, where I may eat the Passover with my disciples?"' [15]And he will show you a large upper room, already laid out; and prepare for us there." [16]And the disciples went out and came into the city, and found exactly what he had told them, and prepared the Passover. [17]And when evening came he arrives with the twelve. [18]And as they were reclined at table and eating, Jesus said, "Amen, I tell you that one of you will hand me over, one who is eating with me." [19]They began to be distressed and to say to him, one by one, "Surely not I?" [20]And he said to them, "One of the twelve, the one who dips in the same dish along with me. [21]Because indeed the Son of Man goes away, just as has been written concerning him; but alas for that man by whom the Son of Man is handed over; a good thing for that man if he had not been born." [22]And as they were eating he took a loaf and, giving thanks, broke it and gave it to them, and said, "Take it: This is my body." [23]And, taking a cup and giving thanks, he gave it to them, and all drank from it. [24]And he said to them, "This is my blood of the covenant, which is being shed for many. [25]Amen, I tell you, henceforth I will most surely not drink of the yield of the vine until that day when I drink it with you, new, in the Kingdom of God."

[26]And, having sung a hymn, they went out to the Mount of Olives. [27]And Jesus says to them: "You will all be caused to falter, because it has been written, 'I shall strike down the shepherd, and the sheep will be scattered.' [28]But after I am raised, I shall precede you into Galilee." [29]But Peter declared to him, "Even if all will be made to falter, still I

q. Actually, the sacrifice of the paschal lamb occurs on the day before the feast.

shall not." ³⁰And Jesus says to him, "Amen, I tell you that today, this very night, before the cock crows twice, you will deny me three times." ³¹But he said more vehemently, "Even if it should be necessary for me to die with you, I most assuredly will not deny you." And so said all.

³²And they come to a place whose name is Gethsemane, and he says to the disciples, "Sit down here while I pray." ³³And he takes Peter and James and John along with him, and he began to be overwhelmed and to suffer distress. ³⁴And he says to them, "My soul is in anguish, to the point of death; remain here and keep watch." ³⁵And going a little ahead he fell on the ground and prayed that, if it is possible, the hour might pass him by, ³⁶And said, "Abba,"—Father—"for you all things are possible; take this cup away from me; yet not what I will, but rather what you will." ³⁷And he comes and finds them sleeping, and says to Peter, "Simon, are you sleeping? Could you not keep watch for one hour? ³⁸Keep watch and pray, that you might not come to trial; truly, the spirit is eager, but the flesh is frail." ³⁹And going again he prayed, speaking the same words. ⁴⁰And on coming he again found them sleeping, for their eyes were becoming very heavy, and they did not know what answer they might give him. ⁴¹And he comes the third time and says to them, "Sleep some more and rest; it is far off . . .ʳ—The hour has come. Look: The Son of Man is delivered over into the hands of sinners. ⁴²Arise, let us be going. Look: The one handing me over has come near." ⁴³And immediately, while he was still speaking, Judas, one of the twelve, ar-

r. ἀπέχει (*apechei*): a word that, in this context, is notoriously obscure. In the transitive, it would normally mean "keeps [something] away," "holds [something] off," or, alternatively, "desists from," "abstains from," "holds off from"; in the intransitive (which it appears to be here), it would normally mean "is far away from," "is distant," or even "extends from"; in the case of certain financial transactions it can mean "is paid in full." Traditional translations, since Jerome, have taken it here to mean "it is enough," "it suffices," though that is a dubious reading. Some take it to be a question—"Is [the hour] far off?"—one that is immediately answered in the negative, or to be a statement—"It is (yet) far off"—one that is immediately contradicted. I have elected the last solution, though with no particular confidence.

rives, and with him a crowd with swords and bludgeons from the chief priests and scribes and elders. [44]Now the one handing him over gave them a sign, saying, "Whomever I should kiss is he; seize him and lead him securely away." [45]And, coming, he immediately approaches and says to him, "Rabbi," and kissed him affectionately. [46]And they laid hands on him and forcibly seized him. [47]But a certain one of those standing beside him, pulling out his sword, struck the chief priest's slave and cut off his ear. [48]And Jesus, speaking aloud, said to them, "You came out to arrest me, as though against a bandit, with swords and bludgeons? [49]Each day I was with you in the Temple teaching, and you did not seize me — that thus, instead, the scriptures might be fulfilled." [50]And abandoning him all fled away. [51]And a certain young man, wearing a linen garment over his bare flesh, followed along with him, and they seize him forcibly; [52]And he, leaving the linen garment behind, fled away naked.

[53]And they led Jesus away to the chief priest, and all the chief priests and the elders and the scribes assemble. [54]And Peter followed him from afar, until he was within, in the courtyard of the chief priest, and he was sitting together with the attendants and warming himself at the light. [55]And the chief priests and the entire Council sought out evidence against Jesus, in order to put him to death, and found none. [56]For many testified falsely against him, and the testimonies were not in agreement. [57]And some, standing up, testified falsely against him, saying: [58]"We heard him saying, 'I will tear down this sanctuary made by hand and after three days I will erect another not made by hand.'" [59]And, even so, their testimony was not in agreement. [60]And, standing up amidst them, the chief priest asked Jesus, "Do you answer nothing to what these men attest against you?" [61]But he was silent and answered nothing. Again the chief priest questioned him and says to him, "You are the Anointed, the Son of the Blessed One?" [62]And Jesus said, "I am; and you will see the Son of Man sitting at the right hand of the Power and coming with the clouds of the sky." [63]And the chief priest, tearing his tunics, says, "What need do we still have for witnesses? [64]You heard the blasphemy. How does it seem to you?" And they all adjudged him to be

liable to death. ⁶⁵And some began to spit upon him and to cover his face and strike him with their fists and say to him, "Prophesy!" And the attendants seized him with slaps. ⁶⁶And, as Peter was below in the courtyard, there came one of the chief priest's maidservants, ⁶⁷And, seeing Peter warming himself, she looked at him intently and says, "You were also with the Nazarene, Jesus." ⁶⁸But he denied it, saying, "I neither know nor understand what you are saying." And he went outside into the forecourt; ⁶⁹And the maidservant, seeing him again, began to say: "This man is one of them." ⁷⁰And again he denied it. And again, a little later, the bystanders said to Peter, "Truly you too are one of them; for you are a Galilaean." ⁷¹And he began to curse and to swear: "I do not know this man of whom you speak." ⁷²And immediately a cock crowed for the second time. And Peter remembered the phrase as Jesus had spoken it to him: "Before the cock crows twice, you will deny me three times"; and, cowling himself,ˢ he wept.

CHAPTER FIFTEEN

¹And immediately, early in the morning, the chief priests prepared a consultation with the elders and scribes and the whole Council and, having bound Jesus, they led him away and handed him over to Pilate. ²And Pilate asked him, "You are the king of the Judaeans?" And in reply he says, "You say it." ³And the chief priests accused him of many things. ⁴And Pilate again asked him, "Do you give no answer? Look how many

---

s. ἐπιβαλὼν (epibalōn): a present participle that would normally mean "casting upon," "laying upon," "covering," "setting over," or, alternatively, "going directly toward," "throwing [oneself] upon," "eagerly desiring." Many traditional renderings take it here to mean "thinking thereon," but that is almost certainly wrong. Some scholars think that it may mean "throwing [himself] upon [the ground]." Others take it to mean "rushing away," "driving [himself] out." Still others, with whom I (hesitantly) concur, take it to mean "covering [his head with his mantle]," or some similar gesture, either as an expression of emotional turmoil or (as seems likely) so as to conceal his grief from bystanders who might yet accuse him of being one of Jesus's followers.

things they accuse you of." ⁵But Jesus answered nothing more, so that Pilate was amazed. ⁶Now at a festival he released to them one prisoner, whomever they requested. ⁷And the one called bar-Abbas was bound together with the rebels, those who had committed murder during the insurrection. ⁸And the crowd went up and began to request he act toward them as he usually did. ⁹And Pilate answered them, saying, "Do you wish that I might release to you the king of Judaeans?" ¹⁰For he knew that the chief priests had handed him over through malice. ¹¹But the chief priests agitated the crowds, so that he might instead release bar-Abbas to them. ¹²And in reply Pilate again said to them, "What then should I do with him you call the king of the Judaeans?" ¹³And again they cried out, "Crucify him!" ¹⁴But Pilate said to them, "Why, for what evil did he commit?" But they cried out the more, "Crucify him!" ¹⁵And Pilate, deciding to appease the crowd, released bar-Abbas to them, but having flogged Jesus he handed him over that he might be crucified.

¹⁶Then the soldiers led him inside into the courtyard, which is to say the Praetorium, and they call together the whole cohort. ¹⁷And they clothe him in purple and, plaiting a thorn crown, they placed it around him, ¹⁸And they began to salute him: "Hail, King of the Judaeans"; ¹⁹And they battered his head with a rod and spat on him, and going down on their knees they made obeisance to him. ²⁰And when they had mocked him they stripped off the purple and put his clothing on him. And they lead him away so that they might crucify him. ²¹And they press into service a certain passerby coming in from the field, Simon the Cyrenian, the father of Alexander and Rufus, so that he might carry his cross. ²²And they bring him to the place Golgotha—which, being interpreted, means Skull's Place. ²³And they gave him wine infused with myrrh; but he did not take it. ²⁴And they crucify him, and portion out his garments, casting a lot upon them regarding who would take what. ²⁵And it was the third hour and they crucified him. ²⁶And the epigraph of the charge inscribed against him was: "THE KING OF THE JUDAEANS." ²⁷And they crucify two bandits with him, one at his right

and one at his left. [²⁸And the scripture was fulfilled that said, "And he was numbered with the lawless."] ²⁹And the passersby blasphemed against him, wagging their heads and saying, "Ah, the one tearing down the sanctuary and building it up in three days—³⁰Save yourself by descending from the cross." ³¹And the chief priests likewise, sharing in the mockery with the scribes, one with another, said, "He saved others, himself he cannot save; ³²Let the Anointed, the king of Israel, descend from the cross, so that we may see and believe." Those crucified along with him upbraided him also. ³³And, when the sixth hour came, darkness fell over all the land, until the ninth hour. ³⁴And at the ninth hour Jesus cried out in a loud voice, saying, "*Eloi, Eloi, lama sabachthani?*"—which, being interpreted, means, "My God, my God, why did you forsake me?" ³⁵And some of those who were standing there, hearing this, said, "Look, he calls Elijah." ³⁶And one of them—having filled a sponge with vinegar and placing it around a rod—ran and gave it to him to drink, saying, "Leave off, let us see if Elijah comes to take him down." ³⁷But Jesus, letting out a great cry, expired. ³⁸And the veil of the sanctuary was rent in two, from top to bottom. ³⁹And the centurion who was standing by opposite him, seeing that he had thus expired, said, "Truly this man was a god's son." ⁴⁰Now there were also women watching from afar, among whom were Mary the Magdalene, and Mary the mother of James the Small and Joses, and Salome, ⁴¹Who had followed him and attended on him when he was in Galilee, and many others who had come up with him into Jerusalem.

⁴²And now that evening had come—since it was the day of Preparation, which is the day before the Sabbath—⁴³There came Joseph from Arimathaea, an honored member of the Council who was himself also awaiting the Kingdom of God; taking courage, he went in to Pilate and requested the body of Jesus. ⁴⁴But Pilate was amazed that he should have died already and, summoning the centurion, asked whether he had died as yet; ⁴⁵And learning it from the centurion he gave the corpse to Joseph. ⁴⁶And, having purchased linen cloth, he took him down and wrapped him in the linen and placed him in a tomb that had been hewn

out of the rock, and rolled a stone against the tomb's door. ⁴⁷And Mary the Magdalene and Joses's Mary watched where he was laid.

CHAPTER SIXTEEN

¹And when the Sabbath had passed, Mary the Magdalene and James's Mary and Salome purchased spices so that they might come and anoint him. ²And very early on the first day of the Sabbath-week they come to the tomb, as the sun is rising. ³And they said to one another, "Who will roll away the stone from the door of the tomb for us?" ⁴And looking up they see that the stone has been rolled back—for it was extremely large. ⁵And entering the tomb they saw a young man sitting to the right, clothed in a white robe, and they were amazed. ⁶But he says to them, "Do not be amazed. You seek Jesus the Nazarene, who has been crucified. He has been raised; he is not here. Look: the place where they laid him. ⁷But go tell his disciples and Peter that he precedes you into Galilee; there you will see him, as he told you." ⁸And, going out, they fled from the tomb, for trembling and bewilderment had taken hold of them; and they said nothing to anyone; for they were afraid.

[⁹Now, rising early on the first day of the Sabbath-week, he appeared first to Mary the Magdalene, from whom he had cast out seven demons. ¹⁰She went and announced it to those who had been with him as they were mourning and weeping; ¹¹And they, on hearing that he lives and was seen by her, did not believe. ¹²But thereafter he was made manifest in another form to two of them who were walking, as they were going into the countryside; ¹³And they, going away, announced it to the rest; they did not believe them either. ¹⁴Later he was made manifest to the eleven themselves as they were reclining at table, and he reproached their unbelief and the obduracy of their hearts, because they had not believed those who had seen him after he had been raised. ¹⁵And he said to them, "Going forth into all the world, proclaim the good tidings to all creation. ¹⁶The one having faith and being baptized will be saved, but the one not having faith will be judged. ¹⁷And these signs will closely accompany those having faith: In my name they will exorcize demons, they will speak in new languages, ¹⁸They will take hold of snakes and, if they drink anything lethal, it will in no way harm them, they will lay hands upon the ill and they will be well." ¹⁹So then, after speaking to them, the Lord Jesus was taken up into heaven and sat to the right of God. ²⁰And going forth they made their proclamation everywhere, the Lord working with them and confirming the word through the signs accompanying them.]ᵗ

t. The final twelve verses of the Gospel are set apart here because they are a somewhat later addition, absent from the text known to the earliest Church Fathers. Whether they were added to compensate for the abruptness of Mark's conclusion (intentional or accidental) or to replace a lost original ending (which is not unlikely, given the hazards afflicting the transcription and preservation of manuscripts in late antiquity) we cannot say. That they were not written by Mark, however, is beyond serious doubt.

The Gospel
According to Luke

CHAPTER ONE

¹Since many have set their hands to laying out an orderly narrative regarding the events that have been brought to fulfillment among us, ²Just as those who were eyewitnesses from the beginning, and who became servants of the word, passed it on to us, ³It seemed a good thing that I also, having exactingly traced out everything from the beginning, should write it out in order for you, most exalted Theophilus, ⁴So that you might recognize the reliability of the accounts you have been taught.

⁵In the days of Herod, king of Judaea, there was a certain priest, Zacharias by name, from the priestly order of Abijah, and his wife came from the daughters of Aaron, and her name was Elizabeth. ⁶And both were upright before God, conducting themselves impeccably in all the commandments and ordinances of the Lord. ⁷And they had no child, because Elizabeth was barren, and both were well advanced in their days. ⁸Now it happened that, when it was his order's turn in the presence of God, and as he was serving as priest, ⁹It fell to him by lot—as was the custom of the priesthood—to enter the sanctuary of the Lord and burn incense. ¹⁰And all the main body of the people was outside praying during the hour of the incense. ¹¹And an angel of the Lord appeared to him, standing to the right of the altar of the incense. ¹²And seeing him Zacharias was alarmed, and fear descended upon him. ¹³But

the angel said to him, "Do not be afraid, Zacharias, for your supplication has been heard, and your wife Elizabeth will bear you a son, and you shall declare his name to be John; [14]And for you there will be joy and delight, and many will rejoice at his birth. [15]For he will be great in the Lord's eyes; and he must not drink wine or fermented drink, and he will be filled with a Holy Spirit even from his mother's womb, [16]And he will turn many of the sons of Israel to the Lord their God; [17]And he will go forth in his presence, in the spirit and power of Elijah, to turn the hearts of fathers to their children and to turn the wayward to the wisdom of the upright, to prepare a people made ready for the Lord." [18]And Zacharias said to the angel, "In what way shall I know this? For I am old and my wife is well advanced in her days." [19]And in reply the angel said to him, "I am Gabriel, who stand before the presence of God, and I was sent to speak to you and announce these good tidings to you; [20]See then: You shall be silent and unable to speak till the day these things take place, because you did not trust my words, which will be fulfilled at their proper time." [21]Now the people were waiting for Zacharias, and they were amazed that he was taking so much time in the sanctuary. [22]And when he came out he was unable to speak to them and they knew he had seen a vision in the sanctuary; and he was gesturing to them, and remained mute. [23]And it happened that when the days of his service were completed he departed to his house. [24]And after these days his wife Elizabeth conceived, and kept herself concealed, saying: [25]"Thus the Lord has done for me, in the days when he looked to remove the censure that is mine among men."

[26]In the sixth month, the angel Gabriel was sent from God to a city in Galilee whose name was Nazareth, [27]To a virgin betrothed to a man whose name was Joseph, and the virgin's name was Mary. [28]And going in to her he said, "Hail, favored one, the Lord is with you." [29]And she was greatly distressed at his words and pondered what sort of greeting this might be. [30]And the angel said to her, "Do not be afraid, Mary, for you have found favor with God. [31]And see: You will conceive in your

womb and will bear a son, and you shall declare his name to be Jesus. [32]This man will be great and will be called Son of the Most High, and the Lord God will give him the throne of his father David, [33]And he will reign over the house of Jacob throughout the ages, and of his kingdom there will be no end." [34]And Mary said to the angel, "How shall this be, as I have intimacy with no man?" [35]And in reply the angel told her, "A Holy Spirit will come upon you, and the power of the Most High will overshadow you; hence the offspring will be called holy also, a Son of God. [36]And look at your kinswoman Elizabeth: She also conceived a son, in her old age, and this is the sixth month for her who had been called barren; [37]Because nothing, of all the things I have said, is impossible with God." [38]And Mary said, "See: the slave of the Lord; may it happen to me as you have said." And the angel departed from her. [39]And during those days Mary went up in haste into the hill country, to a city of Judah, [40]And entered the house of Zacharias and greeted Elizabeth. [41]And it happened that when Elizabeth heard Mary's greeting the baby leapt in her womb, and Elizabeth was filled with a Holy Spirit, [42]And with a great cry she called out and said, "Blessed are you among women, and blessed the fruit of your womb. [43]And is this happening to me—that the mother of my Lord comes to me? [44]For look: As the sound of your greeting entered my ears, the baby in my womb leapt in joy. [45]And how blissful she who has faith, for from the Lord will come fulfillment of what she has been told." [46]And Mary said, "My soul proclaims the Lord's greatness, [47]And my spirit rejoices in God my savior, [48]Because he looked upon the low estate of his slave. For see: Henceforth all generations will bless me; [49]Because the Mighty One has done great things to me. And holy is his name, [50]And his mercy is for generations and generations to those who fear him. [51]He has worked power with his arm, he has scattered those who are arrogant in the thoughts of their hearts; [52]He has pulled dynasts down from thrones and exalted the humble, [53]He has filled the hungry with good things and sent the rich away empty. [54]He has given aid to Israel his servant, remembering his mercy, [55]Just as he promised to our fathers, to Abraham and to his seed, throughout the age."[a] [56]And Mary stayed with her about three months, and returned to her house.

[57]Now for Elizabeth her time of bearing reached its term, and she gave birth to a son. [58]And her neighbors and relatives heard that the Lord had so lavishly bestowed his mercy on her, and they rejoiced with her. [59]And it happened that on the eighth day they came to circumcise the little child, and they were calling him by the name of his father Zacharias. [60]And speaking out his mother said, "No, he shall instead be called John." [61]And they said to her: "There is no one from your family who is called by this name." [62]And they gestured to his father concerning what he might wish him to be called. [63]And, requesting a tablet, he wrote, "John is his name." And all of them were amazed. [64]And on the instant his mouth and tongue were set free, and he spoke, blessing God. [65]And fear came upon all who dwelled around them, and all these stories were talked about throughout the whole hill country of Judaea, [66]And all those hearing them took them to their heart, saying, "What then will this little child be? For surely the hand of the Lord was with him." [67]And his father Zacharias was filled with a Holy Spirit and prophesied, saying, [68]"Blessed be the Lord God of Israel, because he has visited his people and bought their liberation, [69]And raised a horn of salvation for us in the house of David his servant—[70]As he said through the mouth of his holy prophets of old—[71]Salvation out of the hands of our enemies and out of the hand of all who hate us, [72]To work mercy with our fathers and to remember his holy covenant, [73]The oath he swore to Abraham our father, to grant that we, [74]Having been delivered without fear from our enemies' hands, might worship him, [75]In holiness and justice before his presence for all our days. [76]And now you, little child, will be called a prophet of the Most High; for you go forth before the presence of the Lord to prepare his ways, [77]To give to his people a knowledge of salvation in the forgiveness of their sins, [78]Through our God's inmost

a. Or "until the Age."

mercy, whereby a dawning from on high will visit us, [79]To shine upon those sitting in darkness and death's shadow, so to guide our feet into the path of peace."

[80]And the little child grew and became mighty in spirit, and he was in the desert places till the days when he was openly proclaimed to Israel.

CHAPTER TWO

[1]Now it happened that in those days an edict went out from Caesar Augustus that all the inhabited world should be enrolled in a census. [2]This, the first enrollment, took place when Quirinius was governing Syria.[b] [3]And all went to be enrolled, each to his own city. [4]And so Joseph went up from Galilee, out of the city of Nazareth, to Judaea, to the city of David, which is called Bethlehem, since he was from the house and lineage of David, [5]To be enrolled with Mary, who was betrothed to him, and who was pregnant. [6]And while they were there it came about that the days of her bearing reached their term, [7]And she gave birth to her son, her firstborn, and she wrapped him in swaddling cloths and laid him in a manger, because there was no room for them in the lodge. [8]And there were shepherds in the countryside there, dwelling out in the fields and keeping guard in the night over their flock. [9]And an angel of the Lord stood before them and the glory of the Lord shone around them, and they were afraid, greatly afraid. [10]And the angel said to them, "Do not fear; for see: I bring to you good tidings of a great joy, which will be for all the people, [11]Because today, in David's city, a savior was born to you who is the Anointed Lord. [12]And this is a sign for you: You will find a baby wrapped in swaddling cloths and lying in a manger." [13]And suddenly there appeared with the angel a throng of the

b. Quirinius was governor in Syria in AD 6–7, which would place Christ's birth considerably later than Matthew's Gospel claims (inasmuch as Herod the Great died in 4 BC).

heavenly army, praising God and saying, [14]"Glory to God in the highest places and peace on earth among men of good will." [15]And it happened that, as the angels departed from them into heaven, the shepherds said to one another, "Let us go now to Bethlehem and see this story that has unfolded, which the Lord has made known to us." [16]And hastening they went and found both Joseph and Mary, and the baby lying in the manger as well; [17]And seeing them they revealed what they had been told concerning this little child. [18]And everyone who heard was amazed at the things reported to them by the angels. [19]But Mary kept all these things in her heart, pondering them. [20]And the shepherds went back glorifying and praising God for all they had heard and seen, just as they had been told.

[21]And when eight days had been completed it was time to circumcise him, and his name was declared to be Jesus, the name pronounced by the angel before his conception in the womb.

[22]And when the days of their purification were completed, in keeping with the Law of Moses, they took him up to Jerusalem to present to the Lord—[23]As has been written in the Law of the Lord: that "Every male that opens the womb shall be declared holy to the Lord"—[24]And to offer a sacrifice—in keeping with what is stated in the Law of the Lord: "A pair of turtledoves or two nestling pigeons." [25]And look: There was a man in Jerusalem whose name was Symeon, and this was a man upright and pious, eagerly awaiting the consolation of Israel, and a Holy Spirit was upon him; [26]And it had been made known to him by the Holy Spirit that he would not die before he should see the Anointed of the Lord. [27]And he came in the Spirit into the Temple; and as the parents brought in the little child Jesus, so that they could do for him what was customary according to the Law, [28]He took him in his arms and blessed God and said, [29]"Now you release your slave in peace, Master, in keeping with your word; [30]For my eyes have seen your salvation, [31]Which you have made ready before the face of all peoples, [32]A light for a revelation to the gentiles and a glory for your people Israel." [33]And his father and mother were marveling at the things being said about him. [34]And

Symeon blessed them and said to his mother Mary, "Look: This one is appointed for the fall and the rise of many in Israel, and as a sign that will be spoken against—³⁵And your own soul a sword will also pierce— so that the considerations of many hearts may be revealed." ³⁶And there was Anna, a prophetess, daughter of Phanuel of the tribe of Asher—she was advanced in days, a great many—who had lived with her husband for seven years after her maidenhood, ³⁷And for eighty-four years had been a widow: who did not leave the Temple, serving night and day with fasts and supplications. ³⁸And, approaching at the same hour, she openly praised God and spoke about him to those awaiting the liberation of Jerusalem. ³⁹And when they finished everything required by the Law of the Lord, they returned to Galilee, to their own city of Nazareth.

⁴⁰And the little child grew and became strong, being filled with wisdom, and the grace of God was upon him.

⁴¹And each year, at the feast of the Passover, his parents journeyed to Jerusalem. ⁴²And when he had reached twelve years of age they went up for the feast as they were accustomed to do; ⁴³And having finished their days there, and as they were on their way back, the boy Jesus remained in Jerusalem, and his parents were unaware he had done so. ⁴⁴Rather, assuming him to be in the traveling party, they went on their way for a day, then sought him among their relatives and acquaintances, ⁴⁵And, not finding him, they returned to Jerusalem looking for him. ⁴⁶And it happened that, after three days, they found him in the Temple, sitting amid the teachers, both listening to them and posing them questions; ⁴⁷And those listening to him were astonished at his intelligence and at his responses. ⁴⁸And seeing him they were struck with wonder, and his mother said to him, "Child, why have you treated us thus? Look! Your father and I are in horrible distress seeking you." ⁴⁹And he said to them, "Why did you seek me? Did you not know that it is necessary for me to be in the home of my Father?ᶜ ⁵⁰And they did not understand what he had said to them. ⁵¹And he went down with them and came to Naza-

---

c. Or "about my Father's affairs," or "among my Father's own."

reth, and was obedient to them. And his mother treasured all these sayings in her heart. ⁵²And Jesus progressed in wisdom and age and favor before God and men.

CHAPTER THREE

¹Now in the fifteenth year of the reign of Tiberius Caesar, when Pontius Pilate was governing Judaea, and Herod was tetrarch of Galilee, and his brother Philip was tetrarch of the region of Ituraea and Trochonitis, and Lysanias was tetrarch of Abilene, ²While Annas and Caiaphas held the high priesthood, a word of God came to John the son of Zacharias in the desert. ³And he went into all the region round about the Jordan proclaiming a baptism of the heart's transformation, for the forgiveness of sins, ⁴As it is written in the book of the sayings of Isaiah the prophet: "A voice of one crying out in the wilderness: 'Prepare the Lord's way, make straight his paths. ⁵Every ravine shall be filled and every mountain and hill shall be made low, and whatever is crooked shall become straight, and the rough roads shall become smooth; ⁶And all flesh shall see the salvation of God.'"

⁷So he said to the crowds going out to be baptized by him, "Brood of vipers, who divulged to you that you should flee from the wrath that is coming? ⁸Bear fruits, then, worthy of a change of heart; and do not think to say among yourselves, 'We have Abraham as father'; for I tell you that God has the power to raise up children to Abraham from these stones. ⁹And even now the axe is laid to the root of the trees; and thus every tree not bearing good fruit is felled and thrown into fire." ¹⁰And the crowds questioned him, saying, "What then should we do?" ¹¹And in reply he said to them, "Whoever has two tunics must share with him who has none, and whoever has food must do likewise." ¹²And tax-collectors also came to be baptized, and they said to him, "Teacher, what must we do?" ¹³And he said to them, "Collect nothing more than you are required to." ¹⁴And men serving in the army also questioned him, saying, "And we too, what should we do?" And he told

them, "Neither extort from, nor falsely accuse, anyone; and be contented with your wages." ¹⁵And as all were waiting in expectation, and were debating in their hearts concerning John—whether "He might perhaps be the Anointed"—¹⁶John spoke aloud to everyone, saying, "I indeed baptize you in water; but there comes one mightier than I, regarding whom I am not fit to loosen the thong of his sandals; he will baptize you in a Holy Spirit and fire; ¹⁷Whose winnow is in his hand, and he will thoroughly purge his threshing floor, and will gather his grain into the storehouse, and will burn away the chaff with inextinguishable fire." ¹⁸Thus, then, with many and various exhortations, he proclaimed the good tidings to the people; ¹⁹But Herod the tetrarch, having been censured by him concerning Herodias, his brother's wife, and concerning all the wicked things Herod had done, ²⁰Crowned all those things with the addition of this: He shut John up in prison.

²¹And it happened that when all the people were being baptized, and Jesus had been baptized and was praying, heaven was opened, ²²And the Spirit, the Holy one, descended in the corporeal form of a dove, and a voice came out of heaven: "You are my Son, the beloved, in you I have delighted." ²³And, when he set out, Jesus was himself about thirty years old, being the son—so it was supposed—of Joseph, son of Heli, ²⁴Son of Matthat, son of Levi, son of Melchi, son of Jannai, son of Joseph, ²⁵Son of Mattathias, son of Amos, son of Nahum, son of Esli, son of Naggai, ²⁶Son of Maath, son of Mattathias, son of Semein, son of Josech, son of Joda, ²⁷Son of Joanan, son of Rhesa, son of Zerubbabel, son of Shealtiel, son of Neri, ²⁸Son of Melchi, son of Addi, son of Cosam, son of Elmadan, son of Er, ²⁹Son of Joshua, son of Eliezer, son of Jorim, son of Matthat, son of Levi, ³⁰Son of Symeon, son of Judah, son of Joseph, son of Jonam, son of Eliakim, ³¹Son of Melea, son of Menna, son of Mattatha, son of Nathan, son of David, ³²Son of Jesse, son of Obed, son of Boaz, son of Sala, son of Nahshon, ³³Son of Amminadab, son of Admin, son of Arni, son of Hezron, son of Perez, son of Judah, ³⁴Son of Jacob, son of Isaac, son of Abraham, son of Terah, son of Nahor, ³⁵Son of Serug, son of Reu, son of Peleg, son of Eber, son of Shelah, ³⁶Son of Cainan, son

of Arphaxad, son of Shem, son of Noah, son of Lamech, ³⁷Son of Methusaleh, son of Enoch, son of Jared, son of Mahalaleel, son of Cainan, ³⁸Son of Enos, son of Seth, son of Adam, son of God.

CHAPTER FOUR

¹And Jesus, full of a Holy Spirit, returned from the Jordan, and was guided in the wilderness by the Spirit, ²Being tempted for forty days by the Slanderer. And during those days he ate nothing, and when they had reached their end he was hungry. ³And the Slanderer said to him, "If you are God's Son, command that this stone become a loaf of bread." ⁴And Jesus answered him, "It has been written that 'Man shall not live upon bread alone.'" ⁵And, leading him upward, he showed him all the kingdoms of the inhabited world in a single instant of time. ⁶And the Slanderer said to him, "To you I will give all this power and the glory of these things, because it has been delivered over to me and I give it to whomever I wish. ⁷Therefore, if you prostrate yourself before me, it will all be yours." ⁸And in reply Jesus said to him, "It has been written, 'You shall make obeisance to the Lord your God and him only shall you adore.'" ⁹And he led him to Jerusalem and stood him upon the pinnacle of the Temple, and said to him, "If you are God's Son, cast yourself down from here, ¹⁰For it has been written that 'He will command his angels concerning you, to keep guard over you,' ¹¹And that 'Their hands will bear you up, that you may not strike your foot against a stone.'" ¹²And in reply Jesus said to him: "It has been said, 'You shall not put the Lord your God to the test.'" ¹³And, having exhausted every temptation, the Slanderer departed from him until an opportune time. ¹⁴And Jesus returned to Galilee in the power of the Spirit, and a rumor concerning him went forth through the whole region. ¹⁵And he taught in their synagogues, being praised by all.

¹⁶And he came to Nazareth where he had been brought up and, as he was accustomed to do, he entered the synagogue on the day of the Sabbath and stood up to read. ¹⁷And a scroll of the prophet Isaiah was

handed to him, and having opened the scroll he found the place where it was written: [18]"A Spirit of the Lord is upon me; hence he has anointed me to announce good tidings to the destitute, he has sent me out to proclaim release to captives and sight to the blind, to send the downtrodden forth in liberty, [19]To proclaim the Lord's acceptable year." [20]And, having closed the scroll and returning it to the attendant, he sat; and the eyes of everyone in the synagogue were gazing at him. [21]And he began by saying to them, "Today, in your ears, this scripture has been fulfilled." [22]And all professed their admiration for him and were amazed at the words of grace coming out of his mouth, and they said, "Is this man not Joseph's son?" [23]And he said to them, "Surely you will quote me this parable: 'Physician, heal yourself'; the things we heard were happening in Capernaum, do them here as well, in your native country." [24]And he said, "Amen, I tell you, no prophet is accepted in his own country. [25]And I tell you in truth, there were many widows in Israel in the days of Elijah, when the sky was sealed up for over three years and six months, as a great famine took place over all the land, [26]And to none of them was Elijah sent except to a widowed woman of Sarepta in Sidon. [27]And there were many lepers in Israel during the time of Elisha the prophet, and none of them was cleansed except Naaman the Syrian." [28]And all in the synagogue were filled with rage when they heard these things, [29]And rising up they drove him outside the city, and led him to the edge of the mountain on which their city was built so as to throw him down; [30]But he passed through their midst and went away.

[31]And he went down to Capernaum, a city of Galilee. And he was teaching them on the Sabbath; [32]And they were astounded at his teaching, because his speech had power. [33]And in the synagogue there was a man having the spirit of an impure demon, and he shouted out in a loud voice, [34]"Ah, what is there between us and you, Jesus the Nazarene? Did you come to destroy us? I know who you are, the holy one of God." [35]And Jesus rebuked it, saying, "Be silent and come out from him." And the demon, throwing him down in their midst, came out from him, doing him no injury. [36]And amazement came over everyone,

and they spoke to one another, saying, "What speech is this, that he commands the unclean spirits with authority and power and they come out?" [37]And a rumor concerning him went forth into every place in the region. [38]And rising to leave the synagogue he went into the home of Simon, and Simon's mother-in-law was in the grip of a great fever, and they appeal to him concerning her. [39]And, standing over her, he rebuked the fever and it left her; and, immediately getting up, she waited on them. [40]And, when the sun had set, all those who had persons ailing from various diseases brought them to him; and he, laying his hands on each one of them, healed them. [41]And demons also came out from many, crying out and saying: "You are the Son of God." And, admonishing them, he did not allow the demons to speak, because they knew him to be the Anointed. [42]And when day came he departed and went to a deserted place; and the crowds sought him out, and came to him, and detained him so that he would not go from them. [43]And he said to them: "It is necessary for me to announce the good tidings of the Kingdom of God to the other cities as well, because for this I was sent forth." [44]And he was making his proclamation in the synagogues of Judaea.

CHAPTER FIVE

[1]And it happened that, as the crowd pressed in upon him and listened to God's word, and as he stood by the Lake of Gennesaret, [2]He then saw two boats standing at the lake's edge; and the fishermen, having disembarked from them, were washing the nets. [3]And embarking in one of the boats, which belonged to Simon, he asked him to put out a little from the land; and sitting down he taught the crowds from the boat. [4]And when he ceased speaking he said to Simon, "Put out into the deep, and let your nets down for a haul." [5]And in reply Simon said, "Master, we labored all through the night and took in nothing; but on your word I will let down the nets." [6]And when they did so they ensnared an immense multitude of fishes, and their nets were being torn. [7]And they signaled to their fellows in the other boat that they should come to help

them; and they came, and they filled both boats, so much so that they were sinking. ⁸And seeing this, Simon Peter fell at the knees of Jesus, saying, "Go from me, Lord, for I am a sinful man." ⁹For amazement had seized him and all those with him at the haul of fishes that they gathered—¹⁰And so likewise both James and John, the sons of Zebedee, who were partners with Simon. And Jesus said to Simon, "Do not be afraid; from now on you will be capturing men." ¹¹And, bringing the boats back onto the land, they abandoned everything and followed him.

¹²And it happened that he was in one of the cities, and look: a man covered with leprosy; and seeing Jesus he fell upon his face and implored him, saying, "Lord, if you wish it, you are able to cleanse me." ¹³And stretching out his hand he touched him, saying, "I wish it, be cleansed." And immediately the leprosy left him. ¹⁴And he enjoined him to tell no one: "Rather, go show the priest, and for your cleansing make an offering as Moses commanded, for a testimony to them." ¹⁵But, instead, talk concerning him went about all the more, and many crowds came together to listen and to be healed of their infirmities; ¹⁶But he was withdrawn into the desert places and was praying.

¹⁷And it happened that, on one of those days, he was teaching, and seated there were Pharisees and teachers of the Law, coming from every village of Galilee and Judaea and from Jerusalem; and the Lord's power of healing was with him. ¹⁸And look: men carrying on a pallet a man who had been paralyzed; and they sought to carry him in and lay him before him. ¹⁹And, not finding a way by which they could bring him in, on account of the crowd, they went up onto the roof and lowered him, along with his pallet, through the tiles and into their midst, right in front of Jesus. ²⁰And seeing their faith he said, "Man, your sins have been forgiven you." ²¹And the scribes and the Pharisees began to ponder this, saying, "Who is this man who utters blasphemies? Who is able to forgive sins except God alone?" ²²But in reply Jesus, knowing what they were thinking, said to them, "Why do you reason over these things in your hearts? ²³Which is easier, to say, 'Your sins have been forgiven you,' or to say, 'Rise and walk'? ²⁴But in order that you should know that

the Son of Man[d] has power to forgive sins on the earth . . ." — He said to the paralytic, "I say to you, rise and take your pallet and go to your house." [25]And rising at once, picking up what he had been lying on, he went away to his house glorifying God. [26]And bewilderment took hold of everyone, and they glorified God, and were filled with fear, saying, "We have seen incredible things this day."

[27]And after these events he went out and saw a tax-collector by the name of Levi sitting at the tax-collection house, and said to him, "Follow me." [28]And abandoning everything he rose and followed him. [29]And Levi set a great banquet for him at his home; and there was a great crowd of tax-collectors and others who were reclining at table with them. [30]And the Pharisees and their scribes murmured to his disciples, saying, "Why do you eat and drink with the tax-collectors and sinners?" [31]And in reply Jesus said to them, "Those who are hale have no need of a physician, but rather those who are ill; [32]I have come to call not the upright, but sinners, to a change of heart." [33]And they said to him, "John's disciples fast and pray frequently, as do also those of the Pharisees, but yours eat and drink." [34]And Jesus said to them, "Can you make the sons of the bridal chamber fast while the bridegroom is with them? [35]But the days will come when the bridegroom is taken away from them; and then, in those days, they will fast." [36]And he also told them a parable: "No one tears a patch from a new garment to put it on an old; otherwise, he tears what is new, while the patch from the new will not match the old. [37]And no one puts new wine in old wineskins; otherwise, the new wine will burst the wineskins, and will be spilled out, and the wineskins will perish. [38]Rather, one must put new wine into new wineskins.

---

d. Though "son of man" is simply a good Semitic idiom meaning "a man," by the first century it had long served as the name of a mysterious apocalyptic or eschatological figure (as in the one "like a son of man" who rides in the chariot of God in Ezekiel), and as Christ uses it in the Gospels it should clearly be read as a distinctive prophetic title (though not one whose precise significance can be ascertained).

³⁹And no one having drunk the old desires the new; for he says, 'The old is good.'"

CHAPTER SIX

¹Now it happened that he passed through fields of grain on the Sabbath, and his disciples plucked and ate the ears of grain, chafing them in their hands. ²And some of the Pharisees said, "Why do they do what is unlawful on the Sabbath?" ³And replying to them Jesus said, "Have you not read what David did when he was hungry, as well as those who were with him? ⁴How he entered the house of God and, taking the loaves of the bread of Presentation, which it is unlawful except for the priests to eat, he ate them and gave them to those with him?" ⁵And he said to them, "The Son of Man is Lord of the Sabbath." ⁶And it happened that, on another Sabbath, he entered a synagogue and taught; and there was a man there and his right hand was withered; ⁷And the scribes and the Pharisees observed him closely to see if he heals on the Sabbath, that they might find a way to accuse him. ⁸And he knew their reasoning, and he said to the man with a withered hand, "Rise and stand up in our midst." And, rising, he stood. ⁹And Jesus said to them, "I ask you whether it is permissible on the Sabbath to do good or to do evil, to save a soul or to destroy it?" ¹⁰And, looking around at all of them, he said to him, "Stretch forth your hand." And he did, and his hand was restored. ¹¹And they were filled with unthinking rage, and discussed with one another what they might do to Jesus.

¹²Now it happened that in those days he went out to the mountain to pray, and spent the whole night in prayer to God. ¹³And when day came he summoned his disciples, and chose twelve from among them whom he also named Apostles: ¹⁴Simon, whom he also named Peter, and Andrew his brother, and James and John, and Philip and bar-Tholomaus, ¹⁵And Matthew and Thomas, James the son of Alphaeus and Simon—the one called Zealot—and Judas the son of James, ¹⁶And

Judas Iscariot, who turned traitor. ¹⁷And descending with them he stood upon a level place, along with a large crowd of his disciples, and a great multitude of the people from all of Judaea and Jerusalem and the coastal country of Tyre and Sidon, ¹⁸Who came to hear him and to be cured of their diseases; and those troubled by unclean spirits were healed. ¹⁹And all the crowd sought to touch him, because power went forth from him and healed all. ²⁰And he, raising his eyes to his disciples, said:

"How blissful[e] the destitute, for yours is the Kingdom of God; ²¹How blissful those who are now hungry, for you shall feast; how blissful those now weeping, for you shall laugh; ²²How blissful you when men hate you and when they exclude you and reproach you and reject your name as something wicked, for the Son of Man's sake: ²³On that day, rejoice and leap about; for look: Your reward in Heaven is great; for their fathers accordingly did the same things to the prophets.

²⁴"But alas for you who are rich, for you have your comfort. Alas for you who are now replete, for you will be hungry. ²⁵Alas for those now laughing, for you will mourn and lament. ²⁶Alas for you when all men speak well of you, for in like fashion their fathers did the same things to the false prophets. ²⁷But to you who listen I say, Love your enemies, do well by those who hate you, ²⁸Bless those cursing you, pray for those reviling you. ²⁹To him who strikes you on the cheek turn the other also, and from him who takes your cloak do not withhold your tunic as well. ³⁰Give to everyone who asks and do not ask back from the one taking your things. ³¹And just as you wish men should do to you, do likewise to them. ³²And if you love those who love you, what is your thanks? For even sinners love those who love them. ³³For even if you do good to those who do good to you, what is your thanks? Even sinners do the same. ³⁴And if you lend to those from whom you hope to receive, what thanks have you? Even sinners lend to sinners in order that they may receive an equal return. ³⁵But love your enemies and do good and lend

e. μακάριος (*makarios*): "blessed," "happy," "fortunate," "prosperous," but originally with a connotation of divine or heavenly bliss.

without despairing of it; and your reward will be great, and you will be sons of the Most High, because he is kind to the ungrateful and wicked. [36]Become compassionate, just as your Father is compassionate. [37]And do not judge, and you surely shall not be judged, and do not condemn, and you surely shall not be condemned. Forgive, and you shall be forgiven. [38]Give, and you shall be given: Into your lap they will pour a goodly measure, pressed down, shaken together, and spilling over; for in whatever measure you measure it shall in turn be meted out to you." [39]And he spoke a parable to them as well: "Can a blind man guide a blind man? Will not both fall into a pit? [40]A disciple is not above his teacher; but everyone who is fully trained will be like his teacher. [41]And why do you look at the straw in your brother's eye, yet do not perceive the beam in your own eye? [42]How can you say to your brother, 'Brother, let me take the straw out of your eye,' while not yourself seeing the beam in your eye? Charlatan, first pluck the beam out of your eye, and then you will see clearly how to pluck the straw out of your brother's eye. [43]For there is no good tree that produces diseased fruit, nor again any diseased tree that produces good fruit. [44]For every tree is known by its own fruit; for they do not gather figs from thorns, nor do they pluck a bunch of grapes from brambles. [45]The good man brings forth that which is good from the good treasury of the heart, and the wicked man brings forth that which is wicked from the wicked; for his mouth speaks out of what overflows from his heart. [46]And why do you call out to me, 'Lord, Lord,' and do not do what I say? [47]Everyone coming to me and hearing my words and doing them, I will show you whom he is like. [48]He is like a man building a home, who dug and delved and laid a foundation upon the rock; and a flood came and the river broke upon that home and could not shake it, because it was well built. [49]But the one hearing and not doing is like a man who built his home atop the earth, without a foundation, upon which the river broke and immediately it collapsed, and the ruin of that home was a great one."

CHAPTER SEVEN

¹When he had entirely filled the ears of the people with these discourses of his, he entered Capernaum. ²Now a certain centurion's slave, who was dear to him, was ill to the point of death. ³And hearing about Jesus he sent elders of the Judaeans to him, asking him that he might come and save his slave. ⁴And coming to Jesus they earnestly entreated him, saying: "He to whom you would grant this is worthy; ⁵For he loves our nation and he built the synagogue for us." ⁶And Jesus went with them. And, when he was not far away from the household, the centurion sent friends, saying to him, "Lord, do not trouble yourself, for I am not worthy that you should come in under my roof; ⁷Hence I did not think myself worthy to come to you; but declare it by a word, and let my servant be healed. ⁸For I am also a man set under authority, having soldiers under me, and to this one I say, 'Go,' and he goes, and to another, 'Come,' and he comes, and to my slave, 'Do this,' and he does it." ⁹And, hearing this, Jesus marveled at him and, turning to the crowd following him, said, "I tell you, I have not found such faith in Israel." ¹⁰And, returning to the house, those who had been sent found the slave in good health. ¹¹And it happened that on the next day he went into a city called Nain, and his disciples and a large crowd went with him. ¹²And as he drew near the city's gate, look: A man who had died was being carried out, the only-begotten son of his mother, and she was a widow. ¹³And, seeing her, the Lord was moved inwardly with compassion for her and said, "Do not weep." ¹⁴And approaching he touched the coffin, and those bearing it stood still, and he said, "Young man, I say to you, arise." ¹⁵And the dead man sat up and began to speak, and he gave him to his mother. ¹⁶And fear gripped everyone, and they glorified God, saying: "A great prophet has been raised up among us, and God has visited his people." ¹⁷And this story about him went out into the whole of Judaea and the surrounding region.

¹⁸And John's disciples brought him word concerning all these things. And, summoning a certain pair of his disciples, John ¹⁹Sent to

the Lord, saying, "Are you the one who is coming or should we expect another?" ²⁰And coming to him the men said, "John the Baptist sent us to you, saying, 'Are you the one who is coming or should we expect another?'" ²¹In that hour he healed many of diseases and afflictions and evil spirits, and he granted sight to many who were blind. ²²And in reply he said to them, "Go report to John the things that you have seen and heard: The blind see again, the lame walk, lepers are being cleansed, and the deaf hear, the dead are raised, and the poor are given good tidings, ²³And how blissful is he who is not offended by me." ²⁴And when John's messengers went away he began to speak to the crowds concerning John: "What did you go out into the wilderness to gaze at? A reed being shaken by the wind? ²⁵What rather did you go out to see? A man clothed in soft garments? Look: Those wearing splendid garments and living in luxury are in the houses of kings. ²⁶What, rather, did you go out to see? A prophet? Yes, I tell you, and much more than a prophet. ²⁷This is he concerning whom it has been written, 'See: I send forth my messenger before your face, who will prepare your path before you.' ²⁸I tell you truly, among those born of women no one is greater than John; but a lesser man in the Kingdom of the heavens is greater than he." (²⁹And all the people hearing this who had been baptized with John's baptism, even the tax-collectors, spoke of God's justice; ³⁰But the Pharisees and the lawyers, not being baptized by him, rejected God's will for them.) ³¹"To what, then, may I liken the men of this generation, and what do they resemble? ³²They are like children sitting in a marketplace accosting one another, who say, 'We played flutes for you and you did not dance; we wailed in lamentation and you did not weep.' ³³For John the Baptist has come neither eating bread nor drinking wine, and you say, 'He has a demon.' ³⁴The Son of Man has come eating and drinking, and you say, 'Look: a gluttonous and wine-besotted man, a friend of tax-collectors and sinners.' ³⁵And Wisdom has been vindicated by all her children."

³⁶Now a certain one of the Pharisees requested him to dine with him; and entering the Pharisee's house he reclined at table. ³⁷And look:

There was a woman in the city who was a sinner, and knowing that he is reclining in the home of the Pharisee, and bringing an alabaster phial of unguent, [38]And standing behind, weeping at his feet, she began to make his feet wet with her tears, and she wiped them off with the hair of her head, and fervently kissed his feet and anointed them with unguent. [39]But, seeing this, the Pharisee who had invited him talked to himself, saying, "This man, if he were a prophet, would have known who and of what sort this woman who touches him is, for she is a sinner." [40]And in reply Jesus said to him, "Simon, I have something to say to you." And he says, "Speak, teacher." [41]"There were two men indebted to a certain moneylender: The one owed five hundred denarii and the other fifty. [42]As they had nothing with which to repay, he graciously forgave them both. Which of them, therefore, will love him more?" [43]In reply Simon said: "The one to whom he freely forgave more." And he said to him, "You have judged correctly." [44]And turning to the woman he said to Simon, "Do you see this woman? I entered your home, you did not give me water for my feet; but she washed my feet with her tears and wiped them off with her hair. [45]You gave me no kiss of friendship, but she from the time I entered has not ceased fervently kissing my feet. [46]You did not anoint my head with oil; but she anointed my feet with unguent. [47]By virtue of which, I tell you, her sins—which are many—have been forgiven, because she loved much; but one to whom little is forgiven loves little." [48]And he said to her, "Your sins have been forgiven." [49]And those reclining at table with him began to say among themselves, "Who is this, who even forgives sins?" [50]And he said to the woman, "Your faith has saved you; go in peace."

CHAPTER EIGHT

[1]And afterward it happened that he journeyed through every city and village proclaiming and announcing the good tidings of the Kingdom of God, and the twelve along with him, [2]As well as certain women who had been cured of evil spirits and infirmities: Mary, who was called

Magdalene, from whom seven demons had come out, ³And Joanna, wife of Chuza the steward of Herod, and Susanna, and many others, who provided for them from their own possessions. ⁴Now as a great crowd was gathering and those of every city were journeying to him, he spoke by way of a parable: ⁵"A sower went out to sow his seed. And as he sowed some of it fell beside the path and was trampled down, and the birds of the sky devoured it. ⁶And other seed fell upon a rock and when it sprang up it withered because it had no moisture. ⁷And other seed fell amid thorns, and the thorns, springing up along with it, throttled it. ⁸And other seed fell into the good soil and when grown yielded fruit a hundredfold." Having said these things, he called out, "Let him who has ears listen." ⁹And his disciples asked him what this parable might mean. ¹⁰And he said, "To you it has been given to know the mysteries of the Kingdom of God, but to the rest it is given in parables, that seeing they may not see and hearing they might not understand. ¹¹Now this is the parable: The seed is the word of God. ¹²Those beside the road are those hearing; then the Slanderer comes and seizes the word away from their heart, that they might not have faith and be saved. ¹³And those on the rock are those who hear and accept the word with joy; and these have no root and they have faith for a season and in the season of trial fall away. ¹⁴And that falling into the thorns, these are the ones who hear but who, in going on, are throttled by the anxieties and riches and pleasures of life, and never reach ripeness. ¹⁵And that in the good soil, these are those who, hearing with a fine and good heart, hold fast to the word, and by their constancy bear fruit. ¹⁶Now no one, having lit a lamp, covers it with a vessel or places it beneath a couch; rather he places it on a lamp-stand, so that those who enter may see the light. ¹⁷For nothing is hidden that will not become manifest, nor is anything secret that will not certainly be made known and come into the open. ¹⁸Take care, therefore, how you listen: For whosoever has, to him it will be given; and whosoever does not have, even what he seems to have will be taken from him."

¹⁹And his mother and brothers came to him, and were unable to come near to him because of the crowd. ²⁰And it was reported to him:

"Your mother and your brothers are standing outside, wishing to see you." [21]But in reply he said to them, "My mother and my brothers are those hearing the word of God and doing it."

[22]And it happened on one of those days that, as he and his disciples embarked in a boat, he said to them, "Let us go over to the other side of the lake." And they set forth. [23]And as they sailed he fell asleep. And a windstorm descended upon the lake, and they were being overwhelmed and were in peril. [24]And they went to him and roused him, saying, "Master, master we are perishing." And he, having been awakened, rebuked the wind and the turmoil of the water; and they ceased, and a calm came about. [25]Then he said to them, "Where is your faith?" And, being afraid, they marveled, saying to one another, "Who then is this man, that he commands even the wind and the water, and they obey him?" [26]And they sailed down to the region of the Gerasenes, which lies opposite Galilee. [27]And as he went onto land he was met by a certain man from the city who had demons in him, and who for a considerable time had worn no garment, and who dwelled not in a house but among the tombs. [28]And seeing Jesus, and crying out, he fell prostrate before him and in a loud voice said, "What do I and you have to do with one another, Son of God Most High? I implore you, do not torment me." [29]For he was commanding the unclean spirit to come out from the man. For many times it had seized hold of him, and he had been bound with chains and fetters, and tearing the bonds apart he was driven by the demon into desert places. [30]And Jesus asked him, "What is your name?" And he said, "Legion," for many demons had entered him. [31]And they implored him that he would not order them to depart into the Abyss. [32]And there was a herd of many swine feeding there on the hill; and they implored him to let them enter into those; and he granted them permission. [33]So the demons, on coming forth from the man, entered into the swine, and the herd rushed down the precipice into the lake and was drowned. [34]And, seeing what had happened, the herdsmen fled and reported it in the city and in the fields. [35]And they went out to see what had happened and came to Jesus, and found the man from whom the

demons had departed sitting clothed and in his right mind by the feet of Jesus, and they were afraid. [36]And those who had seen it recounted how the demoniac had been healed. [37]And the whole populace of the surrounding region of the Gerasenes asked him to depart from them, because they were gripped with a great fear. So he, embarking in a boat, went back. [38]And the man from whom the demons had departed begged that he might stay with him; but he sent him away, saying, [39]"Return to your house and relate what God has done for you." And he went off throughout all the city, proclaiming all the things Jesus had done for him.

[40]And when Jesus returned the crowd welcomed him, for all were expecting him. [41]And look: There came a man whose name was Jairus, and this man was a ruler of the synagogue; and falling at the feet of Jesus he implored him to come into his house, [42]Because he had an only daughter, about twelve years old, and she was dying. And as he went with him the crowds pressed in upon him. [43]And a woman who had suffered a discharge of blood for twelve years, [having squandered all her livelihood on physicians,] who could be healed by no one, [44]Approaching from behind, touched the fringe of his mantle, and at once her discharge of blood stopped. [45]And Jesus said, "Who touches me?" And, when everyone denied it, Peter said, "Master, the crowds press in upon and are jostling against you." [46]But Jesus said, "Someone touched me; for I was aware of power having gone forth from me." [47]And the woman, seeing that she was not hidden from view, came trembling and fell down before him, and declared before all the people for what reason she had touched him, and how she had been instantly cured. [48]And he said to her, "Daughter, your faith has healed you; go in peace." [49]As he was yet speaking, someone comes from the home of the ruler of the synagogue, saying: "Your daughter has died; do not trouble the teacher further." [50]But hearing this Jesus answered him, "Do not be afraid; only have faith and she will be saved." [51]And, on coming into the house, he permitted no one to enter with him except Peter and John and James and the girl's father and mother. [52]And all were weeping and beating

their breasts for her. And he said, "Do not weep; she has not died, but sleeps." [53]And they scoffed at him, knowing that she had died. [54]But he, taking hold of her hand, called to her, saying, "Little girl, arise." [55]And her spirit returned, and she at once arose, and he instructed that she be given something to eat. [56]And her parents were astonished; but he enjoined them to tell no one what had happened.

CHAPTER NINE

[1]And having called the twelve together, he gave them power and authority, over all the demons and for curing diseases; [2]And he sent them forth to proclaim the Kingdom of God and to heal diseases; [3]And he said to them, "Take nothing for the road, neither staff, nor leather pouch, nor a loaf of bread, nor silver—nor have two tunics each. [4]And into whatever household you enter, stay there and venture out from there. [5]And whoever should not receive you, on leaving that city shake the dust from your feet as a testimony against them." [6]And setting out they passed throughout the villages, everywhere proclaiming the good tidings and healing. [7]Now Herod the tetrarch heard of all the things taking place, and he was perplexed because it was said by some that John had been raised from the dead, [8]And by some that Elijah had appeared, and by others that one of the prophets of old had risen again. [9]But Herod said, "I beheaded John; but who is this about whom I hear such things?" And he sought to see him.

[10]And when they had returned the Apostles recounted to him the things they had done. And taking them aside he departed in private to a city called Bethsaida. [11]But the crowds, knowing this, followed him; and, welcoming them, he spoke to them about the Kingdom of God, and he cured those who had need of healing. [12]And the day began to decline; and the twelve approached and said to him, "Send this crowd away so that, going to the surrounding villages and towns, they may find provisions, because here we are in a desert place." [13]But he said to them, "You give them something to eat." But they said, "We have no more

than five loaves of bread and two fish among us, unless we go out to buy food for all these people." [14]For there were about five thousand men. And he said to his disciples, "Make them recline in parties of about fifty each." [15]And they did so and made everyone recline. [16]And, taking the five loaves and the two fishes, looking up to heaven, he blessed and broke them; he gave them to the disciples to serve out to the crowd. [17]And everyone ate their fill; and they took up twelve baskets of the fragments left over.

[18]And it happened that, as he was praying alone, the disciples were with him, and he questioned them, saying, "Who do the crowds say that I am?" [19]And in reply they said, "John the Baptist; but others Elijah, and others that a certain prophet of old has risen again." [20]And he said to them, "But you, who do you say that I am?" And in reply Peter said, "The Anointed of God." [21]But, admonishing them, he enjoined them to tell this to no one, [22]Saying: "It is necessary that the Son of Man suffer many things and be rejected by the elders and chief priests and scribes and be killed, and on the third day be raised." [23]And he said to all, "If anyone wishes to come along after me, let him deny himself and take up his cross each day, and let him follow me. [24]For whoever wishes to save his soul will lose it; but whosoever loses his soul for my sake, this one will save it. [25]For what profit is there for a man gaining the whole cosmos but losing—or being deprived of—himself? [26]For whoever is ashamed of me and my words, of this one the Son of Man will be ashamed when he comes in his glory, the glory of the Father and of his holy angels. [27]But I tell you truly, there are some of those standing in this place who most certainly would not taste of death until they see the Kingdom of God."

[28]And it happened that, about eight days after these exchanges, he took Peter and John and James and went up into the mountain to pray. [29]And as he was praying the appearance of his face became different and his raiment became gleaming white. [30]And look: Speaking with him were two men who were Moses and Elijah, [31]Who—appearing in glory—spoke to him about his journey forth, which he was about to

complete in Jerusalem. ³²And Peter and those with him were weighed down by sleep; but waking thoroughly they saw the glory of him and of the two men standing with him. ³³And it happened that, when they parted from him, Peter—not knowing what he is saying—said to Jesus, "Master, it is a good thing for us to be here, and let us make three tabernacles, one for you and one for Moses and one for Elijah." ³⁴And as he was saying these things a cloud came and overshadowed them; and as they entered into the cloud they were afraid. ³⁵And a voice came out of the cloud, saying, "This is my Son, the chosen one, listen to him." ³⁶And, when the voice had gone, Jesus was found alone, and they were silent, and during those days no one told any of the things they had seen.

³⁷And the next day, as they came down from the mountain, it happened that a great crowd met him. ³⁸And look: A man shouted out from the crowd, saying, "Teacher, I beg you to look upon my son, because he is my one and only child, ³⁹And look, a spirit takes hold of him and suddenly cries out and throws him about frothing and, bruising him, scarcely leaves him. ⁴⁰And I implored your disciples that they might exorcize it, and they were unable." ⁴¹And in reply Jesus said, "O faithless and perverse generation, for how long shall I be with you and endure you? Bring your son here." ⁴²But, while he was still approaching, the demon tore at him and convulsed him violently; but Jesus rebuked the impure spirit and healed the boy and restored him to his father. ⁴³And all were utterly astonished at the greatness of God.

And, as everyone was marveling at all the things he had done, he said to his disciples, ⁴⁴"Store these words deep in your ears; for the Son of Man is about to be delivered over into the hands of men." ⁴⁵But they did not understand this statement, and it was veiled from them so that they could not comprehend it, and they were afraid to question him about this remark. ⁴⁶And a debate began among them, concerning who among them might be the greater. ⁴⁷And Jesus, perceiving the reasoning of their heart, took a little child and stood him beside himself, ⁴⁸And said to them, "Whoever receives this little child in my name receives me; and whoever receives me receives the one having sent me. For he who remains the lesser among all, this one is great." ⁴⁹Then, speaking out, John said, "Master, we saw someone exorcizing demons in your name, and we tried to prevent him, because he does not follow along with us." ⁵⁰And Jesus said to him, "Do not prevent him, for he who is not against you is for you."

⁵¹And it happened, as the days leading to his being taken up above were being completed, that he turned his face to the journey to Jerusalem, ⁵²And he sent out messengers before his face, and as they journeyed they entered a village of the Samaritans in order to prepare for him; ⁵³And they did not receive him, because his face was turned toward the journey to Jerusalem. ⁵⁴And the disciples James and John, seeing this, said, "Lord, do you wish that we should command fire to descend from heaven and to destroy them?" ⁵⁵But turning he rebuked them. ⁵⁶And they went to another village.

⁵⁷And, as they went along the road, someone said to him, "I will follow you wherever you go." ⁵⁸And Jesus said to him, "The foxes have holes and the birds of the sky nests, but the Son of Man has nowhere he may lay his head." ⁵⁹And he said to someone else, "Follow me." And he said, "Allow me first to go bury my father." ⁶⁰But he said to him, "Leave the dead to bury their own dead, but you go announce the Kingdom of God." ⁶¹And another also said, "I will follow you, Lord; but first permit me to bid farewell to those at my house." But Jesus said, "No one putting his hand to the plow and then looking to the things behind him is fit for the Kingdom of God."

CHAPTER TEN

¹After these events, the Lord appointed seventy [-two] others, and sent them out two-by-two before his face, into every city and place to which he was about to come. ²And he said to them, "The harvest is great indeed, but the laborers are few; therefore implore the Lord of the harvest that he may cast laborers out into his harvest. ³Go; see, I send you out as lambs among wolves. ⁴Do not carry a purse, or a leather pouch,

or sandals; and do not greet anyone upon the road. [5]And into whatever household you enter, say first, 'Peace be upon this house.' [6]And if there is a son of peace there, your 'Peace' will rest upon him; otherwise, it will revert to you. [7]And remain in that household, eating and drinking meals with them; for the laborer is deserving of his wages. Do not move about from home to home. [8]And into whatever city you enter where they welcome you, eat whatever is set before you, [9]And heal those therein who are ailing, and say to them, 'The Kingdom of God has drawn near to you.' [10]And into whatever city you enter where they do not welcome you, go out into its streets and say, [11]'Even the dust from your city, clinging to us on our feet, we shake off at you; nevertheless, know this: that the Kingdom of God has drawn near.' [12]I tell you that it will be more tolerable for Sodom on That Day than it will be for that city. [13]Alas for you, Chorazin! Alas for you, Bethsaida! For if the deeds of power occurring in you had occurred in Tyre and Sidon they would have changed their hearts long ago, sitting down in sackcloth and ashes. [14]Nevertheless, it will be more tolerable for Tyre and Sidon at the judgment than for you. [15]And you, Capernaum, have you not been exalted to heaven? You shall descend into Hades. [16]Whoever hears you hears me, and whoever rejects you rejects me; and whoever rejects me rejects the one having sent me forth." [17]And the seventy [-two] returned saying, "Lord, even the demons submit to us in your name." [18]And he said to them, "I was watching the Accuser[f] fall like lightning out of the sky.[g] [19]Look: I have given you the power to tread upon snakes and scorpions, and on all the power of the enemy, and nothing at all shall harm you.

f. "The Satan," which is to say, "prosecutor," "accuser," "arraigner."

g. Although later Christian tradition would conflate this verse with Isaiah 14: 12 (where the fallen King Nebuchadnezzar II of Babylon is apostrophized as Hêlêl ben Shahar, "Lucifer Son of the Morning") to produce the idea of the fall of an angel called Lucifer before creation, the reference is actually far more limited. Jesus is simply employing a metaphor to say that the mission of his disciples had been so successful that it had inaugurated the end of the cosmic reign of the Satan (or Accuser); hence, as they were passing through the villages, it was as if Jesus could see Satan toppling from his seat on high.

[20]Nevertheless, do not rejoice in this, that the spirits submit to you, but rejoice that your names have been inscribed in the heavens." [21]In that same hour he became exultant in the Spirit, the Holy One, and said, "I praise you, Lord, because you concealed these things from the wise and clever, and revealed them to infants; yes, Father, because such was pleasing before you. [22]All things have been handed over to me by my Father, and no one knows who the Son is except the Father, and who the Father is except the Son and the one to whom he chooses to reveal him." [23]And turning privately to the disciples he said, "How blissful the eyes seeing the things you see, [24]For I tell you that many prophets and kings longed to see the things that you see and did not see them, and to hear the things you hear and did not hear them."

[25]And look: A certain lawyer stood up to test him, saying, "Teacher, by what deeds may I inherit life in the Age?" [26]And he said to him, "What has been written in the Law? How do you read it?" [27]And in reply he said, "You shall love the Lord your God out of the whole of your heart and in the whole of your soul and in the whole of your strength and in the whole of your mind, and your neighbor as yourself." [28]And he said to him, "You answer correctly; do this and you shall live." [29]But he, wishing to vindicate himself, said to Jesus, "And who is my neighbor?" [30]Taking this up, Jesus said, "A certain man was going down from Jerusalem, and he fell among bandits, who stripped him and rained blows upon him and went away leaving him half dead. [31]And by a coincidence a certain priest was going down by that road and, seeing him, passed by on the opposite side. [32]And a Levite also, coming upon the place and seeing him, passed by on the opposite side. [33]But a certain Samaritan on a journey came upon him and was inwardly moved with compassion, [34]And approaching bandaged his wounds, pouring on oil and wine, and setting him upon his own mount he brought him to a lodge and cared for him. [35]And taking out two denarii on the following day he gave them to the keeper of the lodge and said, 'Take care of him, and whatever you spend beyond this I shall repay you on my return.' [36]Who of these three does it seem to you became a neighbor to the man falling among ban-

dits?" ³⁷And he said, "The one treating him with mercy." And Jesus said to him, "Go and do likewise."

³⁸And as they journeyed on he entered a certain village; and a certain woman by the name of Martha received him into her home. ³⁹And she had a sister called Mary who, sitting also beside the Lord's feet, listened to his speech. ⁴⁰But Martha was distracted by serving so much; and she came and said, "Lord, does it not matter to you that my sister left me all alone to serve? Tell her, therefore, that she should assist me." ⁴¹And in reply the Lord said to her, "Martha, Martha, you are anxious and disturbed about many things, ⁴²But there is need of one thing: for Mary has chosen the good portion, which shall not be taken away from her."

CHAPTER ELEVEN

¹And it happened that as he was praying, when he finished, a certain one of his disciples said to him, "Lord, teach us to pray, just as John too taught his disciples." ²And he said to them, "When you pray, say, 'Father, let your name be held sacred; let your Kingdom come; ³Give us each day our bread for the day ahead, ⁴And forgive us our sins, for we also forgive all who are indebted to us; and do not bring us to trial.'"ʰ ⁵And he said to them, "Among you, what man would have a friend, and would come to him at midnight and say to him, 'Friend, lend me three loaves of bread, ⁶Since a friend of mine has just visited me from the road and I have nothing I might set before him,' ⁷And the one inside would say in response, 'Do not present me with difficulties; the door has already been closed, and my children and I are in bed; I cannot get

h. In the Byzantine Text-type, Luke's version of the Lord's Prayer has been brought into much closer conformity with Matthew's: "[Our] Father [who are in heaven], let your name be held sacred; let your Kingdom come; [your will be done, as in heaven, so on earth]; ³Give us each day our bread for the day ahead, and forgive us our sins, for we also forgive all who are indebted to us; and do not bring us to trial [but rather rescue us from the wicked one]."

up and give you anything.' ⁸I tell you, even if he will not rise and give it to him because he is his friend, still on account of his persistence he will rise and give him whatever he needs. ⁹And I tell you, ask and it will be given to you; seek and you will find; knock and it will be opened to you. ¹⁰For everyone asking receives, and the one seeking finds, and to the one knocking it will be opened. ¹¹And what father among you, if his son will ask for a fish, will hand him a snake instead of a fish? ¹²Or, again, if he will ask for an egg, will instead hand him a scorpion? ¹³If therefore you, being wicked, know to give good gifts to your children, how much more will the Father from heaven give a Holy Spirit to those asking him."

¹⁴And he was exorcizing a demon, and it was mute; and it happened that, as the demon departed, the mute man spoke; and the crowds were amazed; ¹⁵But some of them said, "He exorcizes demons by Beelzebul, the Archon of the demons." ¹⁶And others, testing him, sought from him a sign out of heaven. ¹⁷And he, perceiving their thoughts, said to them, "Every kingdom divided against itself is brought to desolation, and a house divided against itself falls. ¹⁸And, if even the Accuser has been divided against himself, how will his kingdom stand? For you say that I exorcize the demons by Beelzebul. ¹⁹But, if I exorcize the demons by Beelzebul, by what do your sons exorcize? Therefore, they will be your judges. ²⁰But if I exorcize the demons by the finger of God, then the Kingdom of God has come upon you. ²¹When a strong man, well-armed, keeps guard over his own courtyard, his possessions rest peacefully; ²²But, when someone stronger than he vanquishes him, he strips away his panoply, on which he had relied, and divides up the weapons despoiled from him. ²³Whoever is not with me is against me, and whoever does not gather together with me scatters. ²⁴When the impure spirit departs from the man, it passes through all the dry places seeking rest, and finds none. [Then] it says, 'I shall return to my house, from which I departed.' ²⁵And coming it finds it swept clean and furnished in good order. ²⁶Then it goes and brings along seven other spirits more wicked than itself, and entering in it dwells there, and the man's last circumstances become worse than the first." ²⁷And it happened that as

he was saying these things a certain woman raised her voice and said to him from the crowd, "How blissful the womb having borne you and the breasts from which you sucked." ²⁸But he said, "Blissful, rather, those hearing God's word and keeping it."

²⁹And as the crowds pressed in upon him he began to say, "This generation is a wicked generation; it seeks a sign, and a sign shall not be given to it, except the sign of Jonah. ³⁰For just as Jonah became a sign to the Ninevites, so also will the Son of Man to this generation. ³¹The Queen of the South will be raised at the judgment along with this generation and will condemn them; because she came from the farthest reaches of this earth to hear the wisdom of Solomon, and see: Something greater than Solomon is here. ³²Ninevite men will rise at the judgment along with this generation and will condemn it; because at the proclamation of Jonah they changed their hearts, and see: Something greater than Jonah is here. ³³No one having lit a lamp sets it in a hidden place or under the dry-goods basket, but rather on the lampstand, so that those coming in may see the radiance. ³⁴The body's lamp is your eye. When your eye is pure, your whole body is luminous; but when it is baleful, your body is dark also. ³⁵Keep watch, therefore, that the light in you is not darkness. ³⁶If, therefore, your whole body is luminous, having no part dark at all, it will be wholly luminous, as when the lamp illuminates you with its shining.

³⁷Now as he was speaking a Pharisee requests that he dine with him; and going in he reclined. ³⁸But the Pharisee was astonished on seeing that before the dinner he did not first wash. ³⁹But the Lord said to him, "But you, the Pharisees, cleanse the outside of the cup and the dish, but your inside is full of spoliation and wickedness. ⁴⁰Fools, did not the one who made the outside make the inside also? ⁴¹Instead, give away the things that are within as alms, and look: All things are pure to you. ⁴²But alas for you, the Pharisees, because you make the tithe of the mint and the rue and every herb, and neglect God's judgment and love; but these it was necessary to practice, without neglecting those things also. ⁴³Alas for you, the Pharisees, because you love the chief seat in the syna-

gogues and the salutations in the marketplaces. [44]Alas for you, for you are like unseen graves, and the people walking over them do not know it." [45]And in reply one of the lawyers says to him, "Teacher, in saying these things you insult us also." [46]And he said, "Alas also for you, the lawyers, because you burden men with unbearable burdens, while you yourselves do not lay a single one of your fingers upon those burdens. [47]Alas for you, because you build the tombs of the prophets, and your fathers killed them. [48]You, therefore, are witnesses that you consent to your fathers' works, because they killed them and you do the building. [49]Thus also the Wisdom of God said, 'I will send prophets and Apostles to them, and some of them they will kill and persecute,' [50]So that all the blood of the prophets shed since the foundation of the cosmos will be required of this generation, [51]From the blood of Abel to the blood of Zachariah who perished between the altar and the sanctuary; yes, I tell you, it will be required of this generation. [52]Alas for you, the lawyers, because you carried away the key of knowledge; you yourselves did not enter in, and those going in you prevented." [53]And when he had departed from there the scribes and the Pharisees began to oppose him fiercely and to interrogate him on a great many matters, [54]Lying in wait for him to catch something out of his mouth.

CHAPTER TWELVE

[1]Meanwhile, as the thousands in the crowd had congregated so that they were treading on one another, he began first to say to his disciples, "Guard yourselves from the yeast of the Pharisees, which is dissemblance. [2]There is nothing thoroughly veiled that will not be unveiled, or hidden that will not be known. [3]Thus the things you said in darkness will be heard in the light, and what you whisper in private rooms will be proclaimed on the rooftops. [4]And I say to you, my friends, do not be afraid of those killing the body and thereafter having nothing more that they can do. [5]But I shall show you whom you should fear: Fear the one who, after killing, has the power to cast one into the Vale of Hinnom.

Yes, I tell you, fear this one. ⁶Are not five sparrows sold for two pennies? And not one of them is forgotten in God's sight. ⁷Rather, even the hairs of your head have all been numbered. Do not be afraid; you are worth more than many sparrows. ⁸But I tell you, everyone who acknowledges me before men, the Son of Man will also acknowledge him before the angels of God; ⁹And the one denying me before men will be denied before the angels of God. ¹⁰And everyone who will speak a word against the Son of Man, it will be excused him; but the one blaspheming against the Holy Spirit will not be excused. ¹¹And when they bring you in before synagogues and rulers and authorities do not be anxious about how or what you may answer in defense or may say; ¹²For in that hour the Holy Spirit will teach you the things it is necessary to say." ¹³And someone spoke to him out of the crowd: "Teacher, tell my brother to divide his inheritance with me." ¹⁴But he said to him, "Man, who appointed me judge or arbiter over you?" ¹⁵And he said to them, "Be wary and guard against all greed, because one's life does not consist in the abundance of one's possessions." ¹⁶And he told them a parable saying, "The land of a certain rich man yielded well, ¹⁷And he reasoned with himself, 'What shall I do? For I have nowhere to gather in my fruits?' ¹⁸And he said, 'I shall do this: I shall pull down my granaries and build larger ones and I shall gather there all my grain and goods, ¹⁹And I shall say to my soul, "Soul, you have many goods stored up for many years; take your ease, eat, drink, make merry."' ²⁰But God said to him, 'Fool, this night they demand your soul from you; the things you prepare, then, whose will they be?' ²¹Thus is the one storing up treasure for himself but not being rich toward God." ²²And he said to the disciples, "I tell you, therefore, do not be anxious for the soul, what you might eat, or for the body, what you might wear. ²³For the soul is more than food and the body more than clothing. ²⁴Consider the ravens, for they neither sow nor reap, they who have neither storehouse nor granary, and God feeds them. How much more valuable are you than birds? ²⁵And who among you can by being anxious add a cubit to the span of his life? ²⁶If, therefore, you are incapable of the least of things, why are you anxious concerning the rest?

²⁷Consider the lilies, how they neither spin nor weave; but I tell you, Solomon in all his glory was not arrayed as one of these. ²⁸And if God thus clothes the grass, which is in the field today and tomorrow is flung into an oven, how much more so you, you of little faith? ²⁹And you, do not seek after what you might eat and what you might drink, and do not fret. ³⁰For these things all the gentile peoples of the world seek after; but your Father knows what you have need of. ³¹But seek after his Kingdom, and these things will be given you in addition. ³²Do not be afraid, little flock, because your Father has delighted to give you the Kingdom. ³³Sell your possessions and give alms. Make for yourselves purses that do not wear out, an unfailing treasury in the heavens, near which no thief comes and which no moth destroys. ³⁴For where your treasure is, there your heart will also be. ³⁵Let your loins be wrapped and lamps be burning. ³⁶And you, be like men awaiting their lord, whenever he returns from the wedding feast, so that when he comes and knocks they may immediately open up for him. ³⁷Happy those slaves whom the lord will find vigilant when he comes; amen, I tell you that he will gird himself, and will make them recline and will come and serve them. ³⁸And if he comes in the second or third watch and finds them so, happy are they. ³⁹But know this, if the master of the house knew in what hour the thief comes, he would not have allowed his house to be breached. ⁴⁰And you, be prepared, because the Son of Man comes in an hour you do not expect." ⁴¹And Peter said, "Lord, do you address this parable to us, or also to everyone?" ⁴²And the Lord said, "Who is the faithful, the prudent steward, whom the lord will appoint over the household attendants, to give them their rations at the proper time? ⁴³How happy that slave whom his lord, on coming, will find doing so. ⁴⁴I tell you truly that he will place him in charge over all his possessions. ⁴⁵But if that slave says in his heart, 'My lord takes a long time in coming,' and begins to beat the menservants and maidservants, and both to eat and to drink, and to become drunk, ⁴⁶That slave's lord will come on a day he does not expect and in an hour he does not know, and will cut him to pieces and assign him a portion with the faithless. ⁴⁷And that slave who has known his

lord's will, and has not made preparations or acted according to his will, will be beaten with many blows. [48]But the one who has not known, but has done things worthy of a thrashing, will be beaten with few blows. And to everyone to whom much was given, from him much will be demanded, and from the one to whom much has been entrusted they will request far more. [49]I came to fling fire upon the earth, and how I wish it were already kindled. [50]And I have a baptism in which to be baptized, and how hard-pressed I am till it is accomplished. [51]Do you think that I came to give peace on earth? No, I tell you, but rather division. [52]For from now on there will be five in one house divided three against two and two against three; [53]Father against son and son against father will be divided, mother against daughter and daughter against mother, mother-in-law against her daughter-in-law and daughter-in-law against mother-in-law." [54]And he also said to the crowds, "When you see a cloud rising over the west, you immediately say a storm is coming, and so it happens, [55]And when a south wind blows, you say it will be hot, and so it happens. [56]Charlatans, you know how to discern the face of earth and sky, but how do you not discern this season? [57]And why do you not judge what is right even for yourselves? [58]For, as you are going with your adversary to a ruler, take pains to be reconciled with him out in the street, so that he does not drag you to the judge, and the judge hand you over to the officer, and the officer throw you into prison. [59]I tell you, you most surely will not come out from there until you pay the very last pittance."

CHAPTER THIRTEEN

[1]Now some were present at that time who told him about the Galilaeans whose blood Pilate had mingled with their sacrifices. [2]And in response he said to them, "Do you think that these Galilaeans surpassed all Galilaeans as sinners, because they suffered these things? [3]No, I tell you, but unless you change your hearts you will all perish likewise. [4]Or those eighteen upon whom the tower of Siloam fell and killed them, do you think that they surpassed all men dwelling in Jerusalem in guilt?

⁵No, I tell you, but unless you change your hearts you will all perish likewise." ⁶And he spoke this parable: "A certain man had a fig tree planted in his vineyard, and came seeking fruit on it, and did not find any. ⁷And he said to the vinedresser, 'Look, for three years I come seeking fruit on this fig tree and find nothing; cut it down. Why does it even waste the soil?' ⁸But in reply he says to him, 'Leave it this year too, until I can dig around it and spread manure, ⁹And see if indeed it produce fruit in future; but if not, you will cut it down.'"

¹⁰And he was teaching in one of the synagogues on the Sabbath, ¹¹And look: a woman suffering from a spirit of infirmity for eighteen years, and she was bent over and was entirely unable to stand up straight. ¹²And seeing her Jesus called her to him and said to her, "Madam, you have been released from your infirmity." ¹³And he placed his hands upon her and at once she was raised up erect, and glorified God. ¹⁴But in response the ruler of the synagogue, incensed that Jesus had healed on the Sabbath, said to the crowd: "There are six days when it is necessary to work; come, therefore, and be healed on those, and not on the day of the Sabbath." ¹⁵But the Lord answered him and said, "Charlatans, does not each of you untie his ox or his ass from the manger on the Sabbath and lead it away to drink? ¹⁶And this woman, who is a daughter of Abraham whom the Accuser has bound for—look!—eighteen years, should she not be released from bondage on this, the day of the Sabbath?" ¹⁷And when he had said these things all those opposing him were put to shame, and all the crowd exulted at all the glorious things occurring through him. ¹⁸He said, therefore, "What is the Kingdom of God like, and to what may I liken it? ¹⁹It is like a grain of mustard, which a man took and cast into his own garden, and it grew and became like a tree, and the birds of the sky took up lodging in its branches." ²⁰And again he said, "To what may I liken the Kingdom of God? ²¹It is like yeast, which a woman took and hid in three measures of flour, until the whole was leavened."

²²And he traveled on throughout cities and villages, teaching and making his journey to Jerusalem. ²³And someone said to him, "Lord,

is it the case that those being saved are few?" And he said to them, [24]"Strive to enter through the narrow door, because many, I tell you, will seek to enter and will not have the strength. [25]From the time the master of the house rises and closes the door, you then begin to stand outside and to knock upon the door, saying, 'Lord, open it for us,' and in reply he will say to you, 'I do not know you, where you come from.' [26]Then you will begin to say, 'We ate and drank before you, and you taught in our streets.' [27]And, speaking to you, he will proclaim, 'I do not know where you come from; stand away from me, all workers of injustice.' [28]There will be weeping and the grinding of teeth when you see Abraham and Israel and Jacob and all the prophets in the Kingdom of God, but yourselves driven outside. [29]And they will come from east and west, and from north and south, and will recline at table in the Kingdom of God. [30]And look: 'There are those who are last who will be first, and there are those who are first who will be last.'" [31]In that same hour some Pharisees approached, saying to him, "Leave and journey away from here, for Herod wishes to kill you." [32]And he said to them, "Go tell that fox, 'See, I exorcize demons and accomplish healings today and tomorrow, and on the third day I reach my destination.' [33]Moreover, it is necessary for me to journey on, today and tomorrow and the day following, because it is not allowed that a prophet perish outside Jerusalem. [34]Jerusalem, Jerusalem, the one killing the prophets and stoning those sent to her, how often I have wished to gather your children as would a bird her nestlings beneath her wings. [35]Look: Your house is abandoned. I tell you, you most surely will not see me till the time when you will say, 'Blessed is the one coming in the name of the Lord.'"

CHAPTER FOURTEEN

[1]Now it happened that, as he went into the house of one of the chiefs of the Pharisees, they were observing him carefully. [2]And look: Before him was a certain man with dropsy. [3]And speaking out, Jesus addressed the lawyers and Pharisees, saying, "Is it lawful on the Sabbath to

heal or not?" [4]And they were silent. And laying hold of him he healed him and sent him away. [5]And he said to them, "Who is there among you whose son or ox will fall into a pit, and he will not immediately pull it up again on a Sabbath day?" [6]And against this they were powerless to return an answer. [7]And taking note of how they were choosing the chief places at the table, he addressed a parable to those who had been invited, saying to them, [8]"When you are invited by someone to wedding festivities, do not recline at the best place at the table, in case someone more honored than you has been invited by him, [9]And the one who invited both you and him will come and say to you, 'Give place to this man,' and you then will proceed to take the last place. [10]Rather, when you are invited, go and recline at the last place, so that when the one who has invited you comes he will say to you, 'Friend, go up to a higher place'; then there will be glory for you before everyone reclining at table with you. [11]For everyone exalting himself will be humbled, and the one humbling himself will be exalted." [12]And to the one who had invited him he said, "When you prepare a luncheon or dinner, do not call to your friends or your brothers or your relatives or your rich neighbors, lest they invite you in return and it becomes a recompense for you. [13]Rather, when you prepare a celebration invite the destitute, the crippled, the lame, the blind, [14]And you shall be blissful, for they have nothing to repay you with; for it will be repaid you in the resurrection of the just." [15]And, hearing this, one of those reclining at table with him, said to him, "Blissful is he who eats bread in the Kingdom of God." [16]And he said to him, "A certain man prepared a great banquet, and invited many, [17]And sent out his slave at the hour of the banquet to say to those who had been invited, 'Come, because it is ready now.' [18]And as one they all began to decline. The first said to him, 'I have bought a field, and am forced to go out to see it; I ask you, have me excused.' [19]And another said, 'I bought a yoke of five oxen, and I am going to make a test of them; I ask you, have me excused.' [20]And another said, 'I have married a wife and therefore cannot come.' [21]And, approaching, the slave reported these things to his lord. Then, enraged, the master of the house told his slave, 'Go out quickly, into the streets and alleys of the city, and bring in here the destitute and crippled and blind and lame.' ²²And the slave said, 'Lord, what you commanded has been done, and there is still room.' ²³And the Lord said to the slave, 'Go out to the roads and palings and force them to come in, so that my house may be filled; ²⁴For I tell you, not one of those men who have been invited shall taste of my banquet.'"

²⁵And many crowds journeyed along with him, and turning he said to them, ²⁶"If anyone comes to me and does not hate his father and mother and wife and children and brothers and sisters, and even his own soul as well, he cannot be my disciple. ²⁷Whoever does not bear his own cross and come after me, he cannot be my disciple. ²⁸For which of you, wishing to build a tower, does not first sit down to estimate the cost: whether he has enough to complete it? ²⁹So that when he has laid a foundation, and is unable to complete it, those watching him should not begin to mock him, ³⁰Saying: 'This man began to build and was not able to finish.' ³¹Or what king, journeying to another king to engage him in war, does not first sit down and deliberate whether he is able with ten thousand to meet the one who is coming upon him with twenty thousand? ³²And, if not, he will while he is still far off dispatch an embassy to sue for peace. ³³So, therefore, no one of you who does not bid farewell to all his own possessions can be my disciple. ³⁴Salt is a good thing, then; but if salt too becomes insipid, with what will it be seasoned? ³⁵It is fit neither for soil nor for manure; they throw it outside. Whoever has ears to listen, let him listen."

CHAPTER FIFTEEN

¹Now drawing near to him to listen to him were all the tax-collectors and sinners. ²And both the Pharisees and the scribes murmured a great deal, saying: "This man welcomes sinners and eats with them." ³And he spoke this parable to them, saying, ⁴"What man among you, owning a hundred sheep and losing one of them, does not leave the ninety-

nine in the open country and go after the one that has been lost until he finds it? ⁵And finding it he joyfully places it on his shoulders, ⁶And entering the house he calls his friends and neighbors together, saying to them, 'Rejoice with me, because I found my sheep that had been lost.' ⁷I tell you that such will the joy be in heaven over one sinner changing his heart, more than over ninety-nine upright men having no need of a change of heart. ⁸Or what woman possessing ten drachmas, if she loses one drachma, does not light a lamp and sweep the house and seek diligently till she finds it? ⁹And finding it she calls her friends and neighbors together, saying, 'Rejoice with me, because I found the drachma that I lost.' ¹⁰Thus, I tell you, there is joy in the presence of God's angels over one sinner changing his heart." ¹¹And he said, "A certain man had two sons. ¹²And the younger of them said to the father, 'Father, give me the share of the property falling to me.' And he divided his living between them. ¹³And not many days later, the younger son, having collected everything, departed for a far country, and dissipated his property by living prodigally. ¹⁴When he had spent everything a severe famine spread throughout that country, and he began to be in need. ¹⁵And he went and attached himself to one of that country's citizens, and he sent him into his fields to feed the pigs; ¹⁶And he longed to fill his stomach with the carob pods that the pigs ate, and no one gave him anything. ¹⁷And coming to himself he said, 'How many of my father's hired men are overflowing with bread, but I am here perishing from famine. ¹⁸I will get up and go to my father, and I will say to him, "I have sinned against heaven and before you, ¹⁹I am no longer worthy to be called your son."' ²⁰And he rose and went to his own father. And while he was yet far away his father saw him and was inwardly moved with pity, and ran and fell upon his neck and kissed him fervently. ²¹And his son said to him, 'Father, I have sinned against heaven and before you, I am no longer worthy to be called your son.' ²²But the father said to his slaves, 'Quickly bring out the best robe and put it on him, and place a ring on his finger and sandals on his feet, ²³And bring the fattened calf and kill it, and let us sit and have good cheer, ²⁴Because this son of mine was dead and has come to life again, was lost and has been found.' And they began to celebrate. ²⁵But his older son was in a field; and as he came and drew near the house he heard music and dancing, ²⁶And calling one of the servants over he asked what all this might be. ²⁷And he told him that 'Your brother has come, and your father has killed the fattened calf, because he has got him back in good health.' ²⁸But in his response he was indignant and did not wish to go in; and his father came out and pleaded with him. ²⁹But in reply he said to the father, 'Look, for so many years I am slaving for you, and I have never disobeyed a command of yours, and you never gave me a goat so that I could make merry with my friends, ³⁰But when this son of yours came, he who has devoured your livelihood with whores, you killed the fattened calf for him.' ³¹And he said to him, 'Child, you are always with me, and all my things are yours. ³²But we had to celebrate and rejoice, because this brother of yours was dead and came to life, and was lost and has been found.'"

CHAPTER SIXTEEN

¹And he said to the disciples, "There was a certain rich man who had a steward, and the complaint was made concerning him that he was wasting his property. ²And calling him he said, 'What is this I hear about you? Render the account of your stewardship; for you can be steward no longer.' ³And the steward said to himself, 'What may I do? For my lord is taking the stewardship away from me. I am not strong enough to dig and I am ashamed to beg. ⁴I have realized what I may do, so that once I am removed from stewardship they might welcome me into their houses.' ⁵And summoning each one of his lord's debtors he said to the first, 'How much do you owe my lord?' ⁶And he said, 'A hundred baths of oil.' And he said to him, 'Take your bill and quickly sit down and write fifty.' ⁷Then he said to another, 'And how much do you owe?' And he said, 'A hundred *kors* of grain.' He tells him, 'Take your bill and write eighty.' ⁸And the lord praised the dishonest steward, because he acted prudently; for the sons of this age are more prudent in

dealing with their own generation that are the sons of the light. ⁹And I tell you, make friends for yourselves from the Mammon of unrighteousness, so that when it gives out they may welcome you into the tents of the Age.ⁱ ¹⁰Whoever is faithful in the least thing is also faithful in much, and whoever is dishonest in the least thing is also dishonest in much. ¹¹If, therefore, you were not faithful with dishonest Mammon, who will entrust you with true wealth?' ¹²And, if you were not faithful with what belongs to another, who will entrust you with what belongs to us?ʲ ¹³No household slave can be a slave to two lords, for either he will hate the one and will love the other, or he will stand fast by the one and disdain the other. You cannot be a slave both to God and to Mammon." ¹⁴Now all the Pharisees, being lovers of money, heard these things and sneered at him. ¹⁵And he said to them, "You are the ones who are offering justifications of yourselves before men, but God knows your hearts; because that which is lofty among men is an abomination before God. ¹⁶Until John, there were the Law and the prophets; since then the good tidings of God's Kingdom are being proclaimed, and everyone is being forcedᵏ into it. ¹⁷But it is easier for sky and earth to pass away than for

i. Aeonian. Perhaps, however, here meaning only "enduring a long time," or "lasting through this age," or "enduring for life." This is an instance where the settled habit of translating *aiōnios*—here in the plural form, modifying "tents," τὰς αἰωνίους σκηνάς (*tas aiōnious skēnas*)—simply as "eternal" or "everlasting," except in cases where it absolutely cannot have that meaning, serves to veil an ambiguity of the text. It is traditional to read these words eschatologically, as referring to "everlasting abodes" (or some other ethereal phrase that somewhat dissembles the rather homely image of "tents"), and this may well be correct. But it is not at all clear that, at this point in the text, Jesus has taken leave of the "earthly level" of imagery, and he may be speaking literally of shelters in this world that will last a lifetime (one of the possible acceptations of *aiōnios*).

j. Other manuscripts read "what belongs to you." In either case, this phrasing is somewhat obscure.

k. βιάζεται (*biazetai*): While it is traditional to translate this verse as saying that "everyone forces his way into" the Kingdom, the verb βιάζομαι (*biazomai*) much more typically has a passive force. In fact, this is true of its every other instance in either the New Testament or the Septuagint. The tendency to treat it here as active is almost certainly an attempt to bring it into conformity with

a single serif to fall away from the Law. ¹⁸Everyone divorcing his wife and marrying another commits adultery, and the woman divorced by her husband who marries commits adultery. ¹⁹Now there was a certain rich man, and he used to don a purple robe and fine linen and make merry every day in splendid fashion. ²⁰And a certain destitute man by the name of Lazarus had been laid at his gate, covered with sores, ²¹And longing to have his hunger sated with the things falling from the rich man's table; and instead, the dogs came and licked at his sores. ²²And it happened that the poor man died and was carried off by the angels into the Vale of Abraham;¹ but the rich man also died and was entombed. ²³And lifting up his eyes in Hades, being in torment, he sees Abraham far off and Lazarus in his vales. ²⁴And calling out he said, 'Father Abraham, have mercy on me and send Lazarus, so that he might dip the tip of his finger in water and might cool my tongue, because I am in agony in this flame.' ²⁵But Abraham said, 'Child, remember that you received your good things during your life, and Lazarus in the same way the bad things; and now he is comforted here and you are in torment. ²⁶And, besides all that, a great chasm has been firmly fixed between us and you, so that those wishing to pass to you from here cannot, nor may anyone cross over from there to here.' ²⁷And he said, 'Then I ask you, father, that you might send him to my father's house, ²⁸For I have five brothers; thus he might bear witness to them, so they might not also come to this place of torment.' ²⁹But Abraham says, 'They have Moses and the prophets; let them listen to them.' ³⁰But he said, 'No, father

---

the imagery (though not the syntax) of Matthew 11:11–12; yet, curiously enough, even there the same verb carries a passive force, only with "Kingdom" rather than "everyone" constituting its subject. It seems clearly better, then, to read this verse in continuity with 14:21–23 above (and perhaps as an analogue of John 12:32).

1. The word κόλπος (*kolpos*) can mean "bosom" or "womb," but also a great many other things, among them "pocket" or "fold," or "hidden places" or "inward parts," or "bay" or "valley." In the next verse, the noun shifts into the plural, which encourages me to translate the phrase as I have done here; that the place of peace set apart for the righteous in the realm of the dead (Hades) might be depicted as a place of sheltering valleys seems to make perfect sense.

Abraham, but if someone should go to them from the dead, they will change their hearts.' ³¹But he said to him, 'If they do not listen to Moses and the prophets, neither will they be persuaded if someone should arise from the dead.'"

¹And he said to his disciples, "It is impossible that causes of faltering should not come, but alas for the one through whom they come. ²Better for him that a millstone be placed round his neck and he be thrown into the sea rather than that he should cause one of these little ones to falter. ³Keep watch upon yourselves. If your brother sins, admonish him, and if he changes his heart, forgive him. ⁴And if he sins against you seven times a day, and seven times turns back to you saying, 'I change my heart,' you shall forgive him." ⁵And the Apostles said to the Lord, "Increase our faith." ⁶And the Lord said, "If you have as much faith as a grain of mustard, you might have said to this mulberry tree, 'Be uprooted and be planted in the sea,' and it would have obeyed you. ⁷But which of you, having a slave plowing or shepherding, will say to him when he comes in from the field, 'Come at once and recline at table,' ⁸And will not instead say to him, 'Prepare something for me to dine on, and gird yourself and wait on me while I eat and drink, and after that eat and drink yourself.' ⁹Does he give thanks to the slave because he did the things he was commanded to do? ¹⁰So you too, when you do all the things commanded of you, say: 'We are worthless slaves, we have done what we ought to do.'"

¹¹And it happened that as he journeyed to Jerusalem that he also passed between Samaria and Galilee. ¹²And as he entered a certain village ten men with leprosy, who stood far off, met him, ¹³And they raised their voices saying, "Jesus, master, have mercy on us." ¹⁴And seeing them he said to them, "Go show yourselves to the priests." And it happened that, as they went, they were cleansed. ¹⁵And one of them, seeing that he was healed, returned glorifying God with a loud voice,

¹⁶And fell on his face at his feet, thanking him; and he was a Samaritan. ¹⁷And in reply Jesus said, "Were not ten of you cleansed? But where are the nine? ¹⁸Was none found returning to give glory to God except only this man of another people?" ¹⁹And he said to him, "Rise and go; your faith has saved you."

²⁰And when he was asked by the Pharisees, "When is the Kingdom of God coming?" he answered them and said, "The Kingdom does not come as something one observes, ²¹Nor will persons say, 'Look: Here it is' or 'There it is' for look: The Kingdom of God is within you."ᵐ ²²And he said to the disciples, "The days will come when you will long to see one of the days of the Son of Man and will not see it. ²³And they will say to you, 'Look: There it is,' 'Look: Here it is'; do not go off or follow them. ²⁴For just as the flashing lightning illuminates everything below heaven, from one end to the other, such will be the Son of Man on his day. ²⁵But first it is necessary that he suffer many things and be rejected by this generation. ²⁶And, just as happened in the days of Noah, so it will also be in the days of the Son of Man: ²⁷They were eating, drinking, marrying, giving in marriage, right up to the day when Noah entered into the ark, and the flood came and destroyed them all. ²⁸Just as happened, likewise, in the days of Lot: They were eating, drinking, buying, selling, planting, building; ²⁹But on the day Lot departed from Sodom, fire and brimstone rained from heaven and destroyed them all. ³⁰It will be just so on the day when the Son of Man is revealed. ³¹On that day, whoever will be upon the roof while his goods are in his home, let him not come down to collect them; likewise, whoever is in the field,

---

m. ἐντὸς ὑμῶν (entos ᵇymōn): it is occasionally argued that this phrase would be better translated "among you" or "in your midst," especially by those who instinctively prefer social to mystical construals of Jesus's teachings; but this is surely wrong. *Entos* really does properly mean "within" or "inside of," not "among," and Luke, in both his Gospel and the book of Acts, when meaning to say "among" or "amid," always uses either the phrase ἐν μέσῳ (en mesō̦) or just an ἐν (en), followed by a dative plural; and his phrase for "in your midst" is ἐν μέσῳ ὑμῶν (en mesō̦ ᵇymōn), as in 22:27 below. He uses *entos* only here, with a distinct and special import.

let him not turn back to the things behind. ³²Remember Lot's wife. ³³Whoever seeks to preserve his soul, he will lose it; and whoever loses it will preserve it. ³⁴I tell you, on that night there will be two men upon one bed, the one will be carried off and the other spared. ³⁵There will be two women grinding grain together, the one will be carried off and the other spared. [³⁶There will be two men in the field, the one will be carried off and the other spared.]" ³⁷And in response they say to him, "Where, Lord?" And he said to them, "Where the body is, there the eagles will also be gathered."

CHAPTER EIGHTEEN

¹And he told them a parable on the necessity of their always praying and not becoming remiss, ²Saying, "In a certain city there was a certain judge who did not fear God and who had no concern for humankind. ³And there was a widow in that city, and she came to him saying, 'Grant me justice over against my adversary.' ⁴And for some time he would not; but thereafter he said within himself, 'Though indeed I do not fear God, nor do I have any concern for humankind, ⁵I shall grant her justice simply because she bothers me, for fear that at the last she will entirely exhaust me with her visits.'" ⁶And the Lord said, "Listen to what the unjust judge says; ⁷Will not God then surely bring about justice for his chosen ones crying to him day and night, and not delay over them for long? ⁸I tell you, he will swiftly bring them justice. Yet, when the Son of Man comes, will he then find faith on the earth?"

⁹And he also spoke this parable to certain persons who were confident that they were upright while despising everyone else: ¹⁰"Two men went up to the Temple to pray, the one a Pharisee, the other a tax-collector. ¹¹The Pharisee stood up straight and prayed these things about himself: 'God, I thank you that I am not like the rest of mankind—rapacious, unjust, adulterous—or even like this tax-collector; ¹²I fast twice a week and tithe from everything whatsoever that I earn.' ¹³But the tax-collector, standing a good distance off, would not lift his

eyes to heaven, but beat upon his breast, saying, 'God, grant mercy to me, a sinner.' [14]I tell you, the latter rather than the former went down to his house vindicated; because everyone who exalts himself will be humbled, and whoever humbles himself will be exalted."

[15]And they also brought babies to him, so that he might touch them; but seeing this the disciples admonished them. [16]But Jesus called them forward, saying, "Allow the little children to come to me, and do not prevent them; for of such is the Kingdom of God. [17]Amen, I tell you, whoever does not receive the Kingdom of God as a little child shall most certainly not enter into it."

[18]And a certain ruler inquired of him, "Good teacher, by doing what may I inherit life in the Age?" [19]And Jesus said to him, "Why do you say I am good? No one is good except one—God. [20]You know the commandments: Do not commit adultery, do not murder, do not steal, do not give false testimony, honor your father and mother." [21]And he said, "All of these I have kept from youth." [22]But hearing this Jesus said to him, "One thing is still lacking in you; sell everything, whatever you have, and distribute it to the destitute, and you will have a treasury in the heavens, and follow me." [23]And he, hearing these things, became very morose, for he was extremely rich. [24]And, seeing him, Jesus said, "How hard for those possessing wealth to enter the Kingdom of God, [25]For it is easier for a camel[n] to enter through the eye of a needle than for a rich man to enter into the Kingdom of God." [26]And those hearing this said, "Can any of them then be saved?"[o] [27]And he said, "Those things impossible for men are possible for God." [28]And Peter said to him, "Look: We have abandoned all that was ours and followed you."

---

n. The text speaks of a κάμηλος (kamēlos, acc. kamēlon), "camel," but from the early centuries it has been an open question whether it should really be the homophonous (but poorly attested) word κάμιλος (kamilos), "rope," "hawser": a more symmetrical but less piquant analogy.

o. καὶ τίς δύναται σωθῆναι (kai tis dynatai sōthēnai): often translated as "Who then can be saved?" or "Can anyone then be saved?" but I take the import (specifically as regards the τίς) to be "Can any [rich man] then be saved?"

²⁹And he said to them, "Amen, I tell you that there is no one who has left home or wife or brothers or parents or children for the sake of the Kingdom of God, ³⁰Who does not surely receive many times as much in the present time and, in the Age to come, the life of that Age."

³¹And taking the Twelve aside he said to them, "Look: We are going up to Jerusalem, and everything written by the prophets concerning the Son of Man will be accomplished; ³²For he will be handed over to the gentiles and will be mocked and insulted and spat upon, ³³And having flogged him they will kill him, and on the third day he will rise again." ³⁴And they understood none of this, and this message was hidden from them, and they did not know what they were being told.

³⁵And it happened that, as he drew near to Jericho, a certain blind man was sitting beside the road begging. ³⁶And hearing a crowd passing through he inquired what this might be. ³⁷And they explained to him: "Jesus the Nazorean is going by." ³⁸And he cried aloud, saying, "Jesus, son of David, have mercy on me." ³⁹And those leading the way admonished him that he should be silent; but he cried out all the more, "Son of David, have mercy on me." ⁴⁰And, coming to a standstill, Jesus ordered that he be brought to him. And, when he came near, he asked him, ⁴¹"What do you wish I might do?" And he said, "Lord, that I might see again." ⁴²And Jesus said to him, "See again; your faith has saved you." ⁴³And on the instant he saw again, and followed him glorifying God. And all who saw this gave praise to God.

CHAPTER NINETEEN

¹And, having entered Jericho, he was passing through, ²And look: a man called by the name of Zacchaeus, and he was a chief tax-collector, and he was wealthy; ³He wished to see "Who Jesus is," and was not able on account of the crowd, because he was small of stature. ⁴And having run ahead he climbed up into a sycamore tree so that he might see him, because he was just about to pass by there. ⁵And Jesus, as he came to the place, looked up and said to him, "Zacchaeus, be quick, come down, for

it is necessary for me to stay in your house today." ⁶And, making haste, he descended and welcomed him with joy. ⁷And seeing this everyone murmured, saying that "He went in to lodge with a man who is a sinner." ⁸But Zacchaeus stood up and said to the Lord, "Look, Lord, I give half my possessions to the destitute, and if I have taken anything from anyone by falsehood I restore it fourfold." ⁹And Jesus said to him: "Today salvation has come to this house, because he too is a son of Abraham. ¹⁰For the Son of Man came to seek and to save what has been lost."

¹¹And, as they were listening to these things, he added a parable, because he was near Jerusalem and they thought that the Kingdom of God was about to appear all at once; ¹²Therefore he said, "A certain man of noble birth went to a far country to assume a kingdom for himself and to return. ¹³And having called ten of his slaves he gave them two minas, and said to them, 'Engage in trade until I come.' ¹⁴But his fellow citizens hated him, and sent a delegation after him, saying, 'We do not want this man to reign over us.' ¹⁵And it happened that when he returned, having received the kingdom, he ordered that those slaves to whom he had given the money be called to him, in order that he might learn what each had gained in trade. ¹⁶And the first came and said, 'Lord, your mina earned ten minas.' ¹⁷And he said to him, 'Well done, good slave, because you were faithful in the least of things, take authority over ten cities.' ¹⁸And the second came, saying, 'Your mina, lord, made five minas.' ¹⁹And to this one too he said, 'And you shall be set over five cities.' ²⁰And the other came, saying, 'See, lord, your mina, which I kept put away in a napkin; ²¹For I was afraid of you, because you are an exacting man; you take up what you did not lay down, and you reap what you did not sow.' ²²He says to him, 'Out of your mouth I will judge you, wicked slave. Did you know that I am an exacting man, taking up what I did not lay down and reaping what I did not sow? ²³Why then did you not put my money on a banker's table, and then on coming I would have withdrawn it with interest?' ²⁴And to those standing attendance he said, 'Take the mina from him and give it to the one who has

ten minas.' ²⁵And they said to him, 'Lord, he has ten minas.' ²⁶'I tell you that to everyone who has it will be given; and from him who does not have even what he has will be taken away. ²⁷As for those enemies of mine, however, those not wishing me to reign over them, bring them here and slaughter them before me.'"

²⁸And having said these things he journeyed on ahead, going up to Jerusalem. ²⁹And it happened that, as he drew near to Bethphage and Bethany, at the mountain called Mount of Olives, he sent out two of his disciples, saying, ³⁰"Go into the village opposite, on entering which you will find a tethered colt upon which no one among men has ever yet sat, and untie it and bring it. ³¹And, if anyone asks, 'Why are you untying it?' you will answer thus: 'Because the Lord has need of it.'" ³²And, going away, those who had been sent found it just as he had told them. ³³And, as they were untying the colt, its owners said to them, "Why are you untying the colt?" ³⁴And they said, "Because the Lord has need of it." ³⁵And they led it to Jesus and, throwing their cloaks on the colt, they set Jesus on it. ³⁶And as he proceeded people spread their own cloaks on the road. ³⁷And, as he drew near to the path descending from the Mount of Olives, the whole multitude of disciples began joyfully to praise God in a loud voice on account of all the deeds of power they had seen, ³⁸Saying, "Blessed is the king who comes in the name of the Lord; peace in heaven and glory in the highest places." ³⁹And some of the Pharisees from the crowd said to him, "Teacher, admonish your disciples." ⁴⁰And in answer he said, "I tell you, if they should fall silent the stones would cry out." ⁴¹And as he came near and saw the city, he wept over it, ⁴²And said, "If you had known on this day, even you, the things that lead to peace—but now they have been hidden from your eyes, ⁴³Because the days will come upon you when your enemies will erect a rampart against you and will encircle you and will press in upon you on every side, ⁴⁴And will dash you to the ground, and your children within you, and will leave not a stone upon a stone in you, because you did not recognize the time of your visitation." ⁴⁵And entering the Temple he began expelling those who were selling there, ⁴⁶Saying to

them, "It has been written, 'And my house shall be a house of prayer'; but you, you have made it a robbers' den."

⁴⁷And he was teaching each day in the Temple; and the chief priests and the scribes, as well as the preeminent men of the people, sought to destroy him. ⁴⁸And they found nothing they could do; for all the people hung upon him, listening.

CHAPTER TWENTY

¹And it happened that, on one of the days when he was teaching the people in the Temple and proclaiming the good tidings, the chief priests and the scribes, together with the elders, descended upon him, ²And spoke to him, saying, "Tell us by what power you do these things, or who it is who has given you this power." ³And in reply he said to them, "I will also ask you to say something, and tell me: ⁴The baptism of John, was it from heaven or from human beings?" ⁵And they debated among themselves, saying: "If we say, 'From heaven,' he will say, 'Why did you not have faith in him?' ⁶And if we say, 'From human beings,' all the people are persuaded that John was a prophet." ⁷And they answered that they did not know where it came from. ⁸And Jesus said to them, "Neither do I tell you by what power I do these things." ⁹And he began to tell this parable to the people: "A man planted a vineyard, and leased it out to husbandmen and went abroad for a considerable time. ¹⁰And at the proper time he sent a slave to the husbandmen, so that they would yield him some of the vineyard's fruit; but, beating him, they sent him away empty. ¹¹And thereupon he sent another slave, but they, beating and humiliating that one as well, sent him away empty. ¹²And thereupon he sent a third; and this one they also wounded and threw out. ¹³And the owner of the vineyard said, 'What may I do? I will send my son, my beloved; perhaps they will treat him with shamed deference.' ¹⁴But on seeing him the husbandmen reasoned with one another, saying, 'This is the heir; let us kill him so that the inheritance might become ours.'

[15]And, throwing him outside the vineyard, they killed him. What then will the lord of the vineyard do to them? [16]He will come and destroy these husbandmen, and give the vineyard to others." And those listening said, "Let this not happen!" [17]But looking directly at them he said, "What then does this scripture mean: 'The stone that those building rejected, this has become the capstone of the corner'? [18]Everyone who falls on that stone will be shattered; but on whomever it falls, him it will utterly crush." [19]And the scribes and the chief priests longed to lay their hands on him in that very hour, and were afraid of the people; for they knew he told this parable in regard to them. [20]And, observing closely, they sent spies who pretended that they were upright, that they might catch him in something he said, so as to hand him over to the rule and authority of the governor. [21]And they questioned him, saying, "Teacher, we know that you speak correctly and teach, and you are not a respecter of persons, but teach the way of God in truth; [22]Is it lawful or not for us to render tribute to Caesar?" [23]But, perceiving their wiliness, he said to them, [24]"Show me a denarius; whose image and inscription does it have?" And they said, "Caesar's." [25]And he said to them, "Then render Caesar's things to Caesar and God's things to God." [26]And they were powerless to seize upon any utterance of his in the presence of the people and, amazed at his answer, they were silent.

[27]And some of the Sadducees, those who speak against the reality of the resurrection, approached and questioned him, [28]Saying, "Teacher, Moses wrote for us that if anyone's brother dies having a wife, and this brother is childless, that his brother should take his wife and raise up seed for his brother. [29]Now there were seven brothers; and the first, having taken a wife, died childless, [30]And the second [31]And the third took her, and in the same way the seven left no children behind and died. [32]Lastly the woman died also. [33]The woman, then, in the resurrection will become the wife of which of them?" [34]And Jesus said to them, "The sons of this age marry and are given in marriage, [35]But those accounted worthy of sharing in that Age and in the resurrection

of the dead neither marry nor are given in marriage, [36]For they cannot even die any more, for they are the equals of angels,[p] for they are God's sons, being sons of the resurrection. [37]But that the dead are raised even Moses reported in regard to the bush, as he calls the Lord the God of Abraham and God of Isaac and God of Jacob, [38]But he is God not of the dead but of the living; for to him all are alive." [39]And in reply some of the scribes said, "Teacher, you speak well." [40]For they did not again dare to ask him anything.

[41]And he said to them, "How is it that they say the Anointed is David's son? [42]For David himself says in the book of Psalms, 'The Lord said to my lord, "Sit at my right, [43]Until I set your enemies as a footstool for your feet."' [44]David then calls him 'Lord,' so how is he his son?"

[45]And, while all the people were listening, he said to the disciples, [46]"Be wary of the scribes, who wish to walk about in long robes and who cherish salutations in the marketplaces, and the chief seats in the synagogues, and the chief couches at banquets; [47]Who devour the houses of widows and as a pretense make long prayers; these shall receive a severer judgment."

CHAPTER TWENTY-ONE

[1]And looking up he saw the rich putting their offerings into the treasury. [2]And he saw a certain impoverished widow there putting in two lepta, [3]And he said, "I tell you truly that this destitute widow put in more than all; [4]For all of these donated their gifts out of their abundance, but this woman donated out of her poverty all the livelihood she possessed."

[5]And as certain persons spoke about the Temple—that it had been made lovely with beautiful stones and votive gifts—he said, [6]"As for these things you gaze upon, the days will come in which there will be

p. See Acts 23:8; 1 Corinthians 15:40–54; and 1 Peter 3:18–19, 4:6, as well as the footnotes thereto.

left no stone upon a stone that will not be overthrown." ⁷And they questioned him, saying, "Teacher, when will these things be, then? And what will the sign be when these things are about to happen?" ⁸And he said, "Be wary, so that you might not be led away; for many will come in my name, saying, 'I am he,' and 'The time has drawn near.' Do not go after them. ⁹And when you hear of wars and upheavals, do not be terrified; for it is necessary that these things happen first, but the end will not come immediately." ¹⁰Then he said to them, "Nation will be raised against nation and kingdom against kingdom, ¹¹And there will be great earthquakes and in various places pestilences and famines, terrible portents and great signs in the sky. ¹²But before all this they will lay their hands on you and will persecute you, handing you over to the synagogues and prisons, led away to kings and governors for my name's sake; ¹³It will result in you offering testimony. ¹⁴Therefore, put it into your hearts not to rehearse your defense in advance; ¹⁵For I will give you a mouth and wisdom, which none of those prosecuting you will be able to oppose or contradict. ¹⁶And you will be handed over even by parents and brothers and relatives and friends, and they will put some of you to death, ¹⁷And you will be hated by all because of my name. ¹⁸And by no means shall a hair of your head perish; ¹⁹By your endurance you will gain your souls. ²⁰But, when you see Jerusalem surrounded by arms and encampments, then know that her desolation has drawn near. ²¹Then let those in Judaea flee into the mountains, let those inside her walls go out and away, and let those in the countryside not enter her, ²²Because these are the days of retribution, when all the scriptures are fulfilled. ²³Alas in those days for pregnant women and women nursing; for there will be great distress in the land and ire against this people, ²⁴And they will fall by the edge of the sword and will be led away captive to all the nations, and Jerusalem will be trampled upon by the gentiles, until the seasons of the gentiles are fulfilled. ²⁵And there will be signs in sun and moon and stars, and on the earth the distress of nations, in bewilderment at the roar of sea and surf, ²⁶While men faint away from fear and anticipation of the things coming upon the inhabited world; for the powers of the heavens will be shaken. [27]And then they will see the Son of Man coming in a cloud with power and great glory. [28]And, when these things begin to happen, stand up and lift your heads, because your liberation draws near." [29]And he told them a parable: "Look at the fig tree and all the trees; [30]When they break now into leaf, you see for yourselves and know the summer is near; [31]So too, when you see these things happening, you also know that the Kingdom of God is near. [32]Amen, I tell you that this generation most certainly will not pass away until all things occur. [33]The sky and the earth will pass away, but my words shall most certainly not pass away. [34]And regarding yourselves take care, so that your hearts may not become burdened with carousing and heavy drinking and the anxieties of life, and That Day come upon you suddenly, [35]Like a snare; for it will come in upon all who dwell on the face of all the earth. [36]But be on watch at every moment, imploring that you might be able to escape all the things about to happen, and to stand before the Son of Man."

[37]Now during the days he was in the Temple teaching, and during the nights he departed and stayed upon the mountain called the Mount of Olives. [38]And in the early morning all the people came to him in the Temple to listen to him.

CHAPTER TWENTY-TWO

[1]Now the feast of the Unleavened Loaves, which is called Passover, drew near: [2]And the chief priests and the scribes sought a way to destroy him; for they were afraid of the people. [3]And the Accuser entered into Judas, the one called Iscariot, who was one of the Twelve's number; [4]And he went off to confer with the chief priests and officers regarding how he might hand him over to them. [5]And they were elated, and agreed to give him silver. [6]And he consented entirely, and sought an opportunity to hand him over to them away from any crowd.

[7]Now the day of Unleavened Loaves arrived, when it was necessary for the Passover lamb to be sacrificed; [8]And he sent out Peter and John,

saying, "Go prepare the Passover for us, so that we may eat." ⁹And they said to him, "Where do you wish that we should make preparations?" ¹⁰And he said to them, "Look: As you enter the city you will meet a man carrying a clay vessel of water; follow him into the house into which he enters; ¹¹And you shall say to the master of the household, "The Teacher says to you, 'Where is the guest room where I may eat the Passover with my disciples? ¹²And that man will show you a large room already laid out; make preparations there." ¹³And going forth they found it just as he had told them, and they prepared the Passover. ¹⁴And when the hour came, he reclined at table, and the Apostles with him. ¹⁵And he said to them, "With such longing I have yearned to eat this Passover with you before I suffer; ¹⁶For I tell you that I most surely will not eat it again until it has its fulfillment in the Kingdom of God." ¹⁷And taking a cup and having given thanks he said, "Take this and share it among yourselves, ¹⁸For I tell you, I most surely will not drink from the yield of the wine from now until the Kingdom of God comes." ¹⁹And taking a loaf of bread, having given thanks, he broke it and gave it to them, saying, "This is my body, which is being offered for you; do this in my memory." ²⁰And after supping he did likewise with the cup, saying, "This cup is the new covenant in my blood, which is being shed for you. ²¹But look: The hand of him who betrays me is on the table with mine. ²²For the Son of Man does indeed proceed as has been determined; yet alas for that man by whom he is handed over." ²³And they began to ask one another who among them it might then be who was about to do this. ²⁴And a dispute also arose among them regarding which among them seems to be greater. ²⁵So he said to them, "The kings of the gentile peoples dominate them, and those having power over them are called benefactors. ²⁶But not so you; rather let him among you who is greater become as though the junior, and the one governing as though the one serving. ²⁷For who is greater, the one reclining at table or the one serving? Is not the one reclining? Yet I am in your midst as one serving. ²⁸But you are those who have stayed with me through my trials; ²⁹And to you I appoint—just as my Father appointed to me—a Kingdom, ³⁰So that you might eat and drink at my table in my Kingdom, and you will sit on thrones judging the twelve tribes of Israel. [31]Simon, Simon, look: The Accuser has begged to sift you all like wheat. [32]But I have prayed concerning you, that your faith might not fail; and you, when you have returned, strengthen your brothers." [33]And he said to him, "Lord, I am ready to go both to prison and to death with you." [34]And he said, "I tell you, Peter, a cock will not crow this day before you will deny you know me three times." [35]And he said to them, "When I sent you out, without purse and leather pouch and sandals, were you in want of anything?" And they said, "Of nothing." [36]And he said to them, "Now, however, whoever has a purse, let him take it, and a leather pouch likewise; and whoever lacks a sword, let him sell his cloak and buy one. [37]For I tell you that it is necessary for this scripture to be brought to completion in me: 'And he was reckoned with the lawless.' For indeed that which concerns me has its fulfillment." [38]And they said, "Lord, look, we have two swords." And he said to them, "It is enough."

[39]And going out he went to the Mount of Olives, as was his habit; and his disciples followed him too. [40]And coming to the place he said to them, "Pray that you do not enter into trial." [41]And he was withdrawn from them, about a stone's throw away, and kneeling down he prayed, [42]Saying, "Father, it if is your will, take this cup away from me; yet let not my will, but yours, come to pass." [43]And an angel from heaven appeared to him, strengthening him. [44]And, being in anguish, he prayed more fervently; and his sweat became like drops of blood falling to the earth. [45]And rising from prayer, coming to the disciples, he found them asleep from sorrow, [46]And he said to them, "Why do you sleep? Get up, pray that you might not enter into trial." [47]While he was still speaking, look: a crowd; and the one called Judas, one of the Twelve, led them forward, and drew near to Jesus to kiss him. [48]But Jesus said to him, "Judas, do you betray the Son of Man with a kiss?" [49]And seeing what was going to happen, those about him said, "Lord, should we strike out with a sword?" [50]And one of them struck the chief priest's slave and slashed off his right ear. [51]And Jesus, speaking out, said, "Leave off, enough." And

touching the ear he cured him. [52]And, to the chief priests and officers of the Temple and elders coming for him, Jesus said, "You come out with swords and bludgeons as though against a bandit? [53]While I was with you each day in the Temple you did not stretch out your hands against me; but this is your hour, and the rule of darkness."

[54]And having seized him they led him and brought him into the household of the chief priest; and Peter followed from afar. [55]And, when they had lit a fire in the center of the courtyard and sat down together, Peter sat among them. [56]And a certain maidservant saw him seated near the light and, gazing at him, said, "This man was with him also." [57]But he denied it, saying, "I do not know him, woman." [58]And, a short time later, someone else saw him and announced, "You are one of them too." But Peter said, "Man, I am not." [59]And after an interval of about an hour someone else quite emphatically asserted it, saying, "In truth this man was also with him, for he too is a Galilaean." [60]But Peter said, "Man, I do not know what you are saying." And all at once, while he was yet speaking, a cock crowed. [61]And the Lord turned and looked at Peter, and Peter remembered what the Lord said when he told him: "Before a cock crows this day you will three times deny me." [62]And going outside he wept bitterly.

[63]And the men in charge of him ridiculed him, beating him, [64]And covering him with a hood, interrogated him, saying, "Who is he who is sporting with you?" [65]And, blaspheming, they said many other things against him, [66]And when day arrived the people's assembly of elders came together, both chief priests and scribes, and led him away to their Council, [67]Saying, "If you are the Anointed, tell us." And he said to them, "If I tell you, you most surely will not believe, [68]And, if I ask you, you surely will not answer. [69]But henceforth the Son of Man will be seated at the right hand of the Power of God." [70]And they said, "What further need have we of witnesses? For we ourselves have heard it from his mouth."

CHAPTER TWENTY-THREE

¹And, rising up, the whole group of them led him before Pilate. ²And they began to accuse him, saying, "We found this man corrupting our nation and forbidding the paying of the poll-tax to Caesar, and claiming that he himself is an Anointed—a king." ³And Pilate interrogated him, saying, "You are the king of the Judaeans?" And in answer he said, "You say so." ⁴And Pilate said to the chief priests and the crowds, "I find no crime in this man." ⁵But they were insistent, saying: "He agitates the people, teaching throughout all Judaea, starting even in Galilee, right to here." ⁶And hearing this Pilate asked whether this man is a Galilaean; ⁷And, realizing that he is under Herod's authority, he sent him up to Herod, who was also in Jerusalem in those days. ⁸And Herod, on seeing Jesus, was overjoyed; for he had been wishing to see him for a long time, since he had heard about him and hoped to see some prodigy performed by him. ⁹And he questioned him in many words; but he answered him nothing. ¹⁰And the chief priests and the scribes stood there accusing him vehemently. ¹¹And, holding him in contempt and mocking him, Herod, along with his soldiers, cast splendid garments around him and sent him back to Pilate. ¹²And on that very day Herod and Pilate became friends; for previously they were in enmity with one another. ¹³And Pilate, summoning together the chief priests and the rulers and the people, ¹⁴Said to them, "You brought this man to me as one corrupting the people, and look: I have examined him before you and in this man have found no element of the things you accuse him of. ¹⁵But neither has Herod; for he sent him back to us. And look: Nothing has been done by him deserving of death; ¹⁶Therefore I will punish him and release him." [¹⁷For it was necessary for him to release one man to them for the festival.] ¹⁸But they shouted out, the whole crowd altogether, saying, "Take this man and release bar-Abbas to us!" ¹⁹—This man was in prison for an insurrection that had occurred in the city and for murder. ²⁰But again Pilate called out to them, wishing to release Jesus. ²¹But they went on shouting, saying, "Crucify, crucify him!" ²²But he said to

them a third time, "But what evil has this man done? I have found in him no cause for death. I shall therefore punish and release him." ²³But they insisted with loud voices, asking that he be crucified, and their voices prevailed. ²⁴And Pilate decided that what they had demanded would happen; ²⁵And he released the man thrown into prison for insurrection and murder, for whom they had asked, but Jesus he delivered over to their will.

²⁶And as they led him away they seized Simon, a certain Cyrenian, coming from the field, and placed the cross on him to carry behind Jesus. ²⁷And a large multitude of the people followed him, as well as of women who mourned and lamented for him. ²⁸But turning to them Jesus said, "Daughters of Jerusalem, do not weep over me; weep rather for yourselves and for your children, ²⁹For see: Days are coming in which they will say, 'Blessed are the barren, and wombs that have not given birth, and the breasts that have not nursed.' ³⁰Then 'They will begin to say to the mountains, "Fall down upon us," and to the hills, "Cover us over,"' ³¹For if they do these things when the tree is full of sap, what will happen when it is dry?" ³²And two others, malefactors, were also led off with him to be executed. ³³And, when they came upon the place called Skull, they crucified him there, as well as the criminals, one at his right and one at his left. ³⁴And Jesus said, "Father, forgive them; for they do not know what they are doing." And dividing his garments they cast lots. ³⁵And the people stood watching. And the rulers too derided him, saying, "He saved others; let him save himself, if this man is the Anointed, God's chosen one." ³⁶And the soldiers also mocked him, approaching, offering him vinegar, ³⁷And saying, "If you are the king of the Judaeans, save yourself." ³⁸And there was also an epigraph above him: "THIS IS THE KING OF THE JUDAEANS." ³⁹And one of the criminals hanging there insulted him: "Are you not the Anointed? Save yourself and us." ⁴⁰But the other, rebuking him, said, "Do you not fear God, since you are under the same sentence? ⁴¹And we have received a return of the things due for the things we did; but this man did nothing wrong." ⁴²And he said, "Jesus, remember me when you come into your

Kingdom." [43]And he said to him, "Amen, I tell you, today you will be with me in paradise." [44]And now it was about the sixth hour and darkness came over the whole land until the ninth hour, [45]Inasmuch as the sun was darkened; and the veil of the Temple sanctuary was torn down the middle. [46]And crying out in a loud voice Jesus said, "Father, into your hands I commit my spirit." And, saying this, he breathed out his spirit. [47]And the centurion, seeing this happen, gave glory to God, saying, "This truly was an upright man." [48]And all of the crowds that had gathered for this spectacle, seeing what was happening, returned home beating their breasts. [49]But all who had been his acquaintances stood at a distance, along with the women who had accompanied him from Galilee, watching these things.

[50]And look: A man named Joseph, who was a member of the Council, a man good and just—[51]This man had not agreed with the Council and their actions—from Arimathea, a city of the Judaeans, who was awaiting the Kingdom of God. [52]Approaching Pilate, this man requested the body of Jesus, [53]And, taking it down, wrapped it in linen, and placed him in a carven tomb where no one had yet been laid. [54]And it was a day of preparation, and the Sabbath was approaching. [55]And, following behind, the women who had come with him from Galilee saw the tomb and how his body had been laid out, [56]And went back and prepared spices and ointment.

But they rested on the Sabbath, in keeping with the commandment.

CHAPTER TWENTY-FOUR

[1]But on the first day of the week, while it was still very early, they came to the tomb, having with them the spices they had prepared. [2]And they found the stone rolled away from the tomb, [3]And entering they did not find the body of the Lord Jesus. [4]And while they were in confusion over this, look: Two men in clothing shining like lightning stood beside them; [5]And, when they became terrified and turned their faces down to the ground, they said to them, "Why do you seek the living

with the dead? ⁶He is not here, but has been raised. Remember how he spoke to you when he was still in Galilee, ⁷Saying, 'It is necessary for the Son of Man to be delivered into the hands of sinful men and to be crucified and on the third day to rise again.'" ⁸And they remembered his words. ⁹And, returning from the tomb, they related all these things to the eleven and all the others. ¹⁰Now it was the Magdalene woman Mary, and Joanna, and Mary the mother of James, as well as the other women with them, who told these things to the Apostles. ¹¹And in their eyes these reports seemed like nonsense, and they did not believe them. ¹²Then Peter rose and ran to the tomb; and stooping down he saw the linen cloths laid out by themselves; and he left, amazed within himself at what had happened.

¹³And look: On that very day two of them were journeying to a village sixty stadia away from Jerusalem, the name of which was Emmaus, ¹⁴And they were talking with each other about all these events. ¹⁵And it happened that, as they talked and debated, Jesus himself approached and journeyed along with them; ¹⁶But their eyes were constrained so as not to recognize him. ¹⁷And he said to them, "What are these remarks you exchange with one another while walking?" And they stood still with saddened expressions. ¹⁸And in reply one of them, Cleopas by name, said to him, "Are you only a visitor to Jerusalem and ignorant of the things happening in it these days?" ¹⁹And he said to them, "What things?" and they said to him, "The things concerning Jesus the Nazarene, a man who was a prophet, mighty in work and word before God and all the people. ²⁰But the chief priests and our rulers both handed him over for condemnation to death and crucified him. ²¹But we had been hoping that he was the one about to liberate Israel; and, in addition to all this, it has reached the third day since these things occurred. ²²But some women among us also astonished us, having come to the tomb early in the morning, ²³And, not finding his body, came and told also of having seen a vision of angels, who say that he lives. ²⁴And some of those with us went to the tomb, and found it just as the women had said, but did not see him." ²⁵And he said to them, "O fools, and with hearts

slow to believe in all the things of which the prophets spoke: [26]Was it not necessary for the Anointed to endure these things and to enter into his glory?" [27]And, beginning with Moses and with all the prophets, he expounded to them the things concerning himself in all the scriptures. [28]And they approached the village to which they were journeying, and he made as if to journey further on. [29]And they urged him intently, saying, "Stay with us, for it is toward evening, and this day has now set." And he went inside to stay with them. [30]And it happened that, as he reclined at table with them, he took the loaf and blessed it and, having broken it, he shared it with them; [31]And their eyes were opened, and they recognized him; and he vanished from their sight. [32]And they said to one another, "Was not our heart burning within us while he spoke to us on the road, as he opened up the scriptures to us?" [33]And, rising up in that same hour, they returned to Jerusalem and found the Eleven gathered together, along with those who were with them, [34]Saying: "The Lord truly has been raised and appeared to Simon." [35]And they related the things that had happened on the road, and how he had been recognized by them in the breaking of the bread. [36]And as they were saying these things he stood in their midst, and said to them, "Peace be with you." [37]And, alarmed and terrified, they thought they were seeing a spirit. [38]And he said to them, "Why are you disturbed, and why do doubts arise in your hearts? [39]Look at my hands and my feet—that I am myself; touch me and look, for a spirit does not have flesh and bones, as you see I have." [40]And when he had said this he showed them his hands and feet. [41]And while they were yet in disbelief from joy, and were in amazement, he said to them, "Do you have any food here?" [42]And they gave him a piece of broiled fish; [43]And, taking it, he ate it before them. [44]And he said to them, "These are the words I spoke to you when I was still with you: That it is necessary for everything written about me in the Law of Moses and the prophets and the Psalms to be fulfilled." [45]Then he opened their mind to understand the scriptures; [46]And he said to them: "Thus it has been written that the Anointed will suffer and rise again from the dead on the third day, [47]And in his name transformation of the heart and forgiveness of sins will be proclaimed to all the nations, beginning from Jerusalem. [48]You are witnesses of these things. [49]And see: I send forth the promise of my Father upon you; but stay in the city until you are clothed with power from on high."

[50]And he led them out as far as Bethany and, raising his hands, he blessed them. [51]And it happened that while he was blessing them he withdrew from them, and was taken up into the sky. [52]And they returned to Jerusalem with great joy, [53]And they were in the Temple constantly, blessing God.

The Gospel
According to John

━━━━━━━━━━

CHAPTER ONE

[1]In the origin there was the Logos, and the Logos was present with God,[a] and the Logos was god; [2]This one was present with God in the origin. [3]All things came to be through him, and without him came to be not a single thing that has come to be. [4]In him was life, and this life was the light of men. [5]And the light shines in the darkness, and the darkness did not conquer it. [6]There came a man, sent by God, whose name was John; [7]This man came in witness, that he might testify about

---

a. To understand my translation of the first eighteen verses of the Gospel, the reader should refer to "A Note on the Prologue of John's Gospel" in my postscript to this volume. Here in the Gospel's prologue, as well as in the closing verses of chapter twenty below, I adopt the typographical convention of the capital *G* followed by small capitals to indicate where the Greek speaks of ὁ θεός (*ho theos*), which clearly means God in the fullest and most unequivocal sense, and I use one capital letter followed by two lowercase letters to indicate where the Greek speaks only of θεός (*theos*) without the article; but, to make the matter more confusing, I have indicated three uses of the word without article (vv. 6, 12, and 13), all concerning the relation between the divine and the created, in all small capitals, to indicate that it is not clear in these instances whether the distinction in forms is still operative, and whether the inarticular form of the noun is being used simply of God as related to creatures through his Logos. And then, in v. 18, I assume the first use of the inarticular form of *theos* still refers to God in the fullest sense, God the Father, though again the clause in question concerns the relation of creatures to the divine.

the light, so that through him all might have faith—[8]But only that he might testify about the light; he was not that light. [9]It was the true light, which illuminates everyone, that was coming into the cosmos. [10]He was in the cosmos, and through him the cosmos came to be, and the cosmos did not recognize him. [11]He came to those things that were his own, and they who were his own did not accept him. [12]But as many as did accept him, to them he gave the power to become GOD's children—to those having faith in his name, [13]Those born not from blood, nor from a man's desire, but of GOD. [14]And the Logos became flesh and pitched a tent among us, and we saw his glory, glory as of the Father's only one, full of grace and truth. [15]John testifies concerning him and has cried out, saying, "This was he of whom I said, 'He who is coming after me has surpassed me, for he was before me.'" [16]For we all have received from his fullness, and grace upon grace; [17]Because the Law was given through Moses, the grace and the truth came through Jesus the Anointed. [18]No one has ever seen GOD; the one who is uniquely god, who is in the Father's breast, that one has declared him.

[19]And this is John's testimony when the Judaeans of Jerusalem sent priests and Levites to him, so that they might ask him, "Who are you?" [20]And he avowed, and did not deny, and confessed that: "I am not the Anointed." [21]And they asked him, "What then? Are you Elijah?" And he says, "I am not." "Are you the Prophet?"[b] And he answered, "No." [22]So they said to him, "Who are you? So that we may give an answer to those who have sent us, what do you say concerning yourself?" [23]He said, "I am a voice of one crying in the desert, 'Make straight the way of the Lord,' as Isaiah the prophet said." [24]And some who had been sent were of the Pharisees. [25]And they questioned him and said to him, "Why then do you baptize, if you are not the Anointed or Elijah or the Prophet?" [26]John answered them saying, "I baptize in water; among you there stands one whom you do not know, [27]The one coming after

b. That is, the great prophet "like unto Moses" supposedly predicted in Deuteronomy 18:15-20.

me, the thong of whose sandals I am not worthy to untie." ²⁸These things occurred in Bethany beyond the Jordan where John was baptizing. ²⁹The next day he sees Jesus coming toward him, and says, "See the lamb of Godᶜ who is taking away the sin of the cosmos. ³⁰This is he concerning whom I have said, 'A man is coming after me who has surpassed me, for he was before me.' ³¹And I myself did not recognize him, although I came baptizing in water so that he might be made manifest to Israel." ³²John also testified by saying: "I have seen the Spirit descending as a dove from the sky, and he rested on him. ³³And I did not recognize him; rather he who sent me to baptize in water, that one said to me, 'On whomever you see the Spirit descending, and resting upon him, this is he who baptizes in a Holy Spirit.' ³⁴And I have seen and have borne witness that this man is the Son of God."

³⁵The next day John again stood there, and two of his disciples as well. ³⁶And, watching Jesus walking by, he says, "Look: the Lamb of God." ³⁷And the two disciples heard him saying this and followed Jesus. ³⁸And turning around, and seeing them following, Jesus says to them, "What do you seek?" And they said to him, "Rabbi"—which is to say, when translated, "Teacher"—"where are you staying?" ³⁹He says to them, "Come and you will see." So they went and saw where he was staying, and stayed with him that day; it was about the tenth hour. ⁴⁰One of the two men who had heeded John and were following him was Andrew, the brother of Simon Peter; ⁴¹The first thing he does is find his own brother Simon and tell him, "We have found the Messiah" (which, being translated, is "the Anointed"). ⁴²He led him to Jesus. Looking at him, Jesus said, "You are Simon the son of John; you shall be called Cephas" (which is translated as "Peter" [Rock]). ⁴³On the following day he wished to go away into Galilee, and he finds Philip. And Jesus

c. Here, ʰo theos (in the genitive: τοῦ θεοῦ [tou theou]) is used to indicate God the Father, who is clearly God in the fullest sense (allowing me to dispense with typographical devices to indicate different usages); and this rule holds throughout the Gospel, right up to 20:28, where the designation is at last used as a proper address to the Son. Again, see my remarks in my postscript.

says to him, "Follow me." ⁴⁴Now Philip was from Bethsaida, the city from which Andrew and Peter came. ⁴⁵Philip finds Nathanael and says to him, "We have found him of whom Moses wrote in the Law and the Prophets, Jesus son of Joseph, from Nazareth." ⁴⁶And Nathanael said to him, "Can there be anything good out of Nazareth?" Philip says to him, "Come and see." ⁴⁷Jesus saw Nathanael approaching him and says of him, "Look: truly an Israelite, in whom there is no guile." ⁴⁸Nathanael says to him, "Where do you know me from?" Jesus answered and said to him, "Before Philip called you, I saw that you were beneath the fig tree." ⁴⁹Nathanael answered him, "Rabbi, you are the Son of God, you are the king of Israel." ⁵⁰Jesus replied and said to him, "You have faith because I told you I saw you below the fig tree? You shall see greater things than these." ⁵¹And he says to him, "Amen, amen, I tell you, you shall see the heavens open and the angels of God ascending and descending upon the Son of Man."ᵈ

CHAPTER TWO

¹And on the third day there was a wedding feast in Cana of Galilee and the mother of Jesus was there. ²And both Jesus and his disciples were invited to the wedding. ³And, when the wine was exhausted, the mother of Jesus said to him, "They have no wine." ⁴And Jesus says to her, "What, madam,ᵉ is this to me and you? My hour is not yet arrived."

d. Though "son of man" is simply a good Semitic idiom meaning "a man," by the first century it had long served as the name of a mysterious apocalyptic or eschatological figure (as in the one "like a son of man" who rides in the chariot of God in Ezekiel), and as Christ uses it in the Gospels it should clearly be read as a distinctive prophetic title (though not one whose precise significance can be ascertained).

e. γυνή (gynē): "woman" (as distinct from "maiden," "virgin"), "wife." As denoting a married woman and mother rather than an unmarried girl or maidservant, it is a perfectly polite term of respect, a fact that is somewhat obscured in traditional translations that render its vocative use here simply and curtly as "woman."

⁵His mother says to the servants, "Do whatever he tells you." ⁶Now six stone water jars, as prescribed for purification for the Judaeans, were set nearby, each containing two or three measures.ᶠ ⁷Jesus says to them, "Fill the water jars with water." And they filled them to the brim. ⁸And he tells them, "Now pour out a draft and take it to the master of the festivities." ⁹And when the master of the festivities tasted the water that had become wine, and did not know where it came from—though the servants who had drawn the water knew—the master of festivities calls out to the bridegroom, ¹⁰And says to him, "Everyone sets out the fine wine first, and the worse when they have been made drunk; you have saved the fine wine till now." ¹¹This inauguration of signs Jesus performed in Cana of Galilee, and made his glory manifest, and his disciples had faith in him.

¹²Thereafter he went down into Capernaum with his mother and brothers and his disciples, and remained there for not many days.

¹³And the Passover of the Judaeans was near, and Jesus went up to Jerusalem. ¹⁴And in the Temple he found men selling oxen and sheep and doves, as well as installed moneychangers, ¹⁵And, having fashioned a stockwhipᵍ out of cords, he drove all of both the sheep and the oxen out of the Temple; he also spilled out the coins and overturned the tables of the moneychangers, ¹⁶And said to those selling doves, "Take these away from here; do not make my Father's house a house for merchandise." ¹⁷His disciples remembered that it is written, "Zeal for your house will consume me." ¹⁸In reply, then, the Judaeans said to him, "What signs do you show us, since you do these things?" ¹⁹Jesus answered and said to them, "Destroy this sanctuary, and in three days I shall raise it." ²⁰So the Judaeans said, "This sanctuary was built over forty-six years, and you will raise it in three days?" ²¹But he was speaking about the sanctu-

f. Approximately fifteen to twenty-five gallons.

g. φραγέλλιον (*phragellion*): "whip," "scourge," "lash," "riding-whip," or a drover's "stockwhip"—here, definitely the last. In the Greek it is clear that Jesus uses the braided or tied cords simply to herd the sheep and oxen out of the compound, not to thrash the moneychangers.

ary of his body. ²²Thus when he was raised from the dead his disciples remembered that he said this, and they believed the scriptures and this saying that Jesus had uttered.

²³And when he was in Jerusalem during the Passover, at the feast, many had faith in his name, seeing the signs he was performing; ²⁴But Jesus did not entrust himself to them because he knew everyone, ²⁵And because he had no need that anyone should make attestation concerning humanity, for he knew what was in humanity.

CHAPTER THREE

¹Now there was a man, one of the Pharisees, whose name was Nicodemus, a ruler of the Judaeans; ²This man came to him at night and said to him, "Rabbi, we know that you have come as a teacher from God; for no one can produce these signs you perform unless God is with him." ³In reply Jesus said to him, "Amen, amen, I tell you, unless someone is born from above, he cannot see the Kingdom of God." ⁴Nicodemus says to him, "How can a man be born when he is old?" ⁵Jesus replied, "Amen, amen, I tell you, unless a man is born of water and spirit, he cannot enter into the Kingdom of God. ⁶That which is born of flesh is flesh, and that which is born of the Spirit is spirit. ⁷Do not be amazed because I have told you it is necessary for you to be born from above. ⁸The spirit respires[h] where it will, and you hear its sound but you do not know where it comes from or where it goes; such is everyone born of the Spirit." ⁹Nicodemus answered and said to him, "How can this happen?" ¹⁰Jesus replied and said to him, "You are the teacher of Israel and you do not know these things? ¹¹Amen, amen, I tell you that we speak of what we know and bear witness to what we have seen, and you

h. τὸ πνεῦμα . . . πνεῖ (*to pnevma . . . pnei*): "the spirit breathes," "the wind blows," "the breath respires": the wordplay of the Greek is irreproducible in English, so I have elected uniformity of translation, at least for the noun, despite the awkwardness, simply to make it clear that the same word is used at both the beginning and the end of the verse.

people do not accept our witness. [12]If you do not believe what I have told you of things upon the earth, how will you believe if I tell you of things in heaven? [13]And no one has gone up into heaven except the one who has come down from heaven, the Son of Man. [14]And, just as Moses lifted up the serpent in the desert, so it is necessary for the Son of Man to be lifted up, [15]That everyone having faith in him might have the life of the Age. [16]For God so loved the cosmos as to give the Son, the only one, so that everyone having faith in him might not perish, but have the life of the Age. [17]For God sent the Son into the cosmos not that he might pass judgment on the cosmos, but that the cosmos might be saved through him. [18]Whoever has faith in him is not judged; whoever has not had faith has already been judged because he has not had faith in the name of the only Son of God. [19]And this is the judgment: that the light has come into the cosmos, and men loved the darkness rather than the light; for their deeds were wicked. [20]For everyone who does evil things hates the light and does not approach the light, for fear his deeds will be exposed; [21]But whoever acts in truth approaches the light, so that his deeds might be made manifest—that they have been worked in God."

[22]Thereafter Jesus and his disciples came into the territory of the Judaeans, and stayed on there with them and baptized. [23]Now John also was baptizing in Ainon, near Salim, because there were many waters there, and people came and were baptized; [24]For John had not yet been thrown into prison. [25]Thus there arose among John's disciples a dispute with a Judaean over purification. [26]And they came to John and said to him, "Rabbi, the one who was with you on the Jordan's far side, concerning whom you gave testimony, look: This man is baptizing and everyone is coming to him." [27]John answered and said, "A man cannot receive anything unless it has been given to him out of heaven. [28]You yourselves bear witness for me, that I have said, 'I am not the Anointed,' but that 'I have been sent out before that one.' [29]He who has a bride is a bridegroom; but the friend of the bridegroom, standing by and listening for him, rejoices elatedly at the bridegroom's voice. This joy of mine is therefore made complete. [30]It is necessary for that one to in-

crease, but for me to decrease. [31]He who comes from above is above all; he who is out of the earth is out of the earth and speaks from out of the earth; he who comes out of heaven is above all; [32]Whatever he has seen and heard, to this he attests, and no one accepts his testimony. [33]He who accepts his testimony has set his seal that God is true. [34]For he whom God sent speaks God's words; for the Father gives the Spirit without measure. [35]The Father loves the Son, and has placed all things in his hand. [36]He who has faith in the Son has the life of that Age; and the one rejecting the Son will not see life, but God's ire rests upon him."

CHAPTER FOUR

[1]When therefore the Lord learned that the Pharisees had heard of Jesus making and baptizing more disciples than John — [2]Although in fact Jesus himself did not baptize, but rather his disciples did — [3]He left Judaea and departed into Galilee again. [4]And it was necessary for him to pass through Samaria. [5]Thus he comes to a city of Samaria called Sychar,[i] near the plot of land that Jacob gave to his son Joseph; [6]And a font of Jacob's was there. So then Jesus, wearied by the journey, sat down by the font; it was about the sixth hour. [7]A woman comes from Samaria to draw water. Jesus says to her, "Give me a drink." [8]For his disciples had gone away into the city so that they might buy food. [9]So the Samaritan woman says to him, "How do you, being a Judaean, ask for a drink from me, a Samaritan woman?" [10]Jesus answered and told her, "If you recognized God's gift and who it is saying to you 'Give me a drink,' you would have asked him and he would have given you living water."[j] [11]She says to him, "Lord, you have no bucket and the well is deep; so where do you get the living water from? [12]Surely you are not greater than our Father Jacob, who gave us the well, and drank from it

i. In all likelihood, Shechem.

j. ὕδωρ ζῶν (^{b}ydōr zōn): "living water" has something of a multiple meaning here; it means the water of life as well as water that continues to live within one so that one no longer thirsts, but it is also a way of speaking of flowing water.

himself, and his sons and livestock too?" [13]Jesus answered and told her, "Everyone who drinks of this water will thirst again; [14]But whoever drinks from the water that I shall give him will most definitely never thirst, throughout the age;[k] rather the water that I shall give him will become in him a fountain springing up to the life of the Age." [15]The woman says to him, "Lord, give me this water so that I am not thirsty and do not continually come here to draw." [16]He says to her, "Go call your husband and come here." [17]The woman replied and said, "I do not have a husband." Jesus tells her, "You speak well to say, 'I do not have a husband.' [18]For you have had five husbands, and he whom you have now is not your husband; this you have said truthfully." [19]The woman says to him, "Lord, I see that you are a prophet. [20]Our fathers worshipped on this mountain; and you people say that the place where it is necessary to worship is in Jerusalem." [21]Jesus says to her, "Trust me, madam, an hour is coming when you will worship the Father neither on this mountain nor in Jerusalem. [22]You people worship what you do not know, we worship what we know; because salvation is from the Judaeans; [23]But an hour comes, and now is, when the true worshippers will worship the Father in spirit and truth; for indeed the Father looks for those worshipping him so; [24]God is spirit, and it is necessary that those worshipping worship in spirit and truth." [25]The woman says to him, "I know that the Messiah is coming";—the one called Anointed—"when that one arrives he will announce all things to us." [26]Jesus say to her, "I am he: I who am speaking to you."

[27]And at this point the disciples come to him and were astonished that he was conversing with a woman; but no one said, "What do you want?" or "Why are you speaking with her?" [28]The woman, therefore, abandoned her water jar and departed into the city, and tells the people, [29]"Come, see a man who told me everything that I have done; might this not be the Anointed?" [30]They went out from the city and came to him. [31]In the meantime, the disciples implored him, saying,

k. Or "until the Age [to come]."

"Rabbi, eat." [32]But he said to them, "I have food to eat of which you do not know." [33]So the disciples said to one another, "Could someone have brought him something to eat?" [34]Jesus says to them, "My food is that I may do the will of the one who has sent me and may bring his work to completion. [35]Do you not say, 'Four months yet, and then comes the harvest'? I tell you, Look, lift up your eyes and see the fields, because they are already white for harvesting. [36]The reaper is receiving wages and gathering fruit for life in the Age, so that the one sowing and the one reaping may rejoice together. [37]For in this the saying is true: 'That one is the sower and another the reaper.' [38]I have sent you to reap that for which you have not labored, and you have entered into their labor." [39]And many of the Samaritans of that city had faith in him on account of the woman testifying: "He told me all the things I had done." [40]So when the Samaritans came to him they implored him to stay with them, and he stayed there two days. [41]And many more had faith as a result of his teaching. [42]And they said to the woman: "We have faith no longer on account of your talk; for we ourselves have listened and we know that this man is truly the savior of the cosmos."

[43]And after those two days he went from there to Galilee. [44]For Jesus himself had attested that a prophet has no honor in his native land. [45]So when he entered Galilee, the Galilaeans welcomed him, having seen all the things he had done in Jerusalem and at the feast. [46]So he came again to Cana of Galilee, where he made the water into wine. And in Capernaum there was a certain royal courtier whose son was ill; [47]This man, hearing of Jesus coming out of Judaea into Galilee, went to him and implored him to come down and cure his son; for he was about to die. [48]So Jesus said to him, "Unless you people see signs and prodigies, you most certainly do not have faith." [49]The courtier says to him, "Lord, come down before my little child dies." [50]Jesus says to him, "Go, your son is alive." The man had faith in the words Jesus spoke to him and departed. [51]And even as he was going down his slaves met him, saying that his boy lives. [52]He therefore inquired of them the hour at which he became better; so they said to him, "Yesterday the fever left

him, at the seventh hour." ⁵³So the father knew that it happened in that hour at which Jesus had told him, "Your son is alive"; and he and his whole household had faith. ⁵⁴And this was the second sign, which Jesus performed on having come from Judaea into Galilee.

CHAPTER FIVE

¹After these things there was a festival of the Judaeans, and Jesus went up to Jerusalem. ²Now at the sheep's gate in Jerusalem there is a pool, which in Hebrew is called Bethesda, having five porches. ³A great many of the ill lay in them—the blind, the lame, the withered [—waiting for the moving of the waters. ⁴For an angel descended into the pool at a certain time and bestirred the waters; whoever then, after the stirring of the waters, stepped in first was healed of whatever disease he had]. ⁵And there was a certain man there who had had an ailment for thirty-eight years; ⁶Jesus, seeing this man lying there and knowing he had already done so for a long time, says to him, "Do you wish to become healthy?" ⁷The sick man answered him, "Lord, I have no man who might place me in the pool when the water is stirred; rather, as I approach someone else goes down ahead of me." ⁸Jesus says to him, "Arise, take your pallet and walk." ⁹And immediately the man became well, and took his pallet and walked. And on that day it was a Sabbath. ¹⁰So the Judaeans said to the man who had been healed, "It is a Sabbath, and it is not lawful for you to carry the pallet." ¹¹But he answered them, "The one making me well, that one told me, 'Take your pallet and walk.'" ¹²They asked him, "Who is the man telling you, 'Take and walk'?" ¹³But the man who had been healed had no idea who it was; for, there being a crowd in that place, Jesus had withdrawn. ¹⁴Afterward Jesus finds him in the Temple and said to him, "See, you have become well; sin no more, so that something worse may not happen to you." ¹⁵The man went away and told the Judaeans that Jesus is the one who had made him well. ¹⁶And so the Judaeans persecuted Jesus for having done these things on a Sabbath day. ¹⁷But he answered them, "My Father is working right up to the present

moment, and I am working too." [18]On account of this, therefore, the Judaeans sought all the more to kill him, for not only did he break the Sabbath, but he had also called God his own Father, making himself equal to God. [19]So Jesus answered and said to them, "Amen, amen, I tell you, the Son can do nothing from himself, except what he sees the Father doing; for whatever things that one does, these same things the Son likewise also does. [20]For the Father loves the Son and shows him all the things he does, and will show him works greater than these, that you may be amazed. [21]For just as the Father raises the dead and makes them live, so the Son makes alive those whom he wishes; [22]For the Father does not judge anyone, but has given the judgment of all to the Son, [23]That all may honor the Son as they honor the Father who has sent him. [24]Amen, amen, I tell you that whoever hears my word and has faith in the one who has sent me has life in the Age, and does not come to judgment, but rather has crossed out of death into life. [25]Amen, amen, I tell you that an hour is coming—and now is—when the dead will hear the voice of the Son of God, and those who hear will live. [26]For as the Father has life in himself, he also granted it to the Son to have life in himself. [27]And he gave him power to pass judgment, because he is the Son of Man. [28]Do not be amazed at this, for an hour is coming in which all those in the tombs will hear his voice, [29]And those who have done good things will come forth into a resurrection of life, and those who have done evil things into a resurrection of judgment. [30]Of myself I can do nothing; I judge as I hear, and my judgment is just, because I see not my will, but rather the will of the one who has sent me. [31]If I testify concerning myself, my testimony is not true; [32]There is another testifying concerning me, and I know that the testimony he gives concerning me is true. [33]You have sent to John and he has testified to the truth; [34]But I do not take the testimony of a man; rather, I say these things that you might be saved. [35]That man was a lamp that was burning and shining, and you were willing to exult in his light. [36]But I have a greater testimony than John's; for the works that the Father has given me to accomplish, the very works I am performing, testify about me that the Father has sent me. [37]And, the Father having sent me, that one has testified concerning me. You have never heard his voice or seen his form, [38]Nor do you have his Logos[1] abiding in you, for this one whom he sent, in him you do not have faith. [39]Because you think to take hold of the life of the Age, you search through the scriptures; and those are what testify concerning me; [40]Yet you do not wish to come to me in order to take hold of life. [41]I do not receive glory from men, [42]But I have known you: that you do not have God's love in yourselves. [43]I have come in my Father's name and you do not receive me; if another comes in his own name, that one you will receive. [44]How are you able to have faith, receiving glory from one another, yet you do not receive the glory coming from the one God? [45]Do not think that I shall accuse you before the Father; the one accusing you is Moses, in whom you have hoped. [46]For if you had had faith in Moses, then you would have had faith in me; for that one wrote concerning me. [47]But if you do not have faith in that one's writings, how will you have faith in my utterances?"

CHAPTER SIX

[1]Thereafter Jesus went away across the Sea of Galilee, which is to say the Sea of Tiberias, [2]And a large crowd followed him because they saw the signs he had performed upon those who were ill. [3]And Jesus went up upon the mountain and sat down there with his disciples. [4]And the Passover, the feast of the Judaeans, was near. [5]Raising his eyes, therefore, and seeing a large crowd approaching him, Jesus says to Philip, "Where might we buy loaves of bread, so that they might eat?" [6]But this he said to test him; for he knew what he was about to do. [7]Philip replied to him, "Two hundred denarii's worth of bread is not enough for them, even if

---

1. Or "word." I have chosen this rendering of the verse, somewhat diffidently, because the very concept of the divine *Logos* in Jewish and Christian thought of late antiquity is of that mediating divine principle in and by whom the invisible and silent God is seen and heard. See my footnote to 10:35 below, and my remarks on the word *logos* in my postscript.

each take only a morsel." ⁸One of his disciples, Andrew the brother of Simon Peter, says to him, ⁹"There is a lad here who has five barley loaves and two dried fish; but what is that among so many?" ¹⁰Jesus said, "Make the people settle themselves." Now there was plenty of grass in that place. So the men, numbering about five thousand, reclined. ¹¹Jesus, therefore, took the loaves and, having given thanks, distributed them to those reclining, and the fish in the same manner, as much as they desired. ¹²And when they were sated, he tells his disciples, "Gather up the fragments left over, so that nothing is lost." ¹³So they gathered them up and filled twelve baskets with the fragments of the five barley loaves left over by those who had eaten. ¹⁴Therefore the people, seeing the sign he had performed, said: "This is surely the Prophet who is coming into the cosmos." ¹⁵So Jesus, knowing that they were about to come and seize hold of him so that they might make him king, again went away by himself to the mountain. ¹⁶And when evening came his disciples went down to the sea, ¹⁷And, embarking in a boat, they went across the sea toward Capernaum. And darkness had now come and Jesus still had not joined them; ¹⁸And, as a great wind was blowing, the sea was roused. ¹⁹So, having rowed twenty-five or thirty stadia,ᵐ they see Jesus walking upon the sea and coming near to the boat, and they were afraid. ²⁰But he says to them, "It is I, do not fear." ²¹So they were willing to receive him into the boat, and immediately the boat was at the shore to which they had been going.

²²The following day, the crowd standing on the sea's other side saw that there had been only the one boat there and that Jesus had not entered the boat with his disciples, but that the disciples had departed alone; ²³Then some small boats from Tiberias came near the place where they ate the bread [when the Lord had given thanks]. ²⁴When, therefore, the crowd saw that neither Jesus nor his disciples were there, they embarked in the small boats and came to Capernaum in search of Jesus. ²⁵And finding him on the other side of the sea they said to him,

m. Roughly three to four miles.

"Rabbi, when did you come to be here?" [26]Jesus answered them and said, "Amen, amen, I tell you, you seek me not because you saw signs, but because you ate the loaves and were fully filled. [27]Do not labor for perishable food, but for the food that abides unto life in the Age, which the Son of Man will give you; for God has placed his seal on this one." [28]So they said to him, "What may we do so that we may perform the labors of God?" [29]Jesus answered and said to them, "This is the labor of God, that you have faith in him whom that one sent." [30]So they said to him, "What sign, then, do you perform, so that we may see it and have faith in you? [31]Our fathers ate manna in the desert as it is written: 'He gave them bread out of heaven to eat.'" [32]So Jesus said to them, "Amen, amen, I tell you, Moses has not given you the bread from heaven, but rather my Father gives you the true bread from heaven; [33]For the bread of God is the one descending out of heaven and imparting life to the cosmos." [34]So they said to him, "Lord, give us this bread always." [35]Jesus said to them, "I am the bread of life; whoever comes to me most assuredly does not hunger, and whoever has faith in me most assuredly does not thirst—forever. [36]But I have told you that, though you have seen, [37]All whom the Father gives me will come to me, and the one who comes to me I most certainly will not cast out. [38]Because I have descended from heaven so that I might do not my will, but rather the will of the one having sent me. [39]And this is the will of the one who has sent me: that I shall lose nothing out of all that he has given me, but shall instead raise it up on the last day. [40]For this is the will of my Father, that everyone who sees the Son and has faith in him might have life in the Age, and I shall raise him up on the last day." [41]So the Judaeans murmured about him because he had said, "I am the bread having descended out of heaven"; [42]And they said, "Is this man not Jesus, the son of Joseph, whose father and mother we know? How does he now say that 'I have come down out of heaven'?" [43]Jesus answered and said to them, "Do not murmur with one another. [44]No one can come to me unless the Father who sent me should draw him, and I will raise him up on the last day. [45]It is written in the prophets, 'And they shall all be in-

structed by God'; everyone who listens to the Father and takes instruction comes to me. [46]Not that anyone has seen the Father, except the one
who is from God—this one has seen the Father. [47]Amen, amen, I tell
you, the one who has faith has life in the Age. [48]I am the bread of life.
[49]Your fathers ate the manna in the desert and died; [50]This is the bread
descending out of heaven so that one might eat of it and not die. [51]I am
the living bread that has descended out of heaven; if anyone eats of this
bread he will live throughout the age;[n] and the bread I shall give for the
life of the cosmos is my flesh." [52]The Judaeans therefore quarreled with
one another, saying, "How can this man give us [his] flesh to eat?" [53]So
Jesus said to them, "Amen, amen, I tell you, if you do not eat the flesh
of the Son of Man and drink his blood, you do not have life in you.
[54]Whoever feeds upon my flesh and drinks of my blood has life in the
Age, and I will raise him up on the last day. [55]For my flesh is true food,
and my blood is true drink. [56]Whoever feeds upon my flesh and drinks
my blood abides in me and I in him. [57]Just as the living Father sends me
forth and I live through the Father, whoever also feeds upon me, that
very one will live through me. [58]This is the bread that has descended out
of heaven, not such as the fathers ate and then died; whoever feeds upon
this bread will live throughout the age."[o] [59]He said these things while
teaching in a synagogue in Capernaum. [60]Thus many of the disciples,
hearing this, said, "This word is hard; who can listen to it?" [61]But Jesus,
knowing in himself that his disciples are murmuring about this, said to
them, "This causes you to falter? [62]If then you see the Son of Man ascending to where he originally was . . . ? [63]It is the spirit that gives life;
the flesh is of no worth; the words I have spoken to you are spirit and
are life. [64]Yet there are some of you who do not have faith." For Jesus
had known from the outset which are those not having faith and which
is the one betraying him. [65]And he said, "Thus I have told you that no
one can come to me unless it has been granted to him by the Father."

n. Or "until the Age [to come]."
o. Or "until the Age [to come]."

⁶⁶At this many of his disciples departed, going back, and no longer walked with him. ⁶⁷So Jesus said to the Twelve, "Do you not wish to depart also?" ⁶⁸Simon Peter answered him, "Lord, to whom shall we go away? You have the words of life in the Age. ⁶⁹We have both trusted and known that you are the holy one of God." ⁷⁰Jesus answered them, "Did I not choose the twelve of you? And one of you is a slanderer."ᴾ ⁷¹He was speaking of Judas, son of Simon Iscariot; for this one, one of the Twelve, was about to betray him.

CHAPTER SEVEN

¹And after this Jesus walked about in Galilee, for he did not wish to walk about in Judaea, because the Judaeans were seeking to kill him. ²Now the Judaeans' feast of the Tabernacles was near. ³Therefore his brothers said to him, "Leave here and go into Judaea, so that your disciples will see these works of yours that you do; ⁴For no one does something in secret and expects to be in public view; if you do these things, reveal yourself to the cosmos." ⁵For his brothers did not have faith in him. ⁶So Jesus says to them, "My proper time is not yet arrived; but it is always already the proper time for you. ⁷The cosmos cannot hate you, but it hates me because I testify regarding it: that its works are wicked. ⁸You go up to the festival; I am not [yet] going up to this festival because my proper time has not fully come." ⁹And saying these things to them he remained in Galilee. ¹⁰But, when his brothers went up to the festival, he then went up also, not openly but in secret. ¹¹So the Judaeans looked for him at the festival and said, "Where is that man?" ¹²And there was a great deal of murmuring about him among the crowds. Some said, "He is a good man"; but others said, "No, rather he deceives the crowd." ¹³But no one talked of him openly, for fear of the Judaeans.

¹⁴But, when the feast was at its midpoint, Jesus went up to the Temple and taught. ¹⁵The Judaeans were amazed therefore, saying,

p. διάβολος (*diabolos*): "slanderer," "devil."

"How is this man so lettered, not having studied?" [16]So Jesus answered them and said, "This teaching of mine is not mine, but rather that of him who sent me; [17]If anyone wishes to do his will, he will recognize, as far as this teaching is concerned, whether it is from God or whether I speak from myself. [18]Whoever speaks from himself seeks his own glory; but whoever seeks the glory of the one who has sent him, this man is true, and in him is no injustice. [19]Did not Moses give you the Law? And none of you keeps the Law. Why do you seek to kill me?" [20]The crowd answered, "You have a demon; who seeks to kill you?" [21]Jesus answered and said to them, "I performed one work and you all marvel. [22]Thus Moses gave you circumcision (not that it comes from Moses; rather it comes from the Patriarchs); even on the Sabbath you circumcise a man. [23]If a man receives circumcision on a Sabbath day in order that the Law of Moses might not be broken, are you angry because I made a whole man healthy on a Sabbath day? [24]Do not judge by appearances, but instead pass a just verdict." [25]So some of the Jerusalemites said, "Is not this the man whom they are seeking to kill? [26]And look, he speaks openly and they say nothing to him. Did the rulers perhaps know, then, that he truly is the Anointed? [27]But we know where this man is from. But when the Anointed comes no one knows where he is from." [28]So Jesus spoke aloud in the Temple, teaching and saying, "You both know me and know where I come from; and I have not come on my own behalf; but he who sent me, whom you do not know, is true; [29]I know him, because I am from him, and that one sent me." [30]So they sought to seize him, yet no one laid a hand upon him, for his hour had not yet arrived. [31]But many from the crowd had faith in him, and said, "When the Anointed comes, will he perform more signs than this man has performed?" [32]The Pharisees heard the crowd murmuring these things about him, and the chief priests and Pharisees sent Temple guards, in order that they might seize him. [33]So Jesus said, "I am with you but a little time, then I go to the one who sent me. [34]You will seek me and will not find me, and where I am you cannot come." [35]So the Judaeans said to themselves, "Where is this man about to go so that we cannot find him? Is he about to go to the

Diaspora among the Greeks, to teach the Greeks as well? [36]What is this remark he uttered, 'You will seek me and will not find me, and where I am you cannot come'?"

[37]Now on the feast's final day—its great day—Jesus stood up and called out loudly, saying, "If anyone is thirsty, let him come to me, and let him drink. [38]Whoever has faith in me, just as scripture has said, 'Out of his inner parts streams of living water will flow.'" [39]Now he said this in regard to the Spirit, whom those who had faith in him were about to receive; for as yet there was no Spirit, because Jesus had not yet been glorified. [40]Some from the crowd, therefore, hearing these words, said: "Truly this man is the Prophet." [41]Others said, "This man is the Anointed." Yet others said, "Could the Anointed then come out of Galilee? [42]Has not the scripture said that the Anointed comes out of the seed of David, and from Bethlehem, the village where David dwelt?" [43]So a division arose in the crowd on account of him, [44]And some of them wished to seize him, but no one laid hands on him. [45]So the Temple guards came to the chief priests and Pharisees, and these men said to them, "Why did you not bring him?" [46]The Temple guards replied, "No man ever spoke in such a way as this man speaks." [47]The Pharisees therefore answered them, "Have you also been deceived? [48]Has any one from among the rulers or of the Pharisees had faith in him? [49]But this crowd, who are ignorant of the Law, are cursed." [50]Nicodemus, the one who had come to him earlier, being one of them, says, [51]"Does our Law judge the man without first hearing from him and knowing what he is doing?" [52]They answered and said to him, "Are you also from Galilee? Search and see that a prophet is not raised up out of the Galilee."

[[53]And each one went to his house,

CHAPTER EIGHT

[1]But Jesus went to the Mount of Olives. [2]And at daybreak he appeared again in the Temple, and all the people came to him, and sitting down he gave them instruction. [3]And the scribes and the Pharisees

brought a woman who had been caught in adultery and, making her stand before everyone in the open, ⁴Say to him, "Teacher, this woman has been caught in the very act of committing adultery; ⁵Now, in the Law Moses enjoined us to stone such a person; so what do you say?" ⁶(And they said this to test him, so that they might have some accusation to bring against him.) Jesus, however, bending down, wrote upon the ground with his finger. ⁷But, when they continued to question him, he stood up straight and said to them, "Let whosoever among you is without sin be the first to cast a stone at her." ⁸And again, bending down, he wrote on the ground. ⁹And, hearing this, they departed one by one, beginning with the older of them, and he was left alone with the woman before him. ¹⁰And Jesus, standing up straight, said to her, "Madam,�q where are they? Does no one condemn you?" ¹¹And she said, "No one, Lord." And Jesus said, "Neither do I condemn you; go, from now on sin no longer."]ʳ

q. γυνή (gynē): "woman" (as distinct from "maiden," "virgin"), "wife." As it can denote a married woman and mother, it is a polite term, neither dismissive nor condescending; even here it is a form of address that is perfectly gentle.

r. There is little doubt among scholars that the episode of the woman taken in adultery was not written by the same hand that produced the surrounding text. It is not found in the earliest manuscripts of John, or in any Greek or Latin text still extant from before the late fourth century. It is written in a more polished style than the rest of the text, far closer to that of Luke's Gospel than that of John's; and, in fact, in certain Greek and Armenian families of manuscripts the story appears in Luke—where it seems to fit better for a great many reasons—rather than in John. It is also a passage that, in both its Lucan and Johannine exemplars, shifts between different locations in the texts; as placed here in John, it clearly interrupts Jesus's discourse. This does not mean, however, that the episode is some late invention inserted into the text to make Jesus appear more compassionate (not necessarily his most conspicuous characteristic in the fourth Gospel). For one thing, in late antiquity—Jewish, Christian, or pagan—it would have been far more scandalous than commendable in most eyes for Jesus to have allowed an adulteress to go away not only unpunished, but entirely without rebuke. For another, there is good reason to think the episode may in fact be drawn from an older narrative source than the Gospel itself: there is a tale of a very sinful woman that the early second-century Christian Papias mentioned as being part of the lost Gospel of the Hebrews; the Syrian *Didascalia* (from the third century) cites

¹²Jesus spoke to them again, saying, "I am the light of the cosmos; whoever follows me most surely will not walk in darkness, but rather will possess the light of life." ¹³So the Pharisees said to him, "You yourself testify concerning yourself; your testimony is not valid." ¹⁴Jesus answered and said to them, "Even if I myself testify concerning myself, my testimony is valid; because I know where I come from and where I am going; but you do not know where I come from or where I am going. ¹⁵You pass judgment according to the flesh; I pass judgment on no one. ¹⁶But, even if I judge, my judgment is valid because it is not only I, but rather I and the one who has sent me. ¹⁷And in your Law it has been written that the testimony of two men is valid. ¹⁸I am the one testifying concerning myself, and the Father, who has sent me, testifies concerning me." ¹⁹So they said to him, "Where is your father?" Jesus answered, "You know neither me nor my Father; if you knew me, you would have known my Father as well." ²⁰He spoke these words while teaching in the treasury of the Temple; still no one seized him, because his hour had not yet come.

²¹Again, therefore, he said to them, "I am going and you will look for me, and you will die in your sin; where I am going you are not able to come." ²²So the Judaeans said, "Will he kill himself, and that is why

---

"the story of the adulteress"; the *Constitutions of the Apostles* (in a portion probably also from the third century) relates a similar story of a sinful woman whom Jesus refused to condemn; and both Didymus the Blind and Jerome mention the tale as appearing in many manuscripts before the end of the fourth century. Moreover, the earliest texts of John do not merely lack the story; in its place are diacritical marks indicating that something (maybe the same story, maybe something else) has been omitted. Augustine, in fact, aware of the story's absence from many texts of the Gospel, opined that perhaps it had been removed because of the offense it might give to pious souls unable to understand how Christ could excuse so grave a transgression with no more than an exhortation to sin no more. It seems that the story was something of a freely floating tradition, perhaps with very deep roots in Christian memory, one that was not originally firmly associated with any particular Gospel text, but that was inserted in various versions of Luke or John because it was too beautiful and too illuminating of Christ's ministry and person to be left out of the church's lectionary cycle (and hence out of scripture).

he says, 'Where I am going you are not able to come'?" ²³And he said to them, "You are from that which is below, I am from that which is above; you are from this cosmos, I am not from this cosmos. ²⁴Therefore I said to you that you will die in your sins, for if you do not have faith that I AM,ˢ you will die in your sins." ²⁵So they said to him, "Who are you?" Jesus said to them, "To begin with, why am I even speaking to you? ²⁶I have many things to say and many judgments to make regarding you; but he who sent me is trustworthy, and what I have heard from him, this I speak to the cosmos." ²⁷They did not know that he was speaking to them about the Father. ²⁸So Jesus said, "When you lift up the Son of Man, then you know that I AM, and I do nothing from myself; but, just as the Father taught me, I speak these things. ²⁹And the one who has sent me is with me; he did not leave me alone, because I always do the things that are pleasing to him."

³⁰As he was saying these things, many had faith in him. ³¹So Jesus said to the Judaeans who had faith in him, "If you abide in my word, you are truly my disciples, ³²And you will know the truth, and the truth will make you free." ³³And they replied to him, "We are seed of Abraham, and we have never been anyone's slaves; how is it you say we will become free?" ³⁴Jesus answered them, "Amen, amen, I tell you that everyone committing sin is a slave to sin. ³⁵But the slave does not remain in the household for life; the son remains for life. ³⁶If, therefore, the Son sets you free, you will be free indeed. ³⁷I know you are seed of Abraham; but you seek to kill me, because my word has no place in you. ³⁸I speak what I have seen by the Father's side, so do what you have heard from the Father." ³⁹They answered and said to him, "Abraham is our father." Jesus says to them, "If you are children of Abraham, perform the works of Abraham; ⁴⁰But now you seek to kill me, a man who has spoken the truth to you, which I heard from God; Abraham did not do

s. The somewhat abbreviated and enigmatic use here and below of the phrase ἐγώ εἰμι, *ego eimi*, which can usually be rendered simply as "it is I," seems clearly meant to echo God's words to Moses out of the burning bush, and so functions as a somewhat veiled but still nearly unmistakable divine name.

this. ⁴¹You perform the works of your father." They said to him, "We were not born from whoring; we have one Father: God." ⁴²Jesus said to them, "If God were your Father you would have loved me; for I proceeded forth and have come from God; for I have come not from myself; rather that one sent me. ⁴³Why do you not understand my speech? Because you are unable to hear my word. ⁴⁴You come from a father who is the Slanderer; and you wish to do your father's wishes. That one was a killer of men from the beginning, and did not stand upon the truth, because truth is not in him. When he speaks a lie, he speaks from what is proper to him, because he is a liar and the liar's father. ⁴⁵But I, because I speak the truth, me you do not trust. ⁴⁶Who among you arraigns me for sin? If I speak the truth, why do you not trust me? ⁴⁷Whoever listens to the words of God listens to God; the reason you do not listen is that you are not of God." ⁴⁸The Judaeans answered and said to him, "Do we not speak well in saying you are a Samaritan and have a demon in you?" ⁴⁹Jesus answered, "I do not have a demon in me, but rather I honor my Father, while you dishonor me. ⁵⁰But I do not seek my own glory; there is one who seeks and judges. ⁵¹Amen, amen, I tell you, if anyone keeps my word he shall most certainly not see death, throughout the age."ᵗ ⁵²The Judaeans said to him, "Now we know that you have a demon. Abraham died, the prophets too, and you say, 'If anyone keeps my word he shall most certainly not taste death throughout the age.' ⁵³Are you greater than our father Abraham, who died? The prophets died too. Who are you making yourself out to be?" ⁵⁴Jesus answered, "If I give myself glory, my glory is nothing. It is my Father—of whom you say, 'He is our God'—who gives me glory; ⁵⁵And you have not known him, but I know him. And if I say I do not know him I shall be a liar like you; rather, I know him and keep his word. ⁵⁶Your father Abraham was eager to see my day, and he saw and rejoiced." ⁵⁷The Judaeans therefore said to him, "You have not quite reached fifty, and you have seen Abraham?" ⁵⁸Jesus said to them, "Amen, amen, I tell you, before Abraham

t. Or "until the Age [to come]" (here and in the next verse).

came to be, I AM." [59]So they took up stones, in order to cast them at him; but Jesus was hidden and departed from the Temple.

CHAPTER NINE

[1]And, as he was passing along, he saw a man blind from birth. [2]And his disciples questioned him, saying, "Rabbi, who sinned, this man or his parents, that he was born blind?" [3]Jesus answered, "Neither this man nor his parents sinned; but rather that the works of God might be made manifest in him. [4]It is necessary for us to perform the works of the one who has sent me while it is day; the night comes, when no one can work. [5]While I am in the cosmos, I am the light of the cosmos." [6]Having said these things he spat on the ground and made clay from the spittle, and anointed his eyes with the clay, [7]And said to him, "Go wash in the pool of Siloam,"—which means, when interpreted, "Sent Forth." So he went and washed and came back with sight. [8]So the neighbors and those who earlier had seen him and seen that he was a beggar said, "Is this not the one who was sitting and begging?" [9]Some said, "This is he." Others said, "No, but he resembles him." But that man said, "I am he." [10]So they said to him, "How [then] were your eyes opened?" [11]That man answered, "The man called Jesus made clay and anointed my eyes and told me: 'Go to Siloam and wash'; so, going and washing, I saw." [12]And they said to him, "Where is that man?" He says, "I do not know." [13]They lead him—the man formerly blind—to the Pharisees. [14]Now, on the day when Jesus made the clay and opened his eyes, it was a Sabbath. [15]So the Pharisees again asked him how it was he saw, and he said to them, "He anointed my eyes with clay, and I washed, and I see." [16]So some of the Pharisees said, "This man is not from God, for he does not keep the Sabbath." But others said, "How can a sinful man perform such signs?" And there was a division among them. [17]So again they say to the blind man, "Since he opened your eyes, what do you say regarding him?" And he said, "He is a prophet." [18]So, regarding him, the Judaeans did not trust that he had been blind and had then seen, until they had called the

parents of the man who had received sight, [19]And interrogated them, saying, "Is this your son, who you say was born blind? How then does he now see?" [20]So his parents answered and said, "We know that this is our son and that he was born blind, [21]But how he now sees we do not know, nor do we know who opened his eyes. Ask him, he is of age, he will speak for himself." [22]The parents said these things because they feared the Judaeans; for the Judaeans had agreed that anyone who might acknowledge him to be the Anointed would be expelled from the synagogue. [23]For this reason his parents had said: "He is of age; question him." [24]So for the second time they called the man who had been blind and said to him, "Give glory to God; we know this is a sinful man." [25]So the man answered, "Whether he is a sinful man I do not know; I know one thing: that, having been blind, I now see." [26]So they said to him, "What did he do to you? How did he open your eyes?" [27]He replied to them, "I already told you and you did not listen; why do you wish to hear it again? Do you wish to become his disciples?" [28]And they deprecated him and said, "You are a disciple of that man, but we are disciples of Moses; [29]We know that God has spoken through Moses, but we do not know where this man comes from." [30]The man answered and said to them, "Why then, there is something amazing in this: that you do not know where he comes from, and he opened my eyes. [31]We know that God does not listen to sinful men, but if anyone reveres God and does his will, to this man he listens. [32]From the beginning of the age it has not been heard of that anyone opened the eyes of a man born blind; [33]If this man were not from God he could not do anything." [34]They answered and said to him, "You were born utterly in sin and you lecture us?" And they expelled him. [35]Jesus heard that they had expelled him and, finding him, said, "Do you have faith in the Son of Man?" [36]The man answered and said, "And who is he, Lord, that I may have faith in him?" [37]Jesus said to him, "It so happens that you have seen him and also that the one who is speaking to you is he." [38]And he said, "Lord, I have faith"; and he prostrated himself before him. [39]And Jesus said, "I came into the cosmos for judgment, that those without sight may see, and those with sight might become blind."

⁴⁰Some of the Pharisees who were nearby to him heard these things and said to him, "Are we blind also?" ⁴¹Jesus said to them, "If you were blind you would not have sin; but now that you say, 'We see,' your sin remains.

CHAPTER TEN

¹"Amen, amen, I tell you, someone who does not enter the sheep-fold through the gate, but climbs in by another way, is a thief and a bandit; ²But the one who enters through the gate is the shepherd of the sheep. ³To this man the gatekeeper grants entry, and the sheep hearken to his voice, and he calls his own sheep by name and leads them out. ⁴When he has herded out all of his own, he goes before them, and the sheep follow him, because they know his voice; ⁵And by no means will they follow a stranger, but rather will flee from him, because they do not know the voice of strangers." ⁶Jesus pronounced this proverb for them, but they did not understand what the things he was telling them were. ⁷So Jesus spoke again: "Amen, amen, I tell you that I am the sheeps' gate. ⁸All who came before me are thieves and bandits; but the sheep did not hearken to them. ⁹I am the gate; if anyone enters in through me he will be saved, and he will go in and will go out and will find pasture. ¹⁰The thief does not come except so that he may steal and slaughter and destroy; I came that they might have life and might have it in abundance. ¹¹I am the good shepherd. The shepherd, the one who is good, lays down his soul for the sake of the sheep. ¹²He who is the hireling and not the shepherd, to whom the sheep do not belong, sees the wolf coming and abandons the sheep and flees—and the wolf seizes and scatters them—¹³Because he is a hireling and the sheep are no concern of his. ¹⁴I am the shepherd who is good, and I know my own and my own know me, ¹⁵Just as the Father knows me and I know the Father; and I lay

down my soul for the sake of the sheep. ¹⁶And I have other sheep, which are not from this fold; it is necessary for me to lead those also, and they will hearken to my voice, and there will come to be one flock, one shepherd. ¹⁷For this reason the Father loves me: that I lay down my soul, so that I may take it up again. ¹⁸No one has taken it from me; rather I lay it down, and I have power to take it up again; this command I received from my Father." ¹⁹Again there was a division among the Judaeans on account of these words. ²⁰And many of them said, "He has a demon in him and is deranged; why do you listen to him?" ²¹Others said, "These are not the words of a demoniac; can a demon open a blind man's eyes?"

²²Then came Hannukah in Jerusalem; it was winter; ²³And Jesus was walking in the Temple, in Solomon's portico; ²⁴So the Judaeans encircled him and said to him, "For how long are you going to keep a grip on our soul? If you are the Anointed, tell us forthrightly." ²⁵Jesus replied to them, "I have told you, and you do not have faith; the works that I perform in my Father's name, these testify concerning me; but you do not have faith, ²⁶Because you are not from among my sheep. ²⁷My sheep hearken to my voice, and I know them, and they follow me, ²⁸And I give them life in the Age, and they most certainly do not perish throughout the age,ᵘ and no one shall snatch them out of my hand. ²⁹My Father, who has given them to me, is greater than all, and no one can snatch them out of the Father's hand. ³⁰I and the Father are one." ³¹Again the Judaeans picked up stones so that they could stone him. ³²Jesus replied to them, "I have displayed to you many good works from the Father; for which work among them do you stone me?" ³³The Judaeans answered him, "We stone you not on account of a good work, but rather on account of blasphemy, and because you who are a man make yourself out to be God." ³⁴Jesus answered them, "Is it not written in your Law 'I said, "You are gods"'? ³⁵If he called gods those to whom God's Logosᵛ

u. Or "until the Age [to come]."
v. Or "to whom God's word came," or "to whom God's word happened," or "with whom God's Logos was." It was a belief among many Jewish and Christian thinkers of late antiquity that the Logos of God—which is to say, that mediating

came, and the scripture cannot be dissolved, ³⁶How is it that, because I have said I am the Son of God, you say, 'You blaspheme' to one whom the Father sanctified and sent out into the cosmos? ³⁷If I do not do the works of my Father, do not have faith in me; ³⁸But if I do, even if you do not have faith in me, have faith in the works, so that you may know and continue to know that the Father is in me and I am in the Father." ³⁹So they again sought to seize him; and he slipped out of their hands.

⁴⁰And he departed again, across the Jordan to the place where John had earlier been baptizing, and there he remained. ⁴¹And many came to him and said: "John may have performed no sign, but everything whatsoever that John said about this man was true." ⁴²And many there had faith in him.

CHAPTER ELEVEN

¹Now there was a man who was ill, Lazarus of Bethany, from the village of Mary and her sister Martha. ²It was the Mary who had anointed the Lord with unguent, and had wiped off his feet with her hair, whose brother was ill. ³So the sisters sent to him, saying, "Lord, look: He whom you cherish is ill." ⁴And on hearing this Jesus said, "This illness is not unto death, but rather is for the glory of God, so that the Son might be glorified through it." ⁵Now Jesus loved Martha and also her sister and Lazarus. ⁶Even so, having heard that he was ill he then stayed on in the place where he was for two days; ⁷After this he then says to the disciples, "Let us go into Judaea again." ⁸The disciples say, "Rabbi, the Judaeans

divine principle or agency whereby the Father expressed himself in created reality—was the direct subject of all the theophanies and divine visitations narrated in Hebrew scripture; for God in his proper, "Most High" reality was beyond all immediate contact with the created order. For Christians, this meant that these Old Testament revelations of God, from Genesis through Ezekiel and beyond, were acts of the divine Son before his incarnation, as the one who is the "express image" of the Father, and so the one in whom the Father is seen. I have therefore translated the verse as a reference to the Logos of the theophanies. See my remarks on the word "*logos*" in my introduction.

were lately seeking to stone you, and you are going there again?" ⁹Jesus answered, "Are there not twelve hours in the day? If one walks by day, he will not stumble, because he sees the light of this cosmos; ¹⁰But if one walks by night, he stumbles, because the light is not in him." ¹¹He said these things, and thereafter says to them, "Our friend Lazarus has fallen asleep; but I am going so that I might awaken him." ¹²Therefore the disciples said to him, "Lord, if he has fallen asleep he will be saved." ¹³But Jesus had been speaking about his death; yet they thought him to be talking about sleeping in the sense of slumbering. ¹⁴So then Jesus told them forthrightly, "Lazarus has died, ¹⁵And for your sakes I rejoice that I was not there, so that you may have faith; but let us go to him." ¹⁶So Thomas, the one called Twin, said to his fellow disciples, "Let us go as well, so that we may die with him." ¹⁷On arriving, therefore, Jesus found he had been in the tomb for four days already. ¹⁸Now Bethany was near Jerusalem, about fifteen stadia away. ¹⁹And many of the Judaeans had come to Martha and Mary so that they might offer them consolation over their brother. ²⁰So Martha, hearing that Jesus is coming, met him; but Mary sat in the house. ²¹So Martha said to Jesus, "Lord, had you been here, my brother would not have died. ²²Even now, I know that whatever things you ask of God, God will give you." ²³Jesus says to her, "Your brother will rise again." ²⁴Martha says to him, "I know that he will rise again in the resurrection on the last day." ²⁵Jesus said to her, "I am the resurrection and the life; whoever has faith in me, even if he should die, shall live, ²⁶And whoever lives and has faith in me most certainly does not die, throughout the age;ʷ do you have faith in this?" ²⁷She says to him, "I have had faith that you are the Anointed, the Son of God who is coming into the cosmos." ²⁸And saying this she went away and called Mary, secretly telling her, "The teacher is here and he is calling you." ²⁹And she, when she heard this, quickly arose and came to him. ³⁰Now Jesus had not yet entered the village, but was still at the place where Martha had met him. ³¹Therefore the Judaeans who had

w. Or "until the Age [to come]."

been with her in the house consoling her, seeing that Mary arose quickly and went out, followed her, thinking: "She is going to the tomb so that she may mourn there." ³²So Mary, when she arrived where Jesus was and saw him, fell at his feet, saying to him, "Lord, had you been here, my brother would not have died." ³³Therefore, when Jesus saw her weeping, he groaned in his spirit and yielded himself to his turmoil, ³⁴And said, "Where have you laid him?" They say to him, "Lord, come and see." ³⁵Jesus wept. ³⁶So the Judaeans said, "See how he cherished him." ³⁷But some of them said, "Is not this man, who opened the eyes of the blind man, able to bring it about that this man also might not die?" ³⁸So Jesus, again groaning within himself, comes to the tomb; and it was a cavern, and a stone was lying against it. ³⁹Jesus says, "Take away the stone." Martha, the sister of the man who had died, says to him, "Lord, by now it gives off a bad odor; for this is the fourth day." ⁴⁰Jesus says to her, "Have I not told you that if you have faith you will see God's glory?" ⁴¹So they took away the stone. And Jesus lifted up his eyes and said, "I give you thanks that you have heard me; ⁴²And I knew that you always hear me; but I have spoken on account of the crowd standing all around, so that they might have faith that you have sent me." ⁴³And saying these things he cried out in a loud voice, "Lazarus, come forth!" ⁴⁴The one who had died came forth, feet and hands bound with strips of linen and his face wrapped in a cloth. Jesus says to them, "Unbind him and let him go."

⁴⁵Thus many among those Judaeans who had come to Mary and seen what he had done had faith in him, ⁴⁶But some of them went away to the Pharisees and told them what Jesus had done. ⁴⁷So the chief priests and the Pharisees convened a Council and said, "What do we do now that this man is performing many signs? ⁴⁸If we allow him to continue thus, everyone will have faith in him, and the Romans will come and will take away both our holy place and our nation." ⁴⁹But a certain one of them, Caiaphas, who was that year's chief priest, said to them, "You know nothing; ⁵⁰You do not realize that it is expedient for us that one man should die for the people and that the whole nation not perish." ⁵¹Yet

he did not say this from himself, but being that year's chief priest he was prophesying that Jesus was about to die for the nation — ⁵²And not only for the nation, but also that he might gather the scattered children of God into one. ⁵³From that day, therefore, they took counsel so that they might kill him. ⁵⁴So Jesus no longer openly walked about among the Judaeans, but departed from there to a region near the wilderness, to a city called Ephraim, and remained there with the disciples.

⁵⁵Now the Passover of the Judaeans was near, and many went up to Jerusalem from the countryside before the Passover so that they might purify themselves. ⁵⁶So they looked for Jesus and, standing in the Temple, they said to one another, "How does it seem to you? That he will not come to the feast at all?" ⁵⁷And the chief priests and Pharisees had issued orders that, should anyone know where he is, he should report it, so that they might seize him.

CHAPTER TWELVE

¹Therefore, six days before the Passover, Jesus came to Bethany, where Lazarus was, whom Jesus raised from the dead. ²So they prepared a supper for him there, and Martha served, and Lazarus was one of those reclining at table with him. ³So Mary, taking a pint of unguent of pure nard, which was very expensive, anointed the feet of Jesus, and with her hair she wiped his feet off; and the house was filled with the fragrance of the unguent. ⁴But Judas Iscariot, one of his disciples, who was about to betray him, says, ⁵"Why was this unguent not sold for three hundred denarii, and that donated to the destitute?" ⁶But he said this not because he was concerned for the poor, but because he was a thief and, being keeper of the purse, drew on what was deposited in it. ⁷Jesus therefore said, "Leave her, so that she might keep it for the day of my burial; ⁸For you always have the poor with you, but me you do not always have." ⁹So a large crowd of the Judaeans knew that he is there and they came, not only on account of Jesus, but also that they might see Lazarus whom he had raised from the dead. ¹⁰And the chief priests

conspired so that they might kill Lazarus also, [11]Because on his account many of the Judaeans were going over to Jesus and having faith in him.

[12]The next day the great crowd that had come to the feast, hearing that Jesus was coming to Jerusalem, [13]Took branches from the palm trees and went forth to meet him and cried out, "Hosanna, blessed is the one coming in the name of the Lord, and the king of Israel!" [14]And Jesus, having found a young ass, mounted it, just as it is written: [15]"Fear not, daughter of Zion; see, your king comes seated on the foal of an ass." [16]His disciples at first did not understand these things, but when Jesus was glorified they then remembered that these things had been written concerning him, and also that they did these things to him. [17]So the crowd that had been with him when he had called Lazarus forth from the tomb and raised him from the dead bore witness. [18]Hence the crowd also met him, because they heard that he had performed this sign. [19]So the Pharisees said to themselves, "You see that this avails us nothing— look: The world has gone after him."

[20]Now there were some Greeks among those going up so that they might worship at the feast; [21]These men therefore approached Philip, who was from Bethsaida in Galilee, and begged a favor of him, saying, "Lord, we wish to see Jesus." [22]Philip comes and tells Andrew; and Philip and Andrew tell Jesus. [23]And Jesus answers them, saying, "The hour has arrived when the Son of Man is glorified. [24]Amen, amen, I tell you, unless the grain of wheat falling to the ground dies, it remains alone; but if it die it bears plenteous fruit. [25]Whoever cherishes his soul destroys it, and whoever hates his soul in this cosmos will preserve it for life in the Age. [26]If anyone serves me let him follow me, and where I am there my servant will be as well; if anyone serves me, the Father will honor him. [27]Now my soul has been troubled, and what might I say? Father, rescue me from this hour? But for this I have come to this hour. [28]Father, glorify your name." A voice, therefore, came out of the sky: "I both have glorified and will glorify again." [29]So the crowd standing there and hearing this said it was a thunderclap; others said, "An angel has spoken to him." [30]Jesus answered and said, "Not on account of me

has this voice come, but on account of you. ³¹Now is the judgment on this cosmos; now shall the Archon of this cosmos be cast out; ³²And I, when I am lifted up from the earth, will drag everyone to me." ³³And he said this signifying by what kind of death he was about to die. ³⁴So the crowd replied, "We have heard from the Law that the Anointed abides until the Age,ˣ so how is it you say it is necessary for the Son of Man to be lifted up? Who is this Son of Man?" ³⁵So Jesus said to them, "For only a little time longer is the light among you. Walk while you have the light, so that the darkness does not overtake you; and he who walks in the darkness does not know where he is going. ³⁶While you have the light, have faith in the light, so that you might become sons of light." Jesus said these things and, departing, was hidden from them.

³⁷But, though he performed so many signs before them, they did not have faith in him, ³⁸So that the word spoken by the prophet Isaiah might be fulfilled: "Lord, who has trusted our report, and to whom has the arm of the Lord been revealed?" ³⁹For this reason they could not have faith, because again Isaiah said, ⁴⁰"He has blinded their eyes and hardened their heart, so that with their eyes they might not see and with the heart they might not understand and turn, and I will heal them." ⁴¹Isaiah said these things because he saw his glory and spoke concerning him. ⁴²But, nevertheless, even many of the Pharisees did not confess it for fear they should be expelled from the synagogue; ⁴³For they loved the glory of men better than the glory of God. ⁴⁴But Jesus spoke aloud and said, "Whoever has faith in me has faith not in me but in him who has sent me, ⁴⁵And whoever sees me sees him who has sent me. ⁴⁶I have come as a light into the cosmos, so that everyone who has faith in

x. Or "throughout the age" — or "Age." It is difficult to say what is being asserted here, since no such prophecy seems to be advanced in Hebrew scripture. It could, perhaps, mean that the Anointed, in the sense of the king of the restored Davidic line (or at least his posterity), will never disappear from a restored Israel. Or it could mean that the Anointed, in the sense of the Messiah who ushers in the Age to come or the Kingdom of God, will abide until the Age or the Kingdom arrives, or will abide in the Age or Kingdom perpetually.

me might not remain in darkness. [47]And if anyone hears my words and does not keep them I do not judge him; for I came not that I might judge the cosmos, but that I might save the cosmos. [48]Whoever rejects me and does not accept my words has one who judges him: the word that I uttered—that will judge him on the last day. [49]For I did not speak from myself, but rather the Father who has sent me, he has commanded what I should say and what I should speak. [50]And I know that his command is life in the Age. Thus, whatever things I speak, just as the Father has told me, so I speak."

CHAPTER THIRTEEN

[1]Now before the feast of the Passover, Jesus, knowing that his hour had come—that he might pass from this cosmos to the Father—having loved his own in the cosmos, he loved them to the end: [2]And, as the evening meal was taking place—now that the Slanderer had put it into the heart of Judas Iscariot, son of Simon, that he should betray him—[3]Knowing that the Father had placed all things in his hands, and that he came forth from God and is under way to God, [4]He rises from the supper, and places his mantle aside and, taking up a towel, wrapped it around his loins; [5]Then he pours water into the basin and began to wash the disciples' feet and began to wipe them off with the towel wrapped about his loins. [6]Thus he comes to Simon Peter; he says to him, "Lord, are you washing my feet?" [7]Jesus answered and said to him, "You do not yet understand what I am doing, but hereafter you will understand." [8]Peter says to him, "Most surely, throughout the age,[y] you will not wash my feet." Jesus answered him, "Unless I wash you, you have no portion with me." [9]Simon Peter says to him, "Lord, not my feet only, but also my hands and head." [10]Jesus says to him, "One who has been bathed has no need to wash [except for his feet], but is entirely clean; and you are clean, but not all among you." [11]For he knew who was to betray him;

y. Or "unto the Age [to come]."

for this reason he had said, "Not all among you are clean." [12] Therefore, when he had washed their feet and taken up his mantle and again reclined at table, he said to them, "Do you know what I have done for you? [13] You address me as 'Teacher' and 'Lord,' and well you speak, for such I am. [14] So if I, the Lord and the teacher, have washed your feet, you are obliged to wash one another's feet; [15] For I have given you an example so that, just as I have done for you, you may do as well. [16] Amen, amen, I tell you, a slave is not superior to his lord, nor is a messenger superior to the one sending him. [17] If you know these things, how blissful you are if you do them. [18] I do not speak in regard to all of you; I know those I have chosen; but so that scripture might be fulfilled: 'He who eats my bread has lifted up his heel against me.' [19] I tell you from this moment, before it happens, so that when it happens you may believe that I AM. [20] Amen, amen, I tell you, he who welcomes whomever I might send welcomes me, and he who welcomes me welcomes the one who has sent me." [21] Having said these things, Jesus was troubled in spirit and testified and said, "Amen, amen, I tell you that one of you will betray me." [22] The disciples looked at one another, confused as to whom he means. [23] One of his disciples, whom Jesus loved, was reclining at table close beside Jesus. [24] So Simon Peter nods his head at this one and says to him, "Ask who it is that he is talking about." [25] So that one, leaning back on Jesus's chest, says to him, "Lord, who is it?" [26] So Jesus answers, "It is the one for whom I shall dip a morsel of food and give it to him." So, dipping the morsel, he gives it to Judas, son of Simon Iscariot. [27] And then, following behind the morsel, the Accuser[z] entered into that one. So Jesus says to him, "What you do, do quickly." [28] But none among those reclining at table knew why he told him this; [29] For some thought that, inasmuch as Judas kept the purse, Jesus is telling him, "Buy what we need for the feast," or that he should give something to the destitute. [30] So, having received the morsel, that one immediately departed; and it was night.

z. "The Satan," which is to say, "prosecutor," "accuser," "arraigner."

[31]When, therefore, he had departed, Jesus says, "Now has the Son of Man been glorified, and God has been glorified in him; [32][If God has been glorified in him,] God will also glorify him in himself, and will glorify him immediately. [33]I am with you yet a little while, little children; you will seek me, and just as I said to the Judaeans I now also say to you: Where I am going you cannot come. [34]A new commandment I give you: that you love one another. [35]By this everyone will know that you are disciples to me, if you have love for one another." [36]Simon Peter says to him, "Lord, where are you going?" Jesus answered, "Where I am going you cannot follow now, but you will follow later." [37]Simon Peter says to him, "Lord, why can I not follow you now? I will lay down my soul for you." [38]Jesus answers, "Will you lay down your soul for me? Amen, amen, I tell you most assuredly, a cock will not crow before you deny me three times.

CHAPTER FOURTEEN

[1]"Do not let your heart be troubled; have faith in God and have faith in me. [2]In my Father's house there are many places of rest. Would I otherwise have told you that I am going to make a place ready for you? [3]And if I go and make a place ready for you, I am coming again and will take you along with me, so that where I am you might be also. [4]And you know the way to where I am going." [5]Thomas says to him, "Lord, we do not know where you are going. How do we know the way?" [6]Jesus says to him, "I am the way and the truth and the life; no one comes to the Father except through me. [7]If you had known me you would also have recognized my Father. From this moment you know and have seen him." [8]Philip says to him, "Lord, show us the Father, and for us that suffices." [9]Jesus says to him, "I am with you for such a long time, Philip, and you have not known me? Whoever has seen me has seen the Father. How can you say, 'Show us the Father'? [10]Do you not believe that I am in the Father and that the Father is in me? The words that I utter to you I do not speak from myself; but the Father, abiding

in me, performs his works. ¹¹Have faith in me, that I am in the Father and that the Father is in me; or else have faith on account of the works themselves. ¹²Amen, amen, I tell you, whoever has faith in me, the works I perform he will perform also, because I am going to the Father. ¹³And whatever you request in my name, this I will do, so that the Father might be glorified in the Son. ¹⁴If you ask anything of me in my name, I will do it. ¹⁵If you love me, you will keep my commandments. ¹⁶And I shall entreat the Father, and he will give you another Advocate, that he may be with you throughout the age,ᵃᵃ ¹⁷The Spirit of truth, which the cosmos cannot receive because it neither sees nor knows it; you know it because it abides with you and will be within you. ¹⁸I shall not leave you orphans; I am coming to you. ¹⁹Just a little while and the cosmos no longer sees me, but you see me; because I live, you too will live. ²⁰On that day you will know that I am in my Father, and you are in me, and I am in you. ²¹Whoever has my commandments and keeps them, that one is the one who loves me, and whoever loves me will be loved by my Father, and I will love him and will manifest myself to him." ²²Judas— not Iscariot—says to him, "Lord, what has happened then, that you are about to manifest yourself to us and not to the cosmos?" ²³Jesus answered and said to him, "If someone loves me, he will keep my word, and my Father will love him, and we will come to him and will make our home with him. ²⁴Whoever does not love me does not keep my words; and the word that you hear is not mine but rather that of the Father who has sent me. ²⁵These things I have spoken to you while remaining with you; ²⁶But the advocate, the Spirit, the Holy One, which the Father will send in my name, he will teach you everything and will remind you of everything I have told you. ²⁷Peace I leave you, my peace I give to you; I give to you not as the cosmos gives. Do not let your heart be troubled, neither let it be afraid. ²⁸You heard that I told you that I am going away and am coming to you. If you had loved me you would have rejoiced that I am going to the Father, because the Father is greater

aa. Or "until the Age [to come]."

than I. ²⁹And now I have told you before it happens, so that when it happens you might have faith. ³⁰I will no longer speak much with you, for the Archon of the cosmos is coming—and he has no hold in me—³¹But so that the cosmos may know that I love the Father, and that just as the Father has commanded me so I do. Arise, let us go from here.

CHAPTER FIFTEEN

¹"I am the true vine and my Father is the husbandman. ²Every branch in me that does not bear fruit he takes away; and every branch that bears fruit he trims clean so that it might bear more fruit. ³You are already clean because of the word I have spoken to you. ⁴Remain in me—and I in you. Just as the branch cannot bear fruit from itself unless it remain in the vine, so neither can you unless you remain in me. ⁵I am the vine, you are the branches; the one remaining in me and I in him, this one bears plentiful fruit, because apart from me you can do nothing. ⁶Unless someone remain in me he is like the branch that has been cast outside and has withered, and they gather them up and cast them in the fire, and they are burned. ⁷If you remain in me and my words remain in you, ask whatever you wish, and it shall happen for you. ⁸By this my Father has been glorified: that you bear plentiful fruit and will become my disciples. ⁹As the Father has loved me I have also loved you; remain in my love. ¹⁰If you keep my commandments, you will remain in my love, just as I have kept my Father's commandments and remain in his love. ¹¹I have spoken these things to you that my joy may be in you and your joy may be made full. ¹²This is my commandment: that you love one another as I have loved you. ¹³No one has greater love than this: that he should lay down his soul for his friends. ¹⁴You are my friends if you do what I command you. ¹⁵I call you slaves no longer, because the slave does not know what his lord is doing; but I have called you friends, because everything I have heard from the Father I have made known to you. ¹⁶You did not choose me, but I chose you and appointed you, so that you should go and should bear fruit, and your fruit will last, so that

whatever you might ask in my name he might give you. ¹⁷These things I command you so that you love one another. ¹⁸If the cosmos hates you, you know that it has hated me before you. ¹⁹If you were of the cosmos, the cosmos would have loved its own; but since you are not of the cosmos, the cosmos therefore hates you. ²⁰Remember the word that I spoke to you: A slave is not superior to his lord. If they persecuted me they will persecute you as well; if they kept my word they will keep yours as well. ²¹But all these things they will do to you on account of my name, because they do not know the one who has sent me. ²²Had I not come and spoken to them they would have borne no sin; but now they have no excuse for their sin. ²³Whoever hates me also hates my Father. ²⁴If I had not performed among them the works that no one else had performed, they would have borne no sin; but they have both seen and hated both me and my Father. ²⁵And thus might the passage written in the Law be fulfilled: ²⁶When the advocate comes, whom I shall send to you from the Father, the Spirit of truth who comes forth from the Father, he will testify concerning me; ²⁷And you too must testify, for you are with me from the beginning.

CHAPTER SIXTEEN

¹"I have spoken these things to you so that you might not be caused to falter. ²They will make you exiles from the synagogue; and an hour is coming in which everyone who kills you thinks he is offering a service to God. ³And they will do these things because they have known neither the Father nor me. ⁴But I have spoken these things so that when their hour arrives you may remember that I told them to you. At first I did not tell you these things, since I was with you. ⁵But now I am going away to the one who has sent me, and not one of you asks me, 'Where are you going?' ⁶But, because I have spoken to you, grief has filled your heart. ⁷But I tell you the truth, it is for your own good that I should go away. For if I do not go away the Advocate surely is not coming to you; but if I go I shall send him to you. ⁸And when he comes he will

prove the cosmos wrong concerning sin and concerning righteousness and concerning judgment: [9]Concerning sin, because they do not have faith in me; [10]And concerning righteousness, because I am going to the Father, and you no longer see me; [11]And concerning judgment, because the Archon of this cosmos has been judged. [12]I still have many things to tell you, but right now you cannot bear them; [13]But when that one comes, the Spirit of truth, he will guide you on the way to all truth; for he will not speak from himself, but will speak what he hears, and he will announce to you things to come. [14]That one will glorify me, because he will receive from what is mine and will announce it to you. [15]All that the Father has is mine; that is why I said that he receives from what is mine and will announce it to you. [16]A little while and you see me no longer, and a little while again and you will see me." [17]Therefore some of his disciples said to one another, "What is this that he is telling us: 'A little while and you see me no longer, and a little while again and you will see me'? And: 'Because I am going to the Father'?" [18]So they said, "What is this that he is saying, this 'little while'? We do not know what he is saying." [19]Jesus knew that they wished to question him and said to them, "Are you asking one another this, because I said, 'A little while and you do not see me, and a little while again and you will see me'? [20]Amen, amen, I tell you that you will weep and will lament, and the cosmos will rejoice; you will feel anguish but your anguish will become joy. [21]The woman, when she is giving birth, feels anguish because her hour has come; but, when she produces the child, she no longer remembers the suffering on account of the joy that a human being has been born into the cosmos. [22]And so now indeed you feel anguish; but I shall see you again, and your heart will rejoice, and no one takes your joy away from you. [23]And on that day you will not ask me any question. Amen, amen, I tell you, whatever you request of the Father he will give you in my name. [24]Until now you have not asked anything in my name; ask and you will receive, that your joy might be complete. [25]I have spoken these things to you figuratively; an hour is coming when I will no longer speak to you in figures, but will make open proclamation to you concerning the Father. [26]On that day you will ask in my name, and I am not saying to you that I will implore the Father on your behalf; [27]For the Father himself loves you because you have cherished me and have had faith that I come forth from God. [28]I came forth from the Father and have come into the cosmos; I am leaving the cosmos again and am going to the Father." [29]His disciples say, "See, now you speak openly, and utter no figure of speech. [30]Now we know that you know all things and have no need that anyone should question you. By this we have faith that you came forth from God." [31]Jesus answered them, "Now you have faith? [32]See: An hour is coming—has indeed come—when you are scattered, each one to his own home, and you leave me alone; and I am not alone, because the Father is with me. [33]I have spoken these things to you so that you might have peace in me. In the cosmos you have suffering; but take heart—I have conquered the cosmos."

CHAPTER SEVENTEEN

[1]Jesus spoke these things and, lifting up his eyes to the sky, said, "Father, the hour has come; glorify your Son, so that the Son might glorify you, [2]Just as you gave him power over all flesh, so that you have given everything to him, that he might give them life in the Age. [3]And this is life in the Age: that they might know you, the sole true God, and him whom you sent, Jesus the Anointed. [4]On earth I glorified you by completing the work that you have given me to do. [5]And now, Father, glorify me by your side with that glory I had by your side before the cosmos was. [6]I disclosed your name to the men whom you gave to me out of the cosmos. They were yours and you gave them to me, and they have kept your word. [7]Now they know that all the things you have given me, however many, are from you. [8]Because the words that you gave me I have given to them, and they accepted them, and knew truly that I came forth from you, and they had faith that you sent me forth. [9]I make supplication on their behalf; I do not make supplication on behalf of the cosmos, but rather on behalf of those you have given to me, because

they are yours. [10]And all that is mine is yours, and what is yours is mine, and I have been glorified in them. [11]And I am no longer in the cosmos, and they are in the cosmos, and I am coming to you. Holy Father, keep them in your name, which you have given me, that they may be one just as we are. [12]When I was with them, I protected them in your name, which you gave me, and guarded them, and not one of them perished except the son of perdition, so that the scripture might be fulfilled. [13]But now I am coming to you, and in the cosmos I speak these things so that they might have the joy that is mine made full within them. [14]I have given them your word, and the cosmos hated them, because they are not of the cosmos, just as I am not of the cosmos. [15]I pray not that you should take them out of the cosmos, but that you should keep them away from the wicked one. [16]They are not of the cosmos, just as I am not of the cosmos. [17]Make them holy in the truth; the word that is yours is truth. [18]Just as you sent me forth into the cosmos, I sent them also forth into the cosmos. [19]And on their behalf I make myself holy, so that they also may be made holy in truth. [20]But I make supplication not for them only, but also for those having faith in me on account of their word, [21]That all may be one, just as you, Father, are in me and I in you, that they too might be in us, so that the cosmos may have faith that you sent me forth. [22]And I have given to them the glory you have given me, that they may be one just as we are one: [23]I in them and you in me, that they might be brought to completion in one, so that the cosmos might know that you sent me forth, and loved them just as you loved me. [24]Father, I wish that they too, those you have given to me, might be with me where I am, that they might see my glory, which you have given me, because you loved me before the foundation of the cosmos. [25]Righteous Father, the cosmos also did not know you, but I knew you, and these know you have sent me forth; [26]And your name I have made known, and will make known to them, so that the love with which you loved me may be in them, and I in them also."

CHAPTER EIGHTEEN

¹Having said these things, Jesus went forth with his disciples across the Kedron, which flows in the winter, to where there was a garden, which he and his disciples entered. ²Now Judas, who was handing him over, also knew the place, because Jesus often met with his disciples there. ³So Judas, taking a detachment of soldiers and officers from the chief priests and Pharisees, comes there with torches and lamps and weapons. ⁴Jesus, therefore, knowing about all the things descending upon him, went forth and says to them, "Whom do you seek?" ⁵They answered him, "Jesus the Nazorean." He says to them, "I AM." ⁶Thus, when he said "I AM" to them, they stepped backward and fell to the ground. ⁷So again he inquired of them, "Whom do you seek?" And they said, "Jesus the Nazorean." ⁸Jesus replied, "I have told you that I AM; so, if you are seeking me, allow these to go." ⁹—So that the word that he had spoken might be fulfilled: "Those whom you have given me, I lost none of them." ¹⁰Simon Peter, therefore, having a sword, drew it and struck the high priest's slave and hacked off his right ear; and the slave's name was Malchus. ¹¹So Jesus said to Peter, "Put the sword in its sheath; the cup that the Father has given me, shall I not most surely drink it?"

¹²So the detachment of soldiers and the chiliarch, along with the officers of the Judaeans, seized Jesus and bound him, ¹³And led him first to Annas; for he was the father-in-law of Caiaphas, who was that year's chief priest; ¹⁴Now it was Caiaphas who had advised the Judaeans: "It is expedient that one man die on behalf of the people." ¹⁵And Simon Peter and another disciple followed Jesus. And that disciple was known to the chief priest and entered along with Jesus into the chief priest's courtyard, ¹⁶But Peter stood outside at the gate. So the disciple who was known to the chief priest went out and spoke to the girl keeping the gate, and conducted Peter in. ¹⁷So the maidservant keeping the gate says to Peter, "Are you not also one of this man's disciples?" He says, "I am not." ¹⁸And the slaves and the officers were standing there, having made a charcoal fire because it was cold, and they were warming themselves;

and Peter was also with them, standing there and warming himself. ¹⁹So the chief priest interrogated Jesus concerning his disciples and concerning his teaching. ²⁰Jesus answered him, "I have spoken openly to the cosmos; I always taught in synagogue and in the Temple, where all the Judaeans congregate, and I spoke nothing in secret. ²¹Why do you question me? Question those who have listened to what I told them; look: They know the things I have said." ²²And, as he said these things, one of the officers standing nearby struck Jesus a blow to the face, saying, "This is how you answer the chief priest?" ²³Jesus answered him, "If I spoke amiss, bear witness to the wrong; but, if well, why do you beat me?" ²⁴So Annas sent him bound to the chief priest Caiaphas. ²⁵Now Simon Peter was standing there warming himself. So they said to him, "Are you not also one of his disciples?" He denied it and said, "I am not." ²⁶One of the chief priest's slaves, a relative of the man whose ear Peter cut off, says, "Did I not see you in the garden with him?" ²⁷So again Peter denied it, and immediately a cock crowed.

²⁸So they led Jesus from Caiaphas to the Praetorium; and it was just before dawn; and they did not enter the Praetorium, so that they should not be defiled but might instead eat the Passover. ²⁹So Pilate went outside to them and says, "What accusation do you bring against this man?" ³⁰They answered and said to him, "If this man were not doing evil we would not have handed him over to you." ³¹So Pilate said to them, "You take him and judge him according to your Law." The Judaeans said to him, "It is not legal for us to kill anyone." ³²—So that the word spoken by Jesus, indicating by what death he was about to die, might be fulfilled. ³³So Pilate went back into the Praetorium and summoned Jesus and said to him, "You are the king of the Judaeans?" ³⁴Jesus answered, "Do you say this on your own, or did others speak to you about me?" ³⁵Pilate answered, "Am I a Judaean? Your nation and your chief priests handed you over to me; what have you done?" ³⁶Jesus answered, "My Kingdom is not of this cosmos; if my Kingdom were of this cosmos my subjects would have struggled so that I should not be handed over to the Judaeans; but for now my Kingdom is not from here." ³⁷So Pilate said to

him, "Are you then a king?" Jesus answered, "You say that I am a king. I was born for this, and for this have I come into the cosmos: that I might testify to the truth; everyone who belongs to the truth hearkens to my voice." ³⁸Pilate says to him, "What is truth?" And, having said this, he went outside again to the Judaeans and tells them, "I find absolutely no case against him. ³⁹But it is a custom among you that I should release one of you at the Passover; do you want me to release the king of the Judaeans, therefore?" ⁴⁰So again they cried out, saying, "Not this man, but bar-Abbas!" (And bar-Abbas was a bandit.)

CHAPTER NINETEEN

¹So Pilate then took Jesus and flogged him. ²And the soldiers, having plaited a crown from thorns, placed it on his head, and threw a purple cloak around him, ³And went up to him and said, "Hail, king of the Judaeans!" And they gave him blows to the face. ⁴And Pilate went outside again and says to them, "Look: I am bringing him out to you, so that you might know that I find no case against him." ⁵So Jesus came outside, wearing the thorn crown and the purple cloak. And he says to them, "Look at the man." ⁶When, therefore, the chief priests and officers saw him they cried out, saying, "Crucify! Crucify!" Pilate says to them, "You take him and crucify him; for I find no case against him." ⁷The Judaeans answered him, "We have a Law, and according to the Law he ought to die because he has made himself out to be God's Son." ⁸When, therefore, Pilate heard this statement he was more afraid, ⁹And again went into the Praetorium and says to Jesus, "Where are you from?" But Jesus did not give him an answer. ¹⁰So Pilate says to him, "Do you not know that I have the power to release you and the power to crucify you?" ¹¹Jesus answered, "You had no power over me whatsoever were it not given you from above; for this reason he who handed me over to you bears the greater sin." ¹²Thereafter Pilate sought to release him; but the Judaeans cried out, "If you release this man you are

not a friend of Caesar." [13]So Pilate, hearing these words, brought Jesus outside and sat upon a tribune's seat at a place called Stone Pavement, or rather Gabbatha in Hebrew. [14]Now it was the Preparation day of the Passover, and was around the sixth hour; and he says to the Judaeans, "Look at your king." [15]So they cried out, "Take him, take him, crucify him!" Pilate says to them, "Shall I crucify your king?" The chief priests answered, "We have no king other than Caesar." [16]So then he handed him over to them, so that he might be crucified.

So they took Jesus, [17]And bearing the cross for himself he went out to what was called Skull's Place, which in Hebrew is called Golgotha, [18]Where they crucified him, and with him two others—one on this side, one on that, and Jesus in between. [19]And Pilate also inscribed a titular notice and affixed it to the cross; and what was written was: "JESUS THE NAZOREAN THE KING OF THE JUDAEANS." [20]Many of the Judaeans, therefore, read this title, because the place where Jesus was crucified was near the city; and it was written in Hebrew, Latin, and Greek. [21]So the chief priests of the Judaeans said to Pilate, "Do not write, 'The king of the Judaeans,' but rather that 'That man said, I am king of the Judaeans.'" [22]Pilate answered, "What I have written, I have written." [23]So the soldiers, when they crucified Jesus, took his garments and made four shares, one share for each soldier, with the tunic left over. For the tunic was seamless, woven as a whole from the top down. [24]So they said to one another, "Let us not tear it, but rather cast lots over whose it shall be"—this that the scripture might be fulfilled: "They divided my garments among themselves, and over my raiment they cast a lot." [25]Now beside the cross of Jesus there stood his mother, and his mother's sister Mary the wife of Clopas, and Mary the Magdalene. [26]Therefore Jesus, seeing his mother and the disciple whom he loved standing by, says to his mother, "Madam, look at your son." [27]Then to the disciple he says, "Look at your mother." And from that hour the disciple took her for his own. [28]After this, Jesus, knowing that everything had now been completed, in order that the scripture might be fulfilled, says, "I am thirsty."

²⁹A vessel full of diluted wine was placed there; so, putting a sponge soaked in the wine around a hyssop, they brought it up to his mouth. ³⁰When, therefore, Jesus had taken the wine, he said, "It has been completed." And lowering his head he delivered up his spirit.

³¹So that the bodies might not remain on the cross on the Sabbath—for, since it was the day of Preparation, that Sabbath's day was a high holy day—the Judaeans asked Pilate that their legs might be broken and that they might be taken down. ³²So the soldiers came, and broke the legs of the first and of the other crucified with him; ³³But when they came to Jesus, seeing that he had already died, they did not break his legs. ³⁴But one of the soldiers jabbed at his side with a lance, and immediately blood and water came out. ³⁵And the one having seen this has testified, and his testimony is true, and that man knows that he is speaking truthfully, in order that you might have faith. ³⁶For these things happened in order that the scripture might be fulfilled: "Not a bone of his shall be broken." ³⁷And, again, another scripture says, "They shall gaze on him whom they pierced." ³⁸Now, after these things, Joseph of Arimathea—being a disciple of Jesus, but in secret out of fear of the Judaeans—requested of Pilate that he might take the body of Jesus away; and Pilate permitted this. So he came and took away his body. ³⁹And Nicodemus came as well—the one who had first come to him by night—bringing a mixture of myrrh and aloes, about a hundred litra[ab] in weight. ⁴⁰So they took the body of Jesus and wrapped it in linen cloths with the aromatic spices, as is the custom for interment among the Judaeans. ⁴¹Now in the place where he was crucified there was a garden, and in the garden a new tomb in which no one had ever yet been laid; ⁴²So, on account of the Judaeans' day of Preparation, they put Jesus there, because the tomb was nearby.

ab. Roughly seventy-five pounds, an enormous quantity.

CHAPTER TWENTY

¹Now early on the first day of the Sabbath-week, while it is still dark, Mary the Magdalene comes to the tomb and sees that the stone has been removed from the tomb. ²So she runs away and comes to Simon Peter and to the other disciple, him who Jesus loved, and says to them, "They took the Lord out of the tomb and we do not know where they put him." ³So Peter and the other disciple went forth and came to the tomb. ⁴And the two of them were running together; and the other disciple ran ahead more quickly than Peter and came to the tomb first, ⁵And bending down he sees the winding sheets lying there, but he did not enter. ⁶And so Peter comes following after him and entered the tomb; and he sees the winding sheets lying there, ⁷And the kerchief that had been on his head not lying together with the sheets, but apart, folded up in a place of its own. ⁸So the other disciple, the one having come first to the tomb, also entered, and he saw and had faith; ⁹For as yet they did not know the scripture: that it is necessary for him to rise again from the dead. ¹⁰So the disciples went away home again. ¹¹But Mary stood outside by the tomb weeping. As she was weeping, then, she bent down into the tomb, ¹²And sees two angels in white sitting there, one at the head and one at the feet of where the body of Jesus had lain. ¹³And they say to her, "Madam, why are you weeping?" She says to them: "They took away my Lord and I do not know where they put him." ¹⁴Saying these things, she turned back around and sees Jesus standing there, and did not know that it was Jesus. ¹⁵Jesus says to her, "Madam, why are you weeping? Whom do you seek?" She, thinking that he is the gardener, says to him, "My lord, if you have carried him off, tell me where you put him, and I will take him away." ¹⁶Jesus says to her, "Mary." Turning, she says to him in Hebrew, "Rabbouni" (which means "Teacher"). ¹⁷Jesus says to her, "Do not cling to me, for I have not yet ascended to the Father; but go to my brothers and tell them: I ascend to my Father and your Father, and to my God and your God." ¹⁸Mary the Magdalene comes to the disciples, announcing: "I have seen the Lord," as well as the things he told her.

[19]When, therefore, it was early evening of that first day of the Sabbath-week, and where the disciples were the doors had been sealed for fear of the Judaeans, Jesus came and stood in their midst and says to them, "Peace to you." [20]And, saying this, he showed them both his hands and his side. Thus, on seeing the Lord, the disciples were overjoyed. [21]So [Jesus] again said to them, "Peace to you. As the Father has sent me, I also send you." [22]And, saying this, he breathed upon them and says to them, "Receive a Holy Spirit. [23]For those whose sins you let go, they are let go; those you hold fast, they have been held fast."

[24]But one of the Twelve, Thomas (which meant "Twin"),[ac] was not with them when Jesus came. [25]So the other disciples said to him, "We have seen the Lord." But he said to them, "Unless I see the mark of the nails in his hands and put my hand into his side, I will most certainly not have faith." [26]And eight days later his disciples were again inside, and Thomas with them. The doors being sealed, Jesus comes and stood in their midst and said, "Peace to you." [27]Then he says to Thomas, "Bring your finger here and look at my hands, and bring your hand and put it into my side, and cease to be faithless, but be faithful instead." [28]Thomas answered and said to him, "My LORD and my GOD."[ad] [29]Jesus says to him, "You have faith because you have seen me? How blissful those who do not see and who have faith."

[30]Of course, Jesus performed many other signs as well before the disciples, which have not been recorded in this book; [31]But these ones have been recorded so that you might have faith that Jesus is the

ac. Δίδυμος (*Didymos*).

ad. ὁ κύριός μου καὶ ὁ θεός μου (*ho kyrios mou kai ho theos mou*): Here, Thomas addresses Jesus as *ho theos*, which unambiguously means "God" in the absolute sense (see my remarks on John's prologue in the postscript). He addresses him also as *ho kyrios*, again with the honorific article, which also happens to be the Greek rendering of the Hebrew *Adonai* in the Septuagint, the preferred textual circumlocution for God's unutterable name, the tetragrammaton (YHWH). Thomas's words here, then, appear to be the final theological statement of the Gospel at its "first ending."

Anointed, the Son of God, and that in having faith you might have life in his name.

CHAPTER TWENTY-ONE[ae]

[1]Thereafter Jesus again manifested himself to the disciples on the Sea of Tiberias; and this was the manner in which he manifested himself: [2]Simon Peter, and Thomas (which means "Twin"),[af] and Nathanael of Cana in Galilee, and the sons of Zebedee, and two other of his disciples were together. [3]Simon Peter says to them, "I am going to fish." They say to him, "We are coming with you as well." They went out and embarked in the boat, and they caught nothing during the night. [4]But now, as it was becoming early morning, Jesus stood on the shore; but the disciples did not know that it was Jesus. [5]So Jesus says to them, "Little children, do you have any fish?" They answered him, "No." [6]So he said to them, "Cast the net out on the starboard side of the boat, and you will find some." So they cast it out, and they were no longer able to haul it in on account of the great number of fish. [7]Hence that disciple whom Jesus loved says to Peter, "It is the Lord." So Simon Peter, hearing that it is the Lord, tied his coat round his waist, for he was undressed,[ag] and flung himself into the sea; [8]But the other disciples came in the small boat, for they were not far from the land, but about two hundred cubits away, hauling along the net full of fish. [9]When, therefore, they had disembarked onto the land, they see a charcoal fire laid out and a fish lying on it, as well as a loaf of bread. [10]Jesus says to them, "Bring some of the fish that you have just caught." [11]Simon Peter

ae. The Gospel clearly reaches a natural conclusion at the end of chapter twenty; chapter twenty-one is, most scholars believe, a slightly later addition to the text, a sort of theological (and rather dreamlike and lovely) coda.

af. Δίδυμος (*Didymos*).

ag. The Greek γυμνός (*gymnos*) means "naked" or "lightly clad," and here almost certainly means wearing only a loin covering or an inner tunic. No observant Jew would have entirely disrobed out of doors.

went up and dragged along the net, full of a great many fish—a hundred and fifty-three; and, though there were so many, the net was not torn. ¹²Jesus says to them, "Come, break your fast." None of the disciples dared ask him, "Who are you?"—knowing it is the Lord. ¹³Jesus comes and takes the bread and gives it to them, and likewise the fish. ¹⁴This was now the third time that Jesus was manifested to his disciples as having been raised from the dead.

¹⁵When, therefore, they had breakfasted, Jesus says to Simon Peter, "Simon son of John, do you love me more than these?"ᵃʰ He says to him, "Yes, you know that I love you." He says to him, "Feed my little lambs." ¹⁶A second time, he again says to him, "Simon son of John, do you love me?" He says to him, "Yes, Lord, you know that I love you." He says to him, "Shepherd my flocks." ¹⁷The third time he says to him, "Simon son of John, do you cherish me?" Peter was aggrieved that this third time he had said, "Do you *cherish* me?" and he told him, "Lord, you know all things, you know that I cherish you." Jesus says to him, "Feed my flocks. ¹⁸Amen, amen, I tell you, when you were younger you tied your clothes about yourself and went walking about wherever you wished; but when you grow old you will stretch out your hands and someone else will tie your clothes about you and will take you where you do not wish." ¹⁹And he said this signifying by what death he will give glory to God. And, saying this, he tells him, "Follow me." ²⁰Turning, Peter sees the disciple whom Jesus loved following behind—he who also had leaned on his chest at supper and said, "Lord, who is he who betrays you?" ²¹So, seeing this one, Peter says to Jesus, "Lord, and what of this one?" ²²Jesus says to him, "If I wish him to remain until I come, what is that to you? Follow me." ²³Thus it is that the claim went forth to the brethren that this disciple is not to die; but Jesus did not say to him that

ah. Often read as meaning "Do you love me more than you do these others?" or even "Do you love me more than these others do?," it is equally (and perhaps more) likely that it means "Do you love me more than these things?"—that is, the things of this age.

he is not to die, but rather: "If I wish him to remain until I come, what is that to you?"

²⁴This is the disciple who testifies concerning these things and who has written these things, and we know that his testimony is true. ²⁵And there are many other things that Jesus also did, which, were they written down one by one, I think the cosmos itself would not contain the books that would be written.

The Acts of the Apostles

BY LUKE

CHAPTER ONE

¹I produced an earlier treatise, O Theophilus, concerning every-thing Jesus initiated, both as a practice and as a teaching, ²Until the day when he was taken above, having issued instructions through a Holy Spirit to the Apostles he had chosen, ³To whom, after he had suffered, he showed himself alive by many irrefutable proofs, being seen by them over a period of forty days and telling them things about the Kingdom of God; ⁴And, meeting with them, he enjoined them not to depart from Jerusalem, but rather to "Await the promise of the Father, which you heard from me: ⁵Because John indeed baptized of water; but you will be baptized in a Spirit, the Holy one, not many days hereafter." ⁶So, then, coming together they questioned him, saying, "Lord, are you restor-ing the kingdom of Israel at this time?" ⁷He said to them, "It is not for you to know the times or seasons that the Father has set by his own au-thority, ⁸But you will receive power when the Holy Spirit comes upon you, and you will be my witnesses both in Jerusalem and in all Judaea and Samaria, even to the end of the earth." ⁹And saying these things, as they were watching, he was taken up, and a cloud took him from their eyes. ¹⁰And as they were staring at him ascending into the sky, look: Standing beside them were two men in white garments, ¹¹Who said, "Galilaean men, why do you stand looking at the sky? This Jesus who has thus been taken up from you into the sky will come in the way you

saw him going to the sky." [12]They then returned to Jerusalem from the mountain called Mount of the Olive Grove, which is near Jerusalem, a Sabbath's walk away. [13]And when they came in, they went up into the upper room where they were staying: Peter and John and James and Andrew, Philip and Thomas, bar-Tholomaeus and Matthew, James son of Alphaeus and Simon the Zealot and Judas son of James. [14]These devoted themselves constantly to prayer, with a shared intensity of feeling, together with the women and with Mary the mother of Jesus and with his brothers.

[15]In those days Peter, standing in the midst of the brethren (and the crowd of names, taken all together, was about a hundred and twenty), said, [16]"Men, brothers, it was necessary that the scripture be fulfilled, which the Spirit, the Holy one, spoke beforehand through the mouth of David concerning Judas, who became a guide for those who arrested Jesus— [17]For he was numbered among us, and had a share in this ministry— [18]So that from the reward for his injustice this man purchased a field and, having fallen prone in the middle of it, he burst apart and all his entrails were poured out; [19]And this came to be known to all the inhabitants of Jerusalem, so that the field came to be called Akeldama"— which, in their language, means "Field of Blood"— [20]"For it is written in the Book of Psalms, 'Let his estate be deserted, and let there be no one dwelling therein,' and 'Let another take over his office' . . . [21]So it is necessary that, out of those men who accompanied us during the whole time that the Lord Jesus went in and out among us— [22]Beginning with John's baptizing until the day he was taken up from among us—one of these should become a witness to his resurrection." [23]And they proposed two: Joseph, called bar-Sabbas, who was also called Justus, and Matthias. [24]And, praying, they said, "You, Lord, knowing the hearts of all, show us which one of these two you have chosen [25]To take a place in this ministry and apostolate, which Judas deserted for a place of his own." [26]And they cast lots over them, and the lot fell to Matthias, and he was reckoned together with the eleven Apostles.

CHAPTER TWO

¹And, when the day arrived that completed the fifty after Passover, they were all gathered together in one place; ²And suddenly there came a noise like a turbulent wind borne out of the sky, and it filled the whole house where they were sitting, ³And there appeared before them tongues as of fire, which parted and came to rest, one each upon each one of them, ⁴And they were all filled with a Holy Spirit, and they began to speak in other tongues, as the Spirit gave them to utter. ⁵Now dwelling in Jerusalem were devout Judaeans from every nation under the sky; ⁶And on the advent of this noise the multitude gathered, and were confused because each one heard them speaking in his own language. ⁷And they were amazed and astounded, saying, "Look, are not all of these who are speaking Galilaeans? ⁸And how is it that each of us hears his own language, the languages in which we were raised—⁹Parthians and Medes and Elamites, and those living in Mesopotamia, both Judaea and Cappadocia, Pontus and Asia; ¹⁰Phrygia and Pamphylia, Egypt and the parts of Libya abutting Cyrene, and visitors from Rome; ¹¹Both Judaeans and proselytes, Cretans and Arabians—we hear them declaring the great deeds of God in our tongues?" ¹²And all were amazed and entirely at a loss, saying to one another, "What does this portend?" ¹³But others, ridiculing them, said: "They are full of sweet new wine." ¹⁴But Peter, standing up along with the eleven, raised his voice and addressed them:

"Judaean men, and all of you staying in Jerusalem, let this be known to you, and lend your ears to my words, ¹⁵For these men are not drunk, as you suppose, as it is the third hour of the day; ¹⁶Rather, this is what was declared through the prophet Joel: ¹⁷'And in the last days it shall happen, says God, that I will pour forth from my Spirit upon all flesh, and your sons and your daughters shall prophesy, and your young men shall dream dreams; ¹⁸Yes, in those days, I will pour forth from my Spirit even upon my male slaves and upon my female slaves, and they shall prophesy, ¹⁹And I will send prodigies in the sky above and signs in the earth below, blood and fire and clouds of smoke. ²⁰The sun shall be turned into darkness and the moon into blood before the great and re-splendent day of the Lord arrives. ²¹And it shall happen that everyone, whosoever it is, who calls on the name of the Lord shall be saved.' ²²Isra-elite men, listen to these words: Jesus the Nazorean, a man validated by God among you by feats of power and prodigies and signs that God performed in your midst through him, as you yourselves know— ²³This man—delivered up by the determined counsel and with the foreknowl-edge of God—you killed, affixing him with nails, employing the hands of men without the Law: ²⁴Him whom God raised up, releasing him from the torments of death, because it was not possible for him to be restrained by it. ²⁵For David says of him, 'I saw this Lord always before me, because he is on my right, so that I might not be shaken. ²⁶There-fore my heart was gladdened and my tongue rejoiced, and now my flesh will also raise its tent upon hope, ²⁷Because you will not abandon my soul to Hades, nor will you allow your hallowed one to see decay. ²⁸You have made known to me the paths of life, with your face you will fill me with delight.' ²⁹Men, brothers, it is permissible to speak openly to you about the patriarch David: that he both died and was buried, and his tomb is in our midst to this day; ³⁰So, being a prophet and knowing that God swore him a pledge that one from the fruit of his loins would sit on the throne, ³¹He saw it in advance and spoke about the resurrection of the Anointed: that neither was he abandoned to Hades nor did his flesh see decay. ³²God raised this Jesus up, of which we are all witnesses: ³³Having therefore been exalted to God's right side, and receiving from the Father the promise of the Spirit, the Holy one, this he poured out—which you both see and hear. ³⁴For David did not ascend into the heavens, yet he says, 'The Lord said to my lord, sit down at my right side, ³⁵Until I set your enemies as a footstool for your feet.' ³⁶Therefore let the whole house of Israel know with certainty that God has made him both Lord and Anointed—this Jesus whom you crucified."

³⁷And, hearing this, they were pierced in heart and said to Peter and the rest of the Apostles, "What may we do, men, brothers?" ³⁸And Peter

said to them, "Change your hearts, and let each of you be baptized upon the name of Jesus the Anointed, for the forgiveness of your sins, and you will receive the gift of the Holy Spirit. ³⁹For the promise is to you and to your children and to those far away, as many as the Lord our God will call to himself." ⁴⁰And with many words more he testified to them and exhorted them, saying, "Be saved from this perverse generation." ⁴¹So those who accepted his word were baptized, and that day about three thousand souls were added, ⁴²And they devoted themselves stead-fastly to the Apostles' teachings and communal life, in the breaking of bread and in prayers. ⁴³And reverence came to every soul; and through the Apostles came many wonders and signs. ⁴⁴And all those who had faith were at the same place and owned all things communally, ⁴⁵And they sold their properties and possessions, and distributed to everyone, according as anyone had need. ⁴⁶And from day to day they steadfastly remained in the Temple in concord of spirit and, breaking bread in one house after another, they shared their food in gladness and simplicity of heart, ⁴⁷Praising God and enjoying the favor of all the people. And day by day the Lord added those who were being saved to their company.

CHAPTER THREE

¹Now Peter and John were going up to the Temple at the ninth hour, the hour of prayer. ²And a certain man was being carried in, one blind from his mother's womb, whom they used to place at the door of the Temple called "Lovely" each day to beg alms from those entering the Temple: ³Who, on seeing Peter and John about to enter the Temple, asked for a gift of alms. ⁴And Peter gazed at him, as did John, and said, "Look at us." ⁵And he turned his attention to them, expecting to get something from them. ⁶And Peter said, "I possess no silver or gold; but what I do have, this I give you: In the name of Jesus the Anointed, the Nazorean, walk." ⁷And grabbing him by the right hand he raised him; at once, his feet and ankles were made firm, ⁸And leaping up he stood and walked and entered the Temple along with them, walking and leap-

ing and praising God. ⁹And all the people saw him walking and praising God; ¹⁰And they recognized him—that this was the one sitting by
the Temple's "Lovely Gate" to receive alms—and they were filled with
astonishment and bewilderment at what had happened to him. ¹¹And,
as he clung to Peter and John, the people rushed to them all together
in utter astonishment, at the colonnade known as "Solomon's." ¹²And,
seeing this, Peter spoke out to the people: "Men, Israelites, why are you
amazed at this man? Or why do you stare at us, as if we had made him
walk by our own power or piety? ¹³The God of Abraham and Isaac and
Jacob, the God of our fathers, glorified his servant Jesus whom you
handed over and disowned before the face of Pilate when that man had
resolved to release him; ¹⁴But you disowned the holy and upright one,
and asked for a man who was a murderer to be released to you, ¹⁵And
you killed the leader on the Way of Life,ᵃ whom God raised from the
dead, of which we are witnesses. ¹⁶And his name, through faith in his
name, gave strength to this man—whom you see and recognize—and
the faith that comes through it gave him this perfect health, right here
in front of you all. ¹⁷And now, brothers, I know that you acted out
of ignorance, as did your leaders as well; ¹⁸But thus God fulfilled that
which he announced beforehand through the mouth of all the prophets:
that his Anointed would suffer. ¹⁹So change your hearts and turn about,
so that your sins may be expunged, ²⁰So that times of renewal may come
from before the face of the Lord, and he may send the Anointed who
was appointed for you beforehand, Jesus, ²¹Whom heaven must hold
until the times of that Restoration of all thingsᵇ of which God spoke

a. According to Acts, believers in Christ, before coming to be known as
"Christians," spoke of themselves simply as followers of "the Way," or as those
who had chosen the Way of Life.

b. ἄχρι χρόνων ἀποκαταστάσεως πάντων (*achri chronōn apokatastaseōs
pantōn*): this trope of the "universal apokatastasis" or "Restoration of all things"
appears also at Matthew 17:11, where it is depicted as the work of Elijah, who must
precede the appearance of the Son of Man (and who, says Jesus, has already come
in the person of John the Baptist). Here, the phrase may have acquired a more
cosmic dimension. In later Christian thought it would come to refer not only to

through the mouth of his holy prophets an age ago. ²²Indeed, Moses said that 'the Lord your God will raise up for you a prophet like me from among your brothers; you must listen to him concerning everything, whatsoever he shall say to you. ²³And it shall be that every soul, whoever it is, who does not listen to that prophet will be eradicated from the people.' ²⁴And all the prophets—all who spoke from Samuel onward—also announced these days. ²⁵You are the sons of the prophets and of the covenant that God made with our fathers, telling Abraham, 'And in your seed all the families of the earth shall be blessed.' ²⁶And God, having raised up his servant, sent him to you first, to bless you by turning each of you from your wicked ways."

CHAPTER FOUR

¹And, while they were speaking to the people, the priests and the captain of the Temple and the Sadducees came up to them, ²Immensely disturbed that they were teaching the people and proclaiming resurrection from the dead in Jesus, ³And laid hands upon them and put them under guard until the following day; for it was now evening. ⁴But many of those who had heard the discourse had faith, and the number of men grew to about five thousand.

⁵Now the following day it happened that their rulers and elders and scribes were gathered together in Jerusalem, ⁶As well as Annas the chief priest and Caiaphas and John and Alexander and as many as there were of the chief priest's family; ⁷And, having made them stand in their midst, they asked, "By what power or in what name did you do this?" ⁸Then Peter, filled with the Holy Spirit, said to them, "Rulers and elders of the people, ⁹If today, on account of a good deed done to an infirm man, we are being interrogated as to how he has been healed, ¹⁰Let it be known to all of you and to all the people of Israel that in the name

---

the final reconstitution of the cosmos, but also (for some) to the final salvation and glorification of all of creation and of everyone therein.

of Jesus the Anointed, the Nazorean—whom you crucified, whom God raised from the dead—by this name this man stands before you completely healed. [11]This is the stone despised by you, the builders, which has become the capstone of the corner. [12]And there is salvation in no one else; for there is no other name given among men under the sky by which we must be saved." [13]And, seeing the audacity of Peter and John, and perceiving them to be unlettered and common men, they were amazed, and recognized that they had accompanied Jesus, [14]And, seeing the man who had been healed standing beside them, they had no demurral to make. [15]So, having commanded them to go outside from the Council, they conferred with one another, [16]Saying, "What may we do with these men? For it is obvious to everyone inhabiting Jerusalem that a remarkable sign has come about through them, and we cannot deny it; [17]But, so that it should not be any further spread about among the people, let us warn them under threat no longer to speak in this name to any men." [18]And, summoning them, they enjoined them not to speak or teach in the name of Jesus at all. [19]But, in reply, Peter and John said to them, "Judge for yourselves whether it is upright before God to listen to you rather than to God; [20]For we are unable not to speak of the things we have seen and heard." [21]And they, having made additional threats, released them, finding that—on account of the people—they had no way to punish them; for everyone gave God the glory for what had happened; [22]For the man upon whom this sign of healing had come was over forty years old. [23]And, on being released, they went to their own company and reported what the chief priests and elders had said to them. [24]And they, having listened, lifted their voices to God with one accord and said, "Master, you are he who made the sky and the land and the sea and all the things that are in them, [25]Who spoke by a Holy Spirit through the mouth of your servant, our father David, saying, 'Why did the gentiles rage and the peoples devise vain intrigues? [26]The kings of the earth drew up ranks and the rulers gathered together against the Lord and against his Anointed.' [27]For in truth both Herod and Pilate, along with the gentiles and peoples of Israel, conspired in this city against your holy servant Jesus, whom you anointed, [28]To do what your hand and your counsel designated should happen in advance; [29]And now, Lord, consider their threats and grant it to your slaves to speak your word with all boldness, [30]By stretching forth your hand so that healing and signs and wonders may occur through the name of your holy servant Jesus." [31]And, as they were making their supplications, the place in which they were gathered was shaken, and they were all filled with the Holy Spirit, and they spoke the word of God with boldness.

[32]And both the heart and the soul of the multitude of those who had come to have faith were one, and no one said that any of the possessions belonging to him was his own, but everything was owned among them communally. [33]And the Apostles of the Lord Jesus bore witness to the resurrection with great power, and great grace was upon all of them. [34]For neither was anyone among them in need; for as many as were proprietors of lands or households were selling them and bringing the profits of the things sold, [35]And laying them at the feet of the Apostles, and there was a redistribution, to each according as anyone had need. [36]And Joseph, who was called bar-Nabas by the Apostles (which, translated, means "Son of Consolation"),[c] a Levite and a Cypriot by birth, [37]Owned a field, and when he had sold it he brought the proceeds and placed them at the Apostles' feet.

CHAPTER FIVE

[1]But a certain man by the name of Ananias, together with his wife Sapphira, sold a piece of property, [2]And he kept some of the proceeds for himself (his wife also being aware of this), and brought along a certain portion of it and placed it at the feet of the Apostles. [3]But Peter said, "Ananias, why did the Accuser so fill your heart that you lie to the Spirit, the Holy One, and keep some of the proceeds from the land for

c. In fact, the name has no such meaning, nor is there any plausible etymology suggesting such a meaning, in Aramaic, Hebrew, Greek, or Latin.

yourself? ⁴So long as it remained unsold, did it not belong to you? And once sold was it not in your power? Why was such a deed put into your heart? You did not lie to men, but to God." ⁵And, on hearing these words, Ananias fell down and yielded up his soul; and great fear came over all who heard of it. ⁶And the young men rose and shrouded him and, carrying him out, buried him. ⁷Then an interval of about three hours elapsed and his wife, not knowing what had happened, came in. ⁸And Peter spoke aloud to her: "Tell me whether you sold the land for this much." And she said, "Yes, for this much." ⁹And Peter to her: "Why was it agreed between you to try the Spirit of the Lord? Look: at the door, the feet of those who have buried your husband; they will carry you out also." ¹⁰And at once she fell down at his feet and yielded up her soul; and, coming in, the young men found her dead and, carrying her out, buried her beside her husband. ¹¹And great fear came over the entire assembly and over everyone hearing of these things.

¹²And many signs and wonders occurred among the people through the hands of the Apostles; and all, in a common spirit, were in Solomon's Portico, ¹³But no one else dared to join them; rather, the people praised them; ¹⁴And more were added to those having faith in the Lord, great numbers of both men and women, ¹⁵So that they even brought the ailing out into the streets and laid them on pallets and mats, in order that at least Peter's shadow might be cast over some of them as he went by. ¹⁶And a multitude also gathered from the cities around Jerusalem, bringing the ill and those tormented by impure spirits, all of whom were healed.

¹⁷And, rising up, the chief priest and all who were with him—those constituting the sect of the Sadducees—were filled with jealousy, ¹⁸And laid hands on the Apostles and put them in the public jail. ¹⁹But during the night an angel of the Lord opened the doors of the prison and, leading them out, said, ²⁰"Go, stand in the Temple, and speak all the words of this Life to the people." ²¹And, having heard this, they entered the Temple around dawn. And, when the chief priest and those with him arrived, they convened the Council and all the assembly of the elders of

the sons of Israel, and sent to the jail to have them brought in. [22]But, on arriving there, the Temple guards did not find them in the prison; and when they returned they reported this, [23]Saying: "We found the jail shut quite fast, and the prison guards stationed at the doors, but on opening it we found no one inside." [24]And, on hearing these words, both the captain of the Temple and the chief priests were utterly at a loss over them, unable to say what would come of this. [25]But someone came and alerted them: "Look: The men whom you put in prison are standing in the Temple and teaching the people." [26]At that the captain, along with the Temple guards, brought them in—not by force, because they were afraid of the people and feared that they might be stoned—[27]And, leading them in, they made them stand before the Council. And the chief priest interrogated them, [28]Saying, "Did we not issue you an order, commanding you not to teach in this name? And look: You have filled Jerusalem with your teaching, and you wish to impute this man's blood to us." [29]And in reply Peter and the Apostles said, "It is necessary to obey God rather than men. [30]The God of our fathers raised Jesus, whom you killed, hanging him upon a tree; [31]God exalted this man to his right side as a prince and a savior, that he might give Israel a change of heart and forgiveness of sins. [32]And we and the Spirit, the Holy one that God gave to those obeying him, are witnesses to these things we say." [33]And those listening were cut to the core, and resolved to kill them. [34]But, standing up in the Council, a certain Pharisee by the name of Gamaliel, a teacher of the Law revered by all the people, ordered that the men be put outside for a little while, [35]And said to them, "Men, Israelites, consider among yourselves what you intend to do to these men. [36]For before, in days past, Theudas arose claiming to be someone, to whom about four hundred men became attached—who was killed, and all of those who obeyed him were dispersed and came to nothing. [37]After that, in the days of the census, Judas the Galilaean arose and drew people along behind him; and that man perished, and all who obeyed him were scattered. [38]And now I say to you, stand back from these men and leave them; for if this movement or this work is from men it will be destroyed; ³⁹But if it is from God you will not be able to destroy them; you might even turn out to be men who are battling against God." And they were persuaded by him. ⁴⁰And, having summoned the disciples, they beat them and commanded them not to speak in the name of Jesus, and released them. ⁴¹Thus they departed from before the face of the Council, elated because they had been deemed worthy to suffer disgrace on behalf of the name; ⁴²And every day, in the Temple and from house to house, they did not cease teaching and proclaiming the good tidings of Jesus the Anointed.

CHAPTER SIX

¹Now in those days, as the disciples were growing in number, a murmur of complaint arose against the Hebrews from the Hellenists,ᵈ because their widows were being neglected in the daily ministry. ²And the Twelve, having summoned the whole company of the disciples, said, "It is not acceptable for us to neglect the word of God to serve at tables. ³Now, brothers, seek out seven men attested to be full of spirit and wisdom, whom we will assign to this task; ⁴But we will keep to prayer and to the ministry of the word." ⁵And this counsel was pleasing in the eyes of the whole company, and they elected Stephen, a man full of faith and of a holy spirit, and Philip and Prochorus and Nicanor and Timon and Parmenas and Nicolaus, a proselyte from Antioch, ⁶Whom they stood before the Apostles; and, having prayed, they laid hands on them.

⁷And the word of God spread, and the number of the disciples in Jerusalem was enormously multiplied, and a large group from among the priests submitted to the faith.

⁸And Stephen, full of grace and power, performed great marvels and signs among the people. ⁹And certain members of the so-called Synagogue of Freedmen—including Cyrenians and Alexandrians and those

d. That is, Jews who spoke Greek rather than Aramaic, being children of the Diaspora.

from Cilicia and Asia—rose up in argument with Stephen, ¹⁰And were powerless to withstand the wisdom and the spirit with which he spoke. ¹¹Then they suborned some men to say: "We have heard him uttering blasphemous words against Moses and God." ¹²And they agitated the people and the elders and the scribes; and, confronting him, they seized him and led him to the Council, ¹³And they produced false witnesses who said, "This man incessantly makes pronouncements against [this] holy place and the Law; ¹⁴For we have heard him saying that this Jesus the Nazorean will destroy this place and will change the customs that Moses delivered to us." ¹⁵And all those sitting on the Council, gazing upon him, saw his face to be like the face of an angel.

CHAPTER SEVEN

¹And the chief priest said, "Is this how things are?" ²And he said:

"Men, brothers and fathers, listen. The God of glory appeared to our father Abraham when he was in Mesopotamia, before he dwelled in Haran, ³And said to him, 'Depart from your land, you and your kin, and come into the land that I shall show you.' ⁴Then, departing from the land of the Chaldeans, he dwelled in Haran. And, after his father died, he removed himself to this land in which you now dwell, ⁵And gave him no inheritance in it, not even a foot's length of it, and promised to give it as a possession to him and to his seed after him—when he had no child. ⁶And God spoke thus: that his seed 'will be a sojourner in a land belonging to others, and they will enslave and mistreat it for four hundred years; ⁷And, the nation for which they will slave,' said God, 'I shall judge; and thereafter they will depart and will worship me in this place.' ⁸And he gave him a covenant by circumcision; and so he sired Isaac and circumcised him on the eighth day, and Isaac Jacob, and Jacob the twelve patriarchs. ⁹And the patriarchs, moved to envy, sold Joseph away into Egypt; and God was with him, ¹⁰And rescued him from all his afflictions, and gave him favor and wisdom before Pharaoh, king of Egypt, and before his whole household. ¹¹But a famine descended upon the whole of Egypt and Canaan, and a great affliction, and our fathers found no sustenance. ¹²But Jacob, having heard there was grain in Egypt, first sent out our fathers; ¹³And on the second occasion Joseph was made known to his brothers, and Joseph's kin were revealed to Pharaoh. ¹⁴And Joseph sent and called for his father Isaac and his kin, seventy-five souls in all. ¹⁵And Jacob went down to Egypt, and he died, and our fathers too, ¹⁶And they were translated into Sychem and were placed in the tomb Abraham had bought for a sum in silver from the sons of Emmor in Sychem. ¹⁷And, as the time of the promise that God had made to Abraham drew near, the people grew and multiplied in Egypt, ¹⁸Until another king arose over Egypt who did not know Joseph. ¹⁹This man, deceitfully outwitting our race, forced our fathers to expose their infants, so that they would not survive. ²⁰At which juncture Moses was born, comely to God, who for three months was reared in his father's house; ²¹And, when he had been exposed, Pharaoh's daughter picked him up and reared him as her own son. ²²And Moses was indoctrinated in all the wisdom of the Egyptians, and he was powerful in his utterances and works. ²³But, when he had fully attained forty years of age, it came upon his heart to visit his brothers, the sons of Israel. ²⁴And, seeing one of them being treated unjustly, he came to his defense, and exacted justice for him by striking down the Egyptian. ²⁵Now, he assumed his brothers would understand that God would grant them salvation by his hand; but they did not understand. ²⁶And on the succeeding day he appeared to them as they were fighting, and would have reconciled them in peace, saying, 'Men, you are brothers; why do you mistreat each other?' ²⁷But the one who was mistreating his neighbor pushed him away, saying, 'Who appointed you as a ruler and a judge over us? ²⁸Do you intend to kill me just as you killed the Egyptian yesterday?' ²⁹And at this word Moses fled and became a sojourner in the land of Midian, where he sired two sons. ³⁰And when fully forty years had passed there appeared to him in the wilderness an angel within a flame of fire, in a thorn bush. ³¹And, seeing this, Moses was amazed at the vision, and as he approached to investigate it there came a voice from the Lord: [32]'I am the God of your fathers: the God of Abraham and Isaac and Jacob.' But Moses, growing tremulous, dared not look. [33]And the Lord said to him, 'Untie the sandals from your feet, for the place upon which you stand is holy ground. [34]I have looked and seen the oppression of my people in Egypt, and have heard their groaning, and I have come down to rescue them; come now, then, I will send you forth to Egypt.' [35]This Moses—whom they rejected, saying, 'Who appointed you a ruler and a judge?'—this man God sent, by the hand of the angel who appeared to him in the thorn bush, as both a ruler and a liberator. [36]This man led them out, performing wonders and signs in the land of Egypt, and in the Red Sea, and in the wilderness for forty years. [37]This is the Moses who said to the sons of Israel, 'God will raise up for you, from among your brothers, a prophet like me.' [38]This is he who was in the assembly in the wilderness, with the angel speaking to him on Mount Sinai, and with our fathers—he who received living oracles to give to you, [39]He to whom our fathers had no intention of becoming obedient, but whom rather they pushed away, and in their hearts turned back to Egypt, [40]Saying to Aaron, 'Make for us gods who will lead the way before us; for Moses, who led us forth out of the land of Egypt, what has become of him we do not know.' [41]And in those days they made a calf and led a sacrifice up to the idol, and reveled in the works of their hands. [42]And God turned and delivered them to the worship of the army of the sky, as has been written in the book of the prophets: 'House of Israel, have you offered me slaughtered offerings and sacrifices for forty years in the wilderness? [43]And you took along the tent of Moloch and the star of the god Rephan, the figures that you made in order to prostrate yourselves before them; and I will exile you beyond Babylon.' [44]Our fathers had the Tent of Witness in the wilderness, just as he who spoke to Moses also commanded him to fashion it, according to the model that he had seen: [45]Which our fathers, who inherited it, also brought in with Joshua at the conquest of the gentiles, whom God drove out from before the face of our fathers, until the days of David, [46]Who found favor before God, and sought to find a tabernacle for the house of Jacob. ⁴⁷And Solomon built a house for him. ⁴⁸But the Most High does not dwell in something made by hands; as the prophet says: ⁴⁹'To me the sky is a throne, and the earth my feet's footstool; what house will you build for me?' says the Lord, 'Or what place of rest for me? ⁵⁰Has not my hand made all these things?' ⁵¹You who are stiff-necked and uncircumcised in hearts and ears, you always oppose the Spirit, the Holy One: as your fathers, so also you. ⁵²Which of the prophets did your fathers not persecute? And they killed those who made proclamations in advance regarding the righteous one, of whom you now have become betrayers and murderers: ⁵³You, who received the Law through ordinances of angels,ᵉ and did not keep it."

⁵⁴And, hearing these things, they were cut to their hearts, and ground their teeth at him. ⁵⁵But, being full of a Holy Spirit, gazing into the sky, he saw God's glory, and Jesus standing at God's right hand, ⁵⁶And he said, "Look, I see the heavens opened and the Son of Man standing at God's right hand." ⁵⁷And crying out with a loud voice they covered their ears and rushed upon him, all in one mind, ⁵⁸And throwing him outside the city they stoned him, and the witnesses shed their robes at the feet of a young man called Saul, ⁵⁹And they stoned Stephen, who prayed and said, "Lord Jesus, receive my spirit." ⁶⁰And going down on his knees he cried with a loud voice, "Lord, do not charge them with this sin." And saying this he fell asleep.

e. εἰς διαταγὰς ἀγγέλων (eis diatagas angelōn): perhaps "by angelic ordinances," or "by [God's] commands to angels," or "through [God's] deputations of angels." The phrase is strange, and interpretation is complicated by the reality that, in late antique Judaism, it was common to understand all of God's dealings with creation as conducted not immediately, but only through angels who seemingly enjoyed a certain autonomy or defectibility in regard to how they discharged their missions, and who perhaps delivered the Law to Israel in a form proportional to their own limited powers. Thus for Paul, in Galatians 3:19–20, the Law "having been ordained by angels" (διαταγεὶς δι' ἀγγέλων [diatageis di' angelōn]), "in the hand of an intermediary [Moses]," is holy but still inferior to God's direct promises. And in Hebrews 2:2–4 the Law merely spoken through angels is not yet equal to, or as final as, the word spoken directly by the Lord.

CHAPTER EIGHT

¹And there was Saul, approving of his destruction.

And on that day a great persecution broke out against the assembly in Jerusalem. And all but the Apostles were dispersed throughout the territories of Judaea and Samaria. ²And devout men helped to bear Stephen away and performed loud lamentations over him. ³But Saul wreaked havoc upon the assembly, entering house after house, hauling off both men and women and delivering them to prison.

⁴So those who had been scattered went all about, proclaiming the word of the good tidings. ⁵And Philip, going down to the city of Samaria, proclaimed the Anointed to them. ⁶And, with one accord, the crowds paid attention to what was said by Philip, as they listened to him and saw the signs that he performed. ⁷For many of those having impure spirits in them, shouting out in a loud voice, came out;ᶠ and many who were paralyzed and lame were healed; ⁸And there was a great deal of rejoicing in that city. ⁹Now, previous to this, a certain man by the name of Simon had been practicing magic in the city and astonishing the people of Samaria, presenting himself as someone great, ¹⁰To whom everyone, from small to great, gave heed, saying, "This man is the Power of God, which is called Great." ¹¹And they gave him their attention because, for a considerable time, he had amazed them with his feats of magic. ¹²But when they believed Philip, as he proclaimed the good tidings concerning the Kingdom of God and the name of Jesus the Anointed, they were baptized, men and women both. ¹³And Simon himself also had faith, and having been baptized he attached himself to Philip and, seeing the signs and the great feats of power taking place, he was amazed. ¹⁴And the Apostles in Jerusalem, hearing that Samaria welcomed the word of God, sent Peter and John to them, ¹⁵Who went down and prayed over

f. Whether intentionally or by inadvertence, the Greek text speaks of those possessed by impure spirits (or, really, those "possessing" such spirits) as the ones who "came out" as a result of exorcism.

them, so that they might receive a Holy Spirit; ¹⁶For as yet it had not descended upon any of them, and they had been baptized only in the name of the Lord Jesus. ¹⁷Then they laid hands on them, and they received a Holy Spirit. ¹⁸And Simon, seeing that the Spirit is imparted by the laying on of the Apostles' hands, offered them money, saying, ¹⁹"Give me this power too, so that whomever I lay my hands upon, he might receive a Holy Spirit." ²⁰But Peter said to him, "To perdition with your silver, and with you, because you imagined you could procure God's gift with money. ²¹You have no part or lot in this matter, for your heart is not right before God. ²²So turn your heart away from this wickedness of yours, and implore the Lord that this design in your heart might be forgiven you; ²³For I see you are galled with bitterness and fettered in iniquity." ²⁴And in reply Simon said, "Implore the Lord for me, that none of the things you have said may befall me." ²⁵So, when they had finished bearing witness and speaking the Lord's word, they returned to Jerusalem and declared the good tidings to many villages of the Samaritans.

²⁶But an angel of the Lord spoke to Philip, saying, "Arise and go southward on the road leading down from Jerusalem to Gaza." This is wilderness. ²⁷And, arising, he went. And look: An Ethiopian man, a eunuch—a courtier of Candace, Queen of the Ethiopians, one who was in charge of all her treasury—had gone to Jerusalem to worship, ²⁸And was returning, and was seated in his chariot and was reading the prophet Isaiah. ²⁹And the Spirit said to Philip, "Approach this chariot and accompany it." ³⁰And, running up, Philip heard him reading Isaiah the prophet, and said, "Do you really understand the things you are reading?" ³¹And he said, "Unless someone will guide me, how indeed could I?" And he invited Philip to come up and sit with him. ³²Now this was the passage of scripture he was reading: "He was led like a sheep to slaughter; and just as a lamb is silent before its shearer, so he does not open his mouth. ³³In his humiliation, he was robbed of a fair hearing. Who will tell of his posterity? For his life is taken from the earth." ³⁴And, speaking directly to Philip, the eunuch said, "I ask you, about whom does the prophet say this? About himself or about some-

one else?" ³⁵And opening his mouth Philip, beginning with this scripture, announced to him the good tidings of Jesus. ³⁶And, as they were traveling along the road, they came upon some water, and the eunuch says, "Look, water. What prevents me being baptized?" [³⁷And Philip said, "It is possible, if you have faith with all your heart." And in reply he said, "I have faith that Jesus the Anointed is God's Son."] ³⁸And he commanded the chariot to stand still, and they went down to the water, both Philip and the eunuch, and he baptized him. ³⁹And when they came up out of the water a Spirit of the Lord seized Philip away, and the eunuch did not see him again, for he went on his way rejoicing. ⁴⁰But Philip found himself in Azotus and, passing through it, he proclaimed the good tidings to all the cities, until he came to Caesarea.

CHAPTER NINE

¹But Saul, still snorting out menaces and slaughter at the Lord's disciples, approaching the chief priest, ²Requested letters from him to Damascus for the synagogues, so that if he discovered any persons belonging to the Way he might lead them in bonds to Jerusalem, men and women alike. ³Now, as he journeyed, it happened that he drew near Damascus, and suddenly there flashed around him a light from the sky, ⁴And falling upon the ground he heard a voice saying to him, "Saul, Saul, why do you persecute me?" ⁵And he said, "Lord, who are you?" And he said, "I am Jesus, whom you persecute; [it is hard for you to kick against the prods." ⁶And, trembling and amazed, he said, "Lord, what do you will that I should do?" And the Lord said to him, "] Arise, however, and go into the city, and you will be told what it is necessary to do." ⁷And the men journeying with him stood speechless, clearly hearing the voice, but seeing no one. ⁸And Saul was lifted up from the ground, but when his eyes were opened he saw nothing; and, leading him by the hand, they brought him into Damascus. ⁹And he was blind for three days, and neither ate nor drank.

¹⁰Now in Damascus there was a certain disciple by the name of

Ananias, and in a vision the Lord said to him, "Ananias." And he said, "See, Lord, it is I." ¹¹And the Lord to him: "Rise, go to the street called Straightway and, in the household of Judas, inquire after a Tarsean by the name of Saul; for, see, he is praying, ¹²And [in a vision] he has seen a man by the name of Ananias entering and laying hands upon him, so that he may see again." ¹³But Ananias replied, "Lord, I have heard from many persons about this man: how many offenses he committed against your holy ones in Jerusalem; ¹⁴And here he has authorization from the chief priests to put all those who invoke your name in bonds." ¹⁵But the Lord said to him, "Go, because this man is a vessel chosen for me, to bear my name before [the] gentiles and kings and the sons of Israel; ¹⁶For I shall show him how many things it is necessary for him to suffer on behalf of my name." ¹⁷And Ananias went off and entered the household and, laying hands on him, said, "Brother Saul, the Lord Jesus has sent me, he who appeared to you on the road by which you came, so that you may see again and be filled with a Holy Spirit." ¹⁸And immediately scales, as it were, fell away from his eyes, and he saw again, and getting up he was baptized, ¹⁹And accepting food he grew stronger.

And he was with the disciples in Damascus for some days, ²⁰And immediately he proclaimed Jesus in the synagogues: that "This man is the Son of God." ²¹And all those who heard him were astonished and said, "Is this not the one who wreaked such carnage in Jerusalem on those invoking this name, and who had come here for just that, so that he could put them in bonds and bring them before the chief priests?" ²²But Saul was infused with more power, and confounded the Judaeans living in Damascus, marshaling arguments that this man is the Anointed. ²³And, when a good many days had passed, ²⁴The Judaeans conspired to kill him; and their intrigue was known to Saul. But they also kept close watch on the gates, both day and night, so that they could destroy him. ²⁵But his disciples took him by night and lowered him through the wall in a basket. ²⁶And on arriving in Jerusalem he attempted to become an associate of the disciples; and everyone was afraid of him, not believing him to be a disciple. ²⁷But bar-Nabas, taking hold of him, led him to the

Apostles, and he recounted to them how he had seen the Lord on the road, and that he had spoken to him, and how in Damascus he had spoken boldly in the name of Jesus. ²⁸And he was with them in Jerusalem, coming in and going out, speaking boldly in the Lord's name, ²⁹And he both spoke to and debated with the Hellenists; and they attempted to kill him. ³⁰But, knowing this, the brethren took him down to Caesarea and sent him out to Tarsus.

³¹So the assembly throughout the whole of Judaea and Galilee and Samaria had peace, being built up and advancing in the fear of the Lord, and it grew in numbers by calling on the Holy Spirit.

³²Now it happened that Peter, going about everywhere, went down as well to the holy ones dwelling in Lydda. ³³And there he found a certain man by the name of Aeneas who was paralyzed, prostrate on a pallet for eight years. ³⁴And Peter said to him, "Aeneas, Jesus the Anointed heals you; get up and smooth out your beddings for yourself." And at once he got up. ³⁵And all those living in Lydda and Saron who saw him turned to the Lord. Now in Joppa there was a certain disciple by the name of Tabitha—³⁶Which, translated, means "Gazelle";ᵍ she was full of good works and of the giving of alms. ³⁷And it happened during those days that, being ill, she died; and having washed her they placed her in an upper room. ³⁸Now, Lydda being near Joppa, the disciples—hearing Peter is there—sent two men to him, imploring him, "Do not delay in coming over to us." ³⁹And Peter, rising up, went with them; when he arrived they led him up into the upper room, and all the widows were standing by, weeping and showing him the tunics and robes that Gazelle had made when she was with them. ⁴⁰And, thrusting them all outside, Peter went down on his knees and prayed, and turning to the body he said, "Tabitha, arise." And she opened her eyes and, seeing Peter, sat up. ⁴¹And, giving her his hand, he raised her up and, calling to the holy ones and to the widows, he presented her alive. ⁴²And it came to be known throughout the whole of Joppa, and many had faith in the Lord. ⁴³And

g. Δορκάς (*Dorkas*).

it happened that he remained in Joppa with a certain Simon, a tanner, a good many days.

CHAPTER TEN

¹Now a certain man in Caesarea by the name of Cornelius—a centurion from a military cohort called the Italic, ²A devout man and one who along with all his household revered God, donating many alms to the people and always supplicating God—³Clearly saw in a vision, around about the ninth hour of the day, an angel of God coming in to him and saying to him, "Cornelius." ⁴And, gazing at him and growing terrified, he said, "What is it, lord?" And he said to him, "Your prayers and your almsgiving have risen up as a memorial offering before God. ⁵And now send men to Joppa and summon back a certain Simon, who is also called Peter; ⁶This man is lodged with a certain Simon, a tanner whose household is by the sea." ⁷And as the angel who was speaking to him departed he called two of the household slaves and a devout soldier from among those in constant attendance on him, ⁸And, explaining everything to them, sent them to Joppa. ⁹And the next day, as they were journeying and approaching the city, Peter ascended around the sixth hour up to the roof to pray. ¹⁰And he became hungry, and wished to taste some food; and as they were preparing it an ecstasy came upon him, ¹¹And he beholds the sky opened, and an object descending, like a great sheet being let down to the ground by four corners, ¹²On which were all the quadrupeds and reptiles of the earth and birds of the sky. ¹³And a voice came to him: "Arise, Peter, sacrifice[h] and eat." ¹⁴But Peter said, "Certainly not, Lord, for I have never eaten anything profane and impure." ¹⁵And again, for a second time, there came a voice to him: "Do not deem profane what

---

h. θῦσον (*thyson*): often translated here, somewhat less disturbingly, as "slay" or "slaughter"; but the verb θύειν (*thyein*) always means "to sacrifice" to the gods or to God, "to offer up" or "to slay" the sacrificial victim. Jews and Christians alike may have been reluctant to eat meats offered to pagan gods; but every animal slain for the table was still consecrated to God.

God has made pure." ¹⁶And this happened three times, and at once the object was taken up into the sky. ¹⁷And, as Peter was wondering within himself what the vision he had seen might be, look: The men who had been sent by Cornelius, inquiring after the household of Simon, were standing at the gate, ¹⁸And calling out they asked, "Is Simon, also called Peter, perhaps lodged here?" ¹⁹And as Peter was pondering the vision the Spirit said, "See, two men are seeking you; ²⁰But rise and go down, and go with them, hesitating over nothing, for I have sent them." ²¹And descending Peter said to the men, "See here, I am he whom you are seeking; what are you here for?" ²²And they said, "Cornelius, a centurion, a just man and one who reveres God, and one in high repute with the whole nation of the Judaeans, was enjoined by a holy angel to summon you to his house and to listen to words from you." ²³So, calling them in, he gave them lodging. And the next day he arose and departed with them, and some of the brethren from Joppa accompanied him. ²⁴And the next day he entered Caesarea; and Cornelius was waiting for them, having called together his relations and intimate friends. ²⁵And, as Peter was coming in, Cornelius came to meet him, fell at his feet, and prostrated himself. ²⁶But Peter raised him up, saying, "Stand up; I too am a man." ²⁷And, conversing with him, he went in, and finds a gathering of many persons, ²⁸And said to them, "You understand how impermissible it is for a Judaean man to associate with or approach a person of foreign extraction; God also showed me that I must not call any man profane or impure; ²⁹So in fact, on being summoned, I came without raising any objection. I ask, therefore, for what reason did you summon me?" ³⁰And Cornelius said, "Four days ago, at this, the ninth hour, I was in my house praying, and see: A man was standing before me in shining raiment, ³¹And he says, 'Cornelius, your prayer has been heard and your alms-givings have been remembered before God. ³²Send to Joppa, therefore, and call for Simon, who is also called Peter; this man is lodged by the sea in the household of Simon, a tanner.' ³³So I sent to you at once, and you have been so good as to come. So now here we all are in the presence of God, to listen to all the commands you have been given by the Lord."

³⁴And, opening his mouth, Peter said, "In truth, I perceive that God is not a respecter of persons; ³⁵Rather, in every people, whoever reveres him and performs works of righteousness is accepted by him; ³⁶The word that he sent to the sons of Israel, proclaiming the good tidings of peace through Jesus the Anointed—this one is Lord of everyone . . . ³⁷You know the story of what took place throughout the whole of Judaea, starting out from Galilee after the baptism that John announced: ³⁸Jesus, the man from Nazareth, how God anointed him with a Holy Spirit and with power—who went about doing good and healing all those under the power of the Slanderer, because God was with him; ³⁹And we are witnesses of all the things that he did, both in the country of the Judaeans and in Jerusalem—whom in fact they killed, hanging him up upon a tree. ⁴⁰This one God raised up on the third day, and granted that he become manifest, ⁴¹Not to all the people, but to us, witnesses previously appointed by God, who ate and drank with him after he rose again from the dead; ⁴²And he commanded us to proclaim to the people and solemnly to testify that this is the one marked out by God as judge of the living and the dead. ⁴³To this one all the prophets bear witness: Everyone having faith in him is to receive forgiveness of sins through his name." ⁴⁴While Peter was still uttering these words, the Spirit, the Holy One, fell upon all those listening to the discourse, ⁴⁵And the faithful among the circumcised, as many as had accompanied Peter, were astonished, because the gift of the Holy Spirit has been poured out even upon the gentiles; ⁴⁶For they heard them speaking in tongues and praising God's greatness. Then Peter spoke up: ⁴⁷"Can anyone forbid the water for baptizing these persons, who have also received the Spirit, the Holy One, just as we did?" ⁴⁸And he instructed them to be baptized in the name of Jesus the Anointed. Then they asked him to remain for a few days.

CHAPTER ELEVEN

¹Now the Apostles and brethren living throughout Judaea heard that the gentiles too were receiving the word of God. ²And when Peter

went up to Jerusalem some of the circumcised disputed with him, ³Saying, "You went indoors with men who have foreskins, and ate along with them." ⁴And Peter explained it to them from the beginning, saying, ⁵"I was in the city of Joppa praying, and in an ecstasy I saw a vision, a certain shape descending like a great sheet having been let down from the sky by four corners, and it came right up to me, ⁶Gazing into which I perceived and saw the quadrupeds of the earth, and the wild beasts and the reptiles, and the birds of the sky. ⁷And I also heard a voice saying to me, 'Get up, Peter, sacrifice[i] and eat.' ⁸And I said, 'Certainly not, Lord, for nothing profane or impure has ever entered my mouth.' ⁹And a voice answered a second time out of the sky, 'Do not deem profane what God has made pure.' ¹⁰And this happened three times, and everything was lifted into the sky again. ¹¹And see: All at once three men were standing at the household where I was, having been sent to me from Caesarea. ¹²And the Spirit told me to go with them, hesitating at nothing. And these six brethren came with me as well, and we went into the man's house. ¹³And he recounted to us how he had seen the angel standing in his house and saying, 'Send to Joppa and summon Simon, who is also called Peter, ¹⁴Who will speak words to you by which you may be saved, you and all your household.' ¹⁵And as I began to speak the Spirit, the Holy One, fell upon them, as upon us also at the beginning. ¹⁶And I remembered the word of the Lord, how he said, 'John indeed baptized in water, but you will be baptized in a Holy Spirit.' ¹⁷So, if God gave them a gift equal to the one he also gave us when we had faith in the Lord Jesus the Anointed, who was I that I might hinder God?" ¹⁸And, hearing these things, they quieted down and gave glory to God, saying, "Then God has also given the gentiles a turning of the heart toward life."

¹⁹Therefore those who had been dispersed by the persecution that had occurred in connection with Stephen journeyed on to Phoenicia and Cyprus and Antioch, speaking the message to Judaeans only, and to no one else. ²⁰But some of them were Cypriot and Cyrenian men

---

i. θῦσον (*thyson*): see the note to 10:13 above.

who, on coming to Antioch, spoke to the Greeks as well, proclaiming the good tidings of the Lord Jesus. [21]And the hand of the Lord was with them, and a great many had faith and turned to the Lord. [22]And word regarding these things reached the ears of the assembly that was in Jerusalem, and they sent out to Antioch bar-Nabas, [23]Who, on arriving and observing the grace of God, was exultant and exhorted all of them to remain with the Lord with firm purpose of heart, [24]For he was a good man, and full of a Holy Spirit and faith; and a considerable throng was added to the Lord. [25]And he went out to Tarsus to look for Saul, [26]And on finding him brought him to Antioch. And it happened that they too gathered together with the assembly and gave instruction to a considerable throng of people, and that in Antioch the disciples assumed the title "Christians" for the first time.[j]

[27]And in those days prophets came down to Antioch from Jerusa-

---

j. χρηματίσαι τε πρώτως ἐν Ἀντιοχείᾳ τοὺς μαθητὰς Χριστιανούς (chrēmatisai te prōtōs en Antiocheia, tous mathētas Christianous). The followers, that is, or party, or representatives of the Christ, the Anointed. The grammar is slightly obscure here. The verb chrēmatisai is an active infinitive, as are the two preceding verbs, all dependent upon the dispositive intransitive ἐγένετο (egeneto): "it happened that . . ." It could possibly, therefore, be translated as "they [bar-Nabas and Saul] first called the disciples 'Christians' in Antioch," though there is sound palaeographical evidence that the active voice of the verb could carry a passive sense, so that the sentence might be rendered "the disciples were first called 'Christians' in Antioch" (by others, presumably). Others argue, and I have chosen here to take this line, that the active was often used as a tacit reflexive, meaning something like "to style oneself" or "to give oneself the title," in the way that a business concern might name itself. And a very few—noting that the verb χρηματίζω (chrēmatizō) was used classically to mean "to deliver an oracle," as the Pythia or some other prophet or prophetess might do when consulted by a suppliant, and that even in the New Testament it is occasionally used specifically to mean a divine revelation or admonition (e.g., Matthew 2:12; Luke 2:26; Acts 10:22)—have suggested that the phrase means something like "the disciples were first named 'Christians' by divine revelation in Antioch"; this, however, is something of a stretch. It should be noted that there is a certain oddity to the very word Christianos, since it is not a natural Greek nominalization; rather, it is a Latin nominalization transliterated into Greek, and Latin was certainly not the common tongue of first-century Antiochenes.

lem; [28]And one of them, by the name of Agabus, stood up and through the Spirit gave a sign that a great famine was about to occur all over the entire inhabited world (which did happen, in the time of Claudius). [29]So each of the disciples, insofar as any had the resources, decided to send supplies for ministering to the brethren dwelling in Judaea—[30]Which indeed they did, sending them to the elders by the hand of bar-Nabas and Saul.

CHAPTER TWELVE

[1]Now at that time Herod the king applied his hands to oppressing certain members of the assembly. [2]And he executed James, the brother of John, by the sword. [3]And, seeing that this was pleasing to the Judaeans, he made the additional move of arresting Peter—and these were days of Unleavened Bread—[4]Whom he seized and placed in prison, handing him over to be guarded by four quarternia of soldiers, intending to bring him up before the people after the Passover. [5]So Peter was held in the prison. But prayer was being offered up to God ardently on his behalf by the assembly. [6]And, on the night just before Herod was going to bring him out, Peter was sleeping, bound with chains between two soldiers, and sentries were set before the doors, guarding the prison. [7]And look: An angel of the Lord descended upon it, and a light shone within the building; and, striking Peter's side, he roused him, saying, "Rise up, quickly." And the chains fell away from his hands. [8]And the angel said to him, "Tie your clothes about you and put on your sandals." And he did so. And he says to him, "Throw your robe about yourself and follow me." [9]And, going out, he followed him, and he did not realize that what was going on with the angel was real, but thought he was seeing a vision. [10]And, passing through the first prison enclosure and then the second, they came upon the gate of iron leading into the city, which opened for them by itself, and they went out and along one street, and immediately the angel departed from him. [11]And, having come to himself, Peter said, "Now I know that the Lord

truly did send out his angel and did rescue me from Herod's hand, and from everything the Judaean people anticipated doing." ¹²And, having realized this, he came upon the household of Mary the mother of John (also called Mark), where many were gathered together and praying. ¹³And when he knocked at the door of the outer gate a maidservant by the name of Rhoda approached to listen, ¹⁴And, in her joy at recognizing Peter's voice, she failed to open the gateway, and instead ran inside and announced that Peter was standing at the gate. ¹⁵And they said to her, "You are raving." But she insisted emphatically that it was so. So they said, "It is his angel." ¹⁶But Peter persisted in knocking; and when they had opened up they saw him and were amazed. ¹⁷And, gesturing with his hand for them to be silent, he related to them how the Lord had led him out of the prison, and said, "Report these things to James and the brethren." And going out he went off elsewhere. ¹⁸Now when day had come there was no little commotion among the soldiers: "So what has become of Peter?" ¹⁹And Herod, looking for him and not finding him, interrogated the guards and ordered that they be disposed of;ᵏ and, going down from Judaea to Caesarea, he stayed there. ²⁰Now he was in a hostile frame of mind toward Tyrians and Sidonians; but they came to him in a united spirit and, having won over the royal chamberlain Blastos, they sued for peace, because their territory was fed by the royal territory. ²¹And on an appointed day Herod, clad in royal raiment and seated on the tribunal, delivered a public address to them; ²²And the local inhabitants cried out, "A god's voice, and not a man's!" ²³And at once, since he had not given God the glory, an angel of the Lord struck him a blow; and, being devoured by worms, he expired.

²⁴And the message of the Lord spread and became more abundant. ²⁵And bar-Nabas and Saul returned from Jerusalem, having completed their ministration, bringing with them John (also called Mark).

---

k. ἀπαχθῆναι (*apachthēnai*): "be led away," "be taken off": a verb Luke uses of those being sent off to execution, such as Christ (Luke 23:26).

CHAPTER THIRTEEN

¹Now in Antioch, among the assembly that was there, there were prophets and teachers: both bar-Nabas and Symeon (who was called Black);¹ also Lucius the Cyrenian, Manaen, who had grown up along with Herod the tetrarch, and Saul. ²And, as they were conducting a religious service to the Lord and fasting, the Spirit, the Holy One, said to them, "Now set bar-Nabas and Saul apart for me, for the work to which I have called them." ³Then, having fasted and prayed and laid hands upon them, they sent them off.

⁴So, sent out by the Holy Spirit, they went down into Seleucia, and from there sailed off to Cyprus, ⁵And coming into Salamis they proclaimed God's word in the synagogues of the Judaeans; and they also had John with them as an aid. ⁶And passing through the entire island to Paphos they found a certain Judaean man, a sorcerer^m and false prophet, whose name was bar-Jesus, ⁷Who attended the proconsul Sergius Paulus, an intelligent man. This man, summoning bar-Nabas and Saul, wished to hear the word of God. ⁸But Elymas the sorcerer (for such is his name when translated)^n opposed them, seeking to turn the proconsul away from the faith. ⁹But Saul (who was also "Paul"),^o filled with a Holy Spirit, gazed at him and said, ¹⁰"O you, full of all deceit and all villainy, son of the Slanderer, enemy of all righteousness, will you not cease twisting the Lord's straight paths crooked? ¹¹And

l. Νίγερ: the Latin name Niger, which means "black," transcribed into Greek.

m. μάγος (*magos*): the same word Matthew used to described the Magians from the East who visited the child Jesus, but here with what had become the more common meaning in the Greek-speaking world.

n. The claim here, as written, seems to be that the name Ἐλύμας (Elymas) means "sorcerer," but neither the Greek name itself nor any known Semitic root of which it might be a homonym or paronym has such a meaning. It certainly cannot mean that Elymas is the Greek "translation" of bar-Jesus.

o. This may simply mean "who was also known as Paul," and Luke may merely be casually mentioning Paul's "Christian name" for the first time; but it may also mean that he has the same name as the proconsul.

now see the Lord's hand upon you, and you will be blind, not seeing the sun for a season." And at once a mist and a darkness descended on him, and he went about seeking for those who would lead him by the hand. ¹²Then, seeing what had occurred, the proconsul had faith, being moved to wonder by the Lord's teaching.

¹³And, setting sail from Paphos, those in Paul's party came to Perga in Pamphylia; and John departed from them and returned to Jerusalem. ¹⁴And, passing on from Perga, they arrived in Psidian Antioch and entered the synagogue on the Sabbath day and seated themselves. ¹⁵And after the reading of the Law and the Prophets the synagogue leaders sent to them, saying, "Men, brothers, if among you there is any word of exhortation for the people, speak." ¹⁶And Paul, rising and gesturing with his hand, said, "Men, Israelites, as well as you Godfearers,ᴾ listen! ¹⁷The God of this people Israel chose our fathers, and exalted the people during the sojourn in the land of Egypt, and with arm upraised led them out of it, ¹⁸And bore with them for a period of about forty years in the wilderness, ¹⁹And having overthrown seven nations in the land of Canaan he ceded them the land as an inheritance, ²⁰For about four hundred and fifty years. And thereafter he gave them judges, until Samuel the prophet. ²¹And from that point they requested a king, and God gave them Saul son of Kish, a man from the tribe of Benjamin, for forty years. ²²And, on removing him, he raised up David as king over them, in testimony to whom he also said, 'I have found David son of Jesse, a man after my own heart, who will do all the things I have willed.' ²³From this man's seed God, according to his promise, brought to Israel a savior, Jesus, ²⁴When John, going before his face, in advance of his advent, had preached a baptism of the heart's transformation to all the people of Israel. ²⁵And as John came to the end of his course he said, 'What do you suppose me to be? I am not he. But look: He comes

p. οἱ φοβούμενος τὸν θεόν (*ʰoi phoboumenos ton theon*): "those revering God" or "Godfearers" were gentile proselytes who attended the synagogues as "hearers" of scripture, but who had not as yet been circumcised or fully initiated into the community.

after me, the sandal of whose feet I am not worthy to untie.' ²⁶Men, brothers, sons of Abraham's race, as well as those Godfearers among you, the word of this salvation was sent to us. ²⁷Because those living in Jerusalem and their rulers, not recognizing this man and putting him on trial, fulfilled the utterances of the prophets that are read aloud every Sabbath, ²⁸And finding no case for his death they petitioned Pilate for him to be destroyed; ²⁹And when they had brought all the things written about him to completion, they took him down from the tree and laid him in a tomb. ³⁰But God raised him from the dead: ³¹He who over a course of many days appeared to those who had accompanied him up from the Galilee to Jerusalem, who are [now] his witnesses to the people. ³²And we proclaim to you the good tidings, that the promise made to our fathers—³³That God has fulfilled it for us the children, raising Jesus up, as is also written in the second Psalm: 'You are my son; today I have begotten you.' ³⁴And, since he raised him up from the dead, never again to return to decay, he has spoken thus: 'I will give to you the hallowed things assured to David.' ³⁵For which reason he also elsewhere�q says, 'You will not allow your holy one to see decay.' ³⁶For indeed David, having served God's purpose in his own generation, fell asleepʳ and was added to his fathers and saw decay; ³⁷But he whom God has raised has not seen decay. ³⁸Therefore let it be known to you, men, brothers, that through this man forgiveness of sins is proclaimed to you, ³⁹And by this man everyone who has faith is made righteous,ˢ in everything regarding which you could not be made righteous by the Law of Moses. ⁴⁰So beware, lest what the prophets said should happen to you: ⁴¹'Look, you contemptuous ones, and marvel, and perish, because I am performing a work in your days, a work in which you will certainly not have faith, though someone declare it to you.'" ⁴²And, as they were leaving, they begged them that these matters be explained to them dur-

q. Literally, "in another [Psalm]."
r. Or "having served in his own generation by the will of God, he fell asleep," or "having served God's purpose, he fell asleep with his own generation."
s. Or "vindicated."

ing the period before the next Sabbath.ᵗ ⁴³And, when the synagogue had dispersed, many of the Judaeans and the proselytes worshipping there followed Paul and bar-Nabas, who spoke to them and persuaded them to hold fast in the grace of God. ⁴⁴And on the coming Sabbath nearly the whole city was gathered to hear God's word. ⁴⁵And on seeing the crowds the Judaeans were filled with a sense of rivalry, and abusively contradicted the things Paul was saying. ⁴⁶Both Paul and bar-Nabas, speaking up boldly, said, "It was necessary for God's word to be spoken first to you; since you reject it, and pass judgment on yourselves, as being not worthy of the life of the Age, look: We are turning to the gentiles. ⁴⁷For the Lord has commanded us thus: 'I have set you up to be a light for the gentiles, for salvation to the ends of the earth.'" ⁴⁸And hearing this the gentiles were elated and gave glory to the Lord's word, and as many as were disposed to the life of the Age had faith; ⁴⁹And the Lord's word was borne through the whole country. ⁵⁰But the Judaeans incited those women worshippersᵘ who were of high degree, as well as the city's leading men, and started a persecution against Paul and bar-Nabas, and expelled them from their borders. ⁵¹But they, shaking off the dust of their feet at them, came into Iconium, ⁵²And the disciples were filled with joy and a Holy Spirit.

CHAPTER FOURTEEN

¹Now in Iconium they happened to enter the synagogue of the Judaeans together, and they spoke, and thus a great number of Judaeans and Greeks had faith. ²But the Judaeans who were resistant aroused and

---

t. εἰς τὸ μεταξὺ σάββατον (*eis to metaxy sabbaton*): this is oddly phrased, and is usually translated as "on the next Sabbath"; on the other hand, since *metaxy* really means "in between," and "Sabbath" can simply mean "week," it may be read as "during the intervening week [till the next Sabbath]," and the next verse might be taken as the congregation encouraging Paul and bar-Nabas to continue their discourse in the present.

u. That is, again, gentile proselytes of Judaism.

poisoned the souls of the gentiles against the brethren. ³So for some considerable time they continued on, speaking boldly about the Lord who—allowing signs and wonders to happen by their hands—testified to the message of his grace. ⁴But the population of the city was divided, and some were with the Judaeans, but others with the Apostles. ⁵And, when there was a sudden rush on the part of both gentiles and Judaeans, as well as of their leaders, to abuse and stone them, ⁶They became aware of it and escaped to the Lycaonian cities of Lystra and Derbe and the surrounding region; ⁷And they were there, proclaiming the good tidings. ⁸And in Lystra there sat a certain man incapacitated in his feet who, lame from his mother's womb, had never walked. ⁹This man listened to Paul speaking—who, gazing at him and seeing he had the faith to be saved, ¹⁰Said in a loud voice, "Stand up straight upon your feet." And up he leapt and walked. ¹¹And the crowds, seeing what Paul had done, raised their voice, saying in Lycaeonian, "The gods, transformed into the likenesses of men, have descended to us"; ¹²And they called bar-Nabas Zeus, and Paul Hermes (since he was the principal speaker). ¹³And the priest of Zeus, situated just outside the city, brought bulls and garlands to the gates, intending to sacrifice with the crowds. ¹⁴But on hearing this the Apostles bar-Nabas and Paul rent their garments and rushed out into the crowd, crying aloud, ¹⁵And saying, "Men, why are you doing these things? We are human beings too, subject to the same feelings as you, proclaiming the good tidings to you so that you will turn from these empty things to a living God, who made the sky and the land and the sea and everything in them, ¹⁶Who in generations past let all nations go on their own ways; ¹⁷And yet he did not leave himself unwitnessed to—acting benevolently, giving us rain from the sky and fruitful seasons, filling our hearts with nourishment and with joy." ¹⁸And in saying these things they just barely restrained the crowds from sacrificing to them. ¹⁹And Judaeans from Antioch and Iconium came up and won over the crowds, and they stoned Paul and dragged him outside the city, thinking he had died. ²⁰But when the disciples gathered around him he arose and went into the city. And the next day he departed with bar-Nabas for Derbe. ²¹And, proclaiming the good tidings to that city and having made a good many disciples, they returned to Lystra and to Iconium and to Antioch, ²²Strengthening the souls of the disciples, exhorting them to persist in faith, and telling them that "We must endure many afflictions to enter the Kingdom of God." ²³And, having appointed elders for them in every assembly, they committed them with prayer and fasts to the Lord in whom they had had faith. ²⁴And passing through Pisidia they came to Pamphylia, ²⁵And speaking the word in Perga they came down to Attalia, and from there sailed off to Antioch, ²⁶From where they had been committed to God's grace for the task they had accomplished. ²⁷And, having arrived and bringing the assembly together, they reported the things God had done with them, and reported that he had opened faith's door to the gentiles. ²⁸And they stayed not a little while with the disciples.

CHAPTER FIFTEEN

¹And some, coming down from Judaea, taught the brothers that "Unless you are circumcised according to the custom of Moses you cannot be saved." ²And, when Paul and bar-Nabas had no small measure of contention and argument with them, they appointed Paul and bar-Nabas, along with some others among them, to journey up to the Apostles and elders in Jerusalem concerning this question. ³So, having been sent on their way by the assembly, they passed through both Phoenicia and Samaria, relating at length how the gentiles had been converted and exciting great joy in all the brethren. ⁴And, having arrived in Jerusalem, they were welcomed by the assembly and the Apostles and the elders, and reported the things that God had done with them. ⁵But some of those who had come to have faith who were from the sect of the Pharisees stood up from among them, saying: "It is necessary to circumcise them and charge them to keep the Law of Moses."

⁶And the Apostles and the elders gathered together to look into this matter. ⁷And, when a great deal of examination had taken place, Peter

rose and said to them, "Men, brothers, you are aware that, from days long past, God chose the gentiles among you to hear the word of the good tidings through my mouth, and to have faith. ⁸And the God who knows hearts bore witness, giving them the Spirit, the Holy One, just as he did us, ⁹And made no distinction between us and them, purifying their hearts through faith. ¹⁰Why, therefore, do you now put God to the test, so as to place upon the neck of the disciples a yoke that neither our fathers nor we were strong enough to bear? ¹¹Rather, we have faith we shall be saved by the grace of the Lord Jesus, in the way that they too will be." ¹²And the whole company became silent and listened to bar-Nabas and Paul relate the signs and wonders God had performed among the gentiles through them. ¹³And, after remaining silent, James spoke up, saying, ¹⁴"Men, brothers, listen to me. Simon has declared how God first saw to it that he would take a people for his name from the gentiles. ¹⁵And the words of the prophets agree with this, just as has been written: ¹⁶"'After these things, I will return and rebuild the fallen tabernacle of David, and will rebuild its ruins and erect it again, ¹⁷So that the rest of humankind might seek out the Lord, even all the nations, those upon whom the name of the Lord has been invoked,' says the Lord who does these things, ¹⁸Known from an age ago.' ¹⁹Hence my verdict is not to cause difficulties for those among the gentiles turning to God, ²⁰But rather to write them, telling them to abstain from the pollutions of idols, and from whoring, and from anything strangled, and from blood. ²¹For Moses has men who preach him in every city, being read aloud in the synagogue every Sabbath since the times of generations long past." ²²Then it was resolved by the Apostles and elders, together with the whole assembly, to send some men chosen from their midst—Judas (the one called bar-Sabbas) and Silas, leading men among the brethren—to Antioch along with Paul and bar-Nabas, ²³By whose hand they sent a letter: "The Apostles and the elder brethren send greetings to those brethren throughout Antioch and Syria and Cilicia who come from among the gentiles. ²⁴Since we have heard that some of our number, to whom we gave no orders, have troubled you with teachings unsettling to your souls, [saying you must be circumcised and be observant of the Law,] ²⁵It occurred to us, having reached a common accord, to send chosen men to you, along with our beloved bar-Nabas and Paul, ²⁶Men having handed over their souls for the sake of the name of our Lord Jesus the Anointed. ²⁷We have therefore sent Judas and Silas, and they will communicate the same to you verbally. ²⁸For it was resolved by the Holy Spirit and by us to impose upon you no greater burden than these necessities: ²⁹To abstain from things sacrificed to idols and from blood and from things strangled and from whoring, by keeping yourselves from which you will be doing well. Farewell."

³⁰They therefore, being dismissed, went down to Antioch and, assembling the community, delivered the letter. ³¹And having read it they were elated at the encouragement. ³²And Judas and Silas, being themselves also prophets, encouraged and fortified the brethren with a good deal of teaching; ³³And when they had labored for a while they were dismissed by the brethren with a "Peace" to those who had sent them out. [³⁴Nevertheless, it pleased Silas still to remain there.] ³⁵But Paul and bar-Nabas stayed in Antioch teaching and, along with many others, proclaiming the good tidings of the word of the Lord.

³⁶And after some days Paul said to bar-Nabas, "Let us return, then, and visit the brethren throughout all the cities in which we announced the word of the Lord—how are they holding on?" ³⁷But bar-Nabas wished also to take along John (the one called Mark); ³⁸Paul did not think it fitting, however, to take someone along with them who had deserted them in Pamphylia and who had not accompanied them in their labor. ³⁹And it became a discord so sharp as to separate them from one another; and, taking Mark, bar-Nabas sailed off to Cyprus. ⁴⁰Having chosen Silas, however, Paul departed, commended by the brethren to the grace of the Lord; ⁴¹And he went through Syria and Cilicia, fortifying the assemblies.

CHAPTER SIXTEEN

¹And he also came down to Derbe and to Lystra. And look: There was a certain disciple there—a son of a Judaean woman who was a believer, but with a Greek father—by the name of Timothy, ²Who was well spoken of by the brethren in Lystra and Iconium. ³Paul wanted this man to journey forth with him, so he took him and, on account of the Judaeans living in those places, circumcised him; for all of them knew that a Greek was his father. ⁴Now, as they passed through the cities, they delivered the teachings that the Apostles and elders in Jerusalem had decided they should keep. ⁵Thus the assemblies were fortified in the faith and increased daily in numbers.

⁶And they passed through the territory of Phrygia and Galatia, being prevented by the Holy Spirit from speaking the word in Asia; ⁷And coming to Mysia they attempted to enter Bithynia, but the Spirit of Jesus did not permit them to do so; ⁸So, passing Mysia by, they came down to Troas. ⁹And a vision appeared to Paul during the night: A certain Macedonian man was standing there and supplicating him and saying, "Cross over to Macedonia and help us." ¹⁰So, when he saw the vision, we immediately sought to depart for Macedonia, concluding, "God has called us to proclaim the good tidings to them."

¹¹And setting sail from Troas we ran a straight course to Samothrace, and on the next day to Neapolis, ¹²And from there to Philippi, a colonyᵛ that is the principal city of that part of Macedonia. ¹³And on the day of the Sabbath we went outside the gate, beside a river where we supposed there was a place for prayer, and sitting down we spoke to the women gathering there. ¹⁴And a certain woman by the name of Lydia, a dealer in purples from the city of Thyatiraʷ who worshipped God,ˣ listened to us—one whose heart the Lord opened to listen to the

v. A colony of Rome, that is.

w. That is, Tyrian purples: cloth richly colored with Tyrian porphyry dye, of which Thyatira was one of the major producers.

x. That is to say, she was, in all likelihood, a gentile "Godfearer."

things spoken by Paul. ¹⁵And when she and her house were baptized she extended an invitation, saying, "If you have adjudged me to be faithful to the Lord, come into my house and stay there." And she urged us. ¹⁶And it happened that, as we were going to the place of prayer, a certain slave girl who had a Python spirit^y in her met us, one whose soothsaying brought considerable profit to her masters. ¹⁷Following behind Paul and us she cried aloud, saying, "These men are slaves of God Most High, who are proclaiming a way of salvation to you." ¹⁸And she did this over many days. But Paul, becoming quite perturbed and turning around to the spirit, said, "I command you in the name of Jesus the Anointed to come out of her." And it came out at that very hour. ¹⁹And her masters, seeing that their hope of gain had departed, seized hold of Paul and Silas and dragged them before the rulers in the marketplace, ²⁰And bringing them to the generals^z said, "These men, being Judaeans, are causing enormous havoc in our city, ²¹And they are advocating customs that are not lawful for us, being Romans, either to accept or to practice." ²²And the crowd joined in against them, and the generals tore the garments from them and ordered their flogging, ²³And, laying many strokes upon them, threw them into prison, charging the jailer to keep them there securely— ²⁴Who, having received such a charge, threw them into the inner prison and fastened their feet in wooden stocks. ²⁵And at about midnight, as they were praying, Paul and Silas sang hymns to God, and the prisoners listened to them; ²⁶And suddenly there was a great earthquake, so that the jail's foundation was shaken; and at once all the doors were opened, and everyone's fetters came loose. ²⁷And the jailer, having wakened from sleep and seeing the doors of the prison opened, had drawn his sword and was about to kill himself, supposing the prisoners

y. Python was the dragon or great serpent slain by Apollo at Mount Parnassus, at whose southwestern spur Delphi is located; and the prophetess who delivered the oracle at Delphi was known as the Pythia. By the time of the writing of Acts, a "python" was a common name for a spirit of clairvoyance.

z. An honorific title given the two chief magistrates of Philippi, who enjoyed the full powers of a self-governing colonial authority.

to have escaped. ²⁸But Paul shouted in a loud voice, saying, "Do yourself no harm, for we are all here!" ²⁹And calling for lights he rushed in, and becoming tremulous he fell down before Paul and Silas, ³⁰And conducting them outside he said, "My lords, what must I do to be saved?" ³¹And they said, "Have faith in the Lord Jesus, and you and your house shall be saved." ³²And they spoke the word of God to him, along with all those of his household. ³³And at that hour of the night he took them and washed their wounds, and at once he and all his people were baptized, ³⁴And bringing them up to the house he set out a table for them, and rejoiced along with the whole household at having come to have faith in God. ³⁵And when day had come the generals sent over staff officers, saying, "Release those men." ³⁶And the jailer announced these words to Paul: "The generals have sent for you to be released. So depart now, and go in peace." ³⁷But Paul said to them, "Having publically beaten us, who are Roman men, without a conviction in court, they threw us into prison; and now they surreptitiously expel us? No indeed; rather, let them come and escort us out themselves." ³⁸And the staff officers reported these words to the generals. And, on hearing that these men are Romans, they were afraid, ³⁹And came and implored them, and escorted them out and asked them to leave the city. ⁴⁰And departing from the prison they entered Lydia's home and, seeing the brethren, gave them encouragement and departed.

CHAPTER SEVENTEEN

¹And, traveling through Amphipolis and Apollonia, they came to Thessalonika, where there was a synagogue of the Judaeans. ²And, as was his custom, Paul went into them, and on three Sabbaths discussed the scriptures with them, ³Explaining and demonstrating that "It is necessary for the Anointed to suffer and to rise again from the dead," and that "This man is the Anointed: Jesus, whom I proclaim to you." ⁴And some of them were persuaded and threw in their lot with Paul and Silas, as well as both a large complement of Greek worshippers and not a

few of the most prominent women. ⁵But the Judaeans [who did not have faith]—becoming jealous and bringing along some loutish men from among the idlers in the marketplace, and gathering together a horde—set the city in riot and, marching to the household of Jason, demanded they be brought before the people; ⁶But, not finding them there, they dragged Jason and some of the brethren to the city rulers, crying: "These men, having turned the entire inhabited world upside down, have arrived here as well—⁷Whom Jason has welcomed; and all these men act in defiance of the decrees of Caesar, saying that Jesus is another king." ⁸And they put the crowd in a turmoil, as well as the city rulers who heard these things; ⁹But, exacting a fee from Jason and the rest as surety, they released them. ¹⁰And immediately the brethren dispatched both Paul and Silas to Beroia by night, and when they arrived they went into the synagogue of the Judaeans. ¹¹And these were of nobler birth than those in Thessalonika and received the word with complete eagerness, examining the scriptures every day to see whether these things were so. ¹²Many of them had faith, therefore, as did also many Greek noblewomen, and not a few men. ¹³But, when the Judaeans from Thessalonika learned that the word of God was being proclaimed by Paul in Beroia also, they came and agitated the crowds and stirred them up. ¹⁴And at that point the brethren immediately sent Paul away, to journey as far as the sea. But both Silas and Timothy remained there. ¹⁵And those escorting Paul led him as far as Athens and departed, taking instructions to Silas and Timothy that they should join him as quickly as possible.

¹⁶And, while Paul was waiting for them in Athens, his spirit within him was incensed, for he saw the city full of idols. ¹⁷So he debated with the Judaeans and the worshippersᵃᵃ in the synagogue, and every day in the marketplace with those who chanced to be there. ¹⁸And some of the Epicurean and Stoic philosophers came across him as well, and some said, "What would this seed-pecking ditherer like to say?" But others

aa. That is, again, gentile "hearers" of the Law.

said, "He seems to be a herald for foreign daemons";[ab] for he was proclaiming Jesus and the resurrection. [19]And they laid hold of him and led him to the Areopagus,[ac] saying, "Can we learn this new teaching expounded by you? [20]For you are introducing some things strange to our ears; so we would like to learn what these things are." [21]Now, all the Athenians and the local resident aliens have leisure for nothing but discussing or listening to the latest thing. [22]And Paul stood in the middle of the Areopagus and said, "Athenian men, I observe how exceedingly reverent you are toward the daemonian[ad] in everything; [23]For as I was walking along and looking over the objects of your devotions I even found an altar on which was inscribed, 'To a GOD UNKNOWN.' What you revere in ignorance, therefore, this I announce to you. [24]The God who made the cosmos and everything in it, this one—being Lord of heaven and earth—does not dwell in sanctuaries made by hand; [25]Needing nothing, neither is he aided by human hands—he who gives life and breath to all things; [26]And he made every race of men out of one, to live all over the face of the earth, appointing them their epochs and setting the boundaries of their habitations, [27]So that they might seek God— though they might perhaps grope their way toward him to find him, even though he is not far from any one of us. [28]For in him we live and move and are, as indeed some of the poets among you have said: 'For we too are his offspring.'[ae] [29]So, being God's offspring, we ought not to suppose the divine to be like gold or silver or stone, a graven product of human craft and concept. [30]Thus God, having overlooked the times of ignorance, now calls aloud to all human beings everywhere to change their hearts, [31]Because he has set a day on which he will soon judge

ab. That is, "divine spirits" or "gods."

ac. The Ἄρειος πάγος (*Areios pagos*), the "Hill of Ares," "Mars Hill," an elevation west and somewhat north of the Acropolis that was often used for public assemblies.

ad. Again, the reference is to δαίμονες (*daimones*), "divine spirits" or "gods," a word that would become opprobrious in Christian usage as the gods of the nations were progressively demoted to the status of "demons."

ae. A quotation from the *Phaenomena* of the Stoic poet Aratos (c. 315–240 BC).

the inhabited world through a man whom he marked out, offering an assurance to everyone by raising him from the dead." ³²But on hearing of resurrection from the dead some scoffed; others however said, "We will listen to you again concerning this." ³³So Paul departed from their midst. ³⁴But some men stayed with him and had faith, among them Dionysius the Areopagite[af] and a woman by the name of Damaris, and others along with them.

CHAPTER EIGHTEEN

¹Thereafter, departing from Athens, he came to Corinth. ²And discovering a certain Judaean by the name of Aquila—a native of Pontus who had recently arrived from Italy with his wife Priscilla because Claudius had commanded all Judaeans to leave Rome—he approached them; ³And since he practiced the same trade he stayed with them, and they engaged in their work (for they were skilled tentmakers). ⁴And he discoursed in the synagogue on every Sabbath, and persuaded both Judaeans and Greeks. ⁵But, when both Silas and Timothy came down from Macedonia, Paul was pressed upon by the word, testifying to the Judaeans that Jesus was the Anointed. ⁶And, when they opposed and insulted him, he shook out his garments and said, "Your blood on your head; I am clean; henceforth I shall go to the gentiles." ⁷And departing from there he entered the home of a certain reverer of God[ag] by the name of Titius Justus, whose household was next door to the synagogue. ⁸And the synagogue's ruler Crispus, along with his whole household, had faith in the Lord, and many of the Corinthians listened, had faith, and were baptized. ⁹And in a vision in the night the Lord said to Paul, "Do not be afraid, but speak out and do not keep silent, ¹⁰Because I am with you, and no one shall set upon you and do you harm, for in

af. That is, a member of the Council of the Areopagus, a public juridical tribunal.

ag. That is, again, a gentile adherent of Judaism.

this city I have a good many people." ¹¹And he settled there for a year and six months, teaching God's word among them. ¹²But, when Gallio was proconsul of Achaia, the Judaeans with one accord set upon Paul and brought him to the tribunal, ¹³Saying, "This man is urging people to worship God outside the Law." ¹⁴But as Paul was about to open his mouth Gallio said to the Judaeans, "O you Judaeans! If it were actually some malfeasance or some criminal wickedness, it would be reasonable for me to bear with you; ¹⁵But if it is a question concerning a teaching and terminologies and a Law of yours, you shall deal with it yourselves; I have no intention of being a judge in these matters." ¹⁶And he expelled them from the tribunal. ¹⁷And everyone seized hold of Sosthenes, the synagogue's ruler, and thrashed him before the tribunal; but none of this was of concern to Gallio. ¹⁸And Paul, having stayed on for many days yet, took leave of the brethren and sailed off to Syria—and Priscilla and Aquila with him—having shorn his head in Cenchria (for he took a vow). ¹⁹And they went down to Ephesus, and there he left them and entered the synagogue and debated with the Judaeans. ²⁰But when they asked him to remain a while longer he refused, ²¹And took his leave, saying, "God willing, I shall return to you"; and he set sail from Ephesus, ²²And disembarking at Caesarea he went up and paid a call on the assembly, then went down to Antioch; ²³And when he had spent some time there he departed; and, passing through the Galatian region and Phrygia in an orderly sequence, he gave encouragement to all the disciples.

²⁴And a certain Judaean by the name of Apollos, Alexandrian by birth, an eloquent[ah] man with a great command of the scriptures, came to Ephesus. ²⁵This man had been instructed in the Way of the Lord and, fervent in spirit, he spoke and taught accurately about things regarding Jesus, while knowing of only the baptism of John; ²⁶And this man began boldly speaking out in the synagogue. And, on hearing him, Priscilla and Aquila took him to their place and explained the Way of God to

---

ah. Λόγιος (*logios*): "eloquent," "cultured," "learned."

him more accurately. ²⁷And, when he wished to proceed onward into Achaia, the brethren, feeling encouraged, wrote to the disciples to welcome him—who, when he got there, made a great contribution to those who by grace had come to have faith; ²⁸For he confounded the Judaeans in public debate with great rhetorical power, demonstrating through the scriptures that Jesus is the Anointed.

CHAPTER NINETEEN

¹Now while Apollos was in Corinth it happened that Paul, having traversed the upland region, came to Ephesus and found some disciples there, ²And said to them, "When you came to faith, did you receive a Holy Spirit?" And they said to him, "We have not even heard that there is a Holy Spirit." ³And he said, "Into what, then, were you baptized?" And they said, "Into John's baptism." ⁴And Paul said, "John baptized with a baptism of the heart's transformation, telling the people that they should have faith in the one coming after him—which is to say, in Jesus." ⁵And on hearing this they were baptized in the name of the Lord Jesus. ⁶And, as Paul laid hands on them, the Spirit, the Holy One, came upon them and they both spoke in tongues and prophesied. ⁷And they were about twelve men in all. ⁸And joining the synagogue he spoke boldly, discoursing upon the Kingdom of God, and persuasively, over a period of three months. ⁹But when certain persons grew obdurate and restive, maligning the Way before the main congregation, he withdrew, restricting the disciples from them, debating every day in the school[ai] of Tyrannus. ¹⁰And this continued for two years, and thus all the inhabitants of Asia, both Judaean and Greek, heard the word of the Lord. ¹¹And God, through Paul's hands, performed extraordinary deeds of power, ¹²So that kerchiefs and aprons were even brought away

---

ai. σχολή (scholē): literally, "leisure," which is to say, "those with leisure," gathering as a rule for lecture and debate in an open hall. The identity of Tyrannus is otherwise unknown; he may have been either a teacher or the patron of the hall, and so in all likelihood a pagan.

from contact with his skin and placed upon the ill and they were ridded of their diseases, and the spirits, the wicked ones, departed from them. ¹³And some among the itinerant Judaean exorcists also attempted invoking the name of the Lord over those having wicked spirits in them, saying, "I adjure you by the Jesus whom Paul proclaims." ¹⁴And there were seven sons of a certain Sceva, a Judaean chief priest, who were doing this. ¹⁵And in reply the spirit, the wicked one, said to them, "Jesus I [indeed] know of, and Paul I recognize; but who are you?" ¹⁶And the man in whom the wicked spirit dwelt leapt upon them and, overmastering them both,ᵃʲ thoroughly defeated them, so that they escaped naked and wounded. ¹⁷And this came to be known to all those living in Ephesus, Judaeans and Greeks alike, and fear descended upon all of them, and the name of the Lord Jesus came to command great force. ¹⁸And many of those who believed came forward confessing and openly acknowledging their deeds. ¹⁹And a considerable number of those practicing occult arts gathered up their books and burned them in front of everyone; they reckoned their value and found it to be five thousand silver pieces. ²⁰So the word of the Lord spread mightily and prevailed.

²¹Now, these things having been accomplished, Paul resolved in his spirit to go to Jerusalem, passing through Macedonia and Achaia, saying: "After I get there I must also see Rome." ²²And sending two of those attending him, Timothy and Erastus, into Macedonia, Paul delayed for a time in Asia. ²³Now, at about that time there arose no small turmoil in regard to the Way. ²⁴For a certain silversmith by the name of Demetrius, who fashioned silver shrines to Artemis, provided no little trade for artisans—²⁵Whom he convened, along with workers in related trades, and said, "Men, you are aware that our earnings come from this trade, ²⁶And you see and hear how this fellow Paul, not only

aj. κατακυριεύσας ἀμφοτέρων (*katakyrievsas amphoterōn*). Whether Luke really means to say "both" (either to suggest that only two of the seven brothers were present at the time or to suggest that the demoniac assaulted only two of the seven), or is instead using the word catachrestically to mean "the lot of them," is impossible to determine.

in Ephesus but in practically all of Asia, has persuaded and perverted a considerable throng, saying that they whom hands bring into being are not gods. ²⁷Now, the danger is not only that our business might come into disrepute, but that the Temple of the great goddess Artemis[ak] might be esteemed as nothing, and that it is even about to be deprived of the magnificence proper to her whom the whole of Asia and the inhabited earth adores." ²⁸And hearing this, and filled with passion, they cried out, saying, "Great is Artemis of the Ephesians!" ²⁹And the city was filled with confusion, and they rushed into the theater with one accord, clutching Gaius and Aristarchus, Paul's Macedonian traveling companions. ³⁰But when Paul wanted to go into the mob the disciples would not permit him; ³¹And even some of those Asiarchs[al] who were his friends sent him word, urging him not to present himself at the theater. ³²Various persons were shouting out different things; for the assembly[am] was in a state of confusion, and most of them had no idea for what reason they had gathered. ³³And, as the Judaeans were pushing Alexander forward, some in the crowd offered him suggestions; and Alexander, waving his hand, wanted to offer a defense before the people. ³⁴But, as they knew him to be a Judaean, a united outcry of "Great is

ak. The Artemision (Temple of Artemis) in Ephesus—here in its third and most glorious iteration—was indeed one of the ancient world's "seven wonders," and according to Antipater of Sidon the most impressive among them. The sacred site long antedated the Greco-Roman syncretism that would convert the resident "Great Goddess" or "Great Mother" of Ephesus into a special manifestation of the lunar goddess Artemis (or Diana), and so did the sacred iconography of the Temple idol that, according to Luke—but to no other extant ancient source—the Ephesians believed to have fallen from Zeus on high (see v. 35 below).

al. Perhaps these are members of the Common Assembly of Asia in Ephesus; but the word's generally attested meaning is that of priests of the imperial cult of Roma installed in Asia.

am. ἐκκλησία (ecclēsia), which would usually mean a legislative assembly, but may here refer simply to the crowd as a whole; it might also mean that an official municipal assembly was seated in the theater, or was summoned there by the public demonstration, since in v. 39 the municipal clerk uses the word again with the clear meaning of a legal deliberative body, while in v. 41 he brings the episode to an end by, it seems, an official dissolution of the session.

Artemis of the Ephesians!" rose from them for roughly two hours. [35]But when he had quieted the crowd the municipal clerk said, "Men, Ephesians, who is there among men who does not in fact know that the city is warden of the Temple of the Great Artemis, and of that which fell from Zeus? [36]These things being indisputable, then, you must be quiet and do nothing rash. [37]For you have brought here these men who are neither temple thieves nor blasphemers of your goddess. [38]If indeed Demetrius and the artisans with him have a suit against anyone, the assizes are open and there are proconsuls; let them plead their case against one another. [39]But if you seek anything further it will be resolved in the legally constituted assembly. [40]For, indeed, because of today we are in peril of being arraigned for insurrection, there being no rationale by which we shall be able to explain this mass dissension." [41]And saying this he dissolved the assembly.

CHAPTER TWENTY

[1]Now when the disturbance had ceased Paul, summoning the disciples and giving them encouragement, took his leave and departed on his journey to Macedonia. [2]And, having passed through those parts and given them many words of encouragement, he came into Greece, [3]And he made his home there for three months. When he was about to set sail for Syria, a conspiracy was formed against him by the Judaeans, and he decided to go back through Macedonia. [4]And accompanying him were Sopater the son of Pyrrhus, a Beroean; and Aristarchus and Secundus, who came from among the Thessalonikans; and Gaius, a Derbean; and Timothy; and the Asians Tychicus and Trophimus. [5]And these men, going on ahead, waited for us in Troas; [6]And after the days of Unleavened Bread we sailed away from Philippi and in five days came to them in Troas, where we stayed seven days. [7]And on the first day of the Sabbath week, as we were gathered together to break bread, Paul addressed them and—as he was about to leave the next day—continued his discourse until midnight. [8]Now there were a considerable number of lamps

in the upper room where we were assembled. ⁹And a certain young man by the name of Eutychus, sitting on the window ledge and being carried down into deep sleep as Paul's disquisition went on and on, was upended in his sleep and fell from the third floor, and was lifted up a corpse. ¹⁰But Paul went down and fell upon him and, holding him close, said, "Do not be horrified; for his soul is in him." ¹¹And, going back up and breaking bread and talking at great length until it was light, he thus departed. ¹²And they led the boy away alive, and were comforted in no small measure. ¹³And we, going on ahead to the boat, set sail for Assos, intending to collect Paul there; for so it had been arranged, as he intended to go there by foot. ¹⁴And when he met us at Assos we brought him on board and came to Mitylene; ¹⁵And sailing away from there on the following day we arrived off Chios, and on the next day crossed over to Samos, and came to Miletus on the day after that. ¹⁶For Paul had chosen to sail past Ephesus, so as not to lose time in Asia; for he was making haste to be in Jerusalem for the day of Pentecost, if it was possible for him.

¹⁷And sending word from Miletus to Ephesus he summoned the elders to the assembly. ¹⁸And when they came to him he told them, "You know that, from the first day I set foot in Asia, I was with you the entire time, ¹⁹Slaving for the Lord with all humility and with tears and with the trials befalling me on account of the intrigues of the Judaeans, ²⁰While holding back nothing of benefit to you; by preaching to you and teaching you, publically and in one house after another, ²¹I gave full testimony, to Judaeans and Greeks alike, concerning a change of the heart toward God, and concerning faith in our Lord Jesus. ²²And now look: I am going to Jerusalem, bound by the Spirit, knowing nothing of what will meet me there, ²³But only that in every city the Spirit, the Holy One, testifies to me, saying fetters and afflictions await me. ²⁴But I do not count my soul precious to me, so long as I may finish my race and the ministry to bear witness to the good tidings of God's grace that I received from the Lord Jesus. ²⁵And now look: I know that all of you, among whom I have traveled about proclaiming the Kingdom, will see my face no more. ²⁶Therefore, today I attest to you that I am clean of

everyone's blood; [27]For I did not hold back in declaring God's will to you. [28]Watch over yourselves and over all the flock, of which the Spirit, the Holy One, has set you as supervisors, to shepherd God's assembly, which he purchased by his own blood. [29]I know that after my departure baleful wolves will come in among you, and will not spare the flock, [30]And that there will arise from among you men who will say perverse things in order to drag away the disciples after themselves. [31]So take heed, remembering that for three years I did not cease admonishing each of you, night and day, with tears. [32]And now I commend you to the Lord and to the word of his grace, which has the power to establish a house and bequeath the inheritance to all who have been made holy. [33]I coveted no one's silver or gold or clothing; [34]You yourselves know that these hands have provided for my needs and for those who are with me. [35]I have revealed all to you: how, laboring in this very way, you must care for the infirm, and must remember the words of the Lord— that he said, 'It is a blissful thing to give rather than to receive.'" [36]And, having said these things, he went down on his knees and prayed with all of them. [37]And there was considerable weeping on everyone's part, and they draped themselves over Paul's neck and kissed him, [38]And their greatest suffering came from his having stated that they will see his face no more. And they escorted him to the boat.

CHAPTER TWENTY-ONE

[1]Now, having torn ourselves away from them, we at last set sail and, taking a direct course, came to Cos, and to Rhodes the next day, and to Patara from there; [2]And having found a ship making the crossing over to Phoenicia we embarked and set sail. [3]And, sighting Cyprus and keeping it off the port side, we sailed to Syria and came down to Tyre, since the ship was unloading cargo there. [4]And, finding the disciples, we remained there for seven days; and they, through the Spirit, told Paul not to go up to Jerusalem. [5]But when we completed our days there we left and went on our way, and all of them, along with their wives and

children, escorted us all the way out of the city; and, going down on our knees and praying, ⁶We exchanged our farewells with one another; then we embarked on the ship and they returned to their homes. ⁷And when we had finished our voyage from Tyre we arrived at Ptolemais and, greeting the brethren, stayed with them a single day. ⁸And setting off the next day we came to Caesarea and entered the house of the evangelist Philip, who was one of the Seven,ᵃⁿ and stayed with him. ⁹Now this man had four virgin daughters given to prophesying. ¹⁰And we remained for several days. And a certain prophet by the name of Agabus came down from Judaea, ¹¹And approached us and took Paul's cincture and, having bound his own feet and hands, said, "The Spirit, the Holy One, says these things: In Jerusalem the Judaeans will bind the man to whom this cincture belongs and hand him over to the gentiles." ¹²And, having heard this, both we and those residing there implored him not to go up to Jerusalem. ¹³Then Paul replied, "What are you doing, weeping and breaking my heart? For I am prepared not only to be bound, but even to die in Jerusalem for the name of the Lord Jesus." ¹⁴And when he was not persuaded we—having said, "Let the Lord's will be done"—fell silent.

¹⁵And, when those days had passed, we readied ourselves and went up to Jerusalem; ¹⁶And some of the disciples from Caesarea went with us as well, bringing along a certain Mnason, a Cypriot and a disciple from early on, with whom we would be able to lodge. ¹⁷And when we were in Jerusalem the brethren welcomed us joyously. ¹⁸And the next day Paul went along with us to James, and all the elders were present. ¹⁹And having greeted them he related one by one the things God had done among the gentiles through his ministry. ²⁰And hearing this they gave glory to God, but also said to him, "Brother, you see what myriads of believers there are among the Judaeans, and they are all zealous for the Law; ²¹And regarding you they have been told that you teach apostasy from Moses to all the Judaeans living among gentile peoples,

an. That is, one of the "deacons" or "ministers" chosen to serve at table so that the Apostles would be free for other things.

instructing them not to circumcise their children or to follow his customs. ²²So what to do? [A crowd will doubtless gather,] For they will at all events hear that you have come. ²³So do this, as we advise you: There are four men among us who have taken a vow; ²⁴Take these men, be purified along with them, pay for them to have the head shaved, and then everyone will know that there is nothing to the rumors as far as you are concerned, and that instead you follow and safeguard the Law as well. ²⁵And as regards the believers among the gentiles we have written to them with our decision that they should abstain from anything sacrificed to an idol, and from blood, and from anything strangled, and from whoring." ²⁶Then Paul, the next day taking the men and having been purified with them, went into the Temple and declared what the full term of the days of purification would be, at which time the offering would be made for each of them.

²⁷Now, when the seven days were nearly at an end, the Judaeans from Asia, seeing him in the Temple, roused the entire crowd and laid hands on him, ²⁸Crying out, "Men, Israelites, help! This is the man who is giving everyone everywhere teachings against the people and the Law and this place, and who has also even brought Greeks into the Temple and profaned this sacred site." ²⁹(For earlier they had seen in his company Trophimus the Ephesian, whom they assumed Paul had brought into the Temple.) ³⁰And the whole city was stirred up, and the people came running together and laid hands on Paul and dragged him outside the Temple, and the doors were immediately shut. ³¹But as they were trying to kill him word reached the chiliarch of the cohort that the whole of Jerusalem was in turmoil; ³²And he immediately took soldiers and centurions and went running down to them; and on seeing the chiliarch and soldiers they ceased battering Paul. ³³Then the chiliarch approached him and placed him under arrest and ordered him bound with two chains, and inquired, "Who might this be, and what is it he has done?" ³⁴But different members of the crowd were shouting out different things, and such was the tumult that he could discern nothing trustworthy; so he commanded that he be brought into the garri-

son. [35]And when he was on the steps he was carried by the soldiers, on account of the crowd's violence; [36]For the mass of the people was following after, crying out, "Take him away!" [37]But Paul, when about to be led into the garrison, says to the chiliarch, "Is it licit for me to say something to you?" And he said, "You know Greek? [38]Are you not the Egyptian, the one who in days past created unrest and led four thousand men from the assassins[ao] out into the desert?" [39]And Paul said, "I am actually a Judaean man, a Tarsian, a citizen of no mean city in Cilicia; and I request that you allow me to address the people." [40]And, when he gave him permission, Paul stood on the steps and beckoned to the people with his hand; and, when a great hush descended, he addressed them in the Hebrew dialect, saying,

CHAPTER TWENTY-TWO

[1]"Men, brothers and fathers, listen now to my defense before you." [2]And on hearing that he was addressing them in the Hebrew dialect they comported themselves more quietly. And he says: [3]"I am a Judaean man, having been born in Tarsus in Cilicia, but I was reared in this city; having been trained in the Law of the fathers with exacting precision at the feet of Gamaliel, I was—just as all of you are today—a zealot for God, [4]One who persecuted this Way to the death, binding and delivering men and women alike to prison: [5]As is attested for me by even the chief priest and the Council of elders as a whole, from whom I secured letters to the brethren and journeyed to Damascus, in order to bring those there to Jerusalem in chains so they could be punished. [6]But it so happened that, as I was journeying along and approaching Damascus, a great light from the sky shone about me, at about midday, [7]And I fell to the ground and heard a voice saying to me, 'Saul, Saul, why do you persecute me?' [8]And I replied, 'Who are you, Lord?' And he said to

ao. That is, violent Judaean zealots, here called *Sicarii* (dagger-bearers, assassins).

me, 'I am Jesus the Nazorean, whom you persecute.' [9]Now those who were with me did in fact see the light, but they did not hear the voice of him who was speaking to me. [10]And I said, 'What may I do, Lord?' And the Lord said to me, 'Arise and go into Damascus, and there you will be told everything that has been arranged for you to do.' [11]And, as I could not see on account of the glory of that light, I went into Damascus being led by the hand by those who were with me. [12]And a certain Ananias, a man devout in his adherence to the Law, having heard reports of me from all the Judaeans living there, [13]Came to me and stood by me and said, 'Saul, brother, look up.' And in that hour I looked up at him. [14]And he said, 'The God of our fathers foreordained you to know his will and to see the righteous one and to hear a voice from his mouth, [15]For you will be a witness for him to all men regarding the things you have seen and heard. [16]And why do you delay now? Arise, be baptized and wash away your sins, calling upon his name.' [17]And it happened that, having returned to Jerusalem and praying in the Temple, I fell into an ecstasy, [18]And I saw him speaking to me: 'Be quick and leave Jerusalem, for they will not accept your testimony concerning me.' [19]And I said, 'Lord, they are aware that throughout the synagogues I have been imprisoning and beating those who have faith in you; [20]And even when the blood of your witness Stephen was being shed I myself kept an eye on the cloaks of those who were killing him.' [21]And he said to me, 'Go, for I will send you out to nations far away.'" [22]And they listened to him as far as this statement, but then raised their voice, saying, "Rid the earth of such a man! For it is not fitting for him to live!" [23]And, as they were crying out and casting off their cloaks and throwing dust into the air, [24]The chiliarch commanded that he be led into the fort, directing that he be interrogated with scourges, so that he could properly determine for what crime they were crying out against him in this manner. [25]But, as they were stretching him out with the thongs, Paul said to the centurion standing there, "Is it legal to flog a man who is a Roman and who has not been convicted?" [26]And on hearing this the centurion approached the chiliarch, saying, "What are you about to do? For this man is a Roman." ²⁷And the chiliarch approached and said to him, "Tell me, are you a Roman?" And he said, "Yes." ²⁸And the chiliarch replied, "I purchased that citizenship at an enormous price." And Paul said, "But I in fact was born with it." ²⁹Immediately, therefore, those who had been about to interrogate him stood back; and the chiliarch, on realizing that he was a Roman and had been put in chains, also became frightened.

³⁰So the following day, wishing to ascertain what it was he was being denounced for by the Judaeans, he released him and ordered the chief priests and the whole Council to assemble; and, having led Paul in, he set him in their midst.

CHAPTER TWENTY-THREE

¹And, gazing at the Council, Paul said, "Men, brothers, up to this very day I have lived for God in all good conscience." ²And Ananias, the chief priest, ordered those standing beside him to strike his mouth. ³Then Paul said to him, "God is about to strike you, you whitewashed wall; and you sit passing judgment on me according to the Law while you, transgressing the Law, order me to be struck?" ⁴And those standing by said, "You insult the chief priest?" ⁵And Paul said, "I did not know that he is the chief priest, brothers; for it is written, you shall not speak evil of a leader of your people." ⁶And Paul, recognizing that there was one party from the Sadducees and another from the Pharisees, cried out in the Council, "Men, brothers, I am a Pharisee, a son of Pharisees, and I am on trial for hope in resurrection of the dead." ⁷And when he said this there arose a discord between Pharisees and Sadducees, and the whole assembly was divided. ⁸For the Sadducees say there is no resurrection—neither as angel nor as spirit—while the Pharisees profess both.^{ap} ⁹And a great uproar arose, and some of the scribes from

---

ap. Σαδδουκαῖοι μὲν γὰρ λέγουσιν μὴ εἶναι ἀνάστασιν μήτε ἄγγελον μήτε πνεῦμα, Φαρισαῖοι δὲ ὁμολογοῦσιν τὰ ἀμφότερα (*Saddoukaioi men gar legousin mē einai anastasin mēte angelon mēte pnevma, Pharisaioi de ^bomologousin ta amphotera*): usually translated as meaning that the Sadducees did not believe in

the Pharisees' party stood up and created strife, saying, "We find nothing evil in this man. What if a spirit spoke to him, or an angel? [Let us
not strive against God.]" ¹⁰And when a great dissension broke out the
chiliarch, fearing Paul might be torn apart by them, commanded the
soldiery to go down and seize him out of their midst and bring him to
the fort. ¹¹And, coming to him the following night, the Lord said, "Take

---

resurrection *or* in angel (s.) *or* in spirit (s.), while the Pharisees believed in "all
of these." There are both historical and grammatical grounds for doubting this
reading. The existence of a Jewish sect in the first century that did not believe in
resurrection makes perfect sense, inasmuch as the very idea of resurrection was
a fairly late aspect of Jewish thought, almost certainly imported from Persia; but
the existence of a Jewish sect that did not believe in angels and spirits is certainly
an historical impossibility (though Luke was a Greek and might not have known
this). The phrasing also somewhat discourages the conventional translation. Not
only are the words "angel" and "spirit" in the singular (which could perhaps mean
"any angel or spirit" or "angel and spirit as an abstract principle," but which would
still not be the most felicitous way of phrasing the matter in Greek), but the final
word of the sentence, ἀμφότερα (*amphotera*), really does mean "both [of two],"
and there are not many examples of Luke using Greek words catachrestically
(then again, just four chapters above, at 19:16, the text *may* misuse the same
word). Also, even though μή is sometimes paired with μήτε (in place of the
more common pairing of one μήτε with another) to mean "neither . . . nor . . . ,"
here it seems natural to read the more typical formula of "μήτε . . . μήτε . . ." as
forming a couplet distinct from the subject of the immediately preceding μή ("to
be no resurrection"), as an elucidation thereof. On the other hand, the repeated
mention of "a spirit or an angel" in the next verse may be intended to emphasize
again the difference between Pharisaic and Sadducaic beliefs, and the cause of
dissension between them. So my translation here is offered only tentatively.
Whatever the case, though, this passage may be read as reinforcing a point that
is made at several other places in the New Testament (Matthew 22:30; Mark 12:
25; Luke 20:36; 1 Corinthians 15:40-54; 1 Peter 3:18, 4:6): that those late antique
Jews and early Christians who believed in resurrection did not, as a rule, think of
it as simply the "reanimation" of—a restoration of psychē to—a "fleshly" corpse,
but saw it as an emergence into a new life beyond the fragile "animal" bond of
soul and flesh, life in a spiritual or even "angelic" form. In Hellenistic Jewish and
much early Christian usage, the word "spirits" is often used to refer to angels
and demons, as distinct from disembodied human souls, precisely because these
former are creatures who do not subsist in an "animal" or "psychical" manner,
comprising soul and flesh.

heart. For just as you bore witness to me in Jerusalem, so too must you bear witness in Rome." ¹²And when day came the Judaeans made a compact, placing themselves under bane, saying they would neither eat nor drink till they should kill Paul. ¹³And there were more than forty who took this shared oath, ¹⁴Who approached the chief priests and elders and said, "We have placed ourselves under bane, cursing ourselves to eat nothing till we should kill Paul. ¹⁵Now you, then, along with the whole Council, inform the chiliarch that he should bring him down to you because you intend to examine his case in greater exactitude; and we are prepared to kill him before he gets close." ¹⁶But Paul's sister's son, hearing of the intrigue, came and entered the fort and told Paul about it. ¹⁷And Paul summoned one of the centurions and said, "Take this young man up to the chiliarch, for he has something to report to him." ¹⁸So, taking him, he led him up to the chiliarch and says, "The prisoner Paul summoned me and asked me to bring you this young man, who has something to say to you." ¹⁹And, taking hold of his hand and retiring into private, he asked, "What have you to report to me?" ²⁰And he said, "The Judaeans have conspired to ask you whether you would bring Paul down to the Council tomorrow, as though intending to make more exact inquiries concerning him. ²¹So do not let them persuade you, for, from among those who have placed themselves under bane neither to eat nor to drink till they kill him, more than forty men are lying in wait for him, and are now ready, and are awaiting this promise from you." ²²So the chiliarch dismissed the young man, enjoining him, "Divulge to no one that you have reported these matters to me." ²³And summoning two of the centurions he said, "Get two hundred infantry and seventy cavalry and two hundred pikemen ready to go to Caesarea at the third hour of the night, ²⁴With beasts standing by as well, so that they can get Paul mounted and convey him safely to the governor Felix." ²⁵He wrote a letter of this sort: ²⁶"Claudius Lysias to his excellency, Governor Felix: Greetings. ²⁷This man having been seized by the Judaeans and about to be killed by them, I came with my soldiers and rescued him, having learned that he is a Roman; ²⁸And, wanting to understand fully for what cause they arraigned him, I took him down to their Council; ²⁹I found him to be under accusation in regard to questions of their Law, but charged with nothing meriting death or chains. ³⁰And when it was disclosed to me that there was a plot against the man I immediately sent him to you, and commanded that his accusers make their case against him before you." ³¹So the infantrymen, as they had been appointed, took Paul and led him through the night to Antipatris, ³²And the next day returned to the fort, leaving the cavalrymen to proceed onward with him—³³Who, entering Caesarea, delivered the letter to the governor and presented him with Paul. ³⁴And, having read, he asked what province he comes from and, learning it was Cilicia, ³⁵Said, "I will give you a hearing when your accusers arrive," and commanded he be kept under guard in Herod's praetorium.

CHAPTER TWENTY-FOUR

¹And after five days the chief priest Ananias came down, along with some elders and a certain trial lawyer, Tertullus, who briefed the governor against Paul. ²And, when he was called, Tertullus began to make allegations against Paul, saying, "Because of you we have enjoyed a great deal of peace, and on account of your foresight restorations of order have come to this nation, ³Which we welcome, in everything and everywhere, with all gratitude, most excellent Felix. ⁴But so as to detain you no further I beseech you, in your forbearance, to grant us a brief hearing. ⁵For we having found this man pestilential, and provoking insurrections among all the Judaeans throughout the inhabited world, and a ringleader of the heresy of the Nazoreans—⁶Who also attempted to desecrate the Temple, and whom we seized [⁷—But the chiliarch Lysias arrived in great force and conducted him out of our hands—], ⁸From whom, when you have examined him, you will be able to ascertain everything of which we accuse him." ⁹And the Judaeans joined in too, asserting that these things were true. ¹⁰And, when the governor had signaled him to speak, Paul answered, "Knowing you have been a judge of

this nation for many years, I gladly offer my apology for myself. [11]You can verify that it is no more than twelve days since I went up to Jerusalem to worship. [12]And neither in the Temple, nor in the synagogues, nor anywhere throughout the city did they find me debating or drawing a crowd; [13]Nor can they provide you evidence concerning the things they accuse me of. [14]But this I confess to you: that, in keeping with the Way—which they call a heresy—so I worship the ancestral God, believing everything in accord with the Law and written in the prophets, [15]Keeping hope in God that—as they themselves anticipate—a resurrection of both the just and the unjust is about to occur. [16]In this too I myself strive always to keep a conscience void of offense against God and human beings. [17]And after many years I came, bringing along alms to my people and offerings, [18]In the course of which—having been purified, and with neither crowd nor commotion—I was discovered in the Temple [19]By some Judaeans from Asia, who ought to be present and accuse me before you if they have anything against me. [20]Or let these men themselves tell what malfeasance they found when I stood before the Council—[21]Unless it concerns that single protest I cried out as I stood among them: 'I am being tried before you today in regard to resurrection of the dead!'" [22]But Felix, who had a fairly accurate knowledge of the Way, put them off, saying, "When the chiliarch Lysias comes down I will make my determination on your case." [23]He commanded the centurion to keep him and to allow him license, and to forbid no one among his own acquaintances to attend him. [24]And arriving after some days with his wife Drusilla, who was a Judaean woman, Felix sent for Paul and listened to him regarding faith in Jesus the Anointed. [25]And as he held forth concerning justice and temperance and the judgment about to come, Felix grew anxious and replied, "Go away for now; and later, when I find an occasion, I shall send for you." [26]At the same time, he was also hopeful that he might receive money from Paul; and so he sent for him fairly frequently and conversed with him. [27]And, when two years had elapsed, Felix was succeeded by Porcius Festus; and, wanting to appear gracious to the Judaeans, he left Paul in bondage.

CHAPTER TWENTY-FIVE

¹So Festus, having arrived in the eparchy, went after three days up to Jerusalem and Caesarea, ²And the chief priests and premier men among the Judaeans presented him with charges against Paul and entreated him, ³Asking him as a favor that he summon him to Jerusalem (plotting to kill him on the road). ⁴Festus, therefore, replied that Paul was to be held in Caesarea, and that he was himself about to depart: ⁵"So," he said, "those of you able to do so go along with me, and if there is anything amiss in the man let them accuse him." ⁶And, having stayed with them no more than eight or ten days, he went down to Caesarea, took a seat on the tribunal the following day, and commanded Paul be brought. ⁷And when he arrived the Judaeans who had come down to Jerusalem stood around, bringing numerous and grave charges against him, which they were unable to prove, ⁸While Paul offered his defense: "I have committed no sin, either against the Law of the Judaeans, or against the Temple, or against Caesar." ⁹But Festus, wishing to grant the Judaeans a favor, said in reply to Paul, "Do you want to go up to Jerusalem and be judged before me there concerning these things?" ¹⁰And Paul said, "I am standing before Caesar's tribunal, where I should be judged. I have done the Judaeans no wrong, as you are in fact very well aware. ¹¹So if I have done any wrong, and done anything deserving of death, I do not protest dying; but, if there is nothing to these things they accuse me of, no one can surrender me to them. I appeal to Caesar." ¹²Then Festus, having consulted with the Council, answered, "You have appealed to Caesar; to Caesar you shall go."

¹³And, when some days had passed, Agrippa the king and Bernice arrived in Caesarea, greeting Festus. ¹⁴And, when they had stayed there some days more, Festus laid the matter of Paul out before the king, saying, "There is a certain man whom Felix left behind in bonds, ¹⁵Concerning whom, when I came to Jerusalem, the chief priests and the elders of the Judaeans preferred charges, requesting a verdict against

him—[16]To whom I replied that it is not the custom of the Romans to hand over any man before the accused has faced his accusers and been given an occasion for a defense concerning the charge. [17]Thus, when they had come here with me, I made no delay; the next day I took a seat on the tribunal and commanded the man to be brought—[18]Concerning whom the accusers stood and charged him with none of the wicked things I anticipated, [19]But rather had certain questions for him regarding their own superstition, and about a certain Jesus who had died and whom Paul asserted to be alive. [20]And I, being at a loss regarding how to conduct an examination concerning these matters, asked if he wanted to go to Jerusalem and be judged there regarding these things. [21]But, when Paul appealed to be held over for the decision of the Augustus,[aq] I commanded he be held till I might send him to Caesar." [22]And Agrippa said to Festus, "I have been inspired also to listen to this man for myself." "Tomorrow," he says, "you will hear him." [23]So the next day, when Agrippa and Bernice came with great pomp and entered the audience chamber along with chiliarchs and the city's leading men, and when Festus had given the order, Paul was brought. [24]And Festus says, "King Agrippa, and all you men who are present here with us, you see this man concerning whom the better part of the Judaeans all petitioned me, both in Jerusalem and here, crying out that he should live no longer. [25]And I found him to have done nothing deserving of death; but when this man himself appealed to the Augustus I decided to send him— [26]Concerning whom I have nothing definite to write to the lord. Hence I have brought him out before you—and before you especially, King Agrippa—so that when there has been an examination I might have something I could write; [27]For to me it seems unreasonable, when sending a prisoner, not also to give some sign of the charges against him."

aq. ὁ Σεβαστός (*ho Sebastos*), the Greek equivalent of Augustus, which here is simply a formal title of the emperor (in this case, Nero).

CHAPTER TWENTY-SIX

¹And Agrippa said to Paul, "You may speak on your own behalf." Then, stretching forth a hand, Paul offered his defense: ²"Concerning the things of which I am accused by Judaeans, King Agrippa, I consider myself blessed in being about to offer my defense today before you, ³Especially as you are an expert regarding all of the customs and the controversies peculiar to the Judaeans; hence I beseech you, magnanimously, to listen to me. ⁴So, then, all the Judaeans know the manner of my life since youth, which from the first has been in my nation and in Jerusalem, ⁵Having known me in the past—if they are willing to attest to it—to have lived as a Pharisee from the first, according to the most exacting sect of our religion; ⁶And now I stand being judged on account of hope in the promise made to our fathers by God—⁷To which our twelve tribes hope to attain, earnestly worshipping night and day—in regard to which hope, O king, I am accused by Judaeans. ⁸Why is it judged incredible by you that God raises the dead? ⁹Thus indeed I used to think within myself that I should do many things to oppose the name of Jesus the Nazorean—¹⁰Which in fact I did in Jerusalem, and I also sealed up many of the holy ones in prisons, having received that authority from the chief priests, and I cast a vote for their execution, ¹¹And often, throughout all the synagogues, I punished them, coercing them to blaspheme, and—raging against them exorbitantly—I persecuted them all the way into foreign cities—¹²In the course of which, while journeying to Damascus with authority and a commission from the chief priests, ¹³I saw upon the road at midday, O king, a light from the sky brighter than the sun, shining around me and those journeying with me; ¹⁴And, when we had all fallen to the earth, I heard a voice saying to me in the Hebrew dialect, 'Saul, Saul, why do you persecute me? How hard for you to kick against goads.' ¹⁵And I said, 'Who are you, Lord?' And the Lord said, 'I am Jesus, whom you persecute. ¹⁶But stand on your feet; for it is for this that I have appeared to you, to ap-

point you a minister and a witness, both of the things you have seen of me and of the things I shall make appear to you, [17]Rescuing you from the people and from the gentiles, to whom I am sending you, [18]To open their eyes, to turn them away from darkness toward light, and away from the power of the Accuser toward God, that they may receive forgiveness of sins and an inheritance among those made holy by faith in me.' [19]Whereupon, King Agrippa, I was not disobedient to the heavenly vision, [20]But I exhorted first those in Damascus and in Jerusalem, as well as in all the territory of Judaea and the nations, to change their hearts and to turn to God, performing works worthy of the heart's transformation. [21]On account of these things Judaeans, having seized me in the Temple, tried to kill me. [22]Thus, having up to this day received aid from God, I stand bearing witness to small and great alike, saying nothing beyond what both the prophets and Moses said to be about to happen: [23]That the Anointed would suffer, and that he—as the first in the resurrection of the dead—is about to proclaim a light to the people and to the gentiles alike." [24]But, as he was offering these apologies, Festus says in a loud voice, "You are raving, Paul! So much learning is driving you mad!" [25]"Your excellency Festus," he says, "I am not raving, but speaking words of truth and sense. [26]For the king understands all about these things, and I speak before him with confidence; because I am convinced none of this escapes his notice, for it has not been done in a corner. [27]Do you believe the prophets, King Agrippa? I know that you believe." [28]And Agrippa to Paul: "You persuade me that in a little while you will make me a Christian." [29]And Paul: "Would to God, I pray, that—in a little while and for a great while—not only you but all those hearing me today would become even such as I am—except for these bonds." [30]Both the king and the governor rose, along with Bernice and those seated with them, [31]And went out and spoke to one another, saying: "This man is doing nothing deserving of death or fetters." [32]And Agrippa said to Festus, "This man could have been released had he not appealed to Caesar."

CHAPTER TWENTY-SEVEN

¹And when it was decided that we should sail to Italy they delivered Paul, as well as some other prisoners, to a centurion from the Augustan Cohort^{ar} by the name of Julius. ²And, embarking in a ship from Adramyttium about to launch out for ports along the coast of Asia, we set sail; with us was Aristarchus, a Macedonian from Thessalonika; ³And on the next day we landed at Sidon, and Julius treated Paul with kindness and allowed him to visit friends to get his needs provided for. ⁴And putting to sea from there we sailed alee of Cyprus, since the winds were countervailing, ⁵And sailing the open sea off the coast of Cilicia and Pamphylia we came down to Myra in Lycia. ⁶And, having there found an Alexandrian ship sailing for Italy, the centurion embarked us in it. ⁷And over several days, sailing slowly and coming off the coast of Cnidus with difficulty—inasmuch as the wind did not abate for us—we sailed alee of Crete, opposite Salmone, ⁸And sailing past it with difficulty we arrived at a certain place called Fair Havens, near which lay the city of Lasea. ⁹And when considerable time had passed, and the voyage was now perilous because the fast had gone by as well, Paul offered a warning, ¹⁰Saying to them, "Men, I see that the voyage will soon be accompanied by violence and great loss, not only for the cargo and ship, but for our souls." ¹¹But the centurion was persuaded by the pilot and the ship's master rather than by Paul's words. ¹²And, since the port was an inhospitable one for wintering in, the counsel taken by the majority was to sail on from that place, in hope of somehow reaching Phoenix—a port of Crete facing southwest and northwest—in order to winter there. ¹³And, believing they had achieved their purpose when a south wind gently blew in, they weighed anchor and sailed along the coast of Crete. ¹⁴But not much later a turbulent wind called the Nor'easter beat down ¹⁵And, the ship being taken hold of and unable to run in the face of the

ar. The Cohors Augusta ($\sigma\pi\epsilon\hat{\iota}\rho\alpha\ \sigma\epsilon\beta\alpha\sigma\tau\acute{\eta}$ [*speira sebastē*], in Greek) was principally stationed in Syria and was largely composed of Syrian recruits.

wind, we gave way and were carried along; [16]And running alee of a certain islet called Clauda we were hardly able to secure the skiff; [17]Having hoisted it, they employed stays to undergird the ship; and, fearing they might be driven into the shoals, they lowered tackle; and thus they were borne along. [18]And, as we were violently storm-wracked, the next day they jettisoned freight, [19]And on the third day they threw the ship's gear overboard with their own hands. [20]And when over the course of many days neither sun nor stars appeared, and with no small storm setting in, all hope that we might be saved was now taken away. [21]And then, when they had abstained from food for a long while, Paul stood up among them and said, "O men, you should have heeded me and not sailed to Crete, and not come to this disaster and deprivation. [22]And now I exhort you to be in good spirits: for the ship will be lost, but not one soul. [23]For there stood by me this night an angel of the God to whom I belong and whom I serve, [24]Saying, 'Do not fear, Paul; you must stand before Caesar; and see: God has given you all those who sail with you.' [25]So take heart, men; for I have faith in God that it shall be just as was told me. [26]But we shall need to run aground on some island." [27]When the fourteenth night of our being carried about the Adriatic came, the sailors came around midnight to suspect that they were approaching some country. [28]And on taking soundings they read twenty fathoms; and having moved a little further along, and taking soundings again, they read fifteen fathoms; [29]And, fearing they might at some point run upon hard reefs, they dropped four anchors astern and prayed for day to come. [30]And when the sailors sought to flee from the ship and lowered the skiff into the sea, pretending that they intended to drop anchors off the bow, [31]Paul said to the centurion and soldiers, "If these men do not remain aboard ship, you cannot be saved." [32]Then the soldiers cut off the skiff's ropes and let it fall away. [33]And, as day was about to come, Paul implored everyone to take some food, saying, "This is the fourteenth day that you have continued on without food, anxious, eating nothing. [34]So I beg you to take some food; for this is the beginning of your rescue; for no hair on the head of any of you shall perish." [35]And saying these things, and taking a loaf of bread, he gave thanks to God before them all and broke it and began to eat. ³⁶And, their spirits improving, all of them took food as well. ³⁷Now, those of us in the ship were two hundred and seventy-six souls in all. ³⁸And, when they were sated with food, they lightened the ship, jettisoning the grain into the sea. ³⁹And when day came they did not recognize the land, but they did make out a certain bay that had a strand, onto which they resolved to drive the ship if they could. ⁴⁰And, cutting loose the anchors, they abandoned them to the sea, at the same time cutting the rudder's cords and raising the foresail into the wind, and held course for the strand; ⁴¹But, entering a stretch where the two tides met, they drove the vessel on; and the prow, having run upon the bar, remained fixed, and the stern was shattered by the blast. ⁴²Now the soldiers were of a mind to kill the prisoners, so that none of them could swim off and escape; ⁴³But the centurion, determined to save Paul, forbade them their purpose, and commanded those who were able to swim to dive out and be the first to make for the land—⁴⁴And the rest either on planks or on items from the ship. And thus it happened that everyone escaped to land.

CHAPTER TWENTY-EIGHT

¹And, having been saved, we then discovered that the island is called Malta.ᵃˢ ²And the barbarians extended us extraordinary kindness; for when they had lit a fire they welcomed all of us, on account of the rain that had set in and on account of the chill. ³And when Paul had gathered a load of kindling and was placing it on the fire a viper came out of it as a result of the heat and fastened onto his hand. ⁴And when the barbarians saw the creature dangling from his hand they said to one another, "This man is surely a murderer whom—even though he was saved from the sea—Justice has not permitted to live." ⁵But, shaking the beast off into the fire, he suffered no harm; ⁶And they expected that he would

as. Μελίτη (Melitē).

soon swell up or fall down dead; but, waiting in suspense a considerable time and seeing nothing unusual happen to him, they changed their minds and said that he was a god. [7]Now, in the vicinity of that place were estates belonging to the island's chief man, Publius by name, who welcomed us in and lodged us hospitably. [8]And it so happened that Publius's father was prostrate from fevers and dysentery; Paul went in to him and, praying and placing hands on him, cured him. [9]And when this occurred the rest of those on the island who were suffering from ailments also came forward and were healed—[10]Who lavished plenteous honors on us as well, and supplied the ship with our needs when we put out to sea.

[11]And after three months we embarked on a ship that had wintered at the island: an Alexandrian craft with the Dioscuri[at] as its ensign. [12]And landing at Syracuse we remained there three days, [13]From which we tacked away and arrived at Rhegium. And, with a south wind rising after the first day, we arrived at Puteoli on the second, [14]Where we found some of the brethren and were prevailed upon to stay with them for seven days; and thus we went to Rome. [15]And from there the brethren—having heard of our affairs—came as far as Appii Forum and Tres Tabernae[au] to meet us; seeing them, Paul thanked God and became encouraged. [16]And when we came to Rome [the centurion handed over the prisoners to the garrison; but] Paul was allowed to lodge by himself, with a soldier guarding him.

[17]And it happened that, three days afterward, he summoned the leading men of the Judaeans; and, when they had gathered, he said to them, "Men, brothers, having done nothing contrary to the people or

at. That is, the Gemini or Celestial Twins, Kastor and Polydeukes (Castor and Pollux in Latin), sons of Zeus by Leda, according to the dominant legend, and brothers of Helen. The Gemini were patron protectors of travelers—sailors and seaborne travelers especially—and their cult was particularly popular in Alexandria.

au. "The Forum of Appius" and "Three Taverns" were two towns along the Appian Way, roughly forty and thirty miles from Rome, respectively.

customs of the fathers, I was delivered in bonds from Jerusalem into the hands of the Romans—¹⁸Who, having examined me, were of a mind to release me, since there was in me no guilt warranting death; ¹⁹But when the Judaeans demurred I was forced to appeal to Caesar—not that I have any charge to lay against my nation. ²⁰For this reason, therefore, I called for you, to see and speak to you; I bear this chain about me on account of the hope of Israel." ²¹And they said to him, "We have not received letters concerning you from Judaea, nor has any of the brothers come to report or speak anything wicked regarding you. ²²And we consider it worth hearing from you what you think; for what is known to us regarding this sect is that it is denounced everywhere." ²³And, arranging a day with him, they came to him in his lodgings in greater numbers, to whom he bore witness, expounding the Kingdom of God, and arguing from both the Law of Moses and the prophets, from morning to evening, to persuade them concerning Jesus. ²⁴And some were persuaded by what was said, ²⁵And others did not have faith; and they were sent away disagreeing with one another, after Paul had made one statement: "The Spirit, the Holy One, spoke well to your fathers through Isaiah the prophet, ²⁶Saying, 'Go to this people and say, "Hearing, you shall hear but most certainly not understand; and, looking, you will look but most certainly not perceive; ²⁷For this people's heart has grown obdurate, and with their ears they have listened ponderously, and they have shut their eyes: lest they should ever see with the eyes and hear with the ears and understand with the heart and turn about, and I should heal them."' ²⁸So let it be known to you that this saving thing of God's has been sent to the gentiles; and they will listen." [²⁹When he said this, the Judaeans departed, debating among themselves a great deal.]

³⁰And he remained a whole two years in his own rented lodgings and received all who came to him, ³¹Proclaiming the Kingdom of God and teaching the things concerning Jesus the Anointed, with all boldness and without hindrance.

The Letter to the Romans

BY PAUL

CHAPTER ONE

¹Paul, a slave of the Anointed One Jesus, called an Apostle, having been set apart for God's good tidings, ²Which he promised in advance through his prophets in sacred writings ³Concerning his Son—born from David's seed according to the flesh, ⁴Marked out by resurrection of the dead as God's Son in power according to a spirit of holiness—Jesus the Anointed, our Lord,[a] ⁵Through whom we have received grace

---

a. The syntax of verses 3 and 4 (the latter especially) is somewhat confusing in the Greek, though clearly Paul is attempting a parallel construction: born *from* David's seed (ἐκ σπέρματος Δαυίδ [*ek spermatos David*]) according to the flesh (κατὰ σάρκα [*kata sarka*]) yet marked out *from* resurrection of the dead (ἐξ ἀναστάσεως νεκρῶν [*ex anastaseōs nekrōn*]) according to a spirit (or Spirit) of holiness (κατὰ πνεῦμα ἁγιωσυνης [*kata pnevma ᵇagiōsynēs*]). It is not clear, however, precisely what the phrase ἐν δυνάμει (*en dynamei*) modifies or how it should be construed: Does it refer to an attribute of Christ's Sonship, to the manner in which he is marked out, or to the special power that comes from the Spirit of holiness? And is it better taken, then, as "in," or "by," or "with" power? And the phrase ἐξ ἀναστάσεως νεκρῶν (*ex anastaseōs nekrōn*) is often rendered as if we may presume an ἐκ ("out of," "from") before the νεκρῶν, which would yield the traditional construction "resurrection from the dead (pl.)"; but the literal translation is "resurrection of the dead (pl.)," and various critics have read it as meaning either that Jesus has been marked out as God's Son "by" the eschatological sign of universal resurrection, or that he has been marked "out from" the universal resurrection by being raised in the present, or that he has been marked out "since" the resurrection—and then, if the last of these, it could

287

and, for his name's sake, a mission for consent to faith among all the gentiles, ⁶Among whom you too are included, you who are called Jesus the Anointed's own—⁷To all in Rome, who are beloved of God and called to be holy: grace to you and peace, from God our Father and from Lord Jesus the Anointed.ᵇ

⁸Firstly, I give thanks to my God through Jesus the Anointed for all of you, because your faithfulness is proclaimed in all the cosmos. ⁹For God—whom I worship in my spirit, in the good tidings of his Son—is my witness to how unceasingly I remember you ¹⁰Always in my prayers, asking whether now somehow, by God's will, I might have a clear path to come to you. ¹¹For I long to come to you, that I might give you some spiritual gift so that you may be made firm—¹²That is, rather, to be comforted along with you, through one another's faith, both yours and mine. ¹³I do not want you to be ignorant, brothers, that often I have intended to come to you—and have been prevented right up to the present—so that I might gather some fruit among you too, just as among the other gentile peoples. ¹⁴Both to Greeks and to barbarians, both to sages and to fools, I am a debtor; ¹⁵So, as far as is possible for me, I am eager to proclaim the good tidings to you who are in Rome too. ¹⁶Because I am not ashamed of the good tidings; for it is the power of God for salvation to everyone having faith, to the Judaean first, then also to the Greek. ¹⁷For in it God's justice is revealed, from faith to faith, as has been written: "And the upright shall live by faithfulness."

¹⁸For God's vehemence against all the impiety and injustice of human beings, who by injustice suppress the truth, is revealed from heaven, ¹⁹Because what is known of God is manifest among them; because God made it manifest to them. ²⁰For from the creation of the cosmos his invisible things are clearly descried, understood from the things made: both his everlasting power and his deity; so they are without de-

---

mean either "since [his] resurrection [from] the dead" or "since [the general] resurrection of the dead [began with him]."

b. Or perhaps "from God, Father of us and of Lord Jesus."

fense, [21]For, knowing God, they did not give him glory and thanks as God, but instead grew inane in their reasoning, and their witless heart was darkened. [22]Having pretensions to be wise, they became imbeciles, [23]And exchanged the glory of the incorruptible God for a likeness of the image of a corruptible man, and of birds, and of quadrupeds, and of reptiles; [24]Hence God handed them over in the desire of their hearts to impurity, the disgracing of their bodies amongst themselves—[25]They who exchanged God's truth for a lie, and adored and worshipped the creation rather than the Creator who is blessed unto the ages; amen. [26]Thus God delivered them to the passions of disgrace; for even their females exchanged natural use for what is contrary to nature, [27]And the males also, in the same way, abandoning natural use with the female, burned in their longing for one another, males performing shameful acts among males, and receiving in turn within themselves the requital befitting their deviancy. [28]And, as they did not deem it worthwhile to acknowledge God, God surrendered them to a reprobate mind, to do indecent things, [29]Having been filled with every injustice, wickedness, avarice, vice; full of envy, murder, strife, deceit, boorishness; whisperers, [30]Slanderers, haters of God,[c] licentious, overweening, braggarts, contrivers of evils, defiant of parents; [31]Witless, faithless, ruthless, merciless—[32]Though knowing God's decree that those who do such things are deserving of death, they not only do them, but give approval to those engaging in these same practices.

CHAPTER TWO

[1]So you are without defense, O man—everyone who judges—for in that you judge another you condemn yourself; because you who judge engage in the same practices. [2]But we know that God's judgment on

c. θεοστυγεῖς (theostygeis): a θεοστυγής (theostygēs) (s.), originally—and technically—was someone hated by God or the gods; by the Hellenistic period, however, the term had acquired an active connotation as well and could be used as a synonym for μισόθεος (misotheos), a hater of God or the gods.

those doing such things is in accord with truth. ³And do you, O man—you who judge those doing such things while also doing them—reckon that you will escape God's judgment? ⁴Or do you disdain the abundance of his kindness and forbearance and magnanimity, ignorant that God's kindness leads you to the heart's transformation? ⁵Yet you store up indignation for yourself—in accord with your obduracy and impenitent heart—on a day of indignation and of a revelation of the just judgment of God, ⁶Who will requite everyone according to his deeds: ⁷To those who by perseverance in good work seek after glory and honor and incorruption—the life of the Age;ᵈ ⁸But to those of selfish ambition, who are also defiant of truth and yet compliant with injustice—indignation and vehemence. ⁹Distress and anguish upon the soul of everyone applying himself to what is evil—Judaean first, then Greek; ¹⁰But glory and honor and peace to everyone applying himself to what is good—Judaean first, then Greek. ¹¹For with God there is no respecting of persons. ¹²For as many as have sinned without the Law will perish without the Law; and as many as have sinned within the Law will be judged by the Law; ¹³For those who hear the Law are not upright before God; rather doers of the Law will be proved upright. ¹⁴For, whenever gentiles who do not have a law do the things of the Law by nature, they who do not have Law are a Law to themselves: ¹⁵They who exhibit the work of the Law inscribed in their hearts, their conscience also bearing witness with them, and the thoughts between one another making accusation or even offering defenseᵉ ¹⁶On the day that, according to my good tidings, God judges men's secrets through the Anointed One Jesus. ¹⁷But if you bear the name of Judaean and rely on Law and boast in God, ¹⁸And know what is willed, and attempt exceptional things, having re-

---

d. The grammar of this verse is peculiar in that all the nouns and the single modifier are in the accusative, and hence it might be natural to read "life of the Age" (ζωὴν αἰώνιον [zōēn aiōnion]) as the object of the "seeking"; the syntax, however, is roughly parallel to that of the following verse, where the two nouns at the end are in the nominative and so clearly represent God's requital of sin.

e. Paul's syntax here is less than perspicuous.

ceived instruction from the Law, [19]And having also persuaded yourself to be a guide to the blind, a light to those in darkness, [20]An instructor of the foolish, a teacher of infants, having in the Law the very shape of knowledge and of the truth . . . [21]Do you who teach another not therefore teach yourself? You who preach not to steal, do you steal? [22]You who say not to commit adultery, do you commit adultery? You who abominate idols, do you rob temples? [23]Do you who boast in the Law dishonor God by transgressing the Law? [24]For "God's name is blasphemed among the gentiles because of you," as has been written. [25]For circumcision does indeed have value if you happen to practice the Law; but if you happen to be a transgressor of the Law your circumcision has become a foreskin. [26]If, therefore, "Foreskin" keeps the just requirements of the Law, will not his foreskin be reckoned as circumcision? [27]And "Foreskin" (physically speaking), fulfilling the Law, will adjudge you—on account of scripture and circumcision—the transgressor of Law. [28]For he is not a Judaean who appears to be so, neither is circumcision something apparent in the flesh—[29]Rather, the Judaean is one in secret, and circumcision is of the heart—in spirit, not letter—whose praise is not from human beings but from God.

CHAPTER THREE

[1]What then the Judaean's advantage, or what "Circumcision's" profit? [2]A great deal, in every way! Firstly, indeed, they were entrusted with God's oracles. [3]What then? If some were unfaithful, will their infidelity annul God's fidelity? [4]Let it not be so! But let God be truthful and every man a liar, as has been written: "So that you might be vindicated in your words and may prevail when you are judged." [5]And if our injustice secures God's justice, what shall we say? That the God who enforces this indignation is unjust? (I speak in human terms.) [6]Let it not be so! Else how will God judge the cosmos? [7]Yet, if through my falsehood God's truth overflowed to his glory, why am I still also judged as a sinner? [8]And why not (as we are slandered, and as some claim we

say): "Let us do evil things that good things may come?"—on them the verdict is just . . .[f] [9]What then? Are we more excellent?[g] Not at all. For we have already charged both Judaeans and Greeks, all alike, with being under sin. [10]As has been written: "There is none just, not one; [11]There is none who understands, there is none who seeks God; [12]All turned away—together became useless; there is no one practicing kindness, there is not even one"; [13]"Their throat is an opened grave, with their tongues they worked deceit, the venom of asps behind their lips"; [14]"They whose mouth is gorged with curses and bitterness"; [15]"Swift their feet to shed blood, [16]Ruin and misery in their paths, [17]And they knew no path of peace"; [18]"There is no fear of God before their eyes." [19]And we know that the Law, whatsoever it says, speaks to those within the Law, so that every mouth may be stopped up and all the cosmos might become accountable to God. [20]For all flesh will be vindicated before him not by observances. For through Law—full knowledge of sin.

[21]But now God's justice has been manifested apart from Law, being attested by the Law and the prophets, [22]And, by the faithfulness of [Jesus] the Anointed, God's justice is for everyone [as well as upon everyone] keeping faith; for there is no distinction: [23]For all have sinned and fall short of God's glory, [24]Being made upright as a gift by his grace, through the manumission fee paid in the Anointed One, Jesus: [25]Whom God set forth as a place of atonement[h] through faith in his blood, as

f. In the Greek, the syntax of the verse is a barely distinguishable blur and might more literally be rendered as follows: "And why not as we are slandered, and as some claim we say that 'Let us do evil things that good things may come?' on whom the verdict is just[?]" Those on whom the verdict is just are, presumably, the slanderers.

g. προεχόμεθα (*proechometha*): this could mean either "do we excel over (others)?" or "are we excelled over (by others)?" Either interpretation could be defended from Paul's argument.

h. ἱλαστήριον (*hilastērion*): technically, a word that could mean either "expiation" or something "expiatory," but that in the standard Greek rendering of Hebrew scripture had the special meaning of the Mercy Seat covering the Ark of the Covenant (hence "place of atonement").

a demonstration of his justice through the dismissal of past sins [26]In God's clemency—for the demonstration of his justice in the present season—that he might be just and show him who is of Jesus's faith to be upright.[i] [27]Where, therefore, the boasting? It has been excluded. By what law? That of observances? No, rather by faith's law. [28]For we reckon a man as vindicated[j] by faithfulness, apart from observances of Law. [29]The God of Judaeans only, and not also of gentiles? Yes, of gentiles also, [30]Since the God who both vindicates[k] "Circumcision" from faith and "Foreskin" by faith is one. [31]Do we then abolish Law through faith? Let it not be so! Rather, we establish it.

CHAPTER FOUR

[1]Then what shall we say that Abraham—our forefather according to flesh—discovered? [2]For, if Abraham was vindicated by observances, he has a boast—although not before God. [3]For what does scripture say? "And Abraham had faith in God, and it was accounted to uprightness on his part." [4]But to someone who labors the reward is reckoned not according to grace but according to what is owed; to someone not laboring, however, [5]But placing faith upon him who makes the impious upright, his faithfulness is accounted to uprightness, [6]Just as David says concerning the bliss of the man for whom God takes account of uprightness apart from observances: [7]"How blissful they whose Lawless ways are excused and whose sins are covered over; [8]How blissful the man whose sin the Lord in no way takes into account." [9]Does this bliss pertain to those of the circumcision, then, or to those of the foreskin also—since we say that faithfulness was accounted to uprightness for

i. In vv. 21–26 what is rendered here by the words "righteousness" and "justice" (or by "upright" and "just") are in the Greek the same word; there is no single term in English that quite captures both dimensions of the word's meaning simultaneously. See my remarks on *dikē* and *dikaios* in my postscript.
j. Or "rectified."
k. Or "rectifies."

Abraham? [10]How then was it taken account of? When he was in circumcision or with a foreskin? Not in circumcision, but with a foreskin; [11]And he received a sign of circumcision, a seal of the uprightness of his faithfulness during the time when he had had a foreskin, so that he might be the father of all those who have faith while in possession of a foreskin, so that [this] uprightness might be accounted to them, [12]And a father of circumcision not only to those coming from circumcision, but also to those who walk in the steps of our father Abraham's faithfulness when he had a foreskin. [13]For the promise to Abraham or to his seed that he should be heir to the world came not through Law, but through the uprightness of faithfulness. [14]For, if the heirs are so by Law, faithfulness has been evacuated and the promise annulled; [15]For the Law brings wrath; but, where there is no Law, neither is there transgression. [16]Hence it is from faithfulness, and thus according to grace, so that the promise should be firm for all seed: not only for that of the Law, but for that of the faithfulness of Abraham (who is father to us all, [17]As has been written: "I have appointed you father of many nations") before him in whom he had faith—God, who gives the dead life and calls forth the things having no existence as having existence—[18]Who, against hope, placed his faith upon hope, so that he might become father of many nations, in keeping with what had been said: "Such shall be your seed."[1] [19]And, without weakening in faith, he recognized that his body had died (being about a hundred years old), and recognized the death of Sarah's womb, [20]Yet he did not falter through infidelity to God's promise, but rather was made strong by faith, giving glory to God, [21]Being fully persuaded as well that what he has promised he is also able to do. [22]Therefore it was accounted to uprightness on his part. [23]And not only in regard to him was it written that it was accounted to him, [24]But also in regard to us, to whom it is to be accounted—for those being faithful to him who has raised Jesus, our Lord, from the dead, [25]He who was de-

---

1. The syntax of vv. 14–18 possesses a tenuous coherence at best.

livered over on account of our transgressions and raised on account of our vindication.[m]

CHAPTER FIVE

[1]Having, therefore, been vindicated[n] by faithfulness, we have peace before God through our Lord Jesus the Anointed, [2]Through whom we have also gained access [by faithfulness] to this grace wherein we have stood, and boast on the hope of God's glory—[3]Though not only that: rather, we boast in afflictions, knowing that affliction brings about endurance; [4]And endurance, proven character; and proven character, hope; [5]And hope does not prove an embarrassment, because God's love has been poured out in our hearts through a Holy Spirit that has been given to us; [6]The Anointed, indeed, when we were yet weak, died in due season on behalf of the impious. [7]For rarely will one die on behalf of an upright man; or no, perhaps on behalf of a good man one does indeed risk dying; [8]But God shows his own love to us in that, while we were yet

m. ὃς παρεδόθη διὰ τὰ παραπτώματα καὶ ἠγέρθη διὰ τὴν δικαίωσιν ἡμῶν (*ʰos paredothē dia ta paraptōmata kai ēgerthē dia tēn dikaiōsin ʰēmōn*): a difficult verse. Generally, in a case like this, the word διά (*dia*)—when followed by an accusative, as it is here in both instances, in a clearly parallel construction—would be translated "because of," "on account of"; but theological tradition has been reluctant to treat the two sides of the parallel as equivalent, preferring to believe that Paul is saying in the former instance that Christ was delivered over to death "as a result of" our transgressions, but in the latter instance that Christ was raised from the dead "for the purpose of" our "justification." In English, the convenient solution is simply to translate διά as "for," which can be taken in either sense. But this obscures the problem of the original text, because this second sense of "for" does not correspond to the typical use of the word διά. It is quite possible, therefore, that Paul—unaware of the fastidious theological concerns that would be attributed to him in later centuries—meant the parallelism to be taken in what appears to be its plain sense: to wit, that the death and resurrection of Christ do full justice to both sides of our condition: his death to our transgressions, his resurrection to our faith's righteousness.

n. Or "rectified."

sinners, the Anointed died on our behalf. ⁹So much the more, therefore, shall we—having now been vindicated° by his blood—be saved
from the indignation. ¹⁰For if, being enemies, we were reconciled with
God through his Son's death, so much the more shall we—having been
reconciled—be saved through his life—¹¹Though not only that: rather,
boasting also in God through our Lord Jesus [the Anointed], through
whom we have received reconciliation.

¹²Therefore, just as sin entered into the cosmos through one man,
and death through sin, so also death pervaded all humanity, whereupon
all sinned;ᴾ ¹³For prior to the Law there was sin in the cosmos, but when

o. Or "rectified."

p. Διὰ τοῦτο ὥσπερ δι᾽ ἑνὸς ἀνθρώπου ἡ ἁμαρτία εἰς τὸν κόσμον
εἰσῆλθεν καὶ διὰ τῆς ἁμαρτίας ὁ θάνατος, καὶ οὕτως εἰς πάντας ἀνθρώπους
ὁ θάνατος διῆλθεν, ἐφ᾽ ᾧ πάντες ἥμαρτον (Dia touto ᵇōsper di᾽ ᵇenos anthrōpou
ᵇē ᵇamartias eis to kosmon eisēlthen kai dia tēs ᵇamartias ᵇo thanatos, kai ᵇoutōs eis
pantas anthrōpous ᵇo thanatos diēlthen, eph᾽ ᵇō; pantes ᵇēmarton). A fairly easy verse to
follow until one reaches the final four words, whose precise meaning is already
obscure, and whose notoriously defective rendering in the Latin Vulgate (in quo
omnes peccaverunt) constitutes one of the most consequential mistranslations in
Christian history. The phrase ἐφ᾽ ᾧ (eph᾽ ᵇō;) is not some kind of simple adverbial
formula like the διὰ τοῦτο (dia touto) ("therefore") with which the verse begins;
literally, ἐφ᾽ ᾧ means "upon which," "whereupon," but how to understand this is
a matter of some debate. Typically, as the pronoun ᾧ is dative masculine, it would
be referred back to the most immediate prior masculine noun, which in this case
is θάνατος (thanatos), "death," and would be taken to mean (correctly, I believe)
that the consequence of death spreading to all human beings is that all became
sinners. The standard Latin version of the verse makes this reading impossible,
for two reasons: first, it retains the masculine gender of the pronoun (quo) but
renders θάνατος by the feminine noun mors, thus severing any connection that
Paul might have intended between them; second, it uses the preposition in, which
when paired with the ablative means "within." Hence what became the standard
reading of the verse in much of Western theology after the late third century: "in
whom [i.e., Adam] all sinned." This is the locus classicus of the Western Christian
notion of original guilt—the idea that in some sense all human beings had sinned
in Adam, and that therefore everyone is born already damnably guilty in the eyes
of God—a logical and moral paradox that Eastern tradition was spared by its
knowledge of Greek. Paul speaks of death and sin as a kind of contagion here, a
disease with which all are born; and elsewhere he describes it as a condition like

there is no Law sin is not taken account of. [14]Yet death reigned from Adam till Moses, even over those who did not commit sin similar to the transgression of Adam, who is a figural type of the one about to come. [15]As the transgression, however, not so the grace bestowed: for if by the transgression of one the many died, so much the more did God's grace and the gift in grace of the one man Jesus the Anointed overflow to the many. [16]The gift, moreover, comes not as though through one who sins; for, from one—the verdict for condemnation; from many transgressions, however—the grace bestowed for rectification.[q] [17]For if, by the one's transgression, death reigned through the one, so much more will those receiving grace's abundance and the gift of righteousness reign in life through the one Jesus the Anointed— [18]So, then, just as by one transgression unto condemnation for all human beings, so also by one act of righteousness unto rectification of life for all human beings;[r]

---

civil enslavement to an unjust master, from which we must be "redeemed" with a manumission fee; but never as an inherited condition of criminal culpability. It has become more or less standard to render ἐφ' ᾧ as "inasmuch as" or "since," thus suggesting that death spread to all *because* all sinned. But this reading seems to make little sense: not only does it evacuate the rest of the verse of its meaning, but it is contradicted just below by v. 14, where Paul makes it clear that the universal reign of death takes in both those who have sinned and those who have not. Other interpretations take the ἐφ' ᾧ as referring back to Adam, not as in the Latin mistranslation but in the sense that all have sinned "because of" the first man; this, though, fails to honor the point Paul seems obviously to be making about the intimate connection between the disease of death and the contagion of sin (and vice versa). The most obvious and, I think, likely reading is that, in this verse, a parallelism (something for which Paul has such a marked predilection) is given in a chiastic form: just as sin entered into the cosmos and introduced death into all its members, so the contagion of death spread into the whole of humanity and introduced sin into all its members. This, as we see in Romans and elsewhere, is for Paul the very dynamism of death and sin that is reversed in Christ: by his triumphant righteousness he introduced eternal life into the cosmos, and so as that life spreads into the whole of humanity it makes all righteous (as in vv. 15–19 below, or as in 1 Corinthians 15:20–28).

q. Or "vindication."

r. This is one of those many verses in Paul more honored in the paraphrase than in the literal rendering. From the context, one can tell what he is saying:

[19]For, just as by the heedlessness of the one man the many were rendered sinners, so also by the obedience of the one the many will be rendered righteous.[s] [20]But Law was introduced in order that the transgression might abound; and, where sin was abundant, grace was superabundant, [21]In order that, just as sin reigned in death, so also grace might reign by righteousness for life in the Age through Jesus the Anointed, the Lord.

CHAPTER SIX

[1]What shall we say then? Should we persist in sin so that grace might abound? [2]Let it not be! We who have died to sin, how shall we still live in it? [3]Or are you unaware that we—as many as were baptized into the Anointed One, Jesus—were baptized into his death? [4]Thus, by baptism into death we were buried with him in order that, just as the Anointed was raised from the dead by the Father's glory, so we

---

that just as one transgression (or the transgression of one man) brought condemnation to all human beings, so by one rectifying act (or the rectifying act of one man) all human beings receive a rectification of life (meaning either a rectification of their lives or a rectification imparted by the life of the risen Christ). The actual Greek text, however, is not only so terse as to be practically a shorthand jotting, but ungrammatical as well; if anything, my translation here somewhat veils the rushed brokenness of the original. The strict proportionality of the formulation, however, is quite clear, here and in the surrounding verses: just as the first sin brought condemnation and death to *absolutely everyone*, so Christ's act of righteousness brings righteousness and life to *absolutely everyone*. Whether intentional or not, the plain meaning of the verse is that of universal condemnation annulled by universal salvation.

s. The use of the definite article here and elsewhere must be scrupulously observed, in keeping with the traditional way of formulating the distinction between the unique singular and the comprehensive plural in Greek (which a language without articles, like Latin, cannot reflect): not, that is, "one" (in the sense of "someone") and "many" (in the sense of a mere plurality of "someones"), but "*the* one" (in the sense of the unique and irreplaceable, an irreducible singular) and "*the* many" (in the sense of all and everyone, the indivisible totality of all particulars). As in the prior verse, the proportion uniting both halves of the formulation is that of the particular and the universal, both in sin and in salvation.

too might walk in newness of life. ⁵For, if we have become of a kin-dred natureᵗ in the similitude of his death, we shall at least also be of the resurrection;ᵘ ⁶Knowing this: that our old man was co-crucified, in order that the body of sin might be destroyed so that we should be enslaved to sin no longer; ⁷For the one who has died is absolved from sin. ⁸And, if we died with the Anointed, we have faith that we shall live together with him; ⁹Knowing that the Anointed, having been raised from the dead, dies no more: his death no longer dominates. ¹⁰For in that he died he died to sin once and for all; but in that he lives he lives to God. ¹¹So also we reckon ourselves to be dead to sin, yet also living for God in the Anointed One, Jesus. ¹²So do not let sin reign in our mor-tal bodies, for the purpose of obeying its lusts; ¹³Neither present your bodily members to sin as weapons of iniquity; rather, present your-selves to God as those alive from the dead, and your bodily members to God as weapons of justice, ¹⁴For sin shall not dominate; for you are not under Law, but rather under grace. ¹⁵What then? Should we sin be-cause we are not under Law but under grace? Let it not be! ¹⁶Do you not know that, to whomever you give yourselves as slaves in obedience, to him you are slaves, whether of sin for the sake of death, or of obedience for the sake of uprightness? ¹⁷But grace be to God that you were slaves to sin, but that you were obedient from the heart to the pattern of the teaching to which you had been entrusted. ¹⁸And having been liberated from sin you were enslaved to righteousness. ¹⁹I speak in human terms on account of the frailty of your flesh; for, just as you presented your bodily members as slaves to impurity and lawlessness for lawlessness' sake, so now present your bodily members as slaves of righteousness for the sake of sanctification. ²⁰For when you were slaves of sin you were

---

t. Or "planted together," "grown together."

u. Paul's Greek so condenses the consequent second half (the apodosis) of this verse that its correspondence to the conditional first half (the protasis) becomes extremely grammatically elliptical. He means, it seems obvious, that "if we have become of kindred nature in the image of his death, we shall at least also be [of kindred nature in the image] of [his] resurrection."

free from righteousness. ²¹So what fruition did you have back then? Over which things are you now ashamed? For the end of those things is death. ²²Yet now, having been liberated from sin and enslaved to God, you have your fruition, for the sake of sanctification, and the end is life in the Age. ²³For sin's wages are death; but God's bestowal of grace is the life of the Age in the Anointed, Jesus our Lord.

CHAPTER SEVEN

¹Or are you unaware, brothers—for I speak to those knowing the Law—that the Law dominates the man for whatever time he lives; ²For the wife who is subject to a husband has been bound by Law to the living man;ᵛ but if the husband dies she has been released from the husband's Law. ³Hence, if she takes up company with another man while the husband is alive, she will be styled an adulteress; but if the husband dies she is free from the Law, so that in having taken up company with another man she is not an adulteress. ⁴Thus, my brothers, you too were made dead to the Law through the body of the Anointed so that you might come to be with another, the one who has been raised from the dead in order that we might bear fruit for God. ⁵For when we were in the flesh the passions of sin, which came through the Law, acted in our bodily members for the purpose of bearing fruit for death; ⁶But now we have been released from the Law, having died wherein we were imprisoned, so that we slave in newness of spirit and not in scripture's obsolescence.

v. In this and the following verse, the word translated variously as "wife" and "woman" is γυνή (gynē), while that translated as either "husband" or "man" is ἀνήρ (anēr); in the ancient world, full adulthood and the married state were very nearly interchangeable concepts, especially for women, as, to a great degree, were the concepts of marriage and sexual union. The word ὕπανδρος (ʰypandros) can be rendered "married," but its literal meaning is "under a husband" or "under a man."

⁷So what shall we say? The Law is sin? Let it not be! Rather, I did not know sin except through Law; for I did not even know about covetousness except that the Law said, "You shall not covet." ⁸But sin was seizing an opportunity through the commandment, for apart from the Law sin is dead. ⁹Now, once I was alive apart from Law; but when the commandment came sin sprang to life ¹⁰And I died; and the Law that is for life—this I found to be for death; ¹¹For sin, seizing the opportunity through the commandment, thereby deceived and killed me. ¹²Thus the Law is holy; and the commandment is holy and just and good. ¹³So the good became death for me? Let it not be so! Rather, sin, so that it might be made manifest as sin, was bringing me death through the good, so that through the commandment sin might become sinful to the point of excess. ¹⁴For we know that the Law is spiritual, but I am fleshly, having been sold in subjection to sin. ¹⁵Because I do not know what it is that I accomplish; because what I wish, this I do not do; instead, what I hate, this I do. ¹⁶But so long as I do not do this, what I wish, I am in agreement with the Law—that it is good. ¹⁷But now no longer am I at work, but rather the sin that dwells within me. ¹⁸For I know that in me—that is, in my flesh—dwells nothing good; for it is present in me to will, but not to accomplish, the good; ¹⁹For I do not do the good I wish; instead, the evil I do not wish, this I do. ²⁰But if what I do not wish, this I do, then no longer am I operating, but rather the sin that dwells within me. ²¹Thus I discover the law that, when I am desirous of doing the good, ²²The evil presents itself to me. For I delight in God's Law according to the inner man, ²³But I see a different law in my bodily members warring against the Law of my mind and taking me captive by the law of sin that is in my members. ²⁴I am a man in torment—who will deliver me from the body of this death? ²⁵Grace to God through Jesus the Anointed, our Lord. So then I myself am a slave in mind to God's Law, and yet in flesh to the law of sin.

CHAPTER EIGHT

¹So now: no condemnation for those in the Anointed One, Jesus. ²For the law of the spirit of life in the Anointed One Jesus freed you from the law of sin and death. ³For the thing that is impossible for the Law, in which it was weak on account of the flesh—God, having sent his own Son in a semblance of the flesh of sin, also (as regards sin) condemned sin in the flesh, ⁴In order that the Law's just ordinance might be fulfilled in us who walk not according to the flesh but according to spirit. ⁵For those who exist according to flesh incline the mind to the things of the flesh; but those according to spirit, the things of the spirit. ⁶For the mental inclination of the flesh is death; but the mental inclination of the spirit is life and peace; ⁷Hence the mental inclination of the flesh is enmity to God; for it is not subordinated to the Law of God, nor indeed can it be; ⁸For those existing in flesh cannot be pleasing to God. ⁹But you are not in flesh, but rather in spirit, since God's Spirit dwells in you. But if one does not have the Spirit of the Anointed, this one is not his. ¹⁰But, if the Anointed is in you, the body is dead on account of sin, and yet the spiritʷ is life on account of uprightness. ¹¹But if the Spirit of the one who has raised Jesus from the dead dwells in you, he who raised the Anointed One Jesus from the dead will also make your mortal bodies live through the indwelling of his Spirit in you.

¹²So then, brothers, we are indebted to the flesh, to live according to flesh. ¹³For if you live according to the flesh, you are about to die; but, if you put the deeds of the body to death by spirit, you will live. ¹⁴For as many as are led by God's Spirit, these are God's sons. ¹⁵For you did not receive again a spirit of slavery to fear, but rather received a spirit of adoption in which we cry, "Abba, Father!" ¹⁶The Spirit itself testifies along with our spirit that we are God's children. ¹⁷And, if children, heirs as well; on the one hand, God's heirs and, on the other, co-heirs of the Anointed, since we co-suffer in order that we may be co-glorified.

w. Or "Spirit."

¹⁸For I reckon the sufferings of the present time to be of no worth before the coming glory that will be revealed to us. ¹⁹For the earnest expectation of creation anxiously awaits the revelation of the sons of God. ²⁰For creation was made subordinate to pointlessness, not willingly but because of the one who subordinated it, in the hope ²¹That creation itself will also be liberated from decay into the freedom of the glory of God's children. ²²For we know that all creation groans together and labors together in birth pangs, up to this moment; ²³Not only this, but even we ourselves, having the firstfruits of the spirit, groan within ourselves as well, anxiously awaiting adoption, emancipation of our body. ²⁴For in hope we have been saved, but a hope seen is not hope; for why hope for what one sees? ²⁵But, if we hope for what we do not see, we anticipate by perseverance. ²⁶And likewise the spirit also gives us aid in our infirmity; for we do not know what we ought to pray for, but the spirit itself makes intercession with unutterable groans, ²⁷And he who searches out the heart knows what the spirit's mind is, for in accord with God it makes intercession on behalf of the holy ones. ²⁸And we know that, for those loving God, all things work together for good to those called according to a purpose. ²⁹Because those he knew in advance he then[x] marked out in advance as being in conformity[y] to the image of his Son, so that he might be firstborn among many brothers;[z] ³⁰And those he marked out in advance, these he then called; those he called, these he

x. καί (*kai*) (here and in the rest of vv. 29–30): "also," "even"; but, in a consecutive series or consequent construction, properly read as indicating sequence: "then . . . and then . . ."

y. Generally interpreted as "to be conformed to," a reading that much theological tradition has ratified; but, if this is Paul's meaning, he has somewhat too hastily elided a preposition, or verb, or both; as it stands, the phrase seems equally well (or more naturally) to mean that those whom God foreknew he then marked out as persons already conformed or conformable to the image of his Son. Much depends upon whether the prior "delineation" or "demarcation" of this conformity is understood as determining it or merely setting it apart.

z. Compare 1 Peter 1:1–2.

then proved righteous;[aa] and those he proved righteous, these he then glorified. [31]What then shall we say about these things? If God is for us, who is against us? He who did not even spare his own Son, [32]But rather delivered him over on behalf of all of us, how shall he not grace us with all things along with him? [33]Who will make an accusation against God's chosen ones? God is the one who vindicates: [34]Who is the one who condemns? The Anointed One, Jesus? He who has died — or, rather, he who was raised? Who is at God's right hand? Who also intercedes for us? [35]Who will separate us from the love of the Anointed? Affliction or anguish or persecution or famine or nakedness or peril or the sword? [36]As has been written: "For your sake we are being put to death all day long, we were reckoned as sheep for slaughter." [37]Rather, in all these things we more than conquer through the one who has loved us. [38]For I have been persuaded that neither death nor life nor angels nor Archons[ab] nor things present nor things imminent nor Powers, [39]Nor height nor depth nor any other creature will be able to separate us from the love of God that is in the Anointed, Jesus our Lord.

aa. Or "made righteous," in both instances.

ab. ἀρχαί (*archai*): "rulers," "principalities," "archons," perhaps "archangels"; the reference is not to earthly rulers but to celestial spirits or angelic beings governing the nations, in whom most of the peoples of late antiquity believed in one form or another, and who were quite prominent in Jewish apocalyptic tradition (influenced by Persian thought). The same is true almost certainly of the δύναμεις (*dynameis*), "Powers" also mentioned in this verse (in some manuscripts directly following ἀρχαί). Here, moreover, the text is full of associations with the complicated angelology and demonology of late antique Judaism and Christianity, dependent to a large degree on such intertestamental texts as 1 Enoch and the book of Jubilees. One should not assume, incidentally, that these superterrestrial powers were understood *simply* as fallen beings; elsewhere in Paul's thought (Galatians 3:19 in particular) there seems to be a mention of angels who function as deputies of God, and yet perhaps do so ineptly or recalcitrantly; and there is even a suggestion (not necessarily intended as irony) that an angel might deliver a false gospel (Galatians 1:8). Moreover, central to Paul's eschatology is the certainty that in the Age to come creation will be freed from subjection to all celestial powers and ruled solely by Christ and, through Christ, the Father (see, especially, 1 Corinthians 15:24–28).

CHAPTER NINE

¹In the Anointed, I speak truth, I do not lie, my conscience testifying along with me in a holy spirit ²That I harbor immense sorrow and unceasing pain in my heart; ³For I have been praying that I myself be something accursed by the Anointed for the sake of my brothers, my kindred according to flesh, ⁴They who are Israelites: theirs the filial adoption and the glory and the covenants and the Lawgiving and the worship and the promises, ⁵Theirs the fathers, and from them— according to the flesh—the Anointed; blessed unto the ages the God over all things, amen.ᵃᶜ ⁶Not, of course, that God's word has proved ineffectual. For not all of those who come from Israel are Israel, ⁷Nor are all of them children because they are Abraham's seed. Rather: "Through Isaac will seed be named for you." ⁸That is: not the children of the flesh, these children of God; rather, the children of the promise are reckoned as seed. ⁹For this is the word of promise: "I will come in due time, and there will be a son for Sarah." ¹⁰And not only this, but Rebecca also, having conceived by one man, our father Isaac—¹¹For they, not yet having been born, or having engaged in any good or bad

---

ac. A verse whose syntax and uncertain punctuation make it liable to a variety of interpretations. It can be read, as it is here, as if the "Anointed" comes at the end of a sentence or clause, followed by a doxology. Or it could be read: "the Anointed, who is God over all things, blessed unto the ages, amen." Or (though less plausibly), "the Anointed, over all things; blessed be God unto the ages, amen." Or (less plausibly still), if a scribal error transformed the plural genitive pronoun ὧν (*ʰōn*) ("of whom") into the present participle ὢν (*ōn*) ("being"), the last phrase may complete the list of Israel's special prerogatives begun in v. 4: "theirs the God over all things, blessed unto the ages, amen." Theological tradition favors the first of these alternate renderings; but, though Paul in Philippians speaks of Christ's equality with God, and though Christ's divinity is obviously indubitable for him, he nowhere else speaks of Christ simply as ὁ θεός (*ʰo theos*), "God" specified by the definite article, which it seems likely was for him (as for most of his contemporaries) a privileged name for the Father. Moreover, the concluding "amen" seems to indicate a doxological, not a predicative, formulation.

practices, so that God's purpose in electing might remain, [12]Coming not from observances but from the one calling—it was told her, "The greater shall be slave to the lesser"; [13]Just as has been written, "Jacob I loved, but Esau I hated."

[14]What then shall we say? Is there injustice with God? Let it not be so! [15]For he tells Moses, "I will have mercy on whomever I have mercy, and I will pity whomever I pity." [16]So, then—neither of the one willing nor of the one running, but of the God showing mercy. [17]For scripture says to Pharaoh, "For this very thing I raised you forth, so that in you I might display my power, and so that my name might be proclaimed abroad in all the earth." [18]So, then, he has mercy on whom he wishes, and hardens whom he will. [19]So you will say to me, "Why does he still assign blame? For who has thwarted his purpose?" [20]But no, O man, who are you who argue against God? Will the thing molded say to the molder, "Why did you make me thus?" [21]Or does the potter not have the power to make from the same mass of clay both the vessel for honor and the one for dishonor? [22]And what if God, though disposed[ad] to display his indignation and make known what is possible for him, tolerated with enormous magnanimity vessels of indignation, suitable for destruction, [23]In order that he might also make known the wealth of

---

ad. θέλων (thelōn), "wishing," "intending": the present participle here taken as a "participle of concession," which both the syntax and the logic of Paul's argument make the most plausible reading. Hence, the verse should be translated as if Paul were asking not whether God perhaps wished to display his indignation, and *therefore* prepared vessels of wrath, but rather whether God, *although* inclined to show his indignation against sin, *nevertheless* tolerates vessels suitable for destruction, so that he will instead be able to display his mercy when the time comes for raising up vessels of mercy to fulfill his purposes. The other reading is often abetted by taking the past participle κατηρτισμένα (katērtismena), which modifies "vessels of indignation," as meaning "prepared" or "fashioned" *for the purpose of* destruction, as though equivalent to something like προκατασκευαστά (prokataskevasta), "fashioned in advance [for]"; but really it should probably be taken here as "suited to," "perfect for," "fit for." In a sense, however, as this whole passage is conditional in form, and is finally negated as a counterfactual below in 11:32, perhaps it is not a matter of crucial moment exactly how one reads it.

his glory upon vessels of mercy that he had already prepared for glory, [24]Whom—us—he called not only from the Judaeans but from the gentiles as well? [25]As he also says to Hosea, "I will call the people not mine 'my people,' and her who is not loved 'Beloved'"; [26]And, "It shall be in the place where it was said [to them], 'You are not a people of mine': there they will be called sons of a living God." [27]But, on Israel's behalf, Isaiah cries, "Though the number of Israel's sons be as the sands of the sea, the remainder will be saved. [28]For the Lord will execute a decree, completing it and abbreviating it [—in justice, because a decree abbreviated—] upon the earth." [29]And just as Isaiah has previously said, "Had not the Lord Sabaoth left us a seed, we should have become as Sodom and been made like Gomorrah."

[30]What then shall we say? That gentiles, not chasing after righteousness, seized hold of righteousness—albeit a righteousness coming from faithfulness—[31]While Israel, chasing after a Law of righteousness, failed to catch up to the Law? [32]Why? Because not out of faithfulness, but rather out of observances, they stumbled over the "stone of stumbling," [33]Just as has been written, "See: I set in Zion a stone of stumbling and a rock for faltering, and whoever has faith on him will not be put to shame."

CHAPTER TEN

[1]Brothers, my heart's fond desire[ae] and prayer to God on their behalf is for salvation. [2]For I testify of them that they have a zeal for God, but not according to knowledge; [3]For, not knowing God's justice and seeking to set up their own, they did not become subject to God's justice. [4]Because the end of the Law is the Anointed, for the purpose of uprightness for everyone having faith. [5]For Moses writes of the Law's

---

ae. εὐδοκία (*evdokia*): "good pleasure," "good will," "delight," here (as in a few Septuagintal usages) meaning "fond desire," "a thing dearly wished" (as, of course, the phrase "good pleasure" once meant in English).

uprightness that: "The man who does these things will live by them."
⁶But the uprightness coming from faithfulness speaks thus: "Do not say in your heart, 'Who will ascend into heaven?'"—that is, to bring the Anointed down—⁷"Or, 'Who will descend into the abyss?'"—that is, to bring the Anointed up from the dead. ⁸What does it say, rather? "The utterance is near you, in your mouth and in your heart"—that is, the utterance of the faith that we proclaim. ⁹Because, if you confess with your mouth, "Jesus is Lord,"ᵃᶠ and have faith in your heart that God raised him from the dead, you shall be saved. ¹⁰For one has faith in the heart for uprightness and confesses with the mouth for salvation. ¹¹For the scripture says, "No one who has faith in him will be put to shame." ¹²For there is no distinction between Judaean and Greek. For the same one is Lord of all, with riches for all who call on him. ¹³For "Everyone who invokes the name of the Lord shall be saved." ¹⁴How may they invoke one in whom they did not have faith? And how may they have faith in one of whom they have not heard? And how may they hear apart from someone proclaiming? ¹⁵And how may they proclaim unless they were sent forth? Just as has been written: "How lovely the feet of those [announcing glad tidings of peace and] proclaiming glad tidings of good things." ¹⁶But not all heeded the good tidings. For Isaiah says, "Who had faith in our report?"ᵃᵍ ¹⁷So, faith is from hearing, and hearing is by the utterance of the Anointed. ¹⁸But I say, "Did they not hear?" No indeed: "Their speech went out to all the earth, and their utterances to the ends of the inhabited world." ¹⁹But I say, "Did Israel not know?" First, Moses says, "I will provoke you to envy against a non-nation, I will provoke you to anger against a witless nation." ²⁰And Isaiah grows bold and says, "I was found by those not seeking me, I became manifest

af. Or "confess the Lord Jesus."
ag. ἀκοή (akoē) can mean both a "spoken report" and an "act of hearing," and Paul uses the same word in both v. 16 and v. 17 (which might just as well be rendered ". . . faith is from a report . . ."). The word is echoed by the verb ὑπακούω (ʰypakouō) ("heed," "obey," "submit to what is said and heard") in v. 16.

to those not asking after me." ²¹And to Israel he says, "The whole day long, I stretch out my hands to an intractable and gainsaying people."

<h3 style="text-align:center">CHAPTER ELEVEN</h3>

¹Therefore I say, "Did God reject his people?" Let it not be so! For I too am an Israelite, of Abraham's seed, of the tribe of Benjamin. ²God did not reject his people, whom he knew in advance. Or do you not know what scripture says regarding Elijah, how he made a plea with God against Israel? ³"Lord, they killed your prophets and razed your altars to the ground, and I was left behind alone and they seek my soul." ⁴Yet what does the divine oracle tell him? "I reserved seven thousand men for myself, those who did not bend the knee to Baal." ⁵So, then, in the present time too a remnant has arisen according to the election of grace. ⁶And if by grace, then no longer from observances, since grace were then no longer grace. [And if from observances, it is no longer grace, since then observance were observance no longer.] ⁷What then? The mark Israel aims at, this it did not hit, but "Election" did hit it; and the rest were hardened. ⁸As has been written, "God gave them a spirit of stupor, eyes that do not see, and ears that do not hear"—right up to the present day. ⁹And David says, "Let their table come to serve as a snare and as a net and as a stumbling-block and as retribution for them, ¹⁰Let their unseeing eyes be darkened, and their back forever bent down."

¹¹So I say: Did they stumble that they might fall? Let it not be so! Rather, through their error comes salvation for the gentiles, so as to provoke them to envy. ¹²But if their error is enrichment for the cosmos and their discomfiture enrichment for the gentiles, how much more so the full totalityᵃʰ of them? ¹³But I speak to you, the gentiles: insofar as I am indeed Apostle of the gentiles, I extol my ministry, ¹⁴In case I might somehow provoke my flesh to envy and might save some of them.

ah. πλήρωμα (*plērōma*): "plenitude," "full number," "entirety," "whole complement," "totality."

¹⁵For if their rejection is reconciliation for the cosmos, what is their acceptance except life from the dead? ¹⁶And if the firstfruits is holy, the whole mass of dough is too; and if the root is holy, the branches are too. ¹⁷But if some of the branches were broken off and you, being wild olive, were grafted in among them and became a partaker in the richness of the olive-tree's root, ¹⁸Do not exult over the branches; rather, if you do exult, you do not support the root, but rather the root you. ¹⁹Therefore you will say, "Branches were broken off that I might be grafted in." ²⁰Fair enough. They were broken off by faithlessness and you have stayed in place by faithfulness. Do not be haughtily minded, but fearful. ²¹For if God did not spare the natural branches, neither will he spare you. ²²See, then, God's kindness and severity: severity upon those who have fallen, but God's kindness upon you if you abide in that kindness; otherwise you too will be cut off. ²³And they too, if they do not persist in faithlessness, will be grafted in; for God is able to graft them in again. ²⁴For if you were cut from an olive wild by nature and, contrary to nature, grafted into a cultivated olive, how much rather will these, in keeping with nature, be grafted into their own proper tree. ²⁵For I do not want you, brothers, to be ignorant of this mystery, lest you be arrogant in yourselves: that a hardness has come upon one part of Israel until the full totality[ai] of the gentiles enter in, ²⁶And thus all of Israel shall be saved, just as has been written, "The one who delivers will come out of Zion, he will turn away impiety from Jacob, ²⁷And this is the covenant on my part with them, when I take away their sins. ²⁸On your account, as regards the good tidings, they are enemies; and yet, on account of the fathers, as regards election, they are beloved. ²⁹For God's bestowals of grace and vocation are not subject to a change of heart. ³⁰For, even as you once did not trust in God but have now received mercy through their mistrust, ³¹So they now also have not trusted, to the end that, by the mercy shown you, they now also might receive

---

ai. Again, πλήρωμα (plērōma): "the total number," "the entirety."

mercy. [32]For God shut up everyone in obstinacy so that he might show mercy to everyone.[aj]

[33]O the depth of God's richness and wisdom and knowledge! How inscrutable his judgments and untraceable his paths! [34]For "Who has known the Lord's mind? Or who has become a counselor to him?" [35]Who has given him anything in the past and will have it repaid him? [36]Because from him and through him and to him is everything; to him the glory, unto the ages, amen.

CHAPTER TWELVE

[1]Therefore I implore you, brothers, by God's mercies, to present your bodies as a living, holy, acceptable sacrifice to God, your rational worship; [2]And do not be configured to this age, but be transformed by renewal of the intellect, so you may test the will of God, which is good and acceptable and perfect.

[3]For, by the grace given me, I say to everyone among you not to be more haughtily minded than your thinking ought to be, but rather let your thinking conduce to sober-mindedness, as God has apportioned a measure of faithfulness to each. [4]For, just as we have many members in one body, yet the members do not all have the same function, [5]So we who are many constitute one body in the Anointed, and are mem-

---

aj. This is the conclusion to the question of 9:14 above, which prompts the long, difficult series of reflections that end here, and which is posed in its most troubling conditional form at 9:22 (*what if* those who have erred or stumbled are merely vessels of wrath, whose only function is to provide a contrast to vessels of mercy?). At 11:11, however, Paul affirms that those not elected for service on the basis of divine foreknowledge, though they have stumbled, nevertheless will never fall; and at 11:12 and 25 he affirms that the estrangement of the elect and "those who stumble" is a temporary providential arrangement that allows the "full totality" of Jews and gentiles alike to enter in; and here, finally, he affirms that there is then no actual distinction of vessels of wrath from vessels of mercy: rather, *all* are bound in sin and *all* will receive mercy.

bers each one of one another; [6]And having different gracious gifts, according to the grace given us: if prophecy, according to the proportion of faithfulness; [7]If service, in serving; if a teacher, in teaching; [8]If one who exhorts, in exhortation; one who distributes, in liberality; one who directs, in diligence; one who engages in acts of mercy, in joyousness. [9]Love is without dissemblance. Abhorring wickedness, clinging to the good, [10]Devoted to one another in brotherly love, giving preference of honor to one another, [11]Not slothful in zeal, fervent in spirit, slaving for the Lord, [12]Rejoicing in hope, enduring in affliction, persevering in prayer, [13]Providing for the needs of the holy ones, pursuing hospitality—[14]Bless those who persecute, bless and do not curse—[15]To rejoice with those rejoicing, to weep with those weeping—[16]Being of the same mind toward one another, not loftily minded, but instead associating with the lowly—do not fancy yourselves sages—[17]Repaying no one evil for evil, providing things in good countenance with all human beings. [18]If possible for you, be at peace with all human beings. [19]Do not exact justice for yourselves, beloved, but yield place before anger; for it has been written, "'The exacting of justice is mine, I will requite,' says the Lord." [20]But rather, "If your enemy hungers, feed him; if he thirsts, give him drink; for in doing this you will heap coals of fire on his head." [21]Do not be vanquished by evil, but vanquish the evil with the good.

CHAPTER THIRTEEN

[1]Let every soul be subordinate to higher authorities. For there is no authority except under God, and such as exist are subordinated to God. [2]So he who opposes authority has opposed God's ordination; and those who have made opposition will invite a verdict upon themselves. [3]For the rulers are a terror not for the good deed, but for the evil. Do you wish not to dread authority, then? Do what is good, and you will receive its praise; [4]For it is God's servant to you for the good. If, however, you do evil, be afraid; for not without a purpose does it carry around a short-sword. For it is God's servant, exacting justice against the prac-

titioner of evil, on account of outrage. ⁵So, to become subordinate is a necessity, not only on account of outrage, but on account of conscience as well. ⁶So, then, pay taxes also: For they who attend constantly to this very matter are God's ministers. ⁷Render to everyone the things owed: to whom tax, tax; to whom dues, dues; to whom reverence, reverence; to whom honor, honor. ⁸Owe nothing to anyone, except to love one another; for whoever loves the other fulfills the Law. ⁹For "You shall not commit adultery," "You shall not murder," "You shall not steal," "You shall not covet," along with every other commandment whatsoever, are summed up in this saying: "Love your neighbor as yourself." ¹⁰Love does not work evil against the neighbor; hence love is the full totality[ak] of the Law. ¹¹—This, moreover, knowing the time: Now is the hour for you to be roused from sleep, for our salvation is nearer now than when we came to faith. ¹²The night is far advanced, and the day has drawn near. So let us cast away the deeds of the darkness and don the armaments of the light. ¹³Let us walk becomingly, as in daylight, not in revels and inebriations, not in copulations and debaucheries, not in strife and envy; ¹⁴Rather, array yourselves in the Lord Jesus the Anointed, and take no forethought for the lusts of the flesh.

CHAPTER FOURTEEN

¹Now welcome the one who is weak in faith, not in order to reach verdicts on disputes. ²One man believes in eating all things, while one who is weak eats vegetables. ³Let not the one who eats hold the one who does not eat in disdain, and let not the one who does not eat judge the one who does eat. ⁴Who are you to judge another's house-servant? He stands or falls by his own lord; and he shall stand because that lord is able to make him stand. ⁵One man esteems one day above another day, but another esteems every day; let each be fully convinced in his own mind. ⁶Whoever is mindful of the day minds it for the Lord's sake; [and

---

ak. πλήρωμα (plērōma).

whoever is not mindful of the day is unmindful of it for the Lord's sake;] [7]For none of us lives for himself, and none dies for himself; [8]For if we live we live for the Lord; or if we die we die for the Lord. So, whether we live or die, we are the Lord's. [9]For to this end the Anointed died and lived, that he might be Lord of both dead and living, [10]And why do you judge your brother? Or, indeed, why do you hold your brother in contempt? For we shall all stand before God's judgment seat. [11]For it has been written, "'As I live,' says the Lord, 'every knee shall bow to me, and every tongue shall joyfully praise[al] God.'" [12]Therefore each of us will give an account of himself [to God].

[13]So let us no longer judge one another, but let us arrive at this judgment instead: to place before the brother no stumbling-block, or a snare that causes one to trip. [14]I know and have been persuaded by the Lord that nothing is profane in itself except to the one who reckons something to be profane—it is profane for him. [15]For, if your brother is caused distress on account of food, then you are no longer proceeding in accord with love. [16]So do not let the good be blasphemed by you. [17]For the Kingdom of God is not eating and drinking, but rather justice and peace and joy in a holy spirit; [18]For the one who slaves for the Anointed in this is delightful to God and approved of by human beings. [19]Let us therefore pursue the things belonging to peace and the things belonging to mutual edification. [20]Do not ruin the work of God for the sake of food. Indeed, all things are pure; yet for the one who eats it is something evil because a stumbling-block—[21]A good thing neither to eat meat nor to drink wine, nor anything upon which your brother stumbles [or is caused to fall or is weakened]. [22]The belief you hold to for yourself, hold it before God. How blissful he who does not judge himself by what he approves of. [23]But the one who has doubt has been

---

al. ἐξομολογήσεται (*exomologēsetai*): the verb ἐξομολογέομαι (*exomologeomai*) means "confess openly," "acknowledge," with the additional connotation (especially in biblical Greek, as here in Paul's use of the Septuagintal text of Isaiah 45:23) of "praise gladly," "give fullest thanks," "joyfully proclaim."

judged, whether he eats or not, because it is not out of faithfulness; and everything that is not out of faithfulness is sin.

[1]Now we who are able ought to give support to the infirmities of those who are incapable, and not please ourselves. [2]Let each of us please his neighbor for the sake of what is good, for edification; [3]For even the Anointed did not please himself; rather, as has been written, "The reproaches of those reproaching you fell upon me." [4]For whatever things were written in the past were written for our instruction, so that we might have hope through endurance and through the scriptures' consolations. [5]And may the God of endurance and consolation grant that you be of the same mind one with another, according to the Anointed One Jesus, [6]In order that, in sameness of feeling, you might glorify the God and Father of our Lord Jesus the Anointed with a single mouth.

[7]For this reason, welcome one another, just as the Anointed One welcomed us also, for the glory of God. [8]For I say that the Anointed became "Circumcision's" servant on behalf of God's truth, for the purpose of confirming the promises of the fathers, [9]And so that the gentiles might glorify God on mercy's account, as has been written: "I will therefore joyfully praise you among the gentiles, and will sing psalms to your name." [10]And again it says, "Rejoice, gentiles, with his people." [11]And again: "Praise the Lord, all the gentiles, and let all peoples sing him praises." [12]And again Isaiah says, "There will be Jesse's root, and one rising up to rule gentiles; on him the gentiles will hope." [13]And may the God of hope fill you with all joy and peace in hope by the power of a Holy Spirit.

[14]But concerning you I have been persuaded, my brothers—even I myself—that you, having been filled with all knowledge, are yourselves replete with goodness also, and are able to admonish one another. [15]And I have written in part more boldly so as to give a reminder to you, by the grace granted me by God, [16]So that I might be a minister of

the Anointed One Jesus to the gentiles, making the sacrifice of God's good tidings, so that the offering up of the gentiles might be acceptable, having been consecrated by a Holy Spirit. [17]I have, therefore, a boast in the Anointed One Jesus regarding the things pertaining to God. [18]For I shall not dare to speak of things not accomplished by the Anointed through me for the gentiles' submission in word and deed, [19]By power of signs and wonders, by power of [God's] Spirit; thus I have fulfilled the good tidings of the Anointed, from Jerusalem and in a circuit as far as Illyricum, [20]Thus earnestly striving to announce the good tidings where the Anointed has not been called by name, so that I should not build upon another's foundation, [21]But rather, as has been written, "They, to whom nothing concerning him was announced, shall see; and they who have not heard shall understand"; [22]For which reason I have been hindered so many times from coming to you; [23]But now, having nowhere left in these regions, and for several years having had a longing to visit you, [24][I shall come to you] whenever I journey to Spain; for I hope to look upon you as I pass through, and there to be sent onward by you, if I might be replenished by you first. [25]But for now I am journeying to Jerusalem, ministering to the holy ones, [26]For Macedonia and Achaia thought it good to make some communal contribution[am] for the destitute among the holy ones in Jerusalem. [27]For they thought it good, and they are indebted to them; for, if the gentiles have shared in their spiritual things, they are obliged to minister to them in fleshly things. [28]Having finished this, then, and having delivered them these fruits under seal, [29]I shall depart for Spain by way of you; and I know that, in coming to you, I shall come in the fullness of the blessing of the Anointed. [30]Now I implore you, [brothers,] through our Lord Jesus the Anointed and through the Spirit's love, to strive along with me in prayers to God on my behalf, [31]So that I might be delivered from those

am. κοινωνία (koinōnia): literally, "communion," "commonality," "common sharing"; here and in 2 Corinthians 9:13, Paul uses the word to mean a charitable donation from one Christian assembly to another, in a way that seems to invoke the apostolic church's community of goods described in the book of Acts.

in Judaea who are distrustful, and my ministry to Jerusalem might be acceptable to the holy ones, [32]In order that, coming to you in joy by God's will, I might rest with you. [33]And the God of peace be with all of you; amen.

CHAPTER SIXTEEN

[1]Now I commend to you our sister Phoebe, who is [also] a minister[an] of the assembly in Cenchrae, [2]So that you may welcome her in the Lord in a way worthy of the holy ones, and may assist her regarding whatever thing she may need from you; for she has been a protectress[ao] of many, myself included.

[3]Give greetings to Prisca and Aquila—my fellow laborers in the Anointed One Jesus, [4]Who risked their own neck on my behalf, to whom not only I, but all the assemblies of the gentiles also, give thanks— [5]As well as to the assembly at their home. Greet my beloved Epenetus, Asia's firstfruits for the Anointed. [6]Greet Mary, who has undertaken many labors for you. [7]Greet my kinsfolk and fellow prisoners Andronicus and Junia,[ap] who are especially notable among the Apostles, and

an. διάκονος (*diakonos*): "servant," "minister," "attendant," "deacon."

ao. προστάτις (*prostatis*): "protectress," "champion," "leader," "someone at the forefront."

ap. Ἰουνιᾶν (*Iounian*), the accusative form of the name Junia, of whom nothing is known beyond this passing reference, but whose sex was uncontentiously acknowledged throughout the patristic period (tradition assumed that Andronicus and Junia were husband and wife). John Chrysostom, for instance, opined that Junia must have been a woman of superlative wisdom, inasmuch as Paul accords her the title Apostle. In later centuries, however, some anxiety was occasioned by that title being attached to a woman; and, in projecting later, more rigidly precise understandings of apostolate and episcopacy back upon Paul, some writers started claiming that the reference was actually to a man named Junias or Julias (supposedly a diminutive of Julianus). As far as we can tell, the first to make this argument was Giles of Rome (c. 1243–1316), who probably knew no Greek; but the argument remains popular to this day among those eager to make the church safe for misogyny. It can safely be dismissed as nonsense, however, inasmuch as there is no instance anywhere in the vast literary remains

who were in the Anointed before I was. [8]Greet my beloved Ampliatus in the Lord. [9]Greet Urbanus, our fellow laborer in the Anointed, and my beloved Stachys. [10]Greet Apelles, proved in the Anointed. Greet those coming from Aristobulus's household. [11]Greet my kinsman Herodotus. Greet those from Narcissus's household who are in the Lord. [12]Greet Tryphaena and Tryphosa, who labor strenuously in the Lord. Greet beloved Persis, she who has undertaken many labors in the Lord. [13]Greet Rufus, chosen by the Lord, and also his mother and mine. [14]Greet Asyncritus, Phlegon, Hermes, Patrobas, Hermas, and the brothers along with them. [15]Greet Philologus and Julia, Nereus and his sister, and Olympas, and all the holy ones along with them. [16]Greet one another with a holy kiss. All the assemblies of the Anointed greet you.

[17]I implore you, brothers, watch out for those who create divisions and stumbling-blocks opposed to the teaching you have learned, and avoid them; [18]For men of that sort do not slave for our Lord the Anointed, but rather for their own guts, and by blandishments and flatteries deceive the hearts of the guileless. [19]For your submission has gone abroad to everyone; so I rejoice over you, but I wish you to be wise in respect of what is good, but guileless in respect of what is evil. [20]And the God of peace will soon crush the Accuser beneath your feet. The grace of our Lord Jesus be with you.

[21]Timothy, my fellow laborer, greets you, as do Lucius and Jason and my kinsman Sosipater. [22](I, Tertius, who am writing out this letter in the Lord, greet you.) [23]Gaius, host to me and to the whole assembly, greets you. Erastus the city's treasurer greets you, and also brother Quartus.[aq]

[[24]The grace of our Lord Jesus the Anointed be with all of you; amen.]

---

of antiquity, or of any period within the Greek or Latin tongues, of Junias as a masculine name. Junia the Apostle was a woman.

aq. The most trustworthy manuscripts end the letter here, and most scholars regard the verses that follow (in part because of certain linguistic anomalies) as later additions.

[²⁵Now to him who is able to establish you firmly in accord with my good tidings and the proclamation of Jesus the Anointed, according to a revelation of the mystery held in silence through time's ages,ᵃʳ ²⁶But now made manifest by prophetic scriptures and by the ordination of the God of the ages,ᵃˢ made known to all the gentiles for the purpose of the submission of faith, ²⁷God alone wise, through Jesus the Anointed—to him be the glory, unto the ages. Amen.]

ar. "Aeonian times." The phrase χρόνοις αἰωνίοις (*chronois aiōniois*) could mean "during times ages past" or "during times ages long."

as. "The aeonian God."

The First Letter to the Corinthians

———

BY PAUL

¹Paul, by the will of God called Apostle of the Anointed One Jesus, and brother Sosthenes, ²To God's assembly that is in Corinth, to those sanctified by the Anointed One Jesus, called holy ones, along with all of those who in every place call upon the name of Jesus our Lord—theirs and ours: ³Grace to you and peace from God our Father and Lord Jesus the Anointed.

⁴I give God thanks always concerning you for the grace of God given you in the Anointed One Jesus, ⁵Because you have been enriched in everything by him, in all discourse and all knowledge, ⁶Just as the testimony of the Anointed was confirmed in you, ⁷So that you should not be wanting in any gracious gift, waiting upon the revelation of our Lord Jesus the Anointed, ⁸Who will also, on the day of our Lord Jesus [the Anointed], confirm you as blameless till the end. ⁹God is faithful, by whom we were called into communion with his Son Jesus the Anointed, our Lord.

¹⁰Now, brothers, I implore you by the name of our Lord Jesus the Anointed that you all profess the same thing, and that there be no schisms among you, but that you might be joined together, in the same mind and of the same purpose. ¹¹For concerning you, my brothers, it

has been disclosed to me by Chloe's people that there are dissensions among you. [12]Now I say this: that each of you says either "I am of Paul" or "I am of Apollos" or "I am of Cephas" or "I am of the Anointed." [13]Is the Anointed portioned out? Was Paul crucified on your behalf, or were you baptized in Paul's name? [14]I give thanks that I baptized none of you except Crispus and Gaius, [15]So that no one may say that you were baptized in my name. [16]And I also baptized the household of Stephanas; beyond that, I do not know if I baptized anyone else. [17]For the Anointed gave me a mission not to baptize, but rather to proclaim the good tidings—not in sophisticated speech, lest the cross of the Anointed be made void.

[18]For the word of the cross is folly to those who are perishing, while to those who are being saved it is God's power for us. [19]For it has been written: "I will bring ruin to the wisdom of the wise, and the cleverness of the clever I will thwart." [20]Where is the wise man? Where the scribe? Where the dialectician of this age? Has not God made foolish the wisdom of the cosmos? [21]For since, in God's wisdom, the cosmos did not know God by wisdom, God thought it well to save the faithful by the foolishness of a proclamation. [22]Since Judaeans ask for signs while Greeks seek wisdom, [23]And we proclaim the crucified Anointed One—both a stumbling-block to Judaeans and a folly to the gentiles, [24]But to those who are called, Judaeans and Greeks alike, the Anointed One, God's power and God's wisdom. [25]Because God's foolish thing is wiser than human beings, and God's weak thing stronger than human beings. [26]For look at your vocation: that not many are wise according to flesh, not many powerful, not many well-born; [27]Rather, God chose the foolish things of the cosmos in order that he might shame the wise, and God chose the weak things of the cosmos in order that he might shame the mighty, [28]And God chose the lowborn things of the cosmos and the things treated as nothing, the things that have no being, in order that he might nullify the things that do have being, [29]So that no flesh at all might boast before God. [30]And you are his in the Anointed One Jesus, who for us became wisdom from God, uprightness and sanctification

and the fee for emancipation, ³¹So that, as has been written, "Let the one who boasts boast in the Lord."

CHAPTER TWO

¹And on coming to you, brothers, I came announcing God's testimony to you not according to some preeminent discourse or wisdom.^a ²For I decided when among you to know of nothing except Jesus the Anointed, and him crucified. ³And I came to be with you in frailty and in fear and in considerable trembling, ⁴And with my speech and my proclamation not in persuasive words of wisdom, but rather in a demonstration of spirit and of power, ⁵So that your faith might be not in men's wisdom but rather in God's power.

⁶But we speak wisdom among the perfected, though not wisdom of this age or of this age's Archons, who have been brought to nothing; ⁷Rather, we speak of God's wisdom in a mystery, which has been hidden away, which God has marked out in advance for our glory before the ages, ⁸Which none of this age's Archons knew; for had they known they would not have crucified the Lord of glory; ⁹Rather, as has been written, "Things that eye has not seen and that ear has not heard and that have not risen up upon the heart of a human being, whatsoever God has prepared for those who love him." ¹⁰For God has given us revelation by the Spirit; for the Spirit searches all things, even the depths of God. ¹¹For who knows the things of men except the man's spirit, which is within him? So also no one has known the things of God except the Spirit of God. ¹²And we received not the spirit of the cosmos, but rather the Spirit that is from God, so that we might know the things graciously given us by God. ¹³Which things we also speak not in words taught from human wisdom, but rather in those taught by a Spirit, combining

---

a. καθ' ὑπεροχὴν λόγου ἢ σοφίας (*kath' ʰyperochēn logou ē sophias*): or "vaunting" or "masterfully persuasive" language or wisdom, of the sort practiced by Sophists or masters of rhetoric.

things spiritual with things spiritual. [14]But a Psychical man[b] does not receive the things of God's Spirit; for to him it is folly, and he is unable to know them, since they are discerned spiritually. [15]The Spiritual man,[c] moreover, discerns all things, yet is discerned by no one. [16]"For who has known the mind of the Lord, who will give him instruction?" And we have the mind of the Anointed.

CHAPTER THREE

[1]And I was able to speak to you, brothers, not as to Spiritual men but rather as to fleshly men, as to infants in the Anointed. [2]I gave you milk to drink, not food; for you were not capable then. But neither now are you [yet] able, [3]For you are still fleshly. For, wherever there is jealousy and strife among you, are you not fleshly and proceeding in a human manner? [4]For whenever someone says, "I am Paul's" while another says, "I am Apollos's," are you not being human beings? [5]So what is Apollos? And what is Paul? Servants through whom you came to faith, even as the Lord gave it to each. [6]I planted, Apollos watered, but God caused the growth. [7]Hence neither the one planting nor the one watering is anything, but rather the God causing the growth. [8]Now he who plants and he who waters are one, and each will receive his own reward, in keeping with his own labor. [9]For we are God's fellow workers;[d]

b. ψυχικός (*psychikos*): here is the first appearance of an antithesis, crucial to Paul's larger argument, especially in chapter fifteen, between "psychical" life (which comes from *psychē* or, in Latin, *anima*: hence also "animate" or "animal" life) and "pneumatic" or "spiritual" life (which is of a radically different nature).

c. πνευματικός (*pnevmatikos*): not "spiritual" in the vague sense in which we use that term, but referring to a special condition—and perhaps special status within the early church—probably that of someone filled with and transformed by God's Spirit, and so living according to *pnevma* rather than *psychē*.

d. συνεργοί (*synergoi*): This distinctively Pauline teaching of a "synergism" between God and humans, and of a final trial by fire of the works thus produced, leading either to condign rewards or to salvation by way of that purging fire (vv. 10–17 below), is the fullest picture provided in Paul's writings of the criteria and nature of eschatological judgment.

you are God's tilth, God's building. [10]According to the grace of God given to me, I laid a foundation like a wise master builder; but another builds upon it. But let each one be vigilant of how he builds. [11]For no one can lay another foundation beside the one laid down, which is Jesus the Anointed. [12]Now, if on this foundation one erects gold, silver, precious stones, woods, hay, straw, [13]Each one's work will become manifest; for the Day will declare it, because it is revealed by fire, and the fire will prove what kind of work each person's is. [14]If the work that someone has built endures, he will receive a reward; [15]If anyone's work should be burned away, he will suffer loss, yet he shall be saved, though so as by fire. [16]Do you not know that you are God's Temple and that God's Spirit dwells within you? [17]If anyone ruins God's Temple, God will bring him to ruin; for God's Temple—which you are—is holy.

[18]Let no one deceive himself: If anyone among you thinks to be a wise man in this age, let him become foolish in order to become wise. [19]For the wisdom of this cosmos is folly before God. For it has been written, "He catches the wise in their craftiness." [20]And again: "The Lord knows the ponderings of the wise, that they are vapid." [21]Hence let no one boast in human beings; for all things are yours, [22]Whether Paul or Apollos or Cephas or cosmos or life or death or things past or things imminent—all yours—[23]And you the Anointed's, and the Anointed God's.

CHAPTER FOUR

[1]So let a man account us servants of the Anointed and stewards of God's mysteries. [2]Here, moreover, it is required that among stewards one be found faithful. [3]And for me it is a very small thing that I am judged by you, or subject to a human day;[e] but I do not judge myself. [4]For I am conscious of nothing against myself; yet not by this have I been shown to be righteous; rather, the one judging me is the Lord. [5]So

e. A human day of judgment, that is.

then do not judge anything before the proper time, till the Lord come, he who will both shed light upon the things that are hidden and make the counsels of hearts manifest; and then the praise will come to each from God.

⁶Now, brothers, for your sake I have reshaped these matters in the direction of myself and of Apollos, in order that in us you may learn not to vaunt beyond what has been written, so that no one, on one man's behalf, bluster at another. ⁷For who regards you as exceptional? And what do you have that you did not receive? And, if in fact you received it, why did you boast like someone not receiving it? ⁸Now you are surfeited; now you have been made rich; without us, you reigned—and a profitable thing indeed that you reigned, so that we also might reign with you. ⁹For I think God has demonstrated that we Apostles are the very last, doomed to death, because we became a spectacle to the cosmos, to men and angels alike. ¹⁰We are fools for the Anointed's sake, but in the Anointed you are sages; we are weak, but you are mighty; you are admired, but we are without honors. ¹¹Right up to the present hour we hunger and thirst, and are denuded and buffeted about and have no place of rest, ¹²And labor on, working with our own hands; when reviled, we bless; when persecuted, we endure; ¹³When slandered, we politely entreat. We have become like the refuse of the cosmos, like the scurf of all things, right up till now.

¹⁴I write these things not to make you abashed, but rather as though admonishing my beloved children. ¹⁵For although in the Anointed you have ten thousand schoolboys' chaperons, yet you do not have many fathers; for in the Anointed, by the good tidings, I sired you. ¹⁶Therefore I implore you, become my imitators. ¹⁷For this very reason I have sent you Timothy, who is my beloved and faithful child in the Lord, who will in the Anointed One [Jesus] remind you of my ways, just as I teach them everywhere in every assembly. ¹⁸Now some have been blustering as though I might not be coming to you; ¹⁹But I shall come to you shortly, if the Lord wills, and will ascertain not what the blusterers say, but instead what their power is. ²⁰For the Kingdom of God is not

in speech, but rather in power. [21]Which do you want? That I come to you with a rod, or in love and a spirit of gentleness?

CHAPTER FIVE

[1]It is generally reported that there is whorishness among you, and whorishness of a kind not found among the gentiles—such as a certain man taking his father's wife. [2]But you are huffish, and not instead mournful, so that the one committing this deed might be removed from among you; [3]For I indeed, being absent in body but present in spirit, have already judged the one who brought this about, just as though I were present: [4]When you and my spirit have assembled in the Lord's name with the power of our Lord Jesus, [5]To deliver such a man to the Accuser[f] for destruction of the flesh, so that the spirit might be saved on the day of the Lord. [6]Your boasting is not a seemly thing. Do you not know that a little leaven leavens the whole batch of dough? [7]Purge away the old leaven, so that you might be a new batch, just as though you are unleavened. For indeed the Anointed, our Passover, has been sacrificed. [8]So let us keep the feast not with the old leaven or with a leaven of evil and wickedness, but with unleavened loaves of unmixed purity and of truth. [9]I wrote to you in a letter not to associate with the whorish[g]—[10]Not entirely meaning with the whorish of this cosmos—or with the acquisitive and rapacious, or idolaters, since you ought to go out from the cosmos. [11]But now I have written to you that, if anyone bearing the name of brother is a whoring or acquisitive man, or an idolater, or vituperative, or a drunkard, or rapacious, not to keep his company—not to eat with such a man. [12]For what is it for me to pass judgment on outsiders? Do you not judge insiders? [13]But God will judge the outsiders. "Expel the wicked man from your midst."

f. "The Satan," which is to say, "prosecutor," "accuser," "arraigner."
g. πόρνοις (*pornois*): a *pornos* was often a catamite, or boy prostitute, but here Paul is clearly using the term to mean anyone guilty of sexual wantonness.

CHAPTER SIX

[1]Does anyone among you who has a case against another dare to be judged before the unjust, and not before the holy ones? [2]Or do you not know that the holy ones will judge the cosmos? And, if the cosmos is judged by you, are you not worthy to pass judgment in minimal matters? [3]Do you not know that you will judge angels, to say nothing of the things of this life? [4]So, if indeed you obtain court adjudications on this life's affairs, do you install on the bench those who have no standing in the assembly? [5]Shame on you, I say. Is there then not one wise man among you—not one—who will be able to reach a decision upon his brother in your midst? [6]Instead, a brother obtains judgment over against a brother—and this before unbelievers? [7]In fact, then, it is already a total defeat on your part that you have lawsuits with one another. Why not instead suffer injustice? Why not instead be deprived? [8]Rather, you practice injustice and you deprive, and you do this to brothers. [9]Or do you not know that the unjust will not inherit God's Kingdom? Do not be led astray. Neither the whoring, nor idolaters, nor adulterers, nor feckless sensualists,[h] nor men who couple with catamites,[i] [10]Nor thieves, nor the acquisitive, nor drunkards, nor

h. μαλακοί (*malakoi*). A man who is *malakos* is either "soft"—in any number of opprobrious senses: self-indulgent, dainty, cowardly, luxuriant, morally or physically weak—or "gentle"—in various largely benign senses: delicate, mild, congenial. Some translators of the New Testament take it here to mean the passive partner in male homoerotic acts, but that is an unwarranted supposition.

i. ἀρσενοκοῖται (*arsenokoitai*). Precisely what an *arsenokoitēs* is has long been a matter of speculation and argument. Literally, it means a man who "beds"—that is, "couples with"—"males." But there is no evidence of its use before Paul's text. There is one known instance in the sixth century AD of penance being prescribed for a man who commits *arsenokoiteia* upon his wife (sodomy, presumably), but that does not tell with certainty how the word was used in the first century (if indeed it was used by anyone before Paul). It would not mean "homosexual" in the modern sense of a person of a specific erotic disposition, for the simple reason that the ancient world possessed no comparable concept of a specifically homoerotic sexual identity; it would refer to a particular sexual behavior, but

the vituperative, nor the rapacious will inherit God's Kingdom. [11]And some of you were these very things; yet you were washed—yet you were made holy—yet you were made upright in the name of the Lord Jesus the Anointed and by the Spirit of our God.

[12]All things are lawful to me—but not all are beneficial. All things are lawful to me—but I will not be overpowered by any of them. [13]Foods for the stomach and the stomach for foods—but the Lord will reduce both it and them to nothing. And the body is not for whoring but for the Lord, and the Lord for the body; [14]And God raised the Lord and will also raise us by his power. [15]Do you not know that your bodies are the Anointed's members? Shall I then take the Anointed's members and make them a prostitute's members? Let it not be! [16]Or do you not know that the man joined to a prostitute is one body? "For the two," he says, "will become one flesh." [17]And the one joined to the Lord is one spirit. [18]Flee from prostitution. Every sort of sin is external to the body; but the one who whores sins against his own body. [19]Or do you not know that your body is a temple of the Holy Spirit within you, which you have from God, and that you are not your own? [20]For you were bought at a price, so glorify God in your body.

CHAPTER SEVEN

[1]Now, concerning those matters of which you wrote: It is a good thing for a man not to touch a woman; [2]But, on account of prostitution, let each man have a woman of his own, and let each woman have a man

---

we cannot say exactly which one. The Clementine Vulgate interprets the word *arsenokoitai* as referring to users of male concubines; Luther's German Bible interprets it as referring to paedophiles; and a great many versions of the New Testament interpret it as meaning "sodomites." My guess at the proper connotation of the word is based simply upon the reality that in the first century the most common and readily available form of male homoerotic sexual activity was a master's or patron's exploitation of young male slaves.

of her own.ʲ ³Let the man render to the woman what is owed, and likewise also the woman to the man. ⁴The wife does not exercise authority over her own body, but rather the husband; and likewise too the husband does not exercise authority over his own body, but rather the wife. ⁵Do not deprive one another, except by common consent for an appropriate period, so that you might have leisure for prayer, and then come together again so that the Accuser might not test you through [your] incontinency. ⁶Now I say this as a lenient concession, not as an ordinance. ⁷I want all human beings to be just like me; but each has his own gracious gift from God: one thus, another thus.

⁸Now, to the unmarried and the widows I say: good for them if they also remain as I am; ⁹But, if they cannot remain continent, let them marry; for it is better to marry than to be afire. ¹⁰And regarding the married, I enjoin—or, rather, not I, but the Lord—a woman not to be separated from her husband ¹¹(Though, if she is in fact separated, let her either remain unmarried or reconcile with her husband), and a man not to divorce his wife. ¹²And to the rest I say—I, not the Lord—if any brother has an unbelieving wife, and she consents to live with him, let him not divorce her; ¹³And if any woman has an unbelieving husband, and he consents to live with her, let her not leave the man. ¹⁴For the unbelieving husband has been made holy by the wife, and the unbelieving wife has been made holy by the brother; else your children are impure—yet they are now holy. ¹⁵But, if the unbeliever separates, let the separation happen; in such circumstances, the brother or the sister is not enslaved; for God has called you in peace. ¹⁶For how do you know, woman, whether you will save the man? Or how do you know, man, whether you will save the woman?

¹⁷Only as the Lord has apportioned it to each one, as God has called each one, so let one walk. And thus I ordain in all the assemblies. ¹⁸Let

j. Again, the words for "man" and "woman" are the same as those for "husband" and "wife."

no one who was circumcised when he was called have it covered over by stretching;[k] let no one who had a foreskin when he was called be circumcised. [19]The circumcision is nothing, the foreskin is nothing—but rather keeping God's commandments. [20]Each one in the calling by which he was called, let him abide therein. [21]If a slave when called, do not accustom yourself to it; rather, if you can indeed become free, make the most of it. [22]For the slave who has been called in the Lord is the Lord's freeman; likewise, the freeman who has been called is the Anointed's slave. [23]You were purchased at a price; do not become slaves of human beings. [24]Each whereby he was called, brothers, therein let him abide by God's side.[l]

k. A painful operation undergone by some Hellenized Jews who wanted to hide their circumcision (which was apparently regarded as an unseemly form of self-exposure) so that they could participate in nude athletic contests, public exercise, or public bathing.

l. Vv. 20–24 are usually read as continuing the preceding verses' theme of remaining in the condition one was in (either circumcised or uncircumcised) when called by God, rather than as describing the new situation that makes circumcision or uncircumcision a matter of indifference. Thus, in v. 20, the phrase ἐν τῇ κλήσει ᾗ ἐκλήθη ... μενέτω (en tē; klēsei [b]ē; ... menetō), which means "let him remain ... in the calling by"—or "in"—"which he was called," is taken as meaning that one should remain in the social station one occupied *before* being called by God, rather than (as I have taken it) that one should now live according to the divine calling *by which* one was called. Similarly, in v. 21, the phrase μή σοι μελέτω (mē soi meletō) is usually taken as meaning simply that the slave should not "care about"—fret or concern himself over—his slavery; but the verb typically means "care" more in the sense of "exercise," "apply oneself to," "become practiced at," "become accustomed to" (which is how I read it). Moreover, the rest of the verse is usually read as a counterfactual or hypothetical parenthesis, ending with an admittedly obscure injunction (μᾶλλον χρῆσαι [mallon chrēsai]: "make more use" or "rather, use [it]"), rather than as the completion of the positive instruction of the verse's first part; thus it is often taken to mean something like either "make yourself even more useful when free" or even "rather than become free, work harder as a slave." Then v. 22 is taken not as an explanation of why Christians are beyond mastery and slavery, but of why masters and slaves need not be concerned over their relative stations in the unredeemed world. But then the final injunction of v. 23 must be read as either a strange non sequitur or a singularly feeble admonition against emotional or spiritual subservience. My

²⁵Now, concerning the virgins, I have no ordinance from the Lord, but I offer an opinion as someone who has received from the Lord the mercy to be faithful. ²⁶This, then, I suppose to be a good thing on account of present necessity: that it is good for a man to be as is. ²⁷Have you been bound to a wife? Do not seek divorce. Have you been divorced from a wife? Do not seek a wife. ²⁸But if you do indeed marry you do not sin, and if the virgin marries she has not sinned; but such persons will have great affliction in the flesh, and I am sparing you. ²⁹But I say this, brothers: The time has been made short; so that, henceforth, even those who have wives might be like those having none, ³⁰And those who weep like those not weeping, and those who rejoice like those not rejoicing, and those who buy like those possessing nothing, ³¹And those who make use of the cosmos like those who do not exploit it; for the frame of the cosmos is passing away. ³²But I want you to be free from care. The unmarried man cares about the Lord's things: how he might please the Lord. ³³But the married man cares about the things of the cosmos: how he might please his wife. ³⁴And he is torn. And the unmarried woman or the virgin cares about the Lord's things, in order that she might be holy in both body and spirit; but she who is married cares about the things of the cosmos: how she may please her husband. ³⁵But I say this for your convenience: not in order to throw a halter over you, but for the purpose of what is seemly, and for the purpose of unwavering attendance upon the Lord without distraction. ³⁶But, if someone is considering behaving in an unseemly manner toward his virgin, if she is past pubescence and it ought to happen, let him do what he wills; he is not sinning, let him marry.ᵐ ³⁷But he who stands firm in his heart,

rendering of these verses is based on the assumption that they unfold a continuous line of reasoning about the new reality in which Christians are called to live—a line of reasoning echoed in Paul's letter to Philemon, enjoining the latter to welcome his former slave Onesimus no longer as a slave, but as a brother.

m. This verse is a thicket of grammatical and syntactical ambiguities. It is not certain whether the adjective ὑπέρακμος (hyperakmos) refers to the virgin or her potential husband, as its gender is indeterminate. Nor is it certain that it means "post-pubescent," rather than "past her [or his] youth," or "sexually mature";

having no necessity, but who has authority concerning his own will and has reached this decision in his own heart to keep his virgin, will do well. [38]Thus he who marries his virgin does well, and he who does not marry does better. [39]A wife has been bound for however long a time her husband lives; but, if the husband is laid to rest, she is free to be married to whomever she wants, so long as it is in the Lord. [40]But she is more blessed, in my opinion, if she remains as is; and I also think I have God's Spirit.

CHAPTER EIGHT

[1]Now, as regards sacrifices to idols, we know that we all possess knowledge. Knowledge inflates, but love builds; [2]If someone thinks he has known something, he has not yet known as he ought to know; [3]But if anyone loves God, this one is known by him. [4]As regards eating from sacrifices made to idols, we know that an idol within the cosmos is nothing, and that none is God except the One. [5]For even though there are those who are called gods, whether in heaven or on earth (as indeed there are many gods and many lords), [6]Yet for us there is one God, the Father—out of whom come all things, and we for him—and one Lord, Jesus the Anointed—through whom come all things, and we through him.[n]

---

some interpreters even take it to mean a state of being erotically excitable. Nor, indeed, is it certain that the phrase I have rendered as "it ought to happen" does not really mean something like "so [she or he] ought to become." The phrase "his virgin" is also obscure; usually taken to mean the man's fiancée—the young woman to whom he has been betrothed by arrangement of the parents—a few interpreters believe that the man in question is the father and that "his virgin" means his daughter, in which case the end of the verse should be read not as "let him marry" but as "let him give her in marriage." This seems unlikely; the first verb in the verse, ἀσχημονεῖν (aschēmonein), could perhaps be read as "to fail to do right by" or something of the sort, but its typical connotation is "to disgrace oneself" or "to behave in a shameful way."

n. Paul should be taken fairly literally in these two verses: He really means that, in a sense, there are such things as "gods" in heaven and earth, though as

[7]But the knowledge° is not within everyone; and some, because of habitual association with the idol right up to the present moment, eat such food as is sacrificed to the idol, and their conscience—being weak—is defiled. [8]But food will not remand us over to God; neither are we wanting if we do not eat, nor do we abound if we eat. [9]But be watchful, so that this license of yours should not become a stumbling-block to the weak. [10]For if someone sees you, who possess knowledge, sitting down in an idol's temple, will not his conscience, being weak, be encouraged to eat the sacrifices offered to idols? [11]For the one who is

a pious Jew and Christian he would more naturally call them angels or demons. Most Jews, Christians, and educated pagans of late antiquity drew an absolute distinction between, on the one hand, the spiritual or divine powers that rule the nations and inhabit the cosmos and, on the other, the one God who is the source of existence from whom everything comes forth (gods no less than other limited beings). For Paul, these "powers on high," "archons," and so on are the gods worshipped by the several nations, but are ultimately only angelic governors of the cosmos, often either rebellious or incompetent; this seems to include even the angel governing Israel, who, according to Galatians, delivered a defective version of the Law to Moses. In Paul's time, the idea of angelic "gods of the nations" would have been, for instance, an unproblematic interpretation of Deuteronomy 32:8–9, which describes God as dividing the nations among the "sons of God [El]," as well as 32:43, in which these same sons of God, along with the nations they govern, are called to make obeisance to God (in the Rabbinic Masoretic Text of the Hebrew, which is a later synthetic redaction, the phrase in v. 8 becomes "sons of Israel," but in the Septuagint—the favored text of Paul and much of the Greek-speaking Diaspora—it was still "sons of God" or perhaps, in some copies, "angels of God"; and in v. 43 the Masoretic Text omits the reference to the sons of God and the angels of the nations altogether, though, again, they are still present in the Septuagintal version). As will emerge in chapter fifteen below, it is a large part of Paul's understanding of the gospel that these cosmic "gods" have been conquered and placed in proper order by Christ and will, at the end of time, be handed over in proper subordination to the Father so that God may be "all in all."

o. γνῶσις (gnōsis). Here, Paul reflects on the difference between those who possess gnosis, therefore understanding that they need not fear contamination from heathen sacrifices, and those who do not, therefore still in thrall to fear of the cosmic powers. This distinction between "gnostic" and less fully enlightened members of the church was not at all uncommon in Christian and para-Christian circles in the early centuries; but, as v. 1 above makes clear, for Paul this is not some sort of ontological distinction among believers.

weak is destroyed by your knowledge, the brother for whose sake the Anointed died. [12]So, when you sin against the brothers and wound their conscience, you sin against the Anointed. [13]Hence, if a food causes my brother to falter, I will eat no flesh at all, throughout the age,[p] so that I might not cause my brother to falter.

CHAPTER NINE

[1]Am I not a free man? Am I not an Apostle? Have I not seen our Lord Jesus? Are you not my work in the Lord? [2]If I am not an Apostle to others, I nevertheless surely am to you; for you are the seal of my mission in the Lord. [3]This is my defense to those who interrogate me. [4]Do we not have license to eat and drink? [5]Do we not have license to bring along a sister as wife, as the rest of the Apostles do also, as well as the Lord's brothers and Cephas? [6]Or do only I and bar-Nabas have no license not to labor? [7]Who ever serves as a soldier while paying his own wages? Who plants a vineyard and does not eat its fruit? Or who shepherds a flock and does not partake of the milk? [8]I say these things not as a human being—or does not the Law say these things too? [9]For in the Law of Moses it is written: "You shall not muzzle an ox while it is treading the grain." Is God preoccupied with the oxen? [10]Or does it speak of all cases generally, for our sake? For it was written for our sake, because the plowman ought to plow in hope—as well as the creature treading grain in hope—of partaking. [11]If we sowed spiritual things among you, is it a great matter if we should reap fleshly things from you? [12]If others partake of your license, how much more so we? Yet we did not exploit this license, but rather tolerated everything, so that we might not impose an obstacle to the Anointed's good tidings. [13]Do you not know that those who perform the Temple rites eat from the Temple? That those attending at the altar are partakers from the altar? [14]So also the Lord ordained that those proclaiming the good tidings live from the good

p. Or "until the Age [to come]."

tidings. ¹⁵But I have exploited not a single one of these things. And I did not write these things so that it might thus be done for me; for it is good to die rather than that anyone make my boast empty. ¹⁶For, if I proclaim the good tidings, no boast belongs to me. Because a necessity is laid upon me; for it is a woe to me if I do not proclaim the good tidings. ¹⁷Because, if I do this willingly, I have a reward; if unwillingly, however, I have been entrusted with a stewardship. ¹⁸What then is my reward? That, when proclaiming the good tidings, I may propose the good tidings free of charge, so as not to exploit my license in the good tidings.

¹⁹For, being free from all, I enslaved myself to all, that I might gain yet more. ²⁰And to the Judaeans I became as a Judaean, that I might gain Judaeans; to those subject to the Law, as one subject to the Law—while not being subject to the Law—that I might gain those subject to the Law; ²¹To those without the Law, as one without the Law—though being not without God's law, but rather subject to the law of the Anointed—that I might gain those without the Law; ²²To the weak I became weak, that I might gain the weak; I became all things to all persons, that in every case I might gain some of them. ²³But I do everything for the sake of the good tidings, that I might become a co-partaker thereof.

²⁴Do you not know that all of those racing in a stadium do indeed run, yet one receives the prize? Run, then, so that you might win. ²⁵But all those who compete exercise self-control in all things: they so that they might receive thereby a perishable crown, while we an imperishable one. ²⁶Thus, accordingly, I do not run aimlessly; thus I do not box as if thrashing the air; ²⁷Rather, I beat my body down, and lead it about slavishly, so that in proclaiming to others I myself might not be disqualified.

CHAPTER TEN

¹For I do not intend you to be ignorant, brothers, that all our fathers were under the cloud and passed through the sea, ²And all were baptized into Moses in the cloud and in the sea, ³And all ate the same spiri-

tual food, [4]And all drank the same spiritual drink—for they drank of the spiritual rock that followed behind, and the rock was the Anointed. [5]Nevertheless, God was not delighted with most of them, for they were scattered in the desert. [6]Now these things have become typological figures for us, so that we should not lust after evil things, as indeed those men lusted. [7]Neither let us become idolaters, like some of them; as has been written, "The people sat down to eat and to drink, and stood up to revel." [8]Neither let us go whoring, as some of them whored—and in a single day twenty-three thousand fell. [9]Neither let us tempt the Lord, as some of them tempted—and they were destroyed by serpents. [10]Neither murmur, as some of them murmured—and were destroyed by the Slayer. [11]Now these things happened to them figuratively, and were written for the purpose of our admonition,[q] for whom the ends of the ages have arrived. [12]Hence let him who thinks he stands be watchful lest he fall. [13]No temptation has seized you other than what is human; but God is faithful, he who will not let you be tempted beyond your capacity, but who along with the temptation will furnish the way out, so that you may be able to endure.

[14]Therefore, my beloved ones, flee from idolatry. [15]I speak as to sagacious men; judge what I am saying. [16]The cup of blessing that we bless—is it not communion with the blood of the Anointed? The loaf of bread that we break—is it not communion with the body of the Anointed? [17]Because of one loaf, we who are many are one body, for we all partake of the one loaf. [18]Look at Israel according to the flesh:[r] are

q. As should be obvious, Paul frequently allegorizes Hebrew scripture; the "spiritual reading" of scripture typical of the Church Fathers of the early centuries was not their invention, nor just something borrowed from pagan culture, but was already a widely accepted hermeneutical practice among Jewish scholars. So it is not anachronistic to read Paul here as saying that the stories he is repeating are not accurate historical accounts of actual events, but allegorical tales composed for the edification of readers.

r. Readings or practices "according to the flesh" are those to which Paul opposes interpretations according to the spirit, which is to say, allegorical readings.

not those who eat the sacrifices partakers of the altar? ¹⁹What then am I to say? That a sacrifice made to an idol amounts to anything? Or that an idol amounts to anything? ²⁰Or rather that the things they sacrifice [they sacrifice] to daemonic beings,ˢ and not to God? I do not intend you to become communicants of daemonic beings. ²¹You cannot drink from the cup of the Lord and the cup of daemonic beings; you cannot partake of the table of the Lord and the table of daemonic beings. ²²Or do we provoke the Lord to jealousy? Are we mightier than he?

²³All things are lawful—but not all are expedient; all things are lawful—but not all edify. ²⁴Let one seek not what is his own, but rather what is for the other. ²⁵Eat everything sold in the meat market, without making inquiry into anything out of conscientiousness; ²⁶For "The earth is the Lord's and the fullness thereof." ²⁷If any of the unbelievers issues you an invitation and you intend to go, eat everything set before you, making no inquiry into anything out of conscientiousness. ²⁸But should anyone say to you, "This is a temple sacrifice," do not eat, for the sake of the one alerting you as well as for conscience's sake— [For "The earth is the Lord's and the fullness thereof."] ²⁹Not, I mean, one's own conscience, but that of the other person; for why is my freedom judged by another's conscience? ³⁰If I am by grace a partaker, why am I maligned because of what I give thanks for? ³¹So, whether you eat or drink, or do anything whatever, do all things to God's glory, ³²Just as I too am

s. The Greek word δαίμων (*daimōn*) originally meant a heavenly "god" or a lesser "divine spirit" presiding (generally from above) over certain areas of natural or human life. By late antiquity, δαίμονες (*daimones*) were often understood as divine beings inhabiting the heavens and mediating between this world and the highest divine reality. In biblical Greek the word generally has an opprobrious connotation, and refers to wicked divinities or powers. The δαιμόνιοι (*daimonioi*) ("daemonic powers," "daemonic beings") to which Paul here refers are probably those superterrestrial angelic governors who are the "gods" of the nations. Or, if he is drawing on intertestamental angelology and demonology (of the sort found in 1 Enoch or the book of Jubilees), he may be referring to the "spirits" of the *nefilim*—the gigantic children of the fallen angels or "Watchers" who coupled with human women—that haunt this world as "demons" until the day of judgment.

conciliatory to all persons in all matters, seeking not my own advantage but rather that of the many, so that they might be saved.

CHAPTER ELEVEN

¹Become my imitators, just as I am the Anointed's.

²And I praise you because you have remembered me in all things and hold fast to the traditions just as I delivered them to you. ³But I want you to know that every man's head is the Anointed, and a wife's head the husband, and the Anointed's head God. ⁴Every husband who has his head covered when he is praying or prophesying shames his head. ⁵But every wife who has her head uncovered when she is praying or prophesying shames her head;ᵗ for it is one and the same thing as its being shaven. ⁶So if a wife is not covered let her be shorn as well;

---

t. Paul is addressing a situation that had evidently arisen specifically in the church of Corinth, where certain women, when publically praying or prophesying in the assembly, removed their cover from their heads and exposed their hair. There have been many elaborate discussions of these verses (4–16), but both the issue and the energy with which Paul addresses it may be easily understood if one recall that he belonged to a culture of extreme modesty, in which a woman's full and lustrous head of hair was regarded as among the chief beauties of her sex; hence, a woman's uncovered head in public, and especially in places of worship, was seen both as an ostentation and as an ill-mannered provocation (rather as, today, immodest dress is discouraged in many places of worship). Paul's long, symbolic justifications for demanding more traditional behavior from Corinthian Christian women are notoriously tortuous, and at times obscure. And his arguments from marital hierarchy (hardly a contentious issue in an age when— in addition to the force of universal cultural custom—society was unpoliced, households lived by a labor economy, and young girls were married to fully grown men) are no sooner introduced than they disintegrate in the solvent of his (for his time) quite remarkable sexual egalitarianism (vv. 11–12). Finally, he is forced to appeal instead to a natural sense of propriety and seemliness, and his anxieties become quite clear when he explains (v. 15) that, whereas a man adorns his head with a "wraparound" covering ($\pi\epsilon\rho\iota\beta\acute{o}\lambda\alpha\iota o\nu$ [*peribolaion*]) and so should remove it in order to approach God in humility, a woman's adornment is a natural endowment that cannot be removed, and so should be covered if she too is to humble herself before God.

but, if it is a hideous thing for a woman to be shorn or shaved, let her be covered. [7]For a man ought not to be covered at the head, as he exists as the image and glory of God; but the wife is a husband's glory. [8]For man is not out of woman, but woman out of man.[u] [9]For indeed man was not created on account of the woman, but rather woman on account of man. [10]Therefore a woman ought to keep ward upon her head on account of the angels.[v] [11]Then again, in the Lord there is neither woman apart from man nor man apart from woman; [12]For, just as the woman is out of the man, so too is the man through the woman, and all things are out of God. [13]Judge among yourselves: Is it proper for a woman to pray to God uncovered? [14]Does not nature herself teach you that if in fact a man lets his hair grow luxuriant it is a dishonor to him? [15]But if a woman lets her hair grow luxuriant it is a glory to her? Because her hair has been given to her instead of a mantle. [16]But, if anyone is inclined to be argumentative, we do not have such an established custom, and neither do God's assemblies.

[17]And in delivering this message I do not offer praise, because you

u. Or, perhaps, "One is a husband not because of a wife, but a wife because of a husband."

v. No one knows what this verse means. The phrase ἐξουσίαν ἔχειν ἐπὶ τῆς κεφαλῆς (*exousian echein epi tēs kephalēs*) can be translated as "have authority upon the head" or "have power . . ."; and this may be taken as meaning simply that she should exercise control over her head (some have taken it as meaning that she should "have a [symbol of her husband's] authority upon her head," but that is almost surely wrong, since the formula ἐξουσίαν ἔχειν, which is frequently used in the New Testament, has such a meaning nowhere else in the text). But the matter is complicated by the reference to the angels. Most interpreters think Paul's meaning is that the angels are present when Christians worship and that a woman should not offend against decency in their august presence; but a few think he is referring to fallible angels, "powers" looking down from on high, who (as in the story of the "sons of God" in Genesis 6:4) are susceptible to the beauty of the "daughters of men." In the latter case, the phrase ἐξουσίαν ἔχειν refers to a woman covering her head as an apotropaic "power" for warding off the lustful gaze of the "gods." This reading seems implausible, because Paul only rarely uses the word "angel" of these defectible celestial governors (he does so, if at all, only in Galatians). My translation attempts to split the difference.

convene not for the better, but for the worse. [18]For in fact I hear, firstly, that there are schisms among you when you convene in assembly, and some part of this I believe. [19]For indeed there must be sects among you, so that those that are approved might become manifest among you [as well]. [20]When you convene in the same place, therefore, it is not to eat the Lord's supper; [21]For, in eating, each proceeds with his own supper, and one man goes hungry while another is besotted. [22]For do you not, in fact, have households for eating and drinking in? Or do you despise God's assembly and humiliate those who have nothing? What should I tell you? Shall I praise you? In this matter, I offer no praise. [23]For from the Lord I received what I also delivered to you: that the Lord Jesus, on the night in which he was betrayed, took a loaf of bread, [24]And, having given thanks, broke it and said, "This is my body, which is [being broken] for your sake; do this for my remembrance." [25]Likewise, after supping, the cup also, saying, "This cup is the new covenant in my blood; do this as often as you drink, for my remembrance." [26]For as often as you eat the loaf and drink the cup, you announce the Lord's death until he come. [27]Thus, whoever eats the loaf or drinks the cup of the Lord unworthily will be answerable for the Lord's body and blood. [28]But let a man prove himself and so eat of the loaf and drink of the cup; [29]For the one who eats and drinks while not discerning the body eats and drinks judgment upon himself. [30]Thus among you many are weak and infirm, and a considerable number have fallen asleep, [31]But if we examined ourselves we should not be judged; [32]But, in being judged by the Lord, we are corrected by the Lord, so that we might not have a verdict passed upon us along with the cosmos. [33]So, brothers, when convening to eat, wait for each other. [34]Should anyone be hungry, let him eat at home, so that you not convene for judgment. And the remaining matters I shall set in order whenever I come.

CHAPTER TWELVE

¹Now, brothers, as regards spiritual things, I do not intend you to be ignorant. ²You know that, when you were gentiles, in whatever way you were led, you were being guided away to voiceless idols. ³Hence I am letting you know that no one speaking in God's Spirit says, "Jesus is accursed," and no one is able to say "Jesus is Lord" except in a Holy Spirit.

⁴Now there are differences in the graces bestowed, but the same Spirit; ⁵And there are differences of ministries, and the same Lord; ⁶And there are differences of operations, and the same God who makes active all things in all persons. ⁷But to each is given the Spirit's manifestation for some benefit. ⁸For to one a word of wisdom is given by the Spirit, and to another a word of knowledge by way of the same Spirit, ⁹To another faith, by the same Spirit, and to another graces and healings bestowed by the same Spirit, ¹⁰And to another realizations of deeds of power, to another prophecy, and to another the discernment of spirits, to another varieties of tongues, and to another interpretation of tongues: ¹¹And one and the same Spirit makes all of these active, distributing to each appropriately, as it will. ¹²For—just as the body is one and has many members, yet all the members, while being many, are one body—so also the Anointed; ¹³For indeed, by one Spirit we were all baptized into one body, whether Judaeans or Greeks, whether slaves or freemen, and all of us were given one Spirit to drink. ¹⁴For indeed the body is not a single member, but many: ¹⁵If the foot says, "Because I am not a hand, I am not of the body," it is not for this reason not of the body. ¹⁶And if the ear says, "Because I am not an eye, I am not of the body," it is not for this reason not of the body. ¹⁷If the whole body is an eye, where is hearing? If the whole is hearing, where the scenting? ¹⁸But now God has situated the members, each one of them, in the body as he has willed. ¹⁹And if all were one member, where the body? ²⁰Yet now, in fact, many members but one body. ²¹And the eye cannot say to the hand, "I have no need of you"; or again the head to the feet, "I have no need of you." ²²Rather, much more necessary are the members of the

body that seem weaker, ²³And those that we think less honorable to the body we wrap about in more abundant honor, and our unseemly parts wear a more abundant decorum, ²⁴But our presentable parts have no need. Rather, God assembled the body, giving more abundant honor to that which is in want, ²⁵So that there be no division in the body, but that instead the members have the same care one for another. ²⁶And if one member suffers, all the members co-suffer; if a member is glorified, all the members co-rejoice. ²⁷And you are the Anointed's body and partial members, ²⁸And God has indeed assigned persons their place in the assembly: Apostles first, prophets second, teachers third, then powers, then the gracious gifts of healings, aids, governances, varieties of tongues. ²⁹Are all Apostles? Are all prophets? Are all teachers? Are all powers? ³⁰Do all have graces bestowed for healings? Do all speak with tongues? Do all interpret? ³¹But be zealous for greater gifts of grace.

And to you I show a yet more excellent path:

CHAPTER THIRTEEN

¹If I speak in the tongues of human beings and of the angels, but do not have love, I have become resounding brass and a clanging cymbal. ²And if I have prophecy and know all the mysteries and all the knowledge,ʷ and if I have all faith, of such a sort as to remove mountains, but do not have love, I am nothing. ³And if I distribute all my possessions, and if I hand over my body so that I may be burned, and do not have love, I am profited nothing. ⁴Love is magnanimous, love is kind, is not envious, love does not boast, does not bluster, ⁵Does not act in an unseemly fashion, does not seek for things of its own, is not irascible, does not take account of the evil deed, ⁶Does not rejoice in injus-

---

w. τὰ μυστήρια πάντα καὶ πᾶσαν τὴν γνῶσιν (*ta mystēria panta kai pasan tēn gnōsin*): Paul's use of the article—"*the* mysteries," "*the* knowledge"—may suggest that he is not speaking of mysteries and knowledge in general, but of a special knowledge possessed by only those initiated into them (this would, in fact, have been the common understanding of *mystēria*: literally, "things kept closed").

tice, but rejoices with the truth; ⁷It tolerates all things, has faith in all things, hopes in all things, endures all things. ⁸Love never fails; but if there are prophecies, they will be made ineffectual; if tongues, they will cease; if knowledge, it will be made ineffectual. ⁹For we know partially and we prophesy partially; ¹⁰But, when that which is complete comes, what is partial will be rendered futile. ¹¹When I was an infant, I spoke like an infant, I thought like an infant, I reckoned like an infant; having become a man, I did away with infantile things. ¹²For as yet we see by way of a mirror, in an enigma, but then face to face; as yet I know partially, but then I shall know fully, just as I am fully known. ¹³But now abide faith, hope, love—these three—and the greatest of these is love.

CHAPTER FOURTEEN

¹Pursue love, and be zealous for spiritual things, and especially that you may prophesy. ²For whoever speaks in a tongue is speaking not to humans, but rather to God; for no one hears him with understanding, but he speaks mysteries in spirit; ³But whoever prophesies speaks to human beings, with edification and encouragement and solace. ⁴Whoever speaks in a tongue edifies himself; but whoever prophesies edifies the assembly. ⁵Now I want you all to speak in tongues, but would prefer that you should prophesy; and the one who prophesies is greater than the one who speaks in tongues, unless he interpret, so that the assembly might receive edification. ⁶But now, brothers, if I come to you speaking in tongues, what profit do I provide you if I do not speak to you either in a revelation or in knowledge or in prophecy or [in] teaching? ⁷Yet inanimate things that emit a voice—whether a pipe or a lyre—if they do not yield a distinction among the voices, how will what is being piped or what is being played on the lyre be recognized? ⁸For, indeed, if a trumpet emits an obscure voice, who will get himself ready for battle? ⁹So you also, unless by the tongue you provide an utterance that is easily discerned, how will what is being said be recognized? For you will be speaking to air. ¹⁰There are, as it happens, so many kinds of voices in

the cosmos, and nothing is voiceless; [11]If, therefore, I do not know the voice's force, to the speaker I shall be a barbarian and to me the speaker will be a barbarian. [12]So you also, since you are zealous for spirits, seek that you may abound for the edification of the assembly. [13]So let him who speaks in a tongue pray that he may interpret. [14]For if I pray in a tongue my spirit prays but my mind is unfruitful. [15]Which is it, then? I shall pray with the spirit and I shall also pray with the mind; I shall hymn with the spirit and I shall also hymn with the mind. [16]Otherwise, if you bless [in] spirit, how will the one who occupies the station of the novice say "Amen" to your thanksgiving, inasmuch as he does not know what you are saying? [17]For you are indeed doing well at giving thanks, but the other is not edified. [18]I thank God, I speak in tongues more than all of you; [19]Yet in assembly I elect to speak five words with the mind, in order that I may give instruction to others, rather than tens of thousands of words in a tongue. [20]Brothers, do not become children in your minds; rather, as regards malice be as infants, but in your minds become fully formed. [21]In the Law it has been written that: "'By those of other tongues and by the lips of others I will speak to this people, and even so they will not hear me,' says the Lord." [22]Thus tongues are for the purpose of a sign, not to the believers but to the unbelievers, but prophecy not to the unbelievers but to the believers. [23]If, therefore, the whole assembly should convene, and all speak in tongues, and novices or unbelievers come in, will they not say you are maniacs? [24]But if all are prophesying, and some unbeliever or novice enters, he is convicted by all, he is judged by all, [25]The hidden things of his heart become manifest, and so he will fall on his face and worship God, declaring that God is actually among you. [26]So what is it, brothers? Whenever you convene, each has a psalm, each has a teaching, has a revelation, has a tongue, has an interpretation; let all things be for edification. [27]If anyone speaks in a tongue—by two or at most three, and each in turn, and let one interpret; [28]But, if there is no interpreter, let him keep silence in assembly and let him speak to himself and to God. [29]And let two or three prophets speak, and let the others discern; [30]But if there is revelation to another who is sitting down, let the first be silent. ³¹For you can all prophesy singly, in order that all may learn and all may be consoled. ³²And prophets' spirits are subordinate to prophets, ³³For he is the God not of disorders but of peace, as in all the assemblies of the holy ones. . . .

[³⁴Let the women in the assemblies be silent, for it is not entrusted to them to speak; rather let them be subordinate, as the Law also says. ³⁵But, if they want to learn anything, let them inquire of their own husbands at home, for it is an unseemly thing for a woman to speak in an assembly.]ˣ

x. These verses are a considerable textual problem, as they clearly constitute an interpolation that breaks the flow of the text, and that seems written in a voice unlike Paul's, and that contradicts other passages in Paul. Simply on its face, the argument reads coherently only when these verses are removed: Paul is talking about speaking in tongues and prophecy, and about which communicates God's word to those outside the inner circle, and about how to maintain order and clarity in the enunciation of the gospel. In fact, the insertion is so awkward that it obviously interrupts a single thought: Paul exhorts the Corinthians to heed the example of all the churches (v. 33) and then (v. 36) emphasizes his point with the rhetorical question of whether, instead, they think the gospel their exclusive property. The interpolated verses not only make no sense here; they deprive the surrounding verses of the sense that unites them. From a broader perspective, moreover, it is absolutely clear from the discussion on women's head-coverings in chapter eleven above, and particularly at 11:5, that Paul fully expects women to speak and prophesy in church, and clearly approves of the practice so long as women do not provocatively flaunt their "glorious" hair while doing so. And, in fact, the whole tenor of Paul's genuine writings is one of almost unprecedented egalitarianism with regard to the sexes (Galatians 3:28 being perhaps the most famous instance, but 7:4 above being no less extraordinary for its time). Moreover, the palaeographic evidence is suggestive: A good number of the earliest Western texts of the New Testament locate these verses not after v. 33, but after the now traditional final verse of the chapter (v. 40) instead—though there they constitute no less abrupt an interruption of Paul's argument. A Greek manuscript from the twelfth century (*Minuscule 88*) does the same, though with editorial markings that seem to suggest that these verses might be better placed as they are here. And the sixth-century *Codex Fuldensis* (arguably the nearest thing to a critical edition produced in the late antique West) places an editorial

³⁶. . . . Or did God's word come from you, or has it reached you only? ³⁷If anyone thinks himself a prophet or a Spiritual One,ʸ let him recognize that the things I am writing to you are a commandment; ³⁸But if anyone is ignorant, let him be ignorant. ³⁹Therefore, my brothers, be zealous to prophesy, and do not forbid speaking in tongues; ⁴⁰But let all things be done becomingly and in orderly fashion.

CHAPTER FIFTEEN

¹Now, brothers, I apprise you of the good tidings I proclaimed to you, and which you received and in which you stand, ²Through which you are also saved if you hold fast to the word of those good tidings I proclaimed to you; otherwise you have believed in vain. ³For, among the very first things, I delivered to you what I had also received: that the Anointed died because of our sins, in accord with the scriptures, ⁴And that he was entombed, and that he was raised on the third day in accord with the scriptures, ⁵And that he was seen by Cephas, then by the Twelve; ⁶Thereafter he was seen by over five hundred brothers at one time, of whom the majority remain till now, though some have fallen

---

notation after v. 33, directing the reader to the foot of the page, where our vv. 37–40 are written out a second time, either to suggest that the questionable verses might better be placed thereafter or to note that the text might better be read without those verses at all. Most tellingly of all, perhaps, a fourth-century Greek manuscript, *Codex Vaticanus*, has an editorial mark between v. 33 and these verses, which seems to indicate a textual *dubium*, regarding either the questionable verses themselves or their placement in the text. In any event, the best critical scholarship regards these verses as a later and rather maladroit interpolation, perhaps drawn from 1 Timothy 2:11–12; and the evidence preponderantly indicates that they are almost certainly spurious.

y. πνευματικός (*pnevmatikos*): Paul may here mean merely a "spiritual" man in a general sense, though not in the emptily general sense in which we today might use such a term; but in some early Christian and para-Christian circles it was not uncommon for certain members of the congregation, called pneumatics, to constitute a sort of special class of believer, possessed of fuller hidden knowledge, or privy to more direct divine inspiration; and this distinction may have been observed in the apostolic age.

asleep; [7]Thereafter he was seen by James, then by all the Apostles; [8]And last of all, as if by a miscarried baby, he was seen by me also. [9]For I am the least of the Apostles, who am inadequate to be called an Apostle, because I persecuted God's assembly; [10]And I am what I am by God's grace, and his grace to me did not become void; rather, I labored more abundantly than all of them—though, rather, not I, but the grace of God that is with me. [11]So, whether I or they, as we proclaim so also you have believed.

[12]But if the Anointed is proclaimed—that he has been raised from the dead—how is it some among you say that there is no resurrection of the dead? [13]Now, if there is no resurrection of the dead, then neither has the Anointed been raised; [14]And if the Anointed has not been raised then our proclamation is vain, and your faith vain; [15]And also we are found to be false witnesses of God, because we testified of God that he raised the Anointed, whom he did not raise if the dead are not raised; [16]For, if the dead are not raised, then the Anointed has not been raised either; [17]And if the Anointed has not been raised your faith is futile: you are still in your sins. [18]And then those who have fallen asleep in the Anointed have perished. [19]If we have had hope in the Anointed only within this life, we are the most pitiable of men. [20]But now the Anointed has been raised from the dead, the firstfruits of those who have fallen asleep. [21]For, since death comes through a man, resurrection of the dead also comes through a man. [22]For just as in Adam all die, so also in the Anointed all will be given life.[z] [23]And each in the proper order: the Anointed as the firstfruits, thereafter those who are in the Anointed at his arrival, [24]Then the full completion, when he delivers the Kingdom to him who is God and Father, when he renders every Principality and every Authority and Power[aa] ineffectual. [25]For he must reign till he puts all enemies under his feet. [26]The last enemy rendered ineffectual is death. [27]For "He subordinated all things beneath his feet." But, when it

z. Compare Romans 5:18.
aa. Again, Paul is referring here to the heavenly governors of the nations.

says "all things" have been subordinated beneath his feet, it is clear that this does not include the one who has subordinated all things to him. [28]And, when all things have been subordinated to him, then will the Son himself also be subordinated to the one who has subordinated all things to him, so that God may be all in all.[ab] [29]Otherwise, what will they be doing who are being baptized on behalf of the dead?[ac] If the dead are not raised at all, why are those baptized on their behalf? [30]And for what are we imperiled at every hour? [31]I die daily, as surely, brothers, as the boast I have regarding you in the Anointed One, Jesus our Lord. [32]If for human ends I fought wild beasts in Ephesus, what is the profit to me? If the dead are not raised, "Let us eat and drink, for tomorrow we die." [33]Do not go astray: "Bad associations corrupt good customs." [34]Become sober, in upright fashion, and do not sin; for some harbor ignorance of God. Shame on you, I say.

[35]But someone will say, "How are the dead raised, and with what kind of body do they come?" [36]Ridiculous man, what you sow is not made alive unless it dies; [37]And, whatever it is you sow, you are not sowing the body that is going to come into being, but a naked grain—perhaps of wheat, or of something else; [38]But God gives it a body as he has willed, and to each one of the seeds a body of its own. [39]Not all

ab. This is the fullest depiction of Paul's eschatological vision anywhere in his writings. He describes three phases in the life-giving reconciliation of all things to God: Christ's resurrection, then the salvation of those who already belong to Christ at the time of his *parousia* ("presence," second coming), and finally the full completion of this universal renewal (perhaps on the far side of that purging fire of judgment described at 3:10–15 above), when all things and persons will have been "set in order beneath" Christ, including the celestial powers (who will be rendered powerless, not—as the verb often is, but probably ought not to be, translated—"abolished"), and then the whole of the cosmos will be returned in its fullness and perfect order to the Father by Christ.

ac. The practice of Christians receiving baptism on behalf of other persons who died unbaptized was evidently a common enough practice in the apostolic church that Paul can use it as a support of his argument without qualification. And the form of the Greek (ὑπὲρ τῶν νεκρῶν [*hyper tōn nekrōn*]) leaves no doubt that it is to just such a posthumous proxy baptism that he is referring.

flesh is the same flesh; rather, indeed, one is that of human beings, another is flesh of beasts, another is flesh of birds, and another is flesh of fishes. [40]Both heavenly bodies and earthly bodies—but the glory of the heavenly is different, while that of the earthly is different again. [41]One glory of the sun, another glory of the moon, and another glory of the stars; for star differs from star in glory. [42]Thus also the resurrection of the dead: it is sown in perishability, it is raised in imperishability; [43]It is sown in dishonor, it is raised in glory; it is sown in weakness, it is raised in power; [44]It is sown a psychical body, it is raised a spiritual body.[ad] If there is a psychical body, there is also a spiritual. [45]So it has also been written, "The first man Adam came to be a living soul," and the last Adam a life-making spirit. [46]But not the spiritual first, but rather the psychical, the spiritual thereafter. [47]The first man out of the earth—earthly; the second man out of heaven. [48]As the earthly man, so also those who are earthly; and, as the heavenly, so also those who are heavenly; [49]And, just as we have borne the image of the earthly man, we shall also bear the image of the heavenly man. [50]And I say this, brothers: that flesh and blood cannot inherit the Kingdom of God; neither does perishability inherit imperishability. [51]Look, I tell you a mystery: Not all of us shall fall asleep, but all of us shall be changed, [52]In an instant, in a glance of an eye, at the final trumpet; for the trumpet will sound, and the dead will be raised imperishable, and we shall be changed. [53]For this perishable thing must clothe itself in imperishability, and this mortal thing must clothe itself in immortality. [54]And, when this perishable thing shall clothe itself in imperishability and this mortal thing clothe itself in immortality, then will the saying that has been written come

ad. The distinction is between a σῶμα ψυχικόν (*sōma psychikon*) (a body literally "ensouled," "animated," or "animal," given life by *psychē*, the "soul" or organic "life-principle") and a σῶμα πνευματικόν (*sōma pnevmatikon*) (a body that is of a "spirited" nature, or constituted from or made to live entirely by deathless spirit, *pnevma*). As is even more clear in the succeeding verses, this is also a distinction between earthly and heavenly origin; and, as is clearest of all in v. 50, resurrection for Paul is not a simple resuscitation of the sort of material body one has in the fallen world, but a radically different kind of life.

to pass: "Death has been swallowed up in victory. [55]Where, death, is your victory? Where, death, is your sting?" [56]Now death's sting is sin, and sin's power is the Law; [57]But thanks to God who gives us victory through our Lord Jesus the Anointed. [58]So, my beloved brothers, become steadfast, immovable, ever abounding in the Lord's work, knowing that in the Lord your labor is not in vain.

CHAPTER SIXTEEN

[1]Now, concerning the collection for the holy ones—just as I ordained for the assemblies of Galatia, so you do as well. [2]On the first day of the week, let each of you place in treasury whatever profit has accrued to him, so that there be no collecting at the time when I arrive. [3]And, whenever I arrive, whatever men you give approval to in your letters, these I shall send to carry your gracious gift to Jerusalem; [4]And, if it is suitable for me to go as well, they shall journey with me. [5]And I shall come to you whenever I come through Macedonia; for I am passing through Macedonia, [6]And perhaps I shall stay with you, or even spend the winter, so that you may send me onward to wherever I might go. [7]For I do not intend to see you yet, in passing, because I hope to remain with you for some time if the Lord permits. [8]But I shall remain in Ephesus until Pentecost; [9]For a great and effectual door has opened for me, and many oppose me. [10]Now, if Timothy comes see that he comes to be with you without fear; for he labors at the Lord's work, as I also; [11]So let no one despise him. But send him onward in peace, so that he might come to me; for I am awaiting him along with the brothers. [12]Now, concerning brother Apollos, I implore him a great deal that he should come to you along with the brethren; and he has not been at all disposed to come to you now, but he will come to you whenever he has an opportunity. [13]Keep watch, stand in the faith, be manly, be strong, [14]Let all your affairs be in love.

[15]Now I implore you, brothers, consider the household of Stephanas—that it constitutes Achaia's firstfruits, and that they have de-

voted themselves to the service of the holy ones—[16]So that you might also be subordinate to such persons, and to everyone who joins in the work and labors. [17]And I rejoice at the presence of Stephanas and Fortunatus and Achaiachus, that they supplied what you were lacking. [18]For they refreshed my spirit and yours. So give such persons recognition.

[19]The assemblies of Asia greet you. Aquila and Prisca, along with the assembly at their household, send you many greetings in the Lord. [20]All the brothers greet you. Greet one another with a holy kiss. [21]The greeting of Paul (in my own hand). [22]If anyone does not cherish the Lord, let him be accursed. *Marana-Tha!*[ae] [23]The grace of the Lord Jesus with you. [24]My love with all of you in the Anointed One Jesus.

ae. "May he come!" (Aramaic).

The Second Letter to the Corinthians

———————

BY PAUL

¹Paul, by God's will an Apostle of the Anointed One Jesus, and brother Timothy, to God's assembly that is in Corinth, together with all the holy ones throughout the whole of Achaea, ²Grace to you and peace from God our Father and Lord Jesus the Anointed.

³Blessed be the God and Father of our Lord Jesus the Anointed, the Father of mercies and God of all comfort, ⁴Who comforts us in our affliction, so that we might be able to comfort those in every affliction through the comfort with which we are ourselves comforted by God. ⁵Because, just as the Anointed's sufferings abound in us, so also through the Anointed our comfort abounds. ⁶And if we suffer affliction it is for the sake of your comfort and salvation; or if we are comforted it is for the sake of your comfort, which is at work in the endurance of those same sufferings that we too suffer. ⁷And our hope on your behalf is firm, since we know that, as you are communicants in the sufferings, so also in the comfort.

⁸For I do not want you to be ignorant, brothers, regarding the affliction that came our way in Asia: that we were placed under excessive pressure, beyond our power, of such a kind that we even despaired of living; ⁹But we held the sentence of death within ourselves, so that we should be trustful not of ourselves, but of God who raises the dead: ¹⁰Who has res-

cued and will rescue us from so great a death—in whom we have hoped that he will rescue even yet—¹¹And you cooperating by your prayer on our behalf, in order that thanks might be given on our behalf by many for the gracious gift bestowed on us by numerous persons.

¹²For this is our boast, the witness of our conscience: that we have conducted ourselves in the cosmos, and toward you especially, in holiness and in God's sincerity, [and] not in fleshly wisdom but rather in God's grace. ¹³For we do not write any things for you other than what you can read, or indeed fully understand, and I hope you will understand it all the way to the end, ¹⁴Just as you have understood us in part; because we are your boast—just as you are ours for the Day of our Lord Jesus.

¹⁵In this confidence, moreover, I elected to come to you, so that you might have a second grace, ¹⁶And to pass through to Macedonia by way of you, and to come to you again from Macedonia, and be sent on my way by you to Judaea. ¹⁷So, then, when I reached this determination, did I do so lightly? Or do I choose the things I choose in a fleshly way, so that I might say both "Yes, yes" and "No, no"? ¹⁸Yet, as God is faithful, our word to you is not a "Yes" and a "No." ¹⁹For the Son of God, Jesus the Anointed, who was proclaimed among you by us—by me and Silvanus and Timothy—did not become a "Yes" and also a "No"; rather, in him came "Yes." ²⁰For, however many God's promises may be, in him there is the "Yes"; therefore, through him there is also our "Amen" to God. ²¹But he who fortifies us along with you, and who has anointed us, is God, ²²The one who has also sealed us, and given us the pledge of the Spirit in our hearts.

²³Now, on my soul, I call upon God as a witness that, by not coming to Corinth yet, I was sparing you—²⁴That we do not dominate your faith, but are fellow agents of your joy—for you stand by faith.

CHAPTER TWO

¹But within myself I reached the decision not to come to you in grief again. ²For, if I cause you grief, then who will cheer me except

the one who is being caused grief by me? ³And, confident as regards all of you that my joy belongs to you all, I wrote this very thing so that I should not receive grief from those who should cause me joy. ⁴For I wrote to you out of much affliction and anguish of heart, through many tears, not in order that you should be caused grief, but rather so that you should know of the love I have for you in such abundance. ⁵And if anyone has caused grief he has caused grief not to me but rather, partly (lest I impose a burden), to all of you. ⁶For such a one, this penalty by the majority suffices; ⁷Hence, instead, you should graciously forgive and give aid, so that such a man might not be engulfed in excessive grief. ⁸Therefore I implore you to confirm your love for him; ⁹For I have written also to this end, so I might know, as regards you, whether it has been proved that you are obedient in respect to all things. ¹⁰Now, whomever you graciously forgive, I do also. For, indeed, what I have forgiven—if I have forgiven anything—is because of you, before the person of the Anointed, ¹¹So that we might not be plundered by the Accuser.ᵃ For we are not ignorant of his devices. ¹²But when I came to Troas for the purpose of the good tidings of the Anointed, and a door was opened for me by the Lord, ¹³I had no rest in my spirit when I failed to find my brother Titus; rather, bidding them farewell, I departed into Macedonia. ¹⁴But grace to God, who is always leading us in a triumphal procession, and through us making the fragrance of his knowledge manifest in every place; ¹⁵Because we are the Anointed's sweet fragrance for God, among both those who are being saved and those who are perishing, ¹⁶To the latter an odor from death to death, yet to the former from life to life. And who is adequate to these things? ¹⁷For we are not hawking God's word, as so many do; as out of sincerity, rather—as from God, rather—we speak in the Anointed, before God.

a. "The Satan," which is to say, "prosecutor," "accuser," "arraigner."

CHAPTER THREE

[1]Are we beginning again to commend ourselves to you? Or do we need letters of recommendation, as some do, either to you or from you? [2]You are our letter, which has been inscribed in our hearts, known and read by all human beings, [3]As it is manifest that you are a letter from the Anointed, ministered to by us, written not by ink but rather by the Spirit of a living God, not on tablets of stone but on tablets of hearts of flesh.

[4]And we have such confidence toward God because of the Anointed. [5]Not that we are competent to reckon anything regarding ourselves; rather, our competency is from God, [6]Who also made us competent as ministers of a new covenant, not of scripture but of spirit; for scripture slays but spirit makes alive. [7]But, if death's ministry by way of scriptures engraved in stones came with glory, so that the sons of Israel were unable to gaze on the face of Moses on account of his face's glory—which is being abolished—[8]How shall the ministry of the spirit not come with more glory? [9]For if there is glory to the ministry of condemnation, the ministry of vindication abounds much more in glory. [10]For even that which was made glorious, compared to the glory that exceeds it, has not been made glorious in this degree. [11]For, if by glory that which is being abolished—much more in glory that which endures. [12]Having such a hope, therefore, we venture considerable boldness, [13]Unlike Moses, who put a veil on his face so that the sons of Israel should not gaze intently toward the end of what is being abolished. [14]Instead, their thoughts were coarsened. For right up to the present day that same veil remains drawn over the reading of the old covenant, it not being revealed that in the Anointed it is abolished. [15]Rather, to this day, when Moses is being read a veil lies upon their heart; [16]But whenever it turns to the Lord the veil is removed. [17]Now the Lord is the Spirit, and wherever the Spirit is there is freedom. [18]But all of us with face unveiled, mirroring the Lord's glory, are being transformed into the same image, from glory to glory, as by the Lord's Spirit.

CHAPTER FOUR

¹Therefore, having this ministry as recipients of mercy, we do not grow weary, ²But rather have renounced the things hidden in shame, neither proceeding by guile nor falsifying God's word; instead, by making the truth manifest, we commend ourselves before God to every human conscience. ³And if our good tidings have been veiled, they have been veiled from those who are perishing, ⁴Those in whom the god of this age blinded the thoughts of the faithless, so that the illumination of the good tidings of the glory of the Anointed—he who is God's image—should not shine out. ⁵For we proclaim not ourselves, but Jesus the Anointed as Lord, and ourselves as your slaves for Jesus's sake. ⁶Because the God who says, "Light shall shine out of darkness" is the one who has shone in our hearts, for illumination of the knowledge of God's glory in the face of the Anointed.

⁷But we have this treasure in vessels of clay, so that the power's excellence might be God's, and not come from us; ⁸In every way afflicted yet not crushed, perplexed yet not despairing, ⁹Persecuted yet not forsaken, cast down yet not perishing, ¹⁰Always bearing in the body the dying of Jesus, so that Jesus's life might be made manifest in our mortal flesh. ¹¹For we the living are always being delivered over to death on account of Jesus, so that the life of Jesus may also be made manifest in our mortal flesh. ¹²Hence death is operating in us, but life in you. ¹³And, having the same spirit of faithfulness—in keeping with the scripture: "I had faith, therefore I spoke"—we both have faith and thus also speak, ¹⁴Knowing that he who raised the Lord Jesus will also raise us with Jesus and will present us along with you. ¹⁵For all things are for your sake, so that the grace that has spread out through ever more persons might make thanksgiving abound to God's glory. ¹⁶Hence we do not grow weary; but, if indeed our outward man is wasting away, still our inward is being renewed day by day. ¹⁷Because for us the transitory lightness of our affliction is bringing about, ever more exorbitantly, the Age's weight of glory. ¹⁸Not looking to things seen but instead to things not

seen; for the things seen are for but a season, but the things not seen are of the Age.

<h3 style="text-align:center">CHAPTER FIVE</h3>

[1]Now we know that, if the tent that is our earthly home is destroyed, we have a building from God, a home of the Age, in the heavens, not made by hands. [2]For herein we groan, fervently longing to clothe ourselves about in our dwelling from heaven, [3]Inasmuch as, in being clothed, we shall not be found naked. [4]For indeed in this tent, being burdened, we groan, since we do not wish to unclothe ourselves, but rather to clothe ourselves, so that what is mortal may be swallowed up by life. [5]Now he who wrought us for this very thing is God, the one who has given us the pledge of the Spirit. [6]Therefore, being always confident, and knowing that when at home in the body we are away from home, separated from the Lord— [7]For we walk by faith, not by what is seen— [8]And we are confident and think it better to depart from home, out of the body, and come home to the Lord. [9]For which reason it is also our ambition, whether at home or away from home, to be delightful to him. [10]For we must all of us appear before the tribunal of the Anointed, so that each may be requited for the things he did, whether good or deplorable.

[11]So, knowing the fear of the Lord, we are persuading people, and we are made manifest to God; and I hope to have become manifest in your consciences. [12]We are not commending ourselves to you again, but instead giving you occasion for boasting on our account, so that you may have something for those who boast of things that are superficial and not in the heart. [13]For if we are deranged it is for God; if we are sound of mind it is for you. [14]For the love of the Anointed constrains us, having reached this judgment: that one died on behalf of all; all then have died; [15]And he died on behalf of all so that the living should live no longer for themselves, but for the one who has died and been raised on their behalf. [16]Thus, from now on, we know no one according to the

flesh, even though we have known the Anointed—yet know him now no longer—according to flesh. [17]Hence if anyone is in the Anointed he is a new creation; the old things have passed away; look: They have become new. [18]And all things come out of God, who through the Anointed has reconciled us to himself, and has given us the ministry of reconciliation: [19]So that God was in the Anointed reconciling the cosmos to himself, not accounting their trespasses to them, and placing in us the word of reconciliation. [20]Therefore, we are ambassadors on the Anointed's behalf, of such a kind that God makes supplication through us: for the sake of the Anointed, we implore, be reconciled to God. [21]For our sake he made the one who knew no sin into sin, so that in him we might become God's righteousness.

CHAPTER SIX

[1]And, cooperating with him,[b] we also implore you not to receive God's grace in vain; [2]For he says, "In an acceptable time I heard you, and on a day of salvation I helped you." Look: Now is an acceptable time. Look: Now is a day of salvation. [3]—Providing no stumbling-block in any matter, so that the ministry should receive no censure, [4]But instead commending ourselves in everything as God's ministers, in immense endurance, in afflictions, in necessities, in narrow straits, [5]In welts, in jails, in riots, in labors, in sleepless nights, in days of hunger, [6]In chastity, in knowledge, in magnanimity, in honesty, in a holy spirit, in unfeigned love, [7]In a discourse of truth, in God's power; by righteousness' armaments, on our right and our left, [8]Through glory and dishonor, through censure and praise; as both deceivers and truthful

---

b. συνεργοῦντες (*synergountes*): "coworking," "acting with"; here, in keeping with Paul's characteristic language of the "synergy" of divine and human works, the word should be read in continuity with the final verses of the previous chapter, where Paul speaks as God's ambassador, through whom God implores the Corinthians to be reconciled with him. Hence, Paul and his companions are *synergountes* with God, not merely "fellow workers" with the Corinthian church.

men, [9]As both unknown and fully known, as both dying and — see! — we live, as both chastened and not put to death, [10]As aggrieved yet ever rejoicing, as destitute yet enriching many, as both having nothing and possessing all things.

[11]Our mouth has been opened to you, Corinthians, our heart has grown expansive; [12]You are not constrained by us, but you are constrained in your own inward parts; [13]But, as a fair exchange (I am speaking as to children), become yourselves expansive as well.

[14]Do not come to be disparately yoked with the faithless; for what do uprightness and lawlessness share, or what communion has light with darkness? [15]And what concord is there of the Anointed and Beliar, or what portion is shared by a faithful with an unfaithful person? [16]And what assent does God's sanctuary give to idols? For we are a living God's sanctuary; just as God has said: "'I will dwell and walk among them, and I will be their God, and they shall be my people. [17]Therefore come out from their midst and be set apart,' says the Lord, 'and do not touch anything impure; and I will welcome you in.'" [18]"'And I will be as a Father to you, and to me you shall be as sons and daughters,' says the Lord almighty."

CHAPTER SEVEN

[1]So having these promises, beloved ones, let us purify ourselves from every pollution of flesh and spirit, perfecting holiness in fear of God. [2]Make space for us; we have done no one an injustice, have corrupted no one, have plundered no one. [3]I do not say this for the purpose of condemnation; for I have already said that you are in our hearts, to live with and to die with. [4]With me there is great boldness toward you, with me great boasting over you; I have been filled with comfort, I overflow with joy at our every affliction. [5]For, indeed, when we came into Macedonia our flesh had no rest, as we were instead afflicted in every way: battles without, fears within. [6]But God, who comforts the downcast, has comforted us by Titus's arrival; [7]And not only by his ar-

rival, but also by the comfort with which he had been comforted regarding you—by him reporting to us your ardent longing, your lamentation, your zeal on my behalf—so that I rejoiced even more. ⁸Because if, in fact, I caused you grief by a letter, I feel no contrition; and if I did feel contrite—[for] I see that that letter did grieve you, if only for an hour—⁹I now rejoice: not that you were grieved, but that you were grieved into a change of heart; for you were caused Godly grief, so that you might in no way receive damage from us. ¹⁰For Godly grief brings about a change of heart, leading to a salvation that cannot be regretted; but the grief of the cosmos brings about death. ¹¹For look at what earnestness this very experience of Godly grief has produced in you, not to mention apologetics, and ire, and fear, and ardent longing, and zeal, and the exacting of justice. ¹²Indeed, then, if I wrote to you it was neither for the sake of the one who committed the wrong nor for the sake of the one who was wronged, but so that your earnestness on our behalf might be made manifest before God. ¹³So we have been comforted. And, in addition to our comfort, we rejoiced still more abundantly in Titus's joy, because his spirit has been given rest by all of you. ¹⁴For, if I have made any boast to him regarding you, I was not embarrassed; rather, just as we spoke everything to you in truth, so also our boasting came to be the truth for Titus. ¹⁵And his inner self is disposed abundantly toward you as he recalls the obedience of all of you, how you welcomed him with fear and trembling. ¹⁶I rejoice that in everything I am confident in you.

CHAPTER EIGHT

¹Now, brothers, we apprise you of the grace of God that was given in the assemblies of Macedonia: ²That, amid a very great deal of trying affliction, the abundance of their joy and their profound poverty yielded abundance in the richness of their generosity; ³That according to their power—even beyond their power, as I can attest—of their own accord, ⁴With a great deal of pleading, they implored us for the grace and the

community of the ministry to the holy ones, ⁵And not as we had anticipated. Instead they gave themselves first to God, then to us by God's will, ⁶In consequence of which we beseeched Titus that, as he had already begun, so also he should make this grace complete for you as well. ⁷Rather, as you abound in everything—in faith and speech and knowledge and all diligence and love from us to you—so may you abound in this grace as well. ⁸I say this not by way of a command but rather, by the diligence of others, proving your love genuine as well. ⁹For you know of the grace of our Lord Jesus [the Anointed]: that, being rich, he impoverished himself so that you might be enriched by his poverty. ¹⁰But I offer an opinion on this; for this is beneficial to you—you who a year ago already began not only to act, but to will it; ¹¹But now complete the action so that, just as the eagerness to will it, so also the completion, out of what you possess. ¹²For, if the eagerness is already there, it is accepted according to what one has, not according to what one does not have. ¹³Because relief for others is not intended to be distress for you, but follows from equality: ¹⁴At the present juncture, your abundance is for their lack, so that their abundance may be for your lack, in order that there might be equality, ¹⁵As has been written, "Whosoever [gathered] much had nothing in excess, and whosoever [gathered] little had no shortage."

¹⁶But grace to God who places this same diligence on your behalf in Titus's heart, ¹⁷Because in fact he received the request, and being more diligent he went out to you of his own accord. ¹⁸And with him we sent the brother who is renowned for the good tidings throughout all the assemblies—¹⁹And not only that, but who has been handpicked by the assemblies as our traveling companion in this gracious gift that is being administered by us, for the sake of the Lord's glory and of our eagerness, ²⁰Making this provision so that, as regards this bounty being administered by us, no one might make an accusation against us; ²¹For we pay attention to the things that are seemly not only in the Lord's eyes, but also in the eyes of human beings. ²²And with them we sent our brother, whom we have often proved to be diligent in many things, and

much more diligent now on account of his great diligence toward you. ²³As for Titus: my partner and fellow worker on your behalf; as for our brothers: the assemblies' Apostles, the Anointed's glory. ²⁴Thus give them a demonstration of your love and of what we boast on your behalf in the presence of the assemblies.

CHAPTER NINE

¹For indeed, as regards the ministry for the holy ones, it is super-fluous for me to write to you; ²For I know of your eagerness, of which I boast to Macedonia regarding you—that Achaea has been making preparations for a year past, and that your zeal has stirred up the major-ity—³And I sent the brothers, so that our boasting over you should not be made vain in this area, so that you might be prepared just as I have said, ⁴So that in this confident undertaking we—to say nothing of you—should be put to shame if Macedonians should come with us and find you unprepared. ⁵Therefore I thought it necessary to entreat the brethren that they proceed onward to you and arrange in advance the blessing promised by you, so that it might be ready as a blessing and not as plunder. ⁶And this: Whoever sows sparingly will also reap sparingly, and whoever sows for blessings will go reaping for blessings. ⁷Each one as he has chosen in the heart, not from grief or from neces-sity; for God loves a happy giver. ⁸And God is able to make all grace abound for you so that, having self-control at all times in everything, you may abound in every good work, ⁹Just as has been written, "He has scattered, has given to the poor, his justice abides throughout the age."c ¹⁰For he who provides seed for the sower will both supply bread for food and multiply your seed, and also increase the fruits of your righteous-ness, ¹¹Being enriched in everything for the purpose of all generosity, which brings about thanksgiving from us to God. ¹²For the ministry of this service not only supplies the wants of the holy ones, but also over-

c. Or "until the Age [to come]."

flows in many thanksgivings to God; [13]Because of the proof given by this ministry, they are glorifying God for the obedience of your confession of the Anointed's good tidings, and for the generosity of this communal sharing with them and with all, [14]And with prayer on your behalf they long after you, on account of God's surpassing grace upon you. [15]Thanks to God for his indescribable gift.

CHAPTER TEN

[1]Now I, Paul myself, implore you by the gentleness and equitableness of the Anointed—I who am indeed humble when among you in person, but bold toward you when away—[2]And I beseech that, when I am present, I shall not be bold with that self-assured frankness I anticipate venturing toward some who think we walk, as it were, according to the flesh. [3]For, though we walk about in flesh, we do not go into battle according to the flesh—[4]For the weapons of our campaign are not fleshly, and yet are (through God) powerful enough to overthrow fortresses—we who are overthrowing argumentations, [5]And every high rampart reared against the knowledge of God, and taking every concept captive for subjection to the Anointed, [6]And holding ourselves ready to exact justice for every disobedience whenever your obedience reaches fulfillment.

[7]See the things right before your face. If anyone has convinced himself he is the Anointed's own, let him reconsider this for himself: that, just as he is the Anointed's, so also are we. [8]For even if I should boast more extravagantly regarding our authority, which the Lord gave for the sake of edification and not for your overthrow, I shall not be put to shame—[9]Lest I seem as though I am trying with my letters to intimidate you. [10]"Because, in fact," says someone, "his letters are weighty and powerful, but his bodily presentation is weak and his speech is deplorable." [11]Let such a man count on this: that what we are in epistolary discourse when absent, such we are as well in action when present. [12]For we do not have the audacity to class or compare ourselves with

some of those who are recommending themselves; but they—in measuring themselves by themselves and comparing themselves to themselves—gain no insight.[d] [13]But we will not boast without measure, but according to the measure of that province whose measure God has apportioned us—which extends even as far as to you. [14]For we are not overextending ourselves, as though our reach did not extend as far as to you, for we were also the first to come to you with the good tidings of the Anointed, [15]Not boasting without measure in others' labors, but harboring the hope that among you, when your faith is increased, we may be enlarged—as far as our province is concerned—into overflowing, [16]So as to proclaim the good tidings to places beyond your boundaries, not boasting about what has already been done in another's province. [17]And "Let whoever boasts boast in the Lord"; [18]For that man—he who commends himself—has not been approved, but rather the one whom the Lord commends.

CHAPTER ELEVEN

[1]I should hope that you will bear with a little bit of foolishness on my part—but, of course, you *are* bearing with me. [2]For I am jealous for you with God's jealousy, for I betrothed you to one husband, to present to the Anointed as a pure virgin; [3]And I am afraid lest somehow, just as the serpent deceived Eve by his wiles, your thoughts should be seduced away from singleness [and purity] for the Anointed; [4]For if indeed someone comes proclaiming another Jesus, one whom we did

---

d. The final words of this verse ("they . . . gain no insight") are absent in Western textual tradition; and, since the plural participles ("measuring," "comparing") could equally well modify either the "we" of Paul's ceremoniously plural self-reference or the "they" of those who recommend themselves, the verse would then mean that Paul measures himself by himself, rather than by those who are promoting themselves at his expense in the Corinthian church. But the Greek text uniformly attests to the presence of those final words, and (especially given how very unlike Paul it would seem for him to speak of himself as his own proper measure) the reading I have assumed seems to me the preferable one.

not proclaim—or you receive another spirit, one that you have not received—or another proclamation of good tidings, one that you have not accepted—you are bearing with it well. [5]For I do not reckon that I am in any way less advanced than these Superlative Apostles—[6]And, though indeed incompetent in speaking, yet not in knowledge, but rather in every way having made ourselves clear to you on all things. [7]Or did I commit a sin in abasing myself so that you might be exalted, insofar as I proclaimed God's good tidings to you free of charge? [8]I robbed other assemblies, receiving wages for ministering to you, [9]And, when present with you and in need, I was a burden to no one, because the brothers coming from Macedonia supplied what I lacked; and in every way I kept, and will keep, myself from being a burden to you. [10]The Anointed's truth is within me: that this boasting of mine shall not be fenced in within Achaea's climes. [11]Why? Because I do not love you? God knows . . . ! [12]But what I am doing I shall continue doing, that I might obviate the occasion for those who want an occasion by which they might also appear to be like us in what they boast of. [13]For such men are pseudo-Apostles, deceitful workers, transforming themselves into Apostles of the Anointed. [14]And no wonder! For the Accuser himself transforms himself into an angel of light. [15]No great thing, then, if his ministers transform themselves into ministers of righteousness— they whose end will be in accord with their works.

[16]I repeat, let no one think me mad; or else welcome me even if as a madman, so that I too might boast a little. [17]What I speak, I speak not according to the Lord, but rather as though—by the very confidence of the boasting—in madness. [18]Since so many boast according to the flesh, I too shall boast. [19]For, being of sound mind, you bear gladly with madmen. [20]For you bear it if someone enslaves you, if someone devours you, if someone seizes you, if someone stirs you up, if someone clouts you across the face. [21]With shame I say that it seems we have been weak; but, however anyone might dare, in my madness I say: I dare also! [22]Are they Hebrews? I too. Are they Israelites? I too. Are they Abraham's seed? I too. [23]Are they ministers of the Anointed? Being mad, I say: the more

so I—in labors abundantly, in jails abundantly, in scars exceedingly, in deaths frequently. [24]Five times, I received the "forty-minus-one"[e] from the Judaeans, [25]Thrice I was beaten with rods, once I was stoned, thrice I was shipwrecked, I have toiled a night and a day upon the deep; [26]Frequently in journeys on the road, in perils on rivers, in perils from bandits, in perils from my own kind, in perils from gentiles, in perils in the city, in perils in the desert, in perils on the sea, in perils from false brothers, [27]In toil and hardship, in frequent sleepless nights, in famine and thirst, in frequent fasts, in cold and nakedness; [28]Quite apart from the things that come from outside—the daily obstructions in my path—there was the anxiety over all the assemblies. [29]Who is weak, and I am not weakened? Who is caused to falter, and I do not burn? [30]If I must boast, I will boast of things belonging to my weakness. [31]The God and Father of the Lord Jesus, who is blessed unto the ages, knows I am not lying. [32]In Damascus, the ethnarch of King Aretas had the city of the Damascenes placed under guard in order to apprehend me, [33]And I was lowered in a basket through a window in the wall and eluded his hands.

CHAPTER TWELVE

[1]It is necessary to boast—not of course a beneficial thing—but I will proceed to visions and revelations from the Lord. [2]I knew a man who is in the Anointed, one such as was rapt up all the way into the third heaven fourteen years ago—whether in the body I do not know, whether out of the body I do not know—the Lord knows. [3]And I knew of one such man—whether in the body or whether out of the body I do not know, God knows—[4]That he was rapt up into paradise and heard unutterable words, which it is not lawful for a human being to speak. [5]I shall boast on such a man's behalf, but on my own behalf I shall not boast, except in my weaknesses. [6]For, should I want to boast, I shall not

e. Thirty-nine lashes with the flagellum—a particularly severe beating, potentially fatal or disabling.

be mad, for I shall be speaking the truth; but I refrain, so that no one will overestimate me, going beyond what he sees of me or hears from me, [7]And from the extraordinariness of my revelations. Hence, so that I should not be excessively exalted, a thorn in the flesh was given to me, an angel of the Accuser, so that he might buffet me about, so that I might not be excessively exalted. [8]As for this, three times I implored the Lord that it might depart from me. [9]And he said to me: "My grace is sufficient for you; for power is perfected in weakness." Therefore, I shall instead most gladly boast in weaknesses, so that the power of the Anointed might overshadow me. [10]Therefore I delight in frailties, in insults, in exigencies, in persecutions and ordeals on behalf of the Anointed; for when I am weak, then I am powerful.

[11]I have become mad; you compelled me. For I ought to be commended by you. Because in nothing was I less advanced than the Superlative Apostles, even if I am nothing. [12]Indeed the Apostles' signs were accomplished among you in all patient endurance, by signs as well as by marvels and by deeds of power. [13]For what is there in which you are inferior to the rest of the assemblies, except that I did not encumber you with myself? Graciously pardon me for this injustice! [14]Look: I am ready to come to you this third time, and I will not be a burden; for I am seeking not your things, but you. For the children ought not store treasure for the parents, but the parents for the children. [15]But I will most gladly spend—and be spent out—on behalf of your souls. If I love you more abundantly, am I loved less? [16]So be it. I did not burden you. But, being wily, I took you with guile. [17]Any one of those I sent to you, did I plunder you through him? [18]I implored Titus and sent the brother with him; did Titus plunder you? Did we not walk in the same spirit? Not in the same steps?

[19]Have you been thinking all this time that we are offering you a defense? We speak before God in the Anointed; and all things, beloved ones, are for the sake of your edification. [20]For I am afraid lest, in coming, I might find you to be not such as I wish, while I am found by you to be not such as you wish—lest there be strife, jealousy, ve-

hemences, rivalries, slanders, whisperings, blusterings, disturbances—
²¹Lest when I come again my God may humble me before you, and I shall lament over many of those who have previously sinned and who are impenitent over the impurity and whoring and licentiousness they committed.

CHAPTER THIRTEEN

¹I am coming to you this third time. "Every word shall be verified by the mouth of two and three witnesses." ²I have already told you, and I foretell—just as when I was present the second time, now also in being absent—to those who previously sinned and to everyone else, that if I come again I shall not be sparing, ³Since you seek proof that the Anointed is speaking in me, he who is not weak toward you, but who is powerful within you. ⁴For indeed he was crucified out of weakness, but he lives out of God's power. For we also are weak in him, yet shall live for you with him, by God's power. ⁵Test whether you yourselves are in the faith, prove yourselves; or do you not yourselves perceive that Jesus the Anointed is in you, unless you are unproven? ⁶But I hope that you will know that we are not unproven. ⁷Now we pray to God that you do nothing evil, not so that we may appear to be proven, but so that you may do the good even if we should appear to be unproven. ⁸For we have power not against the truth, but rather for the sake of the truth. ⁹For we rejoice when we are weak and you are powerful; this we pray for as well: your restoration. ¹⁰Therefore I write these things while absent, in order that when present I might not have recourse to severity, in keeping with that authority that the Lord gave me for the sake of building up and not for tearing down.

¹¹As for the rest, brothers, rejoice, be restored, be encouraged, be of the same mind, be at peace, and the God of love and peace will be with you. ¹²Greet one another with a holy kiss. All the holy ones greet you.

¹³The grace of the Lord Jesus the Anointed and the love of God and the community of the Holy Spirit be with all of you.

The Letter to the Galatians

BY PAUL

¹Paul, an Apostle sent out not from human beings, nor by a man, but rather by Jesus the Anointed, and by God the Father who has raised him from the dead, ²And all the brethren who are with me, to the assemblies of Galatia: ³Grace to you and peace from God our Father and Lord Jesus the Anointed, ⁴Who has given himself on behalf of our sins so that he might deliver us from the present evil age, according to the will of our God and Father, ⁵To whom be the glory unto the ages of the ages; amen.

⁶I am astounded that you are so quickly defecting from the one who has called you by [the Anointed's] grace, toward an alternative proclamation of "good tidings"—⁷Which is no alternative at all, except that there are certain persons who are agitating you, and seeking to reverse the Anointed's good tidings. ⁸But, even if we or an angel out of heaven should proclaim [to you] good tidings that differ from what you received, let him be accursed. ⁹As I have just said, and now say again, if anyone proclaims good tidings to you differing from what you received, let him be accursed.

¹⁰For am I now prevailing upon human beings, or upon God? Or am I seeking to appease human beings? If I were still appeasing human beings, I should not have been a slave of the Anointed. ¹¹For I apprise you, brothers, that the good tidings proclaimed by me are not of human

origin; ¹²For neither did I receive it from, nor was I taught it by, a human being—by way, rather, of a revelation from Jesus the Anointed. ¹³For you have heard of my conduct when I was inside Judaism: that I persecuted and besieged God's assembly with such extravagance, ¹⁴And was progressing in Judaism beyond many contemporaries among my people, being exorbitant in my zeal for my ancestral traditions. ¹⁵But when God, who had set me apart from my mother's womb and had called me by his grace, was pleased ¹⁶To reveal his Son in me, so that I might proclaim the good tidings regarding him among the gentiles, I did not immediately take counsel with flesh and blood, ¹⁷Nor did I go up to Jerusalem to those who had been Apostles before I had, but instead departed into Arabia, then returned to Damascus. ¹⁸Then, after three years, I went up to Jerusalem to visit Cephas and remained with him for fifteen days; ¹⁹But I saw no other of the Apostles except James, the Lord's brother. ²⁰And the things I write to you—see!—before God, I am not lying. ²¹Then I entered the climes of Syria and Cilicia. ²²And I was not known by face to the assemblies of Judaea that are in the Anointed. ²³And they heard only that "The one formerly persecuting us now proclaims the faith that he besieged." ²⁴And they glorified God in me.

CHAPTER TWO

¹Then, after fourteen years, I went with bar-Nabas up to Jerusalem again, taking along Titus also; ²And I went up in accord with a revelation; and I laid out before them the good tidings that I proclaim among the gentiles, but did so privately to those in high esteem, lest I run—or had run—in vain. ³Yet not even Titus who was with me, though he is a Greek, was compelled to be circumcised; ⁴But because of false brethren secretly brought in, who stole in so as to spy upon our freedom, which we have in the Anointed One Jesus, so that they could enslave us—⁵To whom we did not yield in subordination for even an hour, so that the

truth of the good tidings might remain with you. . . .ᵃ ⁶And from those who were esteemed as something—precisely what sort of something at that time does not matter to me (God does not take a man at his face)ᵇ— for to me these estimable men had nothing to add; ⁷Rather, to the contrary, seeing that I have been entrusted with the good tidings for those of the foreskin, just as has Peter for those of the circumcision—⁸For he who was operating in Peter for a mission to those of the circumcision was also operating in me for the gentiles—⁹And, recognizing the grace given to me, James and Cephas and John—who appeared to be the pillars—gave their hands in fellowship to me and to bar-Nabas, that we should go to the gentiles and they to the circumcision, ¹⁰If only we should remember the poor—the very thing, indeed, that I was eager to do. ¹¹But when Cephas came to Antioch I opposed him to his face, because he was being contemptible. ¹²For he ate with the gentiles before certain men came along with James; when they had come, however, he withdrew and separated himself, in fear of those from the circumcision; ¹³And the rest of the Judaeans [also] joined him in his theatrical charlatanry, so that even bar-Nabas was carried away by their dissimulation. ¹⁴But, when I saw that they were not proceeding straightforwardly regarding the truth of the good tidings, I said to Cephas in front of everyone, "If you who are a Judaean live as a gentile and not as a Judaean, how is it you require the gentiles to become Judaean?" ¹⁵We who are naturally Judaean, and not sinners coming from the gentiles, ¹⁶And who know that a human being is vindicatedᶜ not by observances of Law but by the faithfulness of the Anointed One Jesus—even we have placed our

a. Paul's syntax here is even more vagrant than usual.

b. πρόσωπον ὁ θεὸς ἀνθρώπου οὐ λαμβάνει (*prosōpon ᵇo theos anthrōpou ou lambanei*): "God does not take hold of a man's face," which renders a Semitic idiom meaning the act of a man in authority taking and raising (out of partiality) the face of one man among many kneeling in supplication. Paul's meaning is that God does not have favorites.

c. Or "rectified," here and in the following.

faith in the Anointed One Jesus, so that we might be vindicated from the faithfulness of the Anointed and not from observances of Law, because no flesh at all will be vindicated from observances of Law. ¹⁷But if, while seeking to be vindicated in the Anointed, we were also to be sinners ourselves, is the Anointed then a minister of sin? Let it not be so! ¹⁸For if I rebuild the very things I demolished I contrive to make myself a transgressor. ¹⁹For by Law I died to Law so that I might live to God. I have been crucified along with the Anointed. ²⁰And I live no longer, but the Anointed lives within me; and the life I now live in the flesh I live by the faithfulness that is of God's Son, who loves me and delivered himself up on my behalf. ²¹I do not reject God's grace; for if vindication^d is by Law then the Anointed died for nothing.

CHAPTER THREE

¹O, witless Galatians, who has bewitched you [so as not to obey the truth], before whose eyes Jesus the Anointed has been so vividly portrayed [among you] as crucified? ²This alone I want to learn from you: Did you receive the Spirit from observances of Law or from faith's obedience?^e ³Are you so witless? Having begun in spirit, are you being finished in flesh? ⁴Did you suffer so many things in vain, if indeed it is in vain? ⁵So is he imparting the Spirit to you and performing deeds of power among you as a result of the Law's observances or of faith's obedience? ⁶Just as "Abraham had faith in God and it was accounted to righteousness on his part." ⁷Know then that those coming from faith, these are Abraham's sons. ⁸And the scripture, foreseeing that God would prove the gentiles righteous^f from faithfulness, proclaimed to Abraham in advance the good tidings that "In you all the

---

d. Or "rectification."

e. ἐξ ἀκοῆς πίστεως (*ex akoēs pisteōs*), which might also be translated as "from a hearing of faith," "from a report of faith," "from faith's heedfulness," or "from heedfulness to faith."

f. Or "make the gentiles righteous."

gentiles will be blessed." [9]So those coming from faith are blessed along with Abraham, who had faith. [10]For as many as come from observances of Law are under a curse; for it has been written: "Accursed is everyone who does not persevere in doing the things written in the book of the Law." [11]But it is obvious that before God no one is vindicated[g] by Law, because "The upright will live by faithfulness." [12]And the Law is not from faith, yet the one who does these things will live by them. [13]The Anointed redeemed us from the Law's curse, becoming a curse on our behalf, because it has been written: "Accursed is everyone hanging upon a tree."[h] [14]So that in Jesus the Anointed the blessing of Abraham might come to the gentiles, so that we might receive the promise of the Spirit through faith. [15]Brothers, I am speaking in human terms. All the same, once a human covenant has been ratified, no one nullifies or amends it. [16]Now the promises were spoken to Abraham and to his seed. It does not say, "and to the seeds," as in the plural, but as in the singular instead: "and to your seed," who is the Anointed. [17]And I say this: The Law—having come into being four hundred and thirty years afterward—does not revoke a covenant previously ratified by God, thus abolishing the promise. [18]For if the inheritance comes from Law, it no longer comes from a promise; but God graced Abraham with it by a promise. [19]Why, then, the Law? Ordained by angels in an intermediary's hand, it was given as a supplement, on account of transgressions, till such time as the seed to whom it was promised should come. [20]Now, the intermediary does not belong to one party, and yet God is one. [21]Is the Law therefore opposed to the promises [of God]? Let it not be! For, if a Law had been given that was capable of imparting life, righteousness really would have come from Law; [22]But the scripture imprisoned all things under sin so that the promise—from the faithfulness of Jesus the Anointed—might be given to those having faith. [23]But before faith

g. Or "rectified."

h. ἐπὶ ξύλου (*epi xylou*): "upon wood," "upon a beam," "upon a stake," "upon a tree," "upon a gallows."

came we were held under guard, under Law, kept imprisoned for the faith that was about to be revealed. ²⁴Thus the Law has become our custodial guide[i] to the Anointed, so that we might be proved righteous from faithfulness; ²⁵But, the faith having come, we are no longer under a custodial guide. ²⁶For you are all God's sons through the faithfulness within the Anointed One Jesus; ²⁷For as many of you as were baptized into the Anointed have clothed yourselves in the Anointed. ²⁸There can be neither Judaean nor Greek, there can be neither slave nor freeman, there cannot be male and female, for you are all one in the Anointed One Jesus. ²⁹But, if you are the Anointed's, then you are Abraham's seed, heirs according to a promise.

CHAPTER FOUR

¹But I say that, for however long a period the heir is an infant, he is no different from a slave, even though he is the lord of everything; ²Rather, he is subject to legal guardians and estate stewards until the term appointed by the father. ³So also we, when we were infants, were enslaved in subjection to the Elementals of the cosmos;[j] ⁴But when the

i. παιδαγωγός (*paidagōgos*): not a "paedagogue" in our sense, but the male slave (a sort of male governess) who would lead a schoolboy to school and back home again, and keep an eye on him.

j. τὰ στοιχεῖα τοῦ κόσμου (*ta stoicheia tou kosmou*): "the elements of the cosmos," "the principles of the cosmos," perhaps "the elemental spirits of the cosmos." It is an obscure phrase, made not much clearer by what follows. Some take it as meaning simply the material constituents of the world, or the "flesh" of the "psychical" or "animal" body, or perhaps lifeless idols. "*Stoicheia*" can also refer to the most "elementary" aspects of language, which a child must learn before advancing to written words; for some, this suggests that Paul is likening all religions before Christ's advent to children's earliest lessons, in much the same way that he describes the Law as a schoolboy's custodian. From the immediate context, I find this an extremely plausible interpretation. But the phrase might also refer to the "Elementals," as in my rendering: elemental spirits of the (fallen) world, or even those spiritual powers on high who govern the nations, who in Paul's cosmology do indeed hold the world in thrall, and who have been defeated by Christ; they may even be understood as those fallen angels of the natural

fullness of time had come God sent forth his Son, coming to be from a woman, coming to be under the Law, [5]So that he might redeem those under Law, in order that we should receive filial adoption. [6]And, since you are sons, God sent forth his Son's Spirit into our hearts, crying, "Abba!"—Father! [7]Thus you are no longer a slave, but a son; and, if a son, also an heir through God.[k]

[8]But back then, indeed, being ignorant of God, you slaved for those who by nature were not gods; [9]Now, however, knowing God— or, rather, being known by God—how is it you are turning again to the weak and impoverished Elementals, for which you wish anew to slave again? [10]You observe days and months and seasons and years. [11]I fear for you, lest I have labored among you in vain.

[12]Brothers, I implore you, be as I am, because I too am as you are. You have done me no injustice; [13]And you know that I proclaimed the good tidings to you the first time on account of an infirmity of the flesh, [14]And the trial that was visited on you by my flesh you neither held in contempt nor spurned, but instead you welcomed me as God's messenger, as the Anointed One Jesus. [15]Where therefore is your blessing? For I attest to you that, if possible, you would have gouged your eyes out and given them to me. [16]So, in telling you the truth, have I thus become your enemy? [17]They are zealous for you not in a seemly way, but want instead to alienate you, [18]So that you might be zealous for them. But it is a good thing to be zealous always for what is good, and not only when I am present with you, [19]My children, for whom I am again suffering the pangs of birth until the Anointed is formed in you; [20]And I wanted

---

world who, according to the book of Jubilees, fathered the *nefilim* (monstrous giants) on human women, and thereby all the demons who haunt this world. This interpretation also strikes me as a plausible reading within the larger context of Paul's theology of this age and the Age to come, and of Christ's conquest of the "principalities and powers"; and I believe that vv. 8–10 make this reading a sound one (though, even there, Paul may simply be speaking of the "weak and impoverished material elements" from which idols are made). (See also Colossians 2:8 and 1 Peter 3:18–19 and my footnotes thereto.)

k. Some texts read "an heir of God through Christ."

to be present with you right now, and to change my tone of voice; for I am at a loss regarding you.

²¹Tell me, you who want to be under Law, do you not listen to the Law? ²²For it has been written that Abraham had two sons, one from the maidservant and one from the freewoman. ²³But [indeed] the one from the maidservant was born according to the flesh, and the one from the freewoman through the promise. ²⁴These things are told allegorically;¹ for these are two covenants—the one from Mount Sinai, giving birth for slavery, is Hagar. ²⁵And this Hagar is Mount Sinai in Arabia, and corresponds to present-day Jerusalem, for she slaves along with her children. ²⁶But the Jerusalem above, who is our mother, is free; ²⁷For it has been written, "Be glad, O you barren woman who bear no children; break forth and shout, you who suffer no birth pangs; because the desolate woman's children are far more plentiful than those of her who has a husband." ²⁸And you, in the manner of Isaac, are children of a promise. ²⁹But just as, back then, the one born according to flesh persecuted the one according to spirit, so now also. ³⁰But what does the scripture say? "Cast out the maidservant and her son, for by no means shall the maidservant's son inherit along with the freewoman's son." ³¹Hence, brothers, we are not the maidservant's children, but the freewoman's.

CHAPTER FIVE

¹The Anointed freed us for freedom; stand fast, then, and do not again be restrained by slavery's yoke.

²Look, I Paul tell you that if you come to be circumcised the Anointed will profit you nothing. ³And again I attest to every man who becomes circumcised that he is obliged to perform the whole of the Law. ⁴You who are proved righteousᵐ by Law have been severed from

---

1. Again, one should not assume that Paul does not mean precisely what he says, and does not take the tale to be essentially (not merely secondarily) allegorical. His interpretive habits are rarely literalist.

m. Or "made righteous."

the Anointed, you have fallen from grace. [5]For we—in spirit, from faith—eagerly hold onto hope of righteousness. [6]For in the Anointed neither circumcision nor a foreskin is of any avail, but rather faithfulness made actual through love. [7]You were running well; who hindered you, so that you are not persuaded by truth? [8]What persuades you is not coming from the one who calls you. [9]A little leaven leavens the whole mass of dough. [10]In the Lord, I am confident in you that you will be of no other mind; but the one who is perturbing you, whoever he may be, will bear the judgment. [11]Now, brothers, if I am still preaching circumcision, why am I still being persecuted? The scandal of the cross, then, has been annulled. [12]Would that they who are causing you agitation might just castrate themselves!

[13]For you were called to freedom, brothers; only let this freedom not serve as an occasion for the flesh; rather slave for one another by love. [14]For the whole Law is summed up in a single utterance; to wit: "You shall love your neighbor as yourself." [15]If, however, you bite and devour one another, watch that you are not destroyed by one another. [16]Now I say, walk in spirit and you most certainly will not bring the longings of the flesh to pass. [17]For the flesh longs in opposition to the spirit, and the spirit in opposition to the flesh, inasmuch as they are opposed one to the other, so that you might not do as you would wish. [18]But if you are led in spirit you are not under Law. [19]Now what the works of the flesh are is obvious: whoring, impurity, licentiousness, [20]Idolatry, witchcraft,[n] enmities, strife, jealousy, rages, rivalries, dissensions, heresies, [21]Envies, inebriations, carousals, and things of that sort, regarding which I tell you in advance—just as I have said in the past—that those doing them will not inherit God's Kingdom. [22]But the fruit of the spirit is love, joy, peace, magnanimity, kindness, goodness, faithfulness, [23]Gentleness, self-mastery; against such things there is no

---

n. φαρμακεία (*pharmakeia*): literally, "the making of drugs" or "of medicines," but also a name for witchcraft, which was understood as largely involving the concoction of poisons, abortifacient drugs, and magic potions.

law. [24]Now those belonging to the Anointed One Jesus have crucified the flesh, along with the passions and the lusts. [25]If we live in spirit, let us also be aligned with spirit. [26]Let us not become vainglorious, provoking one another, envying one another.

CHAPTER SIX

[1]If indeed, brothers, a man is caught in some trespass, you the Spiritual Ones° restore such a man in a spirit of gentleness, keeping watch over yourself so that you too might not be tempted. [2]Bear one another's burdens and thus you will fulfill the law of the Anointed. [3]For, if anyone thinks himself to be something while being nothing, he is deceiving himself. [4]But let each test his own work, and then he will have his boast in himself alone, and not in someone else; [5]For each will bear his own burden. [6]Let the one who is receiving instruction share all good things in common with the one who is giving the instruction. [7]Do not be led astray: God is not mocked. For whatever a man may sow, this he will also reap; [8]Because the one sowing in his own flesh will reap perishability from the flesh, but the one sowing in the spirit will reap life in the Age. [9]And let us not be remiss when doing what is seemly; for, in not relenting, we shall reap in the proper season. [10]So, then, when the season is ours, let us work the good for all, and most particularly for the household of the faith.

[11]See with what large letters I have written to you with my own hand. [12]As many as want to be in good countenance in the flesh, these are urging you to be circumcised, just so that they are not persecuted for the cross of the Anointed. [13]For they who are circumcised do not keep the Law themselves, yet they want you to be circumcised so that

o. οἱ πνευματικοί (*hoi pnevmatikoi*): probably not "spiritual" in a general sense, and certainly not in the vague sense in which we use that term today, but referring to a special condition—and perhaps special status within the early church—of one filled with and transformed by God's Spirit, and living according to *pnevma* rather than *psychē*.

they may boast in your flesh. [14]May I, however, boast in nothing except the cross of our Lord Jesus the Anointed, through whom the cosmos has been crucified to me and I to the cosmos. [15]For neither circumcision nor having a foreskin means anything, but rather a new creation. [16]And as many as proceed in line with this rule, peace and mercy upon them, and upon the Israel of God.

[17]Henceforth let no one cause me trouble; for I bear the marks of Jesus in my body.

[18]The grace of our Lord Jesus the Anointed be with your spirit, brothers; amen.

The Letter to the Ephesians

———

ATTRIBUTED TO PAUL

CHAPTER ONE

¹Paul, by God's will an Apostle of the Anointed One Jesus, to the holy ones who are [in Ephesus] and who have faith in the Anointed One Jesus: ²Grace to you from God our Father and Lord Jesus the Anointed.

³Blessed be the God and Father of our Lord Jesus the Anointed, who in the Anointed has blessed us with every spiritual blessing in the heavenly places, ⁴As he chose us in him before the foundation of the cosmos, that we might be holy and immaculate before him in love, ⁵Marking us out in advance for filial adoption to himself through Jesus the Anointed, according to his will's delight, ⁶For the praise of the glory of his grace, with which he graced us in the Beloved One, ⁷In whom— by whose blood—we have the fee for liberation, the forgiveness of trespasses, according to the riches of his grace, ⁸Which he has caused to abound for us in all wisdom and understanding, ⁹Making known to us the mystery of his will, which was his purpose in him, ¹⁰For a husbandry of the seasons' fullness, to recapitulate all things in the Anointed, the things in the heavens and the things on earth: in him ¹¹In whom we too received our lot, being marked out in advance according to the purpose of the one who enacts all things in accord with the counsel of his will, ¹²So that we, who first hoped in the Anointed, might be for the praise of his glory: ¹³In whom you too—hearing the word of the truth, the good tidings of your salvation, and having faith in him—were sealed with the

Spirit of the promise, the Holy One, ¹⁴Who is an earnest of our inheritance until the liberation fee is paid for what has been procured, for the praise of his glory.

¹⁵Hearing, therefore, of the faithfulness in the Lord Jesus that is among you, and of the love for all the holy ones, I too ¹⁶Do not cease giving thanks on your behalf, making a remembrance in my prayers, ¹⁷So that the God of our Lord Jesus the Anointed, the Father of glory, might give you a spirit of wisdom, and of revelation by a full knowledge of him, ¹⁸The eyes of your heart having been illumined, so that you should know what the hope in his call is, what the riches of his glory's inheritance in the holy ones, ¹⁹And what the extravagant glory of his power toward us who have faith, in accord with the operation of the strength of his might, ²⁰Which he has enacted in the Anointed, raising him from the dead and seating him at his right hand in the heavenly places, ²¹Far above every Rule and Authority and Power and Lordship,ᵃ and every name being named not only in this age, but in that about to come; ²²And he has ordered all things under his feet, and has given him headship over all things in the assembly, ²³Which is his body, the plenitude of the one filling all in all.

CHAPTER TWO

¹And you, being dead in your trespasses and sins, ²In which you used to walk, in accord with the age of this cosmos, in accord with the Archon of the Power of the air, of the spirit now operating in the sons of disobedience, ³Among whom we all also formerly conducted ourselves in the lusts of our flesh and in our thoughts, and were by nature children of ire just like the rest— ⁴But God, being rich in mercy because of that great love of his whereby he loved us, ⁵And we being dead in trespasses, he gave us life along with the Anointed—you are saved by grace— ⁶And in the Anointed

a. Again, these are names for the celestial spiritual or angelic powers governing the cosmos.

One Jesus co-raised us and co-seated us in the heavenly places, [7]In order that in the ages he might show forth the extravagant richness of his grace, in kindness toward us in the Anointed One Jesus. [8]For you are those who in grace have been saved by faithfulness: And this, God's gift, is not from you, [9]Nor from observances, so that no one may boast. [10]For we are his artifact, created in the Anointed One Jesus for good works, which God prepared in advance so that we might walk in them.

[11]Therefore, remember that you, formerly gentiles in flesh—the ones called "Foreskin" by the so-called "Circumcision" in flesh (of the handmade variety)—[12]That at that period you were without the Anointed, having been aliens to the polity of Israel and strangers to the covenants of the promise, without any hope, and godless in the cosmos. [13]But now in the Anointed One Jesus you who were once far away have come to be near, through the blood of the Anointed. [14]For he is himself our peace, who has made the two into one and shattered the interposing wall of partition—the enmity—in his flesh, [15]Having abolished the Law consisting in commandments in ordinances, that in himself he might fashion the two into a single new human being, making peace, [16]And might by the cross reconcile the two to God in one body, killing enmity in himself; [17]And he came announcing the good tidings of peace, to you who were far away, as well as to those who were nearby, [18]Because through him we both have access in one Spirit to the Father. [19]In this way, then, you are no longer strangers and sojourners, but are instead fellow citizens with the holy ones, and are members of God's household, [20]Having been built upon the foundation of the Apostles and prophets, the Anointed One Jesus himself being the cornerstone, [21]In whom every edifice that is built grows into a holy Temple in the Lord, [22]In whom you also are together being built up in spirit into God's dwelling place.

CHAPTER THREE

[1]For this reason, I Paul am the prisoner of the Anointed One Jesus on behalf of you the gentiles—[2]If indeed you have heard of the steward-

ship of God's grace given to me for your sake: ³That the mystery was made known to me by a revelation, as I briefly wrote you before—⁴Regarding which you can, by reading of it, understand my insight into the mystery of the Anointed—⁵Which was not made known to the sons of men in other generations as it has now been revealed in spirit to his Apostles and prophets: ⁶That the gentiles are fellow heirs, and fellows in a single body, and fellow participants in the Anointed One Jesus through the good tidings, ⁷Of which I became a minister by the gift of God's grace, which was given to me by the operation of his power. ⁸This grace was given to me, the least of all the holy ones, to proclaim to the gentiles the good tidings, the unfathomable riches of the Anointed, ⁹And to cast light upon what constitutes the stewardship of the mystery that from the ages had been hidden in God, who has created all things, ¹⁰In order that, through the assembly, the manifold wisdom of God might be made known to the Archons and Powers in the heavenly places, ¹¹According to the purpose of the ages, which he fashioned in the Anointed One Jesus our Lord, ¹²In whom, through his faithfulness, we have boldness and access in confidence. ¹³Therefore I ask you not to grow faint during my afflictions on your behalf, which is your glory. ¹⁴By grace of this, I bend my knees to the Father, ¹⁵From whom every kindred fatheredᵇ in heavens and on earth receives its name, ¹⁶So that, by the riches of his glory, he might grant you to be made mighty with power in the inward man by his Spirit, ¹⁷That the Anointed might dwell in your hearts by faithfulness, having been rooted and grounded in love, ¹⁸So that you might have the strength to grasp, along with all the holy ones, what breadth and length and height and depth is, ¹⁹And to know the love of the Anointed that exceeds knowing, so that you might be filled to all the fullness of God. ²⁰Now, to the one who, by the power operating within us, is able to do superabundantly more than all the

b. πατριά (*patria*) (from πατήρ [*patēr*], "father"): "lineage," "patrilineal descent," or a "family," "people," or "tribe" derived from a single forefather. The point here is that every family, clan, or people ultimately derives its lineage from the one God who is Father of all.

things for which we ask or of which we think, [21]To him be the glory in the assembly, and in the Anointed One Jesus, unto all the generations of the age of the ages; amen.

CHAPTER FOUR

[1]Therefore I, the Lord's prisoner, implore you to walk in a way worthy of the call by which you were called, [2]With all humility and gentleness, with magnanimity, bearing with one another in love, [3]Endeavoring to keep the unity of the Spirit in the bond of peace: [4]One body and one Spirit, just as you were called in your calling's one hope; [5]One Lord, one faith, one baptism; [6]One God and Father of all, who is over all and through all and in all. [7]And grace has been given to each one of us according to the measure of the gift of the Anointed. [8]Which is why it says, "Having ascended on high, he took a host of captives prisoner, he gave gifts to human beings." [9]Now, what does this "he ascended" mean if he did not descend into the earth's lower parts? [10]The one descending is the same one also ascending far above all the heavens, so that he might fill all things. [11]And he granted it to some to be Apostles, and some prophets, and some evangelists, and some shepherds and teachers, [12]For the restoration of the holy ones for the work of ministry, for the building up of the body of the Anointed, [13]Until all of us come to the unity of the faith and of the full knowledge of God's Son—to the perfect man—to the measure of the fullness of the Anointed—[14]So that we might no longer be infants, wave-tossed and carried about by every wind of teaching, by men's sleight of hand, by villainy attendant upon error's wiliness, [15]But rather, speaking truth in love, we may in all things grow into him who is the head, the Anointed, [16]From whom all of the body—fitted together and knitted together by every joint provided, according to its operation, in the measure proper to every single part—effects the body's growth, for the sake of building itself up in love.

[17]This, therefore, I tell you and testify in the Lord: You are no

longer to walk as the gentiles walk, in the irreverent frivolity of their mind, [18]Being darkened in intellect, having been estranged from God's life, through the ignorance that is within them because of the petrification of their heart, [19]Who, having become unfeeling, gave themselves over to wantonness, for commerce in all impurity, in acquisitiveness. [20]Not thus, however, were you instructed regarding the Anointed, [21]If indeed you have listened to him and been taught in him—as in Jesus there is truth; [22]As regards former conduct, you are to shed the old man, the one corrupted by the lusts of deceit, [23]And to be renewed in your intellect's spirit, [24]And to don the new man, the one created by God in the righteousness and holiness of the truth.

[25]Therefore, shedding the lie, let each one of you speak the truth to his neighbor, because we are one another's corporal members. [26]Be indignant and yet do not sin; do not let the sun set on what provokes your anger, [27]Neither give the Slanderer a place. [28]Let the thief no longer steal, but instead let him work, accomplishing something good with his own hands so that he might have it to share with the person in need. [29]Out of your mouth let no foul utterance proceed, but instead whatever is good for needed edification, that it might impart a grace to those listening. [30]And do not grieve the Spirit, the Holy One of God, by which you were sealed with a seal for a day when the fee for liberation is paid. [31]Let all bitterness and animosity and indignation and clamoring and defamation be removed from you, together with every evil. [32]And become helpfully kind to one another, inwardly compassionate, forgiving among yourselves, just as God also graciously forgave you in the Anointed.

CHAPTER FIVE

[1]Become imitators of God, therefore, like beloved children, [2]And walk in love, as the Anointed also loved you and gave himself up on our behalf, an offering and sacrifice to God, for the aroma of a sweet fragrance. [3]But whoring, and every impurity or acquisitiveness—let it

not be named among you, as befits holy persons—[4]Nor foul conduct and imbecile chatter and flippancy, which are unbecoming things—but instead thanksgiving. [5]For be cognizant of this: that no whoring or impure or acquisitive man—someone who is an idolater—has an inheritance in the Kingdom of the Anointed and of God. [6]Let no one deceive you with empty words; for on account of these things God's ire is coming upon the sons of disobedience. [7]So do not be participants in them; [8]For back then you were darkness, but now, in the Lord, you are light; walk as children of light—[9]For the light bears fruit in all goodness and righteousness and truth—[10]Proving what it is that is delightful to the Lord, [11]And do not have a share in the fruitless works of darkness, but rather, indeed, reprove them, [12]For it is shameful even to speak of the hidden things that take place among them; [13]But all things reprobate are made manifest by the light; [14]For everything made manifest is light. Therefore it is said, "Arise, sleeper, and stand up from among the dead, and the Anointed will shine upon you."

[15]So be scrupulously watchful of how you walk, not as unwise, but as wise persons, [16]Redeeming the season, because the days are wicked. [17]Do not be witless, therefore, but instead understand what the Lord's will is. [18]And do not get drunk on wine, in which there is profligacy, but be filled instead with spirit, [19]Speaking to yourselves in psalms and hymns and spiritual odes, singing and psalming with your heart to the Lord, [20]Always giving thanks for all things to the God and Father in the name of our Lord Jesus the Anointed.

[21]Being stationed under[c] one another in reverence for the Anointed,

---

c. The verb here and in the following verses, ὑποτάσσω ([h]ypotassō), literally means "subordinate," in the sense either of "arranging under" or of being "sub-ordinated to"; but it can also mean being "stationed under the shelter" of something or someone, like a horse tethered beneath an awning, or simply being "assigned" to someone. In the case of wives and husbands, the issue here does not seem to be merely one of domestic authority (which in the first century would have been regarded as a matter of positively banal obviousness), but also one of reciprocal service and protection. Hence, the verb has a very different

²²The wives to their own husbands as to the Lord, ²³Because a husband is head of the wife even as the Anointed—himself the body's savior—is head of the assembly. ²⁴But, just as the assembly is stationed under the Anointed, so also the wives to their husbands in everything. ²⁵Husbands, love your wives, just as the Anointed loved the assembly and gave himself up on her behalf, ²⁶So that he might make her holy, purifying her by the washing of water, by a word, ²⁷So that he might present the assembly to himself glorious, having no stain or wrinkle or anything of that sort, that she might instead be holy and unblemished. ²⁸So [too] the husbands ought to love their wives like their own bodies. He who loves his own wife loves himself; ²⁹For no one ever hated his own flesh, but rather nourishes it and keeps it safely warm, as the Anointed does for the assembly, ³⁰Because we are members of his body. ³¹"For this reason a man shall leave his father and mother, and shall cling to his wife, and the two shall be for one flesh." ³²This mystery is a great one, but I am speaking about the Anointed and the assembly. ³³Nevertheless, let every single one of you love his wife even as himself, and the wife see that she revere her husband.

CHAPTER SIX

¹Children, heed your parents in the Lord; for this is right. ²"Honor your father and mother"—which is the first commandment that includes a promise: ³"So that it may go well with you, and that you may

---

connotation than does, say, ὑπακούω (ʰypakouō), which is used in the next chapter of the obedience of children to parents or of slaves to masters. In the world of late antiquity a household was under the authority of the paterfamilias; but it is also the case that, in an unpoliced society, households were often small fortresses with bolted outer gates and inner doors, wives were often much younger than their husbands, and male labor was the foundation of most of the economy. So, here, a husband's reciprocal responsibility to his wife—who is under the shelter of his household—is to lay down his life for her, on the model of Christ's self-sacrificial headship.

be on the earth a long time." ⁴And fathers, do not provoke your children to anger, but bring them up in the Lord's rearing and admonition. ⁵Slaves, heed your fleshly lords as though the Anointed, with reverence and trembling, in your heart's simplicity, ⁶Not by affecting slavishness before people's eyes, like someone obsequious to human beings, but as slaves of the Anointed, doing God's will from the soul, ⁷Slaving with a good will, as though for the Lord and not for human beings, ⁸Knowing that whatever good thing each man does, this will be rewarded him by the Lord, whether a slave or a freeman. ⁹And, lords, do the same to them, refraining from making threats, knowing that both their Lord and yours is in the heavens, and with him there is no respecting of persons.

¹⁰As for the rest, be empowered by the Lord and by the force of his might. ¹¹Put on God's panoply, so that you are able to withstand the Slanderer's wiles, ¹²Because we are wrestling not against blood and flesh, but against the Archons, against the Powers, against the Cosmic Rulers of this darkness, against the spiritual forces of wickedness in the celestial places. ¹³Therefore, take up God's panoply, so that on the evil day you might be able to resist and, having accomplished all things, take your stand. ¹⁴Take your stand, therefore, girding your loins with truth, and donning the breastplate of justice, ¹⁵And pulling up the straps under your feet in preparation for the good tidings of peace, ¹⁶Above all taking up the shield of the faith, with which you will be able to quench the flaming darts of the wicked one; ¹⁷And put on the helmet of salvation, and the sword of the spirit, which is God's utterance, ¹⁸By all prayer and supplication, praying in spirit in every season, and keeping watch on it in all perseverance, and in supplication on behalf of all the holy ones, ¹⁹And on behalf of me, that speech might be given me when I boldly open my mouth to make the mystery of the good tidings known— ²⁰On behalf of which I am an ambassador on a chain, so that while attached to it I might speak boldly, as it is necessary for me to speak.

²¹Now, so that you also know my affairs, what I am doing, Tychus— the beloved brother and faithful minister in the Lord—will apprise you

of everything, [22]Whom I sent to you for this very reason, so that you might know about our affairs and might give your hearts encouragement.

[23]Peace to the brethren, and love with faith from God the Father and Lord Jesus the Anointed. [24]Grace be with all those who love our Lord Jesus the Anointed in incorruption.

The Letter to the Philippians

BY PAUL

[1]Paul and Timothy, slaves of the Anointed One Jesus, to all the holy ones in the Anointed One Jesus who are in Philippi, together with supervisors and ministers; [2]Grace and peace to you from God our Father and Lord Jesus the Anointed.

[3]I give my God thanks for your every remembrance, [4]At all times, in my every supplication on behalf of you all, making the supplication with joy [5]At your communion in the good tidings from the first day till now, [6]Confident in just this: that he who initiated a good work in you will bring it to completion by the time of the Anointed One Jesus's Day— [7]As it is right for me to think this in regard to all of you, for I have you in my heart, both in my chains and in defending and confirming the good tidings, all of you being fellow participants in my grace. [8]For, God is my witness: how I long for you with the inmost affections of the Anointed One Jesus. [9]And this I pray: that your love might abound yet more and more in full knowledge and in all percipience, [10]So that you discern the things that are exceptional, in order that you might be pure and blameless on the Anointed's Day, [11]Having been filled with the fruit of uprightness that comes through Jesus the Anointed, to the glory and praise of God. [12]And I wish you to know, brothers, that my circumstances have indeed conduced to the advancement of the good tidings, [13]Such that it has become obvious in the whole of the praetorium and

to everyone else that my chains are for the Anointed, [14]And most of the brethren in the Lord, made confident by my fetters, dare to speak God's word with more abundant fearlessness; [15]Some indeed proclaim the Anointed out of envy and strife, and some out of good will: [16]The latter out of love, knowing that I am placed here to defend the good tidings; [17]The former proclaim the Anointed out of rivalry, impurely, thinking to add affliction to my fetters. [18]To what end? Notwithstanding which, the Anointed is proclaimed in every way—whether in pretense or in truth—and in this I rejoice; yet I shall rejoice also [19]Because I know that, through your supplication, this will result for me in salvation, and provision by the Spirit of Jesus the Anointed, [20]As accords with my ardent expectation and hope that I shall be made ashamed by nothing, but that instead the Anointed shall be magnified in my body, with all boldness—as always, so also now—whether by life or by death. [21]For, to me, to live is the Anointed and to die is a gain. [22]Yet, if it be to live on in the flesh, this means fruitful labor for me; and which I shall choose I do not know. [23]And I am straitened between the two, having the desire to depart and be with the Anointed, for this is better by far; [24]And yet it is more expedient to remain in the flesh on your account. [25]And this I know with confidence: that I shall remain and continue on with all of you, for the sake of your advancement and joy in the faith, [26]So that, by my being present with you again, your exultation over me might abound in the Anointed One Jesus.

[27]Only be good citizens, in a way worthy of the good tidings of the Anointed One, so that I—whether coming and seeing you or being absent—hear of your affairs: that you stand in one spirit, striving together in the faith of the good tidings with one soul, [28]And without being terrified in any way by adversaries—which is a sign of ruin for them, but of salvation for you, and this from God; [29]Because for the Anointed's sake it has been granted you not only to have faith in him, but also to suffer on his behalf, [30]Having the same struggle that you saw in me, and that you now hear of in me.

CHAPTER TWO

¹If, therefore, there is in the Anointed any comfort, if any consolation of love, if any communion of spirit, if any inward affections and feelings of pity, ²Make my joy full, so that you may be of the same mind, having the same love, together in soul, minding one thing—³Nothing according to rivalry or according to vainglory, but rather in humility esteeming each other as far better than your own selves, ⁴Each looking not to his own concerns, but rather each to the concerns of others. ⁵Be of that mind in yourselves that was also in the Anointed One Jesus, ⁶Who, subsisting in God's form, did not deem being on equal terms with Godᵃ a thing to be grasped,ᵇ ⁷But instead emptied himself,ᶜ taking a slave's form, coming to be in a likeness of human beings; and, being found as a human being in shape,ᵈ ⁸He reducedᵉ himself, becoming obedient all the way to death, and a death by a cross. ⁹For which reason God also

a. τὸ εἶναι ἴσα θεῷ (*to einai isa theō̜*): a somewhat obscure phrase. Literally, perhaps, it might be translated as "the [state of] being equal to God," the whole infinitive phrase functioning as a single substantive. But the form of the predicate "equal," ἴσα, is the neuter plural, not the masculine singular (ἴσος [*isos*]). And the plural neuter traditionally has a number of distinctive uses: in a very formal legal sense, for instance, it can denote equality of rights, privileges, and duties (the "equal things" common to all enfranchised citizens); or it can mean "equal shares" or "fair shares" (a connotation that would perhaps fit neatly with the word ἁρπαγμός [ᵇ*arpagmos*], which precedes it in the Greek text of the verse: see following note).

b. ἁρπαγμός (ᵇ*arpagmos*), a word that typically means "something seized" or "stolen," "plunder," but that might also have much the same connotation here as ἅρπαγμα (ᵇ*arpagma*), a "windfall" or perhaps "prize." Or perhaps it should be read as "something to be clung to" or "held onto," a prize Christ might have jealously kept to himself, but which instead he relinquished in "emptying" or "impoverishing" himself for us (see following note).

c. ἑαυτὸν ἐκένωσιν (ᵇ*eavton ekenōsen*): "emptied himself," "impoverished himself," "divested himself."

d. σχήματι . . . ὡς ἄνθρωπος (*schēmati . . . ᵇōs anthrōpos*). The word σχῆμα (*schēma*) means "shape," "figure," "form," but also often has the meaning of "appearance" or "outward aspect" (as opposed to "inward reality").

e. ἐταπείνωσεν (*etapeinōsen*): "reduced," "lessened," "lowered," "humbled," "abased."

exalted him on high and graced him with the name that is above every name, [10]So that at the name of Jesus every knee—of beings heavenly and earthly and subterranean—should bend, [11]And every tongue gladly confess that Jesus the Anointed is Lord, for the glory of God the Father.

[12]Thus, my beloved ones, just as you have always been obedient (not as if only in my presence, but a great deal more so in my absence), work out your own salvation in reverence and trembling, [13]For it is God who is making active within you both the willing and the working of that which is dearly desirable. [14]Do all things without murmurings and disputations, [15]That you might come to be blameless and inviolate, children of God, without fault amid a twisted and perverse generation, among whom you shine as luminaries within the cosmos, [16]Holding forth life's word, so that the boast may be mine on the Anointed's Day that I neither ran in vain nor labored in vain. [17]But, if indeed I am a votary libation poured out upon the sacrifice and the liturgy of your faith, I rejoice, and I rejoice along with all of you; [18]And you likewise: rejoice and rejoice along with me.

[19]And I hope in Lord Jesus to send Timothy to you shortly, so that in knowing of your affairs I too might be stout of soul. [20]For I have no one equal to him in soul, who will genuinely care about your affairs; [21]For all seek after the things that concern themselves, and not the things of the Anointed One Jesus. [22]But you know the proof of him: that, like a child with his father, he slaved with me in the good tidings; [23]This one I therefore hope to send as soon as I see how things stand with me; [24]And I trust in the Lord that I too shall come shortly. [25]But I deemed it necessary to send you Epaphroditus, my brother and fellow worker and fellow soldier, as well as your Apostle and attendant to my needs, [26]Inasmuch as he has been longing after all of you, and has been worried because you heard that he was ill. [27]For he was indeed ill, very nearly to death; but God had mercy on him, and not only on him but on me as well, so that I might not have grief laid upon grief. [28]I have sent him all the more eagerly, therefore, so that on seeing him again you might rejoice, and so that I might be less grieved. [29]So welcome him in

the Lord with all joy, and hold such men in honor, [30]Because he drew extremely near to death, risking his soul for the Anointed's work, so that he might supply what your ministry to me was as yet lacking.

CHAPTER THREE

[1]As for the rest, brothers, rejoice in the Lord. For me, writing the same things to you is not something troublesome, but is steadfastness toward you.

[2]Watch out for the dogs, watch out for the evil workers, watch out for the "In-cision"[f]—[3]For it is we, those worshipping and boasting in the Anointed One Jesus by the Spirit of God and not trusting in flesh, who are the Circumcision—[4]Although I do have trust in flesh as well: if any man thinks to trust in the flesh, I more so, [5]With my circumcision at eight days of age—of the race of Israel, the tribe of Benjamin, as well as a Hebrew coming from Hebrews, as regards the Law a Pharisee, [6]As regards zeal a persecutor of the assembly, as regards the uprightness that is found within the Law a man who came to be blameless. [7]But the things that were to me a gain, on account of the Anointed I have deemed these to be a loss. [8]But, in fact, I also deem everything to be a loss on account of the excellence of the knowledge of the Anointed One Jesus, my Lord, on whose account I lost all things, and deem them to be excrement, so that I might gain the Anointed, [9]And be found in him, having as mine not the righteousness that comes from Law, but that which comes through the faithfulness of the Anointed, the righteousness of God resting upon faithfulness, [10]That of knowing him, and the power of his resurrection, and communion in his sufferings, being conformed to his death, [11]If only I might somehow attain to that "ex-surrection" that is from the dead.[g] [12]Not that I have obtained it already,

f. ἡ κατατομή (*katatomē*): literally, an "incision" or "carving into" the surface of something, or the cutting of a notch or groove. Here it is used as a mocking equivalent for περιτομή (*peritomē*), "circumcision."

g. τὴν ἐξανάστασιν τὴν ἐκ νεκρῶν (*tēn exanastasin tēn ek nekrōn*):

or have already been perfected, but I press onward, that perhaps I might seize that for which I myself was seized by the Anointed One Jesus. [13]Brothers, I do not yet reckon myself to have seized hold, save of one thing: Both forgetting the things lying behind and also stretching out to the things lying ahead, [14]I press onward to the mark, for the prize of God's call above in the Anointed One Jesus. [15]Let, therefore, as many of us as are perfected be of this mind; and if you are of another mind, God will also reveal this to you; [16]Regardless of what we have attained to, let us fall into line with the same thing, [let us be of the same mind]. [17]Become my fellow imitators, brothers, and pay attention to those walking thus, just as you take your example from us. [18]For many—of whom I have spoken to you often, and speak now also, shedding tears—walk as enemies of the Anointed's cross—[19]Whose end is ruin, whose God is their guts and whose glory is in their shame, whose mind is on earthly things. [20]For our citizenship is in the heavens, from which we also eagerly await a savior, Lord Jesus the Anointed, [21]Who will transfigure the body of our abjectness, conformed to the body of his glory by the operation of his power for setting all things in order under himself.

CHAPTER FOUR

[1]Therefore, my beloved and dearly desired brothers, my joy and crown, take your stand in the Lord thus, my beloved ones.

[2]I beseech Evodia and Syntyche to be of the same mind in the Lord. [3]And, yes, I ask you, my true yoke-fellow, take care of those women who struggled along with me in the good tidings, with Clement and with the rest of my fellow workers as well, whose names are in life's book. [4]Rejoice in the Lord always; I will say it again: Rejoice! [5]Let your fairness be known to all human beings. The Lord is near. [6]Do not be anxious about

---

ἐξανάστασις can mean either "arising from" or "removal"; but the root ἀνάστασις (*anastasis*) means "resurrection," and so the entire phrase might be rendered as "that *out*-resurrection that is *out of* the dead." The play on words is not much less ponderous in the Greek.

anything, but rather in everything let your petitions be known to God by prayer and supplication, accompanied by thanksgiving. [7]And the peace of God that surpasses every mind will keep watch over your hearts and your thoughts in the Anointed One Jesus. [8]As to the rest, brothers, whatever things are grand, whatever right, whatever pure, whatever lovely, whatever of good repute—if there be any virtue and be any praise—[9]Ponder these things. Those things that you learned and received and heard and saw in me, put these into practice; and the God of peace will be with you.

[10]And I have rejoiced greatly in the Lord that you have now, at last, revived your thoughtfulness on my behalf—inasmuch as, even though you have indeed been thoughtful, you have had no opportunity. [11]Not that I am speaking as a result of want; for I have learned to be self-sufficient, whatever the circumstances I am in. [12]I know both how to be lowly and how to abound; I have been initiated into all mysteries—both how to be sated and how to be famished, both how to abound and how to suffer want. [13]I have strength for all things in him who gives me the power. [14]Nevertheless, you did nobly in together keeping communion with me in my affliction. [15]And know also, you Philippians, that when I departed from Macedonia, at the very start of my proclamation of the good tidings, in the matter of giving and receiving not a single assembly kept communion with me save you alone, [16]For you sent to me even in Thessalonika, more than once supplying my need. [17]Not that I am seeking a donation; rather, I am seeking fruit whose increase is credited to your account. [18]But I have all things and I abound; I have been filled, having received from Epaphroditus the things issuing from you, a sweet fragrance's aroma, an acceptable sacrifice, well-pleasing to God. [19]And my God will fill your every need according to his riches, in glory, in the Anointed One Jesus. [20]And to our God and Father be the glory, unto the ages of the ages; amen.

[21]Greet every holy one in the Anointed One Jesus. The brethren who are with me greet you. [22]All the holy ones greet you, and most especially those from Caesar's household.

[23]The grace of the Lord Jesus the Anointed be with your spirit.

The Letter to the Colossians

ATTRIBUTED TO PAUL

CHAPTER ONE

¹Paul, by God's will an Apostle of the Anointed One Jesus, and brother Timothy, ²To the holy and faithful brethren in the Anointed in Colossae: grace and peace to you from God our Father.

³We give thanks to God, Father of our Lord Jesus [the Anointed], praying about you always, ⁴Having heard of your faithfulness in the Anointed One Jesus, and of the love that you harbor for all the holy ones, ⁵Because of the hope stored up for you in the heavens, of which you have already heard in the word of the good tidings' truth, ⁶Which has come to you—as it has to all the cosmos, bearing fruit and growing, just as in you since the day when you first heard it and fully knew God's grace in truth, ⁷Just as you learned it from our beloved fellow-slave Epaphras, who is a faithful minister of the Anointed on your behalf, ⁸And who has made clear to us your love in spirit.

⁹Hence we also, since the day we heard this, do not cease to pray on your behalf and to ask that you may be filled by the full knowledge of his will in all wisdom and spiritual understanding, ¹⁰To walk in a way worthy of the Lord, wholly pleasing, bearing fruit in every good work and growing in the full knowledge of God, ¹¹Being empowered with every power by the might of his glory, for all endurance and longanimity, with joy, ¹²Giving thanks to the Father who has made you fit for participation in the holy ones' allotment in the light, ¹³Who delivered

us from the power of the darkness and translated us into the Kingdom of his love's Son, ¹⁴In whom we have the price of liberation, the forgiveness of sins, ¹⁵Who is the image of the invisible God, firstborn of all creation,^a ¹⁶Because in him were created all things in the heavens and on earth, the visible as well as the invisible (whether Thrones or Lordships or Archons or Powers);^b all things were created through him and for him; ¹⁷And he is before all things, and all things hold together in him, ¹⁸And he is the head of the body, of the assembly—who is the origin, firstborn from the dead, so that he might himself hold first place in all things—¹⁹For in him all the Fullness was pleased to take up a dwelling,^c ²⁰And through him to reconcile all things to him, making peace by the blood of his cross [through him], whether the things on the earth or the things in the heavens. ²¹And you, back then, had been aliens and enemies in thought, through wicked deeds, ²²Yet now he has effected reconciliation by a death, in the body of his flesh, to present you holy and blameless and irreproachable before him, ²³If you indeed abide in the faith, established and steadfast and not moved away from hope in the good tidings that you have heard proclaimed to every creature under heaven, of which I Paul became a minister.

²⁴Now I rejoice in sufferings on your behalf, filling in the things be-

a. πρωτότοκος πάσης κτίσεως (*prōtotokos pasēs ktiseōs*): perhaps "of every creature the firstborn" or "born prior to all creation [every creature]." This last reading may accord best with the following verse's assertion that all things were created in Christ.

b. Again, these are all titles for the invisible spiritual powers—angelic or daemonian—who hold sway over this cosmos.

c. εὐδόκησεν πᾶν τὸ πλήρωμα κατοικῆσαι (*evdokēsen pan to plērōma katoikēsai*): The verb "was pleased" (εὐδόκησεν) here seems naturally to take "all the Fullness [*Plērōma*]"—divine? creaturely? both?—as its subject, but perhaps God the Father or Christ is the subject intended. Moreover, πᾶν τὸ πλήρωμα is neuter, but as the sentence continues to unfold in the following verse the present participle "making peace" (εἰρηνοποιήσας [*eirēnopoiēsas*])—which should take the same subject—is masculine. This may simply be a case of personification, or perhaps the subject at that point has casually and somewhat ungrammatically shifted to Christ, consequent upon the preceding phrase.

longing to the Anointed's sufferings that are lacking in my flesh, on be-half of his body, which is the assembly, ²⁵Of which I became a minister according to God's stewardship, which I have been given for your sake, to fulfill God's word, ²⁶The mystery that has been hidden from the ages and from the generations, but that has now been made manifest in his holy ones, ²⁷By whom God wished to make known what the wealth of this mystery's glory is among the gentiles, which is the Anointed within you, the hope of glory, ²⁸Whom we proclaim, warning every human being and teaching every human being in all wisdom, so that we may present every human being as perfected in the Anointed; ²⁹For which I too struggle, according to his operation working within me in power.

CHAPTER TWO

¹For I want you to know how great a struggle I have for your sake, and for that of those in Laodicea, and for so many who have not seen my face in the flesh, ²So that their hearts, being joined together in love, might be encouraged onward toward all the riches of full cer-tainty in understanding, for full knowledge of the mystery of God, of the Anointed, ³In whom are all the hidden treasures of wisdom and of knowledge. ⁴I say this so that no one may beguile you with plausible talk. ⁵For though I am indeed absent from you in the flesh, I am still with you in spirit, rejoicing, and seeing your orderliness and the stead-fastness of your faithfulness to the Anointed.

⁶Therefore, just as you received the Anointed One, Jesus the Lord, walk in him, ⁷Having been rooted and built up in him, and being con-firmed in the faith just as you were taught it, abounding in thanksgiving. ⁸Watch that there be no one who robs you by way of philosophy and empty deceit according to the traditions of human beings, according to the Elementals of the cosmos,ᵈ and not according to the Anointed;

---

d. τὰ στοιχεῖα τοῦ κόσμου (*ta stoicheia tou kosmou*): "the elements of the cosmos," "the principles of the cosmos," perhaps "the elemental spirits of the

⁹Because in him dwells all the Fullness of deity bodily,ᵉ ¹⁰And you are those who have been made full in him who is the head of every Rule and Power, ¹¹In whom also you were circumcised with a circumcision not accomplished by hand, through the shedding of the body of the flesh, through the circumcision of the Anointed, ¹²Buried with him in baptism, by which you were also raised along with him by the faithfulness of the operation of the God who raised him from the dead; ¹³And, while you were dead in trespasses and in your foreskin of flesh,ᶠ he gave you life along with him, forgiving all trespasses, ¹⁴Expunging what is written by hand against us—contrary to us—in ordinances, and has removed it, out of the way, nailing it to the cross; ¹⁵Stripping the Archons and Powers, he exposed them in the open, leading them prisoner along with him in a triumphal procession.

¹⁶Therefore, let no one judge you for eating and drinking, or for

---

cosmos." It is an obscure phrase, and it is not elucidated in what follows. Some take it as meaning simply the material constituents of the world, or the "flesh" of the "psychical" or "animal" body, or perhaps lifeless idols. "*Stoicheia*" can also refer to the most "elementary" aspects of language, which a child must learn before advancing to written words; for some, this suggests that all human traditions are here being likened to a children's earliest lessons. But the phrase might also refer to the "Elementals," as in my rendering: elemental spirits of the (fallen) world, or even those spiritual powers on high who govern the nations (as in v. 10 below), who hold the world in thrall but who have been defeated by Christ; they may even be understood as those fallen angels of the natural world who, according to the book of Jubilees, fathered the *nefilim* (monstrous giants) on human women, and thereby all the demons who haunt this world. This interpretation also strikes me as a plausible reading within the larger context of the Pauline theology of this age and the Age to come, and of Christ's conquest of the "principalities and powers." (See also Galatians 4:3 and 1 Peter 3:18-19 and my footnotes thereto.)

e. As in 1:19 above, the formula πᾶν τὸ πλήρωμα (*pan to plērōma*), but here identified specifically as "all the Fullness *of deity*" (θεότητος [*theotētos*]).

f. The image here can easily be missed, especially if the pudency of traditional translations substitutes the word "uncircumcision" for "foreskin." Paul seems not to mean simply that his readers were once uncircumcised in body, but that their flesh itself (as opposed to spirit) constituted a "foreskin" that was removed by a circumcision not accomplished by hand, baptism into Christ and the new covenant (vv. 11-12 above).

taking part in a festival or in a new moon celebration or in Sabbaths; [17]These are a shadow of things to come, but the solid body thereof is that of the Anointed. [18]Let no verdict be passed against you by anyone affecting humility and a religion of the angels, venturing upon visions he has never had, blustering aimlessly by the mind of his flesh, [19]Not holding to the head from whom all the body—furnished and knitted together by its joints and ligatures—will grow with a growth from God.

[20]If with the Anointed you died away from the Elementals of the cosmos, why are you submissive to ordinances, as though living in the cosmos—[21]"Do not handle" or "taste" or "touch" [22]Things that are all reduced to decay in being used up—according to the injunctions and teachings of human beings? [23]Which things indeed—though having a reputation as wisdom on account of affected religion and mental lowliness and lavish neglect of the body—are of no real value against indulgence of the flesh.

CHAPTER THREE

[1]If, therefore, you were raised together with the Anointed, seek the things above, where the Anointed is sitting at God's right hand; [2]Set your mind on the things above, not the things on earth. [3]For you have died and your life has been hidden with the Anointed in God; [4]When the Anointed, our life, is made manifest, then you too will be made manifest along with him in glory.

[5]So mortify those bodily members that are on earth: whoring, impurity, passion, malign desire, and acquisitiveness (which is idolatry), [6]On account of which things God's indignation is coming, [7]And in which things you used to walk, back then when you lived by them; [8]But now you must put it all away: indignation, animosity, malice, blasphemy, obscene speech from your mouth; [9]Do not lie to one another, having shed the old man along with all his practices, [10]And having donned the new man, who is renewed in full knowledge, according to the image of the one creating him, [11]Where there is no Greek and Judaean, Cir-

cumcision and Foreskin, barbarian, Scythian, slave, freeman; rather, the Anointed is all things and is in all. [12]Therefore, as God's chosen ones, holy and beloved, put on inward compassion, honesty, humility, gentleness, magnanimity—[13]Upholding one another and forgiving one another if anyone should have a complaint against anyone . . . just as the Lord forgave you, so you also—[14]And, above all of these, love, which is the bond of perfection. [15]And let the Anointed's peace rule in your hearts, to which you were indeed called in one body; and become thankful. [16]Let the word of the Anointed dwell within you richly, teaching and admonishing each other in all wisdom, in psalms, hymns, spiritual songs, singing in grace within your hearts to God; [17]And everything you do whatsoever, in word or in deed, do all things in Lord Jesus's name, giving thanks to God the Father through him.

[18]Wives, station yourselves under[g] your husbands, as is fitting in the Lord. [19]Husbands, love your wives and do not be bitter toward them. [20]Children, obey your parents regarding all things, for this delights the Lord. [21]Fathers, do not provoke your children, so that they might not be dispirited. [22]Slaves, obey your lords according to the flesh in regard to all things, not by affecting slavishness before people's eyes, like someone obsequious to human beings, but in sincerity of heart, revering the Lord. [23]Whatever you do, work from the soul as for the Lord and not for human beings, [24]Knowing that you will receive the reward of the

g. The verb here, ὑποτάσσω ([h]ypotassō), literally means "subordinate," in the sense either of "arranging under" or of being "subordinate to"; but it can also mean being "stationed under the shelter" of something or someone, or simply being "assigned" to someone. In the case of wives and husbands, the issue here does not seem to be merely one of domestic authority (which in the first century would have been a matter of positively banal obviousness), but also one of reciprocal service and protection. Hence, the verb has a very different connotation than does, say, ὑπακούω ([h]ypakouō), which is used two verses below of the obedience of children to parents. In the world of late antiquity a household was under the authority of the paterfamilias; but it is also the case that, in an unpoliced society, households were often small fortresses with bolted outer gates and inner doors, wives were often much younger than their husbands, and male labor was the foundation of most of the economy.

inheritance from the Lord. You slave for the Lord, the Anointed. [25]For the one acting unjustly will suffer the wrong he has done, and there is no respecting of persons.

CHAPTER FOUR

[1]Lords, provide the slaves with what is right and fair, knowing that you also have a Lord in heaven.

[2]Persevere in prayer, keeping watch in it with thanksgiving, [3]Praying together for us as well, in order that God might open a door to the word for us, to speak the mystery of the Anointed, on account of which I have also been put in bonds, [4]So that I make it clear, as it is necessary for me to speak. [5]Conduct yourselves in wisdom toward outsiders, redeeming the season: [6]Your speech always with grace, seasoned with salt, to know how you should answer each man.

[7]All my affairs will be made known to you by Tychicus, the beloved brother and fellow minister and fellow slave in the Lord, [8]Whom I sent to you for this very thing, so you might know of our affairs, and so he might comfort your hearts, [9]Along with Onesimus, the faithful and beloved brother who is one of you; they will make known to you all the things here.

[10]Aristarchus, my fellow captive, greets you, as does Mark the cousin of bar-Nabas (concerning whom you have received instructions—if he comes to you, welcome him), [11]As well as Jesus—the one called Justus—who are my only fellow workers for God's Kingdom from among the Circumcision, and who have become a comfort to me. [12]Epaphras greets you, he who is one of you, a slave of the Anointed One Jesus, always wrestling in prayers on your behalf, that you might stand perfect and be brought to your full measure in all God's will. [13]For, as regards him, I attest that he suffers considerable distress on behalf of you, and of those in Laodicea and those in Hierapolis. [14]Luke the physician, the beloved, greets you, as does Demas. [15]Greet the brethren in Laodicea, as well as Nymphas and the assembly at her house. [16]And, when this let-

ter is read before you, make sure that it is also read in the assembly of the Laodiceans, and that you also read out the one for Laodicea. [17]And say to Archippus, "See to the ministry that you received in the Lord, so that you might fulfill it."

[18]The greeting by my—Paul's—hand. Remember my fetters. Grace be with you.

The First Letter to the Thessalonikans

BY PAUL

¹Paul and Silvanus and Timothy to the assembly of the Thessaloni-kans, in God the Father and Lord Jesus the Anointed: grace and peace to you.

²We always give thanks to God concerning you, making mention unceasingly in our prayers, ³Remembering the working of your faithfulness and the labor of your love and the patience of your hope in our Lord Jesus the Anointed before our God and Father, ⁴Knowing of your choice,ᵃ brothers beloved by God, ⁵Because our good tidings came to you not only in word, but also in power and in a Holy Spirit and with great assurance—just as you know what sort of men we came to be on your account when among you. ⁶And you became imitators of us and of the Lord, having received the word with the Holy Spirit's joy, even though in a great deal of affliction, ⁷So that you became a model for all those in Macedonia and Achaea who have faith. ⁸For the word of the

---

a. ἐκλογή (*eklogē*): "choice," "selection," "collection." Usually read here as referring to God's "election" of the Christians in Thessalonika, but perhaps referring instead to their decision to believe, or even perhaps to a collection of goods that they, like other churches to whom Paul wrote, had made for support of other churches or of missions like Paul's.

Lord has not sounded out from you only in Macedonia and Achaea; rather, your faithfulness to God has been communicated in every place, so we need say nothing; [9]For, as regards us, they themselves proclaim what sort of entrance to you we had, and how you turned to God from the idols, to slave for a God living and true, [10]And to await his Son out of the heavens, whom he raised from the dead: Jesus, who delivers us from the approaching ire.

CHAPTER TWO

[1]For of our entrance in among you, brothers, you yourselves know that it has not come about in vain; [2]Rather, having previously suffered and been insulted in Philippi (as you are aware), we were bold in our God to speak God's good tidings to you amid a considerable struggle. [3]For our appeal came not from error or from impurity or with guile. [4]Rather, just as we have been approved by God to be entrusted with the good tidings, so we speak, so as to please not human beings but the God who tests our hearts. [5]For neither at any time did we come with words of flattery (as you know), nor with any motive of acquisitiveness (God be our witness), [6]Nor seeking glory from human beings, either from you or from others, [7]Though it lay within our power as Apostles of the Anointed to place a burden upon you; but rather, when among you, we became gentle, just as a nurse might cherish her own children; [8]In this way, longing for you, it pleased us to give you not only God's good tidings, but our own souls, because you came to be beloved by us. [9]For you remember our labor and toil, brothers: Working night and day so as not to place a burden on any of you, we proclaimed God's good tidings to you. [10]You are witnesses, and God also, in how pious and upright and blameless a manner we behaved toward you who have faith, [11]As you know—toward each one of you just like a father toward his own children, [12]Exhorting and consoling you and attesting that you should walk in a way worthy of God, who calls you into his own Kingdom and glory. [13]And for this reason we also unceasingly give thanks to

God that, when you received the word of God that you heard from us, you received not a word of human beings but rather a word—as it truly is—of God, who also operates within you who have faith. [14]For you, brothers, became imitators of the assemblies in Judaea in the Anointed One Jesus, because you too suffered the very same sort of things from your own fellow-countrymen as they did from the Judaeans in turn— [15]They who killed the Lord Jesus and the prophets and who also drove us out, displeasing God and opposed to all human beings, [16]Hindering us from speaking to the gentiles so that they might be saved, thus always replenishing their own sins. And the ire has at last overtaken them.

[17]But we, brothers, bereaved of you for an hour's breadth—in face, not in heart—we were yet more abundantly eager in our great desire to look upon your face. [18]For which reason we had wanted to come to you—indeed I, Paul, more than once—and the Accuser[b] hindered us. [19]For what is our hope or joy or crown or boast before Lord Jesus, in his presence, if it is not in fact you? [20]For you are our glory and our joy.

CHAPTER THREE

[1]So, bearing it no longer, we were content to be left alone in Athens, [2]And sent Timothy, our brother and God's fellow worker in the good tidings of the Anointed, to fortify you and to encourage you in your faithfulness, [3]So no one should be wagged about[c] by these afflictions. For you yourselves know that we are appointed for this, [4]Because even when we were with you we foretold to you that we were about to suffer affliction, as indeed happened (as you also know). [5]So I also, no longer bearing it, sent to gain knowledge regarding your faithfulness, for fear the Tempter had somehow tempted you and our labor had been reduced

b. "The Satan," which is to say, "prosecutor," "accuser," "arraigner."

c. σαίνεσθαι (*sainesthai*): the passive infinitive of the verb σαίνω (*sainō*), which properly refers to the wagging of a dog's tail, and by extension to fawning or cringing behavior; it can also refer to making someone glad or to deceiving or beguiling someone. How it should be read here is uncertain.

to vanity. [6]But now Timothy has come to us from you and announced to us the good tidings of your faithfulness and love, and announced that you always keep a good remembrance of us, longing to see us as we also you. [7]We were therefore encouraged regarding you, brothers, in all our anguish and affliction, on account of your faithfulness, [8]For we live now so long as you stand in the Lord. [9]For what thanks can we give to God as regards you, in return for all the joy with which we rejoice before God on your account, [10]Night and day praying to excess to see your face and to restore the imperfections of your faith? [11]And may our God and Father himself, as well as our Lord Jesus, direct our path to you; [12]And the Lord cause you to increase and abound in love for one another, just as we also for you, [13]To confirm your hearts as blameless in holiness before our God and Father, in the presence of our Lord Jesus, with all his holy ones.

CHAPTER FOUR

[1]Therefore, brothers, as to the rest, we beseech and entreat in the Lord Jesus that, just as you have learned from us the manner in which you must walk and please God, and just as you do indeed walk, so you should excel at it still more. [2]For you know what injunctions we gave you through the Lord Jesus. [3]For this is God's will, your sanctification: for you to abstain from whoring, [4]For each one of you to know how to take possession of his own vessel[d] in holiness and honor—[5]Not in lust's passion like the gentiles who do not know God—[6]So that no one transgress upon or plunder his brother in this matter, because the Lord is the one who exacts justice for all such things, as we have told you in the past and have solemnly attested. [7]For God did not call us to impurity, but in holiness. [8]For that very reason, whoever rejects this is rejecting not

d. σκεῦος (*skevos*): "vessel," "implement," sometimes "sarcophagus." Most interpreters take this to be a reference to the body (as its verbal form does in 2 Corinthians 4:7), but some think it to be a direct translation of the Hebrew *kelî*, used in some Rabbinic sources as a term for one's wife.

a man, but God, who indeed gives you his Spirit, the Holy One. ⁹Now, as regards brotherly love, my writing to you is something of which you have no need; for you are taught to love one another by God. ¹⁰And indeed you put it into action toward all the brethren in the whole of Macedonia. But we entreat you, brothers, to excel at it still more, ¹¹And to make it your ambition to be quiet and to occupy yourselves with your own affairs and to work with your own hands, just as we enjoined you, ¹²In order that you may conduct yourselves decorously toward outsiders and may have need of nothing.

¹³Now we do not wish you to be ignorant, brothers, regarding those who sleep, so that you might not grieve like those others who have no hope. ¹⁴For if we believe that Jesus died and rose again, so will God also, through Jesus, bring along with him those who sleep. ¹⁵For this we say to you, in a word from the Lord: that we who are alive—those remaining till the Lord's arrival—shall by no means have precedence over those who have slept; ¹⁶Because the Lord himself—with a word of command, with an archangel's voice, and with a trumpet of God—will descend from the sky, and the dead in the Anointed will be first to rise again; ¹⁷Then we the living who remain will be seized together with them among clouds, into the Lord's escort through the air; and thus we shall be with the Lord always. ¹⁸So comfort one another with these words.

CHAPTER FIVE

¹Now, brothers, you do not need to be written to regarding the times and the seasons; ²For you are yourselves keenly aware that the Lord comes like a thief at night. ³When they are saying "peace and safety," it is then that ruin comes upon them suddenly, like the pregnant woman's birth-pang, and they cannot escape by any means. ⁴But you, brothers, are not in darkness, that the day should overtake you like a thief; ⁵For you are all sons of light and sons of day. We are neither of night nor of darkness; ⁶So let us not sleep like the rest, but let us be vigilant and sober. ⁷For those who are sleeping sleep by night, and those

who are drunk are drunk by night; [8]But we who are of the day, let us be sober, donning a breastplate of faithfulness and love, and hope of salvation for a helmet; [9]For God has appointed us not for ire, but rather for obtaining salvation through our Lord Jesus the Anointed, [10]Who died for us so that we, whether we are vigilant or we sleep, may live with him. [11]So, comfort one another, and each edify the other—as indeed you do.

[12]Now we entreat you, brothers, to recognize those who labor among you and who are set over you in the Lord and who admonish you, [13]And hold them in high esteem in love because of their work. Be at peace among yourselves. [14]And we exhort you, brothers, admonish the idle, encourage the faint of soul, support the weak, be magnanimous with all. [15]See to it that no one return evil for evil; rather, always pursue the good, in regard to each other and in regard to all. [16]Always rejoice, [17]Pray incessantly, [18]In everything give thanks; for this is God's will toward you in the Anointed One Jesus. [19]Do not quench the spirit; [20]Do not disdain prophecies; [21]And test all things; hold fast to what is good; [22]Abstain from every appearance of wickedness. [23]And may the God of peace himself make you holy with absolute completeness, and may the whole of you—spirit and soul and body—be preserved blamelessly at the arrival of our Lord Jesus the Anointed. [24]The one who calls you—who will surely do it—is faithful.

[25]Brothers, pray for us [also].

[26]Greet all the brethren with a holy kiss. [27]I adjure you by the Lord that this letter be read to all the brethren.

[28]The grace of our Lord Jesus the Anointed be with you.

The Second Letter to the Thessalonikans

ATTRIBUTED TO PAUL

CHAPTER ONE

¹Paul and Silvanus and Timothy to the assembly of the Thessalonikans, in God our Father and Lord Jesus the Anointed: ²Grace and peace
to you from God the Father and Lord Jesus the Anointed.

³We ought always to give God thanks regarding you, brothers, as is
a worthy thing, because your faithfulness grows beyond measure, and
the love of all of you—each one for the other—increases, ⁴Such that
we ourselves boast about you in God's assemblies, on account of your
patience and your faithfulness in all your persecutions, and in the afflictions you endure: ⁵A clear indication of the justice of God's judgment
in finding you worthy of God's Kingdom (on behalf of which you also
suffer), ⁶Since it is just on God's part to repay those afflicting you with
affliction, ⁷But you who suffer the affliction with repose in our company
at the revelation of the Lord Jesus from heaven, along with the angels
under his power, ⁸In a flaming fire, exacting justice upon those who do
not know God and do not heed the good tidings of our Lord Jesus—
⁹Who will pay the just reparation of ruin in the Age, coming from the
face of the Lord and the glory of his might ¹⁰On that day when he
comes to be glorified by his holy ones and to be worshipped with wonder by all those who have been faithful (because our witness to you was

trusted). [11]For which reason we do indeed pray for you always—that our God may deem you worthy of this calling and may fill every intention of goodness and work of faith with power, [12]So that the name of the Lord Jesus might be glorified in you, and you in him, according to the grace of our God and of Lord Jesus the Anointed.

CHAPTER TWO

[1]Now, brothers, we implore you—as regards the arrival of [our] Lord Jesus the Anointed and our being gathered together to him— [2]That you neither be quickly shaken in mind, nor disturbed by a spirit or a discourse or a letter (purporting to be from us) to the effect that the Day of the Lord has come. [3]By no means allow anyone to delude you that the apostasy would not come first, and the man of lawlessness—the son of perdition—be revealed: [4]The one who is an adversary, and who exalts himself over everything called a god or object of worship, so as to seat himself in God's Temple, proclaiming that he himself is a god.[a] [5]Do you not remember that, when I was still with you, I used to tell you these things? [6]And now you know what restrains him, so that he may be revealed at his proper time. [7]For the mystery of lawlessness is already operating; one alone is restraining it, right up until he is taken out of the way. [8]And then the lawless one will be revealed, whom the Lord [Jesus]

---

a. Precisely who this "lawless one" was understood to be we do not know. He seems clearly modeled upon some fairly notorious precedents. The Seleucid tyrant Antiochus IV Epiphanes (c. 215-164 BCE) had installed an idol in the Jerusalem Temple—perhaps Zeus, or perhaps Ba'al—and sacrificed swine to it. This is the Abomination of Desolation of which the book of Daniel speaks in veiled language. The Roman emperor Caligula (12-41 CE) had also threatened to place an image of himself as Zeus in the Temple, but was assassinated before the plan was accomplished. Whatever the case, in later Christian generations the figure of this lawless man would be combined with the "antichrist" or "antichrists" of 1 and 2 John and the "beast" of Revelation to produce the legend of "the Antichrist" who will arise in the last days.

will take away by the Spirit[b] of his mouth, and will bring to nothing by the revelation of his arrival: [9]The man whose arrival is brought about by the operation of the Accuser,[c] with all power and with signs and marvels of falsehood, [10]And with all the deceit of iniquity for those who are perishing, because they did not welcome the love of the truth so that they might be saved—[11]And hence God sends them delusion's operation, so that they believe the lie, [12]So that all who did not have faith in the truth, but instead took pleasure in injustice, might be judged.

[13]And we ought to thank God always, brothers, regarding you who have been loved by the Lord, because God chose you as a firstfruit for salvation, in holiness of spirit and faithfulness to truth, [14]To which he also called you by our good tidings, to obtain the glory of our Lord Jesus the Anointed. [15]So then, brothers, take your stand, and hold to the traditions you were taught, either by discourse or by one of our letters. [16]And our Lord Jesus the Anointed himself, as well as God our Father who has loved us and has by grace given us the comfort of the Age and a good hope, [17]May he comfort your hearts and make you steadfast in every good deed and word.

CHAPTER THREE

[1]As for the rest, brothers, pray concerning us that the Lord's word may race on and be glorified (as indeed it has been with you), [2]And that we may be delivered from outlandish and wicked men, for the faith is not everyone's. [3]But the Lord—who will make you firm and guard you from the wicked one—is faithful. [4]And regarding you we are confident in the Lord that you are doing, and will do, those things we command. [5]And may the Lord direct your hearts into God's love and into the Anointed's perseverance.

b. Or "breath."
c. "The Satan," which is to say, "prosecutor," "accuser," "arraigner."

⁶Now, brothers, I enjoin you in the name of the Lord Jesus the Anointed to draw back from every brother who walks idly and not according to the traditions you received from us. ⁷For you yourselves know how you ought to imitate us, because we were not idle when among you, ⁸And we ate bread not as a gift from anyone, but rather by labor and struggle, working night and day so as not to place a burden upon any of you; ⁹Not that we did not have the authority; rather, it was so that we might give ourselves to you as a model, for you to imitate us. ¹⁰For even when we were with you we enjoined this of you: that if anyone should not wish to work, neither let him eat. ¹¹For we hear of some who walk in idleness among you, not doing any work, but just working themselves about;[d] ¹²And we enjoin and exhort such men in Lord Jesus the Anointed that, working in silence, they eat their own bread. ¹³And you, brothers, do not be remiss in doing good. ¹⁴And if anyone does not heed what we say in this letter, give a sign not to mix with this man, so that he might be made ashamed; ¹⁵Even so, do not deem him an enemy, but rather admonish him as a brother. ¹⁶And may the Lord of peace himself always give you peace in every way. The Lord be with all of you.

¹⁷The greeting of my hand—of Paul—by which I sign every letter: Thus I write. ¹⁸The grace of our Lord Jesus the Anointed be with all of you.

---

d. περιεργαζομένους (*periergazomenous*): literally, "working around," "working all about," which has the connotations of "wasting time," "wasting work," or even "being busybodies."

The First Letter to Timothy

ATTRIBUTED TO PAUL

CHAPTER ONE

¹Paul, an Apostle of the Anointed One Jesus according to a command of God our savior and of the Anointed One Jesus, who is our hope, ²To Timothy, true child in faith: grace, mercy, peace from God the Father and the Anointed, our Lord.

³Just as I urged you when I went into Macedonia—to remain in Ephesus, so that you might enjoin certain persons not to teach different doctrines, ⁴Nor to devote themselves to myths and interminable genealogies, which produce curious inquiries rather than God's stewardship in faith. ⁵Now the goal of the command is love from a pure heart, and a good conscience, and unfeigned faithfulness, ⁶From which some persons, missing the mark, have turned away to idle talk, ⁷Desiring to be teachers of Law, understanding neither what they are saying nor what they are so confidently affirming. ⁸Now we know that the Law is good, if one use it lawfully, ⁹And we know this: that Law is laid down not for an upright person, but for the lawless and disorderly, for the impious and sinful, for the unholy and profane, for parricides and matricides, for killers of men, ¹⁰For the whorish,ᵃ for men who couple with

---

a. πόρνοις (*pornois*): a "*pornos*" was typically a catamite, or boy prostitute, but in the Septuagint—and probably here—the term is used to mean anyone guilty of sexual wantonness.

catamites,[b] slave-dealers, liars, perjurers, and for whatever else opposes sound teaching, [11]In keeping with the good tidings of the glory of the blissful God with which I was entrusted. [12]I am grateful to him who empowers me, the Anointed One Jesus our Lord, because he deemed me faithful, placing me in ministry, [13]I who was formerly a blasphemer and persecutor and overweeningly violent; but I was shown mercy because I was ignorant when I acted in faithlessness. [14]And the grace of our Lord was superabundant in faith and love in the Anointed One Jesus. [15]This saying is trustworthy and worthy of all acceptance: that Jesus the Anointed entered the cosmos to save sinners, among whom I am foremost; [16]But for this very reason I was shown mercy: so that in me, the foremost, Jesus the Anointed One might demonstrate total magnanimity, as a model to those coming to faith in him for life in the Age. [17]Now to the King of the ages, the incorruptible invisible only God, honor and glory unto the ages of the ages; amen. [18]I commit this command to you, Timothy my child, according to the earlier prophecies about you, so that by them you might wage the good war, [19]Holding to faithfulness and good conscience, by casting which away some have caused shipwreck in respect to the faith, [20]Among whom are Hy-

---

b. ἀρσενοκοίταις (arsenokoitais). Precisely what an arsenokoitēs is has long been a matter of speculation and argument. Literally, it means a man who "beds"—that is, "couples with"—"males." But there is no evidence of its use before the New Testament. There is one known instance in the sixth century AD of penance being prescribed for a man who commits arsenokoiteia upon his wife (sodomy, presumably), but that does not tell us with certainty how the word was used in the first century (if indeed it was used by anyone before Paul). It would not mean "homosexual" in the modern sense, for the simple reason that the ancient world possessed no comparable concept of a specifically homoerotic sexual identity; it would refer to a particular sexual behavior, but we cannot say exactly which one. The Clementine Vulgate interprets the word arsenokoitai as referring to users of male concubines; Luther's German Bible interprets it as referring to paedophiles; and a great many versions of the New Testament interpret it as meaning "sodomites." My guess at the proper connotation of the word is based simply upon the reality that in the first century the most common and readily available form of male homoerotic sexual activity was a master's or patron's abuse of young male slaves.

menaeus and Alexander, whom I remanded to the Accuser[c] so that they might be taught not to blaspheme.

CHAPTER TWO

[1]First of all, therefore, I encourage petitions, prayers, intercessions, thanksgivings to be made on behalf of all human beings, [2]On behalf of kings and of all who hold preeminence, so that we might lead a tranquil and quiet life in all piety and solemnity. [3]This is a good and acceptable thing before our savior God, [4]Who intends all human beings to be saved and to come to a full knowledge of truth. [5]For there is one God, and also one mediator of God and human beings: a human being, the Anointed One Jesus, [6]Who gave himself as a liberation fee for all persons, the proof rendered at their own proper times:[d] [7]For which I was appointed as a herald and Apostle—I am telling the truth, I am not lying—and instructor of gentiles in faith and truth. [8]Therefore, I desire the husbands in every place to pray, lifting up holy hands without anger or dissension. [9]Likewise the wives to adorn themselves in well-ordered apparel, with modesty and prudence, not with braids and gold or pearls or extravagantly costly raiment, [10]But rather with what befits women professing reverence for God: good works. [11]Let a wife learn in quietude, in all orderly compliance; [12]But I entrust it to a wife neither to teach nor to wield authority over her husband, but to abide in quietude, [13]Because Adam was formed first, then Eve, [14]And Adam was not deceived; rather the woman, being deceived, came to be in transgression;

c. "The Satan," which is to say, "prosecutor," "accuser," "arraigner."

d. τὸ μαρτύριον καιροῖς ἰδίοις (*to martyrion kairois idiois*): a phrase of some considerable obscurity. It may mean a "proof" or "witness" that has been rendered "in its due season" (or, literally, seasons), or "in their own times," or "in his own times," or "in its own times." My suspicion (and it is no more than that) is that τὸ μαρτύριον serves as a complement of ἀντίλυτρον (*antilytron*)—the manumission fee paid to redeem someone from slavery—in the preceding phrase, and that it refers to the legal writ (or even "receipt") for emancipation, given in the "due times" of those being set free (that is, given when their terms of enslavement end).

¹⁵But she will be saved through the bearing of children, if they abide with temperance in faith and love and holiness.

CHAPTER THREE

¹This is a trustworthy counsel: If anyone aspires to oversight, he is desirous of a good work. ²So it is necessary for a supervisor to be irreproachable, a husband of one wife, temperate, reasonable, orderly, hospitable to strangers, with an aptitude for teaching, ³Not addicted to wine, someone who does not resort to blows but is instead forbearing, not belligerent, not fond of money, ⁴A good leader of his own house, with all dignity, having children in compliant orderliness ⁵(And, if one does not know how to govern his own house, how will he take care of God's assembly?), ⁶Not a neophyte, so that he might not, delirious with arrogance, fall into the judgment of the Slanderer—⁷And he must also have a good repute from outsiders, so that he might not succumb to calumny or to a snare of the Slanderer. ⁸—Necessary likewise for ministers to be dignified, not duplicitous, not overly given to wine, not given to the sordid desire for financial gain, ⁹Guarding the mystery of the faith with a pure conscience. ¹⁰And let these men first be tested and then, being without reproach, let them serve as ministers. ¹¹—Necessary likewise for their wives to be dignified, not slanderers, sober, faithful in all things. ¹²Let ministers be husbands of one wife, leading their children and their own houses well. ¹³For those who minister well obtain a good rank for themselves, and great confidence in the faith that is in Jesus the Anointed. ¹⁴I write these things to you, though I hope to come to you shortly, ¹⁵So that if I am delayed you might know how you need to comport yourself in God's house, which is the assembly of a living God, a pillar and support of the truth. ¹⁶And confessedly the mystery of piety is great—who was manifested in flesh, proved righteousᵉ in spirit, seen

---

e. ἐδικαιώθη (*edikaiōthē*): here employing the same verb that is traditionally translated as "justified" when applied to human beings, but that in all cases

by angels, proclaimed among nations, an object of faith in the cosmos, taken up in glory.

CHAPTER FOUR

[1]Now the Spirit expressly says that in the latter times some will apostatize from the faith, devoting themselves to spirits that lead astray and to teachings of daemonic beings, [2]By the charlatanry of liars, cauterized in their own conscience, [3]Issuing commands not to marry, to abstain from foods—things that God created to be received with thanksgiving by those who have faith and who have fully known the truth. [4]For everything created by God is good, and nothing that is received with thanksgiving is to be cast away, [5]For it is made holy by God's word and by prayer. [6]In laying these things down for the brethren, you will be a good minister of the Anointed One Jesus, nourished on the words of the faith and by the good teachings you have followed. [7]But reject profane and anile myths. And train yourself for piety; [8]For bodily exercise is profitable for a short time, but piety is profitable for all things, holding promise for the present life and for that to come. [9]This saying is trustworthy, and worthy of all acceptance. [10]For we labor and struggle to this end, because we have hoped in a living God who is the savior of all human beings, especially those who have faith. [11]Enjoin and teach these things. [12]Let no one hold your youth in disdain, but instead become a model for the faithful in speech, in comportment, in love, in faithfulness, in purity. [13]Until I come, devote yourself to public reading, to exhortation, to teaching. [14]Do not neglect the gracious gift that is within you, which was given to you through prophecy accompanied by a laying-on of hands by the company of elders. [15]Ponder these things; be absorbed in them, so that your advancement may be apparent to all. [16]Be attentive to yourself and to the teaching. Persevere in

---

properly means either "proved righteous" or "made righteous" (here, presumably, the former).

these things; for, in so doing, you will save both yourself and those listening to you.

CHAPTER FIVE

[1]Do not rebuke an older man, but address him as a father, younger men as brothers, [2]Older women as mothers, younger women as sisters, in all purity. [3]Honor widows who are really widows. [4]But, if any widow has children or grandchildren, let those persons learn to show piety toward their own house and to repay their forebears with due requitals; [5]Now she who is a widow in reality, and who has been left all alone, has placed her hope in God and perseveres in petitions and prayers night and day; [6]But she who is living profligately, though living, has died. [7]And enjoin these things, so that they may be without reproach. [8]And if anyone does not provide for his own, and especially for his household, he has denied the faith—is indeed worse than faithless.

[9]Let a widow be put on the rolls when she has reached no less than sixty years of age as a wife of one man, [10]Having received attestation for good works: whether she has raised children, whether she has been hospitable to strangers, whether she has washed the feet of holy persons, whether she succored the afflicted, whether she complied with every good work; [11]But refuse younger widows, because, if they grow libidinous while belonging to the Anointed, they want to marry, [12]Inviting judgment because they have cast aside their prior fidelity;[f] [13]And at the same time they also learn to be idle, going about to all the households— and not only idlers, but gossips and meddlers also, talking about things that are improper. [14]Therefore, I counsel younger women to wed, to bear children, to be mistresses of households, to give the enemy no pretext for the sake of slander; [15]For some have already turned away in the Accuser's train. [16]If any woman of faith harbors widows, let her give

f. τὴν πρώτην πίστιν (*tēn prōtēn pistin*): "the first faith," "the earlier trust," "the prior pledge."

them relief, and let the assembly not be burdened, so that it may give relief to those who really are widows. ¹⁷Let those elders who preside well be accounted worthy of double honor, especially those laboring at discourse and teaching. ¹⁸For the scripture says, "You shall not muzzle an ox when it is treading grain" and "Worthy is the worker of his pay." ¹⁹Do not entertain an accusation made against an elder except upon the word of two or three witnesses. ²⁰To those who sin, make your reproof in front of everyone, so that everyone else may be daunted. ²¹I solemnly attest, before God and the Anointed and the chosen angels, that you are to keep these things without prejudice, doing nothing out of partiality; ²²Lay hands on no one hastily, neither have communion in the sins of others; keep yourselves pure. ²³No longer drink water, but instead use a little wine for the sake of your stomach and of your frequent ailments. ²⁴Some men's sins are evident from the first, leading the way to judgment, while some men they pursue close behind; ²⁵Similarly, works that are good are evident from the first, while those that are otherwise cannot be hidden.

CHAPTER SIX

¹As many as are under yoke as slaves, let them esteem their own masters worthy of every honor, so that God's name and teaching should not be blasphemed. ²And those who have masters who have faith, let them not think slightly of them because they are brothers, but let them slave yet better for them, because the recipients of that good work are persons faithful and beloved. Teach and exhort these things.

³If anyone teaches otherwise, and does not consent to these sound words, which are those of our Lord Jesus the Anointed, and to the teaching that accords with piety, ⁴He has become deluded with arrogance, understanding nothing; but he has a sickness for controversies and verbal battles, from which come envy, strife, blasphemies, wicked suspicions, ⁵Constant quarrels by men of corrupt mind and deprived of the truth, supposing piety to be a means of gaining a livelihood.

[Withdraw from such men.] ⁶But the great profit is piety accompanied by self-sufficiency; ⁷For we have brought nothing into the cosmos, neither obviously can we carry anything away; ⁸But, having things to eat and things to wear, we shall be satisfied with these. ⁹But those who want to be rich are falling into temptation and are ensnared by many witless and injurious longings, which plunge human beings into ruin and destruction. ¹⁰For the love of money is a root of all evils, in reaching out for which some have wandered from the faith and pierced themselves about with many pains. ¹¹But you, O man of God, flee from these, and pursue righteousness, piety, faithfulness, love, endurance, gentleness. ¹²Struggle in the good struggle of the faith, lay hold of the life of the Age, for which you were called and for which you confessed the good confession before many witnesses. ¹³Before the God who makes all things live, and before the Anointed One Jesus who bore witness to the good confession in the time of Pontius Pilate, I enjoin ¹⁴That you keep the commandment, immaculate, irreproachable, until the radiant appearing of our Lord Jesus the Anointed, ¹⁵Which he will display in his own proper times, the blissful and only Dynast, the King of those who reign and Lord of those who exercise lordship, ¹⁶He who alone possesses immortality, dwelling in unapproachable light, whom none among human beings has seen or can see, to whom the honor and might of the Age; amen. ¹⁷To those who are rich in this present age, command them not to be high-spirited, and to vest hope not in the hiddenness of riches,ᵍ but rather in God, who richly provides us all things for enjoyment, ¹⁸To work the good, having their riches in good deeds, readily giving away, communalists,ʰ ¹⁹Storing for themselves the treasury of a

g. ἀδηλότητι (*adēlotēti*): the common translation of ἀδηλότης (*adēlotēs*) is "uncertainty," but principally in the sense of "obscurity," "unclarity"; literally, it means "what is not manifest" or "not evident." Here I suspect it means simply the hiddenness of riches stored away in private possession.

h. κοινωνικούς (*koinōnikous*): this is often translated as "generous," "liberal," or "sharing"; but, more properly, κοινωνικός (*koinōnikos*) refers to something held in common trust or communally owned; applied to a person, it might better

good foundation for the future, so that they may take hold of the life that is real. [20]O Timothy, guard the deposit, turning away from the profane inanities and antitheses of what is falsely named knowledge, [21]In professing which some have missed their aim as regards the faith.

Grace be with you.

be translated either as "belonging to the community" or "sharing his property in common." In fact, it would probably be accurate to render the term here as "communists."

The Second Letter to Timothy

ATTRIBUTED TO PAUL

CHAPTER ONE

¹Paul, an Apostle of the Anointed One Jesus by the will of God, according to a promise of the life that is in the Anointed One Jesus, ²To Timothy, beloved child: grace, mercy, peace from God the Father and the Anointed One Jesus our Lord.

³I am grateful to God—whom I worship from my ancestors with a pure conscience—that I keep remembrance of you in my petitions, night and day, ⁴Yearning to see you, having been reminded of your tears, so that I might be filled with joy, ⁵Calling to memory the unfeigned faithfulness in you, which previously resided in your grandmother Lois and your mother Eunice, and which I am convinced also resides in you. ⁶For which reason I remind you to fan the flame of the gracious gift of God, which is within you through the laying-on of my hands. ⁷For God gave us a spirit not of cowardice, but of power and of love and of moderation. ⁸Therefore, do not be ashamed of the witness of our Lord, or of me his prisoner, but be fellow sufferers of evil for the sake of the good tidings, by the power of God, ⁹Who has saved us and called us with a holy calling, not according to our observances, but according to his own purpose and grace, which is given to us in the Anointed One Jesus from before the times of the ages,ᵃ ¹⁰But which is now made manifest by the appear-

---

a. "Aeonian times."

ing of our savior the Anointed One Jesus, abolishing death, and having brought life and incorruption to light by the good tidings, ¹¹To which I was appointed as a herald and an Apostle and a teacher; ¹²For which reason I suffer these things as well, but am not ashamed, for I know in whom I have had faith, and I am convinced that he is able to guard my deposit for That Day. ¹³Hold on to the model of the sound words that you heard from me, in faith and in the love that is in the Anointed One Jesus; ¹⁴Guard the good deposit by the Holy Spirit dwelling within us. ¹⁵You are aware of this: that all those in Asia have turned away from me, Phygelus and Hermogenes among them. ¹⁶May the Lord bestow mercy on the house of Onesiphorus, because he often refreshed me and was not embarrassed by the chain binding me; ¹⁷Rather, on arriving in Rome he diligently sought and found me—¹⁸May the Lord grant it to him to find mercy from the Lord on That Day—and you are well aware of the matters he took care of in Ephesus.

CHAPTER TWO

¹So you, my child, be empowered by the grace that is in the Anointed One Jesus, ²And those things that you have heard from me—by way of numerous witnesses—commit these to faithful men who will be competent to teach others. ³Be a fellow sufferer of evil, like a good soldier of the Anointed One Jesus. ⁴One who serves as a soldier is disentangled from life's affairs, so that he might execute what the one who enlisted him in the army pleases. ⁵And if, indeed, a man competes as an athlete he does not receive the crown unless he competes lawfully. ⁶The husbandman who labors should be first to partake of the fruits. ⁷Think what I am saying, for the Lord will give you understanding in all things. ⁸Remember Jesus the Anointed raised from the dead, of the seed of David, in keeping with my proclamation of the good tidings; ⁹For which I suffer evil, even to the point of being put in chains as an evildoer; but God's word has not been enchained. ¹⁰Therefore I endure all things for the sake of those who are chosen, so that they might obtain

the salvation that is in the Anointed One Jesus, along with the glory of the Age. [11]This saying is trustworthy: For, if we died with him, we shall also live with him; [12]If we endure, we shall also reign with him; if we shall deny him, he will also deny us; [13]If we are unfaithful, he remains faithful, for he cannot deny himself. [14]Give reminders of these things, solemnly pledging before God not to engage in verbal battles, which lead to nothing useful, but bring catastrophe to those hearing them. [15]Hasten to present yourself proven to God, a worker unashamed, cutting the word of truth straight. [16]And shun profane inanities, for they will lead on to more impiety, [17]And their talk will eat away like a gangrene—among these are Hymenaeus and Philetus, [18]Who missed their aim as regards the truth, saying the resurrection has come already, and they have overturned certain persons' faith. [19]But God's foundation stands firm, bearing this seal: "The Lord knows those who are his own" and "Let everyone naming the Lord's name stand away from injustice." [20]Now, in a great household there are vessels not only gold and silver, but wooden and earthen as well, and some are for worthy occasions and others for common; [21]So, if someone purifies himself of these latter, he will be a vessel for worthy employment, having been made holy, well useful to his master, having been prepared for every good work. [22]And flee youthful lusts and—along with those who call on the Lord from a pure heart—pursue justice, faith, love, peace; [23]But refuse imbecile and untutored questions, knowing that they breed fights; [24]And a slave of the Lord must not engage in fights, but must be gentle toward all, able to teach, forbearing, [25]Correcting opponents leniently, in case God might perhaps give them a turning of the heart toward a full knowledge of truth, [26]And they might recover their sobriety, slipping from the snare of the Slanderer, having been caught by him to do his will.

CHAPTER THREE

[1]And know this: that in the last days there will be difficult times; [2]For human beings will be lovers of self, lovers of money, shamelessly boast-

ful, arrogant, blasphemous, disobedient to parents, ungracious, unholy, ³Lacking natural affection, implacable, slanderous, intemperate, savage, without love of the good, ⁴Traitorous, reckless, delirious with conceit, lovers of pleasure rather than lovers of God, ⁵Holding to piety's form but rejecting its power. And turn away from these men. ⁶From this sort of men come those who creep into homes and captivate little women burdened with sins and carried away by diverse lusts, ⁷Always studying and never able to arrive at a full knowledge of truth. ⁸And, just as Jannes and Jambres opposed Moses, so these men also oppose the truth, depraved in mind and reprobate as regards the faith. ⁹But they will advance no further, for their foolishness will be quite evident to all, just as those men's came to be. ¹⁰But you have closely followed my teaching, conduct, purpose, faith, magnanimity, love, endurance, ¹¹Persecutions, sufferings (such as befell me in Antioch, in Iconium, in Lystra)—what persecutions I endured, and out of them all the Lord delivered me! ¹²And in fact all who seek to live piously in the Anointed One Jesus will be persecuted, ¹³While wicked men and seductive imposters will continue their advance toward the worse, leading astray and going astray. ¹⁴But, as for you, continue in the things you have learned and been persuaded of, knowing those from whom you learned them, ¹⁵And knowing that from infancy you have known sacred scriptures, which can give you wisdom leading to salvation through faith in the Anointed One Jesus. ¹⁶Every scripture is divinely inspired,ᵇ and profitable for teaching, for reproof, for correction, for training in righteousness, ¹⁷So that the man of God may be fitted completely, having been fitted out for every good work.

CHAPTER FOUR

¹ Before God and the Anointed One Jesus, who is about to judge living and dead both by his appearing and by his Kingdom, I solemnly

b. θεόπνευστος (*theopnevstos*): "God-breathed," "God-inspired."

adjure: ²Proclaim the word; be faithful to it in season and out of season, reprove, admonish, exhort with all magnanimity and instruction. ³For a season will come when, having a tickling at the ear, they will not tolerate sound teaching, but will heap up teachers attuned to their own preferences, ⁴And in fact will avert the ear from the truth, and will be diverted toward myths. ⁵As for you, though, be sober in all things, suffer evil, do the work of an evangelist, fulfill your ministry. ⁶For I am already being poured out in libation, and the time of my departure has arrived. ⁷I have struggled the good struggle, I have finished the race, I have kept the faith. ⁸As for the rest, the crown of justice is laid up for me, which the Lord, the just judge, will award me on That Day—and not only me, but also all who have loved his appearing.

⁹Hasten to come to me in short order, ¹⁰For Demas, loving the present age, abandoned me and went to Thessalonika, Crescens to Galatia, Titus to Dalmatia; ¹¹Luke alone is with me. Take Mark along and bring him with you; for he is useful to me in ministering. ¹²And I sent Tychicus to Ephesus. ¹³When you come, bring the cloak I left in Troas with Carpus, as well as the books, the parchments especially. ¹⁴Alexander the coppersmith showed me many evils; the Lord will reward him according to his deeds, ¹⁵Against whom you too be on guard, for he opposed our discourse strenuously. ¹⁶At my first public defense, no one came to be beside me, but all abandoned me; may it not be counted against them. ¹⁷But the Lord stood by me and empowered me, so that through me the proclamation might be fulfilled and all the gentiles might hear, and I was rescued out of a lion's mouth. ¹⁸The Lord will deliver me from every wicked deed and will save me for his heavenly Kingdom—to whom be the glory unto the ages of the ages; amen.

¹⁹Greet Priscus and Aquila and the household of Onesiphorus. ²⁰Erastus remained in Corinth, but Trophimus I left ailing in Miletus. ²¹Hasten to come before winter. Eubulus and Pudens and Linus and Claudia and all the brethren greet you.

²²The Lord be with your spirit. Grace be with you.

The Letter to Titus

ATTRIBUTED TO PAUL

CHAPTER ONE

¹Paul, a slave of God and an Apostle of Jesus the Anointed One according to the faith of God's chosen ones, and according to the full knowledge of truth that accords with piety, ²In hope of the life of the Age, which God, who does not lie, promised before the times of the ages,[a] ³And who in his own due times made his word manifest by a proclamation, with which I was entrusted by the command of God our savior, ⁴To Titus, a true child by virtue of a faith held in common: grace and peace from God the Father and the Anointed One Jesus our savior.

⁵For this reason I left you in Crete: so that you might set right the things still needing to be done, and might appoint elders in each city as I enjoined you—⁶If there is anyone who is irreproachable, husband of one wife, having faithful children, not under accusation of profligacy, not insubordinate. ⁷For it is necessary that a supervisor, as God's steward, be irreproachable—not self-willed, not vehement, not addicted to wine, not someone who resorts to blows, not prone to the sordid desire for financial gain—⁸But must instead be hospitable to strangers, a lover of the good, of sound mind, just, holy, self-controlled, ⁹Holding to the trustworthy word, in keeping with what he has been taught, so that he might be able both to encourage by sound teaching and to convince

---

a. "Aeonian times."

opponents. ¹⁰For there are many unruly men, vain talkers and deceivers, especially those of the circumcision, ¹¹Who must be muzzled, who overturn whole households, teaching things they should not for the sake of sordid financial gain. ¹²One of them, one of their own prophets, has said, "Cretans are always liars, evil beasts, idle gluttons." ¹³This testimony is true. For this reason, rebuke them cuttingly, so that they might be sound in the faith, ¹⁴Not heeding Judaean myths and commandments from men who turn away from the truth. ¹⁵To the pure all things are pure; but to the defiled and faithless nothing is pure; instead, their mind and conscience are both defiled. ¹⁶They profess to know God but deny him by their deeds, being abominable and recalcitrant and reprobate toward every good work.

CHAPTER TWO

¹But, as for you, say things that are marked by sound teaching: ²Older men are to be sober, solemn, sensible, sound in faith, in love, in perseverance; ³Older women likewise reverent in demeanor, not slanderers, not enslaved by an excess of wine, teachers of the good, ⁴So that they might train the young women to be lovers of their husbands, lovers of children, ⁵Sensible, pure, working in the household, stationed below their own husbands, in order that God's word should not be maligned. ⁶Likewise, urge the younger men to be sensible, ⁷In all things showing yourself a model of good works; when teaching, exhibiting incorruptibility, dignity, ⁸And sound speech, beyond reproach, so that any opponent may be embarrassed, having nothing ill to say of us. ⁹Slaves are to be ordered under their own masters in all things, to be well-pleasing, not argumentative, ¹⁰Not pilfering, but rather demonstrating all good faith, so that in all things they may give adornments to the teaching of God our savior. ¹¹For the grace of God has appeared, giving salvation to all human beings, ¹²Teaching us that we, in rejecting impiety and the desires proper to the cosmos, may live sensibly and rightly and piously

in the present age, [13]Awaiting the blissful hope, and the appearing of the glory, of the great God and of our savior, the Anointed One Jesus, [14]Who gave himself on our behalf so that he might buy us out of all lawlessness, and might purify for himself a people of his very own, zealous for good works. [15]Say these things, and exhort and reprove with all the power of command; let no one hold you in contempt.

CHAPTER THREE

[1]Remind them to be ordered under rulers, under authorities, to obey authority, to be ready for every good work, [2]To speak evil of no one, not to be belligerent, showing gentleness to all human beings. [3]For in the past we ourselves were also witless, disobedient, led astray, enslaved to various lusts and pleasures, passing our lives in malice and envy, hateful, hating one another; [4]But when the kindness and love for humankind of God our savior appeared—[5]Not from exercises in rectitude that we ourselves had performed,[b] but according to his mercy—he saved us by a washing of regeneration and a renewal of a Holy Spirit, [6]Which he shed upon us richly through Jesus the Anointed One, our savior, [7]So that, having been made righteous[c] by his grace, we might become heirs according to hope of life in the Age. [8]This is a trustworthy saying, and I want you to affirm these things forcibly, so that those who have been faithful to God may set their minds on perseverance in good works. These are things good and profitable to human beings. [9]But shun foolish debates and genealogies and strife and battles about Law, for they

b. οὐκ ἐξ ἔργων τῶν ἐν δικαιοσύνῃ ἃ ἐποιήσαν ἡμεῖς (*ouk ex ergōn en dikaiosynē*, *ᵇa epoiēsan ᵇēmeis*). It is the word "observances," "exercises," or "works," and not the performing of them, that is qualified as being "in rectitude," "in righteousness," "in uprightness." The formulation suggests that the "righteousness" in question is the "right requirements" of the Law of Moses, and that the works are then ritual and legal observances.

c. Or "proved righteous."

are unprofitable and vain. [10]Avoid a sectarian man after a first and a second admonition, [11]Knowing that such a man is perverse and is sinning, having passed judgment on himself.

[12]Whenever I shall send Artemas or Tychicus to you, hasten to come to me in Nikopolis, for I have decided to winter there. [13]Be diligent in sending Zenas the lawyer and Apollo onward, so that they should want for nothing. [14]And let our people also learn how to maintain good works for pressing needs, so that they might not be unfruitful.

[15]All those who are with me greet you. Greet those who love us with faithfulness. Grace be with all of you.

The Letter to Philemon

―――――――

BY PAUL

¹Paul, a prisoner of the Anointed One Jesus, and brother Timothy, to Philemon, a man beloved to us and a fellow worker with us, ²And to sister Apphia, and to Archippus our fellow soldier, and to the assembly that is in your house: ³Grace and peace to you from God our Father and from Lord Jesus the Anointed.

⁴I thank my God always, making mention of you in my prayers, ⁵Hearing of the love and faithfulness that you have toward the Lord Jesus and toward all the holy ones, ⁶So that your communion in the faith might become effective by a full knowledge of every good thing that is within us for the Anointed's sake, ⁷For I have had a great deal of joy and comfort over your love, brother, because the inward parts of the holy ones have been refreshed by you. ⁸Therefore, even though in the Anointed I have plenty of confidence in commanding the proper thing from you, ⁹For love's sake I instead beseech you: Being such as I am—old man Paul—and now a prisoner of the Anointed One Jesus as well, ¹⁰I implore you regarding my child Onesimus, whom I begot in my chains—¹¹Someone who was formerly useless to you but who is now of use to you and to me, ¹²Whom I have sent back to you—him, which is to say what is innermost to me—¹³Whom I had intended to keep with myself so that he might on your behalf minister to me in the fetters of the good tidings—¹⁴But I was unwilling to do anything without your consent, so that your goodness might be not a result of compulsion, but

something voluntary. ¹⁵For perhaps it is for this reason that he departed for an hour, so that in return you might have him for the Age,ᵃ ¹⁶No longer as a slave, but something beyond a slave, a beloved brother—to me especially, but how much more so to you—both in flesh and in the Lord. ¹⁷Therefore, if you hold me to be a companion, welcome him as you would me. ¹⁸And if he in any way has wronged you or is indebted to you, reckon it to me; ¹⁹I, Paul, have written it with my hand: I will repay (not to mention to you that you are indebted to me for your very self). ²⁰Yes, brother, let me have from you a benefit in the Lord; refresh my inward parts in the Anointed.

²¹I write to you confident of your compliance, knowing that you will do even more than I say. ²²At the same time, moreover, prepare a lodging for me; for I hope that, by your prayers, I shall be graciously granted to you.

²³Epaphras, my fellow captive in the Anointed One Jesus, greets you, ²⁴As do Mark, Aristarchus, Demas, Luke—my fellow workers.

²⁵The grace of the Lord Jesus the Anointed be with your spirit.

a. Perhaps "in return you might have him for life." To be precise, the phrase is ἵνα αἰώνιον αὐτον ἀπέχῃς (ᵇina aiōnion avton apechēs): "that in return you might have him [as] *aeonian*." Paul could mean that Philemon can now welcome Onesimus back as a fellow heir of the Age to come; but it may also be the case that this verse is a play upon Exodus 21:6, the Septuagintal Greek version of which uses the word *aiōn* to mean the lifetime of a slave who elects to remain with his master permanently—though in this case, as the following verse says, Onesimus returns as a companion for life *not* as a slave, but as a brother in Christ.

The Letter to the Hebrews

AUTHOR UNKNOWN

CHAPTER ONE

¹God, having of old spoken to the fathers by the prophets, in many places and in many ways, ²At the end of these days spoke to us in a Son, whom he appointed heir to all things, and through whom he made the ages: ³Who—being a radiance of his glory and an impress of his substance, and upholding all things by the utterance of his power—took his seat at the right hand of the Majesty in the places on high once he had accomplished a purification of sins, ⁴Becoming as far superior to the angels as the name he has inherited surpasses theirs in distinction. ⁵For to which of the angels did he ever say, "You are my Son, this day I have begotten you"? And again, "I shall be a Father to him, and he shall be a Son to me"? ⁶And again, when he brings the firstborn into the world, he says, "And let all of God's angels make obeisance to him." ⁷And, as regards the angels, he says, "The one who makes his angels spirits,ᵃ and his ministers a flame of fire." ⁸But, as regards the Son: "Your throne, O God, is unto the age of the age, and the rod of rectitude is the rod of his Kingdom. ⁹You have loved justice and hated lawlessness; therefore God, your God, has anointed you, above your fellows, with the oil of gladness." ¹⁰And: "You, Lord, at the beginnings laid the earth's foundation, and the heavens are works of your hands; ¹¹They will perish, but

a. Or "winds."

435

you perdure; and all will grow old like a garment; [12]And you will furl them up like a mantle, and like a garment they will be changed; but you are the same and your years will not fail." [13]And to which of the angels has he at any time said, "Sit at my right hand until I set your enemies as a footstool for your feet"? [14]Are they not all ministering spirits, sent forth into service for those about to inherit salvation?

CHAPTER TWO

[1]Therefore it is needful for us to heed more abundantly the things that have been heard, so that we might not drift away. [2]For, if the word spoken through angels proved unalterable and every transgression and disobedience received a just requital, [3]How shall we escape if we neglect so great a salvation, one that, having received a commencement declared by the Lord, was confirmed for us by those who heard it, [4]God also bearing witness along with them by signs and wonders, and by various deeds of power and impartations of a Holy Spirit, in accordance with his will?

[5]For not to angels did he subordinate the world that is coming in, about which we are speaking. [6]And at some point a certain person has borne solemn witness, saying, "What is a man that you remember him? Or a son of man that you watch over him? [7]You made him something just a little less than angels, you have crowned him with glory and honor, [8]You have set everything in order under his feet." For in this subordination of all things he left nothing not ordered under him. But at present we do not yet see all things ordered under him. [9]But we see Jesus, who was made just a little less than angels, having been crowned with glory and honor on account of suffering death, so that by God's grace he might taste of death on behalf of everyone. [10]For it was fitting for him, on account of whom all things are and by whom all things are, to perfect through sufferings the originator of their salvation, who has led many sons to glory. [11]For both he who makes holy and they who are made holy all come from one—for which reason he is not ashamed to call them

brothers, [12]Saying, "I will proclaim your name to my brothers, in the midst of the assembly I will hymn you." [13]And again: "I will put my trust in him." And again: "See, I and the children whom God has given me." [14]Inasmuch, therefore, as the children have blood and flesh in common, he too shared in these same things, so that by death he might render the one holding the power of death—that is, the Slanderer—ineffectual, [15]And might liberate those who had all their lives been bound in slavery by fear of death. [16]For surely he does not reach out to[b] angels, but rather reaches out to the seed of Abraham. [17]Hence it was necessary to become like his brothers in all things, so that he might become a merciful and faithful high priest of God's affairs, in order to make expiation for the people's sins. [18]For, inasmuch as he himself has suffered in being tried, he is able to help those enduring trials.

CHAPTER THREE

[1]Therefore, holy brothers, sharers in a heavenly calling, carefully consider Jesus, the apostle and high priest of our confession, [2]Being faithful to the one making him so,[c] as Moses had also been in [the whole of] his[d] house. [3]For this one has been counted worthy of greater glory than Moses, by the same degree as the honor of a house is exceeded by that of its builder. [4]For every house is built by someone, but the one who

---

b. ἐπιλαμβάνεται (*epilambanetai*): literally, "takes," "lays hold of," "attains to," "reaches," "comes within the reach of," "seizes." Various scholars take the letter to be speaking of Christ either "taking on" the nature of human beings, or "reaching out to aid" human beings, or "becoming available" to human beings, or "seizing hold of" human beings.

c. τῷ ποιήσαντι αὐτόν (*tō, poiēsanti avton*): literally, "to the one making him." "Arians" of every Christian epoch have fastened upon this verse as perhaps meaning that the Son was created by the Father; but, dogmatic issues aside, the verb *poiein* frequently means "make" in the sense of "appoint as," and here the meaning seems quite clear: Christ is faithful to the God who appointed him as "apostle and high priest," just as Moses had been appointed to serve in God's house.

d. That is, "God's."

has built all things is God. ⁵And, while "Moses was faithful in the whole of his house as an attendant," in testimony of the things later to be spoken, ⁶So was the Anointed over his house, but as a Son—he whose house we are, if we hold fast to the confidence and the boast of our hope [, firm until the end]. ⁷Therefore, as the Spirit, the Holy One, says, "Today, if you hear his voice, ⁸Do not harden your hearts as in the rebellion, on the day of temptation in the wilderness, ⁹When your fathers tempted me with a test, and saw my works for forty years; ¹⁰Hence I was provoked by that generation, and I said, 'Always they go astray in the heart, and they do not know my paths,' ¹¹So in my indignation I swore, 'They shall not enter into my rest.'" ¹²Watch, brothers, that there shall never be in any of you the wicked heart of faithlessness, in apostasy from a living God, ¹³But rather encourage one another every day, for as long as it is still called "today," so that none of you might be hardened by sin's deceitfulness—¹⁴For we have become partakers of the Anointed if indeed we cling to the origin of our assurance, firm to the end—¹⁵By saying, "Today, do not harden your hearts, as in the rebellion." ¹⁶For who are they who heard and rebelled, except all of those who came out of Egypt, led by Moses? ¹⁷And with whom was he angry for forty years, except those who had sinned, whose corpses dropped in the wilderness? ¹⁸And to whom did he swear that they "shall not enter" his rest, except to those who had disobeyed? ¹⁹And we see that they were unable to enter on account of faithlessness.

CHAPTER FOUR

¹Therefore, as the promise of an entry into his rest has been left open, let us be afraid lest any of you should appear to have fallen short of it. ²And indeed, just like them, we have had good tidings proclaimed to us; but the word that was heard did not profit them, not having been mingled with faith in those who heard it. ³For those who have had faith enter into rest, just as he said: "So in my indignation I swore, 'They shall not enter into my rest.'" And yet the works have been accom-

plished since the foundation of the cosmos. ⁴For somewhere he has spoken thus concerning the seventh day: "And on the seventh day God rested from all his works"; ⁵And again, at this juncture: "They shall not enter into my rest." ⁶Therefore, inasmuch as it remains for some to enter in, and those who formerly received the good tidings did not enter in on account of disobedience, ⁷He again marks out a certain day as "today," saying through David (after so much time had passed), as had been said before, "Today, if you hear his voice, do not harden your hearts." ⁸For, if Joshua had provided them rest, he would not thereafter have spoken about some other day. ⁹So there yet remains a Sabbath rest for God's people; ¹⁰For whoever has entered into his rest has also rested from his works, as did God from his. ¹¹Let us strive, therefore, to enter into that rest, so that no one should fall, after the same pattern of disobedience. ¹²For the word of God is living and active, and sharper than any two-edged sword, piercing so deep as to separate soul and spirit, both joints and marrows, and is a discerner of a heart's reflections and thoughts; ¹³And there is no creature not manifest before him, but all things are naked and laid bare before the eyes of him to whom we are accountable.

¹⁴Therefore, having a great high priest who has passed through the heavens, Jesus the Son of God, let us cling to the confession. ¹⁵For we have a high priest who is not incapable of suffering along with our weaknesses, but rather one who has been tested in all things like us, without sin. ¹⁶Let us therefore approach the throne of grace with boldness, so that we may receive mercy and may find grace for help in due season.

CHAPTER FIVE

¹For every high priest who has been taken from among human beings is appointed on behalf of human beings as regards matters relating to God, so he might offer gifts and sacrifices for sins, ²Being capable of feelings of mildness toward the ignorant and erring, since he is himself also beset by frailty, ³And because of this he must make

offerings for sins—as for the people, so also for himself. ⁴And no one assumes the honor of himself; rather, it is the one called by God, even as Aaron was. ⁵So, also, it was not the Anointed who gave himself the glory of becoming high priest, but instead the one who said to him, "You are my Son, today have I begotten you." ⁶Just as he says in another place as well: "You are a priest unto the Age,ᵉ according to the order of Melchizedek." ⁷Having in the days of his flesh, with a mighty outcry and tears, offered up both supplications and entreaties to the one who was able to save him from death, and having been heard on account of his reverence, ⁸He learned obedience from the things he suffered, even though he was a Son; ⁹And having been perfected he became a cause of salvation in the Age for all who are obedient to him, ¹⁰Having been designated by God a high priest according to the order of Melchizedek.

¹¹Concerning this we have an abundance of things to say, and it is difficult to explicate since you have become lethargic as listeners. ¹²For indeed, though by this time you ought to be the teachers, you again have need of someone to teach you the most elementary principles of God's oracles, and have come to require milk, not solid food. ¹³For everyone who feeds on milk is without experience in the word of righteousness, since he is an infant; ¹⁴But solid food is for full-grown men, whose sensibilities have been trained by use to discern both good and evil.

CHAPTER SIX

¹Therefore, departing from the elementary message about the Anointed, let us press onward to full maturity, not establishing yet again the foundation: of turning the heart away from dead observances, and of faithfulness toward God; ²Instruction regarding baptism, as well as the laying-on of hands, resurrection of the dead, and the judgment of the Age. ³And this we shall do, if God permit. ⁴For it is impossible— regarding those who have been illuminated, and having tasted of the

e. Or "throughout the age."

heavenly gift, and having become partakers in a Holy Spirit, ⁵And having tasted the goodness of God's word and the power of the Age to come, ⁶And then having fallen away—to restore them to a changed heart, since they are themselves re-crucifying the Son of God and subjecting him to open disgrace. ⁷For the land that drinks in the rain frequently falling upon it, and that yields pasturage useful to those for whose sake it has been cultivated, receives a blessing from God; ⁸But if it yields thorns and thistles it is worthless, in fact very nearly a curse, whose end is to be burned. ⁹Yet, brothers, even though we speak in this way, regarding you we are persuaded of things that are better, and that bring salvation. ¹⁰For God is not unjust, so as to forget your work and the love that you have shown toward his name in having ministered—and in ministering—to the holy ones. ¹¹And we desire each of you to demonstrate to the end the same earnestness for a full assurance of hope, ¹²That you might become not dullards, but rather imitators of those who, through faithfulness and longanimity, are inheritors of the promises. ¹³For God, when making the promise to Abraham—since he had no one greater by whom to swear—swore by himself, ¹⁴Saying, "Surely, then, blessing I will bless you, and multiplying I will multiply you." ¹⁵And thus, being long-suffering, he obtained what was promised. ¹⁶For men swear by what is greater, and the oath made as confirmation is an end to all dispute; ¹⁷Wherein God, wishing to demonstrate more plenteously the immutability of his resolve to the heirs of the promise, interposed with an oath, ¹⁸So that, by way of two immutable realities, we who have fled for refuge should have a mighty encouragement to lay hold of the hope set before us: ¹⁹Which we have as an anchor for the soul, safe and unyielding; and which also enters within the veil, ²⁰Where Jesus entered as a forerunner on our behalf, having become a high priest according to the order of Melchizedek until the Age.ᶠ

f. Or "throughout the age."

CHAPTER SEVEN

¹For this "Melchizedek"—King of Salem, priest of the Highest God, who met Abraham returning from the slaughter of the kings and blessed him, ²To whom Abraham apportioned a tenth of everything—is interpreted firstly as "King of Righteousness," and yet also as "King of Salem," which is to say, "King of Peace." ³Without father, without mother, without genealogy, having neither beginning of days nor end of life, and being likened to the Son of God, he remains a priest in perpetuity. ⁴Now contemplate how great this man was, to whom even the patriarch Abraham gave one-tenth his spoils. ⁵And indeed, those of the sons of Levi who receive the priesthood have a commandment to take, by the Law, a tenth from the people—that is, from their brothers, even though they have come from the loins of Abraham; ⁶And yet he, who does not trace his genealogy from them, received a tenth from Abraham, and blessed the one who had received the promises. ⁷And it is altogether incontrovertible that the inferior is blessed by the superior. ⁸And here, in the one instance, mortal men receive a tenth; yet there, in the other, it is attested that he lives on. ⁹And even Levi, who received the tenth, has so to speak paid the tenth through Abraham; ¹⁰For he was still in the loins of his forefather when Melchizedek met him. ¹¹If, then, perfection had come through the Levitical priesthood—for thereupon the people had received the Law—what need was there still for another priest to arise according to the order of Melchizedek, and to be denominated not according to the order of Aaron? ¹²For, when the priesthood has been transposed, there also of necessity comes about a transposition of law. ¹³For he concerning whom these things are said is part of another tribe, from which no one has served at the sacrificial altar; ¹⁴For it is quite clear that our Lord sprang from Judah, a tribe in regard to which Moses said nothing about priests. ¹⁵And this becomes all the more plentifully evident when another priest in the likeness of Melchizedek arises, ¹⁶One who has become such not according to the law of a fleshly commandment, but according to the power of an indestructible life. ¹⁷For it

is attested that "You are a priest unto the Age, according to the order of Melchizedek." [18]For there comes about both the annulment of a previous commandment, on account of its weakness and uselessness—[19]For the Law perfected nothing—and also the introduction of a better hope, whereby we draw near to God. [20]Inasmuch as it did not come without an oath—for those men became priests without an oath, [21]Whereas he did so with an oath, made by the one telling him, "The Lord has sworn, and will not change his mind, 'You are a priest unto the Age'"—[22]By just so much also has Jesus become a surety of a better covenant. [23]And even those who became priests are many in number, because they were prevented from continuing by death, [24]Whereas he, because he abides unto the Age,[g] has a perpetual priesthood; [25]For which reason also he is able to save the entirety of those who approach God through him, as he lives forever to intercede on their behalf. [26]For just such a high priest was fitting for us: holy, innocent, undefiled, set apart from sinners, and having been exalted higher than the heavens, [27]One who has no need, like those high priests, to offer up sacrifices daily, first on behalf of his own sins and then on behalf of the people's; for this he did once and for all in offering up himself: [28]For the Law appoints men who are weak as high priests, but the word of the oath that was made after the Law appoints a Son made perfect[h] unto the Age.[i]

CHAPTER EIGHT

[1]The principal point of these remarks, then: We have just such a high priest, one who has sat down at the right hand of the throne of the Majesty in the heavens, [2]A minister of the Holy of Holies and of that true tabernacle that the Lord—not some human being—erected. [3]For every high priest is appointed to offer both gifts and sacrifices; hence

g. Or "throughout the age."
h. Or "consecrated."
i. Or "throughout the age."

it was necessary for this one also to have something he could offer. [4]If he were on earth, then, he would not in fact be a priest, since there are those who offer the gifts according to the Law, [5]Who worship in a symbol and a shadow of the heavenly places, just as Moses was admonished when he was about to complete the tabernacle: "See," it says, "you shall make all things according to the pattern shown you upon the mountain." [6]Yet now he has obtained a ministry that is superior, by as much indeed as he is mediator of a better covenant, legislated upon better promises. [7]For, if the first one had been free of fault, no place would have been sought for a second one. [8]For, placing blame upon them, it says, "'See, the days are coming,' says the Lord, 'and I will complete a new covenant upon the house of Israel and upon the house of Judah, [9]Not according to the covenant I made with their fathers on the day I took their hand to lead them forth out of the land of Egypt; for they did not abide in my covenant, and I turned my regard from them,' says the Lord; [10]'Because this is the covenant that I shall ordain with the house of Israel after those days,' says the Lord, 'placing my laws in their minds, and I will inscribe them upon their hearts, and I will be God for them and they will be a people for me. [11]And by no means shall they give instruction—each to his neighbor and each to his brother—saying, "Know the Lord," because all will know me, from the least of them to the greatest, [12]Because I will be merciful toward their unrighteousness, and I will certainly remember their sins no more.'" [13]In saying "new," he has made the first one obsolete; and whatever is becoming obsolete and growing old is near to vanishing away.

CHAPTER NINE

[1]So, then, the first had both ordinances for worship and also a worldly sanctuary. [2]For a tabernacle was fashioned, in whose first part, which is called the Holy Place, there were the lampstand and the table and the loaves of presentation; [3]And behind the second veil was a tabernacle called the Holy of Holies, [4]Containing a gold altar of incense and

the Ark of the Covenant covered about on all sides with gold, in which there was a gold jar holding the manna, as well as the rod of Aaron that had borne buds, and the tablets of the covenant, [5]And above it cherubim of glory overshadowing the seat of atonement—things concerning which there is not now the time to speak in detail. [6]Now, these things having been thus arranged, the priests are always going into the first tabernacle, performing the rites of worship, [7]But only the high priest into the second, once in the course of the year, not without blood, which he offers for himself and for the people's ignorances—[8]The Holy Spirit thereby indicating that the way into the Holy of Holies had not been made manifest while the first tabernacle was standing, [9]Which is a parable for the present time, according to which both gifts and sacrifices were being offered that were incapable of perfecting the worshipper in conscience, [10]As they concerned only foods and drinks and various ritual ablutions—ordinances of flesh, imposed until a time of reform.

[11]But when the Anointed had appeared as high priest of the good things that have come to pass through that greater and more perfect tabernacle not made by hand—not, that is, of this creation—[12]Not by blood of goats and calves, but by his own blood, he entered once and for all into the Holy of Holies, having obtained an emancipation payment for the Age. [13]For if the blood of goats and bulls and a heifer's ashes, in sprinkling those who have been made profane, provide a sanctification that purifies the flesh, [14]How much more will the blood of the Anointed, who through a Spirit of That Age[j] offered himself unblemished to God, purify our conscience from dead observances, for worship of a living God! [15]And therefore he is mediator of a new covenant, so that—a death having come to pass for the transgressions that occurred under the first covenant—those who are called might receive the promise of the inheritance of the Age.[k] [16]For where there is an attested covenant, proof of the death of the covenant's testator must nec-

j. "An aeonian Spirit."
k. "The aeonian inheritance."

essarily be adduced; [17]For a covenant is enforced in respect of those who are dead, since it is never in force while the testator of the covenant is alive. [18]Neither, therefore, was the first covenant consecrated without blood. [19]For, when every commandment according to the Law had been spoken to the people by Moses, he took the blood of the calves and the goats, along with scarlet wool and hyssop, and sprinkled the book itself, as well as all the people, [20]Saying, "This is the blood of the covenant that God enjoined for you." [21]And likewise he also sprinkled both the tabernacle and all the vessels of the ministry with the blood. [22]Indeed, according to the Law nearly everything is purified by blood, and without the shedding of blood there is no remission. [23]It was therefore necessary for the representations of the heavenly things to be purified by these sacrifices, but the heavenly things themselves by better than these. [24]For the Anointed entered not into a Holy of Holies made by hand, a mere figural copy of the true one, but into heaven itself, now to appear in God's presence on our behalf—[25]And not so he might offer himself often, like the high priest entering the Holy of Holies year after year with another's blood, [26]As then it would have been necessary for him to suffer often, from the foundation of the cosmos; now, rather, he has appeared just once, at the consummation of the ages, to abolish sin by the sacrifice of himself. [27]And just as it is reserved to human beings to die once, and thereafter judgment, [28]So also the Anointed, having been offered once in order to take away the sins of many, will appear a second time, apart from sin, to those awaiting him for salvation.

CHAPTER TEN

[1]For the Law—containing a shadow of the good things to come, and not the very image of those realities—can never, through those same sacrifices that they continually offer every year, perfect those who approach. [2]Would they not have ceased to be offered otherwise, inasmuch as the worshippers, having once been purified, would no longer have a conscience bearing any sins? [3]Instead, through them there is a yearly

reminder of sins. [4]For it is impossible for the blood of bulls and goats to take away sins. [5]Hence, on entering the cosmos, he says, "Sacrifice and offering you did not desire, but you prepared a body for me; [6]You did not delight in burnt offerings and sin offerings. [7]Then I said, 'See, I have come—it is written of me in a chapter of a book—to do your will, O God.'" [8]When, above, he says, "Sacrifices and offerings and burnt offerings and sin-offerings you neither wish nor delight in"—which are offered according to Law—[9]He has then said, "See, I have come to do your will." He takes away the first so that he may establish the second. [10]By that will we have been made holy, through the offering of the body of Jesus the Anointed once and for all. [11]And every priest stands daily to minister and to offer the same sacrifices frequently, which can never take sins away; [12]And yet this one, having offered one sacrifice for sins in perpetuity, sat down at God's right hand, [13]Waiting since then till his enemies are set as a footstool for his feet. [14]For by a single offering he has perfected those who are being made holy for all time. [15]And the Spirit, the Holy One, also testifies to us; for after having said, [16]"'This is the covenant that I will dispose for them after these days,' says the Lord, 'placing my laws in their hearts, and I will inscribe them on their mind,'" [17]He then adds, "By no means will I still remember their sins and their lawless deeds." [18]And, where these have forgiveness, there is no longer an offering for sin.

[19]Therefore, brothers, having the confidence to enter into the Holy of Holies by the blood of Jesus—[20]By a way fresh[1] and living, which he opened for us through the veil, which is to say, through his flesh—[21]As well as a Great Priest over the house of God, [22]Let us approach with a true heart in faith's full certainty, hearts that have been washed clean of a wicked conscience by sprinkling, and with our body having been washed clean with pure water; [23]Let us cling unwaveringly to our hope's

---

1. πρόσφατον, *prosphaton*: "fresh," "not decomposed," "recent": here, perhaps, having a connotation extending both to the present force of the new covenant and the incorruptibility of Christ's body.

confession; for he who has promised is faithful. ²⁴And let us consider how to incite one another to love and good works, ²⁵And not neglect to gather ourselves together, as is the custom of some, but instead give encouragement—and all the more so as you see the Day drawing near. ²⁶For, if we sin willfully after receiving full knowledge of the truth, a sacrifice for sins no longer remains, ²⁷But instead a certain terrifying expectation of judgment, and the fervency of the fire that is about to consume the adversaries. ²⁸Anyone disregarding the Law of Moses dies without mercies on the word of two or three witnesses; ²⁹How much worse a punishment, do you think, will he deserve who has trampled upon the Son of God, and who has profaned the blood of the covenant by which he was made holy, and who has insulted the Spirit of grace? ³⁰For we know the one who has said, "The exacting of justice is mine, I will repay"; and again: "The Lord will judge his people." ³¹It is a dreadful thing to fall into the hands of a living God. ³²But recall the former days in which, having been enlightened, you endured a considerable struggle with sufferings: ³³On the one hand by being made into a spectacle by insults and afflictions, on the other by being in communion with persons who in this way were overturned; ³⁴For you both suffered along with those in chains and also accepted the seizure of your own possessions with joy, knowing that you had a better and permanent possession. ³⁵So do not cast away your confidence, which has for its recompense a great reward. ³⁶For you need to persevere so that, having done God's will, you may receive what is promised. ³⁷For "In just a very little while, he who is coming will come, and will not delay, ³⁸But my righteous one will live by faith, and if anyone should shrink back my soul does not delight in him." ³⁹But ours is not a shrinking back toward destruction, but faithfulness for preservation of the soul.

CHAPTER ELEVEN

¹Now faithfulness is the substance of things hoped for, the evidence of unseen realities. ²For the ancients were commended for this. ³In faith

we rationally perceive that the ages were composed by an utterance of God, so that the things that are seen have not been made from the things that are manifest. ⁴In faith Abel offered God a more excellent sacrifice than did Cain; through that faith he was attested righteous, God bearing witness to his gifts, and through it he still speaks, even though he has died. ⁵In faith Enoch was translated, so as not to see death, and he was not found because God had removed him. For before this translation he was reputed as one in whom God delighted. ⁶And without faith it is impossible to be pleasing; for the one who approaches God must have faith that he is, and that he becomes a giver of rewards to those who seek him. ⁷In faith Noah, being reverent, having been divinely warned regarding things not yet seen, constructed an ark for his house's salvation, whereby he passed a verdict upon the cosmos and became an heir of the righteousness that comes by faithfulness. ⁸In faith Abraham, being called to go forth to a place he was about to receive as an inheritance, obeyed and went forth, not knowing where he was going. ⁹In faith he sojourned in a land of promise, as in a foreign land, dwelling in tents with Isaac and Jacob, his fellow heirs of the same promise; ¹⁰For he was looking forward to the city that would have foundations, whose architect and builder is God. ¹¹In faith, when Sarah was herself sterile, he also received the power to sow his seed, even beyond his life's proper season, since he deemed him who had made the promise to be faithful.ᵐ ¹²And hence they were born from one man—and he

m. The syntax of this verse is somewhat unclear. It is usually read as if Sarah is the subject of the sentence: "In faith Sarah also, being herself sterile, received power for conceiving seed, even beyond her life's proper season, since she deemed him who had made the promise to be faithful." A number of New Testament scholars have argued for the reading I have offered, however, on grounds I find convincing, if not decisive. Most significant among them is the consideration that the phrase καταβολή σπέρματος, *katabolē spermatos*, which I have rendered "sowing [his] seed," does literally mean something like "dissemination," "casting down seed," and typically refers to the part played by the man in engendering a child (in fact, I know of no exception to this in any other text). Moreover, both the preceding and the following verse concern the story of Abraham, and

a man who had died away—like the stars of heaven in their multitude, and as innumerable as the sand at the lip of the sea. [13]All of them died in faith, not having obtained the things promised, but having seen and hailed them from afar, and they acknowledged themselves to be foreigners and sojourners on the earth.[n] [14]For those who say such things make it quite evident that they are seeking a fatherland. [15]And indeed, had they thought back to the one from which they had departed, they might have had occasion to return; [16]But now they yearn for a better one, which is to say, a heavenly one. Hence God is not ashamed of them, of being called their God; for he has prepared a city for them. [17]In faith Abraham, being tested, offered up Isaac; he who had in fact received the promises was offering up an only son, [18]He to whom it had been said, "In Isaac seed shall be reckoned to you," [19]Having reasoned that God was able to raise him up even from the dead—from which he did indeed, figuratively, receive him. [20]In faith also Isaac blessed Jacob and Esau, in respect to things to come. [21]In faith Jacob, as he was dying, blessed each of the sons of Joseph and, leaning on his staff, made obeisance to him. [22]In faith Joseph, as he was reaching his end, called to mind the exodus of the sons of Israel and issued orders regarding his bones. [23]In faith, when Moses was born, he was hidden by his parents for three months, because they saw that he was a charming child, and they did not fear the king's edict. [24]In faith Moses, when he had grown up, refused to be called a son of Pharaoh's daughter, [25]Choosing to be ill-treated along with God's people rather than to hold onto a temporary enjoyment of sin, [26]Esteeming the reproach of the Anointed a greater wealth than the treasures of Egypt; for he was looking off to the reward. [27]In faith he left Egypt, not having feared the king's anger; for he persevered, as seeing the invisible one. [28]In faith he performed the Passover and the

---

this verse seems clearly to be part of a continuous reflection on the example of Abraham's faith.

n. Or "in the land."

sprinkling of the blood, so that the Destroyer of the firstborn should not touch them. ²⁹In faith they passed through the Red Sea as though through dry land, in having attempted which the Egyptians were swallowed up. ³⁰By faith the walls of Jericho fell, having been encircled for seven days. ³¹In faith Rahab the prostitute did not perish with those who had disobeyed, having welcomed the spies with "Peace." ³²And what more might I say? For time will fail me if I recount the tales of Gideon, Barak, Samson, Jephtha, both David and Samuel, and the prophets, ³³Who through faithfulness conquered kingdoms, effected justice, obtained promises, stopped lions' mouths, ³⁴Quenched fire's power, escaped swords' edges, gained strength out of weakness, became mighty in war, caused foreign armies to yield. ³⁵Women received back their dead by resurrection; and others, not accepting this deliverance, were pounded like drum-skinsᵒ so that they might obtain a better resurrection; ³⁶And others underwent trial with mockeries and floggings and, still worse, chains and prison; ³⁷They were stoned, were sawn asunder, [were tried,] were murdered with the sword; they wandered in sheepskins, in goatskins, impoverished, afflicted, maltreated, ³⁸They of whom the cosmos was not worthy, wandering in deserts and mountains and caverns and holes in the ground. ³⁹And all of them, though reputed for their faithfulness, did not obtain the thing promised, ⁴⁰God having foreseenᵖ something better with regard to us, so that they should not be made complete without us.

o. ἐτυμπανίσθησαν, *etympanisthēsan:* the verb τυμπανίζω, *tympanizō,* refers to beating a drum (τύμπανον, *tympanon*), but it is also related to the verb τυμπανόομαι, *tympanoomai,* which refers to being stretched out like a drum-skin. I suspect that more abstract translations (such as "and others . . . were tortured") fail to capture a very precise image, calling to mind martyrs under the Seleucids like Eleazar in 2 Maccabees 6:19–30, who was stretched out on a device called a *tympanon,* a "drum"—probably the wrack or the wheel—to be "broken" (beaten to death).

p. Or "provided."

CHAPTER TWELVE

¹Therefore, we also, having so great a cloud of witnesses surrounding us, having with such ease put off every encumbrance and the sin besetting us, let us run the contest set before us, ²Looking ahead to Jesus the leader and finisher of faithfulness who, preferring the joy that lay before him, endured a cross, disdaining its shame, and has sat down at the right hand of the throne of God. ³So ponder him who endured so much hostility against himself from sinners, so that you should not grow weary, fainting in your souls. ⁴You have not yet, in struggling against sin, resisted till you bleed, ⁵And you have forgotten the exhortation that addresses you as sons: "My son, neither make light of the Lord's discipline nor faint when you are reproved by him; ⁶Because whom the Lord loves he disciplines, and every son whom he adopts he lashes." ⁷So endure discipline; God is dealing with you as with sons; for what son is there whom a father does not discipline? ⁸And if you are without discipline, of which all come to have a share, then you are bastards and not sons. ⁹Moreover, we have had fathers of our flesh who were disciplinarians, and we respected them; shall we not be far more subordinate to the Father of the spirits, and live? ¹⁰For they indeed imposed discipline for a few days as they deemed fit; he does so for our benefit, so that we might participate in his holiness. ¹¹Of course, no discipline seems a joy in the present, but rather something grievous; and yet afterward, for those who have been trained by it, it yields a peaceful fruit of righteousness.

¹²So make your limp hands and slackened knees stiff again, ¹³And make straight trails for your feet, so that the one who is lame might not be turned away but might instead be healed. ¹⁴Pursue peace with all, and holiness, without which none will see the Lord, ¹⁵Watching so that no one lag behind God's grace, so that no root of bitterness should spring up to cause disturbance and the many be defiled by it, ¹⁶So that there be no whoring and profane person, like Esau who parted with his rights of primogeniture for a single meal. ¹⁷For afterward, as you know, he

was rejected when he wanted to inherit the blessing, though he sought it with tears, for he had found no room for a change of heart. ¹⁸For you have not come to something tangible and set ablaze with fire, and to deep gloom, and to a storm, ¹⁹And to a trumpet's echo, and to a voice uttering words whose hearers begged that no further word be imposed upon them; ²⁰For they could not bear what was commanded: "Should even a beast touch the mountain, it must be stoned." ²¹And what appeared was so dreadful that Moses said, "I am terrified and trembling." ²²Rather you have come to Mount Zion and to the city of a living God, a heavenly Jerusalem, and to myriads of angels, ²³And to [a full gathering and] an assembly of the firstborn, enrolled in the heavens, and to God the judge of all, and to spirits of the righteous who have been perfected, ²⁴And to Jesus the mediator of a new covenant, and to a blood for sprinkling that bespeaks something better than that of Abel. ²⁵See to it that you do not refuse the one who speaks; for if they who refused the one who warned them on earth did not escape, how much less we if we turn away from the one doing so from the heavens: ²⁶Whose voice back then shook the earth, but now has given a promise, saying, "Once more I will shake not only the earth, but also heaven." ²⁷Now, this "once more" indicates the removal of things that are shaken, as things that have been made, so that the things unshaken might remain. ²⁸Therefore, receiving an unshakable Kingdom, let us have grace, by which we may worship God as delights him, with reverence and awe, ²⁹For indeed our God is a consuming fire.

CHAPTER THIRTEEN

¹Let brotherly love abide. ²Do not neglect hospitality to strangers; for thereby some have entertained angels unawares. ³Remember those in chains as though you were chained with them, those maltreated as though you too were yourselves in their body. ⁴Let marriage be honored by all, and the marriage bed undefiled; for God will judge the whoring

and adulterous. [5]Let it be your way to be devoid of any fondness for money, being satisfied with whatever things are present, for he has himself said, "I will never desert you, nor will I ever forsake you." [6]So we are emboldened to say, "The Lord is a helper to me, I will not be afraid; what shall a human being do to me?"

[7]Remember your leaders, who spoke God's word to you; contemplating the result of their conduct, imitate their faithfulness. [8]Jesus the Anointed is the same yesterday and today and unto the ages. [9]Do not be carried about by various and strange teachings; for it is good for the heart to be made firm by grace, not by foods, which do not profit those who are occupied with them. [10]We have an altar of sacrifice, from which those who worship in the tabernacle have no authorization to eat. [11]For the bodies of those animals whose blood, on behalf of sins, is brought into the Holy of Holies by the high priests are burned outside the camp; [12]Thus Jesus also suffered outside the gate, so that he might make the people holy by his own blood. [13]So let us go forth to him outside the camp, bearing the reproach directed at him; [14]For here we have no abiding city, but instead seek the one about to come. [15]Through him, therefore, let us always offer up a sacrifice of praise to God; this is the fruit of lips confessing his name. [16]And do not neglect beneficence and communal ownership; for with such sacrifices God is delighted. [17]Comply with and submit to your leaders, for they stand vigil on behalf of your souls as men who render an account, so that they may do this with joy and not groaning; for the latter is profitless for you. [18]Pray for us, for we are convinced we have a good conscience, intending to conduct ourselves well in all things. [19]And I exhort you to do this still more copiously, so that I might be restored to you sooner.

[20]Now may the God of peace—who by blood of a covenant for the Age has led the great shepherd of the flocks up from the dead, our Lord Jesus—[21]Equip you with everything good for doing his will, making within us what is delightful before him through Jesus the Anointed, to whom be glory unto the ages of the ages; amen. [22]And I exhort you,

brothers, bear with the word of this exhortation, for indeed I have written to you with brevity. [23]Know that our brother Timothy has been released, with whom I shall see you if he should come sooner. [24]Greet all your leaders and all the holy ones. Those from Italy greet you.

[25]Grace be with you all.

The Letter of James

¹James, a slave of God and of Lord Jesus the Anointed, to the twelve tribes in the Diaspora: Greetings.

²Consider it all joy, my brothers, whenever you might fall into various trials, ³Knowing that the testing of your faithfulness produces perseverance. ⁴And let perseverance have its operation in full, so that you may be perfect and whole, lacking nothing. ⁵But, if any of you lacks wisdom, let him ask for it from the God who gives to all unreservedly and without reproach, and it will be given to him. ⁶But let him ask in faith, not hesitating, for he who hesitates is like a wave of the sea driven by the wind and tossed about. ⁷For let that man not presume he will receive anything from the Lord: ⁸A man divided in soul, fickle in all his ways. ⁹And let the lowly brother exult in his elevation, ¹⁰But the rich man in his abasement, because he will pass away like a flower in the grass; ¹¹For the sun rose with a scorching heat and withered the grass, and its flower fell away, and the loveliness of its face perished; thus also will the rich man fade away amid his undertakings. ¹²How blissful the man who endures trial, because—having become proven—he will receive the crown of the life that he has promised to those who love him. ¹³Let no one who is being tempted say, "I am being tempted by God"; for God is incapable of temptation by evil things, and himself tempts no one. ¹⁴But everyone is tempted by his own desire, being drawn away and enticed;

[15]This desire, having conceived, gives birth to sin, and sin fully grown bears death as its offspring. [16]Do not go astray, my beloved brothers.

[17]Every good act of giving and every perfect gift is from above, descending from the Father of the Luminaries, with whom there is no alternation or shadow of change. [18]Having so resolved, he gave birth to us by a word of truth, so that we should be a kind of firstfruits from among his creatures.

[19]Know this, my beloved brothers: Let every man be swift to listen, slow to speak, slow to indignation; [20]For a human being's indignation does not accomplish God's justice. [21]Hence, putting away every defilement and surfeit of evil, receive in gentleness the implanted word, which can save your souls. [22]And become doers of the word, and not only hearers, thus deluding yourselves. [23]Because, if anyone is a hearer of the word and not a doer, he is like a man observing the face he was born with in a mirror; [24]Because he has observed himself and gone away, and has immediately forgotten what he was like. [25]For the one who has gazed intently into the perfect law, which is one of freedom, and has stayed there next to it, becoming not a forgetful listener but instead a doer of work—this one will be blissful in what he does. [26]If anyone fancies himself religious while not bridling his tongue, but instead deceiving his own heart, his religion is empty. [27]Pure and undefiled religion before the God and Father is this: to watch over orphans and widows in their affliction, to keep oneself unstained by the cosmos.

CHAPTER TWO

[1]My brothers, hold to the faith of our Lord of glory, Jesus the Anointed, without any respecting of persons. [2]For if a man were to enter your synagogue with gold on his fingers and in splendid attire, and a destitute man in begrimed attire were also to enter, [3]And you were to look at the one wearing the splendid attire and say, "Here, be finely seated," and were to say to the destitute man, "Stand over there"

or "Seat yourself below my footstool," [4]Have you not discriminated among yourselves, and become judges whose deliberations are wicked? [5]Listen, my beloved brethren: Has not God chosen the destitute within the cosmos, as rich in faithfulness and as heirs of the Kingdom he has promised to those who love him? [6]But you have dishonored the destitute man. Do not the rich oppress you, and haul you into law courts as well? [7]Do they not blaspheme the good name that has been invoked upon you? [8]Now, if you fulfill what, according to scripture, is a royal law—"You shall love your neighbor as yourself"—you are doing well; [9]But if you are respecters of persons you are committing a sin, being convicted by the Law as transgressors. [10]For whoever keeps the whole Law, yet falters in one thing, has become answerable for everything. [11]For he who has said, "Do not commit adultery" also said, "Do not commit murder." Now, if you do not commit adultery yet do commit murder, you have become a transgressor of Law. [12]Speak and act like persons about to be judged by a Law of freedom. [13]For the judgment on the one who has shown no mercy will be merciless; mercy triumphs over judgment. [14]What is the profit, my brothers, if someone claims to have faith but does not have works? Is faith able to save him? [15]If a brother or a sister are[a] naked or lacking in daily food, [16]And one of you says to them, "Go in peace, be warm and sated," but you do not give them the body's necessities, what is the profit? [17]So also faith by itself, if it does not have works, is dead. [18]Yet someone will say, "You have faith and I have works." You show me your faith without the works, and I will show you faith by my works. [19]You have faith that God is one? You are doing well. Even the daemonic beings have that faith, and they tremble. [20]But are you willing to recognize, O you inane man, that faith without works yields nothing? [21]Was not our father Abraham made righteous[b] by works, offering up his own son Isaac on the sacrificial altar? [22]You see that faith cooperated with his works, and by the works the faith was

a. *Sic.*
b. Or "proved righteous."

brought to completion, [23]And the scripture was fulfilled: "And Abraham had faith in God, and it was accounted to righteousness on his part," and he was called a friend of God. [24]You see that a human being is made righteous[c] by works, and not by faith alone. [25]And, likewise, was not Rahab the prostitute also made righteous[d] by works, sheltering the messengers[e] and sending them forth by a different path? [26]For just as the body without spirit[f] is dead, so also faith without works is dead.

CHAPTER THREE

[1]Not many of you should become teachers, brothers, as you know that we shall receive a greater judgment. [2]For we all falter in numerous ways. If anyone does not falter in speech, he is a perfect man, able also to bridle his whole body. [3]And, when we insert bridles into the mouths of horses to make them comply with us, we also direct their whole body. [4]And look at how ships, which are so enormous and which are driven by powerful winds, are directed wherever the pilot's impulse determines by a tiny rudder; [5]So also the tongue is a small bodily member, yet it boasts of great things. See how immense a forest so tiny a fire ignites. [6]And the tongue is a fire, iniquity's cosmos, defiling the whole body, and setting aflame the wheel of generation, and being itself set aflame by Hinnom's Vale. [7]For every nature[g] — both of beasts and of birds, both

c. Or "proved righteous."

d. Or "proved righteous."

e. ἀγγέλους (*angelous*): one of the few instances in the New Testament where "angel" is used with its strictly literal meaning.

f. Or "breath." Whereas most of the writers in the New Testament tend to use the word *psychē* to speak of the innate principle of life within us and *pnevma* to name a distinct principle (such that, for instance, 1 Thessalonikans 5:23 can speak of spirit, soul, and body as three distinct aspects of human beings), here James apparently uses *pnevma* for the principle of corporeal life, almost certainly as the Greek equivalent of the *neshamah* ("breath," "spirit") that God breathed into Adam in Genesis 2:7.

g. Or "natural kind," "species," in both cases.

of reptiles and of creatures of the sea—is being tamed, and has been tamed, by human nature, ⁸But from among human beings there is no one able to tame the tongue: a restless evil full of lethal venom. ⁹With it we bless the Lord and Father, and with it we curse human beings who have been born according to God's likeness; ¹⁰Out of the same mouth comes blessing and curse. It is not fitting, my brothers, that these things happen thus. ¹¹Does the fountain issue forth from the same spout as both sweet and bitter? ¹²Can a fig tree produce olives, my brothers, or a vine figs? Neither can what is salty produce sweet water. ¹³Who among you is wise and knowledgeable? Let him display his works by comely conduct in wisdom's gentleness. ¹⁴But, if you harbor bitter jealousy and selfish ambition in your heart, do not boast and speak falsely against the truth. ¹⁵This is not the wisdom that descends from above, but is earthly, natural, daemoniacal; ¹⁶For where there are jealousy and selfish ambition, there is disorder and every squalid deed. ¹⁷But the wisdom from above is first of all pure, then peaceable, reasonable, accommodating, full of mercy and good fruits, impartial, unfeigned. ¹⁸And the fruit of righteousness is sown in peace for those who make peace.

CHAPTER FOUR

¹Where do the conflicts and where do the battles among you come from? Is it not from there—from the pleasures waging war in your bodily members? ²You desire and you do not have; you murder and covet and you are unable to obtain; you fight and wage war; you do not have because you do not ask; ³You ask and do not receive because you ask in an evil fashion, so that you might spend on your own pleasures. ⁴You adulteresses, do you not know that friendship with the cosmos is enmity with God? Whoever therefore resolves to be a friend of the cosmos is rendered an enemy of God. ⁵Or do you think it in vain that the scripture says, "The spirit that has dwelt within us yearns to the point of envy"? ⁶But he gives greater grace. Hence it says, "God opposes the arrogant but gives grace to the humble." ⁷Therefore, be subordinate to

God, but oppose the Slanderer and he will flee from you. ⁸Draw near to God and he will draw near to you. Cleanse your hands, you sinners, and purify your hearts, you double-souled men. ⁹Be distressed and mourn and weep; let your laughter be turned to mourning and your joy to dejection. ¹⁰Be humbled before the Lord and he will lift you up. ¹¹Do not speak against one another, brothers. Whoever speaks against a brother or judges a brother speaks against Law and judges Law; if you judge Law, you are not a doer of Law, but a judge. ¹²There is one Lawgiver and judge, he who has power to save and destroy. But who are you who judge your neighbor?

¹³Come now, you who say, "Today or tomorrow we shall journey into this city, and spend a year there, and engage in commerce, and make a profit": ¹⁴You who do not know what your life will be like on the morrow—for you are a vapor, appearing for a short while and then vanishing—¹⁵You should instead say, "If the Lord will it, we shall both live and also do . . ." this or that. ¹⁶But now, in your pretentiousness, you boast; all such boasting is wicked. ¹⁷Therefore, when someone knows to do the good and does not do it, it is sin for him.

CHAPTER FIVE

¹Come now, you who are rich, weep, howling out at the miseries that are coming for you: ²Your riches have spoiled and your garments have become moth-eaten; ³Your gold and silver have corroded, and their corrosion will serve as testimony against you and will eat your flesh like fire. You have kept treasure in the last days. ⁴Look: The wages of the workers who have reaped your lands, which have been unfairly held back by you, clamor aloud, and the outcries of those who have reaped have entered the ears of the Lord Sabaoth. ⁵You lived on the earth in dainty luxury and self-indulgence. You have gorged your hearts on a day of slaughter. ⁶You have condemned—have murdered—the upright man; he does not oppose you.

⁷So, brothers, be long-suffering until the arrival of the Lord. Look:

The farmer awaits the precious fruit of the earth, remaining patient over it until it receives the early and the late rains.[h] ⁸You be patient too, strengthen your hearts, for the Lord's arrival has drawn near. ⁹Do not murmur against one another, brothers, so that you might not be judged—look: The judge is standing before the doors! ¹⁰Brothers, take the prophets who spoke in the name of the Lord for an example of suffering evil and of patience. ¹¹Look: We consider those who persevere blissful. You have heard of Job's endurance and you have seen the ending that came from the Lord—that the Lord is lavishly compassionate and merciful. ¹²But before all else, my brothers, do not swear—neither by the heaven nor by the earth nor by any other object of oaths; rather let your "Yes" be "Yes" and your "No" be "No," so that you may not fall under judgment. ¹³Is anyone among you suffering evil? Let him pray. Is anyone of good cheer? Let him sing psalms. ¹⁴Is anyone among you ill? Let him summon the elders of the assembly, and let them pray over him, having anointed him with oil in the name of the Lord. ¹⁵And the prayer of faith will save the one who is ailing, and the Lord will raise him up, and if he should be someone who has committed sins it will be forgiven him. ¹⁶Therefore fully acknowledge your sins to one another, and pray on one another's behalf, so that you might be healed. An upright man's petition, when it is put into effect, is very powerful. ¹⁷Elijah was a man, with feelings like ours, and he prayed a prayer that it might not rain, and no rain fell upon the earth for three years and six months; ¹⁸And again he prayed, and the sky gave rain, and the earth brought forth her fruit.

¹⁹My brothers, if anyone among you should stray from the truth, and anyone should turn him back, ²⁰Be aware that the one who turns a sinner back from the error of his way will save his soul from death and will cover over a multitude of sins.

h. The Greek, in an idiomatically casual manner, lacks the word "rain" or "rains," but the reference to the seasonal cycle of the region is clear.

The First Letter of Peter

AUTHOR UNKNOWN

CHAPTER ONE

¹Peter, an Apostle of Jesus the Anointed, to the sojourners of the Diaspora in Pontus, Galatia, Cappadocia, Asia, and Bithynia, who were chosen ²According to the foreknowledge of God the Father,[a] by a sanctification of spirit for obedience and for a sprinkling of blood of Jesus the Anointed: May grace and peace be multiplied for you.

³Blessed be the God and Father of our Lord Jesus the Anointed, who through the resurrection of Jesus the Anointed from the dead regenerated us according to his plenteous mercy for a living hope, ⁴For an imperishable and undefiled and unfading inheritance kept in the heavens for you, ⁵Who through faithfulness are protected by God's power for a salvation ready to be revealed in the last time, ⁶In which you greatly rejoice, even though just now you are (if need be) grieved by a variety of trials for a little while yet, ⁷So that the proof of your faithfulness—far more precious than gold that perishes, though it be proven by fire—might be found, leading to praise and glory and honor at the revelation of Jesus the Anointed, ⁸Whom you love without seeing, in whom—having faith, although not now seeing—you exult with ineffable and glorious joy, ⁹Obtaining the end of your faithfulness: salvation of souls. ¹⁰The prophets, who prophesied concerning the grace

a. Compare Romans 8:29–30.

coming to you, inquired about and diligently investigated this salvation, ¹¹Seeking what—or what kind of—season the Anointed's Spirit within them was indicating when it predicted sufferings for the Anointed, and the glories to come thereafter; ¹²It was revealed to them that they were ministering not to themselves, but to you, in these things: things that have now been announced to you by those who have proclaimed the good tidings to you through a Holy Spirit sent forth from heaven— things into which angels long to look.

¹³So, girding up the loins of your mind, being sober, vest your hope completely in the grace being brought to you in the revelation of Jesus the Anointed, ¹⁴As children of obedience, not fashioning yourselves according to the desires of your former ignorance. ¹⁵But, as he who called you is holy, you yourselves be holy too, in every behavior, ¹⁶For it is written, "You shall be holy because I am holy." ¹⁷And, if you invoke as "Father" him who judges according to each person's work, without personal partiality, then pass the time of your sojourn in reverent fear, ¹⁸Knowing that your liberation from the futile conduct of life handed down by your fathers was bought not with perishable things—silver or gold—¹⁹But rather with precious blood of the Anointed, as of an unblemished and immaculate lamb, ²⁰Having been foreknown before the foundation of the cosmos, yet having been made manifest in the last times for the sake of you ²¹Who, through him, have faith in the God who has raised him from the dead and has given him glory, so that your faith and hope might be in God. ²²Having by obedience to the truth purified your souls for unfeigned brotherly love, love one another fervently from a pure heart, ²³Having been regenerated not from perishable—but rather from imperishable—seed by a living and abiding word of God. ²⁴For "All flesh is as grass, and all its glory as a flower of the grass. The grass withers and the flower falls away, ²⁵But the Lord's utterance abides through the age."ᵇ And this is the utterance of the good tidings proclaimed to you.

b. Or "until the Age [to come]."

CHAPTER TWO

¹Therefore, having put away all malice, and all guile, and imposture, and envies, and all slanders, ²Crave the unadulterated milk of reason like newborn babes, so that you may thereby grow into salvation, ³If you have indeed tasted that the Lord is wholesome. ⁴Approaching him—a living stone rejected by human beings yet chosen as precious by God—⁵You yourselves, also like living stones, are being built up as a spiritual house, for a holy priesthood to offer spiritual sacrifices acceptable to God, through Jesus the Anointed. ⁶Because this is contained in scripture: "See: I lay a stone in Zion, a chosen, precious cornerstone, and the one who places faith on it most certainly will not be made ashamed." ⁷To you who have faith, therefore, it is precious; but to those who do not have faith, "A stone that the builders rejected, this has come to be the capstone of the corner"; ⁸And: "A stone of stumbling and a rock of faltering"; they stumble on the word, which they indeed, being unpersuaded, were set on doing.ᶜ ⁹But you are a chosen kindred, a royal priesthood, a holy nation, a people held in peculiar possession, so that you may openly proclaim the virtues of the one who called you out of darkness into his wondrous light—¹⁰Who back then were not a people, but who are now a people of God—who were not pitied, but who have now been pitied.

¹¹Beloved ones, I exhort you as sojourners and resident aliens to abstain from fleshly desires, which wage war against the soul, ¹²Keeping your conduct comely when among the gentiles so that, whatever thing they arraign you for as evildoers, they might from the good deeds they have observed glorify God on a day of his visitation.

¹³Be subordinate to every human institution for the Lord's sake, whether to a king as your superior, ¹⁴Or to governors as those who have

---

c. οἳ προσκόπτουσιν τῷ λόγῳ ἀπειθοῦντες εἰς ὃ καὶ ἐτέθησαν (ᵇoi proskoptousin tō̧ logō̧ apeithountes eis ᵇo kai etethēsan): not, that is, that some were "appointed to stumble" in the sense of "preordained" by God, but rather that some have, by their disobedience or mistrust, set themselves to stumble.

been sent by him to exact justice from evildoers and to praise those who do what is good; [15]For this is God's will: to silence the ignorance of the foolish by doing the good, [16]As free persons—and not as persons using that freedom as a cloak for evil, but rather as slaves of God. [17]Give honor to everyone, love the brotherhood, revere God, honor the king. [18]You who are domestics, order yourselves under your masters with all reverence, not only the good and gentle, but the perverse as well, [19]For, if anyone who suffers unjustly endures his grief out of conscientiousness toward God, it is a grace. [20]For what renown is there if, when you sin and are thrashed, you endure it? But, if you instead endure when doing good and suffering, this is a grace before God. [21]For to this you were called, because on your behalf the Anointed suffered also, leaving behind a model so that you should follow his steps: [22]"Who committed no sin; neither was guile found in his mouth"; [23]Who, when reviled, did not revile in return; who, in suffering, did not issue threats; who delivered himself to him who judges justly; [24]Who himself, in his body, bore our sins upon the tree, so that, having died to sin, we might live for justice—"by whose scarring you were healed." [25]For you were like sheep going astray, but now you have turned back to the shepherd and overseer of your souls.

CHAPTER THREE

[1]Likewise, you wives, order yourselves under your own husbands so that, if any of them are unpersuaded by the word, they will be won over without any word by the conduct of their wives, [2]Observing your pure conduct in reverence; [3]Let your adornment not be external— plaiting your hair and wreathing yourselves in gold, or wrapping yourselves in mantles—[4]But rather the hidden human being of the heart, in that imperishable reality of the gentle and quiet spirit, which in God's eyes is something lavishly opulent. [5]For thus also the holy wives of the past, whose hope was in God, adorned themselves, being stationed under their own husbands, [6]As Sarah obeyed Abraham, calling to him

as lord—she whose children you have become in doing good and in not being afraid of anything alarming. ⁷Likewise, you husbands, cohabit knowledgeably, as with a weaker—the feminine—vessel, rendering honor as to those who are also fellow heirs to the grace of life, so that your prayers not be hindered. ⁸And finally: All of you be of the same mind, sympathetic, with fraternal love, tenderly compassionate within, of humble mind, ⁹Not repaying evil for evil or insult for insult but rather, to the contrary, giving a blessing; because you were called for this, so that you might inherit a blessing. ¹⁰For: "Whoever wishes to love life and to see good days, let him restrain his tongue from evil, and his lips, so that they utter no deceit, ¹¹And let him turn away from evil, and do good; let him seek peace and pursue it; ¹²For the eyes of the Lord are on the righteous, and his ears toward their petition, but the face of the Lord is set against those who do evil."

¹³And who is the one who will harm you if you are zealous for what is good? ¹⁴But if indeed you suffer for the sake of righteousness, how blissful you. "And do not fear their terror, neither be troubled," ¹⁵But in your hearts hallow the Anointed as Lord, ready always to offer a defense to everyone who asks you for an account of the hope within you, ¹⁶Yet with gentleness and respect, harboring a good conscience, so that, whatever they arraign you for, those who spitefully abuse your good conduct in the Anointed might be made ashamed. ¹⁷For it is better to suffer for doing good, if God's will so ordains, than for doing evil. ¹⁸For the Anointed also suffered, once and for all, a just man on behalf of the unjust, so that he might lead you to God, being put to death in flesh and yet being made alive in spirit,ᵈ

d. θανατωθεὶς μὲν σαρκί, ζῳοποιηθεὶς δὲ πνεύματι (*thanatōtheis men sarki, zō̗opoiētheis de pnevmati*): This is a parallel construction using modal datives to indicate the manner or condition in which, on the one hand, Christ died and, on the other, he was made alive. Translations that attempt to insert a reference to the Holy Spirit here defy not only the sense of the verse, but also its syntax. Here, as elsewhere in the New Testament (see Acts 23:8 and 1 Corinthians 15:40–54, along with my notes thereto), the distinction between this life and the life of the resurrection is one between two distinct and (in some sense) antithetical states of

¹⁹Whereby^e he also journeyed and made a proclamation to the spirits in prison, ²⁰To those in the past who disobeyed while God's magnanimity bided its time, in the days of Noah when the ark was being fashioned,^f

---

being: "flesh" and "spirit." It would not be misleading to translate this clause as "being put to death *as* flesh and yet being made alive *as* spirit"; this might, in fact, clarify the logic of the verse that follows (see note *e* below).

e. ἐν ᾧ (*en* ^bō_i): The conjunctive phrase is somewhat obscure, but what seems the plainest meaning is that, because Christ was made alive "as spirit" or "in spirit," he was now able to travel to the "spirits in prison" (regarding whom, see footnote *f* below). This visit is depicted as following Christ's resurrection to new life, not as a "descent into Hades" during the interval between cross and resurrection.

f. These are notoriously obscure verses, but the difficulty they pose is often exaggerated. While below, at 4:6, the text speaks of "the dead" as having been "evangelized," the language here is of Christ "making a proclamation" to "the spirits." This is because at this point the reference is not to human beings who have died, but to angels or daemonic beings imprisoned until the day of judgment (they are mentioned also in 2 Peter 2:4–5 and Jude 1:6). During the intertestamental period, before the "official" canon of Hebrew scripture was generally established for either Jews or Christians, among the most influential holy texts for both communities were visionary books such as 1 Enoch and Jubilees, which (among many other things) recount the apostasy and punishment of various angels and their offspring in the days after the expulsion of Adam and Eve, and the evils these angelic dissidents visited upon the world—the ultimate consequence of which was the flood, sent by God to rescue the world from the iniquity they had set loose. The idea of a pre-cosmic fall of the Archangel "Lucifer" or "Satan" was a later development of Christian thought (see Luke 10:18; 2 Peter 1:19; Revelation 22:6, and my footnotes thereto); in the flood narratives known to the earliest Christians, the only angelic rebellion was that of those "sons of Elohim," or angels, who, according to Genesis 6:2, were drawn by the beauty of "the daughters of men" to wed them; and according to these texts the mysterious "*nefilim*" of Genesis 6:6 (understood as monstrous giants) were the children sired by these angels on human women. According to 1 Enoch there were two hundred of these sons of Elohim, or "Watchers," who abandoned God's heavenly court, led by a Watcher called Semyâzâ; they not only became fathers of the nefilim, but taught their human wives to practice sorcery; and one of them, Azâzêl, taught humanity how to make weapons, jewelry, and cosmetics (with predictably dire results). On being informed of these transgressions by four of his Archangels, God sent the Archangel Michael to imprison the celestial dissidents in the darkness below and to slay the nefilim; but the ghosts of the

by which a few—that is, eight souls—were brought safe through the water, ²¹Which also prefigures the baptism that now saves you—which is not a removal of the filth of flesh but rather the pledged consent^g of a good conscience to God—through resurrection of Jesus the Anointed, ²²Who is at God's right hand, having journeyed into heaven, angels and Authorities and Powers having been made subordinate to him.

CHAPTER FOUR

¹Therefore, the Anointed having suffered in the flesh, arm yourselves with the same mind, for he who has suffered in flesh has rested from sin, ²So as to live the time that remains in flesh no longer for the desires of human beings, but for God's will. ³For the time that has passed away was sufficient for carrying out the purpose of the gentiles,

---

nefilim then became the demons that now haunt the world. According to the book of Jubilees, the angels who became enchanted with the beauty of human women were angels of a lower order assigned to govern the natural elements and kinds of this cosmos. In that version of the tale, the celestial angels imprisoned these fallen cosmic angels in the dark below to await the final judgment, while the nefilim were driven to fall upon and kill one another. After the flood, however, the ghosts of the nefilim were still wandering the earth as demons under their leader, Mastema or Beliar (assuming these are the same figure). When God ordered these bound in prison as well, Mastema prevailed on him to allow a tenth of their number to continue roaming the world till the last day, so as to test humanity and punish the wicked; and thus Mastema comes to serve as "a satan" (that is, an Accuser) in this age. The reference to Christ journeying to these spirits to make his proclamation to them seems to echo the account of Enoch journeying to their abode in order to proclaim God's condemnation upon them (in chapters 12–15 of 1 Enoch).

g. ἐπερώτημα (eperōtēma), most properly a "question" or "inquiry," or sometimes a "request," but also occasionally meaning an answer to a question issued by someone of superior authority (which is to say, a humble answer), in some cases meaning a formal obligation or covenant, including the pledge of assent or promise made in response to a formal question ("Do you promise to discharge . . . ?" "Yes, I promise . . ."). Thus, in the Code of Justinian it appears as the Greek equivalent of the Latin *stipulatio*, and it might also be said to approximate the meaning of *sacramentum* (in the proper sense of an oath of allegiance or solemn vow).

having journeyed along in licentious behaviors, lusts, wine-soaked revels, carousals, drunken debauches, and abominable idolatries. ⁴For this reason they who malign you think it strange you do not run along with them into the same engorged flood of profligacy—⁵They who will give an account to him who is ready to judge living and dead. ⁶Because it was for this that the good tidings were proclaimed to the dead, that though judged in flesh according to human beings they might live in spirit according to God.ʰ

⁷Now the end of all things has drawn near. So be sound of mind and sober, for the sake of prayers; ⁸Above all, have fervent love for one another, for love covers over a multitude of sins, ⁹Being hospitable to one another without murmuring, ¹⁰Ministering to one another—each as he has received a gracious gift—as good stewards of God's manifold grace; ¹¹If anyone speaks, do it as with oracles from God; if anyone ministers, do it as from a strength that God supplies: so that God may be glorified in all things through Jesus the Anointed, to whom be the glory and the might unto the ages of the ages; amen.

¹²Beloved ones, do not be surprised at the cauterizing fire among you—which comes to you as a trial—as though it were something strange that is happening to you; ¹³Rather, rejoice, inasmuch as you have had communion with the sufferings of the Anointed, so that you may also rejoice exultantly at the revelation of his glory. ¹⁴If you are reviled in the name of the Anointed, how blissful you, because the Spirit of glory and of God rests upon you. ¹⁵For let none of you suffer for being a murderer or a thief or an evildoer, or for being a meddler in the affairs of others—¹⁶Yet, if for being a "Christian," let one not be ashamed, but instead glorify God by this name. ¹⁷For it is the time for

h. This, the locus classicus of the ancient Christian teaching of Christ's harrowing of Hades, is definitely a reference to the gospel having been preached (εὐηγγελίστη [evēngelisthē]) to the dead (νεκροῖς [nekrois]), and not (as some willfully distorted renderings have made it) to an evangelization of men and women who have since died.

judgment to commence with the house of God; and, if it starts with us, what will the end be for those who are recalcitrant to God's good tidings? [18]For, "If the upright man is just barely saved, where will the impious and sinful man show up?" [19]So then indeed, let those suffering according to God's will commit their souls to a faithful creator by doing what is good.

CHAPTER FIVE

[1]I therefore exhort the elders among you, as a fellow elder and witness to the sufferings of the Anointed, as well as a communicant in the glory that is about to be revealed: [2]Shepherd God's flock among you, watching over it not under constraint, but willingly, in accord with God, not from the sordid desire for profit, but eagerly, [3]Not as dominating those allotted you,[i] but becoming models for the flock instead; [4]And when the chief shepherd appears you will receive the unfading crown of glory. [5]Likewise, you younger men, place yourselves in order under elders; and all of you array yourselves in humility toward one another, because "God opposes the proud, but to the humble he gives grace."

[6]Therefore, be humbled under the mighty hand of God, so that he may exalt you in due season, [7]Casting all your worry upon him, because your affairs are of concern to him. [8]Be sober, be vigilant. Your adversary the Slanderer prowls about like a roaring lion seeking whom to devour—[9]Whom you must oppose, steadfast in the faith, knowing that the same kinds of sufferings are being visited in full upon the company of your brethren within this cosmos. [10]And may the God of all grace, who in the Anointed has called you to his glory—once you have suffered for a little while—himself mend, confirm, strengthen, establish you. [11]To him be the might unto the ages of the ages; amen.

[12]I wrote to you briefly through Silvanus, who is in my estimation a

---

i. Or perhaps "the things allotted" or "the inheritances."

faithful brother, giving exhortation and attesting that this is God's true grace; stand fast therein. [13]She, your fellow elect in Babylon, greets you, as does my son Mark. [14]Greet one another with a kiss of love.

Peace to all of you in the Anointed.

The Second Letter of Peter

AUTHOR UNKNOWN

CHAPTER ONE

¹Simon Peter, a slave and Apostle of Jesus the Anointed, to those who have obtained a faith equally precious to our own, through the justice of our God and of our savior Jesus the Anointed: ²Grace and peace be multiplied for you by a full knowledge of God and of Jesus our Lord, ³Just as his divine power has given us all the things pertaining to life and piety, through the full knowledge of him who has called us to his own glory and virtue, ⁴Whereby he has given us his precious and majestic promises, so that through these you may become communicants in the divine nature, having escaped from the decay that is in the cosmos on account of desire. ⁵And for this very reason also, having brought along all your earnestness, supplement your faith with virtue, and virtue with knowledge, ⁶And knowledge with self-mastery, and self-mastery with perseverance, and perseverance with piety, ⁷And piety with brotherly affection, and brotherly affection with love. ⁸For, when these things are in you and are increasing, they render you neither idly barren nor barrenly unfruitful for the full knowledge of Jesus the Anointed; ⁹For the one in whom these things are not present is blind, gazing with closed eyes,ᵃ

---

a. μυωπάζων (*myōpazōn*): often translated here as "shortsighted" or "blinking," the word literally means "closed-gazing" or "gazing with closed eyes" or perhaps "gazing with blinkered eyes."

imbibing forgetfulness[b] of the purging of his old sins. [10]Therefore, brothers, be eager instead to make your calling and your election firm; for in doing these things you will surely never fall. [11]For thus the entrance into our Lord and savior Jesus the Anointed's Kingdom in the Age shall be lavishly provided you.

[12]Hence will I always be ready to remind you about these things, even though you know them and have been fully confirmed in the truth that is present. [13]And I deem it right, so long as I am within this tent, to rouse you by a reminder, [14]Knowing that the shedding of my tent is imminent, as our Lord Jesus the Anointed has indeed made clear to me; [15]And I shall also strive to have you at all times, after my going away, make a remembrance of these things. [16]For we were not following after cleverly devised myths when we apprised you of the power and the advent of our Lord Jesus the Anointed, but had instead been eyewitnesses to his majesty. [17]For, when he had received honor and glory from God the Father, a voice was borne to him from the Majestic Glory—thus: "This is my Son, my beloved one, in whom I have delighted"; [18]And we heard this voice borne out of heaven when we were with him on the holy mountain. [19]And we have the still firmer prophetic word, of which you do well to take heed, as to a lamp shining in a dreary place, till day should dawn and Phosphoros[c] arise in your hearts, [20]Knowing this before all else: that no prophecy of scripture comes from a private interpretation; [21]For at no time was any prophecy produced by a human

b. λήθην λαβών (lēthēn labōn): "receiving forgetfulness," "taking forgetfulness," but perhaps in the sense of drinking in the waters of Lethe.

c. Phosphoros, the "Light-Bringer" (Hêlêl in Hebrew, Lucifer in Latin), is the Morning Star (Venus as seen before dawn). Jesus is also identified with this same "Star of Morning" at Revelation 22:16. Though later Christian tradition would conflate Isaiah 14:12 (where the fallen King Nebuchadnezzar II of Babylon is apostrophized as Hêlêl ben Shahar, "Lucifer Son of the Morning") and Luke 10:18 (where Christ describes the missions of his disciples as causing Satan to fall from the sky "like lightning"), and thus produce the idea of the fall of "Lucifer" before creation, in the New Testament texts every association with the Morning Star is a good one, and the only person identified with the star "Lucifer" is Christ.

being's will; rather, human beings spoke from God when they were borne along by a Holy Spirit.

CHAPTER TWO

[1]Yet there arose false prophets among the people as well, just as there will also be false teachers among you who will secretly introduce destructive heresies, even denying the master who has purchased them, bringing swift destruction upon themselves; [2]And many will follow their licentious ways, by whom the path of truth will be blasphemed; [3]And in acquisitiveness they will traffic with you in fabricated discourses— upon whom the verdict passed long ago does not tarry, and their destruction does not slumber. [4]And if God did not spare the angels who sinned, but rather cast them into Tartarus in bonds of nether darkness, held there for judgment,[d] [5]And did not spare the ancient cosmos, but preserved the eighth person, Noah, a herald of justice,[e] having brought a flood upon the cosmos of the impious, [6]And by burning the cities of Sodom and Gomorrah to ashes condemned them to ruin, having provided an illustration for those about to commit impiety, [7]And having rescued Lot, a righteous man oppressed by the lascivious conduct of the lawless— [8]For that righteous man, dwelling with them day after day, was tormented in his righteous soul by observing and hearing of their lawless deeds— [9]The Lord knows how to rescue the pious from trials and to keep the unrighteous guarded in confinement[f] for a day of judgment,

d. The reference here is to those angels or daemonic beings who are, according to Jewish and Christian belief in the intertestamental and early Christian era, imprisoned until the day of judgment (as recounted, for example, in 1 Enoch and the book of Jubilees). They are mentioned also in 1 Peter 3:19–20 and Jude 1:6. See my footnote to 1 Peter 3:20.

e. Though Genesis records only that Noah was a righteous man, there was a well-established Jewish and early Christian tradition of describing him as a prophet or preacher of righteousness who had tried to bring his contemporaries to repentance.

f. κολαζομένους τηρεῖν (*kolazomenous tērein*): usually translated as "to hold

¹⁰And especially those who follow after flesh in a desire for scandalous pollution, and who hold lordship in contempt—bold, self-willed, they do not tremble when they defame the Glories,ᵍ ¹¹Whereas angels, who are greater in strength and power, do not bring a defamatory condemnation against them before the Lord. ¹²But these men, like unreasoning animals born in a state of nature, on the way to capture and decay, uttering defamations in matters of which they are ignorant, will indeed perish in their corruption, ¹³Suffering wrongs as the reward of wrongdoing: deeming it a pleasure to carouse through the day, they are stains and blemishes, reveling in their deceits as they feast with you, ¹⁴Having eyes full of adulteryʰ and incessant in their sins, seducing labile souls, possessing a heart trained in acquisitiveness, children of a curse; ¹⁵Forsaking a straight path, they have gone astray, following on the path of Barlaam son of Bosor, who loved the wages of iniquity, ¹⁶But who was rebuked for his personal transgression by a mute jackass that, speaking in a human voice, restrained the prophet's madness. ¹⁷These men are waterless springs and storm-driven mists, for whom the darkness's nether gloom has been reserved [unto the Age]. ¹⁸For, loudly uttering bloated prolixities, they use flesh's desires to lure back into lascivious

---

them while they are being tormented" or "to hold them while still chastising them" or something equally awkward. But the most proper meaning of κολάζω (kolazō) (even though it is also typically used to mean "chasten" or "punish") is "dock" or "hold in check," while that of τηρέω (tēreō) is "keep under guard," and in this construction the meaning is clear: God knows both how to rescue the pious from their trials and also how to prevent the unrighteous from escaping the judgment that awaits them.

g. This is almost certainly a reference to angels, and perhaps to a special order of angels. These "Glories" or "Glorious Ones" (perhaps identified with the stars) are mentioned as members of God's heavenly court in 2 Enoch 22:7. See also Jude 1:8.

h. μοιχαλίδος (moichalidos): the genitive of μοιχαλίς (moichalis), a word that actually, as a substantive, means "adulteress," but that the text here apparently uses as a synonym for μοιχεία (moicheia), "adultery" (though it may just be possible that the intended image here is that of licentious men gazing in lust at an adulterous woman).

behaviors those who had truly escaped from persons of aberrant conduct, ¹⁹Promising them freedom while being themselves slaves of corruption; for by whatever someone has been vanquished, to that he is enslaved. ²⁰For if—having escaped the defilements of the cosmos by a full knowledge of the Lord and savior Jesus the Anointed and yet having become entangled in them again—they are vanquished, the last things have become worse for them than the first. ²¹For it was better for them not fully to have known the path of righteousness than, having known it fully, to turn back from the holy commandment delivered to them. ²²The proverbial truth of "a dog having returned to its own vomit, and a washed sow to wallowing in a mire" suits them precisely.

CHAPTER THREE

¹Beloved ones, I am writing you a second letter; in them I rouse your pure mind with a reminder ²To remember the words spoken in the past by the holy prophets, and the commandment of the Lord and savior through your Apostles, ³Knowing this before all else: that in the last days scoffers will come to scoff, proceeding according to their own desires, ⁴And saying, "Where is his promised arrival? For since the fathers fell asleep all things remain as they were from creation's beginning." ⁵For this is concealed from those who wish it so: that the heavens long ago existed, and the land was constituted out of water and through water, by the word of God, ⁶By which the world back then perished, flooded by water; ⁷And by that same word now the heavens and earth are stored up for fire, reserved for a day of judgment and of ruin for the impious among human beings. ⁸But do not let this one thing be concealed from you, beloved ones: that with the Lord one day is as a thousand years and a thousand years as a single day. ⁹The Lord is not delaying what is promised, as some reckon delay, but is magnanimous toward you, intending for no one to perish, but rather for all to advance to a change of heart. ¹⁰But the Lord's Day will come like a thief; on it, the heavens will pass away with a rushing sound, and the elements

will be dissolved, burning away, and earth and the works therein will not be found. ¹¹With all these things being thus dissolved, what kind of persons ought you already to be, in holy conduct and piety, ¹²Anticipating and hastening the arrival of God's Day, by which the blazing heavens will dissolve and the burning elements will melt? ¹³But we, in accord with his promise, look forward to new heavens and a new earth, in which justice dwells. ¹⁴Therefore, beloved ones, anticipating these things, be eager to be found immaculate and unblemished by him in peace, ¹⁵And deem our Lord's magnanimity to be salvation, just as our beloved brother Paul, according to the wisdom vouchsafed him, also wrote to you, ¹⁶And just as he does in all his letters when speaking in them about these things—wherein there are some things that are difficult to understand, which the untutored and unstable distort (as they do to the rest of the scriptures too), to their own ruin. ¹⁷You, therefore, beloved ones, knowing this beforehand, be on guard so that you should not fall away from your own steadfastness by being led off along with the lawless in their straying; ¹⁸And grow in grace and knowledge of our Lord and savior Jesus the Anointed. To him be the glory, both now and unto the Day of the Age.ⁱ

i. εἰς ἡμέραν αἰῶνος (eis ᵇēmeran aiōnos): a formula not used elsewhere in the New Testament, probably meaning something like "until that day when the Age to come arrives."

The First Letter of John

ATTRIBUTED TO
"JOHN THE ELDER"

CHAPTER ONE

¹What was from the origin, what we have heard, what we have seen with our eyes, what we have gazed upon and our hands have touched concerning the Logos of Life[a]—²And the Life was made manifest, and we have seen, and bear witness to, and announce to you the Life of the Age, which was present with the Father[b] and which was made manifest to us—³What we have seen and heard we also announce to you, so that you may also have communion with us. And our communion is indeed with the Father and with his Son Jesus the Anointed. ⁴And we write these things [to you] so that our[c] joy might be made full.

⁵And this is the message that we have heard from him[d] and an-

---

a. The prologue to this letter seems quite consciously to echo the prologue of the fourth Gospel in many ways, not only by its initial invocation of what was "from the beginning" or "from the origin" (ἀπ᾽ ἀρχῆς [*ap' archēs*]), nor even by its immediate mention of a *logos*, but by speaking of that logos as belonging to a kind of life that is identified in the next verse as being "present with" God the Father in his divine aeon or "Age" (see footnote *b* below). Hence my choice not to render *logos* here as "word," but rather to leave it untranslated.

b. πρὸς τὸν πατέρα (*pros ton patera*), which may well be an intentional echo of the πρὸς τὸν θεόν (*pros ton theon*) ("present with God") of John 1:1.

c. Some versions of the text read "your."

d. It is unclear here whether the subject is "Father," "Son," or "Logos."

nounce to you: that God is light and in him is no darkness whatsoever. [6]If we say we have communion with him, yet walk in darkness, we are lying and not practicing the truth; [7]If we walk in the light, as he himself is in the light, we have communion with one another, and the blood of Jesus his Son purges us of all sin. [8]If we say we have no sin we lead ourselves astray and the truth is not in us. [9]If we confess our sins, he is faithful and just, so that he may forgive us our sins and purge us of all iniquity. [10]If we say we have not sinned, we make him a liar and his Logos is not in us.

CHAPTER TWO

[1]My little children, I write these things so that you do not sin. And if anyone sins we have an advocate with the Father, Jesus the Anointed, the righteous one; [2]And he is an atonement for our sins, and not only for ours, but for those of the whole cosmos. [3]And, by this, we know that we have known him: if we keep his commandments. [4]Whoever says, "I have known him" and does not keep his commandments is a liar, and the truth is not in him; [5]But whosoever should keep his word, in him the love of God has truly been perfected. By this we know that we are in him: [6]Whoever says that he abides in him ought himself to walk just as he walked.

[7]Beloved ones, I am writing no new commandment to you, but an old commandment that you have had from the beginning; the old commandment is the word that you heard. [8]Then again, I am writing a new commandment to you, which is true in him and in you, because the darkness is passing and the true light is already shining. [9]Whoever claims to be in the light and hates his brother is in the darkness right up till now. [10]Whoever loves his brother abides in the light, and in him there is no occasion for faltering; [11]But whoever hates his brother is in darkness, and walks in darkness, and does not know where he goes off to, because the darkness has blinded his eyes. [12]I am writing to you, little children, because your sins have been forgiven through his name.

¹³I am writing to you, fathers, because you have known him from the beginning. I am writing to you, young men, because you have vanquished the wicked one. ¹⁴I have written to you, little children, because you have known the Father. I have written to you, fathers, because you have known him from the beginning. I have written to you, young men, because you are strong, and the Logos of God abides in you, and you have vanquished the wicked one. ¹⁵Do not love the cosmos or the things within the cosmos. If anyone love the cosmos, the love of the Father is not within him; ¹⁶Because all that is in the cosmos—the lust of the flesh and the lust of the eyes and the vainglory of living^e—is not from the Father, but from the cosmos. ¹⁷And the cosmos is passing away, as well as its desire, but whoever does the Father's will abides unto the Age.^f

¹⁸Little children, this is a last hour; and, just as you have heard that an antichrist^g is coming, many antichrists have arisen even now; there-

---

e. Here the noun is βίος (*bios*): "life" or "manner of living." This must be distinguished from the word translated as "life" in most of the text—ζωή (*zōē*)—which is used to name the divine life or life of the Age to come that Christ brings into the world.

f. Or "throughout the age."

g. The figure of an "antichrist" (ἀντίχριστος) appears in the New Testament only in 1 and 2 John, and—though in time this figure would be combined with the "man of lawlessness" of 2 Thessalonians and the "beast" of Revelation to produce the legend of "*the* Antichrist" who will rule the nations in the last days—here the precise reference is considerably more obscure and probably considerably less grand. In part, the difficulty of knowing exactly what that reference is lies in the prefix "anti-," which in Greek does not necessarily mean "opposed to" (although it often does). It can also simply indicate equivalence (an ἀντίθεος [*antitheos*] is not an antagonist of God, but an equal of the gods), or reciprocity (in the sense of one thing that is exchanged for another), or correspondence (in the way that an antitype—ἀντίτυπος—corresponds to an original type). And in many cases it means a substitute: either in the purely benign sense of a representative or deputy (an ἀντίφορτος [*antiphortos*] is simply a proconsul, and an ἀντίβασιλευς [*antibasilevs*] is merely a regent who governs during an interregnum, or perhaps a viceroy); or in the malign sense of an imposter or a usurper of someone else's role. It is in this last sense, in all likelihood, that the formula of an "antichrist" should be understood: a false anointed one. This may also explain the sense in which such a figure had been predicted. The promise in Deuteronomy 18:15–20

fore we know that this is a last hour. [19]They *went out from* us, but they did not *come from* us—for if they had come from us they would have remained with us—so that it might instead be made manifest that none of them at all comes from us. [20]And you have an unction[h] from the Holy One, and you all have knowledge.[i] [21]I have written to you not because you do not know the truth, because you do know it, and no lie comes from the truth. [22]Who is the liar except the one who denies that Jesus is the Anointed? This is the antichrist: one who denies the Father and the Son. [23]No one who denies the Son has the Father; the one who confesses the Son has the Father also. [24]As for you, let what you have heard from the beginning abide in you. If what you have heard from the beginning abide in you, you also will abide in the Son and in the Father. [25]And this is the promise that he has promised us: the life of the Age. [26]I have written these things to you in regard to those who are leading you astray. [27]And as for you, the unction that you received from him remains within you, and you have no need for anyone to teach you; rather, as his unction teaches you about all things, and is true and is no lie, you must abide in him, just as it has taught you.[j]

[28]And now, little children, abide in him, so that when he is made manifest we may have confidence, and not be driven from him by shame

---

that another prophet "like unto Moses" would arise comes with a warning against the false prophet who leads people away from worship of the true God. For many Jews and Christians alike in this period, both "the Prophet" (as in John 1:21) and an opposed "false prophet" had become fixed figures in apocalyptic imagination. Here, perhaps, the arrival of not only one, but several false prophets is taken as an indication that the end is near. Or perhaps, more simply, an antichrist or "spirit of antichrist" (see 4:3 below) is simply a "denier of Christ," as in v. 22 below. 2 John describes an antichrist as one who, more specifically, denies that Christ "has come in the flesh" (see my footnote to 2 John 1:7), but precisely what that means, and whether it is relevant to how the word is used in 1 John, cannot be determined.

h. χρῖσμα (*chrisma*), here and below (v. 27): probably "anointing," but perhaps "oil," "unguent," or "balm" (hence the ambivalence of my rendering).

i. Some versions of the text read "and you know all things."

j. The exact meaning of this verse is all but impossible to determine exactly in the Greek, in any of its textual variants.

at his arrival.[k] [29]If you know that he is righteous, you know that everyone who practices righteousness has been born out of him.

CHAPTER THREE

[1]See what kind of love the Father has given us so that we might be called children of God—and we are. Therefore the cosmos does not know us, because it did not know him. [2]Beloved ones, now we are children of God, and what we shall be has not yet become apparent. We know that when he appears we shall be like him, because we shall see him as he is. [3]And everyone who has this hope in him makes himself pure, just as that one is pure. [4]Everyone who commits sin practices lawlessness also; and sin is lawlessness. [5]And you know that he appeared so that he might bear sins away, and in him there is no sin. [6]Anyone who abides in him does not sin; anyone who sins has not seen him, nor has known him. [7]Little children, let no one lead you astray; whoever practices righteousness is righteous, just as that one is righteous; [8]Whoever commits sin is from the Slanderer, because the Slanderer has been sinning from the beginning. For this the Son of God appeared: that he might dissolve the works of the Slanderer. [9]No one born out of God commits sin, because his seed abides in him, and he is unable to sin, because he has been born out of God. [10]By this, the children of God and the children of the Slanderer are made manifest: No one who does not practice righteousness is of God, nor anyone who does not love his brother. [11]For this is the message that you have heard from the beginning: that we should love one another, [12]Unlike Cain, who was of the wicked one and slaughtered his brother. And for what reason did he slaughter him? Because his works were wicked, but his brother's works righteous. [13]Do not be amazed, brothers, if the cosmos hates you. [14]We know that we have passed over from death into life, because we love our brothers. Whoever does not love abides in death. [15]Everyone who hates

k. Or "in his presence."

his brother is a murderer, and you know that no murderer has the life of the Age abiding in him. [16]In this we have known what love is: that that one laid down his soul on our behalf; and we ought to lay down our soul on behalf of our brothers. [17]But should anyone have the means of living[1] in this cosmos, and see his brother in need, and inwardly close himself off from him, in what way does God's love abide in him? [18]Little children, let our love be not in talk or on the tongue, but in action and truth. [19]By this we shall know that we belong to the truth, and assure our heart before him: [20]That, if our heart should offer condemnation, God is greater than our heart, and knows all things. [21]Beloved ones, if our heart offer no condemnation, we have confidence toward God, [22]Because we receive from him whatever we might ask, because we keep his commandments and do the things that are pleasing in his sight. [23]And this is his commandment: that we should have faith in the name of his Son Jesus the Anointed, and should love one another, just as he gave us a command to do. [24]And whoever keeps his commandments abides in him, and he in that one; and by this we know that he abides in us: from the Spirit that he has given us.

CHAPTER FOUR

[1]Beloved ones, do not have faith in every spirit, but test the spirits— whether they are from God—because many false prophets have gone out into the cosmos. [2]By this you know the Spirit of God: every spirit that confesses that Jesus the Anointed has come in flesh is from God, [3]And every spirit that does not confess Jesus is not from God; and this is the one belonging to the antichrist, which you have heard is coming, and which is now already in the cosmos. [4]You are from God, little children, and have vanquished them, because the one that is in you is greater than the one that is in the cosmos. [5]They are from the cosmos;

---

1. Again, βίος (*bios*)—"worldly life," "livelihood," "means of living"—as distinct from ζωή (*zōē*).

therefore they speak from the cosmos and the cosmos listens to them. ⁶We are from God; the one who knows God listens to us; he who is not from God does not listen to us. From this we know the spirit of truth and the spirit of error.

⁷Beloved ones, let us love one another, because love is from God, and everyone who loves has been born out of God and knows God. ⁸Whoever does not love has not known God, because God is love. ⁹By this, the love of God was made manifest in us, because God has sent his only Son into the cosmos so that we might live through him. ¹⁰Herein is love: not that we loved God, but rather that he loved us and sent his Son as atonement for our sins. ¹¹Beloved ones, if God loved us so, we ought also to love one another. ¹²No one has ever looked upon God; if we should love one another, God abides in us and his love has been made perfect in us. ¹³By this we know that we abide in him and he in us: because he has donated to us from his Spirit. ¹⁴And we have seen and attest that the Father has sent the Son as savior of the cosmos. ¹⁵Should anyone confess that Jesus is the Son of God, God abides in him and he in God. ¹⁶And we—we have come to know and have faith in the love that God has in us. God is love, and whoever abides in love abides in God, and God abides in him. ¹⁷Hereby love has been made perfect with us, so that we might have confidence on the day of judgment that, just as he is, so also are we in this cosmos. ¹⁸In love there is no fear; rather, the love that is perfect casts out fear, because fear carries chastisement, and whoever fears has not been perfected in love. ¹⁹We love because he first loved us. ²⁰If anyone should say, "I love God," and hate his brother, he is a liar; for the one who does not love his brother, whom he has seen, cannot love the God whom he has not seen. ²¹And we have this commandment from him: that the one who loves God must also love his brother.

CHAPTER FIVE

¹Everyone who has faith that Jesus is the Anointed has been born out of God, and everyone who loves the one who engenders loves the

one who has been engendered by him. ²By this we know that we love the children of God: when we love God and carry out his commandments. ³For this is the love of God: that we keep his commandments; and his commandments are not burdensome, ⁴Because everything that is born out of God conquers the cosmos; and this is the victory that has conquered the cosmos: our faithfulness. ⁵And who is the one who conquers the cosmos if not the one who has faith that Jesus is the Son of God? ⁶This is the one who comes through water and blood: Jesus the Anointed; not by the water only, but by the water and by the blood; and the Spirit is the one that testifies, because the Spirit is the truth. ⁷For those bearing witness are three: ⁸The Spirit and the water and the blood, and the three are of one accord. ⁹If we accept the testimony of human beings, the testimony of God is greater. For this is the testimony that God has attested regarding his Son. ¹⁰Whoever has faith in the Son of God has the testimony within him. Whoever does not have faith in God has made him out a liar, because he has not had faith in the testimony that God has attested in regard to his Son. ¹¹And this is the testimony: that God has given us the life of the Age, and this life is in his Son. ¹²Whoever has the Son has this life; whoever does not have the Son of God does not have this life.

¹³I have written these things to you who have faith in the name of the Son of God, so that you may know that you have life in the Age. ¹⁴And this is the confidence that we have toward him: that if we ask anything in accord with his will, he hears us. ¹⁵And if we know that he hears us we know that, whatsoever we ask, we have the boons that we have asked of him. ¹⁶If anyone sees his brother committing a sin that does not lead to death, he should make supplication, and he will give him life—for those committing sins not leading to death. There is sin that leads to death; I do not say that he should make petitions concerning that. ¹⁷All iniquity is sin, and there is sin that does not lead to death. ¹⁸We know that no one who has been born out of God sins; rather, whoever is born out of God keeps watch over himself, and the wicked one does not touch him. ¹⁹We know that we are of God, and that the whole cos-

mos rests entirely upon the wicked one.^m ²⁰And we know that the Son of God has come and has given us understanding, so that we may know the one who is true; and we are in him who is true, in his Son Jesus the Anointed. This one is the true God and Life in the Age.

²¹Little children, guard yourselves against the idols.

---

m. ὁ κόσμος ὅλος ἐν τῷ πονηρῷ κεῖται (^ho kosmos ^holos en tō̦ ponērō̦ keitai): literally, "the whole cosmos lies in the wicked one." This is a common idiom: κεῖσθαι ἔν (keisthai en)—"to lie in"—someone is to be entirely dependent upon him, or to be entirely within his power.

The Second Letter of John

———

BY "JOHN THE ELDER"

[1]The Elder to the elect Lady and her children, whom in truth I love, and not I alone, but all those who have known the truth, [2]Because of the truth that abides in us and will be with us unto the Age.[a] [3]Grace, mercy, peace will be with us from God the Father and from Jesus the Anointed, the Father's Son, in truth and love.

[4]I was overjoyed to have found some of your children walking in truth, just as we have received a commandment to do from the Father. [5]And now I make a request of you, Lady, not as if writing you a new commandment, but rather one that we have had from the beginning: that we love one another. [6]And this is love: that we should walk according to his commandments; this is the commandment, just as you have heard it from the beginning, so that you might walk therein. [7]For many deceivers have gone forth into the cosmos, those who do not confess that Jesus the Anointed has come in flesh.[b] This is the deceiver and the antichrist. [8]Look to yourselves, that you not lose the things we have accomplished, but rather receive a full reward. [9]Everyone who goes on ahead and does not abide in the teaching of the Anointed does not have

a. Or "throughout the age."

b. This may mean that an antichrist is specifically someone who teaches a "docetic" view of Christ: that is, the view that the divine Son never truly assumed a fleshly or "psychical" body—being divine and therefore beyond the defilements of matter—but only appeared to have done so.

God; the one who abides in the teaching, this one has both the Father and the Son. [10]If anyone comes to you and does not bring this teaching, do not receive him into the household and do not bid him welcome; [11]For whoever bids him welcome has communion in his wicked works.

[12]Having many things to write to you, I did not wish to do so by paper and ink; rather, I hope to come to you and speak mouth to mouth, so that our joy might be made full. [13]The children of your elect sister greet you.

The Third Letter of John

BY "JOHN THE ELDER"

[1]The Elder to beloved Gaius, whom in truth I love.

[2]Beloved, I pray that you are doing well in regard to everything, and are in good health, just as your soul does well. [3]For I was exceedingly joyful when some of the brothers came and attested to the truth that is yours, just as you are walking in truth. [4]I have no joy greater than these things: that I hear that my children walk in truth. [5]Beloved, you discharge whatever labors you might perform for the brothers faithfully—and this for foreigners, [6]Who have attested to your love before the assembly; you will do well in having sent them onward in a manner worthy of God; [7]For they went forth on behalf of the name, taking nothing from the gentiles. [8]We ought, therefore, to support such men, so that we might become fellow workers in the truth.

[9]I wrote something to the assembly; but Diotrephes, who cherishes his preeminence among them, does not receive us. [10]For this reason, if I come, I shall remind you of his deeds, which he enacts while prattling about us with wicked words; and, not content with these things, he also does not receive the brothers, and prevents those who would do so, and expels them from the assembly.

[11]Beloved, imitate not what is bad, but what is good. Whoever does what is good is from God. Whoever does what is bad has not seen God. [12]Testimony has been given on behalf of Demetrius by everyone, and

by the truth itself; and we testify as well, and you know that our testimony is true.

[13]I had many things to write to you, but I do not wish to write to you by means of ink and pen; [14]But I hope to see you presently, and we shall speak mouth to mouth.

[15]Peace to you. The friends greet you. Greet the friends by name.

The Letter of Judas

[1]Judas, a slave of Jesus the Anointed and brother of James, to those who are called, those beloved of God the Father and preserved by Jesus the Anointed: [2]Mercy and peace and love be multiplied for you.

[3]Beloved ones, though at pains to write to you about our common salvation, I had need to write to exhort you to contend for the faith delivered once and for all to the holy ones. [4]For certain men have crept in, those who had long ago been predicted for this judgment,[a] impious men, translating the grace of our God into wantonness[b] and denying our only master and Lord, Jesus the Anointed. [5]But I am determined to remind you—although you once knew all this—that Jesus,[c] having saved

a. προγεγραμμένοι εἰς τοῦτο τὸ κρίμα (progegrammenoi eis touto to krima): perhaps "under proscription for this judgment," or "prescribed to this judgment," or "publically announced for this judgment," or "summoned to this judgment," or even "given notice regarding this judgment." The verb προγράφω (prographō), which literally refers to writing something out in advance, has a certain fluidity of meaning. In much biblical Greek it is used to refer to the act of making a prediction, but it can also mean giving a public notice (πρόγραμμα [programma] or προγραφή [prographē]), sometimes of a list of the condemned; and sometimes it can mean issuing a summons or an injunction, or appointing something, or even placing something or someone at the head of a list.

b. The most common interpretation of this phrase is that there were men teaching an antinomian form of faith, according to which grace so liberates the saved from the prescriptions of the Law that even its restrictions on sexual behavior can be set aside.

c. Ἰησοῦς (Iēsous): that is, "Jesus," which is the Greek rendering of Joshua (Yeshua). Many texts, especially of the Byzantine type, have "Lord" here, and

a people from the land of Egypt, secondly destroyed those who were faithless; [6]And angels who did not maintain their own position of rule, but instead deserted their proper habitation, he has kept in everlasting chains under nether gloom for the judgment of the Great Day;[d] [7]Just as—in the same manner as these—Sodom and Gomorrah and the cities thereabout, who whored about and went in pursuit of other flesh,[e] provide an example by undergoing the just requital of fire from the Age.[f] [8]Yet in the same way these dreamers defile flesh, and treat lordship with

---

a few have "Christ God," but the best textual evidence favors "Jesus." Most scholars who accept this nevertheless find the verse problematic, recognizing that—even if the author might have seen Jesus as the preexistent divine Son, and seen the acts of God in Hebrew scripture as being executed through the Son— talk of Jesus acting in the events of the book of Exodus is without much precedent or analogue in early Christian literature. Alternatively, perhaps the name should be rendered "Joshua." I have hesitated to do so only because this passage seems to be the first in a series of descriptions of episodes of divine punishment of sinners (see vv. 6–7), rather than a simple warning that the one who saves the righteous is also the one who will punish the iniquitous. And in Exodus Joshua is not explicitly involved in the liberation of Israel from Egypt—though he soon appears as Moses's lieutenant and chief warrior. And the mention of the destruction of the faithless might refer to Joshua's presumed participation in the slaughter of the Israelite idolaters after the fashioning of the golden calf (Exodus 32:17–35), or perhaps simply to his campaign against the Amalekites in Rephidim (Exodus 17:8–16), or even to his conquest of Canaan.

d. The reference here is to those angels or daemonic beings who are, according to Jewish and Christian belief in the intertestamental and early Christian era, imprisoned until the day of judgment (recounted, for instance, in 1 Enoch and the book of Jubilees). They are mentioned also in 1 Peter 3:19–20 and 2 Peter 2:4. See my footnote to 1 Peter 3:19–20. This is the one place in the New Testament, incidentally, in which an image of otherworldly punishment (though only of fallen angels and demons) is accompanied by the Greek word that properly means "eternal" (δεσμοῖς ἀϊδίοις [desmois aïdiois]: "everlasting chains"), though even here the phrase seems to mean only that the chains are infrangible, inasmuch as they are "everlasting" only *until* the day of judgment.

e. σαρκὸς ἑτέρας (sarkos ᵇeteras): This could mean sexual relations with neighbors rather than with spouses, or with strangers (such as the angelic visitors of Lot), or with partners forbidden by the Law (for instance, persons of the same sex), or even with beasts.

f. "Aeonian fire."

contempt, and defame the Glories.ᵍ ⁹Yet when the Archangel Michael contended with the Slanderer, arguing over the body of Moses, he did not dare to bring a defamatory condemnation against him, but instead said, "The Lord rebuke you."ʰ ¹⁰But as for these men—on the one hand, they defame whatever things they have not perceived; and, on the other, whatever things they do understand—in a natural way, like unreasoning animals—by these they are corrupted. ¹¹Alas for them, for they have traveled the path of Cain, and for profit have abandoned themselves to the error of Balaam, and have perished in the sedition of Korah. ¹²These are the hidden reefs lurking in your love-feasts, joining in the feasting without fear, shepherds tending themselves, waterless clouds carried off by the wind, autumnal trees bearing no fruit, having twice died, uprooted, ¹³Wild waves of the sea foaming over with their shames, wandering stars for whom the darkness's nether gloom has been reserved until the Age.ⁱ ¹⁴And Enoch, the seventh from Adam, prophesied about these men as well, saying, "See: The Lord has come amid myriads of his holy ones, ¹⁵To execute justice upon all and to put every soul to shame for all their works of impiety, which they have committed impiously, and for all the harsh things that impious sinners have spoken against him."ʲ ¹⁶These men are murmurers, querulous, following after their own lusts, and their mouth utters overblown words, lavishing their obsequiousness on "personages" for the sake of gain.

¹⁷But you, beloved ones, recall the words previously spoken by the Apostles of our Lord Jesus the Anointed, ¹⁸For they told you, "In the last time there will be scoffers, following after their own desires for im-

g. This is almost certainly a reference to angels, and perhaps to a special order of angels. These "Glories" or "Glorious Ones" are mentioned as members of God's heavenly court in 2 Enoch 22:7. See also 2 Peter 2:10.

h. The most likely source from which this episode is drawn is the intertestamental text *The Testament of Moses* or *The Assumption of Moses* (though these may in fact be distinct texts), of which only fragments remain. Such, at least, is the report of certain early patristic writers.

i. Or "throughout the age."

j. 1 Enoch 1:9.

pious things." ¹⁹These are those who cause divisions, psychical men, not possessing spirit.ᵏ ²⁰But you, beloved ones, building yourselves up in your most holy faith, praying in a holy spirit, ²¹Keep yourselves in love of God, awaiting the mercy of our Lord Jesus the Anointed for life in the Age. ²²And have mercy on those who suffer doubt, ²³Yet also save them by seizing them out of fire; but have mercy on them in fear,ˡ hating even the inner tunic stained by flesh.

k. Despite its long history of often vague and misleading translations, this verse clearly invokes the distinction between *psychē* and *pnevma* (soul and spirit) as principles of life, and between "psychics" and "pneumatics" as categories of persons. There is most definitely no reference here to the Holy Spirit: given the construction of the sentence, the absence of the definite article alone makes this certain; and the reasoning of the sentence makes it all the more so. See 1 Corinthians 2:14 and 15:44–47, along with my footnotes, as well as my remarks on the words *psychē* and *pnevma* in my postscript.

l. ²²καὶ οὓς μὲν ἐλεεῖτε διακρινομένους, ²³οὓς δὲ σῴζετε ἐκ πυρὸς ἁρπάζοντες, οὓς δὲ ἐλεεῖτε ἐν φόβῳ (²²*kai ᵇous men eleeite diakrinomenous*, ²³ᵇ*ous de sō₂zete ek pyros ᵇarpazontes, ᵇous de eleeite en phobō₂*): These lines present a number of interpretive difficulties, in part because of the obscurity of their phrasing, and in part because they exist in a number of variants. My translation follows from the preferred Critical Text reading, but even then deviates both from the standard text and from the standard reading (perhaps implausibly). Many take these verses as constituting a threefold formulation for dealing with those led astray: "Toward some who suffer doubt have mercy; and save others by snatching them from fire; and toward yet others have mercy with fear." The Majority Text has διακρινόμενοι (*diakrinomenoi*) in place of διακρινομένους (*diakrinomenous*), which might yield something like "have mercy discriminatingly"; and the Majority Text also offers a simpler reading of the next verse: "²³And save some in fear, seizing them out of fire, hating even the inner tunic stained by flesh." The Majority Text, moreover, has in its favor that it uses the imperative ἐλεεῖτε (*eleeite*), rather than ἐλεᾶτε (*eleate*) (and I have substituted the former for the latter above); certainly *eleate* seems like an anachronism in the current versions of the Critical Text (at least, I am unaware of any other comparably ancient text that employs it). *Diakrinomenous* can also mean "disputing" rather than "doubting," and indeed several ancient manuscripts have neither *eleate* nor *eleeite*, but rather ἐλέγχετε (*elenchete*), which can mean either "refute" or "convince." Still other versions, attested by several patristic citations and confirmed by the manuscript known as P72, offer a terser but perhaps more lucid iteration of both verses: "²²Seize some out of fire, ²³And have mercy in fear on some who doubt."

²⁴And to him who has the power to guard you against stumbling and to stand you before his glory without blemish, in exultation, ²⁵The only God our savior, through Jesus the Anointed our Lord, be glory, majesty, and authority, before every age, both now and unto all the ages; amen.

It is unlikely that the tangled history of the transmission of these verses will ever be convincingly reconstructed, absent a number of significant palaeographic discoveries.

The Revelation of John

BY "JOHN THE DIVINE" OF PATMOS

CHAPTER ONE

¹A revelation from Jesus the Anointed, which God gave him, to show his slaves what things must occur extremely soon, and he signified this by sending it out through his angel to his slave John, ²Who attested to the word of God and the witness of Jesus the Anointed, regarding as many things as he saw. ³How blissful both that lector of and those listeners to the prophecy who also abide by the things written therein; for the time is near.

⁴John to the seven assemblies that are in Asia: grace and peace to you from the one who is and who was and who is to come, and from the seven Spirits that are before his throne, ⁵And from Jesus the Anointed, the faithful witness, the firstborn of the dead, and the Archon of the kings of the earth. To the one who has loved us and has loosed us from our sins by his blood, ⁶And has made us into a Kingdom, priests to his God and Father—to him be the glory and the might unto the ages of the ages; amen.

⁷Look: He is coming with the clouds, and every eye will see him, and they who pierced him and all the tribes of the earth will beat their breasts in lamentation because of him. Yes, amen!

⁸"I am the alpha and the omega," says the Lord God, "the one who is and who was and who is coming, the Almighty."

⁹I, John, your brother and fellow communicant in the affliction and Kingdom and endurance in Jesus, happened to be on the island called Patmos for the sake of God's word and of witnessing to Jesus. ¹⁰On the Lord's day I happened to be in spirit and I heard a voice as loud as a trumpet behind me, ¹¹Saying, "Write what you see in a book and send it to the seven assemblies—to Ephesus and to Smyrna and to Pergamum and to Thyatira and to Sardis and to Philadelphia and to Laodicea." ¹²And I turned to look toward the voice that spoke to me; and, having turned, I saw seven gold lampstands, ¹³And amid the lampstands one like a son of man[a] garbed down to his feet and girdled around at the chest with a golden cincture, ¹⁴And his head and hair were as white as wool—a white like snow—and his eyes like flames of fire, ¹⁵And his feet like fine brass, as if fired in a furnace, and his voice was like a sound of many waters, ¹⁶And he held seven stars in his right hand, and a sharp two-edged sword coming out of his mouth, and his face was like the sun shining at full strength. ¹⁷And when I saw him I fell down at his feet like a dead man; and he placed his right hand on me, saying, "Do not be afraid: I am the first and the last, ¹⁸And the one who lives and who became dead and—see!—I am alive unto the ages of the ages, and I have the keys of death and of Hades. ¹⁹Therefore, write down the things you have seen and the things that are and the things about to occur thereafter. ²⁰The mystery of the seven stars you saw upon my right hand and the seven gold lampstands—the seven stars are angels of the seven assemblies, and the seven lampstands are seven assemblies.

CHAPTER TWO

¹"Write this to the angel of the assembly in Ephesus: 'The one who wields the seven stars in his right hand, who walks amid the seven lampstands, says this: ²"I know your works, and your labor and endurance, and that you cannot bear evil men, and have tested those who claim to

a. That is, "a man."

be Apostles and are no such thing, and have found them to be false, [3]And you have endurance, and have borne up because of my name, and have not grown weary. [4]But I hold it against you that you abandoned your first love. [5]Therefore remember from where you have fallen, and change your heart, and practice the works you practiced at first; and, if not, I am coming to you, and will remove your lampstand from its place—unless you change your heart. [6]But this you do have: that you hate the works of the Nicolaitians,[b] which I hate as well. [7]Whoever has an ear, let him hear what the Spirit says to the assemblies. To the one who conquers, I shall grant it to him to eat from the tree of life, which is in God's paradise."'

[8]"And to the angel of the assembly in Smyrna write: 'The first and the last, who became dead and who lived, says these things: [9]"I know your affliction and destitution, and the blasphemy of those who call themselves Judaeans and are not, but who are instead a synagogue of the Accuser.[c] [10]Do not fear the things you are about to suffer. See: The Slanderer is about to cast some of you into prison so that you may be tested, and you will suffer affliction for ten days. Be faithful unto death and I will grant you the chaplet[d] of life. [11]Whoever has an ear, let him

b. Some early patristic commentators identified the Nicolaitians as a gnostic sect of an especially antinomian variety; but whether this is accurate cannot be ascertained.

c. It is traditional (or, at any rate, instinctive) to assume that this is a condemnation of certain Jews or Jewish authorities outside of the Christian movement, who are therefore allegedly not "true Jews." But some scholars think it possible that the accusation is aimed instead at gentiles (such as Paul's gentile converts) who believe that, by virtue of becoming Christians, they have become Jews without having to keep the Law. And, indeed, the author of Revelation does at times seem very much a Jewish Christian—observantly Jewish, in all likelihood—whose chief concern seems to be God's elect within the twelve tribes of Israel and the divine restoration of Jerusalem.

d. The στέφανος (stephanos) of which John speaks here and below is not really a "crown" in the sense that we use it (a somewhat hypertrophied diadem or circlet, proper for kings); it is a (military or athletic) victor's wreath or chaplet, his "laurels," sometimes of gold or silver. The emperors of Rome traditionally

hear what the Spirit says to the assemblies. The one who conquers will by no means be harmed by the second death."'

¹²"And to the angel of the assembly in Pergamum write: 'The one who has the sharp two-edged sword says these things: ¹³"I know where you dwell—there where the throne of the Accuser is—and that you hold fast to my name, and did not renounce my faith even in the days of Antipas, my witness, my faithful one, who was killed right by your side, there where the Accuser dwells. ¹⁴But I hold a few things against you, because you have some persons there who hold onto the teachings of Balaam, who taught Balak to throw down a snare before the sons of Israel, to eat sacrifices offered to idols, and to engage in whoring. ¹⁵So also, similarly, you have persons holding to the teaching of [the] Nicolaitians. ¹⁶Therefore change your hearts; and, if not, I am coming to you quickly, and will wage war on them with the sword in my mouth. ¹⁷Whoever has an ear, let him hear what the Spirit says to the assemblies. I will impart to the one who conquers some of the hidden manna, and will give him a white stone, and a new name inscribed on the stone, which no one will know except the one who receives it."'

¹⁸"And to the angel of the assembly in Thyatira write: 'The Son of God, who has eyes like a flame of fire, and his feet like fine brass, says these things: ¹⁹"I know your works and love and faith and ministry, as well as your endurance, and your last works are more plentiful than your first. ²⁰But I hold it against you that you tolerate the woman Jezebel, who calls herself a prophetess, and she teaches and deceitfully persuades my slaves to whore about and to eat sacrifices offered to idols. ²¹And I gave her time so that she might change her heart, and she does not wish to turn her heart away from her whoring. ²²Look: I cast her down onto a sickbed, and those who commit adultery with her into great affliction, should they fail to turn their hearts from her works; ²³And her children I will strike down with death, and all the assemblies

_____
wore such a chaplet specifically as an alternative to the royal diadem of the pre-Republican kings.

shall know that I am the one who searches kidneys[e] and hearts, and I will pay out to you each according to your works. [24]But I say to the rest of those in Thyatira, however many do not hold to this teaching—who have not plumbed the Accuser's depths, as they say—I am not heaping another burden upon you; [25]Nevertheless, hold onto what you have until I shall come. [26]And the one who conquers, and who abides by my works until the end, to him I will give power over the gentiles—[27]'And he will shepherd them with a rod of iron: they are shattered like clay vessels'—[28]Just as I also received it from my Father; and I will give him the Morning Star.[f] [29]Whoever has an ear, let him hear what the Spirit says to the assemblies."'

CHAPTER THREE

[1]"And to the angel of the assembly in Sardis write: 'The one who has the seven Spirits of God and the seven stars says these things: "I know your works—that you have won a name for being alive, yet you are dead. [2]Be vigilant, fortify the things that remain that are moribund, for I have not found your works to be fulfilled in the eyes of my God; [3]Remember, therefore, how you have received and listened, and keep watch and change your hearts. Should you not be vigilant, then, I shall come like a thief, and you surely would not know at what hour I shall come upon you. [4]But you have in Sardis a few who can be named who did not sully their garments, and they shall walk with me in whites, because they are worthy. [5]The one who conquers shall thus be wrapped in white garments, and I most certainly will not expunge his name from the book of life, and I will acknowledge his name before my Father and before his angels. [6]Whoever has an ear, let him hear what the Spirit says to the assemblies."'

e. Not only in the Bible, nor only in antiquity, but even into early modernity, the kidneys were often understood as the seat of the affections.

f. See 2 Peter 1:19 and my footnote thereto; see also 22:16 below.

⁷"And to the angel of the assembly in Philadelphia write: 'The holy one, the true one, who holds the key of David, the one who opens—and none shall close—and who closes—and none opens—says these things: ⁸"I know your works. See: I have provided an opened door before you, one that none can close, for you have small power, yet you have kept my word and not denied my name. ⁹See: I make a gift of some from the synagogue of the Accuser—those who say they are Judaeans, yet are not, but are lying. Look: I will make it so that they shall come and prostrate themselves before your feet, and they shall know that I have loved you. ¹⁰Because you have kept my instruction to endure, I will also keep you from the hour of the trial that is about to come upon the whole inhabited world, to test those who dwell upon the earth. ¹¹I am coming very quickly; hold fast to what you have so that no one take your chaplet. ¹²The one who conquers, I will make him a pillar in the sanctuary of my God, and he shall surely not go out of it any longer, and I will inscribe upon him my God's name and the name of my God's city—the New Jerusalem descending out of heaven from my God—as well as my new name. ¹³Whoever has an ear, let him hear what the Spirit says to the assemblies.'"

¹⁴"And to the angel of the assembly in Laodicea write: 'The Amen, the witness faithful and true, the originᵍ of God's creation, says these things: ¹⁵"I know your works—that you are neither hot nor cold. I would that you were cold or hot. ¹⁶Thus, since you are lukewarm, and neither hot nor cold, I am about to vomit you from my mouth. ¹⁷For you say, 'I am rich, and have been enriched, and need nothing,' and you do not realize that you are someone wretched and pitiable and destitute and blind and naked. ¹⁸I counsel you to buy gold refined by fire from me so that you may be rich, and white garments so that you may be clad and the shame of your nakedness may not be made manifest, and salve to anoint your eyes so that you may see. ¹⁹As many as I love I rebuke and

g. ἀρχή (archē): "beginning," "origin," "first principle," "foremost," "sovereign."

discipline; so be zealous and change your heart. ²⁰Look: I stand at the door and knock; should anyone hear my voice and open the door, I will enter in to him, and I will dine with him and he with me. ²¹The one who conquers, I will grant it to him to sit with me upon my throne, just as I also conquered and sat with my Father on his throne. ²²Whoever has an ear, let him hear what the Spirit says to the assemblies."'"

CHAPTER FOUR

¹Thereafter I looked, and see: an opened door in the sky, and the first voice that I had heard, the one like a trumpet, spoke with me, saying, "Come up here and I shall show you things that must occur hereafter." ²Immediately I came to be in spirit, and look: A throne was set in heaven—and one sitting on the throne, ³And the one sitting there like stone of jasper and carnelian in appearance—and a nimbus,ʰ like emerald in appearance, encircled the throne—⁴And, all around the throne, twenty-four thrones, and sitting on the thrones twenty-four elders clad in white garments, and on their heads gold chaplets. ⁵And from the throne come lightning flashes and noises and peals of thunder—and burning before the throne are seven lampstands, which are God's seven Spirits; ⁶And before the throne it was like a sea of glass, like crystal; and in the midst of the throne and in a circle around the throne were four animals,ⁱ full of eyes front and back. ⁷And the first animal was like a lion, and the second animal like a calf, and the third animal possessing a face like a man's, and the fourth animal like an eagle in flight. ⁸And the four animals—each and every one of them having six wings—are full of eyes, around and within, and they have no rest, day and night, saying, "Holy, holy, holy, Lord God the Almighty, who was and who is and who is to come!" ⁹And whenever the animals will give glory and honor and thanks to the one sitting on the throne, who lives unto the ages of

h. Or "rainbow."
i. Or "living things."

503

the ages, [10] The twenty-four elders will fall down before the one sitting on the throne, and will make obeisance to the one who lives unto the ages of the ages, and will cast their chaplets before the throne, saying, [11] "Worthy are you, our Lord and our God, to receive the glory and the honor and the power, because you created all things, and by your will they were and were created."

CHAPTER FIVE

[1] And in the right hand of the one sitting on the throne I saw a book with writing on its inner and outer sides,[j] sealed with seven seals. [2] And I saw a mighty angel proclaiming in a loud voice, "Who is worthy to open the book and loose its seals?" [3] And no one in heaven or upon the earth or below the earth was able to open the book or look at it. [4] And I was weeping copiously because no one was found worthy to open the book or to look at it. [5] And one of the elders says to me, "Do not weep; look: The lion of the tribe of Judah, the root of David, has conquered, so as to open the book and its seven seals." [6] And in the midst of the throne and the four animals, and in the midst of the elders, I saw a suckling lamb[k] standing, like one that had been slaughtered, having seven horns and seven eyes—which are God's seven Spirits sent forth into all the earth—[7] And he came and took it from the right hand of the one sitting on the throne. [8] And when he had taken the book the four animals and the twenty-four elders fell down before the suckling lamb, holding each a lyre, and gold libation-dishes[l] full of incenses, which are the prayers

j. The "book" here is a scroll, not a codex.

k. Not an ἀρνός (*arnos*) or an ἀρνήν (*arnēn*)—a "lamb"—but an ἀρνίον (*arnion*)—literally, a "little lamb" or "lambkin" (or, alternatively, a "sheepskin"), a term most properly applied to a lamb that is still nursing. Perhaps John means a lamb in only a rather general sense, but given the farraginous nature of the imagery of Revelation, it would be unwise to presume to know for certain.

l. A φιάλη (*phialē*) (*patera* in Latin) is a dish, pan, or saucer, but in the context

of the holy ones. ⁹And they sing a new song, saying, "Worthy are you to receive the book and to open its seals, because you were slaughtered and by your blood you made a purchase for God from every tribe and tongue and people and nation, ¹⁰And have made them into a kingdom and into priests for our God, and they will reign upon the earth. ¹¹And I looked, and I heard the noise of many angels in a circle around the throne, and around the animals and the elders, and their number was myriads of myriads and thousands of thousands, ¹²Saying with a loud voice, "The suckling lamb who has been slaughtered is worthy to receive the power and riches and wisdom and might and honor and glory and blessing." ¹³And I heard every creature that is in heaven and on the earth and below the earth and on the sea, and all the things among them, saying, "To the one who sits upon the throne and to the suckling lamb be the blessing and the honor and the glory and the might unto the ages of the ages." ¹⁴And the four animals said, "Amen," and the elders fell down and prostrated themselves.

CHAPTER SIX

¹And I watched as the suckling lamb opened one of the seven seals, and I heard one of the four animals saying, as with a sound of thunder, "Come." ²And I looked, and see: a white horse, and the one sitting upon it had a bow, and a chaplet was given to him, and he went forth in conquest, so that he too might conquer. ³And when he opened the second seal I heard the second animal say, "Come." ⁴And another horse went forth, the color of flame, and it was granted to the one who sat upon it to remove peace from the earth and—so that they might kill one another—a great sword was also given to him. ⁵And when he opened the third seal I heard the third animal say, "Come." And I looked, and

of worship or devotion it is a broad, shallow dish or chalice, usually with a central boss, used for pouring out libations or burning incense.

see: a black horse, and the one sitting upon it holding a pair of scales in his hand. [6]And amid the four animals it was as if I heard a voice saying, "A choinix[m] of wheat for a denarius, and three choinixes of barley for a denarius, and do no harm to the oil and the wine." [7]And when he opened the fourth seal I heard the fourth animal's voice saying, "Come." [8]And I looked, and see: a pale green horse, and the name for him who sat atop it was Death, and with him followed Hades, and authority was granted them over a fourth of the earth to kill by sword and by famine and by death and by the wild beasts of the earth. [9]And when he opened the fifth seal I saw below the sacrificial altar the souls of those who had been slaughtered for the sake of God's word, and for the sake of the witness that they had borne. [10]And they were crying out in a loud voice, saying, "How long, O master, the holy and the true, will you not judge and exact justice for our blood from those who dwell upon the earth?" [11]And to each of them was given a white robe, and it was told to them that they should rest a little while longer, till both their fellow slaves and their brothers—who are about to be killed just as they had been—should reach their full complement. [12]And I looked when he opened the sixth seal, and there came a great earthquake, and the sun became as black as hair-sackcloth, and the moon became wholly like blood. [13]And the stars of heaven fell to the earth, as a fig tree shaken by a great wind sheds its wild figs, [14]And the sky receded like a scroll being rolled up, and every mountain and island was moved from its place. [15]And the kings of the earth and the great men and the chiliarchs and the rich and every slave and freeman hid themselves in the caves and among the rocks of the mountains, [16]And they say to the mountains and the rocks, "Fall upon us and hide us from the face of the one who sits upon the throne, and from the anger of the suckling lamb, [17]For the Great Day of their ire has come, and who is able to withstand it?"

m. Slightly less than two pints.

CHAPTER SEVEN

¹After this I saw four angels standing on the four corners of the earth, restraining the four winds, so that no wind might blow on the earth or on the sea or on any tree. ²And I saw another angel ascending from the sunrise, holding a seal of a living God, and he cried in a loud voice to the four angels—they to whom it had been granted to harm the earth and the sea—³Saying, "Do not harm the earth or the sea or the trees, until we should seal the slaves of our God upon their foreheads." ⁴And I heard the number of the ones sealed: a hundred and forty-four thousand sealed, from every tribe of the sons of Israel: ⁵From tribe Judah twelve thousand who had been sealed; from tribe Reuben twelve thousand; from tribe Gad twelve thousand; ⁶From tribe Asher twelve thousand; from tribe Naphtali twelve thousand; from tribe Manassah twelve thousand; ⁷From tribe Symeon twelve thousand; from tribe Levi twelve thousand; from tribe Issacher twelve thousand; ⁸From tribe Zebulun twelve thousand; from tribe Joseph twelve thousand; from tribe Benjamin twelve thousand who had been sealed. ⁹After these things I looked, and see: a great crowd that no one was able to number, from every nation, and from tribes and peoples and tongues, standing before the throne and before the suckling lamb, clad in white robes, and date palms in their hands, ¹⁰And they cry out in a loud voice, saying, "Salvation to our God who sits upon the throne, and to the suckling lamb." ¹¹And all the angels stood around the throne in a circle, and around the elders and the four animals, and fell on their faces before the throne and made obeisance to God, ¹²Saying, "Amen, the blessing and the glory and the wisdom and the thanks and the honor and the power and the might to our God unto the ages of the ages; amen." ¹³And one of the elders spoke out, saying to me, "These who have been clad in the white robes, who are they and where did they come from?" ¹⁴And I said to him, "My lord, you know." And he told me, "These are the ones coming out of the great tribulation, and they have washed their robes and whitened them in the blood of the suckling lamb. ¹⁵For this

reason they are before God's throne, and worship him day and night in his sanctuary, and the one sitting on the throne will spread a tabernacle over them. [16]No longer will they hunger, nor any longer thirst, neither surely shall the sun beat down upon them, nor any scorching heat, [17]Because the suckling lamb in the midst of the throne will shepherd them and lead them the way to springs of life's waters, and God will wipe away every tear from their eyes."

CHAPTER EIGHT

[1]And when he opened the seventh seal, a silence fell in heaven for about half an hour. [2]And I saw the seven angels who stood before God, and seven trumpets were given to them.

[3]And another angel came and stood on the sacrificial altar holding a gold thurible, and many incenses were given to him, so that he might offer them with the prayers of the holy ones upon the gold sacrificial altar before the throne. [4]And from the angel's hand the smoke of the incenses rose up before God along with the prayers of the holy ones. [5]And the angel took the thurible and filled it from the fire of the sacrificial altar and cast it onto the earth, and there came peals of thunder and noises and lightning flashes and an earthquake.

[6]And the seven angels who held the seven trumpets prepared themselves, so that they might sound the trumpets. [7]And the first sounded the trumpet, and there came hail and fire mingled with blood, and it was cast onto the earth; and one third of the earth was burned, and one third of the trees were burned, and all green grass was burned. [8]And the second angel sounded the trumpet, and it was as if a great mountain burning with fire were cast into the sea; and one third of the sea became blood, [9]And within the sea one third of the creatures that had souls[n] died, and one third of the ships were destroyed. [10]And the third angel sounded the trumpet, and a great star fell out of heaven burning

n. That is, simply, "living creatures."

like a torch, and it fell upon one third of the rivers and upon the springs of the waters; [11]And the star's name is called Wormwood. And one third of the waters turned into wormwood, and a great many human beings died from the waters because they were embittered. [12]And the fourth angel sounded the trumpet, and one third of the sun was struck, and one third of the moon, and one third of the stars, so that one third of them might be darkened, and the day—one third of it—should not appear, and the night likewise.

[13]And I looked, and I heard a solitary eagle that was flying in midheaven say in a loud voice, "Alas, alas, alas for those who dwell on the earth, on account of the trumpet-blasts that yet remain from those three angels who are about to sound their trumpets!"

CHAPTER NINE

[1]And the fifth angel sounded the trumpet, and I saw a star that had fallen out of heaven to the earth, and it was given the key to the well of the abyss, [2]And he opened the well of the abyss, and smoke arose from the well, like smoke from an immense furnace, and the sun and the air were darkened by the well's smoke. [3]And locusts came forth from the smoke into the earth, and power was given to them like the power that the earth's scorpions possess. [4]And it was told to them that they should not harm the grass of the earth or any greenery or any tree, but only those human beings who do not have God's seal upon their foreheads. [5]And it was granted them not that they should kill them, but rather that they should be tormented for five months, and their torment is like the torment from a scorpion when it stings a man. [6]And in those days human beings will seek death and will by no means find it, and they will long to die, and death flees from them. [7]And the likenesses of the locusts resembled horses prepared for war, and it was as if upon their heads there were chaplets, as if of gold, and their faces were like faces of human beings, [8]And they had hair like the hair of women, and their teeth were like those of lions, [9]And they had thoraxes like cuirasses of

iron,[o] and the sound of their wings was like a sound of chariots drawn by many horses, charging into war, [10]And they have tails and stings like scorpions, and in their tails is their power to harm human beings for five months. [11]They have the angel of the abyss as a king over them, he whose name in Hebrew is Abbadon,[p] while in Greek he bears the name Apollyon.[q] [12]The first woe has passed—look: There are two woes yet to follow thereafter.

[13]And the sixth angel sounded the trumpet, and I heard a single voice coming from the [four] horns of the gold sacrificial altar before God, [14]Saying to the sixth angel who held the trumpet, "Release the four angels who are chained at the great river Euphrates."[r] [15]And the four angels, who had been prepared for the hour and day and month and year, were released so that they might kill one third of humankind. [16]And the number of the soldiers of the cavalry—for I heard their number—was two myriads of myriads.[s] [17]And thus in the vision I saw the horses and those seated upon them, who had fiery and hyacinthine[t] and sulfurous cuirasses, and the heads of the horses are like the heads of lions, and out of their mouths come fire and smoke and sulfur. [18]By these three calamities—by the fire and the smoke and the sulfur coming out of their mouths—one third of humankind was killed. [19]For the power of the horses is in their mouths and in their tails, for their tails are like serpents, having heads, and with them they do harm. [20]And the remainder

o. *θώρακας ὡς θώρακας σιδηροῦς* (*thōrakas hōs thōrakas sidērous*): thus the same Greek word in both instances. A *θώραξ* (*thōrax*) is literally a "cuirass" or "corselet," but from at least the time of Aristotle it was used to mean (as in English) the thorax of an arthropod (a lobster or insect). Admittedly, given the outlandish imagery of Revelation, the text could indeed mean that the locusts are wearing armor about their torsos, but it seems as natural to read it as meaning that their exoskeletons are like iron at the throat and breast.

p. "Destruction."

q. "Destroyer."

r. See 13:3, 18; 16:12; 17:10–11 below and my footnotes thereto.

s. That is, two hundred million.

t. In ancient Greek this could mean a color either like that of sapphire or like that of amethyst.

of humanity, those who were not killed by these calamities, still did not turn their hearts away from the works of their hands, so as not to prostrate themselves before daemonic beings and before the gold and silver and bronze and stone and wooden idols, which can neither see nor hear nor walk, ²¹And neither did they turn their hearts away from their murders or from their sorceries or from their whorings or from their thefts.

CHAPTER TEN

¹And I saw another mighty angel descending out of heaven, garbed in a cloud, and a nimbus upon his head, and his face like the sun, and his feet and legs[u] like pillars of fire, ²And holding in his hand a small book laid open. And he placed his right foot upon the sea and his left upon the land, ³And he cried out in a loud voice, like a lion roaring. And when he cried out the seven peals of thunder spoke out in their own voices. ⁴And when the seven peals of thunder had spoken I was about to write, but I heard a voice out of heaven saying, "Place a seal on the things the seven peals of thunder spoke, and do not write them." ⁵And the angel whom I saw standing on the sea and on the land lifted his right hand to heaven, ⁶And swore by the one who lives unto the ages of the ages—who created the heavens and the things therein, and the earth and the things therein, and the sea and the things therein—that there will be no more time.[v] ⁷Rather, in the days of the seventh angel's voice, when he is about to sound the trumpet, God's mystery would also be finished, just as he proclaimed in his good tidings to his slaves the prophets. ⁸And the voice that I heard out of heaven was speaking with me again and saying, "Go, take the opened book in the hand of the angel who stands upon the sea and upon the land." ⁹And I went away to the angel, telling him to give me the small book. And he says to me, "Take and devour it, and it will

u. πόδες (*podes*): literally, "feet," but also meaning (as is obviously the case here) the whole of the legs together with the feet.

v. Which is to say, no more delay.

embitter your stomach, but in your mouth it will be sweet as honey." ¹⁰And I took the small book out of the angel's hand and devoured it, and in my mouth it was sweet as honey, and when I had eaten it my stomach was embittered. ¹¹And they say to me, "It is necessary for you to prophesy regarding many peoples and nations and tongues and kings."

CHAPTER ELEVEN

¹And a reed like a measuring rod was given to me, saying, "Rise and measure God's sanctuary and the sacrificial altar and those prostrating themselves therein, ²And leave out the courtyard that is outside the sanctuary, and do not measure it, because it has been given to the gentiles, and they will trample the holy city for forty-two months. ³And I shall grant it to my two witnesses, and they will prophesy for twelve hundred and sixty days clothed in sackcloths." ⁴These are the two olive trees and the two lampstands standing before the Lord of the earth. ⁵And, should anyone wish to harm them, fire comes out of their mouth and consumes their enemies; and, should anyone wish to harm them, he must necessarily be killed in this way. ⁶These have the authority to close the sky, so that no rain might fall during the days of their prophecy, and they have authority over the waters, to turn them to blood and to strike the earth with every kind of calamity as often as they might wish. ⁷And, whenever they shall complete their testimony, the beast that rises up out of the abyss will wage war on them, and will conquer them, and will kill them—⁸And their corpse on the open street of the great city (which is spiritually^w called Sodom and Egypt), where their Lord was also crucified. ⁹And representatives from the peoples and tribes and tongues and nations look upon their corpse for three and a half days, and they do not allow their corpses to be placed in a tomb. ¹⁰And those dwelling on the earth gloat over them and merrily celebrate, and they will send one another gifts, because these two prophets tormented those who dwelt

w. Often used to mean "allegorically" or "figuratively."

on the earth. ¹¹And after three and a half days a spirit[x] of life from God entered within them, and they stood on their feet, and a great terror fell upon those looking upon them. ¹²And they heard a loud voice out of heaven saying to them, "Come up here," and they rose up into heaven in the cloud, and their enemies watched them. ¹³And in that hour a great earthquake occurred, and one tenth of the city fell, and seven thousand names of human beings were killed in the earthquake, and the rest became terrified and gave glory to the God of heaven.

¹⁴The second woe has passed—look: The third woe comes quickly.

¹⁵And the seventh angel sounded the trumpet, and there came loud voices in heaven, saying, "The kingdom of the cosmos has become the Lord's and his Anointed's, and he will reign unto the ages of the ages." ¹⁶And the twenty-four elders seated before God on their thrones fell on their faces and made obeisance to God, ¹⁷Saying, "We thank you, Lord God the Almighty, who are and who were [and who are to come], because you have taken your great power and have reigned, ¹⁸And the gentiles were indignant, and your ire has come, and the time for the dead to be judged, and for giving the reward to your slaves the prophets and to the holy ones and to those who revere your name, the small and great, and for destroying those who destroy the earth." ¹⁹And God's sanctuary in heaven was opened, and the ark of his covenant was seen in his sanctuary, and there came lightning flashes and noises and peals of thunder and an earthquake and a great hailstorm.

CHAPTER TWELVE

¹And a great sign was seen in heaven: a woman garbed with the sun, and the moon beneath her feet, and on her head a chaplet of twelve stars, ²And she was pregnant, and she cries out, enduring birth-pangs, and in an agony to give birth. ³And another sign was seen in heaven, and look: a great flame-hued dragon who had seven heads and ten horns and

x. Or "breath."

on his heads seven diadems, ⁴And his tail drags along one third of the stars of heaven, and he cast them onto the earth. And the dragon stood before the woman who was about to give birth so that, when she should give birth, he might devour her child. ⁵And she bore a son, a male child, who is about to shepherd all the gentiles with a rod of iron, and her child was seized away to God and to his throne. ⁶And the woman fled into the wilderness, there where she has a place prepared by God, so that they might nourish her for twelve hundred and sixty days. ⁷And war broke out in heaven: that of Michael and his angels waging a war with the dragon. And the dragon and his angels waged war, ⁸And did not prevail, nor was any place still found for them in heaven. ⁹And the great dragon was cast down, the ancient serpent, the one that is called Slanderer and Accuser, the one that leads the whole inhabited world astray—it was cast down into the earth and its angels were cast down with it.ʸ ¹⁰And I heard a loud voice in heaven saying, "Now has come about the salvation and the power and the Kingdom of our God, and the authority of his Anointed, because the prosecutor of our brothers, the one prosecuting them before our God day and night, has been cast down. ¹¹And they conquered him by the blood of the suckling lamb and by the word of their testimony, and they did not love their own soul all the way to death. ¹²For this reason be glad, O heavens and those tabernacling therein; alas for the earth and the sea, because the Slanderer has descended into you with a great rage, knowing that he has little time." ¹³And, when the dragon saw that he had been cast down into the earth, he pursued the woman who had given birth to the male child. ¹⁴And the two wings of the great eagle were given to the woman so that she might fly to the wilderness, to her place, there where she is nourished—for a season, and for seasons, and for half a season—away from the serpent's face. ¹⁵And from his mouth the serpent spewed forth water like a river

y. These images of an angelic war in heaven later entered into Christian imagination as a depiction of the pre-cosmic defeat and exile of rebel angels; but here, as is especially evident in the verses that follow (10–12), the imagery concerns an event still in the future.

behind the woman, so that he might cause her to be carried off by the river. ¹⁶And the earth aided the woman, and the earth opened its mouth and swallowed the river that the dragon had spewed from his mouth. ¹⁷And the dragon was enraged over the woman, and went off to wage a war with the rest of her seed, who keep God's commandments and hold to the witness of Jesus; ¹⁸And he stood on the sand and the sea.

CHAPTER THIRTEEN

¹And I saw a beast rising from the sea that had ten horns and seven heads, and on its heads blasphemous names. ²And the beast that I saw was like a leopard, and its feet were like a bear's, and its mouth was like a lion's mouth. And the dragon gave it his power and his throne and great authority. ³And it was as if one of its heads had been slaughtered, entirely dead, and its deathblow was healed.ᶻ And all the earth followed after the beast in wonder, ⁴And they made obeisance to the dragon, because he had given authority to the beast, and they made obeisance to the beast, saying, "Who is like the beast, and who can wage war on

---

z. Though Revelation is written in the coded language of apocalyptic literature, and many of its more recondite references are irrecoverably lost to the past, on the whole its symbolism is not difficult to penetrate. It is concerned principally with the Roman Empire, the city of Rome itself, the emperors of Rome, and Jerusalem—both its destruction and its future divine restoration— as well as the final vindication of believers in Jesus as the Messiah. As the seven heads of the beast are generally reckoned (on the basis of clues liberally scattered throughout the text) as seven successive or nearly successive emperors, the reference to one who was wounded by the sword but who lived is almost certainly a reference to Nero, who was generally reported to have died a suicide by the sword in 68 CE, but who had become a legendary figure in the first century, believed by many still to be living in secret (probably among the Parthians, beyond the Euphrates) till he should return with armies from the east to take the empire again. Tacitus, Suetonius, Cassius Dio, and Dio Chrysostomos all reported that occasional pretenders had arisen claiming to be Nero returned. As Nero was remembered by Christians and others as a persecutor and tyrant, the prophecy of his return was one that in certain quarters had acquired a positively eschatological significance (see 16:12 below and my footnote thereto).

him?" ⁵And it was given a mouth speaking grand things and blasphemies, and it was given authority to act for forty-two months. ⁶And it opened its mouth in blasphemies against God, to blaspheme his name and his tabernacle—those tabernacling in heaven. ⁷And it was granted to it to wage war with the holy ones and to conquer them, and it was granted authority over every tribe and people and tongue and nation. ⁸And all those dwelling on the earth will make obeisance to him, everyone whose name has not been written in the book of the suckling lamb who has been slaughtered from the foundation of the cosmos.ᵃᵃ ⁹If anyone has an ear, let him hear. ¹⁰"If anyone is for captivity, to captivity he goes; if anyone is to be killed by a sword, by a sword he is to be killed." Here is the endurance and faithfulness of the holy ones.

¹¹And I saw another beast rise out of the earth, and it had two horns like a suckling lamb, and spoke like a dragon. ¹²And it exercises all the authority of the first beast in the latter's presence, and brings it about that the earth and those dwelling in it shall make obeisance to the first beast, whose deathblow was healed. ¹³And it performs great signs, such that it even makes fire descend from heaven to the earth in front of human beings. ¹⁴And, by the signs it has been granted to perform before the beast, it leads those dwelling on the earth astray, telling those dwelling on the earth to make an image for the beast that bears the sword's wound and that has lived. ¹⁵And it was granted it to give a spiritᵃᵇ to the beast's image, so that the beast's image might speak as well,ᵃᶜ and might bring it about that as many as might not make obeisance to the beast's image should be killed. ¹⁶And it brings it about for everyone—the small and the great, both the rich and the destitute, both

aa. It is not clear whether "from the foundation of the cosmos" modifies the word "written" or the word "slaughtered."

ab. Or "breath."

ac. This was something of a hieratical parlor trick in various of the pagan temples and shrines of late antiquity. The theurgic summoning of spirits into devotional statuary—animating them or speaking through them or both—was apparently accomplished in many cases with automata, or hidden mechanical devices, or hidden speaking trumpets.

the free and the slaves—that they should give them a mark impressed on their right hand or on their forehead, ¹⁷So that no one could buy or sell except whoever had the mark—the name of the beast or the number of its name. ¹⁸Here is the wisdom:ᵃᵈ let whoever has a reasoning mind calculate the number of the beast, for it is the number of a man. And its number is six hundred and sixty-six.ᵃᵉ

CHAPTER FOURTEEN

¹And I looked, and see: the suckling lamb standing upon Mount Zion, and with him a hundred and forty-four thousand who have his name and his Father's name written upon their foreheads. ²And I heard a sound out of heaven like a sound of many waters and like a sound of loud thunder, and the sound I heard was like lyrists playing upon their lyres. ³And they sing, as it were, a new song before the throne and before the four animals and the elders, and no one could learn the new song

ad. A phrase that often means specifically a hidden or veiled wisdom or truth, requiring special knowledge or discernment.

ae. In some very ancient manuscripts, the number is six hundred and sixteen. The numerological practice of "calculating the number" (ψηφίζειν τὸν ἀριθμόν [psēphizein ton arithmon]) of a name or word, or *gematria* in Hebrew, is based on the simple contingency that most written ancient languages used a single alphanumeric system in which numbers were represented by letters, which thus allowed one to add up the numeric value of a name to produce a cipher (or, as was typically the case, a mystic sum). Many names can add up to 666 or 616, of course, especially given the fluidity both of ancient spelling and of differing conventions of transliteration from one language to another, and any number of theories have been ventured regarding whose name lies behind the "number of the beast." But the most plausible of these theories (again, based on all the other clues in the text) is that it refers to the Greek for Nero Caesar—Nerōn Kaisar— transliterated into Hebrew as "Nrvn Qsr" (one of the ways in which it could be written). This might also explain the variant sum of 616, since the same name in Latin lacks the terminal Greek *n* for Nero, which in being transliterated as "Nrv Qsr" would neatly subtract 50 from the total sum of the letters. But this is merely a very suggestive and attractive theory, one that solves certain problems but that also depends upon considerable speculation.

except the hundred and forty-four thousand who had been purchased from the earth. ⁴These are they who were not defiled with women, for they are virgins; these are they who follow the suckling lamb wherever he may lead. These have been purchased from among human beings, a firstfruit for God and for the suckling lamb, ⁵And in their mouth no lie was found; they are immaculate [before God's throne].

⁶And I saw another angel flying in mid-heaven who had the good tidings of the Age to proclaim to those sitting upon the earth, and to every nation and tribe and tongue and people, ⁷Saying in a loud voice, "Revere God and give him glory, for the hour of his judgment has come, and prostrate yourselves before the one who makes the heaven and the earth and sea and springs of waters." ⁸And another angel, a second one, followed, saying, "Fallen, fallen, Babylon the Great who has given all the gentiles to drink from the wine of the vehemence of her whoring." ⁹And another angel, a third one, followed them, saying in a loud voice, "If anyone makes obeisance to the beast and its image, and receives an impress on his forehead or on his hand, ¹⁰He shall drink also from the wine of God's vehemence, mixed undiluted into the cup of his ire, and will be tormented by fire and sulfur before the holy angels and before the suckling lamb. ¹¹And the smoke of their torment rises for ages of ages,ᵃᶠ and the ones who make obeisance to the beast and its image have no rest day and night, as does anyone who might receive the impress of its name. ¹²Here is the endurance of the holy ones who keep the commandments of God and the faith of Jesus. ¹³And I heard a voice out of heaven saying, "Write: 'How blissful the dead who henceforth die in the Lord. "Yes," says the Spirit, "so that they shall rest from their labors, for their works follow along with them."'"

---

af. εἰς αἰῶνας αἰώνων (eis aiōnas aiōnōn). Everywhere else in Revelation, when John is speaking of final or everlasting things, he employs the standard phrase εἰς τοὺς αἰῶνας τῶν αἰώνων (eis tous aiōnas tōn aiōnōn), with the definite articles: "unto *the* ages of *the* ages." Here alone the articles are omitted, perhaps producing a weaker and more indefinite formula, one that might be read as meaning "for a very long time."

[14]And I looked, and see: a white cloud, and seated upon the cloud one like a son of man who had a gold chaplet on his head and a sharp sickle in his hand. [15]And another angel came forth from the sanctuary, crying out in a loud voice to the one sitting upon the cloud, "Thrust forth your sickle and reap, for the hour to reap has come, for the earth's harvest has grown dry."[ag] [16]And the one sitting on the cloud heaved his sickle over the earth, and the earth was reaped. [17]And another angel came forth from the sanctuary in heaven, also holding a sharp sickle. [18]And another angel came forth from the sacrificial altar, one who had charge over the fire, and spoke out in a loud voice to the one holding the sharp sickle, saying, "Thrust forth your sharp sickle and gather the clusters from the vine of the earth, because its grapes have reached their full ripeness." [19]And the angel heaved his sickle into the earth and gathered the vine of the earth and cast it into the great winepress of God's vehemence. [20]And the winepress was trodden outside the city, and blood came out of the winepress, as high as the horses' bridles, a distance of sixteen hundred stadia.[ah]

CHAPTER FIFTEEN

[1]And I saw another great and wonderful sign in heaven: angels who had seven calamities—the very last ones, because in them God's vehemence reached its end. [2]And I saw, as it were, a sea of glass mingled with fire, and those who were victorious over the beast and its image and its name standing upon the sea of glass holding lyres from God. [3]And they sing the song of Moses the slave of God and the song of the suckling lamb, saying, "Great and wonderful are your works, Lord God the Almighty, just and true are your ways, the King of the gentiles! [4]Who, Lord, would not revere—and will not glorify—your name? Because you

ag. ἐξηράνθη (exēranthē): literally, "has been parched" or "has withered," but here meaning that the grain has matured, having passed from green and moist to pale and dry.

ah. About 180 miles.

alone are hallowed, because all the gentiles will come and make obeisance before you, because your acts of justice have been made manifest."
⁵And thereafter I looked, and the sanctuary of the tabernacle of the testimony in heaven was open, ⁶And the seven angels who had the seven
calamities came forth from the sanctuary, clad in bright clean linen and
girdled with golden cinctures around their chests, ⁷And one of the four
animals gave the seven angels seven gold libation-dishes filled with the
vehemence of the God who lives unto the ages of the ages. ⁸And the
sanctuary was filled with smoke from God's glory and from his power,
and no one could enter into the sanctuary until the seven calamities of
the seven angels had reached their end.

CHAPTER SIXTEEN

¹And I heard a loud voice out of the sanctuary saying, "Go and
pour out the seven libation-dishes of God's ire into the earth." ²And
the first departed and poured out his libation-dish into the earth, and
an evil and pernicious ulceration developed upon those human beings
who bore the impress of the beast and who made obeisance to its image.
³And the second poured out his libation-dish into the sea, and it became blood, like that of a dead man, and every life's soul—the things
in the sea—died. ⁴And the third poured out his libation-dish into the
rivers and the springs of waters, and it became blood. ⁵And I heard the
angels of the waters saying, "You are just, you who are and who were
[and who will be], the holy one, because you have judged these things,
⁶Because they have shed the blood of holy ones and prophets, and you
have given them blood to drink, as they merit."ᵃⁱ ⁷And I heard the sacrificial altar saying, "Yes, Lord God the Almighty, true and just are your
judgments." ⁸And the fourth poured out his libation-dish upon the sun,
and it was granted to itᵃʲ to scorch humankind in fire. ⁹And humankind

ai. Literally, "you have given them blood to drink, they are worthy."
aj. Or "to him."

was scorched by a great heat, and they blasphemed the name of the God who had power over these calamities, and they did not turn their hearts to giving him glory. [10]And the fifth poured out his libation-dish onto the beast's throne, and its kingdom became dark, and they gnawed their tongues from the anguish, [11]And they blasphemed the God of heaven from their pains and their ulcerations, and did not turn their hearts away from their deeds. [12]And the sixth poured out his libation-dish onto the great river Euphrates, and its water dried up, so that the way was prepared for the kings who come from the sunrise.[ak] [13]And I saw coming out of the mouth of the dragon and out of the mouth of the beast and out of the mouth of the false prophet three impure spirits like frogs. [14]For they are spirits of daemonic beings who perform signs, which go forth to the kings of the whole inhabited world so as to assemble them for the war of the Great Day of God the Almighty. [15]"Look: I am coming like a thief; how blissful the one who remains vigilant and keeps his clothes on, lest he walk naked and they see his shame." [16]And he assembled them at the site that in Hebrew is called Armageddon. [17]And the seventh poured out his libation-dish upon the air, and a loud voice from the throne came out of the sanctuary, saying, "It is done." [18]And there came lightning flashes and noises and peals of thunder, and a great earthquake occurred—such an earthquake—one so great—as had not occurred since humanity had come to be upon the earth. [19]And the great city came to be broken into three parts, and the cities of the gentiles fell. And Babylon the Great was remembered before God—to give her the cup of the wine of the vehemence of his ire. [20]And every island fled, and no mountains were found. [21]And a great storm of hail-stones the weight of talents[al] descends from the sky upon humankind,

ak. One very early and prevalent version of the legend of Nero's return (as reflected, say, in the fourth and fifth books of the *Sibylline Oracles*) was that Nero was living among the Parthians and would return leading armies from the East.

al. The standard weight of a talent varied among different currency systems, but in the time of the New Testament the common heavy "talanton" was about

and humankind blasphemed God from the pounding of the hail, for its pounding was extraordinarily violent.

CHAPTER SEVENTEEN

[1]And one of the seven angels holding the seven libation-dishes came and spoke with me, saying, "Come, I shall show you the verdict upon the Great Whore who sits upon many waters, [2]With whom the kings of the earth have whored, and those who dwell on the earth became drunk with the wine of her whoring." [3]And he bore me away in spirit into a wilderness, and I saw a woman sitting upon a scarlet beast, wholly covered with blasphemous names, which had seven heads and ten horns. [4]And the woman was clad in purple and scarlet, and gilded with gold and precious stone and pearls, holding in her hand a gold cup filled with abominations and with the impure things of her whoring, [5]And written on her forehead was a name, a mystery: "BABYLON THE GREAT, THE MOTHER OF THE WHORES AND THE ABOMINATIONS OF THE EARTH." [6]And I saw the woman drunk on the blood of the holy ones and on the blood of the witnesses of Jesus. And, seeing her, I marveled in utter astonishment. [7]And the angel said to me, "Why were you astonished? I shall tell you the mystery of the woman and of the beast that bears her, the one that has the seven heads and the ten horns. [8]The beast that you saw was, and is not, and is about to rise from the abyss, and is going to destruction; and they who dwell on the earth, whose name has not been written in the book of life from the foundation of the cosmos, will be astonished on seeing that the beast was and is not and will presently be. [9]Here is the mind possessed of wisdom: The seven heads are seven mountains, there where the woman sits upon them, and are seven kings. [10]The five have fallen, the one is, the other has not yet come, and when he has come he must remain for a little while. [11]And the beast that

---

130 pounds. In the old, traditional Roman system, a talent was a little over 70 pounds.

was and is not, he is himself also an eighth, and is one of the seven, and goes to destruction.^{am} ¹²And the ten horns that you saw are ten kings who have not yet received a kingdom, but receive authority as kings along with the beast for one hour. ¹³These have a single resolve,^{an} and they give their power and authority to the beast. ¹⁴These will wage a war with the suckling lamb and the suckling lamb will conquer them, because he is Lord of lords and King of kings, and those with him are called and chosen and faithful." ¹⁵And he says to me, "The waters that you saw, where the whore sits, are peoples and crowds and nations and tongues. ¹⁶And the ten horns that you saw, and the beast, these will hate the whore, and will render her desolate and naked, and will eat her fleshes,^{ao} and will consume her with fire; ¹⁷For God placed it in their hearts to accomplish his purpose, and to accomplish a single purpose, and to give their kingdom to the beast, until God's words shall be completed. ¹⁸And the woman whom you saw is the great city that holds reign over the kings of the earth."

CHAPTER EIGHTEEN

¹Thereafter I saw another angel descending out of heaven who had great authority, and the earth was illuminated by his glory. ²And he cried out in a mighty voice, saying, "Fallen, fallen, Babylon the Great, and she has become a habitation of daemonic beings and a prison for every impure spirit and a prison for every bird that is impure [and a prison for every beast that is impure] and detested, ³Because all the gentiles have drunk of the wine of the vehemence of her whoring, and the kings of the earth have whored with her, and the merchants of the earth have grown rich from her power and wanton luxuriance." ⁴And I

am. That the eighth beast, who is yet to come, is also one of the previous seven—who was, yet now is not—is another indication that the text here presumes the legend of Nero's return.

an. Or "mind," or "thought," or "intelligence," or "intention."

ao. *Sic:* a somewhat archaic use of the plural form.

heard another voice out of heaven saying, "Come out of her, my people, so that you might not share communion in her sins, and might not suffer any of her calamities, ⁵For her sins have been heaped up to heaven, and God has remembered her injustices. ⁶Requite her even as she has requited, and redouble it, twice times her own deeds; in the cup she has mixed, mix twice as much for her. ⁷To whatever degree she has glorified herself and luxuriated, give her torment and grief in that same measure, because in her heart she says, 'I sit as queen, and I am not a widow, and I shall most certainly see no sorrow.' ⁸Hence in a single day her calamities will come—death and sorrow and famine—and she will be consumed by fire, because the Lord who judges her is mighty. ⁹And the kings of the earth, who whored and luxuriated with her, will weep and wail over her when they see the smoke of her conflagration, ¹⁰Standing far off, out of terror at her torment, saying, 'Alas, alas, the great city, Babylon the mighty city, for in a single hour your judgment has come.' ¹¹And the merchants of the earth weep and grieve over her, because no one buys their cargo any more—¹²Cargo of gold and of silver and of precious stone and of pearls, and of fine linen and of purple and of silk and of scarlet, and every citrine wood and every ivory vessel, and every vessel of the most precious wood and of bronze and of iron and of marble, ¹³And cinnamon and cardamom and incenses and perfumed unguents and frankincense, and wine and oil and fine wheat flour and grain, and beasts of burden and sheep, and of horses and of carriages and of bodies and souls of human beings. ¹⁴'And the ripened fruit of your soul's desire has departed from you, and all the sumptuous and splendid things have passed away from you'—and surely they shall find them no more. ¹⁵The merchants of these things, who have been made rich by her, will stand far off, out of terror at her torment, weeping and grieving, ¹⁶Saying, 'Alas, alas, the great city, which is clad in fine linen and purple and scarlet, gilded with gold and precious stone and pearl, ¹⁷For in a single hour such enormous wealth was rendered desolate.' And every ship's pilot, and all those under sail to any destination, and sailors, and as many as toil on the sea stood far off, ¹⁸And cried out on seeing the smoke of her conflagration, saying, 'Who is like the great city?' ¹⁹And they threw dust on their heads and cried out, weeping and grieving, saying, 'Alas, alas, the great city, wherein all who have ships on the sea were enriched by her opulence, for in a single hour she was rendered desolate.' ²⁰Rejoice over her, O heaven, and you the holy ones and the apostles and the prophets, because God has pronounced the verdict of your judgment against her."

²¹Then a mighty angel picked up a stone like a great millstone and cast it into the sea, saying, "Thus, with a sudden rush, Babylon the great city will be cast down, and will certainly no longer be found; ²²And certainly no sound of lyrists and musicians and flutists and trumpeters shall any longer be heard in you; and certainly no craftsman of any craft shall any longer be found in you; and certainly no sound of a mill shall any longer be heard in you; ²³And certainly no lantern's light shall any longer appear in you; and certainly no voice of bridegroom and bride shall any longer be heard in you—for your merchants were the great men of the earth—for by your sorcery all the gentiles were led astray. ²⁴And in her was found blood of prophets and holy ones, and of all those slaughtered upon the earth."

CHAPTER NINETEEN

¹Thereafter, it was as if I heard a loud noise of a large crowd in heaven saying, "Alleluia, the salvation and the glory and the power be to our God! ²For his judgments are true and just, because he has judged the great whore who defiled the earth with her whoring, and exacted justice for the blood of his slaves at her hand." ³And a second time they said, "Alleluia, and her smoke rises up unto the ages of the ages!" ⁴And the twenty-four elders and the four animals fell down and made obeisance to the God who sat on the throne, saying, "Amen, alleluia!" ⁵And a voice came forth from the throne, saying, "Praise our God, all his slaves, [and] those who revere him, the small and the great!" ⁶And it was as if I heard a noise of a large crowd and a sound of many waters

and a sound of mighty peals of thunder, saying, "Alleluia, because our Lord God the Almighty has reigned! [7]Let us rejoice and exult, and we shall give him the glory, for the marriage of the suckling lamb has come, and his wife has made herself ready!" [8]And it was granted her that she be clad in bright, clean, fine linen—for the fine linen is the righteous deeds of the holy ones. [9]And he tells me, "Write: 'How blissful those called to the supper for the marriage of the suckling lamb.'" And he says to me, "These are God's true words." [10]And I fell down at his feet to make obeisance to him. And he says to me, "See here, no! I am a fellow slave along with you and with your brothers who hold to the witness of Jesus; make obeisance to God. For the witness of Jesus is the spirit of prophecy."

[11]And I saw heaven opened, and look: a white horse, and the one sitting on it called Faithful and True, and he judges and wages war in justice. [12]And his eyes are [like] a flame of fire, and on his head are many diadems, he who has a written name that no one except him knows, [13]And who has been clad in a robe deep-dyed[ap] in blood, and his name is called the Logos of God.[aq] [14]And the armies [who were] in heaven followed him on white horses, clothed in bright, clean, fine linen. [15]And from his mouth comes forth a sharp sword, so that with it he might strike the gentiles; and he will shepherd them with a rod of iron; and he treads the winepress of the wine of the vehemence of God the Almighty's ire. [16]And on the robe and on his thigh he has a name written: King of Kings and Lord of Lords.

[17]And I saw one angel who stood in the sun, and he cried out in a loud voice, saying to all the birds flying in mid-heaven, "Come, gather

ap. βεβαμμένον (*bebammenon*). Some texts have "sprinkled" or "spattered" instead, but this is the more convincingly attested reading.

aq. The image of God's Logos as a fierce warrior sent into the earth from God's throne is found also in Wisdom 18:15–16. This is a very different understanding of the "mediating principle" of the Logos from the much more metaphysical version found in the prologue of the fourth Gospel.

to the great supper of God, [18]So that you may eat fleshes[ar] of kings, and fleshes of chiliarchs, and fleshes of the mighty, and fleshes of horses and of those sitting upon them, and fleshes of everyone, both freemen and slaves, both small and great." [19]And I saw the beast, and the kings of the earth, and their armies assembled to wage war with the one who sat upon the horse and with his army. [20]And the beast was seized, and with it the false prophet who had performed before it the signs by which he had led astray those who had received the impress of the beast, and who made obeisance to its image; the two of them were cast alive into the marsh[as] of the fire, of the one burning with sulfur.[at] [21]And the rest were killed by the sword of the one sitting on the horse, that which came forth from his mouth, and on their fleshes all the birds were gorged.

CHAPTER TWENTY

[1]And I saw an angel descending from heaven, holding in his hand the key to the abyss and a great chain. [2]And he seized the dragon, the ancient serpent, who is a Slanderer and the Accuser, and bound him for a thousand years, [3]And cast him into the abyss, and shut it and sealed it over him, so that he should no longer lead the gentiles astray until the thousand years are finished; thereafter he must be set loose for a little while. [4]And I saw thrones, and they sat upon them, and judgment was given to them, as well as the souls of those who had been decapitated

---

ar. *Sic:* in each instance here and in v. 21 below.

as. In ancient usage (unlike modern Demotic Greek), a λιμνή (*limnē*) was not generally much like anything we would properly call a lake today; originally it simply meant a marshy standing pool by the sea or by a large river, and then came to be used of any marshy pond or mere. In very antique usage (Homer, for instance), the term could be used as a poetic trope for the sea; but John does not give the impression of being someone possessed of a classical education.

at. Here, the grammar of the text is somewhat confusing, as the phrase "the one burning" is in the feminine and therefore refers back to the word *limnē*, "marsh," but has shifted awkwardly from the accusative to the genitive.

on account of the witness of Jesus and on account of God's word, and who did not make obeisance to the beast or to its image, and did not receive the impress on their forehead and on their hand; and they came to life and reigned with the Anointed for a thousand years. ⁵Until the thousand years had elapsed, the rest of the dead did not have life. This is the first resurrection. ⁶How blissful and holy the one who has a share in the first resurrection: over these the second death has no power; instead they will be priests of God and of the Anointed, and will reign with him a thousand years.

⁷And when the thousand years have elapsed, the Accuser will be released from his prison, ⁸And will go forth to lead astray the gentiles in the earth's four corners, Gog and Magog, to assemble them for the war, they whose number is like the sand of the sea. ⁹And they marched across the earth's broad expanse and encircled the camp of the holy ones and the beloved city, and fire descended out of the sky and consumed them. ¹⁰And the Slanderer who led them astray was cast into the marsh of fire and sulfur, where the beast and the false prophet are also, and they will be tormented day and night unto the ages of the ages.

¹¹And I saw a great white throne and the one who sat upon it, from whose face the earth and sky fled away, and no place was found for them. ¹²And I saw the dead, the great and the small, standing before the throne, and books were opened; and another book—the one of life, that is—was opened; and, from the things written in the book, the dead were judged according to their works. ¹³And the sea yielded up the dead within it, and Death and Hades yielded up the dead within them,ᵃᵘ and they were judged, every one of them, according to their works. ¹⁴And Death and Hades were cast into the marsh of fire. This—the marsh of fire—is the second death. ¹⁵And, if anyone was not found written in the book of life, he was cast into the marsh of fire.

au. It was a common belief in antiquity, shared by pagans and Jews alike, that the souls of those who die on earth descend to Hades, but the souls of those who perish at sea descend to a place below the waters, or wander the waves as ghosts.

CHAPTER TWENTY-ONE

¹And I saw a new sky and a new earth, for the first sky and the first earth have passed away, and the sea no longer is. ²And I saw the holy city, a New Jerusalem, descending out of heaven from God, made ready like a bride adorned for her husband. ³And I heard a loud voice from the throne saying, "Look: The tabernacle of God is with human beings, and he will tabernacle with them, and they will be his peoples, and God himself will be with them [as their God], ⁴And he will wipe away every tear from their eyes, and no longer will there be death, no longer will there be sorrow or lamentation or pain, for the first things have passed away." ⁵And the one who sat upon the throne said, "Look: I make all things new." And he said, "Write, because these words are trustworthy and true." ⁶And he said, "It is done. I am the alpha and the omega, the beginning and the end. To the one who thirsts I will give freely from the fountain of life's water. ⁷The one who conquers will inherit these things, and I will be a God to him and he will be a son to me. ⁸But, for those who are craven and faithless and abominable and murderers and the whorish and sorcerers and idolaters and all the liars, their part is in the marsh burning with fire and sulfur, which is the second death."

⁹And one of the angels holding the seven libation-dishes filled with the seven last calamities came and spoke with me, saying, "Come, I shall show you the bride, the wife of the suckling lamb." ¹⁰And he bore me away in spirit onto a great and holy mountain, and showed me the holy city Jerusalem descending out of heaven from God, ¹¹Which had God's glory, her luster being like costliest stone, like jasper stone, of crystalline clarity, ¹²And had a wall great and high, which had twelve gates, and twelve angels at the gates, and twelve inscribed names, which are [the names] of the twelve tribes of the sons of Israel—¹³Three gates to the east and three gates to the north and three gates to the south and three gates to the west—¹⁴And the wall of the city had twelve foundations, and in them the twelve names of the twelve Apostles of the suckling lamb. ¹⁵And the one who was speaking with me had a gold measur-

ing reed, so that he could measure the city and its gates and her wall. [16]And the city lies foursquare, and her length as great as her breadth. And with the reed he measured the city as twelve hundred stadia;[av] its length and breadth and height are equal. [17]And he measured its wall as a hundred and forty-four cubits, according to the measure of a human being, which was the angel's measure.[aw] [18]And her wall's enclosure was jasper, and the city pure gold like pure glass, [19]The city's foundation having been adorned with every precious stone: the first foundation jasper, the second sapphire, the third chalcedony, the fourth emerald, [20]The fifth sardonyx, the sixth carnelian, the seventh chrysolite, the eighth beryl, the ninth topaz, the tenth chrysoprase, the eleventh hyacinth, the twelfth amethyst. [21]And the twelve gates were twelve pearls—each one of the gates made from a single pearl—and the street of the city pure gold, like transparent glass. [22]And in her I saw no sanctuary, for the Lord God the Almighty is her sanctuary, as well as the suckling lamb. [23]And the city has no need of the sun or the moon—that they should shine in her—for the glory of God illuminated her, and her lantern is the suckling lamb. [24]And the gentiles[ax] will walk about by her light, and the kings of the earth bring their glory [and worth] into her. [25]And her gates shall most certainly not be closed by day, for night will not exist there; [26]And they bring the glory and the worth of the gentiles

av. About fourteen hundred miles.

aw. A cubit is reckoned as the length of a forearm, and here the text appears to mean that the angel is using a measuring reed corresponding to the human standard, though the phrasing is too elliptically curt to be certain. It could instead mean "by the human—or, rather, the angelic—measure" (and the text has given us to believe that angels can come in very large sizes indeed).

ax. The Byzantine Text reads "the nations of the saved," but this is clearly an emendation of the text, and a fairly maladroit one, meant to make the eschatological imagery seem more consistently *eschatological*. The language used here echoes the prophetic picture (drawn from Isaiah, Micah, and Jeremiah) of a restored Jerusalem and a new earthly age in which the peoples of other nations will come to worship Israel's God, rather than a final dispensation beyond all history.

The Revelation of John

into her. ²⁷And nothing profane, and no one who^{ay} causes abomination and falsehood,^{az} may by any means enter therein, except those written in the suckling lamb's book of life.

CHAPTER TWENTY-TWO

¹And he showed me a river of life's water, bright as crystal, coming forth from the throne of God and the suckling lamb. ²In the middle of her street, and on either side of the river, was a tree producing twelve harvests of fruit, yielding its fruit each month, and the leaves of the tree are for a healing of the gentiles. ³And no longer will there be anything accursed; and the throne of God and the suckling lamb will be therein, and his slaves will worship him, ⁴And they will see his face, and his name will be on their foreheads. ⁵And there will be no more night, and they have no need of lantern light and sunlight, because the Lord God will shine upon them, and they will reign unto the ages of the ages.

⁶And he said to me, "These words are trustworthy and true, and the Lord God of the spirits of the prophets sent his angel to show his slaves things that must occur shortly." ⁷"And look: I am coming quickly. How blissful the one who keeps the words of the prophecy of this book."

⁸And I John am the one hearing and seeing these things. And when I heard and saw, I fell down before the feet of the angel showing me these things to make obeisance. ⁹And he says to me, "See here, no! I am a fellow slave along with you and with your brothers the prophets and with those who keep the words of this book; make obeisance to God." ¹⁰And he says to me, "Do not seal up the words of this book's prophecy; for the time is near. ¹¹The wrongdoer, let him still do wrong; and whoever is foul, let him still be befouled; and whoever is upright, let him still do what is right; and whoever is holy, let him still be made holy." ¹²"Look: I am coming quickly, and with me is the recompense I have to render

ay. Or "nothing that."
az. Or "and no falsehood."

to each, according to what his work is. [13]I am the alpha and the omega, the beginning and the end." [14]How blissful are those who wash their robes,[ba] so that they shall be given sanction for the tree of life, and may enter by the gates into the city. [15]Outside are the curs and the sorcerers and the whorish and the murderers and the idolaters and everyone who loves and practices falsehood.

[16]"I Jesus sent my angel to attest these things to you for the assemblies. I am the root and the offspring of David, the bright Morning Star."[bb]

[17]And the Spirit and the bride say, "Come." And let the one who hears say, "Come." And let the one who thirsts come; let the one who wishes take freely of the water of life.

[18]I testify to everyone who hears the words of this book's prophecy: If anyone should add to them, God will add to him the calamities that have been written about in this book; [19]And, if anyone takes away from this prophecy's book, God will take away his share from the tree of life and from the holy city that are written about in this book.

[20]The one who attests these things says, "Yes, I am coming quickly." Amen, come, Lord Jesus.

[21]The grace of the Lord Jesus be with all.[bc]

ba. In the Byzantine Text this reads "those who do his commandments," but the evidence for the version in the Critical Text (translated here) is quite imposing; this phrase, in fact, refers back to 7:14 above. The change in the text may simply be the result of a scribal error, and one very easy to understand: given the crowded and undifferentiated lettering of the ancient manuscripts, it is not difficult to see how the original text, "οἱ πλύνοντες τὰς στολὰς αὐτων" ([b]oi plynontes tas stolas avtōn), might have been misread or misheard as "οἱ ποιοῦντες τὰς ἐντολὰς αὐτοῦ" ([b]oi poiountas tas entolas avtou).

bb. See 2 Peter 1:19 and my footnote thereto; see also 2:28 above.

bc. Some texts say, "with all of you," some others say, "with all the holy ones," and various texts add a final "Amen."

Concluding Scientific Postscript

A Note on the Prologue of John's Gospel
An Exemplary Case of the Untranslatable

There may perhaps be no passage in the New Testament more re-sistant to simple translation into another tongue than the first eighteen verses—the prologue—of the Gospel of John. Whether it was written by the same author as most of the rest of the text (and there is cause for some slight doubt on that score), it very elegantly proposes a theology of the person of Christ that seems to subtend the entire book, and that perhaps reaches its most perfect expression in its twentieth chapter. But it also, intentionally in all likelihood, leaves certain aspects of that theology open to question, almost as if inviting the reader to venture ever deeper into the text in order to find the proper answers. Yet many of these fruitful ambiguities are simply invisible anywhere except in the Greek of the original, and even there are discernible in only the most elusive and tantalizing ways. Take, for example, the standard render-ing of just the first three verses. In Greek, they read, ¹Ἐν ἀρχῇ ἦν ὁ λόγος, καὶ ὁ λόγος ἦν πρὸς τὸν θεόν, καὶ θεὸς ἦν ὁ λόγος· ²οὗτος ἦν ἐν ἀρχῇ πρὸς τὸν θεόν· ³πάντα δι᾽ αὐτοῦ ἐγένετο, καὶ χωρὶς αὐτοῦ ἐγένετο οὐδὲ ἓν ὃ γέγονεν. (¹*En archē̱ ēn* ᵇ*o logos, kai* ᵇ*o logos ēn pros ton theon, kai theos ēn* ᵇ*o logos;* ²ᵇ*outos ēn en archē̱ pros ton theon;* ³*panta di᾽ avtou egeneto, kai chōris avtou egeneto oude* ᵇ*en* ᵇ*o gegonen.*) I am aware of no re-spectable English translation in which these verses do not appear in more or less the same form they are given in the King James Version: "¹In the beginning was the Word, and the Word was with God, and the Word was God. ²The same was in the beginning with God. ³All things were made by him; and without him was not any thing made that was made." Read thus, the Gospel begins with an enigmatic name for Christ, asserts that he was "with God" in the beginning, and then unambiguously goes on to identify him both as "God" and as the creator of all things. Apart from that curiously bland and impenetrable designation "the Word," the whole passage looks like a fairly straightforward statement of Trinitarian dogma (or at least two-thirds of it), of the Nicene-Constantinopolitan variety. The average reader would never guess that, in the fourth century, those same verses were employed by all parties in the Trinitarian debates in support of very disparate positions, or that Arians and Eunomians and other opponents of the Nicene settlement interpreted them as evidence *against* the coequality of God the Father and the divine Son. The truth is that, in Greek, and in the context of late antique Hellenistic metaphysics, the language of the Gospel's prologue is nowhere near so lucid and unequivocal as the translations make it seem. For one thing, the term *logos* really had, by the time the Gospel was written, acquired a metaphysical significance that "Word" cannot possibly convey; and in places like Alexandria it had acquired a very particular religious significance as well. For the Hellenistic Jewish philosopher Philo, for instance, it referred to a kind of "secondary divinity," a mediating principle standing between God the Most High and creation. In late antiquity it was assumed widely, in pagan, Jewish, and Christian circles, that God in his full transcendence did not come into direct contact with the world of limited and mutable things, and so had expressed himself in a subordinate and economically "reduced" form "through whom" (δι' αὐτοῦ [*di' avtou*]) he created and governed the world. It was this Logos that many Jews and Christians believed to be the subject of all the divine theophanies of Hebrew scripture. Many of the early Christian apologists thought of God's Logos as having been generated just prior to creation, in order to act as God's artisan of, and archregent in, the created order. Moreover, the Greek of John's prologue may reflect what was, at the time of its composition, a standard semantic distinction between the articular and inarticular (or arthrous and anarthrous) forms of the word *theos:* the former, ὁ θεός (*ʰo theos*) (as in πρὸς τὸν θεόν [*pros ton theon*], where the accusative form of article and noun follow the preposition), was generally used to refer to God in the fullest and most proper sense: God Most High, the transcendent One; the latter, however, θεός (*theos*) (as in καὶ θεὸς ἦν ὁ λόγος [*kai theos ēn ʰo logos*]), could be used of any divine being, however finite: a god or a derivative divine agency, say, or even a divinized mortal. And so early theologians differed greatly in their interpretation of that very small but very significantly absent monosyllable. Now it may be that the article is omitted in the latter case simply because the word *theos* functions as a predicate there, and typically in Greek the predicate would need no article. Yet the syntax is ambiguous as regards which substantive should be regarded as the subject and which the predicate; though Greek is an inflected language, and hence more syntactically malleable than modern Western tongues, the order of words is not a matter of complete indifference; and one might even translate καὶ θεὸς ἦν ὁ λόγος as "and [this] god was the Logos." But the issue becomes at once both clearer and more inadjudicable at verse 18, where again the designation of the Son is *theos* without the article, and there the word is unquestionably the subject of the sentence. Mind you, in the first chapter of John there are also other instances of the inarticular form where it is not clear whether the reference is the Father, the Son, or somehow both at once in an intentionally indeterminate way (as though, perhaps, the distinction of articular from inarticular forms is necessary in regard to the inner divine life, but not when speaking of the relation of the divine to the created realm). But, in all subsequent verses and chapters, God in his full transcendence is always *ʰo theos;* and the crucial importance of the difference between this and the inarticular *theos* is especially evident at 10:34–36. Most important of all, this distinction imbues the conclusion of the twentieth chapter with a remarkable theological significance, for it is there that Christ, now risen from the dead, is explicitly addressed as *ᵇo theos* (by the Apostle Thomas). Even this startling profession, admittedly, left considerable room for argument in the early centuries as to whether the fully divine designation was something conferred upon Christ only *after* the resurrection, and then perhaps only honorifically, or whether instead it was an eternal truth about Christ that had been made manifest *by* the resurrection. In the end, the Nicene settlement was reached only as a result of a long and difficult debate on the whole testimony of scripture and on the implications of the Christian understanding of salvation in Christ (not to mention a soupçon of imperial pressure).

Anyway, my point is not that there is anything amiss in the theology of Nicaea, or that the original Greek text calls it into question, but only that standard translations make it impossible for readers who know neither Greek nor the history of late antique metaphysics and theology to understand either what the original text says or what it does not say. Not that there is any perfectly satisfactory way of representing the text's obscurities in English, since we do not distinguish between articular and inarticular forms in the same way; rather, we have to rely on orthography and typography, using the difference between an uppercase or lowercase *g* to indicate the distinction between God and [a] god. This, hesitantly, is how I deal with the distinction in my translation of the Gospel's prologue, and I believe one must employ some such device: it seems to me that the withholding of the full revelation of Christ as *ᵇo theos*, God in the fullest sense, until the Apostle Thomas confesses him as such in the light of Easter, must be seen as an intentional authorial tactic. Some other scholars have chosen to render the inarticular form of *theos* as "a divine being," but this seems wrong to me on two counts: first, if that were all the evangelist were saying, he could have used the perfectly serviceable Greek word *theios;* and, second, the text of the Gospel clearly means to assert some kind of continuity of identity between God the Father and his Son the Logos, not merely some sort of association between "God proper" and "a god." Here, I take it, one may regard chapter twenty as providing the ultimate interpretation of chapter one, and allow one's translation to reflect that.

Translating Certain Words
An Irregular Glossary

In order to avoid misunderstandings or, worse, a surfeit of long and repetitious footnotes, I thought it best to explain my renderings of certain words here for the curious. In some cases my choice of translation—or, in one case, my refusal of a choice of translation—might seem somewhat eccentric, or even perhaps a little perverse; but I can honestly say that all my decisions have been made in good faith and on what I consider the soundest principles. I have also allowed my thinking on certain terms to be shaped by—in addition to the studies of many modern biblical scholars—the readings offered by certain ancient authorities who, to my mind, possessed at once all the necessary attributes of trustworthy exegetical guides: complete linguistic proficiency, penetrating exegetical insight, and genuinely redoubtable theological powers: Origen, Gregory of Nyssa, and Theodore of Mopsuestia (among others).

1. The first word is αἰώνιος (*aiōnios*), which in most traditional translations is rendered as "eternal" or "everlasting," except in the many instances where such a reading would be nonsensical. And I have discovered that there are many Christians whose sometimes furious objection to any other rendering revolves around a single verse, Matthew 25: 46. After all, in the original Greek of the New Testament, there really are only three verses that seem to threaten "eternal punishment" for the wicked (though, in fact, none of them actually does), and many who are doctrinally or emotionally committed to the idea of eternal torment for the unelect would feel gravely bereaved if the delicious clarity of the seemingly most explicit of those verses were allowed to be obscured behind a haze of lexical indeterminacy. To these I can say only that, if they really wish to believe in the everlasting torment of the reprobate, they are perfectly free to do so, whether there is any absolutely unquestionable scriptural warrant for doing so or not; but, then again, even

the Greek word typically rendered as "punishment" in that verse raises problems of translation (see below, and see my footnote to Matthew 25: 46). More to the point, there are three immense difficulties that militate against the traditional rendering of *aiōnios* in the New Testament.

The first is that there is a genuine ambiguity in the term in Greek that is impossible to render directly in an English equivalent. *Aiōnios* is an adjective drawn from the substantive αἰών (*aiōn*, or aeon), which *can* sometimes mean a period of endless duration, but which more properly, throughout the whole of ancient and late antique Greek literature, means "an age," or "a long period of time" of indeterminate duration, or even just "a substantial interval." Its proper equivalent in Latin would be *aevum*. At times, it can refer to an historical epoch, to a time "long past" or "far in the future," to something as shadowy and fleeting as the lifespan of a single person (in Homer and the Attic dramatists this is its typical meaning), or even to a considerably shorter period than that (say, a year). It can also, as it frequently does in the New Testament, refer to a particular universal dispensation: either the present world or the world to come or a heavenly sphere of reality beyond our own. Moreover, the adjective *aiōnios*, unlike the adjective ἀΐδιος (*aïdios*) or adverb ἀεί (*aei*), never clearly means "eternal" or "everlasting" in any incontrovertible sense, nor does the noun *aiōn* simply mean "eternity" in the way that the noun ἀϊδιότης (*aïdiotēs*) does; neither does *aiōnios* mean "endless," as ἀτέλευτος (*atelevtos*) or ἀτελεύτητος (*atelevtētos*) does; and, in fact, there are enough instances in the New Testament where the adjective or the noun obviously does not mean "eternal" or "eternity" that it seems to me unwise simply to *presume* such meanings in any instances at all. Where it is used of that which is by nature eternal, God in himself, it certainly carries the connotation that, say, the English words "enduring" or "abiding" would do in the same context: *ever*lasting. But that is a connotation by extension, not the univocal core of the word. A perfect example of the word's ambiguity can be found in Romans 16:25–26, where in successive verses it is used first of "times ages past" or "times ages-long" (χρόνοις αἰωνίοις [*chronois aiōniois*]) and then of "the eternal God" or "the enduring God" or even perhaps "the God of Ages" (τοῦ αἰωνίου θεοῦ [*tou aiōniou theou*]), though practically no translation gives any clue that the same word is being used in both formulations. I might add, moreover, that this uncertainty regarding the proper acceptation of *aiōnios* in the New Testament is anything but a reflex of modern faddish revisionism. If one consults the literary remains of Greek-speaking Jewish scholars of late antiquity, for example, one will find few instances of *aiōn* or *aiōnios* used to indicate eternal duration: for both Philo of Alexandria (an older contemporary of Jesus) and Josephus (born within a decade of the crucifixion), an "aeon" is still only a limited period of time, usually a single lifetime, but perhaps as much as three generations. And the same is true of Christian thinkers of the early centuries. Late in the fourth century, John Chrysostom, in his commentary on Ephesians, even used the word *aiōnios* of the kingdom of the devil specifically to indicate that it is *temporary* (for it will last only till the end of the present age, he explains). In the early centuries of the church, especially in the Greek and Syrian East, the lexical plasticity of the noun and the adjective was fully appreciated—and often exploited—by a number of Christian theologians and exegetes (especially such explicit universalists as the great Alexandrians Clement and Origen, the "pillar of orthodoxy" Gregory of Nyssa and his equally redoubtable sister Makrina, the great Syrian fathers Diodore of Tarsus, Theodore of Mopsuestia, Theodoret of Cyrus, and Isaac of Ninevah, and so on, as well as many other more rhetorically reserved universalists, such as Gregory of Nazianzus). Late in the fourth century, for instance, Basil the Great, bishop of Caesarea, reported that the vast majority of his fellow Christians (at least, in the Greek-speaking East with which he was familiar) assumed that "hell" is not an eternal condition, and that the "*aiōnios* punishment" of the age to come would end when the soul had been purified of its sins and thus prepared for union with God. Well into the sixth century, the great Platonist philosopher Olympiodorus the Younger could state as rather obvious that the suffering of wicked souls in Tartarus is certainly not endless, *atelev-*

539

tos, but is merely *aiōnios;* and the squalidly brutal and witless Christian emperor Justinian, as part of his campaign to extinguish the universalism of the "Origenists," found it necessary to substitute the word *atelev-tētos* for *aiōnios* when describing the punishments of hell, since the latter word was not decisive. Early in the eighth century, John of Damascus delineated four meanings of *aiōn,* the last of which—"eternity"—is offered as not an intrinsic, but merely an imputed, connotation, presumed whenever the word is used of something (like the Age of God's Kingdom) known to be endless; and even then, John affirms, the true eternity of God is beyond all ages. As late as the thirteenth century, the East Syrian bishop Solomon of Bostra, in his authoritative compilation of the teachings of the "holy fathers" of Syrian Christian tradition, stated simply as a matter of fact that in the New Testament *le-alam* (the Syriac rendering of *aiōnios*) does not mean eternal, and that of course hell is not endless. And the fourteenth-century East Syrian Patriarch Timotheus II thought it uncontroversial to assert that the *aiōnios* pains of hell will come to an end when the souls cleansed by them, through the prayers of the saints, enter paradise. Conscious of the problems the word *aiōnios* presents, some Anglophone translators have in the past chosen simply to use an Anglicized version of the Greek word, "aeonian," and thereby avoid the issue of its precise meaning altogether. Others have ventured such neologisms as "age-during." Even, however, if I did not regard the effects thus produced as a little silly, I would find either an unsatisfactory solution, for a number of reasons—and this brings me to the second difficulty.

In the Gospels there are instances where the substantive *aiōn* and the adjective *aiōnios* are juxtaposed or associated in a single image or utterance (most directly in Mark 10:30 and Luke 18:30). This obvious parallel in the Greek is invisible in almost every English translation. For a long time, I considered translating *aiōnios* as "enduring" or "lasting," the latter, I confess, because the "last" in "lasting" seemed the best I could do at insinuating into the text some faint echo of a hint of the eschatological resonance of the word—its clear reference to the Kingdom of God, "the Age to come" — in several contexts. But, in the end, I feared the loss of that vital and theologically portentous echo. I might have decided simply upon "age-long," admittedly. Ultimately, though, I decided that to treat *aiōnios* as denoting only duration (whether eternal or limited), rather than a certain quality or dimension of reality as well, would still fail to cast any light upon the connection between *aiōn* and *aiōnios* in the text as a whole (especially in the fourth Gospel, where the adjective *aiōnios* seems clearly to indicate a qualitatively different — rather than successive — frame of reality, the divine sphere rather than the earthly). And this brings me to the third difficulty, which may be the most significant.

Jesus of Nazareth, as presented in the Gospels, was a first-century Galilaean who spoke Aramaic and could read Hebrew (if he could speak any *koinē* Greek, he certainly did not do so when teaching his disciples or preaching to the multitudes in Galilee and Judaea); and, if the sayings attributed to him in the Gospels are indeed faithful transpositions of his words into Greek equivalents, then there can be no doubt that the words *aiōn* and *aiōnios* correspond to various forms and uses of the Hebrew *olam* or the Aramaic *alma*, both of which most literally mean something at an immense distance, on the far horizon, hidden from view, and which are usually used to mean "age," or "period of long duration," or a time hidden in the depths of the far past or far future, or a "world" or "dispensation," or even "eternity," and so on; but it can also mean simply an extended period, and not necessarily a particularly long one, with a natural term. Moreover, the Septuagint — which, in its various forms, was the Bible for much of the early church, and which provides nine-tenths of all the quotations from Hebrew scripture found in the New Testament — serves as something of a guide to how various expressions of the Jewish concept *olam* or *alma* were typically rendered in Greek (for instance, in Deuteronomy 15:17 *olam* is used to indicate the period of the life of a slave, and in the Septuagint version of that passage is rendered as *aiōn*). There really is no word in Hebrew that naturally means "eternity," either temporal or atemporal, or any word that naturally means "forever"; the claim occasionally made by champions of the received view—that both *aiōn* and *olam* in scripture mean "eternal" typically rather than defectively—is not merely logically impossible to verify, but simply false. There are, however, metaphoric, circumlocutory, or hyperbolic words and phrases that convey the idea of an extremely long period, which may even be endless in duration (but which, then again, may not be); and these locutions are recognizable just below the surface of certain standard Greek phrases in the Septuagint and the New Testament. Behind *aiōn* lies *olam* (if we confine ourselves to the Hebrew forms), and behind various constructions of *aiōn* lie corresponding constructions of *olam*. For instance, εἰς τὸν αἰῶνα (*eis ton aiōna*)—often translated as "forever" but literally meaning "unto the age" or "until the age" or "into the age" or "throughout the age"—is the equivalent of *le-olam* or *ad-olam* ("unto the age" or "until the age"). The phrase εἰς τοὺς αἰῶνας τῶν αἰώνων (*eis tous aiōnas tōn aiōnōn*)— often translated as "forever and ever" or something similar, but literally meaning "unto the ages of the ages"—and the related ὁ αἰὼν τῶν αἰώνων (*ho aiōn tōn aiōnōn*), "the age of the ages," represent something like the Hebrew *le-olam va-ed* ("unto an age and beyond") or *le-olamei-olamim* ("unto ages of ages"). More important here, however, the age to which many uses of both *aiōn* and *aiōnios* refer is clearly the *olam ha-ba*, "the Age to come": the age or world of God that is coming to this earth, the Age of the Kingdom or of that reality now hidden in God. In the Greek of the New Testament, this is often rendered as ὁ αἰὼν ἐρχόμενος (*ho aiōn erchomenos*), "the coming age," or ὁ μέλλων αἰών (*ho mellōn aiōn*), "the age about to come," or, more simply and mysteriously, ἐκεῖνος αἰών (*ekeinos aiōn*), "that age." And that coming age must be distinguished from the *olam ha-zeh*, "this present age," which in Greek is οὗτος καιρός (*houtos kairos*) or οὗτος αἰών (*houtos aiōn*), "this time" or "this age"; or ἐνεστὼς καιρός (*enestōs kairos*) or ἐνεστὼς αἰών (*enestōs aiōn*), "the present time" or "the present age"; or ὁ νῦν αἰών (*ho nyn aiōn*), "the age now." It is almost certainly the case that in the New Testament, and especially in the teachings of Jesus, the adjective *aiōnios* is the equivalent of something like the phrase *le-olam*, but also the case that it cannot be neatly discriminated from the language of the *olam ha-ba* without losing something of the theological depth and religious significance it possessed in the time of Christ. New Testament scholars as theologically diverse as Marcus Borg and N. T. Wright have suggested that translators might do well in many or most instances to render *aiōnios* as "of the age to come"; in fact, in Wright's own translation of the New Testament he does just this wherever he deems it appropriate (though his resolve inexplicably deserts him at the crucial juncture of Matthew 25:46). I have not quite followed suit. Somewhat more vaguely, perhaps, I have generally rendered *aiōnios* as "of" or "in" either "that Age" (*ekeinos aiōn*) or "the Age," using the unqualified noun alone to suggest a long, if indeterminate, duration, but using the upper-case letter to suggest something of its eschatological or otherworldly resonance. Only in a few cases, where the context warrants, have I used a different rendering. Wherever the word *aiōnios* appears in the text in a distinctive construction, I have indicated the fact in a footnote, for clarity's sake.

2. The next word is γέεννα (*gehenna*). In the New Testament there is no single Greek term corresponding to the Anglo-Saxon "hell," despite the prodigality with which that word is employed in traditional English translations, and no term at all that quite corresponds to the picture of hell — a kingdom of ingenious tortures ruled by Satan — that took ever more opulent and terrifying mythical shape in later Christian centuries. Rather, there is "Hades," the realm of the dead beneath the earth, corresponding to the Hebrew *Sheol* (where, for instance, both "Dives" and Lazarus await the end of all things, or where perhaps disembodied souls heard the gospel from Jesus before his resurrection, and so on); there is "Tartarus" (once, in 2 Peter 2:4), a name drawn from pagan Greek lore referring to a place of postmortem imprisonment and punishment, and most especially to the prison of the Titans, but in the New Testament referring not to some sort of final "hell" of perpetual torment, but solely to the subterranean prison where fallen angels and

demonic spirits are held until the day of judgment; and then there is "the *gehenna*," the Aramaic form of the Hebrew *Ge-Hinnom*, "Valley of Hinnom" (originally the *Ge-ben-Hinnom*, "Valley of Hinnom's Son"). This last term appears eleven times in the synoptic Gospels (seven in Matthew, three in Mark, and one in Luke), and only once in the rest of the New Testament (in the Letter of James). Precisely why this valley to the south and west of Jerusalem had by Christ's time become, in apocalyptic literature and Rabbinic tradition, a name for a place of punishment or purification or both (*usually* after death) is difficult to tell. Scripture and tradition say that the Tophet was there, the place of child sacrifice for worshippers of Moloch and Ba'al, a practice attested in Leviticus, 2 Chronicles, 2 Kings, Isaiah, and Jeremiah; and while there is as yet little archaeological evidence supporting the claim, the association of the Ge-Hinnom with the sacrifice of infants to evil gods was well established long before the Christian period. There is also some small evidence in the valley's southwest reaches that it might have been a place of tombs and (after the arrival of the Romans) of crematory grounds. There is as well a mediaeval tradition, which may be based on older accounts, that the valley served as a rubbish tip and charnel ground, where refuse was burned and where animal and human corpses were left as carrion, but again the archaeological evidence for this is lacking; perhaps in favor of this possibility, however, are Christ's words as reported in Mark 9:45–48, where he describes the valley in terms of the description in Isaiah 66:24 of human corpses being consumed by inexterminable worms and inextinguishable fires (neither of which, incidentally, is described as either otherworldly or eternal in nature). Then again, these same images also fit well with Jeremiah's vision of the Ge-Hinnom gorged with corpses—the "valley of slaughter"— as a result of God's historical punishment of Jerusalem and of those Israelites who had worshipped false gods and sacrificed their babies, using the king of Babylon as the instrument of his wrath; and, indeed, some very formidable New Testament scholars over the years, noting the seemingly more than incidental echoes of Jeremiah in the teachings of Jesus, have concluded that the language of the gehenna in the synoptic Gospels really referred to the historical "wrath" and "judgment" that many could see descending on Israel in Jesus's own time (culminating in the fall of Jerusalem and destruction of the Temple in AD 70), rather than to a cosmic Day of Judgment yet to dawn. After all, Jesus in the Gospels clearly states that the "eschatological" events he prophesies will come to pass during the lifetime of some of his listeners. But we really do not know precisely how this valley became a metaphor for divine punishment, in this world or the next, or exactly what the image's figural function in Christ's evangel was.

Neither do we know with great certainty precisely what meanings and connotations the term would have had for Jesus or for his listeners. Before, during, and soon after the time of Jesus, it was common parlance among a great many sects and schools, and was understood sometimes as a place of final destruction, sometimes simply as a place of punishment, and sometimes as a place of purgatorial regeneration. The two dominant rabbinical schools of Christ's time, that of Shammai and that of Hillel, both spoke of it as a place of purification or punishment for a limited period, but both also taught that for the incorrigibly wicked there would or could be a state of eternal or final shame, remorse, suffering, or ruin; Shammai had a somewhat grimmer view of the number of the ultimately lost (about a third of humanity, on some accounts), whereas Hillel had a far keener sense of the power of God's mercy to save. For Shammai, the gehenna was principally a refiner's fire for those souls neither incorrigibly wicked nor blamelessly good, and those subjected to its pains would ultimately be raised up to paradise. Hillel apparently thought of the gehenna as a place of final punishment and annihilation (body and soul) of the utterly depraved, but thought their number extremely small. And rabbinical tradition says that it is from Hillel that what became the standard Rabbinic view—that no one can suffer in the gehenna for more than twelve months—originally comes; the idea at least goes back as far as Rabbi Akiva, in the generation just after Christ. But, really, we do not know whether Jesus advanced a similar view of the gehenna's fire, or what duration he might have assigned to the sufferings of those committed to it, or how metaphorically or literally he or his listeners might have understood its imagery. Clearly, though, metaphor was his natural idiom, and so it seems unlikely that his language here should be assumed to be any more literal than his language of ovens or harvests or threshing floors or the closed doors of feasts. And later Christian tradition casts no real light on the issue, given the diversity of views that prevailed in the early centuries of the church, and the total absence of any language of the gehenna, or of any kind of lasting postmortem torment, in the earliest Christian documents we possess, the letters of Paul. As for whether Jesus viewed that fire as one of final destruction or one of purification, this too is difficult to say with certainty. The former possibility seems in keeping with the apparently "annihilationist" images frequently employed by Jesus—chaff and darnel weeds and dead branches being consumed in an oven (if these are metaphors for sinners rather than, as certain patristic exegetes believed, for their sins)—as well as with his talk of the gehenna's power to destroy both body and soul. The latter possibility, however, could explain those same images equally well while also, at the same time, making sense of certain other metaphors used by Jesus in the Gospels to describe the punishments that follow from divine judgment: to wit, if remanded to the prison, "you shall most certainly not emerge from there *until* you repay the very last pittance" (Matthew 5:26; cf. Luke 12:59); the unmerciful slave is "delivered . . . to the inquisitors *until* he should repay everything owing" (Matthew 18:34); some wicked slaves "will be beaten with many blows" and others "beaten with few blows" (Luke 12:47, 48); "*everyone* will be salted with fire," the fire in question being explicitly that of the gehenna, and salting being a common image of purification and preservation—for "salt is good" (Mark 9:49-50). It might also explain why the Greek word used for "punishment" in Matthew 25:46 is κόλασις (*kolasis*)—which typically refers to remedial punishment—rather than τιμωρία (*timōria*)—which typically refers to retributive justice (it might not, however, since by late antiquity *kolasis* had *perhaps* become somewhat less specific in connotation). And, if one regards Paul's language as a reliable reflection of the teachings of the apostolic church, one might take 1 Corinthians 3:12–15—which distinguishes not between the saved and the "damned," but only between those who (their works passing the test of fire) merit rewards in the Age to come and those who (their works failing that test) will instead have to be saved "as by fire"—as at least a suggestive gloss. Or, then again, one could take the gehenna in the sense sanctified by so much of the Eastern Christian mystical tradition as a metaphor for how the soul that seals itself against love of God and creatures experiences the saving glory of God: as, that is, a "flame" of exterior chastisement rather than a "light" of transfiguring grace. But that is a spiritual interpretation, not an historical reconstruction. As for the remaining possibility, that the gehenna is a name for a place neither of annihilation nor of purification, but of eternal conscious torment—the God of love's perpetual torture chamber—for this rather repellant idea there is easily the least evidence in the Gospels (if any); but the notion may have some substantial precedent in Jewish intertestamental apocalyptic literature, such as the Book of Enoch, as well as in some early Rabbinic traditions, and it accords with most later Christian readings of that sole suggestive verse, Matthew 25:46 (especially after the fifth century). One might also suppose that other images of exclusion used by Jesus—locked doors, outer darkness, wailing and the grinding of teeth—are descriptions of a literally perpetual state of existence after death, of which there can be no end and from which there is no hope of deliverance through purification. And one can perhaps *assume* that the "inexcusable" sin of blasphemy against the Spirit, mentioned in all three synoptic Gospels, is one for which the penalty exacted must be everlasting, rather than one *necessarily* leading to either annihilation or purification. But the texts do not actually say any of that, and again, the absence of any hint of such a notion in the Pauline corpus (or, for that matter, in the fourth Gospel, or the "Catholic Epistles," or those very early doctrinal and confessional texts the *Didache* and Apostles' Creed, or the writings of the Apostolic Fathers . . .) makes the very concept nearly as historically suspect as it is morally unintelligible. Moreover, to read back into these texts *either* the traditional view of dual and in some sense synchronously eternal postmortem destinies *or* the developed high mediaeval Roman Catholic view of an absolute distinction between "Hell" and "Purgatory" would be either (in the former case) a dogmatic reflex rather than an exegetical necessity or (in the latter) an act of simple historical illiteracy. But I leave it to readers to reconcile the various eschatological passages of the New Testament with one another, or not, as they choose; the most I can do is offer an observation about two of the greatest and most brilliant Church Fathers of the later fourth and early fifth centuries. The Greek-speaking Gregory of Nyssa, who was a universalist and who simply assumed the purgatorial view of the gehenna, was able to unite all the various biblical images and claims in a fairly seamless synthesis in his writings, omitting nothing known to him as Christian canon. Conversely, the Latin-speaking Augustine, who took very much the contrary view, was far more selective in his use of scripture, was dependent on often grossly misleading translations, and had to expend enormous energy on qualifying, rephrasing, and explaining away a host of passages that did not really conform well to the theological system he imagined he had found in Paul's writings. This is, if nothing else, instructive. For myself, at any rate, I have translated "the *gehenna*" as "the Vale of Hinnom" or "Hinnom's Vale," keeping the proper name (which would have been audible to Jesus's listeners) but using the somewhat daintily pretentious "vale" to insinuate a hint of gauzy otherworldliness into the image (since by Jesus's time it was clearly no longer *simply* a geographical designation, but a metaphor with an enormous range of associations and connotations).

3. The next term is Ἰουδαῖος (*Ioudaios*)—or Ἰουδαῖοι (*Ioudaioi*) in the plural—which is usually rendered "Jew" or "Jews," except in places where "Judaean" or "Judaeans" seems better to fit the context: again, a perfectly justifiable practice, but also one that inadvertently introduces a distinction into the text that would not have been entirely intended

by the authors. The books of the New Testament were written in an age in which national, ethnic, religious, and racial identities were not arranged in the often pernicious categories that came to hold sway in subsequent centuries; and it would be a severe distortion of the texts of the New Testament to allow these later developments to cast a shadow backward onto a time innocent of the evils of mediaeval or modern history. For example—and the most striking example—the Gospel of John has often been accused of anti-Semitism, despite the anachronism of the very concept. Where English readers are accustomed to reading the Gospel as referring, often opprobriously, to "the Jews," the original text is usually referring to the indigenous Temple and synagogue authorities of Judaea, or to Judaeans living outside Judaea, or even to "Judaeans" as opposed to "Galileans" (see, for instance, John 7:1). The Gospel definitely reflects the disenchantment of Jewish Christians in Asia Minor with those they saw as having expelled them from the synagogue, and later Christian culture certainly often took this as an excuse for anti-Jewish violence and injustice, but it would be absurd to impute to the Gospel the sort of religious prejudices born in later generations, or certainly the racial ideologies that are so much a part of the special legacy of post-Enlightenment modernity. I have rendered the word as "Judaean" or "Judaeans" throughout, even where that sounds somewhat awkward, and even in places where "Jew" or "Jews" would be an utterly anodyne or bracingly affirmative translation. After all, the general extension of the term "Jews" to all who worshipped Israel's God meant principally that their cultic life was focused on the Temple in Jerusalem. Again, my rationale for doing this, and for ignoring my own twinge of reluctance whenever it produced a somewhat inept construction, is that I thought it better to preserve the unity of the word and the concept in the language of the ancient authors than to impose distinctions that would make the texts conform more readily to our cultural categories (and historical sins).

4. The next word is λόγος (*logos*), which in certain special instances is quite impossible for a translator to reduce to a single word in En-

glish, or in any other tongue (though one standard Chinese version of the Bible renders *logos* in the prologue of John's Gospel as 道 (*tao*), which is about as near as any translation could come to capturing the scope and depth of the word's religious, philosophical, and metaphoric associations in those verses, while also carrying the additional meaning of "speech" or "discourse"). To be clear, in most contexts in the New Testament, *logos* can be correctly and satisfactorily rendered as "word," "utterance," "teaching," "story," "message," "speech," or "communication." In the very special case of the prologue to John's Gospel, however, any such translation is so inadequate as to produce nothing but a cipher without a key. Few modern readers or, for that matter, readers in any age could be expected to be cognizant of the complexities of late antique metaphysics, or to be familiar with the writings of Hellenistic Jewish philosophers like Philo of Alexandria (c. 25 BC–c. AD 50), or to be much acquainted with the speculative grammar of Hellenistic Judaism's "Wisdom" literature. And so they could scarcely be aware of the vast range of meanings the word *logos* had acquired by the time John's Gospel was written, many of which are unquestionably present in its use in the prologue. Over many centuries *logos* had come to mean "mind," "reason," "rational intellect," "rational order," "spirit"; as well as "expression," "manifestation," "revelation"; as well as "original principle," "spiritual principle," and even "divine principle." Really, the full spectrum of its philosophical connotations could scarcely be contained in a single book. In the special context of late antique, Greek-speaking Judaism, and particularly in the work of Philo, the word had come to mean a very particular kind of divine reality, a secondary or derivative divine principle proceeding from the Most High God and mediating between God and the created order. There was a shared prejudice among many of the philosophical systems of late antiquity to the effect that the highest God, God proper, in his utter transcendence could not interact directly with or appear immediately within the created order; hence it was only through a "secondary god" or "expressed divine principle" that God made the world and revealed himself in it. It was assumed by many

Jewish and then Christian thinkers that the theophanies of the Jewish scriptures were visitations of the Logos, God's self-expression in his divine intermediary or Son, as Philo called him. To an educated reader of the late first or early second century, the Logos of John's prologue would clearly have been just this divine principle: at once the Most High God's manifestation of himself in a secondary divine moment, and also the pervasive and underlying rational power creating, sustaining, and governing the cosmos. For all of which reasons, I have chosen not to translate the word at all in the first chapter of John — or in, more controversially, John 5:38, 10:35; or in, yet more controversially, 1 John 1:1, 10; or in, most controversially of all, Revelation 19:13 (though perhaps for somewhat different reasons in this last case). In certain usages, the word is so capacious in its meanings and associations that it must be accounted unique; any attempt to limit it to a single English term would be to risk reducing it to a conceptual phantom of itself.

5. The next word is the verb προορίζειν (*proörizein*), which has traditionally — as a result of the Vulgate Latin translation — been rendered as "to predestine." This is simply incorrect (though some inferior lexica over the years, taking their lead from traditional theological usage in the West, have incorporated it in their definitions of the verb). The word ὁρίζειν (*horizein*) (whence our word "horizon"), means "to demarcate," "delineate," "to mark out as a boundary," "to distinguish," "to sort," "to define," "to assign," "to plan out," "to make determinate," or "to appoint"; and *pro-horizein* is simply to do this in advance. It certainly possesses none of the grim, ghastly magnificence of the late Augustinian concept of "predestination": an entirely irresistible predetermining causal force, not based on divine foreknowledge but rather logically prior to everything it ordains, by which God infallibly destines only a very few to salvation and thereby infallibly consigns the vast majority of humanity to unending torment. Thus, in two of the six instances of the verb's use in the New Testament (Romans 8:29–30), Paul — blissfully innocent of later theological developments and anxieties — explicitly treats this divine "pre-demarcation" as *consequent* upon

divine foreknowledge, and does so without any qualification or notice-able pangs of theological conscience. (1 Peter 1:1–2, more concisely, says the same thing.) Of the very few instances of the verb or its cognate noun προορισμός (*proörismos*) in Greek literature before the New Tes-tament (I am aware of only two), it carries no connotation of predes-tination. More tellingly, none of the Greek-speaking Church Fathers ever read the word as having such a connotation, or even seemed to sus-pect that such a reading was a possibility. The Augustinian understand-ing of "predestination," for all its epochal significance for later Western Christian thought, is a late fourth-century theological innovation, the inadvertent invention of a Paul who never existed, a theological acci-dent prompted by a defective Latin translation and the temperamental idiosyncrasies of a single sullen genius (with at times a singularly dismal understanding of the "good news"). No matter what one's theology, the traditional rendering is simply insupportable. I have therefore trans-lated the verb, with bland literality, as "to mark out in advance."

6. The next word is ἄνθρωπος (*anthrōpos*), which means "man" or "human being," but which is not simply another word for ἀνήρ (*anēr*) ("man" strictly in the sense of an adult male). Like the German *Mensch* (as distinct from *Mann*), it is a masculine noun that, used in either the definite singular (to mean "the man" or "that man") or the indefinite singular (to mean "a man"), would typically refer only to a male; but, used in the singular as a categorical designation, it can mean "man" in the sense of "mankind" or "humanity"; and, used in the plural, it can refer to human beings in general. I have not striven in this translation for "inclusive language," at least where it would involve altering the text. For one thing, I would dislike the pretense that the text does not use the sort of language that it does, and I think readers can be trusted to know that these are first-century writings. Moreover, mine is not a version written for liturgical or homiletic purposes, but an attempt to make the original text visible through as thin a layer of translation as I can con-trive to superimpose upon it. So, in a few places where a late modern phrase like "human being" or "human person" would have seemed jar-

ringly awkward, I have yielded to the sirens of euphony and used "man" or "men"—quite unrepentantly in certain instances (no impulse of conscience, however fervent, could cause me to sacrifice as grand, ancient, poetic, and mysterious a title as "Son of Man" in favor of "Human" or "Child of Humanity" or something equally insipid). Again, I trust readers not only to have a sense of the realities of cultural history, but also to be able to distinguish between substantial and empty gestures. All that said, however, in every instance where it proved both possible and agreeable to do so, I have employed the term "human being" or something similar. In some cases I find this a very happy way of adding what I take to be a needed emphasis to certain phrases, especially those in which the plural noun is modified by the adjective "all." For some reason—possibly simply on account of our settled habit of hearing certain biblical phrases as saying what we expect them to say—we often fail to notice some of the more striking and radical theological formulations that appear in the New Testament; and somehow using phrases like "all human beings" or "every human being" seems to make them more audible to us than does the use of the more familiar "all men" (or even "all persons"). I am thinking of such verses as Romans 5:18; 1 Timothy 2:4, 4:10; Titus 2:11 (when translated correctly), as well as of the light they cast upon such similar or related verses as John 12:32; 1 Corinthians 15: 22; 1 Timothy 2:6; and 2 Peter 3:9.

7. The next word is ἔργα (*erga*), plural of ἔργον (*ergon*), which means "work," "task," "skill," "labor," "operation," "handiwork," or "business"; or, more simply, "work" in the sense of "deed," "act," or "feat"; or, in certain special contexts, a ritual action to be performed or a duty to be discharged. In most cases in the New Testament, the word refers simply to discrete actions, labors, or deeds, and my translation reflects that. There are some special instances in Paul's letters, however, in which the "works" in question are specifically "works of the Law"—that is to say, obligations imposed by the Mosaic code, like circumcision, Sabbath obligations, or kosher laws—and so I have rendered *erga* as "observances" (which is one of the standard renderings of the word when used

in connection with religious obligations). I do this principally because, removed as most of us are not only from the ritual life of first-century Judaism, but also from the idiom Paul shared with many of his contemporaries, we tend to forget what the principal religious issues were for him. And, perhaps needless to say, there is a long tradition of reading Paul as though his concerns were entirely different: Where he drew a distinction between, on the one hand, the righteousness or rewards that one can achieve through such observances (which, incidentally, he affirms) and, on the other, the righteousness God takes account of entirely in respect of one's faithfulness (which God graciously rewards), many Christian theologians down the centuries (at least in the West) have taken him to be drawing a distinction between, on the one hand, the divine blessings one wins through one's good deeds (which supposedly Paul denies are possible) and, on the other, the entirely gratuitous graces bestowed by God without any prevision of or attention to one's moral deeds at all (else grace were not grace). This is clearly an error, and introduces an antithesis into Paul's thought of which his writings betray no consciousness (see, for example, Romans 2:7–14). Taken to its extreme (which, logically, it always has to be) it leads to an absurd situation: Not only is one obliged to read Paul's teaching as diametrically opposed to the theology of "judgment according to works" clearly enunciated by Jesus in the Gospels, by the Letter of James, by the book of Revelation, and so on (however this has been dissembled by a long tradition of forced readings), but one is also obliged to read Paul's teaching as diametrically opposed to itself, since he too clearly affirms "judgment according to works" (see Romans 2:1–16, 4:10–12; 1 Corinthians 3:12–15; 2 Corinthians 5:10; Philippians 2:16; and so on). And, for those who presuppose a perfect theological consistency in the New Testament, it can lead to even more ungainly exegetical contortions, such as John Calvin's weirdly endearing practice of treating Christ's more demanding moral counsels in the Gospels (his advice to the rich young ruler, his exhortation to his disciples to be perfect as their Father in heaven is perfect, and so on) as exercises in irony (for surely, reasoned Calvin, Jesus cannot mean that our good deeds are relevant to our election, or that we should strive for spiritual perfection). Certainly, Paul affirms that it is God who gives the power and grace necessary for the soul to perform good works, and that without God creatures can achieve nothing; but he never suggests either that this power and grace are irresistible predestining forces, or that good works are not genuinely criteria by which God weighs souls in the balance (and determines, perhaps, whether they are to be rewarded for their works or instead are to be saved through the fire by which their works will be consumed). One may view the relation between divine grace and human effort in Paul's thought in whatever way one wishes (though the Eastern Christian language of *synergeia*—synergy—seems clearly to be nearest to Paul's own thought and language). But what one certainly ought not to do is mistake Paul's distinction between faithfulness of the heart and works of the Law for an opposition between mere personal belief and concrete moral effort. For him, as for other writers in the New Testament, human beings are justified—that is, "proved righteous" or "made righteous" (see below)—"by works, and not by faith alone" (James 2:24).

8. The next word is ὑποκριτής (*ʰypokritēs*)—or ὑποκριταί (*ʰypokritai*) in the plural—which is understandably usually translated as "hypocrite" or "hypocrites." But in the Greek of the first century the word did not *quite* mean what "hypocrite" has come to mean to us: a person whose actions belie his words, or whose moral character contradicts his professed moral principles. The word originally designated a public interpreter or expounder of a text, one who declaimed verse, a rhapsode, or an actor playing a role on stage. As a term of abuse, it meant simply one who dissembles or deceives, or one who is putting on a performance to impress or beguile others. I have rendered the word variously in this translation, as context dictates, but in most instances have rendered it as "charlatan" or "charlatans."

9. The next word is the plural noun ἔθνη (*ethnē*), which can mean "nations," "peoples," or "gentiles," and which I have translated as one or another of these as context dictates. It is as well to note, however, that

behind these three English words, wherever they appear in the text, there is only a single Greek word and so, arguably, only a single concept.

10. The next word is actually a pair of words: λύτρον (*lytron*) and ἀντίλυτρον (*antilytron*). The former appears only twice (Matthew 20:28; Mark 10:45) and the latter only once (1 Timothy 2:6), and they are effectively synonymous. There are also occasional verbal formulations derived from the same root. Each refers to Christ in his role specifically as *redeemer* and is traditionally translated "ransom." Though this is not wrong, it does not quite convey the full meaning that the word, in either of its forms, carries in the text. We often fail to appreciate how often the language of salvation in the New Testament employs the imagery and terminology of contemporary civil law regarding slavery. A *lytron* or *antilytron* is, in that context, the required fee for the emancipation of a slave, paid to the slaveholder in order to secure legal manumission. In the earliest centuries of Christian thought, the meaning of the word was still obvious to all readers; the only question of theological moment regarding this manumission fee was to whom we ought to imagine it had been paid: to the devil, our principal slaveholder, so to speak, or to death, the household of our bondage. But, as the centuries flowed on and Christianity spread into other lands, cultures, and languages, the original meaning was occasionally lost sight of, so much so that some Christians came to imagine that the word referred to a ransom paid to God the Father by the Son, to appease God's righteous wrath, or to repair his injured dignity, or to yield tribute to the awful majesty of his sovereignty. That idea is entirely alien to the way the word is used in the New Testament; there is no suggestion there that, in Christ, God pays God off, or God rescues us from God; rather, the work of salvation is depicted as a single, unified act of rescue, whereby God the Father, through the Son, redeems (that is, "buys back") his children from the slavery into which they have been sold, even at the most terrible of costs (the death of the divine Son). So I have rendered it by such phrases as "the price of liberation" or "fee for emancipation," and so on, and have rendered its verbal correlates accordingly.

11. Next comes a cluster of words springing up around a common root: the adjective δίκαιος (*dikaios*), which can be translated as "just," "right," "righteous"; the noun δικαιοσύνη (*dikaiosynē*), which can be translated as "righteousness," "justice," "what is correct," "what is proper," "rectitude"; the verb δικαιόω (*dikaioō*), which can be translated as "make just," "make right," "rectify," "correct," or alternatively, as "prove just," "show to be right," "vindicate"; and all other words related to the noun δίκη (*dikē*), usually rendered as "justice," "rightness," "correct custom." Here I have had to betray my prejudice for formal consistency of translation. To begin with, in regard to the adjectives and nouns, it is not always easy to decide, when translating a particular passage or a particular author, whether it is better to use words like "just" and "justice" or words like "righteous" and "righteousness," given the connotations of each. The nearest we come to words that split the difference are "right," "correct" or "what is right," "uprightness," "rectitude," "correctness"; and I have employed some of these where it seemed wise to do so. In the world of the New Testament, religious and legal identity—or religious and legal obligation—were not distinct concepts, as they usually are for us. But in some instances it is clear that the context is more juridical than religious or moral, and in other instances that the opposite is true, and I have simply made as prudent a choice as I could in each case regarding which word to use. Moreover, there are two special problems of translation that have required firm decisions on my part precisely where I would have preferred indecisive vacillation. First, in most translations of the New Testament the word *dikaiosynē* is rendered as "righteousness"; but it often carries the specific connotation of "ritual propriety" or "what is legally correct," and in the Bible it carries the even more specific connotation of "what is correct according to the Law (of Moses)"—as in the Septuagint's version of Isaiah 26:2, or as in Matthew 3:15; where appropriate, I have attempted to make this clear. Second, the word *dikaioō* is usually translated as "justify"—or, in its passive construction, as "to be justified"—but this does not really capture either of the word's proper meanings *exactly*, at least

not in modern English; and in fact, as a theological term, "justification" has over the centuries acquired so many questionable connotations that it is more likely to obscure the original authors' intentions than to reflect them. Again, *dikaioō* can mean *either* "rectify," "set right," "correct" *or* "vindicate," "prove right," "show to be just"; and it is not always clear, especially in Paul's letters, which of these senses should predominate, since arguments can often be made for either. In reality, I believe, he used the word in both senses, according to context. Of course, from the early fifth century onward, one stream of Western theology came to treat Paul's use of the verb (or of its Latin equivalent, *justifico*) as meaning some sort of merely formal or forensic imputation of righteousness, rather than either a real corrective transformation or a real evidential vindication—an interpretation, arguably, that reached its most extreme expression in certain of Augustine's late writings and in the sixteenth- and seventeenth-century theologies of figures like John Calvin and Cornelius Jansen. But nothing in the word's history allows for such a meaning *intrinsically*, and there is nothing in Paul's arguments that encourages such a reading (despite our habit of reading and translating Paul through the prism of Augustinian tradition). In the end, I found myself constrained to choose between "rectify" and "vindicate" (or similar locutions) in each particular instance of the word's use.

12. Another uniradical cluster of words comprises both the noun πίστις (*pistis*), often rendered as "faith," and the verb πιστεύω (*pistevō*), often rendered as "to believe" or "to have faith." All I wish to emphasize here (and in my translation) is that πίστις can mean both "trust" *in* something and the "trustworthiness" *of* something, and can even (somewhat combining these two connotations) be understood as "fidelity" or "faithfulness." And πιστεύω does not really mean "to believe" in an impartial and merely intellectual way, but "to vest faith in" or "to have trust in" something or someone, and sometimes even "to entrust" either oneself or something at one's disposal to another. I have tried to do justice to these connotations in my translation.

13. Next comes κόσμος (*kosmos*), which I have for the most part

chosen not to translate (in the traditional way) as "world," but simply to transliterate as "cosmos." The effect is often perhaps a bit jarring. But, while there are instances in the text where the word functions as an equivalent of οἰκουμένη (*oikoumenē*), the inhabited world of human beings, it more frequently means the whole of the created order, the heavens no less than the earth. It certainly carries this latter meaning in some crucial and occasionally unsettling ways in many verses in John's Gospel, Paul's letters, and elsewhere. It is good, for example, to be reminded that in the New Testament, and in Paul's theology in particular, both slavery to death in sin and final liberation from death in divine glory are described as cosmic—not merely human—realities, taking in the whole of creation. Moreover, the word "world" as we use it today simply does not capture what is most essential to the ancient concept of "cosmos," a word that most literally means "order" or "arrangement" or even "loveliness of design." For us, the "world" is either merely the physical reality of nature and society "out there," or it is the human sphere with all its attendant moral and historical contingencies. For the late antique cultures from which the New Testament came, the "cosmos" was quite literally a magnificently and terribly elaborate *order* of reality that comprehended nature (understood as a rational integrity organized by metaphysical principles), the essential principles of the natural and animal human condition (flesh and soul, for instance, with all their miseries), the spiritual world (including the hierarchies of the "divine," the angelic, and the daemonic), the astral and planetary heavens (understood as a changeless realm at once physical and spiritual), as well as social, political, and religious structures of authority and power (including the governments of human beings, angels, celestial "daemons," gods, terrestrial demons, and whatever other mysterious forces might be hiding behind nature's visible forms). It is a vision of the whole of things that is utterly unlike any with which most of us are today familiar, and that simply does not correspond to any meaning of "world" intuitively obvious to us. For the author of 1 Peter or of 1 John, for instance, to tell his readers to have nothing to do with the "cosmos" is to say something far more comprehensive, imponderable, and astonishing than that they should avoid vice and materialist longings, or that they should withdraw from society. It seemed better to me to risk oddity of expression than to risk losing sight of these truths.

14. Next, μετάνοια (*metanoia*), a word traditionally translated as "repentance," but whose literal meaning is a "change of mind," or "of thinking," or "of intention," or "of the heart." "Repentance" is a word that today carries none of those connotations naturally; for us, it is a largely negative term that means something like "regret and repudiation," both of which may be some part of the special meaning of μετάνοια in the New Testament, but which say nothing of the real inner transformation that is a far larger part of the word's sense; μετάνοια and its correlative verb μετανοέω (*metanoeō*) have a positive and genuinely transitive power, such that at various times the New Testament uses the formulation of a μετάνοια εἰς (*metanoia eis*), an interior change "*toward*" (God, salvation, life, full knowledge, or so on). Admittedly, in modern English idiom neither "change of mind" nor "change of heart" carries quite the hortatory moral force or rhetorical vigor of the Greek word, but either is more accurate than the now dully conventional "repentance." My only difficulty here was deciding whether I should use a term like "mind" or "thinking" to emphasize the ratiocinative element of the concept, or should instead speak of the "heart" in order properly to emphasize the affective element. I elected the latter, but with the qualification that the heart should be understood in the classical sense, as the seat of both the intellect and the passions. And, as the syntax of particular verses warrants, I have used "change" or "turn" or "transformation" to indicate the *meta-* in *metanoia*.

15. The next word is ψυχή (*psychē*), which in most versions of the New Testament is translated in a great variety of ways, in each instance as context seems to dictate. This is a perfectly fair practice, since, again, there is no single English equivalent for the word that could possibly comprise the full range of its connotations and nuances. The inevitable result of this, however, as is the case in any translation of a conceptu-

ally rich or ambiguous term, is that what appeared to the author of the original to be a complex but coherent unity of meaning becomes for the translator, and those dependent on his or her labors, a cloud of associations—or, really, of dissociations. *Psychē* can mean "life" or "principle of life," or can mean "soul" in the sense of "enlivening force," or can mean "soul" in the sense of "conscious mind" or "self." Its nearest equivalent in Latin is *anima*, meaning both principle of the body's life and soul in the sense of personal identity or self. Thus, for instance, when Paul distinguishes in 1 Corinthians 15:44-46 between the body human beings possess in this age and that which they shall receive in the Age to come, he speaks of the former as a dissoluble and perishable composite of flesh and soul, a σῶμα ψυχικόν (*sōma psychikon*), but of the latter as an imperishable unity, a σῶμα πνευματικόν (*sōma pnevmatikon*): an "animal" or "psychical body," on the one hand, and a "spiritual" or "pneumatic body," on the other. The substantive *psychē*, however, I have rendered as "soul" throughout, even in those cases where this produces somewhat ungainly phrasing. I was prompted to do this by my perhaps overly scrupulous principle that what the original author considered a conceptual unity the translator should try not to convert into a multiplicity of distinct concepts; but I was prompted also by my desire that my translation reflect the text's origin in an age when the very idea of physical life was still not only inseparable from, but even identical to, the idea of the soul—when, that is, the principle of organic life and the principle of thought, sensation, and spiritual personality were understood as one and the same principle. And this seems to me a doubly important consideration in light of what I take to be some of the defective theological scholarship of the past (especially within certain Protestant critical traditions of the nineteenth and twentieth centuries). At one time it was fashionable to note that in ancient Hebrew scripture there is no concept—or at best only a somewhat shadowy and attenuated concept—of a "soul" separable from corporeal existence, and then to assert rather boldly that the same was true of the Judaism of Christ's time and so also of Christian scripture. This is false. In the intertestamental period, when Judaism was well developed in the direction of what we now know as Rabbinic tradition, and had been absorbing and synthesizing Persian and Greek styles of thought for centuries, most Jews (with the exception, apparently, of "mortalist" Sadducees), like most gentiles (again, with some exceptions), were well accustomed to thinking of the soul as in some sense discrete from the flesh, able to persist in some conscious condition after the death of the body. None of them thought like modern Cartesians, admittedly, but most of them understood *psychē* as we now use the word "soul": as simultaneously what makes us alive and what makes us who we are.

At certain points—for instance, 1 Corinthians 2:14 or Jude 1:19— I have rendered the adjective *psychikos* or ψυχικοί (*psychikoi*) (the plural form) simply as "psychical," fully aware of how odd that looks. My reason for doing so is that, in the Greek of the original text, the word sometimes obviously reflects a distinction between persons whose natures are "psychical" or merely "ensouled" and persons who, as Jude puts it, "have spirit" or even "have *a* spirit." But most translations distort these verses so violently that their original meaning has become quite invisible. In the verse from Jude, for instance, most translators render *psychikoi* as vaguely as possible—as "natural," say, or "sensual"— and then capitalize the word "spirit" as though it were a straightforward reference to the Holy Spirit (which it certainly is not). Precisely how Jude or his readers would have understood this distinction is uncertain, but it is there in the text all the same. Today we tend to think that such divisions among persons, or even among Christians within the church, were among the more exotic eccentricities of the para-Christian or "gnostic" movements of the second century and after. But, even if the word "gnostic" is useful as a general designation for groups outside the ecclesial mainstream, their language on this matter was in continuity with language used by early Christians of just about every stripe. Jude may not have conceived of such a distinction as some sort of ontological division between different kinds of human beings, but he certainly did see it as a division between different states of sanctification or "spiritual" progress, and he may well have believed that "spirit" is a special property acquired by progressive sanctification. (And, frankly, we cannot be certain that all the so-called gnostics saw the matter much differently.) Which brings me to the next word.

16. That is, πνεῦμα (*pnevma*), "spirit," which (like the word for "spirit" in so many tongues) most literally means "wind" or "breath." My principal remark here is that in many passages in the New Testament, and especially in some of Paul's letters, it is impossible to tell whether the author is speaking of human "spirit" or of God's "Spirit." At certain crucial junctures, again in Paul's letters, the absence of a clear distinction seems almost intentional. Traditionally, translators choose how the reader should understand the word in moments of uncertainty by either capitalizing it or leaving it in the lowercase; and far too often the word is capitalized when it probably ought not to be. A particularly good example of this is Galatians 5:17, where Paul (whose anthropology is considerably more "dualistic" than it is currently fashionable to admit) is clearly speaking of an opposition between the desires of "the flesh" and of "the spirit" *within each human being,* but where most English translations quite presumptuously and unintelligibly describe an opposition between "flesh" and "the [Holy] Spirit." Another, equally good example is 1 Peter 3:18, where "flesh" and "spirit" are again (somewhat dualistically) opposed to one another in the form of modal datives—the one indicating the manner of Christ's death, the other the manner of his resurrection—but where, again, many translators have tried to turn the latter into a reference to the Holy Spirit, even though both the syntax of the Greek text and the logic of the author's argument make such a reading impossible (among other things, it renders unintelligible the claim of the following verse: see my footnotes to those verses). Yet another example is Jude 1:19, which I have discussed in the section immediately above. And still another might be John 6:63. In any event, in my rendering I have been considerably more chaste in my use of the capital *s* than most translators have been in the past. As a general rule, I have done it in cases where the word *pnevma* is accompanied by a

definite article, in a way that indicates that it is specifically the Spirit of God that is being spoken of. I have also used the capital *s* in many places where the article is absent but where something more than "spirit" in a vague and abstract sense is meant, and where, again, the reference is to a "Spirit" who comes from God. But in several places my judgment on the matter is only a best guess, and reflects a distinction that is not always clearly present in the text. There are numerous instances—in the latter chapters of Romans, say—where the text speaks of "spirit" and even "holy spirit," and it is all but impossible to say whether divine or creaturely spirit is at issue. (How, for example, is one to translate Romans 6:27? How is one to understand it?) Moreover, I can only caution the reader, though without much in the way of further exegetical clarity, not to assume the fully developed theology of the Holy Spirit as enunciated in later church councils when reading the New Testament. I might also add that, at a few points—1 Corinthians 2:15, 3:1, 14:37; Galatians 6:1—I was tempted to render πνευματικός (*pnevmatikos*), or its plural form πνευματικοί (*pnevmatikoi*), simply as "Pneumatic" (as a substantive), but feared this might have the absurd effect of summoning up images of tires or drills or bustlines; still, I wanted to make clear that Paul appears in those passages almost certainly to be speaking of a special class of "spiritual persons" within the body of the church, so I resorted to the same dubious strategy of capitalization that I have just so rudely deplored (but to a very different end). Again, the fear of any hint of "proto-gnosticism" in Paul's letters leads some scholars to reject the conclusion that Paul ever speaks of such a special class of Christian; but the text makes it fairly unavoidable, and it would probably be best for those who suffer such anxieties to remember that Paul's understanding of the distinction need not be thought of as "proto-gnostic," so much as later "gnostic" appropriations of such language might be thought of as "post-Pauline." (Paul even, after all, seems to hint that there are especially advanced Christians who, unlike neophytes in the faith, possess "gnosis.")

17. Then there is σάρξ (*sarx*), which literally means "flesh" and which I translate as "flesh" (I also translated its associated adjective σαρκικός [*sarkikos*] as "fleshly"). This might not seem an exactly daring decision on my part, but in many translations any number of circumlocutions are frequently employed precisely to avoid rendering this word literally. It has become something of a fashion over the past century for theologians to insist almost exclusively on the "worldliness" of Christianity, or on how exuberantly it affirms the material order—the material body especially—as the good creation of God, or on how radically the early Christian view of corporeality supposedly differed from that of more "Hellenistic" or "gnostic" or "idealist" schools of thought. And so, just as the word *pnevma* is often capitalized and thus "divinized," so as to hide instances where it is actually being used to indicate a "good" principle of "spirit" set over against the "bad" principle of "flesh," so *sarx* is often rendered by some sort of theologically sanitized circumlocution like "sinful human nature" or "fallen human nature" or "the mortal body." Both this practice and the theological platitudes inspiring it should be eschewed at every juncture. It is true that there is nothing like an *absolute* dualism in the New Testament, of the sort that would suggest that the physical world is ultimately evil, or that the Age to come will not involve a redemption of the whole created order; but, even so, there is at least a very strong *provisional* dualism clearly present in much of the New Testament, and when the text speaks of "flesh" in opprobrious terms it is not employing a vague metaphor, for which some less upsetting abstraction may safely be substituted. As both 1 Corinthians 15:40-54 and 1 Peter 3:18, 4:6 make quite clear—and as Matthew 22:30; Mark 12:25; Luke 20:36; and perhaps Acts 23:8 all powerfully suggest—many early Christians understood the difference between the mortal body and the resurrected body (whether Christ's or ours) as the difference between earthly flesh and a kind of life that has transcended the flesh (for, as Paul says, "flesh and blood cannot inherit the Kingdom of God"). At times, the early Christians, no less than their pagan

or "gnostic" contemporaries, had a somewhat jaundiced view of "this cosmos" or "this age," as well as of "this body of death," not merely as moral dispensations, but as physical realities.

18. Next comes πορνεία (*porneia*), along with the related substantives πόρνη (*pornē*) and πόρνος (*pornos*). *Porneia* means "prostitution" or (more bluntly) "whoring," but in most traditional translations it is rendered as "fornication." Perhaps, historically speaking, this is very nearly a distinction without a difference. In the first-century world, and especially in Judaea, casual sexual encounters were not a readily available form of recreation; women did not enjoy the liberty (or the safety) to go about in many public places, and certainly had little desire to court the disastrous social and personal consequences of premarital or extramarital liaisons. Most men seeking sexual release outside of marriage generally had to pay for the service. Even so, the word's meaning is precise and ought not to be obscured. Similarly, a *pornē* was a female prostitute and a *pornos* a boy prostitute or hired "catamite," and prostitutes of both sexes were more often than not slaves. In the former case, most translations of the New Testament do in fact render the term accurately as "harlot" or "whore." In the latter case, however, they generally settle on "fornicator." Admittedly, there is a complication here, inasmuch as *pornos* is used at many junctures in biblical Greek to mean not a catamite, but rather a man who uses prostitutes of either sex; even so, the traditional rendering makes neither meaning obvious. I should also note that all of these words have a certain indelicacy about them, and so I have generally used a coarser word like "whoring" or "whore" rather than something blander, like "prostitution" or "prostitute."

19. Finally, μακάριος (*makarios*), which is generally translated as "blessed" or "happy" or "fortunate," and which indeed means all of these things. But it is also a word whose original connotations included something like "divine blessedness" or "the bliss of the gods," and which well into late antiquity suggested a special intensity of delight and freedom from care that the more shopworn renderings no longer quite capture (at least not to my ear). I expect that for many readers this will

prove the most insufferable decision on my part for a number of reasons, and one that will be written off as expressing a perverse aversion to common phrases or a desire slyly to introduce a hint of Asian mysticism into the text, but I have elected to render the word as "blissful" (and I remain entirely impenitent in having done so).

Notes on Authorship

Regarding the issue of how I have assigned the authorship of the various books of the New Testament, I can only say I have followed what I regard as the most credible current scholarship. For the most part, however, this is not so much a matter of identifying who wrote what, but of clearly indicating the depths of our ignorance on many questions. Most scholars are in agreement that seven of the letters traditionally attributed to Paul are indisputably authentic—in the most likely chronological order, 1 Thessalonians (or, as I prefer to render it, Thessalonikans), Galatians, 1 Corinthians, Philemon, Philippians, 2 Corinthians, and Romans—though some doubt the authenticity of even 1 Thessalonians and Philippians (but on rather feeble grounds). Otherwise, the books of the canon are of uncertain authorship, and in some cases are pseudonymous; in one case, Hebrews, the text is simply anonymous (see below). Even the four Gospels were given their names probably only in the second century, and the stories that came to surround those names are legendary at best. The author of the earliest of them (written around AD 70 perhaps) is known to us as Mark, but whether this was indeed his name we do not know, and even if it was we still do not know who he really was. The evangelist called Matthew, whose Gospel was written perhaps a decade or two later, was not the disciple of Jesus who bore that name, but someone who had to rely on a combination of Mark's text (in structure and content) and on independent collections of *logia*, or "sayings," in order to construct his narrative, and who amplified at length upon the originals. The probably single author of both the third Gospel (chronologically perhaps the latest written) and the book of Acts—which together constitute almost a third of the New Testament—is known to us as Luke (though neither the Gospel nor Acts uses the name), and tradition tells us that he was a gentile Christian, a physician, and a companion of Paul. The first two of these claims may well be true, but a great many scholars believe that in all likelihood the third is not, despite certain passages in Acts written in the first person plural. For one thing Paul's own brief references to his personal story contradict Luke's narrative. For another, Luke's Gospel is also transparently built upon and redacts Mark's, and draws on *logia* traditions (many, but not all of which, he shares with Matthew). The dominant critical estimate, for what little that may ultimately be worth, is that Luke's books come from the late first or even early second century. There are also signs in Luke's Gospel of a sophisticated and purposeful theological sensibility, one that even prompts the author to amend the record—or, perhaps, to select alternative features of the tradition—in accord with his theological concerns. For instance, where Mark and Matthew tell us that the centurion below the cross saw in Jesus the son of a god (probably not, as commonly translated, God's Son), Luke tells us the centurion paid tribute only to a "righteous man"; where Matthew and Mark (quoting Psalm 22) record Christ's cry of godforsakenness from the cross, Luke (quoting Psalm 31 instead) reports only that he peacefully yielded up his spirit into his Father's hands. And it is fair to say that, among all the writers of the New Testament, none places a greater emphasis on the social and even political dimensions of the gospel: In Luke's rendering of the beatitudes, it is not the "poor in spirit" who are blessed, but simply "the poor," while in his corresponding list of "woes" the rich are informed that they had their comforts in this life and will have none in the Age to come; it would be difficult to imagine a more subversive social and economic manifesto than Mary's "Magnificat"; Jesus in the synagogue at Nazareth proclaims the fulfillment of Isaiah's prophecy regarding God's rescue of the poor, the imprisoned, and the oppressed as his mission; the parable of the rich man and Lazarus is clearly a condemnation not simply of the former's dissipations, but of his hoarding of the wealth he should be giving to the destitute; Jesus instructs the rich young ruler to sell his possessions and distribute the money to the poor not as an act of perfection *in addition* to what is needful for entry into the Kingdom, but as the one deed *yet lacking* in his pursuit of salvation; and Luke's description in Acts of the early church's communism of goods in Jerusalem is one that good Christians have striven heroically for the better part of two millennia to pretend not to notice. It is Luke who bequeathed to later Christian centuries the best-loved portrait of Jesus and of the early faith, and no writer in Christian history did more to make Christ and his gospel something immediate and even radiant in the Christian imagination; and yet, even so, we do not know who he actually was. As for the fourth Gospel—believed by many to have been written in the last decade of the first century and later attributed to John—its principal author (there were certainly more than one) was not the disciple of Jesus named John; many, however, believe that the book at least comes from a community descending from John's mission and teachings, as the text seems to suggest at such places as chapter nineteen's description of the piercing of the crucified Christ's side, or at the close of the Gospel's added "second conclusion" (the dreamlike coda of chapter twenty-one). Moreover, the author was clearly more concerned with making a complex theological statement about who Christ was than with offering an ostensibly documentary history. His Gospel does not unfold an historical narrative consistent with that of the other three: It depicts Christ's ministry as stretching over at least three years, rather than the single year or less of the synoptic Gospels, and as comprising several visits to Judaea and Jerusalem rather than one; it seems to depict Jesus as a man in his forties (8:57), rather than as the younger man suggested by the historical chronology of Matthew and Luke; it rearranges the order of certain events, placing the cleansing of the Jerusalem Temple at the beginning rather than at the end of Christ's ministry, and situating the crucifixion on the eve of the Passover rather than on the day itself (hence recording no Passover seder and so no Last Supper); it reports at enormous length prayers addressed to the Father by Jesus in private on the eve of the crucifixion, of which there could clearly have been no witness and in which there is no trace of the "agony of Gethsemane"; it describes Jesus as bearing his own cross to Golgotha, rather than Simon of Cyrene doing it for him; and so on. And, as a whole, it is obviously meant as a theological document rather than as a simple record of events. Hence, it is the most mysterious of the Gospels and its author the most mysterious of the evangelists.

And so it goes. Of the "Pauline" letters that most scholars believe were not written by Paul himself, 2 Thessalonians, Ephesians, and Colossians do boast substantial coteries of scholars convinced (as a minority report) of Pauline authorship. But, while 2 Thessalonians echoes Paul's style somewhat, it seems also to be consciously structured upon the genuine 1 Thessalonians; in many respects, also, it seems to be a late text, written in response to realities that arose after Paul's time (in particular, the unexpectedly long delay of Christ's *parousia*). What is more significant still, it contains eschatological claims of striking exactitude that are not only found nowhere else in the Pauline corpus, but that seem almost impossible to reconcile with the eschatological language and motifs of the indubitable letters. The overall impression of the letter is that it emanates from a somewhat idiosyncratic faction within the next generation or two of the early church, a faction in which an elaborate anagogy of the last days had begun to develop in place of the much simpler Pauline vision of an imminent return of Christ and transformation of the cosmos. But that may be *only* an impression.

As for Ephesians and Colossians, it is generally recognized that the style and language of both letters differ somewhat from those of the definitely authentic letters, and that there are certain apparent novelties of theology and vocabulary in both. But arguments from consistency of style, which can always be misleading, are especially perilous in the case of authors who dictated their texts to amanuenses (as was, of necessity, the common practice in late antiquity), because those amanuenses may have exercised varying degrees of editorial discretion over the final products; and it is questionable that we actually possess a sample size of Pauline texts large enough to make such judgments wholly credible. Arguments from consistency of thought, moreover, can often fail to take into account just how much a single thinker's "system" can develop over time. And there can be something insidiously circular about them as well: The scholar who has reached some conclusion regarding "how Paul thought" or "how Paul wrote," based on a small number of texts interpreted by criteria that may be more arbitrary than that scholar realizes, then finds material in other canonically Pauline texts that seems at odds with that conclusion; so, rather than qualify his initial judgments, he dismisses the evidence. To take one obvious example, the authenticity of Colossians has often been denied by some scholars on the grounds that it seems to contain doctrines (a strong "moralism" of good works, for instance) incompatible with those found in the authentic letters. That, however, is where a trap may have been laid. What those scholars generally mean is that Colossians seems somewhat hard to reconcile with Paul's authentic letters *as interpreted by magisterial Protestant tradition*. But the problem with this is that (pardon my bluntness) those traditional Protestant readings of Paul are demonstrably wrong. In the late Augustinian understanding of nature and grace that was exaggerated by, and then became the dominant grammar of, the sixteenth-century Reformation systems, Paul supposedly inveighed against belief in "justification" (meaning "unmerited extrinsic imputation of righteousness") through "works" (meaning all kinds of human efforts, religious *and moral*), and insisted instead on justification through "faith" (meaning intellectual and emotional assent to Jesus as Lord and savior), by the grace of a "predestination" not based on any divine foreknowledge of human "merits." But Paul taught nothing of the sort. Instead he taught that human beings cannot be "justified" (that is, "proved" or "made righteous") by "works of the Law" (such as circumcision or kosher dietary practices), but only by a "faithfulness" that necessarily entails "works" of love—good deeds—in respect of which one will be judged and either rewarded or "punished" (or, better perhaps, "purged"). The power to perform such works is indeed a gift of grace, but for Paul it is one that unites us to God in a real "synergy" (such that we can become, as he likes to say, *synergoi*, "workers-together-with" God). Moreover, as for why some are "marked out in advance" (certainly not "predestined") for God's mission to the cosmos (for mission, that is, not for salvation), Paul in Romans 8 clearly describes God's decision as contingent upon divine foreknowledge (and much theological tradition for centuries has gone through agonizing contortions trying to reverse the clear meaning of those verses). All of which is quite unsettling if one has been raised to believe in a stark antithesis between "works-righteousness" and faith, or between grace and works, or between divine and human merits, or between divine "sovereignty" and human effort; but Paul was not a Lutheran, or Calvinist, or even Augustinian. And so, when the Paul of the authentic letters is freed from the Paul of theological myth, it turns out that Colossians not only says nothing different on these matters at all, but does not even necessarily sound any distinctly different intonations. None of this is to deny the scrupulousness of most modern New Testament scholarship on these texts, but I would caution against accepting its verdicts too credulously. I confess that before I began this translation I had casually accepted the judgment that Ephesians and Colossians were not written by Paul; by the time I had finished it, I had not entirely come around to the opposite conclusion, but I had come to believe that many doubts regarding their authenticity are based on poorer stylistic evidence than is generally claimed, as well as on theological arguments that may say more about certain scholars' theological presuppositions than about the rather unsystematic, late antique "system" of thought to which Paul actually held. There are genuine questions to be raised about the provenance of the letters—for instance, Ephesians frequently appears to have been written by someone who did not share Paul's conviction that Christ's return was imminent—but the solvency of many of those questions may turn out in the end to be rather thinner than has come to be assumed. Whatever the case, even if Ephesians and Colossians are not works of Paul himself, they are nevertheless very much of his "school" and expand faithfully upon his theological vision. Perhaps they were constructed from Pauline fragments by later editors, or were produced either by amanuenses working from particularly rudimentary dictations or by disciples under his directions, or were reconstructions of Pauline teachings by later disciples, or were simply better redacted and edited than the earlier letters; we simply cannot know.

Other "pseudo-Pauline" letters, by contrast, truly are more remote in theological and moral sensibility. The three so-called Pastoral Epistles—1 and 2 Timothy and Titus—may well have been written by a single author, and in many respects they develop themes in Paul's theology, such as the universal saving will of God in Christ; but they appear in some ways to be products of a period in the church's institutional history somewhat later than Paul's time (the early second century probably), seem stylistically unlike Paul's unquestioned writings (the prose is better, the vocabulary more Hellenistic and less Septuagintal), and seem at odds with certain of Paul's more astonishingly radical views, such as the equal spiritual dignity of masters and slaves, or of men and women (especially if, as textual evidence makes very likely, the famously dissonant passage of 1 Corinthians 14:34–35 is an interpolation). Even so, no less eminent a New Testament scholar than Luke Timothy Johnson has made a case for their Pauline authorship; and, while I do not find the argument convincing, I cannot quibble with its pedigree. I am quite prepared, moreover, to believe that all three of the pastorals contain real Pauline materials, revised and amplified upon by later followers.

In the end, then, I suppose I would characterize the various skeptical arguments regarding the Pauline *dubia* thus: The cases against Ephesians and Colossians are not without weight, but are probably weaker than it has become common to assert; those against 2 Thessalonians are extremely (and to my mind decisively) strong; those against the Pastoral Epistles are nearly insuperable; but those against 1 Thessalonians and Philippians are so weak as to be practically self-refuting.

As for Hebrews, in language, substance, and theological intention it could scarcely be more incandescently unlike the letters of Paul, though it is as brilliant as the greatest of them. It also exhibits a command of Greek that, as was generally recognized from the early centuries in educated Eastern Christian circles, is vastly beyond Paul's own; in respect of style alone, to ascribe the letter to Paul is about as credible as ascribing a novel of Anatole France to Maurice Leblanc or a travel memoir of Patrick Leigh Fermor to Erskine Caldwell. But the text's acceptance into the canon of the New Testament was delayed in some parts of the Christian world by uncertainty regarding its origin; so, at the very least, its eventual general attribution to Paul, however incredible, served to dispel doubts about its canonical propriety. Really, though, as Origen said in the third century, only God knows who truly wrote it.

Of the other non-Pauline epistolary books, or Catholic Epistles, the letter of James comes nearest to giving us a clear picture of its author. At least, there is no reason to doubt that he was indeed the leader of the Christians in Jerusalem a decade or two after Christ; he may even have been, as tradition asserts, the brother of Jesus, though the letter makes no such claim. He clearly was a Jewish Christian writing to other Jewish Christians whom he still regarded as Jews, in some sense answerable to the Law of Moses (he even at one point, for what it is worth, refers to the Christian assembly not as an *ekklēsia* but as a synagogue, though most translations hide that fact from view). Regarding the identity of Judas—or as he is more customarily known, for delicacy's sake, Jude—and regarding what exactly provoked him to write his short, exasperated letter, we know next to nothing. As for the three letters of John, they may have been the work of one man; at least the second and third seem to have been, both having been composed by someone identifying himself as "the Elder." But most scholars properly deny that the author of any of them was the same John who wrote the fourth Gospel, or the John of Patmos who wrote Revelation, or John the Apostle. There are stylistic similarities, however, between the Gospel of John and the first of the Johannine letters, and it seems reasonable to suppose that, even if they were not the work of the same hand, they emanated from a close community of shared discourse, and that the latter text is written in a fairly deft imitation of the voice of the former. As for the two letters ascribed to Peter (the second being probably the latest New Testament text by a good margin), they were certainly written by two different authors, neither of whom was either the disciple of Jesus or the first leader of the church in Rome. Admittedly, some scholars have tried to argue for a kind of "indirect authenticity" for the first letter, suggesting that it may contain genuine teachings of the Apostle communicated to, and then paraphrased by, a disciple fluent in Greek; but the case against authenticity is far stronger. No credible scholar argues for the authenticity of the second letter, however; it is an extremely late writing, incorporating a great deal of the Letter of Jude practically verbatim.

I suppose, having said all of this, I should pause to say also that I understand that there are those who object quite fiercely to such statements, and even regard them as implicit denials of the truthfulness of scripture or of sacred tradition. But the evidence supporting some of them is quite substantial, and most of it is drawn directly from the texts themselves, and the scholarship is not, at its best, flimsy or capricious. All Christians believe that the New Testament is divinely inspired; but any coherent account of what this means must involve an acknowledgment that God speaks through human beings, in all their historical, cultural, and personal contingency. For those, however, who not only believe that scripture is inspired, but who are also deeply committed to "literalist," "inerrantist," or "dictational" understandings of inspiration, all the words of the Bible must be understood as direct locutions of God, passing through their human authors like sunlight through the clearest glass, and the canon of the New Testament—even though it took a few centuries to concresce into its present form, and has never really existed as anything but a shimmering cloud of countless variants—must be understood as a flawlessly immediate communication, in its every historical and lexical detail, of the teaching of the Holy Spirit and of the faith of the apostolic church. That has never been the only, or even the dominant, Christian understanding of scriptural inspiration; many modern Christians, in fact, might be quite surprised at the speculative boldness and critical diffidence with which some of the greatest exegetes of Christian late antiquity and the Middle Ages approached the Bible. Still, it is a view of scripture that has had adherents, whether reflective or instinctive, in every epoch, and that with the rise of the fundamentalist movement of the twentieth century has spread far and wide in an especially acute and virulent form. I imagine that, for such believers in "verbal inspiration," the suggestion that the authors of some of the books of the New Testament were not in fact who they represented themselves as being must seem especially intolerable. It is unlikely, moreover, that it will assuage the distress of the aggrieved textual literalist to observe that such pseudonymy was a common and even marginally acceptable practice in late antiquity, and that religious and speculative texts were often written "in the voice" of authorities long dead or even merely legendary, and that—by antiquity's more generous standards of "authenticity"—a text composed of redacted or rearranged materials by an author, or even merely composed by disciples of his school, could still be attributed to him. The only assurance I can offer readers situated anywhere along the spectrum of the various exegetical tendencies is that this translation is the work of someone who believes in divine inspiration, if not in "verbal inspiration" or in the literal factual accuracy of every discrete feature of these texts, and that my judgments regarding their authorial history have had no effect whatsoever on my treatment of their words. I have attempted to render all of them into English with as much fidelity as possible, even when this has meant breaking with prevailing convention, because my conviction is that my principal responsibility is to whatever divine truth shines in and through them. Insofar as I have failed in that respect—and inevitably one must fail, to some degree—I ask the reader's pardon. And insofar as I have succeeded—and I think I have, to some degree—it would be presumptuous to ask for praise; but I do hope this translation will, for many readers, help to cast new light on his or her understanding of the origins and contents of Christian faith. And I repeat my assertion, which may seem slightly incredible, that I have tried not to advance any theological or ideological agenda, but rather to capture in English as much of the suggestiveness and uncertainty and mystery of the original Greek as possible, precisely in order to prevent any prior set of commitments from determining for the reader in advance what it is that the text *must* say (even when it does not).

Anywhere But Here

Anywhere
But Here

by

Mona Simpson

Alfred A. Knopf   New York   1987

THIS IS A BORZOI BOOK
PUBLISHED BY ALFRED A. KNOPF, INC.

LIBRARY OF CONGRESS CATALOGING-IN-PUBLICATION DATA

SIMPSON, MONA.
  ANYWHERE BUT HERE.

  I. TITLE.
PS3569.I5117A8 1986   813'.54   86-45282
ISBN 0-394-55283-0

Manufactured in the United States of America

First Edition

The author wishes to thank the Corporation of Yaddo, the MacDowell Colony, VCCA,
the Transatlantic Henfield Foundation, The Beard's Fund, the Kellogg Foundation,
and The Paris Review for their support during the writing of this book.
Also, the author would like to thank Allan Gurganus, Elizabeth Hardwick, Robert
Asahina, Robert Cohen, Lionel Shriver, and George Plimpton for multiple and
generous readings.

A NOTE ON THE TYPE

This book was set in a modern adaptation of a type designed by the first
William Caslon (1692–1766), greatest of English letter founders. The Caslon face, an artistic, easily read type, has enjoyed two centuries of ever-
increasing popularity in our own country. The first copies of the Declaration of Independence and the first paper currency distributed to the citizens
of the newborn nation were printed in this type face.

Composed by Graphic Composition, Inc., Athens, Georgia
Printed and bound by The Haddon Craftsmen, Inc., Scranton, Pennsylvania
Designed by Marysarah Quinn

For Joanne,
our mother,
and
my brother Steve

There are three wants which can never be satisfied;
that of the rich wanting more, that of the sick, wanting
something different, and that of the traveler, who says,
"anywhere but here."

—*Ralph Waldo Emerson*

Contents

Ann

1

Anywhere

We fought. When my mother and I crossed state lines in the stolen car, I'd sit against the window and wouldn't talk. I wouldn't even look at her. The fights came when I thought she broke a promise. She said there'd be an Indian reservation. She said that we'd see buffalo in Texas. My mother said a lot of things. We were driving from Bay City, Wisconsin, to California, so I could be a child star while I was still a child.

"Talk to me," my mother would say. "If you're upset, tell me."

But I wouldn't. I knew how to make her suffer. I was mad. I was mad about a lot of things. Places she said would be there, weren't. We were running away from family. We'd left home.

Then my mother would pull to the side of the road and reach over and open my door.

"Get out, then," she'd say, pushing me.

I got out. It was always a shock the first minute because nothing outside was bad. The fields were bright. It never happened on a bad day. The western sky went on forever, there were a few clouds. A warm breeze came up and tangled around my legs. The road was dull as a nickel. I stood there at first amazed that there was nothing horrible in the landscape.

But then the wheels of the familiar white Continental turned, a spit of gravel hit my shoes and my mother's car drove away. When it was nothing but a dot in the distance, I started to cry.

I lost time then; I don't know if it was minutes or if it was more. There was nothing to think because there was nothing to do. First, I saw small things. The blades of grass. Their rough side, their smooth, waxy side. Brown grasshoppers. A dazzle of California poppies.

I'd look at everything around me. In yellow fields, the tops of weeds bent under visible waves of wind. There was a high steady note of insects screaking. A rich odor of hay mixed with the heady smell of gasoline. Two or three times, a car rumbled by, shaking the ground. Dry weeds by the side of the road seemed almost transparent in the even sun.

I tried hard but I couldn't learn anything. The scenery all went strange, like a picture on a high billboard. The fields, the clouds, the sky; none of it helped because it had nothing to do with me.

My mother must have watched in her rearview mirror. My arms crossed over my chest, I would have looked smaller and more solid in the distance. That was what she couldn't stand, my stubbornness. She'd had a stubborn husband. She wasn't going to have a stubborn child. But when she couldn't see me anymore, she gave up and turned around and she'd gasp with relief when I was in front of her again, standing open-handed by the side of the road, nothing more than a child, her child.

And by the time I saw her car coming back, I'd be covered with a net of tears, my nose running. I stood there with my hands hanging at my sides, not even trying to wipe my face.

My mother would slow down and open my door and I'd run in, looking back once in a quick good-bye to the fields, which turned ordinary and pretty again. And when I slid into the car, I was different. I put my feet up on the dashboard and tapped the round tips of my sneakers together. I wore boys' sneakers she thought I was too old for. But now my mother was nice because she knew I would talk to her.

"Are you hungry?" was the first thing she'd say.

"A little."

"I am," she'd say. "I feel like an ice cream cone. Keep your eyes open for a Howard Johnson's."

We always read the magazines, so we knew where we wanted to go. My mother had read about Scottsdale and Albuquerque and Bel Air. But for miles, there was absolutely nothing. It seemed we didn't have anything and even air that came in the windows when we were driving fast felt hot.

We had taken Ted's Mobil credit card and we used it whenever we could. We scouted for Mobil stations and filled up the tank when we found one, also charging Cokes on the bill. We dug to our elbows in the ice chests, bringing the cold pop bottles up like a catch. There was one chain of motels that accepted Mobil cards. Most nights we stayed in those, sometimes driving three or four hours longer to find one, or stopping early if one was there. They were called Travel Lodges and their signs each outlined a bear in a nightcap, sleepwalking. They were dull motels, lonely, and they were pretty cheap, which bothered my mother because she would have liked to charge high bills to Ted. I think she enjoyed signing *Mrs. Ted Diamond*. We passed Best Westerns with hotel swimming pools and restaurants with country singers and we both wished and wished Ted had a different card.

Travel Lodges were the kind of motels that were set a little off the highway in a field. They tended to be one or at the most two stories, with cement squares outside your room door for old empty metal chairs. At one end there would be a lit coffee shop and a couple of semis parked on the gravel. The office would be near the coffee shop. It would have shag carpeting and office furniture, always a TV attached by metal bars to the ceiling.

Those motels depressed us. After we settled in the room, my mother looked around, checking for cleanliness. She took the bedspreads down, lifted curtains, opened drawers and the medicine cabinet, and looked into the shower. Sometimes she took the paper off a water glass and held the glass up to see that it was washed.

I always wanted to go outside. My mother would be deliberating whether it was safer to leave our suitcase in the room or in the locked car; when she was thinking, she stood in the middle of the floor with her hands on her hips and her lips pursed. Finally, she decided to bring it in. Then she would take a shower to cool off. She didn't make me take one if I didn't want to, because we were nowhere and she didn't care what I looked like in the coffee shop. After her shower, she put on the same clothes she'd been driving in all day.

I went out to our porch and sat in the one metal chair. Its back was a rounded piece, perhaps once designed to look like a shell. I could hear her shower water behind me, running; in front, the constant serious sound of the highway. A warm wind slapped my skin lightly, teasing, the sound of the trucks on the highway came loud, then softer, occasionally a motorcycle shrank to the size of a bug, red taillights ticking on the blue sky.

I acted like a kid, always expecting to find something. At home, before supper, I'd stood outside when the sky looked huge and even the near neighbors seemed odd and distant in their occupations. I'd watched the cars moving on the road, as if by just watching you could understand, get something out of the world.

At the motel, I would walk around to the back. I'd stand looking at the field, like any field. The back of the building was ordinary, brick, with glass meter gauges. There was a gas tank lodged on a cement platform, pooled with rusty water. The field went on to where you could see trailers and a neon sign for Dairy Queen in the distance.

The near and the far, could have been anywhere, could have been our gas tank, our fields and sky at home. Our yard had the same kinds of weeds. Home could have been anywhere too.

"Ann. A-yun," my mother would be yelling, then. It all ended, gladly, when she called me from the door. She was finished with her shower and wanted to go for supper at the coffee shop. Our day was almost done. And we enjoyed the dinners in those coffee shops. We ordered the most expensive thing on the menu and side dishes and beverages and desserts. We were anxious, trying to plan to get all the best of what they had. We rolled up our sleeves, asked for extra sour cream and butter. We took pleasure in the scrawled figures added up on the green-lined bill.

Mornings, we always started out later than we'd planned. The manager ran the credit card through the machine and filled the form out slowly. My mother drummed her nails on the counter top, waiting. Then she sighed, holding the credit card form in both hands, examining it a second before signing. "Okay," she said every time she handed the paper back, as if she were giving away one more thing she'd once had.

We'd drive off in the morning and I'd look again, at the plain building, the regular field. I'd forget the land. It was like so much other land we'd seen.

My mother had clipped out pictures of houses in Scottsdale, Arizona. We loved the colors: pink, turquoise, browns, rich yellow. The insides of the houses had red tiled floors, clay bowls of huge strawberries on plain, rough wooden tables.

We went out of our way to go to Scottsdale. When we got there, my mother drove to the Luau, a good hotel, one they'd listed in *Town and Country*. I sat in a chair on one side of the lobby while she went up to the desk. She came back and whispered me the price.

"What do you think? It's a lot but maybe it's worth it once to just relax."

"I think we should find somewhere cheaper."

"There might not be a Travel Lodge in town," she said. "Well, think, Pooh-bear-cub. It's up to you. What would you like to do?"

"Let's find out if there's a Travel Lodge."

She sighed. "Okay. I don't know how we're going to find out. There's probably not. In fact, I'm pretty sure. So what do you think? What should we do?"

I worried about money. And I knew it was a bigger system than I understood. I tried to pick the cheaper thing, like a superstition.

"There's a telephone. Maybe they have a phone book." We were standing in the dark Polynesian lobby. A phone hung in the corner.

She did the looking and it was there, Travel Lodge, with a boxed ad showing the bear sleepwalking, in the yellow pages, listed as being on Route 9. "Nine where?" my mother said, biting her fingernail, clicking the other hand on the metal shelf. "Now, how the heck am I going to find that? It says right out of town, yeah, I'll bet. I didn't see anything, coming in."

"We don't have to go there." I felt like I'd done my duty, checking. I looked around the lobby. It seemed nice. I was beginning to hope she picked here.

"Well, come on." She pulled her purse strap over her shoulder. "Let's go. We'll go there. We should." She had that much worry, apparently.

But driving to the Travel Lodge, not even halfway there, in town, at an intersection near a gas station, we had an accident. My mother rear-ended a car on a red light.

I was sitting on a curb of the intersection, pulling at grass behind me banking the closed filling station. Nearby, the cars were pulled over to one side and a police car with a flashing red light was parked, making traffic go around them. The policeman stood writing things down as he talked to my mother.

She was moving her hands all around her hair and face. Then she folded her arms across her chest, but one hand couldn't stand it, it reached up to tug at her collar.

"I was going to just stay at that hotel, I *knew*. I was tired. I know myself. Now, God, tell me, really, how long do you think it will take to be fixed?" She bit a nail.

The policeman looked into the dark gas station. "Problem is, it's a weekend," he said.

My mother looked at me and shook her head. The policeman walked over to the other driver. She was a woman in shorts and a sleeveless shirt. She seemed calm.

"See, I'm not going to listen to you anymore," my mother said. "Because I know best. You try and save a few pennies and you end up spending thousands." She exhaled, shoving out a hip.

It was ten o'clock and finally getting cooler. We were hungry, we still hadn't eaten dinner. The other woman, having taken the numbers she needed, left, waving good-bye to us and to the policeman.

"Calm down, Adele," she said to my mother.

My mother pulled a piece of her hair. "Calm down, well, that's easy for you to say. Jeez, calm down, she says, when she's going to sue, she'll get her kids' college educations out of this, I know how it's done."

The woman laughed and slammed her car door shut. She rolled down her window. "Barry's Hanover might have a mechanic in on Saturday," she called to the policeman.

"Mom, I'm hungry." My rump was cold and it seemed we might be there all night.

"Well, we have to stay," she said. "If we'd just checked in, then we'd be there now, probably eating, no, we'd be finished. We'd probably be having dessert. But now we have to wait."

"For how long?"

"I don't know."

The policeman came over to us, still holding his notebook. "We've done all we can do until tomorrow," he said. "Now I'll take you wherever you want to go and you can just leave the car here and call in the morning and have her towed."

"They're probably not even going to have room left at the hotel now," she said to me.

The policeman had freckles on his arms and his hands, like my mother. He put the notebook in his back pocket. "Now, you are both welcome to stay with my wife and I for the night, if you're worried. There's plenty of extra room."

"Oh, no, thank you, though, we couldn't."

"Because it wouldn't be any trouble. And my wife makes a mean apple pie." He looked at me.

"Thank you, but no, really." My mother inspired offers like that, often. I didn't know until I was older how unusual that is. "But would you mind dropping us off at the Luau?"

"Yes, ma'am," he said. "Nice place."

We both sat in the backseat while he drove. The windows were covered with chicken wire. "I just hope they still have room," my mother said, stretching her fingers out on the seat and looking down at their nails.

The thing about my mother and me is that when we get along, we're just the same. Exactly. And at the Luau Hotel, we were happy. Waiting for our car to be fixed, we didn't talk about money. It was so big, we didn't think about it. We lay on our stomachs on the king-sized bed, our calves tangling up behind us, reading novels. I read *Gone With the Wind*. Near the end, I locked myself in the bathroom, stopping up my face with a towel. After a while she knocked on the door.

"Honey, let me in, I want to tell you something!" I made myself keep absolutely still. "Don't worry, Honey, she gets him back later. She gets him again in the end."

We loved the swimming pool. Those days we were waiting for our car to be fixed, we lay out from ten until two, because my mother had read that those were the best tanning hours. That was what we liked doing, improving ourselves: lying sprawled out on the reclining chairs, rubbed with coconut suntan oil, turning the pages of new-bought magazines. Then we'd go in the pool, me cannonballing off the diving board for the shock of it, my mother starting in one corner of the shallow end, both her arms out to the sides, skimming the surface as she stepped in gradually, smiling wide, saying, "Eeeeeeeee."

My mother wore a white suit, I swam in gym shorts. While I was lying on a chair, once, she picked up my foot and looked down my leg. "Apricot," she said.

At home, one farmer put in a swimming pool, fenced all around with aluminum. That summer, Ben and I sat in the fields outside, watching through the diamond spaces of the fence. Sometimes the son would try and chase us away and throw rocks at us, little sissy pieces of gravel.

"Public property!" we screamed back at him. We were sitting in Guns Field. We kids all knew just who owned what land.

Every afternoon, late, after the prime tanning hours, we went out. Dressing took a long time. My mother called room service for a pitcher of fresh lemonade, told them not too much sugar, but some sugar, like yesterday, a pinch, just enough so it was sweet. Sweet, but a little tart, too. Come to think of it, yesterday tasted a little too tart, but the day before was perfect. This was all on the telephone. My mother was the kind of customer a waitress would like to kill.

We'd each take showers and wash our hair, squeezing lemons on it before the cream rinse. We touched up our fingernails and toenails with polish. That was only the beginning. Then came the body cream and face cream, our curlers and hair sprays and makeup.

All along, I had a feeling we couldn't afford this and that it would be unimaginably bad when we had to pay. I don't know what I envisioned: nothing, no luck, losing everything, so it was the absolute worst, no money for food, being stopped on a plain cement floor in the sun, unable to move, winding down, stopping like a clock stopped.

But then it went away again. In our sleeveless summer dresses and white patent leather thongs, we walked to the district of small, expensive shops. There was an exotic pet store we visited every day. We'd been first drawn in by a sign on the window for two defumed skunks.

"But you can never really get the smell completely out," the blond man inside had told us. He showed us a baby raccoon and we watched it lick its paws, with movements like a cat but more delicate, intricate features.

More than anything, I wanted that raccoon. And my mother wasn't saying no. We didn't have to make any decisions until we left the Luau. And we didn't know yet when that would be.

In a china store, my mother held up a plain white plate. "Look at this. See how fine it is?" If she hadn't said that, I wouldn't have noticed anything, but now I saw that it was thin and there was a pearliness, like a film of water, over the surface.

"Granny had a whole *set* like this." She turned the plate upside down and read the fine printing. "Yup, this is it. Spode."

I remembered Granny almost bald, carrying oats and water across the yard to feed Hal's pony. But still, I didn't know.

"Mmhmm. You don't know, but Granny was very elegant. Gramma isn't, she could be, but she isn't. We're like Granny. See, we belong here, Pooh-bear-cub. We come from this."

I didn't know.

A week after the accident, we had good news. The bill for our car was far less than we'd thought and my mother paid ninety dollars, off the record, to fix the other woman's fender. They both agreed not to contact insurance companies.

This was all great except it meant we were leaving. The car would be ready in a day. My mother sat on the edge of the bed, filing her nails, when she put down the telephone receiver, gently. "There's still a few things I'd like to see here," she said.

We went out to the pool and tried not to think. It seemed easy, lying on towels over warm cement. I'd gotten tan, very dark, the week we'd been there. My mother had freckles and pink burns on her cheeks and shoulders, and her hair was streaked lighter from the sun. That day, my mother got up and went inside before I did. She had to be careful in the sun.

I was in the pool, holding onto the side, kicking my legs in the water behind me. I was worried about my knees. Lately, I'd noticed they were fat, not knobby and horselike, the way my mother's were. So I was doing kicks to improve them. Around the pool, other women slouched in deck chairs. I thought about my knees again. At least tan fat looked better than white fat, I was thinking.

Then my mother called me. "We're going to see a house," she said, shoving a towel into my hand. "Hurry up and jump in the shower."

We waited, clean and dressed, outside the Luau. My mother told me that a real estate agent named Gail was picking us up. There was something in her tone, she didn't want to explain. So I went along with it as if it was nothing out of the ordinary. And there in Scottsdale, it really wasn't. It had been so long since anything was regular.

Suddenly, Gail was there and she honked. I climbed into the backseat and my mother sat next to her in front. They talked quickly, getting to know each other. My mother said we were just moving, from Bay City, Wisconsin, and that she was looking forward to the warm air.

"I couldn't stand another winter." She rolled down her window and glanced outside. "I love Scottsdale, the dryness."

Gail Letterfine was very tan with light gray hair, bright clothes and turquoise Indian jewelry. "You're going to love this house, it's absolutely cream of the crop. I haven't had anything like this to show for over a year."

She drove us to the top of a hill. The land was brown, dirt. There were no lawns. I just sat in the backseat, not saying anything. I wished I had *Gone With the Wind*. I knew I shouldn't say anything, in case I contradicted my mother. I could tell she was lying, but I wasn't sure. And I didn't know why. She liked me to talk, around strangers, like a kid. But I was mad, sort of. So I just stared out the window.

Gail Letterfine parked the Mustang on the pebbled lot near a fountain. Pennies overlapped and glittered on the bottom. Just from where we were, I could tell this was something we'd never seen before. We didn't have houses like this in Bay City. A maid opened the door, a woman I knew was a maid from her black short dress and white apron. We'd never seen a maid before, in person, at least I hadn't, I didn't know anymore about my mother. When we got along, it seemed we knew everything about each other. But now, I felt like my mother glossed over things. She knew how nervous I could be.

The maid went to get someone else. Gail Letterfine opened a door and it was a closet. "Coat closet," she said, loudly, as if it were her own house.

The living room was huge, with red clay tile floors and high ceilings. There were long windows on two walls and you could see outside, down the hill. There was no furniture except a black grand piano and chairs against the walls.

The woman of the house came to meet us. Considering where she lived, she looked like an ordinary person. She had plain brown perma-nented hair and a nice face. She was wearing a gray dress and stockings.

Gail Letterfine introduced her and the woman took us through her house. Out windows, we saw the backyard, brown and dry, with an oval turquoise swimming pool. Clay pots of strawberry plants stood with thick, heavy berries hanging down over their rims. Every time we entered a room, the woman stood in the doorway while Gail Letterfine pointed out features. In the kitchen, Gail opened every cupboard, where we saw canned soup and Jell-O mixes just like in my grandmother's house. Gail went on about the sink, the refrigerator and the stove. Then she started in on the plumbing. From the way my mother shifted, you could tell she was less than interested.

"What about your appointments?" My mother cupped her hand around a painted Mexican candleholder on the kitchen table. "Are they for sale, too? Because they all go so well, they're what *make* the house."

I wondered where she'd learned that word. The woman shook her head. "No, I'm sorry." My mother liked the woman who lived here, her quietness. There was something tough in Gail Letterfine. With her espa-drille, she was now pointing to the molding around the kitchen floor. My mother would rather have talked to the woman in the gray dress. Perhaps that's why we'd come here, because my mother missed her friends.

The bedrooms and bathrooms were regular-sized.

"Our daughter's room," the woman said, in the last doorway on the hall. "She's gone off to college."

My mother nudged me, "This would be yours." We wandered into the adjoining bathroom, which had a vanity and a makeup mirror. Starfish and shells cluttered the tile rim of the sunken tub. My mother frowned at me, "Not bad."

They walked back down the hallway to the dining room. The woman in the gray dress had, quietly, offered them tea, and my mother answered quick and loud, "I'd love some."

I stayed in the room. Outside, water slapped the edges of the swimming pool. A light breeze was making waves. I sat on the hard single bed with stuffed animals bunched up by the pillow. Two pompons fluttered on the bulletin board.

I leaned back and imagined the girl away at college. I thought if I lived here, with this bed and this bulletin board, the regular desk and dresser, I would have this kind of life. Nothing to hide. The girl left her room and went to college and people could walk through and see it.

I actually breathed slower and believed my mother had changed her mind about California, that we were really going to live here, in this house.

It was nice lying on that bed, listening to the soft shuffle of water through the window screen. I felt like sleeping. Then a few minutes later, I woke up hungry. I got up and went down the hall. I was thinking of the woman in the gray dress. For some reason, I thought she would give me cookies and a glass of milk.

They were sitting around the dining room on beige chairs. My mother's knees rested together and her calves slanted down, parallel, mirroring the woman's across the room. My mother was sipping her tea, holding it a long time to her lips, appreciating it.

"Could we put in a bathhouse? I'd love a little cabana out there."

Gail Letterfine lifted her silver glasses, which were attached and hooked behind her ears on a thin silver chain, and wrote down my mother's questions in a hand-sized notebook.

"You'd need a permit." She tapped the arm of her chair with a pen. "That's not hard."

"But I would like to know."

"Who can I call? Let me see. Oh, I got it. Mangold."

My mother floated up to where I was at the sliding glass doors. She rummaged her hand through my hair.

"But you like it," Gail Letterfine said, slamming the notebook closed.

"Well, my husband's coming in next week, and of course, he'll have to see it, too."

"Of course," said the woman in the gray dress, nodding as if she understood perfectly.

"But I'm sure he'll like it." My mother nodded, too. "I think this is the one." She lifted her eyes to the high corners of the room. "Mmhmm, I'm sure of it. What do you think, Ann?"

I was reeling, as if I'd just woken up to trouble, when she said her husband. The sentence went through me like a toy train, three times around the track and no time, coming in, could I picture it right. Ted sure wasn't coming. Not after we'd used his credit card like we had.

"I'm hungry, Mom," I said. I was disappointed by the woman in the gray dress, too. I felt like I'd been promised food and then not given it.

My mother ran her hand through my hair again. "Well, we better be off and get this little one something to eat." She smiled. She liked it when I said bratty, kid things in front of other people. We both did. It made us feel normal. She liked people to think she spoiled me.

On the way back to town, Gail Letterfine drove us to see Frank Lloyd Wright's work site in the desert, Taliesin West. I didn't see what the big deal was. They were excavating. There were huge piles of dirt, like you saw at home where they were developing for the new highway, and dust around everywhere. It was so hot, the piece of thong between my toes stung the skin.

"I love the atmosphere," my mother said, tilting her face up to the sun before naturally drifting indoors, to the air-conditioned gift shop. That was one thing about my mother, why she was fun; she valued comfort. We never had to stay in museums too long. If we didn't like something, we left and went somewhere else, like a restaurant. She wasn't too strict about discipline.

Metal bells of all sizes hung from the gift shop ceiling. "People come from all over the world to buy these bells," Gail Letterfine said. "You're lucky to get them at that price. They're going to be collector's items."

My mother bought one, taking a long time to pick the size. "Won't it look nice in the house?" She winked at me.

I scowled.

Gail took us out to a late lunch. We ate a lot, we each had desserts, extras. We acted the way we did at motel diners, not minding the prices, but this was an elegant restaurant, and expensive. They weren't going to take our Mobil credit card. My mother argued primly when Gail tried to pay the bill and I kicked her, hard, under the table. That night, my mother made me watch while she rolled down her stockings and put her fingers on the bruises. She said she'd known all along Gail would insist. And Gail had, tearing the bottom strip off the bill. "It's a write-off, you know," she'd said. "No prob."

She'd left us in front of the Luau.

"So tomorrow morning, I'll bring a contract to breakfast. Just a work sheet. So we can start talking terms. Toot-a-loo," Gail called, waving her plump hand as she drove away.

We watched her car go. All of a sudden it seemed sad, leaving Scottsdale. Suddenly, I really did like Gail.

"Well," my mother shrugged. "We really don't need dinner, that was plenty. Should we just walk around a little?"

We ambled down the streets slowly, because we were full from eating too much and because it was late afternoon and there was a light, warm breeze and because we were leaving tomorrow. My mother led me through an archway, to some shops on an inside courtyard. She found a perfume maker, a blind man, who blended custom fragrances. He showed us essences of oils, leaves, grasses and flowers.

"All natural," he told us.

He kept the essences in small glass bottles lined up on glass shelves. I dawdled while he worked with my mother. He mixed drops of oils on a glass plate, then rubbed them on the inside of my mother's arm with the tip of an eyedropper.

Finally, they got what they wanted. I had to laugh. The mixture was lily of the valley, wild penny rose, lilac and ordinary lawn grass.

"It's like my childhood," my mother said, holding out her arm. "What I grew up around. Smell."

They decided to call it Joie d'Adele and my mother ordered a hundred and fifty dollars' worth, eight little bottles, the smallest batch he made. She asked if he could mix them overnight, because we had to leave Scottsdale the next morning. He was an odd-looking man. His face hung large and white, creamy. He wore brown clothes and he moved slowly, with his head turned down. But he liked my mother, you could tell. Some people did. You could see it. Strangers almost always love my mother. And even if you hate her, can't stand her, even if she's ruining your life, there's something about her, some romance, some power. She's absolutely herself. No matter how hard you try, you'll never get to her. And when she dies, the world will be flat, too simple, reasonable, too fair.

As soon as we got out of the store, we started fighting about the money.

"We can't afford *that*," I whined, turning on one foot to face her. "A hundred and *fifty* dollars! For perfume! Plus the car and the hotel!"

"Well, you should talk, how much do you think your raccoon is!"

We'd made our way, walking and yelling, to the pet store, where the baby raccoon hunched in the window, his paw stalled in a bowl of water.

"He's a hundred and he eats! He'd eat up fifteen dollars a week in food, at least! The perfume would last, it would last me five years probably. I take care of things and they last. You see what I wear. I haven't bought one new thing in years. But they were all good to start with."

That was a total lie. She bought things all the time. I stood knocking on the glass, trying to make the raccoon look at me. I'd been thinking of starting my new school with the raccoon, riding a bike with him wrapped around my shoulders.

"So, I guess we can't afford him either, then," I said.

"Just remember, I'm the one who has to catch a man in this family. I'm the one who has to find you a father."

"You can buy perfume in California."

"No, not like this. There are only three in the world like him. One is in Italy and the other is in France. He's the only one in the United States."

"According to him."

"Stop kicking stones like that, you're ruining your sandals. And when they go, we can't afford another pair."

We both understood that neither of us would get what she wanted, the raccoon or Joie d'Adele. It was fair that way, both deprived.

That night we packed. My mother wrapped the Taliesin bell with care, bundling it several layers thick in hotel towels. When she paid our bill it was higher than we expected. "Three hundred." She frowned, raising her eyebrows. "It's a good thing we didn't get that raccoon, you know?"

Gail Letterfine was due to pick us up at nine o'clock for breakfast. We were gone, far away in Nevada, before the sun came up.

A lot of times, I've thought about it and I feel bad that I didn't let my mother buy her perfume. For one thing, I feel bad for the guy, early in the morning, trusting, having his eight bottles of Joie d'Adele carefully wrapped. Now I'd like to smell it: lily of the valley, penny rose, lilac and grass. It's been years since we've been home. He must have been very hurt that we duped him. He might have assumed the worst and he would have been wrong about that; my mother really had liked him. It was only me.

Years later, when we were living in California, we read his obituary in *Vogue*. It said he'd been the only living custom perfume maker in the States, so he had been telling us the truth. Apparently, he hadn't trained anyone under him. If they'd listed the name of an apprentice, I'd have sent away and surprised her.

"Awww, we should have bought some from him, remember when I wanted to get some of his perfume?" my mother said, when she showed me the little article. "It would probably be worth something now."

"By now, it'd be all gone."

The weather changes quickly on my mother's face. She shrugged, nose wrinkling. "You're right."

But I do feel bad about it, still. That bell is precious to her. She's moved it everywhere; that bell has hung, prominently, in the now-long series of her apartments.

"People come from all over the world for the Taliesin bells. We're lucky to have one. They're collector's items." I've heard my mother say that fifty times. She believed every word Gail Letterfine told us, as if we were the only people in the world who lied.

It did something for my mother, every time she let me off on the highway and then came back and I was there. She was proving something to herself. When she drove back, she'd be nodding, grateful-looking, as if we had another chance, as if something had been washed out of her.

Years ago, when I was small, she chased me to the kitchen table and swiveled between her long arms on each side of it.

"Now where are you going to go?" she'd said.

This was when we were all living in my grandmother's house back at home.

I ducked under the table and saw everyone's legs. Jimmy's blue uniform slacks, Ben's bare knees with scrapes and white scars, my grandmother's stiff, bagging, opaque, seamed orange stockings in black tie-up shoes, my mother's tall freckled legs in nylons. The muscles in her calves moved like nervous small animals. I knew I couldn't get away. So I lunged out and grabbed my uncle's blue legs, holding on hard, sobbing in yelps, not letting go. I thought Jimmy was the strongest one there. Carol stood with her back to us, wiping the counter with a sponge.

Jimmy ran his hand over my head and down my spine. He hugged me hard, but then he pried my fingers off and pulled me away from him. His face was blank and large. "I have to let your mother have you."

My mother was screaming, "Jimmy, you give her to me. She's my child. Mine."

Jimmy pushed me forward with his knuckles on my back, and then she had me. When she shook me against the refrigerator, Ben ran out the door. None of them looked while we fought. They turned their backs. Jimmy left then, too, the screen door slamming. Carol followed, shaking her head, and they were gone—a family.

I fought back, I kicked and bit and pulled hair. I fought as if I were fighting to live. She always said I turned animal, wild. And there was something in that. I could feel something, the way my lips went curled on my teeth, the backs of my knees.

Later, I'd be in bed, swollen and touchy, not moving, and the house would seem absolutely still. The sheet felt light, incredibly light on my skin. My grandmother made up her own bed for me, with new sheets dried out on the line. They helped me after, but then I didn't care anymore.

When I was better again, up and running around, my mother still hadn't forgiven me. She drew it out. Those days she ignored me, came in the house like a stranger, as if she had no relation. She left me to my grandmother's care. She'd roll up her pants from the ankles and push up her shirt sleeves to show her cuts and bruises.

"Look what she did to me," she told the mailman on the porch. "She's wild. A little vicious animal."

Maybe it was the same as later, for her it was all one circle, coming back to the same place, when we made up. In the middle of the night, she woke me and wanted to talk. She looked hard into my eyes, sincere and promising, touched me where I didn't want her to touch, told me again and again that she'd never leave me, when I wasn't worried that she would.

"Okay," I always said.

The last time my mother let me out by the side of the road was in Nevada. I don't know why she stopped after that, maybe just because we were almost to California. It was different to let me out on the highway than it would be someplace we lived. I was old enough to get in trouble.

That last time in Nevada was different, too. Because she left me out on the road just a mile or two up past an Arco station. I could see the building in the distance. She let me off and drove out of sight, but this time I didn't cry. I started walking, in the ditch, back towards the filling station. I wanted to make a phone call.

There are more important things than love, I was thinking. Because I didn't want to talk to Benny then, he was just a year older, there was nothing he could do.

I got to the gas station. I didn't have any money, but my mind was made up. I went over to a teenage boy who was leaning against a pump, sucking an empty Coke bottle, and asked if I could borrow a dime. He dug into his jeans pocket and pulled one out.

"Don't have to pay me back. You can keep it." When I was walking to the corner of the lot, to the telephone, he said, "Hey. Hey, girl. Where're you from?"

The dime activated the telephone and I told the operator collect call from Ann. Then I stood there waiting for the phone to ring. The static of the line was enough: I could see the old black phone, where it sat on the kitchen counter, breathing silently before it rang. I knew the light there this time of day, the way the vinyl chairs felt, warm and slick from the sun, on your thighs. I thought of the cut cake under the clear glass cover, frosting melting down onto the plate, like candle wax. The empty hallways were clean, roses in the carpet down the middle, strips of wood floor showing at the edges. Clean white lace covered all the dark wood surfaces in the house. Out windows, the yard moved, never still, shimmering, the fields rustled a little, the old barn that used to be a butter factory just on the edge of view.

The phone rang once. I heard it going through the empty house. Maybe my grandmother was out in the yard or at the Red Owl. She could be watering at the cemetery. I was sure, then, no one would be home. And Ted would be working, Jimmy might be on the road.

"Hullo?" My grandmother's voice sounded so exactly like her that I almost hung up. For the first time, the telephone seemed miraculous to me. I looked around at the poles and wires on the dry hills. We were anywhere. I didn't know where.

"Collect call from Ann?" the operator said. "Will you accept the charges?"

"Why sure. Ann, tell me, where are you?"

"I'm fine. I'm in Nevada."

Then the operator clicked off the phone. It was like other people on the old party line, hanging up.

"Well, tell me what you've been doing." She was perplexed. I could hear, she was trying to find out if I was in trouble.

"I don't know. Nothing much. Driving."

There was a billboard across the highway, the paper peeling off, flapping. It was a family, in a red car, advertising the state of Nevada.

"Well, are you having fun?"

"Yeah, I guess."

"Tell me, is there anything you need, Ann?"

That made me wince, so I couldn't say a word. I held the phone a foot away from me. I wanted to go home, but I couldn't ask for a thing. It was too hard to explain.

The house there seemed small then, still and away from everything. I tried to get my normal voice.

"No, I just called to say hello."

"Well, good. That's fine. We sure do miss you around here." She was tapping something. She kept her nails long, filed in ovals and unpolished. She tapped them against her front teeth. "Is your ma nearby?"

"She's in the bathroom," I said.

"Well, I love you. We all do." Then she was quiet from the embarrassment of having said that.

"Bye."

"Shouldn't I hold on a second and talk to your ma?"

"Nah, she takes a long time in there. With her makeup, you know."

"I suppose she hasn't changed then."

"No."

I hung up the phone and the house back at home closed again, silent and private. I couldn't see inside anymore. It was small and neat, far away. I sank back against the outside wall of the phone booth, letting the wind come to my face. There were low blue hills in the distance.

"Hey, girl, wanna take a ride?"

I crossed my arms and began to say no, but just then my mother's car started coming back over the horizon and so I turned and waited. She slowed down up the road where she'd left me.

Maybe that was why this was the last time it happened: because I wasn't there. The car crawled, slowly, towards the station. She was look-ing for me. I stood kicking the pavement, in no hurry for her to get there. The fields were plain and dry. Air above the tar pavement shimmered in ankle-deep waves. In a bucket by the pumps, water sparkled, dark and bright.

When my mother saw me, she stopped the car and got out.

"Ann, you nearly scared me to—"

The boy whistled. I smiled and stared down at the blacktop. He was looking at my legs.

"Ann. Get in the car," my mother said.

In my seat, I still saw him. I closed my fist around the dime.

"Who were you calling, tell me."

She was looking at me, waiting. I had to answer.

"No one."

She sighed and started the car.

"Just hold your horses until we get there, okay? Your grandmother's old, leave her be. She hasn't got that long anymore."

I dragged my cupped hand out the window and the moving air felt solid, like a breast.

She was better. I could tell. She drove evenly and her shoulders dropped. Her foot pumped gradually, modulating the speed.

"Are you hungry?" she said. "'Cause I am. I could go for a little some-thing."

All those times on the highway, it was doing something. I lost time there in the ditches, waiting. Minutes out of my life. It was as if I had millions of clocks ticking inside me and each time one stopped. I left one clock, dead and busted, on the gravel by the side of the road, each time.

I didn't say anything. The highway was clean and straight. I rested back in my seat.

"Huh, what do you say, Pooh?" She was trying to make up.

I held out, I was quiet. She clutched the steering wheel and the blood drained from her knuckles. I squeezed my fist. I could feel my palm sweating as if it would rust the metal of the dime. I wouldn't look at her.

But thinking was too hard. She was my mother and she was driving and we were almost to California.

I was quiet as long as I could be, but she would still have me for a long time. It was easier to talk.

"There's a sign," I said, finally. "A Travel Inn Hobo Joe's."

"Hungry?" she said, glad and loud.

I thought of the french fries, the chocolate malteds, as much as I wanted from the menu. "Starving," I said.

2

Bel Air Hotel

I wonder what we looked like then, that day we drove over into California. My mother could probably still tell you what we were wearing. I remember she looked at me and then at herself in the rearview mirror as we neared the border. She wriggled in her seat.

That morning, she'd shouted, "Look at those fields. Should we stop, Annie? I think they're tomatoes. Yep. They are. Look at those beefsteaks!" She'd skidded to a stop that would have been dangerous if the highway hadn't been so empty. We'd climbed out and picked tomatoes, eating them right there in the field.

We stole vegetables all across America, anything we could eat without cooking. My mother spotted the trucks.

"Oh, Ann. Look. Sweet peas," she'd say. The trucks of peas were open-backed, the vines clumped in bundles. We followed those trucks anywhere, turning off into towns we'd never heard of and then waiting till the first stoplight, when my mother sent me out with a five-dollar bill to the driver. The windows of the cabs were high and I had to jump to knock. The drivers never touched our money. They shrugged and smiled and said, You go on ahead, take what you want, then. And we loaded up the whole backseat of the car, from the floor to the roof, with the sweet, heavy-scented vines.

Sometimes on the highway, loads of peas would drop off the truckbeds and bounce on the concrete like tumbleweed. We pulled onto the gravel shoulder and ran out and chased them, laughing on the hot empty road, the flat country still on all sides of us.

That last morning in Nevada we'd bought nine melons, big melons, each too heavy for one hand. We'd tasted samples from toothpicks on ragged, wet paper plates. We'd never imagined how many kinds of melons there could be. And they were all sweet.

But when we crossed the Nevada border some men made us stop. We couldn't take our melons into California. It was still not noon and already hot. We pulled onto the shoulder of the road. When the man told us we couldn't bring our melons in, my mother stood out of the car and cried. She talked to him, saying the same things again and again, while he shook his head no. He seemed to have all the time in the world. A green fly landed on his forehead and it took him a good forty seconds to lift up his hand and shoo it. I backed the car onto the grass and started hauling out melons. My mother screamed. I was twelve years old. I wasn't supposed to know how to drive.

We didn't have a knife or anything. We split the melons open, smashing them on the legs of the sign that said WELCOME TO CALIFORNIA and we stood on the concrete platform eating them, the juice spilling down our arms.

Our shirts were still sticky and sweet smelling, but the bad, sour side of sweet, when we drove into Los Angeles. My mother had called ahead for reservations at one of the hotels she'd read about, but she wouldn't go there right away.

"Huh-uh. Look at us. And look at this car. We can't go like this. We're going to clean up a little first."

"They're used to it, they're a hotel, aren't they?"

"Honey, the Bel Air isn't just a hotel." She had the tone she always had when she was too tired to fight. "You'll see."

"Why can't we wash up there?"

"*Because.* That's why. You just don't. Listen to me once in a while." Then it seemed she'd brought me all the way to California just to make me mind.

She parked in front of a restaurant near the campus of UCLA. "This looks like a good little place. And we can have a bite to eat. Hamburger Hamlet, it's called. Cute."

She took our gingham dresses from the trunk. They were still in their dry-cleaning cellophane. Two men leaned against the building. They had tie-dyed sheets spread out on the sidewalk with buckles and leather belts for sale. We stood there staring down, entranced. They were slow and graceful, smoking.

"What are you looking at? Come on," my mother said. The ladies' room was upstairs in the restaurant. "Those kids are on drugs," she whispered. "They're hooked on marijuana." My mother had read about drugs.

She always read the magazines. Now she listens to talk radio. But even then she knew what drugs were.

In the rest room my mother plugged her steam rollers into the wall socket and unpacked her cosmetics and soaps, lining them up on the counter. She used the row of sinks as if this was her own huge dressing room. She turned on a hand dryer and touched up her nails, holding them under the warm air.

She washed, shaved her underarms and ripped open a fresh package of nylons. She clipped the hot rollers into her hair. She stood in pantyhose and a bra, starting on her makeup. She didn't dally, watching other people. Strangers touched their hands under thin streams of water in the sink farthest from us and my mother didn't notice. She was driven. The will to be clean.

"Ann," she called then, looking for me in the mirror. I was standing by the door. "Comemeer."

"My name is Heather," I said. While we were driving she told me I could pick a new name for myself in California. It would be my television name.

"Heather, then. You know who I mean." She sniffed me. "You smell," she said, and handed me a towel. "Let's have some scrubbing action. Get undressed and hurry it up."

I washed standing on one leg, the other foot on my knee, swishing the towel around lightly. Other women disciplined their eyes to look away from us, cut a hole in the air and avoided falling into it again.

They saw me as a Theresa Griling. It's a long story, this girl I knew at home. I was beginning to understand how someone could become a long story.

My mother didn't notice the other women, but she saw that I was embarrassed. All of a sudden she saw that. And it must have seemed like a defeat. She'd driven all that way and now we were here and I was ashamed of her.

She sighed one of her sighs. "Comemeer," she said. She brushed blush on my cheeks. "Listen. Nobody cares, do you hear? They don't give a hoot. They can think we wanted to wash up before we eat. They can see we've been traveling. They don't want you to stay dirty."

I must have looked pale standing there, because she pushed some lipstick over my lips. They were chapped and I wouldn't stand still, so she smeared a little and licked her finger to clean the edge of my mouth. I ran over to the sink and spit. I tasted her saliva, it was different from mine.

I felt something then, as I stood watching my spit twirl down the drain. I wanted to get away from her. There was nowhere I could go. I was twelve. She'd have me six more years.

My mother examined us in the mirror and sighed. She held my chin up and looked at us both. She'd been right. We did look much better. She gathered our things back into the suitcase and snapped the buckle shut. "See, all done," she said. "Doesn't it feel good to be clean?"

We found eight car washes in Westwood that afternoon but they were all the drive-through kind. My mother wasn't going to trust them with our Lincoln. She would now, but we were new then.

"You wouldn't do it by *hand*?" She was standing on the blacktop talking to a boy who looked as if she were asking for the world. "I mean, I'll pay you. *Ex*-tra. I just don't want those hard detergents on it. They'll hurt the finish." She ran her hand on the car top. It was still smooth and new. This was a long time ago.

"You can wash it yourself, lady," the boy said, walking off. He walked with his head tilted slightly back, as if he owned the sky.

My mother sat down again in the car. "You know, I guess we could," she said. "I guess we could do it ourselves." She started to unpack the backseat.

"Heather, go." She gave me a five-dollar bill. "Give him this and say we want rags for the windows and stuff to clean the seats. Oh, and ask if they have a little vacuum cleaner, too. Go on."

She already had our one suitcase out and the trunk open. My mounted child's ice skates were on the pavement next to a tire.

The boy stood hosing off the wheels of a Jeep. "Hurry up," my mother yelled, but I kept sluffing. I didn't care about the car being clean. If it was mine, I'd have just left it dirty. She would say I never learned to take care of a thing.

I stood with the five-dollar bill stuck in my hand, looking down at the cement ramps by the gas pumps.

"Could we please buy rags and cleaning stuff and also possibly rent a vacuum cleaner?"

The kid laughed. "What kind of cleaning stuff?"

I shrugged. "For the outside and for the seats."

"Gonna do it yourself, huh?"

"She wants to."

He put the hose down, not turning it off, so a stream of water dribbled down the blacktop. He stuffed a bucket with rags and plastic bottles. "You have to pull up here for the vacuum. You just pull on up when you ready."

"Thank you."

"I don't know how much to charge you for this stuff. Five dollars probably be too much. You not going to use that much fluid."

"She might. You better take it."

He laughed. "She might, huh? She always like that?"

My top lip pulled down over my teeth. "Oh, no, she's usually not that bad. We just moved here. Just today."

"Oh, I see. Well, makes sense. Anxious to get the car cleaned, huh?"

"Yeah."

But we kept looking at each other, his chin tucked down against his neck and his eyes dropping open, until my mother called.

"Heather, hurry it up. It's already four o'clock."

"That your name, Heather?" He picked up his hose again.

"Yeah," I said. "Thanks."

Torches flared on both sides of the road that led to the Bel Air Hotel. The path wound in and out of woods. My mother drove real slow. She parked underneath the awning. I moved to get out but she stopped me and told me to wait. She rested her hands on the steering wheel the way she used to for years on top of my shoulders. The valet came and opened the doors, her door first and then mine. She wasn't shy to relinquish the car now. There was nothing embarrassing in it. It was clean. The leather smelled of Windex.

At the desk a man shuffled through his book. "We've put you in the tower, which is a lovely room, but there's only one bed. A double. I'm afraid it's all we have left."

My mother let a frown pass over her face, for appearances. We'd slept in doubles all the way across America. She didn't like to sleep alone. I did. She was frowning for me to see, too.

"That will be all right." She shrugged.

Following the valet to our room, we let ourselves relax. I bumped against the wall and she let me bump because I was clean. The stucco seemed to absorb amber evening light.

We walked through an outdoor courtyard. There was a small café; white tablecloths, white chairs, the distant slap and shuffle of late swimmers. People at the tables were drinking, lingering in daytime clothes.

We climbed stone steps to the tower. My mother tipped the valet and then closed the door behind us. I crossed my arms over my chest. She looked at me and asked, "What's the matter with you now? Don't tell me even this doesn't satisfy you."

She stood looking around the room. And it was a beautiful hotel.

But I was thinking about us on our hands and knees, our butts sticking out the car door, scrubbing the melon juice stains off the leather. The afternoon canceled out now. My mother was not that way. She could hold contrasts in her mind at once. She must have found me horribly plain.

"It's nice," I said.

A green and white polished cotton canopy shaded the four-poster bed. My mother kicked her shoes off and collapsed. I sat on the window seat, my leg swinging over the side. My jacket hung on the back of a chair where I'd left it. She hooked it with her bare foot and brought it to her face. Then she tried it on, adjusting the collar, turning it up.

I looked at her—she was standing on the bed, barefoot, her toenails polished a light shade of pink, glancing in the mirror. "Take my jacket off," I said, cranking the window open. It wasn't warm but my arm was pumping as if I needed air.

"It fits me. You don't know what a cute little shape I have, for a mother. Pretty darn good for my age."

"Can we afford this place?" I wasn't looking at her anymore. My face was out the window, gulping the night. I watched the waiters move, beautifully, around the glows of candles on the little tables. One man cupped his hand over a woman's to light a cigarette. My mother's fingers spidered on my back.

"I'll worry about that, okay? I'm the adult and you're the child. And don't you forget that."

"Don't I wish I could."

"Well, you can. So start right now." She laughed, half a laugh, almost a laugh.

"I'm hungry."

"Should we call room service?"

"No, I want to go out."

I hardly ever said things like that. I was afraid I would be blamed for wanting too much, but that night it seemed I had to go outside. I didn't like being just with my mother all the time. You were alone but she was there. My mother must have felt that too, but I think it was one of the things she liked about having a daughter. You never were all alone.

"I don't know, I'd just as soon have something here, now that we're parked and all. To tell the truth, I'm sick of this driving. You don't know, you haven't been doing it, but it tires you. You can't believe how my shoulders feel. They ache, Heather-honey, they really ache. Twenty-one, twenty-two, let's see, we left the fifth, do you realize, we've been on the road sixteen days. No, the fifth to the, today's—"

"We can go here. You don't have to drive. There's a restaurant down there."

Her head turned. She looked a little startled; she always did when she was interrupted from one of her long songs. "Oh, okay. Fine. That's fine. It's just this driving, seventeen days, day in, day out, eight hours a day behind that wheel and boy, you feel it, you feel it right—"

I stood up and walked to the door, my jacket hooked on one finger. "Let's go."

"Well, would you just wait a second, please, and let me wash my face? And I want to put on a little bit of makeup."

I sat on the steps and listened to her vigorous washing. She slapped her face, her feet thumping on the bathroom floor.

"It's going to be a few minutes," she said.

And it was. The sky went from deep blue to purple to black in the time it took my mother to get ready. I sat on the steps watching other people come to the café, sit down and drink, clinking their glasses together. I saw a man reach across a table and rummage underneath a woman's hair, as if there were something to find.

My mother was humming, standing with her back to me.

When she stepped outside, I sniffed loudly to let her know I didn't like perfume. I was wearing my regular afternoon clothes, and she'd put on a long dress, with a slit up the back. She was the adult, I was the child. She wore pearls and heels, her hair was teased two inches out from her face.

I rolled up the sleeves of my shirt. I have the kind of arms you roll sleeves up on. My mother is softer, plush.

"Well," she said, making noises around her, the pearls, the cotton swishing, "are we ready?" She was talking in an octave higher than her normal voice, a voice to be overheard.

"What do you think?" I shoved my hands in my pockets and started down the stairs. She clattered behind me.

"Wait, wait, would you? Go a little slower, please. You don't know what it's like up here. I mean on these heels." She put her hands on my shoulders. "My balance isn't what it should be. It's fine, in the morning, I'm fine. But by this time of day, you're just going to have to slow down. Please."

"Why do you wear them, then?"

"Honey, you know. They look nice." She caught up to me and grabbed my arm, falling a little. "At my age, they expect you to have a little height. And who knows, maybe I'll meet someone tonight, you never know. And I'd hate to meet the right man when I had on the wrong shoe."

But my mother seemed to gain balance when we waited at the café entrance. I was glad to be with her then. I was glad to have her in those shoes. I stood close by her, when I was shy.

"Two for dinner?"

"Please," she said, her chin high, following him. She knew how to do these things.

We got a small table at the edge of the courtyard with its own glowing candle, like the rest. We didn't look at each other at first, we looked at the people around us. I didn't see any free men for her.

My mother opened the menu. "Wow," she whispered, "a wee bit pricey."

"Room service would be just the same."

"Not necessarily. But that's okay. We're here now, so fine. Well, I know what I'm having. I'm having a glass of wine and a cup of soup." Even that was going to be expensive.

"I'm hungry," I said. I was mad. I wasn't going to have any soup or salad. If we could afford to stay here then we could afford to eat, and I was going to eat.

The waiter came and my mother ordered her glass of wine and cup of soup. "Is that all, ma'am?"

"I think so. We had a late lunch."

I ordered a steak and began answering the waiter's long string of questions. Baked potato. Oil and vinegar. Beans instead of rice.

My mother kicked my shin, hard, under the table.

"Didn't you want a hamburger? I don't know if you saw, but they have them."

"No, I'd rather have a steak."

"Oh, okay, fine. Whatever you want. It's just that you said you wanted a hamburger. You said it this afternoon."

Then the waiter left us alone. My mother leaned over the table and whispered. "Didn't you see me winking at you, you dummy? Didn't you feel me kick? I can't afford this. What do you think you're doing? Jesus. You saw what I ordered, didn't you? Don't you think I'm hungry? Am I supposed to starve myself so you can have a steak?"

"Why didn't you order yourself a steak?"

"Boy," she said, "I can't believe how dumb you are sometimes. We can't *afford* this."

"So why are we here? Why aren't we somewhere we can afford? I asked you upstairs and you said I shouldn't worry, that you were the adult and I was the child."

"Well, children order hamburgers when they go out to expensive restaurants. That's all they're allowed to order."

"Then, why didn't you change it? Go ahead. Tell the waiter I can't have my steak."

"I don't believe you. You shouldn't have ordered it! You felt my foot under the table, you just wanted your steak. Well, fine, you can have it now and you'd better enjoy it, because believe me, it's the last steak you'll get for a while."

She sank back into her chair, her arms lapsing on the armrests. Our waiter arrived with her wine.

"Everything all right?"

A smile came reflexively to her face. "Lovely, just lovely."

She'd had it with me. She pretended that she simply wasn't hungry. As if not wanting things was elegant, but wanting them and not being able to get them was not.

She leaned over the table again.

"If you were so hungry, why didn't you order more at lunch? You love hamburgers. You usually always order a hamburger."

"I do not *love* hamburgers."

"Yes you do." She sighed. "Why can't it ever just be nice? Why can't we ever just have a nice, relaxing time?"

"In other words why can't I just want a hamburger, why can't I want what you want me to want. Why don't I always just happen to want the cheapest thing on the menu."

"That's what I do, why can't you?" she said. "Don't you think *I'm* hungry after all that driving?"

"You can have some of mine."

"No." She shook her head. "I don't want any. It's yours. You ordered it, now you eat it." She looked around the café. "There's nothing for me here. I wanted to just stay in and have something quick from room service. Not get all dressed up. I just wanted to relax for once."

Our food came and I stopped looking at her. I started cutting my steak. It was thick and glistening with fat. I put all four rounds of butter in the baked potato. Steam rose up in spirals. Then I shook on salt, spooned in sour cream. It looked delicious. She took a sip of her soup.

"So how is it?"

I said fine, still looking at my plate.

"How's the salad? You haven't touched the salad."

"Uh-huh," I said, still eating.

"Try the vegetables, you need those vitamins." She put down her spoon. "Would you like a taste of my soup? It's delicious, really, these little bits of carrot. They're grated very finely. I wonder what they use. It tickles your throat when it goes down, like lots of little sparks."

She was even smiling.

"No thank you," I said.

She did the talking while I ate. "You know, you're really right. This is a lovely place. Lovely. The pool over there, can you hear it? That little glup, glup, glup? And this air. I love these warm, dry nights. I wonder how cold it gets in winter. I know we won't need really heavy coats, coats like we had at home, but do you think we'll even need any? Light coats? Sort of raincoat-ish? I'd love to have a trench."

Then I set my silverware down. I guess I was finally full. Now I looked around, too, and up at the starless sky. "The air is nice," I said.

"Are you finished with that?"

"What? Oh, the steak?"

"I thought if you were I'd try a bite."

I shoved the whole plate over to her side. I passed her the salad and the dish of vegetables.

"Oh, no, I just want a little bite."

"Try the vegetables. They're very good." I knew if she finished my dinner, that would be the last I'd hear about the bill.

She sighed and settled in her chair. "Oh, it is. Very, very good." She leaned over and whispered to me. "You know, for what you get, these prices really aren't so bad. This is enough for the two of us, really. You know?"

Later the waiter came for our plates. All that was left was parsley. "I'll take that," my mother said and grabbed the sprig from his tray. He must have thought we were starving. But my mother really always had liked parsley.

"Will that be all? Or can I get you some dessert and coffee?"

My mother winked. "No coffee, please. But I think we'd like to see a menu for dessert. And would you like a glass of milk, Young Lady?"

I looked up at the waiter. "I'd like coffee please. With cream and sugar."

He left, to bring the dessert tray. My mother looked at me suspiciously and smiled. "Ann, now tell me, when did you learn to drink coffee? Were you just bluffing or did you learn? Look me in the eye and tell me true."

We shared the cup when it came. She took a sip, then I took a sip.

"With you," I said. "I learned from you."

I could see her looking at me, wondering. But she let it go and she let the bill go, too. Now, I'm glad she did. You grow up and you leave them. She only had me six more years.

3

The House on Carriage Court

We were leaving the house on Carriage Court and Ted the ice skating pro. We'd met Ted when we took skating lessons, first to firm my mother's thighs, then just for fun. All day the air conditioners in the arena hummed like the inside of a refrigerator. On the door of my locker hung a picture of Peggy Fleming; on my mother's, Sonja Henie. Framed photographs of Ted during his days with Holiday on Ice hung in the main office, next to the list of hourly prices. In them, he didn't look like himself. He was young. He had short, bristly hair and a glamorous smile. His limbs stretched out, starlike, pointing to the four corners of the photographs. The lighting seemed yellow and false. In one of the pictures, it was snowing.

In spring, three years before we left, my mother had gone to Las Vegas and married Ted. She came back without any pictures of the wedding and we moved into the house on Carriage Court. She said she hadn't wanted a big wedding, since it was her second marriage. She'd worn a short dress she already had.

When my mother and Ted came home from Las Vegas they took me for a ride in Ted's car. He turned into a development on the west side of the Fox River and they told me they'd bought a new house. Before, we'd lived all our lives with my grandmother.

"Guess which," my mother had said, looking back at me from the front seat. Ted drove a white Cadillac, with a maroon interior and roof.

I knew, I could tell from their faces. They'd bought the rectangular house with no windows. "I hope it's not that one," I pointed. "Because that one looks like a shoebox." They didn't say anything, Ted just kept driving. Finally, my mother sighed.

It turned out a young architect had built it. He loved the house. He was only leaving because the house was too small for another child.

After we moved into the house on Carriage Court, my mother and I stopped taking lessons. Ted could fill up the ice with other students and that way he made more money. I quit skating altogether. Eventually, my mother stopped, too. Then Ted went to the rink himself every day, like any other man going to a job.

My mother and I seemed different in the new house. I was always in trouble. Neither of us could remember a time anymore when I wasn't always in trouble. There were rules. We were not supposed to open the refrigerator with our hands, which would smear the bright, chrome, new handle, but by a sideways nudge from an elbow. "Here," my mother demonstrated, showing me how to pull my sleeve over my fist like a mitten if I really had to touch the handle with my hand. Now that she was married, my mother decorated the inside of the refrigerator. All our jars were lined up according to size.

Sinks and faucets were supposed to be polished with a towel after every time you used them. Then the towel had to be folded in thirds and hung up again on the rack. Ted went along with all this, I suppose because he loved her.

And now that we lived on our own, we had the same thing for dinner every night: thick, wobbly steaks, which my mother served with baked potatoes. She also gave us each a plate-sized salad. Ted thought salad dressing was gauche, so we sprinkled the lettuce with salt and red wine vinegar. We didn't have any furniture in the house, except for two beds. We sat on a bed and balanced the plates on our laps.

My mother read health books. She read books by Gaylord Hauser about how he kept movie stars on sets in California looking fresh at four in the afternoon by serving them health food protein snacks. She served us protein snacks. Once a week, she broiled a châteaubriand, which Ted sliced for her. She arranged the pink rectangular pieces on a plate and kept them in the refrigerator under a sheet of Saran Wrap. We ate them cold, with salt. She made us steak tartare for breakfast. She bought ground tenderloin and mixed it with pepper and capers and two egg yolks. We ate breakfast at the counter, standing up. We spread the meat on buttered whole wheat toast.

There were nights I remembered before they were married, when Ted and my mother had eaten late in the gray television light of my grandmother's living room. They sat in chairs with standing TV trays. I saw them when I came down for a glass of water. Then, the rare, thick steaks, moving on their plates when they touched them with knives, running with the shiny, red-gold juice, seemed to make my whole face swell with longing.

Now, in the new house on Carriage Court, I wanted anything else. All meat tasted the same to me. It tasted the way my skin tasted, like a sucked piece of my own arm. I asked my mother for tuna casserole. But she only laughed.

She told me other people ate tuna because it was cheap. Plus it wasn't healthy. Anyway, she and Ted liked meat.

"Very few men are as clean as Ted," my mother told her friend Lolly. There was nowhere to sit in the new rectangular house on Carriage Court, so they stood, holding their coffee cups. Lolly was another woman from Bay City who'd gone away to college and then come back home to her mother. The way my mother sighed and drummed her fingers on the bare wall, it made you think she was a little sorry Ted was so clean. She might have wished he weren't always malleable. She sighed again. Still, she wasn't sure. There was a row of unpacked brown boxes, and I perched crosslegged on one of them. "I'm neat," my mother said, "I just always have been. I can't *stand* messes."

That was a total lie. But Lolly nodded, sipping her coffee. I was thinking of the inside of my mother's purse, of all my mother's purses. In the house on Lime Kiln Road, she'd kept them in a closet, lined up on a shelf. In each one was a nest of old things, brushes, hair, bobby pins, makeup spilled and then hardened, so that the old orange powder and ink stained the lining, broken pencils, scraps of paper, little address books, all worn and woven together into something whole. But no one saw inside them except me.

"Honey, if I've told you once, I've told you a hundred times, don't sit on those boxes, for God's sakes! You don't know what's inside where! I swear, if I open them and find broken dishes, you're going to go out and work to buy new ones."

I jumped off and went to the kitchen. I had no doubt that I'd always be in trouble from now on. There were so many things to remember. Even when I tried I made mistakes. A minute later, I was in trouble in the kitchen for eating grapes from their stems, instead of breaking off my own little cluster.

My mother reached down, out of nowhere in the morning, and laid her cool hand like an envelope on my forehead.

"Where does it hurt?" We didn't have a thermometer in the house on Carriage Court; she would have to decide. She worked and she always ran late in the morning, so she would have to settle this fast.

"All over," I said. "My throat."

She was looking out the window, running through the day ahead, far away, in the out-of-town school. She didn't want to make a mistake. Well, it could never hurt to rest, she seemed to be thinking. She sighed. "Okay, stay here and sleep. Just stay home. Tomorrow, I'll write you a note."

Now that we lived in the new house, I stayed home alone when I was sick. The moisture from my mother's hand felt good on my forehead and the distant slamming of the front door sounded like relief in my side. I spread out in my bed and moved, falling slowly into another red warm sleep. It was familiar to be sick, I was returning to a place already known. Turning in bed, under the cool sheets, all the sick days seemed the same, crystallized like cabins along one lake, spanning all my childhood years. Outside the smallest hung my red and blue plaid jumper, my first-grade Catholic school uniform, and in a corner my grandmother stood shaking a thermometer, reading it by the window light, where a beating humming-bird fed at the red glass dropper just on the other side of the screen. In another cabin, I was nine and pretending to be sick: the distant bell rang, faintly, and a test was being given in the gray-green public school. In the fourth-grade trailer, children handed papers back from the front of every row. The harder glittering objects of my healthy passions expired in my exhaustion. I loved the familiar here. The nicked wood of my old dresser, the kitchen table from Lime Kiln Road. I wanted my own mother's hand.

When I woke up, snow fell softly at the window and the black and white television was on. Lucy and Ethel were trying to steal John Wayne's footprints from the cement outside of Grauman's Chinese Theatre in old Hollywood.

I stayed in bed and watched the reruns and time fell off in half-hour segments. Then I got up to get something to eat. The kitchen was dry and bright with sun. It was late morning. Everyone was out to work. I made a big breakfast to make me feel better. I scrambled eggs and mixed up frozen orange juice. I finished and went back to my room. I wasn't sure anymore if I was sick or not.

And then I heard the noon bell from school. Out my window, there was an aluminum fence and a vacant lot two yards down. I saw my friends from school come back on the path for lunch, their parka hoods down, their black rubber boots unbuckled and flapping.

I ducked. I didn't want them to see me. I wasn't sick enough not to care.

I decided in the glittering noon light that I would get dressed and go to school. I'd tell my teacher I was sick in the morning but I felt better now. I would bring a note from my mother tomorrow. Afternoon was easier anyway. Geography and science and an hour of reading before I would come home, at three o'clock with the others.

I went to my dresser and got tights. Standing up too fast made my head spin and I had to sit down on the bed for a while before it was still again. Then I went to my closet and pulled on a dress over my head. I felt dizzy and hot inside, but I went to the bathroom and brushed my hair. I could hardly feel it. It was like brushing someone else's hair. I steadied my hand on the cool tiles.

I went to the front closet and got on boots and my coat and mittens— I wanted to be all ready to go. I stacked my schoolbooks up on the kitchen counter, my pencil case on top. I stood in the closet and rummaged through my mother's and Ted's coat pockets for money. I took a dollar from Ted's jacket, the paper folded and soft as a Kleenex, and put it in my mitten. Then I sat down in our only chair, waiting for it to be time.

I was floppy in the chair. I felt whatever strength I had seeping out into the upholstery. The walk would be the hard thing, then I would be at my desk at school. Finally, it was time to go. Early, but time. I got up and went to the kitchen to get my books. I was counting things off. I took the balled gray string with my key from my pocket and locked the door behind me. I walked down our driveway to the street. The snow had soaked into the ground already. The plowed, wet pavement seemed very bright.

With each step I felt less sure of myself. I felt myself walking like my grandmother walked, as she stood up out of her car when there was ice on the drive, dizzy.

I turned around and went back home. I closed the door behind me and locked it, pulled off my boots and hung up my coat. I took my clothes off and got into bed again. I fell into a light, warm sleep. Now I didn't care.

I woke up later, hearing the shouts of my friends on the path, coming home from school. They looked fine, themselves, through for the day. You weren't finished with a sick day at three o'clock. You didn't get through being sick until the next morning. I'd still be wearing my same pajamas tonight when my mother and Ted came in from outside. I felt the back of my neck under my hair. I turned on the TV again for the after-school cartoons.

It was dark then and I was glad, because all the other kids would be inside, doing homework and getting ready for supper. There was something about the stillness of our house, though. It was empty and dry and I wished my mother would come home.

The front door slammed. I knew it was my mother, not Ted, from the way she moved around in the kitchen, the double echo of her high heels. I heard the pan I'd left on the stove clatter against the porcelain of the sink. The refrigerator door opened and closed. Then her footsteps were coming and she stood in my doorway, clicking on the overhead light. I was still watching television, another "I Love Lucy," an older one back in New York.

"So what did you do all day?" She looked over the room, her hands on her hips. "Besides making a mess. I thought you might at least vacuum or do a little *something* around here. I can't do everything, you know. I can't work and shop and clean and then come home and clean up again after you. You could've eaten a can of tuna, like I do for lunch, but no, you had to dirty a pan and there's crumbs all over the counter." She clicked the TV off and I felt the loss of the small apartment, the tiny furniture, like a quick pain.

"I'm sick, Mom."

"You're not that sick. I'm sick too, I have a sore throat and I still went to work. Now, come on, get up and you're going to clean that kitchen."

Maybe I should have vacuumed. I could have. Maybe I wasn't that sick. There were obvious things I didn't seem to see. I never in a million years would have thought of vacuuming.

I started doing the dishes. It was easy. I felt warm inside and dizzy. I kept scrubbing and scrubbing at the pan, looking out the window into the dark. The water felt good on my hands.

My mother came up behind me and touched my hair. "I'm sorry for yelling like I did. I guess I'm tired, too, you know? We both just need a rest."

. . .

We weren't popular on Carriage Court. My mother and Ted didn't talk to other people. You saw the others out grilling in their front yards and settling sprinklers on the grass after dark, but my mother and Ted stayed inside. Our first summer, a posse of three fathers from the end of the block came to tell Ted how to mow the lawn. I stood behind the screen door, listening. They were all nice, looking at their hands while they talked, their shoes shuffling on the porch. Ted was nice, too, inviting them in for a drink.

When the men moved towards the door I ran to my room and cried. From the open windows I heard the shouts of a kickball game starting up. I wouldn't go outside then, everyone would know. They must have known already. They probably thought of me as the girl with the overgrown lawn.

A little while later my mother came in and sat next to me on my bed. "Aw, honey, I know just how you feel."

I pushed her and she faltered and fell off, onto the floor. It took a moment to get up. "Oh." She was genuinely shocked. I studied my hand. I was surprised, too. I didn't think I'd pushed her that hard. She looked at me again, brushing off her white sharkskin slacks. "Oh, you little monster."

Her arm came near my face and I hit her.

After that, she left. I heard the two of them moving in the kitchen, but no one came to my room. The house seemed unusually quiet, I could hear the refrigerator humming. Finally, I got tired of being in bed and walked to the garage. I took out the lawn mower. We had the thin, manual kind you pushed, because my mother thought they were more elegant. We had a black one. My mother hated the noise that motors made, mowing.

It was really hard. I'd cut an uneven row of four feet, when Ted tried to take it from me.

"I'll do it, Ann."

My mother stuck her head out the screen door, holding the handle, as if, now that I'd hit her, she was afraid. "Annie, he made arrangements with the Kokowski boy to do it tomorrow morning. It's all set. We even paid him already."

But I couldn't think of anything else except getting the lawn done then. Ted had to pry my fingers one by one off the black handle. I was surprised when he held them, palms up, in his hand. The fingers and knuckles were red and scraped; I was bleeding. He looked down into my face, not letting go.

"Take it away from her, Ted." My mother, still inside, poked her head out, yelling. "She'll kill herself with it. Look at her, she's going crazy."

Ted's voice was gentle, almost a whisper. "I know you want it done now. I understand that. But I'll do it. Let me do it." I thought there was something wrong with his smile, though, his teeth looked like a zipper.

I stepped back, crossing my arms. I was looking down at my tennis shoes. The right one was ripped over the toes and there were grass stains, too.

Ted was stronger than I was. Each of his lunges mowed a five-foot row evenly.

"Oh, Ted, don't now," my mother called. "Why? We already paid him."

"It's all right, Adele. It won't take me long."

She let the screen door drop shut. "I just don't see why she always has to get her way. Every time she throws a tantrum, we give in."

I ran to the end of the block to the kickball game. When the Kokowski boy stole second base, he saw Ted on our lawn.

"Hey, your stepdad's mowing your yard. I was supposed to do it tomorrow."

"You better give him his money back," I said.

"So, how come he's doing it now? He sure waited long enough before."

"Want to fight over it?"

He said no, forget it, even though he was bigger than I was. I'm glad he did because the way I was right then I know I could have hurt him.

I lay on my stomach on the kitchen floor, drawing. My mother moved at the counter, washing food. It was four o'clock on a Sunday and the world, from our windows, stayed still.

For a long time, I colored my picture. All my drawing took a long time. I didn't like there to be any white left on the page. My third-grade nun had tacked my pictures up on the bulletin board in the hall. She had dunked my head over a drawing on a table to see the first place, blue ribbon in the crafts fair. She told me I was the best artist in primary school because I was patient. Then another boy moved to the district, a boy they didn't like because he couldn't sit still and because he wore clothes that were too small for him. Tim drew all the time, on everything. He could pencil psychedelic drum sets on the edge of his lined paper in three minutes and they pulsed against your eyes. Nobody else thought he was any good, but I didn't mind moving so much when we went to Carriage Court, because of Tim. I knew he was better.

I still drew at home, on the floor, and my mother never looked at the pictures. No one saw them except me.

That day she was standing at the window by the sink and I stopped. I put all my crayons away in the box and turned over the picture to the floor. Her shoulders were jumping.

I went over and touched her. She didn't seem to notice. "Mom," I whispered, ever so quiet, not wanting to disturb anything.

Then she looked down at me. "Was it better just the two of us?" She bit her lip, then shoved knuckles into her wobbling mouth. I looked up at her, still holding the end of her sweater. She'd stumped me, guessed what I always meant. If it was still just the two of us, we were going to move to California. So I could be a child star on television.

But I thought of Ted, then, the familiar sound of his car coming up our driveway, everything the way it was.

"Tell me, Bipper, were you happier without this man?"

"He's nice," I said.

"Do you really think so?"

I nodded, eagerly. We took the afternoon to make a surprise; we were both dressed up when he came home at seven for supper, the kitchen floor was waxed and glistening like ice. We must have seemed expectant, heads tilted, beaming, when he came to the door.

He looked from one of us to the other, bemused. "What's up?"

"Dinner in a sec," my mother said. She opened the broiler, poked the meat.

Then Ted did what he always did, he carried the black and white TV in from my room to the kitchen and flicked on the news. I crowded near my mother to fix the plates.

"Do you think he sees?" I said. Everything in the kitchen was clean and polished. We'd opened a new box of Arm & Hammer baking soda in the refrigerator.

"Absolutely." She nodded. "Comemeer." She walked over to a clean place on the counter. When I'd put away my picture, in a cupboard, she must have found it. Now she was looking down hard at it. I had been drawing grass, the individual stalks. There was still a field of white. It was only half finished.

"I thought it would be of me," she said.

I was in trouble all the time now.

On weekends, my mother and Ted slept late. I always snuck outside before they woke up. "A-yun," my mother called me one Saturday, yelling from the porch like other mothers. I wouldn't have gone in, but there was a whole kickball team of kids looking at me who went running when their mothers called.

"Be right back." I dropped the ball, knowing, as I said it, what the chances of that were.

My mother, seeing me, pulled her head back into the house like a turtle and slammed the door. Ted's car was gone from the driveway, that was bad. I walked slowly, staying out as long as I could. She stood just inside the door, in the entry hall. Even though it was a cool, bright day, our house seemed stale, as if the air was old. My mother was wearing nothing but Ted's old gray sweat shirt that she slept in.

"You really think you're the cat's meow, don't you," she said, looking at me and shaking her head. "You think you can just play, while I work and work and work. Sure, that's what mothers are for, isn't it, to slave away so you can have a nice house and clothes and food in the refrigerator when your friends come over. Sounds pretty good. Well, I'm sorry to tell you, but you're not going to get away with that anymore. You're going to have to start pulling your own weight."

Through the kitchen windows, the sky was clear and young, the palest blue.

"It's my fault too, I spoiled you. I should have let you cry when your father wanted to go dancing. I should've gone with him."

I started walking and her nails bit into my arm.

"Oh, no you don't. You're not going anywhere. You're going to stay right here and clean, for a change. You can see what I do all day Saturday and Sunday and that's my vacation. I work all week while you're playing."

"I go to school," I said.

She bent down over the vacuum cleaner. Hoses and brushes sprawled over the kitchen floor.

It was the same vacuum cleaner we'd always had, the Electrolux my father had given me rides on when I was a child. He'd pulled me on it all over my grandmother's house, bumping from the carpets onto the floors. We got it for free because it was my father's sample, when he worked as a vacuum cleaner salesman. "You go over EACH square FIVE times. THEN you move on to the next one." The kitchen was the only room in the new house that didn't have wood floors. The floor was black and white linoleum, checkered. It went on and on. There must have been hundreds of squares. I was counting up one side, to multiply with the other. "See, now watch carefully." My mother put all her weight into banging the long brush against the molding. Her legs moved with bitter, zealous energy.

"Mom, it's one o'clock. Why don't you put on some pants."

"Because *I've* been working all day, that's why, Little Miss."

"You've been sleeping is what you've been doing. And you go to anybody else's house and their mother's wearing pants. I don't care what you do, I just think it's ugly, that's all."

"Well, then, I'll tell you, Honey. Don't look. Because I'll wear whatever I want in my own house that I pay for—"

"Gramma paid for it."

"Ooo, you little—" She lifted the vacuum cleaner nozzle over her head ready to swing, but I jumped back and then she sucked in her breath. "Oh, no. No. You're not going to provoke a fight so you can run outside and get out of your chores. Oh, no you don't. You're a smart kid, but your mother's smarter. Now here. You take it. Let me watch you."

She turned the vacuum cleaner on again. I picked up the handle and brushed it softly against the floor, my ears dull to the noise. Next door, someone was mowing their lawn.

"Come on, let's get some muscle in there. Boy, you can't do anything right, can you?" She grabbed it out of my hand and started banging the metal brush up against the wall again, her whole body slugging. "See, that's the way. Now, do it."

A few seconds later, she called from the back of the house, shouting over the noise of the machine. "Five times. And remember, I'm checking. So it better be clean. Or else you're just going to do it over again."

I looked down at the floor. I thought of the years in front of me when I would still need a mother. The hundreds of black and white squares. And I vacuumed hard, slamming the baseboards.

After six squares I looked behind me at the kitchen floor. Rows and rows and rows times five. I heard water running for my mother's bath. The rushing water sounded musical, tempting. I looked back once and decided, I'm not going to do this. I left the vacuum cleaner going so she'd still hear the noise and I ran outside.

It wasn't the same as before. I didn't play kickball, because my mother could call me there. I ran the other way, past the vacant lots down to where they were building the new highway. In the woods, I remembered I could slow down. My blood was still jumping in the backs of my knees. Below, yellow bulldozers crawled in the sand. Sometimes men hiked up and gave us dollars to keep our eyes on the surveyor's stakes, not to let anyone pull them out. The woods were going for the new highway, but we helped the men for a dollar.

I lay down and put my hands up beneath my head. Clouds moved slowly. I lay there, chewing on a piece of grass. I closed my eyes and tried to forget about myself. When it got dark I'd have to go home. I'd be in trouble again.

A rainy day after school, four, four thirty. Something in my throat. I was alone in the house. They wouldn't be home until six or seven. The house was empty. The kitchen was dry and clean, no food in the refrigerator. It was a night we would go out to eat. Outside, it seemed damp. I sat in my bedroom, in the back of the house, facing backs of things. Fences, other people's yards. There was nothing in my room but one bed and the old TV.

I took my clothes off and I sat on my bed, looking at myself. I hadn't made my bed that morning, so it was a mess of sheets and the wool blanket. The old TV on the floor, a portable black and white, was playing softly, on to a comedy from the fifties. I had the volume turned down low so all I heard was the rise of the same laugh. I'd look at the screen then, when I heard it, and watch the actors, a man and woman staring at each other. It was the same gray and white light, the television, as the sky outside, the rain on the window. I felt my arms and legs, from my shoulders to my elbows, my knees, down to my arches. I was thin, slight.

It seemed damp in the house and I was alone.

I went to my mother's bathroom and I took an oily compact mirror from her makeup bag. Back in my room, the warm blanket felt good on my skin then. I held the greasy mirror, looking at myself.

I felt colder then. I hid the mirror under the blanket and rubbed my legs from the hip bones down to my ankles, the outsides. I clasped my fingers around my ankles. I was alone. Alone. No one was watching me. I didn't feel like I would go anywhere anymore, like California. I knew I'd stay here in the back of the house, facing the backs of things.

My mother looked out the window while she warmed up the car. Anything not to see me. When she got mad enough at me, she took me to my grandmother's house.

Even in my dreams, when I was chased and running, I saw yellow lights in a kitchen, the blue back of my grandmother's dress as she bent over to reach a low cupboard. My grandmother was almost always home.

My mother slowed the car when we turned onto the old road. The sky was darker, the road was uneven, there were no streetlights, only stars. We heard wind in the tall trees. When we walked inside, my grandmother was sitting at the kitchen table, her silver glasses low on her nose, picking the meat out of hickory nuts, collecting the soft parts inside a glass jar.

The plates she used for every day were white with a faded gold line around their rims. The china was scratched from knives and some of the plates were chipped, but I'd known them all my life. She brought out a blueberry pie from the cupboard, still in the square pan, covered with tinfoil, the blueberries black and glistening, caught in a net of glaze like a dark and liquid lace.

My mother sighed, exhausted, holding her coffee cup and looking around the room. It was a place where she recognized everything, the position of the house on the land, the stars out the kitchen windows and the clean, ironed hairpin lace doilies. She did not like the house, she would never have chosen it, but it was the only place I saw her thin shoulders fall, where she hooked her jacket on a peg instead of buttoning it up around a hanger. Her legs swung under the table and her smile came easily to me, no matter what I'd done, no matter how bad I'd been. She was tired and home.

We heard the distant running noise of the highway and the nearer etch-

ing of the crickets by the side of the house, and in the kitchen, the refrigerator and fluorescent lights hummed.

"I was watching Welk," my grandmother said.

"Oh, should we go in there, Mom?"

"Ugh, no, it's all reruns. I've seen it before."

My mother stood up when she thought she should go, slowly, as if she
didn't want to. The beds here were made with tight sheets dried on a line
outside and then ironed. You could hear the wind through the walls. But
she had to go. She was grown up and married. We waited for a moment by
the screen door, looking at the car. My mother had to go out and get in it.
She turned on all her lights. The car glowed like a lit cage. We watched
until we couldn't see her anymore.

In the downstairs bedroom, there were hundreds of pajamas and nightgowns in the dresser drawers, most of which had never been worn. People
gave them to my grandmother for Christmas and her birthday and Mother's Day. When her husband was alive, she'd received them on anniversa-
ries, too.

"I don't know what it is about me that makes them think of pajamas."
She lifted up a pink gown from a box. "Look at this. I don't wear such
fancy stuff. I wish she'd come and take it back."

My mother had tried to outdo the others, with silks and quilted satin,
crocheted inserts, ostrich plumes and matching robes.

"It must be something about me," she frowned.

I picked cotton men's pajamas, my grandfather's, like the ones my
grandmother wore. The huge legs dragged on the floor and the elastic
hung loose around my waist.

We had cornflakes before bed. We didn't talk. The train whistled,
gone as soon as it was there, shaking the ground, moving north. The upstairs smelled of fresh-cut pine. It had been like that for years. I looked
out the window on the landing. The oak leaves were close and big like
hands; between them you could see stars.

I heard the toilet flush, then footsteps to the back door, where my
grandmother called in her dog, shutting the screen again, when he was
shaking against her ankle. She snapped the porch light off. The dog's tail
beat against the wall as she talked him into settling down. She bent down
in the corner, patting him. He always had huge particles of brown lint in
the corners of his eyes. I suspected she let him sleep upstairs with her
when she was alone.

"Yas, yas, you, sure, you're a good dog, yas sure, yas you are. Sure,
that's a good dog, down, go down, yas. At's a good Handy, yas."

She paused for breath every few seconds on the stairs and I heard her
hand clasp the banister.

"Are you asleep?"

"No."

"Are you too warm or too cold?"

"No."

"I can get you a blanket."

"No thank you. I'm fine, Gramma."

She lowered herself slowly, the boards creaking under her, to her knees. She poked her elbows in on the bed and said a prayer. From across the room, it was just words. Then she rattled her pan under the bed and crawled in.

"Well, it does feel good to be in B-E-D."

"Yes."

"Well, good night then."

"Night."

When my grandmother said I love you, which she did only rarely, she waited a long time in the dark. Time enough passed so that I stopped waiting for it, and I would be almost asleep and then she said I love you in an unwavering, normal voice. I thought she said it that night. But I didn't really know if I heard it or not, I could have been asleep, dreaming, so I never answered. My grandmother was so shy.

The next morning, when I woke up, I heard her moving around the kitchen, getting pans out of the oven drawers. Wind was blowing upstairs near my bed, branches were beating against the walls. The crackling sound of the radio came up through the floor. It was dark out the windows. I woke up hours earlier than I ever did at home. My grandmother cut a piece of buttered toast into four squares and arranged them around a yellow scrambled egg. My grandmother's eggs came out the way they were supposed to, not like my mother's. At home, we each made our own breakfast. We spread steak tartare on toast or stood at the open refrigerator and ate cold châteaubriand. My mother cooked the steaks at night and Ted sliced them, so we'd always have protein in the house. The kitchen in my grandmother's house was old-fashioned, with pale yellow cupboards and mint green trim. At home we had all the modern features. But I was more comfortable here at my grandmother's. Still, I didn't know if I would have wanted it to be my house.

The radio was on and there was a storm. We thought of driving up to Lake Erie for the washups. My grandmother and I collected rocks. We'd found minerals and geodes in caves and cracked them open ourselves. When my grandmother took her European tour she brought a chisel and came home with rocks from all the famous places. She wrapped them in colored tissue paper and taped labels to the bottoms on the airplane. Rock from the Acropolis, Rock from Pillar of the Coliseum, Rome. Sometimes we drove to small Indian towns around Bay City for their museums. We'd met rock hounds, old women with pointed sneakers and no socks, their skin gathering at their ankles in tiny folds like nylons, on Lake Michigan, bending over the gray sand, looking for petoskeys.

"Well, should we call your ma?"

"She's not up yet." I was looking at the big round clock over the refrigerator. In the new house, we had to go wandering around to alarm clocks to see if one had the right time. I'd dig Ted's watch out of his pocket in the closet. There was a tiny black traveling alarm by my mother's bed. She slept with one arm draped over it.

"We could call her from up there, I suppose. 'Course then what can she say?"

"Can we take Handy?" I asked. My grandmother got Handy the way she'd gotten all her dogs; Handy was our dog first. I'd wanted a dog because I had a crush on our morning paper boy. I used to take the garbage out when I saw him coming up Carriage Court. But I thought it would look more natural to be walking a dog. After a while, though, my mother decided I wasn't taking good enough care of Handy and besides, he made a mess. She decided that the dog needed more room to run, so we gave him to my grandmother. My grandmother fussed, saying, Oh, I don't want another dog, what do I want a dog for? Handy was the name we'd given him. My grandmother took our dogs and kept whatever names they had.

"Why sure. Does a wanna ride, Handy? Sure, sure a does." Handy began thumping his tail against my grandmother's ankle.

I put on one of the heavy men's wool jackets still left from when my grandfather wore them out to the mink. We took gloves and scarves and loose, baggy clothes. Neither of us would have dressed like this if we were staying in Bay City. My grandmother wore big cotton housedresses or overalls and flannel shirts the days she stayed home, but she owned nice, tasteful suits, knits, with matching purses and jewelry for the days when she had to drive into town, even for ten minutes, to buy something from the department store or to pick up a roast from the butcher.

The dog whimpered and beat his tail against the vinyl of the backseat, and I sat in front with the map spread out on my legs. In a town we didn't know the name of, we stopped in a Swedish tea shop. "Well, should we call your ma from here? They must be up by now."

I found a cuckoo clock by the cash register. Birds and nests on eaves were carved into the blond wood. It said half past eleven.

"Not for sure," I said, although it was about now that they usually got up on Saturdays. My mother would open the back door and sneak out to the garage with a bag of garbage, wearing only a T-shirt. After she pranced in, she'd stand for a minute at the back door, looking out to the dazzling sunlight on the yard. In summer, the sprinklers would already be going on the lawn next door, making thin rainbows over the grass. But it was raining and they were probably sleeping late. At our house, when we got up on a weekend and there was rain, my mother sighed and we all went back to sleep for a few hours.

We decided not to call my mother until we were farther north, in Michigan. It seemed safer in another state. Walking to the cash register, we passed two men in outdoor clothes with a radio going on their table. "Storm's still up," one said to the other.

My grandmother was a shy person, but she made an effort.

"You're not going to the lake, are you?"

"Yes, ma'am. Up to Erie. Gonna get the washups."

"Why, us too. You must be the real rock hounds."

We followed their truck. We drove and drove, through towns with Indian names, down main streets one block long. We passed a road sign advertising the butter factory that used to rent our old barn; it showed a picture of a Michigan summer: blueberry patches, a bear, high clouds over a lake and dark green pines—the paper peeling off the sign, flapping in the wind. We were halfway to Canada.

We each sat on one of the twin beds, taking turns talking to my mother.

She shrieked so loud my grandmother held the receiver out a foot away. At that distance, my mother's voice sounded hilarious, like a tiny recorded puppet's voice.

"Lake *Ee*-rie. My God, Ted, they're at Lake *Ee*-rie, those two. Well, when are you coming home?"

My grandmother kept the phone away from her.

"Put her on," my mother said, "put on my little wee-bear-cub. I miss my Little Bit."

The corners of my grandmother's mouth lowered. I took the phone. My grandmother and I were both laughing then, and I tried to stifle the sound.

"Pooh-bear, are you there? Are you all right?"

"Yes, Mother, I'm fine."

"Do you have enough to eat, Bear-cub? And what are you wearing? Do you have warm clothes?"

"Yes, Mother."

"Well, you be careful out there on the beach. Don't you dare go at night when it's dark. And be careful of the other rock hounds and watch out for those undertows, because, believe me, Twussy, they can be atrocious, they just pull you right out, I'm telling you—"

"We'll be fine, Mom, we're not swimming, we're just walking on the beach. And we're going down to dinner now, so I have to go."

"Okay, well, have a good time and take care, you two. And hurry home because I miss my little Twussy Thing, Pooh-bear-cub. I'm lonesome just thinking of you way up there."

"Is it still raining where you are?" my grandmother asked.

"Storming. I'm in bed already." My mother giggled.

Downstairs to the dining room, my grandmother and I could hardly walk.

"Well, how do you feel, you little, you little Pooh-bear-cub, you," my grandmother said. "Oh ye gods."

"My little Twussy Bear, I'm soo lonesome, sigh." We kept bumping into each other, and then against the walls.

"We shouldn't talk like this," my grandmother said, trying to pull her face straight. "But oh, the things she says. Twussy bear. Now what is a twussy bear?"

Ten at night and the storm was still going. We sat in the dining room in a corner, next to a window. Finally, we were quiet. That was what always happened when we talked about my mother. First, we couldn't stop laughing, we were hysterical with talk. Then it burned out and we each sat quiet, alone.

"Gramma, was she always like this?"

My grandmother turned and looked out the window. Her profile was sharp and even, like faces of men on backs of coins. Outside, waves opened and lit the shore. Rain splattered on the glass.

"Oh, there was always something not quite right about her. Something a little off. She wasn't quite all there."

"Even when she was a little girl?"

"I've thought that to myself a thousand times, and I just don't know anymore." A waitress brought a basket of bread to our table. We knew it was warm. Neither of us touched it. "I think even when she was real small, there was always something missing."

I looked around the room. There were rock hounds at most of the other tables. Canvas bags and flashlights lay next to their feet.

We ordered big meals: fried steaks with pats of butter melting on top and peach pie, warm, under cream, on a soft, dissolving crust. "Nutmeg," my grandmother said, tasting it. "Good." Afterwards, we both drank coffee. The times I'd tasted my mother and Ted's black instant espresso, I spit it out. But we drank cup after cup with cream and sugar and it was delicious, sustaining us, as we waited for the storm to clear. The waitress kept circling the room with the silver pot.

In every person's face, there is one place that seems to express them most accurately. With my grandmother, you always looked at her mouth. Her teeth seemed to balance at the very tips of each other, just touching, her lips held and nervous while she listened to a question.

"Oh, no, we're just amateurs, shucks no," she said, frowning, to a table of women at our left. In groups, she was the shyest one at first, always, but eventually they looked to her to start them laughing. The ladies at the table promised to wake us up if the storm broke.

"That's room nineteen?" one of the women shouted, as we stood up to leave.

"Us, why no," my grandmother teased, "but Elma, you go and knock on nineteen in the middle of the night and just see what the gentleman says. And tell us what you find there." The women were still laughing as we walked away.

We went to feed Handy two pieces of steak we'd wrapped in a paper napkin and to let him outside by the car to make. But he whimpered in the rain, so my grandmother spread newspapers from the trunk over the backseat floor. When we left, we felt sorry for him staring out the car window. With his paws up, he looked tiny and pitiful, wet; his head, with the hair packed down, seemed no bigger than my fist, the size that's supposed to match a human heart. We took him under my poncho and carried him to our bathroom, where he beat his tail against the door. "Ugh, you are a wet thing, you," my grandmother said, lifting him onto her jacket.

The wind was still blowing when we finally went to bed. At the very northern edge of land, where it was dark and late and storming, sleep seemed the easiest state to exist in. I went to sleep there fully trusting the world not to harm me. I don't know if I ever felt that safe, before or again. My hands lay softly on the bed that night, my ear to the pillow as if that was where the comforting sound of rain came from. We were far away. I liked going to sleep knowing it was cold and no one was outside and we were so far away from anywhere else where the sky might be clear and other people might be living other lives.

When we woke up the next morning the storm had broken and the air was sweet. There was only a light rain. We dressed quickly and took our equipment from the car. I carried Handy in my poncho. It was still dark, but the sky was lightening a little over the lake. In the distance, we saw spots of other flashlights. Waves shellacked the sand and brought new rocks and driftwood. The lacy foam receded and we tracked down, looking for agates, banded with gray and blue, the colors of the air here. They were everywhere in the sand, caught in the masses of seaweed. We walked slowly, our eyes careful on the ground. Every few minutes one of us would stop, bend down and pick up a stone. We found agates and arrowheads and just granite smoothed by water. We each came over to see when we found one, held it in our hands under the flashlight. My grandmother walked to wash hers in the water first. I licked mine to see and then put it in my cheek, sucking, until I found a new one.

It was as if the stones renewed us. We could have walked and walked, bending down forever on that beach. There were miles to study. Handy ran along near us, going ahead, then looking back, his barks soft and lost in the louder noise of waves. I hadn't seen an ocean yet, but this lake seemed enough. We couldn't see the other side, but we knew over the pencil gray line of the horizon was Canada. Canada—just the sound of the name. It seemed it could end all our problems.

A man at a filling station kept looking at my grandmother. It bothered me. He leaned on the front of the car and he took a long time to wash the windshield. My grandmother blushed a little when he stared. She picked up the Kleenex box on the car seat between us and set it down again.

"Gramma, why is he looking at you funny?"

She shrugged. "Well, shucks if I know."

Then I remembered something. There was a picture of my grandmother when she was young, wearing a white lace dress, her braids ending in two pencil points at her waist. She was holding a black dog with a huge ribbon around its neck. My mother and my aunt Carol said she was beautiful. They said they felt in awe of her. I'd never seen it. To me, she just looked like a grandmother.

"That guy likes you, Gramma."

"That old fellow. Shucks no, he's too old for me."

But when the man filled the tank, he kept looking in through the window, the nozzle in his hand. My grandmother gripped the steering wheel and she looked down at the spokes, her mouth working, smiling in spite of trying to frown.

"It's Chummy with that Public Service hat." My grandmother walked to the window and pulled back the curtain every time we heard a car. Public Service was the name of the gas and electric company in Bay City. The men wore yellow hardhats. She meant it wasn't my mother.

Then she pointed with her fingernail where I should erase. My homework spread over the kitchen table. She stood behind me, checking the arithmetic of my problems, her glasses low on her nose.

The back of my hand was in my mouth, something I'd done all my life. It drove my mother crazy. When I was young, I bit my nails and she pretended to give me a manicure, rubbing my baby fingers with quinine. It worked, but the gesture simply adjusted itself. Now I moved my lips over the back of my hand. This made my mother more upset. "I should have let her stick with the nails, who cares if she ruined them and had ridges all her life like Juney Miller, it'd be better than this," she told Lolly once. "Ann, take that mouth off of your hand. You're going to get thick awful lips like a Negro. If you do that where other people can see you, they're going to think something's really wrong with you. And I don't think you even know when you're doing it anymore."

"Yes, I do."

"No, you don't. You think you do, but I've seen you doing it when you thought you weren't."

My grandmother watched and didn't say anything. I did another page of problems and she looked over it, checking my additions and multiplications in the old math.

"We have fun," she said. "I know you like it by me."

Then we heard my mother's car in the driveway. My grandmother touched my hair, just then. That was the kind of thing she almost never did.

"I know you haven't got it the easiest with your ma. I know how she can be. I know it."

I looked down at my sheet of problems. I said, "Sometimes," and then my voice stopped.

"I know, I know it, but shhh now."

The screen door banged and my mother rushed in, with Handy beating around her ankles.

"Well, hello, hello." My grandmother collected my school papers together. We sat around the kitchen table. My mother rested her chin on her hands. She fiddled with her bracelet. She seemed tired again.

"So, tell me, what did you two do?"

We told her little bits. We drove up to Lake Erie, we had supper and went to bed. When we woke up, the storm was over. My grandmother took out our rocks from the canvas bag and spread them on the counter. She wrote labels and taped them on rocks while we talked. She'd finish them before I had to go. When we walked out to the porch, a rusty streak of red held in the sky. It was one of those dusks that was cool but not cold, the sky so brilliant it made the houses and barns, everything built, look small.

We stood on the porch, in no hurry to leave, while my grandmother took the leash down to walk Handy. As soon as she lifted it off the peg, Handy jumped up on her, yelping.

"Ya, you be quiet, you," she said with a false sternness.

The highway was barely visible but we heard the constant running noise of travel. My mother was wearing a straight cotton dress with a cardigan and I had on dungarees. It seemed to me then, as we stood there, for a long time on the verge of leaving, that we shouldn't have really had to go. Something had gone wrong.

My mother and I should have both been girls who stayed out on the porch a little longer than the rest, girls who strained to hear the long-distance trucks on the highway and who listened to them, not the nearer crickets. We would have been girls who had names in their heads: Ann Arbor, Chicago, Cheyenne, San Francisco, Portland, Honolulu, Los Angeles; girls who looked at the sky and wanted to go away. We would have been the kind of girls who thought we, more than other people, saw the sadness of things, the poignance of lush darkness around stars, but who finally sighed and, calling the dog with a mixture of reluctance and relief, shut the door and went in home.

My grandmother looked at me as my mother slid into the car. "Go on, get in now," she said.

But she wanted me and I wanted her and she couldn't have me because I was my mother's. She was too old to take care of me. She would die before I was grown.

As we backed out of the driveway she bent down to Handy. My mother turned on our lights.

My mother was born on an old kitchen table, now in the basement, cluttered with tools. Her high school dresses hung packed together over her red ukelele in the upstairs closet, the closet with one high window that showed sky and clouds and telephone wires. Her father's mink sheds stood rusting in the field out back. My mother blamed the house on Lime Kiln Road for things gone wrong in her life. She had hated being so far in the country, she remembered walking miles in the snow to Saint Phillip's Academy, the sound of her boots the only sound for an hour in the hollow, blue air. She had felt embarrassed, bringing boyfriends from college to a dead-end road, when the car had to pass by Griling's house, junk and old auto parts in the front yard, and children whose matted hair made their eyes look huge and hereditarily dumb.

"Well, who could I meet? Out here? Gram talks about Ellie's June this, Ellie's June that, well, I remember when June was in high school, Ellie bought the smallest little house in DePeer and June grew up with all the doctor's kids and lawyer's kids. They could have moved, too, but no, Gram and Dad stayed there. And look at June now. Look who she married. And she didn't even go to college."

"She married an undertaker. And now she's got twelve kids."

"Listen, it's the undertakers who make all the money these days. More than the doctors even. They don't have to pay the malpractice insurance."

"So would you want twelve kids?"

"I think I would." She said that quietly, shy. "I always wanted a big family. I think I would have liked to be a homebody."

That shut me up.

. . .

"So did you really have fun, tell me true, I won't tell her. Did you really have fun or was it just all right?" She bumped over a curb. "Whoops."

Then the car was coasting, and she let me turn the radio on. "It was all right," I said.

She was intent, looking at me. There was something about when she looked at me, it made me blush, I couldn't help it. It always seemed like I was lying, no matter what I said. The blood poured to my cheeks. "What did you have to eat? Did you have a steak up there or just those Polish pasties?"

"We had pasties."

She made a face. "Well, I broiled a château," she said, moving the wheel with one hand, easy. "We'll see that you have a good steak tonight."

A week later, my mother ran to my room. She'd told my grandmother what I'd said and they'd fought on the telephone, my grandmother cried. "Ann, tell me true now, did you lie to me, because she said you had New York steaks, the best they had on the menu up there, and she paid twenty dollars for it." She looked at me, shaking her head. "Don't do that Ann, don't play us against each other. She's my mother, too," she said.

The winter I was six years old, my mother was gone. She went to California, without me. My grandmother and I talked to her on the telephone in the kitchen, asking her when she'd come home. She told us she was recovering. I pictured her in a white hospital like a kitchen, with violets in a water cup. "Not yet," I told the nuns at school when they asked if she was home. They asked at the end of the day when we stood in line, waiting for the bell to ring. They touched the top of my head and their palms felt cool and dry. Every day my grandmother's Oldsmobile would be banked right in front of the school, waiting. She leaned over and opened the door and inside it was warm, the motor running.

One day, a friend from my school came over and we ran through the fields chasing monarchs with butterfly nets and my mother called and said she was coming home. "Just when you had your friend and played nice," my grandmother said, putting down the phone. The jars of butterflies sat all over the counter tops and on the kitchen table, holes punched in their tin lids. Their wings seemed to beat as we breathed.

The day was there then and I was scared. I didn't want her to come. I waited outside, I was wearing all white—white shorts, white T-shirt, white anklets and white sneakers—and when I saw the car coming down the road, I hid behind the garage in a lilac bush. I didn't want her to see me.

But then—then the car door slammed and before she had to come look for me, I ran out and she was there and I was at her legs and she was young and beautiful and so much fun and my mother again.

"My baby's all white, oh, you smell, you smell like perfume."

The white VW gleamed in the sun and she carried me, hers again, my legs sticking out from her back. I felt sorry for my grandmother that day, moving around the kitchen in a blue print dress, there was flour all through the yellow light, she was baking, rolling out dough. She cut around our fingers, making cookies the size of our hands, all day she looked down at her work on the table, because I was not hers to watch anymore.

For a long time, I didn't like Ted. He seemed to get in our way. Before Ted, my mother and I were waiting, preparing. We were going to go to California.

My mother taught me how to diet and smile right so all my teeth showed and to practice, looking in the mirror. I knew how to eat right so if a Hollywood agent came to Bay City, he would pick me. I thought of it every meal. Every meal I didn't chew with my mouth open because I didn't want the Hollywood agent to pick another girl.

But then, my mother went to Las Vegas and married Ted, and in the new house she didn't talk about California anymore.

She gave me her old Sears jacket and she bought herself a new one. It was a zip-up jacket, too big for me, mustard-colored, plain. I walked around in it after school, in the fields, the underdeveloped parts of the new neighborhood. I thought I would just stay there in a plain jacket and no one would ever see me. My mother had told me I was a girl with potential, but now it seemed nobody would ever know.

One night we were driving—my mother and Ted in the front seat, me in the back, to the Lorelei for prime rib. I sat by the dark window and didn't say anything. We passed intersections, the colored lights slick on the road.

"Ann," Ted said to me from the front seat, looking in his rearview mirror, "your mother tells me you'd like to be on television."

I sank further down into the jacket, I could feel my neck flush with blood. She'd told what I wanted. I was ashamed. I was embarrassed to want something like that.

"I know a man who works at WBAY. I can ask him to get you on a local commercial, would you like that?"

My mother leaned her arm on the seat divider. "Just think, you'd be on TV."

Something opened like a clam in my chest. I felt so happy.

"Yes," I said.

"All right, I'll talk to him."

My mother raised her eyebrows and clicked her tongue. "Here's hoping."

We kept driving in the dark but it was different. I watched the red disks throb on stakes by the side of the road. I looked for the skeletal antennas of the radio stations out in the fields, in the country, broadcasting through the night. We felt safe together in Ted's car, we could feel ourselves moving.

I got Mary Griling to come to Carriage Court. It was easy because I was older. I drew her a map and she rode after school on her brother's bike that she had to stand up on so her feet reached the pedals. At our house on Carriage Court, we had a new Instamatic camera. We still didn't have any furniture, but my mother and Ted bought equipment. We had the camera and a radio that picked up international channels. We set the large radio, with the antenna extended, in the middle of the living room floor.

I got kids to come to our house and I took pictures of them. Younger kids, eight- and nine-year-old boys. Mary was the first girl. I didn't know why I did it. It was just one of the things I did.

Mary was different from the other Grilings. Her collars were straight and her dark hair fell evenly onto her shoulders. My grandmother said she was lucky she was pretty, that could help her, God knew nothing else would. I'd watched her coward little kicks during football games, and in school I'd seen her stand by the window, watering plants on the ledge. Careful, she always seemed to be concentrating. I didn't live on Lime Kiln Road anymore and I didn't go to the same school anymore either. But once when I was there playing tag, I held Mary's wrist and pulled her by a tree. Clouds moved above us, it was going to rain before supper.

She came after school before it was dark, that still time of day. I took her through our empty house to the big bathroom, the one my mother and Ted used, and locked the door. I told her she had to do what I said. I told her to take off her shirt and stand by the wall.

I said the same thing to the boys. I was always amazed when they did it. People are so easy to boss.

Mary looked down and unbuttoned carefully, her chin tucked against her collarbone like a bird cleaning itself. I took a picture. Her bare chest was incidental; what I liked were her shoulders curling down, her distracted eyes as she stood with her hands hanging useless at her sides.

They all looked up at me while I did it. They seemed frightened, their faces sunk back, except their eyes. I asked them to lie on the long, fake-marble counter by the sink. They always looked so serious.

Mary rubbed her tennis shoes off, one by one, toes pushing down the soft heel of the other shoe. Kids are so shy. She was lying there, looking up at me, her eyes large and muscular, wet like a fish's eyes. That was what made me want to touch them, that tremble. Some flinch. They were afraid of me. The boys tried to look brave, setting their teeth, breathing in. It's amazing the power people give you. Mary Griling just lay there, her face flattened, I could do anything to her and she looked up at me, weakly and kind, a nerve pulsing in her cheek. The muscles gathered in her stomach. My fingers turned heavy and sensitive, as if all my blood poured down to their tips. I lifted the elastic band of her skirt and looked down at her face. She was peering at me, more and more humbly, the veils of her eyelids closing, knowing she was giving herself up. I could have reached down and killed her, she was just lying there, trusting me.

"The others did this, too?" Her rib bones rose, the highest part of her body. She pulled her stomach in, shy.

"Yes." I'd said there was a club, all the girls on Lime Kiln Road. I didn't tell her there were boys.

I had Mary, good little Mary, serious Mary Griling who worked hard to be neat, to do well in school, in my house alone. She was lying there under my hands. I touched the pancake of her breast and something fluttered beneath my flattened palm. Then I pushed her skirt and her underpants down to her ankles. She flinched while I took the pictures. I was watching her face turn funny.

"Is that enough pictures?"

"Okay." I put the camera under the counter, where my mother stored the Ajax and extra soap. But she still stayed there and I looked at her. The tiny muscles of her upper thighs clinched when I touched her. She looked at me as if my finger was on the wet muscle of her heart. Then I licked my finger. It tasted like flour. I put my hand in her mouth and ran two fingers over the bumps of her gums. I felt like I owned her, then. With the boys it took longer. I stood over them until they shuddered and cried, biting their lips until they bled, arching up and down on the counter, in my hands.

She sat up, sideways, with her legs hanging down and then she jumped. I looked back at her, her buttocks pressed towards each other as if she could feel me watching. She dressed against the wall, in the corner.

"Does your father see you undressed?"

She was clasping the top button of her blouse. "No," she said, guarded but obedient, duty-bound to answer.

"Want me to help you?" Her shirt hung down, lopsided.

"I can do it by myself."

I was thinking of Griling's messy house, the junk in the front yard, piles in the closets. She finished dressing. Her collar folded down, even. I smoothed it carefully, against her neck. She looked up, not knowing if she should be afraid of me.

"You can't tell anybody about today," I said. "I won't show the pictures."

"All right," she said, not sure.

Then she left, walking in one line through the kitchen to the front door. As I watched her go, she seemed to collect mystery again, to draw it back into her small body. Her head was dark as she rode down our street on her brother's wobbly bike. The boys always looked over their shoulders at me, asking, dipping their eyes. I knew they'd be back, I didn't wonder. I hadn't had a girl before because I worried they would tell their mothers. But Mary Griling had no mother.

"I'm really bleeding," my mother said, turning to me in the car. "It's just all over. And thick." My mother said absolutely anything to me. It was as if she were alone.

"I don't want to hear about it," I said, "and could you please keep your eyes on the road." We were driving from my grandmother's house, just the way we did a hundred times after she married Ted and we moved away. The stars were small and dim through the windshield. I sat against my car door, worrying.

I had homework for the next day. We turned off our old road and onto the highway, we drove by barns and silos, we passed a high blinking radio antenna in a deserted field. Then I remembered that my science book, which I needed, was in my locker at school. That made me exhausted. I couldn't possibly finish.

"I have a Super in and a Kotex and it's still going right through. I can feel it. Yech." She made a gagging face. "You'll never believe what that man did. I still can't believe it. Open the glove compartment, Honey."

When I didn't, she reached over and opened it herself. "There. Look at those bills. Those are all our bills, Annie, *un-PAID*. You need clothes, I need clothes, I don't have anything, I go to work in that old junk, in rags, five, ten, fifteen years out of date. I should really go to work looking a little nice, too. But this man, with my money, with our money, goes out and buys himself a new car. Yeah, uh-huh, you can imagine, Annie? He thinks he needs a new used Cadillac. The old one wasn't good enough."

"Could you please be quiet?"

"I'll say what I want in my car," she said. "Don't get fresh with me now, Ann, because I can't take it from you, too. And you should know a little about these things."

She jerked the steering wheel and the car bumped over a curb, turning.

"Where are we going?"

"We're driving past the Lorelei."

The Lorelei was the restaurant near the ice skating rink where the three of us used to go on Sundays for prime rib. They were supposed to have the best prime rib in Bay City, thick and tender. Now Ted ate there without us, after night skating. We drove slowly into the gravel parking lot. Across the road was the pale green dome of the arena, BAY CITY painted in large black letters.

"There's his car," I pointed. Ted's maroon and white Cadillac was in its usual spot.

My mother pulled behind it and turned the motor off. She walked out and peered in at his dashboard. "There he is. That man. Oooh, when I think of it. The dirty devil."

"How do you know he bought a new car?"

"How do I know, they called me, that's how I know. Van Boxtel Cadillac called and said, Well, you must know about the gold Cadillac, it's all set, ready to go. I laughed and said, No, I didn't know a thing about any car. But then I drove out and saw it there on the lot. A gold Cadillac, barely used. A '65."

I still didn't say anything. My mother started up the engine again and tried harder.

"Do you know what this means, Honey? This means no money for us. No clothes, no toys, no nothing. This is it. He's spent all your money, what should have been for your lessons and your clothes."

"So, why don't you go in and talk to him if you're so upset."

That seemed to subdue her. "No, that wouldn't be a good idea." She shook her head, turning the ignition. "He's in there drinking with his friends, he wouldn't say anything in front of them. I know this man. This man is a creature of habit. I'm just going to go home and go to bed. And you, too. Don't say a word about any of this, do you hear me? Not a word, young lady. See, I'm not going to tell him they called, so he won't know I know. We'll just wait and see how he tells me, we'll just see how he tries. Now do you understand? Not one word. Because that could spoil everything. *Every*thing.

"Let's set the alarm for five and get up then. Come on, Pooh, we'll be fresher in the morning. Our minds will think faster."

We were never done with our work, it seemed, all those years with Ted.

We fell asleep, alone in the house. But I didn't sleep good sleep anymore, the way I had when I was younger, at my grandmother's. Now, I had cowering sleep. I snuck under the covers, exhausted, stealing time and comfort I didn't deserve.

It was the fourth or fifth time that winter I'd lost my key. My mother was furious when she drove her car up the driveway and saw me, sitting on the porch. She slammed her door and marched out.

"Your lights," I said.

"Damn." She almost fell, she turned around so fast. "You're ten years old, Ann, you ought to be able to keep one key."

She opened the door and let us in. I stood in the front hall, stamping my feet. My mother set the thermostat up. My hands had swelled and turned red.

"Somebody's going to break in one of these days with your lost keys and then you know where we'll be. In the poorhouse."

"There is no poorhouse in Bay City."

She sighed. "I'm going to have to string it around your neck. And how would you like that, for all your kids to see?"

"Go ahead." I started for my bedroom, then turned around. "What happened with the Cadillac?"

She sighed again. "I don't know. I just don't know yet."

When I first saw the '65 Cadillac, snow was blowing in tiny balls across the gold roof. The Cadillac sat like a huge painted egg on our driveway. There was one streetlamp in front of our yard and as I walked up the road, I could see the glass and chrome glitter. I went up close. It had molded fins and I walked the length of the car, running my hands on the sides, brushing down snow. I pulled off my mitten. Through the windows, the inside looked safe and closed and tended like a home. I lifted up the chrome door handle and it gave with a soft click. Ted never locked things. His office in the arena, his cars; in summer he left our back door wide open. Inside, it smelled rich. I didn't sit down because my clothes were wet and my boots were muddy with slush. The car had thick tan carpets and no plastic mats. I reached over and opened the glove compartment. It was there, what I was looking for and afraid to see: Ted's glasses, folded together in the beaded case that said LAS VEGAS IS FOR LOVERS. The car was his, definitely. I closed the glove compartment and then I shut the door, lifting the handle so it would fall quietly.

I was afraid to go in the house. I would have stayed in the car, but I didn't want my wetness to ruin the leather. I did what I did all summer. I went around the garage to the side of the house and listened against the wall. In summer, if I heard fighting, I wouldn't go inside.

I had my own key, another copy, stuffed with the string down my pocket, and I let myself in. No one called when the door slammed and I stamped my boots in the front hall. The kitchen was dark and the counters were dry and perfectly clean. I opened the refrigerator. There were only jars of things and one head of lettuce in a plastic bag. I guessed we were going out for dinner.

"I'm home," I said and then I heard something in my bedroom at the back of the house. It was dark in there, it took my eyes a second to adjust.

"I AM your little lotus blossom." My mother was banked on my bed-spread, talking baby talk, with a light mohair blanket thrown over her. "Won't you get your lit-tle lotus blossom a glass of wa-wa?"

She still hadn't seen me.

"Get up, Mom, it's suppertime." I switched on the overhead light. Ted was sitting on my bed next to her as if something was wrong. All of a sudden, I thought she was sick. Perhaps this was what happened when people were dying. She still didn't notice me. She smiled up at Ted, her face swaying. "Wa-wa for the lit-tle lotus flowa."

Ted turned to me. "Your mother is drunk," he said, smiling his zipper smile. "She's had too much to drink."

"I am not drunk!" she screamed as Ted stood up to go to the kitchen, to get her a glass of water.

"You're disgusting," I said, looking straight down at her. Then I took dry clothes into the bathroom and locked the door.

Later, Ted knocked and asked if I wanted McDonald's. I said no, I was going to take a bath.

I packed a blanket and pillow in a brown paper grocery bag and put on my boots and coat over pajamas. I stuffed my robe in the bag, too. It was nine o'clock and our whole house was dark and asleep. I slipped out the front door and walked towards the Cadillac. There was a new lawn of snow on the ground. I knew my mother's car in the garage would be safer, but it was old and the seats were vinyl and one of the windows wouldn't go all the way up. Besides, the doors would be locked.

I wanted the Cadillac. I sat on the front seat and let my legs dangle outside while I pulled off my boots. I laid my robe and then the blanket and pillow on the backseat and I wrapped the boots in the thick brown paper bag. Then I crawled low so no one could see me and pushed the locks down into the doors.

I felt safe there with the snow falling in one bank on the slanted back windshield. The leather warmed under me. The streetlamp lit the snow. I closed my eyes and thought about driving all night on a dark road, the car moving smoothly, my mother and father sitting in front, my mother's arm falling down over the seat on my stomach, patting my hands under the blanket, telling me to Don't worry, go to sleep, it's still a long ways away. They would wake me up when we came to California, before, so I could see us crossing over, riding in.

Then I jerked the way I sometimes do and it feels like my heart should stop but doesn't. The streetlight was glaring and now it was hot in the car. It was still night. I took off my pajamas and sat, naked, in the driver's seat, with my hands on the wheel, making it swivel. I slid down to reach, but I was afraid to touch the pedals with my feet. I thought I might make the car go. I could feel the leather sticking to the moisture of my skin. I wondered if my body would leave a stain. I moved my thighs and my arms as if I were making an angel in the snow. That way my print wouldn't be recognized. I would seem to be someone larger.

Then I heard a noise. There's a difference with the things you imagine, that make you jerk in your sleep, and the things you know are real. I crowded down in the footspace and put my pajamas on again. I took my boots out of the paper bag and pulled them on my bare legs. They were heavy rubber boots, much wider than my legs. When I sat up, I saw it was the snowplow, dragging chains, coming down our street, mowing the banks like hedges on either side, blocking all the driveways.

I ran back in the house and to my room. The alarm clock was still ticking, too early to ring. My mom and Ted's door was closed and I could hear them inside, breathing. No one knew I had been gone. I couldn't fall asleep again, so I dressed for school. I sat on the kitchen floor against the refrigerator and worked on my homework. I noticed the kitchen windows coming light and I was still working. It seemed like I had endless hours. I worked out all my math problems and copied them over on a new sheet of paper, the numbers neat like houses on blue lines. I read my reading, called "The Sound of Summer Running," about a boy who didn't have money for new sneakers. Finally, I was finished. I stacked my books up in a neat pyramid and sharpened all the pencils in my case.

For the first time I could remember, I was ready to go to school. All of a sudden, I was starving. I pulled up my knee socks and went to the sink. Ted had remembered to defrost. There was a two-pound package of ground sirloin in the sink, the blood running in jagged lines down the white porcelain.

While I was spreading the meat, my mother walked in, wearing black tights with a hole in one toe and a tartan plaid skirt, looking at her side, tying the matching sash. Ted walked out behind her, all dressed, saying Good morning, Ann, and nodding as he buttoned up his coat. He didn't eat breakfast with us anymore. He drove to the Lorelei and ordered eggs.

We stood at the window over the sink, watched him stamp to the garage and come out with the shovel.

"Look at the size of those icicles," she whispered. "It's like a wonderland. I'd like to chop off a few and keep them in the freezer." We both watched Ted shovel the driveway. He waved when he trudged up and leaned the shovel against the garage. We could see him through the windshield, unfolding his sunglasses and putting them on. He backed the Cadillac out slowly and as panels of snow fell off, it looked like something huge, coming up from underwater.

"It really is a beaut."

I was eating my steak tartare standing up. "So I guess you're not mad about the car anymore." It was still early, but I wanted to be at school before the bell rang for once.

"Oh, Ann, I was all wrong about that. We were wrong about him, we really were. You know what he was going to do—he was going to drive it home and say, Here, Adele, Happy Anniversary."

I sat against the wall, to pull on my boots.

"Really, Ann, we should be ashamed of ourselves. He really only meant the best. We spoiled his surprise."

I heard my mother in the living room click the radio on. Then she came galloping into the hall, saying, "Snow day, put your books away, school's out, snow day! Go out for me once and just hit those icicles with the shovel. We can take them out in summer, on a tray, with fruit around, wouldn't *that* be a centerpiece?"

"You're so *tan*, Ron," my mother was saying. Ron Hanson was Ted's friend from Holiday on Ice. His hair was bleached blond, with tinges of green, he laughed from his waist, placing one arm over his stomach as he bent down, and he had effeminate hands with long, spoon-shaped fingers. My mother talked about him endlessly with Lolly. But Ted was a reserved man with few friends. The three years we lived in the house on Carriage Court, we saw Ron every winter Holiday on Ice came through Bay City. This time, they were in from California and so Ron was staying in our back ironing room.

Now he was in the kitchen, leaning against the counter, with my mother and Ted, drinking. I could hear their ice cubes shifting in their glasses.

"It's those pills, I'm telling you, Adele, you should get them, you really should. You and I have the same skin, that same, pay-yull skin."

I was in the bathroom, standing on the rim of the tub with my arms up gripping the shower curtain rod for balance, so I could look at my body in the mirror. It didn't look to me like me. There were smudges of fat where I didn't feel fat. Water in the tub was gulping out after my bath. I kept looking, trying to look a different way.

"What's the name of those pills?" my mother said. I stopped and stepped down onto the rug. Didn't she know pills that changed your skin, things like that, were dangerous?

"I just call them pigment pills, that's what they really are. But it's a prescription. I'll write it down for you. I found a man who'll give them to me, but they're not inexpensive. They're rather dear, in fact." He laughed. I imagined his hand on his red shirt, his thin fingers spreading.

My mother knocked on the bathroom door. I picked up a brush and ran it through my tangles to be doing something.

"Open up." She rattled the doorknob. "It's locked. Honey, I've told you, don't lock this door. It's dangerous. If something happened to you in the tub, we couldn't get in."

"What's going to happen to me in the tub?"

She was standing, looking at me in the mirror. She smiled and patted my naked butt. She cupped her hand and ran it down my thigh.

"Don't."

She looked down at me. "Why don't you run out there and say good night a second. Go on."

I looked at her as if she were totally crazy. "No."

"Go on. Why not? Don't you think they've ever seen a naked little girl before?"

"I'm ten years old, if you haven't noticed."

"Well, you're still a little girl to us. At our age."

"In case you don't know, it's not very nice to walk around naked. People don't do that, Mom."

"Oh, come on, a little girl with a cute little bod like yours, it's just cute, that's all." It made me wince, hearing her say Lolly's word. She ran one finger under my arm to my elbow and smiled, secretively. Then she stiffened up again. "Go ahead. Come on, Ann, do it for me."

"Why."

She sighed, impatient at having to explain herself. "Because I'd just like them to see what a cute little shape you have. Come on, won't you please, Ann? Just run out. Just for a second."

"Forget it," I said. I had my pajamas there, folded on the toilet seat top. I put them on, buttoning up all the buttons.

My mother sighed. "Boy, I can see you're almost into the terrible teens. Can't ask you to do anything anymore."

I put on my robe and tied the belt, tight. "I will, however, go in and say good night."

My mother followed me into the kitchen, still looking down at me with pride. Her gaze was like a leash as we walked. Ron and Ted leaned on the counter. We still didn't have any furniture in the house.

Ron was holding up a hinged metal fish whose sides shimmered like dark mother-of-pearl. He said he found it in Baja. I asked Ron if, when he went back to California, he would buy us one of the fish if we gave him money now. I'd noticed that most people would give me the thing when I said that. They'd just give it to me. Adults relinquished shiny, pretty things to children. They were embarrassed to be caught liking them too much. I could see Ron looking into the segmented fish, deciding. He wanted to keep the fish—he wanted it that much. It hurt him, the thought of giving it up. I decided then that this made him different from other people. He loved his toy the way a child would.

"I'll get you one if I ever go there again," he said.

"Ron, are you married," I blurted.

"Now, Annie, what do you think?" he said. His eyelashes dipped down, teasing. "Of course I'm not married. I'm waiting for you to grow up."

I ran to my bedroom, screaming.

That night my mother came to my bed and just sat down. It woke me, I could feel her looking at me. I bent my knees under the cover and sat up. She pulled the blanket down off my shoulder, down one side. She pulled one knee out and looked up and down my leg. "You are a long-limbed beauty," she whispered. "You're my jewel. I have to take you somewhere they can see it."

A clear night, my mother and I piling into the car to drive to dinner.

"What about the TV commercial?" I said.

It took her a minute to look at me. She was distracted. Then she sighed. Ted was back in the house, getting something. She leaned from the front seat, her face working, eyebrows, mouth.

"So be nice to him. Play up to him a little. I bet if you're real cute and quiet, he'll do it for you. Don't kid yourself."

"Why can't I ask?"

"I wouldn't. Just be real cute and make him *want* to help you. You've got to learn to make men want to do you favors."

When he came into the car, I asked. "Ted, what ever happened with, you were going to ask a man you know if I could be on a commercial for TV."

He looked over at my mother sharply. She stared straight ahead, hands on her lap.

"Oh, Honey, I did ask him and he said that none of them were made locally, they get them from Chicago and then they dub in the Bay City names. They don't make them here."

"So I can't do it."

"No, I'm afraid not."

"He could, he could get you on if they made them here, but they don't make them here," my mother said, scolding.

"Oh."

A year before we moved to California, I asked my mother for a bikini. Theresa Griling couldn't get one because her older sister who planned their money said her suit from last year was still good. My mother took me shopping downtown, but Shreve's didn't have real bikinis. All the two-piece suits came up too high and most of them had white pleated skirts. When we'd tried on bathing suits, we both stared at me in the store mirrors. In a bathing suit I looked older. "Oh," she said once and put her hand on my waist. I shirked away then. I couldn't have said why, but it felt weird, that touch. It moved as if her hand were burrowing in. After that, I said I didn't want to try on any more.

Then one day I rolled my bike into the kitchen and Lolly was standing there holding a bikini.

"Malibu-wear," my mother said, putting her hands in the bottom, spreading it open between her fingers. "This is the real bikini, all right. Try it on. I put it on me and it was a little small, so it should be just right for you."

I changed in the bathroom with the door closed and walked out, suddenly cold.

"Very shall-we-say-svelte." Lolly and my mother looked at each other, talking over my head.

"What do you think?"

"Love it," said Lolly.

"Comemeer." My mother kneeled down on the black and white linoleum floor and pulled the bottom up as if she were shaking me into it. She pinched the shoulder straps and looked at Lolly. "Just a nip or two on each side.

"Okay, my little Bipper," she said, tapping my butt as punctuation. I was dismissed. "Very cute. Adorable, in fact. Why not, you know. If you've got a cute little body, why not show it?"

Lolly slapped her own butt hard and the cotton made a soggy sound. "This bod needs some work. A good two weeks of diet and exercise before I'm ready for show and tell."

I rode my bike to the public swimming pool with Theresa and Benny. They both still lived on Lime Kiln Road. Every morning that summer, Ted drove me across town before he went to work, turned in the bumpy dead-end road and left me off. I always walked slowly up the yard to my grandmother's house. I liked the minutes alone there. The trees, bushes with shiny leaves—I remembered everything.

I thought I had been happy when we'd lived in the white house, out in the country. But I was dumber then, there were things I didn't know, even about downtown Bay City, where my mother took me to a boutique called The Id. I didn't know if I could be as happy here now, as happy as I had been once. I kicked the gravel stones up the driveway.

Benny lived over the long yard in the next house. Like everything on Lime Kiln Road, I had known him all my life. His mother and father were always Carol and Jimmy. Benny was pale, with thick white-blond hair and scrapes and scars on his skin.

I remembered sitting with Benny on my grandmother's eaves trough, saying our first words. My mother had taught me to say yellow, but Benny said lello. Lello was Benny's color and Benny had to be right. Our parents thought of us as exact opposites and marveled that we played together so well. For years we were together, me trailing behind, always a year younger. I behaved better at school; I was quiet, meticulous, but Benny knew things, the things kids were supposed to know. He was a genius at running and accidents. He could run fast and hard as if his lungs were pure and inexhaustible.

In schoolrooms, he knocked things over. He was accident prone. Once, jumping off the garage roof trying to fly with two paper kites tied onto his arms, he cut himself over the eye. Mothers on Lime Kiln Road loved Benny. You could see him with a white bandage on his forehead, sitting on a front porch, reading or tossing a ball to some rapt younger kid. For a long time he tried to teach Netty Griling how to read.

He knew the names of things. Bugs, trees, things on the radio, parts of machines. He seemed born knowing how to drive. Later, he danced easily, he could throw a perfect stone, a football, he understood rock 'n' roll.

These things mattered, they counted, we both knew. I admired him, he would always be older.

Theresa and I rode behind Benny. Every mile or so he would lazily turn back and circle around to us. It was a clear warm day with soft nimbus clouds drifting in the sky. I had the new bikini rolled up in my towel. At the pool, we paid a quarter for a wire basket and changed in wooden cubicles where the half-size doors were old and chipped and the concrete floor was gritty. You pinned the safety pin, with the number on it, somewhere unnoticeable, like the side of your suit. In the cubicle, all of a sudden I was surprised how small the bikini was. I stayed there awhile tracing a name cut into the pink faded door.

Theresa gasped. "You got a new suit, a bikini." She poked her elbow into my side. "Why didn't you tell me?"

I shrugged, all of a sudden not wanting to be noticed.

We lay in the sun for a while and it was the way it always was. We had to rub the white cream from a silver foil tube on Benny's shoulders and Benny's nose: Benny burned. I went dark. With the new bikini, you could see my tan line. I snapped the elastic of the bottom. My grandmother, my aunt Carol, my mother—all of them looked at me in summer as if I were amazing. They all freckled in our family, freckled and burned. I was dark from my father.

Benny ran to the line at the diving board, and Theresa and I moved back to the metal fence and put our hands behind us. Then we jumped in, cannonballs, our arms hugging our knees.

Something amazing happened then, to the spot I jumped in, the spot of blue in the pool. I was underwater, coming up, and there was a swarm of boys around me, touching, pushing, patting my breasts with their flat hands. Legs and arms were on all sides of me. I felt as if I couldn't get out; they were touching me up and down. I splashed, pushing my shoulders up for air, for breath, and the world changed and stood still, when I came above the water, splashing, trying to move towards the cement side. Something had my leg and was pinching the muscle of my calf. I saw the stillness of the sky, the pale green high water tank with Bay City written on its belly in black letters. I was alone.

I pulled on the metal steps trying to climb and their hands were on my legs. One was pulling my bikini bottom.

I screamed up, "Help me, these guys!" to the lifeguard on a white chair.

I didn't have time to think, I just pulled with my arms. Above me, the lifeguard moved one dark leg over the other. The bottoms of his feet were yellow. He picked up a white whistle off his chest and finally blew it. By then I was out, stepping, making my first footprint on the concrete lip.

"Okay, guys, knock it off," he said.

In the green water, the star-shaped cluster split and disappeared. Their skin looked white and strange, fishlike under the surface. I stood on the concrete, my arms across my chest, looking up at the lifeguard. I was back to myself. This was Ashwaubenon Pool in Prebble Park; I'd been here before, all summer, days and days. I kept standing there, waiting for the lifeguard to talk to me. He was motioning at the deep end, where a boy's arms were beating the air, as he tried to get to the side.

I looked at the shadows in the green water. For a second, for a split second, I had opened my eyes and with the pressure of resistance underwater, for a second, the thought had come, *they like me*, and it was warm and the water was soft and enclosing and I was someone else, being directed, floating.

Theresa hauled one leg up out of the pool; she padded, dripping, and stood next to me. The lifeguard finally looked down and shrugged. "You know, you're asking for it in that suit. If you don't want it, don't ask for it." He grinned. His legs were swinging beneath his chair. It was the first time I'd thought of the bikini; that was what had been different.

We lay down on our towels again, by the fence, and closed our eyes. You could feel yourself drying, just under the wind. I listened to the pumps below the concrete, the steady machines.

Benny stood dripping on us. "What happened?"

I kept my eyes closed and pretended to be asleep. Theresa sat up on her towel and told him.

"I know you're awake." Benny kicked me with a wet foot. His feet were so white. He was frowning. "Those guys are creeps."

"Saint Agnes creeps," Theresa said. None of us ever went to Saint Agnes. It was the rich Catholic school.

Theresa and I turned on our stomachs and opened a magazine and Benny went to buy us all Dreamsicles. Theresa took her sister's magazines; they were swollen and frilled from having been wet and dried so many times. Underwater, those guys were faceless, swirling around like sharks. They still poked up, sometimes, laughing. But I was safe, things were the same, while I stayed on the concrete. It would only change in the water. When Benny came back, the Dreamsicles were already melting inside their paper wrappers.

"Here." He threw his balled-up T-shirt into my lap.

Theresa carried my pin and hers and waited at the counter to get our baskets. She came in the stall with me when I changed. The ordinary dry shorts and top felt good. Then we were standing outside, against the metal bars by our bikes, waiting for Benny. Theresa touched the inside of my elbow. "You better not wear that suit again here."

"He owns the *very* largest real estate company in Bay City." My mother smiled to herself. "And it's growing. Boy, are they growing."

She moved the wooden spoon in the pitcher of lemonade as if her arm were some electric appliance.

"So, why are we going over there? Are we buying a new house?"

"Shhh," my mother said, her eyes casting down the hallway to detect Ted, who hadn't left for the day yet. Ted taught skating classes now on Saturdays and Sundays. He was hardly ever at home. I looked down to the empty rooms. I wouldn't have minded a new house, that was for sure. Two years and we still didn't have furniture. For a while, they'd said they were going to put in a pool, but that fell through, too. Most of what my mom and Ted planned didn't work. It turned out they couldn't get the bulldozers in to dig the pool without going through another yard. And when they asked the neighbors, they said no.

"No, silly, shush." She looked around the small yard, then, at the two trees, the fence. "He's just a friend of mine, that's all."

It took her a long time to get ready. She touched up her finger- and toenails with light pink polish. We drove to the old section downtown. My mother explained that the company had bought a house for its office and remodeled. We walked up the stone pathway and Dan Sklar opened the door, even before we knocked. Wind chimes hung over our heads on the porch.

The office was empty, he was the only one there and he didn't offer to show us around. My mother leaned against a desk and smiled at him. "Well, so, how are you?" she said. Her bright voice made me angry, she had a way of smiling and looking at the other person and paying absolutely no attention to me.

Dan Sklar slumped over as he stood. He looked like a tired person. His small nose was sunburned and peeling.

"The Japanese gardens in front look fan-tastic," my mother said, leaning back and crossing her arms. "They're gorgeous, very elegant. Just like they are over there."

Over where? I wondered for a minute, and then I knew what she meant. I looked at her. There she went again. She'd never been to Japan. She looked down at the rug, into the shag.

"Have you been there?" he asked.

"Mmmhmm."

I knew better than to say, When? or anything, and anyway, what did I care. She'd lie to me, too, in a minute. She was like that.

We were standing by a sliding glass door. Outside, young maples moved slightly, trembling in the stillness. My mother picked up a paperweight and held it in her hand. "A-yun," she said, still looking at the paperweight, turning it, making it snow. "You didn't get a chance to really see the rock garden. Dan's rebuilt a re-yall authentic Japanese rock garden outside." Vowels and consonants rolled and spiked in her mouth, and her eyebrows lifted as if she were talking to a very young child. "Why don't you go out and explore."

I just looked at her. Then at him. It was getting so I always turned to the other person to help protect me against what she said.

But he nodded at me, weakly. "There's a waterfall in back," he offered.

"I don't want to go outside," I said. I pretended to be dumb.

"Oh, well, okay," she said, looking down at the carpet. She lifted her eyes then, up in a straight line to Dan's face. She tossed her head and took a breath.

"Why?" she said.

He couldn't have missed the sharpness in her voice. But his eyes meandered out the glass doors, to the garden. It was high summer, just turning.

"Huh?"

"Why."

"Why don't I want to go outside?"

"Yes. Why don't you want to go outside?"

I shrugged. "I guess I don't feel like it. Is it like a federal case, I have to have a reason?"

"It's just a nice day and I thought you might like a little sun, that's all." She exhaled through her teeth. "But, no, not you, anything to be contrary, to be the center of attention."

Dan Sklar's head turned. His breath came out of his mouth so slowly, it was like something ticking.

"Adele," he said, "leave her."

But then the same thing happened that always happened, when someone tried to stick up for me.

"No, I'm not going to leave her because she's going to have to learn."

Dan Sklar swiveled his chair so he was completely facing out the window. We could see his back and his hands. He'd picked up string from his desk and he was lacing it, cat's cradle, through his fingers. Behind him maple leaves fluttered and moss on the ground seemed wet. Then my mother made a face at me. The face was like a mask: sour and menacing, recognizable, at the same time. The lines around her mouth carved deeper. Her cheeks pushed out, round and young. She looked like she was innocent and just now saw me for what I was: a devil.

I walked across the carpet, quiet—because of my sneakers. I opened the sliding doors and moved outside past Dan Sklar. He didn't matter anymore. He wasn't going to help.

The sun was weak but a definite yellow on the sidewalk. This part of town was still, today, and empty. As soon as I was outside, I was glad. I didn't know why I hadn't left earlier, I should have. It was like stepping into another room, with clean, aquatic light and thinner air. Across the street was a small bank and its empty parking lot. Down the road, pigeons sat on the painted game circles of the playground at Saint John's School, where I used to go. The spires of the steeple intersected with telephone wires.

Then I heard my name. Dan Sklar slumped in the open door, his arm above him on the wall. "Ann, there's a pond with goldfish down on your left, and in back, there's a waterfall."

"And all over the sides, he's planted flowers. Oh, and Ann, you'll never believe, there are lily pads on the pond. Remember, when you were a teensy-weensy girl, we used to go see the farms and the lily pads?"

I just stared.

She was talking to him. "We were living at Mom's and she was always the first one up at five or six, you know. So we just jumped in the car and went to see the farmers milking their cows. And she used to love lily pads, where the wee little frogs sat."

I stayed where I was sitting, on a stone. I drew my knees up and hugged them. "Okay," I said.

They shut the sliding glass door and pulled the beige curtains closed. My mother poked her head out once more.

"Ann, be careful where you step. Don't squash any flowers. Look where you're going."

The wind chime moved above the door as if someone was running their fingers through it. This old neighborhood was near Saint Phillip's Academy, the Catholic high school where my mother had gone. She had taken me to Dean's, the place she'd gone after school for hamburgers and malts—that was around here, too. I felt in my pockets, even though I knew already, I didn't have any money. I could walk off, but then I'd only be in more trouble later and there wasn't anywhere much I could go. There was a car lot a few blocks away. From where I was, I could see the string of flags rippling.

I tried to be very still and forget about myself. I pictured a refrigerator sitting in Griling's dump, the sun on its dry white sides.

Then a boy I knew from my old school rode by on a bicycle. Paul, whose father was a beekeeper. I didn't want him to see me. For two years, he had sat behind me in the row of small desks at my old school, where I went before Ted and the house on Carriage Court. It was possible he would go by and not know me. It was years now since we were in school together. I stayed, crouched there on the rock, like the Land O Lakes Indian. A fly settled on my arm, but I didn't move.

He looked at me and kept walking his bike. Then, a few squares of sidewalk later, he looked back and stood there. "Ann," he said. "You're Ann August, aren't you?"

I stepped forward, my hands conscious and awkward at my sides. We sat down on the steps together by the goldfish pond. There was a patch of smooth black pebbles. I took a handful and pitched them in one by one.

"You're at Oak Grove now," he said.

"Yeah. Public school."

"I see your cousin around. Ben. I used to come over to your house in first grade, I remember once we caught butterflies."

"Yeah, I remember that." I was embarrassed all of a sudden. I didn't want him to ask what I was doing here.

He was hitting two rocks together. "You were living with your grandmother then, out there. You told me once you liked your cousin better than me."

"I'm sorry."

He shrugged. "Doesn't matter. We were just little kids."

"Do you still live on a bee farm?"

"Yup. Got a thousand more bees now than we did then." He opened his hand and counted on his fingers. "Clover, alfalfa, wildflower, orange blossom, grass"—his fist was closed—"and mixed. I get out honey myself now. I have my mask and my gloves and my own colony."

"My grandfather had mink," I said, stupidly.

"Yup, I remember the sheds."

We both just sat there with our elbows on our knees and our chins in our hands.

"I guess I better go now," he said, standing. "Do you ski?" he asked suddenly, looking at me while he kicked the kickstand up on his bike.

"No."

"Oh," he said. "I ski now."

I nodded. Nothing seemed surprising. I fingered the concrete sidewalk, still cool despite the thin yellow from the sun. I liked him but I was glad he was going, because I didn't want him to be there when my mother and Dan Sklar came out.

It was a long time. I walked around to the back, telling myself that when I'd stepped on every stone, when I'd seen and said the name of every flower, they would be finished and we could go home. But then I was finished and nothing happened. Birds sat on the telephone wires not moving, even when I threw stones.

One of the stones landed with a loud ringing on the roof of a car parked across the street. I felt that sound in my heart. I waited then, terrified and stiff, to be caught. But time stayed still, the rectangle of sun, like a room around the parked car, changed, slowly sliding into shade.

Then the old heavy trees on the street began rustling and it started to rain. I skipped to the door then, holding my elbows in the other palm, like eggs. Sure, she would come out now.

But she didn't. I watched the birds fly off telephone wires into the dark trees. The wind chimes on the porch clattered wildly. The pond of goldfish ruffled up and stayed itself at the same time, like the skin on a pan of milk, scalding.

I walked to our car, getting soaked. The rain felt like dull needles. The doors were locked. I stood for a moment looking into the dry, kept inside of our car. My book was there. Then a line of lightning cracked the sky and I ran back to the porch. I put my ear to the wall and I didn't hear anything moving. It seemed impossible now that my mother was inside; still, our car was there. I couldn't seem to hold the two things in my mind at once.

A few minutes later, there was a strange light, slanting as if it came from the ground behind the house. I still sat, damp, in the porch shade. But everything in the yard, stones, the black telephone wires, our car, the tiny, waxy, mossy flowers, seemed to shine hardly, as if their colors were only painted and there was metal inside them.

The sun was in the sky again and the dark clouds, now marbled and veined with light, moved fast. Once, my grandmother had been driving with her husband in the old Ford. They drove into a storm. I always thought of them at one place on the black highway, a firm yellow stripe down the middle, my grandfather with his glasses at the wheel, my grandmother, in a blue dress, looking down at her hands in her lap, and the car, half in rain, the back half dry in sunlight. She'd told me that once and I thought of it a lot. It was just one of those things I used.

I sat in a square of sun, pitching stones in the pond again, trying to rouse a goldfish. They never came to the surface, but sometimes one turned underwater, a quick apostrophe of flame, like sun on a coin for a second, then extinguished again by the green. I looked up and followed the telephone wires, down the road to the string of flags marking the car lot. Something about the stillness of the air made it already late afternoon. My clothes were almost dry now, except for the elastic of my underwear and the rims of my sneakers.

Finally, then, while I was still looking at clouds between telephone poles, printing my thoughts in black square letters on the sky, the door closed behind me and my mother came out alone.

She smiled hugely and stopped a moment, rolling her head and smelling the air. "Mmmph," she said. Then she looked down and found me. She wasn't angry anymore. She stuck her arm out in the air, her hand open, and clicked her tongue—the way she had when I was little. It was a signal for me to come running and take her hand.

But I only stood up slowly.

"Do you have any coins?" I said.

"Coins?" she repeated, not changing her face—the stupid smile was still there. "Why? Do you feel like running over to Dean's?"

I thought of that a second, the silver glistening behind the soda fountain, and the day seemed to close up, small again. We'd get into our car and go, normal. I could taste the beginning of sweetness at the back of my throat.

"But before that, for here. To throw into the goldfish pond."

She stepped lightly over to where I was. She was wearing white patent leather thongs and her pink toenails looked like the washed insides of shells.

She looked in her wallet, but there were no coins. Then she lifted her whole purse to one side and shook it so everything fell to the corner. She rummaged and extracted a dime and a quarter. She gave me the quarter.

"Go on, it'll work even better," she said. "The more money, the faster you get your wish."

My mother looked around the yard. "Isn't this fantastic," she said. Her smile stayed, too big, as if she couldn't stop it.

"It's all right." I shrugged.

"Well, I think it's really great. The authentic Japanese. Really, really great." Then I knew what it was—that smile and the way she was talking—it was as if she was proud.

She closed her eyes and threw in the dime. It landed half on a lily pad, and wavered on its edge a moment before sliding under. She was crouched down so her sharkskin slacks hiked up and I saw the shaved nubs of blond hair on her ankles. Even her ankles had freckles. She was mumbling to herself, moving her lips the way she did when she said prayers. There was a flat, gold leaf on the pavement. She picked it up, examined it against the sky, then set it on the thinly pleated water. We both knelt down watching it move.

A long time ago, once, my mother drove me far, I don't know where it was, to a brick hospital, just the two of us. It was on a long lawn, like the dairy, a low, brick building that went on as far as you could see. We parked in the parking lot in back. My mother told me she had to have a test for TB. I was young enough to misunderstand.

"For TV? For TV?" I kept saying. "You have to have a test for TV?"

"No," she said. She was distracted.

I had to wait, sitting in the lobby on a chair, while she went somewhere else. A long time later, she came out in a wheelchair, a nun in a white habit pushing it behind her. "Come on, Ann," she said, without turning her head to me. The nun didn't say anything; they both looked forward. I hurried up to go and ran a little to keep next to them. The nun left us for a moment in a long hallway. There were glass showcases on both walls. I held onto a small piece of my mother's sleeve.

"See, I'll have to come and live here," she said. She looked at the handiwork in the cases and sighed. "I guess I'll learn how to knit and crochet and make things like that. That won't be so bad. I suppose I'll like it after a while."

She looked down at her hands and smiled.

"What about me?" I said it quietly, almost a whisper, and just then a huge roaring started in my head.

"You'll get used to it. I won't be able to take care of you anymore, I'll be too weak. But I'll knit something for you, maybe a sweater. You can come and visit. Mmhmm. I think I'll knit you a sweater."

The nun came back and said, "We'll have the results on Thursday." Thursday, Thursday stuck in my mind, a purple word.

The nun wheeled my mother to a cement ramp outside the building. My mother stood up and took her purse from next to her on the wheelchair. It was a white patent leather purse with gold clasps. We started walking to our car. My mother looked back, once, at the nun in her white habit, the veil moving a little in the breeze as she turned. The roaring was still in my head, in back of one ear, and I didn't say anything. It was spring that day, there were irises and daffodils planted along the edges of the hospital lawns. There was a watery breeze like on Easter. My mother drove home and never mentioned any of it again.

. . .

I was sitting on my bed, watching television. My mother came into the room. "Oh, there you are, I called you, didn't you hear me." She rubbed away a tear with a cuff. "You scared me. You know yesterday I was watching you from his sliding glass doors, and you were just standing there on that long grass by the sidewalk, you weren't even in the nice garden, sort of shuffling your sneakers on the ground, in that jacket, with your hands in your pockets and your head down. I saw you looking like that, unhappy, sluffing around like a little old man, and I thought, nothing is worth it, you're my jewel. Honest, Honey, you are. You're my absolute precious, long-limbed jewel. I have to get you somewhere they can see you." Her face folded and she started crying. "In that plain old jacket, with your head down, kicking, I thought to myself, here's this beautiful, long-limbed girl with potential stuck in a nothing town. You look like a boy in those jeans and that scruffy jacket, some boy at a gas station in some no-where place."

One day, I came home from school and the house was furnished. It had everything. I walked from room to room, switching on lamps and sitting on sofas. I ran my hands over the polished tabletops. The house had still been empty that morning.

When my mother came home she explained that it was only rented and temporary. She didn't like the blue and green color scheme, but it was the best they had. She and Ted wanted to invite the family over for Thanksgiving.

For three days we shopped. Ted went to work every morning, as usual, but my mother and I drove to the country to buy pumpkins. We placed orders at butchers' and bakeries. My mother said she'd give me a note for school saying I was sick.

My mother's sister Carol lifted her eyebrows, her hands modest in her lap, counting the different kinds of forks and knives fanning out on both sides of her plate, while her husband Jimmy started a story. All of Jimmy's stories were about sex or machines. The same thing with his jokes.

"This widow was lonely," he was saying, "so she goes to her husband's grave and digs up his you-know-what and nails it in her bedroom so it sticks up through the floor. She makes a little trapdoor for it, so, during the day, she can put it down. You know, for company."

"Oh, Jimmy, not with the kids here." Then she looked at me and laughed. "You know, you just can't stop him." Carol was eleven years older than my mother. She looked like a country woman, with her tight curls and undistinguished color of brown hair.

My grandmother shook her head as if she'd just tasted something bitter. "I don't like to hear such stuff." Her voice thumped like the weight of her footsteps when she walked around her house at night.

My mother carried in a pewter soup tureen. She bent over the candles, serving. The soup was from fancy cans we'd bought in the gourmet department of Shreve's, cans imported from France. "It's madrilene," she announced. Jimmy was rolling back his sleeves, still telling his story, but in a softer voice. Jimmy had respect for a few things. One of them was food.

He winked. "And so another guy, a neighbor, he catches on. He looks through her window one night and sees. So he goes in the next day with a saw and a shovel and two-by-fours and he builds himself a little room under the floor where her husband's thing is. He throws that out."

"He doesn't bury it properly?" My cousin Hal carefully unfolded his napkin on his lap, over his knees. Hal was thin and straight, all right angles. You could tell Hal hated his father.

"Okay, say he buries it."

"So," my mother said, sitting down. She smiled and slowly lifted a spoonful of soup to her lips.

"The house looks very nice, oh, so much better," Carol said.

"Every night, he crawls into his spot and he's ready. And so they do it. And this goes on a few months. And then one night, she comes with a knife"—and Jimmy lifted one of his own knives, the butter knife, for emphasis—"and she goes, okay, Harry, come on, we're moving. I bought us a new house."

"Dad," Hal said.

"They're at it again." Carol's head twitched back and forth, resigned.

"No more now," my grandmother said. "You had to have your one, so now you've had it."

Jimmy Measey was still laughing, sputtering, repeating the gesture with his knife. "Come on, you're going to a new house, fella."

He looked over at Benny, who was pretending to smile like he understood. Benny got this smile whenever his dad looked at him, a thin smile you felt you could wipe off with a rag. When Benny was little, his father used to tease him around other people. Once we were sitting at a restaurant, out for steak dinners. Jimmy kept telling Benny how good chopped sirloin was, how that was what he should really want, how nothing in the world was as delicious as chopped sirloin. Jimmy thought that was wildly funny, tricking Benny out of his steak, making fun of him for not knowing the names. Benny had that same wan smile then, when the whole family was laughing, as a waiter set down his hamburger. Benny was afraid of his father.

"What's this, tomato broth?" Jimmy said.

"It's madrilene," Ted said quietly, looking down.

"Yeah. S'good." Jimmy speared a lemon slice with his fork. "Now what am I sposed to do with this?"

Carol nudged him. "Just leave it, Jimmy. Leave it on your plate."

Hal smiled deliberately at my mother.

The next two courses came on small, hand-painted plates. Everyone finished the endive salad and the salmon mousse before my mother. She smiled and talked, eating slowly, looking at each bite before she put the fork in her mouth. She was really enjoying herself. It made me happy. Then Ted cleared the small plates and followed my mother into the kitchen.

"Don't you want us to hold onto our forks, Del?" Carol was asking.

My mother shouted back. "No, there's plenty clean. Just look to the left of your plate."

I brought out the pâté, each plate garnished with a limp-stemmed violet from the refrigerator. We'd paid fifty cents each for them at Debago's nursery.

Jimmy looked at his watch. "It's been almost two hours and all she's done is make me hungry."

When I set down their plates, Carol and my grandmother giggled and shook their heads. Jimmy lifted his violet. In his big hand it looked like a specimen, something dead.

"Addie, what's this flower for? Am I supposed to eat it?" he yelled into the kitchen.

"Shhh," I said.

My grandmother frowned. "It's like those fancy little butters you two used to get from the factory, such little portions," she whispered.

Then my mother glided in and they all hushed. She was beaming. Ted stood behind her, pulling out her chair. She still thought her dinner was a success. I looked at her cheeks, high and proud, and I bent over and started eating my pâté. It tasted delicious. I felt like telling her people laughed. They were hungry. But it was so good and she was happy. Why couldn't they just wait?

"So, tell me, how is your work, Adele? How do you like the new school?"

My mother sighed. Whenever my grandmother asked her questions, she sighed and she slumped back into her chair. "Well, Mom, I don't like that drive out there every day in my old car with the window that doesn't roll up. Ann knows. But these administrators are bright, just out of college, most of them. It's a good team." She looked down at her hands on the tablecloth. "I have plenty to do this weekend still. Those darn reports. Ann, maybe tomorrow we'll drive downtown to the library and both just work."

Jimmy Measey was talking to Ted about moving the water softener store to Three Corners, because they were tearing up the road for the new highway.

Ted never talked about his own work at all, as if he were embarrassed. I didn't blame him. It didn't exactly seem like a job. My mother once told me Ted was an orphan.

My mother rustled in her chair and stood up. "Ted, could you please come in and carve? And Ann, would you mind taking our plates?" We both stood up beside her, the family. I felt behind us they were laughing at the way we did things. It seemed unbearable for my mother not to know. She was trying so hard.

In the kitchen, I tugged her arm. "Mom, I think they're really hungry. It's getting late."

"Well, I hope they're hungry." She'd stepped out of her shoes and she was leaning with both hands on Ted's shoulder, watching as he cut. "Oh, it's perfect. Just pink enough. Per-fecto. Honey, you take the bread basket out. Go."

"It's prettinear ten o'clock. Ugh, I don't like to eat so late." My grand-mother smiled at me then, as if it were all right to complain about my mother. I was supposed to know she didn't mean me too. But I felt so sorry for my mother. I wanted them all to leave, before she knew any-thing.

"Ta-da," my mother said, setting down the platter of sliced steak and new potatoes. Her face stalled, waiting for compliments.

"Well, that looks very good," my grandmother said.

"Adele, you don't mean to tell me that after all this time, we're not even going to get a turkey," Jimmy said, laughing but not really.

My mother looked around the table at each of us as if the lights were just turned on. She looked down to Ted, as if for help.

"Jimmy, this is châteaubriand, ordered five days ahead from the butcher down at Krim's, at eight ninety-nine a pound, it's the best meat you can buy in the whole world, I hope that's good enough for you."

"Come, let's shush and eat," my grandmother said.

"Well, Adele, it is Thanksgiving. It's ten o'clock, we have been sitting here since five waiting. If you'd told us, sheesh, we could have had it at our house. Carol would have baked a turkey."

My mother's chair screeched across the floor. She left, running into the other room, her dress a black swatch in the hall. "You can't do anything right with them," I heard her sobbing, as Ted followed. He was smiling his awkward, zipper smile when he stood up.

Benny and I both sat, very straight, with our hands on our laps.

"Oh, Jimmy, if you would only once just be quiet. You know how she is."

"Carol, I don't care what's wrong with your sister, I want a turkey on my Thanksgiving, all right? And if we can't eat now, you can get your purse and we'll go." Jimmy stood up, stuffing a slice of meat from the platter into his mouth with a hand, his napkin still tucked in his collar. Blood dripped on my mother's tablecloth.

Hal got up, making a noise with his chair and walked down the hall towards my mother.

"Should I fix you each a plate?" My grandmother looked back and forth between Benny and me. The food was resting in the center of the table. Parsley and lemon slices garnished the potatoes. It was a beautiful platter, neat like a field.

Benny told her no.

"We're old enough to wait," I said.

Jimmy shook his head, looking at me. "Your mother."

It seemed we waited a long time, still there, and then I heard Ted's voice, shaped and kind, like a curve around my mother. "Before it gets cold," he was saying. They came back, Ted and Hal on either side of my mother. Standing, her face lit with the candlelight where she'd been crying, my mother seemed beautiful and strange and I felt sorry I hadn't run back to her with Ted. She wasn't looking at me now.

"Shall we eat before it's cold?" she said. "Hal, why don't you start the vegetables and I'll serve."

We ate quietly, careful.

"It's wonderful, Adele. This whole meal has been wonderful," Hal said.

"Yes, it's very, very good."

"Thank you," my mother said, primly.

Jimmy leaned back in his chair. "Well, Adele, for the very best meat available in the world at eight ninety-nine a pound, I'll tell you something. It's not bad."

My mother's face hung in the air a second while we waited. Then it grew to a slow smile. She couldn't help but laugh. She looked over at Carol. "I don't see how you put up with him."

"Well, you know, Adele, sometimes I don't either. Sometimes I just don't know either."

They never went to bed that night. I heard them. They moved from room to room on the new furniture, the way people turn over and change positions while they dream. I think they were amazed. They had been married three years but they had never had any furniture.

The next morning my mother came in and sat on the edge of my bed. She looked at the room behind her.

"I think he's running around," she said. She was nodding her head in assent with herself.

"Who is?"

"Shhh. I'm sure of it."

"You're nuts." I turned around to go back to sleep.

Her hand pried my shoulder up. "I don't care if he is, I hope he is. If we caught him with another woman, boy, that would really be it. That would really help."

"What?"

"In court. Then we'd get everything and we could move." She shook her head. "It's no more than I deserve, Gramma paid for the house, it should be mine. She's *my* mother."

"What are you talking about?"

She looked down at her foot. A slipper dangled off the bottom, she was bouncing it on her toes. "Today, at noon, Horst is going to call and ask him out with some girls. We'll just see what he says. I'll bet he goes."

"Who's Horse?"

"You know, Horst, downtown. The tailor. He's the one who took up your raincoat."

The morning was slow and pretend. We all stayed around the house, doing nothing in the kitchen. My mother offered to cook Ted an egg. He refused, but he stood next to her and let her pour him more coffee. She made me cinnamon toast. That was the kind of thing she never did. She hated white sugar. We all ate the leftover château straight from the refrigerator. One of us would open the door and leave it hang while we stood chewing.

Then, at noon, the phone rang.

"It's for you, Ted." My mother handed him the receiver and walked to the stove. My mother rubbed the same spot on the counter, over and over, with her dish towel. I sat where I was, blowing the sugar on my plate, then writing my name with a finger.

"No," Ted said, into the phone. "I'm not interested in that."

Then he was off. He took his coffee cup from where it was on the counter and went back to the screen door hinge he'd been trying to fix. I walked into the living room. All the candles had melted down, the wax flat on the plates like fried eggs.

"So, what was that all about?" my mother asked.

"It was Horst."

"What did he want?"

"Nothing. He wanted to go out somewhere."

"Oh, well, are you going?"

Ted put the screwdriver down. "Adele, you heard what I told him."

"Oh, well, I was just wondering. I mean I was right here, are you sure your answer wouldn't have been different if I wasn't around just then?"

I went back to look in their bedroom. The bed was tight and un-touched. They never had gone to sleep.

A nun's flashlight carved out a cave in the darkness and we followed. The old orphanage had closed. Now, they'd built an annex on the west side of the Fox River, small wooden cabins where older girls, girls who'd been in trouble, lived by themselves, four of them with one nun. My mother and Lolly and I walked through the woods to a benefit dinner in one of the cabins.

My mother nudged me. At the small round table there were candles, that was most of what we could see. The windows were dark and it was dark outside.

All around us girls hovered in white high-necked blouses, their long hair pulled back in plain liver-colored rubber bands, lipstick a little over their lips and dabs of nail polish on their nylons. They seemed tall and awkward, they didn't know what to do with their hands. They'd made our meal and they hovered, waiting to take our plates away and wash them. But I knew sometime, once, they were bad. When one leaned down to pour coffee, my mother touched her sleeve and asked a question. She looked up, distracted, and then explained. As a project, they'd made the centerpieces. Ours was an old 45 record melted down, that's how they got the edges to frill. They put the candle in the hole.

My mother nudged me and whispered. "You could do that."

After school, downstairs, I lay in the cool basement. There was a bed with an old bedspread and a television. I lay on my stomach and watched the reruns in the cool dark. I heard my mother coming down the stairs. She had a load of laundry in her arms. The pipes banged, as she set the ma-chine going. Then she came towards me.

"What are you doing down here? Why do you always come down here when you could watch the big TV upstairs? Are you ashamed of some-thing?" She was talking a certain way. I kept looking at the TV, not mov-ing, though a commercial came on.

"And why do you bounce up and down like that with your hips, people don't do that, it's vulgar."

I still didn't answer. I was barely breathing.

"Did someone fuck you?" She said the word long, with air in it. I wasn't allowed to say it. "They did, didn't they? I can tell. Tell me, Ann, who did, tell me, who fucked you. Because they really ruined you."

I saw her then like an animal, her teeth huge in her face, her body stiff and small. Her feet clicked on the cement basement floor and she moved back and forth with her hands on her hips, her head bent forward, stalk-ing. She wouldn't come any closer. It was as if I had a smell. I made myself stay the same.

"No," I said.

"Come on, tell." Her eyebrows lifted and fell once and she kept her smile. She was excited. "Tell me who did it to you, who fucked you."

I still didn't look at her. "Oooooh," she came towards me with her arm. "Stop twitching like that."

I got up and walked past her to the stairs. She grabbed my arm and I shoved her away. "Leave me alone," I said. She made marks on my skin. "What's wrong with you."

"Nothing's wrong with *me*," she yelled at my back. "I go upstairs in my own house. I'm clean. I don't twitch. I have nothing to be ashamed of."

I locked myself in the bathroom. In a few minutes, she knocked and scraped on the door.

"Ann, come out here a second.

"Ann, I have something to tell you. There's something we have to talk about.

"Open this door. Otherwise, otherwise, I'm going to open it, I'll get the key."

Circles. My head was against the cool tiles of the bathtub. The door had a gold metal doorknob. There was no keyhole, there couldn't be a key. She said she was going to get a key. But there was no keyhole, there couldn't be a key. But she said there was a key.

I pressed myself into the corner, like something molded there. I tried not to hear, not to think. And then, after, there was always a lightness, a feeling of air inside, like you are an impostor, eating only the appearance of things, living in holograms of light. There in the corner, almost gone, I had one feeling above my stomach, like a flutter. No one but me could ever know about this time, not if I wanted love.

Later, Ted came home and everything was normal again. My mother acted nice to me, she made sautéed mushrooms for over our steaks. She seemed to have forgotten. I watched her, but it seemed rinsed away, all gone. We were friends again, I was her daughter, she liked me. And I was relieved, happy in some recovered way. She picked up my hand and squeezed it. And all evening, there was that lightness. I wasn't hungry, I wasn't interested, I wasn't tired.

I didn't want anything. I'd lost my attraction for gravity and I couldn't get it back by myself. I knew it would always be there again in the morning, after sleep. But for that night, I didn't care. I didn't want a thing.

We drove past the shopping center, the used car lot and my public school, out on the highway, to where it wasn't developed yet. And then when we were at the place we'd gone for the benefit dinner, the place for girls, my mother let me out on the ditch by the side of the road and turned around and drove away. I stood waiting for her to come back. I was sure she would come, but I was trembling anyway. I couldn't control my teeth, my hands. I didn't have anything with me, money, anything. I took off my mitten. Inside was one soft worn dollar bill, pale from washing.

I was just wearing my jacket and jeans. I sat on a post. I didn't see my mother's car coming back. I watched the other cars in the distance, each one was a sink of hope, I squinted my eyes so I thought it was ours and let myself feel the sweetness of belief wash over me, but then it would come close and be green or red or yellow or blue, and all the time, inside, I really knew.

I thought of going somewhere. I looked behind me at the woods. The snow was melting on the ground. The tree trunks seemed to all rise, black, from the same level plane. It was hard to look at them. It was late afternoon, their black bark looked lush, holding gold on their thin sides. They glinted like fish in the air and soon it would be dark.

Then down the road, on my side, coming towards me, two girls were walking on the gravel, their hands in their jacket pockets. Their heads were down. I couldn't see any more from where I was. Their feet kicked up clouds of dust. I thought they were coming for me. They were girls who lived here in the woods, in those cabins, and my mother had told them I was bad and they were coming. At the exact same time and with a feeling like a finger pressing down, leaving an impression on my heart, I knew that they were coming for me and I knew that I was imagining it, that they weren't, they didn't know me.

I bolted. I saw a flash of metallic blue, but then I was on the other side of the highway, up the embankment, in the woods, before the blue car passed. I stopped for a moment, still. All my life I'd imagined one death— slow motion, a clear day, pale blue sky, white clouds and a dull gray high-way, a yellow stripe, the long bounce off a rounded blue fender, then the soft fall, dead, then nothing. All in sunlight. I'd never told anyone and I wondered if every person carried their own death with them, like some-thing private and quiet, inside a small box.

I started to walk in the woods, still looking down for a white car on the highway. I knew where I would come out, on the other side. I didn't think past that. At the road, I could hitch. The sky was white and blue now. The trees had lost their gold.

When I came out I was on another highway. Trucks and cars passed by. I'd never hitchhiked before. As bad as my mother thought I was, I hadn't really done much. I was still too scared.

A truck zoomed by and the wind almost knocked me over. I stepped up and stuck out my thumb. I looked ahead of me. Three women, mothers, drove past without picking me up, and I looked down at myself and thought how I must look. My jeans were splattered with mud. Then a truck came and stopped. Feet above me, the cabin door sprang open. The man said he was going as far as the bridge. The seats were leather and cracked, I could feel the tape on the backs of my thighs. The whole cabin smelled of oil. It was a long, easy ride. We passed Dan Sklar's office and I saw a white car like my mother's outside on the street, and Saint Phillip's empty playground. The sky was colored with feathery pink clouds when I got out.

"Say, where're you going?" he said, when I stepped down.

For the first time I thought he might be dangerous. He wore a pale brown uniform with darker brown piping and a clover with his name, BUD, over his left breast pocket.

I jumped down the three steps and pushed the door shut. My ankle twisted and I landed in a puddle. I started running and didn't look behind me. Suddenly, lights flooded the place between me and a brick wall. It was the truck moving and I turned around, stuck.

His head was in the rolled-down window.

"Girl, where are you going? I don't like to let you off like this. It's getting dark."

I looked at my shoes. They'd gone from white to brown with streaks of mud and coal, in just one day.

"I'm going to my grandmother's house."

"She live around here?" His head moved back and forth.

We were downtown, by the quarry. There were old stores here, small stores with gray worn wooden doors and bars across the screens, the only color labels from the orange companies. Ruby Beauty, Sacramento, Indian River.

Two huge piles across the water, the bright soft yellow of sulfur and the smaller mounds of coal; he was staring.

"Yeah," I said.

He waited a minute as if he were deciding whether to believe me. His face stayed in the window. He had short white hair and wide bones. I thought I saw him wince. He was thinking he was acting selfish, he shouldn't leave me, but he wanted to get where he was going.

The small red lights of the truck flashed on and he turned.

I'd lived in Bay City all my life, but I'd never seen this corner. I fingered the dollar in my mitten. I went into the grocery store and the door tinkled above me. It was dark inside except for the wide, white iceboxes along the one wall.

I stood by the cash register, choosing. I bought a package of Milk Duds, a piece of beef jerky and a bottle of chocolate milk with a straw. I opened up my folded dollar and I gave it to the man. He waited while I stood there, before he slid off the wooden stool, butt by butt, to stand.

Then I climbed the cement steps to the bridge. This was somewhere my mother could be driving and see me. She'd brake the car, get out— the world would stop in light. There was no one else on the sidewalk. My footsteps were soft in the dark, I could hear them. Cars flowed in one stream, their small red lights like sequins. For a second, they looked to me like dark separate muscles of one long thing, then they were cars again. I took my mitten off so I could feel the steel metal sting of the banister. There was a three-foot wire mesh fence and I could see through to water. Smoke came from the tailpipes, it was cold enough to hold in the sky. The noise was steady. I looked down. There was splintering ice on the rushing, dirty brown water. It looked like root beer when you took the lid off in the summer.

On the other side factories lined the river as far as you could see. The sky was still a luminous blue. Small windows in the factories showed yellow. And on the ground, trucks, dumpsters, plows and cranes stood still, parked on the coal lots, their orange shapes scattered, left cranked up in open positions, empty-handed. Dirt fell in a fountain from one of the cranes like a huge timer.

Then I looked down again. The sidewalk I was walking on now, halfway across the water, was steel mesh, too, I could see down through it, and then it was as if something uncorked in me, the air rushing inside my ears. I looked at my dirty sock and my dirty shoe from the puddle and the sound of water below was like the reflection and echo of something, and I stopped. I closed my eyes.

Cracks on sidewalks, red lines of ants, uneven places, grass growing up around concrete, the worst thing is you are alone. You always know. When you can't even sink, you can't stop, you can't let yourself. The dream of stopping, the desire, is like a pill. There is no one to hold your dead weight, so you always come back to yourself and you have to move again, your right foot and your left, the same.

I bit my lip until I tasted blood and gripped one hand over the other. One step and one step and one step. The underneath roar and the creak of steel were loud like sound in one closed room running in lines over itself. I bit the Milk Duds like pellets. I felt my tooth; there was a chip. That made me incredibly sad. I kept the piece in my hand. It seemed singularly important that I have it and not lose it to the water. Finally, I was light, a feather on the other side, ground again. I walked by the dark coal plant, I kept walking. I could smell the coal, it smelled like winter. An old neighborhood, these were bad streets, every block the flashing lights of a tavern. A brilliant Schlitz sign, water falling, white and blue, tripping over itself, behind it, I saw that the sky had gone dark. Then I was on the highway, on the shoulder, in fields, unused earth.

. . .

The earth creaked, I stepped on a branch, above me the sky shifted like a wooden door. It started to rain and the drips were themselves and echoes all around me. Along the road, there were stakes with shiny reflector disks to keep the cars from running off. I walked in the marshy ditch, passed the bowling alley, taverns, long fields between lights. There was an old red brick hotel where they put chairs out in the summer, in front of each door. Once the son was my grandmother's paper boy.

In the gravel car lot of the Starlight, a pickup backed out and a guy rolled his window down and whistled and I started running through the field. By the tracks, there were woods, birch and pine. It was very dark now. I knew where I was. But there were noises all around me. I kept biting the hard Milk Duds. I promised I wouldn't look back; I felt touches on my shoulder blades; there was air, different from other air. Some air was curved and shaped like an arm, with viscous weight when it touched you. It touched behind your knees, your neck, the soft part of your cheek that bruises. I was walking over a mulch of disintegrating leaves. There were warm spots and long cooler corridors, as in a house, but I was walking fast, tripping. The points in the sky were stars.

I came to a clearing. A weaker light showed through. The trees were high and feathered; they sighed and dripped, scraped and wheezed, shifted their weight. Finally, I stepped out. There was a long field, water coming out of a cement pipe that we crawled through in summer. Past that was the railroad track.

My cheek brushed against a cattail and I saw my foot sink into a puddle. When I pulled it up out of the swamp, I heard water. The weeds moved under the dark surface like swollen hair. I pulled the cattail hard with my hand and the silver seeds blew off onto the tall grass like scattered wishes. I sat on a rock and took off my shoe, pulled down my sock. Sitting still the noises were louder. There was one sound, loud and continuous. Air has a voice like water, but I didn't know if it was the wind or a faraway train or trucks on the highway. I didn't know if there'd ever been such a thing as silence. The wind rippled on my arms. It was always there, the sound, like inside a shell, but you had to move and then stop to hear it.

I walked with one shoe. I got over the pipe with my knees. The mud of the other side felt silky, good, on my bare foot. Then I was at the tracks. The moon was a long way down, centered between the two ties. I balanced on the rails. The smooth metal was good on my foot. It would take me to the end of Lime Kiln Road.

I kept going and going with my eyes closed, my own sounds, a scuff and a meech, two steps, endless, echoing in my ears, indistinguishable now from the outside, the way the lines of the sky and land finally merge at night and then go on and on, ringing forever.

There was a train. I was in the ditch, holding on, shaking, deaf and blind. After, a long time after, I was cold and wet. My heart was still beating, loud, like underwater.

Then I was at my grandmother's door. The house was dark and quiet, cool, wrapped in wind. I heard branches ticking against the high windows like fingernails. I decided to sleep in the Oldsmobile. I didn't want to wake her up. There was something perfect about her sleep.

The dark in the garage was a different, grayer dark, there was no light inside the blackness. There was a deep scent of rainwater and earth from the geranium planters, filled with soil and roots. Each summer, she took them to the cemetery, planted. I found the handle of the Oldsmobile door and lifted it. I went around to the other side, but the doors were locked. I could see the shapes of the lawn mower, the old hand plow, Benny's dirt bike, all the tools hanging on the wall. Then there was real noise, outside, metal, and the wind taking the garbage can lid down the drive. Something was in the garbage. I pressed myself against the old wood wall and waited. There was a long screeing sound. Raccoons. I stepped outside. Their handlike paws moved intricately below them, as they looked up at me. Their fingers worked without them, over the garbage as if it were jewelry, precious, expensive things.

I stood on the hard grass of the yard and started calling.

"Gramma. Gramma. Gramma."

I kept going and going. Now was too late to stop. I heard my voice coming from all over, the wood of the roof, the high tenting trees, a wind from the railroad tracks, crickets in the fields, all the sounds started anywhere but in me.

A light at the top of the staircase flicked on. My grandmother stood at the small window and opened it.

"Who's there?"

"It's me."

"Who are you?"

But the light pulled off and she was coming down the stairs. Then the kitchen was chalky yellow, the same room I'd seen by itself in dreams, and the dog barked inside the door.

My grandmother opened the screen an inch. "Is it?"

"Gramma."

"Oh, good gracious, come in."

Then it was over like any dream, I was cleaned, I was warm, I was safe. I was wearing loose silk pajamas my great-great-aunt Ellie gave to Carol for Carol's honeymoon at Niagara Falls in 1946, the elastic big on

my waist. I pulled the covers up in the small cold bed while my grandmother sat downstairs in the kitchen corner, calling Ted on the telephone,
telling him she had me here.

"Your mom's not home," she said, kneeling in front of her bed, shoving
the pan underneath with the regular sureness of a cook. "Lan-knows
where she is. Ted says she's out somewhere looking for you."

We each sighed and went to sleep. Later, we heard noise. Doorbells
rang from two places through the house. Someone was at the front door.
It was not the kind of house where you went to the front door. Even the
hoboes in summer knew to use the back. I stood up to the window and
the sky was lit with a huge moving stripe of light.

"Shhh, just stay down where you are. I'm going to go to the hall window to see. If anyone comes, you just run in the attic."

She walked slowly and pulled on the light by the window.

"That's your mom down there. Ye gods, who knows what all she's got
with her. You just sleep. I'm going to tell her she can just come back in
the morning."

I walked to the high window. My mother was standing where I had
been on the lawn, her hands on her hips, staring up at the house. She
looked small. She was wearing her suede jacket and her sunglasses were
still on the top of her head. Dan Sklar stood behind her, his shoulders
curling down. The light was coming from the top of a squad car. Two
policemen crowded on the porch. Then I heard my mother shouting
through the walls.

"Just let me have her, you don't know what I've been through tonight!
She scared me near to death. I almost had a heart attack, I can still barely
breathe."

"You can have her in the morning then. She's here fine, now. Just leave
her sleep."

"Mom, she's mine, she's not yours. Give her to me." My mother was
beating her jacket pocket with a fist.

My grandmother closed the door, I heard the bolt locking. The policemen shifted their feet, their fingers in their belt loops. Then they all left
and it was quiet again.

The inside of the tin bread box, the polished silver metal, was bright with
sun, brighter in the creases. The outside was pink and smooth, painted. I
stood for a long time, looking into the metal, the sparks of light in the tin,
playing.

The screen door rang and my mother stood there to pick me up. My
mother acted nice to me then. It was just us in the car, she and me, and it
was early. She drove fast on the highway, the sun was bright, but still cool.

We sat on the same side of the booth in the restaurant on top of

Shreve's. Our knees touched under the fabric of our skirts. I was wearing
funny clothes, a skirt of Aunt Carol's, my mother's college sweater from
the upstairs closet.

The waiter stood for a long time, pouring champagne into our orange
juice, and we leaned forward, watching the glasses.

"So. I think it's time we really think about going." My mother smiled
at me. Our seat was by the window, over the Fox River. The bridge was
splitting in half, the huge metal sides lifting in the air, for a boat to go
through underneath. From where we were it was all silent choreography,
light blues and darker blues, steel.

"What?"

"We've been talking about it a long time, I think we should really go."

"Could Ted get a job out there?"

My mother put her cup down in her saucer too hard. A pool of dark
water filled the plate to its rim. "He's not coming with us." She shook her
head. "You and I are really elegant. We can pass. He couldn't fit in there.
Not in a million years."

The champagne and orange juice bubbled in quaint, tall glasses. Two
tiny paper umbrellas rested on the ice cubes. When we raised the glasses
and toasted, the backs of our fingers touched.

My mother called the Los Angeles School System. She stood with a yellow
note pad next to her, talking on the phone in the kitchen. I was home,
too. My mother had called us both in sick. While she held the receiver,
saying, "Mmhmm, mmhmm, yes, mmhmm," her hand thumped against
her side.

Then, when she hung up, she started hopping around the kitchen,
clapping.

"Yippee! We're going to make it, Ann-honey. You just see. We are. I
know it."

"What did they say?"

"Well," she started, kneeling down next to me and gathering her
breath, picking up my hand. "It looks like I'm going to get a job. He said
to me, *Well*, for someone with your credentials and experience, there
should be a spot, for sure, somewhere in the system. I just have to send
all my things in. You know, my papers. God, I'm going to have to work on
that. But, let me tell you, Ann, he was impressed. You don't know, but
your mom's pretty special. Really, Ann, you don't know, but not many
women my age have an MA."

She looked down at her hands. She was shy about it. I felt, I don't
know, kind of proud.

She stood up. "Say, remember that boy from TV who was here once
for the Cerebral Palsy telethon? Let's just give his agent a call and see

about getting you on a series. Let's see, it was Ellen Arcade in Riverside, I think." My mother had a long, perfect memory.

She sucked in her breath when she got off the phone. I was absolutely still; I knew the less excited I looked, the faster she would tell me.

"Well. She *said* there's not a thing she can do while we're here. *But,* she said, the minute we get to LA, to call and she'll make us an appointment."

We skated around, skidding over the black and white floor in our socks, our hands clasped together in the center as we spun.

"So what do you think, Ann? Isn't it something? Everything just seems to be falling right!"

When we stopped spinning, I was so dizzy I collapsed against the kitchen counter and hit my head. I remembered the rented furniture, the kitchen which seemed so still and permanent and permanently ours, branded by afternoon light. We would be leaving. The house on Carriage Court wouldn't be our house anymore. That made me sad and tired with the burden of decisions. We wanted too many things.

Then, there was a contest. The spring before we left, the Red Owl Grocery Stores gave you one stamp every time you bought your groceries. They had new bags printed, saying YOU MAY HAVE ALREADY WON. You had to get an A, B, C, D and an E stamp, with consecutive numbers on them. The winner would get ten thousand dollars. My mother and I didn't really become interested until we had a consecutive A and B. Then, we got a C.

We stood outside the Red Owl Grocery Store pasting the stamp in and looking at our card. I licked it and smeared it on, and my mother pressed it down with her thumb. Our grocery bags sat around us on the parking lot.

"Oh, I think we're going to win, Ann, I can just feel it." My mother sighed before she opened her wallet, carefully, to slip the card in. "On second thought, why don't you keep it."

I slid it in my back pocket and felt the tiny raised shape of it under the denim.

Ted sat watching TV when we ran in. We showed him our card, climbing over him, on the couch. He smiled. "They're not going to let you win. The thing's rigged. They just want to get you in the store to spend your money."

"Yeah, mmhmm," my mother said, shaking her head and winking at me behind his back.

Three or four times a night, my mother would think of some small item we needed and we would get in the car and drive to another Red Owl. Ted would shake his head and smile when we decided to have hot fudge sundaes at midnight and when we drove to the other side of town to buy the ice cream and, at another Red Owl, the fudge. When we came back, he'd lift his book down from his face and look at us, bemused. He wasn't absolutely convinced we wouldn't win.

So the night we came racing from the car with thirty dollars' worth of groceries we didn't need and the fourth consecutive number, the D, he smiled and examined the book. In his subdued way, Ted was becoming excited for us.

Before I fell asleep, my mother tickled my back. I lay facing the wall.

"What would you like when we get the ten thousand, I suppose I should say if," she said.

"Go to California," I said, "and boots."

"Do you really want to go to California?"

"Yes."

"Well, maybe when we get the money, we'll just move." I thought I knew what my mother was thinking from the light way her fingers drummed and swirled on my back, her wrist dragging behind. She was thinking of the beach, the wide road dipping down to the ocean, all the things we'd seen on television. But she worried. She pinched my shoulders to keep me awake. "Would you like that, honey?"

"Yes."

"Sure?"

"Yes."

"Okay, good. I would, too, I think. I think I would too."

We bought marshmallows, detergent, whole wheat bread, Rock Cornish hens for the freezer, shish kebab skewers, new sponges, herbal teas, raisins for me to take to school, but we still didn't get the fifth consecutive number on our stamps. We didn't even see an E. We began to talk and compare with people around us in the checkout lines.

Ted became smug with renewed conviction. "That's it," he said, laughing, his arms bursting up extravagantly like a jack-in-the-box, suppressed too long. "They let you come just so close and then you go buy up the store, hoping you'll get the last number."

That was the night we came home with seven bags. My mother nodded, agreeing with Ted. She sighed when we'd hauled the bags in. We still had all those groceries to put away.

"He's right, you know," she whispered to me later, sitting on my bed. "Sure, they're going to try and rig it. If they let you win, they're going to have to pay up. This way the people keep coming in and buying. Of course, they'd rather have you lose. And I think he's right—I don't think there's an E in Bay City. Uh-uh. But I have an idea. Probably a lot of people here have everything but the E. So I thought tomorrow I could call in sick for both of us and we can drive up to Door County and go to a few Red Owls there."

"Okay," I said, grateful, looking up into her eyes. My mother was so smart. I felt excited, lying in my bed.

We didn't tell Ted. We wanted to come home that night with the completed card and surprise him. Mr. Know-it-all. We waited until he left in the morning and then I ducked down under the dashboard until we drove out of the neighborhood. All the kids were walking to school, I didn't want them to see me. I wouldn't be there all day, it made me feel creepy.

But it was all right as soon as we were on the highway. Fifty miles north and we started stopping at every little town and asking where the Red Owl was. Penfield, Egg Harbor, Fish Creek, Kiwaunee, Sturgeon Bay; we bought small items at each one; gum, razors, toothpicks, matchsticks, new soap. We walked into each store several times, taking each thing separately to a different cash register.

"What if they see?"

"Just say you forgot. You went out to the car and thought, Damn, and just remembered. So you ran in again."

In a little town named Malta, we got an E. It wasn't the right E, it wasn't consecutive, but it was our first E. We went to Malta's three Red Owls, in each aisle, hoping we'd get the right E, E 56614. We picked the items carefully, superstitiously, as if the difference between a package of ovenproof tin foil and a box of animal crackers would make the difference in our lives.

My mother sighed, opening the clasp of her purse. "We're running out of money," she whispered. We made our final choices, taking a long time. Holding the things in my hand, I believed they each had magic, a destiny, souls of their own. My mother chose a tin of anise candies. I picked a set of sixty-four crayons. "When are you going to use those?" My mother sighed, but she let me buy them.

We met outside, from our separate cash registers. After six more purchases in Malta, we had one more E, but not the right E, *the* E. My mother broke down. We walked through the store once more, this time both of us in the same register line.

"Look," my mother said to the checkout girl. There was a kind of laugh she used when she asked for something outrageous, a helpless, this-is-crazy-but kind of noise. "You won't believe this, but we just need one E. We need E 56614. Then, if we get that, all we'd need is the C. If you have it in there, could you just please give it to us? We've got the three already, and we only need two more. She's not going to let me go home without it."

My mother pressed down on my foot, hard, with her shoe. She looked at me for the lie. We already had the C.

The girl said she was sorry but the stamps came in an order, a mixed-up order, but she had to give us the top one in her pile.

"Oh, couldn't you please just look through your stack a second and see?"

"No," the girl said.

"Please, I'll give you ten dollars." My mother held the money in her hand and the girl stood shaking her head no. She looked sadly and clearly ahead of her into the keys of the cash register. "No, I'm sorry, ma'am, but I can't."

In back of us a woman was bumping her metal shopping basket forward. "That line's moving twice as fast and this is the eleven or under," she said. "Meanwhile I pay the baby-sitter at home."

My mother took her money back. "Come on, Ann, let's go."

"That's three eighty-nine for the groceries, ma'am."

"Forget the groceries," my mother said. She was mad. She was always mad when she couldn't convince someone to make an exception for us. We climbed into the car and she slammed her door. "That dummy. 'No, I ca-yunt,'" she mimicked.

We drove home and both took naps until dinnertime. After, when we were watching television, Ted looked at us each and said, "Well, aren't we going to have our nightly run? What'll it be? Dessert? Charcoal for next summer's barbecues?"

Ted was hopeless. "Very funny," my mother said, keeping her eyes on the set.

My mother fell in love with a car. It was a used car, but barely used, a beauty. It was only a year and a half old. My mother said the owner had only driven it once a week to go to church. A dealer was selling it, but it was still parked on the owner's curving driveway.

After we gave up on the contest, we drove out to buy ice cream cones at Dean's every night. We rode by the car, after. My mother smiled and shivered slightly whenever she spoke of the car. It had a white exterior, a white roof and two navy blue lines, thin as pencil marks, running down its sides. I always felt like tracing them with my fingers. It was a Lincoln Continental Mark III.

"I think it's the most elegant car in the world right now," my mother said. We'd parked a few houses down and we climbed out to look closer. It was a private driveway, so we kept very quiet, walking. There were dark bushes on either side. The neighborhood was still and lush, perfumed with fallen roses. The dark seemed to gather, secret in the hedges. There was a haze of dusk in their pointed intricate branches. The car had a light tan, creamy interior and an elaborate dashboard with polished wood panels. We pressed against the windows to see more. My mother softly tried the door and grimaced at me, quickly, when it opened in her hand. We slipped in. I was on the driver's side. We each sat in our seats for a minute, I rested my hands on the wheel.

"It even smells good," my mother whispered, "feel the leather." We ran our hands over it, lightly. Then we got out and gently closed the doors again. We each turned back to look at the house we were walking away from. It was large and old and closed.

"Apparently, she's in her sixties," my mother said. "A very dignified woman, I've heard, *very*. He's a dentist. Now, Gramma could be more like that, she could dress up a little and join clubs. But she'd rather just stay out there in her old clothes and make her own little supper and rake her leaves." She sighed. "She's really a loner, you know, Ann? And she'll always be that way, until the day she dies."

We drove past the car every night that spring. The first week in June the weather turned. It was cool when we walked with our ice cream cones from Dean's to the car. My mother switched on our heat.

"Listen, there's something we have to decide." Her tone seemed more solemn than usual, there was something older and sweet in it. It was what she would someday become. "We can afford either the Lincoln or California, with the money we have saved and what I'll get from the Teacher's Retirement Fund. But we can't have both." We stared out the windshield in front of us, licking our ice cream cones, placid as cows. She'd said that softly, as if she were apologizing. "Now, if we get the car," she went on, "we'd still have the house and remember, Honey, we're at the top, here. There, you'd always be one of the poorer kids. I won't be able to compete with the families who have fathers. So, you have to think what you want, Honey. It's up to you."

Sometimes it seemed years, it had been known between us, decided, we were going to California. But we'd never really said it. It was our secret, a nighttime whispered promise. Now we were sitting in the car in the waning summer daylight, early evening. My mother shifted her ice cream cone to her left hand and started the ignition again, driving with her right. We rode slowly through Bay City. The air was moist now as I dragged my hand out the window. I was wearing clothes I'd had for a long time.

Spells can be broken by the person who started them. Some things, once spoken in the daylight, can never be the same. I didn't want to leave, but I didn't want to give up California, either. I never wanted to move from my seat. I wanted my mother to keep driving and driving. She was talking, humbly now, mentioning rent, school systems, putting the house on the market. "Dan Sklar would handle it for me," she said.

But if we stayed, we wouldn't have California anymore. We couldn't whisper at night about moving there when we were sad. We'd never believe it again.

My mother had given me choices all my life and I'd never learned to choose. I always tried to figure out first if there was a way I could have both things. My mother's face was obvious. I'd learned a long time ago to pick the thing she hadn't picked, the one she didn't want. That way she would get me both, because she couldn't bear to give up what she wanted for me.

My mother loved that car. She had to have it, I knew she wouldn't be able to relax until we bought the Lincoln. She pulled up slowly and parked in front of the house with the Lincoln in the driveway. She looked over at me, down into my face. "What do you think, Ann? Which do you want?"

"California," I said.

"Rather than the Lincoln?"

"I think so."

"Well, be sure now. Think a minute."

"I'm sure."

Her hands dropped from the steering wheel to her lap. She stuffed the napkin from her cone in the car ashtray. "Okay." We both looked out the windshield at the darkening bushes. "You really think you can make it on TV?"

"Yes." My hands clutched the car seat under me. I was bluffing, I didn't know anything. I was twelve. I had no idea if there was anything I could do.

"Okay," she said, apparently satisfied. She looked relieved. She backed the car slowly and turned around. "All righty. Well, then, I guess we're going."

We both went solemn. We drove and didn't say anything. I kept thinking of her asking face, peering down at me, and how now she was settled, looking straight out into the dark. It already seemed too late to change our minds. When we pulled into our driveway, a light was on in the neighbor's garage and the door was up. One of the older boys lifted the hood of a car open, he was bending into it, searching the machine parts with a flashlight. I knew what would happen to him, to the people who stayed.

We came out of the Red Owl carrying grocery bags and the cars had their lights on already. It was drizzling slightly and the brown paper bags were damp by the time we got to the car. I had on Benny's junior varsity jacket; it was big and warm, the sleeves too long for me.

My mother sighed once and looked around. That was all. We stood a moment with the groceries on the car top before she opened the doors.

You look at a place differently when you're leaving. I jammed my hands into the deep felt pockets of Benny's jacket.

"You know we can still change our minds." My mother started the car and sat back in her seat. We both put our hands near the heating vent.

We drove out into the traffic. It was still early, five o'clock, and not yet dark. The wet pavement made the car wheels hiss and the drivers ahead of us went slow and cautious.

"I know."

My mother turned onto the highway and pulled on our lights. "Okay, okay," she said to herself, when a passing car honked and blinked. She wasn't going the direction of home, but I didn't care, I didn't have anything to do. We'd both started the year in Bay City knowing we wouldn't finish. I liked wearing Benny's jacket. I felt the inside, serrated seam. We were going over the bridge, the steel underneath roared every ten feet, it was like hearing the hollow height and water. Then we were on the other side of town and my mother drove out to the cemetery.

People were coming home from work, there was traffic. We turned off the road, through a black, wrought-iron arch and then under the trees. My mother's car bumped on a groove, meant to make cars go slow. It always seemed quiet in the cemetery, and that evening there were no other cars. Green vertical pumps stood every few feet on the lawn, to fill cans with water, and most of the boxes were planted. The grass was shiny, bright green under the drizzle.

My mother slowed and parked as close as we could get to her father's stone. It was alone, the only one on a small slope between two oak trees. The other land was all bought for our family.

It was a pink granite stone, smooth on the edges, polished. Years ago, in summer, when we'd come to water the geraniums, Benny and I had slid down the sides. Now, my mother and I stayed in the car with the rain coming down over the windows. My mother left the heat on but turned the motor off. She kept her hands on the steering wheel.

"Should we go out?" I said, after a little while.

She shook her head slowly, no, over the steering wheel, her chin puckering into a frown.

I shifted in my seat, inside Benny's jacket, and looked out the windshield; there was fog on the ground, blurring the distant lights down the hill and behind us on the road. The trees above us were dark and heavy; they seemed very old.

Finally, my mother pulled the lights on again and we drove out, the long way, down the winding path. It was the only time I'd been to the cemetery with my mother. I wondered if she came by herself.

· · ·

We worked on the house. We painted my bedroom floor white and hung curtains to match my flowered bedspread. Ted fixed the fireplace. Now, my mother bought fresh flowers and candy to put out in bowls in the living room. The house was nicer than it had ever been, so people would buy it. But it wouldn't last. We had to mop up my white floor each time before people came to see the house, the new bedspread in my mother and Ted's room wrinkled like a sheet if anyone sat on it. The days we'd stayed around the house, though, cleaning and painting and fixing things, were when Ted and my mother and I got along best, most like a family.

After summer school, once, I was in my room, in play clothes, leaning over to tie the laces on my sneakers. Ted knocked on the door. He was home early, he wasn't usually home at that time.

He sat on my bed next to me. For a while, he didn't say anything. It made me think that in all this time, he and I hadn't been alone much. Just the two of us, we didn't know what to say.

He held his hands in his lap and looked at them. "Your mother is leaving me," he said. "I suppose you already know that."

The tiles of the floor, painted white, spun when you looked at them too hard. It was cool in this room. My room touched the farthest back in the yard.

"Ann, do you know what a homosexual is?" He looked at me hard, waiting, like the teachers wait, a whole side of their heads still, after they ask a question in school. "Well, a homosexual is a man who likes men better than women. Your mother is saying that I'm a homosexual and when you're older and she tells you that, I want you to know it wasn't true."

"Okay."

"That wasn't the reason."

I couldn't look at him. "What is the reason?" I mumbled.

"What?"

"If that's not the reason, so what is the reason then?"

I sat next to him looking down at the floor.

"I don't know, Ann. You'll have to ask your mother. Someday you'll just have to ask your mother. Maybe she'll tell you."

We kept sitting there, on my bed, staring at the wall. Then he picked up my hand.

"I'm sorry to see you go, Ann. Because in the years we've lived together, I've grown to love you. I've come to think of you as my own daughter."

I smiled to myself and tried to keep it from showing. My chest felt warm, as if he'd given me something important to keep. I didn't want to move, I was sitting in a small square of sunlight.

"I'm going to miss you," he said.

I looked down at the floor between my sneakers. Ted was an orphan. My mother had told me he didn't know who his real parents were, but every Christmas he sent a nutted fruitcake, carefully wrapped, to his foster parents in upstate New York. He sent it early so it would be sure to get there on time.

The sky in the windows, that had been plain and blue when I'd started to put my shoes on, was bright and almost dark now. I didn't want to go outside anymore. Then we both heard my mother's car bolt up the drive, the slam of her door. Ted dropped my hand back in my lap.

Lolly and my mother sat in the basement, laughing. They'd made a pitcher of Bloody Marys and it stood on top of the washing machine. They were sorting my mother's old suitcases of things into boxes. All we could take with us was what would fit in the car. Stuff my mother owned but didn't know where to put lay on a carpet in the basement. I sat on the top step where they couldn't see me.

"He's left and gone back and left and gone back. And he knows if he did, she could ruin him."

"You mean she'd get half of everything."

"Half, more than half, the house, *ev*-erything that he's worked so hard for and built up himself from scratch. I don't blame him for wanting to hold onto it."

At night, I walked back down to the basement where they'd been. I pulled a string to turn on the light. It was just one bulb. I rummaged through the cardboard boxes. In the pile marked *Take* were my baby skates and an old suitcase monogrammed with my father's initials. The handle was broken and a dog collar buckled through the two metal loops. Inside was a jumble of my first-grade printing exercises, whole pages filled with small and capital *E*'s, a white photo album with a yellow pressed bud rose in it, a list of classmates who might like me, a faded Band-Aid–colored hospital identification band from when my mother was in Saint Peter and Paul's for me, photos of me naked with a beach ball in little cardboard frames—I quickly flipped them shut, then I found a yellowed onionskin paper report on me.

> Ann is an average child. Her teeth have white marks, possibly from a fever in infancy, making her inappropriate for close-up facial photography. Her hair and olive skin are rich and promising, and her long bones might bode well, but her expressions are sometimes blank and unpredictable. In play skits, with other children, she was sometimes shy and melancholy, looking off somewhere into the distance. Other times, she became aggressive and out of control.

The report was a tissue carbon, on letterhead stationery, green on yellowed white. Ann Hatfield August. Age 2½. The Glory Jones Agency on

Park Avenue in Chicago. I held it in my hands and read it over and over again, as if there might be more about me. I didn't remember any of it. I didn't know I'd ever been in Chicago.

It was a watery day, windy, not raining yet but it would, and I was walking to Three Corners. I waited on the old cracked sidewalk, outside the wire fence of Saint John's School. Mary Griling was going to meet me at ten o'clock. I didn't know how she'd get out of her classroom, recess wasn't until 11:15. I guess she said she needed to go to the lavatory. Anyone would have believed Mary.

Chalky yellow light came from all the windows in the old red brick school. Dry leaves blew up against the fence by my feet. I felt in my pockets. Mary's passion this year was for marbles. The popular girls in her class were girls whose fathers worked in the ball bearing factory up the Fox River in Pulaco, girls who brought huge, shiny ball bearings to shoot with. They called them steelies. I had a steelie and a package of colored cat's-eyes.

I stood there and cars went by and then finally I saw her, coming out in her indoor clothes, a jumper, a white blouse, knee socks and clean, polished saddle shoes. Her collar was neat and crisp, folded down like two envelopes. She had her badge pinned to her jumper over her left breast-bone; it was a silver metal eagle on a white satin ribbon. Mary was awarded it in assembly for being the best female pupil in her class. She ironed the satin ribbon at night and put the pin back, fresh, every morning.

The sharp leaves touched our legs through our socks as they blew against the fence while we talked. I gave her the marbles and steelie and she put them in her pocket, keeping her hand there, holding them. We scuffed our shoes on the pavement.

"I guess you better get back," I said.

"Yes."

"Remember those pictures I took a long time ago in our new house?"

"Uh-huh."

"I'll get rid of them, burn them someplace."

"Okay."

"I'm sorry."

She shrugged. "I don't care."

"Just go ahead and find Benny if you want anything," I said. "Don't be afraid of him."

"I won't. I like Benny."

I never said anything to the rest of them, to the boys. She stood there and I put both hands on the shallow indentations of her shoulders. We kissed softly, both of us, the way I'd seen my cousin Hal kiss my mother once, looking at her mouth, so carefully, as if he were afraid he could miss.

. . .

"This way, we won't have the house, but we'll have a car to let people know who we are a little," my mother was saying. She'd managed to get the Lincoln Continental after all. "Maybe out there where everyone's in apartments, it goes a little more by the car. Because we won't have a house or anything, but maybe this will help. They can see we came out of something."

When we slid into the new car, it smelled like lemon wax. The leather moved below us, soft and rich. We both wriggled, shrugging, to adjust ourselves. It felt like our bodies would make permanent impressions, the leather seemed that moist. My mother opened her purse and took out a bag with two long leather gloves in it. She held each of her hands up, taking a long time pulling them on.

Then it was an Indian summer day and everything was already done. We stood in front of our house on Carriage Court, alone, light, carrying nothing, already packed. Ted had left for the rink very early. The house was empty and clean, the windows washed. Everything inside had been accounted for. The grass was cut. There was a stake with an orange SKLAR REALTY—FOR SALE sign stuck in the front lawn.

"Comemeer," my mother said, "I want to show you something." We were standing on the front sidewalk, by the new car, which glistened in the sun. I didn't want anyone, any of the neighbors, to step out of their house and see us. Across the street, the garage door was rolled up and one of the boys stood over a work table. A radio came on. I just didn't want him to ask anything we would have to answer.

My mother lifted the lid off a garbage can and grabbed the back of my neck. Her other fist held a fan of pictures over the can like a hand of cards. She dunked my head gently.

"I was packing your closet and I found these."

In the pictures, Mary looked simple, very young. She was much older now. The boys looked frightened and excited, eyebrows pushed together, dark uneven lips. The boys seemed guilty, caught. My mother peered down, looking at me looking at them. Her voice was very gentle, as if she were afraid.

"Don't ever do that again, Honey. Seriously. It's against the law. Because they could really sue you and put you in jail if the parents ever found out."

The garbage cans were clean, hosed off, and ferns bright with new tight fronds curled against them.

"What for?"

"Just because." She shook her head. "They just could. Take my word for it. And believe me, they would. So don't ever do that again, Honey, because you could get in big, big trouble. Really."

She ripped the photographs into pieces. They'd yellowed, they looked old and simple. Mary, in them, was nothing, just so young.

"We'll forget about it," she said, quietly, letting them fall into the garbage can. Then, she bent down and retrieved the torn bits. "Actually, let's not leave them here. You never know who looks around. We'll throw them out somewhere else, on the road." She unclasped her purse and dropped the shiny scraps of paper inside.

Then we walked down to the car, stopping on the lawn. My mother frowned. "You know you were right when we moved in. It is an ugly house. It really isn't anything much. Just a little shoe box with no windows."

I turned around and looked. It didn't look to me like a shoe box anymore.

The leather smelled new and old at the same time as we sank down into the car's front seat. My mother seemed nervous, driving. She hadn't told the family about the Lincoln Continental and now they'd all see it. They'd have to. When we turned onto the gravel of Lime Kiln Road from the highway, the sky was blue, the clouds white and thin, the telephone poles pitch-black. High leaves on the trees glittered, sharp, dark green. The sky was a deeper blue than most pale summer skies and the wind moved like bright transparent banners around the branches. My grandmother's house looked trim and neat as we drove up the driveway, the dark front bushes shiny. Birds sat on the tin tops of the mink sheds on the lawn, the cornfield was yellow and dry. Behind the old barn that once housed the butter factory, the highway looked dull, pure gray. And when we drove up and parked, my grandmother and Carol came out of the house. They seemed drawn to the car. Carol and Jimmy each touched it, running their hands over the sides.

My grandmother didn't say anything. She smiled with her teeth together and she was squinting, the way she did in the sun.

"What's that, a Lincoln Continental?" Jimmy said to my mother.

"Mark III," my mother said.

She had packed neatly, and with an eye for color. Through the windows the inside looked spare and orderly. The trunk was full and the backseat had only our best suitcase, and on the tan leather, there was a printed red box and each of our summer sweaters. That was all we were taking with us to California for the whole rest of our lives.

Hal was gone already, at boot camp in Texas. The night before he'd left for the air force, I'd sat on his lap, pretending to shoot beebee guns in the air. I had looked outside over the dry lawns. All our lives we'd collected skeets from the fields. It was supposed to be good when you found a whole one.

Inside, the kitchen was buzzing with sun. It was after eleven in the morning. Jimmy Measey had already driven to breakfast at Bob's Big Boy on the highway, then to the water softener store and back again. Carol stood pouring coffee for everyone while my grandmother served squares of rhubarb pie, just made this morning, still warm. Jimmy sat on a high stool drumming his hands on the table.

That summer, because we were leaving, I'd stayed afternoons and watched, trying to learn how to bake. The crust must be made in the morning; the parts not set, but the flour, lard and water mixed on the kitchen table, rolled out thin on the cutting boards. Nothing was measured, nothing kept. My grandmother washed and picked over the fruit, chopped the rhubarb, peaches, tossed in handfuls of berries and beat up eggs and sugar and fresh nutmeg in a blue bowl. Maybe vanilla, if we remembered. We poured the liquid into pie crusts, lining the square tin pans, and it smelled as clean as milk. We dallied over the crusts, ruffling the edges with two wet fingers for a long time. When they were in the oven, there was a fine dust of white flour in the air. I'd watched and studied, taking notes.

"Would you like milk?" Carol set the glass down, hard, in front of me on the table. Then she walked to the counter and wiped her hands on her apron. She seemed to be trying not to get in anyone's way, she stood studying her knuckles.

Carol would have my grandmother to herself now. My mother eyed Carol suspiciously, a little bitter, as she slowly ate her square of rhubarb pie, examining each piece on her fork before she put it in her mouth, as if it were a complicated wonder.

And Carol looked at her sister, who still had her figure, a young face. (Why was it—she seemed to be puzzling—that Adele's face stayed clear long past the age when Carol's and all Carol's friends', women who used masks and facials and creams, accepted lines?) Who knew what Adele could get for herself, what we could do in California? We already had the new car and Carol must have wondered where we got the money for that. (Later, she would hear from the former owner, the dentist's wife, who belonged to clubs, about the matter of delinquent payments.)

But my mother's optimism must have seemed stamped on her clothes and even on mine, like labels. Carol glanced down shyly at herself, leaning against the counter, and she slouched, looking frumpier. She rubbed at her mouth with a napkin, as if she had eaten something sweet and oily and there were crumbs on her face that would stay no matter how hard and how many times she washed. Her thighs rubbed against each other as she walked and she seemed to wish we would leave. She moved as if she hardly ever thought about her body from the waist down. She paid no attention to her legs. Except when she saw my mother.

But it would only be a little while now. Carol closed her eyes and when she opened them she looked out the window. She could wait, she knew, she must have said it to herself without words, she was a waiter, she always had been, always would. The oblong silver water tank gleamed like the Goodyear blimp on the grass, in the untimely sun. Carol would have remembered Benny and me in our baby sunsuits climbing on the rough silver, scratching our chubby legs. It was all so new to us then. "It's funny what kids like," Carol said, "the most ordinary things, like water." Water tanks, things after a while my mother and I forgot and didn't even see anymore. Carol shook her head. It was too bad for Benny that I would be gone. All summer, Carol had found Graham crackers hidden in stacks in Benny's room, when she'd gone in to dust. She hadn't said anything. She'd left them.

Carol must have known she would always change the towels, screens in summer, storm windows in fall, the plain things, putting both hands on Benny's shoulders; only when she thought of that, she probably pictured his squirmy body below her fingers and a small boy escaping under the kitchen table. Now, to touch Benny's shoulders, Carol had to reach. And he would still grow more.

My grandmother wasn't young either, and when she was old and when she could no longer take care of herself, Carol would be right there, right next door, here. Carol would come every morning for coffee and ask her what she wanted to do that day, in the same careless, flat inflection our grandmother had used with her and she had used talking to her own children.

Carol would keep her mother clean, she would keep the sheets fresh and smelling of rainwater. Every day she'd come and push the windows open. She would take the time to wash the doilies on the windowsills underneath the African violets and iron them, just to put them back again where they'd been. Never in a million years would my mother do that. No matter what she said.

When the sky clouded and turned gunmetal gray with the blue, Carol would walk by herself over the back lawn in a hurry to the clothesline between the two pines. She would put the wooden pins in her pockets and her mouth and fill her arms with sheets.

These were chores my mother and I had done, had dreamed about doing always, but now we wouldn't anymore. We wanted other things.

When my grandmother was old, I would be away at college, my mother could be anywhere and Carol would be there, here, home. We already knew it that day. It worked out like numbers in arithmetic. Carol was already wide in the hips, she and my grandmother went to the same girl at the Harper Method Beauty Shop every Friday, a standing appointment, for the same all-around-the-head permanent curls. Carol's face had become rounder, with kindness, as she'd grown into middle age. Her voice had the bland, even quality of an unselfish nun. It was only around my mother she had an edge.

And my mother, tasting the coffee go bitter and dry in her mouth, having eaten her two pieces of pie, felt full and still sure there was not enough. She stared at the half pie left in the tin pan. Carol was always born first. Her mother already had a daughter when she was born.

It was almost noon and there was a breeze lifting the thin summer curtains off the sills. My mother set her cup in its saucer and it trembled, chiming a little as she looked around the kitchen. Simple views. A corner. The refrigerator. Broom closets, the clean white stove. The mangle. With her chin in her hands, she closed her eyes a second, perhaps believing that if Carol were not next door (the dark darker, the edges of her eyelids tight), her husband, the Arab, my father, gone nowhere, a new hard star in the night sky, it would have been only herself, she would be staying home with her mother. She would be the one. The night sky chipped with light would be bordered with windowsills like a framed doily.

Then she opened her eyes and all the silver in the kitchen—faucets, fixtures, the tin bread box, handles on the cupboards—was glistening with maintenance and care and it would someday be Carol's and if my mother wanted it more than everything, if she picked the first star in the sky every night of her life and wished, she still could not have it, ever.

The screen door slammed and it was Benny. He stamped in, heavy on the floor, hands at his sides, grinning. He wore glasses now, small glasses with thin gold rims. He was shy because he had a present. Just Benny in the room, standing, tall and awkward, breathing like a light lift of sawdust, seemed to let Carol's shoulders relax. He justified the position of the land.

I took my present from his hand. He hadn't wrapped it. He'd been over in the garage, working, he'd finished just this second. It was a metal box, tin, with a hinged lid. Inside was a cushion of blue satin. I kept staring into it, I didn't want to look anywhere else, it was perfect.

"It's for jewelry."

"He made that all by himself." Carol nodded.

Benny and I ran outside, to the lilacs and the pussywillows behind the garage. We were too old to play anymore. We just stood there, our bare arms long and weak, kicking dirt. Our parents were coming out now, down the porch to the car. We could hear the dog yapping at their heels.

"Oh, you shush now, you," my grandmother said to him. I imagined her bending down, patting his back. He had to be quiet. He would be here forever; in a minute, we would be gone.

They couldn't see where Benny and I were and they hadn't thought yet to call or look. We were behind the garage, in the bushes, left alone a secret there. There was wind that day that seemed to make you want to move; I thought after we drove away that Benny would start running. The sky was plain and clear, the air where we were was old. There was nothing in the birdbath. Everything was in its place just where it was.

Suddenly, we heard our mothers, each of them, calling our names.

"Ben-ny."

"Ann. Ann."

They were calling loud, as if we were farther away than we were. Their two voices echoed in the air off the trees. They must have been cupping their hands. We looked at each other, suddenly scared, and hard. We had a minute—they thought we had farther to come—before they would start looking for us.

Then it was black and Benny was hugging me and we were dizzy, turning, standing up. That was something about Benny, always. He could hug you so hard, hanging on as if he were dying, falling off the spinning planet, out of the earth's fall, and his fingernails bit into you and you were there, black, for a second.

We fell to the ground then and apart. We opened our eyes on the grass. I looked at him one second, then ran to my mother.

"Well, well, there you are." They were slow still, by the car, a family in a picture, in blue and white sailor suits, the dresses rustling in the breeze. Then I saw behind her glasses my grandmother was crying, the tears slow on her skin like drops of water on a peach. My bike was leaning against the garage, my bike that Benny was going to give the Grilings.

We stood by the car with the door open, the wind was there all around us, we heard a thin distant constant moving wind. My grandmother came in close. Everyone else was farther back, like croquet balls, anything colored and still, scattered on the grass.

There were three pairs of shoes, my grandmother's, my mother's and mine, all white. "Here," she said, and far above, she handed my mother a blue envelope. "It's nothing much, just go buy yourself one of those little portable televisions with it once you get there."

Her hand slapped against the skirt of her dress to call her dog away, away from the white wheels of our car, us, the open window, the gravel white and sparkling as we were driving away.

"Well, remember," she said, and then there was just the wind louder and the indifferent changing sky and Benny was running somewhere on the edge of the lawn and I saw nothing and we were gone.

Lillian

4

The Age of the Year

My mother had seven sisters and they all lived near us in Malgoma. I can still remember them on my hands: Hattie, Clara, Ruth, Irene, Alma, Ellie and Jen. My mother was Ida, right in the middle. They were all married except Ruth, and Ruth lived at home with their father. So each one had her own house. Once a week I went to those houses because they'd decided I could make piecrusts. They used to say you were born with a feel for it, like with gardening, especially there near the water where the air changed so much day to day. Their mother was one such a one and Hattie, but Hattie had arthritis. I never used a recipe. I just mixed flour and water, sugar and lard, sometimes a speck of spice or nuts. It would take me all morning every Saturday, going from house to house. The aunt would generally sit with me, talking, and doing something else, sewing or sorting the wash. There was a lot more housework in those days. You had to do everything by hand.

I carried notes between the sisters. They sent everything back and forth—recipes, gossip, what the one was making for supper that night. And if someone spilled something that made a stain, she'd write a note and ask what would take it out. They were each different but they all got along. You don't see that so much anymore, close sisters. Alma was the pretty one. She wasn't the youngest, but she was a baby. She was always the father's favorite and the others knew it. They envied her, especially Ruth, who stayed there cooking his meals and cleaning up after him, but they never held a grudge. They were just the opposite. They fawned over her.

I remember the older ones brushing out and braiding her hair. She would just sit there and let them fuss. Alma loved to be touched. Sometimes, when I was there, she held out her arm and asked me would I tickle her. But she had her share of hard luck, too. She married a vaudeville piano player and he was gone a lot, always on tour. First he was in John Johnson's band, then it was Hans Hansen. And by the end, she lost all her hair, poor Alma. I used to visit him in the nursing home. Alma had passed away long ago. He still had his two pictures—one of her, with her long hair, and one of him with his band. They aren't allowed to have anything in there, so his doctor prescribed two shots of whiskey a day, that was Frank's best medicine. Even into his eighties Frank was still a handsome man. The ladies there liked him too and they tried to get him to play the piano. But he was a loner. He said, what do I want with those old biddies? And every time I visited, he'd tell me the same stories again and again. He'd fingered those two pictures so much, the edges were ruffled like fluted pies.

Each one of the sisters had a real different kitchen. It was like having eight houses, I knew my way around each one. I knew where to find the sifters, where they hid the cherry bounce. We had the smallest house. It was only my father and my mother, my brother Milton and me. My father was a welder and they worked long hours. And when he was home, he was a quiet man. My mother really ruled the roost. I don't think she was too proud of him, either. I think she wanted him to be something better. I know she would have liked to have more children. She played the piano, she embroidered such hairpin lace on the pillowcases and sheets, she made all her own doilies. I suppose she thought she would have made a good doctor's wife or banker's wife. But she only had us. So she paid a lot of attention to Milton, she spoiled him. He was her favorite and he was a pretty boy. It would just have to be a boy that got those curls. And such blond, blond hair. He had long eyelashes too. I didn't have hair like that, mine was straight as a board, until I learned how to braid it. Then it curls when you take it out. Now it's been braided for so many years it curls by itself. I wouldn't know how to make it straight again.

The place I grew up was fifty miles from here. Now it seems like the next town over, but then there were five or ten villages in between. None of them have names anymore. They were just carriage stops really, a hotel and a drugstore and a few houses. There was that huge fire in the canning factory, that closed down Pulaco and Suaminee. And the rest, the people just moved, I suppose. They had to leave to find work. A few farms are still standing, but most of those houses look empty.

We were a small family for that time—all those around us had more. And I always wished for a sister. Then, for a while, we had another girl in our house. I was down by the railroad tracks cutting pussywillows for a tablesetting, one night. It was in the fall, around five o'clock, just before supper. There was a girl and a cat behind her, walking on the coals. We were out there a little while and then a storm came real quick and it started pouring. I turned to go home, but when I looked back, the girl was still there, on the rails. I shouted, did she want to come with me to my house? She didn't look like she heard me, so I went down and took her wrist and then she understood. She followed me, both of us running. I held the pussywillows close to my side and she was carrying that cat up under her dress.

It took us awhile to decide she was dumb. She was filthy dirty, you could see when she was inside under the light, with coal on her arms and face. She had long black hair, all matted. It was thick hair, so when you looked down into it, under the lamp, there were all different colors, blues and greens. I remember that because we brought her into the bathroom and washed her in our big tub. Milton carried in the hot water from the stove and helped us hold her down. You wouldn't believe the ants that came out of that heavy hair, thick streams into the water.

"How old are you?" my mother shouted at her. "Do you hear me now, say if you understand." The girl just stared straight ahead. She looked pitiful and small in our big tub. We figured out that she couldn't talk. She looked to be about seven or eight, she was the same size as I was, and we had no idea where she came from. We thought someone may have just left her off, migrants, maybe, going south for the winter. She was pretty then, once we'd fixed her up. We'd washed her and combed her hair and put her in one of my dresses, like a doll. I'd tried to keep the cat out in the yard, with my boot, but she wanted him in, so he was drinking milk from a saucer, under the kitchen table.

The next day my mother and I went to the convent. We knew there was a nun who taught the deaf. They all went to school together in Malgoma, the deaf, the blind, I suppose they were lucky to go to school at all then. We waited at the door while the novice went to get Sister Mary Bead. We had a cherry kuchen with us; we never went anywhere without something baked. We told the Sister about the girl and she said she'd take her into her class and then we had to pick a name. My mother said Louise. That was what she had wanted to name me, but my father thought it sounded like an old woman. Too much like one of those sisters you already have, he'd told her. I wanted to call the girl Penny and they let me have my way. I suppose so she was more like a sister.

Sister Mary Bead used an old one-room school, with a stove in the corner and a dunce cap up on a bureau. I went to regular school with three rooms. Three rooms was big stuff in those days. Not everyone went to school then. Some of the farmers needed their kids to stay at home and help out. And if they lived too far in the country to walk, they stayed home, that's all there was to it. And in school, it was nice, the older ones helped the little ones. I always had my brother Milton in my class.

On the way home for noon lunch, Milton and I stopped to pick up Penny. Sometimes we stood in the doorway and watched. They went very very slowly. It wasn't noisy like our class. Sister Mary Bead held something up in her hand and the class—there were only four or five there— would try to say the word. Paper. Pencil. Ordinary things. They'd make funny, strange sounds trying to say it. I suppose it's different learning to say a word if you've never heard it.

Then one day in December, I went there by myself. It was a blizzard and my mother had kept Milton home. I walked, reciting my poem to keep my feet from freezing. Did we learn the poems! I must have known fifty. "The small rain down must rain." When I stood at the door Sister Mary Bead was holding up an orange. It was like a little globe in that classroom, against the blackboard and her brown and white habit. Then there weren't oranges like now in the supermarkets, so you can get them all year round. They had to ship them in freight trains from California and Florida and they only came in around Christmas. And even then, they were expensive. Milton and I each got one in our stocking and that was it for the year. But oh, did they taste good. They were darker, almost a red, and heavy with juice. They tasted sweeter then. It was a special meal for us Christmas morning; when our presents were open, there was still something left.

For a long time, Sister Mary Bead stood in front of a teacher's desk, holding up the orange. Strange sounds came from her pupils, every time she said the word. Penny sat with her hands clasped in front of her on the wooden desk. She was louder than the others. I could understand what she said, more than I could the rest, but maybe it was because I was used to her. Outside the windows, snow was falling as if it were stitching such even seams on the darkness and the wood stove whispered in the corner. They spoke in unison and their voices wobbled, almost like singing. By the end, the sound of the class seemed rounder, finished, like a word. Then Sister Mary Bead took out a pearl-handled knife and peeled the orange, holding it in one hand, between her thumb and first finger. The skin came off in one curled ribbon. And they passed it around among themselves, down the rows of desks, and each one took only a section, so there was more than half left at the end. Sister Mary Bead offered it to me. I took a section, too.

We all went to church on Sundays and there we had to be good, because any one of the sisters could shush us or slap our hands, it was like having eight mothers looking down on us from all over. And they were each one tall. All we knew then was that Penny didn't like church. She didn't want to go. At first my mother just made her. But then, once the service was on and we were all kneeling, singing the hymns, Penny scooted out. We couldn't get up and chase her. After supper, that day, she came home again, all dirty and full of burrs. The next Sunday, it was the same thing. She left when my mother walked up for communion. That day, when we went home, a blueberry pie was missing from the kitchen. I'd baked two pies that morning and left them to cool on the mangle.

Later on, we found cans and mason jars missing from the cellar. Ellie's husband, my uncle Shaw, worked for the Great Lakes Railroad Company and he got us dented cans for almost nothing. They couldn't sell them in the stores but what was inside was still good. And we did our own canning from the garden every fall. We didn't notice in the cellar for a long time, though, and Penny was probably going into it every Sunday. She stopped coming to church altogether and Sister Mary Bead told my mother just to leave her be.

Wherever Penny went, that black cat followed along. The cat slept under her desk at school and up on the foot of her bed. We named the cat Silk, but I don't remember anyone ever saying its name. Then one day that spring, the cat bit Penny on our porch. It bit her in two places, on the calf and just above the knee. She came in bleeding and crying, choking noises we'd never heard before. Right away, Milton said, Where is that cat? He understood the cat would run away. Well, the bites were nothing, they weren't deep. We washed and bandaged them and she was all right, they'd heal, but she was frantic all night over that black cat. When she was in the tub and we were cleaning her off, she tried to get up and go outside after it. She slipped away from us—she was so darn skinny and slippery then with soap—and my mother had to stand at the top of the stairs and yell for Milton to catch her. He got her, naked on the front lawn, and carried her upstairs kicking.

My mother sent me with a note to the doctor, this was before we had telephones. The doctor was just Ross Smittie, Clara's husband. I went in through the back door, the way I always came to their kitchen. Their kitchen was the biggest and they had a new pantry, all black and white tiles and cookie-cut woodwork. I told them what happened and right away he said he worried about rabies. He walked back over with me and looked at Penny's leg. He said she'd have to have rabies shots, one each day for fourteen days, unless we found the cat.

I think maybe holding her naked and kicking like that had given Milton ideas. They were such opposites, the two of them; him so white and her dark. But every day, the minute school was out, he went running in the woods to look for that cat. See, if we had the cat, they could test him for rabies. But after three days were up, we hadn't found him and Penny had to start in with the shots. The doctor walked every day to our house. He stood by the window filling his syringe. Ugh, I hated to see that yellow liquid flowing from the little bottle. They were such long long needles. Penny would lie back on my bed while he kneaded her stomach and then pressed the needle in, her legs hanging down over the dust ruffle, still as if they were dead. All that time, she never once cried.

Wouldn't you know it, Milton found the cat two days after the shots were done. And that was when we found out everything. Penny wasn't alone, she had a father. He was living in the foundations of an old house out by the railroad depot. He had a tent strung over the top for a roof and down inside he got the furnace working. He cooked his meals right there.

Milton said he found all our dented cans, empty, piled up neat in one corner. The man was apparently clean. But Milton hadn't said anything to him; he'd turned around and run home, without even taking the cat. He'd been scared to death, he said, he'd never seen anyone so ugly.

So a group of men went, my father, the doctor, three or four of the other sisters' husbands. They left that same night, with lanterns, the doctor carried Penny piggyback. It was summer already and warm late. My mother and Milton and I stayed out on the porch, shucking corncobs, waiting.

And when they came back, they had a story to tell. Penny's father could talk and hear. The men explained about having to test the cat, that there was a possibility it was rabid and the man was happy to give him up. The man had offered them coffee—coffee my father recognized as ours from the dented Holloway tin. He told them they were Oneidas from up near Locknominee. Penny was half Indian, her mother was dead. Then he showed them what he called his laboratory and in there he had needles and alcohol, all such stuff, and books. Ross Smittie was amazed. Penny's father had performed plastic surgery on himself, he'd remade his own face. His tribe of Oneidas had always thought he was the ugliest man they ever saw. Even when he was a little boy, they wouldn't look at him. He had lived with his wife, she was a runaway from the orphanage in Traverse City, outside the tribe, but in those same woods. Then when his wife and two Oneida children died of polio, the Indians decided it was him. His own people stoned him and chased him away. He took Penny and they left—they got a ride on a cart with some gypsies up to Michigan, they picked cherries with the migrants all summer and then they rode the freight trains here. But what was really so hard to think was that this man found a way to sneak into the public library at night—see, he was afraid for people to see him—and read up all about plastic surgery. He wanted to remake his face to be better. He got a hold of needles and suture somehow and from studying those books, he changed himself. I suppose he used mirrors to see. He said it took months, most of the winter. He had to wait for one part to heal before touching another. And he did it. Well, you can imagine the ruckus—Ross Smittie wanted to call in reporters from the newspaper and write to other doctors from all up and down the state to come and see. He said it was a miracle the man hadn't killed himself, but there were no infections Ross could find, only clear, healed scars.

Now that there was a big to-do, they moved to Clara's house, Penny and her father and the cat. They had more room there and it was nicer, I suppose. There was a write-up with a picture in the newspaper and a couple other doctors came to see. But it all died down, because the truth was, he still had such an ugly, ugly face. It was scary, I could see how the people were scared.

In all the hoopla for him, nobody did anything with that cat. Finally, my mother went over one day and got him. She had him tested and there were no rabies. But at that time they had to kill the animal to test him for rabies. They cut their heads off. I suppose they found the rabies somewhere in the brain. And we knew just where they put the animals, too, in a big metal drum out in a field of the dump. We sat on the porch that day thinking of the drum, our cat inside limp like a rag.

It was summer and school was out and so I only saw Penny on Saturday mornings when I went over to Clara's to make crusts. Penny knew more words and now she could read lips. She put her hand right up against your mouth to feel while you were talking. Her fingers always had a taste, what was it, like apricots, I think. Well, Milton was prettinear all the time over there. He had a real crush. Clara teased about it, she said he chased Penny around in the backyard, pulled her skirt up to see her panties. They were just kids, eight or nine years old, but ooh, was my mother mad. That's the only time during all those years I saw her mad at him. She got mad at me plenty, I was clumsy and knocked things over and she didn't think I was quick as I should have been, but she always thought Milton was perfect. To her he was really something.

She gave him a spanking with a willow switch on the kitchen table with his pants pulled down. I watched and he cried, oh ye gods, he cried, you could hear him two yards down. Then after, while he was resting in his bedroom, sulking, she went right to work mixing the batter for his favorite cake. We could smell it coming up from the oven; I sat with Milton on his bed trying to make him laugh, pushing his kneecaps through the covers.

"Smell," I said and we both sniffed the air. "She's already trying to make up with you. She likes you better."

Well, that made him smile, it just came out like he'd been holding still purposely before.

"It's 'cause I'm a boy," he said. He was glad it was true, but I suppose he felt bad for me. He knew it wasn't fair.

"I know," I said. And there we both sat.

He got his cake but she told him that he was forbidden from playing with Penny ever again. He did it anyway, they snuck. My mother never caught them that I know of. I saw them once in Swill's barn. I followed him and lay on the ground, looking in one of those low windows. They were close enough so I could hear most everything they said. They were playing doctor.

She lay down on a bale of hay the way she used to on my four-poster bed. He pushed her blouse up and the band of her skirt down. He kneaded her stomach and I watched her muscles jump and sink under his hands.

"And all around the mulberry bush, the monkey chased the weasel. And all around the mulberry bush, pop goes the weasel."

At pop, he stuck a finger down in her belly. That's all they did, again and again. Lying on that prickly hay, I got bored, but I was afraid they'd hear me if I stood up. I wanted them to be done with it, so I could leave, but every time I looked in again, I got a feeling like goose bumps, I wished it was my stomach giving under his hands like dough and me submitting without ever once crying. But I'd been around all his life. Milton hardly ever noticed me.

Then that fall a circus came to town. We all went to see. They had a big green and white striped tent in a field. It was Indian summer and it was hot. I got sick from being in there, Lan-knows what all we ate, and my father took me outside the tent so I could throw up in the grass. I remember the stagehands standing smoking, the stars and their lit cigarettes and fireflies near the ground by the ropes.

When the circus left, Penny and her father went with them. The two brothers who ran the circus gave him a job. He had a side tent with a two-hundred-twenty-pound lady, and a banner that said MAN WHO RECON-STRUCTED HIS OWN FACE. Ross Smittie wrote the story that was going to be painted on a placard. They made a wooden cutout for his face.

The day they left town, Milton and I got up early. Milton shook me awake. There was still dew on the ground when we went out to the barn. Milton rode me on the handlebars of his bike. It was the only time I remember us sneaking together like that. In the barn, he'd found a litter of kittens. He had a cardboard box and we filled it with hay, then lifted the kittens in one by one. Their eyes were still just bulges grown over with fur. I had to hold the mewing box on my lap on the bumpy road home.

My mother didn't come, she didn't want anything to do with it, she and the sisters all thought circus people were dirty and they were none too sorry to see them leave. But my father walked us to the parade, one on either side. The elephant led, then the carts, then the zebras my mother said were painted ponies. When we saw Penny and her father on the back of a covered wagon, we waved and Milton ran to catch up with them. He gave her the box of kittens and that was the last time we ever saw them.

I've often wondered about that and whether that might be why Milton turned out the way he did. I suppose he loved her like kids do and then her going off all of a sudden, away into nothing, as if she'd hardly ever been there. Sometimes people did that then, it was harder to communicate; they'd just disappear and you'd never see them again and it was like they were dead. Worse than dead. You didn't even know a place where they were buried.

Something else happened to Milton that I didn't know at the time and it might explain some, too. My mother told me fifty-odd years later. I guess once, when Milton was a little boy, this was before Penny, when he was real young, my mother was in the kitchen canning peaches. We had two peach trees in our backyard and they had big good peaches. She used to put them up in mason jars and she made jam. It must have been a Saturday morning because I was somewhere else, baking. My dad would have been out at work. Our kitchen was nice; it was a mint green with nice white counters. We had a white mangle by the window, with a doily. My mother was proud of her kitchen. It faced the backyard and it was sunny and it was always spic and span, real clean. She polished so all the silver on everything and the white of the sink and stove just shone.

Well, it was a summer day and she was canning and I suppose the mason jars, some filled already, some waiting, were lined up on the counters. The peaches boiled in a big white pot on the stove. I was at an aunt's house, my father was at work and Milton sat on the kitchen table, swinging his legs below him. He'd just gotten a splinter from lifting the crate he wasn't supposed to touch, the crate that held the milk bottles on our porch. He'd wear just his knickers, no socks, and his bare legs would dangle from the table. He liked to sit like that. She took the splinter out with a needle and a knife. She was good at it. She could get deep ones in one piece and it only hurt for a second.

She told me she didn't know what happened but the weather changed outside. One minute it had been raining and then it was fair and drops lit up against the window. She had been looking there at a spiderweb outside shining with colors. Milton had his eyes squeezed shut. "Is it going to hurt?" he asked her. She laughed because it was all over. She showed him the sliver on her palm.

"Lil, I was so happy all of a sudden, I don't know what came over me." She said all at once she felt real happy alone by herself and with Milton. I guess she sat down on a chair and took him in her lap—and my mother wasn't that way. She told me, he hung onto the back of her neck and started kissing her and she was distracted, thinking of something else I suppose or nothing, not thinking, and she didn't know how much later, maybe a minute, she realized her eyes were closed and she had been kissing Milton like a man. Their mouths were open and he tasted like peaches, she said. She supposed they both did. He was sucking her chin like nursing again almost. She pulled him against her shoulder then and shuddered when she thought what she was doing. She said she found her hand just laid soft over his britches. It all seemed terrible, wrong, like an accident. Then she set him on the floor, stood herself back at the stove and slapped her hands together. She used to do that whenever she finished something, even when she got real old. It was a habit with her.

And nothing happened. The day went on, no one knew, I suppose she finished her canning. And later on, when she thought about it again, it didn't seem to matter so much. Milton had gone outside and played in the afternoon, it was just one minute in the kitchen, in with so many others. He was so young, too, she didn't suppose he'd remember anything. And at that age, they didn't know yet what you are and aren't supposed to do. After a while, she said, she didn't think about it anymore. She wasn't even sure it happened. Or maybe only a few seconds.

But when she finally told me, she said she sometimes wondered if it could be the reason why Milton went away. She didn't know, it wasn't much, she said she sometimes had a feeling. What did I think? Did I think it could have mattered, something less than a minute, so many years ago?

"Oh, no, shucks no, Milton is Milton," I told her. We sat in my kitchen then. "He always wanted to go away. He wanted to see the world and now I suppose he's seen it."

That seemed to make her feel better. She nodded. "Yes, I suppose he is seeing it."

We were drinking tea that day and we stopped talking. She was already old, in her eighties. But I still sometimes wonder whether that might have had something to do with it. Because Milton always loved his momma, he loved her but he had to get away.

There was a boy who came and helped my dad with the yard. That was Art. He lived on the other side of town, poorer than we were. He was a year older and that seemed like a lot to me then. One night, he baby-sat for us, it was in summer, and my aunt Ruth was having a garden party. My mother and father left, all dressed up, carrying a rhubarb pie I'd baked that morning, a deep dish, with a fancy lattice crust. Rhubarb grew in our ditches, all over. It was like a weed. Milton and I used to hide in it when we were real little, behind those huge leaves. It grew bigger than we were then. In summer, we ate it for a snack, just plain. We dipped the stalks in a bowl of sugar before each bite and the sugar would get real pink.

That night we had to be in our beds early, when it was still light out. I could hear water dripping down from the pump onto the cement in front of our house. Then Art walked into my room. I don't know why, maybe I went down first and asked for a glass of water, but he sat in my little rocker, with his bare feet on the curved runners. I'd never seen that before. All my boots were dainty, lined up pointed straight front in the closet. He told me a story. Oh, and I just loved it. I still remember how it went. He said an old hobo and some kids were playing down by the tracks and in one of those fields, they found a trunk. And the trunk had three compartments. They opened the first compartment and there was ice cream in it. And they all ate and ate the ice cream. And then the kids went home. And when they came back the next day they ate more ice cream—

they figured out no matter how much they ate, there was still the same amount left. It was a magic chest. Things didn't get used up. The ice cream knew how to replenish itself.

Well, so then they opened the second compartment and it was filled with all kinds of candy. And that was what we loved. The kids ate and ate loads of candy and it was still full to the brim when they went home. The next day they opened the third compartment and that was full of golden coins. They ran their hands through the coins and laughed. They filled their pockets until they bulged and they ran home to their families. The hobo waited until the sun was down and came back to the chest with a sack. He filled the sack with coins and ate candy and ice cream until he couldn't eat any more and then he jumped on a train. He remembered the stop, he wrote the name of the station down on the inside of his cuff, so he could always come back and get more. He vowed to himself never to tell anyone about the magic trunk, even if he fell in love and found a wife. But he died that very same night. Thieves came into the car he was riding and killed him for the money. They filled their own bags with the golden coins and threw his body in the sack, by the side of the tracks.

The kids who had found the chest made a pact; they could each use it, take as much as they wanted, but they could never tell anyone about it, ever. And they kept their word and always went back and took from it. Their families and friends wondered how they got their treasures; in fact, the families worried. They each had a secret idea: each one decided he would tell his own child about the chest, so that after he died, his family wouldn't go without. When they were children and first found the chest, they were two boys and a girl. And later, the men watched anxiously over their wives, waiting for them to show, and the woman prayed and prayed to have a child, but she couldn't have one. They each died true to their word, childless. And there was a drought in the place where they'd lived and the town got poorer and poorer, but no one else knew about the magic chest and there it sat in the field, full to the brim with ice cream and candy and golden coins.

Lan-knows where he got that story, I suppose someone told it to him. I just loved to think about it, I pictured that chest out there in the field, like my mother's big steamer trunk in the basement, and it always made me happy. I suppose when you're a kid like that, just going to sleep at night, you think, even though you know better, Well, maybe you can find it. Art sat on my bed and wrote my name on my back with his fingers. L-I-L-L-I-A-N. He traced each letter big and I felt it through the cotton of my nightgown. His letters made big circles that put me to sleep.

I suppose that was when I first started to like him. It happened slow, he was always around, you didn't really notice it. I don't think he really thought anything of me then, I was just a little kid to him. Most of the older boys had a few younger ones to follow them around and help, if they were the least bit nice. That's the way we did it. I suppose he knew I had a crush, if he ever thought about it, but no one took those things for much. I saw him every day around our house and this wasn't for a month or two, this was years. And he saw me every which way—with leaves in my hair, all dirty, when we helped him rake and burn, dressed up nice for church, when I first learned to put on rouge. Heck, he still gave Milton and me our bath together, so he saw me that way too.

Milton and I both thought he was just the greatest thing we ever saw and we followed him around when he'd let us. They used to shoot rifle practice in a field back of Swill's barn. We weren't allowed when they had guns, but we'd listen from our porch at night and the next morning before breakfast, Milton and I would go and see if we could find skeets in the field. We found plenty of broken pieces, but we didn't want those, we needed whole ones, ones somebody had missed. When we found one, oh, then we thought we had a prize. We brought them home and gave them back to Art, the next time he came around. He never said anything about it, he just smiled and took it with him in his pocket. I suppose they just threw them in the air again the next time they shot, after all our hard looking.

I think the thing that finally made him look at me, like a girl not just some little kid, was a picture. There were traveling photographers in those days, just like musicians—the little towns couldn't support such stuff on their own. There wasn't the business. But once a year they'd come and line us all up outside of school, the girls together. Cameras were huge then, big wooden boxes, and they brought their own umbrellas and all. When I was a senior, after the class picture, the photographer asked if he could come to my house and take some more pictures of me alone. Well, I had to ask my mother and then I went the next day and said, Why sure.

When he came to our house, my mother had us all ready. I was wearing a white lace dress, all pressed and starched and my boots were polished so the buttons shined. She'd braided my hair and pinned it and she'd dressed up Milton too. All the furniture in the house had been oiled. She had flowers from the garden set out in silver vases. My little dog, Blackie, had a big blue satin ribbon around his neck. My mother asked the photographer if he didn't want to take Milton in the picture, too, but he said no, and so it was just me sitting on the piano bench, holding Blackie on my lap. He came around the next day with the picture all mounted on fancy black paper and he left it with us. It was nice of him. My mother had already been figuring out how she could scrape together the money from our food allowance, but he just gave it to us and went on his way.

Then, after that, every time anyone walked into the house, they had to see my picture. Why sure. I was big stuff then for a week or two. And that's when they all got the idea that I was pretty. I was just a little runt before, but now they all thought I was swell. I could tell, because they treated me a little different. Even my mother, she was careful. She looked at me more. It made her think of me better. Everyone but Milton. It didn't make one bit of difference to him, one way or the other. He didn't care what I looked like.

But what I worried about was with Art. You know, at that age, you don't think so much about your family. You think they'll always be around and you can forget about them for a while. Art was the one I wanted to look at the picture. And he finally did. All that summer, I palled around with Art and his crowd of older kids. They were from big families most of them and they had to work—they picked strawberries for Swill, the nurseries could hire kids cheaper then than the migrants—and after their day, we'd all do something. They'd be tired from kneeling under that hot sun, so we'd just walk around town, maybe buy an ice cream if we had a little money. Then ice cream was more of a treat, they made it in molds, like cookies, so you'd get a new shape every time. A clover or a heart or a flower. And each one would be a different flavor.

And then on the weekends we had our real fun. We went swimming in the quarry or down by Baird's Creek. We'd each take a sandwich and a towel and we'd wear our bathing suits under our dresses and hike out there. We hung our dresses on the branches alongside the creek. I loved to swim, that feeling of getting all wet and drying off so quick in the sun, and then sliding in again.

We could have gone on like that forever. We didn't worry then, like kids do now. Both my daughters worried so much about themselves. More than I ever did. And the granddaughter is the worst, yes you are, it's the thighs one week, and of course the breasts aren't big enough, next thing you know, it's the knees or the ankles. Pretty soon it'll be the ear, you just wait.

We were too shy to think about our bodies. And we wore bathing suits that came almost to our knees, so you couldn't see much anyway. I still have mine; it's a blue with white buttons, I don't know why I keep all such stuff.

And in the country, there where we were, it was quiet. Quieter than it is anywhere now. We didn't have the cars and the trucks or the highways. Once in a very long while we'd hear a train go by and you'd stop whatever you were doing and listen because it was a change. It always seemed sort of sad, a train, but an everyday sadness. To me it did. It made you think of the things you didn't know. Most of all day it was silent, except what noise we made ourselves, diving in the water, splashing. I remember lying flat on a rock for hours under a tree that would sway, just the littlest bit, in the breeze. We could have gone on like that for years, and it was my fault that we didn't. That was my one big mistake, but what did I know?

For my seventeenth birthday, I made a big cake and we had a party. It was just girls, that was the way they did it, with ribbons hanging from the ceiling, and all the aunts came. My mother's old steamer trunk sat in the front parlor, repapered inside, and they each brought something for me to take along to college. I'd already gotten in for the next year, at the Catholic college in Marquette, it was all set I was going to go.

I suppose I was so puffed up from the party and everyone giving me something that I said yes when I really shouldn't have. When Art came that night and gave me his present—it was a black pin, I still have it—he asked would I go swimming with him the next day and I said yes.

And wouldn't you know, sure, that was when it happened. He was young, too, just eighteen, he didn't know any better. He'd never been alone with a girl before, except maybe his sisters. First we swam and then after, it was still morning, we were lying on that rock, under the tree. The way the branches moved, the air went on your skin like from a fan. All of a sudden he came and lay on top of me and I didn't know what was what. All the time I was growing up, I thought a soul lay in your chest, I even thought I knew what it looked like. It was a wide, horizontal triangle like a yoke, made out of white fog, like clouds are. I thought married people had babies by somehow pressing their chests together so their souls touched. That's how dumb I was. That was as much as I knew. I was pretty sure it had something to do with kissing, and so I was careful we didn't kiss. I hadn't really pictured more than that—but there it was, our chests felt real warm and pressed next to each other, so I could feel his sharp bones. It was uncomfortable, but not an altogether bad feeling either.

Then the other began. Neither of us said anything. I was afraid to move, I was ashamed of how much I didn't know. That's how dumb I was. And he was different, too, I was afraid of how his face looked, stern and sealed like a stranger's, like a profile of a man you see a distance away, working up on a power line.

He started rubbing me all over and I knew you weren't supposed to let them touch you. I didn't know exactly why and to tell you the truth, I didn't know how to stop it. Then he reached under my back and opened my swimsuit. Then all of a sudden, I was a little smarter, because I knew enough to know it shouldn't go much below the waist. At first it didn't. Then he reached down by my left leg and went up under the band around one thigh. It hurt, like something sharp, the edge of a thing. I kept hoping nothing more would happen. Then he pulled the suit down so above my waist was bare. Right away, I thought, all right, that's done now, just as long as he doesn't pull it down any further. I kept thinking like that, nervous, until it was all off. Then when he was right there, over me, I understood more. I cried a little, I suppose most people do, especially like me when they don't know what's coming and feel that first burning, oh it hurts, but then it went on and on and I closed my eyes and all I thought of was my mother.

I thought of her room. I could exactly picture the furniture. The high bed, square and neat, with the white chenille spread, the tassels just touching the floor, the mirror, the white bureau, the one fern and then the white curtains, blowing at her windows. I had gone into my mother's room alone in the afternoon. The white walls had a bluish color, like light around an egg. I thought of my mother with my father in that room and the white cotton nightie she wore to bed and how she must have wanted to touch her soul to his and I tried to feel that way and be that way with Art, my chest pressed right under his, collapsing, so we could both feel the warm.

And that's when I got pregnant with Carol, from that one time. We did have bad luck, that I'll say. I had wanted it, though, I was thinking of it. Wanting it made the pain seem important, for that one second the whole thing seemed holy, like a sacrifice. Maybe you get pregnant easier when you think like that.

My mother and father sure weren't happy. Oh, no. My mother had worked hard saving and fixing up my college trunk and she never liked Art so well anyway. She wanted Milton and I both to marry better families, families she knew. Cousins even.

I got married in a dark blue dress. My mother didn't come, but I went home after, alone, she wouldn't let him in the door again. She was just wearing a housedress. She was sweeping when I came in. I half kissed her, she moved her cheek away and for a long time I remembered her face inside the oval glass of the door. I felt my braid swish on my back as I walked down the path. She was watching me and I left that day. Art met me down the road. Art was scared too, but there we were married. We had no choice but to do it.

For him it was a kind of adventure. And he never did have to go to a war. He went and tried to enlist for the first one. They sent him back because he was too young. Then, by the second, he was too old already. I was born in May 1900, Art in 1899, so between us, one was always the age of the year. And he had an idea that we had more fun somehow because it was the beginning of a century. He told that to Adele once and oh, was she mad. We had the whole century in front of us. He always liked gadgets, balloons, fireworks, everything new. See, I didn't learn all his crazy ideas till then when I was stuck with him.

We moved sixty miles to Bay City and at first we lived on top of a

to stretch out the meat. I still have that metal box of recipes we used then, things we cut from the paper.

Carol changed Adele and watched her, everything. Carol was always serious. I thought because we had her so young, she stayed afraid of things. I was afraid when I was pregnant with her. That Tinta said her mother took up mail-order watercolor lessons only once in her life, when she was pregnant with Tinta, and here Tinta turned out to be a painter! And I suppose, too, when Carol was little, she could tell how scared I felt. She always kept quiet, that didn't worry me because I was like that, too, but really, I think she had a hard time of it. She was always short and dark, and then she would have Art's big nose. Neither you or Adele have that nose but Carol sure enough got it.

And everything Carol didn't get, Adele did. When I think of it it makes me mad. Because we were older then and then we really wanted a child. We were the right age then for one. And we had more money. Art never really took the time to spend with Carol when she was little, he was building up the business and those years we were so poor, scraping and saving, but later, when Adele was born, he could like a baby, he'd come in and play with her, oh, for hours. When she was still in diapers, he'd carry her out to see the mink.

And of course Adele would just be pretty. She always had blond, blond hair—she got that from my mother—and such perfect creamy skin. Just like Milton. She didn't get the freckles until later. She's the only one of all of us who got my·mother's long legs. And dimples. And so you can imagine she had the clothes and the kids over and the parties. Able Hansen had moved in by then and they had kids she could play with. And Amber had Phil and Lacey, where when Carol was growing up, there was only Chummy, and Carol was always too shy to play much with a boy. Carol used to stay inside by me.

Adele, when she was old enough, trouped out there with the worst of them, a real tomboy. She was always a regular dickens, into everything, in the swamps, all full of coal from the tracks, whatever they could find to collect dirt and tear their clothes, they found. Of course, those years I had a wash machine already, in the basement, back of his Polynesian bar. When Carol was little she had to be careful to keep whatever she had nice, because if that went, there wasn't the money for new. Adele had a horse when she was thirteen, fourteen, that's what that shed in back was from. That's where Adele kept her horse. It wasn't fair and I know it. It just never was fair. Adele got more.

But even with that, there was always something not quite right with her. I remember there was something far back, I think even when she was a baby. She was never all there. She did odd things even when she was

store. It was all new people. I wrote to my mother and dad, one letter a week for more than a year before she would even answer me. I don't think she ever really forgave me. She had to some later, when she was sick and living with me. But she never liked Carol because of it. As if Carol could help what we did.

Then a year after we left, Milton ran away. That must have been hard on my mother. He went off to San Francisco to join the merchant marines. From what I heard after, we were the only ones in Malgoma who were the least bit surprised. And when I knew, it seemed right, it made sense. He had always wanted to get away. Even when he was a little, little boy and I had to watch him, he'd crawl off the blanket, under the fence, out of the yard, away from where he was supposed to stay.

Milton's birthday is September first, the same as our Adele's. And they are a lot alike, so I've often wondered if there isn't something to that. There's one such a one like Milton in every family. One who thinks he has to get away.

We lived above a little grocery store, which was a help to me with the baby. Art was gone all day and some at night, too, he was just starting up, trying to make a go of it, and he was still young enough to want some fun. So I took the baby downstairs and sat in the store with Mrs. Sheck. She knew babies, she had three schoolchildren of her own. She'd hold Carol, too, and we'd talk all day about babies, she'd show me one little product or another. We got through.

Art began as a photoengraver just when they were starting up the newspaper. He worked Sundays and all night sometimes to get it out when he was supposed to. I still have the first year of newspapers all bound up in such a book, this big. I should call the museum, see if they want the old thing. I just haven't wanted to lug it out to the dump.

Then, when we'd saved a little money, after the first few years, we bought the land for this house. We rode all over, looking at land. I picked out this spot for the oak tree. I liked that big tree in the front yard. The land was cheap then and this was nowhere. We were the first on Lime Kiln Road. Art bought past where the barn is now and all the way down to the tracks.

"That swamp?" I said. "What are you ever going to do with that swamp?"

I should have kept my big mouth shut, because now that land is worth a lot of money. It was outside of the city limits, part of a new little town, Ashland they were calling it then. Art was already thinking he wanted enough land so when Carol grew up she could build and live here, too. He was hoping if we built a nice house, others who wanted to live in the country and were just getting a start would move out. He thought we could all pitch in and help with the work, women and men. The newspaper gave him his ideas. He started town meetings and they drew up a plan for every house to have sewer and water and electricity.

Then he got into the mink and was that a lot of work. He built that barn in back prettinear by himself. And they were temperamental, those mink. If you didn't do every little thing just right, they could die and then you were out.

By that time, too, other people built on our road like Art wanted. Mack Griling moved in down where they are now and he built a house, and the Brozeks came across the road. They built a house and that little apartment above the garage, for her brother who was in the navy, for when he came home.

See, all the time Carol was growing up, we were so busy, thinking of other things, trying to make a go of it.

And we were still so young. Lot of other people our age didn't have children. I made friends with the other mothers, though, even if they were older. Amber Brozek across the street—she had Chummy—and I was even friends with Mack's first wife. Tinta was her name and ooh, was she a pack rat, every inch of that house was full of junk. And she painted paintings too yet, all of them landscapes from around here. So every little spot on the wall that wasn't full already, she covered with one of her paintings. Some were so small like a postcard. That end of the road was never any good. I was sorry they moved there, I still am. Ugh, I didn't like going with Carol into all that dust and dirt, you knew there were plenty of germs. I don't think Tinta ever cleaned. And when she opened a drawer once, I saw she had her clothes all rolled up in little balls. But, still, she was a neighbor too, and we didn't have very many. Amber and I went with our babies once a week or so for tea. We'd dress Carol and Chummy in their oldest clothes before we walked down and then, after, we'd let them play in the dirt. That's when they made their mud pies. They loved that, sure. And then we plunked them right down in the tub.

Art hired two men to help him out with the mink. Only one was married, the other still lived at home. Art palled around with them, after work too. They used to go to the Morley Meyerson Building, it's not there anymore, but it was one of the first old buildings, right along the river. They climbed up to the top, five stories, and they jumped off the roof into the Fox River. The Fox River was clear in those days, cold, but you could swim in it. The bay, too. People swam all over in summer. And they had the nice beaches. Now that's all gone because of those darn paper mills. But they give the people the jobs, that's the thing. I didn't like to hear it, Art taking risks like that, five stories, and me with a daughter barely walking at home, but I knew he had to get it out of his system somehow, being young. And so I didn't say anything. We wives didn't say too much. I

suppose he had to have his fun, too. He worked very hard for his money. And we were lucky. Lots weren't as lucky as we were.

When my father died, we hired detectives to go find Milton. We had to hire detectives when Dad died and then again for my mother. They found him in a one-room over a tavern in San Francisco. The detectives had a picture we gave them and they said right away, coming off the ship, they knew it was Milton. He still had those yellow curls. But I hardly recognized him anymore, he changed so. He was a real solid man at the funeral, people looked and wondered, is that Milton? He had to borrow one of Art's suits and it hardly fit him. He wasn't thin anymore. But he did still have those curls. If we hadn't found him and sent him money to come home, he never would have known his father was dead. He stayed for a while and worked on the mink farm, but that didn't go. He didn't like that. I suppose he'd been around the world prettinear by then, he'd seen all kinds of things. He was used to more excitement. And he drank. As soon as he had a little money saved up, he'd go blow it in the taverns. I remember once it was Thanksgiving. He had gone the night before, from tavern to tavern by taxi, and when we were just sitting down for Thanksgiving, he staggered up the road. He was shaking when he came in and he asked Carol to get him a glass full of whiskey. She was eight or nine then and she did it. She got him a water glass full and he just gulped it down. And the way he ate, he was a nervous person. He ate real fast and greedy. He never used to be like that. I suppose on the ship maybe they had to be. Then, after us, he went home to Malgoma and lived with Granny for a while and that was a disaster, too.

A year or so later, after he'd left again, he sent us a big coconut, with painting on it. That gave Art the idea for the Polynesian bar in the basement, oh ye gods. Yes, we have Milton to thank for that, the colored lights and all. The fish was our fault, that was from Florida. I wanted to go to Florida, and he caught it there and had it stuffed. And every once in a while, we got a postcard from Milton. I stopped reading them because I found out things I didn't necessarily want to know. He went on about the Silver Slipper, oh, he ranted, he must have been drunk when he wrote some of those. I wouldn't be the least surprised.

Carol was eleven years old by the time we had Adele. Everything was different by then. Adele was born in 1929, she was a child in the depression years, but she was too little to tell. By the time she was old enough to know anything, we had some money again. And she got plenty, much more than Carol.

Carol was like a little mother, such a help to me. Those years, for a long time, we had hamburger every night and we did all kinds of things with it, Hamburger Surprise, Hamburger Supreme, Hamburger Royale. We mixed in potatoes and ketchup, different canned vegetables, anything

real, real little. I often feel bad that we spoiled her and I know we did spoil her, but I think there was something else the matter, always.

Of course with two daughters so far apart in age, you have to expect they'll be different. And we had some good times, too, the family. When we first got the car, we'd drive to Kewaunee and stop at the old dime store and buy the girls those little wax bottles with syrup in them. They made them to look like little Cokes. And we'd have picnics on the beach all day long. Once we sent the girls off to Mackinac Island. They took the train up to Michigan and then a ferry—it was a big trip for them. I remember them all dressed up with their lipstick on, going. I'm still glad we planned that, that was nice for them. There haven't been too too many times when they were close, as sisters.

Adele was alone then for a long time when Carol went into the army. She was my only one at home. Of course, when she was that age, out of high school, Adele went to college, the works. These days they go to graduate school and get so smart you can't even talk to them anymore. But when Carol finished with high school, we didn't have the money for college, so she had to stay home and work. I still feel bad about it. Because she would have liked that, too, she would have gotten something out of it. I've told her many times, I'd pay for her now to go, but she doesn't want to be in with those young kids.

When the war came, she went into the Wacs and she was overseas, so I suppose she saw something there, too. I know there was a fellow she liked over in France. Both of my daughters went in for the foreigners. I suppose they wanted something a little different. I always wonder if it wasn't from Milton that they got the idea.

Oh, it was a shock for me when I first found out Carol had signed up. She was twenty-four, but I wasn't ready yet to lose a daughter. I was home baking one day in the kitchen, I had a sponge cake in the oven and I went out to get the mail. And there was a summons for Carol. It was wartime already, but they didn't enlist the women. She must have signed herself up and never said a word. Well, there was no more deciding about it, like it or not. It said she had to report, with her clothes, to boot camp in Cedar Rapids, Iowa, December 18. Before Christmas. Carol worked downtown then, at the Harper Method Beauty Shop, and I called her on the telephone. And I said, "What in heavens did you do?"

But she just kept still. That's the thing with the quiet ones. They can do it to you, too. Finally, she said she'd written away because she wanted information.

And here she was stuck, before she knew it. And wouldn't it just be Art's Elk night. He joined with a couple other fellows from the mink. I called the Elk Lodge and they wouldn't tell me where he was, only that the men had gone out to have fun. Oh, that made me mad. Well, I had an idea. There was a house on Irwin Street that was never any good. I'd heard the men out by the mink cages talk and laugh about it and then they always hushed up when I came near.

So I took the bus and then walked the eight or ten blocks towards the bay. That neighborhood has never been good and it still isn't. That house is still there, it's a supper club now. Small's Paradise. Then, it was for the men to go and see a show. They had a stage in the living room. Lan-knows how much they paid to get in and then I suppose they got stuck for drinks too. Well, I looked in at the window and I couldn't see anything. The grass came up to my knees, they must never have cut it, and I tore my stockings on a thistle. Then I just walked right in. I'm still sorry I did. That taught me a lesson. I'd never seen the things that I saw that night on the stage. There was a woman up there with a donkey. Yes, a donkey, and they were doing just what you'd think, the worst you could imagine. I wouldn't have thought it was possible. It made me sick just to see it. They did that here in Bay City. Carol's Jimmy says they still have stuff like that going on down in Mexico.

I saw Art's face for a moment before he saw me. He was leaning forward from a table with two other fellows, laughing.

Well, sure enough, Carol went into the army—there was nothing we could do—and I got myself used to the idea. Art and I never talked about it. I went on, same as usual, but after that I kept the whole business of the Wacs between Carol and me. We talked about it, we got her clothes and cosmetics and toiletries packed. It was the first time I had a project like that alone by myself—before we'd done everything together. And I didn't want him getting funny with me anymore either. Not after what I saw. Not if that's what he thought of me.

But then after a while you forget. Carol went away and we got letters home, from camp first and then from the base. Adele was getting to be a teenager, lovesick around the house. She went with her girlfriend to see *Gone With the Wind* and they were fits and sighs and giggles in every corner, after, all secrets.

Pretty soon we were back to the usual, but then sometimes at night in bed, he'd be breathing on top of me, I'd have my chin tucked over his shoulder, looking at the ceiling, the way we did, and I couldn't think of my mother anymore. Our room now looked just like hers, the same white everywhere. I'd think of the girl with the donkey, she had such dark legs, like an Indian almost or a gypsy, and she was wearing something like a red girdle. Her eyes the way she looked straight ahead without blinking, opened all the way open, I wondered if she could be blind.

. . .

I was glad enough never to have more children. Two was enough, and then the grandchildren. I suppose when you have daughters, you end up with the families. I think when you have boys, they go off and make a start by themselves, but your daughters always come back to you. They bring their children home.

Carol is like me. She went into the army, then pretty soon after the war, she came home and went back to work at the beauty shop. And we had some fun then too. We miniature golfed and we gave each other manicures. Then she met Jimmy at the country club and not too long after they were engaged. When they got married, we had the reception right here, we put tables out in the backyard. They built the house next door. Amber's Chummy did the same thing when he got married; he and June built on the lot next to the old Brozeks. So Chummy and Carol ended up both next door to their mothers. Carol always worked, she kept the books for Jimmy at the water softener store and she was a very good mother with her sons. The only thing I wonder is if she didn't make the same mistake I did, having them too far apart. But she and I get along. We still do.

Adele I will never understand. She was seventeen when Jimmy and Carol got married, old enough to be jealous.

But then Adele went away to college and did she have the clothes. And shoes and furs, you can't imagine. And they needed formals and she could never wear the same one twice. Oh, she got plenty, believe me. And even in college with all that she had—and she was in a sorority, she won some beauty prize, she was the lilac queen of this or that, she was on the dean's relief committee, her picture in the paper—all that wasn't enough for her. She got in with that Lolly, and sure enough they got themselves in trouble. Oh, it was a big scandal, I'm still ashamed. They went up and posed half-naked for a fellow who put out topless bathing suits. They wore them in pictures for a mail-order catalog. Someone Jimmy worked with saw it, Carol didn't even want to tell me. Now, why would she want to do a thing like that?

Then after college she wanted to stay and get her master's degree. She went out to California, the first time in 1954. I remember because that was the year Art got sick. He had cancer of the colon. I thought it was because he wouldn't take the time, when he was out with the mink, to come and go to the bathroom when he had to. He worked so hard, he would just wait and hold it. But now his brother and two sisters died of it too, so it must have been in the family. He was young to be so sick, only fifty-five.

We had to go to the Mayo Clinic and the doctors there did what they could. But they told us it wouldn't be long. They couldn't say just how much, but less than a year, they were almost sure of it. So right away, we called Adele—we had a hard time getting her, too—and we asked her to

come home. And she wouldn't. I never understood why she didn't then—
because she and Art were always close, he did loads for her. She was just
like Milton. So far away and her own father dying. She kept postponing
and postponing, she said she had a test, then her orals. I was scared she
wouldn't make it before he died, and oh, he wanted to see his Del. And
for months there at the end, he wasn't so good. But she did make it.
That's one thing I have to say for Adele. She is lucky.

Then right after Art passed she wanted to marry this Hisham. I probably should have stood up to her more, but I didn't know either. I was just
plain tired after a year of nursing him. And it's not easy to stand up to her.
She gets mean when she doesn't have her way. I'll tell you, many times
I've been afraid of her.

That last summer before Art died, Carol and I drove out by the bay
and picked a stone. He had worked very hard all his life for his money and
I wanted to get him a nice stone. I was glad that I could. So then after I
spent lot of time planting flowers. I went out almost every day to water.
And it is a nice stone. I always think that pink granite is the prettiest. It
stays.

You want to know about your mother and I suppose that's natural, sure, a
person wants to know about their family and you haven't had too too much
of one. But I don't know what I can tell you. She's always been a mystery
to me, too. I just don't know about her.

Well, after they were married, they moved around for a while, here in
Bay City, always renting. They got a lot of Granny's nicest furniture and
her good china dishes and I'd like to know what they did with it all, because Adele hasn't got any of it anymore. Then they were flying back and
forth from his family in Egypt, too, I think for a while they thought they
might live over there. But your mom couldn't take it. She couldn't eat the
food. The food that was their equivalent to butter, she couldn't keep
down.

I was there once too, oh, she wanted me to go and see his family.
When I went on the tour with Em, I stopped on the way back from Aus-
tria. I'll tell you everything was so dirty, everywhere was dust and they
just sat outside in their dirt. She said his parents were real wealthy like
kings over there, but not that I could see. It was just so very very dirty.

Your mom got pregnant over there. I'll tell you, Ann, you're lucky to
be healthy, because your mom was real sick when she came home. I didn't
believe her when she told me she was seven months. She was down to
nothing, eighty or ninety pounds. She said she couldn't eat the food over
there, she couldn't keep it down. I suppose that's why you turned out
small, because your dad was tall, six foot something. And then you were

early, in an incubator. Your dad made it just a few weeks before you were born. I remember him down by the sidewalk and the little bit of lawn outside Saint Peter and Paul's. He was smoking a cigarette and looking up at the windows, I suppose trying to see in your ma's.

He was a funny one, the things he said. You couldn't always understand him. "So congratulations," I said to him. "How does it feel to be a father?"

And he was always shaking his head. "Beauty is a betrayal," he said. "It's always for itself, never for you." Now do you know what that meant? I didn't either. I still don't.

For a while when you were a baby, they lived in one of those little cottages by the bay. Well, I don't suppose you'd remember, you were real small yet then. You lived in that red cottage at the end. He taught classes over at Saint Norbert's College, but he couldn't make a go of that. He made a speech out there once and they all said it sounded just the slightest little bit on the communistic side and they didn't ask him back the next year. Then, he was selling Volkswagens and pretty soon, Jimmy got him started with the vacuum cleaners.

Once I went over to visit your mom in that cottage. It was during the day, and your dad wasn't there, he was out working, I suppose. Well, here it was middle of winter and you were toddling around in just a diaper. On that bare floor. With no socks or shoes. And there was hardly any heat in those cabins, either. Well, we went to the bureau and got a little jumpsuit to put on you. But when we came to the feet, Adele told me she didn't have any shoes for you. She told me, "Hisham says that babies don't need shoes." Well, over there, the babies probably don't *get* any shoes.

So I don't think you had the easiest time. But then I suppose it didn't hurt you. I went out that day and bought you socks and shoes, three or four pair. I thought that would last a little while.

Then it wasn't too long and you all moved in by me. I suppose they couldn't keep up with the rent on that cabin. And the house wasn't so empty anymore then, the way it was with Art gone. I think it was better for you, too. We had Benny right next door, he was just a year ahead, and even when you were both babies, you always played together nice.

How old were you, three or four, when your dad left? He came and went a couple of times—Adele gave him money to fly back and forth from Egypt, they thought he could get money from his parents, but I don't think that ever came to much. Then, the last time, he charged up all those bills. That time he went to California. I guess he thought he could get famous there. He was a handsome man. For a long time, I watched for his face on the television. The bills started coming a couple weeks after he left. Then we knew he wouldn't come back. Expensive luggage, tailored suits, shirts, shoes, socks, hankies—I suppose everything he thought he'd need for a big, fancy trip. He and Adele were good for each other that way—they both liked to live high on the hog.

Well, I just paid the bills, we didn't want the talk. We paid it all, and it was steep, and then that was the end of it. And not too long after, my own mother got sick, your granny. So I had to go down to Malgoma and settle her things and move her up to my house. Oh, was I mad. Before I got there, just the week before, two such antiquers, young men, came and cleaned her out. She gave them her best pieces for almost nothing. Between what Adele got and sold Lan-knows where and those antiquers, there was hardly anything left. But there were two things I wanted. The piano was still there, that I used to practice on when I was a girl, and it had such a nice round bench. I wanted that bench. And above the piano hung one frame with eight oval holes cut out of the paper and pictures of the eight sisters inside.

Well, my mother was a tough one, such a one. Two things I wanted, neither worth much, and she wouldn't give them to me. She made sure the piano and the piano bench and that picture stayed with the house when she sold it. That was the way she wanted it to be, and what she wanted she got. When she came to live with me, she was the boss, even sick. You probably don't remember her much because those years she stayed to herself. She didn't like kids anymore. She just didn't have the patience. I used to buy presents for Ben and you at Christmas and try and say they were from her, but she shouted from the den, no, no, they're not from her, she didn't buy you anything. And she wouldn't come in and see the Christmas tree. She stayed alone in her room. Do you remember we had goose for Christmas? Granny always liked goose.

Then Carol's Hal got that horse. Oh ye gods. Hal always had a scheme and it never went right, ever. He was sixteen years old and we went to a church bazaar, here at Saint Phillip's. They were auctioning off a pony. I remember I fought that day with your mom because once we got there and each gave in what we brought, your mother and that Lolly started giggling and giggling. Oh, they thought something was so funny.

"Well, what are you laughing at," I said. "Why don't you let us all in on the joke."

It turned out those two had baked a pie and when they were done and it was in the oven, they figured out they'd forgot to put in sugar. They each thought the other had put it in. But then when they took it out of the oven, it looked just fine, and so they brought it and gave it in anyway.

I told them that wasn't at all nice and that just made them giggle some more. Ugh, when they got started, watch out. I was thinking, Well, what if a poor family bought that pie, one that really couldn't afford it, but just said, oh, the money goes to the church and it would be a nice dessert for

Sunday supper. And then they got that sour thing. Well, I let them laugh and I went all over, to all the booths, and tried to buy that pie back. But I couldn't find it, no, somebody must have bought it already. I just hope to God it was a family that could afford to throw it out.

For years already, Hal had been collecting silver dollars. Whenever any of us got one in our change, we'd save it for Hal, for his collection. When they announced the winner of the big auction that day at the bazaar, they said Hal's name for the pony. Carol almost fainted. "What am I going to do with a horse?" she said. He'd spent all those silver dollars on that pony, seventy-three of them. He thought he'd take the neighborhood kids on rides for a nickel or a quarter and that way earn some money! He always had a scheme. I told him, if he'd just once hold onto his money.

It was a brown and white spotted pony, not trained or anything. Some farmer must have donated it. We called him Silver Dollar. Well, pretty soon, when it didn't all pan out the way he'd thought—there weren't many kids in the neighborhood and they didn't want to pay to ride that pony, it was slow, they could go quicker on a bike—Hal lost interest in it. We had to nag him even to feed it and brush its hair. It lived in that old shed where Adele's horse had been.

Wouldn't you just know, Granny was the one who took care of it. She got up at five every morning and hauled out that big pail of water and oats. She was the one who brushed that pony. Even after they took the leg off, she hobbled out there on crutches. She was a tough one, such a one.

I'm still sorry I let them take that leg, I think that's why she died. She just didn't want to live anymore when she couldn't move around. They said her heart was like a girl's, she could have lived lots longer. But she'd had the tumor in the leg. That they had to get rid of. Those last months were hard, with her in bed, I got up all hours of the night, changing the bedpan, she was so ashamed, she wouldn't let anyone but me in there. And then she was losing her hair, too. She was a proud, proud woman. It was hard for her.

She died on your seventh birthday, in the morning, before any of you were awake. I wasn't sorry. She'd lived a long, long life, she was ninety-one when she died and she didn't really want any more. I was up with her all night. We didn't talk much. We weren't ever close and she wasn't one to pretend. But I'd taken good care of her all that time and she knew it. She never had bedsores, she always had her things around her, I fixed her just what she wanted to eat. She had to admit I'd been good to her. And I was glad to have done it. Then when she died, at five thirteen in the morning, she looked happy, she got this big smile and her hands just opened at her sides. Carol was there then, too, she saw it. And then I knew, that was the end of something.

Adele and I talked and we decided to go ahead with your party. Why not, it didn't make any difference to you kids and she had everything already planned. She had a cake from the bakery in the icebox. And because Granny was so old, we weren't sad. She would be happier where she was.

So I sat on the phone to the funeral parlor and with the priest. And then again, too, we had detectives looking for Milton. They'd been looking this time for weeks already. And I saw outside the kitchen window, Hal taking you kids for rides on Silver Dollar. He went round and round the garage, so slow. I suppose your mom paid him something, that was probably the only time he made his money on that horse. Not long after Granny died, we had to give the horse away. Some people on a farm took him, where they had little kids. They came in a truck and got him.

You were wearing white that day. A white eyelet blouse and shorts and white anklets and white tennies. I remember from the picture: you had a big white bow in your hair. Your mom planned a nice party for you. Some of Chummy and June's came, Hansens, and that Stevie Felchner, whose parents rented the little orange cottage in back by the barn, and those Griling kids. You can see in the picture, after all these years, you can still see how the other little children look clean and had decent clothes and shoes and those Grilings didn't. There were the two girls your age, Theresa and Mary, and the one they didn't have too much longer, that retarded girl, Annette, who went away to school for them up in Okonowa. I remember they each brought you presents. Everyone's was nice, something the mothers bought and wrapped, except the Grilings'. They each brought something they'd just bought, in the bag from the store. I suppose the dad or whoever gave them their money, gave each one fifteen cents or a quarter and they each went in and picked out what she wanted. I don't remember what Theresa or Mary brought anymore, jacks or something, you know, a regular present. But this Netty brought you such a cellophane bag of chocolate candies. I suppose that's what she would have liked for herself. She couldn't play with toys much. But it was a warm day and they were all outside and I suppose she was carrying it around, holding it in her hands, and by the time you opened your presents, hers was all melted, just one gooey bag of chocolate and the kids laughed.

Your mom had all kinds of things planned: games, pin the tail on the donkey, she'd bought firecrackers that came out like red, white and blue parachutes you kids could chase across the yard. So while you were all busy with that, she came in and found me. She had a supper planned for the kids after, she'd ordered that cake from the bakery a week ahead. She had sparklers and those black firework snakes for you kids to light after you ate.

She came and told me about Netty's chocolates; we both felt so bad.

"Pyuk," she said, holding the bag up and dropping it, with a thud, in the wastebasket. "Mom, you don't think you could just whip up some-thing chocolate for a cake, so we could take it out and say it was made from Netty's candies? You wouldn't have the time?"

"Why sure," I said, "but won't Annie expect the storebought? She knows you went to pick it up." The cake from the bakery was real fancy, I bet she paid quite a bit for it. She'd brought one of your crayon pictures of a swimming pool and they'd copied that, with the frosting.

She said she'd take you aside and explain. You always were good like that, she could talk to you and tell you the truth. She knew you wouldn't cry or fuss or throw a tantrum like a lot of children would. You were ma-ture, more than Benny was. Carol couldn't talk to Benny like that. Your mom talked to you almost like a grown-up.

"We can have the other with Benny and Hal tomorrow," she said.

And I was glad to do it. When someone dies, it's like you've been hit hard in the stomach; you lose your breath for a moment and everything stops. Then when it all comes back, you have an empty house. I'd made the phone calls first thing in the morning. Now there was nothing left to do. The house seemed so big and quiet. And do you know what I did? I fetched that bag of chocolate from the wastebasket, it was sealed with such a cardboard strip on top, it was perfectly good, just melted, and I used that as the start of your cake. And believe me, I'm telling the truth, did that cake ever turn out good.

I took my time. I had all afternoon. I baked three layers and then while they were cooling on the mangle, I made a filling with nuts and a separate maple frosting. Your mom had the idea to put seven sparklers in like candles, and we lit them just before she carried it out.

We'd set up two card tables in the backyard, and your mom had cov-ered them with paper tablecloths. Red, white and blue. Everything had to match. It was just dusk then and Carol and Hal were there too, and your mom and Lolly and we all sat down and had that cake on paper plates. Your birthday is in June and the mosquitoes mustn't have been too bad then yet, because we stayed out late and watched while you kids drew with your sparklers on the air. You and Benny played tick-tack-toe, but whichever one won, it always faded before you could draw the line through. Ben was teaching Netty to write her name. She wrote the same letters over and over. She had the letters right, but she was too slow. I went and made a pot of coffee to bring out and we ladies kept drinking the coffee and eating the cake. Then, one by one, at eight or nine o'clock, the mothers would step out on the porches and call their kids home, and family by family, they'd go. First Hansens, then Stevie Felchner, then finally June came over to get hers. Pretty soon all the mothers had called their kids in, except the Grilings, and they looked embarrassed because they had no mother. That little Mary got the older ones by the sleeves and they said they better go home, too, their father would be missing them. And by the time we folded the card tables up and went in, all that cake was done for.

I've thought about that many times. That was good of your mother to think of, on that day when she had so much to do. That Netty went away, I don't know, a year or two later. I remember when they came and took her in the car. I watched by the window. It was two women with short hair, they looked like church women, and just an ordinary car.

Ann

5

South of Wilshire

When we moved to California, we didn't know anybody. For the first three weeks, we stayed at the Bel Air Hotel, but that was too expensive, so we moved to another, smaller hotel on Lasky Drive. Lasky was one of the quiet, mildly commercial streets south of Wilshire Boulevard in Beverly Hills. It seemed to be a clean hotel, inhabited mostly by older single people who rented by the month. Our room in the Lasky House had a double bed with a faded, flowered bedspread, gray carpeting and old wooden venetian blinds.

We went to the same place for dinner every night, the Hamburger Hamlet in Westwood, and we tried to sit in the same booth. We ordered the same food every night, too. There was enough else new in our lives.

"Well, it *is* beautiful." My mother sighed as we drove away from the Lasky House and Beverly Hills and the car coasted down a hill on wide, bright Wilshire Boulevard into the sun. Tall, glorious apartment buildings stood on both sides of the street, their stripes of window catching light from the late, red, falling sun. We saw young boys in huge white leather tennis shoes on skateboards. Two rabbis walked on the sidewalk with a three-year-old girl in a pink dress. A couple in sweatsuits jogged.

We didn't know how they could do it; live, eat, look like that. For us, it seemed so hard.

My mother was going to be a special education teacher in the Los Angeles Public School District and her classes started a day before mine. We got up early when it was still dark. She took a long time dressing and left an hour to drive. As she went out to the elevator, she told me to stay inside our hotel room. I asked if I could just walk around the block.

"Honey, I've got a lot on my mind. Just do what I say this once."

So I made the bed and stayed in the room, watching TV, pretending I was an actress on each of the shows. I kept calling the desk to ask the time. I wanted to go out but I didn't. Here I was too scared to disobey.

And when my mother finally came back, something was wrong. She knocked things over, moving quickly. It seemed everything had changed.

I didn't even know if we'd get dinner. She exhaled, snapped on the over-head light, kicked her shoes off and began undressing, hanging her good clothes neatly in the closet.

She looked at me for the first time that afternoon. "You won't believe what I've been through today, you just won't believe it," she said. Then she went back to undressing.

Except for the overhead light, it was dark in the room because the blinds were down. We never raised the blinds. We didn't want anyone on the street to be able to see us.

"I can't teach there, Honey. They sent me to Watts. That car going in the parking lot with barbed wire all around. They have electric fences. I'm telling you, Ann, we're lucky I'm alive."

Her voice sounded small. I'd never heard her so scared. It made me feel light in my stomach. I lifted up an edge of the blind. It was reddish outside, dark only in the centers of bushes.

"They have a big wire fence around the school, it's like a prison. They give you a card you put in to open the gate. And Annie, those kids were like this, taller than I am." She was standing in just her bra and under-pants. She whispered, "And all black. I can't go back there, Ann."

"Don't other people go, too? I mean, what about the other teachers? It couldn't be that bad."

"With this car? Wait'll you see. They scratched it. Somebody scratched it with a piece of broken glass. He must have taken something and gone all the way down the side. One day there and the car's ruined. You'll see." She sat on the bed and turned off the overhead light, even though it was only five o'clock and reddish outside. We could still hear the day from the sidewalk below, other people's day.

"Won't they send you somewhere else, somewhere safer?"

"I doubt it. They're probably all booked. School's started. They've got their staffs lined up. See, that's how they get you. That's what this school system does. They get the poor person from out of town and stick them there in the ghetto, where no one else will go. And I suppose they can get away with it. People come all the way out here, and then what are they going to do? And if it's a man and he has a family to support? But I'm too old for that, Honey. I'm sorry, Honey, but that I just can't do for you."

I remembered how we were the day we found out. We whirled around in our stocking feet, our hands together in the middle, screaming "Weeeeeeeee!" We'd been alone in the house on Carriage Court, skidding on the black and white checked kitchen floor, no one heard us. When we stopped, she had looked shy. "You don't know, Annie, but there aren't many women my age who have an MA," she'd said.

She probably remembered that too, and it made everything worse. We felt like dupes now, for having been proud. And she probably went back to thinking what she usually thought about herself, that she wasn't quite right in the world.

"We'll have to go home if I can't get another job. I can't work in that school, Honey. I'd get hurt. I wouldn't get out alive."

"Are you just not going to go tomorrow?" Tomorrow was my first day of school. I didn't even know if we were having dinner. I started to hang my clothes up, too, neat in the closet. I always get neat when I'm scared.

"I'm calling first thing in the morning, believe you me. We'll set the alarm. But the other teachers said, sure, they wanted to leave, too. Everyone wants to get out of there. I'll tell them I just can't teach there and see what they do. And otherwise, I guess I'll look for another job."

I didn't say anything for a while.

"I don't even know where to look here. I mean the LA School System is it, they're all over. I don't know, but I need to make money. We have to live."

It was still only afternoon, but I pulled on the T-shirt I slept in and crawled under the covers. My mother sighed and sat down next to me. We had the one double bed and I always stayed on my side, near the edge. She shook my foot through the blanket.

"Come on. Get up, Honey. Let's go get a bite to eat."

I had to know. "Do we have enough money?" I asked. "If you're not going to have a job?"

"Well," my mother tried to laugh. "We have enough for one dinner, silly. Don't worry so much. Come on. It'll work out. I don't know how, but it will."

I felt something like a metal bar in my chest as I stood up, going from my heart to my neck.

But outside the Lasky House, there was a breeze. The air was bright and cool. I looked at the other people walking on the sidewalk. They seemed amazing to me. Then, I saw the scratch on our Lincoln. We both looked away from it.

"Should we try somewhere new, closer, or would you rather just go to the old place?"

"Hamburger Hamlet," I said.

We ordered sunflower sandwiches, the same thing we ate every night. They were cheese, tomato, and sprouts on wheat bread with little porcelain dishes of sunflower seeds on the side. They had always enchanted us. We knew from the menu that the mayonnaise was safflower. But tonight the sandwiches weren't wonderful. They were food. When we'd finished the sandwiches, we ate every sunflower seed from the small white porcelain bowls.

We drove past the long strips of park in Beverly Hills, lawns that separated the commercial district from the lush, residential streets above. Papery late summer poppies bloomed, red and tall, moving in the little breeze.

"One of these nights I'm going to come with a scissors when it's dark and cut a bunch of those." My mother laughed a little, mimicking the mischievous vigor she'd always had, effortlessly, in Bay City. It was a weak try. We were both far too afraid to do anything like that here. And if we did steal the flowers we would have no vase to put them in, nothing but the paper-wrapped water glass in our hotel bathroom.

The next day was my first day of school and I had to go anyway, even knowing we might not stay. My mother was driving to the Los Angeles School District office to try and talk to someone. We both wore our best clothes. My best dress from Wisconsin was navy blue wool, with a red belt, a little hot for this weather, but my mother said to wear it anyway. "They always remember what you wore your first day." While she dabbed makeup on in the bathroom, I pulled up my first pair of navy blue nylons. At home in Bay City, we girls all bought our own nylons at K-Mart down the new highway. We hid them in our school lockers, changing out of our knee socks from home every morning. When my mother finished her own hair, she braided mine and tied on a red ribbon.

"Are those kids going to *school* like that?" My mother peered over the steering wheel to get a better look. We were early, parked across the street. "They look like they're going to the beach."

They wore long, wide-bottom jeans, ragged at the ends from dragging on the ground, leather sandals and T-shirts. The girls' hair fell down over their faces onto their arms and backs, thinning to points at the ends like vines, as if it had never been trimmed.

"I have to change," I said. "I want to go back to the hotel."

My mother shook her head slowly. "We don't have time, Honey. I have to get going and, anyway, you'd be late. You don't want to be late your first day. And I wouldn't send you to school looking like that, I wouldn't."

"I'll walk back."

"There'll be the nicer kids and those girls will be wearing dresses. Believe me, Annie, I know. Go on, you look real cute. Really, or I wouldn't tell you."

I got out, carrying my clean new notebooks. It was nothing like schools in Wisconsin. It was old. The plain stucco walls were painted pink. All the roofs were red tile. There was a square steeple, as if it had once been a church.

Everything seemed strange: the small, old desks, the pale but bright blue walls. I thought it might always seem odd to me; I might leave before it ever grew normal. From where I sat in the class, I could see a palm tree, its huge leaves fluttering a little near the window.

Two girls in my class wore dresses, but I could already tell that they weren't the ones I wanted to know. I liked the thin girls with long panels of hair like curtains on both sides of their faces. They smiled and laughed, knowing things. But I wasn't even sure if I'd come back here tomorrow. I thought of my mother somewhere asking the LA School District for a different school. I imagined her in the district office like a court, pleading her case. She was asking for our two lives. The person who decided was a man. He sat and listened behind a large, wooden teacher's desk; he played with a pencil between two fingers. She was standing in high heels, pacing, occasionally running her hand through her hair, pushing it back. She moved precariously, in those heels. He deliberated, listening. The sleeves of his judge's robe dragged on the desk. She talked on and on, a whine in her voice. At moments, she broke into a cry, while he sat calmly looking down at his clean hands.

The teacher asked me a question and I said, I'm sorry, I lost my place.

She moved on, kindly, to the next person. Finally, the lunch bell rang. I followed behind the crowd down to the basement cafeteria, but I didn't have any money, so I walked around to some trees in front of a smaller playground, with low gym equipment for the little kids. The air was hazy, hot but not clear, and cars moved on Wilshire, a block away. I didn't know if I would ever like it here. It wasn't the way I'd imagined.

I stood there, looking at the empty painted playground toys. I was thinking of my mother, where she was. Two girls walked up in front of me. One was tall and messy, messy hair, knee socks too thin for her legs and a large mouth. The other was small. They were the two girls wearing dresses.

"You new?" the big one said.

"Yeah."

"Where do you live?"

I knew the right answer. But I didn't live on Roxbury or Camden or Rodeo, or on any of those streets with the pretty names. I didn't live anywhere.

"I don't know," I said. "I don't remember the name of the street."

The big girl bent over her open palm, concentrating. "Is it above or below Santa Monica?"

I shrugged. She used the lines on her palm as a map. "Say this is Wilshire, the next big street is Santa Monica and above that is Sunset. You don't know which one you're closer to?"

"I think Sunset, but I'm not sure."

The bigger girl looked down at the small one. "She probably lives near Sunset."

A bell rang then and we moved towards the door.

"What does your father do for a living?" the taller girl said, her hand on my arm.

Two answers came to me. "He's a doctor," I told them. The first thing I'd thought was, He's dead.

The teacher stood drawing a map with colored chalk on the board, her dress lifting to show her strong, tan legs as she reached, and outside, a buzz saw tore the air. I read the part in the book and I liked it. School was so easy. I had darker things; the judge's sentence on my mother and me, the word no. I would have given anything that day to be twelve and I was twelve.

The two girls in dresses turned up next to me in the hall, after the last bell rang. Now that I'd lied to them, they bugged me. I wished they'd go away.

"You know what you could do to be really pretty? I think you'd be really pretty except for your teeth are crooked. You should get them straightened." She looked at the smaller girl. "Don't you think she'd be pretty with even teeth?"

The smaller girl nodded avidly.

"You should go to an orthodontist and get braces."

In the surprise of sun, I was wondering where I could walk that wouldn't show I was going south of Wilshire. I'd never thought about my teeth before. I'd always thought my teeth were fine. I'd looked at my face hundreds of times in the mirror, looking at it different ways for when I would be on television. Always, the best angles were ones only I saw. When I was alone and no one else could see. Now I worried about my teeth. I made my mouth go narrower.

Then my mother's car pulled over by the curb and I was so glad to see it, I ran and got in and she started driving before she even said anything. It was something she'd picked up from the summer. She drove to relax now, just anywhere, just to drive. We rode through the quiet residential streets with big houses and green slatted tennis courts. We both liked to look at those houses. What my mother had thought before in Bay City was true; it helped to have a car we weren't ashamed of. There was so much else we had to hide.

"Well," she sighed. "It looks like we can stay. They gave me another school in West Covina. I went out there this afternoon and saw it already. It's in the Valley, it's a long drive every day, but it's a white school, middle-class, all houses. So, I guess we'll have to really start looking for an apartment."

"Isn't that good? Aren't you happy?"

"Well, I'm tired. It's an hour and twenty minutes there, and another hour and a half back. I've been driving all day. Let's go get an ice cream cone."

We parked in front of the Baskin-Robbins and my mother gave me five dollars to buy our cones. She would never go in herself. At night, she said she wasn't dressed well enough and she didn't want to run into anyone. As if we knew anyone to run into. But today she had on her best suit.

We tried to meet people. My mother asked about kids at school and about their parents, but nothing seemed to come of it. We called a family named the Flatows, who'd moved from Bay City a few years ago, when Mr. Flatow's company transferred him to Beverly Hills. In Bay City, their family owned an expensive children's clothing store. I remember shopping there with my mother when I was little. The saleslady would take out a drawer full of socks which were all your size and they would be folded up so they looked like colored eggs.

My mother and I sat in their apartment for an hour, having tea. They lived south of Wilshire, too. They had a daughter a year younger than me, but she left to go to a dog show a few minutes after we arrived. Her parents asked my mother about news in Bay City and my mother told them what she could, but they didn't seem to know the same people. They praised the Beverly Hills High School, where we kids would all eventually get to go, and encouraged us to drive by. "It's like a college campus," they said as we left. Nothing came out of that visit, either. We didn't see them again.

We met Julie Edison the way we'd met other real estate agents. My mother called and said we were looking for a house. Weekends, we toured Beverly Hills mansions for sale. We saw houses with five bathrooms and only one bedroom, houses with tiny kitchens and ballrooms, a house that had once belonged to William Holden. We saw where the Monkees lived for a while. We walked through houses with more than one real estate agent. That was when we were living at the Bel Air Hotel. When we moved to the Lasky House, all of them but Julie stopped calling. She kept showing us houses, and the places she took us to were smaller and smaller. Finally, she showed us a house we really liked.

It was a normal house, with two bedrooms, just above Santa Monica Boulevard on an old, unimposing street. None of the houses were big or fancy. This one was white brick with a red chimney and bushes out in front. It had two stories, a fireplace, a nice kitchen with windows looking over the backyard. We fell in love with the house.

We'd seen it twice already. It was the picture I held in my mind at night when I was trying to fall asleep. My mother told Julie what she'd told other real estate agents, other times: that we'd come ahead to start looking, but we were waiting for a husband to join us. After a while, my mother stopped returning Julie's phone messages. They came on little pink slips the man behind the reception desk handed us when we walked into the Lasky House. My mother stuffed them in her purse.

While we licked our ice cream cones at night, we drove by the house. Once, my mother parked in front. We just stared.

"It really is a beauty, isn't it? It's small, but elegant. It has charm, more charm than a lot of these that have been added onto and added onto so they end up one big hodgepodge. I'd do it all in white wicker and chintz. It's really the perfect little place for two girls. And in the winter, we could make fires in the fireplace. We could go to the woods and collect pine-cones, remember how nice they burn?"

"But we can't afford it, can we?"

She sighed. "I don't see how. But who knows, we'll see."

"It's a hundred thousand dollars. How much is that you'd have to put down?"

"I don't know, twenty, thirty."

"And we don't have that much?" I had no idea how much money we had.

"Honey, we've got barely enough with what I'm making to pay the Lasky House and our food every night. Plus your school clothes and when we get an apartment, we'll have to give a deposit, plus, plus, plus. I can't do all this on my own."

"So it's out then. We can't afford it."

"I *told* you, we'll see. I just don't know right now. Who knows, Gramma might even give us something."

We parked on the street in front of Julie's condominium, a new high-rise building.

"Now, you know, this might be the last time we see her, once she finds out we don't want the house. She knows she won't get her commission then," my mother said.

We'd called home, collect, to my grandmother many times.

"I know, I don't care."

We sat in the car. It was October and a little cool in the evening. We had the heat on.

"Okay, as long as you know. So you won't be disappointed." My mother hadn't wanted to return Julie's messages. She thought the best thing would be to drop it and just run into her again sometime, later, when we were all set. It was my idea to call.

We rode up the elevator in silence. When she opened the door, Julie was standing, holding a phone to her ear. A thirty-foot extension cord dragged behind her. She ushered us in, smiling, all the while saying, "Right, right," into the receiver. She was wearing a man's long-sleeved shirt rolled up to her elbows and purple panties. Her fingernails looked newly polished. There were cotton balls stuck between her toes.

We sat down primly, waiting for her to get off the phone. We liked Julie.

"So, how are you," she said, as she hung up. "I've missed you, I've been calling."

"Well, we've been busy, haven't we, Ann?" my mother said. "And I have some unhappy news. My husband won't be coming. We've decided to get a divorce."

Julie pounced on the couch beside us, her fingers spreading on my mother's back.

"It looks like he won't be joining us. I've decided to leave and so . . . we're on our own."

"Oh, no, I'm sorry."

"Well, I am too. I'm really sorry for her. And she's being a very brave girl. But I think it'll be for the best. I've really known that for a long time. And I just don't think I can live with him again. I just can't."

"Jesus, let me make some coffee."

My mother said she'd decided to leave; she thought turning down money was a claim in itself. I'm sure to Julie it made no difference. Julie wasn't a snob. She was a practical person. If you had the money, you bought a house. If you didn't, you rented.

"I can't do it, it's just not right," my mother yelled into the kitchen.

"Maybe then it's not bad news," Julie called. "Maybe it's really good news. Or it will be. If you'll be happier."

"I think we will, in a little bit, when we're settled. But unfortunately, I'm afraid it means we won't be able to swing the house. On our own, we just won't be able to do it."

"There'll be other houses again when you can. That one was a partic-ular steal, but if you can't, you can't."

"I'm just sorry for all your trouble."

"Oh, don't be sorry about me, that's my business." Julie squeezed my shoulder. "Ann, I've got a half gallon of Jamoca Almond Fudge in the freezer, why don't you dish it out for us." She yelled after me. "If there're no spoons in the drawer, they're in the dishwasher."

"Oh, none for me, please," my mother said, "I really shouldn't."

"You shouldn't. I shouldn't." Julie slapped a thigh. "Come on, Adele, you *should*."

"Well, a wee bit."

"So, you're going to need an apartment." From her pink lacquered file cabinet, Julie took out a map of Beverly Hills. She squeezed between us on the couch. We each ate our ice cream staring down at the map on the coffee table. We listened and memorized, alert, to all she could tell us.

"The bottom line is you want to keep her in Beverly Hills for the school district. But I think we can do even better than that. In high school—they're all together. But this year, for seventh grade, there's four elementary schools. And if you can get her in with a good group of kids, she can just keep on with them."

"RIGHT," my mother said, hitting the table. "It'll just carry over. That's why I wanted to get her in now, while she's still in the seventh."

Julie traced the map and its districts with her pink fingernail. The names enchanted us. Trusedale Estates and all the long, wide streets with palms down the center belonged to Hawthorne School. Cañon, Rodeo, North Elm Drive.

"I'd try to keep her in El Rodeo. Beverly Vista is mostly apartments. And see, Horace Mann's way over here. That gets into La Cienega."

My mother reached over and ruffled my hair. "We'll keep you in El Rodeo."

Julie snapped her fingers. "I have a friend who has a daughter in seventh or eighth grade in El Rodeo and she's in with a real chic crowd. She's the only one in her group who doesn't live in a house. All the others live above Sunset. Should I call her and ask if she has any advice?"

"Would you?" My mother dabbed the corner of her eye. My mother loved being grateful. She crossed her fingers while Julie dialed. I turned away.

"Okay. Good." Julie stood on one leg with the other foot crushing down a sofa cushion. "She should. Okay. One sec." She looked at us. "She says she should work it in the conversation that she's from Wisconsin. A lot of the new kids are just from other schools in LA and that's a bore. But Wisconsin's different, so see if she can mention that."

Excitement built on my mother's face. She loved social strategy, careful planning. It was one of her lifelong passions.

"Oh, Annie, I've got it," she said, hitting her hands together.

"What."

"You can say, how's this, she can say, Gee, in Wisconsin, where I'm from, by now, by this time of year, I'd be wearing my bunnyfur coat. It'd already be so cold." One of the great prides of my mother's life will always be that when I was ten, I owned a real rabbit coat. "Say, every year I was wearing it by November. Or even October. Say October."

"I'm not gonna say that."

"Why not? Or, let's see, you could say, Boy, is it ever warm here. I wonder if it'll ever get cold enough to wear my bunnyfur coat. In Wisconsin—"

Julie's hand slapped over the mouthpiece again. "And she should be a little shy, aloof. Don't chase them. Let them come to you."

"Yes. Let *them* come to you. Do you hear. Don't PUSH. Wait. Just let them come to you in their own time. Because sometimes you push."

"No I don't."

"Yes, you do. I've seen you."

That was a theme of my mother's. She thought I was too aggressive. She tried to teach me to be feminine. The art of waiting. I thought if she were a little more aggressive, we might know people and have a place to live.

"Why don't you worry about making friends yourself? I don't see why you're so worried about me."

"Where am I going to meet anybody? You're the one who can."

Julie found us a one-bedroom apartment on South Elm Drive, just inside the El Rodeo border. It had nice windows overlooking the street and gold shag carpeting throughout. We lived there with no furniture except a queen-sized Sealy Posturepedic mattress and box spring we'd ordered over the telephone.

My mother was obsessed with paint. The first few weeks, she found spots the painter had missed. She called the landlord, a large-breasted woman who lived north of Sunset and drove down to our building in a brown Mercedes once or twice a week. The landlord had also promised my mother white shutters for the windows. My mother became enraged each succeeding week they were late. She began to doubt that they would ever come. Every day, I arrived home from school before my mother. And when I saw the windows still bare, I got nervous, knowing my mother would yell for a while when she came in from work. She had long, angry telephone conversations with the landlord at night. Sometimes, the landlord put her husband on. I could hear the change in my mother's voice. She was softer with a man.

Finally, the shutters arrived. The landlord had promised white shutters and they were white, but a shade off from the color of the walls. My mother felt heartsick and furious. After two nights of phone calls with the landlord, the same painter came back to repaint.

"It's cheap. She got the cheapest bad paint and slapped it on. With all this cheap stuff around not right, I don't even want to be here. I JUST CAN'T LIVE LIKE THIS!" my mother screamed.

I stood there. I used to make myself peanut butter sandwiches on toasted English muffins and eat them standing up.

The second day the painter came back to match the shutters to the wall, I stayed home sick from school. I wanted to offer him something, but we didn't have the usual things, like coffee. All we had were sunflower seeds and peanut butter and English muffins.

Then the landlord walked in and I hid in the closet. The painter knew I was there, but she didn't.

"Just impossible," I heard her say.

"Oh, she's all right once you get to know her," the painter said. "I think she's really a good person underneath."

I didn't know if he was saying that because I could hear. He and my mother used to talk, though. She'd cry and tell him how frustrated she was, how hard everything was for us here, at the same time pointing to spots on the wall and saying, "Oh, oh, you missed" or "This little bit looks thinner, would you mind, just to even it? Thank you."

"Well, she may be wonderful as a person, but as a tenant, she's a nightmare."

When my mother came home, the landlord was in the front yard talking to the gardener. My mother bounded upstairs to see the painted shutters and then marched down again. "Well, the shutters are better, it's an improvement. But now what about the carpets? They were supposed to be cleaned two months ago. I don't even want to walk around without socks and shoes. They're filthy."

I watched from the window upstairs. The landlord dropped the green hose she'd been holding.

"I mean, Geraldine, I JUST CAN'T LIVE LIKE THIS!"

"Adele, it's been shampooed twice already and let me tell you something. You say you can't live like this, with the shutters a shade off color, and meanwhile you can live in an empty apartment with no furniture, with a daughter in school for three months."

"Well, the furniture's all picked out, it's just WAITING at Sloane's to be delivered. I just want everything RIGHT before it comes."

They talked a while longer in low voices and then the landlord slid into her brown Mercedes and drove way. But she'd gotten to my mother that time. At dinner, in our booth at Hamburger Hamlet, my mother seemed distracted. I tried to talk about different things. She had a piece of her hair between two of her fingers and she kept turning it, studying.

"Split ends," she said, in the middle of my sentence.

I stopped talking and she seemed to notice. She looked up at me. "You know, she's right, Ann, living all these months with no furniture and I'm worried about the carpets. She's right."

I loved her then. I was so glad, that seemed so normal and reasonable. I thought now we might start living the way other people did.

But the next thing that happened was my mother found another apartment. It was smaller, but cheaper and already furnished. "I mean, it's not great furniture, but it could be cute. I can see already. We could make it real cute with some felt draped and different things around," she told me.

So maybe that was it all along. Maybe we just couldn't afford our apartment.

"But she could sue us for the whole rest of the year," my mother said. She was scared about our lease. So we moved out late at night, carrying all our stuff in bags and suitcases to the car and driving to the new apartment in the dark. "I want us all out of here, before she knows." Even without furniture, it took hours before everything we had was moved. We left the bare, almost new mattress and box spring. The studio had only one room, with a small alcove to sleep in, and the alcove already had a bed in it.

When we finished moving, we didn't go to sleep. The new place was still too new and we didn't want to look around carefully, then. We drove out Sunset in the dark to see the beach. We parked on the Pacific Coast Highway, and sat in the car with the doors locked, looking at the waves. We did that whenever things got too bad. You couldn't see much, the ocean was just black, but you could hear the waves and sometimes we saw foam. We waited until it was light and the sand changed and then we drove back to town and had big breakfasts at Nibbler's. My mother called in sick to her school. We were both going to stay home and work on the new apartment.

Then, when it was nine o'clock, we drove right up to the landlord's house. We'd never been inside, but we knew where it was, we'd driven by. I pressed myself hard against my car seat. But then we were there parked in front and my mother was taking off her seat belt, saying, "Okay, here we are. Let's get it over with."

There was a long lawn in front of the house. The grass seemed wet from the night. It was a pinkish brick house with white statues by the drive. There was a fountain but it wasn't running yet. The whole house looked closed as if the people inside weren't up.

"Can I stay in the car?"

"Hon, I think it would be better if we both went. I really do." Her voice was kind. She was being nice. "Come on, Hon. Let's go."

We stood there on her porch, our car far away over the lawn, knocking on the brass knocker. We must have looked like refugees. We'd been wearing the same clothes all night to move, we hadn't slept. I could feel my hair matted in the back.

A maid answered and then we waited for a long time while she went to get the landlord.

Finally, the landlord walked to the door. We'd never seen her like this, she was barefoot, wearing only tennis shorts and a T-shirt. She was obviously surprised to see us, her eyebrows pressed down, but her voice stayed measured and pleasant.

"What can I do for you?"

My mother started shaking her head. "Geraldine, we have to talk. It just hasn't worked out for us, the apartment. The rug, the shutters, everything. And I think I have grounds to get out of the lease, given all that's been done and what was said would be done."

"You want to get out of your lease? Is that what you want?"

"Well, yes, I think given—"

"Fine. I'll be happy to let you out of it. No problem. I'll rip it up right here."

My mother and I looked at each other, following her into an office. The house seemed large, solidly furnished, quiet. It must have been wonderful to wake up in the morning and walk around heavy things like that.

The landlord scribbled on the lease and attached a note to the top, signing it and stapling the pages. "Fine, just let me know when you'll be out."

My mother laughed oddly. "Well, actually, we're already out."

The landlord looked at us fast and hard when she heard that, her head steady in one position, as if we really were crazy. "Okay," she said, slowly. "I'll write you a check for your deposit, then."

"Believe me, Geraldine, we left it clean as a whistle. You can ride right down and look."

Her dark head was already bent down, writing. "I believe you," she said and handed us the check.

The next place was worse. I never liked it. But we cleaned and then we got used to it. At least there was furniture. My mother had plans; she wanted to make new curtains and slipcover the vinyl couch, but for a while we didn't do anything.

We had a loud, cheap alarm clock that rattled on the floor when it rang. Every night, my mother sighed as she set it. She sat on her side of the bed, next to the telephone, naked except for a T-shirt, and handed the clock to me. We never had our work finished, so sleep always seemed a small surrender. Our work was as simple as my homework for school, the books piled up on the tiny, wobbly, dinette table and whatever my mother was supposed to do with the stack of manila files she carried in from the car every evening and then brought back the next morning. Our work was simple, but it hung over us so constantly that we lost track of what exactly it was we hadn't done. We always knew we were behind. So my mother set the alarm for five o'clock. We both felt so tired at night we could excuse ourselves, with the idea of the long empty hours that would hang in front of us when we got up.

I knew when my mother turned and sighed in the night, I had radar for her. I always moved before she inched anywhere near me. I slept with a closed fist full of blankets and sheets. Our life together made me selfish.

We kept the clock by my side of the bed and when it blared out, rattling, in the morning, my mother would turn and say, "Five minutes. Five more minutes."

This happened six or seven times. Then at eight or eight thirty, she'd bolt up to a sitting position and say, "Oh my God," with a low hardness that made my heart stop.

"Hurry up," my mother yelled while I sat on the edge of the bed, pulling on my knee socks. She stood naked, across the room, pinning her hair up into a showercap. She paced. I just looked straight back at her, pulling my sock on slowly.

"Okay, fine, you can make fun, but I'm leaving without you if you're not ready."

I was ready twenty minutes before she was, the same as every morning. I sat on the edge of the bed with my schoolbooks ready on my knees.

"I'm going as fast as I can, Honey."

"I'm going to be late again."

"Well, so am I then, and believe me, my job is more important than the seventh grade."

When we stepped outside, it was already too bright and my mother's heels clicked on the raked cement going down to the garage. As she drove the Continental up, pumping gas with her shoe, it scraped the cement side of the ramp. The space we had to go through was almost exactly the same width as the car and so, every morning, it made an awful, shrieking noise.

"Damn," my mother said.

"Could you please shut up."

"Jeez. You think you've got something a little decent once that you've paid a lot for, and then, before you know, it's just another piece of junk, too."

I did feel bad about the car. I knew how she thought. We were one by one getting the things you needed for a life. We didn't expect to get ahead or get extra things, not since we'd moved. We just wanted what it seemed everybody else already had. But things didn't keep. We'd never have them all at once. It made me think of the junk in Griling's front yard, back on Lime Kiln Road. All those parts of things. I could understand it when my mother sighed. When she did that, some part of me opened and closed again.

.   .   .

I did weird things, too, by myself. At night, when we went to dinner, I said I had to go to the bathroom and walked upstairs to the wall of phones and phone books. The Hamburger Hamlet had thirteen different phone books for LA. I looked in two or three a night—that's as long as I thought I could be gone before my mother would miss me—for the first three letters of my father's name. I'd gone through every phone book and it was never there, but still, any time I was anywhere near a phone book, I had to check again, as if it could be. I was never surprised when I didn't find it. I didn't think about it too much. It was just something I did.

The last day of school before winter vacation, Daniel Swan started walking home with me. I guess like my mother said, it was easier for me to meet people. He was a guy in my class. He always kept a stash of square Kraft caramels in his jacket pocket, sometimes he'd give me one, sometimes not. I didn't want him to see where I lived, so every few blocks, I'd stop and say, This is out of your way.

He'd start ahead of me, digging his hands in his parka pockets. "I'll go a little bit farther."

Finally, we stood in front of my apartment building. "Okay, I'm going to go now." I put out my arm like to shake hands.

But he didn't leave. I didn't invite him in, even though I had my key in my hand, and he didn't ask. Our apartment was on the first floor, you could see our front window. But I didn't tell him which door was ours, or anything, and we just sat on the landing doing nothing. He gave me a caramel and started opening another for himself, the cellophane one small glitter in the dull late afternoon sun.

Then I heard the scrape that was my mother's car going down into the garage. It made an awful sound. I just sat there.

"Hi, you kids!" my mother shouted as she hurried up the ramp, pitched forward because of her high heels. She dabbed the edge of her eye with a sleeve. She was carrying a stack of files, as usual. It was December, but in Los Angeles, December can be like autumn. The air was dull and cool and smelled as if the earth were about to change.

"Hey, why don't you help me carry in groceries!"

We both ran down the concrete to the garage, glad to be told what to do. Then, I was grateful for the car. The leather smelled rich and good. I was glad my mother kept it clean.

My mom had gone shopping, so she could offer us things to drink. She'd been to the Linville Nutrition Center and bought pomegranate juice and carrot juice and celery juice and three kinds of kefir. Daniel seemed used to that kind of thing. When she asked him, he said he wanted peach kefir.

My mother brought out bags of cranberries and brand new needles and threads. She told us she'd seen gorgeous strings of cranberries on a Christmas tree in a store window, prettier than popcorn, and so she thought we should make some. They were opening lots already, all over Westwood, the trees bundled together and stacked against walls.

We sat on the floor and started stringing. It was hard. The needles seemed thin and flimsy against the berries. We pricked our fingers and broke the cranberries and after a half hour, we each had only a short little stringful to show for it.

"Well, we're going to have dinner at the Hamburger Hamlet, Daniel. You're welcome to join us, if you'd like. Or if you can, if your mom's not expecting you."

"But you mean, we're going to give up on the cranberries?"

"I think we should, don't you?"

Daniel stood and wiped his hands on his pants and followed my mother to the sleeping alcove where she pointed to the phone. In the little space between the bed and the wall, there wasn't room for two, so she moved out of the way for him.

"The Witch will still be working, but I'll call the rest of them. They'll be glad I'm not there. More food for them."

"Oh, Daniel." My mother laughed as if that were a joke.

In the living room with just me, she sighed and her shoulders dropped and she looked tired again.

We crowded in our regular booth at Hamburger Hamlet, all three of us.

"Hmmm. They've raised their prices, I see," Daniel said.

Neither of us ever would have said that. It seemed odd and happy for someone to talk about money.

My mother put her menu down and smiled. She was charmed. It was a relief to know other people thought about money, too. "You may have whatever you'd like, Daniel."

"Hmm, I always like their halibut, but it's gone up since the last time I was here."

"Oh, go ahead. Get it," my mother said.

On our week's vacation, my mother and I wandered into a store on Brighton Way and bought two suede jackets to give each other as presents. They were expensive, but they were on sale and my mother said they would be good forever and you need one or two smashing things.

So we had those and there weren't going to be any surprises. We'd received wrapped boxes of presents in the mail from home in the middle of December and we opened them as soon as they arrived.

We didn't know what to do with ourselves during vacation. We saw Julie once and we took an old woman from the Lasky House to the Hamburger Hamlet for dinner. Beverly Hills put up elaborate decorations on the streetlamps, but except for them you wouldn't have known it was Christmas. When we drove out of the commercial district, the long residential streets looked bright as always. The lawns were thick and tended, green, the palms tall and dry, and we heard the hollow thonks of volleys on hidden tennis courts.

My mother said we could get steaks for five dollars at the Charthouse, a new redwood restaurant on the water, so Christmas Eve we drove down to the beach. We argued, I thought the place would cost more. But by that time our car was looping on Sunset over Westwood. From the hills, the pink roofs of UCLA looked quaint.

But I was right. When we stood inside the Charthouse, waiting, my mother raised her eyebrows and said, "Let's go."

I wanted to stay. You could see the waves through a glass wall. It was warm and softly lit, the Beach Boys sang from the corners, a woman had already taken our names.

"I *told* you," I said.

We walked out on the gravel parking lot to our car. "Honey, they've gone up. You used to be able to get a steak here for five, six dollars," my mother said. "Well, anyway, it was a nice ride."

We drove back to the Hamburger Hamlet. Later that night, my mother rewrapped the presents we'd gotten from home in better paper, paper that all matched, and she wrapped our jackets and whatever empty boxes we could find around the house. "Just to make it a little Christmasy." She'd bought thick shiny dark green paper and red satin ribbons.

Then, at ten o'clock, my mother decided she didn't want to do any more decorating until the house was clean. "Let's just stay up and finish it. Then we can wake up in the morning and it'll be all done."

"Can't we do it in the morning? Why don't we just put the felt up and the cookies out and go to bed."

"Well, I don't care what you do but I'm staying up. I couldn't sleep with that kitchen floor the way it is."

"You've slept fine every other night."

"Honey, I'm not going to fight with you just because I want something a little nice once in my life, at Christmas. I'd like to wake up Christmas morning and have the place clean, okay?"

I didn't argue anymore. My mother started on the kitchen and put me in the bathroom. She told me to scrub every tile and then the insides of the tub and the toilet. I was down on my knees with a pail of water and ammonia and a plastic cylinder of Comet. I swiped pieces of dirt and strands of hair from the corners. I stopped for a second and looked down into the toilet water, blue from Comet. Then I went into the kitchen to get something to drink.

My mother knelt, fiercely scrubbing the floor.

"Don't tell me you think you're done already." Some hair fell out of the rubber band and a vein in her forehead was raised. She looked strained and awful, like a dog pulling against its leash.

"I just wanted to get something to drink."

"Oh, okay."

"You bet, okay," I said, carrying my glass back to the bathroom.

"Shhh, the whole building can hear you, these walls are like nothing."

"I don care," I shouted. And then I turned the shower on before she could say anything else.

The bathroom did look nice, the tiles glistened, clean, but there was something about our apartment that still didn't seem worth the work. It felt like a toy apartment, nothing was big enough, and whether it was a little cleaner or a little dirtier, it still wasn't right. That was the thing about working hard on it—while you looked close at one little thing, scrubbing, you forgot. Then when you finished and stepped back, it was always a disappointment you couldn't change more.

At two thirty we quit. We peeled our clothes off right onto the laundry pile. We still didn't have a hamper. It was another thing, like ice cube trays, that other people always had. The clothes smelled the way a refrigerator smells when you defrost it.

My mother sighed when she handed me the alarm. "I set it for six," she said, in the dark. "We'll feel better when it's clean."

We slept a groggy sleep until eleven. When we woke, the apartment was warm.

"Are you up?" my mother said. She sat, hugging her knees under the blanket. From where we were, we could see the opposite white wall, where the paint was cracking, and the bathroom door. "Well, Merry Christmas, Little One. Should we open our presents now or should we best leave them wrapped a while? They look so nice wrapped."

"We can leave them. We know what they are."

"You know, I know I said we'd go out to breakfast but we slept so late I'd almost rather just stay here and finish so it's done. Then we can go to your friends' this afternoon." We had been invited to one Christmas party by a friend of mine from school, who lived near us in an apartment. Her mother and stepfather were giving an open house. It was the only Christmas thing we were doing.

"I'm hungry."

"Have a little eggnog, Hon, and let's get started."

"What do we still have to do?"

"Not too much, really. We've got to vacuum, and especially the closets, because they're full of dust. Then the windows and polish the silver and that's it. Then just decorate." She shrugged. "I just can't really relax until it's done."

For maybe the first time in my life, I went without being asked to the closet and took out the vacuum cleaner. I began in the bathroom, banging on walls.

My mother walked past, still wearing only her sweat shirt, drinking from a carton of eggnog.

I pulled the plug on the vacuum cleaner.

"Could you PLEASE not drink from the carton. Could you just pour it in a glass?"

"I can see you're in a pleasant mood for Christmas."

"There's germs."

"The other one's unopened. Drink from that."

I plugged in the cord again and pounded against the floorboards. A few minutes later, my mother tapped my shoulder. I jumped. "Honey, we should really call home. Let's do that now." She sat on the bed and crossed her legs. "You know, I don't know why they can't call us. It's later there, you know."

I opened the new carton of eggnog, poured some into a glass. I took the carton to the living room closet, where I kept my schoolbooks.

"So did you get the sweater?" my mother was saying, into the phone.

"Let me talk," I said softly.

"You didn't! You've got to be kidding. Well, they sent it two weeks ago! You *didn't* get a sweater? Are you sure? It was a, a brown sweater. Are you sure, a brown sweater, with, let's see, a shawl collar and yellow buttons! Oh, it was beautiful, Mom."

The way she was yelling, my grandmother must have been holding out the phone.

"It's not her fault," I said, but my mother didn't hear me. I was sitting on the floor, gulping. I didn't know if there really was a sweater. I'd never seen it or heard about it. She could have gone and done it without me. But then, why wouldn't it have gotten there? Other people's things always worked.

"It was from Saks. They said it would get there for sure. Oh, I'm sick, I'm absolutely sick. It was a beautiful sweater, gorgeous wool. Oh, and it had pockets. Well, you'll see. It should come any day now."

The sweater never arrived. Neither did Carol's nightgown or Jimmy's scarf or Benny's sweat shirt or Hal's blazer. And my mother did it again and again, every holiday. It got to be a joke with the rest of us, "Did you get the sweater?" And it got so my mother didn't trust the United States Postal Service. If you said you were going to send her a letter, she wanted you to insure it.

We went back to cleaning. Every few minutes, she would stop and shout. "She could do a lot more to help you, you know? You'd think she'd want to help, her own daughter. But no, not her."

By the time the apartment was ready, it was after three. I ran to the kitchen to throw away the dirty paper towels from the windows. The open house at my friend's was from one o'clock until six. We had to hurry.

Then my mother handed me the car keys to get the cedar boughs from the backseat.

"Can we do that later, we're going to miss the party."

"Honey, it's going to take three minutes. This is the very last part. Just let me feel like it's finished, so I can at least think we're going to come back to a clean house. Here. Go on, Ann."

I squeezed the keys in my hand so it hurt and ran outside. The street was deserted and the air was cool so my arms had goose bumps. It felt good. The light was soft and gray, as if it might rain. In another window in the building there was a huge fake tree with colored lights that blinked. An older woman lived there alone and she hardly ever came out.

Most of the cars were gone. I sat inside ours for a while, smelling the clean air from the cedar. I put my hands on the steering wheel. I wished I could drive. I knew how, but my mother would never let me. Benny drove lawn mowers and tractors, over the fields in summer.

I piled all the cedar branches in my arms. Needles fell on the car carpet, but my mother could worry about that later. I didn't care. I dumped the branches just inside the door in one heap.

My mother stood placing her gingerbread house on a polished silver platter. We'd draped a card table with green felt. Then she began sticking the cedar boughs around it for a wreath. She draped cedar boughs on the moldings a foot down from the ceiling, on the bathroom mirror, anywhere she thought they would stick. She was right, they did change the apartment. The air felt like the outside. It seemed the ceilings were higher. You could feel it in your lungs. It was clean.

Finally, she finished. The last cedar branch was placed. We both stood back to admire it.

"Well, there. Now we just have to vacuum up these needles and we're done."

I started stripping my clothes off. It was four o'clock, there wasn't even time to take a shower. I pulled on clean knee socks. "This is the one fun thing we can do for Christmas and it's going to be over in an hour and I'm not sitting here and vacuuming."

"Okay, don't. You don't have to. I'll do it." And she dragged the old Electrolux like a dog out from the closet. And then I knew that she'd never get ready. There wasn't time. Because after that was done and put away, she needed her hour-long regime for dressing.

I yelled so she could hear me over the vacuum cleaner. "I'm going. I'm writing the address down here, so you can come if you want."

"No, don't bother. I won't come. I wouldn't go in alone. I'd really rather just finish here. To tell the truth, Honey, that's what'll make me feel best. Just so I know it's done. But you go on and have a good time." She didn't seem mad.

I walked outside. The clouds were moving fast above me. I jammed my hands in my pockets. I walked down the sidewalk and everything looked closed. You couldn't see inside the apartments. I thought of the door opening, the noise and color when I first walked in. All of a sudden, I didn't want to go. I turned towards my friend's street though, anyway. I'd walk around the block and then see. I walked all the way to the high school. It stood there empty and cool like a castle over the tiered lawns. Two men ran back and forth playing tennis on the green courts. There was no one else around. I was wearing my best jeans, which I'd ironed for this, and high platform shoes and now I wished I had on my sneakers so I could walk over the lawns. For some reason I wanted to put my hand on the pale pink stucco of the school's walls, as if I could leave a handprint. But walking across the wet lawn would have ruined the suede of my Korkease. And I thought of things like that.

I turned towards home and walked slowly. There was no hurry anymore. The apartments looked like everyone had left for Christmas, as if only people who owned houses stayed. I didn't want to see anyone. I started to cry, the tears stinging my skin, for no reason. It was pretty outside and calm and I felt glad to be in new clothes.

When I walked back to our building, I didn't go inside. I sat by our door for a long time, staring at the street. I didn't think about anything, I just didn't want to go in yet.

Finally, the door opened and my mother shrieked. "Oh, Ann. You scared me. I was coming to look for you. How long have you been here?" She wore a coat, opening the door, nothing on her legs. Her hair was still pulled back in the pink rubber band. She was carrying keys.

"Come on, let's jump in the car and just get an ice cream cone."

"Now?"

"Mmhmm. I'm just in the mood."

We turned the heat on and I realized as my mother's coat fell open that she wasn't wearing anything. She was planning to have me run in and get her cone, as always. But the Baskin-Robbins was closed, a small crooked sign in the glass door.

"Damn. Damn, I really wanted one after all that work. We should've just spent the money and had our steaks. And I want an ice cream cone. Damn."

My mother bent over the steering wheel and she wouldn't stop crying. I kept looking out the car windows at the empty street. Then I'd shake her shoulder and say, "Mom, Mom?" but that only made her heave harder.

I took the keys out and walked around to her side of the car. I pushed her over to the passenger door and drove home, dizzy, wobbling some, down the deserted wide streets. My mother was quiet now, her eyes closed.

A long time ago, once, in the cab of Jimmy Measey's red truck, it was a bright afternoon and the fields were blue with snow. On the highway, Benny perched up on his father's lap driving. I remember his green and yellow striped shirt. There were times when we were happy. Then, turning onto our road, Jimmy said, "Ann's turn, Ann, do you know how to drive?"

I said yes, but I was terrified. I didn't know how. I didn't know where things were, anything. I knew we would all die, but then someone lifted me up on Jimmy's lap and I could see: the telephone lines for miles, patches of mud in the field, tall grass poking through, snow sparkling out the windshield all the way to the barn, I was so high up. I turned the wheel with Jimmy's hands outside my hands and felt the car move on the road, as if we were sliding. I could feel Jimmy's weight behind me, his hands hovering on either side. They let me steer, swiveling up the road, the great truck rocking with all of us in it, under the power of my hands.

In front of our apartment, a policeman stopped me. I looked up at him as he bent to our window. He was staring at my mother, crumpled against her door. He asked me where we lived. I pointed. He shook his head, Okay, and tapped my shoulder with a piece of paper rolled up. He let us go and drove away slowly, on the empty, holiday street.

I opened the door with my own key. We left the room dark, except for the tree lights. I went over and took a Christmas cookie, tree-shaped, with red and green sprinkles on top and sat on the felt-covered sofa. My mother hung up her coat and got into bed. I sat there and ate my Christmas cookie, slowly, each bough of the Christmas tree first until it was just a blob. When I was done I looked down at my empty palm and licked off the crumbs.

"Was it over?" my mother said. She was propped up in bed, using both pillows.

"What?"

"Your party."

"I didn't go." I hated admitting that. Instantly, I wished I'd lied.

"I know just how you feel. I'm happiest right here in our own cute little place. Just relaxing. It *is* cute now." She yawned and stretched. She was still wearing her gray nighttime sweat shirt. All that Christmas Day, she never did get dressed.

6

Las Vegas, Disneyland, Egypt

It felt like two hands of air opening inside my chest when my father lifted me on the bottoms of his feet. He lay on his back, his legs sticking up, supporting my belly, his hands holding my hands. I swam in air and light. Kaboosh was what we called that game, Kaboosh, Kaboosh. I didn't know whether it was a word in Arabic or something he made up.

I didn't know anything until he was gone. And then it was like any death: absolute and very slow. My father left while we were still sleeping. He drove away in our brown Valiant, without his vacuum cleaners or vacuum cleaner attachments. He took a new suitcase with new clothes.

The door would have been locked and the air outside must have felt cool. His footsteps would have broken the web of dew on the lawn. The six-fifty train went by every day, setting the bushes and trees trembling in the yard like teacups. Perhaps they surprised him and he looked back at the house, remembering each of our round faces. Rows of old mink sheds sagged in back of the clotheslines, with patched red tented roofs. There may have been sheets, white and fluid, on the line. Everything would have seemed pure and distinct in the waterless, early morning light. He must have rubbed his eyes and then left.

He had to turn at the end of our road, onto the highway, our white house in his rearview mirror shrinking to the size of the building on the back of a penny, then nothing, a spec of dust on the glass. The sound of our car, now his, mixed with the other traffic, which we always heard and would hear, even in sleep.

We woke up late and dizzy the next morning. The sun felt high and generous, soaking the white curtains and softening the corners of the room. Lilacs seemed to beat against the screens.

"Where did he go?" I asked my mother. We were tucking a corner of the white chenille bedspread into the dark wooden frame. Together we bunched the cloth down, her hands pressing over mine.

"He's gone," my mother said.

"For how long?"

"Oh, I don't know." A string of hummingbirds moved on the lilac bush outside, where someone had tied a red scarf. Flies in slow orbits hit against the screens. My mother started ironing. All her summer clothes that year were seersucker and cotton.

"He's gone to California to make us money," she said. "But he'll be coming back."

"When?"

For a moment, her mouth wavered and her face began to lift. Her hands stalled on the iron. She picked up a blouse, held it across her shoulders and then took it to the closet. There was a row of empty hangers. Her chin snapped back into a straight line and she began pushing the iron again, over the perforated pink and white fabric.

"I don't know," she said.

I sat on the floor, waiting. She ironed carefully, starting every blouse at the collar. When the last one was hung up and buttoned again, I asked her what we were going to do.

She didn't answer. She turned off the iron and looked out the window, her hand resting on the dresser. "What, Honey?" she asked a moment later.

"I said, what are we going to do today."

She yawned. "I don't know. I'm a little tired, how about you?" She reached out her hand and found mine. We stood there a moment and then she sat on the bed. "Come on up, let's just close our eyes a minute."

We lay there on our backs. It was where she'd slept with him.

Before we went to sleep, my mother hummed one of my father's tunes. My father wanted to be a songwriter. That was why he'd gone to California. People told him he was a handsome Arab. He thought he could make money in the movies. As far as I know, songwriting was the only one of his aspirations to remain constant for most of his twenties. Later on, he gave up on music, too.

After my father left, my mother and I slept in the same bed. My mother would slide under the sheet, in her slip that she slept in, and tuck her hands under my arms to get warm. That year, my mother went to bed with me after supper and when I crawled out in the morning, she was still asleep. My grandmother and I tiptoed around the house until noon, when she woke up, and then we were quiet again after four, when my mother took her naps.

The three of us drank large quantities of milk. Our milkman delivered two cold bottles every morning. African violets on the mantelpiece thrived, perhaps because my grandmother and I stopped several times a day to check the moisture of their soil with our fingers. The house seemed to stay effortlessly clean.

And while my mother rested, my grandmother and I stole out of the house on expeditions, to see the maple syrup tapped out of trees in fall, to feed ducks and geese cans of corn at the Wildlife Preservation Center in winter, to search in spring for trilliums and wild violets in the fields. Perhaps my grandmother and I could have lived like that forever, moving quietly, playing, she on top of the kitchen table with her cards, me underneath with my colors; but by summer, my mother regained her strength. We watched it happen. One day she stopped taking naps. The next week she didn't go to bed with me after supper. And by that time, she was already bored.

She enrolled the two of us in figure skating classes Saturday evenings. She bought us matching short dresses made of stretch fabric and skin-colored tights. The rink seemed silent, the only sound was a humming, like the inside of a refrigerator. The ice was divided into eight rectangular patches and my mother and I shared one.

We concentrated, our necks bent over like horses', as we followed the lines our blades made. My skates had double runners. Then, at eight o'clock, scratchy music started up on the PA system and we free-skated, wild around the rink.

"This is how you really lose the pounds," my mother called, slapping her thigh, "skating fast."

A man did a T-stop in front of her, shaving a comet of ice into the air. They skated off together, while I stood there, wiping the melting ice from my face. That was the first time we saw Ted.

When the music stopped, my mother pulled me over to the barrier, where we ran our skate tips into the soft wood.

"See, when you're older, you can bring a boy you're dating here to see you skate. He can watch you and think, hey, she's not just another pretty girl. She can really do something." She nodded up to the rows of empty seats. They were maroon velvet, with the plush worn down in the centers. My mother looked at me with a slanted gaze as if, through a crack, she could see what I'd become. I knew what I wanted to be: I wanted to be just like her.

But my mother felt restless, waiting. We drove slowly through the winding streets of the good neighborhoods by the river, her friend Lolly from college in the front seat. We ate soft ice cream cones which melted fast, the chocolate dripping down our shirts.

"Boy, wouldn't you love to live there?" my mother said, slamming on the brakes.

Behind a long dark lawn stood a house with white pillars. "But, go on, Lolly."

They spoke in low voices. "Who would have thought, here in Bay City? Would you, the next time, I mean, before the, shall-we-say, ring? You know what I mean?"

"I know what you mean. And I think I would," my mother said.

"And so do I know what you mean," I yelled from the backseat, although of course I didn't. I just felt left out and I wanted them to stop.

They sipped coffee outside on the back porch. I pretended to be taking apart a lady's slipper, studying it, setting the soft red pieces out on the boards between my legs, so they wouldn't think I was listening. They were talking about how many times a week Lolly should wash her hair and how many shampooings per wash.

My mother sighed and looked out over the fields. Serrated red and yellow leaves stuck in the grass, and all the corn was down.

"So have you heard anything from, a-hem, California?"

My mother didn't talk for a while. I didn't dare look at her. I moved the stem of the lady's slipper up and down on my palm. My father had been gone for two years.

"Ann, go inside and watch TV with Mom," she said finally. "Go sit and keep her company."

I dragged my slippers on the boards. They were quiet until I was gone. My mother had both hands around her coffee cup and she stared down into it, blowing. The living room was dim because all the curtains were closed. I sat on the floor next to my grandmother's legs.

I liked the smell of nylon stockings. They were everywhere in our house: hanging from the shower curtain rod, brushing my face in the bathroom, tucked in the top drawers of dressers next to silver cases of lipsticks, which, at that time, had their own rich waxy smell. The stockings smelled different with legs inside the nylon, they smelled like something burnt.

"Well, now, let's get up and do something," my grandmother said, at the commercial. "Not just S-I-T in front of the TV all day. Should we drive out to the cemetery and water? We can stop at the dairy on the way and you can get your chocolate milk."

"Okay, Gramma," I said.

While my grandmother backed the Oldsmobile out of the garage, I stood on the porch, listening to my mother and Lolly again.

"And so he said, he said to me, Well, come on, Adele, you've been married before. Let's try and see if we like it. Like it? I said, Like it? Well, what happens if I don't?"

My mother and Lolly bent over, hugging their knees, laughing. A hawk drifted in the sky.

"Why is that funny?" I said. "Will someone please tell me what's so funny about that?"

They looked at each other and laughed some more. I started walking to my grandmother's car, my hands trembling at my sides.

"It's something that's only funny for grown-ups," my mother called.

I slammed the door and then turned, smiled at my grandmother. The tin cans we used for watering at the cemetery rattled in the backseat. I was glad we were going because I didn't want my grandmother to stay inside all day and get pale and soft like an old person. She thought she was taking me for my benefit. Neither of us imagined that we were the one in any trouble.

Once, when he was still at home with us, my father tried to mow the lawn. In the morning, he left from the back door, with his black case of vacuum cleaners and vacuum cleaner attachments. My father was a salesman then. He loaded the trunk of the car, our Valiant, the color of root beer Popsicles.

The lawn mower was a piece of furniture, orange metal like a tractor. It was the kind you sat on and rode. Grass sprayed off in a fountain from one side.

My cousin Benny stood on the driveway, bare-legged, fidgeting by the lawn mower. Even as a child, he was always moving. When he had to wait for us, he'd go out in the backyard, with a stick as tall as he was, spinning, and you could run up to him and clap your hands and he wouldn't hear. He was blond as an unlit wick.

"You wanna ride?" Benny's sneaker stuck up against the orange metal, bracing to pull the cord. Jimmy Measey walked out of the garage carrying a tin can of oil. It was still on the ground, empty, after.

"Me?" My father's fingers opened on his chest, lightly. He'd been in Wisconsin five years. In Egypt, where he came from, they had no lawns.

Just then the metal of the screen door rang. My grandmother walked outside with a hoe and a white cotton glove. She wore men's clothes, overalls, plaid shirt, a different plaid scarf. Since her husband died, she'd begun to get up early and she had taken to wearing his clothes.

My father wavered. Jimmy Measey told me later he was trying to impress my grandmother.

"Sure," my father said. He looked down at Benny, touched the chalky yellow of his hair. My father was always sorry I wasn't blond. I looked like him, not my mother. "Would you like to ride along?"

"Can't. Only one person at a time."

"All right."

"Here's the gas, here's the brake," Jimmy Measey explained, swiveling the wheel.

Benny snapped the cord and my father shot off, his backbone a ruler, taking the ride hard. He went in one straight line. All of a sudden, the velvety grass turned bumpy. My father's hand waved, the arm flapping back behind him.

"Hey, get off, slam the brake!" Benny's yell scratched a sharp red line on the sky. I saw it years, a long time, after.

"Jump off," Jimmy Measey said, running after the lawn mower. "Jump."

No one understood what my father was yelling, and he went through the hedge, crashing corn stalks. Finally he fell off. Silky corn hair stuck on his collar when Jimmy Measey caught up to him, on the ground. The mower was still going, towards the barn. Benny chased it. My mother started out of the house then, her high heels catching in the grass.

"I don't know why you didn't just slug on the brake." Jimmy Measey demonstrated, crushing a corncob under his boot, even though my father was walking, towards the house and my mother. Jimmy Measey felt impatient to go, he was late. He liked to drive to Bob's Big Boy on the highway before work and order coffee and unbuttered toast. He liked to sit at the counter and hear the other voices, familiar and unfamiliar at the same time. He'd made a rule for himself, to be in the water softener store by ten. Jimmy Measey was a salesman, too. But he never left. He might have looked at cars on the highway overpass, wishing he were a stranger in one of the small windows, going west. But even in imagination, he always returned, back to Lime Kiln Road.

"What have they done to you?" my mother screamed, but my father shrugged her off his elbow and walked ahead fast and alone.

Benny rode the mower in, his sneakers bouncing up off the sides. Benny loved machines.

Jimmy Measey's hands rocked my shoulders, tilting me back. "You miss your dad, don't you? You miss your daddy, I can feel that in you." We stood outside, by a fire, burning leaves. Jimmy Measey was behind me, I felt all his weight. Benny stood there too, impatient to move, his blue sneaker pawing the ground. Smoke poured into the sky.

My eyes closed, I was dizzy. When I opened them again, we were all still standing, watching the light black ghosts of leaves escape, up into the air. Across the road, a light came on in the kitchen. Old Mrs. Brozek set her table. From where we were, it all looked like wax. Jimmy Measey put his hands over my ears.

"See that hole?" He pointed my head. His fingers pressed into my temples, as if they were denting them. "That's where your dad went through the hedge."

It was an ordinary hole, just a lapse in the dark bushes.

"He's yelling away something in Egyptian, whatever they talk over there. You couldn't understand it. I tried to stop him."

I felt the fat jiggle on Jimmy Measey's belly, warm and deep.

"Practically needed a lasso. He went right through the hedge."

Our oak tree was over a hundred years old. We'd been raking for days. That year the leaves were the size of Benny's and my hands. We'd knelt on the ground, matching them. From the noise in the wind and the silvery outlines of branches swaying, there was something enormous above us. There were still about a million leaves.

We stood there watching leaves collapse and fizzle into light black ash. A rusty sunset streaked the sky for miles, making our houses look small.

"Whenever I look out my sliding glass doors and see that hole, I think of your dad," Jimmy said. "I wonder where he is now."

I'd been staring at the oak tree, the patches of the sky through the fists of dry, curled leaves. They rattled like brown paper bags being crumpled.

"Dad," Benny said, his sneaker rubbing the soft lawn. "When are we going to eat?"

All of a sudden, I thought of my mother and wondered where she was. I left them there and ran inside. My grandmother stood up to her elbows in flour. Flour seemed suspended all through the kitchen, mixing in the soft yellow air. I found my mother sitting on the bathroom rug in a shortie flannel nightgown, tweezing. She was holding a small round mirror up to her face.

"What is it, Honey," she said, studying her left eyebrow.

"Uncle Jimmy asked if I still missed my dad."

Now she was doing the lip. She pulled it down over her top teeth.

"Oh, Honey, you didn't even know your dad. You were too young to really know him. How could you miss him?" She sighed. "When people ask you that, you just say, No, not really, I'm very close to my mom. That's what you say."

"Okay," I said and still stood there.

"I'm the one who misses my dad," she said. "But you never had that real total love. Maybe you're lucky, you know, maybe it'll be better for you. You'll never know enough to miss it."

I walked into Jimmy Measey's house without knocking. I let the screen door slam. Jimmy Measey sat in the kitchen, holding a beer can beaded with water.

"Is Benny here?" I asked.

He lifted the can of beer and took a drink. Then he looked at me, grinning, and held up his hand. "I hit him," he said. "I smacked him a good one." For an instant, he seemed to be licking his lip. Then he swung his chair to face the wall. "He's in the bathroom," he said.

Benny stood on the plush-covered toilet seat examining his cheek in the mirror. There was a big red handprint on his nose and over the left side of his face. He carefully dabbed cold cream on the indentation. He looked solemn as if he were adjusting, as if it would never go away. His mother stood helplessly below, holding up the open jar of cream.

"Jimmy hit him," she said, shaking her head.

Benny turned around to look at me. "I was bad," he said.

I was afraid of Jimmy Measey, but sometimes he was different. He took Benny and me for a walk down to the railroad tracks and when Benny ran ahead and got a milkweed stem, saying "Lookit this, Dad," I wanted to remind Benny of the red handprint and, at the same time, I wished Jimmy was my father too.

Before we'd left the house, my grandmother tied a wool scarf on me, her knuckles hurting under my chin as she made the knot. Benny didn't have to wear a scarf because Jimmy Measey thought we didn't need them, but he let my grandmother put mine on me. I was the women's and Benny was his.

Near the ditch, Jimmy Measey took my hand. His hand felt dry and hard, like a foot. Down the tracks, two kids balanced on one rail, their arms out to the sides. We knew who they were; they were Grilings.

Jimmy Measey rummaged in his pants pocket and took out a dime and handed it to me. "Here." He looked down the tracks. I thought he wanted me to give it to Grilings, so I started running on the coals.

"Annie, no."

"I'll do it, Dad." Benny stooped and left the dime on the rail. The kids were still a long ways down the tracks in what was left of the sun.

We heard from my father in the middle of winter three years after he left. There was a long-distance phone call from Las Vegas and it was him.

"We're going to Disneyland!" my mother said, covering the mouth-piece with her hand. Into the phone, she said she'd take me out of school. We'd fly to Las Vegas and then the three of us would drive west to Disneyland. I didn't recognize the voice when my mother held out the phone. It sounded like someone I didn't know.

I held onto the edges of the kitchen table. I wanted to go to school the next day. I shrugged and wouldn't touch the phone.

"You'll know him when you see him," she said.

We waited three days for our summer linen dresses to be dry-cleaned. "It's going to be hot," my mother warned. "Scorching," she added, with a smile. It was snowing dry powder when we left; we saw only white outside the airplane window. Halfway there, we changed in the tiny bathroom, from our winter clothes to sleeveless dresses and patent leather thongs.

My mother brushed blush on our pale winter shoulders. With her eye pencil, I drew freckles on my nose. It still felt cool in the plane, but my mother promised it would be hot on the ground.

It was. The air swirled with visible heat and dirt. A woman walked across the lobby with a scarf tied around her chest for a shirt.

My mother spotted my father in the crowd and, holding my hand, pulled me towards him. We pretended I recognized him, too. He looked like an ordinary man. He wore tight black slacks, a brown jacket and black leather slip-on shoes. His chin stuck out from his face, giving him an eager look.

He had our brown Valiant parked outside and my mother sat in the front seat. We passed motel swimming pools and the tinge of sky hung over the water like a line of dirt on the rim of a sleeve. My father parked in front of a low pink stucco apartment building. When we walked up, three men crowded on a porch, leaning against the iron banister.

"He told us you had long hair," one said.

"You look like your dad."

"A real brunette."

"She's prettier than her dad."

My father smiled and the gaps between his teeth made him look unintentionally sad, like a jack-o-lantern. He touched my hair, looking down at it, and I knew he was proud of me. I loved him blindly then, the feeling darkening over everything, but it passed.

"Don't you want to introduce your friends to me, too?" My mother pushed our suitcase onto the porch. She smiled the smile she practiced in front of the mirror, sucking her cheeks in to make her bones seem higher.

The men wore V-necked T-shirts and their skin was dark like my father's. The way they bent and leaned and shuffled while they stood made them seem dangerous, like teenagers. My father introduced each man and each man smiled. He said they were his roommates. Then he gave me a present: a package of six different colored cotton headbands. They made me think of Easter eggs. I held the package carefully and didn't tear the cellophane open.

My father worked as a waiter in a hotel restaurant. My mother and I went there for supper, our first night. We ate slowly, watching him balance plates on the inside of his arm. He sat down with us at the end of our meal, while my mother sipped her coffee. He crossed one leg over the other, smoking luxuriously, when my mother leaned closer and whispered in my ear.

"When are we going to Disneyland?" I said, saying what she said to say but somehow knowing it was wrong.

My father put out his cigarette and looked up at my mother. "You're late," he said. "It's Friday. You're four days late."

My mother pushed her hair back with her hand. "Well, we were busy. There were people we had to see. We canceled plenty as it was." My mother could hold her own. "So, when are we going?" she asked gamely.

"When you didn't come Monday, I lost the money I'd saved." He said this matter-of-factly, looking around the room.

"In four days, how?"

"On the tables."

My mother's voice gathered, "You, you can't do this to her."

Back at my father's apartment, they sent me outside to the porch. There was a book of matches on the ground and I lit them, one by one, scratching them against the concrete and then dropping them in the dirt when the flames came too close to my fingers. Finally it was quiet. My father opened the screen door and I went in.

They'd put sheets on the living room couch for me. They both un-dressed in my father's room. My mother looked over her shoulder, while she unzipped her shift. Then she came out to say good night. She looked down at me hard, as if she were trying to judge whether I was young enough to forget things I didn't understand. She sighed, finally deciding it wouldn't matter.

"Now, don't say anything to Gramma that I slept in his room. But there's nowhere else to go here." She rubbed my back absentmindedly for a second.

The next morning my father and I woke up early. We walked to the hotel coffee shop and sat on stools at the counter. I was afraid to ask for anything, so I said I wasn't hungry. My father ordered a soft-boiled egg for himself. We didn't talk. I watched his eyes catch on the uniformed wait-ress, the coffeepot tilting from her hand, a white purse on the other end of the counter. He seemed happy.

He whistled the refrain to his song, a song we all believed would be a hit. I sang along the words to myself. "Oh, Ringo Starr on top of my tree, Oh, Santa bring the Beatles to-oo me." Ringo was my mother's favorite Beatle. "He's so homely he's cute," she always said, clicking her fingers against her thighs when she and Lolly danced in the den.

The egg came in a white coffee cup. He chopped it with the edge of a spoon, asking if I'd ever tasted a four-minute egg. I ate a spoonful and I loved it. No other egg was ever that good. I told my father, hoping we could share it. But he slid the whole cup down, the spoon in it, without looking at me and signaled the waitress for another egg.

Walking back to the apartment, he kicked sand into the air. He turned to me suddenly, as if he'd just then thought of something.

"How do you like school?" he asked.

"Fine," I said. "I like it."

"That's good," he said. Our conversations were always like that, like lighting single matches.

I sat on a towel by the hotel pool while my parents tried to win back our money for Disneyland. When my mother rubbed lotion into my shoulders, she pointed to a woman sleeping on her back, with a washcloth covering her eyes. A child squatted next to her head, brushing the woman's hair with a toy brush. A boy, asleep next to them, had a white bar of soap hanging from a braided cord around his neck; his fingers moved over the soap, as if he were dreaming on it.

"Those kids are in the shows at night. Look at that," my mother said. "The kids make the money and the mother just lounges."

Later, when my parents went into the casino, the little girl pulled the woman's hair.

"Shhhh," the woman said. "And let him sleep. He was up late. Go in the water, Honey."

But the boy woke up and ran onto the diving board, the muscles in his stomach jiggling like a bowl of shaken water. The sound of his yell made the woman sit up and lift the washcloth off her face.

His feet flapped on the surface of the water, then he stopped and shook. His mother and sister and I all stared but he didn't seem to notice us. He seemed to be splashing with other, invisible bodies in the pool.

I watched the boy most of the afternoon, hoping he would look at me. He stood gurgling water, his head tilting up, soaping himself with bubbles from the bar around his neck. His mother would pull to a sitting position every once in a while, taking her sunglasses down from the top of her head, and smile, watching him, look nervously over to his sister; then, having counted each of her children, she would sigh, sinking back to her towel, opening a magazine over her face.

I waded in the shallow end. My mother said I could play with these children so I knew I could, but I didn't know how to start. It seemed too hard. I closed my eyes, tumbling through the water, and thought that when I went home I could write letters to them. Months later, back at my grandmother's house, times when I wasn't even thinking of my father, I felt like writing a letter to that boy. But I didn't even know his name.

"So we'll go to Disneyland next trip," my father said, walking me back from the pool. There were no lawns in front of the parked trailers, but the sand was raked and bordered with rows of rocks. My father's black slip-on shoes were scuffed. He was holding my hand but not looking at me.

"When?"

Suddenly, I wanted the name of a month, not to see Disneyland but to see him. Taking long steps, trying to match his pace, I wanted to say that I didn't care about Disneyland. I dared myself to talk after one more, two more, three more steps, all the way to the apartment. But I never said it. All I did was hold his hand tighter and tighter.

"I don't know," he said, letting my arm drop when we came to the porch.

On the plane home, I held the package of headbands in my lap, tracing each one through the cellophane. My mother turned and looked out the window.

"I work," she said finally, "and I pay for your school and your books and your skates and your lessons."

She picked up the package of headbands and then dropped it back on my lap. "A seventy-nine-cent package of headbands," she said.

I hid behind a tree, watching my grandmother walk down the driveway, the back corner of her scarf whipping in the wind. The red metal flag stood up on the mailbox. I watched her shuffle through the mail and shove it into her pocket. She didn't hold any of the letters in her hand or look at one for longer; that meant there was nothing unusual. Then I ran up to her.

I thought I still wanted to go to California, but later. My blood ticked from running, the damp air touched my temples, the wind was a battle in my sleeves. Twigs lifted off the ground as we headed towards the back-yard, where the wash was still moving on the lines. I helped my grand-mother gather the sheets, collecting clothespins in our mouths and pockets, to carry them in before the rain. The sheets that night felt stiff on our beds, smelling of soil and cold water. When it started to rain, we hauled out our buckets to collect in the yard, under the eaves troughs. My grandmother believed rainwater made our houseplants grow. At night, we listened to the sounds on the roof. It was a different life from my father's, from what we imagined was California. I didn't know whether I watched for the mail because I wanted a letter from my father, or because I was afraid and hoped he would stay away, so we could keep what we had.

At Bob's Big Boy, one day in the summer, my mother and I pressed to-gether in the phone booth and emptied her purse out on the metal ledge. There were hundreds of scraps of paper, pencils, leaking pens, scuffed makeup tubes, brushes woven with a fabric of lint and hair, a bra, and finally, my mother's brown leather address book, with the pages falling out. We wanted to call my father in Las Vegas. It was already over a year since we'd flown there. The number was written, carefully, in brown ink.

My mother dialed, saying Hold your thumbs, here's hoping. She said a quick, mumbled Hail Mary, rounding off the four points of the cross to a touch on her forehead and three quick taps on her chest. I scraped all the coins from the bottom of her purse. When the operator came on to say how much the call cost, my mother lifted me up and I dropped in the money. We both waited, our mouths together by the receiver. A sleeping male voice answered.

"Yeah?"

My mother asked if my father was there.

"No," the man said. "Wrong number. Nobody here by that name."

"Well, do you know where he went? He used to live there, we saw him there."

"Not since I've been here."

"Would one of your roommates know?"

"I've been here the longest."

"Oh," my mother said. "All right."

We called information in Las Vegas then and gave my father's name, but they had nothing listed.

Sunday was the day my mother took over the house. My grandmother woke up early and drove to church. Everyone on our road went to church except us. In the morning, when our neighbors were driving into town, the women holding the clasps of their purses in their laps, Lolly drove on the same highway, in the other direction, with the car radio on, and a box of warm cinnamon rolls open on the passenger seat.

She went to Krim's, Bay City's best bakery, early, before the after-church crowd and bought twelve of the large soft rolls for just us. They were expensive and we loved the extravagance. By the time Lolly stamped to our back door, my mother was up and around the kitchen singing "I'm Gonna Wash That Man Right Out of My Hair" and the pitcher of dark, thick orange juice was slowly filling. It was my job to squeeze the oranges.

Lolly tore open a new carton of cream and walked out to the porch. "So did you try it?" she asked my mother.

With my grandmother gone, they didn't even send me inside when they talked. We ate slowly, on our second rolls each. My mother and Lolly sipped their coffee. They gave me a mugful just to warm my hands. I took small drinks and it tasted like dirt. I was trying to learn to like it.

"Why do you ask?" my mother said.

"I just thought, it seemed last night on the ice, there were some, shall-we-say, new jumps?"

"Well, yes. Mmhmm. I did try it."

"You did?"

I was bouncing my slipper on the edge of my foot, over the side of the porch, and it fell. The ground felt cold when I hopped down to get it.

"Where did you go?"

"Nowhere. Just here."

"In the bedroom, with the troops upstairs? You're kidding. With Mama in the house?"

"We watched Carson. Everyone was asleep."

"And?"

My mother sighed, blowing on her coffee and looking out over the yard. The grass seemed faded and the fall light was whiter than in summer. "It was fine. It'll be fine," she said. Sometimes my mother seemed older.

Lolly scanned her face as if there was something different she couldn't quite put her finger on. Finally, she looked at me as if I knew. My mother seemed slow and collected, it seemed she'd come to some resolution. When the train passed and her coffee cup chattered in its saucer, she looked down and smiled, as if the noise were music.

"So what about California?"

"I don't know," my mother said, looking straight at Lolly, holding her cup in the air, "but with a man like that, who can? Who does know?"

"You haven't heard anything?"

"Not a thing."

"And you don't think you will?"

"Oh, I think so. I'm sure of it, in fact. Someday, he'll have a record out or they'll cast him in a movie and he'll come into some money and, then, I'm sure he'll call us. But who knows when?"

"I know what you mean."

"And she's growing up. I can't just stay here forever." My mother nodded at me.

As soon as she said that, I wished I was younger. I fell out onto the grass and started doing cartwheels. My hair knocked against my cheeks. I walked on my hands.

"Did you see, Mom, did you see me?"

My mother and Lolly both sat with their coffee cups in their laps, not talking.

"Do it again, Honey," my mother said.

Skating the next time, I didn't get off the ice. When the music stopped, my mother and Lolly stepped delicately onto rubber mats at the exit, my mother taking a few last breaths, as if she were leaving precious air. The Zamboni, a machine that cleared the ice, already stood growling at the other end of the rink. I took one last run around the ice, skating as fast as

I could, my arms flailing. The Zamboni followed close behind because the man who drove it believed I needed to be taught a lesson.

It was like being chased by an animal; I heard the thing behind me, I couldn't tell how near it was. I was ready for its paw on my back, to tip me over, any second. My mother stood at the exit yelling and I saw her but I couldn't hear. The Zamboni behind me, I raced, running on my tips, trying not to fall forward because if I did I'd be caught underneath the machinery. I raced for my life, believing I could die and that if I tripped and fell and the Zamboni ran me over, it would be fair, because I shouldn't have been on the ice.

Maybe I wanted to die. I ended up ramming against the barrier at the exit, falling hard into the wood.

And just then, my mother and Lolly looked at each other, turned and walked downstairs. They refused to acknowledge me; they wouldn't encourage such behavior. Besides, my mother felt embarrassed because of Ted. She wanted Ted to think she could make me mind.

I had some pride. Instead of running after them, I stood at the exit, kicking sheets of ice off my blades. Another mother, there to pick up her children, hugged me against her belly, a strong arm pulling me in. She whispered, "Tell me, does your ma hear anything from your daddy?"

"I don't know," I said.

"Awww," Mrs. Bayer whispered, rubbing down my hair.

For a moment, but only for a moment, I let my eyes close.

"You must miss your daddy," she said, her face dropping into a loose expression of pity.

I pulled away. "No."

Taking the skates off on the bench was pure joy. My work was done. My shoes seemed sizes too big for my feet and my ankles felt filled with air. Walking over the thick rubber mats, my body seemed to start at my shins. I was light. I'd done what I could do.

We heard from my father again two years after my mom married Ted. He called my grandmother first. He didn't know about Ted or the house on Carriage Court. He seemed to suppose we stayed the same the years between his phone calls. He told my mother he lived in Reno, with a new wife. So, apparently, he still hadn't made it to California. He told my mother he wanted to take me to Disneyland.

"Well, I don't know. Do you think we'll really get there this time?" She snorted into the phone.

"Oh, no, you don't," my mother said then, after huffs and pauses, impatient sighs. "Nothing doing. I'm not taking her out of school to fly out there alone. Either I come too or she's not going."

My father wanted to have just me. Finally, he agreed to send the money for two tickets. Then, she covered the receiver with her hand. "Ann, his new wife has an eleven-year-old granddaughter. She's never seen Disneyland and they thought they might bring her along. Would you like that or would you rather it be just us?" She whispered, "If you'd rather just us, then say so."

"I'd rather be just us," I said.

My mother took her hand off. "She feels she'd rather not have another child there." I hated the way it sounded like that, loud. I hopped around the kitchen in a circle and yelled, "I don't care. I don't care who comes. Bring her."

"Don't worry, I'm sure he won't bring her," my mother said. We stood in front of the open refrigerator, eating slices of cold châteaubriand. That way there were no dishes to wash. "What do you think, a granddaughter your age. His wife must be as old as Gramma."

"Why couldn't I go alone?"

"Honey, there's a lot of things you just don't know, okay? Believe me, I'm a lot older and I know this man."

She waited and I didn't say anything. I had the salt shaker. I shook on salt.

"Ann, he could get you on a plane to Egypt in a couple hours and who'd ever know? Yeah, you didn't think of that, did you? And let me tell you, you wouldn't like it. They'd get you married and pregnant in no time. Over there, they educate the boys, not the girls. There's no such thing as a high school girl. Your dad was just darn lucky."

My mother and father wanted to take me out of school and fly to Disneyland right away, but Uta, the new wife, insisted we wait for Easter vacation. That gave my mother and me three weeks to shop. We bought new dresses and my first stockings and white gloves.

Then my mother read about something she wanted: a new Sony portable color television. A jewel. They were small; she showed me the picture she cut out of the magazine. She wanted a white one, she felt sure they came in white. The article said they wouldn't be available in the States for another year, but my mother thought they'd have them in California. "I'm sure of it," she said, "it's right across the water from Japan. I bet they'll be all over the stores."

My mother had stopped telling Ted about the things she wanted, because he tried to get them for her and he made mistakes. For Christmas, he'd bought her a console record player instead of a stereo with component parts. He surprised her with a dishwasher, just after she'd bought hand-painted plates. She shuddered talking about what he'd come up with if she told him about the Sony: a big, cabinet-sized Zenith or RCA.

She picked me up after school and we drove downtown to Shreve's. We browsed on the electronics floor, watching all the televisions. They had Sony black-and-whites but no colors. All the colors were huge things, whole varnished cabinets.

"Can I help you," a young woman said, her hands in the pockets of the brown store smock.

"Oh, no, thank you." My mother nudged me as we walked to the parking lot. "We'll have the first one in Bay City."

Ted walked us outside to the aluminum steps of the plane. It was a windy, wet afternoon. My mother hooked my hair behind my ears and then put her hand on her own head. She wanted to go inside the plane, so we wouldn't get mussed, but Ted just stood there and so we waited.

His smile seemed different to me that day, higher on the left side, bent, not like a zipper.

Our airport wasn't large. You could see runways going into the fields and around the perimeters; behind the blinking lights, trees started again, birches and pine. The inside terminal was small, too, with one coffee shop where high school girls worked as waitresses.

"Well, you have fun," Ted said. He laid one arm on my shoulder and his other hand reached under the back of my mother's hair.

She sighed. "Well, I don't know if it'll be fun, I doubt it, but necessary. And it'll be fun for her, you're right, for her it should be fun."

My father sat with his legs crossed, staring as if he wasn't seeing anything, in a plastic, molded airport chair. A woman stood behind him, with a hand on his shoulder. Her other hand was cocked over her eyebrows, as if she was looking for something far away. It seemed they'd been waiting a long time.

"John, is that them?" I heard her say. But John was not my father's name.

Then my mother waved, he stood up and we all met. The granddaughter stood there, too, a girl whose legs were so thin it looked as if something might be seriously wrong. She kept shaking my hand up and down.

The five of us were going to eat right away in a restaurant in Beverly Hills, Uta told us. She had already made the reservation. But first, my mother wanted to use the ladies' room. She asked me to come along.

"Don't feel bad about the granddaughter," she said, in front of the mirror. She brushed out our hair. "Because I'm sure *he* didn't want to bring her. *She* insisted. Did you see how *she's* the one with the money. *She* made the reservation. *She* had the camera around *her* neck. It's like she's the man and he's the woman. So don't feel bad."

They had a rented car and my father drove. He and Uta sat in the front seat. My mother had to climb in the back with the granddaughter and me. Her high heels made it hard to balance, getting in. She put her hands on her lap and smiled right away and you could tell she didn't like this.

"So, Hisham, do you still have the Valiant?"

He chuckled a little. "No, I had to get rid of that."

I thought of our Valiant in a Nevada dump somewhere. Benny was good with cars. Even though he was only eleven years old, he drove up and down Lime Kiln Road in his dad's truck. I'd been to the dump in Bay City where they put the old cars; Griling ran it, walking around with a stick. The machine dump covered two sides of a hill and a long valley. It wasn't just cars, there were old wash machines and refrigerators, their doors open, and warm from the sun. Cats lived on the empty wire shelves.

"I'm calling myself John now," my father said, glancing over at Uta. Uta nodded, looking down at her purse.

"John," my mother mulled. "How come?"

My father shrugged. "People recognize it. They know how to spell it." He laughed. "I'm applying to be a citizen."

Uta took a small white box from her purse and gave it to my father to give me; it was a gold bracelet, with one charm, a tree with turquoise leaves.

"Well, it's real, all right," my mother said, examining it later under the lamp. We stayed at the Disneyland Hotel, my mother and me in one room, them in another. She showed me the tiny stamp of 19K printed on the gold. "It must have been expensive. But it's gaudy, you know, she's got money, but no taste. That's one thing about us, Ann, we have taste. We can go anywhere and they'd think, Hey, what a great-looking mother and daughter. And that's class."

For years, I'd watched "The Wonderful World of Disney" on TV. Sometimes in bed, before I went to sleep, I imagined us—my father with more hair than he had now, my mother's swooped up on top of her head, held with a diamond pin, and me, blond like my mother and prettier than I am—in our old brown car, with rounded fenders, floating down a long canal. A fairy with a wand of flies' wings perched just at our backs, touching the tops of our heads. I'd feel her fingers on my spine and lean against her knee, but I wouldn't turn back to look at her, for fear she wouldn't be there. The brown car drifted slowly and trees above us bent down with the weight of their fruit. When we touched it, it was ours, the way, when you cup your hand outside the window of a moving car, you imagine something solid and then you feel it. We passed animals on the banks of the canal and at one turn, I saw an elephant carrying the Las Vegas circus children dressed in leopard skins and sequins. The lighted castle stood in the distance. The banks of the canal were a simple yellow, the trees green, the sky and water blue. Disneyland looked like the crayoned city I'd drawn on my grandmother's floor when I was a child and we floated in the Valiant, farther and farther in.

I'd wanted to see Disneyland for so long and now I was there. All day the five of us bought things. My father and my mother kept peering down into my face and saying, "Having fun?" I felt like they could see all the things I'd imagined to myself, the private things I'd pictured with my eyes closed, in the dark. I'd shrug and say, "Yeah," and look at the granddaughter. I turned out glad she was there. The two of us got to pick out the restaurants we wanted and what we wanted to order in each one. Nobody talked about money. Uta always paid.

They all kept looking at me and asking what I wanted to do next. I shrugged and said, "I don know." But that made them nervous. My father walked with his hands in his pockets, looking high up, towards the sky. Then he talked to my mother about cutting my hair.

"We've thought of it, but I think it's better long," she said.

He seemed to agree. "No, she'd have to be thinner if it were short."

"Sometimes, I think about bangs," my mother volunteered.

On Saturday, Uta rented a limousine to drive us to a famous restaurant. It was on top of a tall building so we could see lights of the whole city below us. One side was pure black and my father said that was the ocean.

My father spoke French to the waiter—I watched my mother and Uta look at him and sink back in their chairs. There were some things women couldn't do and those were the things my father was good at. My father ordered for all of us, something I'd never heard of, tournedos.

When Uta went to the ladies' room, my mother laughed, leaning over so her face came close to my father's in the reddish light. She picked up the candleholder in her hands and looked up at my father.

"John, I'm trying to see you as a John," she said.

He laughed, moving the salt shaker. The granddaughter looked at me. "When you go home, we can write letters to each other and be pen pals. Will you write to me?"

As I watched my mother laughing, I wasn't sure if it was a real laugh, from happiness, or if it was for our TV.

I was full before my tournedos came. But they were steak and delicious. I asked my father if I could wrap them in a napkin and take it back in a doggy bag. He stamped his cigarette out and looked at my mother, smiling. "No, Ann," he said. "Not here."

My mother joined in quickly, "Oh, no, Honey, not in a place like this."

"Is she yours?" a man asked.

My mother answered, "She sure is, she's my little one." We stood in a dark hallway. Uta was paying someone to find our coats.

"A very pretty child," the man said. He was short and bald, fat, in a dark suit.

"Yes, isn't she? And she's nice, too. She's a real nice girl, aren't you?" My mother stroked my hair.

"No," I said, looking down.

The fat man was not alone. He lifted a silver stole off a woman's shoulders and followed her into the restaurant. My mother bent down to me. "Do you know who that was? *That* was Robert Wise, the producer of *Sound of Music*. Did you see the way he looked at you? You're going to make it, kid. I can't believe it."

"How do you know it was him?"

"Believe me. I just know."

In the lobby, my father spoke to the headwaiter. He took a salt shaker from his left pocket and a matching pepper shaker from his right and gave them to me. "A little memento of tonight."

I said thank you and held them the way he held them, in my coat pockets, and looked up, overly grateful. My father always had nerve.

My mother just smiled grimly and thanked Uta and my father, as we crowded in the backseat of the limousine, my mother's heel catching on the carpet. We felt cowed by their money, both of us.

I worried about the New Sony. We were leaving tomorrow and we hadn't done anything. All day, I brought up the subject of televisions, but the only one who answered was the granddaughter, who told me that her favorite program was "Gilligan's Island" and that we could write to each other what our new favorite programs were in fall when the listings came out.

And it wasn't only my mother, it was me, too. When I slipped my hand in my father's, I wasn't sure why. It seemed easier to have another reason. Otherwise, we felt like fools.

My mother and father and I seemed more like a family that trip than we'd ever been and that was because of Uta, because she thought of things. She took pictures of me with my dad. My mother and father each went along with it, but they didn't seem to like her ideas. They did things because they had to.

It was Uta's idea that my father and I should meet before dinner the last night, so we'd have a chance to be alone. My mother shrugged as Uta suggested it, as if to say, what for, but she didn't have the nerve to do anything. In our room, before I was supposed to go down, she brushed my hair out across my back.

I was nervous. I wasn't used to being alone with my father. I didn't know what to say to him.

"I'll bet they've got one right here," my mother said. "In Disneyland." We both knew what she was talking about.

"I haven't seen any in the stores."

"I think I saw one," she said, winking. "A white one."

"Where?" I'd been looking all week. It was the only thing I'd known to do.

"In one of those little shops downstairs."

"Which one?"

"I'm not sure, exactly. But I saw it."

"What should I do?" I knew I had to learn everything.

My mother shrugged. It seemed easy for her. "Tell him you're saving for it. He'll probably just buy it for you. Suck in your cheeks," she said, brushing blush on my face. She was having fun.

I didn't want to leave the room. I wanted to close my eyes and keep feeling the spokes of the hairbrush on my back. My mother gave me a short push out the door. I tried to remember everything.

I saw my father's back first. He was standing by the candy counter in the hotel drugstore. Every time I saw him I went through a gradual series of adjustments, reconciling the picture I held in my imagination to his appearance, as I recognized him. He was almost bald now. He was heavier than he had once been. His chin still shot out, but it no longer made him look eager. He seemed mildly dissatisfied, bored. His lower lip seemed to hang a fraction too far out, it didn't match his upper lip. He was buying a roll of Life Savers, peeling the wrapping paper off one end. He peeled it in a string.

Then he saw me and smiled. "Would you like anything?" he asked, tilting his head to indicate the rows of candy on the counter.

I thought for one wild moment. I could abandon the plan and say yes. Yes I want a candy bar. Two candy bars. He'd buy me two of the best candy bars there and I could stand and eat them sloppily, all the while gazing up at him. If I smiled, he would smile. He would bend down and dab the chocolate from my mouth with a handkerchief moist with his own saliva.

But I knew I'd remember. And then I would hate my best memory because it would prove that my father could fake love or that love could end, or, worst of all, that love could exist weakly, without the power to dominate a life, his life. And I couldn't believe he'd write me letters, I just couldn't believe it. I thought of my grandmother, years and years, walking out to get the mail.

"No," I said, "I'm saving up my money."

"What?" My father smiled down. He was still unraveling the paper from his Life Savers. He hadn't heard me. I had another chance.

"I'm saving my money for a new Sony portable color television," I blurted.

He had been looking at me and he stopped. He didn't move but he lifted his eyes up to something over my shoulder. Then he glanced at his watch and scanned the drugstore.

"Oh," he said.

I think at that moment he relinquished me to my mother. He was humming "Raindrops Keep Falling on My Head"; he'd been humming all weekend—other people's songs.

On the way home, neither of us mentioned it.

"Look at the mountains," I said.

"Yeah, mmhmm." My mother wouldn't even move her head.

It's funny how we were. The bracelet my father and Uta gave me turned out to be worth money, more than what the televisions cost when they came out a year later. It would have taken a miracle to convince us.

When the plane landed, we didn't even call Ted. We took a taxi home, my mother clicking her nails against the window. When we were inside, she collapsed on the blue-green couch and looked around disapprovingly. Our suitcases lay scattered on the floor.

"You know what he told me when we left? He said after all he did you didn't even say thank you. He said he'd open doors and you'd just walk through, he'd offer to buy you candy and you just said no. Not even no thank you. Just no. I've taught you how to act and what do you do there? Nothing."

The days with my father flashed like cards. I hadn't said no-thank-you.

"And here you use big words all the time and complex sentences. You should hear yourself joking around with Ted. You didn't say ONE BIG WORD the whole time we were there. I couldn't even stand listening to you. Un-huh. Yeah-uh. I don know. You didn't say one smart thing in front of him. Let me tell you, Kid, you sounded dumb."

"My name is Ann," I said.

She turned over and sighed. It sounded like air coming out of a balloon. "Sure, Ann. Call yourself whatever you want, I don't care. Go out and play. Go out and play with your kids."

I opened the refrigerator door and looked. Ted had made a château-briand by himself and sliced it. He'd stacked the rectangles neatly on a plate. Behind me, my mother turned over and knocked the cushions onto the floor. Her shoes dropped, one at a time.

"And you didn't even smile. Here, you're sharp and funny. There you slumped and looked down. And you talk about getting on television. You really just looked like any other kid around here. Well, fine. It's a good thing we're back because I can see now that this is just where you belong. Here with all the mill workers' kids. Well, good."

I walked outside without a jacket, looking for one of my friends. On Carriage Court, kids didn't knock on each other's doors. We just went outside and waited. But no one was there. It was a gray, cold day and it looked like it might rain. I was walking when a mother, from down the street, honked. She rolled down her window and asked if I wanted a ride. I got in the station wagon though I didn't know where I was going. She didn't even ask me. She just dropped me off at the skating rink. By that time it had started raining. The guard nodded as I walked in and from the lobby I saw Ted on the ice. Just then, I realized it was a workday, a school-day, Monday. That was why none of the kids came outside. Ted was giving a lesson, bending down and holding a woman's ankle, pointing her foot into a figure eight.

I walked to his office and took the key for the rental room, from under a certain bench. The rental room was small and covered with cubbyholes, with the sizes of skates painted in yellow. I took a pair of knicked, worn gray fives, with the brown rental stripe in back. When I'd skated, I had my own good skates. In these, the ankles were broken down.

I put them on and ran on points, wobbling because of the skates. Then I stepped onto the ice and skated; I crashed into Ted and held his sweater. He put a hand over my head and told the student something I didn't hear. When I pulled myself off, the student was gone. I opened my eyes and looked up at Ted; it was different than with my father. I couldn't bury my head in Ted's sweater and forget. Here, I knew exactly where I was. Ted was still Ted, standing in front of me. I didn't expect him to understand.

"You're back," he said. That was all. Ted would never know, unless I could find the words to explain myself, one by one. It seemed too hard.

I looked across the empty rink. The ice was gray blue, the hockey lines pale underneath like bruises. My father was gone for good and Ted was just Ted, another man in the world who had nothing to do with me.

"Would you like me to teach you to do loops?" he asked. His teeth were grinding, you could hear that, it was so quiet on the ice.

I couldn't say no because of the way he looked, standing there with his hands in his sweater pockets. He started skating in tight, precise loops. I hadn't figure skated for years and my ankles felt shaky. I was tired. I didn't have the concentration or drive I'd had before; then I'd been trying to improve. Now, the quick, beautiful loops seemed pointless in the empty arena. I glanced up at the stands around us. But Ted's hand was tight around mine and I began to follow his lines on the ice. I didn't know. I thought maybe I could learn.

Ted had an office, deep in the arena, underneath the rink, in a basement hall with no windows. When my mother and I had first met him, his office was like a home. He had an oak wardrobe with clothes, mostly sweaters, all warm things, and a stereo with his favorite records. In the years since he married my mother, those records ended up warped and misplaced, and the office wasn't neat and tended the way it had been. When we left and put the house up for sale, he began to spend all his time there again, sleeping on the cot against the far wall.

I guess that time in Disneyland was the last time I saw my father. I'm not sure. He didn't die or anything. For a long time, we thought we would see him. There wasn't a day. We just never heard from him again. I still wouldn't be surprised if he found us.

7

A Shopping Center Somewhere in the Valley

We used to drive around at night, we didn't have anything else to do. We didn't like to be in our apartment. There weren't places we could sit and do things. If I read my homework on the bed, there wasn't anywhere for my mother to go. The sofa in the living room was old and uncomfortable. I didn't like both of us to be on the bed. So we drove around in the dark. We drove down Sunset and slowly through the quiet northern streets in Beverly Hills. Sometimes we parked and beamed the headlights over one lawn. Houses in Beverly Hills still amazed us.

After we sat for a while, peering out trying to see movement inside the frames of fuzzy, lighted windows far back on a lawn, my mother would sigh and turn on the ignition. "Someday," she'd say.

"Yeah. Right."

"I believe it. We'll have a house. And clothes. You'll have everything a teenage girl could want, Puss." She'd reach over and slap my thigh. I'd move closer to the door, stiffening. "I just have to meet the man and catch him. Should we stop and get an ice cream quick before bed, for a little energy? Maybe it'll even get us up and working. That little sugar in our blood."

One night, we drove to Will Wright's, because my mother was dressed up. It was our favorite ice cream place. You could sit down in it. It was over-priced and old-fashioned, the garden circled with Christmas tree lights all year long. We sat outside in the courtyard at a small, wobbly table; I stuck a wad of gum under the metal base to even it. The round pink top was marble and the chair backs were lacy, heart-shaped wrought iron.

"You know, it's really something, when you think of it. Weather like this in March." That was one of the public things my mother said. When we were out, she only said things that could be overheard.

"Yeah, so."

She gave me a reproaching, corrective smile. "It's nice." She forced a laugh. "In Wisconsin now, you'd be freezing cold. You'd be in your bunny-fur coat."

Ice cream was my mother's favorite food, and in it she loved contrasts. Icy vanilla with scalding hot, hot fudge. Will Wright's served tiny sundaes: little silver dishes with a scoop of exquisite ice cream, flecked with black shavings of vanilla bean. The scoop was the size of a Ping-Pong ball. Two separate porcelain pitchers came with it: one of whole almonds, the other of hot fudge, which my mother spooned on, a bite at a time, to keep the maximum hot-cold contrast.

A tall man swaggered over to our table and, yanking a chair with him, turned it backwards and sat on it like a horse.

"Howdy, ladies," he said, extending his hand. "I was wondering if I could, uh, borrow a match."

"Honey, do you have a match?" If I had had a match, my mother would have killed me.

"Honey, I asked you a question."

"You know I don't."

She smiled at the man. "I'm terribly sorry. I'm afraid neither of us smoke." She rummaged in her handbag. "I sometimes carry them, for candles, but I don't seem to have any just now."

The man stayed. He didn't ask other people around us for matches and he didn't go back to his table in the corner.

"So, my name's Lonnie," he said. "Lonnie Tishman."

My mother stepped on my foot, hard, under the table.

"I'm Adele and this is my daughter, Ann."

"Your daughter? You two look just like sisters."

"Oh, no."

"You sure do. I said to my friend over there, I'll ask those two gals. They look like they'd be smokers."

"I'm twelve years old," I said. My mother kicked me, then pressed her shoe over my foot again, driving in the heel.

My mother and Lonnie Tishman were both moving. He stood up and turned his chair around and sat on it the regular way, then he crossed one leg over the other, like a woman's. He seemed rubbery, all joints. His top leg bounced off the other knee. His fingers drummed on the marble table-top. My mother seemed to be in slow motion, her spoon abandoned on the saucer, her ice cream melting in a puddle, no hot-cold contrast any-more. She gradually realigned herself so everything, her legs, her shoul-ders, her hands, faced him.

I was the only one still. I'd learned when I was young to be very still and not move when I wanted something. I wanted Lonnie Tishman to leave. My knees pressed into each other. Later, I found tender bruises. But he stayed, breathing loudly. Lonnie was a mouth breather.

"So how are you gals tonight?"

"We're great, aren't we, Annie? We were just saying how we *love* this weather. We're new to LA and we really love it."

"Just got here? Where're you from?"

"We're out of Bay City, Wisconsin."

Lonnie slapped his top knee, setting both legs jiggling.

"Golly. Wisconsin."

My mother looked down at the table and lifted the tips of her fingers.

"So, what are you two gals doing out here?"

"Well, I teach. I'm a speech therapist in the LA Public School Sys-tem." There was something tiny about her pride. It killed me, I loved her. "And she's an actress," she said.

I stared down at my ice cream as if eating required all my concentra-tion. They both looked at me hard, as if they were tracing me, drawing outlines on the sky.

Lonnie whistled through his teeth. "She's an actress." His chin fell down and the way his face turned, I could see, in his cheekbones, he was handsome.

"Mmhmm." It sounded like my mother could say more, but wouldn't. It was her imitation of modesty. Of course, there was nothing more to tell. I wasn't an actress. I only wanted to be.

"Whewee, a kid actress, huh? I knew a guy whose daughter was on TV. Little blond kid with the braids down the back. What was that show called. Her name's Linda, I think, or Lisa. Lisa Tannenbaum."

"Do you know her, Honey?"

That was harsh, like a twig snapped at my face. There wasn't any possible way I could have known Lisa Tannenbaum. "No," I said.

"Where do you gals live?" Lonnie pushed his chin close to my mother. He had short bristles on his face, which made me think of an electric field, things crackling, lightning on dry ground. I wished my mother would feel it, too, and pull away. It was something about men. When I was a child, I went to my cousin's house. I locked myself in the bathroom and looked at things. It was all different from ours. I felt something like electricity when I put their towels to my face. I thought it came from men, the smell of men. I imagined it had something to do with shaving.

"In Beverly Hills," my mother said quietly, dropping the words.

"Well, hey, what do you say, why don't we get together sometime."

"Sure," my mother said.

"Why don't you give me your phone number and I'll call you and we'll hook up?"

"We're 273-7672."

Lonnie took a pen from his shirt pocket and wrote our phone number on his wrist. He stood up, shoved the chair in towards the table, pulling the back to his leg. "Well, I'll be a-seeing ya," he said.

My mother put her hand over the bill. "Should we get going?" I'd finished my ice cream; my mother no longer seemed interested in hers. She quickly looked over her shoulder to see he was gone and then bent towards me, her face greedy with excitement.

"You know who that was, don't you?" There was something hard and individual about her face; her beauty was her beauty, her luck was her luck.

"No." I ground a stone under my shoe.

"Didn't you hear him say his name? That was Tishman: Lonnie Tishman. Haven't you seen those signs on Wilshire where they're building? That's all Tishman. They're everything. All the high rises. Those condominiums in Century City where we drove by, don't you remember? I said the top ones would be gorgeous. Who knows, I'll bet he'll give us one of them. He's all over. Believe me. *Ev*-ery-where." There was something about the way she said it. I can't explain.

I knew I was supposed to be glad and excited; if I were excited, it would be like praise. She would shake her hair and bask. But I didn't believe her. He didn't look rich. Something about the way he rubbed his hands on his pants when he stood up.

"You know what this all means, don't you?"

"No."

My mother sighed, dragging her spoon in her coffee. "Boy, can you be dumb sometimes."

I was quiet, knowing I could be. I looked up at the sky and understood, without exactly thinking, that it was late on a school night again, eleven or twelve o'clock, and that I hadn't done my homework and I

wouldn't do it. That tomorrow would be like other days, the hall of my
school with old wooden doors, closing and closing, me coming up the
stairs, alone and late. The sky was a dark blue, through the branches of
the trees. The stars seemed very dim.

"You're going to make it, kiddo. Why do you think he came up to us?"
My mother's voice curved; it was like a hook. She was scolding to get me
back.

"He liked you, I suppose." I hated saying that. Her face lit up from
her eyes.

"You think so?"

"I don know."

"Did you really think he liked me? Tell me, Ann."

"I guess."

"Well, he's going to put you on television." My mother clapped. From
a lifetime of working with children, all my mother's emotions expressed
themselves in claps.

"He's not an agent." I said that, but I could feel the beginning of
something in her insistent, lilting voice. She worked with that voice, as
hard as if she were building something both of us could see. Sometimes,
I felt my mother climbing up a long, long series of stairs, above what
seemed true—my school, the hum of electric clocks behind closed
wooden doors, my steps, late, the messy locker, my books, heavy and
unlooked at, and I followed her to up to the clear air. At the top, there
was a sky, but when she pushed at it, it broke like so many sheets of
colored tissue paper. She began to climb to the other side. I stood still
below, next to her legs, but I could see air, feel the wind, from the other
side.

"Oh, come on. Didn't you hear the way he said, he has a *friend* whose
daughter is on TV? What do you think that meant? He was just testing
you. That was his way of asking, do you really, really want it? You know, a
lot of kids *say* they want to be on television, sure, but then when it comes
right down to it, they don't have the commitment. Not really. We're different. We really do have it. This man's not the agent, but I'll bet his
friend is, the one he was sitting with. I'll bet *he's* the agent and this Tishman's the producer. We'll just have to wait and see, but he has our number. I'll bet you land a TV show. And now it's all in the offing."

"When?"

I pulled closer to her and waited. She didn't have to build anymore or
fight: we were there. Now, she could be slow. I needed every word. I
moved close and watched her face, attentive, like a person holding a bowl,
trying to catch single drops of rain.

She tilted her head for a moment, thinking. Her cheekbones seemed
high, she looked thin, as if the bones in her face were very frail. When I

was little, I'd once held a velvet-lined box with a glass cover, a perfect bird skeleton laid out inside. My grandmother had lifted the lid with her fingernail.

"I would say soon. Very soon."

It was all different now, where we were. I didn't snap or mope or sulk. I sat at the edge of my chair, leaning across the table to be near her. She was distracted, aloof—sure of me.

The night had the same blue perfect air as the inside of a bubble. I felt elated to touch the marble of the table under my hand. I slept that night easily, thoroughly pleased, the knowledge dissolving in me.

Lonnie Tishman called the next day. I answered the phone. I recognized his voice and for a moment I believed it was the call that would deliver me. A sound stage. Cameras. A voice would say, You have been chosen. You. But he just asked, "Your mom around?"

Then the usual came back. Brown doubts and suspicion. The wooden backs of doors.

"It's for you." I shoved the receiver away.

My mother, three feet to the left on the carpet, stood still in her tracks for a full minute. Then she walked the four steps to the night table, breathed in and picked up the phone. The mattress jiggled as she squirmed. She changed her legs, from the left to the right, on top. She laughed, but I could hear she was puzzled. She was trying, with her pauses and tones, to weld whatever he was saying into the shape of a normal date.

"Well, okay, I suppose. But actually, I don't cook very well." With one hand, she redistributed bobby pins in her hair. Her mouth was working. "Oh. Oh. Well, really, it's our kitchen. To tell the truth, I think I'd just as soon go out." This—a more aggressive statement than she liked to make to a man, especially at the beginning—was followed by an avalanche of helpless giggles. "Okay," she said, finally, bouncing her shoe off her toe. "We can do that."

She stood and clapped after she hung up the phone. "What do you know, Ann! We've got a date this Sunday night."

I stayed on the bed, doing nothing.

"Hey, Little Miss, you better paste a smile on that face, because this could just be your big break."

"Oh yeah. How's your date going to be my big break?"

She stuttered a second. Even speech therapists stutter. "He probably wants to check me out first and see if I'll really let you do all this. You know, a lot of mothers wouldn't cart their kids around to rehearsals and tryouts and to the studios. But I will. I really will. And that's probably what he wants to know."

· · ·

We both got haircuts. My mother only let me get a trim, half an inch of split ends, so I was finished a long time before she was. I sat under the turned-off dryer and leafed through old movie magazines. I studied the dotted pictures of dark men. I thought it was possible I'd see a picture of my father.

"So this man wants to hide it," my mother said, to the woman teasing her hair. At the same time, she watched her curls fall around her face in the mirror. She tilted her head to the left. My mother held her face like a jewel, always moving a little to glance off another facet of light. "He doesn't want me to know."

"Could be," the hairdresser said. "There's supposed to be one Tishman brother left and they say he's a little nuts."

"This is the man. I know it."

By the time we left, it was raining outside. My mother took my magazine and tented it over her head as we ran to the car.

"These people play down their money. Because they want you to like them for *them*. Lots of people are probably after him for his money. Sure. And this is his way of testing us." She nodded, preoccupied, as she warmed up the car. "Mmhmm. See, at first, I was upset, because he didn't want to go out to eat, and then when I kind of suggested it, you know, he wanted this Love's Bar-b-que, a really cheap place. No atmosphere or anything. Here, I thought, well, with all his money, he can take me somewhere a little better. But I can see now that he wants to find out if we really like him for *him*."

Again, the car screeched going down into the garage. "After all, we met him in the Beverly Hills Will Wright's. And anybody in there is somebody."

"What about us?" I said.

She shrugged. "You're right."

Sunday was the date. It was all we did. We woke up early, at six, when the alarm clock rang, for once. We cleaned, then shopped. We bought candy to put out in a bowl and things he could drink if he wanted to. In the afternoon, I sat on the bed, watching my mother dress. She'd already taken her bath. She moved around the small floor space in her bra and pantyhose, running from the closet back to the bathroom mirror.

I picked up a book to read, but every two minutes she interrupted, and I was glad to quit again. This was fun.

"Ann-honey, tell me something. Which way, up or down, what do you think? The hair, come on, concentrate a second. Down? Are you sure? Why?"

"Makes your neck look longer."

"It does, good. Are you sure?"

It occurred to me that my mother had never been alone. At home, she'd had Lolly, probably even before I was born. Lolly had always been there, bigger, quiet, sitting on the edge of some bed, watching my mother become shinier and shinier, enclosing more and more light in her body on a dull, late Saturday afternoon, getting ready to give herself, brilliant, to one man. For the first time ever, I felt sorry for Lolly. I remembered her scratchy plaid Bermuda shorts, her head bent, looking down at her big hands. At least I was younger. I could still be pretty myself someday.

I was asleep when they came home that night, but I heard the key work in the door and Lonnie's loud, raucous voice and her hushing him. And then I heard her giggles. That was the worst thing. I was awake then and I waited for it to stop. I wanted him to leave, so it would be quiet again. But he didn't. He never did. For the first time in that apartment, my mother didn't sleep with me in the bed. They opened the sofa; I heard the metal mattress frame scraping the floor.

"Shhh, you'll wake her."

"I forget you've got a child in here."

We'd never opened the sofa bed before. It must have been a dusty mess. The dark green vinyl sofa was a problem. At Christmas, we'd tried to drape it with a bolt of green felt, but it had looked wrong and you couldn't sit on it. We'd finally settled for cleaning it and draping a red mohair afghan over the back.

My mother stood a foot away from me, lifting sheets out of the closet. I held absolutely still. As a child, I'd dreamed of burglars coming in at night from the train. In the dream, I'd have to be still. Later, the burglar lined us up in the cellar. He was stealing our television and my mother blamed it on me. The burglar pointed a rifle at us and Benny saved everything by putting his finger in the hole at the end of the gun.

They must have been making the bed. It sounded like they dropped twenty shoes and tripped over each other each time. It seemed it would never be quiet.

"Shhh," my mother said and then giggled.

"Hell, I thought you said she was asleep."

"Well, she is, but she's a light sleeper."

Another shoe dropped. For what seemed like hours, layers and layers of time, I thought I heard something; the sheets moving, the metal of the bed. The sound of his mouth-breathing changed the whole air. I didn't want to close my eyes.

But I must have finally fallen asleep in the morning, because I missed the alarm. I put my hand over the buzzing clock, to stop the noise, but I didn't reset it. My mother woke up on her own and came and sat next to me on the bed. She moved her hand on the blanket, over my back.

"Get up, Honey. It's time to get ready for school. Upseedaisey. Really, Honey. It's time now."

"Is he still here?"

"He's sleeping."

I pulled the covers and bedspread around me, and walked into the closet. I put my jeans and T-shirt on there. My mother stepped in and grabbed my arm. There wasn't room for two. Our closet was small and full, with clothes on hangers and linens on the shelves.

"Ann, I didn't sleep with him," she whispered. "I mean, I slept with him, but I didn't. He didn't touch me, we just slept. I swear to God, Ann, that's all we did." She lifted her palm up like a child, scout's honor.

"I don't care what you did." I walked around him to the bathroom. There was almost nowhere to walk. Opened up, the sofa bed took the whole room.

My mother followed me to the sink. "Well, I care. And I didn't."

We were alone in the apartment, making my bed. My mother shook a pillow down into the pillowcase. We'd driven to a laundromat in Pacific Palisades. Of course, there were closer laundromats, but my mother had found this one and it was clean and there was a health food snack bar next door. The main thing was my mother didn't want to be seen in a laundromat. In Pacific Palisades, it was okay. We didn't know anybody there. And now that I had friends at school, I felt the same way. I didn't want them to see me doing wash. When we finished my bed, my mother opened the sofa and put sheets on. I didn't help her with that and she didn't ask me.

"The tingling is over. What can I say? That real excitement, the fantasizing—I just don't feel it anymore. So, let's just hope some money comes in on one of his deals so we get a little something. And soon."

Lonnie slept here every night now. We no longer pretended Lonnie was an agent or a producer. Now, it was supposed to be enough that he might have money and give us some, to help us out. And it was enough. We adjusted.

"What about all these buildings that say TISHMAN on the scaffolding? I saw another one today on the way to school. On Roxbury."

She sighed. "Could you come and help me here a second? Just tuck the other side." The sofa bed felt flimsy, metal springs and a three-inch mattress. Sometimes in the night I heard a crash when the metal legs buckled and collapsed. "This man wants to make it on his own. He doesn't want to just be the son of someone who made it big. But I think if one of his deals comes through, if this shopping center makes it, *then* he'll go back to his family and say, See, this is what I could do, alone."

"Are you sure it's even the same family? There're a lot of Tishmans in the phone book."

"Honey, I'm sure."

"How do you know? Did he tell you?"

"Ann, I just know. Okay? You just have to learn that I know some things you don't. Okay? I'm a grown-up."

"At least he could pay rent."

"Honey, he does pay rent. He pays rent on his own apartment in Hollywood."

We'd seen his building. It was dark red brick, old, set far away from the street. Once, after dinner, my mother had stopped there, outside his building, so he could run in and get clean clothes. While we were waiting for him in the car she pressed the button that locked our doors.

"He's never in it."

"Well, let's just cross our fingers and hope it comes through soon, okay, Honey? Because I need it too. Believe me. Believe me, I'm getting tired."

I dropped it.

I developed sores on my head; small red bumps with scabs. My mother thought it was either lice or some weird disease. She decided I'd caught it from Lonnie. She called and made an appointment with a doctor in the Valley, an hour's drive away.

"You never know, people talk. Word gets around. Beverly Hills is really a very small community. And it's not the nicest thing to have, you know." My mother always worried that people would think we were unclean.

After school, we drove to the Valley. Sometimes, I really liked my mother. She drove easily, with one hand, as she pumped the gas with the toe of her high-heeled shoe. We looped on the freeway ramps smoothly. She talked to me and drove almost unconsciously on the six-lane highway with a freedom and confidence anyone at home in Bay City would have admired if they could have seen her. I remembered our first day in Los Angeles, how she'd clutched her whole body an inch away from the steering wheel. Her voice, when she told me to turn off the radio, fell stern and quiet. She'd been afraid for our lives. She'd driven on the right-hand side, almost on the gravel by the high aluminum fence. Her lips had moved and I thought she might have been praying. Now, she changed lanes and told me to look at the sun, just over a Coke sign on a dry hill. There were things to be proud of my mother for. I doubt she ever thought about it, how she'd learned to drive here.

She knew the Valley; she drove out to work every day. I didn't know much about her life without me. And my mother seemed shy and a little ashamed of what she did all day. Driving to the doctor, I asked her what she'd done at school. "Oh, nothing. You know. Just the usual," she said.

I imagined her in a room, plants on the windowsill, with tall boys and fat sloppy girls. With her they would all be timid. I imagined her standing close to them, holding their faces by the chin and looking in their eyes while she said the word. "Say thick. Th-th-th-thick." Their mouths wobbled crumbled sounds, trying to copy her lips.

We were speeding, my window cracked open, the sun a fuzzy line over the brown hills.

"There's my exit," she said, real joy in her voice, as if she were showing me the building where she worked.

The doctor didn't seem horrified by my head. My mother and I always felt calmed by doctors. They made us feel clean, like everyone else. He diagnosed the bumps as scabies, said I could have picked them up anywhere, probably in school, and matter-of-factly wrote out a prescription for Quell Lotion. He told us to wash my hair every day for eight days and put on the pink lotion afterwards. My mother nodded while he explained this, as if she were receiving critical and difficult instructions. That was all. He let us go. We bought the lotion downstairs in the pharmacy and then went for an early supper at the Van Nuys Hamburger Hamlet. We ordered big dinners and we each had dessert. It felt good to be alone, just the two of us.

We could have gone home after that and I could have washed my hair in our shower, but my mother panicked over anything having to do with uncleanliness, and when she panicked, spending money made her feel better, so she took me to her hairdresser. The hairdresser washed and blow-dried my hair so it looked thick and good, and then we had to ruin it, rubbing in the lotion, which made it greasy and rumpled.

"Ever hear from that Tishman fellow?" the hairdresser asked my mother.

"Mmmhmm, sometimes."

The next day she took me to a different beauty parlor.

After my last treatment, it was almost dark when we left the beauty shop. We drove to our apartment to pick up Lonnie, and then we drove farther out into the Valley than I'd ever been. We didn't have time for dinner because we were late. Lonnie had an appointment to meet someone for a business deal. He was supposed to be building a shopping center.

My mother drove and Lonnie sat in the front seat creating a chain reaction, hitting one hand on the other hand, which, in turn hit his knee. My mother let him play the radio while she drove. I was sitting up against the back door with a book open, trying to do my homework. I was trying to improve my life, do what I was supposed to do. My efforts to make myself better never went anywhere. I didn't really believe they would.

The land changed outside our car windows. It was brown and flat, the hills seemed lower, and buildings were small and scarce. It reminded me of little towns in the desert when we drove into California. We stopped at a light and a man in a cowboy hat crossed the road. There were no sidewalks, just highway and gravel on the sides. There were more trucks than cars on the road with us. Gray-brown tumbleweed dotted the hills above the shopping center, where my mother finally slowed the car.

There was a McDonald's in the shopping mall and Lonnie told my mother and me we should wait for him there. When we all got out of the car, he walked in the other direction, towards a bar, where he was supposed to meet his partner. He walked away, rubbing his hands on the front of his pants. We stood on the blacktop and my mother seemed distracted until she said, "Wait here a second, stay right here," and ran up to Lonnie, her purse hitting the side of her thigh as she ran. They weren't far away. "She can wait in the car. She'll study. Are you sure I shouldn't come along?"

I stood still, growing cold up from my feet.

"Hey, hey, comemeer a second, Woman. Let me give you a kiss before I go."

They stood there in the middle of the parking lot like two movie stars, her hair falling over her back and her stockinged heels rising up out of her shoes.

I looked the other way, at the window of a closed knitting store. I felt like I was nothing and I never would be. Then my mother came running back. She slapped her thigh when she stopped. "Come on. Let's hurry it up."

We sat against the inside glass wall of the McDonald's. There was a field on the other side of the highway, except for one gas station, nothing. My mother sipped coffee from a coated paper cup. We thought if we were going to sit here, we'd better buy something and we didn't want to spoil our appetites. My mother pointed on the glass.

"See, over there. That's where they're going to put the shopping center."

"Why?"

"What do you mean, why? So we can make some money, that's why. And buy a house, maybe. So I don't have to run myself ragged—"

"I mean, why there?"

"Oh, I don't know. They know where the best places are. This man is *the* expert on shopping centers. He's already made millions."

The sides of the highway were marked with glowing red circles on three-foot wooden stakes. It was just brown field on the other side, nothing, land that could have been anywhere. I didn't believe it. I couldn't believe Lonnie being in a bar down the mall with some guy would make a shopping center grow there.

I thought of something I hadn't remembered for a long time: the city I'd drawn under my grandmother's kitchen table with crayons. I'd planned houses and swimming pools, buses. I could easily draw for hours, working on one thing for my city. Now I looked outside and imagined the colored structures I'd drawn, huge and built, on the field across the street.

"But there's one already, across the highway. This one."

She sighed, tired and preoccupied. "I don't know, Honey. I'm not the expert. They are."

"What kind of people have business meetings at night, in the middle of nowhere, anyway?"

She didn't get mad. "Shhh, Honey. Just be quiet a minute. I've been working all day and I'm tired." She put her purse up on the plastic table-top and unclasped it. "Here," she said, handing me a dollar. "Go get us french fries. But just a small because we don't want to spoil our appetites. If this meeting goes well, he'll take us out somewhere nice. We'll get you a good steak. Really, Honey."

We were still eating the french fries, not talking, when Lonnie came in, rubbing his palms on the front of his pants.

"Hiya," he said to my mother. He did that a lot, acted as if he was with just one person instead of two. He was wearing the same thing he wore every day. A velour pullover and a blue zip-up vinyl jacket.

I looked out the window at the dull field across the highway. Business-men didn't look like this. Neither did millionaires.

Lonnie was nuzzling his flecked chin against my mother's neck. She hummed "mmmmm" with a noise that sounded vaguely electric.

"So, how's about a little supper?" he said.

"Okay. What do you feel like? Should we stay somewhere around here or head back towards home?" Then, she winked at me from over his shoulder.

"How's about here? I'd take a Big Mac and fries, how 'bout it. How 'bout it, Ann? Hamburger?"

"All right," my mother said, sliding back down onto the plastic chair.

There was an apology in her eyes as she turned and held her face in both hands, but she never would have said anything in front of Lonnie.

"Let's get it to go," Lonnie said, fidgeting at the counter.

My mother's car had changed. She never would have let me bring McDonald's into the cream-colored leather interior. But she let Lonnie. We ate on the way home, my mother asking me to hold her milkshake for her on the freeway.

· · ·

"So what was the gist?" she was saying in the front seat. I had the ashtray in the back lifted and I was trying to read my homework by that little light.

"That's one proud man, I'll tell you," Lonnie said. He lowered his window so a whistle of air came in and he rested his elbow on the glass.

"So, do you think it'll go or not so much?"

"Hey," Lonnie said, beating his hand on his chest so the windbreaker made a rattling noise. My mother was driving, I held her milkshake, Lonnie's hands were free. "What kind of guy do you think I am, anyway? Course it'll go."

"Ann, you can hand me my malt now. Thank you."

I had my book propped as close to the ashtray as it would go. It stayed steady there as long as the car went straight on the freeway. I didn't look up until the book fell.

"This isn't our exit, Mom." We were past Beverly Hills. The streets where we were driving looked dark and unfamiliar.

"We're going to stop at Lonnie's apartment for a second."

Yellow lights shone from his building. My mother and I stayed in the car while he ran out to get a change of clothes. His apartment building looked very old. We had buildings like that in Wisconsin, the orphanage and paper mills along the river. Dark brick buildings, small windows, built in the last century.

"So what happened to our nice dinner?"

She turned the heat on. The doors were locked and the motor was still running. "Honey, I'm trying to get rid of him, too. Don't you think I'm scared? But let me do it slowly. I know how to manage this man."

Someone walked by on the sidewalk, a kid. My mother stiffened, clutching the wheel, watching him all the way away in the rearview mirror.

"I don't even like him anymore, believe me," she whispered. "I think he's on drugs. But he could hurt us, Ann. He's in with people who could really hurt us. Do you know what the Mafia is?"

"Some kind of straw?"

"No, no, that's raffia. Like we had at your birthday party the year with the piñata. That was fun, wasn't it?"

"I don know what it is then." The trees here scared me. Otherwise I would have lied. I didn't like admitting things I didn't know.

"Well, it's gangsters. Awful, awful people. Criminals, but whole gangs together. All over the country. They kill, they cheat, anything. And I think he's part of that. I'm worried for my life. And your life. This other man he met tonight could kill me."

Lonnie started across the lawn, holding his bag in front of him with both arms.

"What about the police?"

"The police can't stop them. Nothing can. So just let me take care of it, okay?"

I didn't say anything, I was too scared. When he came back into the car, with a wash of cold air and the sinister click of the locks after him, it was almost a relief. He was just Lonnie. He'd brought his clothes in a brown paper shopping bag, a white shirt on the top.

In bed that night, trying to sleep, I couldn't get warm. I thought of the shapes of my crayoned drawings, built, on a field of dull grass. I was scared to be in the same room with Lonnie.

We'd driven by Century City on the way home; a few floors stayed lit in the tall buildings. I thought that in offices there, in rooms with typewriters and metal desks, shopping centers were being planned. I believed and I didn't believe my mother. I was beginning to distrust her promises but I still believed her threats. I believed Lonnie was a criminal.

I barely slept that night. And in the morning, I got up when the alarm rang. Light was coming in through our faded Christmas green felt curtains, making delicate lacy patterns over the apartment. My mother and Lonnie were asleep in the middle of the room. Nothing looked so dangerous anymore. I bent down and shook my mother. For once, I wanted us all to be up on time.

"Why don't you get up already so we can eat some breakfast for a change."

"Shhh. He's sleeping. Five more minutes. Please, Hon."

"Fine, I don't care what you do." She turned over and pulled the blanket to her eye.

I took a shower and dressed. Then my mother got up. She stood by the bed, wearing nothing but Lonnie's T-shirt.

"You know, you're not the only person in the world," she said.

"So." I was buckling my shoes. I picked up my books. "I'm leaving."

"Just hold your horses. You have time. I'll be ready in a second. Sit down."

Lonnie was awake now, too. He looked tiny in his white jockey shorts, the leg holes stretched and bagging. He held his slacks out delicately as if he might trip stepping into them. His hair was a mess.

"I'm leaving," I said again.

"Just wait." My mother was yelling. "You'd think SHE's the only person in the world."

"I don't always have to wait for you just because you don't want to get up on time and eat breakfast and live like a normal person. I'm always waiting for you." I guess I was screaming, then.

"Oh, you, you—" My mother came at me, tripping over the huge sofa bed between us. She tripped and hit her knee, which made her madder. "I work, I slave, I run myself ragged, so SHE can live in Beverly Hills, so

SHE can be a movie star, and what do I get? What do I get for thanks? A whole lot of guff from a stinky mouth."

"Who's a movie star," Lonnie said, one leg in his pants, one not.

"Thanks a lot."

"Hey." Lonnie lifted his hand in a grand gesture intended to silence us both. He looked at me, his face slack. "Your mother is a lovely woman," he said, his chin weaving slowly left and right, "you ought to treat her with respect."

My mother was still wearing nothing but the T-shirt, standing with her hands on her hips.

"I'm leaving."

Lonnie staggered up onto the bed, so he stood there, with his pants unzipped. "Hey," he said, loudly, raising his hand again. "Everyone quiet."

He didn't have a chance. Neither of us paid any attention.

"Oh, ohh, you lit-t—"

I was almost to the door when Lonnie jumped down and caught my arm, hard, twisting the skin. "Hey. Listen. I don't want to see you upset your mother like this." He looked back at her, she sat on the bed, crying now.

I twisted away. "Get your hands off me. Don't touch me. I'm leaving and I'm not coming back."

"You go ahead, you should. Go on and get lost. You don't deserve your mother. She's a lovely woman and you're nothing."

"Fuck you!"

My mother followed me to the door but I was already outside, down the sidewalk. She stepped for a moment onto the landing, wearing just the T-shirt, the toes of one foot on the other, shyly, shouting my name.

I kept walking. I heard the door slam and then I heard her shrill voice and Lonnie's low bellow. But they diminished as I walked, replaced by the small sounds of birds, slow tires, the first hammers on a construction site a few blocks away. The air felt kind, mild, windy as it touched my skin. I checked each of my pockets. I had everything I needed for a day. My hair was clean, just now beginning to lift a little as it dried, I had my books, money in my pocket. For once I had left early for school. The clean fronts of apartment houses, cars on the streets, the fountain at the corner of Wilshire and Little Santa Monica, all seemed indifferent and kind.

I'd been taught all my life or I knew somehow, I wasn't sure which, that you couldn't trust the kind faces of things, that the world was painted and behind the thin bright surface was darkness and the only place I was safe was home with my mother. But it seemed safer outside now, safer with indifference than care.

I decided I could go to Nibbler's. I had money, I had time. I could eat breakfast and then go to school. But my mother and the apartment had something on their side, a card to play against the bright, moving air: night. I had nowhere to go.

I kept walking. The air was cool on my skin, a leaf dropped on me— it tingled, the serrated sharpness of its edge like a scratch, then softness, a belly. I turned around. I kept expecting someone to stop me. But no one did and so I kept walking, now afraid to look back at the apartment.

Then I came to the street Nibbler's was on; it seemed large, a decision. I turned. Now if my mother or Lonnie left the apartment, I would be out of sight, gone. I was halfway there when I heard a car behind me that sounded like my mother's. I didn't have the nerve to turn around, because it seemed like something I'd made up, but I bit my lip and stood still. The tires sounded like ours. Then a Mustang pulled in front of me, forest green. My heart fell several inches lower.

I started walking again. I could hardly believe this was me. The noise of Wilshire Boulevard came closer. The day seemed to start in many places, like gears catching and moving, a huge machine. Beverly Hills was a city all of a sudden and I had six dollars and some change. I walked past the glass reflecting door of Nibbler's and stopped at Wilshire Boulevard in front of a purse shop. Then, somewhere behind me a car skidded and I heard heels and my mother was there, grabbing my arm, her fingernails biting my skin.

"Annie, Honey." She hugged me, her rib cage heaving, I felt her breasts move through her blouse. I just stood there and didn't say anything and then it was back to normal. "Let's go and park the car right and we'll have some breakfast at Nibbler's. He's gone, Honey. He's all packed. I told him he had to get out and he's gone. So it's just us again, thank God. I told him when he yelled at you like that, that was the end. No one, not anyone, can get between us." My mother's face seemed shallow and concave, like the inside of a pan.

"I'm hungry," I said. I started walking fast. Now I was thinking of time again, of not being late for school.

"Well, okay, wait a minute." She grabbed my arm. "We have to go a little slower. It's these damn heels." She lifted one foot and pushed something with her hand.

I felt the money in my pockets, the soft paper of the dollars. The buildings were just buildings again, what they seemed, familiar. The city looked beautiful and strong now, bright and silver, like a perfect train, drizzling light off its wheels as it moved. We could hear the fountain splashing behind our backs.

Lonnie was gone and we ate a big breakfast and I still had my money. She paid.

8

A Doctor's Apartment

The cake was my idea. Daniel Swan and I were both bad students, underachievers, according to our mothers. Neither of us did any homework. We were weeks late handing in our maps of Johnny Tremain's Boston. We made the cake with mixes, cut it in the shape of Boston and drew in the streets with a fluted frosting tin. For the first time I could remember, I got an A on something. The class laughed and the teacher left the room and came back with a serrated knife and brown paper towels from the bathroom. She cut the cake in little squares and gave them to the first person in each row to pass back.

They were good. Sweet and airy. That's the thing about mixes; they are good the first day. After that they get hard.

From then on, Daniel Swan and I baked cakes for all our high school projects. We stopped using mixes. We tried out different recipes and our cakes improved. I kept a notebook and wrote to my grandmother to ask why things turned out the way they did, to learn about icing.

There was an annual high school bake sale and everyone was supposed to bring something. So I was at Daniel's house, high in Benedict Canyon, making the Milky Way galaxy, all the planets and planet rings and moons in round cake tins. It was a big project. We mixed a different kind of batter for each planet and they'd all have to be frosted. My mother had bought us the ingredients. She'd taken us to the store the night before. Daniel had raised his eyebrows when the checker totaled the bill.

"That's pretty high. You shouldn't have to do all that, Mrs. August. I can ask the Witch."

"Oh, no, don't be silly, it's your kitchen."

My mother was serious about the cake. Except for the one old woman at the Lasky House and Julie, the real estate agent, my mother didn't have any friends. It seemed easier for me to meet people. I had school. She was hoping for a divorced father. Or a widower, better still. Maybe one where the wife ran away. For good, of course. She didn't know, but she'd already planned what she was wearing. She had a new dress, yellow, with her ivory jewelry and black pumps. She was counting on the auction. And she felt glad I was up at the Swans' baking cakes. "See and this way, we'll at least know the Swans," she'd said.

"I know other people, too."

"Well, I hope," she'd laughed. "And I hope they have fathers. Single."

We slid three round cakes in the oven. I mixed batter for a yellow cake while Daniel melted unsweetened chocolate. There were two ovens, one regular and one microwave, built in. Whatever seemed new and expensive and could be built in, the San Ysidro house had. When I looked at the long row of ingredients, the colored boxes and bags and jars, I felt bad my mother had spent so much money.

"So maybe we can all go together, your family and my family."

"You want to go with the twins and Rod, you go ahead. They're terrible. They're uncivilized."

"And your mom and dad."

"They won't go. Maybe the Witch, but she's probably got something for work. And the Failure'll be in Mexico."

"When's he coming home?"

"Depends on the deal. But probably the end of the month. No. Definitely the end of the month. Because to come home sooner than the end of the month, something would have to go right. And that's impossible."

I sifted. It felt quiet in the house, we were almost alone. The twins were at Scouts and Rod was visiting his best friend, Harold. But from the room off the kitchen, a wedge of bluish light came from the TV and we heard the steam of Darcy's ironing. Riley sat at the low kitchen table, the children's table, doing his homework. His glasses dropped to the bottom of his nose and he sometimes looked at me from over them. At the same time his shoulders shrank down and he sank in the chair under the table, his black high tops sticking out the other side.

"Riley." Darcy pulled him up by the collar. "Get to work now." Riley was Darcy's son and she was harder on him than she was on the Swans. "You children makin another cake?"

It was hard not to smile at Riley. There was something about his face. When you looked at him, you felt like you knew what he was feeling. He was already rich from commercials; the Witch's advertising agency had started him when he was three years old and now he got parts on his own. But Darcy cared about school, too, even though he didn't. We all understood why. He'd have plenty of money. Darcy drove all the Swans and Riley to El Rodeo and the high school in the station wagon every morning.

The house seemed empty while we worked, but it was a house that always felt empty. Dull white ceramic candlesticks with hinged doves stood on the windowsills. Frank Swan was a land developer in Mexico. He took trips down there two months of the year, but nothing had come of them yet, nothing worked. "He doesn't make any money," Daniel simply said. "The Witch makes all the money and the way they spend it, even that's not enough." He called his mother the Witch to her face, but he never would have called his father the Failure.

We both looked around the house while we mixed, grateful and helpless. "It's nice that your kitchen is so good," I said.

"We may as well use it while we have it."

Daniel said the Swans might lease the San Ysidro house and move to another, rented, place, if the Failure's deal didn't come through. They'd lived in a lot of houses before, all rented. This one they had built. I never could talk about our money problems, even though I worried all the time. But Daniel had seen our apartment. It seemed different for us. It was obvious. You could see what we didn't have.

"Here," he said, sweeping the walnuts into a blender. And we watched the dust coming up, whirling against the glass.

When we set the last cakes in the oven, Daniel asked Darcy to watch them for us and we climbed the back steps to Daniel's room. The children's hallway was narrow, littered with socks and T-shirts and baseball cards. Another stairway led to the parents' room. They never came to this part of the house. Paper blinds moved a little from the open window. Outside stood a pool house that was supposed to be for the kids, but so far, it had only one big bean bag chair. Nothing in the San Ysidro house was done yet.

"Last year, somebody paid two hundred dollars for a stupid model of the school. And they didn't even frost the roof, they used licorice."

"Not that we'd get to keep the money."

"No way."

A radio snapped on outside to "Jeremiah was a bullfrog." Home again, the twins splashed in the water. I never got to listen to rock stations and we didn't have a stereo, so I tried to remember what I could. I admired people who knew about songs. It was like dancing, one of those things like being rich or smart in school or good-looking. I always tried to remember and write the names down when I got home. I kept secret notebooks, neat charts, Group, Song, Album, Refrain. I studied these like I never studied school. It seemed people were born with it, you got it like long legs or an older brother.

"Why, what would you buy? More shoes?" Daniel reached over and touched the platform of my Korkease.

I looked down at my feet. I was wearing good socks and shoes, they looked normal, nothing to be ashamed of. I wasn't the least bit insecure about those shoes because they weren't mine. I'd stolen them a week ago from a girl's open locker. I figured I could get away with it because every girl at school wore these same shoes. I had another pair, older and beaten up, with platforms not as high. The shoes cost sixty dollars.

My mother noticed when I had new things but she never asked about them. "They give you that height you need in the thigh," she'd said.

I wore them every day. They seemed like mine now.

"You mean, if they gave us two hundred dollars? I don't know. I guess I'd give it to my mother."

I reached down on the floor and picked up a card of Uranus. Daniel had cards of the planets and constellations. He went with other guys to Mount Pinos every weekend. One of the fathers drove. There was a telescope at the top. I thought skies weren't much to look at, in Los Angeles. I would have liked to see stars.

Then Daniel stretched a rubber band between his hands and stared at it. He sat next to me on the bed. "So when are we going to?"

I knew what he meant. His mouth went a certain way.

"What?" I was a girl.

"You don't know?" He looked at me skeptically, but I wasn't scared. I said what I was supposed to say and anyway, sometimes being caught lying isn't as bad as being caught with the truth. "I can't believe you. You're so naive. Don't you know where babies come from?" Daniel made fake kissing noises.

"Kissing, you mean." I looked down at my feet. My feet looked irreproachable. Packaged. "I think we're too young. I'm not going to do it until college."

"What about more than kissing? When are you going to do that?"

"When I'm thirty."

Daniel snapped the rubber band across the room. "You're hopeless." He picked up his jacket from the floor and took out one Kraft caramel.

"Can I have one?"

He raised his eyebrows. "Ask nicely."

"Can I *please* have one."

He tossed it to me.

We heard Darcy downstairs, opening the oven door and shutting it again. A breeze came from Daniel's window and lifted a paper airplane from his desk to the carpet. There was a sugary smell of caramel on both our breaths.

Daniel stuck out his arm in front of me. "Here, rub my arm."

We scratched the hard tops of each other's arms, from our elbows down to our hands. Another person's fingers feel different on your arm. There seemed to be sparks, tracing down my skin and lasting about as long as something you write with a sparkler holds in the sky. Then Daniel took my leg and pushed my sock down to my ankle, my shoe in his lap. They were precise fine sensations.

When Darcy called us, we jumped and ran. She and Riley were standing in front of the microwave and we stood, too, looking in the glass window watching the pale belly of our cake rise.

The Witch bounded in, calling, "I'm ho-ome," carrying two grocery bags like any mother. Darcy hurried over to help. "Oh, thank you, Darcy, I'm so tired. Hello, Ann, how are you? I bought dates."

The twins ran in from outside and fought for their mother's arms.

"Let's go." I liked the noise and disorganization of a family, but Daniel wanted to be alone. I followed him to the living room. The living room seemed to be why they'd built the San Ysidro house. The kids' bedrooms were tiny like closets, Darcy and Riley's room was normal, even the upstairs master bedroom was just nice. The living room looked like a ballroom; two stories high, and banked on both sides with tall windows. A fireplace grew out of the stucco. The floor was red clay, Mexican tiles.

There was absolutely no furniture unless you call a grand piano furniture. There were niches on the side walls to sit in, but the cushions were put away in a closet.

It was a house for crowds. The Witch and Frank had given a party that winter, a benefit for musicians who'd written a musical called *Year of the Mushroom*. The living room had been lit with candles, torches lined the drive and everyone sat on the smooth floor, listening to the kids in tie-dyed clothes pound the grand piano and shake their heads and sing.

"It's going to be the next *Hair*," my mother whispered.

They planned to perform around the country in mushroom-shaped tents, with seating for five hundred. My mother wrote out a check. I tried to stop her but she was excited. It scared me a little, her attraction to them. She wouldn't have wanted me to be like that.

Daniel and I sat together on the piano bench. Daniel had studied piano for eight years and then quit. The whole reason the Witch liked me was that I somehow got Daniel to practice. The living room was cold. I'd never taken piano or any instrument in my life and my fingers didn't know where to go. Daniel was trying to teach me. He'd played three or four pieces through, after sorting out the dusty stack of music under the piano bench, slapping the books against his thigh.

Then he played this piece. I made him stop. I loved the melody. It made me think of something in nature. This was the piece I wanted to learn.

Daniel wanted to teach me so we could play it together. But it was really hard. We hadn't gotten three bars down yet. My fingers seemed to have no memory. We went over and over the same nine notes, going as far as we could until I made a mistake, but I never got tired of it, because I

loved hearing the melody, even a piece of it, every time. I liked to think
I was learning how to do something, improving myself. Then I saw my
mother's white car pull up outside the front window. She got out, pushed
her hair back with both hands and ran to the door. We slipped off the
bench and walked to the kitchen, passing Riley. Then we heard the sound
of a rough scale. Riley was beginning to take lessons. He wanted to start
a rock band when he was eighteen.

In the kitchen, our mothers each had their hands in a plastic bag of
dates. "Mmmm," my mother was saying.

"Adele, I have to take you down there. They're so cheap. Don't you
think they'd make a nice present, in some kind of basket?"

"With a bow. Absolutely."

"I have so many clients. And they all have to be Christmased."

My mother touched my hair and kissed me. "Hi, Darling."

"You're lucky she lets you kiss. I wouldn't dare touch Daniel,
would I?"

Daniel shrieked and ran around the counter. "Ouch! Stay away from
me, Witch!"

"So, Adele, Ann tells us you ski."

"Well, mmhmm, we really haven't here. To tell the truth, I'm a little
scared of skiing on this western snow. They say it's different."

The Witch pulled up another plastic bag of dates for my mother to
sample. Daniel and I snuck out. They'd talk awhile. We still had time.
"To tell the truth," my mother was saying again, as we skidded through
the dining room on just our socks.

But she didn't tell the truth. To my mother, Cassie Swan wasn't the
Witch, she was a woman who lived north of Sunset on San Ysidro Drive
and so my mother was all dull formality. My mother wasn't scared of western snow. It was money. It was always money.

Daniel said, Move over, and Riley looked at us, over his horn-rimmed
glasses that were too big for his face, and kept on with his scales. "Come
on," Daniel said. Then finally, he shoved Riley off onto the floor, clearing
the piano bench for me. I saw Riley's face for a moment when he fell, he
looked up at me, it was awful, something I never forgot. Then, a minute
later, on the floor, he did a back somersault, and landed, smiling goofy
again, all charm.

Both mothers walked in to watch. They each slid one foot out of one
high heel.

"Isn't that great?" my mother said.

"Daniel could be so good if he'd only practice. If he'd only once stick
to something."

"Oh, he should, he's obviously talented. Obviously."

"I wish he'd listen to you."

Under the piano, Riley bent over, pounding away at the tiles like a keyboard, with his genius for mimicry.

At the cake sale my mother fell in love.

"Did you see when we walked down the hall and he walked down the hall?" I was carrying the square marble cake we'd bought and my mother kept elbowing me in the ribs.

"I looked and I saw this HANDsome man, I mean, boy, is HE good-looking, I mean REALLY, and I thought, Hey, he's not with another woman, he's here alone. He must be divorced or even a widower. I'll bet a widower, the way he walked with his head down. And every few minutes I'd be walking along and he'd sort of look at me, like, Hey, who's she? And I'd sort of look at him and he'd look at me and sort of smile, you know. So then, we were both in front of your cake—say, wasn't that something, a hundred dollars. You should be proud. You and Daniel should both be proud—"

My mother unlocked my door. "Oh, Honey, do we really want to put that gooey thing in our nice car? Let's not, Ann. Really. Why don't you run over and throw it in the trash. There's a can. Nobody's going to know and I can just see if I have to brake, it'll be all over the leather. And that'll never come out."

"I'll hold it on my lap."

"Honey, just throw it out. We can go get ice cream cones if you're hungry for a little something sweet, but I don't want that messy thing in my car. I'm sorry, Ann, but I just can't. I'm not. I have to keep this car nice."

I crossed the street and dumped the cake in a garbage can. It was a good cake, it smelled like mint. A girl named Isabel had made it and her cakes had a reputation for being messy, but good. She used liqueurs in her batter.

"We paid seven dollars for that," I said, when I sat down in the car.

"Oh, Honey, the money's for the school really, not for the cake. Ooops." She braked as a man holding a child's hand walked in front of the car. She was always a distracted driver. "Tell you what. Let's go get ice cream cones. That's better for us anyway."

"I don't want ice cream."

"Well, I think I could go for one. Anyway. Where was I? Oh, in front of your big galaxy. I was standing and he was standing, but not saying anything. And that's when you came up with your friend, and she said, 'Oh, Ann, this is my father, Dr. Spritzer'—that's interesting, isn't it, that she said Dr. Spritzer, not just my dad, she must be real proud of him, obviously. You know, Hon, you should really introduce me as Dr. Adele August in situations like that."

"You're not a doctor."

"I am. I have honorary PhDs from a couple of places."

"Where? I've never seen them."

She sighed, steering with two fingers. "I don't know, packed some-where. Maybe at Gramma's. I really have to get all my things organized. But anyway, it doesn't matter, because you were real cute the way you said it anyway, real nonchalant, just, 'This is my mom.' Really, you did it just right."

"I'm relieved."

"And boy, did HE look then. 'Oh, what kind of doctor are you?' I said, but just real casual."

I'd heard all this—I'd been standing right there, but you couldn't stop her once she'd started. I looked at houses out my window as we drove.

"And when he said, 'Orthodontist,' I said, 'Really. That's funny, be-cause I've been looking for an orthodontist to see if Ann's going to need braces.' Remember, Hon, how you came home your first day and said the girls told you you needed braces? It's a good thing they did. Lucky."

Right there, in front of our cake, Dr. Spritzer had leaned over, taken my head in his hands and opened my mouth. He had doctor's hands. While he held my head, I felt like sleeping.

"Yup, I'm afraid she will," he had said. "She's got some pretty big toofers in that little mouth."

I thought he and my mother should get along. They both used the same dopey slang.

"So, did you hear when he said, 'Bring her in anytime and we'll see what we can do'? And then he sort of winked at me. Real subtle. Sort of half a wink. I suppose he didn't want you kids to see. So. We'll just have to wait. But I think in a week or two I'll call his office and see about braces for my little Bear Cub."

She reached over and patted my knee and I stiffened. She parked in front of Baskin-Robbins.

"You really don't want one? Just a single dip."

"No."

She held out money to me. "Well, I'd like a double, the top scoop chocolate almond, the bottom, pistachio. On a sugar cone."

I just sat there.

"Come on, Honey. Just run in and do this one thing for me. After all I do for you. Go on." She pressed the money into my hand.

In the two weeks before the appointment, we dieted. We ate salads at Hamburger Hamlet for dinner and my mother gave up ice cream alto-gether. The Saturday before the appointment, we went shopping on Rodeo Drive. In one of the dressing rooms, a room that was so big and pretty we could have lived in it, my mother sat down on the love seat and cried, quietly, so the salesgirls hovering in the hallway wouldn't hear. She lifted the beige ticket from the sleeve of a suit she was trying on. It cost seventeen hundred dollars.

"Well, so why don't we go somewhere else?"

"There is nowhere else." She shook her head, unzipped the skirt and began to step out of it. She looked ruefully around the room, glancing at herself from different angles in the mirrors, flexing and arching her foot. She looked over her shoulder at the backs of her thighs. Then she sucked in her cheeks.

"I'm pretty, but that's not enough. Nobody wants a woman my age who doesn't dress."

"I thought he liked you. You said he winked."

"Well, he saw me in the yellow. He only saw me in my best thing."

"Oh, come on."

"Don't kid yourself, he's no different from the rest. He can have anyone he wants, let me tell you. They want rich women. Not a schoolteacher with a child to support."

I started putting the clothes back on their hangers. The skirt kept falling off.

"Just leave it," my mother said. "They'll do it. It's their job."

"I'm just going to cancel," my mother said. "Oooh." She swerved, just missing a garbage can. "I don't have anything decent to wear. He's not going to want me in these old fuddy-duddy clothes."

"Why don't you wear the blue?"

"That's out of date. The collar's no good."

"Well, should I come home or not?" The appointment was for two o'clock, I'd have to miss an afternoon of school.

"Just come home and we'll see. I'm not making any promises. We'll just see."

When I walked in, at noon, my mother's six best dresses were lying out on the sofa. She stood in her lace underwear with her hair in rollers.

"Tell me, Honey, what would the other kids' mothers wear, do you think?" She stood soaping her face with pink organic geranium soap. "What do you want me to wear?" I sat on the arm of the vinyl couch and she sat next to me, still soaping. "I even thought of calling Cassie Swan and asking her. Should we go, Honey, or not? Or should we just cancel?"

She felt frightened of people here. I'd gone to school and made some friends. But she still didn't know anybody. The women we met all seemed to have about twenty times more money than we did. She tried, but it wasn't like with Lolly. My mother thought they would be judging her, picking her over for faults. We'd come all the way here and now she was scared. And she'd had so much courage in Wisconsin.

"Wear the blue, it's pretty," I said. But I wasn't sure either.

"You think? Even with that collar?" My mother looked up at me as if I could save her life.

"I think it's pretty. He won't be looking at your collar."

She went back to the sink to rinse. Then she started on her eyes. Suddenly, she banged her hand down on the counter. "I've got it. I'll wear the Gucci scarf. That'll cover the neckline and then it'll be smashing." She started crying again. "Oh, that's it, Ann, we're going to make it here after all. I know it. I really do."

We stood in the elevator. "Look once, Honey. Do I have any on my teeth?" We'd arrived forty-five minutes early to Dr. Spritzer's building and so we'd eaten hot fudge sundaes in the drugstore downstairs.

"Open a little wider, Honey," Dr. Spritzer said. He looked even better than he had at the cake sale. His good face seemed to pop out of the tight-necked green smock.

"So how did you survive your cake?" he asked my mother over my head.

"Ours was very tasty, actually."

"Let's see here." He moved something suspiciously like a pliers in my mouth. "Well, it looks like she's going to need some braces for da teef, I'm afraid."

"She is." My mother patted my shoulder. "Well, Honey, it won't be too bad. I guess you're just going to have to have them." She tried to look concerned and suck in her cheeks at the same time. "How long will she have to wear them, do you think?"

"We'll just have to see how fast her teeth respond." He shook my jaw. My mother didn't say anything about the price and Dr. Spritzer called a girl named Pam to come over and make a plaster mold of my mouth.

"Hi," my mother whispered. I was asleep, then I opened my eyes and made out the shape of her back. "Are you up? Unzip me, would you? I'm stuck."

She wriggled closer to me on the bed. My fingers felt heavy with sleep and they wouldn't move. Finally, the zipper sprang free in my hands. I opened it down to her underpants. My mother stood and hung up her dress in the closet.

"It feels so good to be out of that. But it was absolutely the right thing, the dress. It was perfect. Couldn't have been better."

It was coming to me: we'd gone to Rodeo Drive and she'd bought a dress for her date with Dr. Spritzer, and now she was home late, and happy.

"How was it?"

She pulled on a T-shirt, then sat down. "Well, you won't believe it, Ann. It was marvelous. Just marvelous. We met for drinks. Here at the Left Bank, we sat at the bar, and he was sort of smiling, you know, and I smiled, and then he said, Hey do you feel like a couple of lobsters? I said sure, why not, and he took me to this place. Ann, we've got to go there sometime, you'd love it, you would ADORE it, but it's expensive. It was RIGHT on the beach. And we got in and everybody knows him there. They all say, 'Oh, hello, Dr. Spritzer, Hi Josh.' And he's short. I didn't realize it before, but he's this little itty-bitty man. It's a good thing I wasn't wearing higher heels. Boy, is that ever lucky, when I think about it. I almost wore the black. Even in these, I came right up to here on him.

"So we talked and talked and we just agreed about everything. I don't know how, I don't know why, but we really clicked, you know? Sometimes that just happens, you just CLICK with someone. And here we were eating these lobsters and you know how they're messy and the butter was dripping down my face, oh, God, I thought, here he's going to remember me with a shiny, buttery chin."

"What time is it?"

My mother went to the front window and pulled the felt curtain and let it close again. There was a damp spot where she'd been sitting on the blanket, darker than the rest of the wool. I rolled over and picked up her underpants from the floor. They were wet. I dropped them back, I didn't want her to see.

"It's pretty late. Almost time to get up. Should we jump in the car and ride down to the beach for a little? The sun will be just coming up. And I bet Alice's would have a good breakfast."

My legs still felt weightless and empty inside.

"I'll just throw on some clothes and we'll go." My mother walked into the bathroom and the toilet seat clicked against the wall. "Should we do that, Honey?" She always left the bathroom door open; she liked to keep talking. The toilet paper roll creaked. "We can get some strong coffee. Come on, get up. We'll have fun. Come on, Ann."

She clapped her hands while I put on jeans and a loose, old sweater, warm clothes I'd feel ugly in at school, when it was light. But now I needed comfort and these clothes made me feel regular.

It was still dark when we drove up, out of the garage. We could just see the shapes of the trees and buildings in the weak street light. My mother turned on the heat. Bundled in soft clothes with my sneakers up on the dashboard, I was glad to be driving. I didn't care how far we went.

My mother crossed Wilshire Boulevard, onto Arden Drive. She slowed and then stopped in front of a house. "This is where his kids live. And the ex-wife, Elaine." The street was dark and empty. We could sit there and stare all we wanted. Beverly Hills seemed as small and innocent as Bay City, as anywhere.

"We should always get up early," I said.

"He put a lot of work into that house. A lot of work and a lot of money. He did that whole hedge, he told me. He says he still goes over to do the gardening."

"You don't think he'll ever want to go back?"

"Oh, no. I'm sure of it. He loves his kids, though. He'll always see his kids, I'm sure. Apparently, he worries about Amy. About her weight. Apparently, she's very insecure."

My mother started the car again and we drove south. Even Wilshire Boulevard was empty.

"I'm going to drive you past his apartment for a second. It's gorgeous inside, absolutely gorgeous. See, he had the big house with the garage and the pool and the yard and all, and he said to me, now, for the first time really ever, he's living alone. So he wanted something small and neat, without a lot of stuff around."

She parked across the street from one of the new Century City high rises and rolled her window down.

"He's up there on the fourteenth floor. See his window?" She craned her neck and bent out.

"No."

"It's dark now," she said, sighing. "He turned his lights off. He's probably gone to bed. Sweet." She smiled to herself.

The car rumbled softly and in the field next to us, already staked for development, light was beginning to come up from the ground. Down Wilshire, in the distance, the Veterans' building gleamed like a knife. We turned up to Sunset and drove on the wide, clean, loopy road for a long time. There's a place where Sunset meets Pacific Coast Highway. You turn at a stoplight and then you're there at the beach. We parked the car alongside the road and got out, to walk. The sand was still more gray than yellow. You couldn't see a sun yet. But it was lighter than it was dark. The water looked choppy. There were whitecaps. It was cold, we kept our hands in our pockets.

Close to the shore, the water seemed clear. The boom of waves crashing and the plate of green water, washing up on the sand, seemed to wipe out what we said and start the world over, new and clean, every minute.

Farther out black figures of surfers moved, appearing from where we were like letters of the alphabet.

"Look at how early they come out. That's great. Can you believe we really live here now?" Our hair blew in front of our mouths. "I'd love a house on the beach someday, Josh says that's what he wants, too. He's had the house in Beverly Hills with the kids, he's done that. Now he'd like something else."

"What about my school?" Beverly Hills kept a strict district. That was why we had to live where we lived.

"There must be a school out here somewhere."

"Do you think he'll want to get married again?"

"I don't know, Ann. We'll have to wait and see. We'll just have to see. He's already paying alimony and child support, you know. And those two will have to go to college, too, still. So I don't know. It was just a first date. Let's hope."

We walked north, against the wind. Sand blew up on my jeans, making a ripping noise.

"He did say, though, at the end, he walked to his balcony and he leaned back and said, Adele, I have never had a first date like this in my life. This was more dynamic and more, close, you know, than any first date in my whole life.

"And I said, I was thinking just the same thing. And it's true. Really, Ann. I never, never really feel anything on a first date. I told him, it usually takes me a long time to get to know someone. But this man really, really cares about me."

"Did he say he loved you?"

"Oh, no, Honey, he couldn't. Adults who've been married before just don't say that to each other right away. That takes a long time."

"A month?"

"Even longer. A year, maybe. That's almost like an engagement, saying that at our age. You might not even say it until you just went, Say, here, I bought a ring."

That made me remember Lolly and her shall-we-say-ring. My mother never got a ring from Ted. They'd decided to put the money towards the house on Carriage Court.

"But he did something. He did something last night that grown-ups do sometimes that shows you really, really care about someone."

"What?"

"Oh, Honey, it's something adults do in bed. But not many people ever do it. It means you really, really like the woman. You'll know when you're older. It just means they're really, really serious about you. They wouldn't do it with just any woman."

"How will I know if you don't tell me!"

"Well, I hope you're not planning to go to bed with anyone for a long, long time, Little Miss. Because, let me tell you, it wouldn't be a good idea with boys your age. The men really still want you to be innocent if they're going to marry you. They may say they don't, but they really do.

It's different with me, Honey, because I've already been married."

"So when I'm married, how will I know?"

My mother laughed. "You'll just know. No one ever told me. The way you know never changes. It'll just happen. And you can tell. You really can." She sighed. "Boy, can you."

Farther up, a line of surfers in black wet suits walked towards the shore. In the shallow waves, they rode one hand on the boards, which bobbed ahead like dogs on leashes.

"So whatever this special thing is that Dr. Spritzer did, my dad didn't do that?"

"Oh, Ann, your father. Honey, your father loved me and he loved you, too, but he's an irresponsible man. It wasn't just us. He left his jobs, everything. He's a selfish, selfish man."

The waves broke huge, about ten feet and rounded like perfect glass.

"But, don't worry, because there'll be other men in our lives. I'll catch another father for you, you just wait. Who knows, maybe it'll be Josh Spritzer. Wouldn't that be fun to have a doctor and a doctor like him, who looks like that? Everybody likes him, Ann."

"Even if you marry him, he won't be my father, though."

"I don't know. I think he would. I'll tell you a father is someone who DOES for you and GIVES to you. Not just take, take, take. I mean, what makes your dad your father? Just a little sperm. And genes. What did he ever do for you?"

I shrugged and pulled my collar up. She was right. I couldn't say anything to that.

"And I'll tell you, if we play it smart with Josh Spritzer, he may end up being THE adoring dad. Just watch. He told me last night that his kids give him OODLES of trouble. You can't even imagine, Ann. These kids really have problems. After dinner, we were having coffee and we talked and talked and talked about how worried he is with Andy. He doesn't even know if Andy can get into college, with his grades, Ann. Can you imagine, with a school like Beverly High and money? You'd think he'd have everything going for him. And he can't even get the grades. Not even for UCLA. But don't say anything to any of your kids. Even to Amy. They're trying to keep it quiet. I really shouldn't be telling you any of this, because he hasn't even told Amy. But he thinks Andy may be on drugs.

"Then, at the end, we were just going to leave, he looked at me and smiled—he's got this huge, bright smile—and he said, 'I've been talking and talking about my kids, and you haven't said a word about yours. You must have problems with Ann, too.'

"And I said, 'Well, no, as a matter of fact, I don't.' He said, 'You don't?' And he looked at me, like this, you know, and said, 'You don't worry about drugs or her getting in with the wrong group of kids or anything?' And I said, 'Well, actually, we have pretty good communication. When she has a problem, she tells me and we work it out together.'

"And let me tell you, he was impressed, Ann. He was thinking to himself, Why aren't my kids more like her? You can bet."

We kept walking. She had no idea. I didn't tell her my problems. But I just jammed my hands farther down in my pockets. I wasn't going to fight now. I liked Dr. Spritzer.

She yawned. "I'm getting hungry. Should we trek up and see if Alice's is open?"

The pier seemed a long way off, but we could see the restaurant, with its shingled turret, from where we were. We started diagonally up the sand.

"Wouldn't you love a dog on the beach? Maybe we should get a dog!" My mother's voice boomed loud. The ocean always made her optimistic.

The sand became darker and dirty, when we got up near the restaurant. We stood and looked until we found our car, more than a mile down, by the side of the road.

My mother slapped her thigh. "Well, we can eat whatever we want and the walk back will work it off. We need that little exercise."

She grabbed my hand, right as I turned from the water, to follow the pebbled path to the door. "You know, we made the right choice, coming here. It was hard at first, but look at us now. Look at you. You're getting braces. With your teeth straight, your face will be just perfect and you're in Beverly Hills High with the richest and the smartest kids in the world. Really, Ann. The very top, top kids in this world. We never could have had any of this in Wisconsin."

She stood looking down at my face, waiting for something.

"I'm hungry," I said.

"You're really going to be somebody some day. These kids you meet now will be your connections, your milieu, for the rest of your life. I only wish I'd had the chances you'll have."

Where we walked in there were overturned chairs stacked on tables. A broom was pitched against the wall. At the front, farther down on the pier, a waitress walked between tables with a coffeepot. Her thongs flapped loudly on the floor.

We took a table next to the window. There was one surfer, far away. "He shouldn't be out there all alone," my mother said. "Do you see another one? They're always supposed to have a buddy."

The waitress came to give us coffee. She didn't ask, she just slapped two mugs down and filled them. The skin on her face seemed tight and her toes looked old with wrinkles. But her hair was bleached white and her legs and arms were downy. She probably wasn't much older than I was. Her name, on a plastic pin, was Dawn.

"Isn't this great being up early? It's just seven now. We're not usually even up yet. Look at that. Did you see that wave? Absolutely amazing."

We ordered huge, sloppy omelettes that came with herbed potatoes and raisin wheat bread.

"We'll get a good breakfast and start the day with protein," my mother said. After one date, we already felt richer.

"So, when are you going to see him again?"

"Next Saturday night. He's going to take me to the opera." My mother sighed. "I'm going to need clothes for all this." She started biting her hand. She did that when she was nervous. It made her look terrible.

We felt rich for about as long as it took us to eat our food. Then the dread came back. All we'd have to do. Our plates lay almost empty; only crusts and the rind of a pineapple slice. It would be light in Dr. Spritzer's apartment now. He would be up, moving around. Loose.

"I'm going to have to have clothes and get my nails done. Let me tell you, Ann, there are plenty of women who'd give an arm and a leg to go out with this man. And they can spend all day in the beauty parlor with the manicures and the hairdressers and the leg waxes. And I just can't."

"But he liked you."

"I know. But let's face it. He saw me in my best thing. The green. And that's really all I have that's new."

"I need clothes, too."

"Oh, no, Honey. You really don't. You're just a child. Remember, I'm the one who has to catch us a man."

"I'm almost fifteen."

"I know you are, but believe me, I'm the one who has to find you a father—you really don't need clothes now. When you really need them is in college. You're not going to marry any of these boys you know now. They don't really get serious about you until college. And don't worry, because by then, you'll have the clothes and a great big house to bring your kids home to. I think we will by then, Ann. I really do."

She stared down at her plate and dutifully ate her crusts.

I looked around the restaurant. Then I saw three girls from my school, their black flippers on the floor next to their feet, their hair wet and combed. I panicked. It felt like my mother at Baskin-Robbins. I didn't want them to see me. They sat across from each other, talking and sipping coffee. I wanted to leave.

"There's some kids from school behind you. But please don't look now," I whispered. Now I hated the clothes I had on.

My mother immediately turned. "Where?"

"Over there, but would you please—"

"Well go say hi to them. Go on, I'll pay the check and you go over and say hi. Go on. You look real cute."

"I don't want them to see me."

"Don't be silly. Go on. You know what it is, it's your insecurity. And you shouldn't be insecure. You look darling. Really."

For a second, my eyes lifted, and at that moment, one of them saw me.

"Hi," she mouthed. "Come on over."

"They see me," I said in a low voice.

"Well, I'll pay the bill, you go on."

While my mother walked to the cash register, I skipped up the two steps to where they were. They pulled over a chair for me. One of them got up and took a cup from the waitress's station and poured me coffee. They moved quickly and easily, rearranging themselves and changing like the waves outside.

Huge breakfasts lay in front of them on the table. They each had omelettes with potatoes. There was a bowl of fruit and yogurt and a large plate of thick french toast with powdered sugar in the middle. They had a side order of ham. I felt hungry again. They must have seen me looking.

"Surfing makes you eat a lot," Leslie said. "We've been here since five."

"They got me out that early."

"Feels good when you're in though."

Windows surrounded the table and the light played now from here, now from over there. They were girls I knew from school, smart girls, who sat near the front of the class and asked questions.

"I better go, I think my mom's ready to leave." She stood by the cash register holding her closed purse in front of her. When I looked at her, she smiled.

"That's your mom? She's a fox."

"You guys surf?"

"Leslie surfs. We swim. It just feels good to be out in the morning. What are you doing here? Having breakfast with your mom? You do that a lot?"

"No, she had a big date last night, her first big date in California. So she woke me up and we came here so she could tell me about it."

Their chins sank on their hands. Their mouths fell loose. They leaned forward on the table.

"She *tells* you?"

I nodded. "We're pretty close."

"Did it go all right?" Leslie whispered. "The date?"

"So far. But you never know. They're so innocent." I turned and looked at my mother. "You could break her heart with a blow dryer—you guys don't want this food?"

"You hungry? Here. We'll order more. Isabelle's got her dad's credit card."

"Do you think she slept with him?"

I nodded. "She did."

Susan gasped, then caught herself. "Today's assembly, you know. We don't have to be there for first section. Until ten. We could give you a ride if you want."

"Yeah. Stay with us."

They picked at their food carelessly.

I walked down to my mother. She smiled at me. For once, it was me who touched her arm.

"See, that wasn't so bad, was it? You looked like you were all having fun up there. I was just watching you. Real cute girls. We'll do something with them once maybe. I'll take you kids out to dinner or a movie."

My mother was walking to the door, as if we were leaving. I followed a little back, trying to slow her. Finally, we were there at the door. She opened it.

"Come on, Pooh."

I shrugged. "There's an assembly today, we can come late, so I'll stay here with them and they'll give me a ride."

My mother's mouth twitched, then remade itself, but differently. "How can those kids drive? They're only fourteen."

"Susan's a junior. She has her license. She got a car for her birthday."

My mother ran her espadrille on the sand. She was outside already.

"I don't know if I want you going back in that car with them. We don't know how she drives, anything. You could be dead." She shook her head. "I'll worry all day. Why don't I just drive you and we'll take them out some other time. I could even bring the bunch of you here to the beach. Some Saturday or Sunday. You kids can lie in the sun. I'll bring a book and go sit by myself a little so you kids can talk alone."

"If you drop me off now, I won't have anything to do until ten."

"You could study in the library. Get ahead with your work."

"I want to stay," I said.

"Oh, okay," she said. "Well, have a good time." She looked enviously back at the restaurant. "I have to get going or I'll be late. You make sure she drives carefully. Okay, promise me that."

"I will."

She walked a few steps then turned back. "Wear your seat belt."

I'd never worn a seat belt in my life. My mother and I never used them. "Okay," I said.

I stood at the door watching her. When I turned back towards the table, I couldn't help thinking of how she was walking alone, all that way back to where our car was.

Carol

9

Happiness and Accidents

When I look at those old pictures I hauled out for you, I see things I didn't see at the time. Mostly Hal, I guess. How unhappy he was. He's always got some goofy expression, holding his fingers up, rabbit ears over your head or making a face. Never anything just sincere or natural. Never a smile. I suppose Hal had it hard. Jimmy traveled three, four days a week those years, when Hal was growing up. He went on the road selling water softeners. Jimmy was Northeastern Regional #1 for Aqua-Max. And even just Brown County is a lot of little towns. I knew his route by heart in those days and I used to keep a little patch from the Wisconsin map torn off and taped up by the telephone. I put pins in it, so Hal would always know where his father was.

Benny was just happier, you can see it, in all the pictures, he's got that grin. That just looks like Benny to me. There he is in his costume by the boat. He was ring bearer for Brozek's wedding. You know, we did a lot, we really did things, when the boys were young. We had the boat and the snowmobile, and then for a long time we went up to the trailer.

We went to Disneyland, the four of us, we drove out in the mobile home. That was the first trailer and it wasn't a big one, but we had fun in it. It had bunk beds where they each slept and a kitchenette. We saw a lot that way, driving. Didn't you go to Disneyland too once with your mom and dad? I thought you and your mom flew out there. She was like that, whatever we did, you had to do, but better. So, if we drove the trailer out, you flew. But it was the same Disneyland we saw once we got there.

We traveled a lot then because Jimmy won trips as bonuses. And did he ever sell the water softeners! That was a good time for us and we liked the water softener people. They had fun. When you went somewhere, like a convention with them, they partied. We'd go out. These people with the Rug Doctor are all Jehovah's Witnesses. And they really sort of stick together. They come with their families, they bring the kids along to everything. And they don't drink or dance, so there's not much you can really do with them. They're nice and all during the lectures and the meetings, but then, after, in the evenings, they don't really socialize with you if you're not one of them.

And you, too, look at you. You're real happy in those old pictures. You can tell you and Benny are friends, even though you're not looking at each other—you're each holding up your toys, he's got his roller skate hanging down and his drum, you've got your deer. And all those packages behind you. Your mom always went overboard at Christmas. I think we still have that dollhouse somewhere in the basement. But look at your eyes and mouth. You look so grateful, like you're almost going to cry. I remember how you were. You and Benny had a good period when you were little, lot of people don't even have that.

I think you did change after your dad left, you and your mom both. Or who knows, maybe it was just getting older and going to school. You seemed quieter. I think you always studied a lot. But you didn't have that smile with the open eyes that you had when you were real small. When you were small, you always looked so grateful, nothing like your mom. I think Benny always kept that, but then Benny had it easier.

I worried about you. We felt bad for you with your mother. We thought you'd be the one to have it hard.

I remember once you wanted to go to school with Benny. He was in kindergarten then, not even real school, and I wrote a note and so you went. And Ann, you loved it, you just always liked school. You wanted to go again, and you went once or twice more. Then they were having a field trip. They were going to go on a bus to see Hansen's Dairy. The teacher sent a note home, the parents had to sign permission, a few days before. Oh crumps, all those years of notes and permission forms, every time you're absent, you have to have an excuse when you're sick to get out of gym. They really are hard on kids. Harder than needs be.

Well, I wrote your name in, too, and signed it, but when you came off the school bus that day, you and Benny both had notes pinned to your sleeves from the teacher. You weren't a five-year-old, she said, you weren't in the class, no, you couldn't come, you'd have to wait until next year. Now that seems mean, doesn't it? I don't know, maybe she had enough in her class already. But you wouldn't think one more would be any trouble. They had those ropes with the loops on them and you kids would each put your hands in one loop and go like that, roped together, when they took you across the street. It looked pretty in spring, when all the girls wore their nice summer dresses. I suppose they took those ropes along on field trips. So they never had to worry about losing you.

I remember telling you that, that you couldn't go to the dairy. You had to stay home. You were just mortified. I said it real fast, I didn't think it would be such a big deal, I was probably doing something else, unloading groceries, who knows what anymore. Well, your chin puckered up and wobbled, I could see you just trying your hardest not to cry and you didn't, not that I saw. You walked out of the screen door, with your hands real stiff by your sides and your head high. Your mother probably taught you that.

But with all your mother's messes, you turned out okay. Our kids were the ones who had the trouble. I will say this, your mom was right about one thing: education.

We didn't put as much stress on school. Hal had good marks all through grade school and the highest in his class on the Iowa Basics. I always thought that was why Adele liked him; she figured they were two of a kind, both smart in this family of averages. Benny always came home with Cs. I tried to help Ben with his schoolwork, but Jimmy didn't care too much. After work, he'd take Ben outside and toss a football until it was time for supper. He thought they should learn more outdoor things. Sports. I suppose that's normal with boys.

I sometimes wish I had a daughter. I would have liked that, I think. You know, going shopping and just talking, the things you do with a girl. You were a little like a daughter when you lived here.

I remember once you had a part in the school play. You were going to be Mary. I guess it must have been the Christmas pageant. I don't know anymore, but it was something they had in the auditorium and they invited all the parents and the grandmas. The mothers were supposed to make the costumes. So your mom was going to send you in your summer sandals and this long muslin robe, just a beige thing, like a bedspread or a curtain really, that your dad left in a closet. It was from where he came from. She didn't make a veil or anything. That was going to be it.

"For Mary?" I said to your mom. "For a boy, maybe, one of the shepherds, but not for Mary."

She always had an answer for you. "Well," she said, "that's what they wear over there, in Jerusalem. That's where it happened, you know."

You couldn't say a thing to that, because she'd been there and I hadn't. That much at least was true. But this was Saint Phillip's in Bay City, Wisconsin, and I *had* been here plenty. I don't care what they wear over there in Egypt, I knew they didn't wear that *here* when they were Mary in the Christmas play. So I bought some nice thick velvet, a remnant, it was a beautiful color with your hair, a deep, rich blue, and I sewed you a gown. She didn't mind, she just shrugged and let me do it. And we made you a white veil and a thing around your neck out of a starched sheet. You looked real nice. Your mom went and clapped and all, but here you were Mary and she seemed distracted. After, she came up and pulled on your collar. "You look like a little pilgrim," she said.

But she was funny because the next year you were an angel and she made a tremendous costume for that. I remember because she did it in Gram's garage and she got that gold glittery paint all over everything. On the lawn mower and the wheelbarrows. Gram said she never had been able to get it off the floor. The cement is still gold under the car.

"And how many people get to drive in on a yellow brick road," your mom used to say. She got it from that Lolly. I didn't think it was so funny. I saw Gram's point.

One of those Griling girls was an angel with you, and your mom made a costume for her, too. Your mom took sheets and old white gloves and your tennies. Each of you had to give a pair of your old tennies. Then she bought big pieces of tagboard and she cut out wings. She untwisted coat hangers and made you each haloes that stuck way up over your heads.

She laid it all out on the garage floor once when Gram was at church and she spray-painted it all with gold. You can still see the angel shape from the cement that's not gold on the floor.

Well, it did look good, just great. You two were the best angels Saint Phillip's had ever seen. I think they even gave you some extra lines to say—I suppose they couldn't have such well-dressed angels just stand there doing nothing. You read real well, nice and clear, even then in the second or third grade.

And after the pageant, the Griling girl came running up to us, crying. I think it was Theresa. They'd gotten Bub Griling to come, the older sister brought him, she was the only one that had any sway, they said she looked like the mother.

Theresa was so proud, here she was in a play and with a nice costume like that and he came, drunk. He went up to the stage practically in the middle of the whole thing and shouted, "Now what did you do to your shoes?"

They had to lead him out, the sisters. I remember the oldest, the pretty one, with that wavy blond hair, she was wearing red shoes. He was yelling, oh you can imagine how Theresa felt on her big day, her family all leaving by the side door because her sisters had to take her father home. And I'll tell you, Ann, he stank.

So Theresa stood by us afterwards, when all the kids went with their own families. And she was heaving and crying because he'd said she'd have to go barefoot the next summer because he wasn't going to buy new ones just because she'd gone and ruined her shoes. Or she could wear them gold, he'd said. He was drunk.

So she tugged at your mom, asking, Will it come out? Could she get it off somehow? Oh, those kids were pushy, but I guess they had to be. He never took care of them and their noses were always running, they looked dirty. You know, you tried to be nice to them, but you finally think, Gee, he doesn't do a thing for them and they're his kids, heck, why should I?

Well, it was the last day of your school before vacation and the assembly was over early and they just let you go. So your mom and I took you and Theresa and Ben down to Shaefer's and bought you all new sneakers for the spring. We told Mr. Shaefer to give them to you each big so your feet could grow a little. It was snowing outside downtown and they put the streetlamps on early, it was a dark, wet day, and we were the only ones in the store. You three walked around the carpet in your new, white tennis shoes. You'd think it was the most exciting thing you'd ever had. You walked so delicately, as if you were stepping on the moon. That was what was nice about little kids. It didn't take much to please you then. Keds sneakers and oh, then you were all set.

You wanted to wear them outside, but we didn't let you—they would have been ruined in that slush. Mr. Shaefer wrapped them up nice, you each got your own shoe box to carry. Your mom insisted she pay for all the tennies and she stood up at the counter, giving him her check.

Theresa wanted to keep her gold shoes. I don't know what she ever did with them, threw them out probably, when she got home. They shed those gold sparkles all over wherever you stepped.

Later on, Mr. Shaefer called, her check bounced and I had to pay it. I never told Jimmy, he would have been mad. He called there at Mom's house first and it was just lucky no one was home and then he called me. So I drove down and gave him the cash that same afternoon. He was real nice about it, quiet. He gave me back the check and I folded it in my purse. I never did tell Adele. I talked to Mr. Shaefer a little while by the counter. He had people in the store that day, trying shoes on their kids. It was right after Christmas, I remember.

I only had a few times I was close with Adele, the way you and Benny were fifteen years. Once, really, that I remember, and that was when we were already grown. I sure remember fighting with her. That's most of what comes to mind.

But once my parents sent us both off to Mackinac Island for a holiday, just the two of us, alone. I think Milton wired the money and said to buy something for the girls. He always thought of us like that, as real little girls, even when we were grown. And we had just a wonderful time there. Your mom was already in college, she was going back for her sophomore year and I already had Hal. We took him with us, in a stroller. And he was good. He was an easy baby. Benny always tried to climb out of things, he hardly ever slept. But you could take Hal anywhere. So I never really felt hampered.

We went up on a Friday and you go from the train to a ferry and then over there on the island they don't have any cars. Just horses and buggies. Apparently, the people did own cars, it wasn't that backwards, they just figured out it was a better tourist spot with the buggies. So they passed a town ordinance banning the cars. Can you imagine! What they won't do to make the money. I think maybe they could have cars in the winter, when the tourists went home, but in summer, when we were there, you didn't see a one.

All the roads were that nice old-fashioned brick. We stayed in the Grand Hotel—there was the one big hotel in the center of everything, with pillars and long white steps going up to it. Oh, Ann, I think they were marble. And the horses and buggies would line up in front. It was real swishy. We came on a Friday night and we got all dressed up in our room, and I mean dressed up, we wore long white gloves that buttoned and gowns when we walked down those stairs. Oh, such stuff we had. Those gloves are probably still in the basement, but where would you ever wear gloves?

We did all kinds of things that week. We walked around, we shopped. Lake Michigan was too cold to swim already, it was Labor Day, the end of the season, just before the summer stuff really closed up. But we'd go and walk along the beach.

I remember one morning I woke up real early. It was the Wednesday, I think, we were taking the ferry home the next evening. Well, Adele always slept in, you didn't want to talk to her until noon, but I was used to getting up early from having a baby. They don't let you sleep. So I dressed real quiet and I dressed him and we took a walk. I left a note for Adele at the desk, to meet me for lunch. There was sort of a special bakery we liked and this was going to be their last day open. Most of the summer people had already left.

It must have been eight or nine in the morning. I pushed Hal in the stroller and we came to this painter by the side of the road, painting the woods. I recognized her because she worked at night in the lobby of the Grand Hotel, drawing portraits in oil pastels. I knew because Adele had had herself drawn in her long gown and gloves. Hal and I had been standing, waiting for her. I'd shookled him, rocking, saying, "See, oh, look, see she's drawing a picture of your Auntie Adele."

The artist was dressed differently now, she just had on pants and a shirt, and a cap, I suppose for the sun. I recognized her but I wouldn't have said anything because I didn't want to be a bother, but she said hello and put down her brush. She had her whole easel and palette set up there. It was really something to see, the spot she was looking at and then the way she'd painted it with her colors. Those silvery birches. It was really something. She had a thermos of coffee and we passed the metal cup between us. I rocked the stroller a little with my foot, to keep Hal quiet.

She said this was what she considered her real work, this outside-painting. She painted the water on the beach, too. I thought that would be hard, don't you think? Because it's always moving. It never keeps still. And she said yes, it was hard, she said she had to look a long time at it.

She did the drawings in the hotel to make her living. She wasn't married or anything and she lived here on the island all year long. She said she painted outside every day she could, when the weather was nice, the summer and fall. Then in winter, she stayed in a garage and made bigger pictures from the ones she'd done all summer. She said every year she felt so glad when it was spring. In summer, sometimes after her work in the hotel, she painted at night, too, by the moonlight. She said she took the ferry over to Traverse City and painted tents at the county fair.

"Tents are so beautiful," she said. I never forgot that. Because they are pretty, but it's not just something you'd think of.

She was short, but you could see she wasn't real young. She must have been about my age and she had a real soft way about her. I remember thinking that she might never marry. And here I was with my baby, you know, and I thought, What a wonderful life. She seemed so independent.

She asked if I'd like her to keep Hal there awhile so I could walk around by myself or take her bike and ride a little. And I said, Okay, sure, why not. I had another sip of her coffee. We finished off the cup and I went and rode on her old black bike. Now when I think of it, that was selfish of me, using up her free time and taking her bike and her coffee, but then with a baby I felt so glad when somebody offered a favor. And I expected other people to ask me things, too. That's the way it was with young mothers.

And it was so nice riding. I was the only one on that road, a nice, wide, blacktopped road with a bright yellow line like chalk down the center, and sumac on both sides. I had on a short-sleeved white blouse and a skirt I'd ironed with a little travel iron that morning in the hotel and I felt the air rush up under my arms, so I must have been going pretty fast. I just pedaled, it felt so good, I don't know how long it had been since I'd ridden a bike. Then pretty soon I came to a big lawn for a school—a new, one-story building with all the windows on the same level. I stopped at the curb to tie my shoe. I was the only one anywhere around. It was a still, bright day. And across the street the sumac and the aspen trees and pines looked to me just like they did in her painting.

Then I stared down at my shoe, on the curb. Where the cement ended, there was ordinary dirt. A fringe of such tough grass started an inch or two in. I rubbed that dirt with my foot. And it was all dotted with such scraps, rubbish. Little bits of paper. Just junk. I don't know what it came from, wrappers, beer tops, junk like you saw everywhere. It made me feel awful, like there was no place special, there would always be this dirt. And what I'd seen before, the pretty thin trees and like in her painting, that seemed a small part where all over there was loads and loads of this dumb dirt. Isn't that for the birds, thinking like that on a holiday? I had to make myself lift my eyes up to those trees again.

. . .

That afternoon we met Adele at the bakery we liked and we stayed a long time after lunch. It was their last day. Kids came over from the mainland to work the summer and they were all going home, back to school, I suppose, their regular lives.

Adele had made up a little paper chart and we were figuring out her schedule of courses. She switched back and forth every which way and we went over and over it. It seemed like a game to me. Economics on Wednesday mornings, English from four to six. And people would walk by and look at Hal and I'd take him up out of the stroller. It was the end of the summer and we had suntans. Adele and I were both young.

We sat there for so long we got hungry again. It was outside, in a little area closed off with a wrought-iron railing. We sipped ice water with flowers frozen in the cubes. Those glasses, I don't know what it was, they were thick maybe, they just felt good in your hand. We ordered coffee and blueberry tarts.

The coffee tasted strong and they brought real cream. And those blueberry tarts were delicious. I remember taking mine out of the little wax paper ruffle and slipping it on the plate. They printed the wax paper with gold and they made the tarts with mounds of blueberries under a currant glaze and custard—then a thick layer of chocolate just above the crust. I wish I had the recipe for those. Adele could probably tell you, just from tasting, what was in it, what spices. But she would never remember anymore.

The paper doilies from under the pastry blew onto the brick patio in a little breeze, they were white with gold fluting. They had gray marble tabletops, with dark green iron chairs.

Hal stood up in his stroller blowing soap bubbles. These were really the last few summer days. At the curb under a tent of green leaves, I watched an old man put his hand under his wife's elbow and ask if she wanted an ice cream. They crossed the street in a diagonal, slow, to the cart on the other side. Michigan chills early. They get the Canadian winds.

That chocolate in the blueberry tarts was such a surprise. Oh, they were good. I've meant to try and make them like that a hundred times, but it would be a lot of work. I even bought those little tart pans, I have them here somewhere. I think they put in something special, nuts, I'm sure, and maybe a little lemon in that crust.

People walked past us and some at other tables stood up and left. We just stayed. Behind Adele, a girl who worked there sat with her legs crossed. Their uniforms were red and white, like candy stripers'. She had her hair pulled back off her face in a plain rubber band and she took a long time smoking a cigarette.

Adele would every once in a while bend down and try and teach Hal something. She'd wave her fingers in front of his face to make his eyes move and say This Little Piggy on his toes.

"He's very bright, Carol," she said. "He'll be a bright, bright boy. You'll see. I'll bet he's reading at two or three."

That meant a lot to me from her, but I tried not to show it. Even being sisters, we were shy sometimes.

"So, you think he'll be all right?" I laughed a little. "Smart like you?"

"Smarter." She sighed. "The boys always are. The lucky dogs."

"So you don't think I did too much the wrong thing marrying Jimmy and staying home."

She nodded her head real slowly. Hal stood up in his buggy. We'd bought him that bottle of soap bubbles with the wand. I held his hands, trying to get him to sit down.

"No, I don't think you did the wrong thing, Carol. I think you'll have a good, happy life."

I never forgot that. My chin swelled, I could feel the blood coming there and my lip was doing something funny—I'd had no idea before I cared so much what she thought. I glanced over to see if she was noticing, but she looked away. I suppose she was worried about herself.

"And I think you will, Adele. You've done so much already, at your young age. You'll get your degree, maybe even go to graduate school. I think you're going to have an exciting, exciting life. You'll go places. I know you will."

She smiled at me, but one of her distant smiles. I suppose she thought there was a lot I didn't know. And there was. Plenty I couldn't understand. She hasn't had the easiest time. I suppose even then she must have worried. You could see. A girl that pretty and nervous, beautiful, really, looking all over, scattered, putting on lipstick there at the table.

"Should we go?" she said.

"No, let's stay." For once I acted like the leader. You'd think I always would have been, but even eleven years older, I never was with her. The waiter strolled by and all of a sudden I felt in a festive mood.

"We'd each like another tart," I said. "Two more. And two more cups of your good coffee." That brought us both back to normal. We laughed and laughed. Adele lowered her voice the way she does when she's joking around, trying to be stern, saying, "Carol, you really shouldn't have," but we both wanted more. She slapped her behind. "Why not?" It was our last day of vacation. We were going home tomorrow and then Adele would leave for college. We had plenty of money, extra. We felt like rich girls. And we didn't worry about weight or health or any of that yet either. We were young. And we were both pretty enough the way we were, we knew that. I was married already. That was the least of our worries.

He brought the coffee first in nice china, with pink morning glories painted on the cups. We poured the cream in, it was that old-fashioned heavy cream, almost brownish, and it just swirled and swirled. We watched it a long time, longer than ever needs be. But then we had the time.

For a while everything seemed to be going good with us. Hal really did seem okay, except in school. We had the trailer at Pine Mountain and we went up every weekend skiing. For once, Hal and Jimmy agreed on a sport and Hal could do it. Ted and your mom drove up, too, and stayed in the lodge, we'd always end up there together. You got to be a good little skier, you had your white bunnyfur jacket, remember your mom bought you that? She took a lot of flack for it, believe me. Gram, everybody, thought she would spoil you.

She and Ted and Jimmy and I were all drinking in the lodge bar the night when we found out Hal broke his arm. Your mom and Ted tried to keep apart a little and have their own social group, but they really couldn't. It was small enough so everybody knew everybody. We each sort of liked someone else. I sat on Paul Shea's lap in that cocktail lounge. Jimmy flirted too, with Barbie Shea. That's really as close as we ever got to anything risqué. But we were all there together, so nothing too much could ever happen.

And one of those nights in the bar, they came and told us Hal broke his arm. Safety patrol was up bandaging him on the slope and they'd have to take him to the hospital for a cast. It was that night skiing—I never liked it. It wasn't safe.

So Hal couldn't ski that whole winter he had the cast. We still drove up every weekend, we had a whole social life there by then, and Hal moped around in the trailer. You were a little wizard. You were a real good skier, jumping down those moguls. Well, Ted was good, and he'd taught you. Benny really couldn't keep up and he was always naturally so good at any sport. But I remember him maneuvering his snowplow. You used to dare him onto the tough slopes with you.

One night we were in the lounge and you came in to find your mother because you'd hurt your nose. You kids had been playing on those metal bars for the lines in front of the lift pass windows. You used to twirl on them like monkey bars and I guess you were turning and you just smacked your nose, hard. You had your hand over your face when you ran in.

Of course, your mom got hysterical. "Oh, no, what did you do to yourself? You've ruined your nose."

She held your face to the side and cried, it was ridiculous, we hadn't been near so upset with Hal's broken arm. She was sure your nose was broken and your whole life was down the drain because now you wouldn't grow up to be pretty and no one would want to marry you.

"I TOLD you not to play on those bars," she kept saying.

"You did not." By that time she had you crying, too, she'd convinced you that you'd ruined your chances for a decent life.

Ted and Paul Shea inspected you. They thought it wasn't broken. Ted ordered your mom another drink. She wanted to call an ambulance and take you twenty miles to a hospital. Paul said they didn't do anything for broken noses, anyway, they just had to heal. It's a good thing Ted was there or God knows what she would have done. I told her, too, it probably wasn't anything but a bump, but she didn't listen to me. With your mom, you really had to be a man for her to listen.

She still thinks you broke your nose that night and that's why she wants to get you a nose job. She blames us for not letting her call the ambulance. She begged me, Carol, tell her, tell her *you* did it and tell her how crooked her nose is. She doesn't believe me. Well, it doesn't seem crooked to me. I told her that and she just sighed, ogh, you know, like everyone's against her.

We skied three winters and the year Hal broke his arm was the last time. That March, towards the end of the snow, when we thought there'd be one or, at the most, two more weekends, Hal skied. He knew he wasn't supposed to. The doctor had told him time and time again. He still had the half cast and a sling on that arm. But he had to ski, he had to show he could do it with one arm.

We all saw him at about the same time. Your mom and I were in a chair lift together going down. We went on the high slope where I was scared to ski, but there was a lodge at the top and I'd wanted to go and have hot chocolate. So your mom had talked the lift man into letting us take it up and back again. We were the only ones on the whole lift going down, all the rest were empty chairs. That's one thing your mom is great at, if you ever want to do something that's not allowed, she can talk the person into it. She gets a kick out of it. Behind us, going up, Jimmy sat in another chair with Barbie Shea. Ted was giving a lesson at the top of the mountain, demonstrating the pole. He punched both poles hard into the snow. Across from him a row of skiers copied. First we saw you and Benny, standing where the moguls were way too high for you. They were just a little smaller than you were.

"Oh, my God, look where they are, Carol," your mother said, grabbing my arm. She leaned so far over the chair tilted and swung and we practically fell out.

You seemed to know you were over your heads. You both moved real slow, snowplowing around the moguls, leaning in so your skis were almost horizontal. You looked like you were afraid to look down. You were going first and Benny followed behind you.

"Now, don't yell. Or they'll get scared and then something *will* happen."

"They should take their skis off and walk down. I'm going to tell them to do it. Ann," she shouted. "Ann. Benny."

The chair lift moved pretty quick though. You looked like you heard us but didn't see where we were. All of a sudden, you were staring somewhere else and then we stared too.

There was Hal on an orange stretcher, with his cast on his chest and the other arm out in the snow. Three Red Cross Safety Patrol boys knelt bandaging his leg. We had to keep riding down the chair lift, we couldn't get out. Ted was skiing down to him, neat smooth slalom jumps. He'd left his class, with their poles stuck in the snow, at the top of the mountain. You and Benny looked down and tried to steer towards him, but you could barely move as it was. Then I looked over my shoulder and I saw Jimmy. He was the only one who didn't know. I saw his hat and the back of his head. He was getting ready to jump off the chair lift.

So then Hal had a broken arm and a broken leg and we didn't ski anymore. He really had a hard time of it. That leg was in a cast eight months. He stayed out of school all that spring and I stayed home from the store, too. He mostly read and I'd watch television in the breezeway, but we would eat together. I liked having him home again. Sometimes Gram would walk over and have a cup of coffee with us. She'd bake a cinnamon ring or a blueberry buckle and carry it over warm, covered with a dish towel.

Then when Hal went back to high school, they took his crutches away and kicked him down, those big boys. They could really be mean. And I don't think he ever caught up after the time he missed for the leg. Then when he finally had the cast taken off, he got in with a bad crowd.

When Hal was a freshman he stopped writing his name. At first it just seemed like some stunt a teenager would pull—but he kept to it so darn long. Then pretty soon he didn't write at all—even those tests with the little blue circles you fill in with a pencil, he turned them all back empty.

So they called us, they said specifically that both parents were supposed to come, so Jimmy and I went, one morning, and talked to the principal. They said Hal should see a psychiatrist and they wanted us to both go, too, the psychiatrist wanted the whole family. Now you read about that a lot, but I'd never heard of it then. Well, that was just too much for Jimmy. He banged his fist on the table and said, "No son of mine is going to any psychiatrist. There's nothing the matter with him. The only thing wrong with him is he's stubborn. And he's lazy." Jimmy took the truck and drove back to the water softener store. I apologized for him, but it didn't really do any good. I walked down those halls and the sound of my heels echoed so. But Jimmy's mind was made up. And when he gets like that, it's no use trying to talk to him. What I remember now about that day are those stone hallways and that I was wearing a hat with a feather on it.

He started up with that Merry. We weren't happy, no family would have been, really, I don't think, if it was their son. It wasn't just that she was poor, that wasn't it. But she was dirty. That was really the thing. When Ben went out with Susie, it was a completely different story. We wouldn't have said a thing if he'd decided to marry her. We would have been glad. And her parents weren't rich either. They both worked. But they were nice people. Clean.

But with Merry's family, it really wasn't so good. You know, you hear things. Her mother was gone somewhere, I don't know where, but she wasn't dead. She lived somewhere up north, Escanaba maybe, working as a waitress. And the father drank. I drove by the house once or twice on the way to the cemetery. They lived on Spring Street and their house was one of the worst. It was an old, gray house and all the basement windows were cracked. We heard that Merry had a sister who was sixteen or seventeen that the father had kicked out. She was living on her own, in an apartment above a store, and still going to the high school. Some at church said she was pregnant. So it wasn't all the nicest.

We probably shouldn't have said a thing. Adele used to call us and yell, DON'T tell him not to go out with her, that'll just make him REBEL. Say, Hey, she's a great girl. Have fun!

And then when he graduated, we thought at least he'd go to college and meet other people. You were still here, when Hal finished high school. We were all at the graduation in the gym, when he was number 563 in his class. Merry wasn't going to college. She was going to stay at home and work in a shop. I think she ended up at McDonald's. Whitewater wasn't much of a school, but we thought he could at least get on his feet there. If he applied himself for a year he could transfer to the University of Wisconsin. But he drove back home almost every weekend and partied with the kids from high school. And that was all during Vietnam. So lots of them were signing up. Their parents couldn't pay for college, so they went in and then when they came back, they had the GI Bill. Griling's boy and all those Brozeks went into the service right after high school. Most all the kids around here signed up—the kids you and Benny played with, too. But see by then there wasn't a war.

Well, in April or May, Hal came home and said he wanted to drop out. After Gram's already paid for the whole semester. We tried to talk him out of it, we all did, Adele came over and talked to him for hours about college education, college education.

"So where did a college education get you?" he said. "It got you married to a college professor who left you with a kid to raise by yourself."

Now God forbid if I said that, but when he did, she laughed.

We found out then, too, that he was flunking—Adele got that out of him, he didn't say that to us, so that pretty much had to be the end of it. So we thought, he could come home and work for a year or two and when he'd grown up a little he'd miss the fun of school and then he could go again and maybe apply himself more.

Then he let out the real bombshell. He wanted to get married to Merry. They were in a hurry. Well, that was almost worse than dropping out. That was permanent. Oh, did we fight. We did everything we could to talk them out of it. And for once we all agreed—your mom and I and Jimmy all thought it would be just dumb for him to marry her so young.

Gram didn't like her either, but she wouldn't say anything. She said he was hearing enough bad from all of us, she could just keep her mouth shut. But she hoped too that we could talk him out of it. "At least wait," she used to say when I'd complain to her. I went over lots during that time and had coffee with her in the middle of the day. Hal was at the store, helping Jimmy. Jimmy thought if he wasn't going to be in school and if he wanted to get married too yet, he'd better learn to earn his keep. And I think Jimmy worked him hard. Every morning, they were yelling and fighting before they even left the house. Oh, it wasn't nice. It was really awful. Benny got real quiet. I suppose he didn't know what to do, he liked his brother and he liked his dad, so he'd get up real early and I'd fix him breakfast before they were dressed. He sort of snuck around, he was afraid to get caught in someone's way.

So I tried to be extra nice to Ben. I'd be up early, anyway. I really couldn't sleep, so I'd get myself up and make a cup of coffee and pretty soon Benny'd come down to the kitchen, all dressed with his books ready. I'd fix him cinnamon toast or an egg and he'd eat it real fast and gulp his milk and then he walked over to Gram's. And Gram would feed him a second breakfast. He had such an appetite and he always stayed thin. It would just be a boy to have those long legs.

We all went over there to her house when it got rough. I'd go in the middle of the morning to have some peace. Jimmy and Hal called me to complain about the other one during the day. Jimmy called from his office and Hal called from a pay phone, but if I didn't answer, they hung up. They wouldn't call me at Gram's. And Gram would fix a pot of coffee and we'd eat a little something. She had her house so nice, she had the two bird feeders hanging, one outside each of the kitchen windows. And every once in a while when we were talking a bird would come. We'd stop and watch.

I told her about how dirty Merry was. You'd think if you were going to meet the parents of the boy you wanted to marry, you'd at least wash your hands, wouldn't you? Even if she wasn't going to take a bath. Her finger-nails were so dirty, I can't tell you. There was a black line under each one. And I told Gram that the once I'd gone over to her house with Hal, there were dishes in the sink, and in the drawers, when she went to get a sweater, I saw everything mixed up, scrambled like in a washing machine.

Gram's teeth rubbed together the way they did when she was nervous. She told me old Tinta Griling, Bub's mother, was like that. She kept her clothes in the drawers rolled up in little balls.

Well, your mom drove over with Ted and talked to Hal. That didn't work. Finally, we had everybody together. We had the priest from Saint Phillip's, your mother, you and Benny were back playing in Benny's room.

Jimmy and I had practically given up. We'd tried everything. They were lots calmer than we were. She sat there on the couch with her short, funny hair and her dirty nails and just acted polite. Can you imagine sitting in your fiancé's house with the parents and everyone telling you they think you're too young? But she wasn't the least bit affected. No, they both said the same thing, they were in love and they wanted to get married.

"So how do you think you're gonna make a living?" Jimmy must have yelled that ten, fifteen times.

And Hal just said he was ready to work, he'd go out and find a job. Merry had been working now a year already. We could see the priest grad-ually coming around to their side. And we couldn't really stop them. They were both of age. They didn't need our permission.

But Adele wasn't going to let it drop. She always thought Hal was like her and she wanted him to go to college and really make something of his life. I suppose we'd already given up on some of that. I couldn't picture him going back to school, really. He hadn't been paying attention most of high school. He'd have so much to catch up. And then we didn't go to college either.

Jimmy and I sat with the priest in the kitchen, I fixed coffee, Jimmy stood looking out the glass doors to the backyard. He was on his second vodka gimlet. We were exhausted. Adele was talking to them in the breezeway. We could hear her, her voice was still energetic after all this time. She seemed so young to me, always.

"So, tell me why, really, you have to get married. Why can't you just keep dating? What's really the big deal?"

"Say we want to go to bed together."

I put my hand over my mouth. That was our Hal. I'm sure the priest heard, but he didn't move, he stared down at his coffee mug. It was still empty. Right away, I poured. Then, for sure he heard the next thing my sister said. When she gets excited, her voice is like a bell.

"So why don't you just go to bed together? Let's face it. It's 1968 and people go to bed together before they're married. Plenty of people. You know that. So why the charade? Go on and go to bed together. Take a roll in the hay."

My sister. With a priest in the house. I said, "Oh, crumps, you never know with her." I thought I had to say something. Jimmy turned from the window, slow and grinning, looking at the priest. I think we were both waiting to see if the priest would say anything.

"Leave it to Adele. She's not shy." Jimmy's grin got bigger. "I say she's right, let 'em go ahead. I wouldn't say the same if it was my daughter. But she's not my daughter."

"Oh, sure, and just wait then till she gets pregnant. That'd be real nice, sure."

The priest looked up at the wall telephone. "Let's hear what they say."

"It's a sin," Merry said.

"We want to be okay in the church." That was our Hal.

"Oh, come on, the church looks the other way. Don't you think plenty of people at Saint Phillip's are going to bed together? Why, sure they are. You should hear the half of it. And the church'll change its mind. A few years ago we couldn't eat meat on Friday, now we go to McDonald's. That's no reason to get married."

She went on and on, long after we stopped. She wanted to write Hal recommendations to the University of Wisconsin, Madison, where he hadn't a chance of getting in. She ran all around town, she lined up an appointment for him to go to a psychiatrist. I don't remember anymore what all she did. She did try to help him. But he wasn't going to listen to anyone. We all said we wouldn't go to the wedding if they had one and so they took the bus up to Escanaba one weekend and got married there.

Jimmy went around saying they were living in sin because they weren't married in the state of Wisconsin, but six months or so later, it wasn't long, when she was pregnant, they had another wedding in the backyard and Gram baked a cake and we all went. So that was the end of it. Hal was working at Fort Adams paper mill then, she was still at McDonald's and they had a trailer over by the airport in that lot the Indians own. Those Indians want to put up a hotel there now. Yah! That's their land, they say. Can you imagine?

And then Hal had to go into the service. It was really one thing after the other. He never had any luck. He ended up enlisting because his lottery number was fifty or sixty something—high up. It was 1969 and he knew five or six boys who'd been killed already. He thought in the air force he had a better chance of staying here and fixing engines or something. Jet mechanic. I don't know, maybe he thought being married would help. It didn't, I don't think. He thought he'd like the air force better than the army or the marines. A lot of his friends from high school were already in. Lot of Bay City boys fought in Vietnam.

Hal had to go to boot camp with Merry still pregnant and that seemed real sad. We thought he wouldn't even see the baby or only once or twice, before he left. Adele had a fit again, oh ye gods, she was on the phone with us every day with a scheme. First she wanted to get some kind of student deferment, then she heard somewhere that you could get out of it if you had them put braces on your teeth, she thought of everything.

But we didn't know if it would even be such a bad thing for him to be in the service. Jimmy thought it might make him grow up. I didn't really know, one way or the other, but he was out of the house and I thought it wasn't our business anymore, so I didn't interfere. But this time Hal went along with Adele. He wanted to get out too. They tried the whiplash and the flat feet and the allergies, and whatever else they could say, but it didn't work. He had to go in.

And after all that fuss, he was only gone nine weeks. He went to the Lackland Air Force Base in Texas at the beginning of the summer. And I guess the boots there didn't fit him quite right. Hal was always flat-footed. I've read now that that could have been helped some if we'd gotten a certain kind of shoe with metal arches when he was little, but we didn't know about that then. Your mom read up on such stuff. So you and Benny had good shoes, Stride Rites, all the most expensive. But then Shaefer said your arches got ruined anyway with some red pumps, real fashionable, that your mother bought you in Milwaukee. So, she might as well have let you wear shoes from K-Mart. The ones from Milwaukee were just as bad.

I guess in Texas they were all marching along in some field. He was overweight then. And they shaved his long hair off right away and put him in something called Motivation. They made them march and march. He lost fifty pounds in that nine weeks. Hal with his flat feet in boots that didn't fit him right and pretty soon he tripped over a pothole and I think he even bumped his head with the rifle. So he wasn't there a week even, and we got a telegram that he was in the hospital, he'd torn a ligament in his leg. And then I guess they let him out and made him march again too soon, before he was really better and so the leg got worse and he fell again, from walking on that bad leg, and that time he slipped a disk, too. And so there he was in the hospital again. He was in for a week or two and then they had him out marching. Every time the leg got worse. They were doing something wrong or maybe just making him march too soon before it was healed, but he said at night his leg would swell up over the knee, as big as a basketball. Finally, the doctors said they wanted to operate on the leg—that was the same leg he'd broken skiing—and he said no, he wasn't going to let them. Well, we wouldn't give permission either, not with what happened to Granny, so he stayed in the hospital there and then they finally let him out. He got honorable discharge, medical deferment. They decided he was costing them too much money.

I often wondered if Hal didn't feel bad about being home. I'll tell you, I was glad, and Gram, too. Jimmy was a little ashamed, he didn't say it, but I knew. I hope to God Hal couldn't tell anything. But with Jimmy it was that he'd been in the war and that he'd always tried to get Hal going with a sport all his life, and it just never took. Hal probably should have been the bookworm type, but he got off on the wrong track with that, too. We didn't talk about it once he was home, but I know there were people who probably teased him, because all around here I could tell from the way they asked that they didn't respect us for it. We told them it was honorable discharge, but they still thought less of us. Chummy had two over there, one in the army, one in the marines. And Bub and Chummy had high school boys planning to sign up right away when they graduated.

You and your mom were gone before our real trouble started. We were worried about you still, thinking you'd be all alone with her in California.

I thought maybe that was where Hal got started with the drugs, down in Texas. You read so much now about the soldiers getting hooked on dope. Lot of them got killed because they were over there high on drugs. The Vietnamese wasn't high, so he shot our boys first. Sure. And now all those little Vietnamese we were fighting against are here in Bay City getting money from the government.

But Hal says they were already in the drugs before he left. We didn't see, we just heard about it later. That's the worst part of being a parent. All the dangerous, important things happen to your children without you. You hear about them later, too late. Apparently, he and Merry were in it together. No, it wasn't just the marijuana. We didn't know anything about it. He had his hair long and wore those dirty jeans, but then they all looked like that. And we didn't go visit the trailer. For one thing, she never invited us, for dinner or a housewarming or anything, so we saw them when Gram had something doing and we all went over there. On Christmas and Easter, we did something. Either at our house or we'd take everybody out. After you and your mom left, there wasn't much of a family.

I'd seen the trailer once or twice. I always told Merry I'd baby-sit for Tina when she was busy and a few times she called and said could I come pick her up. Merry had a job at the canning factory then and that is hard work. They all say it. Hal was on at the paper mill. I think she had a shift so she was working most evenings, too. I was glad to take Tina. I was glad to get her out of there. The trailer was truly filthy. I don't think she ever cleaned. There were candles burnt halfway down on the table and they'd just let the wax go right into the wood. And anywhere you'd step there were clothes all over the floor. I bet they just picked their clothes up off the floor in the morning and put them on.

Now Hal says all that time they were in the drugs, so that explains a lot of it. Things got real bad. Hal said sometimes they'd each go out to bars separately, he and Merry, and leave Tina next door with the neighbor. Oh, that still makes me mad. We would have gladly taken her. We would have loved to and I hate to think who those neighbors were, I saw them once, they were no better than Hal and Merry. The husband had such long wavy hair and those tiny little glasses they used to wear on the bottom of his nose. It still makes me mad to think of it.

But he said they'd each find somebody else at one of those bars and bring them home to the trailer. He said whichever got there first, that one got the bed. And the other couple had the couch. So it wasn't good. And who knows when they remembered to go next door and get Tina—then, in the middle of the night, or in the morning with four people milling around that little trailer. He says when she was still in diapers, just learning to talk, Tina knew the word peyote. I guess they had to tell her when they took her over here or to Gram's just what she could and couldn't say. I asked him lot of times if he gave her anything to take and he says no, but I wouldn't be surprised. Or if Merry did during the day to keep her quiet, while she was tired, from the night shift. They say Bub Griling's mother used to give Bub whiskey when he was a baby to make him sleep. But Tina's all right, she's a smart girl and a good girl, so I guess that's the main thing, whatever happened.

We didn't find out until everyone did. You were lucky you weren't here then. It was all over. Election year and the drugs had been coming in and the kids with the long hair, the hippies, and people got fed up. People had had enough and they wanted to crack down. And wouldn't you know, Hal was the one who got caught.

He says now he was set up and I believe him. But he admits that he was breaking the law. He was taking the drugs and he was selling them. He says they were in it for the money. He thought he could make money fast. And sure, look what happened. But he always had to have a scheme to get rich quick. He couldn't just wait and save like everybody else.

We saw it on TV at the store. It was the whole front page of the *Press Gazette* that night and the big story on the local news. FOUR BAY CITY BOYS ARRESTED IN DRUG TRAFFIC. Hal says one of the people who gave the drugs to him was caught for something else, assault with a deadly weapon, and so they really had him, and he was the one who told.

Gram was down in her kitchen, playing solitaire, and she heard it on the radio and she had the stroke. That was her first stroke. We found her right away because Jimmy drove over from the store to tell her, we were scared she'd see it on the television. Really, that was one of the worst things of my life, seeing Hal on the television. Jimmy said he thought the same thing. We recognized him and we heard it and we just couldn't fit it all together. We were really in a daze then.

Jimmy found Gram leaning over unconscious against the counter with the radio still on. I guess she stood up and went closer to the radio, probably thinking the same thing, Could this really be our Hal? But they gave the address and all. Hal Measey of Oneida Parkway, son of James and Carol Measey, Rural Route #1, Lime Kiln Road.

So we had my mom in the hospital, we didn't know if she was going to make it, we had Hal in jail with a twenty-thousand-dollar bail. And we had to get a lawyer. Well, we mortgaged the house. We did it that same day. Jimmy and I went home, it was three o'clock, we'd left Gram in the hospital, we'd locked the shop, and Jimmy called Shea on the phone. When he got off he looked at me and said, "Carol, we're going to have to mortgage the house. That's the only way we can get that kind of money." I said, "Okay, Jimmy," and we drove downtown to the bank and did it.

By the next day, everyone knew. The women neighbors came over to say they were sorry about Gram and could they help. They didn't say a word about Hal. I'll tell you, they were real funny. And when I think now how long we'd lived there—here we'd been twenty-one years already; they'd known Hal all his life, the way I'd known their kids. It wasn't nice, Ann, it really wasn't nice. They thought we were foolish to put up the house and to this day I think it's the best thing we ever did. That's what turned Hal around, that his father would do that for him.

Later, Hal found out Chummy across the street had called in to the police and said there was something going on over here and so they already had a record of complaints against him. That was when Jimmy and I went away for vacation, from the water softener bonuses. Hal and Merry and Ben would throw a party. Well, I suppose they were a little wild. I never knew because they always had it cleaned up nice by the time I got home. But Hal said he used to see Chummy standing over there at the window, watching, holding his curtain back with one hand. And can you imagine calling in to the police without ever once saying a word to Jimmy when we came home? And I'll tell you, I remember when Chummy was in high school, he was one of those with the hot rods and the fast cars. He was a greaser. You wouldn't know it now, but he went through a period when we were young.

And they all thought we were just crazy to mortgage the house. They said if he skipped town then there we'd be and we wouldn't even have our house. But we didn't think twice, we did it and Hal listened to the lawyer. It was someone who worked with Shea. The other boy in with Hal had the trial and he went to prison. He was in the penitentiary for five years. Hal pleaded guilty—the lawyer said with that judge and a jury and here in Bay City, it just wasn't going to go—but he didn't tell on anybody else. He said he just wouldn't do that because that was the thing that made him get caught. They sentenced him to two years in jail, nights and weekends. He had to check in by seven o'clock and they let him out the next morning to go to work.

And that's when he and Jimmy started to get closer again, because of course, Fort Adams fired Hal when it all came out, and in order to make it so he could leave and work during the day, Jimmy said he'd give him a job at the store. That was around when we were getting out of the water softeners and getting into the pressure cleaners. So Jimmy gave Hal all the soaps. He sold the soaps. And it was a step up for him, I think. He was off the drugs and he had a job again. Merry used to bring Tina in at lunch and they'd sit in the back there and eat. I have to say, she was good. A lot of women would have just let him be, but I suppose she was in on the drugs, too. At least she knew about it. I told them a couple times, I'd give them money so they could go across the street and eat lunch at the Big Boy—he worked so hard all day, he really did—but they didn't want to. They just stayed in that little back room. I suppose they were so down in the dumps they didn't want to see anybody. She'd either pack a lunch or stop at McDonald's and bring them all burgers. So at least he saw Tina every day.

I wasn't at the store too much then because I was taking care of Gram. She came home from the hospital and she wasn't so good. She didn't lose anything, she remembered and she was just like herself, but she shook. She cried more. But that first one wasn't too bad.

And you know, even then, she was just so pretty. You weren't born yet when my dad was alive, but then she was really something. How can I describe her? I don't know, except to tell you that we all knew. It was like a fact of the world and it made a difference. When she came into a room or stepped out onto the porch, you felt special, like something was going on there. And I'll tell you, Ann, I don't know what it is, but we're getting smaller. Granny was a big tall woman with enormous breasts and hips. Her bust was a size D. And Mom was tall too, thin but tall. She was the same size as dad. That's why, when he died, she could just wear his clothes. You know, around the house. And I'll tell you, even in his old overalls that he used to wear out to the mink, she'd be on her knees in the garden, wearing those and an old old shirt and her hair braided and pinned up in the back—and even like that she was beautiful. She was weeding like that once, after the stroke, and the meter reader asked her out on a date. Well, Adele and I were each pretty, I think, but we weren't either of us what you'd really call beautiful. And we are both smaller. I'm five foot four,

she's only an inch or so taller. And even before the mastectomy, I had no
bust, really. And you, you're the shortest yet, smaller than both your parents. And a figure almost like a boy. Maybe that's because your mom
didn't have enough to eat when she was carrying you. I remember they
had you in an incubator. But still your Granny was so tall.

We really weren't friendly with them across the street for a long time. And
then later, we found out when Dicky and Ralph came back from the service—Jay didn't go to Vietnam, the war was over by then, he was too
young—they brought back dope and they got Chummy to try it once
when they were all up north camping. I thought that was something, too.
But I suppose that was the difference those five years made. And who
knows what we would have thought if it had been one of their boys, or
one of Grilings, instead of ours, who was in the trouble?
     Now Hal says he's glad he didn't go to Vietnam. It's the boys who went
who are sorry. He still knows quite a few of them, Brozeks, too, they're
pals now, and he and Merry both knew one who died. And they all say
that none of the ones who went came back the way they were before.

We got through. Even that first stroke of Gram's, it sort of all happened
and we got over it. It wasn't so bad after the shock. We still had plenty of
good times after that. That's when my mom and I got close. That's when
I really got to know her and like her as a friend. We used to take a day and
drive up to Door County and go in all those little stores. Jimmy doesn't
really like to do that. Most men don't. And then we talked more like
sisters. The age difference wasn't so much anymore.
     And Hal changed. He really did. He grew up. He's real thin now, he
runs. I tell him he looks better than he did ten years ago. I was sorry after
all they'd been through together that he and Merry couldn't make a go of
it. And of course, you're always sorry for Tina's sake. But a lot of other
kids are in the same boat, even at Saint Phillip's, and some a lot worse off
than she is. She has two parents who really love her and she knows it. And
they still get along. Merry's real cute now. She works in town at Eche-
verry's. She's got her hair real short. And the way Hal looks at her, I think
he still likes her. But she's got someone else. She remarried. And when
that Bob, he's the new one, was out of work, Hal gave him cleaning jobs
out of the store; he did that until he found something permanent. I see
Merry a couple times a year. She comes when we have a party or to pick
Tina up. And I like her now.
     All those things changed and I was sorry at the time, but I changed
too, and it worked out better than I thought. I had a lot of nice times with
my mother after her first stroke, we still had lot of laughs. Hal used to say
we were terrible parents, oh he said awful mean mean things when we

fought, but he's taken that back. I think he's a real good person now. I'm glad to have him around here. I guess you can forgive just about anything, if you're still nearby, you know.

But with Benny it is just the opposite. It never changed or went away. It's like a stone. It's been years now and it's still there. Now, it's almost like it always was. Some things you never do get over.

Ann

10

Home

Once, a long time ago, we had a home, too. It was a plain white house in the country, with a long driveway, dark hedges rising on either side of it. Years before, my thin grandfather, who wore glasses, a white shirt and suspenders in each of his photographs, had built the wooden house for his family. In the photographs, his mouth is delicate and nervous, framed by deep lines, like his wife's. In summer, they put up green and white striped awnings on all the windows. I can imagine him standing on a clean ladder, my grandmother below in a blue dress, holding the two legs firm, while his white shirt billowed and filled with wind.

My mother and I lived in the house on Lime Kiln Road until I was nine, when she married Ted, the ice skating pro. The years I grew up there, I spent time outside, hidden, where no one could see me, trying to talk to the trees. It seemed then that the land around our house was more than owned, it was the particular place we were meant to be. Sometimes I thought we would stay there forever, that all the sounds of the yard would teach us about the world. But the trees never answered.

My mother had been born there, on an old kitchen table, but she saw it as an ordinary house on a dusty dead-end road off the highway, with a tavern on one side and the Land Bank on the other. It was out of the way, surrounded by unused land. She thought it was chance, bad luck that brought us here. She always meant to move.

For a while though, we rested. We lived with my grandmother.

One afternoon, like so many others, my mother and I lay together on our backs. The room was warm and swimming with light. I propped myself up on an elbow, watching her because I wasn't tired. It took willpower for me to keep still. A smile formed slowly on her face until she was asleep and it seemed as unconscious and without meaning as a dolphin's smile. I knew I shouldn't wake her so I just waited, watching for her to blink her eyes open and remember me again.

Asleep on the white chenille bedspread, her hair fanned out over the pillow, my mother was almost beautiful, prettier than she was the seven or eight times a day she looked in the bathroom mirror. She thought her nose was too long and she wasn't happy with her hair. But asleep, her features settled into a calm order. She had pale skin with freckles on her face and hands and arms and knees. Some of the freckles were much darker than the others, so it seemed you could see through her skin to deeper and deeper layers.

I crept off the bed and tiptoed to my mother's makeup bag on the dresser and stole a brown sharpened pencil to draw freckles on my own arm. It took a long time to make them look real. I wanted to connect the dots on my mother's knee, making pictures, the constellations of the stars, but I was afraid the pressure of the pencil would wake her up.

I was used to waiting. Our life in that house, where the furniture seemed to pin the floors to the ground and dense shafts of sunlight came alive with particles of dust, despite my grandmother's conscientious cleaning, seemed to be a temporary arrangement, like an unscheduled delay in a remote train station, best slept through. My father had never wanted to be there. My mother didn't want to stay either. They thought of it as a place to spend time we would forget about as soon as we left, as if it had never happened. I was the only one who liked it.

And I knew about losing time. Drawing freckles on my arm, I watched the clock on the dresser while my mother slept. I knew if she didn't get up soon, there wouldn't be time to go out and do anything. Then, as my mother's breath stretched and seemed to enter a freer, wider plain of sleep, my grandmother knocked on the door.

"Come now, if you're up. You can come in the kitchen and draw."

I tiptoed out, glancing back at my mother, my head heavy and dizzy from lying down. While my grandmother played solitaire on the kitchen table, I sat on the floor in a rectangle of sun, drawing with my set of sixty-four crayons.

The house stayed quiet except for the hum of the wall clock and the slap and shuffle of my grandmother's cards. I took all my crayons out of the box in direct disobedience of my mother's instructions, to take out one at a time and then put it back. I had a plan for a city, and half of it was already made. I lifted my construction paper from the cupboard. My city had a population of sixty-four and it was somewhere in California. Every family had its own house and yard and every crayon drew its own room. Some of the crayons fell in love. The darkest red was the father of his family, the palest, his youngest child. The Lemon Yellow drew a school bus and was the bus driver every morning. On the side, he grew lemons. Sky Blue painted the sky and filled swimming pools in backyards. Greens worked as landscapers and park builders. They sodded everyone's lawn and planted rows of palm trees on the streets. Shades of gray paved the highways and Yellow Orange painted the divider. Reds made chimneys and grew rose gardens.

I shaved bits from each crayon onto a sheet of wax paper. Today, my city needed a church. The grays made a stone building and I sharpened each crayon to contribute shavings for the windows. The crayons were getting haircuts.

When I had a colored honeycomb of shreds, I folded the wax paper and took it into the other room. I plugged in the iron. My mother's breathing made a high uneven hum. That first year after my father left, she was always resting. Now that I was doing something, I didn't want to wake her. I lay the iron on the wax paper and counted to one hundred. The sheet of paper felt warm and stiff when I lifted the iron. The colors had blurred and become transparent. I carried the paper back to the kitchen floor.

My grandmother looked down at me over her bifocals. "What all have you got there?"

I showed her roads, the school, the parks and the houses. "These are the stained glass windows for my church." I traced the empty arched holes in the building.

Then, when I finished explaining, I stared down at the flecks of color in the linoleum floor. I was embarrassed. I knew I shouldn't have told anyone. This wasn't the way you were supposed to play with crayons.

My grandmother pushed her glasses on closer and looked down at my papers. They were just papers now and a mess of crayons. I scooped up the crayons from their seats on the school bus and started shoving them back in the box.

I turned and asked, "Do you think I'm dumb?"

My grandmother shook her head. "It's good. It shows you have good imagination. I guess you'll turn out smart like your mom and dad."

That moment, relief spread from my chest like a pill finally dissolving. My back was warm. I just sat in the square of sun. I didn't feel like drawing anymore, but I didn't want to move. This was happiness, the warm sun on my bare legs. This was happiness. My grandmother went back to her cards, sweeping them together and shuffling the deck.

"Well, they all came out so it's going to be a good day," she said.

My mother slept. I didn't want her to get up anymore. She could sleep until my father came back and kissed her eyes awake. I didn't draw because I was afraid I would spoil it. I held up my windows to the real window; the sun came through, casting reflections on the white refrigerator door, the light sparking souls in all the colors.

The first real city I ever saw was Milwaukee. My mother and Lolly drove there to go shopping and they took me along. In a huge department store, my mother found a pair of red children's shoes, flat with pointed toes, Capezios just like her own. I wanted everything of mine to be like hers.

The three of us stood staring down at the shoes for a long time, but my mother wouldn't buy them.

When we got home, I threw a tantrum. I felt nothing would be right again until I had those shoes. It was as if I'd lost something, although I'd never seen them before. I'd never imagined there were tall, peaked buildings, a place like Milwaukee. The next day I still felt agitated. I got up early from a bad night of sleep and dressed myself, tied my sneakers and said I was running away to Milwaukee to get my shoes.

"And how are you going to buy them when you get there? You've got no money," my grandmother said. She stood in the kitchen ironing. The ironing board came down from the wall and blocked the doorway. I had to crawl under, brushing her nyloned legs, to get through. The stockings she wore were thicker and orange, you couldn't see her skin.

"I'll get some," I said.

"Well, who do you think is going to give it to you? Sit down, why don't you, and I'll fix you an egg. And let me button your blouse on right."

But nothing my grandmother said was consoling. My grandmother wouldn't understand about fancy shoes. This was between my mother and me. I walked out the screen door and let it slam. A few minutes later, my mother stood on the porch. "Come back here! You get back here this instant!"

I marched over the lawn to the road. I was four years old, I don't know where she thought I could have gone. Everyone on Lime Kiln Road knew me. But she came running across the yard, her bathrobe flapping open, and her fingernails bit into my arm.

"Come on, get back in there." When she pushed me through the kitchen door, a box with the new shoes lay open on the table, the brown paper wrapping ripped apart.

"Are you happy now?"

I just looked at the shoes, the shoes I was going to walk to Milwaukee for. There they were, mine. I was relieved and then they were just shoes again.

"Aren't you going to say thank you, now that you got what you wanted?" My grandmother shook her head, ironing harder.

"You just can't surprise her with anything, Mom, she just won't wait."

I began to know I'd done something wrong. I didn't even want the shoes anymore.

"Well, you've got to teach her. You can't give her every little thing she wants. Let her try and walk to Milwaukee once."

"But then she cries."

"Well let her cry."

That day my mother drove past the dry cleaner's to the edge of town by the river and stopped the car on the side of the road.

"We're at the orphanage," she said. It was a dark brick building with tiny windows at the top of a hill. My mother reached over and opened my door. There was a ditch full of waxy, perfect buttercups.

"I brought you here because I'm telling you, Honey, you can't act the way you've been doing. I'm warning you. This is where you'll end up if I can't make you mind."

I sat as long as I could, looking straight in front of me out the wind-shield, maybe a moment longer, and then my chin wobbled and I started to cry. My head was wet and in my sweatered arms. My mother reached over and tried to hug me in her lap, even though I was too big and she hurt my back against the steering wheel. She started to cry, too, and she kissed me. "Don't worry, my Little Bit, I'll never give you up. Don't you ever worry." Then it seemed as if all she'd ever wanted was to make me cry.

She reached over and closed my door again. The buttercups blurred together now in one smear of color and we could hear crickets starting. Lights came on in the orphanage's small windows. Her face was over me. She looked down at me hard, as if she were looking at her own reflection in water. One of her tears dropped into my eye.

For the millionth time, when we were children, Benny started running through a field, shouting ah-a-ah-a-ah-a-ah-a-ah-a, with his arms out to the sides, until I couldn't hear him anymore. My cousin Benny was always running, he ran anywhere, just to run. Later on, he rode snowmobiles, plows, dirt bikes, motorboats, and cars. I didn't like him running away like that, but I didn't want to scuff behind, looking down at the ground, so I ran too, as if I'd felt like running all along. But Benny could run forever and I got tired. I stopped in my grandmother's yard and lay down to listen to the leaves.

Sometimes I thought I could hear the earth spin and I dug my hands into the ground and held on. The sound of the leaves there went on for-ever, but you had to run and then stop to hear it. The earth was like a shell you put your ear to. Then I turned over and looked straight up to the ceiling of leaves, big as hands, and the spots of blue sky between them. I even put my tongue out to taste the ground; it tasted like rusty metal. But that was as far as it went.

I always wanted more. I ended up running to Benny's house to see if he was home yet. If he wasn't there, I would have gone to look for my mother. The wind was always the same. It was like loving someone who didn't know my name.

Aunt Carol said, yes, Benny was in his room, she would go get him. She opened the sliding glass door, asking would I like to come into the breezeway, but I said no, and leaned against the back of the house. The sky was enormous with pink and gold-veined clouds. It was almost sup-pertime. With Benny on his way to see me, walking through his house, I felt I didn't need anyone, anymore. I didn't mind being alone. I could look at other things. I suppose it would have been that way with my father, if he was there. I looked and as far as I could see, the sky was all there was. I imagined a whole continent of men, stopping and leaning on imple-ments, looking up.

We went to school far away, in town. Benny was a year older, so he went first. A school bus came in the morning, and picked him up at the end of Lime Kiln Road.

On Benny's sixth birthday, Carol wrote a note so I could go to school with him and safety-pinned it to my sleeve. That day the class made hats. I loved it. I glued a lace veil and plastic lilies of the valley to a blue con-struction paper oval. The boys made black top hats. We posed in the after-noon outside the school in our hats. In the photograph, we look old, like tiny country men and women.

Benny and I lay next to each other on our mats during rest period and when we woke up, the teacher brought out a cake in the shape of a lamb, with flaky coconut frosting. My grandmother had baked it that morning and driven it to the school in a box. The teacher passed around napkins with two tiny squares of cake on each one.

The first bite tasted better than anything, it was so sweet and soft. Then I remembered my mother and felt bad, so I wrapped my second piece carefully in the napkin and slipped it into my jacket pocket to take home to her. That day I didn't mind parting with Benny at the edge of our lawns. I had gone somewhere too.

"Well, sit down and tell me what all you did." My grandmother's back was to me as she poured a glass of milk.

"We made hats."

I was feeling the napkin in my pocket, trying to assure myself that the cake was still there. I'd held the piece inside my pocket all the way home on the school bus. I'd held it tight. I was worried now; the napkin was still there, but it seemed empty, the cake must have somehow slipped out. My fingers dug into the pocket, touching every part of the lining. It seemed amazing, impossible. It never occurred to me that I might have crumbled it, holding too hard. Finally, while my grandmother dealt cards for double solitaire, I took the napkin out under the table and spread it open on my thighs. There was nothing but a pile of crumbs.

While my grandmother shuffled, I got up and threw the napkin away. I had nothing to give my mother now, and I wasn't even going to mention it. Without the cake, she wouldn't understand.

. . .

The next year, when I started school, a hygienist came to my class and passed out new boxed toothbrushes.

"How many of you have your own toothbrush already?" she asked.

Most of us raised our hands. The few who didn't kept their hands folded on their desk tops and looked down. But Theresa Griling was bold in her dumbness. She got into trouble because you couldn't humiliate her. When people didn't like her, she dared them.

"I got one that's my brother's, too. It used to be my papa's," she said.

The hygienist sucked in her breath and looked at Theresa Griling as if she'd said something so wrong that the best thing to do was to keep very, very quiet. She walked to Theresa Griling's desk and stacked two more boxes of toothbrushes.

"Kin I have a red and a green instead of two greens?"

The hygienist silently made the exchange. "How many people are there in your family?" she said, then.

"Five, six counting my papa."

"Four, five, six. There. You can give them each a present."

"But my papa don't use one no more."

"*Any*more," the nun said gently, from the back of the room, her beads clicking softly in her hands.

The hygienist smiled enormously at Theresa. "Well, perhaps you can persuade him with your good example how important brushing is. He could lose his teeth prematurely."

"He already did. That's why he don't brush."

We laughed out loud and the hygienist looked around herself, touching her skirt, as if there were invisible flies. Theresa won that time; we could see it. The hygienist lost control. She walked to the front of the room and looked at Theresa with pure hate. The hygienist had huge, square teeth. She pointed to the blackboard where she'd drawn a picture of a cavity. Her face was perfectly colored with makeup. "I'll get you in the end," her large smile seemed to say. She was wearing a neat belted navy blue dress with matching navy blue shoes. Theresa's blouse was yellowed and her gray anklets sank down below the heels of her shoes. I was thinking of Theresa at home, where we lived, the flat fields and long rails.

I told my mother about the hygienist that night. We were driving around by the river and her friend Lolly was in the car with us. "You watch out for those Griling kids, because they are filthy, let me tell you," my mother said. "He is, Bub is. When their mother died and he just let them run around like they do, the city came out and took them away. They put them in the orphanage." She was talking to Lolly now, in the front seat. "And the nuns gave them baths and combed their hair; they said their hair was all matted and one of them had burrs in her skin. And they cleaned them all up and gave them new clothes and fixed their hair nice, you know how the nuns are, but the kids ran away and went home again. And when the social workers came to the house, the kids said they'd rather stay with their dad. No matter how terrible, kids just always want their parents."

"Isn't that funny," Lolly said.

When we came home from Las Vegas, the winter I was seven, my mother seemed to lose interest in me. She spent more time with Lolly. I went outside after school, and stayed sometimes into the dark. I ran and played with the kids on Lime Kiln Road because of Benny. Benny was my cousin and that gave me something.

After school, I skidded into the kitchen, my grandmother flipped up the hood of my sweat shirt and then I ran through the yard to the fields. I met Benny and the other kids from our road down by the tracks where the rails were empty and dull silver as far as we could see. We got down on our heels and hit rocks on the rails while we thought about what we would do. We only played made-up games. We didn't use anything bought. Around us, the country seemed so big. Later, when I moved to Carriage Court, the kids played sports on the street with names: Capture the Flag, Red Rover, Kick the Can.

Finally, we started running. At the top of a hill, Benny turned and fell and rolled with his arms spread open. I lay down and let go after him, my arms crossed tight over my chest like a prayer and we turned, rolling, trusting it all, trusting the swatches of sky to come back, the sweetness of grass in our mouths, the bumps, rocks hitting off our heads, our feet coming unfurled and, finally, Benny and I were tangled together in the soft muddy ditch at the end.

We woke up in each other's arms. We'd played all our lives, but we were conscious now when we unfitted ourselves. We were older. I spit out the grass and my spit was mixed with green. We ran to the top again and this time we skidded, our arms out, our chests falling in front of us, to gravity. We tripped over roots and rocks, the steepness pushing our speed, like a hand on the smalls of our backs. The breath cleaned out of our lungs, we fell, rolling onto our backs, looking up at the sky. We lay in the ditch, holding on, as if our own arms braced the land and air in the hurling speed of the planet's fall. We dug our hands into the soft grass until our nails were crammed with dirt.

Benny crawled over to where I was and sat with his knees on my knees. He held my wrists down and wrestled with me and we turned and fought and as we moved, the ground felt hard under us, like another body.

Then from far away the train whistle started and we all ran back to the tracks. We laid pop bottle tops and nickels in rows and we knelt there with both hands lightly on the rails. There was a humming. The metal was warm, holding in the last sun and giving it back slowly; we lay our cheeks down so whole halves of our faces vibrated with the coming of the train. From our ears to under our chins, it felt like a helmet of air. Benny said we should all close our eyes.

I didn't close mine. I knelt there, the field of vibration growing a thicker layer under my cheek, and watched Benny's face, his eyes shut smooth, his mouth moving as he breathed. It was best to be the last to leave but I wasn't that brave. I went back when Theresa Griling yelled; we were the first to go running up the hill, pulling our hair, screaming, so glad to be free, and scared, shouting the names of the boys still there, and we could see the train then, the big front light like an eye. The boys peeled off one by one, rolling down by the ditch and tripping up again, running.

The train came, a moment of pure vision. You couldn't think, you couldn't move, you couldn't see. That moment of suspense; noise of the highway, shudder of the train before we knew—yes, every day we were forgotten again. The wind pushed up and there was a whirl of steel and colors, the last sun drizzling the rails, and we hung onto the weeds by the road with our fists and the rest of us let go. Your face moved without you, your voice just went as if someone was pulling it out in one string, your body shook and you were left in a heap on the dusty road when the train was half a mile up in front of you, a train again, something you could wholly see, something your eye could end.

We gathered the flattened pop tops in our pockets as if they were money.

My mother and I made up a secret. It started one evening, a usual evening in our house, when my grandmother and I sat watching "Family Affair" on television. A branch beat against the wall. I walked to the window and saw the same blue light cast from front windows over the yards on our road. In every house the TV was on. There was comfort in that.

My mother stayed in the bathroom, wearing only a slip, practicing with makeup. She stood for minutes, fully absorbed, looking at her face in the mirror as she pushed up the cartilage on the tip of her nose. In the kitchen, she had Kris Miss Facial Herbs boiling in a pot. She steamed her pores open and then ran to the bathroom, where she had her mirror. During one of her migrations, she stopped in the living room and stood for a few moments watching TV with us.

"Ann, come here. I want to talk to you for a second."

"You know, you're cuter than Buffy," she whispered, looking down hard, as if she were appraising me. She took my face by the chin and turned it. I stood very still, my arms straight at my sides. She clicked her tongue. "You know, I've been thinking. We ought to get you on TV."

That moment something started.

"Come here." She began to brush makeup on my face, holding my chin with two tight fingers. "Like this." She puckered her lips. "Close. Now open." I felt her warm breath on my eyelids. "Let's see." She stood up to look from different angles. "You're going to make it, kid, I'm telling you, you are going to make it." Then she peered into the mirror and sighed. "And I'm not so bad myself, for a mother."

"You're beautiful," I said, meaning it.

"Do you really think so?" Her face was poised, waiting.

I nodded my head hard, up and down.

"Close your eyes," my mother said, smearing shadow on me with her fingers, so I saw colored lights inside.

We decided we would go to California, but it was our secret. I knew I'd have to be different from other children. I'd have to be better than the other kids to be picked and make all that money. My mother started to read to me from magazines at night. We knew all about the children on television. We knew how much money they made, we knew about the Jackie Coogan law, we knew that the camera adds ten pounds.

"Maybe your dad can even help," she whispered.

The next year at school, Theresa Griling walked behind me in the lunch line and every day she stepped on my heel, crushing my saddle shoe down. We ate at two long tables, watched by a novice who stood at the door.

My mother fixed me lunches that were always too big. I got a sandwich so thick the pieces fell apart when I tried to eat it, two eggs that weren't hard-boiled enough, bakery cookies, a bag of sliced carrots, celery and radishes, a banana, an apple and an orange. On both sides of me at the table, girls had standard lunches: a thin sandwich which pressed down even thinner while they ate, and a Hostess Twinkie. Theresa Griling had just one thing every day: a battered apple or a candy bar, sometimes a chicken leg or one slice of bologna. I longed for the other lunches. I was full after half my sandwich. Even my bag sitting open in front of me was bigger than the other bags. It looked sloppy and wrinkled, like an old elephant's thick leg. I threw most of my lunch out, tossing the whole bag into the garbage bin we passed on our way to the playground. It didn't look like the other lunches and some girls stared at me.

One recess, an older girl tapped my arm while I turned a jump rope. She said the Mother Superior would like to see me in her office. I glanced up from the playground; the sky was bordered and fenced with power lines, planted with three-story buildings and the steeple. The girl led me up two flights of stairs and opened a wooden door.

The Mother Superior stood by a window of honeycomb glass. I knew I was probably in trouble, but I thought it was possible I'd be told I'd done something good enough to change my life. Only, I couldn't think of anything I'd done yet. Maybe a Hollywood agent had come to our lunch-room and seen me eat with good table manners. Then I noticed something familiar on the edge of the Mother Superior's desk: a large, brown, wilted lunch bag, like my own.

The Mother Superior nodded, letting her eyes close. The older girl began, pulling back three fingers.

"First thing. Do you like apples?"

"Yes," I said, not knowing what this meant.

"Do you like . . . oranges?"

"Yes."

Then the bell rang. The older girl held onto her index finger, waiting until the noise stopped. All through the building there was an echo of steps, my classmates marching single file down halls, upstairs and into classrooms.

"Last thing," the girl said. "Do you like bananas?"

Bananas. Bananas. I thought hard, deliberating. The room was still. I was sure the question meant something else and that the answer would determine the rest of my life. If I would be a child star or just me. The older girl and I were breathing together, our ribs moving out in unison, like fish hanging in an aquarium.

"Yes," I said.

The older girl picked up the wrinkled brown bag. "Then, how come, in your lunch today, did you throw out a banana and an apple and an orange?"

The Mother Superior's hands, folded on the desk top, looked smooth as those of a statue. I understood now; I'd been caught. I pictured the garbage bin and all the lunch bags. They must have fished out mine.

The older girl led me down the stairs, past closed classroom doors, to the lunch table. A novice stood there, waiting. They set my bag at the place I ate my lunch every day. I started peeling the orange. I took out all the little packets in my lunch and set them up, like a village.

"Everyone else gets a sandwich and a Twinkie. And that's all. Nobody else gets a fruit."

"Honey, other mothers don't put in the time I do. That's why. I can see now you don't appreciate it. You'd rather have a piece of cheap lunch meat slapped between packaged bread. I stay up late, after working all day, and how many mothers do you think work?"

"Hush now. I'll fix her lunch," my grandmother said. "You two just go to bed."

"Mom, why should you have to, just because she—"

"Let Gramma. I want Gramma to make my lunch."

"Okay, fine. Go ahead. I can see no one needs me around here."

We looked at the door my mother slammed. My grandmother pulled out the cutting board and began to make me a sandwich. My mother was banging drawers shut in the bedroom.

It is always the people like my mother, who start the noise and bang things, who make you feel the worst; they are the ones who get your love. When I opened the door, the lights were off and my mother was already under the covers. I climbed up and crawled over her and as I moved, I hit her knee. It made a creaking sound, like wood.

"Watch it, why don't you?"

I slid under the covers, facing the wall. "I'm sorry, Mom."

She didn't say anything. It was as bad as I'd thought. When it seemed she was asleep for sure, I turned around, put my hands on her shoulders and curled against her spine, but she shuddered, shrugging me off. I couldn't get comfortable. My eyes hurt behind my eyes. My arms didn't seem joined to my shoulders right. I turned and turned. I couldn't seem to do anything to get warm.

Finally, I crept to the bottom of the bed, slipped down and walked out of the room. With each creak of the steps as I climbed, I felt safer and more sleepy. The upstairs was like another house. The air seemed colder and clean. While I was pulling the heavy quilts back to crawl into the small bed, my grandmother's sheets rustled.

"Sleep tight," she said, but maybe I only imagined it.

My mother added coffeecake squares to my lunches, squares she bought specially from Krim's, as if all she remembered about our fight was that my lunches should be better, which to her, meant bigger. One morning that fall, on the school bus, Theresa Griling sat next to me and pressed up close against my ribs. "I heard you got in trouble with the Mother Superior." She shifted in the seat, moving her legs. "I got a bag, you can give me half and I'll trade you for my apple." She held a small, very creased paper bag in her lap. Out of her pocket, she pulled a bruised crab apple, from one of the trees in old Brozek's yard. I had my enormous lunch propped up on my schoolbooks. It stood as high as my head. Then as if she'd been holding out, she produced a Milky Way, the brown wrapper twisted, making white lines, and set it on the bag next to the apple.

"You want my stuff?" I said.

"Sure." She studied the ribbed rubber floor of the bus, she waited after she said it. It was the first time I'd ever seen her like that. She used to stare at me behind my bag on the bus in the morning. There were others who'd looked at me in the lunchroom at school. I'd always thought they were making fun, because my lunch was different and silly. Now I saw: they were hungry.

I nudged Theresa's side and we dug our arms in the bag. From that day on we had a deal.

In the spring, a boy from on television was coming to town for a cerebral palsy benefit. After the rains, posters of his face peeled off telephone poles, next to larger posters of Leonard Nimoy. My mother drove the twenty miles to the telethon through a storm. Inside the Civic Auditorium, on a stage, tables of women answered ringing telephones, taking pledges. The boy from on television walked with the cerebral palsy children, who looked complicated and stiff and fragile, as if you wouldn't know where to touch them.

Leonard Nimoy, in Spock ears, sat in the orchestra pit, next to a huge bin. People lined up around the auditorium to shake his hand and throw in their coins and dollars. My mother nudged me into line. "See that little girl? You're cuter than her. Sit on his lap like that and just ask him how he got into show business. Say you were wondering because you'd like to act, too."

"I don know."

"Go on. You have to get discovered somewhere. Who knows? Maybe it'll be here."

Onstage, the boy from on television stood at the microphone singing. He belted out "Every Little Boy Can Be President," opening his arms toward the cerebral palsy children, who were lined up behind him in a row of plastic chairs. On television, he played Buffy's brother. His real name was Timmy Kennedy.

My mother stuck a dollar into my hand. In front of me two boys in matching shirts pushed each other's chests, fighting for the first place in line. I stood straight, thinking about looking right and talking right. When it was my turn I walked up, but I was afraid to sit on Leonard Nimoy's lap. I stood close enough to smell the foreign, chemical smell of his shaved cheek, a man's smell, like the electricity around Jimmy Measey's towel, and I whispered into his ear. "How did you get started as an actor?"

He turned and looked at me, puzzled. "Just a minute." A child handed him her autograph book and he signed, with big loopy letters, smiling. The line moved forward but I stayed.

"Because I'd like to get into show business, too," I said.

He looked at me a little regretfully. "Oh, Honey, it's a long story. Too long for now." He gave me a sideways hug and then turned back to the line. "Bless you, thank you," he was saying, as I walked out towards my mother. I was ashamed. Leonard Nimoy hadn't taken an interest in me. I wondered if he would have if I'd sat on his lap.

Onstage, the celebrities led the CP children around in a circle. The boy from on television walked bending over, to reach the arms of a much smaller girl. The children sang, in partial, shrill voices, looking at their braced feet as they marched.

> LOOK AT US, WE'RE WALKING
> LOOK AT US, WE'RE TALKING
> WE WHO'VE NEVER WALKED OR TALKED BEFORE
> BUT THE FIGHT HAS JUST BEGUN
> GET BEHIND US EVERYONE
> YOUR DOLLARS MAKE OUR DREAMS COME TRUE
> THANKS TO YOU, THANKS TO YOU
>
> LOOK AT US, WE'RE WALKING
> LOOK AT US, WE'RE TALKING
> IMAGINE WALKING TO THE CANDY STORE . . .

My mother found out what flight the celebrities were taking back to California and we drove to the airport that night. We discovered the celebrities sitting quietly in an upstairs waiting room like other people. Leonard Nimoy had taken his Spock ears off, he was reading a magazine. The boy from on television sat playing checkers. He was wearing a velour shirt with a zipper, just like any other kid. But I knew he wasn't. I'd seen him on television.

His father told my mother that he was a gym teacher and that his family was Mormon.

"Mother used to do all her own canning and of course that's had to stop. One or the other of us travels with him. He has eight brothers and sisters, and they've had to make sacrifices for him to be on the show. So with part of his money, we've taken out insurance policies for each of them."

The father asked the boy to say hello to me. He looked up politely from his checker game and smiled. He seemed anxious to turn back to the magnetic checkers. No matter what my mother said, I wasn't pretty enough.

The boy's father told us that Buffy snubbed Timmy on the set. In real life, she was years older, almost in junior high.

"You wouldn't happen to know a songwriter out there," my mother asked. She said my father's name.

"I can't say that I do." He shrugged.

We watched the airplane wheels start spinning as it ran down the runway. "They must be tired," my mother sighed. When we couldn't see the lights anymore, we walked out to the parking lot. I huddled against the outside of my door. We both felt solemn for a moment, watching the plane in the sky. We both wished we were on it, in one of those small yellow windows.

My mother clapped. "Well, should we go get some sundaes to cele-brate?" She unlocked our doors and rubbed her hands together.

"Celebrate what?"

"Well, I think I should give his agent a call, don't you?"

"What?"

"Didn't you hear me asking him who their agent was? She's apparently *the* agent to go to. All the child stars have her. Her name is Ellen Arcade and she's in Riverside. So I think she's the one we should get for you." My mother bent down closer to the heat vent. "A high school gym teacher," she mused. "What do you know."

Benny could be impatient, but sometimes in summer you saw him taking a long time reading to one of the neighbor kids, a story from her cardboard children's book. He helped littler kids with their math problems, ponder-ing the elaborate boxes of numbers on their papers for hours. He tried to teach everything he didn't understand. If you asked him how he made a stone skip seven times on the surface of a pond, or where he found the birds' nests he carried home, perfectly whole, in two hands while running, how he balanced on water skis, he would shrug and grin, I dunno. He couldn't teach you because he had no idea how he did these things. I once asked him to show me how to dance. We put Hal's 45s on the console in their living room. *Would you like some of my tangerine?* Ben moved and shuffled. "How do you do that?" I looked at myself in Carol's huge, gilt-edged mirror. I was all wrong.

"You're fine, Ann," he said. "Forget it."

Once, at night that summer, Benny rode me on his handlebars, down by the tracks. We let the bike fall on the ground and we walked to the creek. Then Benny ran back to his bike and took off.

He threw me his flashlight so it landed in the field.

I screamed no, but he rode away anyway, the light on the front of his bike farther and farther away like a match going out.

I was afraid of the dark. Benny knew. A dog barked in the far distance. Then the country seemed immense, as if there were only small houses far apart and small clearings around them, not networks of electricity, of sound. It felt like a randomly settled wilderness, where you could disap-pear and no one would know. Then, I picked up the cold flashlight from the ground by my feet, touched the metal, fumbled it on and the night changed. Benny was right. It wasn't him. The world softened instantly in light. For the first time I could imagine angels, the halo looked so real. I walked slowly and the sounds receded to crickets and a hum of far-off power lines. With the flashlight, you could see one thing at a time, the fitted seeds of one weed, a rough milkpod stem.

When I came to our road, I could see the shades of gray with just my eyes. I turned the flashlight off. The fields went on to the bare plain barn, a pure black. The land seemed different at night, another place, belonging to anyone who saw it. The light changed everything, made it look still and permanent, meant, like a city.

At the edge of our lawn, I stood on the worn spots by the mailbox. My thin grandfather and my grandmother, my own mother and Carol had walked exactly here, secrets in their hearts, opening the mailbox door, and now it meant nothing, the dirt had no memory, they were separate days, different years, all our thoughts were gone, lost on air. My grandfather had taken long walks at night. He had walked over his lawn, touching the tops of weeds. In blizzards, he had liked to strap on snowshoes, walk out and listen to the quiet under one of his trees. People we wouldn't recognize, strangers, would touch the land after us, pack down the same earth, without ever knowing how beautiful we found it, how troubling.

Sometimes I thought it was Benny who gave me everything. When I ran into the yellow-lit kitchen, he sat eating an orange. He shrugged.

Every fall, when we went back to school in town, they lined us all up by the nurse's room to test for ringworm. You went in one at a time, to a closet, where two hygienists shone a black light on you. If they found ringworm, they would shave your hair off right there and they'd give you a cap to wear when you walked out into the hall again. You knew the kids at school who had the ringworm, they wore stocking caps until their hair grew back. Sometimes, during a wet recess, you would see a gleam of white skull on the playground, when kids ganged up and pulled a cap off. You'd see the kid snatch it back right away, picking it out of the slush and putting it back on.

In line, in front of the nurse's office, I thought I could feel something on my head. Theresa Griling, behind me, stepped down on the heel of my saddle shoe and I had to bite my lip not to cry. I loved my hair. It was my most prized possession. My mother told me that hardly any other kids in America had hair like mine. It was going to help me get on television. "It's the best hair to have," my mother had whispered. "Your black. The very best."

Walking back, I touched my hair lightly. It had been over in a minute, the black light, the hygienist asking my middle name to fill out her form. In the classroom we were supposed to wait in our seats for all the pupils to return. Sitting there, doing nothing, I thought a terrible thought; my mother herself had blond hair. I looked at the other girls around me, the redheads, the blondes. Maybe they could be beautiful too. The Hollywood agent might not pick me.

Theresa Griling walked into the classroom then, not crying, wearing a stocking cap. She just sat down at her desk.

A nun called the girls from the bottom of a wide scrubbed staircase, the steps soft and nicked and scarred. We were picking up orphans from the orphanage for Christmas. We got two girls every holiday, never the same two, and despite my persistent request for boys. A scraggly, flocked wreath hung at the top of the staircase, over a window.

"Probably donated," my mother whispered, seeing me look at it.

Every holiday, the girls bounded down, slumped over, shy and eager in fancy dresses too light for the season and short socks that they were too old for. They usually had sturdy, women's legs. Their hair was pulled tightly off their foreheads, so their white faces seemed startled, like naked bodies. They looked clean. The nuns didn't care about pretty, but they wanted you to know their girls were clean. The year before, we got Mary and Theresa Griling. Bub had taken off somewhere, to Florida, and they had been in the orphanage again.

This year, their names were Dorie and Diane. My mother, who usually slowed the car to an almost halt in front of every expensive store, made only one stop; we all got out to see the Christmas windows at Shreve's. The orphans stood with their hands in their jacket pockets, their legs turning dull red between their dresses and their socks.

"Isn't *he* lovely?" my mother said. "Aw, look at that little wolf. Wouldn't you just like to bring him home?"

The orphans frowned between their eyebrows. They must have been cold. We stood in front of each mechanical scene too long, like people in a museum who look at each painting for an equal length of time, people not intimate enough to laugh and sigh in relief when they can leave.

My grandmother was rolling out dough on the table when we came in the back door. Carol stood rubbing her hands together, meaning to help. "Well, how do you do, I'm Carol. I'm the mother."

My mother snorted in the corner. She sat there, dialing Lolly on the phone.

"Yes, Adele too, sure. I'm the boys' mother. Now, we haven't had you two before, have we?"

"*No,* Carol," my mother said; then she started whispering into the mouthpiece.

"Oh, no, you're right. Now I see. But this one looks a little, you look a little like one we had last Easter and was she ever a pretty girl. What was her name now? I just can't think of it. Was she a Linda? Well, what is your name?" Carol extended a wet, doughy hand.

"This is Dorie and this is Diane," I said.

"Oh, no, it wasn't a Dorie. I'm sure I would've remembered a Dorie."

My mother snorted again into the phone. She was talking to Lolly about why it had been a good idea not to invite Ted for Christmas. Ted didn't have any family in Wisconsin, and he would be eating at a restaurant. "There's no reason he has to see it all, before," she said. "And he'll get a good prime rib, rare the way he likes it." Lolly seemed to agree.

I took Dorie and Diane upstairs to their bedroom. They had their nightgowns and toothbrushes along in one brown paper bag. Dorie hit the window with the back of her hand.

"You got a lot of room," she said.

Dorie's fingernails looked scrubbed clean, transparent. I'd seen where they lived, the huge rooms with rows of bunk beds in the orphanage. The cement floor in their bathroom sloped down to a metal drain. There were ten sinks, all on one wall. She smelled like dust or the air in a closet. Like something clean but old.

In the living room, Jimmy Measey yelled at Carol for stepping in front of the TV. She was standing next to the window, trapped, bunching the curtain in her hand.

"Well, Jimmy, I just wanted to look a second and see if they had their Christmas tree lights on." She let the curtain go and started to walk back towards the kitchen.

"Wait till the commercial, Carol. You can just stand there and wait," Jimmy said. "Don't you dare move while we've got the ball." Looking straight at the screen, he asked the orphans questions.

"What grade have they got you in over there?

"Do you like it with those nuns?"

They answered quietly, in unison, staring down at the rug.

"Fifth and sixth.

"Yes."

"Are there boys in there with you, too?"

"Yes, but more girls."

"More girls, huh."

"The boys run away."

"How long you been in there?"

Jimmy's eyes followed the game, the slow motion accidents and gentle falls, black and white on the television. While the girls talked, answering his questions, our team intercepted and he began yelling, thumping his knees, as Dorie said she'd been in the orphanage since she was eight years old. When the replay was over, Jimmy turned back. "Oh, 'scuse me. I had to see that. But go on."

"What happened to your parents?" I said.

They looked at each other and shrugged. "Mine are dead. They had a car accident when I was just a little baby," Diane said.

"What about yours?" I asked Dorie.

"I never saw my dad. But my mom's dead. Got to be, I used to get cards from her but not anymore for a long time."

"You remember your mother, you're lucky," Diane said.

"Yeah, me and my mom, we used to get up every morning, go buy the newspaper and a box of Milk Duds. We'd share them. She always had Black Jack gum in her purse."

"What happened to her?"

"Ann, shut your mouth. They'll tell you what they want to tell you," Jimmy said.

Benny walked in, carrying a bowl of potato chips. "Annie loves orphans because when she was little she thought she was one," he said. "She used to go around telling everybody she was adopted because her mother's got blond hair. She used to paint fake freckles on herself so she'd look more like her mom."

A commercial flickered onto the television, a waxed floor, and a woman on her knees. Then a vacuum cleaner, and the woman stood up. Jimmy said, "Okay, Carol, now you can go."

We set a plate of broken cookies out on our shoveled porch. "Oh, Honey, Santa doesn't mind, he likes the pieces," my mother said. "He likes to know we're only *hu*-man."

The new snow blew on the ice under the porch light like tiny balls of styrofoam. I opened a box of C & H sugar cubes from Hawaii for the reindeer. Then we put on our coats and hats and trekked over to Carol and Jimmy's house. Hal led the way, stamping a single channel of footprints in the snow. Benny and I were still light enough to walk on the high crusted banks with our arms out to the sides for balance. It was like walking on water, we stepped softly, feeling the peaks of the ridged banks. We stood as tall as our parents.

Snow lit the dark. It covered the fields as far as we could see. Small, sharp stars seemed embedded deep in the sky and the noise of the highway was muffled and far away. There were only a few headlights, they must have been trucks, long-distance interstates, carrying perishables, winter fruit.

Ahead of me, Carol slammed the screen door and began to pull off her boots. She walked through the house in her nylons, turning on lights.

Carol and Jimmy owned one of the first artificial Christmas trees in the state of Wisconsin. It was expensive and innovative when they bought it, and each year they added new lights. This year, families of colors blinked at different times. Carol passed out Tom and Jerrys, and Jimmy told her to sit down. Then she brought in my grandmother's cookies on a plate the shape of a Christmas tree. She'd made the plate in a ceramics class and Jimmy had installed tiny electric lights around its rim. She set it on a low table near an outlet.

"Now, sit down," Jimmy said.

But she walked on her knees to the tree and selected packages for each of the orphans. The rest of our presents had name tags. She gave Dorie a pink plastic cotton-ball dispenser, a coin purse and a scarf. Diane opened a toy gumball machine and a set of lipsticks made to look like peppermint candy. Lippersticks, they were called.

Carol went shopping for the orphans every year at end-of-the-summer dollar sales. She also kept a cardboard box full of wrapped general presents in the closet, which would do for any occasion. Diane and Dorie sat quietly on the carpet, holding their gifts in their laps.

Hal opened the first large box; it held a snorkel and flippers, a new installment in the series of sports equipment Jimmy bought for his oldest son. Jimmy thought sports would make Hal normal; he immediately ordered Hal to try the flippers on. Carol stood to throw away the tissue paper. "Sit down, Carol," Jimmy said.

My mother gave me a blue velvet skating suit. I ran my finger over one of the embroidered flowers.

"Did you make it?" Dorie said. She was sitting at my mother's knees and staring up at her. My mother liked attention, she liked to be watched.

"Oh, no, Honey, it's much nicer than I could do. It's made in Switzerland," she said. "But don't touch. The velvet's very delicate. Real fine."

My other present was a chemistry set. It looked too hard for me. It said on the box ages eleven through fourteen, and I was only eight.

"What's that you got?" Jimmy took the box from me and studied the drawing inside the lid. It said you were supposed to prick your finger and look at the blood through the microscope. Jimmy rummaged in the box. He lifted a needle, about two inches long, in a sealed clear plastic packet. "Here, give me your finger."

I sat on my hands and shook my head.

He stood up. "You shouldn't even have a chemistry set if you're going to be a baby. If you can't prick your finger, you're not old enough."

"She can grow into it," my mother said.

"You spoil her, Adele. It'll hurt her a second and then it's over."

"Not on Christmas, Jimmy."

He looked at the orphans. "You two, hold out your hands. Come on."

They each opened one hand, slowly, palms up, uncurling close to their bodies.

"See, they're old enough. It'll do her good to see that."

Neither of them cried when he pricked their fingers. He didn't set up the microscope. He couldn't find the glass plates in the box. "Well, it's good for her to see," he said. He left the two drops of dark blood glistening on their fingertips.

Carol lifted up a black lacy slip from a rectangular box.

"Oh, Jimmy, now when am I ever going to wear such a thing. I don't think it'll even fit me."

Jimmy fumed. "If you don't want it, Carol, take it back. The receipt's in the box. Don't tell me about it, just take it back."

"Well, Jimmy, I only meant, I think it's too small. Are you trying to tell me something? Maybe I should go back on that grapefruit diet." She laughed an old woman's laugh. Carol's jokes were like the nuns', there was no mischief in them.

"Look at how nicely it's made," my mother said, fingering a seam. "That's all hand-sewn. It'll be smashing on you, Carol."

"Ogh," Carol said, "I don't know."

My mother shook her head. "She never appreciates anything. And he has nice taste, you know?"

Hal came back, in the flippers, stepping carefully between boxes and wrapping paper. Benny looked up at him; he was sitting in a big chair with his legs dangling down, quiet because he hadn't been given anything yet. Benny would get the flippers, though, he got all Hal's equipment, a few months later, when Hal never used it.

Carol passed Jimmy a small red box and he pulled the ribbon off slowly and let it flutter to the floor. His lips closed as tight as a berry and his cheeks puffed out. What Jimmy wanted and believed he deserved couldn't fit into this box.

Jimmy was our big spender. The Measer, he called himself at Christmas. Every year he waited until the day of Christmas Eve and then he went out and used cash. That year, he'd gone to Shopko and the downtown Shreve's. He'd bought a dishwasher for Carol. It had come in a truck early that afternoon. Jimmy had made it perfectly clear that what he wanted for himself was a new black Easy-boy chair with a lever to adjust the seat back's angle. But he'd snooped around the house and he hadn't found it anywhere.

His cheek trembled when he lifted the white cardboard lid and saw the watch. The watch looked expensive enough to mean that it, and not the chair, was his big present for the year.

"Carol, I already have a watch. You know that, Carol."

"Jimmy, I know you have a watch but I thought . . . here, let me show you, this has an alarm on it. Where are the instructions? He told me at the store how to do it, but—"

"I don't need an alarm on my wristwatch."

My grandmother shook her head and opened her own purse. She passed out sealed envelopes with ironed five-dollar bills to Dorie and Diane. She called Benny and me to come sit next to her and our heads pressed together in the small circle of light. Under the lamp, her unpolished fingernails looked yellowish like pearls. She showed us the new green entries stamped in our savings books. She had an account at the bank for each of us. "See the interest," she pointed, her fingernail tapping the paper. "You're each collecting interest."

Carol was whimpering now, wiping tears with the cuff of her sleeve. "Take those fins off and help me, Hal. Jimmy, I just thought you'd like another watch. At the water softener store, and all over, they said this was the newest thing. And you know you always like the newest thing." She leaned over, scattering the crumpled wrapping paper on the floor, still looking for the instructions to set the alarm.

My mother pressed tiny bottles of perfume into the orphans' hands. "It's what I wear, smell." She pushed her wrist up near their faces and they both bent down, sniffing her arm like puppies nursing.

I went over and stood by Benny. He swung his legs below the chair. His parents were fighting and they hadn't noticed him. Then, Jimmy saw.

"What's the matter, Benny, you didn't get anything from Santa Claus? Look, Ann's comforting him because Benny hasn't got any presents."

Carol stood in the doorway, shaking her head while she zipped up her jacket.

"No," Benny said. He looked down, afraid of his father. I could tell from the way his cheeks went, he was about to cry.

"You just weren't good enough, that's the trouble, Ben. I don't know any other reason that Santa'd forget you. Lookit, Annie's got presents and these two, Diane and I'm sorry, what's your name? They both got presents. What happened to you?"

"Dorie," Dorie said quietly.

Jimmy's voice grew. "You must've been bad."

Then, Carol and Hal struggled in, carrying the enormous Easy-boy chair. It had been in my grandmother's garage, next to the old lawn mower.

"Oh, Carol," Jimmy sighed. His relief seemed great enough to almost equal happiness. They lifted the chair in place and Jimmy sank into it, working the lever, cranking himself up and down.

Now, Carol took out her handkerchief and blew her nose. "Oh, Jimmy, I'm so glad you like *some*thing I got you this Christmas." Carol always carried ironed handkerchiefs and she had unfolded a white one, embroidered with green and red holly.

Jimmy leaned down and picked up the wristwatch. "You'll have to show me how to use this alarm." He buckled it onto his arm.

My grandmother stood up stamping her feet. "It's getting to be time for B-E-D."

Benny was still sitting, clutching the arms of his chair. Jimmy maneuvered the Easy-boy to an upright position. "Oh, listen, Ben, would you do me one favor?" He tossed Benny a set of keys. "Would you go and look in the garage for me? I think I left something there. By mistake."

Benny's face flew into an anxious happiness and he ran out through the breezeway. Then he came back, letting the garage door slam and lunging into Jimmy's arms. I hated to see them like that, pasted to each other, as if you couldn't pull Benny off if you tried.

"Here, you sit down a minute, Carol," Jimmy said, giving her his chair. He followed Benny. The two of them ran into the garage and we heard the motor putting. When the rest of us left, to walk back over to our house, Benny was still in the garage, riding around in circles on his dirt bike. And when we came to our porch, the broken cookies and the box of C & H sugar cubes, which had been under the light, were gone.

I stood at the window and watched Benny's garage, the chalky yellow light seeping out of the seams. I wanted it to be dark again. I heard my grandmother walking through our house, turning off lights. My mother came into our room, slipping her hand underneath my pajama top, and telling me it was time to go to sleep. She led me away from the window and pulled down the shade. I lay banked and quiet on the bed, only breathing, not moving otherwise, trying to feel nothing but her fingernails on my back. The sensations were black, delicious the way a cut can be.

It seemed it would have been easy to die like that, doing nothing, feeling nothing but pleasure, like underwater sounds or lights inside the dark bowls of closed eyes.

But I knew that it would always end and I would need it again and wanting it so made me smaller. After she left, going into her closet and pulling on the light or down to the kitchen to call Lolly, I couldn't summon and recall the pleasure I'd just felt. I couldn't remember pleasure and that was why I needed it so often and succumbed, again and again.

Because it was not easy anymore. The night my mother pushed my pajama top down off my shoulders and felt the soft hairs under my arms, I became less than a baby, a blob, a primitive living thing she could do anything to as long as she fed me with tickles. She liked to pull off the sheet, push down my pajama pants and pat my buttocks, they clenched at her touch. She wanted to look at me and blow air on my tummy with the full pride of possession. She kissed me on the lips and I shirked. When her hand reached down to the elastic of my pajama pants, I stiffened and bucked away from her. "Don't."

"I don't know why not," she said. "Why won't you let me look, you've got such a cute, twussy little patutie. Can't I be proud of your little body that I made?" When she stared at me like that, it seemed she could take something, just by looking.

"Could you talk like an adult, please."

She sighed. I was already beginning to accept the back rubs I needed, with one eye open, guarding myself from my mother taking too much.

I thought of the orphans in the upstairs attic room. They didn't belong to anyone. The nuns had clean dry hands, light on the tops of our heads. I knew nuns.

"Well, good night then," my mother said.

A swallow of cold air came in when she opened the door and left. I thought of the orphanage, worn sheets, the one rough blanket, how in winter they may crawl into a bunk together, both girls thin and dry, one of them might wet the bed.

The next day, at noon, the orphans were served enormous portions, as if they had been underfed all year and this was our one chance to make up for it. During a lull in the conversation, my mother suggested that our family sell the land behind my grandmother's house. That started an argument—my mother against everyone else.

It was an old fight. My mother suggested we put the barn on the market and everyone else started screaming. We kids all were sent to the downstairs bedroom, where we balanced our plates on our knees and tried to cut without tipping them. Dorie and Diane sat with their shoulders touching, making quiet references to the nuns, and to some other girl at the orphanage, as if to remind themselves they had a life.

Before, I'd thought Dorie might have scrubbed her fingernails clean in the cement-floored bathroom to impress us, with her manners, her pleasantness, with how little trouble she would be. She might have lulled herself to sleep thinking of flaky yellow light in a kitchen. But it seemed she was just now understanding that her private wish would not be realized, not only because we would not keep her, but because we were not a family she would want. They both seemed tired, anxious to leave.

In the kitchen, my mother was shouting. "I don't want to be stuck here all my life! I CAN'T LIVE LIKE THIS!"

"Adele, it doesn't have sewer and water. What do you think we could get for it now?"

Dorie spilled a cranberry on the white chenille bedspread. She looked up at us with terror, holding the berry between two fingers.

"Don't worry, we won't tell," I said. Benny reached down carefully to get his milk from the floor. We didn't look at each other. None of us said anything. We just waited, eating as if eating was our duty.

Then Benny mumbled something.

"What?" I said. We were all jumpy.

"Salty. This turkey's salty."

Dorie and Diane walked upstairs to get their brown bag of clothes. Their beds were neatly made. It was as if they'd never been here. Their presents lay on top of the dresser, with the wrapping paper folded underneath.

"Can we leave these here?" Dorie said. "If you could keep them for us, because if we bring them back to Saint Luke's, they'll just get stolen."

"Yeah, someone'll take them for sure," Diane said. "They take everything."

"Took a necklace watch I had from my mother."

"Okay," I said, and then we waited in the backseat of our car. When my mother finally came, she was sniffling and she didn't say a word to us. She slammed the door shut and started driving. I pressed my cheek against the window, knowing as sure as I knew anything that these two girls would never come back to our house to get their presents. My aunt Carol would probably keep them and rewrap them for next year's orphans. They would wait in her closet of all-purpose gifts.

I looked over at Dorie and Diane. I wondered if they knew the minute they stepped out of our house that they would never come back, if they'd already forgotten their presents on the upstairs dresser, or if they kept complicated accounts, cataloging their possessions, remembering the names of the streets they would return to when they left the orphanage, to collect the things that would help them in their new lives.

Their faces told me nothing. They were closed and solemn as if they were counting to themselves.

One night, the last summer we lived on Lime Kiln Road, Hal and his friend Dave drove Benny and me out to Bay Beach. It was a night when the air was moist, almost beginning to rain. I felt a mouth of wet like a kiss on my arm and then nothing as we walked through the crowds looking up at the lighted rides, and I waited, expecting it again.

Hal had money to buy tickets for Benny and me. They came ten for a dollar in a long green paper string. Benny and I wanted the Ferris wheel, we always wanted the Ferris wheel, and while the man strapped us in, with the old soft wooden bar, Hal and Dave stood at the fence.

We went slowly at first, our hands light on the bar, as the car tilted back and forth gently. Other people were still getting in, their bars snapped shut, it wasn't really going yet. Then it started, lifting up from under in one cool swoop of wind and we were swinging at the top, stretching, the tilt knocking air out of us. On the way down, falling softly, all the lighted small houses came closer and more real and then the next time up was faster and faster until it was like breathing, our air sucked in and out, our eyes opening and closing, the blur of landscape and lights and dark trees, and our nails biting into the soft gray wood until, finally, our car coasted down. The man swung open the bar and we walked out, dizzy and light, down the runway, where Hal and Dave stood ready to take our hands and lead us through the dark paths. We were happy to follow then, everything was shaken out of us.

We walked to the pavilion, a damp dim building where we weren't allowed, but Hal knew the way we were, half asleep and happy, we would never tell. There was a big barn door at one end that exhaled a breath of water. The bay started right there, down old wooden steps, cold and deep and dirty in one smell.

Girls and sailors moved on the dance floor, the boys in full white uniform, with hats. More sailors leaned on the refreshment bar that sold hot dogs and Nehi Orange. There was something about those girls. It was their dark lips, the glitter on their ears; their hair was not like our hair, it was thick and it swept up, and their legs looked tiny in their shoes. Dave took me on his back and Hal had Benny's hand as we went through the crowd. We could have been lost but we trusted them.

We walked past the games lined with sailors, where there were machine guns, colored ducks, everything with bolted rifles, and went to watch the bumper cars. We stood there listening to the hard thwacks of cars until the showers of sparks slowed above and the power began to drain. I closed my eyes and opened them again to look up at the sparks on the netted ceiling. The blue and white fire seemed magic, like sparklers, and it held a few minutes after in your eyes.

They took us farther into the woods. It was dark but there were noises all around us. Hal seemed to follow the invisible sounds to a place.

Then we were standing in a clearing on pine needles. I could feel the damp tall trees above us. The stars hung tiny in the sky. There were other people on the ground, five feet away, but we didn't know them. A girl was lying on an old army blanket, her knee out facing me like a face. A guy leaned on top of her. There was a flashlight on the edge of the blanket and the beam hit the marbled orange/yellow bottoms of her feet, hooked over the boy's white back. He fell, grunting, as he drove her into the ground. It happened again and again. That went on for a while and then he screamed, high like a girl, and he was still for a second, his neck lifted, thick and dead, but his right eyelid and right foot were flinching.

He rose to his knees and she still clung onto him. She lifted a few feet
off the ground, her butt spread into separate muscles, her legs around him,
hanging on. One by one, he took her hands off his shoulders and let her
slide back to the blanket. She sat there picking at the wool. She bent
down and I saw her face for a moment. She looked like Rosie Griling. I
thought I recognized her; at the same time, I thought it couldn't be. Her
lip was bleeding, she was pretty. A strand of her hair fell over her mouth.

Then another boy stepped out of his pants and lowered onto her, like
someone starting pushups. He was still wearing his socks and T-shirt. She
rearranged herself under him. I didn't like watching. It felt funny being a
girl.

A flowered dress bunched up under her armpits. Her underwear lay
twisted, a few feet away on the dirt. I looked back at Benny like I wanted
to go home and he put his hands, lightly, on my shoulders. It felt safe and
good to be in layers of old clothes, the same clothes as the boys wore. I
was thinking they would never do this to me, I was family. The girl looked
all yellow and white and the boy kept pushing her down. Another boy tore
open a package of wieners. They got on their knees by the blanket. The
one who was on top of her moved. They passed the package of wieners
between them, someone threw down the cellophane wrapping. It glittered
in the flashlight light. They stuck the wieners in her, first one, then another. She shuddered, then started to sit up, her hands coming to her face.

I turned around and said I wanted to go home.

Nobody had been talking and those boys heard me. They stood and
wiped their hands on their pants. Those boys weren't old. They looked
like regular boys, except we didn't know them. They were dressed in
good warm clothes and they started circling around, their bike wheels
wobbling in the dirt.

Hal lifted me on his shoulders. "We'll go now."

She was still sitting on the blanket, her stomach wet and shiny. She sat
there with her legs sprawled out, patting her belly like a baby, as if someone would have to come and dress her. Her hair fell and covered half her
face.

"Come ON, if you want a ride," one of the boys yelled to her.

She hung her head farther down.

"Where's my lipstick?" she said. She looked up at them and then
around. It seemed the first time she saw the trees.

"We're getting out of here, now," one of them said.

"You guys want her?" He was talking to Hal and Dave, who were still
standing with us on their shoulders. "Go ahead. You can have her. She
likes it." The boy looked back at the girl. "Maybe they'll buy you your
lipstick."

They rode away, handling their bikes roughly, standing up and pulling.

I watched the lights on their handlebars draw jagged paths through the dark and then I closed my eyes against Hal's back.

The last night of summer, Benny and I slept outside. Benny stood there, scuffing his sneakers on our porch, at midnight, when he was supposed to. We took a blanket and a box of Graham crackers and walked across the yard to the hickory tree. Benny had climbed out his bedroom window and left it open. It was easy for me to get away. During that summer, Ted often stayed late, watching television with my mother in the living room. I crawled out of the downstairs bed, when I couldn't sleep, and woke up in the tight, cold twin bed across from my grandmother in the attic. Anyway, my mother wouldn't miss me. She was a heavy, greedy sleeper and nothing woke her.

We settled the blanket on the tall, uncut grass and opened the box of Graham crackers, passing it back and forth. We felt hickory roots under us. There were so many noises; some were insects, some were the highway, and some we didn't know. It seemed busy outside, like daytime, except for the dark.

It wasn't cold. The alfalfa field had been plowed and the corn was all picked, but there was a rich smell, like hay, that seemed to come from the ground. Even though school was starting, the air still smelled like summer. And the sky that night washed low and near us. There were white traces, as if the stars had moved and left trails of themselves, chalk dust on the black.

I chewed the end of a weed. I wasn't tired.

"You shouldn't care, you like school. You're good in school," Benny said.

"I don like it."

"Yeah, you do."

"You have a lot of friends," I said.

Since Theresa and I made friends, other girls didn't talk to me at school. When they invited me to their birthday parties, they didn't invite Theresa. And I was afraid of boys. An older boy had come up to me on the playground and teased me, and I'd hit him so hard his lip bled. He'd told and I'd been in trouble with the Mother Superior again.

"I'm afraid of them at school."

"You have some friends."

"Theresa."

"You get nervous," he said.

"Yeah, I get nervous." I felt relieved and happy, having said that. It seemed unimportant now that I'd ever been nervous and I couldn't imagine feeling afraid again.

"S'cause of your mother."

"What?" I'd never thought of that and it seemed awful, all of a sudden, for us to talk about her that way. And it was such a night, I didn't want anything wrong.

"Your family's different."

"No," I said. "She's fine. It's just me."

"Shhhh." He put his hand on the inside of my wrist, where the pulse is, and he went to sleep like that, his fingers on my arm. Everything outside seemed wonderful to me, and falling asleep took a long time. I kept sliding down in the dark and then my eyes opened again. I don't know what was more amazing: that our land was so changed and beautiful at night, or that it was familiar. It was our old barn, standing crookedly, casting a pure black shadow, and they were our houses in the distance with their porch lights on, but the sky was shining as I'd never seen it and each stalk of long grass seemed to hold an identical stem of moonlight on its side.

I woke up first and watched the daylight come into the sky. I propped up on an elbow. I heard the six-fifty train. I had never seen a sunrise and I've never forgotten that one. I must have moved, because Benny woke up, cranky because he felt cold and sore from sleeping on the ground. He ran home, dragging the blanket behind him. But I was happy. I felt incredibly light, walking over the field. I ate the last Graham crackers from the box. I felt I'd discovered something new that would change me and that my old problems, being nervous and afraid, were gone; already they seemed strange and silly to me.

The fall before we moved to Carriage Court, I wanted to go trick-or-treating with Benny, but my mother said no. She offered to take me in the car; she and Lolly would wait by the curb while I ran with my bag to the doors. But I cried and so she finally let me go.

Theresa Griling came, too, she was the only other girl. Their father had driven back from Florida and they were home again. None of us ever talked about when he was gone. That was when they took Netty away, at the end of the summer when he came home. At the railroad tracks, we all started running across the plowed frozen fields in one line. I could feel the hard ridges through the rubber soles of my tennies. After a while I didn't know where we were. The band of my mask hurt my chin and I had to hold up a bunch of sheet with one hand so I didn't trip.

Then there were dim streets where we didn't know anybody and the boys pressed up to the screen doors first. They were down to the next houses before Theresa and I got our bags open. But the heavy drop of candy in the paper bag was a pleasure, it seemed we were making progress. When we ran, the hard candy knocked on the sides of the bags and the bags banged against our thighs.

Later, we lost the boys and sat on a curb where we couldn't even find a street sign. I don't know how long we stayed there. But finally, the boys came back out of the fields. New guys were with them, riding wobbly circles on bikes. Some of them were smoking.

"Where's Benny?"

"I dunno," someone said. "Went somewhere with David."

"He's supposed to stay with us."

"Who says?"

"My mom."

"Her mom says." The smokers giggled, cigarettes dropping in the dark.

We started running again, Theresa and me in front this time and the guys on bikes bouncing over the fields. Then they came right up next to us, almost hitting us with their wheels.

"Watch out." I didn't know yet what they were doing, I didn't know I couldn't say no, that they didn't care. "That's my foot."

They pushed us down in the dirt and we both screamed. One pulled up my sheet and grinned at me. He had a crew cut and pimples and dirty hair on his upper lip. There was nothing in him that I recognized.

The other guy was pressing down Theresa's shoulders. He leaned over and kissed her, making fake smooching sounds like farts.

"Stop it," I screamed, kicking, before he did anything. My ears were cold and humming. I had a headache like one jagged line. He bent down and clamped his hands over my wrists and he was sitting on my legs. But when I looked up, I thanked God, because there was a circle of boys and I saw Benny.

"Benny. Make him stop."

I was so relieved to see Benny I closed my eyes, but then when I opened them again, he was talking to the guy next to him as if he hadn't seen me.

"Benny!"

But he didn't look down at me. He wouldn't. Then, all of a sudden, I felt it. A cold blade against my cheek, under my hair, on my neck. It was a scissors. The guy was cutting my hair. I heard the scissors clicking, the short, snuffling noises the hair made when it came off. Benny knew about my hair, he knew I'd been growing it all my life. It was unusual. Everyone said that about my hair. It was pure black. It was going to be one of the things that would help me get on television. My grandmother said it was so dark you could see other colors in it. I started to cry, but quiet. I didn't even care about Benny helping me anymore. It was too late. My hair was half gone. I just wanted it to be a dream, but I knew it was true. I just wanted my hair back, that was all I wanted and all I could imagine ever wanting.

The two older guys got on their bikes and rode away. That was the way they were, older kids, worse than lawless. They could just come out, get you alone and hurt you and then ride away. The rest of the guys, our guys, the guys we knew, started running across the uneven field. Theresa staggered up, she was crying, too, but she started following after them.

"Stevie," she was yelling and running, "Stev-vie, you're gonna be in troub-bel, I'm telling Da-ad," but she was falling forward, tripping and then getting up again, heaving harder, and I doubt her brother even heard her, she was so far behind.

I just stayed on the ground till they were far away. There was noise from trucks on the highway somewhere, but I couldn't see it. Then some-body was running back towards me. It was Benny, but I didn't want Benny then. He stood ten feet in front of me and screamed.

"Come on. Get up. You want to stay here all night, that's your busi-ness, but I'm supposed to bring you home."

I'm not going to say anything, I was thinking, I knew I didn't have to. There was nothing anyone could do to me now because I didn't care.

"Please, will you please come on. Just this once." Benny knelt down in front of me, moving his hands, wanting me to look at him.

I was trying to collect all my hair from the ground. The pieces felt light and soft and it was hard to see them in the dark. Mostly, I was doing it by touch. Benny scratched under his sock, but I didn't care what he did. He took off running then, yelling so the rest of those guys didn't go without him. I let him. Let them all go. I was wadding the hair in my hand and then dropping the balls in the bag with my candy. At least they didn't take my candy. The hair wadded up in balls, it was neat, it just made these puffs with air inside. When I reached, my knee touched the scissors. They were still there, little rounded elementary school scissors, the same kind I had at home. They lay open, a thin blue metal. I wasn't going to touch them.

"Come on, you coming or not, last chance!" I thought I heard Benny but I wasn't sure anymore. I was lowering my head to the ground, it was almost there, then there. My head felt intricate like an ant farm. I thought I could hear blood moving in tunnels.

But in a while my joints got wrong. My arms felt twisted in the shoul-der sockets. I knew I'd better get up. It had been a long time, the trucks were still running somewhere and there was nobody else around, there hadn't been anybody for hours maybe. I'd have to do something myself. So I started walking with my bag towards the lights, the nearest lights, which were far away.

Ringing the doorbell, I almost fell asleep and a man came and let me in to use the phone. The kitchen gleamed bright and I didn't even have to think about the number. It was there, the first thing I knew. My mother answered and when she heard it was me, she started screaming. I couldn't listen to it and the phone dropped down so it was just hanging, knocking against the wall.

The man who lived there picked it up. I sat in a kitchen chair. When he put the receiver back on the wall, he told me she was on her way.

"She's got the address and all. It won't be long for you now. You're pretty far from home, you have to be careful on Halloween, you know, the things you read."

A chair skidded back on the linoleum and he was across from me at the table, wearing black plastic glasses, with corn-colored hair. My eyes slumped to sleep. I didn't want to bother with anything, talking, nothing. It seemed she would be there as soon as I opened my eyes.

"Would you like an apple?" Something in his voice made me lift my head and see his hand lingering on one of the apples in a bowl between us. They were red, streaked with beads of other colors, beautiful all of a sudden. I wanted one but I was afraid. I couldn't decide what to do and then lights washed in the front window and I recognized the sound of my grandmother's brakes, like a voice. I thanked God it was my grandmother's car. I ran out with my bag in my arms and got into the backseat. Then we were all inside, my grandmother driving, my mother in the front bending over and looking at me.

"Oh God. Oh, my God, give me strength." She was kneeling on her seat then and pulling the short hair out from my face.

"What have they DONE to you? Who did that, tell me right now, who did that to you. Gram, would you look at her? They've ruined her hair, they've just ruined her. I can't believe it. How could you let them do this to you?

"You were the one, you had to go out. You were so smart, you thought you could keep up with the big kids, well, look at you now, just look at you. Sure, now you cry. Well, you'll have to live with it. It's your head, not mine. How could you let them DO that to you? Couldn't you run and call home? Couldn't you call me? Tell me, Honey, what happened?"

I was lying with my face pressed into the crease of the seat, eating my own breath back like another person's. I could taste the vinyl. I knew my mother would go on and on. She'd just keep yelling and yelling and pretty soon all we'd hear was her voice going up and down like a siren.

It was all noise. She was mad, she hated my weakness and wanted to beat it out of me and then she'd knock her hands against her own chest, killing the air there, too. I felt dry. I was a piece of wood. My grandmother just drove. We did things while my mother felt. We were still. Furniture. She took up the room in the car, sucked all the color out of us, eating the quiet for herself and all we heard was her collection, and we hated it. We could have punctured the air with our hate, it was that sharp, it had been turning for so long.

In the house, my mother marched right to the bathroom and called me. "Ann, come in here a second."

My grandmother grabbed my arm before I went. "Listen here, you, don't you worry. Tomorrow, I'll take you to the Harper Method and she'll give you a good cut. It's good to get rid of that heavy hair, anyway. It'll look real nice short." We stood in front of the bathroom. I gave my grandmother my bag of candy before I went in.

In front of the mirror, my mother combed my hair. She closed the door and locked it.

"I mean, it's what MADE you special. It was your crowning glory. You talk about going to California and auditions for television, well, let me tell you, other kids are cuter. Your hair was what you had going for you. Without it, I just don't think you'll stand out."

She shook her head, pulling a strand of my hair up and letting it fall back on my face, but even then, she couldn't resist looking at herself in the mirror and sucking in her own cheeks.

"People say my eyes are nice." I looked up at my mother.

"Who?"

"Lolly said and the ice skating pro said so too."

"Oh, Honey, they were just saying that. Ted said that, really, because he likes me. Your eyes are green, but some kids have a deeper, richer green. Your green is kind of ordinary."

My mother herself had blue eyes.

The next morning, my grandmother was waiting at the kitchen table. She had braided the hair she found in the brown bag of candy and sewn the two thick braids into the back of a yellow straw hat. "With the hat on, they'll all think you still have your long hair," she said.

I hadn't seen my mother yet.

That afternoon, my mother leaned against our white Volkswagen, her voice high above, far, her eyes on the telephone wires. "I think I may just go away somewhere, California maybe, maybe just away. You don't need me here."

I pulled her blouse, hard, trying to tug her down. Her face tilted up to the sky. "I do, Mom," I said. Her blouse that day was pink gingham, her initials embroidered over the pocket in white, fancy letters. The sky was pale blue, with a few clouds, the telephone poles, brown and scarred. She looked down at me, took off the straw hat and tossed it on the grass. She ruffled my hair. "You do, huh? Well, okay."

It only took the smallest thing. No one else in the world, nothing mattered.

11

Lime Kiln Road

There's a place in Beverly Hills where my mother and I lived for a little more than a year. From the outside the building looks like sandstone. The concrete seems gold, instead of gray, the slight difference in color of sand, when the sun comes out. On either side of the entrance, a molded lion's head holds a brass ring in its mouth.

At night, small lamps hidden in ferns lit the lions' heads. My mother and I always thought the building looked very elegant. For one thing, it was a move up for us, from our furnished studio. The apartments were like ski condominiums—there were six units, two floors each, on either side of a courtyard—and they seemed to be newly built. We felt proud to move in. My mother hired Daniel Swan's twin sisters to help us pack and clean. We threw out our unattractive odds and ends and we lined the new kitchen drawers with checkered paper. We had high hopes. We wanted to live like other people.

The apartment retained a just-built feeling, even after we moved in. Maybe it was because we had no furniture. The long, newly painted white walls of the downstairs and the beige carpet throughout, its nap still even to one side, stayed bare. But it was more. The insides of closets smelled like fresh-cut wood. We moved a bed into each of the bedrooms. My mother's room had built-in dressers; I just stacked my clothes in the closet. Ted's huge radio sat alone on the living room floor downstairs.

We often leaned on the carpeted steps in the middle of the apartment and looked at the light coming in through the porch's glass doors, hitting our living room walls in spikes and patterns, sometimes splintering into colors. We both felt pleased with the apartment, with the fact that there was an upstairs and a downstairs. We kept the bare place very clean. We ate most of our meals out and when we stayed home, we balanced plates on our knees, sitting on the carpeted stairs. I did homework on my bed.

My room had a cubbyhole, where I stored things. A door opened out of the wall, and inside, there was a plywood shelf. Every night, I put my schoolbooks there. Slanted two-by-fours sloped from the ceiling down into the foundations of the house. The boards were rough and unsanded, light wood. Perhaps they kept the closets smelling new. Between beams was nothing. You could put your hand through. I tried to be careful when I laid things on the shelf, so they wouldn't fall.

I don't know why the space was left there. Probably it should have been tamped with insulation or more wood. Perhaps the chute was a carpenter's mistake, someone else's careless harm. I've thought about that odd construction many times because one day that winter, after months and a habit of nervous care, I knocked my elbow on a corner and my jewelry box fell down.

"Why on earth did you put it there? I told you to watch that edge, for God's sakes. You knew it could go right through."

But that came afterwards. First I was just stunned. I didn't know why. I thought, Why would I leave something precious in the only unsafe place in the apartment? Perhaps there was a simple reason: it was a shelf. I had no dresser or desk for small things. But I could have put it on the floor.

It was the thing Benny gave me before I left, a tin box, with a hinged lid. Inside, I'd nested a ring, a handkerchief, a rolled-up list of my friends' names. That chute led to nowhere, there was no basement in that apartment. Things that fell down the chute were irretrievable. I imagined the tin box lying on its hinges like an opened clam, still, on the dirt floor among bare foundation beams.

Several times I went to ask the manager. After we moved out, I walked by the building. I've written letters to the investment company that owns it. I don't know what it would mean to me now, the box and its contents recovered. Ben has been dead for years, the box was a collection of childhood things. Still, it must be there at the bottom of that building like the real ticking heart of a huge machine. You remember the places you've lost to.

The night Ben died, we still lived in the small furnished studio where my mother and I slept in the same bed. She shook me awake, her hands rough and gentle at the same time. She squatted near the floor, rocking on her heels, the phone to her ear. It was still night and she was screaming.

She told me he'd been in a car. Jay Brozek had been driving. Jay had been speeding and he ran into a tree. Jay was fine, just a scratch on his cheek.

A smile grew on my face, I didn't have the strength to stop it. I felt the muscles rippling in my cheeks. Her face went crooked with pity. "Awww," she kept saying, "awww, poor Annie, poor poor Carol." When we hugged, we both squatted on the floor. I tasted her hair, a burnt taste, and her breasts moved against mine through our T-shirts.

We dressed and waited at the Western Union office with our suitcase. Carol wired us money for tickets. It was still dark out, when we drove to the airport. We didn't tell anyone where we were going; my mother phoned in to both our schools and said we were sick. It was a Monday morning. We left our car in the airport parking lot. This was our first trip home since we moved.

In Chicago, we changed to a small, older plane with scratchy, red plaid upholstery on the seats. The stewardesses seemed different, too. I recognized their voices. For the first time I heard that we had accents where we'd come from. It was in the way they said their o's. The stewardesses all wore the same maroon nail polish, matching their uniform belts. Their faces were not as delicate or chiseled as their counterparts' on the coastal flight. Maybe airlines chose stewardesses for features and the larger, less balanced profiles were left here, caught in the narrow local triangle above the ground where they grew up. Those voices, their ready nasal friendliness, sounded homely. And then I thought of how we spoke, my mother and me. I didn't think we talked that way anymore. From then on, I started being careful of my o's.

My mother turned in her seat. "Sounds familiar, doesn't it? Sort of a dumb accent, when you listen. Uneducated," she whispered. She bent over me and peered out the window. "But look at all those little farms. It really is pretty land."

The plane shuddered into its descent. Over the microphone, a stewardess asked us to buckle our seat belts.

Her voice hummed with pride and capability. Theresa Griling had wanted to be a stewardess, either that or a hairdresser someplace where rich people lived, Beverly Hills or Florida. When she'd talked like that, it had sounded brave and dangerous, something I'd never do. But, now these stewardesses seemed perfectly safe. Even in the air, even if they slept with a married pilot when the plane was grounded in Chicago for a snowstorm, even their adventures would be innocent. They would probably end up married and living somewhere within a couple hundred miles of the place they were born. They'd grow firm, righteous, the way good mothers become, their young optimism satisfied and thickened. Even those who'd chosen flight and travel, lightness, the air—you knew, listening to them, they'd never get too far away. Gravity sunk in the bottom of their voices, like the thumping of feet on the ground. Their flights would keep a tight perimeter between Chicago, the Twin Cities and Green Bay. We seemed different, already. I didn't know what would happen to us.

The runways of the Bay City Airport were just clearings in the low woods, rimmed with aspen and pine. When the plane shuddered and rumbled and bumped, we closed our eyes, clinging. When I opened my hand, a few moments later, my mother's nails had bitten in so hard there was blood. We both felt terrified of landing.

We walked into the airport slowly, dragging our one heavy suitcase. We saw Betty Dorris, the fat woman, still standing behind the ticket counter, wearing a blouse with a white ruffled collar. She had written my father's plane ticket when he'd first flown away. Betty Dorris had always liked my mother's men. The last year we'd lived in Bay City, she had invited Ted over to dinner. Now, she wouldn't look at us.

"God," my mother said.

Years ago, in December, my mother and I drove to her house and bought Christmas tree ornaments, styrofoam balls she had covered with velvet and lace. We bought them out of pity and then gave them away.

"I think it's rude that she doesn't say anything. She sees us," I said.

"Oh, of course she does. But you know, it's her way of snubbing me. I suppose she figures Bay City's hers now that I'm gone. Well, she can have it."

We braced ourselves, waiting for someone to find us and take us to a car. We didn't know who it would be. It was a relief not to see them yet. I knew the minute one of them looked at me, it would all begin.

My mother slipped the bag off her shoulder and set it on the floor.

"God, doesn't it all look small?" She looked around and then back at me. "I mean, the airport, everything, just seems TINY."

It's funny how close you get, closer than in life, except for the seconds you touched, and then you were both moving, not seeing, exactly. Looking down at Benny, I thought there was something wrong with the way his nostrils joined his lip. They looked strange and fishlike, inaccurate. I leaned over to kiss him and tasted powder on my mouth and felt the hardness just underneath, like metal.

It was a brass-banded cedar box, lined in pleated pale blue satin. A piece of lace I recognized from my grandmother's house lay under his head. It had always been draped over the davenport.

Carol stood on the carpet in her nylons, her high heels next to her feet, facing forward.

"They used to water the greens," Jimmy was saying. "See, then they let them golf free. So he was there with Susie and a whole group of them. And Jay Brozek was there too, he had his own car. So Ben got in the one car with Susie and all the rest."

"He was *in* the car?"

"He was *in* the other car and then Jay called him and said, Hey, Ben, come on over and ride with me, I'm all alone. So he did."

My mother crossed her arms over her chest and then she wiped her glasses on her silk scarf. She was wearing a black pantsuit, belted. "In the millions," she said, frowning. Pews lined the center of the room, so people gathered at the edges, where floral arrangements stood on the carpet. Smaller bouquets were set on draped tables. "Absolutely, they'll be rich from this."

"He can sue for companionship, for loss of income." Hal bent back his fingers, counting. "He'll be able to retire."

Carol moved from her shoes, which were still planted on the carpet, facing the coffin. "I wanted you to see." She pushed the back of my neck, dunking me over a bouquet of long-stemmed dark roses. They looked tinged, almost black. "From that little Susie." My aunt looked at me. "See, I always said, if Ben grew up and wanted to marry that Susie, we would have been glad, Ann. And they're not rich either, the parents both work. But it's a clean nice family."

The couple who owned Krim's bakery tapped Carol's shoulder. Grilings shuffled behind them.

"When you were little, you always thought you were adopted," Theresa told me, "because your mother had blond hair and you had dark." She reached out to touch my hair, the way she always had, as if black hair were amazing.

I asked Theresa and Mary how they liked the academy. "Fine," they each said quickly. "Good." They had known Benny, too, more than I did the past few years.

They told me Rosie had gotten married and moved to Milwaukee and Stevie had gone into the navy. He was on an aircraft carrier going around the world. Theresa said she planned to enlist in the air force when she graduated. On her coat, she was wearing small tin silver wings, from American Airlines. I recognized them, they had been mine. A stewardess gave them to me once when my mother and I flew home from Las Vegas.

"You're going to join the army and leave Mary all alone?"

"There's my dad," Mary said quickly.

"Air force," Theresa corrected.

Then Jay walked in the back door, flanked on either side by Chummy Brozek and his second wife, Darla, who was so fat she had to make her own clothes. She wore a huge brown smock with regular terry-cloth house slippers.

"She probably can't get shoes that wide," my mother whispered. "Look at that. Each foot is like a little dog."

Jay hovered taller than his father, but his neck wilted, he looked bad in a suit. His dark hair seemed wet and there were cracks and scabs on his lips. You could see the tremble. I stared at the scratch on his cheek. The three of them moved together, sideways, into a pew.

"I know it," Carol said, somewhere behind me.

All our lives, Brozeks had lived on Lime Kiln Road, Chummy delivered Morning Glory milk.

"Older," Jimmy said. "They've got two in the marines, one in the air force. The air force one is stationed somewhere in Germany, the other two are over in Vietnam. But they're all alive."

"He's going to be a pallbearer, Jay is," Hal said.

"No," my mother hissed. She shoved her fist in her mouth.

"That's what we said too, but Benny would have wanted it this way."

I'd never seen her before, but I recognized her from the school photograph my grandmother had sent, with *Benny's girlfriend Susie* written on the white border. They'd met working on a float. They'd stuffed thousands of square toilet paper tissues into chicken wire to make the top of a covered wagon.

"But the phone rang in the trailer and Carol got it. And they told us he'd been in an accident. They had him in the hospital at Bailey's Harbor. We had to decide right then if we wanted to fly him down to a big hospital or let the doctor work on him there. Hell, we didn't know. He was unconscious when we got there. And this dumb doctor is fussing, working on the leg, pinning the leg, and here he's concentrating all his energy on the leg and the heart stops."

"But—," I couldn't finish. I couldn't imagine Benny without a leg.

"I don't think he was too much on the ball. You figure, a country doctor up there."

"A GP probably," my mother murmured.

Carol, still without her shoes, clasped a hand on Jimmy's arm. "Look, both of the parents came and brought that Susie. They work, so they must have both taken off."

"See, if that was you, I would have had you on the next plane to Chicago to *the* best doctor," my mother whispered as Carol and Jimmy walked away. "A specialist. Some dumb country doctor sitting the night shift. No wonder, you know."

"Then he could have died on the plane," I said.

My mother pushed her face next to mine. "That's why we moved. So we could be there, *living* with the very best. Of everything. You should be grateful once in a while, you know? For all I've done for you. You don't see now, but you will someday."

Susie inched into the pew behind Jay, and lay a hand on his shoulder. They were friends, there was a whole system of love and danger nobody who wasn't young would see. I was thinking of Benny speeding in the dark, swimming at night with his friends, holding their cigarettes up over the water. All I'd missed the three years since we'd moved. Undressing

Susie, screwing her on the dirty sand. Things I didn't really know, drinking, drugs. I looked at Hal. There was definitely something. All of a sudden, I felt so jealous: Benny had known everything first. Then, as soon as the return of a breath, I hoped he'd done it all, the things my mother most feared, the worst.

Susie wore suede fringed moccasins, tied around her ankles, under her dress. She had thick ankles and the moccasins made them look thicker, but she didn't seem to know. Benny wouldn't have ever noticed either and that made me think that life here was simpler than ours in California. We felt acutely aware of everything wrong with us. I'd been studying with a guy named Peter from my school, and his maid brought us a tray of cookies. "They're good, you should have some," he'd said, "or on second thought, maybe you shouldn't." The next time I'd stood up and crossed the room to sharpen a pencil, he cupped his hand on my thigh. "That's where you put it on," he'd said. My mother and I weren't the hits we'd hoped to be.

At the back of the room, Hal's wife, Merry, handed Tina over to Hal's arms. Merry and Tina lived in a trailer now, twenty miles up out of town.

"They were nice together, that Susie and Ben. They were good kids." Carol sighed.

"Better than Hal is," Jimmy said.

Behind us, two women were talking about Darla Brozek's cooking, how for a long time, she'd had to cook for twelve every night, five of them big boys. One woman started on Darla's recipe for chicken: you bone and skin two big chickens and lay the meat out in such a glass baking dish. You pour over two cans of soup, cream of mushroom, cream of celery, one of the creams. And then on top of that, she spread out those Pillsbury frozen biscuits and baked at 350 for an hour and oh, was it good.

"The Tet Offensive," Chummy Brozek said. "Yes, a medal. No, Hal never went. He was here the whole time."

I walked over to where Hal was standing, against an accordion wall.

"Where's the gramma?" someone asked.

"They've got her sedated, she's in the hospital." The time she'd seen Hal on television was the first stroke. Since then, she'd had two. The first time, Carol called us and said we didn't have to come home. She was already in the hospital recovering from the second stroke when they'd had to tell her about Benny.

That afternoon, when my mother and I had gone to visit, she seemed indifferent. I sat in the corner of the hospital room, watching as she tossed in her bed, my mother hovering over, saying, "Mom, you look great, how do you feel?" her voice loud and bright, as if my grandmother were deaf.

"Leave me be," she'd said.

. . .

Carol stepped back up into her high heels. People were beginning to leave and she had to stand next to Jimmy and shake their hands. She told Jay where the pallbearers would meet and he looked desperately grateful. He kept repeating, "outside back door, eight o'clock in the morning" as if the words were his duty for the rest of his life.

While Jay walked Darla to the car in the parking lot, Chummy lingered inside. "Go ahead and sue me," he said to Jimmy. "We've paid our premiums all our lives for something like this, first Junie and I paid and now Darla and I do. Go ahead and sue me."

"He'll have to live with this, Jay will," Hal said. "Just like I do."

"What he did is worse," I said. "You didn't kill anybody."

"Didn't get a chance."

He meant the war. Whenever Hal brought up Vietnam, the rest of us didn't say anything.

For a long time we all stood there at the door. We watched people we knew go down the dim hallway into the brightness. It was after Labor Day, but hot outside. We were the last ones there; Carol walked around picking dry flowers from the bouquets. She stepped out of her shoes again. "Do you think we should turn off the lights?"

"They do that," my mother said. "Leave it."

Carol rubbed the arch of her foot. "Do you want me to give you my keys?" she said. "You can drive to Dean's and pick up hamburgers for all of us." She was the only one who could dare talk about food.

I turned so our knees touched through our nylons. "I don't have a license."

"Oh, no, sure, I guess you wouldn't. You're a year younger, always."

We sat near the door a little longer. They gave my mother Jimmy's keys, but we were all of us shy to go out into that brightness.

Carol shook her head. "You know, I just can't help it. He was the one drinking. And now he'll get married and go to college and do all the things." No one answered. "Thank God, we gave Ben the skis last Christmas. At least he got some fun out of that."

My mother shoved her knuckles in her mouth. She wiped an eye with one end of her scarf.

"Oh, Adele, don't, you'll ruin it. Silk stains and that's such a very pretty scarf."

We drove fast, the two of us, windows down, my arm out damming the air, along Bay Highway, past factories and then the fields, in no hurry to get home. I fumbled with the radio knobs. It was September, an Indian summer day, and the fields smelled rich like corn.

We passed Bay Beach and the rides were still going. My mother skidded to a stop and we sat there, parked on the gravel, watching the slow-moving machines.

"Should we just go once?" she said.

Our seat bobbed and then we were high, at the top of the Ferris wheel, suspended while the boy below hurried children down the runway and fastened them in. You could see all the land, in clear geometry, the baby pool set like a gem in cement. The amusement park rides looked quaint and small, painted colors faded and old-fashioned. We were still at the top rocking, tilting. It wasn't falling that scared me, but the slow band of time as you're beginning to go, when you can still see the world in clear patterns, the web of lawns, and your fingernails cut into the soft nicked wood and everything in your body screams Stop. But you're moving.

The car tilted down and I was screaming, probably a long time before I heard it.

When we took her out of the car in the back parking lot of the hospital, the pavement sparkled and she planted her feet far apart, her ankles stiff as if she were on ice. In her room, she felt glad to get out of her clothes. She asked us to close the blinds, the bars of light on the blanket hurt her.

"Don't you want to talk a little before you go to sleep, Mom?" my mother whispered through the metal poles of the bed. "We haven't seen you for so long."

"No," she said. "Let me be."

After the funeral, my mother drove downtown to get her divorce. She took a long time dressing for it. Her lawyer told her there would be problems in the way of bills from Ted's credit card. Ted had ended up paying for our Lincoln. My mother skipped the cemetery. The rest of us went and then followed in a slow caravan back to Lime Kiln Road. Women put on aprons in the kitchen and stood cutting cakes on Carol's counters. Jimmy stayed outside, tending the barbecue pit. Hal lugged things—silver kegs of beer, trays of chicken for the grill. There was one round table under an umbrella where the priest sat with his feet up. He wore white athletic socks under his sandals.

There was a small stand of pines between my grandmother's house and Carol's, in the common backyard. I walked over and stood there, my heels puncturing the dry brown leaves and pine needles. My grandmother once told me that during storms her husband had fastened on snowshoes and trekked out to stand in this grove of trees, watching the snow come down. Protected by the high branches, he stood and watched. She said he loved the silence. The pine smelled sharp and good. This was the place Benny and I buried our pets; a bird with a broken wing we'd fed from an eye-dropper, a lame squirrel. We'd sat in here for hours. We'd felt invisible then, inside a dome of different air. Now it was a few scraggly pines. We'd marked the graves with crosses made from clean licked Popsicle sticks and now they weren't there anymore.

I picked up a handful of dirt and let it fall down off my fingers. Things didn't stay and for no good reason. My father's hole in the hedge was a shabby lapse now, almost grown over, as if the bushes were slightly diseased. I thought about our crosses; wood wouldn't dissolve into the ground, not in five or ten years. No one would take them, but they were gone. Things just disappeared and we weren't even surprised. We didn't expect them to last.

When I walked back to the patio, someone was passing around a large gray rock. "It's a rock from Pikes Peak," Hal said. It was labeled in my grandmother's even penmanship, *Rock From Pikes Peak*. "I took a trip to Colorado and Ben said he wanted a rock from Pikes Peak."

"Oh," the women said, in low voices, as if they were holding a dangerous and beautiful secret.

The rock passed from hand to hand on the back patio, the story repeated in different voices. "He said he wanted a rock from Pikes Peak," Jimmy said.

Right then, I wanted it to take home with me to keep. I wanted it a lot and I couldn't think of anything else for a while.

The women stood in the kitchen again, rinsing the dishes and stacking them. Everything outside seemed very clear, the dark green hedge, the corn, the red barn and the highway overpass. The sky was a tender blue with slow pink clouds. Ordinary objects looked precious and defined the way they do sometimes in cold air. It was still early in the afternoon and it seemed as if nothing would change, as if the fields and light had settled into a permanent weather.

The screen banged and my mother tripped, her heel catching in the netted doormat. She let the air out of her cheeks slowly. She stood on one shoe, the other stockinged foot at her knee, her arms crossed over her chest. I was sitting on the warm white stones of the barbecue pit. I waited for her to find me.

Then she saw me and shrugged. "Well, we're free," she said. "We didn't get much, but it's over. We're single."

The trouble with serenity is that it can turn. The trees seem to lose their souls and look again like painted scenery. You hug your knees and kiss them as if chilled. You pinch yourself. Then you turn to other people, talk, you trust only human beings again, as if nature has abandoned you. Christianity must have been born in twilight.

Only the family and Lolly and the priest still sat outside, on the back patio, when the air began to lose its light. The priest lit a cigarette.

I was thinking of Ben again, I imagined him drinking margaritas, ba- nana daiquiris, the way he danced, stamping his feet, spinning, lightly touching Susie's breasts by the side of the house, driving, speeding in the night. "You can smoke?" I said to the priest.

"Sure."

"He's a super-duper-modern priest," Carol said. "They give guitar masses now. Oh, it's all changed since you left. They go to Michigan on retreats. I've seen this one in blue jeans."

The priest laughed, his soft voice dissolving quickly in the air.

"Can you drink?"

He nodded.

"So can you screw now, too?"

"Ann," my mother said. She and Lolly warmed their hands over the barbecue pit. "I don't know where she learns that language. Two days here. She doesn't talk like that in Beverly Hills."

"Some things haven't changed," the priest said.

Jimmy leaned over the table. "Annie here asked you, Father, because she was interested."

"Oh, Jimmy," Carol said.

It was too early for crickets, but it seemed we could hear the night coming slowly, before the light dimmed, a shifting of the earth. The trees moved as if they were pulling into themselves.

"Oh, and he's a good preacher, too, Ann. You should hear him. They come all the way over from the West Side."

"We go at night now," Jimmy said. "Guitar mass."

"You didn't know your aunt and uncle were such swingers."

"Me, I don't go to church," Hal said. "I pray by myself. God knows what I'm saying. I just ask him straight. None of this bullshit."

Nobody paid any attention to Hal, but that was normal. We were all used to ignoring him.

"Different for you," Hal said, pointing to his daughter, Tina. "You have to pray out loud. And you know why? Because I said so."

"I do," she said.

The five o'clock train came, a long faltering wail in the distance.

"Are you too cold?" Jimmy asked me.

"No, it's okay."

"'Cause I can go get you a sweater. You'd fit in one of his." It broke my heart, Jimmy like that, kind.

"So do you like California?" the priest asked my mother. His forehead had no lines, he seemed so innocent, local.

She shrugged. "Well, yes and no. I do and I don't." Her arms spread out, glamorous, over the pit. "I mean, I work nine hours a day and drive two more and just so we can live in one room where she goes to a decent school. So there's no time, really, or money, for me to have any fun. But, yes, I'm glad to be doing it. I'm glad to be giving her this opportunity."

No one said anything. The ice cubes knocked together in Jimmy's glass. Even Lolly seemed embarrassed, looking down. Our leg waxes, the days of facials, hours in tight pink masks, then the steam room at Elizabeth Arden's. I got to go, too, Saturdays and her date days with Josh Spritzer. The opera dress with windows of sheer fabric, revealing printed scenes of other cloth. Palm Springs, the ocean, the desert. We had fun. But I didn't say anything, either.

Jimmy stood up, he was always the worst with my mother. Carol seemed to have a genetic patience for her.

"Let me tell you something, Adele. We all work too, we—"

"Jimmy, don't," Carol said.

"I'm going to go get another drink." He went in through the sliding glass doors he'd built himself, years ago, when Benny and I were pests, underfoot.

My mother appeared injured. "Well, sure you work, too, but you have the house, you have the trailer—" My mother moved her face, looking around at it all.

I stared at her. "You wouldn't want it," I said.

Lolly reached out and touched my mother's arm.

"Just today, let's not have any fighting once," Carol said.

My mother and Lolly started whispering between themselves. "Well she . . ." my mother was saying, as I moved away.

The night before, we slept in my grandmother's house. We needed to be alone. We'd snooped around, opened drawers just to see the things once again where they'd always been, picked at food in the refrigerator. My mother sat on the kitchen floor with her legs spread out, searching the bottom cupboards for hidden cookies.

"They're in here somewhere." She'd been happy. I could have let her look, but she had this grin that bothered me.

I told her. "She stopped making them years ago."

"No," she said. "Those round flat butter cookies. She hides them in here somewhere."

"With the ground hickory nuts and powder sugar on top." I shook my head. "It hurt her eyes too much to pick the nuts."

"Oh."

An hour later, my mother came and touched my shoulder and said, "How did you know she stopped making those?"

I shrugged. "I just knew."

"Oh. I didn't know that," she said.

Then she called Josh Spritzer. The way she talked there was no possible way he could imagine our kitchen. She sat in the corner, her bare feet up on the vinyl chair. The electric clock above the stove buzzed, the cuckoo thugged, the refrigerator churned and the fluorescent curved tube of lights over the table hummed. The inside of houses in the country were like that then. Because of the silence, like a long throat, outside.

I could tell from the way her voice rose in waves of enthusiasm—too much music, nerve and light—that Josh Spritzer didn't want to be listening. Her breath gathered as she began each sentence. "And my sister, on the day of the funeral, was counting the flower arrangements." She laughed, trying to make it light.

After, she went humming through the house, filing her nails. But the phone call hadn't gone well; when she hung up, she'd stayed where she was and stared ahead at the wall for a full minute.

"Maybe we should go back early, huh?" She stopped in the living room doorway and looked around. "Our life isn't here anymore, you know? It's there."

Tina was fidgeting and when Hal yelled at her, she started to cry. He picked her up, then, and spanked her and her yelps escalated to screaming. Our heads bent down over the table.

"Hal, just leave her be once." That was Carol. "Ogh, Hal, she's overtired."

He pointed, with the hand not holding Tina, to his chest. "She's *my* kid, mine. She's not yours. I'll do what I want with her." Tina stopped crying. She hung still now, limp off his shoulder.

Jimmy was standing at the sliding glass doors. He let them pass.

"I mean, if I'd had half the help *she* did from my father." My mother had been talking to Lolly but her voice rose loud in the pause. "The house and every year a new car."

Jimmy just stood with his drink, inside the open glass doors. "Adele, come here a second."

She looked up. She was sitting on the edge of the stone barbecue pit, a leg swinging over the side. "What for?"

"I want to show you something."

"Show me what?"

"I want to show you the deed and the mortgage for this house I've been paying on for twenty-one years and that I'm still paying."

My mother shook her head. For a moment, I blushed. I thought she was ashamed. But she looked up again. No one could beat my mother.

"You know who helped me when I got married? Nobody."

"Come in here."

My mother started crying. "I'm not going in there with you, Jimmy. You'll hurt me. I know that's what you want."

The priest sat chewing on the end of a weed and the evening train went by, a low crooked moan from the tracks. The young priest looked wistful then, as if he wished he were going somewhere.

Carol stood and held her elbows in her hands. Her mouth opened, but she must have thought better of it. She just shook her head.

"You've got your chance to see. Either look at it or shut up from now on."

My mother lifted her head. "I won't be talked to like that, Jimmy, by you or by anyone. I'm going home to Mom's now, because really, I'm very, very tired."

She started walking. Lolly stayed a moment longer, staring down at the fire. Then, reluctantly, it seemed, she stood and followed my mother over the lawn. A little smoke rose from the pit, and I watched the light from the priest's cigarette.

My mother was almost to my grandmother's porch. Then she turned and called me. She slapped her thigh the way people do calling their dogs in from outside. Lolly stood halfway across the dusky lawn and then she turned and walked to her car. It was almost dark. I stayed in my chair. In back of my grandmother's house the fields spread still and empty. A dirt road ran to the barn, then the highway, above the little houses with yellow lights on for suppertime, where a wagon and a wheelbarrow lay tipped. There wasn't much.

The land—it was the same, only small, the trees seemed lower, the houses simple compared to those we'd seen. Still, I understood things here. I knew how to be comfortable. We weren't doing so well in California.

My mother stood across the yard, her elbows pointing out, hands on her waist, like a harsh letter of some other alphabet. She was waiting for me. And I wouldn't move.

"You can stay here," Carol said, "I'll put sheets on his bed for you." Jimmy nodded and closed the glass doors. They hadn't even been in Benny's room yet. Years later, when I came back on a Greyhound bus, it was exactly the same, his size 14 boy's sweaters folded in the drawers, his model cars on shelves, airplanes hanging on strings from the ceiling.

My mother called me again. Everyone waited. Cars on the highway moved slowly, nothing else changed. The barn looked old, unused for years. My grandmother had seemed tiny in the hospital. I looked down at my legs, in dark pantyhose, good high-heeled shoes. The names and prices of these seemed like secrets I would be embarrassed to tell. I couldn't stay here. There was nothing. I'd be like my mother, always wanting to go away.

I looked up. The priest was still chewing a weed. Carol bit her cuticle, her hand close to her mouth, Hal poked the coals of the fire. I did what they all knew I'd do. I followed my mother.

She yelled over the sound of pipes in the bathroom. "You know, I never realized how backwards they still are. They've got the faucet for hot and the faucet for cold and you can't really ever get it right."

I opened a drawer underneath the telephone on the kitchen counter. The half-sized pencils my grandmother used had ridged tips from the way she sharpened them, with a knife. I'd seen her many times, her broad back hunched in concentration over the wastebasket. Deep in the drawer, I found a folded communion veil, a box of oil pastels, a deck of cards with a scene of Canadian wilderness on their browned backs. There were other things: a tiny Bible with four-leaf clovers pressed inside, so their outlines stained the pages; numerous finished tick-tack-toe games; address labels; glue; a cookie cutter in the shape of a hammer. I flipped through one of the small notebooks. It was mostly grocery lists in faded pencil. *A stick of butter, chicken pie, bread, a vegetable.* Then I came across a list of the names of my grandmother's friends. Mabel, Jen, Ellie, April, Sarah, Jude. The women, now in their seventies, she called the girls. She'd sat down once with this little spiral-topped notebook and one of her soft-leaded, knife-sharpened pencils and made a list of her friends. It was something I'd done in Beverly Hills, where I didn't have many, where we weren't as impressive as we'd hoped. I couldn't stand to think my grandmother ever felt the way I did. From the drawer, I stole an old implement, something I didn't recognize that said Callodean's Tin in wood-burned letters on its side. It was just some old tool that fit the hand but had no use. I wanted it. I slipped it in my pocket.

My mother hollered from the tub. "And who do you think'd take care of you here? Your grandmother's in the hospital, she'll probably die, Carol and Jimmy are being nice, sure, but they'll get over it with their money and you just watch now that they'll have something, they're not going to give it to us. You'd think they'd help me after I've been alone all these years, but will they? No."

"You're selfish." I said it quietly, in the kitchen, but she heard me.

"Oh, I can see, it's you too now. All my life, all I've ever done is give to you and do for you and now you go against me with them, too. Well, I can see from now on, I'm going to give to ME."

I was tired. "I'm not going against you, so let's just be quiet."

"I'm not going to be quiet," she yelled. A second later, she stood dripping in front of me, her face crumpled. "You know I've given you every-

thing I could," she said. She was looking at me, pitiful, I can't describe it.
     "I know," I said. It was true.

We left the next morning, days earlier than our tickets said. We all seemed
subdued when Carol drove past the Oneida land to the airport. I kept
thinking that they'd paid for our plane; we were leaving so soon, they
might feel like they paid for a convenient divorce. But then again, Carol
seemed tired. She probably wanted to be by herself. She was getting like
my grandmother. When something was wrong, they wanted to be closed
up in their houses, alone.
     Carol drove very carefully and slow. Her lips wove, she kept licking
them, and her mouth constantly rearranged itself as if any position felt
uncomfortable. We wanted her to just drop us off, so she could drive right
home, but she wouldn't, she parked and waited until we boarded the
plane.
     Once we were in the air, we felt giddy. We both loved airplanes; they
were like doctors; they made us feel rich and clean. We were dressed in
our best clothes and new stockings charged at Shreve's. No one seeing us
would know anything true.
     In Chicago, we bought magazines. We drank Kahlua and creams. We
felt like busy celebrities rushing home to our lives. And that's the way
Carol must have seen us, too, as she lugged our big suitcase up the ramp,
while we held our short dresses down, walking onto the plane. But when
we landed at LAX, no one was waiting for us and we had to find our own
car parked in the ridiculously complicated system of lots and after we got
home, scraping the car so it shrieked against the concrete embankment of
our driveway, my mother said she didn't want to call Josh Spritzer, that
she'd wait for him to call her. And the phone didn't ring at all that night
or the next night either.

Once that fall, my mother drove with the Witch to Palm Springs. They
came back with bad sunburns and three hundred dollar's worth of dates.
Dates and figs and other dried fruits. Daniel Swan and I sat on the porch
steps of the San Ysidro house, watching them haul the bags in.
     "Come on, kids, give us a hand," my mother called.
     "We're absolutely broke." I turned to Daniel, my cheek on my knee.
     He laughed. "We can beat you there. We're in debt."
     Halfway between home and Palm Springs, a place called Hadley's sold
discounted desert dates (and figs and other dried fruits). My mother decided they were a savings. She and the Witch said they'd freeze them all,
then fix them in cellophane and fancy baskets at Christmas and give them
as presents to the people they worked with.

"Listen, that's part of your job," my mother said, later, as we unpacked the plastic bags into our freezer. "And you don't know how much things cost around Christmas." The new apartment had a clean, large refrigerator. We'd moved not long after we came back from Wisconsin.

My mother got home late that winter, sometimes at nine or ten on school nights. We never had much food in the house, so we went out to dinner. Sometimes, when we felt too tired or broke, we'd skip supper and just go to bed.

I started breaking into the stash of frozen dates. I tore open the plastic bags and stood by the freezer when I was hungry, eating handfuls of them, frozen. My mother began to do it, too. We'd stand in our clean, empty kitchen, the freezer open, chewing hard. It was just something we did in that apartment. Every household has its habits. The dates were good but tough. We worried about chipping our teeth.

By November, all the bags were torn open. Sometimes my mother would shake her head. "A hundred ninety dollars on *snacks*," she'd say and sigh.

But we kept doing it anyway. She did it too. We were hungry a lot of the time.

Even though we both liked that apartment, everything went wrong in it. I invited three girls from school over for dinner and when I put the chicken in the oven, we discovered the gas was turned off. My mother had to go knocking at neighbors' doors until she found one who'd let us cook my chicken. She had to do it, I was too embarrassed.

And around Christmas, the day I had my first real date, my mother called, falling apart, somewhere on the highway.

My date was with an older guy named Ronnie. Daniel Swan and I— kids our age—couldn't drive yet. This guy had a blue Porsche and he skied, he had that white-eyed, raccoon tan. He'd run for school president and I'd worked on his campaign. His mother's greatest ambition was for all her sons to be admitted to Stanford. She'd hired a rock band to play at his campaign parties and she liked me because I'd drawn his campaign poster, a huge oil pastel on butcher paper. Probably as compensation, he'd asked me out.

It was a dark day, cool, even for winter. I rode my bike home right after school and washed my hair, taking an hour to blow-dry, curling it under. Then my mother called.

"It's me, your mother," she said.

"Where are you?"

"I'm on the highway, can't you hear the cars?"

I touched a wall. "Where are you calling from?"

"Boy, are you dumb sometimes. I just told you. I'm at a filling station out in the middle of nowhere. Listen to me. I'm not coming home." Her voice was odd and flat. I tasted metal in my mouth.

While we were quiet then, it came over the phone—the roar of trucks and cars.

"Now, listen. When they call you, I want you to say you don't know anything. And I'm going to tell you now about the insurance policy. The papers are wrapped in tinfoil at the bottom of the freezer. Underneath the dates. You'll get twenty-five thousand dollars for me. So take care of yourself, sweetie. You're going to have to from now on. 'Cause I won't be around. But I know you. You'll manage fine."

I couldn't talk at first. My lip was flickering.

"I'm going to have an accident." Her voice sounded make-believe and serious at the same time.

"Why, Mom?" That was all I could choke out. I looked around the room, the empty walls, the dark windows.

"You don't love me and so I—"

I whimpered. "Mo-om, I do, I love you."

"No, you really don't, Ann. I know. And I've tried, believe me, I've tried. I've done all I can do. And I can't help you anymore. You'll be better off without me. You're strong, you're stronger than you think. I know you. I tried to get us a Christmas tree, I got this huge, big beautiful tree. It was expensive, but I thought, Well, this once we'll really have something nice. At least I can do that for her. Don't you think I've felt bad that I couldn't have furniture for you and give you clothes and money like other parents give their kids? But I couldn't, Annie. I was all alone. I didn't have any man to help me. And I said to them at the lot, I said, Tie it on tight, because I've got a long way to drive. And they said, Yeah, yeah, sure they would. Sure. Well, they didn't. Here I'm driving on the freeway and it falls off. This big beautiful tree bounces on the road and it splintered into a million pieces. And that's where it is, all over the highway. A million smithereens. I paid my last money for it. That tree was forty dollars. I couldn't even do that for you. I couldn't even get you a Christmas. I'm giving up. I'm driving up the coast and off the cliffs at Big Sur. It's supposed to be pretty there. Remember I always wanted to see them? I'm just going to have an accident."

"Mom, please, don't. Please come home. I need you." My voice wasn't the same either. I'd never heard it before. I sounded like her.

"You're just scared," she said. "You don't know what you'll do without me. That's why you think you love me now, but you really don't, you're just scared to be alone."

That stopped me for a second. It seemed true. Then I lost some grip and it started again. I sounded like a baby. "Mom, please, no, no, come home, I'll be good, whatever you want, just please—"

She hung up.

I opened the freezer and grabbed dates from the bags, the biggest, most expensive kind, medjools.

I paced the apartment, eating, watching the phone. I expected her to call again. Ticks of the minute hand followed me, pinpricks on my back. Then I sat on the floor and dialed the highway patrol. I waited a long time for them to answer. A man told me he couldn't say anything for twenty-four hours. "You call the hospitals, they'll tell you the same thing," he said. "But if she ends up there, in Emergency, they generally call you."

"I haven't heard anything."

"No, huh?"

"But she should be home by now. Usually." I obeyed what she said. I didn't tell him she'd called.

"Yes." He cleared his throat. "Course a lot of them they can't identify right away. You say a white Continental? What does the driver look like?"

"Oh, well, she has . . ." My voice went dry. It was very hard, all of a sudden, for me to talk. "Blond hair. Freckles. Blue eyes. She's, I don't know, small. And pretty. She's real pretty." I felt like I was giving him what he needed to take her away from me.

There was an awful pause. "I heard about a Continental and something like that on 1 tonight, but I think it was a redhead. You're just going to have to sit tight and wait. Don't worry, if something's wrong, they'll call you."

I climbed upstairs and took off my new pantsuit. I pulled on a nightgown and crawled into bed, but I couldn't get warm. The alarm clock sat on the floor next to me. It was almost seven and Ronnie was coming to pick me up for the movie at seven. I just waited in bed. I didn't know what would happen.

At seven, I went to the window in my mother's room and looked out over the front door. All the lights were off. I was wearing my nightgown and knee socks and my running shoes. I knelt by the window, listening for the Lincoln. Then I heard a door slam and I knew it was Ronnie's. I would have recognized the sound of ours.

I watched him walk up to the door. He was wearing boots that seemed to bind his legs and turn his feet out. He stood there on our doormat, and with both his hands, he rubbed down his hair; for a moment I felt elated; he liked me. But then the bell echoed through the wall and I ducked down under the window ledge. I didn't move, as if I could be caught.

There was a long silence, but I didn't hear footsteps. It was excruciating. He still stood there at the door. I thought in a panic if the door was locked; it was, I'd checked. He would just stand there and then he would leave. He would have to leave.

I felt like we were breathing together, on opposite sides of the wall. He didn't move, I didn't move. I didn't dare peek out anymore. The doorbell rang again, a long ring, making me shudder.

Then something horrible happened. I heard my mother's car screeching to a halt on the street. I knew it was ours. Suddenly, I felt absolutely furious at the way she drove; she never could learn to use a brake. She'd careen along, looking at everything but the road, and then, a second before a collision, she'd say, "Whoops," and smash on the brakes.

I heard the quick nervous clatter of her heels on the pavement and I crawled fast, galloping on the carpet, to my room to put my clothes back on. My hair was a mess, there wouldn't be time for makeup. I flipped the light on and opened my algebra book. I was zipping up my jeans when I heard the key turning in the door downstairs.

"Uh, Ann. Ann? Where are you, Honey?"

"I'm up here, Mom." I tried to make my voice sound cheerful. I brushed my hair furiously. Then I bent down to buckle my shoe. I went downstairs holding my open book in one hand, I must have looked about as casual as Hamlet. Then I stopped, halfway down, and said, "Oh, um hi, Ronnie."

He jammed his hands in his parka pockets and smiled up at me. He really is cute, I was thinking to myself, and just then I remembered that the entire apartment was empty. I'd thought of that before, this morning, which seemed like years ago now. I'd planned to meet him at the door, dressed and ready, smiling, sailing out with one line, like "We just moved in and our furniture's not delivered yet. Such a pain." But here we were, looking down at the expanse of beige carpet. No furniture, with the exception of Ted's big radio. And that was a danger, too. I could sense my mother veering towards it. I thought I'd die if she turned it on to her easy-listening station, I'd truly die. "Smoke Gets in Your Eyes" with orchestration, or "The Impossible Dream." This night was already way too weird for Ronnie. And his parents owned a rock 'n' roll record company.

He was looking around at the bare walls. "Did you hear me, Ann? I rang the doorbell."

"No," I said. "Just now?"

"Yeah. I rang it twice."

"I don't know, I was studying."

My mother smiled, radiant. "You must have just nodded off for a second. Well." She clapped her hands together. From a life of working with children, my mother believed in applause. "You kids won't believe the tree I've got." She winked at me. "It's more gorgeous than the first one even. But I think I'm going to need some help getting her in."

It felt good to be told what to do. We followed her outside. It was cold, a clear black night, with a few rare stars. I stood on one side of the car and Ronnie leaned on the other. We started untying the ropes. I was just following along. The air seemed tender. I felt so, I don't know, grateful. Like Ronnie and I were still just kids.

"Isn't she a beaut?" my mother said, and looked at me, smiling.

I shrugged and looked down. "It's tied to the fender, too."

My mother sighed. "Gee, I wish I had something in the house. Some hot chocolate or cider." She clapped again. "Say. We could all go out and get a little something. I'll take you kids out for some dessert."

"We're going to a movie, Mom."

"Oh, all right." She rubbed her hands together. "I just thought it would be a nice night for a little something hot. Brrr."

"Actually, I think we missed the movie," Ronnie said, lifting his sweater and looking at a watch. "It's starting now."

The three of us lifted the tree onto our shoulders. We stood it up next to the glass doors. The branches trembled and then fell into place. It was a huge, beautiful tree.

"So, what do you say? Should we go out and grab a bite to eat? I could go for a little something. It's up to you kids. Whatever you want."

Ronnie and I looked at each other.

"Okay with me," Ronnie said, his hands jammed in his pockets again. I said, "Sure."

"Let me just change my clothes and we'll go." My mother ran up the stairs, clapping.

We both leaned against the car door, shuffling our feet on the curb. Ronnie's Porsche was down the block. It gleamed under the streetlamp.

"I'm sorry about tonight," I said.

His lip lifted in one place, as if pulled by a string. It was a kind look. "Is something the matter?"

"My dog died," I said. I didn't have one. "His name was Danny. He got run over."

"You should have told me," Ronnie said.

I bit my lip and my cheeks started shaking. I felt it starting. He stepped closer and rubbed my hair behind my ears.

Then my mother called. "I'm com-ing."

We climbed into our car, the three of us in the front seat.

"Should we have a little music?" my mother said, her hand on the knob.

"No!" I shouted, much too loud. I tried to laugh. "I mean, not now."

Ronnie looked out the window. His face seemed chiseled, set. I knew

I'd blown it for being his girl friend. This whole night was too weird. It would be even worse, when he was home, away from us.

But right then, driving, the dark glass on three sides of us, I leaned my head back on the leather seat, it was one of those times I felt like driving all night. A clear sky, stars, the three of us could drive to Michigan or Canada maybe. Somewhere it would be cold.

12

A Backhouse on North Palm Drive

Not too long after Christmas, we ran out of money and moved. My mother quit her job during the fall teachers' strike and took work as a maid for an entertainment lawyer. We moved on a week Josh Spritzer was away, skiing in Colorado with his children, and we managed to keep the same phone number, so for a while Josh didn't know. We would be working for the Keller family, who lived on North Palm Drive, and we moved into their backhouse, behind the tennis courts.

My mother knew the Kellers because of me. Peter was a boy in my high school, a year younger, who asked me over a lot. Sometimes, his mother offered my mother mineral water when she picked me up, and that gave my mother a chance to talk about Josh. In a way, Nan Keller had been in on my mother's romance with Josh Spritzer from the beginning. The first time she dropped me off at Peter Keller's, we were all standing in the hallway and my mother had said, "Do you think I should have braces put on her? What do you think, Nan, aesthetically. You're the artist." I'd stood there like a horse while the two women pulled at my jaw and examined my teeth and gums. Nan Keller had decided we definitely should.

During the teachers' strike, I told Peter my mother was worried about her job, and that if she was laid off we'd have to move back to Wisconsin. In school the next day he said I could eat dinner at their house whenever I wanted. As if that would help our finances.

I suppose along the same idea, Peter called me up and invited me to his house for Thanksgiving. I said I didn't know, I'd have to ask my mother. When I walked into her bathroom, she was sitting on the rug, polishing her toenails, a magazine propped open against the tub. She clapped her hands when I told her. "He did? Great! Definitely we'll go. What do you mean, say no? We haven't got anything else to do." Josh Spritzer planned to take his children skiing, that time in Canada, Lake Louise.

"I don't know. He didn't mention you." That was hard to say.

But my mother didn't seem to mind. "Oh, well, she must expect me, too. She knows we wouldn't separate on a holiday."

I called back and asked Peter if he meant my mom, too. He said he didn't think so. I yelled upstairs. Now she was running water for a bath.

"Well, tell Peter you'd like to, very much, say, but that you don't think you can because you wouldn't want to be without your mom on Thanksgiving. So you'll have to go with her somewhere else she was invited. Say that."

"Did you hear?" I said.

Peter ran to ask. "Okay," he said, when he came back, breathless. "It's okay. Your mother can come, too."

It was always like that with the Kellers.

The afternoon of Thanksgiving, my mother and I arrived and stood in front of the huge door, checking each other over before we dropped the knocker. "You look really great," she mouthed to me. We both pulled up our pantyhose, still standing there on the porch, hoping none of the other guests would come and see us. Then my mother took a deep breath and knocked.

A maid in a short black dress led us to the drink room, a room entirely paneled in salmon suede. About a dozen people stood eating scampi out of little white ramikins. Only Peter walked over to us. He offered to take my coat.

"Should I give Peter your coat, Mom?" I whispered.

She pulled it over her shoulders. "No, Honey, I think I'll keep it."

Peter's grandmother lounged in the corner, talking about grilles on Rolls-Royces between the years of 1957 and 1970. She had a habit of marrying millionaires, who then died. She'd lost the last one recently, so she was wearing red. Peter told me she always wore red when she was in mourning. She wore black when she planned to leave a man. She believed Rolls-Royces hadn't been the same since 1970. She had three of them, each belonging to a dead husband. She herself drove a Bentley Silvercloud.

Peter also told me that she disapproved of Mr. Keller for being a lawyer, and for being a Russian instead of a Viennese Jew. Not that she herself admitted to being any kind of Jew. Whenever the Kellers fought, Peter's grandmother offered her daughter immediate and lavish refuge in her house, three blocks away on Elevado.

A famous movie star leaned on the salmon-colored wall as Nan Keller talked to him about mineral water.

Mrs. Keller had once been a painter. She sometimes spoke, romantically, of San Francisco, and the Art Students' League. It seemed she remembered painting on the sidewalks near Ghirardelli Square. But her mother, not Bert Keller, had come to fetch her home. Through the suede drink room's archway, we could see several of her recent paintings, standing in the living room. She painted with acrylics on clear huge stretched pieces of lucite, so the paintings served as room dividers as well. They seemed mostly abstract. She favored colors in the family of red. What was recognizable tended to be bloody.

"We bottle our own from a little island we found off of Panama," she was saying to the movie star. "Tell me what you think, Tony. It's not too bubbly. We like it clear." Tony Camden was the movie star's name.

"I'm in speech pathology," I heard my mother say next to me at the table. I noticed she was staring at the movie star, four people removed on the other side. Before I could stop her, she leaned forward, almost knocking over Mrs. Keller's centerpiece, made of bones, goat skulls, orchids and tall, burning beeswax candles.

"May I ask you a question?" she said to the movie star. "Your skin is so wonderful. Is there anything you do for it?"

But the movie star seemed pleased. He looked down at his young wife and she smiled back, lifting a piece of her hair behind an ear. "We have a little secret in our house," he said. "Every morning, Jan squeezes our own fresh orange juice. And we drink it with a tablespoon of cod liver oil and a tablespoon of wheat germ oil."

"Really," my mother marveled. She fumbled in her beaded purse, an heirloom. Then she had a piece of paper.

Mrs. Keller engaged the movie star's young wife in a discussion of tennis, how no one could ever be good unless they'd learned their form when they were seven years old and that's why she told Peter, every day, he should be out there with the machine, hitting balls, he'd be sorry later, he'd grow out of those political tracts he stayed inside reading and then he'd wish he'd learned tennis.

"Excuse me, would you mind saying that again," my mother asked. "I'd like to write it down. Now, it was *one* tablespoon of wheat germ oil, *one* of cod liver oil and that's *in* the orange juice? I see, mixed in the orange juice."

"As Winston Churchill said, anyone who isn't a Democrat before thirty hasn't got a heart. And anyone who's a Democrat after thirty, doesn't have a brain."

Mr. Keller, a dark, lean man with a prominent Adam's apple, was roaming around his living room. He had a hard time sitting still at meals, so he tended to roam, with his pipe, through the house. Odd lamps pointed out at weird angles in the living room, highlighting some object or another as if it were a sort of store window.

"Oh, Isabelle," the movie star's young wife said. "She's not sure if she's a girl or not."

Mrs. Keller shrugged. "I don't know why, she looks great as a girl." Mrs. Keller kept a crystal bell next to her water glass, which she rang to call the maid. "Do you like pumpkin pie?" she asked, suddenly, after the maid had been told to bring out dessert and to corral Mr. Keller back to the table. It was the first question she'd asked my mother all evening.

"Oh, yes, I love it!" my mother cried, believing, as she had all her life, that in situations of some awkwardness, it was best to be enthusiastic.

"Do you," Mrs. Keller said, as the maid wheeled the dessert cart beside her. "Thank you, Marie. Because we honestly don't. All three of us just hate it. And we don't like mince either. Can't stand it. So, I found this recipe for a Portuguese ginger pudding that we serve with a hard sauce. Please tell Marie how much sauce you'd like." She turned up to the maid and spoke to her in Spanish.

My mother waited to start eating her pudding, watching her hostess's spoon, the way she'd been taught when she was a girl. Unfortunately, Mrs. Keller was fussing with the coffee service on the second dessert cart. My mother looked to her right and her left, where people sat eating, and she smiled with anticipation, fanning her dessert napkin out over her thighs and folding her own hands politely on her lap.

Outside, in the open air, walking down the street to our car, my mother grabbed my arm. "Did you *see* Tony Camden, how he kept looking at me? I'd turn the other way and then I'd peek back and he'd look again. This dress was really great. You know, it was expensive when I bought it, but boy, every time I get looks."

"Mom, he's married."

I kicked a wheel of our car, hands in my pockets, stamping. We were shouting because my mother walked eight feet away on a driveway so she wouldn't wet her heels on the grass.

"Boy, he sure is and did you catch how much younger? But I'll tell you, he was attracted to me, Ann. And does HE look great for his age. I'm going tomorrow and get us some wheat germ oil and cod liver oil and we're going to start. Now, what did he say, a tablespoon of wheat germ and a teaspoon of, or no, was it the other way around? Anyway, I have it written down."

She opened her side of the car. We both stood there a second. "Honey, look at the stars. It's a real clear desert night. Dry. Feel that air."

"Mom, open my door. Let me in."

"You're really not romantic, are you?" she said, looking at me, perplexed.

"Just cold."

She shuddered loudly, sliding in the car and turning on the heat. "Brrr. Me, too.

"I'll tell you, Honey, that Peter is in love. The way he looks at you."

"Do we have to drive by Josh Spritzer's tonight? You know he's gone," I said.

"Oh, let's. I feel like a little ride, actually."

The next time I saw Peter Keller in school, he told me, "They all liked you. They didn't like your mother, they thought she was strange, but Tony Camden said you were cute." Peter looked at me with a tilted face, as if he were offering something. I felt like pushing him so he fell hard on the concrete floor of the hallway.

But I didn't. I was scared of them, too. I smiled back and made polite conversation.

I probably picked the wrong time to ask. It was a weeknight and my mother seemed tired. We licked our ice cream cones, driving past Josh Spritzer's apartment. He'd been home from Canada four days and she still hadn't seen him.

"When are we going to call that boy's agent?" I was trying to sound casual. I remembered the boy's name perfectly well. Timmy Kennedy.

"Well, Honey, to tell you the truth, you've got to take off about ten pounds." She slapped her thigh. "Right here. I've been kind of waiting to see when you would, but you just gobble down the milkshakes." That night we'd eaten dinner at the Old World, which claimed to make milkshakes with entirely natural ingredients.

"You're the one who drags us out to get ice cream cones every night."

"Well, one little dip isn't going to hurt."

My mother drove to the Linville Nutrition Center, a wholesale health food store decorated in old-fashioned pink. She bought an electric juicer and huge bottles of cod liver oil and wheat germ oil. The grocery bags said KEEP IN THE PINK.

. . .

"So, I just don't know about this man," my mother said, her legs crossed, leaning out of her chair towards Mrs. Keller. They sat on the terrace overlooking the yard. I'd been on the courts with Peter, trying to learn to hit the ball. Now Peter rallied with his teacher, starting his daily lesson. Mrs. Keller offered me a glass of lemonade from a cart as I sat down, eyeing the court while she poured.

"Hi, Honey," my mother said to me. "He's just not stable, Nan. You know, one minute he says one thing, the next minute, it's something else. I can't plan. Sometimes, I even think of just calling up his psychiatrist and saying, 'Hey, what's going on with this man?'" My mother laughed, an asking laugh.

Mrs. Keller responded with a smile that was less a show of support than an act of charity.

Encouraged, my mother went on. "I'd like to tell his psychiatrist a thing or two."

My back stiffened and I pulled my knees up to my chest. I knew my mother shouldn't have been telling Mrs. Keller those things. Mrs. Keller stirred her drink and put the swizzle stick down on a napkin.

"You know, Adele, he does have a reputation as something of a ladies' man. I'd be careful of him." Her gaze drifted back to the tennis court. "Good shot, Peter," she said softly.

My mother took Mrs. Keller's remark as an invitation for further disclosure. She thought about Josh Spritzer so often she needed to talk. The less she saw him, the more she craved talking. Just saying his name seemed to calm her.

"Well, I heard that too, before I started going out with him. But he wants to change, he told me that at the very beginning. I have to say this for Josh Spritzer, that he WAS honest, he told me he had a fear of commitment. So I suppose, for a while it was fine. But now, I think he's getting scared. He got himself in deeper than he planned."

"Hmm," Mrs. Keller said. "Well, are you seeing anyone else?"

My mother fell back in her chair, her hands loose on the armrests. She could have talked for ten straight hours about Josh Spritzer, speculating, analyzing the intricacies of his character and planning strategy. She would have loved to.

I wondered if she ever thought of Lolly and our old porch, looking over the fields, with the constant running sound of the highway. Maybe that was the real happiness in her life, sitting with a friend, easily plotting, yearning, planning out romances—more than the romances themselves. My mother's two passions were for difficult men and expensive clothing, neither obtained by the usual methods, but with a combination of luck, intuition and calculated risk. She could also talk for hours about how she acquired an Alan Austin green leather coat from a cleaner's in Covina for almost nothing, how an old woman gave her a Chanel suit, twenty years ago.

"Oh, sure," she said, recovering. "A few. There are a few other people." She didn't feel quite happy with that, though. She wanted to turn the conversation back to Josh. She wanted to turn every conversation back to Josh. "But you know, Nan," she whispered, leaning forward, "I really don't care for any of them."

"Well, you never know what'll happen," Mrs. Keller replied. With that, she stood up, carrying her drink, and walked over to the terrace ledge. "Look at those lime trees. We pay a three-quarters-time gardener and I don't know what he does all day. Plants weeds. The help situation is impossible. And when you think, really, of what they get. The pay's not bad and our backhouse is quite a nice place to live, when you consider what's on the market."

"Oh, it's fabulous!" my mother burst out.

We all stood, looking over the yard, Peter and his tennis teacher swinging languorously, the still pool behind them under the trees. No one said anything for a while.

"Well, I suppose we should skedaddle, Ann." My mother slapped her hand lightly on her side.

She left it so Mrs. Keller could insist we both stay for dinner, but Mrs. Keller didn't. She just turned around, mildly smiling. "Good-bye."

When we got desperate for money, my mother decided I was thin enough to see Timmy Kennedy's agent. "Who knows, maybe you'll land a series and then we can buy some decent furniture. Who knows?"

I wore tight ironed jeans and a pale green midriff shirt that left two inches of my belly bare. My hair hadn't been cut for a long time, and the ends of it curled under, so it touched my back on the bare spot. It felt creepy, like fingers there.

We started early because we didn't know exactly how long it would take to get there. Ellen Arcade's office was in Riverside. All the way, my mother just drove and we didn't say anything. I hadn't eaten much since my mother made the appointment. And for the past week, I'd sat out in the sun every afternoon, my towel on the overgrown grass of Roxbury Park.

We stopped at two gas stations in Riverside to get directions. And when we parked on the lot in front of the building, we were still a half hour early. It was a huge gray complex and around it were wasted fields and overpasses. I scooched up on the seat to look into the car mirror. All during the ride, I'd kept my eyes closed and my face aimed at the front windshield so my cheeks would get some color. We both sat in the car awhile, back against our seats. We didn't want to walk in too early.

My mother put some makeup on me. She brushed mascara on my lashes, patted on blush. It was a relief to close my eyes and give my face to her. Then I marked on freckles over my nose, with a sharpened eyeliner pencil. With the car door half open, my mother unzipped her pants and tucked in her blouse again. I bent over from the waist and underbrushed my hair, the way girls in my class were doing it that year.

The agent's office was on the third floor and her waiting room was tiny and full. Black and white glossies of children, signed in loopy, slanted penmanships, crowded the walls. Most of the girls' names ended in *i*'s and several were dotted with hearts. Some of the photographed faces smiled, some pouted, a few even cried. In one, a starburst glittered inside a tear. Around us, children squirmed in their chairs. A Mexican baby screamed in his grandfather's arms. One woman, the obvious mother of four blond, freckled children, patiently knitted.

The receptionist gave my mother a clipboard with a form questionnaire. We filled out my name, age, height and weight. I lied about my weight. My mother said I was a year younger than I was. They also wanted to know what languages I spoke, my grades in school and my measurements. When we turned the form back, we were called in, and the others waited, as if they were used to waiting. Ellen Arcade, a woman in her fifties with blond hair, sat behind a large desk in the inner office, stamping a cigarette out in a glass ashtray. She read over my questionnaire on the clipboard, smiling and nodding along. My mother slid me a complicitous look.

"So, how do you like Beverly High?"

"I like it," I said.

"Well, everything here looks good." She shoved the clipboard in a drawer. "Would you read something for me, Ann?"

After, the agent leaned back in her chair. My mother pressed forward, cheeks lifted, listening.

"She'll need pictures," the agent said. My mother nodded, staring at her. While we sat there, Ellen Arcade called a photographer and made an appointment for me. That seemed lucky, because it cost money. If we'd had to do it ourselves, we wouldn't have. My mother would have changed her mind. With arrangements set, Ellen Arcade looked ready for us to leave. Her arm listed towards us, but my mother wanted to talk. She gripped her chair.

"We're out of Bay City, Wisconsin, and once there was a telethon there and that's where we met Timmy Kennedy. Bay City actually has the biggest CP telethon in the country . . ."

"Isn't that something," the agent said. "He was quite a kid, Timmy."

"Is he still acting?" my mother asked.

"No, he's on the football team at Santa Monica High. Had enough of it." She lit another cigarette, then stood up and held each of our hands in a firm, quick yank. I wanted to say, Wait, does this mean you're taking me?

But all she said was, "We'll be in touch."

We did have the pictures done, and Ellen Arcade selected two for portfolio blowups, which I got to sign. Then nothing happened and the photographer charged my mother a hundred dollars. Which contributed to our financial ruin.

The backhouse was next to the pool behind the tennis courts. It had two big rooms and, up three steps, tiny bedrooms off a hallway and a bathroom with a portable shower. It had been built, originally, to be Nan Keller's studio. But since she rented a loft in Venice, they had made the studio into a game room. A felt-covered pool table stood prominently when you walked in and there was a working pinball machine in the corner. They left what furniture there was for us: Nan's old drafting table, the chairs and a couch. There was no kitchen, but there was a bar with an elaborate soda fountain. We had a half-size refrigerator and we always meant to buy a hot plate.

We moved on a week Josh Spritzer was skiing, so we had only the Swans to help us. At first my mother and I cleaned the big house together. We spent long afternoons fighting upstairs over who got to vacuum and who got to dust. Both of us felt embarrassed and we tried to understand each other's weak points. I never wanted Peter Keller to see me. So my mother did his room and bathroom while he was in school. Then, after a few weeks, I stopped helping. I left it for my mother to do during the day. I went to high school and tried to forget about it.

My mother didn't last long as a maid. It turned out she didn't know how to iron. She spent an hour doing each of Mr. Keller's shirts. He wore two a day, all in shades of white and the palest blue.

"How do you iron your clothes? You must stay up all night," Mrs. Keller asked.

"Well, actually, since we moved and I was working, I dry-clean," my mother said.

Another time, Mrs. Keller found my mother standing in her dressing room, with no possible purpose, her arms crossed over her chest, surveying the rows of dresses and shoes.

"What are you doing here?" Mrs. Keller asked.

"I just made the bed," my mother said. And she had done that—beautifully, with a corner folded down and a water glass of hydrangeas on the end table. The trouble was my mother and Mrs. Keller liked to do the same things, the little touches, graceful additions. Mrs. Keller needed someone good with a mop. It's amazing we lasted as long as we did. Finally, Mrs. Keller found my mother crying in the kitchen with the cook, both of them on their knees looking for the piece of my mother's fingernail that had broken off.

"If I bring it in, he can fix it, he has a sheer, sheer fabric he glues it on with."

The two-hundred-and-fifty-pound cook crawled on the floor, searching, her arm around my mother, to comfort. The roast sat bloody in the sink, uncooked, and the next day Mr. Keller walked over the tennis court to the backhouse and spoke to my mother about the possibilities.

My mother broke down and cried and talked about her master's degree, moving her ring around the finger with the now-patched nail. They discussed other possibilities for speech therapists: private practice, convalescent hospitals. They decided we could stay in the backhouse, but that my mother would get a job and we would pay rent.

For three weeks she worked as a hostess in the downtown split-level Hamburger Hamlet, wearing long skirts and walking through every night in a terror, afraid that someone who knew Josh Spritzer would come in. Finally, Mr. Keller arranged for an interview at the convalescent hospital where each of Peter's stepgrandfathers had lived, briefly, before he died. My mother got the job.

I found a job, too, as a wrapper in a clothing store. I went in every day after school and all day weekends. During the holiday rush, my mother asked the manager and they hired her on, too, for Saturdays. We measured our Saturdays, not from our salaries, but from what we took. The way we did it was easy. I would wrap huge packages and send them down with another customer's bags to the pick-up ramp. My mother would write up a receipt for one small thing. We picked the packages up downstairs when we punched out. It didn't feel like stealing, exactly. We owned clothes now, thousands of dollars' worth. Clothes seemed easy, not a big deal. Once I opened a drawer and found a little cellophane bag of rings, untagged. I took the whole bag. None of it seemed dangerous really, it was just a small thrill, something that made you suck in your breath a moment so your rib bones rose. And when we drove home as it was turning dark and the streetlights flickered on, you could touch the clothes on the car seat next to you and feel like you'd gotten something out of the day, something you could use later.

But even though we both had jobs, we were never good with money. The first time we couldn't pay the rent, my mother called Mr. Keller on the telephone and cried and sent me up to the front house carrying mixed flowers and a check they couldn't cash until two weeks from Wednesday.

Mr. Keller was a kind man. He looked at me, put his hand on my arm, his Adam's apple bobbing up over his collar, and said, "Okay, Ann, tell your mother thanks. And don't you worry, huh?"

As I turned to go, Mrs. Keller called, "Bert, ask Ann if she's had anything to eat."

I was standing at the back door of the kitchen, the door that led to the fenced tennis court, which separated the big house from ours. A cake, with a third cut out, showing its layers, was standing on a cake plate. The smell of roast beef lingered on its tin foil, left, wrinkled on the counter.

I hadn't had anything to eat yet. My mother was so upset about the rent, we hadn't gone to get dinner, but I just said, "No thanks, I'm not hungry."

Not that I was any saint. I scuffed my feet along the tennis court and when I walked in, I plopped down onto the sofa, my hand on my belly.

"What did he say?" my mother asked.

"I'm starving," I said. "My tummy hurts."

"Ann, just tell me what Mr. Keller said. Then we'll get something to eat."

"He said okay."

My mother began to beat her chest with an open hand, like a pigeon preparing to take off. "Oh, thank God. Thank you, God," she said, her head tilted up to the low ceiling.

I groaned. It made me sick when she got grateful. Everybody else had a place to live and you didn't see them thanking God for it.

"Okay, okay. Let's go. You're just not sentimental, are you? Well, I am. I'm thankful when people are nice like that. Get your jacket."

We had the half-sized refrigerator but we never kept much food in it. Every night we went out for dinner.

"Brrr, come on, hop in," my mother said. We parked our car in the alley, behind the backhouse. She stood staring up at the sky. I walked around to my door with my fists jammed in my parka pockets. My mother kept quiet because she was making her wish. Forty-four years old and every night of her life she made a wish on a star.

"It's clear tonight, Ann, look at those constellations." My mother clapped her hands. "It's going to be a great day tomorrow."

A Great Big Beautiful Tomorrow. Many of my mother's enthusiasms could be traced. We turned up the heat full blast in the car and I looked out the window, dreaming to myself. I was always dreaming to myself in those days. I wanted so many things. We drove, slowing the car in front of Josh Spritzer's old house in Beverly Hills and then, not finding his Thunderbird in the driveway, my mother headed towards his apartment in Century City.

"What are you thinking, Bear Cub?"

"Nothing."

"Come on, you can tell me."

"Nothing," I said.

"You know, you could say something once in a while, have a conversation."

It was hard to find restaurants that time of night. Usually, we didn't have cash and not too many places took checks. But we'd go into one of those restaurants with the little metal "No checks, please" plaques over the cash register and sit down and eat a whole meal. At the Old World on Sunset, there was a bulletin board in the back of the restaurant, with all the bounced checks pinned up on it. Two of ours were there. You passed it on the way to the bathroom. When my friends from school wanted to eat at the Old World, I didn't have the nerve to say no, but I sat scared, extremely conscious, the minutes any of them left the table to go to the bathroom.

When the bill came, at the end of a meal, my mother would start writing a check. The waitress would usually look flustered and say, "Oh, but we don't take checks."

"You don't! Why not?"

"We just don't. Restaurant policy. There's a sign there, right where you come in."

"Well, this check is good, I can assure you."

"I'll have to ask the manager."

"Please do get the manager."

My mother would fold her arms and smile at me over the table. I'd shove my chair back and put on my jacket. "I'm going outside."

"Okay, Hon," she'd say. "I'll just be a minute."

Then I'd wait for her, leaning against our car. I let her do it alone.

We didn't say anything about it, but we knew we had to avoid the places we'd ever bounced a check. My mother had two dollars in change and she just shrugged.

"Let's go and see if that little French place is open." There was a place on Pico we liked, a small restaurant, that served food like my grandmother's; sweetbreads and pork roasts. "You get your little soup and your salad and a little dessert. I could just go for that tonight," my mother said. But the windows looked dark when we passed. She sighed. "Should we drive over and get ice cream?"

Some nights we skipped dinner and just ate sundaes. We were usually on diets, so it seemed all right. My mother parked under the trees in front of Baskin-Robbins and felt around the bottom of her purse for stray dollars.

"Here, you run in," she said, pressing three damp dollars into my hand. She would wait in the car with the motor running. I knew which flavors she wanted and extra nuts and whipped cream.

Tonight, though, I minded. "You go in and get them. Why should I always go in?"

"I can't, Ann." There was real panic in her voice. "Someone could see me like this." She was wearing a terry-cloth jogging suit and tennis shoes. Her hair was pulled up in a ponytail.

"Someone could see *me*." I had on sweat pants and a T-shirt and sneakers. My hair was wet because I washed it every night.

"At your age it doesn't matter," she said. "Anyway, you look cute. At my age, they expect a woman to dress up a little. Remember, I'm the one who has to catch a father for you."

"I already have a father."

"Yeah, well, where is he?"

She had me there. "Hell if I know."

"Come on, Ann. Please. Just this once. Run in and get it quick."

"No."

We sat there under the trees. "Please, Honey."

I shook my head. My mother started the car with a jolt and we drove home. For a while, she didn't speak to me, but when I came down to the living room later, for a glass of water, she was standing by the open refrigerator, eating crackers and sardines, wearing the sweat shirt she slept in.

"Want some sardines?"

I shook my head and went back to my room.

"Ann, come and try some. Come on a second. It's good."

I heard her lift out the milk carton and drink from it. I hated it when she drank from the carton. I couldn't stand the idea of her saliva in my milk.

"I don't want any," I yelled. "And I'm trying to sleep."

"Okay," she called back. The crackers made crunching noises. "But it's very good. Very, very good."

I was hungry. My stomach seemed to acquire consciousness. It wanted things. Steaks with melted butter. Fresh rhubarb pie. Being hungry made me cold and slightly dizzy. I remember that feeling of going to bed hungry and waking up light as if it happened more often than it really did. Most of the nights we didn't eat, we could have. We were on diets. We were always on diets and neither of us ever got skinny. But years later, it's hunger we remember.

That night I woke up to find my mother sitting next to me on my bed, looking down at my face. "I was just thinking to myself how lucky I am to have a daughter like you."

None of the rooms in the backhouse had locks. After she left, I got up and shoved my dresser against the door.

My mother's room was right next to mine and the construction of the backhouse seemed flimsy. Even with the door shut, I could still hear her breathe on the other side of the wall. I imagined her curled up, pushing into the plaster, trying to make a cave and bore through.

She knocked on the wall. "Good night, Sweetie."

I slept on the outermost edge of my bed.

Josh Spritzer seemed to be dropping my mother. Her dates with him were down to once every other week. Even now that she had better clothes. And he seemed to be taking more out-of-town vacations.

"I think I *will* call his psychiatrist," my mother said one morning, while I ironed my jeans before school.

There was another man who asked her out. His name was Jack Irwin and his head was flat and bald as a nickel. He lived with his mother, who was almost a hundred and who had lost control. When we went to visit in their apartment once, she wobbled in her chair, her face jiggled, her eyes loose, wandering, her hands opening and closing, roaming the air for substance, finding nothing, and, at the end, her mouth opened to about the size of a penny and she left it there and said, "Eh," not like a question but like a word.

My mother had met Jack Irwin in the convalescent home. His mother had broken a hip. Since those days in Palm Manor, Jack Irwin talked about Solvang all the time. "Lovely little village. Rollicking, rolling green hills. And the Swedes. Everything main-tained by the Swedes." Apparently, he'd been there with his mother in 1961.

"He wants to take me there," my mother said, one night. She'd come home from a date with him and she sat on her bed, curling off her pantyhose. "For a weekend. I can't even kiss him. Could you come here a second, Ann, and undo my bra?"

"I'm in bed."

Then there was the slam of a drawer. "Course I suppose he could do a lot for us, with all his money." She sighed and I could hear her sit down again on the mattress. "He always asks about you, Ann, he thinks it's great you're doing so well in your school. He wants to talk to you about your college."

I heard her settle into bed. "Well, at least it was a good dinner," she said through the wall. "And he'll take us out to breakfast on Sunday."

The weekend they went to Solvang, my mother seemed very grown up. She snapped the buckles of her suitcase shut when she heard his car in the alley. She seemed older. She wore a suit, with her hair pinned up neatly in a bun.

"Here," she said, pressing a twenty-dollar bill in my hand and closing my fingers around it. "That's for food. Call Leslie and go out." When she opened the sliding glass door and Jack was there, we both felt disappointed. He stood, hands at his sides, wearing a plaid jacket and a white turtleneck sweater. Every time, we couldn't imagine beforehand how ugly he really was.

"All set," he said, clicking his heels together.

"I'll try to get you a present," she whispered. When she hugged me good-bye, for some reason I didn't know, I started crying. I wetted my mother's collar.

"Sshhh," she said, kissing me next to the eye. "I'll be back on Sunday."

They both looked slow and proper getting into the car. He lifted the trunk and put in the suitcase and opened her door first. She sat in the passenger seat and folded her hands. I threw myself on the couch and pulled up the mohair blanket. And it was me who usually never cried.

The next morning, Saturday, Peter Keller called me on the telephone from the front house. "I want to kiss your lips," he said.

Peter Keller was a year younger and we rode to school in the same carpool. He wasn't the kissing type.

"What for?"

"I don't know."

"Well, not if you can't think of a better reason than that," I said and hung up.

An hour later, he called back.

"I thought of another reason. I'm wild about your warm lips and I want to squeeze you tight." I heard pages moving, but it didn't sound like a joke.

"Yeah?" I was eating a carton of ice cream from the freezer. My mother had stocked up before she left.

"I want to part your lips with my tongue."

"Yeah?" I dragged the phone to the couch and lay down. "And then what?"

"Can I come over now?"

"Sure," I said. I didn't even think of changing my T-shirt, which was spattered with chocolate ice cream. When I came home from school every day, I took my good jeans off and hung them up in the closet. Peter was one of the kids I played with in my old clothes. If another friend of mine called on the telephone, I'd get rid of him fast. I didn't feel bad about it. He was a grade lower.

When he came to our sliding glass doors, he looked the same as always, his hair capping his face. But he squinted and his hands were opening and closing at his sides.

"So?" I said.

"Maybe we should go out some night?"

"Go out some night? What about what you were saying on the phone? Where did you learn that?"

"From a book," he admitted.

"No," I said. "We're not going to go out some night. Come in. Lie down over there and undress."

I hadn't planned anything, I was making it up as I went along. I felt taller and powerful, like a teacher, reaching up to the top of a clean blackboard.

"All right," he said. He untied a sneaker and held it in his hand. "Don't you want to talk first? It's not even dark out," he said, looking at the doors.

I shook my head. It was a spring day. The wind moved in the tops of the palm trees outside. No one was around. Peter undressed, holding his shirt and pants balled up in his hands, as if he were afraid I was going to take them. His arms hung pitifully at his sides.

"Aren't you going to take yours off, too?"

His underwear looked white and new as a child's. One of the things that amazed us when we'd cleaned the big house was the Kellers' surplus. They all kept drawers of new underwear, some in the packages, un-opened. In the bathroom closets, there were rows of soaps and shampoo, more than one of everything.

"You first," I said.

He sat down on the old blue and red striped couch and pulled off his underwear. Guys are so shy, I was thinking.

"Okay," he said, looking up at me. He took in a breath and held it. He seemed scared, as if I would hurt him. He was very thin and almost hair-less. He seemed frightened, like a woman.

I kicked my tennis shoes off with my heels.

"Lie down," I said.

I sat next to him on the couch. "Okay, you can kiss me, but not my face." He fumbled, trying to take my shirt off, so I stood up and pulled it over my head. I unzipped my jeans and dropped them on the floor. Then I sat on top of him.

He closed his eyes but I didn't. I looked around, out the sliding glass doors, while the veins in his neck rose up like a map. The pinball machine sparkled, metal and glass.

"Have you ever done this before?" he asked.

I hadn't. I hadn't even thought of it. Not even with Daniel Swan, whom I loved. We tickled the backs of each other's arms and I thought of wearing a soft white sweater and Daniel kissing me once on each eye. But I wasn't going to tell Peter Keller.

With Peter, it was different. Touching him was like touching myself. I never thought about him. It was broad daylight.

He sat up, facing me, and took my hand. He looked at me as if this were something big in both of our lives. "Lie back down," I said, pushing his shoulders. It was amazing the way he sunk back. You don't think you can do that to another person.

The air didn't move. I made a ring of my first finger and thumb and took him in my hand. It felt soft, the softest skin I ever touched. I watched. His hands fluttered by his sides. In the slits of his eyes, all I could see was white. He had no anger in him.

I don't know how I knew what to do but I did.

I put him inside me. His eyebrows pushed together as if he was working hard. A sound escaped from him. His face looked pure as something new. I felt it, he felt it. Then he started to move, lifting his hands to my waist.

"Lie still," I said. "I'll do it." Peter's dog rattled the metal garbage cans against the wall outside. I looked down; my own leg, the way it tilted, seemed different, separate from my body.

So this is what it is, I thought, not much. I pulled up to my knees for a second. There was a spit of blood on my leg. At the sight of it, I stopped.

"What's wrong?" Peter asked. "Did it hurt?" His fingers fluttered near my face.

"No," I said, crushing his ten fingers in my two hands and starting again. "No."

His face seemed limp on his neck. It would be so easy to kill another person, I was thinking. You'd just reach down. People just walk up and give themselves away to you.

All of a sudden I started moving and I was going faster and faster and I closed my eyes and then, I wasn't doing it anymore, he was holding my waist and I was afraid, so I tried to be still. I hung onto his shoulders like the edge of something and clung to one word, trying to keep it, quiet. Then, just as sudden, it was still again. And slow. I opened my eyes. My feet flickered the way fishtails sometimes beat a few last moments after they're dead. It was like falling. My arches and my knees ached and I felt light and tired, but I didn't want Peter to know anything.

Then I got up and ran outside to the pool. "Hey," he yelled and started to laugh. "Hey." And then he was next to me in the pool, his arms around me underwater.

"I love you, Ann," he said.

He looked at me, waiting. Flat brown leaves floated on the surface of the pool, beginning to disintegrate. The water below felt thick and filmy. I lifted an arm up to the air and it was shiny, as if in a sheer rubber glove.

"I'm taking a shower," I said. All of a sudden, I climbed out and ran into the backhouse. I latched the flimsy lock on the sliding glass doors. A minute later, when he knocked, I wouldn't answer. I thought of him watching me as I ran, naked, my breasts and thighs jiggling, him seeing that and it making him smile.

But he was naked, too. He must have run through his own yard and somehow snuck back into the big house.

My mother came home that same night. A door slammed, she ran in and flipped the light on in my room. She unlatched her suitcase and started unpacking right there, on my floor.

"I just couldn't do it." She stared at her open suitcase, shaking her head. "I couldn't touch him. I let him kiss me and he swished his tongue around in my mouth and I just couldn't. I practically gagged." She walked to my bed and looked down at me. "I'm sorry, Honey. Even for you, I couldn't do it. We slept in the same bed last night and he'd reach over and touch my side and I'd just cringe. I can't stand that man."

She walked to the bathroom and brushed her teeth. Then, she lifted a purple sundress from her suitcase with two fingers. "Well, here. I brought you a present. I went through a lot to get you this so you better like it. Here. Try it on."

I was thinking of the weak, pale folds of skin, like rippled batter, under Jack Irwin's belly. I thought of his mouth, rolling *r*'s against her ear.

"I don't like it," I said. "I don't want it." I really didn't. It had a low back and frills. I looked at the dress and hated it.

My mother examined the hem herself. After all she'd said, she seemed surprised and hurt that I didn't like the dress. "I picked it out. I think it's adorable. Try it on. You'll see how cute it hangs."

I grabbed it and went in the bathroom to change. When I came out, she touched my bare back, inside the long U of the dress.

"Oh, it's adorable. Go look at yourself. It couldn't be cuter, Honey." She sighed. "Well, at least we've got that. And it is cute, Ann, it really is."

My mother seemed to relax then, as if the dress had been worth it, after all.

That night I couldn't fall asleep again. I got up, it must have been two or three in the morning, took the dress from my closet, balled it in my hands and crammed it down the garbage can in our back alley. It was scary and peaceful out there, dark, with a low wind, moving the palms, making them spill small hard dates on the pavement. The next morning I felt settled and pleased when I heard the clatter of garbage trucks in my sleep. But it was Sunday. The only sounds I could have heard were church bells.

I'd invited Leslie over because I thought my mother would still be gone. Finally she left to drive to the convalescent home. Leslie had never seen our house. She came to the front; I sat, waiting on the curb, and led her through the gate, past the courts, to the backhouse. I'd thought all morning of how I could make it seem the big house was ours.

I did that whenever people dropped me off. They just dropped me outside the big house and I dallied by the fountain and then walked around the block. Mrs. Keller asked that I not use the front gate. We were supposed to walk in from the alley.

Inside the backhouse, I'd shut all the doors, so you could only see the big room. We sat on the old red and blue striped couch, sipping Cokes. I looked at the white closed doors. It seemed to me there could have been long hallways, terraces, dens and bedrooms following off behind them in every direction. I hoped that was what Leslie imagined.

She stared at the pinball machine. "Does it work?" she said.

I nodded.

"Is it just you and your mom, here?"

"I have two brothers," I said. I gestured with my arm up at the closed doors, indicating their rooms, their wings. "But they're at camp." It was April, but I didn't remember that until later.

"Oh," Leslie said.

We played pinball three or four times. I was anxious for Leslie to go, because I hadn't told her my mother had come home. I didn't know how to explain it, and I was afraid she'd walk in and open the doors. Especially now that I'd said that about brothers. Finally, Leslie said, "Since your mom's not home, you want to eat dinner at my house tonight?"

I shrugged. "Sure." I liked Leslie's house. It was pink brick with ivy. Any time of the day, when you walked in, there was a hum of quiet activity somewhere behind doors. Once in the afternoon, while she was changing to tennis clothes, I'd stood and stared at the dining room table, the six chairs.

They were brown wooden chairs. There was something permanent, meant, about their placement, the way the trees had seemed to me, back home. Every day, these chairs waited, absorbing light all afternoon, while in the kitchen, soft clicks and knocks of bowls and the whirring of beaters progressed, the evening meal in preparation. I stared at the back of one chair. It seemed the security of a whole childhood. It stayed there, all day, the wood worn and glossed like a held chestnut.

When Leslie had come down, swinging her racket in the still air, I'd been startled. "I like your chairs," I said.

She shrugged. "These?" She squinted, as if looking at her dining room table and chairs for the first time. A bowl of peaches sat in the center of the table. "You always love everything so much," she said.

That afternoon, I didn't leave my mother a note or anything. We ran up the alley and through the back gate to Leslie's house, over her lawn, into the kitchen door, where she shouted, "Rosario, I'm ho-ome and Ann is staying for dinner."

Later, I remembered: we'd walked around our pool to the alley gate. Leslie had seen our house from the outside, she must have known how small it was.

It got worse with Peter and me. We did it all the time, always sneaking off. I got meaner and meaner. He did everything I told him. Sometimes he just rubbed me. I would turn over on my stomach and he'd rub my legs.

My mother and I were invited to more dinner parties at the Kellers' and for Easter and Christmas and Thanksgiving. My mother started calling Mr. Keller Bert. After that, she always left the rent check on their hall table by the first of every month.

In the big kitchen, afternoons with Peter, I felt free to eat. I ate and ate and ate. Everything I wanted.

And Peter got money from his father to take me to restaurants. Peter's father liked me, Nan Keller didn't. But we rode in taxis to expensive restaurants where I could order anything I wanted. I picked the most expensive thing and two desserts. Peter didn't like desserts, so it looked as if we were each having one. I ate the cake in front of me first and then we switched plates. I worried more about what the waiter would see than what Peter would think of me.

After I was laid off from my wrapping job, I got Peter to buy me clothes. He had a charge account at the store where everyone from our high school bought their jeans. At first, he seemed reluctant. But I showed him the slip. "It just says the price. It doesn't say boys' or girls'. It doesn't even give the size."

We went in every few weeks. I wore a larger and larger size. At the cash register once, Peter patted the swell at the top of my thigh. "We should start playing tennis," he said. I felt furious. He'd touched me like I was something he owned.

"You sound like your mother," I said.

That day as we were leaving the store carrying bags of clothes, we passed a girl from our school named May. She was tall and thin, with long blond hair, wearing a pale blue shirt with clouds on it, and matching blue jeans. Seeing her, I felt a wave of humiliation. I was embarrassed to look the way I looked.

I turned to Peter, urgent. "Let's go to the Konditorei for tea." Tea at the Konditorei meant a silver tray of intricate tidy pastries. Mint green cakes, strawberry kiwi tarts inlaid like mosaic floors. It was four in the afternoon.

"Are you sure you want to?"

"Yeah, why?"

He was watching May's hair sway as she walked up the sidewalk. He looked back down at me. "That's okay. I like you the way you are. I like your ass," he said.

That year, Peter's parents sent him back east to a prep school, with strict instructions for the tennis coach. His mother wanted to get him away from me. But when he came home for vacations, we'd start again. Any time of the day in the small maid's room off the big kitchen, the ironing board in the corner, a faded flowered bedspread that held dust which rose like chalk in the sun.

I was less and less nice. I gritted my teeth. I thought of him as anyone, any boy. But the colder I was, he didn't seem to notice. Holding my waist, when he looked up at me from the bottom of the bed, his eyes half closed in devotion.

During the time he was away at school, I started to have normal dates. Leslie and I traded clothes, I had more than she did, from my job at the store. Some nights, Daniel Swan called me late from the phone in his room and we talked and didn't hang up. We put the receivers by our pillows and fell asleep, to the other's breathing. My mother came to my room in the middle of the night and put the earpiece back in its cradle. She thought it was adorable, but she didn't want to tie up our line all night.

All the while, I had tried to diet. But it wasn't until Peter went away to Exeter that I finally lost the weight. And then it came off effortlessly.

It was a June day, the summer I was leaving. I was lying on my back on the single bed in the maid's room with the window cranked open, so we heard the distant slow thonk-pong of tennis balls as my mother took her lesson, and the occasional rousing bark of Groucho, Peter's dog. My mother took her lessons in the middle of the day, when no one else wanted to use the courts. This doesn't count, I was promising, no one will ever know, I won't tell anyone. I was leaving for college. The east. Rain and yellow slickers in cafeterias. Books. Clean things. I won't ever tell anyone, I was thinking, I'll make him swear not to tell, it'll be as if it never happened, this is only sort-of happening . . .

"Ouch," I said, jerking away.

"What's wrong?"

"Your fingernail, it hurt."

Peter stood up and unlocked the door. He walked into the maid's bathroom. I heard the soft clicking sound of him clipping his nails. When he came back I was standing up and dressed, shorts and a T-shirt over my swim suit.

"I don't want to do that anymore," I said.

"Okay." He sat down on the bed, where we were, spread out his hand on my impression.

"Ever." I walked into the bathroom and closed the door. I felt like I'd lost the day already, though it was still early, just noon. I washed my face and ran the maid's plastic brush through my hair. There was a window over the sink and I looked outside. My mother lunged for the ball, all in whites, all heart. Everything else seemed still, hazy in the heat. The clippings from Peter's fingernails were floating in the toilet bowl. I didn't flush them. I left.

13

A Doctor's Office

"I have to learn this stuff, Mom. Kids at school have stereos, they know the names of all these songs. It comes up."

"Okay, okay, but not loud." She sighed and turned the car radio back on. That was one thing about my mother. She could understand your wanting to fit in. "I can't bear those drummers," she said.

Josh Spritzer still seemed to be dropping us. Her last date with him was almost three weeks ago, on a Wednesday. But we kept driving by his house every night, before we went to Baskin-Robbins. First, we drove past the high-rise apartment. My mother couldn't look for his white T-Bird there because he kept it in an underground garage. You needed a special card to get in, and Josh had never given her one. She had to park on the street. So we craned our necks, counting floors by their balconies in order to find his windows. If my mother saw a light, she sank back in the car seat and exhaled, comfortable at least for an hour.

But now, the windows of Josh Spritzer's apartment looked dark and she leaned over the steering wheel biting her fingernails. I felt furious, all of a sudden, that he didn't have a lamp with an automatic timer.

My mother turned the car around in the middle of the wide Century City boulevard and headed towards the house where Josh's ex-wife and children lived. She snapped the radio off. She drove at sixty miles an hour through the residential streets of Beverly Hills to find the soothing sight of his car in front of his children's house.

"But Mom, even if he is seeing his kids, he's still not seeing you."

"Shhh, be quiet." We raced down Little Santa Monica. My mother knew herself. All she needed tonight was to forget those dark windows—to relax, enjoy her ice cream cone, sleep.

It seemed strange that my mother didn't feel jealous of Josh's ex-wife, Elaine. When Josh visited, he often sat for hours in the living room of the Arden Street house, having a drink with Elaine. We sometimes saw them as we drove by at night, two silhouettes at a low table.

But my mother had very specific fears. As it turned out, she did not consider Elaine Spritzer pretty. Elaine was short, only a little over five feet, with muscular arms and legs. My mother described her hair as frizzy.

The fact that Josh had apparently once found Elaine attractive enough to marry seemed to escape my mother's attention. And I sure wasn't going to remind her. We each held our breath as we went over the bump in Arden Street that would give us a clear view of Elaine Spritzer's driveway. And tonight we were lucky. The T-bird was there.

My mother parked our car in front of Baskin-Robbins and fumbled in her purse for dollars. That night I didn't fight. We felt relieved, it was late, we were both tired.

Nan Keller knocked on our glass doors. She seemed bored now that Peter had gone away to school. And the backhouse we lived in had been built to be her painting studio. Now, she rented a huge loft in a renovated Venice hotel on Market Street, but she seemed to harbor affection for our place. Every time she came inside she looked around at the low ceilings and close walls and smiled as if they reminded her of things.

"I brought you some sketches," she said. "I was just drawing. I thought you might want to take a look."

My mother made a face, scanning the backhouse. The place looked a mess, but we had to let her in. She was our landlord.

They laid the sketches out on the pool table.

"Can I get you anything?" my mother asked, veering towards the half-size refrigerator. "We don't have much, but I can make some lemonade, or I have carrot juice."

Nan Keller waved her off. "We had a dinner at Ma Maison and I'm absolutely stuffed."

"Oh, they're Ann." My mother stopped, seeing the pictures.

"They're *almost* Ann," Mrs. Keller said. "I was sketching other noses, just to see what could happen with a surgeon. I think this one would be fabulous. Turn to the side, Ann." Mrs. Keller pointed, her cool fingernails touching my face. "A little off, here and here. Just straight. I think it would be smashing. See, she's got a little bump from somewhere."

"Her father," my mother mumbled. My mother's hands dug in her pockets and she stared up and down from the sketches to me. She started nodding. "I think you're right, Nan. Just a little and she'd really be something." Her eyes opened wider in awe of my potential.

"It's not inexpensive, but now's the time to do it, the kids all get them in high school, over the summer or even in fall, it's no big deal. You see them at Beverly with bandages, the boys and the girls, no one minds, it's like braces, it's almost a stigma *not* to have them. And then when they go to college, nobody ever knows. And when the braces come off she'll be all set."

"Who would you take her to, Nan?" My mother became studious. It was easy to imagine her in college, with the tortoiseshell glasses, long since replaced with constantly lost contact lenses, her pencil neatly scribbling, following the teacher's instructions. My father had been my mother's professor.

"I don't know, there's a Doctor Brey on Roxbury. He's popular, he did Lexie's daughter, but I think he does all the same nose. It's a nice nose, but it's becoming a cliché, you know?"

"Oh, we don't want that." My mother acted so humble with these people.

My mother and Nan Keller continued to talk about plastic surgeons, those who did one tract nose and those who thought they were artists and wouldn't listen to what you wanted. One took nitrate photographs of his noses before and after and had bequeathed them to the Los Angeles County Museum of Art, where his wife served on the board of directors, active in volunteer fund raising. Another looked like Ernest Hemingway; recently divorced, he lived in Malibu.

I excused myself. "HE sounds good to me," my mother was saying.

Later, when I came down for a Coke from the half-size refrigerator, Nan Keller was still there, sitting on the old red and blue striped couch. On the floor in front of them stood the bottle of Courvoisier we'd moved to all the places we'd lived in California and never opened, my mother not being a drinker. We had the one suitcase we'd taken in our trunk when we left Wisconsin. It was printed with my father's initials, and missing a handle. We'd kept it together with a belt around it and a dog collar clipped to the handle loops. In it, we'd carried a jumble: our precious things and our old ice skates, and this bottle of Courvoisier. We'd taken it all the way from Wisconsin and then from apartment to apartment and now Nan Keller sat drinking it.

"Well, it's only a rumor, but apparently, he's been seen with her by a few people at Hillcrest."

"Damn. That man," my mother said.

"Who are you talking about?"

"This isn't for you, Ann, go to sleep," my mother said, tapping her nail against a front tooth.

I could have killed Nan Keller.

My mother shook me awake the next morning. "Come on, we're cleaning up a little." She squatted down in front of a cupboard, taking out pans and setting them on the floor. The house looked more of a mess than last night. She was wearing her gray sweat shirt and her hair strained up in a ponytail. A sponge rested where she'd started to wash the cupboard. Our suitcase of old photographs, mementoes, my skates from when I was five, lay on the sofa, unzipped. Whenever my mother was upset, she took things apart and unpacked.

She didn't look at me. Her arms rummaged in the cupboard.

"Take that garbage out this minute," she said.

Four bags sagged against the doors. I carried two. I could hear her starting to bump things and yell as I opened the gate to the alley. "A damn thing around here. I work and work and slave . . . who does she think she . . ."

I lifted the other two bags, slower this time. Birds made small noises in the trees. A white truck whooshed on the clean empty road a block away, at the end of our alley. I leaned against the wall, in back of the house. I didn't have anything with me.

"Made of money, it's a thousand for her teeth, now two thousand for her nose and meanwhile, I have nothing, NOTHING!"

I slipped back in and snuck to my closet and took all the money I had, shoving bills in my pocket. It felt good, the slightly oily paper. I crushed it in my fist.

She ran to my room and stood, veering at the door.

"Why don't you go find your father, you treat me like filth after all I've done. I'll tell you why, because you're scared. You'd rather stay and sap me. Sure, your dumb mother will always drudge for you. For your bikinis that you HAD to have and never wore after I bought them for you, and your pictures when you thought you were going to be a movie star. Yeah, uh-huh. Well, you've got another thing coming, kid, because you don't respect me. You don't love me after all I do for you, how hard I work."

She was waiting and I just stood there for a long curved minute, one rotation.

"Oooh, you—" Then she was coming and I backed into the closet, my arms in front of my face. I knew what I had to do to stop her. Talk. But I held still, I wasn't going to move. I was a piece of wood. My body turned empty, porous, that was what got her.

Something hovered on the ceiling, a scrap of cloth, I saw everything below, slowly, indifferent, like the blades of a fan, moving at a constant speed. I didn't want anything. Except to be away, east, somewhere cool. It seemed clear and true. I didn't love her.

She hit me once, bad, my cheek vibrating like hard metal, and I was falling against the closet wall, the brass hook knocked my head and I was thinking, this is it, it's sharp like a deep cut, one red scratch in the sky: she could hurt me so bad we would never forget.

And then it turned adult and clean. This person coming at you, lunging, her mouth opening and closing, teeth an ecstasy, and all of a sudden, you know and then, whack, on your forehead and she's moving and the picture you saw breaks like crystal.

She hates you. She hates you more than anything she is and she's tied until she kills you, it's that deep in her. She will stay. And you know you have to get up. You want to close your eyes and be dizzy, let this blur dark, tasting the blood in your mouth like a steak, and let her come back to you and touch you softly, lead you to your bed, tuck you in, care for you.

Now, still in the closet, but a million miles away (a hawk flying over a blank western sky), you start sobbing. You hear yourself as if it's someone sitting in a chair across the room.

I stood up and shuffled past her to the door. She pressed right behind me, breathing.

"It's me or nothing, kid," she is saying, her voice laughing and crying. She looks at me, slack, her face sags with an intimate apology.

I slide the door shut and I am outside. We look at each other, stunned, for a moment through the glass. Stunned that I would choose nothing.

I slumped in the alley, next to clean garbage cans, mad at myself because I was so weak. My ears were ringing and they seemed to ring through all the other days. Everything looked sharp, the willow branches over the alley fence so brittle they could cut the sky.

"Come on, get in," my mother said. She slid over and opened my door. She moved quickly now, dressed and businesslike. She sat in the driver's seat, the passenger door hung open. Then she got out and stood with her hands on her hips. "They turned off the phone and we have to go down there. So if you want the phone to work, when your kids call, then you better get in."

We sat in silence while she drove. She waited in the car and I went in with our papers, the bills rumpled from being in my mother's purse. She counted out the cash she gave me to the dollar, and then she asked me for change. But she was right. I would have stolen from her.

I just went to the people at the desks and gave them everything. I didn't say a word. My mother would have made excuses, told them our tragic life story, tried to make them like her. But they already knew us, that's why she stayed in the car. I went in every month. They just did it for me, right away, without questions.

When I slid back in, my mother was sitting sideways on the edge of her seat, looking at her profile in the rearview mirror. She pushed the tip of her nose up with a finger.

"I need a little, too. Just a touch off the tip. Nobody'd even know." She sighed. "Maybe we'll both go in."

My mother finally did call Josh Spritzer's psychiatrist and he refused to see her. She succeeded, however, with Josh's son's psychiatrist. She drove to see him at his office, three afternoons a week, each time dressed as if for a date. After a while, Josh Spritzer stopped calling altogether, but my mother nonetheless remained cheerful. She seemed to be home a lot more.

She spent time on our half-size refrigerator. She polished the glass and the plastic and the chrome and she bought expensive jars of things which she lined up, according to size. Vinegar with herbs floating upside down, mustards, chutney, maple syrup. She pared and peeled carrots, celery, jicoma and green beans for a platter on the second shelf. The parsley was arranged in its own ceramic pitcher. An elaborate fruit bowl, the apples polished and decorated with sprigs of mint, daisies poking out between the oranges, held the prime spot on the top shelf. I caught her rubbing brown eggs on her sweat shirt. And above the glistening eggs, she rested a small Steiff toy chicken.

I took an apple one day after school and lay on the couch, eating. I was happy. I liked having all that food.

Just then I heard my mother's car outside in the alley. "Honey," she called. "Come help me, would you?"

The backhouse yard was small enough so we could hear each other from anywhere. In the alley, she bent unloading dark green shopping bags. They were light. I took them all in one hand. Then she stood at her dresser, smiling, concentrating on a small, flat box. She untied the green satin ribbon. She opened the box and held it out to show me. It was a man's tie, deep red, with tiny blue dots.

I shrugged. "What's this?"

She kept grinning. It was the middle of the afternoon. She must have been out shopping all day.

"Isn't it pretty?" She stared down at the folded tie in the palm of her hand. "It's silk."

"Who's it for?"

She sucked in her breath and pulled her chin up. "It's a present, Ann."

So that was how it was going to be. I went to my room and closed the door. A few minutes later, she called me again.

She stood in front of the open refrigerator. "Honey, when you take an apple, take it from down here." She pointed to the produce drawer, crammed full of bagged apples and oranges. "I don't mind you eating, but I arrange the basket so it looks pretty."

I didn't say anything and she kept on.

"Do you understand? Because I'd like to keep it nice. It took me three hours the other day to get this refrigerator decent."

"So you're not working anymore."

"I'm working."

"When?"

She smiled. She wasn't going to tell me. I turned to go back to my bedroom. I kept wanting to hit that smile.

"Don't you worry about that," she yelled. "That's my worry. And believe me, everything's fine. Everything's finally going to be just fine." She started humming to herself and I heard glass clinking, jars being moved inside the refrigerator.

Jack Irwin still called. He took us out to dinner in formal, expensive restaurants I'd never heard of and which didn't seem to require reservations. These restaurants had in common white tablecloths and an extraordinary number of small courses. Everyone in those restaurants seemed old, old waiters in black cotton suits and women in long dresses that showed whole U-shaped sections of their paper-thin, crinkly backs.

Would the young lady like whipped cream on her gâteau, the ancient waiter would ask.

"Yeah, tons," I'd say, loudly. But no one looked at me.

"Yes, thank you," Jack would tell him, "the young lady would like a bit of cream."

The backhouse seemed more tended every day. Like before, when I came home from school, it was usually empty. My mother would rush in an hour or so later, perfectly dressed, with a new haircut or a new blouse or a new color on her nails or a mysterious package which I assumed was another present.

She seemed happier than I'd seen her for a long time, but distracted.

My mother couldn't keep her secret for long. "It's going to be wonderful," she said. She sank down against her car seat after she told me, her chocolate almond cone almost touching her chin. "You're finally going to have everything. We'll have a big house and you'll have all the clothes you want." She said that she and her psychiatrist, a Dr. Leonard Hawthorne, had fallen in love. Apparently, they were going to get married.

Her eyes half closed and she licked the cone neatly, around in a circle.

"And I'll get a car?" I said.

"And you'll get your car," she said.

I still hadn't seen Dr. Hawthorne. He didn't call or come to the back-house. From what I could tell, the only times they met were their after-noon sessions. But that seemed to be enough for her. She remained happy in a talkative way. She'd be dusting the inside of a cupboard, she'd look up and say, "Aren't we lucky, Annie-honey? Aren't you glad something nice happened to your mother after she's worked so hard all these years?"

Every night, she sat at the dining room table—which was Nan Keller's old drafting board covered with a new white cloth—and wrote letters. She used red stationery, red envelopes and a quill pen, which she dipped in white ink. She wore a new, floor-length peach-colored silk robe with cuffs that folded back and a long, round collar.

When she completed a letter to Dr. Hawthorne, she sealed it with beeswax. She'd bought a stamp that said "Joie d'Adele."

For my birthday, I wanted a car. Every kid in LA who didn't have one wanted a car.

My mother kept smiling weirdly and humming before the day. "Don't worry," she said, in a singsong lilt.

The morning of my birthday, she gave me keys. Her face seemed ra-diant, spilling. "Yes," she nodded, "it is," and watched me fly into happi-ness.

A few minutes later, after hugs and giggles, I asked where the car was.

"I wanted to get it today for you, but they couldn't have it till next week. But don't worry, Puss, it's on its way."

"What color?"

She hesitated. "White," she said, then nodding too much. "Mmhmm, it's a white one."

A Tuesday night, she took off her peach-colored robe and dressed again. I thought she wanted an ice cream cone and I got dressed right away, too. I thought she might be coming around to her old habits. I actually missed driving by Josh Spritzer's houses.

But when we slid into the car, she seemed distracted. She didn't talk to me or tell me where we were going. It was eleven o'clock and we drove all the way out to Santa Monica. She parked the car across the road from a high-rise apartment building. Outside, the beach palms moved in the wind.

My mother turned to me quickly, for the first time since we'd left the backhouse.

"Do you have a dollar?"

I felt in my pocket, but I already knew what was there. "I have one dollar, but it's my last money."

"Give it to me."

I kept my hand clutched around the soft paper in my pocket. I sweated and the dollar felt damp. "I need it for school tomorrow."

I knew all the arguments: worked all these years, slaved, she supported, etc. But she didn't even start. She just stuck out her hand. "Come on. Give it to me."

She ran to the building across the street in her high heels. I saw her with a man just behind the glass door. Later, she told me she needed my dollar to tip the doorman. Dr. Leonard Hawthorne lived in the penthouse and she wanted her letter delivered by hand.

She looked relieved and looser when she sank back in the car, her hair messy and glamorous from the wind. She rolled down her window. "Oh, smell that air, would you?" She took a deep breath and for a moment, she seemed like herself again. "Should we run and get an ice cream cone? Oh, we don't have any money, do we? Drat. I could really go for a chocolate almond. Do you think they'd take a check? Why not? Huh? They know us. We've been going for years."

Leslie and I walked, as we did every day during morning recess, down the open plaza of the fourth floor New Building, to buy sweet rolls and coffee in the cafeteria. We'd learned to like coffee. We practiced, drinking it with two packets of powdered cream and four Sweet'n Lows. Every day, we found it delicious again.

During class, I'd rifled through all my pockets and purse, but I had no money. I'd used all my change the week before. I would have to lie.

The sweet rolls smelled warmer and darker that day, they'd just been taken out of the oven, the white sugar frosting melted so they stuck together when the ladies behind the counter lifted them with spatulas from huge tin pans.

"I don't think I'll have one today," I said.

Leslie took two, the heavy rolls flopping on the flimsy paper plates. "Come on, you can't let me get fat alone."

I looked down. This was hard but necessary. We stood in the line to pay. Leslie was pouring our coffee. "No, I don't want anything."

Leslie opened her leather wallet and took out a five-dollar bill. She paid for both of us. "I'm forcing you," she said.

We walked back over the fourth floor terrace slowly, careful not to spill, talking quietly, under the eaves where pigeons nested. I kept looking over at her. Sometimes, like at the Pacific Gas and Electric Company, people seemed so kind. Then I thought the world would be easy. But thinking that confused me about my mother.

"Oh, my mom's getting married," I said. A splash of coffee spilled on my suede shoe.

I lied to people on buses. Dumb lies, only things that didn't matter. I told a man I came from a family of seven children, my father worked in a bakery. The man nodded, not the least bit surprised.

My mother took me along on one of her sprees. We got up early and looked at linen suits on sale. She found one that was rust-colored and I found a blue.

"Aren't these too much?" I said, rubbing the cardboard ticket.

"They'll always be good. They're a classic cut. Really classic."

My mother stood in a pool of light from the high arched windows of the store. The brick floors and vaulted ceiling made us feel peaceful. But she hadn't worked in months. The drawer with our bills wouldn't open, it was packed so full.

"Do we have the money?" I whispered.

"Mmhmm," she said. "I think so. For something of this quality, at this buy, yes."

And I let her walk to the antique bar used as a desk and write a check, for mine, too. On the way out we found purple hats, hundred-dollar purple hats.

"Absolutely adorable," my mother said, flipping one on me.

We bought those, too.

I thought, with all the money we owed, a couple hundred dollars wouldn't make a difference. If I tried to be careful, my mother would just spend it anyway, so I'd collect things now while I could. As if you could stock up on purple hats.

When my mother was upset, she turned graceless. She bumped into corners, her elbows jabbed walls. She hurt herself.

"Damn," I heard her say. It frightened me how much she could pack into that small word.

All her knocks and wandering would end up in my room, but there was nothing I could do except wait. There were no locks on any of our doors. Finally, she came. She wasn't wearing anything but a dirty gray sweat shirt. She squatted on my carpet, barelegged, rocking.

"I don't know, I just don't know. SHE'S the one who had to come to California, SHE was going to be a movie star, and I work and work and slave and it's high time I get something for ME once instead of you, you,

you and more you. And you don't even like me. I can see the way you look at me."

She covered her hand with her sleeve before she hit me.

I used everything, hitting hard, loose, not seeing what I was doing. And in a few minutes she fell off the side of my bed. I was getting stronger than she was.

She stood up and walked to my door. She crossed her arms and spit, her saliva arching over the carpet, falling a foot short of the sheet.

My mother didn't forgive me right away. When I came home from school, she was standing in front of the full-length mirror on her closet door, wearing an unfinished wedding dress. A seamstress knelt pinning the hem. I recognized the ivory beaded satin. It was one of our things from Wisconsin. She'd bought it, years ago, in Egypt.

"What are you doing?" I said.

She wouldn't look away from the mirror. "We're busy now, Ann." I just stood there, watching. The woman crawled around my mother's feet, taking pins out of her mouth and sliding them into the thick fabric. My mother kept changing the position of her mouth and watching the effect in the mirror.

"Look what she did to me." She rolled back her left sleeve. Her arms stretched long and thin, light brown. My mother bruised easily. "Look at those marks. She's like a little animal."

I sat in the alley. A few gates down, three boys pedaled out on bikes, with baseball bats and mitts in their baskets. They still had high light voices and I watched them ride off, pedaling standing, beautiful boys with careless voices.

An hour later, at dusk, my mother marched out and asked me if I wanted to put on a sweater, so we could go have dinner. She didn't seem at all surprised to find me slumped in the alley. I sat there a lot of times now. The dressmaker had gone and my mother looked tired. I pulled on an old sweater and she didn't complain. We both just settled in the car.

"Well, so, what are you thinking?" she said at the restaurant. She propped her face on her fists, tried to smile.

"Nothing."

"Nothing at all?"

I shrugged.

She reached over, put her hand on my forehead. "You're a little warm."

"I'm fine."

"You're just tired." She sighed. "Well, it won't be long now. Pretty, pretty soon, I think, things will be changing for the better. The much better."

"Do you still think you're going to marry Dr. Hawthorne?"

"Mmhmm," she said, reveling in the adjustment of her smile, all the while studying her nails. "No, I really don't think, Honey. I *know*."

I crossed my arms on the table. "So if you're going to marry him, why doesn't he ever call? You never go out on dates."

"Honey, you don't understand." She leaned closer. "It's all part of the therapy. Remember the first time when I was upset? Well, he was bringing me through my father and all that pain. I've suffered a lot, Ann, you really don't know. And then the next time it was your father and that was a hard one, boy, I can tell you. Then I had to go through Ted Diamond. But I'm through it all now. It's over. And he's stopped seeing me, as a patient. It's like he's saying, Hey, you're done. You're finished. Now we can go ahead and just date."

"So when do you think you'll get married?"

"I'd say, oh, about a month. Maybe three weeks, but probably a month."

"When will he start calling and coming over and stuff?"

"Any day now, Honey. Certainly by the weekend."

But he didn't call by the weekend. And the next day, my mother's red envelope, addressed with white ink, came back in our pile of mail on the washing machine top, *Return to Sender* scrawled on it with an ordinary ball-point.

"Give me that," my mother said.

I followed her to her bedroom and watched her slip it in a drawer. I saw a flash of red. "If he's going to marry you, why did he send your letter back?"

My mother gave me a patient look. She opened the drawer and took the letter out again. There were dozens of red envelopes in there.

"Look-it, Honey. This is addressed to *Doctor* Leonard Hawthorne. See." She ran her fingers over the indentations his ball-point pen had made. "See, he doesn't want me to write to the doctor. The *doctor* doesn't want to see me anymore. He wants to know me as Len Hawthorne the man, not the doctor. And believe you me, so do I!"

That night, my mother wrote a long letter to Len Hawthorne, The Man. She addressed it to his home in Santa Monica and used twice as many stamps as necessary.

"This is Adele August. I'd like to—okay, okay. But please. It's an emergency." She sat in her bedroom with the door closed, but I could hear through the wall. That was the day when the envelope addressed to Len Hawthorne, The Man, came back in our mail.

·   ·   ·

Since she'd stopped going to her job, my mother slept in. She almost never woke up before I left for school. Mornings, I stood at the half-size refrigerator, looking at all the food. My mother kept it perfectly clean and well stocked now, as if she feared a surprise inspection. I used to stand in the quiet, light backhouse with the refrigerator door open. I stared at the fruit. I almost didn't want to touch it. I wanted it to stay the way it was, cold and hard, the apples beaded with strings of faceted colors.

Then one morning, my mother was moving behind the soda fountain in her peach-colored robe when I woke up. She made us bananas on cereal. She smiled at me weakly while I ate. "Is that good, Honey?"

"Yeah." When I finished, I brought the bowl to the sink and washed it. We didn't have dish towels, so I dried it with a paper napkin. Then I went to get my books.

"Oh, Ann," my mother called. "Could you please stay home for a while this morning. I'll write you a note. There's something I need you to do."

"I should go to school, Mom." I wanted to go.

"Honey. This is important. I need you to call somewhere."

"Can't I do it now?"

"Honey, it doesn't open until nine."

I sat back down. I thought of missing Nutrition. It wasn't even eight yet.

"You'll be glad you waited. This is for your good, too."

At exactly nine, I said, "Okay, let's do it now."

"Well, just give them a second. I said they *open* at nine. Let them put their things down and get a cup of coffee."

If I rode my bike to school, I'd be there for Nutrition. I said, "I have to go."

"Okay, okay, let me find the number." She was stalling. She knew it by heart. She dialed and handed me the receiver.

"Now, say you need to talk to Doctor Hawthorne. Say your name is Amy Spritzer. Go ahead."

I didn't want to do it, but she was looking at me. A woman said, Good morning and I said, Hello, this is Amy Spritzer, Could I please speak to Dr. Hawthorne? Just a moment, please, she said. It was working.

"What should I say to him?"

My mother's eyebrows lifted. "Is he coming?"

I handed the receiver over. "Hell-ow," she said, in a high, soft voice. "Ye-es."

I went to her purse and took out two dollars, and held them up for her to see. She shoved me away with her hand. It wasn't going well.

"I just felt, really, once more . . . Well, I feel I have some things I'd like to talk to you about. With you. . . . Oh, all right. I know."

She hung up the phone and looked straight at me. "See, he just got in. This wasn't the right time. We should've waited an hour. Damn." She bit her cuticle.

"Mom, if he's going to marry you, why won't he talk to you? People who marry you talk to you."

"You don't understand," she said. "You don't know anything."

I walked outside to where I left my bike. My mother followed me. She stood across the pool, holding her robe closed over her chest.

"You better hope it's true," she said, in a warning voice. "You better hope Leonard Hawthorne loves me, because if he doesn't, believe me, there's nothing for us. Nothing, do you hear, nothing!"

She walked towards me on the cement, and I took off on my bike. I stood up, pedaling, giddy. She couldn't seem to realize, it didn't matter what I thought.

My mother said she was going into the hospital for an operation. Something in her voice made it sound like a lie. I tried to hold my own, I didn't believe her.

There was something about the way she said things, about the way she was vague—it made her always seem wrong. You couldn't be sure. It was hard to tell what my mother did and didn't know. She didn't use facts. But then, things that had seemed to be her whimsy, in the past, back in Wisconsin, things I'd laughed at with the rest of our family, turned out to be true here. Like the way my mother had wanted to get Hal excused from Vietnam by putting braces on his teeth. People had laughed and laughed. But that's what Leslie's brother Dean had done and now he was at Stanford.

"What kind of operation?" I said.

She acted like she didn't want to tell me. Then she lowered her voice to a whisper. "Cancer," she said, as if it were a secret.

"Where?"

She slapped a hand on her left breast. "But never mind, never mind."

She did go into the hospital. She stayed overnight. Jack Irwin drove and I rode along in his car to pick her up. She was wearing her peach-colored robe with a white blanket on her lap when a nurse wheeled her out into the parking lot. I climbed over to the backseat. She acted extremely kind to Jack. And for years that was all I heard about her cancer.

I called Dr. Hawthorne from a pay phone at school and gave the receptionist my real name. He came on the line the same way he did when I'd said I was Amy.

"Yes, Ann, what can I do for you?"

A lot. Too much. That was the problem.

"My mother thinks you're going to get married and I wanted to know if that was true." My voice sounded small, peculiar.

"I could see you at three o'clock. Can you come in then?"

I said I could and I didn't go back to class when the bell rang. I walked around the back of the typing building, where smokers ditched and leaned against the wall. I didn't have a watch. Every few minutes I got up and looked at the clock over the track.

Dr. Hawthorne's office was on the ninth floor of a Century City high rise. I leafed through a newsmagazine in his waiting room. It felt really odd to think how many times my mother had been here. I could imagine her, distracted, twisting and biting a piece of her hair.

Dr. Hawthorne wasn't handsome. He was very thin, he wore glasses, and his mouth seemed to hold a permanent expression of distaste.

I sat down in a large, padded chair and looked around. I waited. I'd already asked him on the phone if he was going to marry my mother. I was waiting for his answer.

But he didn't say anything. "You have a couch and everything," I said finally. I tried to sound normal and kidlike.

He acknowledged my comment with a smile that was more like a wince and then he was silent again. He looked at his hands intently.

"So are you going to marry my mother?"

He shook his head and something collapsed in me, a faint rumble, the beginning of a very long sound. I hadn't known how much I'd believed my mother until just then. Everything was going to be different.

"She sees what she wants to see," Dr. Hawthorne said. He held his hands tentatively, forming a basket of air. "My interest in her has always been strictly professional. I've told her that many times."

My mother hadn't worked for months, those bills jamming the drawer.

"I've done everything I can. I've stopped therapy. I refuse her phone calls. I am denying any pleas for contact. I feel that's the best thing."

I just looked at him.

"In fact," he said, staring at his fingertips, lifting them slightly back, "I haven't received payment for the last five months of treatment."

"I'm sorry," I said. Somehow, that seemed the worst thing yet.

"It would be best for your mother to see another therapist."

"Isn't there anything you can do?" My throat swelled up on the inside, it was hard to talk.

"I feel this is the best thing. The only thing."

"What should I do?" I tried to keep my chin in, tight, to lock my jaws.

"Do you have any contact with your father?"

I was surprised that after all those sessions with my mom, he didn't know. I shook my head.

"No contact?"

I shook it again.

"Well, that makes it harder." He looked at me, squinting. "How old are you?"

"Seventeen."

I found myself concentrating, as he did, on his wrists. His cuffs seemed amazingly white. "Try not to depend on your mother very much. She's not responsible enough to take care of herself, not to mention another person."

My chin wove.

"What are your plans after high school?" he asked finally. I suppose I should have stood up to leave.

"Oh, I don't know. College. Back east maybe." The way I was going now, skipping school, forget it. My grades weren't great. I'd be in more trouble.

"That's shooting pretty high. Well, good for you."

I held onto the arms of my chair. I didn't go. "I don't know what to do." That came out like a yelp. "I mean, I lie sometimes, too. I lie to people I'll never see again, and my friends, they don't really know me."

He looked at his watch, on a thick gold band, loose on his delicate wrist. He seemed to be thinking I was her daughter after all. I was screwed up, too.

"We'll have to stop here." He cleared his throat. "I'm not going to charge you for this session."

I still didn't move. I took off one shoe and pulled down my knee sock and dug into my pockets, collecting all the money. I didn't trust anywhere in the backhouse anymore, so I carried my money around with me.

"Will she kill herself?"

He shook a little, wincing, I guess that I surprised him. He frowned. "I don't think so. Your mother hasn't shown signs of a suicide."

"Oh." I looked at him, grateful for that. "Could you see her one more time and tell her you're not going to marry her? Just once."

I sat there with all the crinkled money from my pockets and straightened the bills on my thigh. I offered to pay for one more time. I guess that got to him. He shook his head again and said he wouldn't take the money. He said the appointment my mother used to have was already filled but when there was a cancellation, he'd have his receptionist call.

I didn't go home. On the high school track field, kids from the four classes competed against each other in sack races and egg relays, an athletic carnival. I found Leslie on the top bleacher, drinking coffee with our sixty-two-year-old French teacher, Madame Camille. Outside the announcer's booth, there was a five-foot stack of white pie boxes, from the House of Pies.

My mother had been so enchanted when we'd first moved to Beverly Hills and driven around at night. In Bay City, every block or two had a tavern, an old house with a sign outside. "Here, you don't see the taverns, they all go out for dessert," she'd said. We had marveled at the House of Pies, Lady Kelly's, all the ice cream stores. My mother felt she was finally in her element.

Exhilarated, sick of being goody-goods, Leslie, Madame Camille and I stole a pie and sat on the bleacher sideways, eating it with our fingers, half watching the colors move on the field below.

Later, an announcement blared over the loudspeaker.

"The junior class is disqualified because several members of that class—you know who you are—stole one of the prizes. It's too bad that just a few people ruined the whole class's fun."

We stood up, stunned. Madame Camille walked precariously on the bleacher in her high heels. "I will buy another pie," she said, lifting her white patent leather purse over her head and moving as fast as she could to the control booth. "I will pay."

I didn't tell my mother I'd seen Dr. Hawthorne. We went out to dinner that night, the same as always, and after, we drove to Baskin-Robbins. Now, the furtive run inside with the five-dollar bill moist in my hand and back to the car parked in the dark, under the trees, carrying the two cones like torches and eating them in the front seat with the heat turned on, listening to my mother sigh and talk about what we'd have in the pretty-soon future, acquired a settled sadness. Those trees dropping blossoms on the car top and my mother not taking them for real because she was wait-ing, waiting to be married and to see them as a wife, a doctor's wife. I knew that I would leave her here, still waiting.

When we called home to ask for money, my mother always had me talk first. My grandmother asked me questions about school. Then, I had to stay near the phone, so close we touched, while my mother begged. My grandmother would ask if we really needed it and I would have to say yes. We'd already gone through the green book of my grandmother's account for me.

Ellen Arcade finally called us. She screamed into the phone. "You didn't *tell* me you knew Cassie Swan, we were talking the other day, and your name came up for this commercial, but we have something even better, there's a series and with the influx of the Iranians, oh, you know, Adele, you read the papers, *any*-way, Ann is just perfect, with her coloring. I want her to read next Wednesday . . ."

My mother held out the phone and we both listened. I scribbled notes of the time and place. It was an address in Westwood on the seventeenth floor. An audition. My mother and I wheeled around the room, falling down dizzy, when we hung up the phone and I stopped eating for the next five days.

The morning of the audition the phone rang while I stood in the shower. I hadn't washed my hair for five days. I'd noticed if I let it get totally horrible first, it looked better after I washed it. My mother was talking; I thought I must have heard wrong. "Two o'clock, okay, let me ask you one more thing," she said. "Not one question? Oh, okay."

I bent over, shaking my hair dry upside down to make it straight. My mother knocked on the door. "Hurry up in there. I need a shower, too."

An hour later, she was dressed. "I'm sorry, Ann, but my work is just more important than your audition. We have to live and you don't even know if you'd get the part. It's your first one, you probably wouldn't. Let's face it, you don't really look Iranian." She stood by the door, her purse over her shoulder.

"You said you'd take me." My face fell loose. "You haven't worked for months."

"Well, Honey, I'm sorry, but something today came up and I just have to go."

"You're not going to take me?"

"Try and call and ask them if they'll schedule it an hour later, and I'll come pick you up if I can when I'm done. But I've got to run. I'm sorry, but I've got to do what's best." Her polished purse, her heels, the patent leather gleamed as she tripped to the car. I heard the gate slamming. I ran outside undressed, banged on the car windows. She opened her door. "See if you can change the time."

"I can't," I screamed.

She shrugged, looked in the car mirror, frowning, then smiling again, arranging her face. Then I guessed. "You're not going to work, you're going to go see Leonard Hawthorne who doesn't even want to marry you or anything; that's where you're going! It's not to work for money. You promised!"

She shrugged again and started rolling up the window. "I'm not going to talk to you while you're like this," she said and drove away, out of our alley.

Peter Keller was in Massachusetts. I called Daniel Swan, but only Darcy and the twins were home, she didn't know where Daniel was. I even called Leslie, but her mom said she was out taking her tennis lesson and I wouldn't have ever said anything like this was important enough for her to hurry and call me back, I never would have done that. When you called Leslie's family, they answered in another zone and you had to kind of respect their slow time. Then it was a half hour to three o'clock and I stuffed my dress and makeup and hair things and all the money I had in bags and ran down to the corner, stopping every few feet in the alley to bend over and underbrush my hair, and when I came to Elevado, I hitched and a milk truck picked me up. This was 1975 and there weren't milk trucks any place in the country anymore, except Beverly Hills had these stores called Jurgensons and for about three times the price of anywhere else, they delivered your food in these white, old-fashioned trucks.

The guy drove me to Wilshire, two blocks from the place, and I took my Korkease off and ran. Then, just before I went up in the building, I was sitting on the curb, buckling my shoes, and I saw this orange, flowered baseball cap with a big bill in the window of a jeans store, on a ladder actually, and I liked it and on a whim, I just went in and bought it for six dollars. It was something I would have never done if my mother had brought me, I would have been checking my makeup in the car, all perfect, and this seemed like something just personally me, and I slammed it on my head and went up the elevator.

I thought once I got there, I could check in with a secretary or casting girl or I didn't know what and then I thought I'd find a ladies' room and go and wash up and change and put on my makeup and everything. But when I walked in, it was this ordinary, glass-doored, impressive-looking office, with a big desk, and a big, manicured blond secretary, and when I said who I was, she said my name into an intercom and in like a second, they showed me into this enormous room with windows and striped thin blinds and a view of the whole world and two men were sitting in chairs, leaning back with shirts and ties, saying my name.

They motioned me over to an empty part of the room and I stood there with all my bags just on the carpet and they were laughing, one of them smoked, he leaned down to light his cigarette again, and said, "So, okay, what have you got in there, in all those bags."

And I don't know what happened, I went dark. Pigeon-toed and knock-kneed, I bent down and started pulling things out of my bags. "A dress, a ladies' room, please. Just because I want to clean up a little doesn't mean I don't, I have Dignity. Yes Dignity, with a capital D. I may not have money, but class." I was tripping, leg over leg, and it went on a long time, I put on makeup without a hand mirror, I changed without a bathroom, pulling my dress over my head, I faked those air machines that blow your hands dry. "There," I said, landing on the floor, my stuff a

strewn pile, my makeup smeared, hair two panels in front of my face.
"Don't you feel better clean? Yes, I do, much, much, better. You can seat
us now, please."

I'd mimicked people all my life, but that was the first time I'd done
her. I looked up again. My legs felt like Gumby. The men had been quiet,
both of them, and now they were laughing. One clapped. I had screamed.
I thought they must have felt terribly sorry for me. But I was a little elated,
too. I knew there was a chance I'd done something good, good enough to
change my life. "Okay," the one with the cigarette said, taking out a gold
case, lighting another. "Do they teach you to read, too, over at Beverly
Hills High?" The whole time there, I forgot I was wearing that orange hat.

When I came out of the building I spent the whole three dollars I had left
on a hot fudge sundae at the Westwood Will Wright's, and I ate it in about
a minute, standing at the takeout counter. I was so hungry all of a sudden.
Then I went to go home. Nobody picked me up on Wilshire, this time,
when I hitched. I stood at the corner of Westwood Boulevard, in front of
two huge office buildings at a bus stop, still carrying my bags. About fifty
people in gray business suits milled, waiting for the bus. I went up to each
one, I swear, each one, I said, "Excuse me, I live in Beverly Hills, I go to
the high school; I lost my wallet and I don't have any money. Could I
possibly borrow forty cents for the bus and if you give me your address I'll
send it back to you?" I got two nods, fast, flickering, almost like sleights
of hand. Other people just looked away, into the hills you couldn't see for
the smog, as if they didn't hear me. I ended up walking home. I got there
at eight o'clock and stood looking in the refrigerator. It was empty. My
mother must have thrown out all the food.

After a while, I knocked, lightly, at her door. "Mom, are we going to get
some supper?"

"Leave me be, Ann. Just go away." Her voice was flat and totally different. I scuffed up to the Kellers' and went in the back and the cook fixed
me a ham sandwich.

What I was afraid of never happened. My mother just talked about Dr.
Hawthorne less and less. In the evenings, she still wore her peach-colored
robe, but she tended to lie on the couch flipping through magazines. I
didn't find any more red envelopes in our mail. I'd been walking around
waiting for the day she'd fall apart. But she didn't. She hadn't with Josh
Spritzer, either.

One afternoon, late, she rushed in dressed up, her white lab coat over
a pantsuit.

"Well, I'm back at Palm Manor and guess what? They gave me a party, they were so glad to get me back. They said no one else they'd had in either convalescent home was good with the people the way I was."

A tear formed on the corner of one eye.

"Control yourself, Mom." I could be such a pill.

She dabbed her eye with a sleeve. "Well, I suppose I understand these old people. A lot of them are out here from the midwest or somewhere else, you know, and here they are in a home. All alone."

"I'm glad you're working again," I said. I was so cold. I walked away to my room. She should just work and make money to pay for my school and clothes and for college. For me to go away. I didn't want to hear about it, about her trying, how she felt. She should just do it and make it look easy.

"'Course I suppose they've got it pretty good there. There's a lot worse, I'll tell you," she said, mostly to herself.

The gas and electricity was cut off again and I stayed home from school to pay the bill. We both did it rotely, something we were used to. Now, the people in Pacific Gas and Electric knew my name.

"I'll catch a father for you yet, Ann, you just wait." My mother patted my knee. We sat parked in front of Baskin-Robbins and she sighed.

"Not for me, anymore. You should look for a husband for you. But I don't need a father anymore." We both knew I would go away in one year.

My mother sat up straighter. "Well, sure you do. For when you're in college, you can have parties and bring your kids home. And just to have a man you can look up to a little and talk."

"Even if you marry someone, he won't be my father. I had a father."

"Yeah, well where is he."

I shrugged. "Anyone else'll just be your husband. I won't really know him that well."

"Just wait and see. You plan too much. You're thinking and analyzing, you've got to learn to just be. And besides, you might like to have a man to look up to, to ask for advice once in a while."

A piece of my mother's hair hung near her ice cream cone. I reached over and hooked it behind her ear.

"I have you."

"Yes, but you need a man, too. You'll see." She started the engine of the car. "Who knows, maybe you'll be better off not growing up with a man all the time. Because with my father, you always compare and nobody else ever has that real closeness you did with him. Maybe you're better off never knowing it. I think so. I think everything's just going to go right in your life."

· · ·

We got the call, union scale, sixteen weeks shooting the first season. The part was Marie Iroquois on "Sante Fe." They'd changed me to an Indian.

We had habits, but we never admitted them. We ate out every night, but every night, it was as if my mother felt freshly surprised that driving in the car and finding a restaurant was, at ten o'clock, our only alternative. We never bought food for the half-size refrigerator anymore. All we had in the house was carrot juice and wheat germ oil.

It was stubbornness. My mother didn't want this to be our life. She'd do it a day at a time, she'd put up with it, but she wasn't going to *plan* for it. We didn't pay bills, we didn't buy groceries, we bounced checks. Accepting our duties might have meant we were stuck forever. We made it so we couldn't keep going the way we were; something had to happen. But the thing was, it never did.

My mother had to pick me up from work now, in Studio City. She came late a lot of times. I'd hang around with this boy, Clark, a guy from the Valley.

It wasn't anything like I'd thought it would be, television. I just had to stand around and say lines, once in a while I got to say one word more than another word to make people laugh, but it didn't really matter what I did. It was work, like my sophomore part-time job in the PE office. Mostly they wanted pictures of black hair. Before, I'd imagined the movies were the center of the world, and people loved you, people like my father came up and saw you and told you you were beautiful. But this was like nothing. The places we shot were in the Valley, just gray lots and studios, trailer dressing rooms. We stood around waiting most of the time. Nobody thought we were anywhere. Even people like Clark, who wanted to be actors, and who walked funny, he sort of bounced to make himself seem taller, they all just wanted to get somewhere else.

But other people, outside television, treated you different. Teenaged girls on Beverly Drive giggled behind, turned shy if I stopped, and looked up at me.

I was still going to leave her. I'd go to college, a clean, safe, normal escape. I'd have the money. Before, she used to tell me I had a trust fund. I asked her about it a lot. The first time, when I was fourteen or something, it was, "Don't worry, I arranged this with your father's family when you were a baby. There was money set aside for your college then, from Egypt."

"Like the whole country of Egypt is just going to send me money."

"Don't worry, I've worked it out. On your seventeenth birthday, it'll come."

The second time, it was, "Well, I'm worried, I haven't heard anything from the Egyptians and I'm very worried." I asked about papers, documents, even names. She had nothing. The next time I asked was the June before Marie Iroquois. We sat in the car, licking ice cream cones. She put her fingers to her throat. "My jewels are your trust, Ann, so just be quiet." Once the checks started from "Santa Fe" I never mentioned it again.

The point of the fight was always, "I don't know why you can't go to UCLA like all these kids I see, they're getting good educations, they're studying to be nurses and lawyers and female doctors. I see them in the convalescent homes."

I had no answer so I didn't give one. And the fights always passed.

I got into a better school than I deserved, with my lousy grades. But even colleges thought you were different if they saw you on TV.

We both knew I would go. We joked about it.

"You know after we've worked so hard all these years, you could really just stay a while and help out a little, so we could get ahead once, you know, after I've worked nights and at Hamburger Hamlet and as a maid, and everything, you know? It wouldn't kill you."

I knew.

Something I found when I was packing to go away: a newspaper clipping, in a shoe box where I kept things, from the *Beverly Hills Courier,* March 2, 1972.

13-YEAR-OLD SEEKS HOME. NEAT, WELL-BEHAVED
OKAY STUDENT. B + PRETTY (DARK HAIR, THIN).
DOES NOT SMOKE AND HAS NO INTEREST IN EXPERIMENTING
WITH DRUGS. PLANNING TO GO TO COLLEGE.
I WOULD HELP AROUND THE HOUSE. MAY BE THE DAUGHTER YOU'VE
ALWAYS WANTED. NO TROUBLE. PO BOX 254.

I remembered I wouldn't let the guy who took my money for the ad open the envelope until I left. He was cute, red-headed, he looked like a college kid and he flirted with me, but after he read my ad, which must have been as soon as I walked out of the office, I didn't want to see him again.

I never went and checked my post office box for replies.

Another time, I rummaged through the jumbled suitcase from home. It was a little library of me. First-grade report cards, average, average, average, one above-average—in penmanship—a list of friends to work on stuck in a book (some who already liked me, some who might), a large photo album with one entry, pressed yellow roses and a faded orange clear hospital identification band. Wisps of hair curled in envelopes. Baby teeth in eyedropper bottles. Beach ball photographs.

I remembered it only dimly, the place on the highway, Kelly's, a small brick store with a house in back. Mostly, they developed film, you parked your car on the gravel and went in to pick up your packet of snapshots. It was a dim rainy day when we went, a carpeted room in back. The man looked young and dull. My mother was the brightest thing there, full of light and authority. I wore an orange raincoat with pink dots over my tiny swimsuit and thongs. I remember them posing me with the beach ball, remember lying on the carpet, arching up, for them to slide the swimsuit off. I don't know, I must have been six or seven. I hated the way my hair looks in the pictures, up in a bun, and my forced big smile, the way my leg tilts, posing. Its funny for me to think of us in that little dim place by the highway, taking nude pictures of a seven-year-old with a colored beach ball. At one point, my mother took a powder puff out from her purse and powdered me.

She still has that little orange and pink raincoat. She keeps it in dry-cleaning cellophane at one end of her closet.

Leslie and I shopped together for college. Used clothing stores on La Cienega for broken-in Levi's, we tried on hundreds from the wooden apple barrels, chose the ones that fit and then tore the knees. We bought tiny used T-shirts with numbers on them which we wore so tight they bound our chests and a strip of skin escaped uncovered above our belts. Her parents kept asking me over to dinner, but her family got on my nerves. It was the same every night. Her father, her mother, her little brother, where they sat, the bowls of food moving around the table like a clock.

They all kept quiet, only Leslie complained. "So why *don't* we do these things, why *don't* we boycott grapes?"

But Leslie's parents never yelled. They remained soft-spoken always. "You have to choose your causes," Leslie's mother murmured, "we can't do everything for everyone. Or we'd be boycotting the whole store. We'd have nothing to eat. Your father and I have chosen the Jews. When you go away to college, you'll find the one or two things that mean the most to you."

Leslie rolled her eyes at me. Later, in her room, she shook her head, "I'm counting the days. Sometimes I think all my mother cares about is getting her nails done and her legs waxed. She's like a mannikin in a store window." That's what I thought of Leslie's mother too, I would have agreed if I didn't know that kids really love their parents.

When we walked downstairs later, a huge fight started between Leslie and her father over Häagen-Dazs. Häagen-Dazs ice cream was just new in the stores. Leslie's parents said they wouldn't spend two dollars on a pint of ice cream, no matter what. Leslie screamed, Dana's father bought it for his kids.

I just wanted to go home. My mom and I sometimes bought two pints and each ate one, right from the carton, with a spoon.

One day I brought the rent check up to the big house. I went through the kitchen and while I stood talking with the cook, Mr. Keller walked in. I realized I'd never seen him in the kitchen. He looked slight there, out of place among the huge stainless steel sinks and counters.

"May I have a word with you, Ann?"

We walked through the living room to the back terrace. We stood looking over the lawn and the tennis court. His face twisted. "Do you have all the money you need, for college?" he said.

I shook my head, yes.

"If you need anything," he said.

I looked back towards the empty house. "Where's Mrs. Keller?" I asked.

"In San Francisco for the day."

Daniel Swan wasn't going anywhere. The San Ysidro house stayed the same: the Failure's deal still hadn't come through in Mexico, the Witch still whipped around the corners like a wind, late and busy. The only one making money was Riley, who had already started a rock band. The summer before we'd been in a commercial together. The Swans weren't moving, but they didn't have the money to send Daniel away to college. He was going to stay at UCLA. He didn't seem to mind. We sat on the steps in back of the house, our heads on our knees, staring at the plain dry canyons. "My grandfather's jewelry business, he sells diamonds, I might do that and make a ton of money. Or I could work in a bank like my cousin. I might do that or developing. I'd like to buy my own boat, then you don't have to worry about anything, a sixty-foot yacht and you could live on it and go around the world."

"What about astronomy? I thought you were going to major in astronomy."

"I'll do that too. I could go to school at night, if I make all that money I won't need a degree, I'd just want the classes, I don't know, I might do anything."

Before I left for college, it seemed my mother was working all the time. One night we parked in front of a house on an empty wide street north of Sunset. The palm trees seemed to whisper over the lawn. "Too bad Idie's dead," my mother said as we made our way up the driveway. A Mrs. Dover invited us into the kitchen. We followed her as she slip-slopped through the cluttered house. "The shanty Irish," my mother mouthed.

I sat next to my mother at the kitchen counter, listening while Mrs. Dover made tea and talked about Melly's heart. Melly's heart this, Melly's heart that. Mrs. Dover moved slowly, like a fat person. Mrs. Dover said she could cook only some things now and not others, now they could walk but never too fast, they took rides but not far and all because of Melly's heart. We listened nicely, my mother smiling as if she understood the moment before Mrs. Dover said it.

"It's all the same heart," Mrs. Dover whispered over the kitchen counter, as if she was afraid of being overheard. "Idie was a year younger when she, you know. He's sixty-five now."

"But you forget, Trish, that he's in good shape." My mother's voice scolded with conviction. I didn't know whether she was telling the truth or not. "Idie was fat, Trish. And she didn't exercise. And do you know what she ate?"

"So you think he'll hang on a while?" Mrs. Dover laughed a short laugh.

"She ate doughnuts. Jelly doughnuts. That's all she'd eat. The dietitian forbade the aides to give them to her but she wouldn't touch anything else. Sure. Jelly doughnuts with powder sugar on top."

"I didn't know that."

"Well, of course. He'll live another ten years, Trish. At least. *At least.* Now, you're the one who needs more exercise. You know, when Melly's seventy-five, he's going to be in good shape and he's going to want a wife in good shape, too."

"You think so?" Mrs. Dover looked up at my mother.

My mother and I ran down the gravel driveway to the car, giggling. She drove fast through the residential streets to the store windows on the way to Baskin-Robbins. "Boy, would you look at that suede suit. Isn't *that* elegant. That's what I need, a few good suits that'll take me anywhere."

"I'm sure it's incredibly expensive." Clothes had been so easy when we worked in a store, like a game, getting more and more, making outfits. Now, they seemed hard and important again.

"Yes, but it's quality. That's what I've always done. I've always bought the best, good fabrics and with a good cut that's really well made. And then it lasts forever."

"Fine if you can afford it in the first place." I worried about my mother managing her money, after I was gone.

She sighed. "You can't even let me have a little fun, imagining, can you?"

.   .   .

As if it were something unconnected to my leaving, incidental, my mother would mention her plans to kill herself.

"I might just drive over . . ."

"You'll get the insurance."

"You'll be *fine*."

"I want you to invest that, it'll be a lot of money."

"You're a survivor."

I did not believe her and I did. I knew my leaving would make a difference, could make a difference.

Anyway I left.

The Saturday after my last shoot for "Sante Fe," I made an appointment to get my hair cut. I told my mother in the morning.

"What are you going to have, a trim?"

"More like a cut."

"Oh, Honey, no. Don't, Ann. You'd be crazy to get more than a little trim. Why do think you got Marie Iroquois, that's what's cute about you, Honey. And don't think that doesn't matter at college, too, believe me. Really, it's the truth, Ann."

"I'm just telling you. For your *information*. I'm not asking for advice. I'm just saying, I'll be gone between eleven and noon. You better find something to do with yourself, that's all."

What she found to do with herself was drive to the beauty shop, sit and read magazines in the front, by the window. I'd never had my hair cut since those boys chopped it off on Halloween when I was eight. Just trims. I'd always had long hair. It had seemed important.

I watched the woman and her scissors in the mirror, the little wet pieces falling everywhere. A circle of hair stuck around my shoulders on the cotton smock and a wider circle fell on the floor. The little pieces felt sharp, they itched my neck.

My mother ran up. "What are you doing? She only wanted a little bit. Oh, Honey, look. You just wanted a trim."

They each stood over me, one of them holding scissors.

"That's not what I said."

"You sure did, that's what you told me at home this morning. You said just a little. She's got six inches off already, it's going to look awful. What are you letting her do to you?"

"Please sit down, Mom." I looked at my hands lying there, on the beauty shop smock. They could have been anyone's hands.

My mother turned to the woman cutting my hair. The woman, pivoting on one foot, leaning close, cut in quick, decisive clips. "Why don't you at least undercut it, so it turns *under*, not up? That's just going to flip up when it dries. It's going to be awful."

"I am undercutting it," the woman said.

"Jeez, Honey, I could have taken you to the man who does me in Glendale. You should see the beautiful cuts. The girls your age come out with this full, long, bouncy hair. And it just curls. He cuts it so it goes under." She picked up a panel of my wet hair and dropped it back onto the cotton smock. "She's thinning it," she said. "You're thinning it."

"I am not thinning it," the woman said.

"May I ask you where you learned to cut hair?"

"Mom."

"I'm just asking her a question. She can tell me."

"I studied in New York and in London."

I smiled for pretentious Westwood, where PhDs worked at the post office and my hairdresser studied in London.

"Where in New York?"

"I studied with Christiane at Michel Heron and with André."

"Oh. I haven't heard of them," my mother said. "Oh, stop, please. You're not going to take any more off, are you?"

"I'm going to shape it, so from the bangs down to the shoulder, it's one line." The woman gestured with her comb. "Okay?"

"Oh, God. I don't know why you do this to me. Well, fine, it's your life. But you just have to rebel, don't you? You have to make yourself ugly. Don't you see, Honey, you're cutting off your nose to spite your face."

"My hair. I'm cutting my hair."

"Are you jealous of me? Is that it? Because, Honey, you shouldn't be. I'm your mother. I can help you. If you'd only let me. You should see the cute cuts they're giving."

She walked out of the border of the mirror. Then she came back. "I can't stand it. I can't sit here and watch her doing that to you."

"You're not sitting," I said.

The woman kept turning on one foot and snipping. The hair was now an inch above my shoulders. I turned and saw my mother in the front of the store. She sat back down in her chair and opened a magazine.

Next to me, a man blow-dried a young girl's hair, pulling the brush tightly away from her face. The two hairdressers smiled. "Is she always this way?" The woman looked at me in the mirror.

"Just about my hair. She always wanted me to have long hair."

The woman turned her blow-dryer on. In a minute, my hair began to look beautiful, a neat thick clean line next to my chin.

My mother appeared in the mirror again, holding her magazine in one dropped hand, moving around the chair, circling me. I wouldn't look at her. She stared at my face in the mirror.

"You'll just let anyone be your mother, won't you? You let anyone but me."

. . .

I never did hear from my father. I used to think, he might see me on TV and write me or call me or something, but nothing ever happened. I don't know, maybe he tried or maybe he didn't have a TV or whatever. I suppose it could have been anything.

I left lightly. Everything my mother wanted, I gave her. She kept all my baby things, my first teeth in bottles, my skates from when I was five years old. There was a work shirt she liked, I gave it to her. She pointed to things and I left them in the backhouse. Anything to get away. And when she took me to the airport, she walked me to where I got on the jet, she walked to where they wouldn't let her come any farther without a ticket and when she kissed me, she looked at me, so I pulled out these new jeans I bought, they were Jag, and Jag was just a new name then, they were like my favorite thing, and she knew it and I gave them to her.

"You may not see me again," she said, real softly, because other people were passing, busy, with little suitcases, and I guess they could hear.

I stuffed the jeans in her hands and she looked at me, eyes all grateful, huge like a pet's. But that night, when I called her from Providence, she answered the phone on the first ring, jangled, and said, Well, the pants didn't fit her, I'd obviously bought them for me not for her and I didn't understand the meaning of a present, I'd never learn how to give.

That night she talked about the insurance policy again, the cliffs of Big Sur. I called her back and she didn't answer and then I called her and couldn't find her for three days until I reached the Kellers, who told me she was out practicing on the tennis courts.

For years, I didn't go home.

Carol

14

The Stone and the Heart

It was like a stone, something in me. The way a hook needles a fish, it hurt when I tried to move away from it. And then it turned and I was worse. Love sunk like that in me once. Like a hook so I couldn't think of anyone else.

It was a long long time, too long. And I was alone, dwelling. I passed Benny's room every day, we kept the door shut and I was the only one who went in. I said I had to clean and I did clean every day, wiping dust with a soaked rag before it ever had a chance to settle. I oiled that old wood dresser, wiped the windowsill. We'd built the house ourselves when we were married, so it showed just how many years had gone, that wood. And then I polished each one of his things. He had that fish hanging on the wall that he caught in Florida, they each had their rifles mounted over his bed, and then there were all his models. He spent hours putting those together when he was little. He had such patience. I started with the hotrods and I dusted them with a real soft piece of chamois and then I stood up on a footstool to do the planes. (He had planes and you had stars. He gave them to you—you put them up yourselves on your ceiling, those glow-in-the-dark stars. I remember because your ma was mad. She wanted me to pay to repaint. But then, later, Gram and I stood in your room once—after you'd gone and moved away—and we figured out those were real constellations. We found Big Bear and the Little Dipper, Pleiades. You must have stood by the window and copied it all down.)

I used to take his shirts and socks out of the drawers and wash them in a special laundry. Then I put them all back where they were. I remembered exactly which T-shirt was on top that first day when I came in, and how each went underneath. It took four hours to clean the whole room and I always felt sorry to leave. I used to pick up that rock from Pikes Peak and just stand in the middle of the room and hold it. Those windows are small, I don't know why, that's the way they were doing them that year we built the house I suppose, so somewhere on the floor, there'd be one small square of light. I slipped off my shoes and stood on the light in my nylons and held that rock and looked down at it. It was an ordinary big rock, gray and dusty. It could have been from anywhere. But it was labeled

Rock From Pike's Peak and Benny had held it, like I was doing. I don't know what I thought I'd get from that stone, holding it like that, in the sun. I looked and looked at it and saw the same thing: the dirt color, gray, the plainness. But I felt like something would come into me through my hands. I understood then the way I don't anymore about religion. It is a matter of concentration, a promise never to let anything else come between. I had that kind of bond, then.

I don't mean going to church and giving charity, none of that, that we still do. I mean the religion that is a private thing, trying to clean yourself out, so you're an empty house, a dustless vessel.

I've lost that. That I don't have anymore.

I spent half my day in that room for a year, the first year. Nobody bothered me much about it. Jimmy kept following his own map. We didn't have too much to do with each other. We'd always had the twin beds that made up together to be a queen. That year, I didn't even bother pushing them to the center in the morning. I started sleeping facing the wall. I liked that sour cold air in the crack. That's how I was then. It tasted to me like hosts on my tongue, dust dissolving.

Then once I was in Ben's room, cleaning, and Mary Griling was riding outside on the lawn mower. Jimmy hired her to help around the yard and I don't know why, with the noise and all, but I dropped the rock I was holding in my hand and it fell and shattered on the floor.

After that, I didn't go into the room. We could keep things the way they were more by not looking than by care. I shut the door then and nobody ever went in. I drove in the car and got a rock from the quarry and taped the label on and put it back. I never once touched it again.

Time hadn't stopped, I just had. The next year, eleven months, Jimmy went in the hospital for the heart. He was one of the first in Wisconsin to have the open heart surgery. I don't remember anymore if I was scared. I still lived in another world; the darkness. I didn't mind the waiting at all and in the hospital, that's most of what it was. I didn't mind anything as long as they left me alone. I'd settle in my chair and sink down and then I'd be off. It was as if I had work to do and when they left me alone I could take it out and begin unraveling and get started on what needed to be finished.

I thought about the leg. I worked that night over so much in my mind and every time it hurt. I was like a person with a loose tooth, running his tongue over the sore place again and again, activating the pain. If it was still there, I wanted to touch it.

We were in the trailer, Jimmy and I, the night they called. We were already asleep. The phone there was on a wall in the dinette. We both got up when it rang, we must have known, it was so late at night and we sat across from each other at that little dinette table.

Jimmy talked in the phone but he held it away, so I heard everything they were saying. Right then we had to choose. We could fly him down to Milwaukee to a big city hospital or keep him where he was, in this little Emergency Room. And we couldn't ask anybody, we didn't have time. I was wearing rollers, I touched them to make sure and then I remember staring at Jimmy's hand and my hand on the dinette table. Both our hands looked familiar and old, like gloves, something you'd wear every day that would take on a shape.

Well, neither of us knew.

And I was surprised, because for all Jimmy's wanting to be the man, he looked at me and asked me what to do. Real even. And I knew he'd listen.

"I don't know, Jimmy," I said. I looked and just begged for him to choose. We saw into each other's eyes and they went back and back and back and neither of us knew. He waited. And so I said, "Maybe we'd best keep him here."

He told the man on the phone and in no time, the next thing I knew, we were in the car, on the highway, driving. I don't know how we ever got our clothes on. Times like that, there are miracles you hardly notice.

I remember riding that night. It was eighteen miles to the hospital and Jimmy drove fast. We were the only car on the road. We didn't say anything to each other, but we had the windows open and I could smell. That was the only time in my life, there in the car, when I really felt the word married. We were married. Other times words like that meant other people.

Outside, earth rushing in, and the wetness of pine. Jimmy turned the radio on to country music, a woman singing, "I Fall to Pieces"; her voice whining like the whine of green air just out the windows, clinging. "Always," she sang. And I felt almost happy.

I'd been to the Emergency Room in Bay City so many times with Benny. He'd had to have stitches, he'd had sprains and once the cast. When he was real small, he'd tried to jump off the garage roof. He wanted to fly like Peter Pan. He had you up there too, but we didn't know. I'd found him, curled and bloody, and raced him off to the hospital in the car.

You had been afraid to jump. You kept so quiet up there that even after we came home in the station wagon, nobody knew to get you down. I fixed cinnamon toast and Benny was watching cartoons in the breezeway, and it was Benny who remembered you all of a sudden.

No one else ever died. Granny didn't. It was the same leg, the left, and they took it off just above the knee. Mom thought a long time whether it was the right thing, but there was a tumor, they had to get it out. They operated in winter. And I remember the shock in spring, when I first saw her walking out with the crutches. She wore big high rubber boots on the one leg and a jacket. But she wasn't wearing any stockings and you could see where the leg ended against the fabric of her skirt. The skirt was blue, a real girlish print, and the leg was white and wrinkled and old. It came to a point and a knot, they tied her skin at the end like a sausage. She went outside every day to feed that pony. But Mom said later what broke her spirit were those crutches. She couldn't ever get used to walking that way. She was ninety-one years old. And once she couldn't be outside, running everything, bossing the world, then she didn't want to live anymore.

With Hal in the army, that was the left leg too. He said those army doctors thought he was crazy, that second time he came out of the hospital. They made him march and at night, when they couldn't see, his knee swelled up to the size of a basketball, and it hurt him. But then, when he went to the infirmary in the morning, it fell down again. They made him march. Finally, he said if they'd give him a camera he'd take a picture. And then those doctors wanted to operate and he said no. Who knows what they would have done, those army doctors. And once he came home, it healed by itself. It still hurts him, when it rains I notice a limp.

Jimmy got to be the strong one, after he'd had the operation. When he came home from the hospital, we both worked together and that's when we really got started in the health. That's how I learned the vitamins, he had to take so many pills every day. I made an effort to do the right things. I took them, too, we changed our whole way of eating. I did everything the way we were supposed to, fruits and vegetables and fibers. I threw out the frying pan. And Jimmy really was good. They told him to lose thirty pounds and he lost it. They told him one drink a day, that's it. And that was it. He had to walk five miles and he did, all the way past the tracks on the new road over on Brozek's land, where they put the developments. He got to know some of the people in duplexes on those spoon-shaped drives. They'd wave at him when they went out to water their lawns. He bought the walking machine and he walks in the laundry room when it's too cold outside. He built muscle, he kept telling me he was in better shape than he had been for years. And I think that gave him a new lease. I think that was the turning around for him.

People told me, after the operation, a heart gets scars and creases, wrinkles, lines like a hand.

He took an interest in new things. He read up on solar. He dreamed the idea for a swimming pool. He'd walk in his aerobics clothes past Brozek's land and come home wanting to sue.

"Not yet," I told him. "Nothing doing."

. . .

I was still in the dark, with a long way to walk before the end. I'd be doing the dishes, my ring on the sill, looking out the window to the backyard and I'd try to imagine how Ben would have walked on the grass, without the leg. Sometimes I'd see him walking on water, crooked over the wavy green. Then I'd have to rub my eyes. I couldn't imagine him with crutches, even limping, I couldn't imagine Ben slow. He always loved speed, for the feel of it. When he was real little, he used to haul a stick in the backyard and spin, he'd go so fast, he wouldn't hear you if you called. He got like that sometimes when he ran. And then later, the machines. The minibike, dirt bike, tractors, lawn mowers, snowmobiles. And then the car. I think, truthfully, Benny sped, too, on those empty peninsula highways late at night, sure. It wouldn't have had to be Jay. It could have been Benny alone. He loved anything that went fast. Nobody could keep up with him.

I thought and I thought and I didn't get anywhere. I felt a place in me where it hurt every time I touched, the stone. It was the darkness I swallowed.

I told myself: he could have died those minutes on the helicopter in the air, between the peninsula and Milwaukee. But the way it was was the only way it was: while that old doctor fooled, fussing with the leg, pinning it, the heart stopped.

You were the one who let Gram see him. When a person thinks the same thoughts again and again, they each take on a shape and a color, almost a taste in your mouth. And my thinking, Well, at least Gramma saw him, was clear relief, like green-white air, antiseptic as an after-dinner mint from a nice restaurant, that cleans out all your head. It let me go on to other things.

That day in the hospital was a court of law. Gram was already in for a stroke and then we'd had to tell her about Benny. And even under the drugs, she was fighting us. She wanted to go and see her Ben.

Her arms pushed up, beating out of the blankets, and Adele was standing on one side, keeping her down. When I watched that I remembered years ago, opening the bathroom door and you were standing in the big clawfoot tub. It was the same thing—you were hitting, fighting to come out, and your mother stood pushing you down.

In the hospital, Gram was yelling. "You let me alone. Get away you." But from the drugs, her voice sounded different, real small and far away. "Get," she said, as if she were spitting out the pit of something.

"Mom, you've got to stay here," Adele said.

"I want to see him once more and I'm going to," Gram was saying, but she really wasn't all right. She bit her own lip so hard it bled. I was on the other side of the barred bed from Adele. I saw that bright blood trickling down her chin and I wiped it off with the hem of my dress.

I think maybe what really hurt Adele was Gram didn't seem the least bit interested to see the two of you. It had been years already since you'd been gone. That, I'm sure of it, was the drugs. She could only think of one thing at a time and that was, going to see him.

You sat away from us all, in a chair in the corner. Your mom stood on the one side of the bed with a young doctor in those mint green clothes they wear. He kept fingering his stethoscope.

I had the priest over by me. He was fingering his beads. But neither of them said anything, they let us fight over her.

I wanted Gram to go. It was selfish, because I didn't really know how sick she was either, but I wanted her to go, no matter what. I wanted Adele out of there, back in California. This was our life here. She'd left it.

"She's got to stay, Carol. She could have a stroke and DIE," Adele said. Right there, over Gramma.

Gramma started crying, fingering her sheet. "I am *not* going to die," she said.

Adele turned to the doctor. It was like an instinct in her, turning to men more than women, looking up, and to MDs more than ordinary men.

The doctor dropped his hands from the stethoscope. He seemed reluctant to say. "We can give her another sedative, but it is a risk."

"Do you really want to go, Mom?" I said. Here I was leaning over and shouting loud as if she were a child. Her hearing was just fine. "You know, if you aren't so good, you don't have to go. Benny would understand."

"OF COURSE he would," Adele interrupted, yelling. "In fact, he'd RATHER. He'd rather you not go."

"I want to go and I'm going," she said. She sat up on the bed. "I told you. I want to see him."

I looked at my priest. He bent his head down so I could see the freckles on his balding head. He prayed.

"Carol, I just don't think she should go. It's not going to help Benny anymore and it could, you know—"

I just didn't know. "I don't know," I said. "I just don't know."

Your mother turned all of a sudden and looked at you. "What do you think, Ann?"

We all looked at you then, in the corner. You were wearing scuffed-up cowboy boots, like they wore around here, and your legs crossed. That was the first time I'd noticed you'd grown up. Your legs were long and you moved your arms like someone definite.

"Let her go," you said. You recrossed your legs, put the other one on top. Your boot was worn down in the heel. "She should go."

"You really think so, Annie?" your mom asked.

And you nodded.

So she had a sedative and we held her, me on one side, Adele on the other. Just that walk from the station wagon to the back door of Umberhum's, it seemed like a long ways. I parked as close as I could to the door. The sun was so bright she couldn't look. We walked real careful but her face was confused, as if she thought her ankles were going in different directions, out of control.

I'd driven by Umberhum's Funeral Parlor a million times, but that day I felt like I owned it. Adele and I almost carried Gram in, she was so light, like nothing on our elbows, as if we were fooling, playing the Emperor's New Clothes, and everyone stepped back, hushing, for no one who was there.

Then her weight seemed to fall back into her in a heap from the sky when she knelt on the pew by the coffin. For the first time she seemed to me an old woman, the way she settled on that pew. She reached over and touched Benny's hand. I was thinking how weak and helpless she looked, that we still had to get her up and back, and maybe Adele was right and this was a mistake. I couldn't tell from her face if she knew anything that was going on. She stayed a long time before we realized she'd fallen asleep.

But it wasn't a mistake. She didn't die, either.

I didn't like anything, anymore, for a long time and that's why I had to go away. I saw the bad in everyone around me. As soon as she was well, my mother bored me. Her life seemed like a windup toy. She traced the same steps, through the same little rooms, bedroom, kitchen, bathroom, every day. She ate her meal off the same dish and then she washed it. And that's all she talked about, what food she put on that same plate in that same kitchen and how much she paid for it.

Hal was worse. Merry left, Tina was gone, they lived in a truck up out of town by the bay, with Merry's new boyfriend. And Hal had a girl, that Patty, who I'd always liked, but he treated her like dirt, like nothing. I saw him hit her, plenty, he used to hold her jaw and slap her. And she didn't even fight back. She just stood there and her bangs shook.

There was nothing I did. I went into the store one day to balance the books. I had a cup of coffee from the Big Boy, I was just going to concentrate down in the darkness and do the numbers of the books. I wasn't going to pay any attention.

Then Hal walked in. "How's Patty?" I said, trying to be nice.

He shrugged. "I only like her because she goes down on me."

I shut the drawer in my desk that was open and got my keys out of my purse. I went out to the car and drove home. For a long time, the books didn't get done.

.   .   .

Adele always called, always asking for money. Once she said she had cancer. She sent Gram a Polaroid of herself opened up, in operation on the
surgery table. I'm not sure why, but I knew right away she was lying. That
made me so mad, she gets you down. It was the first thing Jimmy and I
did together for a long time. We needed to find out for sure. She'd told us
the hospital she'd been in and from them we found the doctor. He confirmed it to us: there was no cancer. My sister was a fine, healthy woman.
Her operation had been purely cosmetic. He turned out to be a plastic
surgeon. Apparently, sometime in college, your mother had silicone im-
plants. One had shrunk and now she was having her breasts evened out.

Well, we told Gram and, that once, Adele didn't get her money.

See, it was around that time I found the stone in me, that hardness I'd
swallowed. I felt it, a cold dark, it pressed back against my fingertips. I
didn't tell anyone, I hoarded, kept it to myself. It stayed under my left
breast, always. The hook was there. As soon as I found it, it stopped
hurting. I touched it many times, to test. I couldn't sit still, I always
wanted to be alone. I excused myself four, five times in an hour to go to
the ladies' room to touch it. I went into a trance like that, I didn't think.
Touching the stone in me.

I went away to their retreats. In the woods in Michigan, Minnesota, I
even drove up to Ontario. Never once to a doctor. For a long time it was
my secret. I read the Bible. I memorized: *the fear of God is clean, enduring
forever.*

We are strangers before thee.

I came to know my own wickedness, how I hoarded. Around campfires
in pine woods, clearings like our own in the Vale of Valhalla, painted
rocks in a circle, I knit and felt alone. The others, nuns and church-
women, fell in together and did good. They darned the priests' socks.
They made potato salad, they gossiped and laughed, washing pots and
pans. I wouldn't join. I prayed. I pleaded for cleansing, there in the north.
I wanted the cold to come and burn the dust, everything impure out of
me. A crystal agate, something forced by fire. I touched the stone while I
prayed, the stone I wanted to save. It was the deepest part of me. My fire.
My good.

But the others complained. Priests took my hands and asked me to
forget. One of them read my palms; the right hand and the left, what you
are and what you were born to be. *There is a time to mourn and a time to
forget.* I yanked back. Father James sat me down and gave me suggestions,
how to make my way with the other women, as if I were an unpopular
girl.

That was when I finally went back home. The women stood in front
of a silver trailer, opening bottles of relish and ketchup for a barbecue. All

of a sudden, they looked mismatched and shabby to me, the nuns in their hiking clothes. Socks under sandals, the red acne scars on their skin, they were women who had never been pretty, women who would never have sons.

I didn't want to scrub with them on the ground, in a campsite. I'd wanted silence and cold, I'd wanted to climb. Gossip, cooking—those nuns played bridge on picnic tables—all that I could have with my own.

I drove home. And when I got there, I knew I'd given in. I was tired, I unloaded all my gear and dumped it in the basement. I made a call for an appointment with the doctor.

And what did I see that first day back from Canada, when I opened the newspaper, but a picture of Ben's little Susie engaged to marry to Jay Brozek. All five of those Brozek boys came back from Vietnam. No one else ever died. The Brozek girls were pretty, three or four of them went to college, all on scholarship. Sheila got married and now she lives across the street. Every year, Christmas Eve, they sent their youngest with a basket of cookies to Gram. Phil and Jimmy talked when they met on the yard, Phil told Jimmy to sue. It got me down.

I cut out the picture and put it under glass on the desk top where I paid my bills. I went into the bath and soaked for a long time. I looked at my breast, felt for the stone. I seemed so different now that I was back and given up, I almost thought it wouldn't hurt, I wouldn't find it. But there it was, rubbery, mobile, the same as when I'd first touched it and I knew then that it was something bad they would take away from me. I'd have to go in the hospital for them to cut it out.

I don't know what I thought, that that Susie wouldn't ever get married. She was only sixteen when it happened. She had to go on and have a life, too. I kept looking at that picture every month when I paid my bills, it's still there, under the glass. And now, you know, it doesn't bother me. Because around the eyes and the mouth, Jay turned out to look like Benny. She must have seen that, too.

I was glad about you but you weren't here. The season you were on TV, we bought a machine to tape your show. During the daytime, I'd put you on and just look at you. I thought of you every once in a while and thought that you'd turned out to be a nice girl. I was glad to have you for a niece. But I never wrote. I could have, I had time. I could have at least sent a card. I should have, I was still too much by myself, I wasn't near as good as I should have been.

You came the one Christmas from college on the Greyhound bus, you saw Hal and Jimmy fight. Gram didn't feel too well, she wouldn't have even stayed up if you hadn't been here, but Hal came late and then he played rough with Tina. Poor Jimmy said, maybe next year we could all get to Florida and Adele could come and meet us there.

And Hal said by next year, he'd be a millionaire and he'd have a helicopter. He said maybe he'd visit us for a day in Florida and then go to Haiti.

That Patty put up with all of it, his drinking, everything, and all the while, she worked too. She typed for a pediatrician. Now, she won't even speak to him, he says, she won't say hello when they run into each other in the mall.

That night, your mom called and I think she felt bad because you were here and she was alone then out in California. Well, she started in on Gram. Did you get the sweater, Did you get this, Did you get that. Oh, we were so used to it by then, it didn't get us down anymore. Gram and I just said no, no, not yet, real quietly, but we blamed it on the Christmas mail, said we were sure it would come tomorrow or the day after. And that seemed to calm her down.

She wanted to talk to Hal and I shouldn't have let her, he'd already been so rude to the rest of us, he was drunk. Well, he got on the phone and all of a sudden, he was yelling, I couldn't hardly even listen, he could be so mean. "You're a liar," he shouted. "You didn't send anything and you know it. That's bullshit. And every year since you've been out there you call and say the same damn thing and you know damn well you didn't do it! I don't care if you don't send anything, just don't give me this bullshit."

Jimmy finally tore the phone away from him. Then I guess you went and talked to her on the extension in the bedroom.

Hal and Patty left that night not so long after, Hal still drunk. He'd been drinking since I don't know when, he'd had a beer in his hand steady since he walked in our door.

And we wanted to keep Tina with us, put her to bed in Ben's room. I said I'd take her home in the morning.

But Hal said no, she was his and she was going with him. He grabbed her like he did by the hair so she was almost crying.

I took that Patty aside and asked her if she couldn't just drive or talk him into staying over and she said, no, she felt the same way, but she didn't dare fight. That really got him started, she said, the best thing she could do was go along with it.

Jimmy couldn't take it anymore, he went into the bedroom and said good night. That was it for him. And you and Gram and I stood like a little chorus huddled together in our boots there under the porch light. Patty sat on the passenger side, her face all flat and sour, and Hal took a long time unlocking his door. He drove a Ford pickup then. I bent down to Tina and said, "Where do you want to sleep tonight? Do you want to drive with your dad like this or should we fix you a nice bed and I can take you over to your dad's house in the morning?"

She wouldn't look at me. She squirmed, from one leg to the other.

"I don't know," she said.

All of a sudden, she went to the bathroom then, standing up, I guess she was scared. She couldn't hold it and Hal glared at me saying, "See, now look what you did. Trying to take my kid away from me."

She looked at the little puddle in the snow by her foot and then she started to cry, late, the way kids do sometimes. "I want to go with my dad," she said. And he hoisted her in and we stood and listened to the motor gunning and then watched the headlights make dizzy paths down the road, much too fast. All night, I jerked at noises, waiting for the phone. But nothing happened. They didn't die. Nobody else ever died.

Do you eat carrots? The doctor told me young girls who have cancer in their families should eat a carrot every day. There's something in it that prevents, the same thing that makes the carrot orange. I eat a carrot every day now and it hasn't come back yet. I go in for X-rays every six months and so far nothing has shown. He says I'm like a normal person again now. But they took so much out because I didn't go in right away. If you ever feel anything, you go right in because they say they can do it now and still save the breast. I wear a falsie and then in Florida, I have a bathing suit with it built right in. But it's in our family, both; the stones and the heart.

Hal went through a lot before he straightened out. For a long time, even when he was young, he always had to have a scheme. He tried to sell things around here to the neighborhood kids, he tried to get them to buy his creepy crawlers, he wanted them to pay to ride that horse. Well, in town, maybe so, but no kids out here were going to pay to get up on a pony.

Then, after Benny, he started taking his vacations out in Colorado. He likes it there. He's always said he might like to move someday. I hope he does, I hope he makes it. Well, he was in at the beginning of Breckenridge, before you heard about it as a place. Then the names you heard all the time were Aspen and Vail, Sugarloaf. Well, he put lots of money in, all his savings, and he borrowed from Gram and from us too, for this development. And it really seemed it ought to go. He went in with five or six others. It was a good idea, but somehow, when it all came through, it turned out the others owned the land and Hal owned the snowplows. And the snowplows broke down and that cost money to repair and pretty soon they rusted. In a couple years, he ended up paying someone else to take them off his hands.

He was behind from that for a long time. But he kept working at the store, ten, twelve hours a day until he got ahead a little. The next thing was those houses. He bought two little houses and he was going to renovate and fix them up and sell for a profit. And he worked on those too, Patty helped, he had Tina over there after school painting. But they were right by the railroad tracks, so nobody wanted to buy. He took a loss on those too.

He started the Chinese restaurant and the Frozen Yogurt and then one time he tried to get the Wisconsin franchise for some new Sony gadget. None of it panned out. He just doesn't have the knack for making money.

It's a good thing Jimmy got him started in the Rug Doctor, so at least he's got that and the pressure cleaners. His plans all came to nothing. He still talked, for years he was going to be a millionaire. Nothing he did ever worked.

Jimmy and I were back to normal, then, we had things in common. The health. We both take the Herbalife vitamins in the morning and we eat our cereal with wheat germ and brewers' yeast. You came quite a few times on your vacations, Gram was always glad about that. Each time, you went home with junk from the basement, nothing valuable, our old coats and Villager sweaters. You like that old stuff, I don't know what you do with all that junk. I kept hoping my old coat would turn up on TV. The once you wore those crazy earrings.

I remember, I overheard Jimmy talking to you in the breezeway. I was coming up from the basement with a load of wash. "She doesn't want to," he said. "Not once since Ben."

I stood still there on those steps. I didn't want to hear more.

"Maybe," you said and I could almost see you shrugging.

The next day, we put you on the Amtrak train, Gram and I. You had a duffel bag and a huge sack of peaches from the yard. That was the time, you told us, you fell in love, you wrote that you stayed up all night with him, eating peaches and watching the stars in the observation car.

Well, I didn't have hair then. I was still wearing the wig. All my burns from the trailer fire healed but I still didn't have my hair back. Such a thin down grew all over my head. I've seen it on some women with cancer.

That night, I stayed up late, Jimmy was out, it was his Elks night, they played poker. He kept up a social life, more than I did. When he came home, I heard him on his side of the room, undressing, hanging his clothes.

"Jimmy, are you hungry?" I whispered.

"You up, Carol?"

He switched the light. I was wearing an old nightie and I still had my wig on. "Let's have some ice cream," I said.

In the kitchen, I spooned out from the carton. He opened the sliding glass doors, never mind the bugs, the air smelled sweet, alfalfa and the hay. It smelled like a million dollars.

"Should we go outside and eat it?"

I took the blanket from the davenport in the breezeway and we spread it on the grass in the backyard. I dug out some Hershey's chocolate syrup back in the pantry from before we started the health. It was a loud summer night. The crickets were loud, the stars were near. Everything was dark around us. Next door, Gram had been asleep for hours, Griling's was dark, too. Bub had been gone quite awhile already then.

All of a sudden we were living on a road with mostly old people. We finished our bowls of ice cream and then Jimmy said, "Want some more?" He went in and brought out the whole carton and we ate from that with our spoons. Then that was done for, too.

I shivered a little and Jimmy rubbed his hands on my arms to warm me. All of a sudden, I felt shabby. It was an old flannel gown and I didn't ever bother with the falsie at night.

We lay down there on the grass and we started to sleep. I didn't know if he'd even want to touch me like that, the way I was. It wasn't like when we were young. But then it started. He put his hands under the nightie and rubbed my legs. He pulled the whole thing over my head. The wig caught on the collar and came off.

"Oh, Jimmy," I said.

"Shhh. Nobody's up."

I felt like our voices were drowned out by crickets. I remembered, I didn't want to kiss. I tucked my chin over his shoulder, I felt our legs moving on each other, crossing, and recrossing, the wetness of the grass.

We did everything but kiss. That seemed silly to us, maybe, kid stuff. When we woke up, it was still the middle of the night and the ground had grown cold beneath us. My shoulder was wrong. Jimmy said his hip hurt. So we lugged everything in and went to bed. We didn't find the wig, but we didn't look hard, I said, just leave it, we'd get it in the morning.

And we went in Ben's room and both slept in his little bed. We seemed smaller that night. In the morning, the whole room turned shades of gray, us too, our arms, our legs. I woke up and went to get breakfast ready, I left Ben's door open, Jimmy was still asleep, and then when I was standing in my robe by the counter mixing a blender drink, I remembered my head. I looked out the glass doors to the backyard and it seemed fresh and strong, the way the fields and grass here get in July. July is really our nicest, and it all looked the same, as if we'd never been there. Then I thought I saw a dark impression in the middle of the lawn. The grass was pretty tall, so it was darker there, crushed down. But I didn't see my wig and I wasn't going to go outside and look for it in daylight.

That morning, Jimmy talked to me, reminding. We paid for Adele's divorce; we were still at the store, trying to make a go of it, get out of the hole. He wanted to retire and build. A swimming pool, a Jacuzzi, the solar, a house in Florida. He wanted to give the Rug Doctor to Hal, for Tina's college education.

I felt something dissolving in me. Jimmy turned, made me look around. "We could have a nice life yet, Carol. We don't have much time left."

I said okay. We sued.

There where we'd slept, that's where Jimmy put in the swimming pool.

I come about once a week and water the flowers. I pray. I talk to him. I talk to Benny all the time. Oh, I don't know, I say, "I suppose you're real disappointed in me, in what I've been doing. You must not be too proud of your mother."

Jimmy wants ashes, he wants to be cremated into that dust. He says I should scatter him in the backyard. He never stops at the cemetery, even when he's driving past. But he doesn't really think Ben is here. I do, see.

Gram had seven strokes in all. After the first one, she snapped back in twenty-four hours. With each one it took a little longer. And she'd lost some by the last. "Ben, aren't you dead yet," she'd say to me, when she thought I was Benny. "Ben, I thought you died, Ben."

That last time, your mom called, she talked to all the doctors in the hospital and she had her doctors in Los Angeles give them orders. Gram had things in her hair, test things, wires she really never should have had to have. And all those years, Adele never visited, never once sent a card. But that was your mom. She yelled at me, ooh, in the hospital, it wasn't nice. But you know, we get along now.

They had to move Gram near the end. That night I stayed up and talked to her. They say the hearing is one of the last things to go. I don't know anymore what I said. That last night, I was holding her hand, she didn't seem happy, her mouth looked bitter and she kept calling Adele, Adele. She cried that name all night before she went.

She had a restless time. She'd turn around and toss and switch back and forth. She couldn't get comfortable. I was there when Granny, your great-grandmother, passed away and she got this big, beautiful smile on her face. And I was waiting for something like that to come to Gram. But it never did. I asked the doctor, I asked, why couldn't that have happened to her, Granny was really sort of a mean woman, and my mother was so good, and the doctor said, everyone does it in a different way. Every one is different.

Benny and my mother and my father all share the one granite stone. Somebody else finally died.

Ann

15

A New Car

Christmases I did nothing. Holidays in repertory houses, huge silver and black, beautiful LA romances on the screen, sipping expensive coffee. I was in love, but I wouldn't go to his house, either. By that time families bugged me. Other people's as much as my own. We'd make out, touching each other's clothes; the same jeans, flannels, soft, worn-in things. We loved the movies; they were black and white, beautiful—everything we needed. We sat in the dark, audiences raucous from displacement, all of us away from home, gay men, foreign students, Jews, laughing wildly at *Sullivan's Travels*, *The Navigator*, or *Seven Chances*, gasping through *Hiroshima Mon Amour*.

No matter what, I wouldn't go to LA.

"Some people remember birthdays," my mother said and hung up the phone.

Finally, my mother and I rented a car in northern California, a compromise. She said she'd always wanted to see the wine country. We sat in the car, my mother straight in her seat, staring at her hands, looking deserving. I told her Leslie lived in Berkeley and I'd call her, she could come with us or not, whatever my mother wanted.

"I thought you said it would be just us."

"That's fine."

"I'd rather be just us," she said.

It was spring. We hadn't seen each other for five years. It was interesting just to look at her.

All day, my mother talked about retirement. "I know just what I want," she said. "I'll do it all in French country. I'll have a brick wall in the kitchen. Just real homey." In a restaurant, she tilted her head. "What's this? Is this Bach? I love Bach. Do you know Des Pres, Honey? Well, I mean, he's dead, but there's this record. I learn these things from Daniel Swan, he's a double major in music at UCLA. You wouldn't believe all the things I'm learning." She nodded in time. "This *is* Bach."

She snuck little pieces of bread into her mouth. "I've already started to get things. For the house," she whispered. "See that blackboard up there? I bought two old school blackboards like that. Even nicer. They're in the Swans' basement. And the pine chests I told you about are for the house, too. They'll eventually go in a bedroom. I have another armoire in Nan's garage. See, and then what I'll do is I'll have a big open kitchen and when you bring your kids home, a boyfriend or someone special, or no, just your kids, you always have nice friends, like Leslie and all of them, I'll have the menu written down on the blackboard so when you come down in the morning it'll all be written out."

"Where are you looking for this house?"

Her cheeks lifted. She folded her arms on the table. "I want somewhere where I can see the mountains and the ocean. The whole wide scope of things. It doesn't have to be a big place, I just want a little house, something simple."

"'Cause aren't houses in LA like a fortune now? I mean, hundreds of thousands of dollars?"

"You wouldn't believe it. Remember that little house I wanted to buy from Julie Edison? Eight hundred thousand dollars, they're asking now. Remember how I used to drive by? I could shoot myself now. I knew that area was going to be big, I knew it, if I'd have only trusted my instincts—"

"But we never had the money."

She seemed clear that day, her face intelligent and thin. Her arms refolded, rueful. "No, you're right. We never had the money. But I do now. And I'm saving. So just wait. Someday your mom'll have a real great place for you to bring your friends home to. By the time you're in graduate school. That's when you really need it anyway. That's when the kids in your generation really start to get engaged. I hear it all the time on 'LA Good-Morning.' They're waiting even up until the thirties. Like my dentist."

"I don't know if I'm going to graduate school. Anyway, I'm living with this guy."

"This Henry." She shrugged. "I wish you'd waited. Pretty soon I'll have something you could really show someone."

"Well, I mean, I don't know if it's going to work out."

"But all the others there in Providence must see you're living with someone, all the real choice boys."

"Nobody really knows."

"Sure they do, don't kid yourself. And they don't respect you for it either, Ann, no matter what they say. A boy doesn't respect you when you give him that for nothing. I just remember when I came home from college, what did I have for a boy to see? Lime Kiln Road. And Grilings."

The waiter came, we ordered dessert.

"Well, I don't know, I'm not tied to LA, either. And I'm getting sick of all the driving. Maybe I'll just end up near you, I've heard Cape Cod and what is it, something Vineyard, is supposed to be gorgeous, they say they're the prettiest beaches in the world. I mean, if you really like it there, if you want to stay."

"I don't know what I'm doing. I'll probably just work for a while, travel around. I might waitress at some truckstop."

"With your advantages." She laughed. "I can't really see you at a truck-stop."

"It could happen."

"Well, don't you dare. You know I worked in a cheese factory all through college. It wasn't so much fun. Speaking of truckstops, I got a letter from Lolly." She unfolded a sheet of peach-colored paper from her purse. After all these years and no trips home, Lolly still wrote to my mother. And I knew for an almost fact, my mother never sent letters. After years of saying her mail was lost, my mother wouldn't trust the U.S. Postal Service. She believed mailboxes in LA were obsolete, that no one picked up from them anymore. She said she opened one and saw cobwebs. If she absolutely had to send something, she'd drive to the post office and pay nine dollars for overnight express. Paying made my mother trust things more.

I'd heard my grandmother complain. "I never get a card, nothing. Even when she calls and I send money, I never even get a card to say thanks." It wasn't exactly laziness. It wasn't that she'd forgotten them. I'd seen my mother trying to write something down. She would sit at the table with a card or a piece of fancy colored paper and she'd write and cross out and finally give up. She had it in her mind that she would get married and be rich and then she could make up for all she didn't send by wiring a plane ticket out for her mother to visit and taking her to see everything and buying presents. That's just the way my mother was.

She smoothed out the soft paper of the Bay City *Press Gazette* clipping; a photograph of Lolly hitting the one-million-dollar mark, lifting her left arm up to a chart. Lolly sold real estate now, she'd gone to school and gotten her license the year we left. "Let me tell you, in Bay City, that must not have been easy. That's a lot of little houses to add up to a mil-lion." My mother scanned the letter. "And she's still having this passion-ate, that's what she calls it, affair with the ex-priest. She lost her virginity at forty-five, can you imagine that?" My mother wrinkled her nose.

"Do you think she'll ever get married?"

"No, I don't think so. I doubt it. But who knows? She does have boy-friends."

"It sounds like they're mostly ordained."

My mother laughed. "You *are* funny, besides being factual."

"Maybe if we'd stayed in Bay City, you could afford a house there."

"Oh, sure, I could buy a house there now, a great house. But I'd never go back. It's really nothing, you know, no culture. Nothing." My mother took a pill bottle out of her purse and broke off a piece of seaweed for each of us. "At my age, believe me, I need all the E I can get."

As we left the restaurant, my mother noticed a weathervane on the wall, an antique deer, she wanted. I told her it looked like a decoration, but she went back in and found the owner. He accepted her check. We carried the deer to the car. "He'll fit in a linen closet," she said. "For the time being."

My mother had gone to an accountant and now she carried a black checkbook the size of a three-ring binder.

We skidded in front of a church. My mother was driving.

"Since when do you believe in God," I said.

She told me she wanted to light a candle for my grandmother. "I go to church every Sunday now. The pink Catholic in Beverly Hills. On Little Santa Monica." This Sonoma church stood empty, plain, with simple pews and a pine altar. But all the candles were either lit or burnt down to the bottom of their glass canisters.

"I'll blow one out and you can light it again."

She shook her head no. "We'll just say a prayer." Then she dragged out her long black checkbook again. "Turn around, would you?" She wrote a check on my back and folded it up, stuffing it through the coin slot.

I didn't have to ask the question.

"Sure, it's charity. It's a deduction, I deduct all these things now. And they'll take my check. Gladly."

She slipped her arm through mine. "You'll never guess who I saw at church last month. Tony Camden," she whispered. "I walked in and I saw this very good-looking head. But I only saw the back. You know. He was in front of me. But I thought to myself, Adele, that's one *very* good-looking back of the head. So I sort of elbowed, genuflecting, you know, I think I was a little late, and I knelt down next to him, and I look and who is it but Tony Camden. He was kneeling holding the pleats of his pants. And I thought, Boy, would I like to know him."

"Mom, he's married."

"Is he still? I'm not sure, I didn't see her. Anyway, so I sort of smiled you know and then it was time to sit up and he sort of looked at me and he smiled and I'd smile again and then when we walked out at the end, it was this huge beautiful day, real clear, you could see the mountains just like that, and we're standing on the steps and he looked at me and said, Bye-bye and I looked at him and said, Bye-bye. So I'll tell you, I'm not missing one Sunday."

Inside a dim, windowless room, on a cement floor, we undressed. A woman with feather earrings handed us rough, chlorine-smelling towels, her heavy hair brushing our arms. We'd stopped at the sign that said "Dr. Hickdimon's Mud Baths." My mother knotted a towel above her breasts, making an easy shift. My mother's brilliance is in a lot of things you notice if you're around a person all the time, but which don't count for much in the world. While we talked, her hands moved through her hair, taking bobby pins from the edge of her mouth, arranging a perfect bun.

"This will be just what we need," she said.

The woman led us to a room with two long bathtubs standing in the middle of the floor. Mud filled them to their thick curled brims and spilled over onto the elaborate claw feet. This wasn't ordinary mud. It seemed blacker, and twigs and roots showed. It bubbled. A wooden plank floated on the surface of each tub.

It took a long time to lower us in. My mother went first. She sat on the plank, her belly falling into a small sag. It was a shock, to see her naked. She seemed both thinner and looser and I noticed on one of her teeth there was a black hairline like a crack in porcelain.

"Eeeeeee," she said, sliding into the mud. Sweat glistened on her forehead like a cobweb.

Her eyes closed. "That feel good?" the woman asked.

"Mmmhmm," my mother murmured.

Then it was my turn. The woman kneeled on the floor and pushed the plank so my legs went down like a seesaw. She covered the rest of me slowly, with handfuls of warm mud. You didn't sink. The mud was too heavy. I could have lifted an arm or a leg but it would have been hard. Underneath you felt a thick cushion, we floated like the wood planks. Over me, the mud was about the same weight a person is, sleeping on top of you.

"We've really come a long way, you know, Ann, when you think about it?" My mother turned, her chin bobbing on the surface, her neck smeared with the mud. Then her eyes shut and she smiled.

I thought of what my mother once said about her dying. She didn't want to be buried with the rest of our family in the cemetery above Prebble Park. She wanted to be mounted in a glass case, like a diorama at the Bay City Museum, only it would be in her grandchildren's house. They would change her clothes and accessories according to the season.

I was with my mother the day she'd thought of wanting a scarecrow. We rode and rode past farms until she found the one she liked. It stood alone, set back in a cropped corn field. We couldn't see it without squinting. The wind still lived in the scarecrow's sleeves. The barn and farmhouse were miles away, tiny in the distance.

She bought the scarecrow from a farmer. He accepted her yellow check. The scarecrow's clothes were faded and patched, the thinnest cotton. "He's really a work of art, you should see in back, the way his overalls have been mended. It's like an old quilt. He's all hand done."

The scarecrow had made my mother think of having herself mounted. It had been a joke in Wisconsin, when she'd been full of mischief, when we drove to the cemetery where our family plots were already owned. Now she'd never go back. She'd probably want to be cremated, scattered on California land, somewhere you could see the ocean and the mountains. She hardly ever made fun of things anymore.

I pushed my hand up to the lip of the tub to find her hand, but I could barely feel through the wet mud. Her hand was like something solid your fingertips hit when you're digging.

I'd been back to Wisconsin a million times, on slow Greyhound buses during college, where there was always one very young woman in back, her hair in a bandanna, hitting her kid, saying "Shit-up," softly before each smack, her voice pure as resignation, the kid wailing, arching higher every time, screaming, all the way to Bay City, where I skipped down, light, onto the snow-dusted pavement in back of Dean's ice cream parlor.

I remember the winter town, my grandmother asleep in the country at nine o'clock. Taking the Oldsmobile and driving by the Fox River; the old, old buildings of the men's Y, buying chili and pie at the lighted diner. I sat on a stool smoking, looking out the window. And liking it so: the yellow streetlamps, coal and sulfur piles, smokestacks by the river. A girl going home to a mill town, the familiarity and the strangeness.

I drove to bars at night. Pool tables. Boys sheepish in army coats, home whole from Vietnam. Some. Bashful with me because they knew I went away. I'd gone to college.

To one I said, "I look much better at home." It felt easy here in the old bars, stained walls, the thick inside air. I knew these boys.

"Jeez, you must look great there because you sure look pretty now."

I almost got arrested for stealing a hot fudge pitcher at Dean's. A manager from somewhere else made me take it out of my purse, hurt my arm when I twisted away. Then I had to walk out of the store, in the aisle between warm glass cases, where the intricate-colored German cookies worth a million dollars blinked.

I always drove the Oldsmobile. My mother had never let me touch our Lincoln, even when I was learning. She felt terrified I would ruin it and then she couldn't get to work. I learned on Daniel Swan's ancient Triumph and on Peter Keller's Mercedes. But my grandmother walked with me to the garage, wearing her plastic rainboots, a clear scarf covering her head, and patiently got in at the passenger side and folded her hands in her lap. The Oldsmobile smelled like my grandmother. The tin cans with their coffee labels worn off that we used for watering at the cemetery rattled in the back seat.

It was a smooth, easy car, heavy on roads.

The last time I went, Carol picked me up at the airport, thin in a lemon-colored pantsuit, taking me to a new American car, a convertible.

"He builds now," she said as we pulled into their gravel driveway. When I stepped out, with my suitcase, Jimmy stood in work boots, on top of the roof, holding huge coils of something silver.

He'd retired from the Rug Doctor and now he built in their wide back-yard.

It was nothing like it had been. There was a laned Olympic swimming pool, a garden, blond rocks planted among petunias, an elevated redwood deck, with a redwood ladder to the hot tub. It looked like pictures of California.

"That's the solar," Carol said. Jimmy stood installing the silver coils to heat the pool year round. He climbed down and shook my hand. His voice seemed breathless all the time now. He'd built everything himself, slowly.

Carol still kept the books for the store and now she also sold the Herbalife, a menu of vitamins she and Jimmy ate every morning at the white dinette table, looking out at the new backyard.

Hal was changed entirely. He was thinner and he'd moved back home, into the tiny bedroom he and Ben had shared when they were growing up. He slept in his own small bed. When I stayed there, I slept in that room too. Every day, Hal woke up and dressed while I was asleep. I heard him moving around; he seemed exceptionally neat now, spare of move-ment. He worked at Three Corners, managing the pressure-cleaning ma-chines, renting out the Rug Doctor. He drove to work before seven in the morning. On the bedside table rested a large, hardback book with a pink padded cover like a Valentine's candy box. *Our Daily Helper*, read the title, and the pink satin ribbon was always placed in that day's prayer.

I told Carol my mother still had both breasts, the last time I'd seen her.

"I thought so," she said. "You know the funny thing is we get along now, your mom and I."

For some reason that made me sad.

·   ·   ·

Mostly, my aunt drove me around places. Museums, antique shops, flea markets, the huge untouched Goodwill and Salvation Army stores by the river. I liked to find old things.

Friday night, we went out for fish fry. The restaurants flew in the fish, frozen, from Canada because the Fox River and the bay were polluted by the paper mills. Carol said the Wildlife Preservation Center had cameras out from the local news; the ducks' beaks twisted, they were born mutated, from eating the polluted fish. "And you should smell the East River, does it stink," she said. "They say it'll take ten years to clean it up."

My grandmother's house, in the yard next door, had been rented.

"A young couple where they both work," Carol said. "He's a floor manager at the Shopko."

I looked at it every day I was there, a dark house with low windows above the ground. The grass had grown tall against the siding. Carol said they hired Mary Griling to mow both lawns.

It made me think of once when I sent my grandmother a blank notebook covered in fabric for a diary. When I helped Carol clean out the house, the dresser drawers, I'd found the book wrapped in wax paper, the pages thick and perfectly white.

I couldn't stand the food, after a day or two it drove me crazy. Not one thing was fresh. The lettuce, the iceberg lettuce, seemed old. Jimmy took us all for dinner at the new Holiday Inn. It was a buffet; sweet wine, too much food, races for the shrimp, everything else overcooked. I hated it and hated myself hating it.

I told Lolly, when she showed me her office. She worked for Dan Sklar now, we walked through his Japanese rock garden, our heels sinking in the moss. I told her how I couldn't stand the Holiday Inn buffet.

"On the west side, oh, you didn't like that? Oh no, hmm, well, that's really my favorite place, they have a new chef over there." She laughed her old sly laugh. "Oh, well, if you didn't like that, you really have outgrown Bay City. Because that's really about the best restaurant there is, here."

Lolly had some kind of diabetic anemia and she had to eat protein every few hours. In the office, she took out a small package of tinfoil from her purse and unwrapped it. It was a cold sliced turkey heart.

Once, from Providence, I'd called information and found Ted Diamond's number. He still had a listing in Bay City. It turned out he was married, with five sons. His wife sounded nice on the phone. When she put him on, he said he was okay, tired. "Your mother," he said with a bad laugh.

·   ·   ·

Carol told me after they'd put in the pool they ran into Ted and the new wife somewhere. A week or two later, it was in summer, the new wife called and asked if she might bring the little boys over to go swimming. They didn't know each other, just that Ted had been married to my mother once. Carol said no she had bridge club and couldn't let them come when she wasn't there because of insurance. The wife had called four or five times again.

Once I found a Christmas card in the mail, one of those pictures, with Ted and the wife and the five little boys dressed in identical red blazers with gold buttons, in front of a big fireplace with five red stockings. The wife had written on the bottom, "Ted sends his love and he'll write you a letter after the new year."

The thing with Ted is I always know where to find him. And, like with most people that way, since I could call him and talk to him any time, I never feel like it.

They all got a kick out of what I wore, their old sweaters, earrings from the thirties and forties. They thought it was hilariously funny.

"I don't bullshit them," Hal said. "Whatever they want to know, I tell it to them straight. I tell them what that life did to me."

Hal lectured at Catholic schools in Bay City, about his troubles with drugs and alcohol. He told seventh and eighth graders how he lived with Merry in their silver trailer on the Oneida lot by the airport and what had happened to him.

I asked if it was still the same in school with drugs, wasn't it different then, with Vietnam, the times.

Hal said no, he knew from Tina there was still temptation.

"Tina, come out here and tell your cousin about the marijuana in school." He looked up at the small, added-on breezeway bathroom, one of Jimmy's projects years ago.

"Can I wait just a minute, Dad, I'm doing my makeup."

"She knows everything," he said. "She knows everything I did and she forgives me."

Hal told me he didn't write the lectures. He improvised. He said before he spoke to a class he needed quiet, he needed to be alone in a room. He said he stood in those coat closets, the white tangled safety patrol belts in a cardboard box on the floor, stacked cases of pencils, the gleaming pale green arm of the paper cutter, waiting to see what would come to his mind, some bit of conversation left from his marriage, some morning, drug-laden, in the dirty trailer.

Then Tina came bounding down the three stairs, the wings of her hair swooping out, her chin tilted up, offering us her face.

Carol followed behind. "Look at her, thirteen years old and a half hour in the bathroom already. When she first told me she wore makeup, I said, not around me you're not, but then I saw what little she did and it does look nice. Isn't it something, but you know, even at her age, I can tell the difference, she really does look better with that little color around the eyes. Even at that young age."

Tina flopped down on the couch and operated the TV by remote control.

"So this year, I'm going all over Ohio, Illinois, Michigan, Minnesota and Nebraska," Hal said. "And they're going to have me do a record."

Jimmy and Carol showed me the blueprint of their home, in Hanger's Cove, Florida. They had a brochure with a model of the houses in four color photos. But their house, though model B, was not really like the picture. Jimmy had built onto it, he'd added a patio and a second breezeway.

"We had to go to court and fight," Carol told me, passing Griling's house. "They wanted to put in a junkyard here on Lime Kiln Road, across from Guns. The city tried."

Bub Griling was dead now, his dump overfilled, rotting, a hazard.

Carol mentioned Indians and the Vietnamese. Part of the old water softener store on Three Corners stood empty. The paint shop that had been there closed. Evenings, Carol and I drove over in the car, to show the storefront to prospective leasers who answered the ad in the *Press Gazette*.

It was a shabby empty space, with concrete floors and low ceilings, not carpeted like the Rug Doctor office next door. Carol and I paced, waiting for a woman who wanted to turn it into a dance studio. The rent was sixty-five dollars a month. "One of these little Vietnamese wanted to rent it. Yah! He wanted to put a fruit market in here and he wanted to write on the window, in *Vietnamese*. Yah! Can you believe that?"

The week I stayed, I couldn't convince Carol and Jimmy that the Vietnamese in Bay City were not the same Vietnamese we'd fought.

She stood, shaking her head, looking at her feet on the floor. "We lose so many boys over there and then they come here and get money from the government. Yah. All those little people. There's lot of them, here, we have the H'mong.

"And the Indians, now they want to put up a hotel, across the highway from the airport. They gave them all that land, to the Oneidas, they said that was their land. Yah! And now they want to put a hotel up. They've got bingo games there every Saturday night already."

Driving through the dark city, I saw apartments; old buildings, pretty like New England, turn-of-the-century stone by the river with glass windows and that yellow light. I'd think of coming here and renting an apartment and living. It seemed amazing, how cheap it was. I could easily afford a pretty place, little rooms off a hallway, an old white stove in the kitchen, crannies, closets, maybe a clawfoot tub. But I couldn't live there, I knew it. The feeling always passed.

Every day, Jimmy got up at eight o'clock the way he had when he drove to the store on Three Corners, ate breakfast and began work at nine. He still took an hour lunch break, the only difference was that now he hiked five miles, doctor's orders. He had a machine to walk on in the laundry room for days when it was too cold outside. In the same room, Carol kept a machine which suspended her in the air, hanging her upside down on a series of metal tubes and bars. She said it helped with her back.

I sat in the breezeway talking to Mary Griling, who'd grown up to be six feet tall. She told me what had happened to everyone on our road.

Of the Grilings, Mary ended up being the one who stayed at home. She took care of her father until he died. Now she lived in the house with her brother and oldest sister, she worked in a computer shop in town.

She said she might go to Florida. "My dad's dead, there's nothing for me here."

"But you're close to your family. To Rosie."

"I am, then I'm not," she said. "I am and I'm not. Not like it was with my dad."

After we'd left, she'd had polio. She limped a little and her smile twisted up to the left. She was still very neat, careful. Theresa was the one who'd gone away.

"Coming tonight, Mare?" Jimmy walked through the breezeway, lifting a tray of chickens for the barbecue. Hal was giving a party.

"Working. But Terry'll come. She'll come with the baby."

"Yah, Theresa's home," Carol said. "She was stationed in Japan and she met a fellow over there who can speak and understand Russian. Oh, and a real handsome boy. So he flies one of those planes out of Japan and listens to what they say over there."

Carol stood on the porch hollering. "Handy! Handy!" She waited, fists on her hips, until the dog came running through the back field. She bent to pat him.

. . .

"You know Ralph Brozek, Jay's brother? Yeah, he was staying at my place, freakin' out right and left, one flashback after another. He couldn't get out of my bathtub once, he thought he was in a ship on fire, that's where all the other guys with him died. I say, 'Hey, my brother's dead, too. They're in the same place.' But I don't know one single person who came back from Vietnam the way they started.

"My mom and pop think I got out because of the leg. But that's not how it happened. Air force was messing with my head. They decided they wanted to operate. I said no, you're not going to operate. This went on, I don't know, six or eight weeks. Then I was lying, they didn't know what I was talking about. I was seeing the shrinkologist. I told them a little fairy tale. Asshole doctors. I told them, I'm going to kill myself. You're going to find me hanging from the rafters. I sat down. I couldn't control my emotions. They sent me home."

We sat on the edge of the patio.

"So what made you religious?" I said.

"I needed more than just what was in this world."

Theresa and I stood breast deep in the hot tub, leaning against the underwater benches with our hands. Theresa was tall now, a woman, no signs of what she had been. She'd left the baby at home with her brother's wife, she grabbed my arm and said we had to talk. We sat for a long time in the hot water, steam rising around us, the party continuing, further on the patio near the pool, a stereo blaring in the solar house.

"I miss the trees," she said. She was holding her elbows and shaking her head. I recognized the expression. "I miss the open space."

She lived outside Kyoto and sometimes her husband was gone, flying, for two or three weeks. She took care of the baby herself. She lived on a base, though she was no longer in the army.

"Just a wife," she said. She told me the Japanese were very good with children, that they revered infants. She said she was studying Ikebana.

I looked at her and understood the crooked smile, the rue. We both sat staring into the dark yards, the old barn a pure black, vacant fields.

"They told me they rented out your gramma's house," she said. "That doesn't seem right." I shook my head. "They're putting my dad's house up for sale, too, and that doesn't seem right either."

The pool gleamed turquoise from underwater lights, tropical plants hung in the bathhouse. "It's so different."

"I guess when you go away, you want it to be the same, but when you stay you want it to change."

In the kitchen, before she walked home, Theresa wrote down her address on a square paint-color sample of Jimmy's. Theresa Lambert, FPO Seattle, 98767, Japan.

"You won't believe it. I bought a re-yall Seth Thomas grandfather clock, *signed*. Do you know how rare they are now? They're in museums, you just can't find them anymore. It's here already, in the closet for now, I don't want anybody to see it and get ideas, these doors are like nothing, but won't that be something when I have my little house? Someday. You won't believe, Honey, how beautiful it is."

She called me a lot, whenever she wanted to talk.

Someone from "Santa Fe" had sued, and they paid us all back royalties.

It was easy, sending the check, signing it over—then it was gone and I was only as poor as anyone else in Providence.

I remembered something I'd forgotten for a long time, the job I'd had in a department store wrapping packages. It was like a TV game show, a bonanza, where all around were prizes. My mother had come in on Saturdays as extra help. In three weeks, we ripped them off blind. We stole slacks, dresses, everything.

I still wear some of those shirts. That's one thing about stealing, you wear something long enough and it seems as though it was always yours. It's the same as if you bought it. Those years, I never felt scared. Now I think it's crazy, the risks we took. We could have been in the backseat of a squad car, booked on felonies, both caught. We did a lot for money, things meant so much to us. And it seemed hard for my mother. Since I've been gone, money has come to me. People have given me things. I always feel a little bad at how hard my mother tries.

The thing I keep thinking, when I remember my mother, is how young she was.

One day I read it in the newspaper, Buffy died. The girl who was an actress that everyone wanted to be when I was nine. She'd been nine too. She looked younger, she played a twin on "Family Affair" with two high blond pigtails. Mattel put out a Buffy doll and they also made one of Mrs. Beasley, Buffy's doll on television. Buffy was famous. When I lived in Bay City, I read everything there was about Buffy. I found an interview with her in *TV Guide*. I remember it said she lived in Pacific Palisades. She talked about working, she said once when she came home her brother had eaten all the strawberries. I knew she had a mother and no father, like me. I thought of her now, enormous, full grown, but with the pale thin legs and white anklets, a nineteen-year-old girl in blond pigtails. I kept thinking of paper around her, the long woman's legs, eerie where they met the white anklets, in a shoe box. She died of a drug overdose in an apartment on the Palisades. I guess she'd never gone too far away.

A while later, my mother talked about a house, how I had to come home and see it.

Finally, I went to LA.

"I have everything," my mother says, hugging me. "There's all different kinds of cheese and a salami in the refrigerator. And fruit. I've got peaches and plums and watermelon and strawberries . . ."

She's still listing fruit as I set down my suitcase and walk over the carpet to the sliding glass doors. We're on the ocean, in Malibu. Waves unroll below us on the sand, muscular and glassy.

"Kiwi and kiwi and kiwi . . ." My mother sticks on kiwi when she runs out of fruits. "Oh, and I have white wine and red wine and Kahlua, I remember you like Kahlua, and gin and tonic. And oh, I have limes."

She is standing behind me, her fingers light on my back. Together, we watch the water. That's one thing about my mother, her capacity for awe.

"Isn't it nice?" she whispers.

All her things are here, the things I've heard about for years, the grandfather clock backed into a corner, hidden by ferns and a Kentia palm.

"I don't want anybody to see it and get ideas," she says.

The pine bench, stripped blond and waxed, stands in front of a couch, antique armoires are set with green Limoges plates, tiny antlers, dried roses and orange peel. She shows me each thing. The Tiffany lamp, its one original petal-glass shade, the other replicated by a glass blower she met in Santa Barbara, every piece collected slowly. I walk around the rooms and touch.

"It's worth three times what I paid," she whispers, her eyebrows lifting.

Sometimes when you walk in a house that has been newly, thoroughly cleaned, you feel light. You're eating, you're lounging on a couch, spreading open the pages of a magazine, but you are a small thing, in the rooms. You're living the way people live inside movies.

The carpet is new and even, the glass perfect. I'm surprised. I guess I'm even impressed.

This is what is in the bathroom: Porthault scallop-edged towels, organic geranium soap, aloe vera shampoo, fennel toothpaste on the spotless counter and a huge shell filled with natural sponges.

. . .

I sit on my mother's bed and let her show me things. The Tiffany lamp, half Tiffany, half Santa Barbara, sheds soft colored light on the wall. My mother's closet could be a museum. Each article is tended. The floors shine with oil, her shoes hang in felt bags, tucked in French cloth shoe-panels. Her dresses fall perfectly and sweaters, from Chanel to Lacoste, are stacked according to color, each in its own clear plastic zipper bag. She seems to own nothing old. Most of my mother's clothes are white.

She sits on her bed, next to the lamp, with her glasses on, mending a torn piece of lace on the hem of my skirt. It caught in my heel; the way I live, I would have left it to rip. I idly pull out one of my mother's drawers. There are rows of unopened Dior stockings, textured, not, sheer to opaque, in all colors, her silk and lace panties and bras. An antique coin silver evening purse, wrapped in a white felt bag, and a sachet, rose petals and orange peel.

"I make those myself," she says.

I'm thinking, my mother has changed. When I lived with her, she was more like me. She could walk out of the house looking perfect, nails buffed and polished, hands soft, everything on her bright, pressed, falling in gentle ruffles and folds, the patent leather purse dark and shining like a mirror, but she left a million little odds and ends behind. Old things, gray stained sweat shirts in the closet, clothes she kept for wearing when she was just with me. She didn't seem to own those anymore. She must have thrown them all out, everything stained. She used to have old purses, each one containing scraps of things, change, matted brushes, pictures, junk. They seem gone now, too.

She must have always wanted to live like this; from one perfect outfit to the next, nothing in between, every day crisp new clothes, nothing to be ashamed of, ever, anywhere. She always loved new things. Someone could always be watching.

The ocean feels so close and loud, I don't want to sleep. We drink Kahlua in tall glasses of milk and my mother tells me secrets about her clothes.

The next morning, the living room is a cage of sun. My mother stands by the oven, wearing white, poking at bagels with a fork.

"I have lox and cod and smoked salmon, and onion, tomato and cream cheese and, let's see . . ."

"You bought this house?" In the daylight, it seems too good. If my mother bought a house with the check I sent her, I imagined it small, a bungalow in the Valley, or towards Riverside, Pasadena. There are a million little LA towns. Tarzana, maybe. But not here.

Her back turns, there is a flinch of movement in her shoulder, under the loose white shirt. She stiffens and pauses a second.

"Mmhmm," she says.

Late afternoon, my mother sews over the hem of my skirt, all around, not just where it tore, to strengthen it. She is humble before the ancient delicate fabric, the new, Japanese style. A servant to a beautiful dress. It feels quiet in the house. Dim light. She is bent over, feet clumped pigeon-toed on the floor, knees pressed together, biting a thread. I drop down and do pushups. She is all deft concentration. The skills she's had forever. She studies careful invisible stitches in the weak light. She puts her glasses on.

"Adele, you have enough food for forty," Daniel Swan says, closing the refrigerator door.

"Here's the pasta and here's lemons," my mother calls.

Daniel unrolls white butcher paper with pink, round pieces of veal on it. There must be thirty medallions.

"That's okay, whatever we don't use, we'll keep." My mother sighs and lightly claps. "So."

I cut a lime for my gin and tonic. We've been drinking for hours. My mother washes vegetables, individually, in the sink, drying each mushroom with a paper towel. She stops, looks at us and smiles. "If I ever have a man around again, he's going to have to cook. You bet."

She moves past us to the table, her caftan brushing the floor. The centerpiece is a three-foot basket of fruit. Apples and oranges, cherries, strawberries, grapes and kiwi spill over the top.

I marvel at the kitchen. Tiny brushes stand next to organic soap, under a framed poster of "All rising to a great place is by a winding stair," Francis Bacon rendered orange and blue by Sister Corita. Herbs in a hanging wire basket, shells. "Blue! Blue! The butterfly counts not months but moments, and has time enough."

Foucon. A holy water ox. Orchids in ferns. An old lamp from Wisconsin. A bowl of lemons.

"Oh, come here, you two. Look." My mother stands on the balcony, letting her wine glass dangle off the rail like a huge jewel.

We watch the waves open, white and then transparent over the sand.

"And look at him, can you see that little porpoise? He's been visiting me all week. He looks just like a rock, but that's him."

My mother's hands move delicately under running water; she's a hard-working cook. But she has no sense of timing. The veal burns, curling up at the edges, smelling like milk. She scrapes the pan and sighs, taking the white butcher paper back out of the refrigerator, for more.

I stir the noodles. My mother put in too many and not enough water.

I know her logic; it is a beautiful, if small, copper saucepan. But the noodles seem to be dissolving.

"Yuk," Daniel says, lifting the spoon. He rummages through the cupboards for a colander. I notice him pausing, on his knees. He holds up a white grocery receipt over a foot and a half long.

I shrug and sponge a line of ants from the counter.

The food arranged on platters at the table, I go to look for my mother. I find her in the bathroom, slowly unpinning electric rollers in front of the mirror. Now she puts on her beads. She wears three strands. She lifts each one and lays it on her chest, then rummages under her hair until she finds the clasp. She doesn't fasten it in front and then tow it around, the way I do, living alone. We stand there like that a long time, watching her hands worry under her hair.

"Ann, make a list for me of what books I should read. Listening to you kids talk is great but I realize I've fallen behind. I just don't have the vocabularies you kids have. I used to. But I spend so much time reading in my field and writing those damn reports. I want to catch up again and really follow what's what in the literature and artistic field."

She looks at me from the other end of the table. "She's really beautiful, isn't she," she says.

"No," I say.

"That's what's so nice about her is she doesn't know. I'm so happy when you're here."

A silence falls like the silence after someone has said they love you. She waits.

The food is terrible, the veal, though perfect looking, is tough, the noodles are the texture of oatmeal. We eat slowly.

My mother stands and claps. "Well, what about dessert? Daniel, what would you like? We have carrot cake and I have everything for hot fudge sundaes, I have vanilla and coffee ice cream, and hot fudge and nuts, I have cream, let me think if I have anything to whip it with."

Now, the scraps of food seem solid on the dark plates. The candlelight makes it all look old.

"We'll do it, Mom. What would you like?"

"I think I'll have carrot cake," she says.

Daniel switches on the overhead kitchen light and my mother turns her chair towards the window.

I stack our dishes in the sink.

"Daniel, we wanted cake," I say.

He's balancing three bowls of ice cream on his arm, and nudging past me to the table. "We're having hot fudge sundaes," he says. I flick the light off again and my mother doesn't say a word about the ice cream, only "Mmmmmm," when she lifts the spoon to her mouth.

"Comemeer," Daniel says. My mother zigzagged, tired and glowing, to her bed. She doesn't usually drink, she never used to. Daniel and I clean the kitchen, the pots and pans, the plates. I start wrapping all the food in sight with Saran.

Daniel opens the garage door and squats on the cement. The carrot cake rests on the floor, untouched, perfect.

"Look." Daniel points.

Then I see it, my eyes adjust to the dimness. Ribbon-thick bands of ants surround the base, tunneling into its sides. The frosting is dotted with dead ones.

The next day, my mother shows me her new car. It is a white Mercedes station wagon, with silver everywhere, tan leather interior, a dashboard more computerized and beautiful than any stereo. She blushes. We are standing outside on the dirt Colony Road, overgrown with weeds. She backs the car, infinitely slowly, from the garage. Two tan, very blond children wearing shorts and bandannas chase a dog, also wearing a bandanna. Everything is bright. By the driveway leans one spent rosebush. I hear a motor churning, somebody's pool.

"When did you?"

She shrugs. "I realized, it was the only car I really liked. I looked at Toyotas and Jeeps, I almost bought a Jeep wagon with the wood sides, you know, but it ended up being more expensive than this was. So . . . I just picked it up last week."

"Why do you want a station wagon?"

She inhales, shuddering. "We-ell, I'd like to drive my grandchildren around someday."

On the long streets of our old neighborhoods in Beverly Hills, new octagonal signs stand on all the lawns. Westec Security: Armed patrol, they read. Armed response.

"Oh, come on, after all they've done for us. Besides, Peter wants to see you, poor Petey, he's been calling every day. He still likes you."

"The Kellers haven't done anything for me."

"Well, they have for me."

Almost a year ago, Nan Keller died in an accident. At Aspen, she was run over by a snowplow. She paused at the bottom of the mountain, between runs. The machine stood idle on top of a pile of plowed snow. Kids had been playing in it and they left the brake open. The plow rolled down the hill, over Nan.

Now, Mr. Keller was suing the ski lodge and arranging a retrospective of her paintings. "I went out with him once," my mother says, "but I just couldn't do it. Ugh. I couldn't kiss him."

When Peter Keller calls, I won't talk. Every time my mother lies, says I'm in the bathroom, in the shower, taking a long bath, steaming. He must think I've become extremely clean.

Daniel pulls the strap of my suit down, then we are kissing.

"I didn't think this would ever happen," he says.

I duck underwater and pull off his suit; it tangles on his feet, but I get it somehow and loop it around my wrist like an enormous bracelet. We kiss hard, imprecisely. We bob. He lifts the elastic away from my leg and he feels enormous, and good, oh so good, inside me. I keep rising to the surface, he pushes my shoulders down.

Then, he yanks out of me, bites the package open, pulls the rubber on underwater. He'd been swimming with it in his hand. Now it starts again, random, hard, real inside me.

"Hi, you two!" My mother stands in yellow slacks and sunglasses on the deck.

"Can she see us?"

"No, we're underwater."

But I can see our legs and stomachs, green but distinct, like hands in clear gloves.

I swim away and Daniel yells, hey, grabbing my ankle. A wave comes up over our shoulders, we're caught in it, tumbling, gasping, clawing the sand bottom, finally bobbing up again, ten feet apart, our hair bunched in our mouths. We can't find Daniel's bathing suit. I hold up my arms so he sees and we both start diving for it, looking.

I stand for a second on the ridged sand, closer in than Daniel. My mother bends over, watering geraniums with a hose on her balcony. "She looks so good in her house."

"The Kellers' house," Daniel says.

I start swimming in, hard, breathing underwater, to get Daniel another suit.

"The thing I like about swimming in the ocean is that you can pee whenever you want," he says.

I guess I should have known. She bought the car instead of a house. She's borrowing the house, maybe renting, whatever.

In the dark, my mother shakes me. "Hurry up, you're really lucky. The grunion are running. I have a schedule."

I pull on jeans and a sweat shirt from the chair. In high school, we went on grunion runs, late night rides to the beach in tiny cars, girls sitting on the boys' laps, our hoop earrings catching in our long hair. But we never saw any grunion. We'd walk on the beach with flashlights a few minutes, then pair off to make out in the sand. I'd always thought the fish were an excuse.

But my mother has a little pamphlet from the Coast Guard. "'The female comes in on one wave and she twirls herself into the sand, so she's upright, half buried and half out. And there she lays her eggs,'" my mother reads. "'Then, the male swims in. He circles around her and deposits his sperm.' If they're lucky, they swim off together on the next wave. But sometimes the female gets stuck in the sand and if she doesn't catch the next wave, she dies, poor thing. She can't breathe, I suppose. Aw."

"Why do people catch them?"

"They're good to eat, I think. I suppose you fry them."

We stand on the balcony and don't see anything. The sand looks the way it always looks, shiny and smooth, dark. My mother bends down to roll up her pants. "Come on," she says.

A few minutes later, she runs back up the redwood stairs, two at a time. "It's thick with them. They're all over. You just can't see them from here." She takes pails from the garage, stepping over the carrot cake, and we fill them with water from the hose. The buckets feel heavy and the slap of water on my leg is cold as we lug them down to the beach.

It takes my eyes a few seconds to adjust. But then, I see them everywhere, wriggling like corkscrews in the sand, silver on one side. The shore comes alive with them.

"You catch them with your hands," my mother yells, running, her arms low to the ground.

Holding a grunion is like holding a muscular beam of moonlight. It's that fast. They try to squirm up out of your fist. Some flop down, slithering back into the dark shellac of water. The ones we catch clap against the sides of our pails.

There are hundreds of them. When you put your foot down in a cluster of grunion, they spread away from you in starlike migration.

I look up at the bowl of the sky, alive with stars and stars. They seem to be wriggling, too, burning holes in the dark. My mother knocks the pail over, giving a slush of fish back to the water. We turn it right and start again. It seems we can go on all night. My hands grow quicker and bold.

Our buckets thump like hearts and we keep running. It seems they will come all night, the wet fish we can touch.

"So you didn't buy a house."

She sighs. "I really want a house in just the RIGHT spot, where I can see the mountains and the ocean, and where there's a little artists' colony and I can take a ceramics class and make stained-glass windows, all these various things. I'm just going to wait until I can afford a real choice place. The house can be little, cute, but small."

"You bought the car, though."

"Yes," she says, cautiously, not sure what she's admitting.

We leave the beating pails on our balcony and take our clothes off there, letting them fall in soft piles. I don't know what time it is. The sand still glitters with grunion. Now I see them everywhere. We run the cold hose water over our bodies, before we go inside.

In the morning, we take showers, still smelling of seaweed. I pack. We step over the carrot cake and the murky buckets of dead black fish in the garage, into the white car in the sun. I bring my suitcase with me. I'm leaving my mother to deal with the stink and dead things when I am gone.

"Today is Sunday. It is the third of March, 1979." There is a sign on the fourth floor of my mother's convalescent home in Santa Monica. The bright crayoned letters continue, "The weather today is mild and sunny. 'Nice.'" I follow my mother through the nursing station where she flips through charts, marking files. She moves with competence, the flaps of her lab coat brisk behind her. Everyone knows her here.

"I told you about Miss Eldridge," she says. "She's the one who had beautiful, beautiful things. This may be hard for you, but it's good, I think. You should see what happens."

My mother told me about Miss Eldridge; she came to Los Angeles from Medford, Oregon, during the First World War and lived with her fiancé, who was in the service. She waited for him and he was killed in the war. Then, she worked all her life as a legal secretary, never married.

The curtain is drawn, separating Miss Eldridge from someone else in the room. What I am not prepared for is her beauty. She sits up on the bed, perfectly clear, her hands the conscious hands of anyone.

"Claire, I told you I'd bring my daughter to come meet you and I brought her. Here she is, here's my Ann."

Miss Eldridge looks at my mother and then at me, and shakes my hand. Miss Eldridge is crying without any noise, and my mother begins to cry too. I go over to a bulletin board and study the pins. There are three postcards. I remember now that Miss Eldridge has no children. "I'll change it again this month," my mother says.

"Thank you for bringing her to see me."

"I told you I would. And I did. I brought her. And now she's off again."

Miss Eldridge nods.

· · ·

We sit in the car.

"She'll never leave there," my mother says, "it's really sad, because she's mentally as clear as you or me."

My mother's open eyes are as motionless and blue as a fish's. "But they don't have it that bad, you know?" She looks down. "I feel like you're always leaving."

"I always come back," I say.

"But not for long."

I shrug. "That's what kids do, they leave."

I only left home once and that was years ago.

My mother drives a freeway to the Valley. She turns onto an exit I don't recognize and slows at a gas station. Across the street is a school, fenced with high aluminum.

She pulls up around the back and then I see it: our own Lincoln, up on cinderblocks.

"Do you want it, Ann? I've had them keep it for you. He says it'll only cost two hundred to spiff it up and it might still run a long time. I've got the keys for you."

She took them out of the glove compartment, but I say no.

"Are you sure? It's a good car still. You just may need it."

But we drive to the airport, leaving it.

In front of the terminal, I gather my suitcase. My mother doesn't want to park in the lot. "Somebody could really bump it, you know? Sit a second, we'll just talk, we'll wait here," my mother says. "You have time."

My flight is not for an hour. We sit, not moving, in the new car.

Against the window, she looks perfect. Her scarf falls and ripples at her collarbone, her hair curls under. For a second, I feel like she is leaving, not me. Then I glance down at her hands.

"My hands are my worst feature," she says. "These age marks. But they're getting better. I put E on them."

We turn and see each other.

She says, "Life is just too little, isn't it?"

"Mom." I kiss her, then I run out of the car.

Carol

16

A Lot of People's Secret

Nobody knows it to this day, but my husband almost killed Hitler. That was the most exciting time of my life, those three years I was in the service. Before and after, I've been pretty much in the ordinary. I've stayed here close to home. My sister has had the excitement; she's been all over, she went to college, did everything. But my big time was during the War.

Before that I was real shy, not like Adele. My mother said even when I was just born, I was always a quiet baby. Apparently, I slept all the time. I didn't wake them at night, nothing. I was real easy. Well, I can attest that Adele was never that way.

I was eleven years old when they had Adele and I didn't even know my mother was pregnant. I was so dumb, naive. Just all of a sudden, I had a ittle sister. I didn't like it much, either. No. I had to baby-sit. I was the one who got up in the middle of the night to change her. And she cried plenty. There was always such an age difference, too. We were never really friends.

My parents didn't tell me anything. I remember when I first started menstruating, I didn't know what it was. I was in church and here I was bleeding. And when I came home I was still bleeding. Well, I was so upset, I didn't know what to think. I told my mother and she said to me, "Didn't anyone ever tell you about that?"

And I thought later, many times, Well, gee, who was ever going to tell me, if my own mother didn't?

When Adele was that age, she had plenty of friends to teach her the ins and outs. She always had a crowd. But I was too shy. I never even had a date or anything and this was in high school. I was so shy that if I walked down a street and a fellow was coming towards me, I'd go all the way around the block to avoid him. Isn't that terrible? I think it is.

After high school, I wanted to go in training to be a nurse. But my mother didn't like the idea of nursing, I don't know why, she just didn't see me as a nurse. I still think I would have liked it.

But she knew someone who did beauty and that woman, a Mrs. Beamer, convinced my mother that beauty was really the thing. So I went to beauty school here downtown and then I worked at the Harper Method

Beauty Shop. It was okay, it wasn't too bad, I didn't mind the work one way or the other and I got in with a nice group of girls.

It did help me with my own hair. Now I can go with once a week in the beauty shop and in between, I keep it up myself. I don't give myself permanents or tint my own hair, but everything else, I do. And when I lost my hair in that trailer fire, I knew how to style the wig.

And I learned a lot there, from the other girls. Upstairs from the beauty shop was a doctor my father knew. The doctor's brother was a veterinarian and my father had him out once or twice a year to look at the mink. Well, this particular doctor treated all the girls who lived at the Silver Slipper. That was a tavern at the end of our road. I'd meet them on the stairs as they went up to see Dr. Shea and we nodded. I'd say hello, they'd say hello to me. We'd seen each other on Lime Kiln Road. Well, eighteen years old and until the girls at the beauty shop told me, I didn't know what they were. My mother never said a word. She told me to stay away from there and I knew my dad was real mad when they opened the Silver Slipper Tavern and put the beer sign up, but I thought he was mad about the drinking.

I don't know why I was like that, so backward. Maybe because of my father. Because of what happened to them, having to get married, he was too protective. And I think they made me scared. Because I remember once, I was in fifth or sixth grade, we were living in the house on Lime Kiln Road and some boys came once and knocked on the door. They were just boys from my class. And my father answered and yelled to my mother. "They're after Carol, keep her upstairs," he said. "They're here after Carol."

Well. I suppose they just wanted to get my homework or for me to come outside and play. Oh, when I even think about it, they're after Carol. So he was a part of it, I'm sure.

Then, around that time, after high school, I first started going out a little. I was nineteen or twenty and I used to go with the girls I met working. We went out to Bay Beach. Then, Bay Beach was still real nice. That green and white pavilion was just new and all painted—it was a Public Works Project, for years the men were there building and then they painted those murals for the ballroom. Franklin Roosevelt came to Bay City when it opened. Now they just have those darn pinball machines and computer games. It's all games where it used to be a dance floor. And I remember, they were just putting in the bumper cars. They already had that little train that went along the beach. We saw beautiful sunsets over the Fox River with the silhouettes of the smoke stacks. Those piles of coal and sulfur would take on colors. The bus went right along the river, north to the bay. You went with the girls on a Friday or Saturday night and the fellows came separately. Our crowd from the beauty shop rode on the bus. There were no dates or anything. You'd just dance. And they got the good bands to come here to Bay City then. Tommy Hill and Sammy Kaye. I remember, Swing and Sway with Sammy Kaye. You'd stand by the sides with your girl friends and the fellows would come and ask you to dance and you'd think, Ooogh, he asked me, so excited. There was no go off in the car and do things, like now. It was a whole different way of life. Not everything sex, sex, sex. And then you went home on the bus again. If you did go out after, you'd go to Dean's and have a sundae with the girls. The boys went somewhere else.

The women from the Silver Slipper were actually older than they'd looked from a distance. They dressed young. I'd thought they were all in their twenties, a little older than I was. Now, up close when they went to the doctor, I could see. They were tired women, coming to middle age. They must have been in their late thirties, one or two were past forty. They had such lined faces. A few looked like Indians and I think those few were the only ones who didn't dye their hair. When they climbed upstairs coming to Dr. Shea's, you could see their dark roots. And they must have done it themselves because no one had ever seen them in Harper Method or Billings', that was the other beauty shop in town then. You could see their veins through their nylon stockings. They always walked looking down, with their hands in their jacket pockets. As if they were ashamed, you know.

The girls at Harper Method told me Dr. Shea gave them birth control. He deloused and deflead them and gave them special shampoo and soap for scabies.

When a woman was sick, Dr. Shea drove out to the Silver Slipper and made a house call. People said when one died, they buried her right there out in back of the tavern, in Guns Field. They didn't even own that land. The girls whispered to me what the rumor was: that he gave those women abortions. Of course that was illegal then. No one seemed to have heard any more details, though, and I know for a fact that there was at least one child there at the time, a boy. He ended up at the orphanage.

Jimmy knew that boy later, one summer they worked together on a farm. He said that boy and some of the others used to do things with the sheep. Isn't that terrible? He said they put the ewe's hind legs in the front of their boots, so she was stuck. They wore such high boots then, up to the knees. And the sheep would sort of buck to get away. Ogh. Jimmy never did that, but I suppose the farm boys used to talk about it, I don't know. See, that's what we thought about sex then: it was either real, real bad and a secret, shameful, or there was none and that was all right. I don't think my mother and father ever really did much of anything. No.

Then, the war broke out when I was twenty-three. It was around

Thanksgiving, I remember, I read something about the Wacs and Waves. Become a Wac, you know, they were recruiting. And I filled out an application and sent away to get their booklet. I didn't tell anyone, I just did it. And then one day this letter comes and says that I'm to be in Cedar Rapids, Iowa, on December 18, no ifs, ands or buts. Then I had to go, I couldn't just change my mind anymore. Well, my mother got that letter and she was furious. She called me at the Harper Method—something she never did, my mother had such respect for any work or school, you know, whatever we were supposed to be doing. Because she never worked herself. She said to me on the phone, "Now *what* did you do?"

But the service was a very good thing for me. It was the first time I really had fun. That's when I finally got to know boys. At boot camp, you had one locker—one locker—and in there you had to keep all your clothes, your two uniforms, your cosmetics, your hairbrush, everything. That was it. And there was one big bathroom with a long mirror—so in the morning we'd all be in there lined up, putting on our cosmetics and fixing our hair. You learned some tricks that way, from the other girls.

The girls came from all over and most of them were nice. I stayed six weeks in boot camp in Cedar Rapids, and then we went to Evanston, Illinois. And there, it was a regular base. There were men everywhere, all around us. There were two of us for every ten of them, so we had a ball. And there in Chicago, we got passes to go to plays and movies and musicals, whatever was going on, you know. So even though I didn't go to college, I still did get to see something. It wasn't as if I stayed home in Bay City and just deteriorated.

I was in communications. We operated teletypes; we all knew Morse code. I can still do my name on the clicker. The boys there in Evanston were in training to be pilots. They had these little yellow planes and the ensigns had to fly them to Jacksonville, Mississippi, and then back up to the carrier in Lake Michigan. There were a lot of deaths in those little yellow planes. And then we had to send the telegrams to the parents. And that was the hardest, I think, for the family, you know. If you lost a boy overseas, that was hard. But to lose him when he was still here in training, before he got a chance to fight, well, then, you couldn't even think he died for something. But when they made it, and most of them did, then they'd come back with their wings and their white uniforms all bright and nice.

I had some of the more interesting work there was for women in the army. But communications was actually my second choice. My first choice was to be up in a watchtower, you did the radar for the planes. And I think that would have been interesting, too. But they were all filled up for that. And there was lots of work that wasn't so good. Some of the girls had to fix engines and that was dirty work. After that you could never get your hands really clean again. That grease stained the cuticle, around the nail. Like the people who work out at the armory say, they can never get that smell off their skin.

By then I wasn't so shy anymore. Then I was dating plenty. There was one warrant officer I dated, he was an Italian and he came from Chicago. Then he was stationed in the South Pacific. He wrote me to wait until he was finished and came home, but then already I was dating someone else. Quite a few of them proposed. I could have gotten married several times. I don't remember anymore why I didn't. I guess it just didn't appeal to me.

They sent our unit over to France. Some went to Hawaii, lots went to the west coast, San Diego, San Francisco, Monterey, and we got to go to Europe. First we went to England, then through the Channel and we ended up stationed in Normandy. Well, over there I met a fellow I did like.

And nobody knows it, but I got married over there. It was a real marriage, in the Catholic Church. He wasn't a Catholic, but he converted for me. He took his first communion the morning we were married. I never did tell Jimmy. He wouldn't like it if he knew. But I'll tell you something—he wasn't even the first. There were two in Illinois before him; an ensign and the warrant officer.

Before I went into the Wacs, I had to have a medical examination. I just went upstairs from the Harper Method to Dr. Shea. And he examined me and he said, "My God, you're still a virgin."

I said, "Well, crumps, what else would I be? What did you think I was?" So even then, it couldn't have been so unusual. But it was a big risk you took every time, because they didn't have birth control pills or anything. I never got pregnant, I guess I was lucky. I've often wondered what would have happened if I'd been pregnant when I came home from Europe. Then I would have had to tell everyone I was married. I don't know, who knows what's for the best.

He was a French Jew, he was born in Paris. But he spoke beautiful, beautiful English. Morgenstern was his name. His father had been one of the moviemakers over there, but when I met him, he didn't know anymore where his mother and father were. He was living with a family who had a farm there in Normandy. They sheltered him. You could tell he shouldn't have been on a farm. He had such slender, slender hands. He was real delicate, you know. But he'd learned to milk goats and make cheese. He joked about it. He'd been there already a year and a half.

After we were married, we went to Paris. I had my discharge and we were both going to go to America. The Americans had France then and we were supposed to take a boat that went to Texas. We had our tickets and all.

There in Paris, he left me in a candy store. I suppose he thought that's where a young wife would like to go. He was going to meet a contact from the Resistance. The man was to give him a handgun. He would go over into Germany and attend a parade from a street corner, where he could almost touch the Führer and then he was supposed to shoot him and run.

He was there that day at the parade, with the gun in his pocket. He told me later, there was a blond girl standing in front of him, with hair that had tints of green underneath the yellow. He didn't know her, but for some reason, he lifted his hand and touched the little girl's hair. Hitler rode by on the car four feet in front of him. He could have reached and kicked the metal of the fender. But instead, he stroked the hair of an unknown child, touching the gun in his pocket.

Hitler rode away, the parade went by, and before he came to fetch me, he slid the gun down the dirty toilet of a public rest room. That afternoon, we left for America, Texas.

All the boat ride, he was sick. Did I say before how weak he was? He wasn't in good health for a long time then already. He couldn't sleep at night and I stayed up with him. He had his coat and my coat and still he couldn't get warm. Later on, he complained about the boat ride. One day, he climbed down to the storeroom. He took me to see: there were rats in the barrels of oatmeal. After that, I never once made my children eat things they didn't want to eat. I had fights galore with Jimmy over that, but for once I stuck to my point.

We landed in Texas in the morning and there was this huge, huge horizon. I had never seen it like that before either. Black men moved with ropes there working the docks; that was something he hadn't seen. And a few minutes later, I was opening my purse for American money to buy chewing gum, my husband's first discovery in the New World.

We took a train from Texas that went all the way up to Wisconsin. Oh, was that something. It was all army. People standing up, women with little children and babies, trying to feed them and change their diapers. And my husband was still real sick. I had to ask people to give up their seat for him. And they did. Quite a few offered. Well, he died right there on that train. Yes, he died. It was the scariest thing that had ever happened to me in my life.

Later, the army did an autopsy and said it was a heart attack, but at that time I didn't know what to think. Here I had this young husband, he was twenty-seven then. He just passed out in his seat. It was mostly all women on that train and they all helped. I just cried and cried. I didn't know what to do. I was twenty-six years old and here I was just married and my husband was unconscious on the train. I couldn't think. All I could imagine was if he would only just wake up. I was so unrealistic. And then the terrible thing was nobody could do anything until the train's next stop.

I still don't know how long that was because the woman in the chair next to him got up and gave me her seat and would you believe, at a time like that, I fell asleep? Yes, I did. I slept.

The next stop was some little place in Oklahoma called Gant. Three of the women, one with children, woke me up and led me out. They kept patting my hand and telling me it would be all right. "Poor dear," I heard them whispering. They got me into a hotel and I didn't even see him. They'd carried him out first and somebody had taken him to the army coroner's office.

They had him cremated. They thought that was the best thing. I've thought many times since, I wish I'd had the presence of mind to see that he was buried. Then there would be some place where I could know he was.

It was nice of those women, they stayed overnight two days with me in that hotel. The morning we left, we took his ashes, they came in such a box like this, and we threw them out in the fields by the tracks. They kept asking me if there was anywhere special I wanted them and I said, no, no, I didn't care and I really didn't. I just wanted to get it over with and get back on the train. You see, I didn't connect them with him. The place in Oklahoma, the box, it was all funny. I felt like I was just going along with it. I knew those stones weren't really him.

Then it was a long ride north on the train and I had a lot of time to think. And I thought and I thought, should I tell my mother and dad that I'd been married. I didn't see what would be the good in it. I'd planned to just bring him home and introduce him, this is my husband. We're married. I knew they wouldn't be so happy about it, but I thought they would like him when they got used to him. Now, there wouldn't be any point.

And I thought I might forget about him faster if I didn't tell anybody. That's what they said in those days. When a girl was jilted, the mother would say, now, stop talking about him and pretty soon, you'll stop think-ing about him too. Now I don't think that's true. I don't think that's true at all. But then I did. I remember straightening my hat and gathering all my things neat together when the train pulled into the South Bay Station. I'd be going home alone, there were people for me, family. I thought the army was another world I'd been in—and in this one it wouldn't be so hard not to mention it. Not just him, the whole war. I didn't really feel like talking about any of it.

Now I wish I'd talked about it then when I could, then right away, when it was natural. So many years later, if you don't forget, if you haven't forgotten like I haven't, you're too ashamed to bring it up. And then it's always your secret. I imagine the war is a lot of people's secret; you know, what happened to them then.

Paul was his name and he was a beautiful boy. He looked real, real young, much younger than I did. It's so long ago now; nobody could be as good as I remember Paul. And you know, it's not a good thing to have a secret like that. Something you care about so much. A person you idealize who's dead. Because it takes away from your regular life. You compare and it doesn't do you any good, because no matter what you want or think, he's dead. You're better off forgetting him and trying to be happy with what you've got.

And here I think of him the way he looked then; well, if he still looked like that, who knows, the way I am now, he wouldn't even want me. But I kept thinking of Paul for such a long time, then I couldn't even stop it when I wanted. Every time I'd have a minute alone, my mind would sort of drift and I would picture things with him. I always imagined that it had been a mistake, that it wasn't his bones and ashes we threw away at Gant and that he stayed in a little hospital there—a small stone building run by nuns. I had the whole thing in my head, oh I was so silly, his room with the plain walls, a cot with a navy blue blanket, just a simple wooden cross above the bed. There were dandelions growing in the grass outside his room. That's what he saw when he looked out the window during that long time he was getting well. And every day, the nurses brought him food and stood there while he ate it. They didn't talk much. They folded their hands on the front of their habits and they looked out the window, too. Sometimes, in that field, there were cows.

Then, I always imagined, he found me. He wrote me a long letter or he called me on the telephone and I had to get rid of my life and of Jimmy. That was never too hard. In my daydream, that part never took too long. Sometimes I confessed and told everyone. And then the priest had to come and tell my parents and Jimmy that since my first husband turned out to be still alive, Jimmy and I weren't really married. On other days, I didn't tell a thing to anyone. I just got in my car before supper and drove away. What I spent the most time sitting and dreaming about was when we'd meet together again. He had thick lips and the top one sort of pulled up over his teeth. If I knew how to be a sculptor, I could still make his face. He had a smooth forehead, no lines, high cheekbones like a woman's, and that straight, plain, even nose. It was with him I understood that just the plain, the regular, was beautiful. It didn't have to be something special. It was just the ordinary, not having anything wrong. I suppose he had what people might call a weak chin. His face came to a point and the chin was small and hard, like the tip of an eggshell.

Oh, I'd close my eyes and think of us pressing together, kissing against the wall in a room. I always pictured behind us, one single bed, made up, the cover smooth. I tried to imagine the first instant, that urgency, and then after that—that ohgh—I couldn't do it anymore, I couldn't picture.

I'd have to open my eyes and be wherever I really was. In the house or the yard, Mom's house or the water softener store. And then the air and the light in the room where I was seemed thicker and staler than before. I remembered each time then he was dead. That went on for a long time, for years. It didn't really stop until Benny was born. And then, I don't know why, it went away. I guess it was hard to want to imagine giving up my babies. And they were Jimmy's after all. And by then, too, it was just such a long, long time.

I don't want to make it all sound bad. I had good times when I came home, too. After V-J Day, the young people flooded back to Bay City. There were lots of parties that winter, lot of dances. It was a happy time. Overall, I think the war was a good thing for a lot of people's social lives. Of course, there were some wounded, but you didn't see them much. And then there were those like Phil Brozek, who went over to Bikini Island. When he came back, he picked up his milk route again that he'd had before the war. The swelling in his legs, the cancer, all that from the radiation, that didn't show until much later.

I met Jimmy on the golf course. He had been in the service, too, in New Guinea and then in Australia. He jokes that he should have met me before the war, when I was still a virgin. He knows that much, that it happened with both of us in the war. He grew up in Bay City, too, and we graduated high school the same year, but I never met him. He went to Central High and I went to Catholic, the Academy. We only met the boys from Premontre. He says he wants to go back to Australia sometime and see how many kids look like him; he says there weren't any women in New Guinea, just those natives, but there in Australia, apparently, they had their fun.

I don't know, do you think I should have married him? I don't know either, I often wonder. Then, at the time, I suppose I thought, why not. I needed something new. Here I was back living at home again, sharing a room with my little sister. And she got into everything—oh, God, was she a snoop. She'd open your mail, go through your drawers, anything. One day she told me she stopped reading my diary because it was too boring to keep her interest up. Oh, she could be a little brat.

And my mother wasn't the same with me, either. I never told her I was married, but she knew something was different, she could tell. That last year, I didn't write as much. At the beginning, I'd sent presents from everywhere, but towards the end, I just wasn't thinking about home anymore. I remember on the train, I was an hour away, and I realized I was coming home with no presents for anybody. I got out at one town, I had only a few minutes, and I bought the first thing I saw that would do—a box of cookie cutters. They were nice cookie cutters, all unusual shapes and good stainless steel, but she must have seen that they were just from around here. But at least I had something to give them when I came off at the station.

I remember that night, the lanterns lit, it all looked real pretty and the town had changed so. I felt happy and sleepy all of a sudden. They took me out to Dean's for a sundae and they had the hot fudge, like it always was, in the little silver pitcher. The sky outside over the river turned violet, the lanterns and the piles of sulfur were that real pretty yellow. And you know, I was almost relieved to be alone. I was so tired I felt like a girl again.

But that didn't last. Pretty soon I couldn't stand it anymore. After all the excitement of the war, the travel, the uniforms—you know, sometimes it was like one long parade, you were always sort of tired and excited and you were usually around so many people—Bay City just didn't seem like much anymore. That first night when I was exhausted, it felt perfect, just the way you'd want a town to be. But then when I got some sleep it seemed too small. And here I was plunked back in the same house on the same road. I was shampooing and styling again at the Harper Method Beauty Shop.

And one thing I can say for Jimmy, he knew how to take a girl out on a date. He always took me to a nice supper and then after we'd do something; we'd go to a club and hear music or we'd go dancing. And every couple of dates I'd get a corsage. I have them all here, pressed in the dictionary. And he always had a big crowd of friends and they gave parties. Twenty, thirty people over for fish fry or chicken bouya. And my parents never did that. We didn't have as many friends.

So we went ahead and got married. We had the service at Saint Phillip's. Jimmy was a Catholic, too, so that was never a problem. I think my mother and dad liked Jimmy, if they didn't, they never said anything. And I was already twenty-eight. Maybe they thought I wouldn't get any better.

And wouldn't you know my little sister managed to ruin my wedding. She was a bridesmaid, with two others, my two best girl friends from the Harper Method. I wore Granny's wedding dress. See, my mother never had one. It was a beautiful dress, that old-fashioned pearl-white satin with a long train. Adele walked behind me holding it up. I remember she had a white dress, too. I'd wanted the bridesmaids in pink or mint green, but no, Adele said it was either black or white. And so the others had to be white, too, they all had to match. She herself got married in a suit, I remember.

It was a small wedding, a hundred, hundred fifty people. We had the reception at my parents' house, in the backyard. We had tables spread out with white tablecloths and white and green balloons tied up in the oak tree. My dad's men from the mink had rented tuxedos and they stood behind the tables pouring champagne. There was champagne everywhere and trays of food. My mother had been baking for days.

She'd made the cake herself. It was a lemon cake inside, real moist and tart, with a beautiful, fluffy white frosting. Adele had decorated it that morning—and I have to hand it to her, it was beautiful, she covered the whole thing with sugared flowers, real flowers, violets and pansies from the yard, and with cookies in shapes from those cookie cutters I brought home. She was always good at such stuff. But then, she didn't want us to cut it. She made them take about a hundred pictures, before she'd let us touch it. We have more pictures of that cake than of the rest of the wedding put together.

I do have a picture of the women, when I threw the bouquet. I still had my big nose in the pictures, so we don't put them out anywhere in the house, but we still take the book down and look at them once in a while. Jimmy says he liked my nose big, he says he didn't mind it.

All Granny's sisters were there from Malgoma and Granny, and all the neighbor women. My mother was wearing a peach-colored dress with a corsage. My dad had bought us each special corsages, he had them in the refrigerator when we woke up that morning.

Well, we didn't have a balcony or anything, so I threw the bouquet from the porch. It was just those couple of steps. In the picture, the ladies are all standing on the grass in a line; the married women closest to me, with their hands at their sides, they're not trying to catch it. My mother is the most beautiful one in the picture and you can barely see her, she's standing behind two of the aunts. She really had a perfect profile, like that on a coin, so even, and her hair grew thick and nice. Even then when it was turning gray, it turned that beautiful silver white. And I think she was happy for me. All that day, I'd looked at her from somewhere, when I was going down the aisle at church, later, on the lawn during the party, and her face was so nice, she was glad for me. She'd worked so hard on all the food and the house. And her cake turned out so good.

In the picture, she's got her hands behind her back and this big gorgeous smile. You hardly ever saw her smiling big like that. She was shy. She wasn't a smiler. You know, of my mother and my sister and me, I was the only one with a regular wedding and it made her happy, I suppose. In the picture, the bouquet is blurred in the air. It looks like I'm throwing it to my mother.

Two of my bridesmaids are in the front, crouched and ready like football players. Their knees bent, their arms out, their eyes are on the bouquet. They were both single girls and my age, they were ready, I suppose. Would you believe I don't know who they are anymore? My two bridesmaids, and I can't remember their names. And Adele is standing there, coy, her hands intertwined together. She is looking down at her shoe in the grass.

And she was the one who caught the bouquet. Seventeen years old and she caught the bouquet, sure enough, and without hardly trying. My dad was mad, he thought she was too young to even be in the line for it and he wanted me to throw it again. But she said, nothing doing. She wouldn't give it back.

Then she pulled her real stunt: she locked herself in the bathroom and took a shower! Well, all those people drinking all afternoon and only the one bathroom in the house. Pretty soon they were lined up into the kitchen. Adele was in there humming in the shower. Oh, ye gods. She washed her hair and set it, and so she was in there a long time, hour, hour and a half maybe. And was I mad.

Some of the men walked up the dirt road and went in the field by the barn. But a lot of people just drove home. The party started breaking up. The neighbors ran down the road to their own bathrooms. My father stamped in and rattled on the doorknob—we were afraid he'd break the door down. That was their worst fight I ever saw. When he couldn't get the door open, he went around to the other side of the house and yelled at her through the window. The next day, we went out and my mother showed me: he trampled her whole bed of lilies of the valley.

Well, it was a hot day and I suppose Adele thought she wanted to cool off. Can you imagine, a hundred fifty people, all drinking, and one bathroom, locking yourself in for over an hour? By the time she came out, most of the people were gone. Pretty much just Jimmy's family and our relatives from Malgoma were still there. And the bridesmaids. My sister always did manage to get herself right in the middle of everything. Jimmy still blames her for ruining our wedding. We were planning to party all night! My dad had set up a record player downstairs, in the basement, and his Polynesian room was all set for dancing. But everyone had gone home already! My mother cooked for the relatives and Jimmy and I went out with the bridesmaids and the ushers to a supper club, Jantzen's. I remember we drank lime bitters.

Really, outside of the war, my life has been pretty much in the ordinary and I suppose that's been okay with me. I don't think I would have liked moving around and always having to look right and talk right, like your mother does. But you know, I wish I had gone to college. I listen to Adele and to you talk and you just say things so very well. You know how to speak nice, you do.

We went to Niagara Falls for our honeymoon, just the typical thing, but we had fun. I remember the first night, I suppose from the excitement of the wedding and the party and then traveling, my period came on. It wasn't due then, it was over a week early. I told Jimmy and he said, okay, and said I should just put my hair up and do whatever I needed to do to get ready before bed. See, he knew, he had sisters. And we each got into our single bed and said good night. Every night then, when we came into the hotel room, he'd look at me and I'd say no, not yet. Then our last night before we had to go home, I winked and said, "Tonight."

I don't remember ever deciding to build right next door to my mom and dad, somehow we just knew that's what we were going to do. The land was there already, so at least we had that. My dad helped a little with the foundation, but mostly Jimmy built this house by himself with one other fellow he hired. He was already in the water softeners then. Sullivan Water Softeners. All those years, it was us against Kinsley. That was the other brand. I remember once after we were in the house, I looked out the window while I was doing the dishes and there were all these silver water softeners, shining like torpedoes, leaning against the back of the house. Well, of course, we put in a water softener and Jimmy gave one to Mom and Dad one Christmas. Adele would have gotten one too, but she was never settled down long enough anywhere.

I suppose if I could do it again, I'd build farther away from my parents. It really was just too close. But then, who knows, if I did it again, if I would even marry Jimmy.

And it was a help to me those first years with Hal, to have my mother right next door. And then when Dad was sick. Your mother was out in California at that time, doing something or other in school. We called and called and she wouldn't come home. She was lucky; she barely made it.

When she finally did come, your dad was up here all the time with her. I liked Hisham, he was a nice fellow. Not responsible, well, you know that, but nice. And oh, he was a very handsome man. Tall and dark, with big, big white teeth. I remember him at Dad's funeral. He didn't like the open coffin. He thought that was such a barbaric thing. In fact, if I'm not mistaken, he fainted. He was with Adele and she bent down to kiss the cheek and I'm pretty sure he fainted. He was just appalled. The Muslims didn't do that, see. Over there, they cremate them. I suppose maybe they don't have the room to bury.

We did something around here that my dad had started and all the neighbors took it up, too. When a baby was born, you planted some kind of bush. If it was a boy, you planted a bush that would have berries, if it was a girl, a bush that flowered. With Hal, we planted raspberries, with Benny, currants. Those raspberry bushes are still here, they've spread. The idea was for the kids to be independent. When they were children they could go outside and eat the berries and pick the flowers. My father always thought of things with big ideas; he thought if worst came to worst someone could live on nuts and berries. And then when someone died, we planted a tree. I don't know why a tree. For my father, my mother wanted two; a hickory and a birch.

When my father died, he left money in his will for me to get my nose fixed. He wrote a letter with it that said he had had a big nose all his life and he'd never done anything about it, but that he'd been the one to give it to me and he wanted me to be able to get mine fixed.

And I did. Here I was already married and with a five-year-old son and I went on the train to Chicago alone to have the surgery. There wasn't anyone who did it in Bay City. It was sort of a scary thing. I thought I'd better have a picture to give the doctor an idea of what I'd like; at the Harper Method we'd always told people to look through the magazines so they could show us what they had in mind. So I had my photograph folded up in my purse. It was a picture of Katharine Hepburn. I thought if I was going to get a new nose, I may as well go for something really good, huh? Why not.

Well, I went and it was really awful. Chicago seemed very different from what I remembered of it during wartime, and I was just alone and out of uniform. I couldn't just go anywhere like I did then. And I suppose, I was older.

I remember the night before, I ate dinner in my hotel room because I had no idea where else to go. Then, I still didn't know what to do, I had the whole night ahead of me, so what did I do, I sat down and wrote a letter to my mother. Oh, I was such a goody-good. I really was. I was really too good.

Then the next morning I woke up and I was so scared. All of a sudden, I liked my nose, and I thought, what if I end up with something worse? But I had the appointment already, the doctor was all lined up and I didn't know if I'd even have to pay him anyway, if I didn't come. So I left the hotel and on the way to the hospital, I walked by such an arcade. They had one of those booths where you put in a quarter and it takes your picture four times and they come out in a strip like an up-and-down cartoon. I took my picture. I decided I wanted four pictures of my nose. I still have them. It really wasn't too great a nose.

The funny thing about the operation was that the doctor put me under, but I could still hear him working—I wasn't completely asleep. I heard crunching noises, like the way my dad ate chicken, he cracked the bones with his teeth and sucked the marrow. Then I heard a clipping, like with a shears.

I'd given him the picture beforehand and he said he'd do his best. He told me he had to work with what was there. And I think he did a good job. I've always been glad I did it.

Still, I'll never be pretty like your mother. She has those long legs from Granny. And one thing I have to say for her, she always did keep up her figure and dress herself nice. She has a knack for that, anything with colors. She has that and my mother and Granny had it, too, but I never did.

I've never been good that way. I never could just put things together the way they do. I've always had to buy the whole outfit.

And Adele always did the exciting things, too. She's been all over, she mixes with the real rich people. She's never been happy with just the ordinary. I don't think she ever really liked Bay City.

She called once when she was in California and said she was going to a party where she was going to meet George Cukor and Katharine Hepburn. Jimmy talked to her, he answered the phone. We didn't know who George Cukor was until she told us, but we knew Katharine Hepburn.

"Katharine Hepburn, Katharine Hepburn!" Jimmy was yelling. I think he'd already had his gimlet. "You know your sister has her nose!" Adele remembered the story, too. And she called the next day and said, yes, she had met Katharine Hepburn and that she was a very icy person, real aloof, and all night she'd sort of stood apart, but then Adele had gone up and said, Excuse me, Miss Hepburn, but I wanted to tell you that my sister has your nose. Adele told the whole story, about me working at the Harper Method Beauty Shop and taking in a picture and all and she said, for the first time that night, Katharine Hepburn smiled. So thanks to my sister, somewhere out there Katharine Hepburn knows that a Carol Measey in Wisconsin has her nose.

Adele

The Course of Miracles

I don't plan anymore. I used to. I used to try to control. Now I just sort of let things go with the flow. I live in the Now. And I find, everything just comes the way it's supposed to.

I've learned To Give Is to Receive. And when I can, when my billings are up, I look around for things for her. Even when I shouldn't, I do. I saw an adorable Calvin Klein black and white evening dress at Robinson's. It isn't cheap, but it is ADORABLE, it would be just smashing on her, and she needs to have one or two good things. It's fine to be the intellectual, but once in a while, you should dress up a little, too.

I even thought of it for me, I drove out at noon and tried it on, but my arms are just too old for it, you need a young arms and back. So I put it on layaway for her, she may as well wear it now when she's young. When you've still got the good arms. And those little white outfits I sent her like mine, they're two twenty-five, two fifty, actually, no, they're two seventy-five.

It's the most important, beautiful, fulfilling thing I've ever done in my life, being a mother. And I look at her and think, Hey, I didn't do such a bad job. But she holds in her fear and her anger, she hasn't learned to let go yet of her fear and just love, the way I do. I have no guilt. Not anymore. I'm living in the Now. I've found a real inner peace and nothing can really disturb it. She hasn't learned to forgive yet. But, you know, I look at her and think, If I was such an awful mother, the way she paints me out to be with her friends, she LOVES to play the poor child, the martyr, POOR, POOR Ann, then she wouldn't be so great, what she is.

I see the kids right here in Beverly Hills where the mothers were too busy with their manicures and their thises and their thats, they never took the time to give the real total love, the emotional closeness I did. I see it, I see it all the time in the convalescent homes. I have two girls, one is nineteen, the other's twenty-six, and neither will ever walk again, from the drugs.

And I started from scratch, from nothing, she saw the house and the dead-end road I grew up on. I was on my own, raising her, when I was her age, who does she think helped me? When I think of what I grew up around, the old mink sheds, a dead-end road—nothing, and I look at what she's had. Beverly Hills High School, college. And the lessons. And the clothes.

I think to myself, How did I get out of there. Other people just stay in the same rut all their lives. It must be something in the genes, our genes, that pushes us ahead. My sister is the totally opposite of me. And yet, it's the gene characteristic that's so incredibly, magnificently universal. That makes me believe there has to be a master plan, a universal power. Something in the genes way back, whether it's centuries ago—and here we are that we, a few of us, all these chromosomes meet and become something. We're all only electromagnetic particles. And so is a rock, a fish, a bird, a butterfly. And that's how you know. That's how I know, that I'm more than just this lifetime.

I'm part of all that went before and all that went after me. These are my beliefs. They're very strong and very deep. I was always different. From the kids I grew up with. I was the same and yet I was different. But then everyone feels that.

Everything was meant to be and if she has to rebel to find her own independent self, then I can let her. And I know what I've done, I know it in my heart, in myself, I know she'll thank me someday.

She could have been a poor nothing girl in a factory town in the midwest. And here she's in with a great crowd, going to the best schools, she can go anywhere, mix with anyone. Absolutely anyone. She's really a member of the intelligentsia, the real cream, the upper crust. And she's there because I got her in when she was young enough to learn. I was already thirty-nine when we moved here. I was young and good-looking. Sure, she's smart and she's pretty and talented—the works, she's got it all, the best of everything, I tell her—but I'll tell you, there are plenty of them there in the midwest who are the same and you'll never see them, because they'll never get out and rise up. Like Lolly. They just sink.

They tried—to make me and more than that, my child, into their mold. I had to let myself and my daughter go free. And mold in another way. I didn't see the joys and the happinesses I felt life offered. If only to look at a sunset or to look at an owl on a fence or to see the glories of Yosemite. I think the real ordinary is just to be simple with yourself. But they weren't simple. They were highly complicated people. They lived by the negatives, rather than love and joy.

My mother could have come out once and visited me. Never once did they think that I could need. That has hurt me. But I also know it was Carol's doing. How selfish people can be! To think they don't have to do anything.

It's very hard to change social classes after a certain age. I have friends, the Swans are lovely really, and Bert Keller, they're very good to me, having me up for parties and dinners and screenings, brunches, whenever I want, really, but I'll never be in the way that she can. You really need the man and the house. And you don't just find a man at my age. They're all looking for a woman who has money. And like Nan Keller used to say, if you don't learn your tennis before a certain age, before you're twenty, you'll never get your form just right. But I'm practicing, with tennis I don't agree, I am learning.

She'll have the big house someday and the husband and the beautiful yard, all of it. And, I'm hoping, grandchildren. I'm ready to be a grand-mother. I think it'll be one of the most satisfying emotionally, I mean, beautiful things. I don't worry about getting old. You're as old as you feel and I feel young. I'm ready for grandchildren right now.

I'm happy here in my little place, I've fixed it up cute. Someday, I'd like to buy, I'd like to have a little house where I can see the ocean and the mountains, real choice. But it has to be the right spot. I'm looking. I'm looking all the time. I'm going to move pretty soon. I'm saving. LA has gotten too big and too busy. I'm sick of all this driving.

And her going to Wisconsin, her doubts, all this playing up how she was poor, working class—I tell her, Honey, you were NEVER working class, your mother always had an MA, that's not working class—at the time, it hurt me, it really just hurt me right here in the heart, when she wouldn't dress up, even once, she wouldn't put on the clothes I sent her FOR ONE DAY, just to please me, but now I understand that was all just rebellion. And I've learned to be patient, not to try and change people. And when you do that, they come around by themselves, quicker than if you try to influence. And she'll never go back to Wisconsin. Never in a million years. She couldn't go back, after Brown. I couldn't either, now. I really couldn't. There's nothing for us there anymore.

I remember all those stinky mink sheds—I used to go there after school and talk with my dad. We'd stand and stick our arms in, real quiet and still, that was how you got the mink to know you. I'm the one who had my childhood there. And I wouldn't go back if you paid me. I'd like to know where my furs are now, though, and my dresses. There's one suit with a green velvet collar and the pinched waist, it's exactly just what they're wearing again now, I'd give anything to know where that is now. But Carol probably threw it out or kept it for herself. That's what happens when you leave.

But it's worth it. You have to just say, you lose a lot of things that should be yours, but it's worth it. They're the ones who are stuck there.

A man? I'd like to meet someone real, real special someday, a man I could really share with, but right now, I'm concentrating on my work. I've got the convalescent homes, my patient load is up again, thank God, and I've got a few other little things, I'm designing a line of clothes for the bedridden, I have a partner and we've hired a designer, this young Japanese boy who's going out with Betsy Swan, and I'm writing a book. I don't go to a lot of parties, I live a very quiet life. I'm actually a very shy person. And before I really want to look for a man, I'm just going to get ME organized first, type up those damn reports, it's the end of the month again.

And I read before bed every night. I've gotten very involved in the spirit, in giving and really feeling a oneness with the world. I read this Course of Miracles and I hope and pray, she'll read them. I sent them all to her for Christmas, with a few other things of course, clothes and a little jewelry. She laughs. They may not be Pulitzer Prize–winners but they show you the fullness and the openness of life. They teach you to give. And let's see, what else? I'm reading Zen, all these various philosophies.

Sure, she's going to rebel.

What I try to tell her is you can be BOTH—you can have the high IQ and the real intellect, you can be the Female Doctor AND you can dress up a little and act a little feminine.

I've done it all these years without a man. Not many women have been father and mother both. And I've been through lots she doesn't even know. There are many things she doesn't know, the things I didn't tell her, just so she wouldn't worry, just so she could be a child. I was in jail once for those damn parking tickets, never again will I let them pile up, but for a while there, I was back in school, getting my new California certification and I just put them in the glove compartment when I got them. Well, it happened twice and the first time, Frank Swan drove right down and paid my bail. But the second time I was there till four in the morning, the Swans were in Mexico, they couldn't reach the Kellers, the Kellers were at a party, four o'clock was when they came home. Well, I was raped by a woman in there. Yes, so there's a lot she doesn't know. I haven't had it easy either.

But I've learned to be at one with the world and to forgive. And since I've let go of my fear, lots of good things have just flowed into my life— all this furniture, the Tiffany, the Seth Thomas—it's all just meant to be.

And I even see her coming around. She visited and I got a place at the beach last year, for all her kids, so they could party. And I watched her with them. I just had to say to myself, leave her be, even with the hair and the bitten nails and all, and the underarms and the legs, ugh, that I really can't go for. But those boys all looked at her, so I guess that's just how they wear it now. I don't think you have to, I think the really great girls now still have the long, thick hair and they wear a little mod jewelry or mod dress, not the punk hair that's going to be out of style in six months, but I just shut my mouth and smiled. And I hoped and prayed that like I did years ago, she'd find her own grace, with her eyes closed.

And I think maybe she is. They all danced out on the sand, with their music and can she ever dance! Well, I suppose with the ballet and the thises and the thats, the cotillions, all I gave her as a child. But I didn't recognize her at first, I looked down from the balcony and thought, who's that? And then I couldn't believe that it was me, I made that beautiful girl.

But she thinks too much, she's so nervous, she has that anxiety, she's got to learn to just BE. And for so long all I heard was bitch bitch, whine whine, that now sometimes, no always. Always her happiness surprises me.

I wish I could have brought her here when she was even younger, so she wouldn't have all these various feelings and yearnings for the midwest and her middle-class roots, but that was her father, not me. I never wanted to stay there. But he left. And now I've got my station wagon ready for my grandchildren. They'll be all this—all Beverly Hills. They'll be born into it—thanks to me.

When I was pregnant with her, we lived in Egypt. I didn't know anything, I was so young. But her father wanted to have a baby and so I thought, okay, maybe that would help him, settle him down. His family was there. They thought it would be wonderful. He had backing. Of course, later he changed his mind about that, too. But I'm over him now too finally. I think I could meet him again now and it wouldn't mean anything to me.

I lost so much weight, I was down to eighty-six pounds at seven months and I flew back. I wanted to be home with my mother. And so I could have her here in America with the very best equipment and hospitals in the world.

You carry a baby in the womb for nine months and then, when they're grown up, they call you collect, when they remember. She has her own life. And that's okay. I've learned to be patient. "Teach only love for that is what you are." The ups and down; I live with it. And I've got a lot ahead of me and a lot to be proud of. I know: she is the reason I was born.